OLD
TESTAMENT
LIGHT

By George M. Lamsa

HOLY BIBLE From the
Ancient Aramaic Text

Idioms in the Bible Explained and
A Key to the Original Gospel

OLD
TESTAMENT
LIGHT

The Indispensable Guide
to the Customs, Manners,
& Idioms of Biblical Times

George M. Lamsa

1817

HARPER & ROW, PUBLISHERS, SAN FRANCISCO
Cambridge, Hagerstown, New York, Philadelphia
London, Mexico City, São Paulo, Singapore, Sydney

Library of Congress Cataloging in Publication Data

Lamsa, George Mamishisho, 1893-
  Old Testament light.

  Originally published: St. Petersburg Beach, Fla.: Aramaic Bible Society, © 1964.
  Includes index.
  1. Bible. O.T.—Commentaries.   I. Title.
BS1151.2.L32   1985   221.7   84-48774
ISBN 0-06-064924-0
ISBN 0-06-064925-9 (pbk.)

85 86 87 88 89 10 9 8 7 6 5 4 3 2 1

TABLE OF CONTENTS

	Introduction	vii
Chapter One	Genesis	1
Chapter Two	Exodus	99
Chapter Three	Leviticus	166
Chapter Four	Numbers	189
Chapter Five	Deuteronomy	223
Chapter Six	Joshua	284
Chapter Seven	Judges	293
Chapter Eight	Ruth	306
Chapter Nine	1 and 2 Samuel	310
Chapter Ten	1 and 2 Kings	343
Chapter Eleven	1 and 2 Chronicles	382
Chapter Twelve	Ezra	393
Chapter Thirteen	Nehemiah	397
Chapter Fourteen	Esther	403
Chapter Fifteen	Job	410
Chapter Sixteen	Psalms	461
Chapter Seventeen	Proverbs	548
Chapter Eighteen	Ecclesiastes	588
Chapter Nineteen	Song of Solomon	603
Chapter Twenty	Isaiah	612
Chapter Twenty-One	Jeremiah	729
Chapter Twenty-Two	Lamentations	784
Chapter Twenty-Three	Ezekiel	793
Chapter Twenty-Four	Daniel	844
Chapter Twenty-Five	Hosea	862

Chapter Twenty-Six	Joel	880
Chapter Twenty-Seven	Amos	885
Chapter Twenty-Eight	Obadiah	898
Chapter Twenty-Nine	Jonah	901
Chapter Thirty	Micah	908
Chapter Thirty-One	Nahum	918
Chapter Thirty-Two	Habakkuk	923
Chapter Thirty-Three	Zephaniah	931
Chapter Thirty-Four	Haggai	936
Chapter Thirty-Five	Zechariah	939
Chapter Thirty-Six	Malachi	957
	Index	963

INTRODUCTION

Throughout the centuries men have written commentaries on the greatest of all books. the Bible. Scholars of all races and colors have in one way or another tried to throw light on the Bible. And yet today people are more eager than ever to understand the book that contains life, light, and truth.

This commentary is based on the Aramaic language and the ancient biblical customs and manner which played an important part in recording God's holy word.

The Aramaic word for commentary is *nohara*, "to throw light" or "to enlighten." In the olden days, because of the fact that words and phrases had several meanings, all important state or royal decrees, treaties, and agreements contained marginal explanations or commentaries in order not to leave any doubt in the mind of the reader [Ezra 4:7].

The purpose of this *nohara*, or commentary, is to throw light on obscure passages in Bible translations, to correct the words which have been mistranslated, and thus to recover the lost meaning of the verses; to explain biblical idioms, metaphors, allegories, customs, and manners which in their ancient context are difficult and unfamiliar to Western minds, but simple for the Easterners to understand. After all, the Old Testament was written first in Semitic languages, for Semitic people, centuries before Greek, Latin, and the present European languages were born. The New Testament was written for the descendants of the same people. And the authors of this sacred literature were moved by the Holy Spirit. They lived in a world of unseen realities.

The Western Bible translators and commentators have done their best in translating ideas from the ancient languages and the style of writing in which they were first written and preached into modern, expressive, and changing languages of our days.

This is not a verse-by-verse commentary. Hundreds of comments which have been written on the obscure passages and mistranslations have been clarified through a direct translation from the ancient Aramaic, Peshitta* Text. (The clear, the simple, the true text.) This is a book for ministers, students of the Bible, and laymen who are eager to understand the meaning of the Scriptures and the ancient customs and manners which con-

* Peshitta means "clear, sincere, straight, true and original." The writings were called Peshitta because they were clear in their original setting.

stitute the background of the Sacred Book. Some of the comments are answers to hundreds of letters which come from sincere men and women.

Indeed what sounds hard, harsh, ambiguous, and difficult in the Bible was easily understood by the people to whom the Bible was written, and is still well understood by the descendants of the races and peoples who, centuries ago, played a dominant part in the world's greatest sacred drama, the Bible. This is because in biblical lands most of the ancient biblical culture, customs, manners, idioms, metaphors, and mannerisms of speech had remained unchanged until the dawn of this century.

This is not all. The way of life and the thinking of the people who lived at the time when the men of God penned this sacred literature were handed down in their context to the present day as though embedded in amber. Indeed, it was divinely ordained that the truth in the Bible should be revealed and written in Semitic languages and preserved in its purity for the generations to come. God always leaves a remnant. God's light always keeps burning amidst darkness, persecution, and suffering, and God's truth endures forever.

The term "Bible" in Western languages means a library. It is derived from Biblos, a small town in Syria where papyrus was manufactured. Thus the Bible as a library contains the inspired writings of the Hebrew prophets and those of the temple and court scribes. Indeed, the Bible is the only large authentic and important surviving library from the past containing sacred books written in a plain alphabet that men can read and understand. Moreover, the Bible contains many volumes which cover various phases of life, such as law, drama, history, poetry, philosophy, art, science, religion, and worship. Indeed, the Bible is a revelation out of this world written in the language of this world.

But in Semitic languages, Aramaic or Hebrew, the term Bible does not mean a library. The Hebrew name of the Holy Bible is *Torah*, which means "the law." The name of the Holy Book in the language of the Hebrew patriarchs, Aramaic, is *Auretha*, derived from *ra*, which means to see through the mind. The adjective of this verb is *reyana*, mind. This is because the spiritual truths cannot be seen by human eye or easily explained in words. They are conceived and understood through the mind and higher intelligence. No other name could have been more suitable for a book containing the laws of God, his ordinances and his moral ethics. As the psalmist puts it, "The Bible is a lamp to our feet and a light to enlighten our dark paths" [Ps. 119:105].

Alaha, God, the essence of life, can neither be seen with our physical eyes nor understood with our human senses, but we can see him as a Father and feel his presence and his divine care just as the sheep feel the presence of the shepherd. This is because what is spiritual and infinite cannot be seen or described in the language of mortal and finite beings. Then again, God being the creator, the eternal Spirit and the whole cannot be portrayed, nor described, nor divided, nor defined by his creations. On the other hand, a spiritual idea cannot be pictured or described in words, but it can be imparted in a parable, an allegory, and in figurative speech. This is why some of the prophets portrayed God as an emperor unapproachable, surrounded by ministers, counselors, and intermediaries. A God with hands, feet, ears, and eyes. A God now happy, now sorry, now angry.

We must not forget that the Israelites were forbidden to draw pictures, carve statues, or make graven images or any other symbols or objects of worship. But the Hebrew prophets found a new way to portray and explain spiritual ideas so that even simple folk could understand them. They used parables and allegories which the people easily understood but never took literally. Indeed, the Jews distinguished between a living man and a dumb and helpless statue. Moreover, they were familiar with the language of their day. When women singers said that Saul had slain his thousands and David his tens of thousands, the people knew that what they meant was that David had slain Goliath and had become a greater warrior than Saul. They knew that it was a poetic song composed by dancing women who had not seen the battle. They knew it was a song of triumph to glorify God.

On the other hand, man's mind is blind to spiritual ideas, just as a blind man cannot perceive colors. God is the spiritual essence and the intelligence which governs the universe. A physical God is man's own idea. God is truth, life, and light; therefore, he must be understood and worshiped spiritually. Moreover, we must not forget that everything which God created was perfect and good. Therefore, God is not the author of evil, nor is evil a reality. There is a human element in the Bible just as there is usually a certain amount of copper or brass in gold. And it is this human ingredient which pictures God, who is the source of love, as angry, sorry, and repenting of the evil he did. On the other hand, in the second chapter of Genesis, the spiritual and immortal being is reduced to a physical and mortal man in order to relate the story of his fall and his transgression against God and the moral law. You cannot portray a spirit eating the forbidden fruit, nor finding itself naked, nor clothed in fig leaves or in skins. In other words, the second story of creation is written to show why man fell from grace.

Moreover, the Bible is the only ancient and authentic written record wherein we see the evidences of God's dealing with man and his interest in him, like a father's interest in his child. Nearly all of the great religions have some kind of diety—a revelation from or mystic communication with a higher power. But none of them can compare to the Sacred Book of the Hebrews with their monotheism, their spiritual and clear concept of God, and his love and direct dealing with men.

About four thousand years ago God appeared to Abraham in a vision and told him that by his seed (teaching) all the nations would be blessed. Two thousand years later Jesus of Nazareth read the holy books which contained these divine promises, studied them, and then fulfilled them, and thus became a Great Light to lighten the world. Despite many changes in the world, wars and persecutions, the rise and fall of many great empires, God's promises never failed, nor were they forgotten by the Jews, who had shed rivers of blood for them.

Today the whole world, one way or another, is leavened with the moral ethics and the truths which centuries ago were revealed to the Hebrew patriarchs and to the prophets who came after them; and at last they were fulfilled by Jesus Christ, who put them into practice. The Jewish moral ethic through Jesus of Nazareth has become the ethic of the whole world. No false promises or testaments could have survived all these centuries, and nothing could have enriched and consoled the hearts of men more than the Bible has.

Thus the Bible is a witness to God's revelations and to his interest in man. The sacred Book may also be called a guidepost to lead men to God. The Bible was written by men who had some experience with God and who had heard his inarticulate voice. The Bible is a book of guidance on all phases of human relations; throughout the centuries man has never been able to dispense with it, and nothing has been able to replace it as a book for guidance, edification, and consolation.

We must not forget that this great sacred literature was revealed in visions and dreams in arid deserts, in caves, and upon the tops of mountains; and that the simple and pious people, like the prophets, believed in visions, dreams, and divine communication. The Israelites were directed and guided in all their wandering in the desert by a great spiritual power which they could not see or touch. This is why a large portion of the Bible is based on visions and revelations. Many of these truths were revealed in symbols and metaphors so that the people may understand them and remember them.

It is not easy to describe ideas such as depression, famine, suffering, joy, or sadness. But they can be revealed in symbols, in dreams, and in visions. One can easily understand the significance of fat cows and lean cows or of blasted ears of wheat and full ears of wheat.

Joseph, being a student of God's word and the interpreter of visions and dreams, knew the meaning of the symbols which Pharaoh had seen in his visions during the night. He knew that the fat cows and full ears of wheat meant prosperity and that the lean cows and blasted ears of wheat meant depression.

Every Bible student should know something about inner-voice visions and dreams and their meaning. He also should distinguish between such men as Elijah, Elisha, and Isaiah and the prodigal son, the good samaritan, the rich man who enlarged his barns, and the angels who appeared to the men of God in visions and dreams. For instance, it was in a dream that Jacob wrestled with the angel [Gen. 32:24-29]. The angel was Esau. The next day Jacob said to Esau, ". . . because now I have seen your face, as I saw the face of an angel, and you were pleased with me" [Gen. 33:10]. In Aramaic pious men are called angels. But real angels are spirits; they have no bodies to wrestle with men. Jacob wrestled in his disturbed mind. He had deceived his brother Esau and, therefore, he had a guilty conscience [Gen. 32:11].

As we have said, a large portion of the sacred Book is based on visions which the men of God saw. It was in a vision that Abraham entertained God and the two angels and God ate meat with him. It was in a night vision that Isaiah saw angels worshiping God. It was in a vision that Ezekiel came in the spirit to Jerusalem and measured the temple. It was in visions and dreams that Daniel saw the rise and fall of many empires.

In biblical days kings, princes, and the people depended on the prophets and on God's revelations for guidance, healing, prosperity, and protection. Moreover, prophets and men of God acted as statesmen and counselors to kings and princes. Both the people and their leaders were looking to God for his help, guidance, and the fulfillment of his promises.

Indeed, in the olden days writing was in its infancy and learned men were few. Therefore the prophets wrote in a simple, pictorial, and clear style devoid of ifs, buts, and other qualifying clauses which often obscure the truth. They wrote in a plain manner, using short sentences, so that the simple and unlearned folk might understand their messages, heed their admonitions, and turn from their evil ways. Indeed, these courageous men of God did not hide anything from the people, neither were they afraid of kings and princes, who were often opposed to God's truth and reforms.

In other words, the authors of the Bible were not interested in literary style or degrees. Their main objective was to impart the revealed truths to the ears and eyes of a people who thought and spoke in simple speech and who counted numerals on their fingers. And yet the beauty and the style of the Bible has never been surpassed. No one has since been able to write or produce such an inspiring and lasting literature.

Nevertheless, the Bible contains many expressions and mannerisms of speech, many local idioms that no foreigner without the knowledge of the background of ancient Semitic languages and of the issues which existed during the times of the author could understand. In the same way, of course, American customs and ways of life are difficult for a foreigner to understand.

For example, three thousand years ago the psalmist wrote: "They that sow in tears shall reap in joy. He who goes forth and weeps, bearing precious seed, shall doubtless come again with rejoicing, bringing his sheaves with him" [Ps. 126:5, 6]. The people who heard these words certainly understood what the psalmist meant. In Palestine every family in one way or another felt the scarcity of bread during the sowing season, when the family food supplies which had been stored in the fall were exhausted and the children at home were crying for bread. Even today in the East the farmers weep as they scatter the precious seed into the ground, while their children at home are starving. But during the harvest season, the tears change to joy, and on the first day of the harvest the people celebrate because bread is abundant and the children are filled and happy.

The people in biblical lands suffer from famine, but the people in America suffer from overeating. Today no American minister or Bible student would ever know why the sower wept as he scattered the seed. American farmers sing while they sow and plant, and they are seldom short of bread. In the United States the only problem is what to do with the surplus wheat and other food supplies.

Paul wrote to Philemon: ". . . put it on my account. I, Paul, have written this with my own hand; I will repay it" [Verses 18-19]. Philemon understood what Paul meant by "put it on my account." In Aramaic it means, forget it. The last part of the verse proves that Philemon owed Paul a great debt, his conversion to Christ. Yet Western commentators have pictured Philemon as a banker and moneylender from whom Paul borrowed money. Today in English we say, "Write it on the cuff."

When one of Jesus' disciples said to him, "Lord, suffer me first to go and bury my father" [Matt. 8:21-22]. Jesus knew that what he meant was, "Let me take care of my father until he dies." Western Bible scholars have been teaching that this man's father had just died and Jesus was not interested in seeing him buried. Had the man's father been dead already he would have been busy burying him instead of listening to Jesus; and Jesus himself might have been one of the mourners.

On another occasion Jesus said, "And if thy right hand offends thee, cut it off and cast it from thee" [Matt. 5:30]. The people who heard this would never cut off hands or feet or pluck out one of their eyes. They knew that what Jesus meant was to do away with stealing, with envy, and trespassing on other men's properties. In many Western countries these idioms were taken literally, but there is no mention in the Bible that any of Jesus' disciples or followers ever inflicted such injuries on their bodies.

It is natural that such idioms should be mistranslated or misinterpreted. And, just as the Aramaic idioms and metaphors are hard for Westerners, so English, French, and German idioms are hard for Easterners to understand. For instance, no Easterner would understand such English phrases as these: "He lost his shirt," "He died on third base," "He was born with a silver spoon in his mouth," "He is in hot water," "He was chewing the rag." Many other such sayings bewilder foreign students.

On the other hand, idioms, metaphors, parables, and poetic phrases when translated from one language into another often lose their original meaning. This is because it is difficult to find equivalent words to give the same shade of meaning. Then again parables are derived from customs of the people which sometimes have no equivalent in other countries. For example, Jesus said, "No one knows when the bridegroom and bride come to the house of the wedding." Westerners do know the hour of the ceremonies, but in the East no one knows the time simply because no one knows when the bridegroom and bride would be bathed and clothed in their wedding garments. At times it may take hours before one can procure water. On the other hand, Easterners are never concerned about the time, nor are they prompt in keeping their engagements. Time is of no particular importance.

Therefore, the reader of the English Bible must remember that he is reading a translation of a translation of a translation of the Holy Bible into a totally alien and modern language—a language which did not even exist when the Bible was written. Thus he is bewildered when he reads contradictory and repulsive sayings. For example, in Matthew's Gospel he is told to love and honor his father and his mother and to love even his enemies, but in the Gospel of Luke he is admonished to hate his father, his mother, his wife, his children and the rest of his relatives in order to be a loyal follower of Jesus. And yet we know Jesus was not a teacher of hatred, b.' a teacher of love. He even reversed a Mosaic ordinance when he said, "Love your enemies and pray for those who hate you" [Matt. 5:44].

The Aramaic word *saney*, hate, is written like the word "put aside" [Luke 14:26]. Indeed, there are many words in Aramaic which have several meanings. For example, the Aramaic word *gmorta*, means "a loaf of bread," "wafer," and "coals of fire." In a liturgical work published in England, it has been translated, "coals of fire" instead of "wafers," and the priest must kiss the coals. These words are written alike, but their meaning is different. And some of these words do not appear in the Old Testament or the Pauline epistles. This is because Jesus used simple words, phrases, and idioms which were not often used by other writers. After all, Jesus was addressing the common people, the unlearned, the ones whom the priests and Pharisees called, "the accursed people."

The Easterners knew that "casting pearls before swine" meant speaking words of wisdom to fools. All these figures of speech are still in use in the Bible lands. But in Western languages words change and, like cars, become obsolete. In the East we still say, "He flew over the river," which means he crossed the river. All languages have similar problems. For example, many English words have several meanings: fresh, peach, led, saw, sow, and light. The meaning of such words is always determined by the context. For years missionaries have been confronted by many difficulties in converting Moslems, Jews, and many other races to Christianity. They don't realize that among the greatest obstacles in the way of non-Christians are the mistranslations and contradictions in various Bible versions. Even ancient Christians in the Near East, Assyrians and Armenians, were horrified when they read in the Bible translations that were given to them that one must hate his father, his mother, his wife, his brother, and his children in order to be a follower of Jesus Christ. Hundreds of Bibles were burned because of such mistranslations.

Some Westerners may say, "When Jesus said thus and so he did not mean it." Such an answer might be acceptable in the West, but not in the East. This is because the Easterners believe that the Bible is the Word of God and they well know that the prophets, Jesus, and his apostles meant what they said. Who are we to say that they meant this but they did not mean that? Then again, Easterners love their fathers and mothers and the rest of their relatives.

We must also remember that both the Old and the New Testaments were written by different prophets and disciples at different periods of history. The five books of Moses were written about a thousand years before the book of Malachi, the last book in the Old Testament. When Moses wrote, he and the Hebrews were wandering in a harsh and waste desert, while Malachi was living and writing under the rule of a mighty and well-organized empire, the Persian Empire, which had championed the cause of the Jews. Moreover, the world had advanced in its culture and its institutions.

Therefore, the readers of the Scriptures must know something about the geographical conditions, political situations, and the influences of the period in which any given portion of Scripture was written. In other words, there were many current issues which both the writer and his original readers understood. There was no need to explain such issues and the underlying causes that had created them.

Today we are living in a mechanized world. The wooden threshing instrument is forever gone; cars, trucks, and planes have replaced donkeys, mules, camels, carts, and oxen. Today because of our scientific knowledge and our abundant supply of wheat, no farmer ties the mouths of his oxen; no one ever sees a donkey's mill or a threshing sledge, and many people have not seen an ass. The women no longer sit behind the stone, grinding their meal. No, most of them do not bother even to cook a meal. And no virgins carry lamps to greet the bridegroom and bride. The day in which wine and milk and butter were stored in sheepskins is gone; the skins are replaced by glass containers which never burst. The whole way of life has changed from biblical days. And the change has left a chasm of 3,500 years between us and the time when some portions of the Bible were written.

This commentary is an attempt to bridge that chasm. It covers hundreds of passages, some of which have lost their meaning through mistranslation; some because idioms are translated literally, and others because of the lack of knowledge of the background, customs, manners, metaphors, issues, and allegories which existed during the time of the writer. Still others are due to the lack of knowledge of the Semitic languages and the subtle and allegorical ways through which the Word of God is interwoven and imparted.

My primary objective in this work, just as it was in *Gospel Light* and *New Testament Commentary*, is to take the reader to biblical lands and to let him see and understand the Bible through Eastern eyes.

Since this work is prepared for all the readers of the greatest of all books, the Bible, I have avoided doctrinal and theological matters. And, as I have said in other works, I believe in Jesus Christ, his divinity, his miracles and wonders, and his power as the Saviour of the world. And it is because of these firm beliefs that I have spent nearly all my life in studying, translating, and commenting on the Bible. I am more interested in putting Jesus' teachings into practice than in arguing about them.

This work, like my former books, is based on the Eastern or Semitic understanding of the Bible, the Aramaic culture from which it sprang, and the Semitic languages in which it was written by the holy prophets who were inspired by God.

I believe that when we know the truth the truth will set us free from doubt, contradictions, controversies, and strife and will unite us for a common cause to hasten the reign of God, the reign of peace, justice, and righteousness for which Jesus and the prophets died.

Today, is the day of decision—a crucial day. We must either save the world or see it destroyed—not by natural disasters and calamities, but by the implements we have devised with our own hands. Nothing but God's arm, God's light, and God's truth, which is in his Book—the Holy Bible—can save us.

The author is grateful to hundreds of men and women who have enabled him to complete this work and his translation of the Bible. He is also grateful to the United States of America and to its free institutions.

George M. Lamsa

CHAPTER ONE

GENESIS

INTRODUCTION

GENESIS is the first book of the "Pentateuch," a Greek translation of the Aramaic or biblical term *Khamsha Seprey di Moshey*, "the five books of Moses." They are also called Torah, the law, or the books of the law of Moses.

Genesis in Aramaic is *Berita*, "the creation." Even though the primary objective of the author of it is to give the Jews the history of their ancestors, he included in his work an account of the creation of heaven and earth and all that are therein. This was necessary in order to give the genealogies of the patriarchs and of Abraham, the father and founder of the Hebrew race, and to picture their ancestral and cultural background and their language and religion. The author traces Abraham's ancestry back to Adam and to the divine promises which God made to Eve [Gen. 3:15].

Evidently, some of the portions of the book of Genesis were handed down orally, others were written during the time of Moses. The whole work was guided by a divine revelation and God's inspiration. The author's aim was not to explain God's creations from a scientific point of view, but to give his people an idea that the Lord God of Israel was the creator of the heavens and the earth and that the pagan gods could not create and therefore were false gods created by men.

There are two accounts of the creation in the book of Genesis. The first is the spiritual account. God acted as a God, creating everything by his command. The second is an explanation or a commentary on the first. For many centuries the two accounts of the creation and other sacred materials were handed down on separate scrolls or tablets; and only after many years were they combined into a single work. Moreover, some of these accounts were written by different scribes. Marginal notes were often incorporated into the text and copied by later scribes. For example: "The prayers of David the son of Jesse are ended" [Ps. 72:20]. This note was written to facilitate the reading of the book. "The burden

1

of Babylon, which Isaiah the son of Amoz did see" [Isa. 13:1]. "The burden of Moab" [Isa. 15:1]. "The burden of Damascus" [Isa. 17:1]. And many other such instances are scribal notes which were copied into the book.

ETERNITY

In the beginning God created the heaven and the earth. Gen. 1:1

This should read, "God created the heavens and the earth in the very beginning." God is the subject of the sentence and the heavens and the earth are objects. The author states that the heavens and the earth were created from the very beginning. That is, before the sun and the moon and the stars were created. In other words the heavens and the earth were created before time.

God alone can reveal to man how and when the heavens and the earth were created. Some scientists place the age of the earth at four billion years. Humanly speaking, four billion years are eternity. Many aspects of the creation will remain a secret which man will never be able to unlock or reveal. Neither Jesus Christ nor the Hebrew prophets tried to explain the mystery of the creation, but they believed that God created them and that God can destroy them if he wishes.

ESSENCE WITHOUT FORM

And the earth was without form, and void; and darkness was upon the face of the deep. And the Spirit of God moved upon the face of the waters.   Gen. 1:2

The earth may have suffered some catastrophic disturbances as the result of inner stresses, such as volcanic eruptions and earthquakes. The surface of the moon reveals such marks of volcanic disturbances. Be that as it may, seemingly the earth was devoid of the forces and equilibrium which make order and life possible.

The first order might have been overthrown just as God overthrew Sodom and Gomorrah (Aramaic, *Amorah*) in the days of Abraham.

Moreover, the formless matter may have been in existence ages before order and life appeared upon the face of the earth. The creation of the firmament, the sun, moon, and stars, made order and time and life possible. In other words, we may conclude that at the outset the earth was not capable of producing life and it lacked precision and harmony. "Behold, the Lord shall destroy the earth and lay it waste and turn it upside down and scatter its inhabitants" [Isa. 24:1]. "I beheld the earth, and lo, it was without form, and void; and the heavens, and they had no light" [Jer. 4:23].

The Aramaic word *yath* means "essence," "being," "existence," and "substance"; Hebrew is *eth*. The Greek is *ousia,* and English "it," implying the origin or substance of a thing.

According to the Eastern text, God first created the essence of the heaven and the earth, and the physical or the material form and order came later. This indicates that the essence of heaven and earth existed from the very beginning. God was always manifested through his spiritual creations, out of which the terrestrial creations came into being.

The second verse literally reads: "And the earth was (or came to be) without form and void"; that is to say, empty or desolate, nothing but confusion and chaos. But the essence or the creative force was there.

The Aramaic *Toh opboh, Heb boho,* and Arabic *bahiya,* means emptiness; that is, empty of form but not lacking an essence. The essence is spiritual, eternal, and indestructible, but the form is changeable, temporary, and destructible and depends on the essence which governs it.

LIGHT

And God said, Let there be light: and there was light. Gen. 1:3

Bahra, "shining," light in this instance, means enlightenment. That is, the light and the knowledge of God and moral law. Darkness in Aramaic is symbolical of ignorance, superstition, and evil.

For many centuries man felt the presence of God or of a great governing force, but he knew little or nothing about his being, the natural forces around him, and the moral law.

The author of Genesis tells us that the sun was created on the fourth day, and yet, there were evening and morning on the previous days. Thus, "first day" or "second day" means a unit of time, or a period based on the then seven known planets. The sun was created on the fourth day, after the trees and grass were created.

Then again, we must remember that the early man knew nothing about our present calendar of 365 days. For many centuries the moon served as the only yardstick for measuring time. Nomad people still rely on the moon for their grazing and migrations. The Hebrews and the Moslems still use the lunar calendar.

The present calendar was developed only after man's scientific knowledge had advanced. That is, when the Babylonian and Egyptian scientists discovered that the sun and not the earth was the center of our solar system. This discovery was made more than twenty centuries B.C., long before Abraham left Ur of Chaldea.

DARKNESS

And God called the light Day, and the darkness he called Night.
And the evening and the morning were the first day.   Gen. 1:5

Darkness is temporal and unreal and is merely the shadow of the earth. There is always sun and light above the earth. And since the darkness is relevant to the spinning of the earth, it cannot exist in the mind of God. But it does exist in man's mind.

Therefore, man saw the difference between the light and the darkness. God sees light. Darkness has no existence in the realm of the spirit. Darkness is relative to the position of the earth with respect to the sun.

Light is symbolic of truth and understanding and darkness is symbolic of ignorance and misunderstanding [Verse 1].

Through enlightenment and God's constant divine revelation and guidance man became aware of his Creator and finally of his own spiritual being and his relation to God.

The darkness or the evil forces still dominate man's mind and obscure his understanding of his Creator and the vast universe in which he lives. But in due time the darkness, or the evil forces, will be conquered by the light of God—the understanding of the spiritual man and the spiritual universe.

FIRMAMENT

And God made the firmament, and divided the waters which were
under the firmament from the waters which were above the firma-
ment: and it was so.   Gen. 1:7

The Babylonians and the Assyrians knew that the air in the firmament and the water in the sea and upon the land were of the same essence or nature. The water in the firmament is thinner or finer than the heavy water in the seas. This division is only relevant to the human mind and human eye. There is also another division: that is of ether and the air.

God's work was always perfect, but difficult to understand; but man's quest for knowledge has revealed many of its secrets. This is because man, being the child of God and made in his image and likeness, has power to analyze and understand all things round about him and above him. Man's knowledge comes from God. That is, God works through him.

VEGETATION, SEEDS, AND TREES

*And God said, Let the earth bring forth grass, the herb yielding
seed, and the fruit tree yielding fruit after his kind, whose seed is
in itself, upon the earth: and it was so.* Gen. 1:11

Vegetation, plants and trees, were created before the seeds thereof.
The plants and trees grow and reach perfection in order to develop and
produce perfect seeds. In other words, plants and trees are more or less
finite, but the seed is somewhat infinite.

The little seed contains all the secrets of the plants and trees, their
color and their design, in a manner that cannot be explained. Then
again, the creative germ in seeds is just as secretive and unknown as
the creative spark in man.

On the other hand, the seed can be kept for a long time and then
planted again. Moreover, the seeds know the secrets of the sun, the
water, and the soil. The seeds know how to harness the sun's rays and
bore into rocks with chemical substances.

TIME AND SEASONS

*And God said, Let there be lights in the firmament of the heaven
to divide the day from the night; and let them be for signs, and for
seasons, and for days, and years.* Gen. 1:14

Prior to the creation of the heavens and earth, time was nonexistent.
Without the creation of the heavens and the earth there would have
been no events, no periods, no phases of the moon whereby to reckon
time. Time and space came into existence during the creation.

Time, days and years, were made by God for man's convenience. In
God's eyes a thousand years are but as yesterday, and one day with God
is as a thousand years. The psalmist says, "A thousand years in thy sight
are but as yesterday when it is past, and as a watch in the night"
[Ps. 90:4]. That is, God, being from everlasting to everlasting, is not
subject to time and space.

The term *zabney,* "time," here means "periods." The term *attwata,*
"signs," refers to the stars and planets which stand in the sky like landmarks on the earth.

Shanah, "year," is a unit of time. The Aramaic word for change is
shani. Shanah denotes the change from one period or season to another.
The biblical day was made up from sunset to sunset. According to the

Hebrew calendar, a day is the period from one sunset to the next. Undoubtedly, this division of time was made after the sun was created and its movements studied by man. All of God's work was finished in six days.

Note, the week is not mentioned in this account of creation. Weeks and other subdivisions in time were made later. Night watches and hours were not known until day and night were further divided and our first calendar was instituted. The first mention of a smaller unit of time occurs in the Bible during the time of King Ahaz. It was known as a degree on the sundial [2 Kings 20:10]. The term *shaa*, "hour," first occurs in Daniel 3:6.

Seasons were familiar to man from the very beginning, just as they are familiar today to savage tribes and to the illiterate nomads who have little or no knowledge of calendars. They rely on the seasons to mark the passage of time.

The sun, moon, and stars were created for days, months, and seasons, but it took man a long time to discover their movements. It took man many centuries before he discovered that the sun is the center of the universe. In the ninth century after Christ an Assyrian bishop (Mar Eshak) wrote a book in which he warned the Christians against the teaching of the Chaldean astrologers that the sun is the center of the universe. The Hebrews believed the earth was the center.

DIVISION IN THE SKY

And God set them in the firmament of the heaven to give light upon the earth,
And to rule over the day and over the night, and to divide the light from the darkness: and God saw that it was good.

Gen. 1:17-18

All these divisions exist only in the human mind. God, being the Light, Spirit, and Truth, cannot behold anything contrary to his nature.

As man grew in wisdom and understanding he began to understand the nature of the forces around him and the purpose of their creation. But in his studies of God's creations or God's work, he studied everything in relation to himself. We often think of darkness as an evil, and yet only during the dark hours of the night can we find rest from our toil of the day and see the glorious works of God, the stars and the planets. In the realm of the spirit all things are good because they all exist of necessity.

DRAGONS OR SEA MONSTERS

And God created great whales, and every living creature that moveth, which the waters brought forth abundantly, after their kind, and every winged fowl after his kind: and God saw that it was good. Gen. 1:21

Tanina means "dragon," metaphorically, a devil. But when used astronomically it means the constellation Draco, one of the major constellations.

The Aramaic word is *leviathan,* a sea monster, and metaphorically, a devil. "Whale" was used here by the King James translators simply because the whale was the only great sea monster with which they were familiar.

IMAGE

And God said, Let us make man in our image, after our likeness: and let them have dominion over the fish of the sea, and over the fowl of the air, and over the cattle, and over all the earth, and over every creeping thing that creepeth upon the earth. Gen. 1:26

Nasha, "man," is derived from the Aramaic word *nishmtha,* "breath," that is, the breath of life. Only in his spirituality and his eternity is man the image and the likeness of God. That is, the breath of God, being spiritual and eternal, makes him spiritual and eternal.

God does not create anything opposite or contrary to himself. God has no hands, feet, or eyes, no flesh; neither does he sleep or walk as he has often been pictured. He is often reduced to human terms in order that man may understand him.

God is spirit and is all-knowing, all-hearing, all-seeing. Therefore, man knows, hears, and sees because of the eternal spirit of God which is in him. Physical man knows nothing more than his own image and likeness, but the spiritual man is constantly conscious of his spiritual likeness and his greatness.

Image in this instance means "likeness" or "resemblance." God has been portrayed as having hands, eyes, ears, feet, and nose in order that man may understand him in relation to himself. God's image is spiritual, that is, characterized by intelligence and knowledge. Earthly man is temporal and mortal, but the spirit of God which dwells in him is immortal and real. Moreover, man is conscious of his Creator and knows evil and good. None of God's other creatures are endowed with this knowledge, nor are they governed by moral law.

Man, being in the image and the likeness of God, has power and dominion over all of God's creations.

ADAM

So God created man in his own image, in the image of God created he him; male and female created he them.   Gen. 1:27

In the preceding verse the name of the man is called *nasha*, derived from the Aramaic word *nishmtha*, "breath"; that is, the breath of life, the spirit of God which dwells in man and which makes him in the image and the likeness of his Creator. In verse 27, the term "man" is used collectively, meaning humanity or mankind.

Adam means "red soil," that is, a man formed out of the ground.

According to the first chapter of Genesis, both Adam and Eve were created spiritually by the word of God just as he had created all other things. That is to say, the spiritual man was not formed out of the dust of the ground. For in the first chapter we read, "God created man in his own image, . . . male and female created he them." God's image has nothing to do with the ground.

The creation of man took place on the sixth day, and everything was perfect and good. In other words man was the last of the creations of God. God blessed them and told them to multiply and gave them dominion over all his creations. Thus, the first chapter gives us a true picture of creation and of God as Creator. Here God gives commands and everything is done according to his will, whereas in the second chapter, God works with his hands like a man.

The second account of creation is a commentary on the first chapter. I believe it is the work of a later writer who tried to explain man's creation in a symbolical manner so that the people might understand it. This account is old and it has a spiritual value. It was placed next to the first chapter simply because it is a commentary on it. Some people believe the second account of the creation contradicts the first, but this is not true. The second account is written figuratively from the human point of view in order to explain the first account, which is spiritual and in which God works as God and not as a man.

The reader must remember that the Bible is a library containing hundreds of writings written at different times by different authors. No inspired Hebrew writer could have thought of God literally mixing soil and forming man out of it. But Hebrew prophets often portrayed God as a man planting vineyards or trees, or doing other manual work.

SEEDS

And God said, Behold, I have given you every herb bearing seed, which is upon the face of all the earth, and every tree, in the which is the fruit of a tree yielding seed; to you it shall be for meat.

Gen. 1:29

Plants, and the seeds thereof, were created on the third day. Note that man was created on the sixth day. The green herbs and fruit-bearing trees were created for food. The early men lived on plants and fruits. Moreover, man had authority over beasts, birds, and creeping things, but man's sustenance was first derived from vegetables and fruits. Eating meat may have come later, when man's needs for food increased, or because of famine.

Later, every moving thing that lives is given for food [Gen. 9:3, 4]. In Genesis 3:21 we read that God made skin garments for Adam and his wife and clothed them with them. The skins might have been the skins of sheep which were slain for food.

Be that as it may, Adam and Eve ate vegetables and fruits at first. Many varieties of edible herbs and fruit trees grow in the region of the Garden of Eden north of Mosul, Iraq. Most of the seeds of the trees and vegetables were carried by the Roman armies to Europe from the Garden of Eden.

GENESIS—CHAPTER 2

The second chapter of Genesis is not a contradiction of the first, but an explanation thereof. The first chapter came to us from a divine source and hence is a divine revelation from God. God talks and acts like a God. He speaks the word and things are done.

In the East, spiritual and abstract things are illustrated in parables, allegories, and metaphors. God is often pictured as a potter who mixes clay and makes vessels. This is the only way to convey the spiritual idea of God and his creations to simple folk who live in desert lands, who had heard about the seas but never had seen one, who had eaten fruit, but never had seen the trees on which it grew. How can one lecture to a desert tribe about a ship without drawing a picture of it and making a small sea to show it floating on the water?

If we think that both chapters of Genesis are the work of the same author and that both are God's revelation, then one chapter contradicts the other.

SIXTH DAY—NOT SEVENTH

*And on the seventh day God ended his work which he had made;
and he rested on the seventh day from all his work which he had
made.*   Gen. 2:2

The Eastern text reads: "And on the sixth day God finished his works
which he had made; and he rested on the seventh day from all his works
which he had made."

The Aramaic word "sixth" is confused with "seventh." Had God
finished his work on the seventh day, he would have been working on
that day, that is Friday which in Aramaic means "the week-end day."
But God finished all his work on the sixth day; therefore, he rested on
the seventh day and blessed it because he did no work on it.

The author of Genesis tells us: "So God blessed the seventh day, and
sanctified it; because that in it he had rested from all his work which
God created and made." Rested in this instance means ceased. God was
not tired of working, but he completed his work.

The Sabbath was strictly observed from 6:00 P.M. [Luke 23:54; John
19:31].

The Jews worked six days but, according to the Mosaic law, they
rested from their work on the seventh day.

"Remember the Sabbath day, to keep it holy."

"Six days shall you labor and do all your work; . . ."

"For in six days the Lord made heaven and earth, the sea, and all
that is in them, and rested the seventh day; . . ." [Exod. 20:8-11].

"Six days you shall do your work, but on the seventh day you shall
rest . . ." [Exod. 23:12].

As we can see from the Holy Scripture, no portion of God's work was
left to be done on the seventh day. The end of his work was on the
sixth day.

Peshitta, the pure, the original, is the only text which reads: "On
the sixth day God finished his work which he had made . . ."

GOD BLESSED THE SEVENTH DAY

*And God blessed the seventh day, and sanctified it: because that
in it he had rested from all his work which God created and made.*
                                                          Gen. 2:3

Some Eastern commentators state that God blessed the seventh day
simply because he did not do any work on that day. The other days
were blessed by the work of his hands. Thus, the Jews observed the

seventh day because God rested from his work and sanctified it. That is, he put it aside as a holy day wherein all men may rest from their work and worship their Creator.

All days in the week are holy, but the Sabbath day was declared to be the most holy because on that day the Lord himself ceased or rested from his work.

During the course of time the Sabbath came to be the most important institution in Jewish religion. Commentaries upon commentaries were written on its observances. Years later it became so sacred that even works of mercy such as healing could not be performed on the Sabbath day [Luke 13:14].

Jesus said, "The Sabbath was made for the sake of man, and not man for the sake of the Sabbath" [Mark 2:27].

THE TERM LORD

And every plant of the field before it was in the earth, and every herb of the field before it grew: for the Lord God had not caused it to rain upon the earth, and there was not a man to till the ground.
Gen. 2:5

Yhowh, Lord, is a new name of God. In the olden days God was known as *El.* In the first chapter of Genesis his name in Hebrew is *Elohim* and in Aramaic *Alaha.*

Yhowh is derived from *Hayah,* "to be," and thus suggests the eternal God as the essence of all life and existence. The term *Yhowh* is so holy that the Hebrews never dared to pronounce it. They used the term *Adonay,* "the Lord."

The Hebrew patriarchs used the term *El.* Jacob called Lus, a town in Palestine, Bethel, the house of God. Isaiah called the Messiah *Ammanuel,* "God is with us." *Elohim* is a later name, and is a plural form. The Hebrews during the time of the conquest of Palestine believed in the existence of other gods, but they maintained that *Yahveh* was the God of gods [Josh. 22:22]. God standeth in the congregation of the mighty; he judgeth among the gods. (Aramaic—"He judges among the angels.")

Again and again, the Hebrews lost their pure concept of monotheism and worshiped pagan gods. But the Hebrew prophets constantly fought against their idolatry.

MIST

But there went up a mist from the earth, and watered the whole face of the ground.   Gen. 2:6

Aramaic reads: "But a powerful spring gushed out of the earth and watered all the face of the ground."

Many lands in the Near East are watered by the mist or *telala*, Hebrew *tal*. Palestine, the land of Moab and the land of Ammon, and many other desert lands still depend on the dew which falls in the early morning for irrigation [Prov. 3:20; Zech. 8:12].

This chapter is the result of God's revelation and man's study of the earth and the universe. All things are revealed in the fullness of time.

The earth existed before the rivers and the brooks. Undoubtedly, the early Babylonian scientists knew that the rivers and streams were formed by the flow of waters back into the seas and oceans from which the mist rises and covers the earth. Where there is no water there are no river beds or courses.

FORMED MAN

And the Lord God, formed man of the dust of the ground, and breathed into his nostrils the breath of life; and man became a living soul.   Gen. 2:7

The creation of man and woman are described in the first chapter. "Male and female created he them." This is recorded as the work of God, *El* or *Elohim*, the universal God. But in the second chapter we read about *Yahveh*, the Lord. This term was known to the Hebrews only after the Exodus from Egypt. The Hebrew patriarchs had never used it. *Elohim* or *El*, the God of Abraham, Isaac, and Jacob, is a universal God, the Creator and the source of life.

But *Yahveh*, the Lord, was a tribal god with limited powers. He was stronger than the lords (gods) of other nations; but at times he was limited to geographical location. He was the Lord of the mountainous areas who could not direct a battle in the plain. The Hebrews in Egypt had lost some of their knowledge of the God of their forefathers. Moses didn't even know the name of the deity of his people until God told him. "I am AHIAH ASHAR HIAH THE LIVING GOD, the One which always has been."

This second account of creation is based on the Jehovistic idea of God, a tribal God. In other words, God is portrayed as a man limited in his powers and knowledge.

GARDEN OF EDEN

And the Lord God planted a garden eastward in Eden; and there he put the man whom he had formed.   Gen. 2:8

The term Eden is derived from *Edan*, "a moment" or "a season"; that is, "time." It also means "pleasant," "delight," and "temporal." Material pleasures are delightful, but they are temporal.

The author of Genesis places the location of the Garden between the two historic rivers, the River Euphrates and the River Tigris. The Garden is the fertile land between these two great rivers in the region north of Iraq (Kurdistan) where vegetables and trees grow without being planted or cultivated. Rhubarb, asparagus, green peas, celery, tulips,[1] a kind of endive, and many other varieties of vegetables grow wild in the basins of these two great rivers. Wheat and cotton also grow in the area. Moreover, grapes, pears, apples, almonds, figs, and walnuts and many other trees are plentiful. Medicinal herbs are also collected here by both native and foreign doctors.

This is why this region was called the Garden of Eden, or Paradise, derived from a Persian word *pardesa*, meaning a "park" or "garden." This region in northern Iraq is like a paradise compared with the parched lands of Arabia, Syria, and Palestine. Water is abundant. Besides the two great rivers, there are many streams and brooks and the climate is temperate, dry, and healthful.

This region became the symbol of a delightful land abounding with trees, vineyards, vegetables, and water. The Garden of Eden was also called the Garden of God. This is because God planted the trees and vegetables and made it beautiful in every way [Ezek. 31:9].

THE TREE OF LIFE

And out of the ground made the Lord God to grow every tree that is pleasant to the sight, and good for food; the tree of life also in the midst of the garden, and the tree of knowledge of good and evil.   Gen. 2:9

In Semitic languages, trees are often symbolic of human beings. Vines mean nations, cedars mean kings. Israel is often called a vine or a vineyard [Isa. 5:1; Matt. 21:33].

The "tree of life" might mean man's progeny, rather than an ordinary tree. The tree of life is not included in the trees which were good for

---

[1] Tulip bulbs are eaten, especially when other foods are scarce.

food. The clause reads, "the tree of life also in the midst of the garden, and the tree of the knowledge of good and evil." These two trees were different from all other trees and therefore were used metaphorically.

The breaking of the divine command against eating from the tree[2] in the center of the garden was to result in the discovery of the tree of knowledge; that is, the knowledge of good and evil, or the moral law. Before this Adam and Eve know only good.

Then again, it was the serpent, Satan [Gen. 3:4-5], who told Eve that eating from the tree in the midst of the garden would endow her with the knowledge of good and evil. Hitherto, Adam and Eve knew nothing about evil, neither is there mention that God created anything evil or likely to cause evil. The Scriptures state that everything which God created was very good [Gen. 1:31].

The breaking of the divine command gave man a wrong concept of sex, which has been the cause of the downfall of man.

Indeed, when Adam and Eve transgressed against the law of God, they did become wise. They found themselves naked and beset with problems and difficulties of life which hitherto had never occurred in their minds. In other words, their eyes were opened to the evil they had created. These passages should not be taken literally.

The breaking of the divine command gave man a wrong idea about the relations of a man and his wife. Intercourse was a necessity and a blessing. God created them male and female, and blessed them, and told them to multiply. But the disobedience to God's command caused Adam and Eve to fall.

It was not the eating of the fruit, but the breaking of the moral law which made Adam and Eve sin.

In the East, parts of the human body are often described metaphorically. A woman is often called a garden. "Awake, O north wind . . . blow upon my garden. . . . Let my beloved come to his garden" [Song of Sol. 4:16].

When the divine command was broken, Eve conceived a child, Cain, who became the first man to shed blood upon the earth. Adam and Eve were not spiritually mature enough to bring a child into the world. They listened to the serpent (evil) instead of listening to God.

[2] Darius, king of Persia, in the fourth century B.C., warned one of his officials who was transferring trees and plants from the region of the Garden of Eden east of the River Euphrates to Asia Minor.

During the Roman occupation of some of the lands adjacent to the Garden area, the Roman generals also transferred many varieties of plants and trees to Italy.

PISON

The name of the first is Pison: that is it which compasseth the whole land of Havilah, where there is gold;
And the gold of that land is good: there is bdellium and the onyx stone. Gen. 2:11-12

The Aramaic reads, *Pishon.* The difference here is due to the Hebrew and Arabic languages where *sh* is often pronounced as *s.*

Havilah might be the region of the River Zab, a tributary of the Tigris. Zab means gold. A metal called beryllium is found here. It has been wrongly translated bdellium. The error was caused by the confusion of the letters *resh* (*R*) with *daleth* (*D*). These two letters are almost identical. There are four rivers which merge together and become the Tigris and Euphrates.

The land of Havilah might be a region in eastern Mesopotamia or in Arabia. The author of Genesis was describing fertile areas or deltas which were suitable for human habitation. There is a river in north-western Iraq called Peshawer.

The names of rivers, like the names of seas and cities, often change. At times, when famous cities were conquered, the conqueror gave them new names.

GIHON

And the name of the second river is Gihon: the same is it that compasseth the whole land of Ethiopia. Gen. 2:13

The name of the second river is Gihon. The Semitic name for Ethiopia is *Cush.* The regions of Midian and Yemen were known as *Cush.* The Ethiopians ruled southwestern Arabia for many years. Gihon might be the Nile which compasses the land of Ethiopia.

Then again, Cush is mentioned in Genesis 10:8 as the father of Nimrod, whose kingdom began in Babylon, and Erech, Accad (Aramic *Accar, Akar*), and Calneh, in the land of Shinar. Cush might originally have been an ancient region in Assyria named after Cush, the father of Nimrod. The present Ethiopia was unknown and uninhabited at this time. Mankind had not yet multiplied and spread over the face of the whole earth. These rivers might be named after the original rivers in and around the Garden of Eden, by the people who migrated from there, as in the case of English and American cities.

HIDDEKEL

And the name of the third river is Hiddekel: that is it which
goeth toward the east of Assyria. And the fourth river is Euphrates.
Gen. 2:14

The Hiddekel (Aramaic *deklat*) is another name for Tigris. *Dekley*
means palm trees. Mesopotamia (Iraq) is noted for date-bearing palms.
About four-fifths of all date palms grow in Iraq.

The Garden of Eden is near the sources of the River Tigris and the
River Euphrates in northern Iraq. Water is symbolic of light and life.
This fertile region was the first to be populated and thus became known
as the cradle of the human race. The inhabitants of this land were responsible for some of the greatest discoveries—notably, the alphabet, the
calendar, the chariot, military organizations, and many scientific discoveries.

The author of the book of Genesis located Eden in a region where
fruits of all kinds and vegetables grew wild. The desert Arabs live on
dates. The mountains are graced with fruit trees, vines, green peas,
rhubarb, celery, and scores of other varieties of vegetables. Moreover,
the climate is ideal and temperate.

Eden means "delight," or "temporal." This region is the most delightful one in that part of the world. "Paradise" is the Persian or Babylonian
word for garden, or an orchard spread on the ground. And "garden" is
often metaphorically used as meaning a wife [Song of Sol. 5:1].

See "Garden of Eden" [Gen. 2:8].

SPEECH

And the Lord God commanded the man, saying, Of every tree
of the garden thou mayest freely eat:
Gen. 2:16

All of God's communication with Adam and Eve took place in a divine
revelation or intuition. As long as Adam and Eve were obedient to God
and perfect, they perceived every command of God.

There was no language at that early time as we have today. All words
and languages were born out of human necessities in a gradual way.

This is also true of the prophets and men of God who, after overcoming their physical weaknesses, communed with God by means of
dreams and divine revelations. God spoke to Abraham, to Isaac, to
Jacob, and to Joseph in dreams and visions. At times the words and
ideas were conveyed in a symbolic language. Adam and Eve could hear
the inner voice speaking to them, guiding them and admonishing them.

GOOD AND EVIL

*But of the tree of the knowledge of good and evil, thou shalt
not eat of it: for in the day that thou eatest thereof thou shalt surely
die.*   Gen. 2:17

There is no record of anything evil being created by God. In the
Scriptures we are told that everything that God created was very good,
and since God is good and everything that he had created was good,
there would be no room for evil. In other words, God cannot be both
the author of good and the author of evil.

Evil was created through man's pride, disobedience, and desire for
power. Man was created with a free will and with ability to choose good
or evil. But man wanted to usurp God's authority and power and become like God. That is to say, man was not satisfied to hold a second
place. He wanted to become a god.

This is because man is never satisfied with his station in life. Even
when he becomes an emperor, he still craves more power and glory.
There is no limit to man's aspirations for wealth, glory, and power.
When a man becomes an emperor, then he craves to be worshiped as a
god. Many kings and emperors have proclaimed themselves deities and
were worshiped by their subjects.

The tree of knowledge of good and evil is sex, which has been the
cause of the downfall of many men and women. Man was to become
mature and spiritual before bringing another man into the world. Adam
and Eve transgressed against the moral law, and the first child they
bore became a criminal [Gen. 2:9].

Anything which is contrary to the law of God brings death and destruction upon man. Death separates man from God.

RIB

*And the rib, which the Lord God had taken from man, made he
a woman, and brought her unto the man.*   Gen. 2:22

The term "rib" metaphorically means "support," a "sustainer" or a
"helper" to stand by man and help him in a cold and hostile world.
The woman was created as a helpmate or as an assistant and, therefore,
she is man's rib because man leans on her just as the human body is
supported by ribs. In the first chapter of Genesis, we are told, "Male
and female created he them" [Gen. 1:27].

Causing of the sleep, surgery, and the rib are used in order to explain
the close similarities between man and woman. They both were created

by God as one. Humanly speaking, they are two, but spiritually, they are one. The woman has an extra rib simply because she needs more room in her body in order to be able to conceive and bear children. A woman is weaker than a man, but not inferior to him. All of God's creations were perfect and good. Both Adam and Eve were created in the image and likeness of God. The woman was blamed for the fall of man. In the East, women are blamed for everything.

LOYALTY TO THE WIFE

Therefore shall a man leave his father and his mother, and shall cleave unto his wife: and they shall be one flesh.   Gen. 2:24

This verse may have been copied from a marginal note revealed to a prophet or a man of God. At this early time, there were neither fathers nor mothers nor other women.

In the East, marginal notes are sometimes incorporated into new texts, especially if the writing is the work of a man of God. Scribes, who are the copyists, generally copy any important material which is written on the margin of the manuscript. In the early days before the scrolls were canonized, new material was inserted into the new scrolls.

The Old Testament was canonized at the Jewish Council of Jamnia about the end of first century after Christ.

According to the second chapter, woman was made from man's rib, and since she was made from man's rib, a man and his wife were one and not two.

Marriage was meant to be monogamous from the very beginning. God created one man and one woman only. Polygamy was a man-made ordinance dictated by man's physical desires and greed for power. Jesus disapproved of polygamy. He said, "Have you not read, that he who made them from the beginning made them male and female?" [Matt. 19:4-6; Mark 10:6-9].

Moreover, man must cleave to his wife, simply because it is not good that a man should be alone or take another man's wife and break his home.

In biblical days princes, kings, and powerful men took the wives of other men by force and deserted their own wives. No matter when this verse was revealed and written, it is one of God's commands. Jesus quoted it and upheld it as an original ordinance of God.

NAKED

*And they were both naked, the man and his wife, and were not
ashamed.*   Gen. 2:25

At this early stage, Adam and Eve knew nothing about sin. Everything which God had created was good and they also were good. Hence,
there was no concept of evil.

Sin, shame, and evil came as the result of transgression against God's
command. As long as the divine command was not broken, sin was
dormant and Adam and Eve were not ashamed of anything. Shame, like
sin, came through disobedience to the law of God. The term "naked"
also means "exposed" or "ashamed." There was nothing wherewith to
hide their sins from the presence of God.

SERPENT

*Now the serpent was more subtile than any beast of the field
which the Lord God had made. And he said unto the woman, Yea,
hath God said, Ye shall not eat of every tree of the garden?*
                                                            Gen. 3:1

Serpent, metaphorically, is another name for Satan, and is often used
in both written and vernacular speech. We often say, "He has been a
snake in my house," which means, "He has been an enemy in my house."
Jesus told his disciples that they could handle serpents, meaning enemies
[Mark 16:18]. The term Satan or "devil" was not known to the early
Hebrews, nor does it occur in the early books of the Bible.

Serpent, in this instance, is a symbol of man's deception and his rebellion against his Creator. Had God told Adam and Eve to eat of the
tree of knowledge of good and evil, they would not have eaten, because
they would have wanted to disobey him.

Man is not a robot to be ordered to do things. It is in his nature and
power to revolt even against his own Creator. This is because man has
the freedom and choice to do good or evil. In other words, the serpent
symbolizes man's false idea of himself, his wisdom, his greatness, and
his creative power. He felt that since he had dominion over everything,
why then should he obey a power greater than himself?

The serpent or snake is used in the place of Satan because the serpent
is the most subtle and wise creature on earth. It takes subtleness and
wisdom to deceive anyone. But no serpent is more wise or subtle than
man himself. Man has dominion over all of God's creations. And nothing
from outside can force man to be good or bad. Man is free to disobey
God or to obey God.

Some Bible authorities say the serpent was used by God as an agent to tempt Adam and Eve. If that is the case, why then should God curse it for fulfilling his mission? On the other hand, the serpent could not have conversed with Adam and Eve. James says, "God tempts no one" [James 1:13]. Temptations come from within.

ASHAMED

And he said, Who told thee that thou wast naked? Hast thou eaten of the tree, whereof I commanded thee that thou shouldest not eat?

And the man said, The woman whom thou gavest to be with me, she gave me of the tree, and I did eat. Gen. 3:11-12

In Aramaic "naked" also means "exposed." The serpent had promised Adam and Eve that when they had eaten from the fruit of the tree in the center of the garden their eyes would be open and they would become as gods, knowing good and evil.

Hitherto, Adam and Eve had known nothing but God. The term "evil" had not occurred to them. Everything which God had created around them was good. But now, when they transgressed God's commandment, they saw the counterpart of good—evil—and therefore they were naked; that is, ashamed. The breaking of any divine command brings remorse and shame.

Hitherto, sex was spiritual, but now physical desires were put above the spirit and the truth. Man had listened to the serpent; that is, the opposition to God's truth. Man was not yet spiritually mature enough to beget a child in his image and likeness.

In the first chapter, man was told to go and multiply and fill the earth, but fill it with perfect men and women. In other words, man was to reproduce a perfect and spiritual offspring like himself. But being disobedient to his Creator, he failed to reproduce his own image and likeness and thus brought sin into the world, and sin resulted in death.

SERPENT

And the Lord God said unto the serpent, Because thou hast done this, thou art cursed above all cattle, and above every beast of the field; upon thy belly shalt thou go, and dust shalt thou eat all the days of thy life:

And I will put enmity between thee and the woman, and between thy seed and her seed; it shall bruise thy head, and thou shalt bruise his heel. Gen. 3:14-15

"Serpent" in this instance means "deception" or "lie." In the olden days the terms "devil" and "Satan" were unknown, but the serpent was metaphorically used as an agent of evil forces. This is because the serpent is sly and wise.

The offspring of woman, Jesus Christ, was to crush its head; that is, evil was to be exposed and destroyed. God created no evil, therefore, evil itself is a falsehood. Jesus called the devil "a liar and father of lies" [John 8:44].

In the fullness of time the Spirit was to have victory and dominion over the flesh, and the spiritual man over the physical man. Messiah Christ was to crush the head of the serpent and save man from evil forces and bring him back to God.

SORROWS

Unto the woman he said, I will greatly multiply thy sorrow and thy conception; in sorrow thou shalt bring forth children; and thy desire shall be to thy husband, and he shall rule over thee.

Gen. 3:16

Sickness and sorrows are the result of sin. Just as God did not create the devil and sin, he is not the author of sickness and sorrows. The Eastern text reads "pain" instead of sorrows.

Disobedience to moral law weakens both man's mind and body and brings sickness and pain. Any departure from the truth brings suffering. We always regret when we do something which we should not have done.

Adam and Eve, after transgressing God's command, found themselves to be mortal and hence powerless. Hitherto, they were like angels, above the flesh and free from physical difficulties. It is the fear of sin and disobedience which gives sin death-power. To a spiritual man, death is a glorification or an ascension.

SORROWS AND THORNS

And unto Adam he said, Because thou hast hearkened unto the voice of thy wife, and hast eaten of the tree, of which I commanded thee, saying, Thou shalt not eat of it: cursed is the ground for thy sake; in sorrow shalt thou eat of it all the days of thy life;

Thorns also and thistles shall it bring forth to thee; and thou shalt eat the herb of the field. Gen. 3:17-18

Sorrows, thorns and sweat in Semitic languages mean difficulties in life. Constructive work is not a curse, and struggle is an élan of life. Man is blessed by the work of his hands. When God planted a garden in Eden, he put the man Adam there to work.

It was the disobedience to God's law, and sin, which made work a curse. The physical desires in life made sin dominant and life difficult and complicated.

Today, man's troubles are not due to his labor, but rather to the material and physical concept of life to which he has enslaved himself. Billions of dollars spent on wars and other useless implements of war, if spent on good things, would have made man's life easy and harmonious had he not fallen from the grace of God and disobeyed God's law and lost the true path of life.

DUST

In the sweat of thy face shalt thou eat bread, till thou return unto the ground; for out of it wast thou taken: for dust thou art, and unto dust shalt thou return.   **Gen. 3:19**

The Aramaic reads: "For dust you are, and to dust shall you return." According to the second chapter of Genesis, which is based on symbolism, mortal man was formed out of the ground and to the ground (soil) he was to return. This is because that which is of the earth is earthly and must return to the earth. But this rejoinder has nothing to do with the spiritual man created in the image and likeness of God. In the first chapter of Genesis, man is not created out of the ground, but out of the Spirit of God, and therefore he must return to God. Dust returns to dust, but the spirit returns to God who gave it [Eccles. 12:7].

This command was a punishment for the breaking of the moral law and profaning the body, which is the temple of the Spirit of God. The disobedience was the breaking of the trust in God's plan of perfect and spiritual creation. Now man and woman were left to rely on their own wisdom and to work their own salvation. Their sin brought death into the world.

BECOME AS ONE OF US

And the Lord God said, Behold, the man is become as one of us, to know good and evil: and now, lest he put forth his hand, and take also of the tree of life, and eat, and live for ever:
Therefore the Lord God sent him forth from the garden of Eden, to till the ground from whence he was taken.
So he drove out the man: and he placed at the east of the garden of Eden cherubim, and a flaming sword which turned every way, to keep the way of the tree of life.   **Gen. 3:22-24**

When the serpent, that is, evil forces, caused Adam and Eve to sin, he promised them that if they ate from the tree which was in the center of the garden, they would not die, but instead they would be as gods, knowing good and evil.

The serpent lied to them. Adam and Eve were to know the difference between good and evil and between obedience and disobedience, but they were not to become gods. Had the serpent's promise been true, he would have eaten from the tree himself. In other words, the serpent was a liar and he had to lie in order to cause the downfall of man.

"Behold, the man is become as one of us," was used sarcastically, quoting the lying words of the serpent. God knew that the fruit from a tree that he had created could not make mortal man a rival and god like himself. All these words were spoken to expose the lies. Adam and Eve were assured by the devil that if they ate from the tree in the certain part of the garden they would know good and evil, and now the serpent might tell them to eat from another tree to become gods.

God would not have created such a tree. Nor would he have been jealous because man might become like himself. All these ideas were put in the mind of man by the devil. The devil was jealous of man because man was created in the image of God and had dominion over all of God's creations.

Evil has no origin. The serpent was used allegorically. Man can create evil which comes back on him. Truth can conquer evil.

CAIN

And Adam knew Eve his wife; and she conceived, and bare Cain, and said, I have gotten a man from the Lord.
And she again bare his brother Abel. And Abel was a keeper of sheep, but Cain was a tiller of the ground. Gen. 4:1-2

Cain (Aramaic *Kain*) is derived from the Aramaic word *kana,* "to gain." The birth of the first child was a gain to Adam and Eve after the heavy loss and disgrace they had suffered in Eden.

The second son was named Abel (Aramaic *Habel*) "nothingness," or "a loss." The inner voice must have told Adam and Eve that they were soon to lose Abel.

Generally, in the East, when a man has two sons, the younger one usually feeds the sheep and the other works in the field raising food for the family. It was natural for Cain and Abel to have diverse occupations; one taking care of the sheep and the other farming.

FIRST OFFERING TO GOD

And in process of time it came to pass, that Cain brought of the fruit of the ground an offering unto the Lord.

And Abel, he also brought of the firstlings of his flock and of the fat thereof. And the Lord had respect unto Abel and to his offering:

But unto Cain and to his offering he had not respect. And Cain was very wroth, and his countenance fell.   Gen. 4:3-5

This is the first mention of an offering made to God. But the book of Genesis was written many centuries after Cain and Abel. Thus, the record of this first offering to God must have been handed down orally from father to son, just as many other biblical narratives were handed down orally when writing was unknown.

The Lord has no respect for persons and, as a loving Father, cannot be partial to his children. There must have been other reasons for the rejection of Cain's sacrifice than the sacrifice itself.

Cain offered the fruits of the ground, and Abel the firstlings of the flock. Both brothers offered what was within the reach of their hands. But Cain was rebellious in his heart. He was the first offspring of Adam and Eve after they had transgressed against the divine law of God. Evil was in his heart. God has no pleasure in animal or meal offerings. What he wants is a pure and sincere heart, and mercy and justice. Cain was born merciless and unjust.

On the other hand, in the East, religious men prefer sheep, rams, and he-goats as offerings; they shun wheat, cheese, and other offerings which are hard to keep. Moreover, Easterners praise the man who proffers meat offerings. They love broiled meat, but they do not care for cereal food.

Thus the rejection of the produce of the ground might be a priestly theory. Cain was conceived in sin and was born a sinner. That is why the Lord rejected his offering and why Cain slew his brother.

CAIN'S FEAR

Behold, thou hast driven me out this day from the face of the earth; and from thy face shall I be hid; and I shall be a fugitive and a vagabond in the earth; and it shall come to pass, that every one that findeth me shall slay me.   Gen. 4:14

Cain's fear of being slain raises the question whether there were other people besides Adam and Eve. Those who maintain that the Eden story is allegorical believe that there must have been other people in the world besides Adam and his family.

When Cain slew his brother Abel, and the Lord drew him out from before his presence, there were only three persons upon the earth; namely, Adam, Eve, and Cain. Seth was not yet born. Cain was afraid to go into the land of Nod, fearing that someone might slay him. Some Bible students maintain that had there been no other people, Cain would not have been afraid, for no one would have found him and slain him.

It is maintained that there were other people east of the River Tigris. The land of Nod in Aramaic means "the land of the wandering tribes." Persia (Iran) is noted for her wandering tribes, the Lors and the Bakhtiari. Even today these nomad people live in tents and wander in search of grass for their large flocks.

Be that as it may, Cain, because of the fear of being slain, asked for God's protection. The last portion of the verse clearly reveals that Cain was afraid that he might be slain in the land of Nod.

Cain had a guilty conscience. He had taken the life of his own brother. Now he was afraid that the blood of his brother would be avenged upon him. He knew that whosoever sheds man's blood, by men shall his blood be shed [Gen. 9:6].

CAIN MARRIED

And Cain went out from the presence of the Lord, and dwelt in the land of Nod, on the east of Eden.   Gen. 4:16

Some Eastern biblical scholars maintain that Cain might have married his sister. Others say Cain married in the land of Nod. The author of the creation story does not cover other areas. The whole scene of the creation is the Garden of Eden.

There is no mention in Genesis that Adam and Eve had any daughters. If not, then Cain must have married a woman from the land of Nod (Persia), or God might have provided a wife for him. Be that as it may, Cain was married. Where he was married, or to whom, is irrelevant. God alone can answer such questions.

When Cain left the Garden of Eden area, which was between the rivers Tigris and Euphrates, he crossed the Tigris into what we call Iran (Persia) where he married and begot children. His descendants, the Canaanites, were noted for their large flocks of cattle. Cain was the father of the roaming tribes who dwell in tents and tend large flocks and herds [Gen. 4:20].

The term "Persian" also means "wanderers," the people who spread out and dwell in tents, moving from one place to another seeking grass and water for their large flocks and herds. In Aramaic, the Persians are

called *Mbadrey*, "the scattered people." Even today millions of them
live the tribal life as of yore.

CAIN BUILT A CITY

*And Cain knew his wife; and she conceived, and bare Enoch:
and he builded a city, and called the name of the city, after the
name of his son, Enoch.*   Gen. 4:17

The Eastern text reads: "He was building a village and he called the
name of the village after the name of his son Enoch, which means rest."
This is the first village which was built by the Canaanites. Hitherto, Cain
and his descendants had been wandering, but now they started to build
a village and engage in agriculture, just as the members of some of the
nomad tribes do today.

The term "city" is wrong. The dwelling place which Cain was building
was no more than a small hamlet to protect him and his family during
the winter and the rainy season.

In those days villages and cities were called by the names of the
patriarchs and founders of the tribes or one of their sons.

Cain alone could not have built a city. What would one lone man and
his wife do with a city, or even a village?

Either there were other people in Nod who received Cain as a prince
and helped him build a city, or his descendants centuries after him built
the city and called it after the name of his son Enoch. The author of
Genesis does not explain how Cain got married and where he found
his wife, but simply says that Cain knew his wife. But there is a hint
that there were other people. The Lord set a mark upon Cain lest anyone finding him should slay him.

MUSIC

*And Adah bare Jabal: he was the father of such as dwell in
tents, and of such as have cattle.*

*And his brother's name was Jubal: he was the father of all such
as handle the harp and organ.*   Gen. 4:20-21

Jabal (Hebrew *yobel*, "moving") is the Arabic word for "mountains."
The nomad tribes in Iran during the summer graze in the mountains
and highlands. Moreover, the mountain people are noted for their large
flocks of sheep, goats, and cattle.

Jubal (Aramaic *yobal*, "to play on a musical instrument") was the
father of the musicians. The descendants of Cain were the inventors

of musical instruments. These instruments were used to frighten wild beasts and snakes and to charm the sheep. This ancient custom still prevails among the nomad shepherds in the biblical lands.

GOD TOOK HIM

If Cain shall be avenged sevenfold, truly Lamech seventy and sevenfold.   Gen. 5:24

"God took him" is an Aramaic idiom which means "he died." In Aramaic and other Eastern languages, the word "death" is repulsive because it denotes the end of life. People say, "He is at rest" or "He sleeps."

When a king, a prince, or a holy man dies, we say, "God has taken him." "He was not" means he was no longer in the flesh. Elijah also went to heaven [2 Kings 2:11].

Enoch was a pious man. He died in his flesh, but his soul turned to God his Creator. Enoch, being a good man who pleased God, died a peaceful death and his soul lives forever. Jesus said, "There are men who stand here who will not taste death, until they see the Son of man coming in his kingdom" [Matt. 16:28].

St. Paul states that by faith Enoch was taken up and did not taste death, and he was not found because God took him [Heb. 11:5]. The Scripture states that no one has gone to heaven except Jesus Christ who came from heaven.

DESCENDANTS OF SETH

That the sons of God saw the daughters of men that they were fair; and they took them wives of all which they chose.   Gen. 6:2

The reference here is to the descendants of Seth, the third son of Adam and Eve. Prior to the flood, all the descendants of Seth were good. But when they began to marry the daughters of men; that is, the descendants of Cain, they forsook God and did evil in his presence.

Man was created in the image and the likeness of God, and as long as he remained good he was the child of God. But when he went astray after pagan gods and married pagan women he lost his spiritual heritage and his divine sonship.

Centuries after, this sonship was regained through Jesus Christ. It is through him that we are called the sons of God and heirs to the kingdom of heaven [Ps. 82:6].

THE AGE OF MAN

And the Lord said, My spirit shall not always strive with man,
for that he also is flesh: yet his days shall be an hundred and twenty
years.   Genesis 6:3

God is never sorry nor is he changeable. He is omniscient and his laws
are from everlasting to everlasting—unchangeable.

Man's span of life or his age shrank simply because a new calendar
was discovered by the Chaldean: a calendar based on the solar system
of 365 days. Hitherto, the age of man was computed by the Lunar
Calendar or a Season Calendar, which were the first two measuring sticks
of time prior to the present calendar which was discovered before the
birth of Abraham. (Season Calendar, see Daniel 4:16.)

The story of the creation is the first portion of the Scriptures which was
handed down orally from one generation to another prior to the discovery
of the calendar and the alphabet. Then again, the world in which the
patriarchs lived was a small world surrounded by seemingly limitless
space devoid of borders and boundaries. On the other hand, man's concept of time was in its infancy. True, God had created the sun, moon and
stars for light and for signs and seasons, days and years. But it took a
long time before man became familiar with the movement of these
heavenly bodies. We are told by ancient Eastern writers that it was a
necessity for travelers by night because of the too intense heat of the day
to study with the naked eye the movement of stars and planets, and thus,
the Chaldeans discovered the calendar of 365 days.

Evidently the age of some of the early patriarchs is based on the Lunar
Calendar and some on the Season Calendar. In those early days a month
was reckoned a year. Even today tribal people still use the Lunar and
the Season (Spring, Summer, Fall, Winter) and moon for grazing, planting and for travel and business.

In the Bible we are told that the Jews had an ecclesiastical calendar of
seven weeks of 150 days. Even now the Jews and the Moslems still use
the Lunar Calendar in their worship.

We know that God never makes mistakes nor regrets what he has
created. The phrase "God was sorry" [verse 6] is a scribal footnote written
on the margin when the scribe saw that the age of man shrank so suddenly as though something cataclysmic had happened. The discrepancy
between the age of the early patriarchs and that of those who came later
caused the scribe to believe that God had changed his mind and thus
reduced man's age to 70, 80, 100 and 120 years. This marginal footnote
was copied later into the integral portion of the Bible. As is the custom
today, many interesting marginal notes are incorporated into the main
body of the writing by the copyist. Since writing material was scarce,
notes were written on the margin of scrolls.

Undoubtedly, the change in the calendar changed man's concept of time. If we were to divide the age of the men who had lived 800 or 900 years by 12, we would find that they lived only 75 or 80 years. And those who lived 300 to 500 years by four seasons of four months each, we would find they lived a normal span of life like people live today. We must remember that all the books of the Bible were not written at the same time nor were all people using a standard calendar. Some of the books were written before man's scientific knowledge was developed.

TWO PAIRS OF ANIMALS

There went in two and two unto Noah into the ark, the male and the female, as God had commanded Noah. Gen. 7:9

Noah saved pairs of animals which were found in Assyria (Mesopotamia). He could not have gone to China, Japan, India, Brazil, and other far-off lands to save a male and female of each species of animal.

Such lands as America, Brazil, and Japan were not known to the Bible writers.

Noah, like the early patriarchs, had been a sheep and cattle breeder. He had to save species of animals on which he and his family depended for food and clothing, and also some of the unclean animals and creeping things [Lev. 11].

In verse two, we are told that Noah was commanded to take by sevens of the clean beasts and by two of the unclean.

The discrepancy between the two accounts—two and seven—is due to two early oral or written documents. Verses 15 and 16 confirm that Noah took two and two instead of seven and seven. The most important thing is that Noah saved the animals for his sons and their descendants. Moreover, Noah obeyed the divine voice and faithfully carried out all of God's commands. So Noah and his family were spared.

HAM

In the selfsame day entered Noah, and Shem, and Ham, and Japheth, the sons of Noah, and Noah's wife, and the three wives of his sons with them, into the ark. Gen. 7:13

Ham (Aramaic *Kham*) is derived from the Aramaic word *khoma,* "heat." In western Aramaic and Arabic *kh* becomes *h.* Hence *Kham* is pronounced and written "Ham."

All the three sons of Noah were of the same color—white—and all of them were living in *Bethnahrin* (Mesopotamia). None of them migrated from his homeland to a far-off land. Assyria was large enough and fertile enough for all three men and their families and flocks to dwell in. Then again, in those early days, roads were unknown and forests were infested with snakes and wild animals.

The three sons of Noah divided the land in which they were living among themselves. Each one of them started grazing in a different direction. Japheth went northward; Shem, being the firstborn, stayed home in Assyria; and Ham went southward, grazing and multiplying. This ancient custom still prevails. When a large tribe splits, its segments move in different directions.

As the tribes continued to migrate they multiplied and again divided and started seeking new grazing lands. As the tribe of Ham or the Hamites migrated southward they found more favorable grazing conditions and water, and the climate was warmer. It took many centuries before the descendants of Ham reached the hot regions of Africa where, because of the climatic conditions, their skin became dark. Their bodies created pigments to protect their skins from the strong and penetrating sun rays. This is also true of the bears. In warm climates bears are dark, while in the Arctic they are white. Today, the Ethiopians are called *Amharik,* "the scorched people." This is because they are dark or burned with the sun's rays.

Some Bible teachers wrongly believe that it was because of the curse that Ham turned black [Gen. 9:25]. No curse can change that color of man which was given to him by his Creator, but heat and cold can cause changes in order to offer man protection. Unfortunately, in the past, all weak and backward people who were enslaved by stronger races were supposed to be the accursed ones and their masters the blessed ones. It was the climate which created the black color and not the curse.

When one travels from the north to the south toward Africa, one can notice the color of the people changing gradually; for example, the Arabs in the north are lighter than the Arabs in the south. And the southern Arabs are much lighter than Arabs and other races in Africa. This is also true of the Teutonic people, such as Germans, British, Swedish, and especially Norwegians. They are very white simply because the sun's rays in the north are weak and indirect. Frenchmen who live in southern France are darker than those in the north. This is also true of the Italians.

THE FLOOD

And the waters prevailed, and were increased greatly upon the earth; and the ark went upon the face of the waters.

And the waters prevailed exceedingly upon the earth; and all the high hills, that were under the whole heaven, were covered.

Fifteen cubits upward did the waters prevail; and the mountains were covered.   Gen. 7:18-20

The Aramaic word *arra* means the earth, a country, land, field, ground, region, soil, and the floor of a house. The term *tabel* is used when speaking of the whole habitable earth or world as a whole.

In the days of Noah most of the parts of the world which we know today were unknown. The land between the Tigris and Euphrates rivers was the only world which Noah and his people knew. Not for many centuries were Palestine and other westward lands inhabited; this took place only after the dispersion and the division of languages [Gen. 11:1-6].

The term *shamaya,* "heaven," also means "skies." No doubt the hills in the region where Noah made the ark were covered with water by the flood. The deluge was so great that it lasted forty days and forty nights. The Tigris and Zab rivers flooded all the inhabited region.

"The mountains under all the heaven" would certainly not include the Himalayas. Had the water risen fifteen cubits above the earth's highest mountains the surface of the ocean would have risen 30,000 feet above its present level. If this was the case, the water could not have receded in one hundred and fifty days. There would have been no place for it to flow. A similar phrase appears in the book of Numbers. When Balak, king of Moab, sent messengers to Balaam, the son of Beor, he said, "Behold, there is a people come out from Egypt: behold they cover the face of the earth" [Num. 22:5]. "Face of the earth" in this instance means the face of the ground near the land of Moab. (The word translated "earth" is *arra.*)

The story of the building of the ark is true. Both pitch and gopher wood are found in Assyria.

Indeed, if all the water in the earth's atmosphere were to fall upon the earth at once, the surface of the ocean would not rise more than a few inches. Of course, God can do anything, but we must realize the early men had a smaller world. Thus, when we think of Noah, we must understand the small world in which he lived.

The fact that the dove brought an olive branch proves that some of the mountains were not covered. No olive trees could have survived one hundred and fifty days under the salty seawater. There are many olive trees in northern Mesopotamia (Iraq).

MOUNTAINS OF KARDU

And the ark rested in the seventh month, on the seventeenth day of the month, upon the mountains of Ararat.   Gen. 8:4

The Eastern text reads: *torai kardu,* "the mountains of Kardu," Kurdistan. This chain of mountains starts from northern Mesopotamia and reaches as far as the Armenian boarder near the Taurus range.

Mount Ararat is the highest mountain in the whole range of mountains in Kurdistan and Armenia. Apparently, the name Ararat was used by the translators of the Bible simply because the whole chain is identified with Ararat.

Apparently, the ark rested on one of the lower mountains east or west of the Tigris, near the small river Zab, and not upon Mount Ararat itself.

Mount Ararat is about 18,000 feet high and difficult to descend from its peak. How would Noah have brought down such animals as elephants, camels, and other large animals when even the expert mountain climber cannot ascend or descend Ararat without ropes?

There is no reason why God should have caused the ark to rest on the peak of such a high and cold mountain where neither people nor animals could descend without danger of disaster.

God can do anything, but he would not do something that would work against his purpose of saving Noah and his family. Mount Ararat, because of its height, was known to Westerners, but the mountains in Iraq where the ark was built were unknown.

OLIVES NOT DESTROYED

And the dove came in to him in the evening, and, lo, in her mouth was an olive leaf plucked off: so Noah knew that the waters were abated from off the earth. Gen. 8:11

Had the whole world been covered with water, the trees would have perished. The ocean water would have mixed with the fresh water and the topsoil would have been destroyed. And had Mount Ararat been covered, from where would the dove have found the branch with the green leaf? No olive trees grow in Armenia. But olives grow in Mesopotamia. Therefore, the ark must have rested upon one of the mountains north of the region where Noah was living; and the olive branch was picked up from a higher region where olives were not covered with water. Of course God could have destroyed the entire globe if he had wanted to do so.

SEASONS

While the earth remaineth, seed-time and harvest, and cold and heat, and summer and winter, and day and night shall not cease. Gen. 8:22

Seasons in the region of the Garden of Eden are very evident. The climate is temperate and it changes four times during the year. The changes from one season to another are very evident, and the weather is not erratic. Both farmers and shepherds know the exact day of the beginning of each season.

Prior to the discovery of the calendar and the division of time into years, months, days, and hours, man's knowledge of time was based on the changes in the seasons. That is, the seasons served as a calendar.

This is the first reference in the Bible to cold and heat and to summer and winter.

The year of 360 days was divided into four seasons of three months each. Three hundred and sixty days can easily be divided into four quarters of 90 days each. Then again, the moon was a great help. The 12 moons were known as the 12 months. The priests and shepherds were guided by the phases of the moon, and the farmers by the seasons.

There are about 30 days in each moon, but for two days the moon cannot be seen with the naked eye. The 12 moons multiplied by 30 will give us exactly 360 days. The five extra days caused errors in the calendar which were later corrected by adding an extra month in some years. The early peoples did not know that the earth makes one complete revolution around the sun in 365¼ days.

ANIMALS GIVEN FOR FOOD

Every moving thing that liveth shall be meat for you; even as the green herb have I given you all things. Gen. 9:3

Seemingly, this commandment was given later when man's needs for food had increased. The green herb was given before [Gen. 1:29].

Man, in the beginning, subsisted on green herbs or vegetables. The grass, the herbs, and the fruit trees were created on the third day, but the living creatures and the animals were created on the fifth day, before man was created.

Evidently, early man, like the animals, lived on the vegetables and fruits which grew around him. Many varieties of vegetables and fruit trees grow wild in northern Iraq. This is why the author of Genesis calls that land the Garden of Eden, which means "a delightful garden." Indeed, this is the only land in the world which is graced with all varieties of vegetables, fruit trees, cotton, and wheat.

It is said that the animals which thrive on the grass are stronger than the wild beasts which live on meat.

EATING OF BLOOD FORBIDDEN

But flesh with the life thereof, which is the blood thereof, shall ye not eat. Gen. 9:4

For many centuries, the Hebrews thought that life was centered in the blood. Four centuries after Abraham blood was forbidden to be eaten as food by an ordinance of Moses. "Moreover, you shall eat no manner of blood" [Lev. 7:26].

This is why atonement was done with blood. The sinner was cleansed by means of the blood of animals offered on his behalf. "For if the blood of bulls and of goats, and the ashes of an heifer sprinkling the unclean, sanctifieth to the purifying of the flesh: how much more shall the blood of Christ . . ." [Heb. 9:13, 14].

Pagans and some Christians eat blood, but the Jews still uphold the Mosaic ordinance and abstain from eating meat with the blood. They eat kosher; that is, clean meat without blood. The Mosaic ordinance was based on this command of God in Genesis 9:4.

VENGEANCE

Whoso sheddeth man's blood, by man shall his blood be shed: for in the image of God made he man. Gen. 9:6

When a man slays another man he commits a crime not only against himself but also against all humanity, for all men were created in the image of God. At the outset God created one man and one woman only [Gen. 1:27].

Thus, when a man kills another man, he destroys himself [Matt. 26:52]. This is why the Lord commanded that he who slays a man shall surely be put to death [Exod. 21:12]. "Whosoever killeth any person, the murderer shall be put to death by the mouth of witnesses" [Num. 35:30].

Life is sacred because man is the image and the likeness of God. So he who destroys a branch of a tree destroys a part thereof. God commanded the man to be fruitful and multiply upon the earth. Thus, any act which reverses this divine plan is contrary to God's order. And the offender, through his disobedience and his evil act, will cut himself off from the living God.

MESHECH

The sons of Japheth; Gomer, and Magog, and Madai, and Javan, and Tubal, and Meshech, and Tiras. Gen. 10:2

Meshech or *Meshak* evidently refers to what is now Moscow, the capital of Russia. The Israelites, like the Assyrians, the Chaldeans, and the Persians, knew about other races about them and those who were far off. The Assyrians had conquered what is known as ancient Armenia and Georgia and other lands adjacent to Russia and the Caspian

Sea. For example, Cathay (China) is mentioned in Numbers 24:24 and in many of the books of the prophets.

In the eighth century B.C., some of the captives from the land of Israel were settled in Iran (Persia), Media, Afghanistan, and other lands in the Middle East. No doubt some of them fled to India, China, and Russia. It was during this period that the Israelites knew of these far-off races.

Then again, the Arameans and the Chaldeans traded with many of the Eastern races. Their ships navigated many seas.

Even today, there are large Jewish colonies in many parts of Russia, the Near East, Middle East, and the Far East. There are also Jews of Indian origin who were converted by the early Jewish settlers in India.

Gomer means Germany; *Magog* means Mongolia; *Madai* means Media (Persia); *Javan,* Greece; and *Tubal,* Tubaliskie.

[See Ezek. 27:13 and 32:26.]

TARSHISH

And the sons of Javan; Elishah, and Tarshish, Kittim, and Dodanim.   Gen. 10:4

Tarshish was an ancient name of a region of southwestern Spain. The region was noted for its wealth of silver, tin, and lead [Jer. 10:9].

The inhabitants of Tarshish were the descendants of Japheth, the third son of Noah. They inhabited the region in Andalusia in southwestern Spain.

The term *Tarshish* is of Aramaic derivation: *Tar,* "door," and *shish* (*shagish*), meaning "rough," "raging sea," "violent." Hence, the Gibraltar, or the door to the raging, mysterious Atlantic Ocean [Comment on Obad. 1:20].

GENTILES

By these were the isles of the Gentiles divided in their lands; every one after his tongue, after their families, in their nations.
                                    Gen. 10:5

The Aramaic term *Ammey,* "Gentiles," is used with various meanings. *Ammey* in Aramaic means "kindred races or peoples." The three sons of Noah were born of the same father and mother, and all of them and their immediate children spoke the same language. But after the dispersion, the descendants of the three sons of Noah scattered northward, southward and eastward. And, consequently, new tribes and new languages were born.

The descendants of Laban, Lot, Ishmael, Esau (Edom), and other kindred people were called Gentiles by the Hebrews. Many of these people, who were the direct descendants of Abraham, revered the Lord God of Israel, but in the course of time most of them sank into paganism. For example, Balaam was a Gentile prophet but he revered the Lord God, the Creator of heaven and earth [Num. 22:7-14]. Laban, the Aramean, also feared the Lord.

The Hebrew prophets predicted that Messiah would bring the Gentiles to God [Isa. 11:10] and be a light to lighten the Gentiles [Luke 2:32].

This term *Ammey*, "Gentiles," should not be confused with pagans and Greeks.

ERECH

And the beginning of his kingdom was Babel, and Erech, and Accad, and Calneh, in the land of Shinar.   Gen. 10:10

The Aramaic reads *Erech* (Iraq) and *Akhar* instead of *Accad*. These kingdoms were all a part of ancient Assyria and Babylon.

In the olden days large fortified cities were known as kingdoms. This is why a king of Assyria, Babylonia, or Iran (Persia) was known as a "king of kings."

The name of Assyria was changed from Padam-Aram to Assyria and later to Mesopotamia. Seemingly, the Arabs had retained the ancient name of the region, Iraq.

Such peoples as the "Summerians" and "Accadians" are not mentioned in the Bible. These names were introduced by Western scholars. Yet, the Bible writers have covered all other peoples. Accad and Shamar are the names of regions in Mesopotamia.

AMORA NOT GOMORRAH

And the border of the Canaanites was from Sidon, as thou comest to Gerar, unto Gaza; as thou goest unto Sodom, and Gomorrah, and Admah, and Zeboim, even unto Lasha.   Gen. 10:19

The Eastern text reads *Amorah* instead of Gomorrah. Evidently, during the course of copying and translating, the letter *aey* or *ayen* was confused with the letter *gamel*. These two letters are very similar in Aramaic, especially when they are placed in the beginning of a word or a noun. The tail of *gamel* is slightly longer than that of *aey*.

Today, in Arabic, this biblical town is called *Amoriah. Amorah* means "the inhabited place." Both Sodom and Amorah were prosperous towns situated on the caravan route southeast of the Dead Sea.

EBER

And Arphaxad begat Salah; and Salah begat Eber.   Gen. 10:24

The term Hebrews is derived from the Aramaic word *Abar,* "to cross over." That is, the lands on the west side of the River Euphrates. Eber was a great-grandson of Shem, 2235 B.C. In Numbers 24:24 Eber is mentioned as a nation, the Hebrews. Some of the descendants of Eber remained in Haran and other places west of Assyria. Eber was the father of the Hebrews. See Num. 24:24 Eastern text, Peshitta.

THE DIVISION OF LANGUAGES

And the whole world was of one language and one speech.
Gen. 11:1

Undoubtedly, the primitive people who lived in the land of Shinar spoke one tongue, the first human language. The division of languages was due to the dispersion of the people from Mesopotamia. It was a slow process. New languages cannot be learned in a day or even in a year. It takes centuries before a new language is born, or a new speech replaces an old speech.

Owing to the height of the tower of Babylon, the builders were unable to hear one another. At that time, elevators, telephones, and other means of communication were unknown. The whole project of building such a high tower in Babylon was done by hand. When a mason called for bricks, they sent him mortar; when he asked for mortar, they sent him timber. The higher the building grew the more difficult, confusing and hopeless became the task of the builders. And when the builders realized that the heavens were not over the clouds and could not be reached, they abandoned the project and started to disperse in different directions.

In Biblical days, heavens were supposed to be a few miles above the earth. This concept still prevails among many primitive people who lack the knowledge of astronomy. They believe that God's abode is above the clouds. The Bible tells us that the Lord came down in the clouds [Numbers 11:25]. God was not afraid of man as the Biblical text may indicate. He knew the building of the tower was in vain, so he revealed to the builders that their task was an impossible one.

The dispersion was due to the grazing situation and the population growth. Pastural lands were divided among the tribes, and some of the tribes grazed southward, some northward, and others westward in search of new pastures. Every time a tribe grew up and became powerful, and its sheep and cattle increased, it divided itself into smaller tribes. These divisions and migrations continued for thousands of years, until most of the face of earth was inhabited.

It was during the course of these migrations that the new dialects were formed, which later became distinct languages. At that early time, writing was unknown and commerce was in its infancy. The tribes were independent and self-supporting. Every tribe, in the course of time, incorporated new words into its dialect, which became a new speech. As new discoveries were made, new words were coined. This is also true in our day. For instance, American men and women who passed on 100 years ago, if they were to arise tomorrow, would find it difficult to converse with their descendants. They would hardly recognize any of our modern English words and idioms.

Even today, in the lands where illiteracy is predominant and where there is little social intercourse and commerce, people living a few miles from one another find it hard to understand the speech of one another. In some areas, every town has its own dialect. For instance, Arabic is one language, but it has numerous dialects. An Arab born and reared in the Arabian desert would find it difficult or even impossible to understand the Arabic language spoken in Tunis or Morocco.

EAST

And it came to pass, as they journeyed from the east, that they found a plain in the land of Shinar; and they dwelt there. Gen. 11:2

Madnekha in Aramaic means "the rising of the sun" or "east." The sun rises from the east and therefore *madnekha,* metaphorically, also means light, and light means truth. Jesus said, "I am the light of the world." God is often called the Light, and the sun is symbolic of God, because it pours out three attributes—light, heat, and color.

On the other hand, *maarba* is derived from *erab,* which means "sun setting," "darkness," or "west." In biblical days therefore people used the word for "east" to symbolize right direction, light, truth, and guidance; and the word for "west" to symbolize darkness or going astray— far off from the light.

"They journeyed from the east," means symbolically they strayed from the true path; that is, they forsook God. This is why the people were confused and continued to wander aimlessly from place to place. When they strayed from the true path they were deceived by the material world on which they relied for guidance and security. When man loses the true way, he wanders after the imagination of his own heart and confronts problems and difficulties which he fails to overcome or solve.

"LET US GO DOWN"

Go to, let us go down, and there confound their language, that they may not understand one another's speech.   Gen. 11:7

Emperors, kings, princes, and high ecclesiastical authorities use the plural pronoun, or the pronoun of respect, when referring to themselves: "we" or "us," instead of "I." This is because they are the representatives of the people [Ezra 4:18]. Therefore, when God speaks of himself, the pronouns of respect "we" and "us" are used. The authors of the Bible believed in one God only, the God of heaven and the earth.

The doctrine of the Trinity, three persons in one, was a new concept—a Greek concept of God. The Hebrews throughout centuries believed in one God, or one person. "Hear, O Israel: the Lord our God is one Lord" [Deut. 6:4; Mark 12:29]. The Israelites were admonished against having another god besides the Lord their God. The whole system of the Jewish religion is based on the unity of God—one God.

The Eastern Christians believe in one God with three attributes, instead of three persons.

ABRAHAM, A BLESSING

And I will make of thee a great nation, and I will bless thee, and make thy name great; and thou shalt be a blessing:
And I will bless them that bless thee, and curse him that curseth thee: and in thee shall all families of the earth be blessed.
                                                    Gen. 12:2-3

The departure of Abraham from his land, Ur of Chaldea, was preordained by God. Abraham was to play a great part in the divine plan and the salvation of mankind.

The divine promise was made before Abraham left his land and his kindred. The reward for Abraham's part was that he would become a great nation and a blessing to all the families of the earth. He was called the blessed of the Lord [Gen. 14:19].

We see that God's plan was a universal kingdom, and Israel was simply an agent in this plan. Before Abraham left his people, all the people of the world were straying from the way of God, including many close kinsmen of Abraham. Thus, God's plan was for all the world. The faith of Abraham was to embrace all the races and the peoples of the earth, and the law which was to be given to his descendants was to be a light to the Gentiles and the Jews.

Therefore, Israel's mission is spiritual and not political. For many years the Hebrew government was under the divine guidance of God. All of this was leading to the coming of the Messiah and was to culminate in a messianic kingdom. The dominion of this kingdom was to be from sea to sea, and from the River Euphrates to the ends of the earth. This kingdom was to embrace all races and peoples in the world.

MAMRE

And Abram passed through the land unto the place of Sichem, unto the plain of Moreh. And the Canaanite was then in the land.
Gen. 12:6

The Eastern text, Peshitta, reads *Mamre;* that is, a "dwelling place" or a temporary settlement like a *dera* where nomad people encamp for a long period of time.

Mamre is near Hebron. Abraham traveled between Shechem in the north country and Hebron in the south, feeding his large flocks and seeking new wells and grazing rights from the native people. *Moreh* is a corrupt form for *Mamre.* The error might have been caused during the transcription of the story from one alphabet into another, which often happens.

ABRAHAM WAS A PETTY RULER

The princes also of Pharaoh saw her, and commended her before Pharaoh: and the woman was taken into Pharaoh's house.
Gen. 12:15

In the East an *emir,* or the head of a large tribe, is looked upon as a petty ruler or a small king, and, when traveling, he is respected and honored by princes and kings of other lands. Thus Abraham, on his arrival in Egypt, had to pay his respects to Pharaoh and his princes. Had Abraham been all alone, the princes and Pharaoh probably would not have noticed him in such a great country as Egypt, even though Abraham was a well-respected *emir,* the head of a large and prosperous tribe.

But both Abraham and his wife Sarah called on the Egyptian emperor, who welcomed them and probably invited them to live in one of his many palaces.

BEAUTY IS DANGEROUS

And he entreated Abram well for her sake: and he had sheep, and oxen, and he asses, and menservants, and maidservants, and she asses, and camels. Gen. 12:17

In Eastern countries, a man with a beautiful wife is not safe. The beauty of his wife may cost him his life. It often happens that the husband is killed and his wife is taken away by princes, kings, or high government officials, just as in the case of Bathsheba and David [2 Sam. 11:15].

Abraham was a Chaldean. The Chaldean women are noted for being fair and beautiful, especially when compared with the dark-skinned Arab and Egyptian women. Then again, Abraham was a stranger in Egypt. And, as an Easterner, he had seen and heard that many men had lost their lives on account of their beautiful wives. He knew that his life would be in danger if Pharaoh should desire to have his wife Sarah.

Therefore, the only alternative was to instruct his wife to pose as his sister. Of course, in reality, Sarah *was* Abraham's half sister. Abraham had to do this, not for the sake of money and favors as it may look, but to save his life and the lives of those who were with him. The whole tribe was in danger of perishing with famine. In other words, Abraham was between the devil and the deep, blue sea.

Seemingly, Pharaoh believed in God, because he was able to commune with God in a dream. God warned him relative to the status of Sarah, and told him to return her to her husband Abraham. It seems that the Egyptians had a moral code and were afraid of punishment for wrongdoings.

Isaac did the same thing when he went to Philistia because of famine. His wife Rebecca was an Assyrian, a fair woman to look at. Isaac instructed her not to tell the people that she was his wife but to say that she was his sister [Gen. 26:6-11]. Abimeleck, king of the Philistines, also feared God. And when God revealed to him that Rebecca was Isaac's wife, he immediately sent her back to him and rebuked Isaac for having deceived him.

SODOM

And Lot lifted up his eyes, and beheld all the plain of Jordan, that it was well watered every where, before the Lord destroyed Sodom and Gomorrah, even as the garden of the Lord, like the land of Egypt, as thou comest unto Zoar. Gen. 13:10

The exact location of Sodom and Gomorrah (Aramaic, *Amorah*) is not known. It must have been either north or south of the Salt Sea.

These two ancient cities must have been visible from Bethel. Some authorities maintain that the location of these cities might have been the marshy place near Mount Sodom.

Modern *Amoriah* is at the northwest corner of the Salt Sea. It might be the ancient *Amorah*.

PITCH PITS

And the vale of Siddim was full of slime pits; and the kings of Sodom and Gomorrah fled, and fell there; and they that remained fled to the mountain. Gen. 14:10

The Aramaic word *kira* means "pitch" or "asphalt." Pitch and other minerals are plentiful around the Salt Sea. Some biblical authorities maintain that the brimstone and fire were caused by the combustion of the inflammable material. Be that as it may, the Lord knew that there would be a disaster and he warned Lot to leave the region in time [Gen. 19:22].

Pitch is found in abundance in Mesopotamia and other parts of the Near East. It was the discovery of pitch in Assyria which helped the English geologist to find the rich oil fields in Iraq. Noah was instructed by God to cover the ark with pitch [Gen. 6:14].

The chariots were unable to operate in the hot plains of Jericho. This is because the pitch melts during the hot hours of the day.

ABRAHAM'S ARMY

And when Abram heard that his brother was taken captive, he armed his trained servants, born in his own house, three hundred and eighteen, and pursued them unto Dan. Gen. 14:14

Abraham was the chief of a large tribe. The author of the book of Genesis gives us the impression that Abraham was head of a family. This is because in the East a tribe is known by the name of the chief thereof. Even today, tribes in Arabia and other parts of the Near East and Middle East are known by the name of their chiefs and their families.

Abraham had many men in his tribe. Some of them were tending sheep, some were herdsmen, and others were performing other duties. Moreover, all the men who worked for Abraham and served as his soldiers had their own sheep and cattle.

Abraham took with him 318 trained warriors and, as he trusted in God, this small force was enough with which to defeat his enemies.

The term "servants" does not mean slaves. In the East, members of the tribe, when addressing their chief, call him "our lord" and speak of themselves as servants. The tribal life is one of the most perfect forms of democracy ever devised by man. The chief of the tribe is looked upon as a father, and he considers all the members of his tribe as his children.

BREAD AND WINE

And Melchizedek king of Salem brought forth bread and wine: and he was the priest of the most high God.

And he blessed him, and said, Blessed be Abram of the most high God, possessor of heaven and earth. Gen. 14:18-19

Bread and wine symbolize friendship and loyalty. Bread is a life-sustaining substance and wine makes men's hearts merry.

Whenever a king, a prince, or a nobleman enters a town, he is greeted by the ruler and the noblemen of the town with bread and salt and other articles of food. In the olden days, wine was probably used because of the lack of water. Today in many parts of the Near East and the Middle East bread, salt, and animals are offered to visiting royalty, government officials, and noblemen as tokens of welcome.

On the other hand, in those ancient countries, restaurants and other eating places are rare. The travelers reach the town thirsty and hungry and, at times, almost starving. This ancient practice is evident throughout the Bible and it still prevails today.

Abraham was a petty ruler, an *emir*, or the chief of a large and powerful tribe. Melchizedek, king of Salem (Jerusalem), came forth with bread and wine to greet him. Abraham and his men were returning from the battle victoriously. But they were hungry and thirsty. Such gifts on these occasions inspired friendship and confidence between the two rulers. Words and praises are forgotten, but gifts and good deeds are remembered.

Melchizedek was a righteous priest and king, and Abraham also was the spiritual and political ruler of his people. This is why Melchizedek called him, "Blessed be Abraham of the most high God. . . ."

When Israel came to the border of the Ammonites and Moabites, they did not meet Israel with bread and water, and the Israelites never forgot it [Deut. 23:4].

When David was fleeing from Absalom, Ziba brought him loaves of bread, raisins, summer fruits, and wine loaded on the asses [2 Sam. 16:1, 2].

MOST HIGH GOD

And blessed be the most high God, which hath delivered thine
enemies into thy hand. And he gave him tithes of all.   Gen. 14:20

All pagan people in Palestine knew that there was a High God; that is,
a greater God than the local deities they served. This concept of a Great
Spirit was prevalent among all pagan peoples and even among the American Indians.

The Aramaic word *merema* means "dwelling in the highest"; that is,
the God whose abode is in heaven. The dwelling place of other gods was
on the earth. The helpless statues and images were crowded in dark and
dim temples and shrines.

Melchizedek is an Aramaic name meaning "the king of righteousness."
Probably he was a member of the Semitic people who had migrated
early into Palestine. Abraham had recognized him as a high priest of a
true religion. The Semites asserted themselves wherever they went. The
descendants of Abraham, Lot, Ishmael, Esau, and Jacob became kings
and princes over other races. Melchizedek must have been a descendant
of one of the Babylonian high priests and a distant kin of Abraham.

Shalem or Salem, like Shiloh, was a place of worship and a meeting
place where people made peace with God and settled their differences
with one another. In the East both priests and high priests act as judges
and arbiters in all legal matters.

AN OATH

And Abram said to the king of Sodom, I have lifted up mine
hand unto the Lord, the most high God, the possessor of heaven
and earth.   Gen. 14:22

"I have lifted up my hand" is an Eastern saying which means "I have
sworn before God." Easterners, when taking an oath, lift their hands
toward heaven and invoke the name of God, whom they make a witness
of the oath, ". . . as a faithful witness in heaven" [Ps. 89:37; 1 Sam.
12:5].

When treaties and agreements were made in the name of God they
were generally respected and kept even by the future generations. Other
treaties and covenants were easily broken and repudiated, just as they
are broken today [Josh. 9:18].

Even today the Moslems and some of the Eastern Christians keep their
sworn pledges and agreements. They lend money to one another on the
strength of their oaths.

LARGE NUMERALS

And he brought him forth abroad, and said, Look now toward heaven, and tell the stars, if thou be able to number them: and he said unto him, So shall thy seed be. Gen. 15:5

In the olden days large numerals such as a hundred thousand, million, and billion were unknown. Even the figure one thousand was only known to the few educated people and army officers. The simple folk who used their fingers when counting could not count beyond one hundred.

The stars in heaven and the grains of sand on the seashore were used when describing a large number such as million or billion.

The term "seed" means both offspring and teaching. The reference here is more to the faith of Abraham (teaching) than to his descendants. In the East many nations and people who had embraced the religion of Abraham spoke of Abraham as their father; that is, their spiritual father, the founder of their religion.

Then again, in biblical days when a man changed his religion he changed his race also. Ruth was a Moabite, but when she accepted the God of Israel, she became a daughter of Abraham.

Even today, Christians in the Near East, when speaking of Abraham, call him "Father Abraham"; that is, the father of the believers [Gen. 17:4]. It was Abraham's faith which counted for righteousness [Gen. 15:6].

Today the spiritual descendants of Abraham are more than all the rest of the people in the world. Christians, Jews, and Moslems are all spiritual descendants of Abraham. They all believe in the God of Abraham.

FOUR CENTURIES

But in the fourth generation they shall come hither again: for the iniquity of the Amorites is not yet full. Gen. 15:16

The Aramaic word *darey* means "centuries." The Eastern text reads "four centuries" instead of "four generations." The Israelites were in Egypt about 430 years [Exod. 12:41]. Four generations would be less than a hundred years. The Aramaic words for centuries, generations, and for conflict or struggle are written alike but pronounced differently. Therefore, such an error is almost unavoidable. [See also Judg. 11:26.]

The same error occurs in Acts 7:5. This error occurs in all Western versions of the Bible and the Massoretic text.

ISHMAEL

And he will be a wild man; his hand will be against every man, and every man's hand against him: and he shall dwell in the presence of all his brethren. Gen. 16:12

Ishmael and his Egyptian mother were driven away by Sarah from the good land which God had promised to Abraham and his posterity. Thus, the Ishmaelites had to dwell in semiarid lands and deserts where water was scanty and grazing poor.

As a nomad people, the descendants of Ishmael had to wander from one place to another seeking water and grass and, like the nomads of today, had to fight for their existence.

While roaming, the tribe transgressed the rights of other tribes and fought against them. The desert people are great fighters. Prior to the advent of Islam, many of the desert tribes had to raid and plunder one another in order to make a living. The raiders were in turn raided and plundered by other tribes. The descendants of Ishmael were found all over the desert, and at times they invaded the lands of their kindred tribes [Gen. 25:18]. Ishmael means "God has heard me"—*shama*, "to hear," and *El*, "God." Abraham was still using the pure Aramaic language which he spoke.

THE WELL OF THE LIVING GOD

Wherefore the well was called Beerlahairoi: behold, it is between Kadesh and Bered. Gen. 16:14

The Eastern text reads *Beer-di-khaya-khizan*, "the well of the Living One who saw me."

Hagar was lost in the vast desert and had given up hope of finding water to save her life. But the Living God, the God of her husband Abraham, had compassion on her. He sent his angel to direct her and assure her of the Lord's mercies upon her and upon her unborn son Ishmael. *Khizan* also means "has seen my affliction" or "has taken care of me."

During this early period the Hebrew tribe spoke the Aramaic language of their forefathers which they had learned from their parents in Padan-Aram, Mesopotamia, and Ur of Chaldea.

EL-SHADDAI

And when Abram was ninety years old and nine, the Lord appeared to Abram, and said unto him, I am the Almighty God; walk before me, and be thou perfect. Gen. 17:1

El-Shaddai is another name of the Hebrew God which signifies might and strength. *El-Shaddai* is the Hebrew word for "the Almighty" [Gen. 49:25]. *El* means "God" and *Shaddai*, "strength and power." The Arabic is *Shaddidon*.

The Hebrews had a purer concept of religion and God. They believed that God had created the heavens and the earth and all that is therein. They knew that their God sent rain upon the earth and caused grass to grow and trees to yield fruit.

On the other hand, they saw that the Gentile gods were nothing but helpless images and idols which could not even remove a fly from their faces.

Thus, the Hebrew God was known as the Almighty, and as the God of gods, the Author of life, and Provider of all human needs.

The name *El-Shaddai* was coined by the Hebrews as a contrast between their God and the helpless gods of the Gentile nations, which had ears but could not hear and eyes but could not see. *El-Shaddai* was all-seeing and all-knowing.

ABRAM

Neither shall thy name any more be called Abram, but thy name shall be Abraham; for a father of many nations have I made thee. Gen. 17:5

Abram, high father, was Abraham's nickname. In the East men and women are known by their first names. The family name is used in deeds and documents only. Then again, when there are two persons or more of the same name, the name of the father is used—Jacob, son of Isaac; or Isaac, the father of Jacob.

Customarily, in the East, young men are called by their nicknames. Even young princes and noblemen are called by their nicknames until they become of age and occupy high positions in life, at which time they are no longer so addressed.

Abram now was the titular head of a large tribe and he was to become the father of many people who believed in God, or the father of the faithful. The Lord addressed him as Abraham because the members of the tribe were no longer to call him Abram. This is also true of Sarai. She was no longer to be addressed by her nickname Sarai, "princess," but was to be called Sarah, "the princess of God" [Gen. 17:15].

SEED—TEACHING

And I will establish my covenant between me and thee and thy seed after thee in their generations, for an everlasting covenant, to be a God unto thee and to thy seed after thee.   Gen. 17:7

"Seed" in Aramaic is a metaphorical term for teaching. In the prayer books of the church of the East, we often read: "The seed which the apostles sowed throughout the world," which means, "The gospel of Christ which they have published all over the world." Moreover, Jesus likened the Word of God to the seed. This is because a grain of seed, if planted, can multiply itself abundantly. This is also true of the Word. A word can be published from one corner of the earth to the other. For example, the words which once fell from the mouth of Jesus and his disciples 2,000 years ago now are published in more than 1,000 languages and dialects.

Thus, the term "seed of Abraham" is not only of the flesh but also of the Spirit, because the promise was made not simply to all the descendants of Abraham but also to the heirs of his faith. Thus, Abraham came to be called the father of the believers or the faithful [Rom. 4:11]. The children of Ishmael and Esau were also the descendants of Abraham, but not the heirs of the promise.

According to the Bible, the house of David, because of David's faithfulness before God, became an heir to the promises of God, or an heir to the divine promise which was made to Abraham. As we have said, all the children of Israel are offspring of Abraham, but not all of them were heirs to the promise.

In the realm of the Spirit, all the children of Abraham who believed in his religion and walked in God's way are children of the promise and heirs to the religion of Abraham. This is also true of the Gentiles who believed in the faith of Abraham, for Abraham is the father of all believers, and God's promise to Abraham is a blessing to all the people of the world.

CIRCUMCISION AS A SANITARY PRECAUTION

And ye shall circumcise the flesh of your foreskin; and it shall be a token of the covenant betwixt me and you.   Gen. 17:11

The primary objective of circumcision was the sealing of the covenant which God made with Abraham and his descendants. Covenants or agreements were sealed with human blood. At times, sheep were slaughtered, roasted, and eaten in celebrating the agreement.

But there must have been other reasons beyond the ancient customs. Abraham and his people were not circumcised when they were in Ur of Chaldea and in Haran. The reason must be that in Ur of Chaldea and in Haran there was abundant water and the people bathed themselves frequently. But in Palestine there was a scarcity of water and the people rarely bathed.

In desert lands where water is scarce, bathing is unknown. Men suffer from skin diseases. The foreskin often suffers from accumulated secretions which at times develop infections.

Then again, in the olden days when passports were unknown, tribal people were known by the marks on their bodies and their language.

BLESS HIM

And I will bless her, and give thee a son also of her: yea, I will bless her, and she shall be a mother of nations; kings of people shall be of her. Gen. 17:16

The last part of the verse, according to the Eastern text, reads: "I will bless him" instead of "bless her." The Aramaic masculine pronoun *ebarkioh* has been confused with the feminine pronoun *ebarkeh*. The reference here is to Isaac who was to be the father of many nations, and kings of the people were to be of his descendants.

Mineh means "from him" and *minah* "from her." The feminine gender is indicated by a dot over the letter *heh*, "h."

Isaac was the ancestor not only of the twelve tribes of Israel but also of the powerful tribes of the children of his first-born, Esau or Edom. God blessed both Sarah and her offspring, Isaac, but the second blessing was bestowed upon Isaac who was to become the father of many nations [Verse 19]. In the East the blessings are generally invoked upon the husband. The wife is blessed through him.

SARAH NINETY YEARS OLD

Then Abraham fell upon his face, and laughed, and said in his heart, Shall a child be born unto him that is a hundred years old? and shall Sarah, that is ninety years old, bear? Gen. 17:17

This episode may have happened years later. For in chapter 20:2, we read that when Abraham went to the south country and dwelt between

Kadesh and Shur, and sojourned in Gerar, Abimeleck, the king of Gerar, sent and took Sarah. Abraham had told her not to say that she was his wife but to say she was his sister, fearing that Abimeleck would slay him and take Sarah, as was often done in the East when a man had a beautiful wife.

Kings and princes generally take young women and virgins, but they respect elderly women, especially women who are ninety years old. Then again, had Sarah been ninety years old when Abraham sojourned in Gerar, he would not have been afraid of Abimeleck slaying him on account of his wife.

Sarah must have been attractive enough in her young years to win the favor of the king of Gerar, who had many wives and could marry as many maidens as he pleased.

We must not forget that many of these stories were handed down orally. Others were written, but when they were compiled they were not always placed according to the order of events.

God had already promised Abraham that Sarah would bear a child the next year [Gen. 18:13]. Therefore, Sarah must have been with child before Abraham went to Gerar.

But we must not forget that in those days, a woman of eighty or ninety was still beautiful and charming. Miriam, the sister of Moses, was about eighty-seven years old when she sang and danced in the Hebrew camp [Exod. 15:20].

GOD WENT UP

And he left off talking with him, and God went up from Abraham.
                                                                    Gen. 17:22

The Aramaic word *ettrim* "lifted up" or "went up" means "went away" [Gen. 18:33].

In the olden days the people believed that God's abode was in the skies or heaven, and that he descended to earth when he communed with people. They did not know that God was everywhere. When they communed with God they thought that God had left heaven and come down. When they prayed to him, they implored him to come down and deliver them. "Let us go down and there confound their language" [Gen. 11:7].

This concept of God prevailed for many centuries. Later the idea was refined by the Hebrew prophets and confirmed by Jesus Christ, who taught that God is Spirit and his presence is everywhere [John 4:24].

DIVINE GUESTS

And the Lord appeared unto him in the plains of Mamre: and he sat in the tent door in the heat of the day;
And he lifted up his eyes and looked, and, lo, three men stood by him: and when he saw them, he ran to meet them from the tent door, and bowed himself toward the ground. Gen. 18:1-2

Easterners rest during the hot hours of the day. In Egypt, Arabia, and other countries where the climate is warm, work is suspended at noon and the people rest and sleep until the day starts to cool.

Chiefs of the tribes, such as Abraham, the rich and the noble, sleep on the shady side of the tent or at door to escape the heat and to enjoy the cool breeze.

While Abraham was resting, in his vision he lifted up his eyes and looked and, behold, three noblemen stood nearby. He thought that they were the chiefs of some of the neighboring tribes who had come to visit with him, as often the desert chiefs do without being announced. So Abraham ran to greet them and offered them Eastern hospitality in inviting them to come into his tent to drink water, to wash their feet, and to rest and eat with him. And after urging them, as an Eastern host does to his guests, they accepted his hospitality.

Abraham and Sarah hastened and made preparations to entertain the three strange guests, not knowing who they were. And after washing their feet according to the custom, they set a table before them. And the Lord, and the two angels who accompanied him, ate meat, bread, and other food which Sarah had carefully prepared. Then, after announcing the birth of Isaac and pronouncing the doom of Sodom and Gomorrah, they departed. And Abraham went a little way with them to see them off.

In chapter 19:27, 28, we read: "And Abraham rose up early in the morning and went to the place where he had stood before the Lord . . . and lo, the smoke of the country went up like the smoke of a furnace." Both Abraham and Lot were informed in a vision about the impending disaster.

God is the Spirit and the Truth. He has no feet to be washed nor does he eat and drink. But in a vision, he appears to men as one of them. Abraham was risen so high in his spirituality that he could thus commune with God.

EASTERN HOSPITALITY

Let a little water, I pray you, be fetched, and wash your feet,
and rest yourselves under the tree.   Gen. 18:4

Washing the feet of the newly arrived guests and giving them water
to drink and food to eat is an old Eastern custom which, in Arabia and
some other places, is still practiced today.

In biblical lands, where the chief occupation was raising sheep and
cattle, roads were bad and in some areas still are bad, dusty, and muddy.
Many people wear sandals, while some travel barefooted. When they
arrive in sheep camps or towns, the host sees that their feet are washed.
Then he seats them on quilts and *namdas* (bed garments made of lamb's
wool), rugs, and other bed clothing in which both the family and the
guests sleep during the night.

The guests' feet are washed to keep the bed clothing clean. Years later,
it became an established custom or ritual and a sign of hospitality.

Simon the Pharisee refused to wash Jesus' feet because Jesus' teaching
was questioned by the temple authorities. But a woman who was a sinner
washed them with her tears [Luke 7:36-50]. Jesus washed the feet of his
disciples [John 13:4-10].

CREAM

And he took butter, and milk, and the calf which he had dressed,
and set it before them; and he stood by them under the tree, and
they did eat.   Gen. 18:8

The Aramaic word *khewtha*, in this instance, means "cream." Pastoral
and tribal people always place cream before their honorable guests. At
times, cream is saved just for this purpose. It would be embarrassing for
a wealthy family not to have cream when an honorable man is entertained. Butter is usually placed before common guests and workers.

The cream made from the milk of sheep and goats is very delicious and
is coveted by the people.

Abraham entertained God and the angels in a vision. They ate and
drank in a vision.

PREGNANCY

And he said, I will certainly return unto thee according to the time of life; and, lo, Sarah thy wife shall have a son. And Sarah heard it in the tent door, which was behind him. Gen. 18:10

The Eastern text reads: "And the Lord said, I will certainly return to you at this time next year, and lo, Sarah your wife shall be with child, and shall have a son. . . ."

The Aramaic word *khaitha* means "with child," that is, when a woman feels that she is pregnant.

The Aramaic word for a midwife is *khaitha,* derived from *khaya,* "to have life." A midwife saves babies' lives. This is why they are called *khayatha* [Exod. 1:15, 17].

Some biblical scholars have confused *khaitha* with *khaiwatha,* wild beasts. [See verse 14, Eastern text.]

HOMAGE TO DIVINE GUESTS

And the men rose up from thence, and looked toward Sodom: and Abraham went with them to bring them on the way. Gen. 18:16

Easterners generally welcome their notable guests and high government officials by meeting them on the way and escorting them to the town or city. When they leave, they accompany them for a few miles to bring them out to the highway. They do this as a token of esteem and respect.

This is more true of the small villages and sheep camps where the roads, being narrow paths, are difficult to find.

Abraham in his divine vision accompanied the Lord and the two angels until he brought them to the highway and saw them off. In his vision he did homage to God as he would do to a desert king or the chief of a tribe. Early in the morning Abraham looked from the place where he had communed with the Lord in his vision and, behold, the cities of Sodom and Gomorrah (*Amorah*) were already burning [Gen. 19:27, 28].

TWO ANGELS IN SODOM

And there came two angels to Sodom at even; and Lot sat in the gate of Sodom: and Lot seeing them rose up to meet them; and he bowed himself with his face toward the ground. Gen. 19:1

The term "angel" in Aramaic also means a "counselor," an "ambassador," a "messenger," and a "preacher." John was asked to write to the angels of the seven churches (preachers or ministers) [Rev. 1:20; 2:1]. An angel also means a "man of God." Angels are spirits.

These were apparently the same angels who had appeared with the Lord to Abraham as he was asleep in the door of the tent. Now they appeared in a vision to his nephew Lot. Lot, in his vision, was seated at the gate of the city when the two pious-looking strangers appeared at the gate. Lot rose up and invited them to come into his house. In the East, when strangers are found at the gate, they are invited into the homes and given food and lodging. This is because hotels are unknown. The people often say, "Today he is my guest; tomorrow I will be his guest." Lot did what any noble Arab chief would do.

The people of the town were so wicked and perverted that they would not spare even an angel. Sodom was a lewd and licentious city where men sought heinous vileness. The wanton men were not to be satisfied with Lot's virgin daughters; they would rather choose to disgrace his honorable guests.

Lot was warned by the angels of the Lord to leave the doomed city at once. The perverted townsmen might one day attack him. There were not even ten pious men to be found in Sodom. Lot, like Abraham, obeyed the voice of God and, directed by the angels, left the city in the early morning and fled to Zoar (Aramaic, *Little*), a little town in the mountains of Moab.

A great many episodes in the Bible are based on the visions which men of God saw. The books of the prophets were based on revelations or visions they saw and at times were told to write them [Hab. 2:2].

EASTERNERS DECLINE INVITATIONS

And he said, Behold now, my lords, turn in, I pray you, into your servant's house, and tarry all night, and wash your feet, and ye shall rise up early, and go on your ways. And they said, Nay; but we will abide in the street all night. Gen. 19:2

Nearly all Easterners decline invitations to eat or to lodge until they are urged repeatedly to come into one's house to eat. The host knows that the stranger does not mean it when he declines the invitation. He knows he needs food and lodging.

It is an ancient Eastern custom to decline an invitation until the host asks at least seven times. The angels of the Lord who appeared to Lot in his vision declined Lot's hospitality, but they knew that Lot would insist that they come with him and spend the night in his house. The vision was so real that Lot was conversing with the angels (spirits) as though they were men.

THE STATUS OF WIVES

And Lot went out, and spake unto his sons-in-law, which married his daughters, and said, Up, get you out of this place; for the Lord will destroy this city. But he seemed as one that mocked unto his sons-in-law.　　　　　　　　　　　　　　　　　　**Gen. 19:14**

In the East the status of a married woman is different from that of a concubine. The phrase, "which married his daughters," is recorded by the author of Genesis in order to show that Lot's daughters were given in marriage to his sons-in-law. Had they been concubines or slaves, their master could not be called son-in-law. For example, King Solomon had seven hundred wives whom he had married, and three hundred concubines who were presented to him as gifts and who had no status as wives. This is also true of Abraham and Hagar; the latter was not a wife. This is why Sarah could easily put her away.

This ancient custom still prevails in many parts of the world where polygamy is still practiced.

LOOKING BEHIND

And it came to pass, when they had brought them forth abroad, that he said, Escape for thy life; look not behind thee, neither stay thou in all the plain; escape to the mountain, lest thou be consumed.　　　　　　　　　　　　　　　　　　**Gen. 19:17**

"Do not look behind" as an idiom means "Do not regret," "forget the past." Lot had chosen the plain of Jordan, the well-watered land which was like a garden and like the fields of Zoan in Egypt, and the arid region west of Jordan was left to Abraham [Gen. 13:10].

Lot, even though faithful to the voice of God, was somewhat reluctant to leave. Some of his daughters were married in Sodom and Gomorrah and had considerable properties in the land. It was not an easy thing not to think of the past in such a fertile valley where one harvest comes after another throughout the year. But Lot was warned by God to leave immediately in order to escape the impending disaster which was to befall the doomed cities. On such an occasion every minute counts.

Lot was also warned not to stay in the plain but to escape to the mountains. This is because the whole region of the plain was to be destroyed with a mysterious fire of chemicals and brimstone. Even an hour of delay would have caused Lot and his family to be engulfed by the great disaster. The whole region of the plain which contained pitch was to be ablaze.

PILLAR OF SALT

But his wife looked back from behind him, and she became a pillar of salt. Gen. 19:26

"She became a pillar of salt" is an Eastern idiom which means, "She had a stroke, or she was paralyzed and dead." In the East, when a man becomes paralyzed or has a stroke, the people say, "He has turned into a rock," or "he has become like a stone."

When Abigail told her husband Nabal that she had given provisions to David and his men, Nabal was so enraged that he had a heart attack. The Bible says: "And his wife had told him these things, that his heart died within him, and he became as a stone" [1 Sam. 25:37]. And yet, Nabal died ten days after [Verse 38]. Had he literally become a stone, he could not have lived for ten days more. These idioms are still in use in the East.

Lot's wife had been reluctant to leave the pleasant gardens and orchards of Sodom. She had doubted her husband's vision and the divine warning. Her sons-in-law had thought Lot had lost his mind and that he was mocking when he told them of the divine warning asking them to leave the city [Verse 14]. Evidently Lot's wife also did not believe the city would be destroyed.

When Lot's wife disobeyed the divine command and stood up and looked behind and saw the city of orchards and lush gardens and everything which had been dear to her heart, on fire, and the smoke rising to the heavens, she had a stroke and she became hard like a block of salt or flint rock, which is also called salt, and she was dead. Such blocks of salt rock are still to be found in Sodom.

The catastrophe and the loss of her daughters, her sons-in-law, and her other relatives were too much for a woman who had been brought up in the luxuries of Sodom and who had no faith in the God of her husband.

The miracle here is that Lot's wife died because of her unfaithfulness and her disobedience to God's command. She was dead, like a pillar of salt. Whether she actually turned into a pillar of salt or not, she was stricken and dead. God could have made her turn into anything.

NO KINDRED LEFT

And the firstborn said unto the younger, Our father is old, and there is not a man in the earth to come in unto us after the manner of all the earth. Gen. 19:31

The Aramaic word *arra*, in this instance, means "land," "region," and "ground," and not "the world."

There were other races in Palestine and Jordan, such as Hittites, Amorites, Philistines, Syrians, and Canaanites. But all these people were pagan and corrupt. All the men and women who belonged to the family or the tribe of Abraham and Lot had perished in Sodom and Gomorrah.

Lot's daughters were unwilling to marry pagan men. Abraham and his tribe were on the other side of the River Jordan.

During this early time all Hebrew patriarchs were opposed to inter-marriage with the natives in Palestine [Gen. 24:1-4]. Then again, Lot's daughters wanted to preserve the posterity of their own family. Had they married pagan men, Lot's name would have been obliterated and his posterity lost forever.

LOT'S DAUGHTERS

Come, let us make our father drink wine, and we will lie with him, that we may preserve seed of our father.

And they made their father drink wine that night: and the first-born went in, and lay with her father; and he perceived not when she lay down, nor when she arose. Gen. 19:32-33

The Hebrews had a code of morals older than the Mosaic law and its ordinances. This code was handed down orally just as the nomad tribes keep oral treaties and preserve moral laws which are handed down from one generation to another.

The Hebrews never married sisters, daughters, and other near kinsmen. Lot's case was dictated by emergencies. Apparently, Lot's daughters had no one of their kindred to marry. They had just fled from Sodom where their relatives and friends had perished in the earthquake. They saw that in order to preserve their posterity, they had to live with their father, Lot.

They knew their father, being a pious man, would not consent to lie with them, so they made him drink wine until he was drunk. Lot knew both of his daughters without perceiving that they had lain with him. When a man is inflamed with wine, he does not know what he is doing. "For wine is a mocker" [Gen. 9:21; Prov. 20:1; 23:20, 21].

ABIMELECK TOOK SARAH

But Abimeleck had not come near her: and he said, Lord, wilt thou slay also a righteous nation? Gen. 20:4

In biblical times when monarchs took new wives, they did not have intimacy with them for a long time. The women were examined, purified, dressed, and prepared to be acceptable to the monarchs. Esther had to wait twelve months to undergo the treatment prescribed for the women [Esther 2:12].

Abimeleck took Sarah, believing that she was a sister of Abraham. (She *was* a half sister and a wife.) Abraham, fearing for his life, had told Sarah not to say she was his wife. When a man had a handsome wife, his life was in danger. But when a man had a pretty sister, he was welcomed and given many gifts.

Evidently, it was during the time of Sarah's preparation and prescribed treatments that the Lord spoke to Abimeleck in a dream at night and warned him that Sarah was the wife of Abraham. The king hastily returned her to her husband, Abraham. Abimeleck had not approached her. In the same way Sarah was also taken by Pharaoh [Gen. 12:15].

ABRAHAM, A PROPHET

Now therefore restore the man his wife; for he is a prophet, and he shall pray for thee, and thou shalt live: and if thou restore her not, know thou that thou shalt surely die, thou, and all that are thine.
Gen. 20:7

All patriarchs and pious men who communed with God in visions were addressed as prophets, seers, or men of God.

Abraham, throughout the latter part of his life, communed with God and remained faithful to him. This is why he was called the father of believers. The prophets were looked upon as representatives of God and were feared more than the priests. Nevertheless, Abraham left no book, delivered no oracle, and never acted as a counselor to kings or as a teacher. Writing in his day was in its infancy and difficult. And Abraham was a chieftain and a prophet. All other prophets either left a book or taught or gave counsel and admonished the people.

The Moslems call Abraham a prophet and his name is listed in the Koran as one of God's prophets.

ABIMELECK, A BELIEVER

And Abimeleck said unto Abraham, What sawest thou, that thou hast done this thing?
And Abraham said, Because I thought, Surely the fear of God is not in this place; and they will slay me for my wife's sake.
Gen. 20:10-11

Many of the peoples in Palestine revered and feared the Lord God of the Hebrews and had an oral or written code which prohibited adultery.

Abimeleck seemingly was a righteous man who respected his neighbor's wife. He had taken Sarah because of her beauty, thinking that she was Abraham's sister. But she was his half-sister and wife.

The nomad tribes practice polygamy, but they respect one another's wives as their own sisters and mothers. A moral code of law must have existed in Palestine, Egypt, and Assyria prior to the Mosaic law. The law of Khomarabi (Hammurabi, king of Babylonia) was written before the days of Abraham. It is the first recorded moral code in human history.

When Abraham prayed to God, Abimeleck was healed. The Lord forgave him because he was innocent and ignorant in the matter.

DECEIVING

And unto Sarah he said, Behold, I have given thy brother a thousand pieces of silver: behold, he is to thee a covering of the eyes, unto all that are with thee, and with all other: thus she was reproved.   Gen. 20:16

The Eastern text reads: ". . . because you have been humbled in the eyes of my people, and because of the other things for which I have reproved you."

Sarah had posed as a sister of Abraham. (She *was* his half-sister as well as his wife.) Because of the stories she had told the people in the palace, she was humiliated. In the East, when a person is humiliated or exposed, the people who stand near him cover their faces on account of reproach and deception. The king paid Abraham one thousand pieces of silver in order to absolve himself of any guilt in the matter, even though he had not touched her, and because Sarah was ashamed in the eyes of the people. It was a reproach.

HAGAR AND ISHMAEL

And God said unto Abraham, Let it not be grievous in thy sight because of the lad, and because of thy bondwoman; in all that Sarah hath said unto thee, hearken unto her voice; for in Isaac shall thy seed be called.   Gen. 21:12

Bondwoman is another term for maidservant. Bondwomen had no status and, therefore, they were not called wives. Some of them were slave women whom men had bought with money or taken captive. They could be dispossessed and put away at any time. Hagar, here, is addressed not as a wife but as a bondwoman; that is, a piece of property.

Seed, in this case means not only "posterity" but also the "teaching" or "faith" of Abraham which was to become the religion of the world whereby all the nations and peoples were to be blessed. That is to say, the messianic promises were to be fulfilled through the descendants of Isaac. Later Esau was rejected and Jacob chosen.

Ishmael was not rejected by God simply because his mother was an Egyptian. Ishmael had no fault in being born of a slave woman. God blessed him and made him a great nation. Many princes came forth from the lineage of Ishmael.

The covenant was made and confirmed with Isaac before his birth [Gen. 17:21]. Ishmael is the ancestor of Mohammed, and the prophet of the Moslem people. Millions of men and women heard of the God of Abraham through Mohammed. Today, the descendants of Ishmael are stronger and far more numerous than those of Jacob [Gen. 17:20; 21:13].

HEAVY BURDENS

And Abraham rose up early in the morning, and took bread, and a bottle of water, and gave it unto Hagar, putting it on her shoulder, and the child, and sent her away: and she departed, and wandered in the wilderness of Beer-sheba.   Gen. 21:14

Even today, travelers in Palestine, Arabia, and other parts of the Near East carry bread and water on a journey. This is because distances between towns are long, and bread and water cannot be easily obtained along the way. Water is carried in a sheep or goat skin.

Jesus and his disciples carried bread on their journeys and at times, when the bread was exhausted, they were hungry.

When Joseph sent his brothers to the land of Canaan to bring their father Jacob to Egypt, he gave them provisions for the journey [Gen. 45:21-23 and Josh. 9:5].

In the East it is not unusual to see a woman carrying a heavy burden with a large child on top of it. Eastern women, during migrations, often carry burdens and place one of their children upon it. Many mothers would hate to see their only child walking while they themselves were carrying only a light burden.

Hagar's burden consisted of ample provisions for the journey, a skin filled with water, and her son Ishmael. The latter is still referred to as a child, though he was thirteen years old when Abraham circumcised him [Gen. 17:25].

On the other hand, Hagar, being a slave woman, Abraham wanted her to carry the child who was awakened in the early morning.

Ishmael, being the only child of Abraham, was spoiled. The sons of princes and rulers seldom walk. They are carried by the servants, or ride on horses or donkeys.

THE WELL FOUND

And God opened her eyes, and she saw a well of water; and she went, and filled the bottle with water, and gave the lad drink.
Gen. 21:19

The well was always there, but Hagar was unable to find it. Her mind was confused and embittered toward her mistress, Sarah, who had expelled her and her only child.

But when she forgot her troubles with Sarah and turned to God and prayed for help, her eyes were opened and she looked around and there was the well.

When our spiritual vision is shut off, our eyes become blind. At times, we fail to see the things which are around us. But when we turn to God our eyes are opened and we are guided to the right way and to sources of help.

BEER-SHEBA

Wherefore he called that place Beer-sheba; because there they sware both of them.
Gen. 21:31

Beer-sheba is an Aramaic compound noun which means "the seventh well." *Beer*, "well," and *sheba*, "seven."

Abraham gave Abimeleck seven ewe lambs as a witness that he had dug the seven wells. The seven of them were the property of Abraham [Verses 29 and 30]. The seven ewes were the reminder of the seven wells which belonged to Abraham.

Water being scanty in Palestine and Arabia, the shepherds fought over the wells. At times princes and powerful chiefs confiscate wells ruthlessly [Gen. 21:25 and 26:15-18].

In Genesis 26:33, the name of the well is called *Shebah*, Hebrew "oath." *Sabaa* in Aramaic means "plenty." Isaac found a prolific well of running water; therefore, the term was given a new meaning. Hebrew was not yet spoken at that time.

GOD OF THE WORLD

And Abraham planted a grove in Beer-sheba, and called there on the name of the Lord, the everlasting God.
Gen. 21:33

The Eastern text more correctly reads: *Alaha di almey*, "the God of the worlds." The Aramaic word for everlasting is *Alam*.

As we see from the previous verses, God had communed with Abimeleck, the king of Gerar, and warned him to return Sarah to her husband, Abraham [Gen. 20:7]. Some years before, God had punished Pharaoh and warned him to restore Sarah to Abraham [Gen. 12:17]. Abraham began to realize that his God was the God of all races and peoples.

Now it was time for Abraham to plant a grove in Beer-sheba and invoke the name of the God of the worlds, the Living and the Everlasting God. Beer-sheba was a good place in which to settle.

Abraham planted the grove, not to worship the trees as the pagans did, but to provide shelter from the sun and fruit for the people who were with him.

Then again, in the East when one plants trees in a place, he becomes the recognized owner thereof. Abraham wanted to have a place to call his own.

ABRAHAM'S VISION

And it came to pass after these things, that God did tempt Abraham, and said unto him, Abraham: and he said, Behold, here I am.
And he said, Take now thy son, thine only son Isaac, whom thou lovest, and get thee into the land of Moriah; and offer him there for a burnt offering upon one of the mountains which I will tell thee of.
Gen. 22:1-2

This episode took place in a vision. God often speaks to men in visions and dreams [Job 33:14, 15]. All God's divine communications with Abraham, Isaac, Jacob, and the prophets were in visions and dreams.

Abraham was living among pagan people who worshiped idols and graves and even sacrificed their children to false deities. In those days, droughts, famines, plagues, and diseases were blamed on certain people. Therefore, the pagans always tried to appease their gods.

Palestine has too many droughts, and the people suffer from famines. Abraham saw other people sacrificing one or two of their children to their gods; so he thought he should do the same. After all, he was living in a pagan land. But it was revealed to him in a vision to offer a ram instead of his only son, Isaac. God tempts no one [James 1:13, 14]. All of man's temptations come from within.

The Lord commanded Abraham to go to the land of Moriah in what is now Jerusalem. It is nearly a three-day journey from Beer-sheba to Jerusalem, but in the vision it takes only a few minutes. The Eastern text reads: *learra di-Amoraye,* "the land of the Amorites."

When Abraham arrived in the land of the Amorites, he saw the place and left the donkey with the servant, and he and his son Isaac went to the high place. Evidently, Abraham saw an altar on the high place and knew that it was the place of worship which God had indicated to him in the vision [Verses 5 and 6].

Moriah might be a corrupt form of *Amoriah*. The letter *aleph* in Semitic languages is a weak letter and is often silent or even omitted in writing.

The locality of the mountain is unknown. The reason for this might be that the place of worship was so well-known that there was no reason to point it out or to name it. The Amorites were a Semitic people. They must have had a place of worship or a shrine on one of the high places to which tribal people went to offer their burnt offerings.

In Chronicles the place is called the Mountain of the Amorites, indicating that it was a shrine on one of the mountains. I believe the reference here is to Jerusalem, the Jebusite city where Solomon later built his great temple [2 Chron. 3:1].

Abraham had visited this city when he defeated the five Mesopotamian kings and Melchizedek, the king of Salem (Aramaic *Shalem*), the priest of the Most High God, brought him bread and wine and blessed Abraham and called him the blessed of the God, the possessor of heaven and earth [Gen. 14:18].

Evidently the Amorites, like other Semitic tribes, worshiped the God of heaven, the same living God to which Abraham went to sacrifice. That is why Abraham was told to go to the land of the Amorites.

Had Abraham, his son Isaac, and his servants actually gone to Jerusalem, Melchizedek, the king of Salem, would have gone to greet Abraham, and his princes and noblemen would have gathered around the altar. Abraham had already met the king of Salem [Gen. 14:18-20]. But there is no mention that Abraham was met by anyone. Nor is there any mention of Sarah, his wife.

Indeed, Sarah would have protested against the sacrificing of her only son, and she would have mourned for him. But the incident took place in a divine revelation [Gen. 22:11-18].

And some days after, Abraham related his vision and the meaning thereof, and from henceforth the Hebrews offered sheep, rams, he-goats, and oxen. But once in a while they offered human sacrifices, too [Judg. 11:34-39].

A KNIFE

And Abraham took the wood of the burnt offering, and laid it upon Isaac his son; and he took the fire in his hand, and a knife; and they went both of them together.   Gen. 22:6

Probably this is the first mention of the knife in the Bible. [See also Gen. 22:10.] Steel knives might have been a new invention and scarce. Sharp flint was used for circumcision [Exod. 4:25].

Iron and steel were in use a long time before Abraham. Noah would have had to have iron and steel instruments in order to build such a large ship (the ark). The Assyrians, the Arameans, and the Babylonians were great pioneers in all scientific fields. They had swords, chariots, and instruments of iron.

FIGURATIVE SPEECH

That in blessing I will bless thee, and in multiplying I will multiply thy seed as the stars of the heaven, and as the sand which is upon the seashore; and thy seed shall possess the gate of his enemies.
Gen. 22:17

These idiomatic expressions should not be taken literally. In biblical days, such large figures as millions and billions were unknown. A thousand, ten thousand, and thousands of thousands were the highest figures which were used by the learned men. The common people counted on their fingers and knew the familiar figures such as ten, twelve, twenty, forty, and a hundred.

"As the stars of the heaven, and as the sand which is upon the sea shore" means "numerous." Of course no one can count the stars or the sand which is on the seashore.

On the other hand, the Hebrews have never been as numerous a people as the Arabs, Chinese, Indians, and Russians.

But the descendants of Abraham are not only those of his posterity; that is, the flesh, but those of the Spirit, also. All the believers in the faith (religion) of Abraham are his descendants [John 8:39; Gal. 3:7].

[See also article on Gen. 24:60.]

ABRAHAM A PRINCE

Hear us, my lord: thou art a mighty prince among us: in the choice of our sepulchres bury thy dead; none of us shall withhold from thee his sepulchre, but that thou mayest bury thy dead.
Gen. 23:6

Abraham was a God-fearing man, looked upon as a prince of God, and revered as a prophet. Abraham was the chief of a powerful tribe which defeated the five kings [Gen. 14:14-20].

Then again, Abraham communed with God, received divine revelations, and gave counsel. This is why he was revered by the native Palestinians.

EASTERN BARGAINING

Nay, my lord, hear me: the field give I thee, and the cave that is therein, I give it thee; in the presence of the sons of my people give I it thee: bury thy dead. **Gen. 23:11**

In the East such statements and generosity are not taken seriously, even though the person might mean what he says. This is because Easterners are habitually extravagant with their remarks, especially when buying and selling.

When they start to converse with a prospective customer, they may say, "It is yours; take it away!" or, "My house is your house!" But the customer knows they don't really mean what they say.

As soon as the seller knows that the buyer is ready to buy, he then starts with a high price, and then they begin to bargain seriously.

In this case, there was no bargaining. Abraham's wife was dead and she had to be buried. Ephron knew that Abraham was not going to bargain in the presence of mourners, nor accept the burial ground gratis; and, being a prince, Abraham would not bury his wife in a burial ground which was not his. Moreover, Abraham knew the custom of the land and the business formalities. Even if Ephron might have meant what he said, he knew Abraham would not accept the field and the cave gratis, and that he would willingly pay a higher price to avoid bargaining. [See also Gen. 25:9; 50:13.]

MATURE MEN

Unto Abraham for a possession in the presence of the children of Heth, before all that went in at the gate of his city. **Gen. 23:18**

"All that went in at the gate of his city" is an idiom which means "all the mature men." In the East the elders spent most of their time at the gate of the city. Parks and other public places are still unknown in walled cities and towns.

Gates of the cities are used as places for public gatherings, loitering, and for conducting business or legal transactions [Ruth 4:1-4]. At the gate of the city one can find his friends, his enemies, and his business associates. War counsels are also held at the gate of the city [1 Kings 22:10 and Gen. 23:10]. Scribes and self-appointed judges are found at the gates, waiting to be called upon to perform services. This custom prevailed until recently.

AN ANCIENT BINDING OATH

And Abraham said unto his eldest servant of his house, that ruled over all that he had, Put, I pray thee, thy hand under my thigh:

And I will make thee swear by the Lord, the God of heaven, and the God of the earth, that thou shalt not take a wife unto my son of the daughters of the Canaanites, among whom I dwell.

Gen. 24:2-3

The Aramaic reads *khasi*, "my girdle." The Easterners wear a girdle on their vests to keep their clothes together and prevent money, bread, and other articles from falling.

Placing of the hand under the girdle symbolizes a solemn and binding oath which cannot be broken. In some instances, when people take an oath, they place their right hand on their heart. In the olden days the heart and kidneys were considered the most holy organs in the body.

This patriarchal admonition was later incorporated in the Mosaic laws and ordinances. The loyal Hebrews or Israelites refrained from marrying Gentile women or giving their daughters in marriage to their sons.

Just as the girdle binds the clothes to the body, so the person is bound with the oath. Then again, the heart is close to the girdle.

MEETINGS AT THE WELL

And he made his camels to kneel down without the city by a well of water at the time of the evening, even the time that women go out to draw water.

Gen. 24:11

In the Fast, springs and wells are the only places where a man can see maidens or married women and converse with them. Easterners seldom look at a strange woman and try to converse with her. The father of a girl or the husband of a woman would resent such repulsive advances.

Nevertheless, at a spring or at a well, one can carry on conversations with both girls and married women under the pretense of being thirsty and asking for water to drink [Gen. 24:45, 46].

Young men purposely go to springs or wells during the evening hours to see the girls they love and, if possible, to converse with them. Moses met his wife at the well [Exod. 2:15-17] and Jacob met Rachel at the well [Gen. 29:2-12]. Eastern poets have composed many songs about lovers who had met at a fountain or a well. When Jesus' disciples saw him talking to the Samaritan woman at the well, they were surprised ". . . and marvelled that he talked with the woman" [John 4:27].

Abraham's servant had trusted in the God of his master who knows all and ordains all. The Lord led him to the right place at the right time, where he met the right woman who was to become the wife of his master's son. God guides all those who trust in him and are willing to be directed.

BETROTHAL CUSTOM

And there was set meat before him to eat: but he said, I will not eat, until I have told mine errand. And he said, Speak on.

Gen. 24:33

When Easterners go on a mission seeking the hand of a maiden for a bridegroom-to-be, they refuse to eat or drink until their request is granted and the father of the bride-to-be gives his consent.

On such occasions, generally in the evening, a party of respectable townsmen calls on the father of the girl and, on their arrival, are greeted warmly and seated. Then food is set before them. But when they are asked to eat, they decline. Then the father of the maiden says to them, "You have come in peace; you have walked over my eyes," which means, "You are most welcome." To this, the chief matchmaker replies, "May God bless you; may your eyes see more light." Then he adds, "We have come to seek the hand of your daughter." If the father is pleased, he says, "My daughter is a pair of shoes before your feet." Then the guests start to eat. But if he is unwilling to give his daughter in marriage, the guests rise up one by one leaving the food on the table untouched. Abraham's servant refused to eat until he saw that his mission had prospered and that Rebekah's father, Bethuel, and her brother, Laban, were willing to give her in marriage to their kinsman, Isaac.

When Laban and his sons consented to give Rebekah to Isaac, then the engagement festivity began [Gen. 24:51-54].

ESPOUSAL CONSENT

And before I had done speaking in mine heart, behold, Rebekah came forth with her pitcher on her shoulder; and she went down unto the well, and drew water: and I said unto her, Let me drink, I pray thee.

And she made haste, and let down her pitcher from her shoulder, and said, Drink, and I will give thy camels drink also: so I drank, and she made the camels drink also. Gen. 24:45-46

When a maiden consents to give a drink to a prospective lover or an emissary of his, it indicates that she is willing to marry.

When Abraham's servant saw that she was not only willing to give him a drink but also offered to give his camels a drink, he did not wait to see her father and brother; he put the earring on her ear and the bracelets upon her arms. Rebekah was divinely informed regarding the man's mission. Both Abraham's servant and Rebekah were divinely guided, because of the faith of Abraham and his loyalty to God. This success was not incidental, as may be seen. Abraham believed in God and prayed for the success of his servant's mission and God granted him his request.

BRIDES ARE BLESSED

And they blessed Rebekah, and said unto her, Thou art our sister; be thou the mother of thousands of millions, and let thy seed possess the gate of those which hate them.　　　Gen. 24:60

The term "millions" was unknown to the ancients, just as the term "billion" was hardly known prior to World War II. Today the figure trillion is known only to mathematicians.

The ancient term used was *rebotha;* that is, the great number "ten thousand." And *riboth-ribotha* meant many ten thousands. At times, these figures were used without the slightest knowledge of numerical value. What they really meant was "May you have many descendants."

Even today, when a girl is given in marriage, she is blessed by the priest and her parents and relatives who wish her happiness, prosperity, and many children. Other figures of speech describing large numbers are, "sand of the sea," "leaves of the trees," and "stars of heaven."

[See article "Figurative Speech," Gen. 22:17.]

SHE HAD DONE

And the servant told Isaac all things that he had done.
　　　Gen. 24:66

The Eastern text correctly reads: ". . . all things that *she* had done." The letter tau, "t," at the end of the verb with two dots under it is the feminine sign. *Ebdat,* "she had done." *Ebdet,* "I have done."

Rebekah gave Abraham's servant water to drink, and she also watered his camels [Gen. 24:18-22]. The servant was relating to his master's son, Isaac, how God had prospered his way and answered his prayer, and how Rebekah had helped him and made her betrothal easy.

SHEBA AND DEDAN

And Jokshan begat Sheba, and Dedan. And the sons of Dedan were Asshurim, and Letushim, and Leummim. Gen. 25:3

Sheba and Dedan were great-grandsons of Abraham from his wife Keturah. They were the grandsons of Zimran, Abraham's son [Compare Gen. 10:7].

Dedanites were kindred of the Midianites and other people who were descendants of Abraham, such as the Edomites and Amalekites. Many Arab tribes in western and southern Palestine trace their ancestry to Abraham. Many of these tribes lived in Teman (southern Palestine), known today as Negeb [Isa. 21:13, 14; Jer. 25:23; Ezek. 27:20].

The Koresh, the most powerful Arab tribe in Mecca, traces its descendancy to Ishmael, the son of Abraham.

BIRTHRIGHT

And Jacob said, Sell me this day thy birthright. Gen. 25:31

In the East the first-born is considered as the heir of his father. He is the one who carries the family tradition; therefore, he receives the largest portion of his father's estate. In biblical days the first-born received a double portion [Deut. 21:15-17].

Selling and buying of the birthright has nothing to do with God's blessing. Nevertheless, Easterners believe that such rights can be transferred from one person to another.

The little stew which Jacob gave to his brother Esau could not have changed God's mind. Jacob was preordained as the heir of his father Isaac by God. That is, God knew that Jacob was more interested in spiritual things and in the family heritage than Esau was. Esau from his childhood was a worldly man, interested in hunting, fighting, and subduing other people by means of his sword and bow. Therefore, Esau had disqualified himself as an heir of his father Isaac. He was not interested in the tribal destiny and the divine plan which ran through the family.

Rebekah knew that her eldest son, Esau, was lenient toward paganism and that her youngest son, Jacob, was religiously inclined. The stew was incidental, but Isaac's blessings gave Jacob strength, wisdom, and a firm belief in the family tradition. On the other hand, God chose Jacob simply because Jacob was the right man. God does not look to seniority, nor is he partial. He sees the inner, the heart only, but man sees the outer.

SATAN

And they digged another well, and strove for that also: and he called the name of it Sitnah. Gen. 26:21

This is the first time that the name of Satan, Aramaic *Satana*, "the adversary," is mentioned in the Bible. The term *Sitnah* is a verbal noun meaning "adversity," of the same root as Satan.

The term "Satan" is derived from the Aramaic word *sata*, "to mislead," "to go astray," "to slide," and "to miss the mark."

Isaac called the name of the well "Satan" simply because there had been so much quarreling and deception over it. The servants of Abimeleck, the king of Philistia, confiscated many of the good wells which the servants of Isaac had dug.

The other well was called *Rakhboth* or *Rehoboth*, "enlarged," because the servants of Abimeleck did not quarrel with him over it.

Anything which is deceitful or unjust and contrary to the truth is called Satan because it is misleading.

A PROLIFIC WELL

And he called it Shebah: therefore the name of the city is Beer-sheba unto this day. Gen. 26:33

Aramaic *sebah* means "plenty," "satisfied," or "filled." This word is different from *shebah*, "seven."

Isaac called the name of the place Ber-sebah, the well with plenty of water. The words *sebah* and *shebah* are very close.

Previously, the place was named Beer-sheba by Abraham because he had dug seven wells [Article on Genesis 21:31].

ESAU'S SPECIAL GARMENT

And Rebekah took goodly raiment of her eldest son Esau, which were with her in the house, and put them upon Jacob her younger son. Gen. 27:15

In the East all noblemen and rich men have an expensive suit which they wear at feasts, banquets, and other special occasions. Some of the parts of the garments are heavily embroidered, especially the sleeves. This goodly apparel is carefully stored by the women to protect it from moths.

Esau was the first-born and the heir to his father Isaac. Therefore, he was entitled to wear a special garment with long sleeves. Rebekah knew that her son, Esau, would wear his special garment on such an occasion and that Isaac might feel it with his fingers. This is why she put the garment on her son, Jacob.

JACOB MEANS "HEEL"

And he said, Thy brother came with subtilty, and hath taken away thy blessing.
And he said, Is not he rightly named Jacob? for he hath supplanted me these two times: he took away my birthright; and, behold, now he hath taken away my blessing. Gen. 27:35-36

Yacob, Jacob, in Aramaic means "heel." The name is derived from *ekba,* "heel." When Jacob was born, his hand took hold of the heel of his twin brother, Esau.

Esau and Jacob struggled together when they were in their mother's womb [Gen. 25:22-23]. Years later, Esau thought that Jacob had held his foot in trying to restrain him from being born first. Now Jacob had taken from him the birthright, the family blessing.

Indeed, Jacob was born to be the heir to his father Isaac and to Abraham. He was interested in the family traditions, its culture, and its peculiar religion; but Esau was interested only in hunting and diversion. Therefore he disqualified himself as an heir and the first-born.

INTERPRETATION OF DREAMS

And he dreamed, and behold a ladder set up on the earth, and the top of it reached to heaven: and behold the angels of God ascending and descending on it. Gen. 28:12

Jacob had taught Joseph to interpret dreams, to explain dark sayings, and to know how to lead the tribe and find grazing and water for the flocks.

Joseph, before he was sold by his brothers, had a dream that offended his brothers and made them hate him. And when he dreamed another dream and related it to his father, Jacob, the latter rebuked him. Jacob knew the meaning of the dream. Jacob was trained by Isaac, and Isaac by Abraham. In those days, knowledge was handed down from father to son.

When dreams and visions were hard to understand, the prophet sought God's aid in interpreting it [Dan. 9:20-24]. But Jacob knew the meaning of the symbol.

A ladder, according to the interpretation of dreams and visions, indicates an understanding, or difficulties overcome. Jacob was fleeing from his brother, Esau, not knowing what the future had in store for him. And while he was on his way to Padan-aram he wondered if he ever would return to his people again.

Jacob, in his vision, saw the angels ascending and descending the ladder which stood between heaven and earth. The angels, in this instance, were symbolic of God's counsel. Jacob was assured that he was to be guided by divine messages and that the Lord would change Esau's heart toward him, and finally reconcile them. Jacob was to attain the highest success and prosperity in the land to which he was fleeing, and later return to his family. He was going to return by the same way and to the same place where he saw the vision, just as the angels ascended and descended the same ladder. Jacob was to return the same way. The heaven and the earth were the two points of difference between Jacob and his brother Esau which would be bridged by understanding.

PILLARS OF STONE

And Jacob rose up early in the morning, and took the stone that he had put for his pillows, and set it up for a pillar, and poured oil upon the top of it. Gen. 28:18

Prior to the Mosaic code of worship, sacred stones and sacred trees were venerated and worshiped by the people. Many of the pagan altars were stones or rocks which had offered some protection to shepherds and wayfarers during the time of heat and severe storms. The trees also offered relief to the thirsty and weary travelers [Judg. 6:19-27].

Many of these ancient stones and trees which once were venerated are still to be found in northern Mesopotamia, Persia, and Arabia. Even today the people revere these sacred stones and trees, and visit them from time to time.

Jacob took the stone which he had used for his pillow and set it up for a pillar, and consecrated it with oil as a memorial for the generations to come, that they might not forget God's goodness and his loving kindnesses to him and his posterity.

SCARCITY OF WATER

And they said, We cannot, until all the flocks be gathered together, and till they roll the stone from the well's mouth; then we water the sheep. Gen. 29:8

In many parts of Palestine and Arabia where wells are not prolific, water is scarce and at times is rationed. The people draw water in turns and the flocks are watered together. The water is drawn in leather buckets and poured out into long troughs constructed of stone or wood.

The shepherds obey the oral laws and respect the rights of their neighbors. Nevertheless, at times, because of the scarcity of water, shepherds quarrel among themselves and kill one another.

Moses, after his flight from Egypt helped Jethro's daughters to water their sheep. He drove other shepherds away [Exod. 2:16, 17].

WAGES

And Laban said unto Jacob, Because thou art my brother, shouldest thou therefore serve me for nought? tell me, what shall thy wages be?   Gen. 29:15

In the olden days, when silver and gold were scarce, dowries and wages were paid in kind; that is, in sheep, cattle, salt, butter, wheat. This ancient custom prevailed until World War I. In many parts of Iran, Turkey, Arabia, and Palestine, both dowries and wages were paid in kind. This is not all. Most of the business was also transacted by the exchange of wheat, butter, cheese, hardware, rugs, and dry goods.

During the time of Jesus some of the laborers were paid in money [Matt. 20:2].

Our word "salary" comes from "salt." During the Roman days, soldiers were paid with salt. Salt still remains as a medium of exchange in some parts of Africa. This is because in some regions salt is precious and hard to obtain.

PRETTY EYES

Leah was tender eyed; but Rachel was beautiful and well-favored.
                                                           Gen. 29:17

The Aramaic reads *rakikhan*, which means "attractive," "pretty," "warm," "sparkling," "charming," "penetrating." In the appraisal, both girls are lovely, one of them pretty-eyed and the other lovely and of good figure; that is, she was well-built. In the East people overlook the defects in a woman's body. They always point out the good qualities which they have.

Probably the error was caused by the confusion of the Aramaic word *ratiban*, "weak," "sick," "watery," with *rakikhan*, "pretty," "charming."

Jacob chose Rachel simply because she was younger and he had met her first at the well and had fallen in love with her.

Indeed, Leah's eyes were not weak or diseased as some Bible students maintain. The Eastern text reads: "And Leah had attractive eyes; but Rachel was beautiful and well favored."

The term *rakikhan,* "attractive," is still used in vernacular Aramaic.

A DOWRY

And Jacob served seven years for Rachel; and they seemed unto him but a few days, for the love he had to her.
And Jacob said unto Laban, Give me my wife, for my days are fulfilled, that I may go in unto her.   Gen. 29:20-21

Even today in northern Mesopotamia (Assyria), men pay a dowry to the father of the bride. The dowry is an ancient custom, as old as the Bible itself. The dowry is paid in money, sheep, cattle, or labor. In that part of the world the people believe that when a man pays for his wife he will appreciate and love her more.

Then again, when a man pays a dowry, it makes divorce difficult. Jacob had neither money, sheep, nor cattle, so he paid with his labor.

In Lower Mesopotamia, Syria, and Egypt the father of the bride pays the prospective bridegroom for marrying his daughter. This is because there are more women than men.

JACOB DECEIVED BY LABAN

And it came to pass, that in the morning, behold, it was Leah: and he said to Laban, What is this thou hast done unto me? did not I serve with thee for Rachel? wherefore then hast thou beguiled me?
                                                    Gen. 29:25

In the East, honeymooning is unknown. After the wedding ceremonies and festivities, which generally last for several days, the bridegroom and the bride sleep in the same room with the rest of the family. At times, there are more than ten families living under the same roof and they all sleep close to each other. In some houses the whole family sleeps in the same bed on the floor; privacy is unknown.

During the wedding feast the bride's face is covered, and the bridegroom seldom sees it. After six or seven o'clock, when it is dark, the lamps in the houses are put out and everybody goes into bed. Not until the day breaks does the man see the face of the woman with whom he has slept.

Jacob has seen Rachel clad in her wedding attire and Leah ministering to the guests. He, therefore, expected Rachel to be in bed with him. But his shrewd uncle, Laban, had put Leah in the bed. Then again, during the wedding feasts there is much confusion and drinking.

Jacob was shrewd, but Laban was more shrewd. Now Laban made Jacob work seven years more for the girl he really loved. On the other hand, most of the Easterners would refuse to give one of their younger daughters in marriage before the eldest was married. Customs and traditions are highly upheld in that part of the ancient world.

PLEADED WITH HER

And Rachel said, With great wrestlings have I wrestled with my sister, and I have prevailed: and she called his name Naphtali.

Gen. 30:8

The Eastern text reads: *Etkashpeth,* "I pleaded with her." That is to say, Rachel had to obtain her sister's consent in order to give her maid, Bilhah, to her husband, Jacob. The Aramaic word for "fought" or "wrestled with her" would be *etkatshet.* The two words are so close that one may easily confuse one with the other.

Jacob's time was divided between Leah and Rachel. Even today in the lands where polygamy is still practiced, the husband visits each of his wives on their appointed day. Rachel had to plead with her sister to permit her to give her maid Bilhah to Jacob. Her desire to have a child born from her maid, Bilhah, prevailed.

BLACK SHEEP

And Jacob took him rods of green poplar, and of the hazel and chestnut tree; and pilled white streaks in them, and made the white appear which was in the rods.

And he set the rods which he had pilled before the flocks in the gutters in the watering troughs when the flocks came to drink, that they should conceive when they came to drink.   Gen. 30:37-38

As there is little use for black wool, black sheep are unwanted in the Near East. White wool can be dyed into red, blue, green, yellow, and black. On the other hand, black is symbolic of death, mourning, and hardship. The people abhor the black. One can often hear people say, "My days have been black" [See also Lam. 5:10 and Jude 1:13].

Invariably, there are a few black rams in the flocks. This is because some of the families who make rugs like the natural black wool more than the dyed wool. But most of the shepherds and sheepowners resent having black rams near their sheep during the mating seasons.

Customarily, during the mating season, shepherds borrow rams from one another. Black rams are borrowed only when there is a need for black wool. When a shepherd wants to get revenge against a family, he will let a black ram mate with white sheep belonging to the family.

How Jacob used the rods to achieve his purpose and to get even with Laban is hard to understand. Thus far, no one has been able to duplicate this feat. God revealed the secret by the means of the rods.

What really happened was: God was on the side of Jacob because Laban had tried to cheat him. The rods which Jacob used were immaterial in this incident. God needed no rods in order that white sheep might bear speckled and spotted lambs, but he wanted Jacob to know that he was on his side. Nor was God a partner in any deceptive plan. Laban got what he deserved and Jacob was rewarded for his integrity, hard work, and faith in the God of his fathers.

WOMEN PURCHASED

Are we not counted of him strangers? for he hath sold us, and hath quite devoured also our money.   Gen. 31:15

"He has sold us," in this instance, means "He has devoured our dowry." The Assyrian and Aramean fathers received a dowry for their daughters. Jacob worked thirteen years for Laban's daughters. And since Jacob married in Laban's house, Laban gave his daughters no presents. The whole dowry of Jacob's hard labor went to him.

The betrothed girl is called *makhirtha,* derived from *makhar,* "to buy as a wife." The imperfect is *nmkhar* or *ymkhar. Makhirtha* means "the purchased one." In the Eastern liturgical books the church is called *makhirthey Damshikha.* The church is the bride, the purchased one of Chirst, who has bought her with his blood.

PAGAN GODS

With whomsoever thou findest thy gods, let him not live: before our brethren discern thou what is thine with me, and take it to thee. For Jacob knew not that Rachel had stolen them. Gen. 31:32

Jacob's father, Isaac, and his grandfather, Abraham, were monotheists. Evidently, Abraham had left Ur of Chaldea simply because of idolatry.

Seemingly, not all the people who came forth with Abraham believed in one God, the God of heaven who had communed with him and commanded him to leave his kinsmen and his land and go into a land which he was going to show Abraham. In other words, Abraham and his own family were the only ones who believed in one God. Nevertheless, God communed with the patriarchs of other families who had also forsaken their land and left with Abraham.

Laban was an idolator. His family had brought some of their gods (images) with them. In those days, gods gave oracles and were often consulted by the leaders of the tribe. Indeed, gods were essential for the tribal people who needed good counsel during their migrations and grazing seasons and for the welfare of the people and the sheep.

It seems that Jacob, even though he had prospered in Laban's house, worried over the presence of pagan gods and it made him long to return to his own people. Jacob was not interested in these gods and never knew that his wife had stolen one of the images from Laban, her father.

COLD AND HEAT

Thus I was; in the day the drought consumed me, and the frost by night; and my sleep departed from mine eyes. Gen. 31:40

The temperature in the northern part of the Arabian desert rises as high as 120 degrees during the day and falls as low as 55 degrees during the night. Therefore, the shepherds who tend their flocks during the day and watch over them during the night suffer from both heat and cold. Faithful shepherds sleep little during the night, for thieves steal and wild animals strike when the shepherd is asleep.

In the East when people say, "I was frozen," they mean, "I was cold." During certain times of the year one can find frost on the ground, yet during the day the temperature of standing water may be very high.

Jacob had been faithful to his father-in-law Laban and had undergone many difficulties and made many sacrifices in order to make good, but his father-in-law had not been fair to him. He had treated him as an hireling.

HEAP OF STONES

And Laban called it Jegar-sahadutha: but Jacob called it Galeed.
Gen. 31:47

The Aramaic text reads: *yagra, di sahdotha,* "the heap of the witness." Jacob called it Galeed, which means "the heap of witness," that is, the witness to a covenant. The heap was to remain as a witness to the compact between Laban and Jacob. *Doka* in Aramaic means "watchman." In Hebrew it is rendered *mizpeh,* "watch."

Mizpeh in Aramaic means, "Let the Lord settle the problems between you and me." Laban had tried to cheat Jacob, and Jacob also was not entirely innocent toward his father-in-law Laban. In a scientific or clever way he had been able to acquire most of his father-in-law's flocks [Gen. 30:37-43].

The heap of stones was built as an everlasting witness to the compact which was made between Laban and his nephew and son-in-law, Jacob. When the heap was built, then they sacrificed sheep and ate and made merry. Laban was divinely warned not to do any harm to Jacob. Moreover, the heap was a reminder forever that Jacob must not despise or mistreat Laban's daughters and Laban was never to seek vengeance against Jacob for his conduct.

The heap became as a boundary line between the descendants of Laban and those of Jacob, never to be transgressed by either one of them. Years later, Gilead became a disputed borderland between Israel and Syria.

GALEED

And Laban said, This heap is a witness between me and thee this day. Therefore was the name of it called Galeed.   Gen. 31:48

Gil-ad, Hebrew *Gilead, Galeed,* is a compound noun, *Gil-adad,* which means "the gully of meeting, celebrating, witnessing, and affirming an agreement."

Galeed is a mountainous country with many valleys and ravines.

Laban used the term *sahdotha,* derived from *sahad,* "to bear witness" to the agreement which was just concluded between Jacob and himself.

Laban and Jacob met and celebrated in this historic land; and each one of them gave a different name to the place. The term "Galeed" or "Gilead" was known to the Israelites prior to the Exodus. "And Machir begat Gilead" [Num. 26:29].

Galeed lies between the Sea of Galilee and the Dead Sea. On the east is the desert and on the south, Moab.

Prior to the occupation of Palestine by Joshua, Galeed was under Sihon, the king of the Amorites, who dwelt east of Jordan; the territory between the Arnon and Jabbok and between Jabbok and the Yarmuk. This mountainous land was given by Moses to the tribes of Reuben and Gad, and to half the tribe of Manasseh. This is because these tribes had large flocks and herds. In Arabic it is called *Jaladah.*

PRESENTS TO APPEASE

And say ye moreover, Behold, thy servant Jacob is behind us. For he said, I will appease him with the present that goeth before me, and afterward I will see his face; peradventure he will accept of me. Gen. 32:20

In the East, when governors, generals, princes, and rulers enter a city they are met by a welcoming party and greeted with lavish presents of silver, gold, sheep, oriental rugs, and other valuable things.

In biblical days, when princes or government officials were angry with the inhabitants of a town, the people brought them presents to appease their anger. The people believe presents appease government officials' anger and will secure favors. "Every one loveth gifts (bribes)" [Isa. 1:23]. Gifts are also offered to judges and governors for favors. "And thou shalt take no gift: for the gift blinds the wise, and perverts the words of the righteous" [Exod. 23:8]. This ancient custom still prevails in many lands. The recipient prefers to call it a "gift."

WRESTLING WITH AN ANGEL

And Jacob was left. alone; and there wrestled a man with him until the breaking of the day. Gen. 32:24

The wrestling was not between Jacob and an angel, but between Jacob and his brother Esau. The news that Esau was on his way to meet him, accompanied by four hundred men, had caused Jacob considerable anxiety. He could not tell how Esau would react when he would meet him. Therefore, Jacob kept pondering about the past, when he had stolen the blessing from his brother.

But Esau was innocent and, as a noble man, had forgotten the shortcomings of his younger brother. In other words, Esau was like an angel. When Esau declined to accept Jacob's present, the latter said to him, ". . . because now I have seen your face, as I saw the face of an angel, and you were pleased with me" [Gen. 33:10 and 32:25-30].

Angels have no physical bodies to wrestle or fight. The illness in Jacob's body was probably caused by the disturbances in his mind—the fear and regrets over his unfair dealings with his brother Esau.

THE TERM "ISRAEL"

And he said, Thy name shall be called no more Jacob, but Israel: for as a prince hast thou power with God and with men, and hast prevailed. Gen. 32:28

Israel is an Assyrian name which means "Prince of God." *Sar* means "prince" and *Eel*, "God."

Jacob in Aramaic means "heel." This name was given to Jacob because during the time of his birth he was holding the heel of his brother Esau. Now when Jacob strove with the angel and prevailed, the angel said to him, "Your name shall be called no longer Jacob, but Israel."

For many centuries all of the ten tribes were called, collectively, Israel. The term "Judah" was only used when the people referred to the tribe of Judah, which was one of the twelve tribes of Israel.

During the time of the conquest of Palestine and the period of the Judges the term "Israel" was used as a national name, like Edom (Esau), Moab, and Ammon. Saul was king over Israel.

But after the division of the kingdom during the reign of Rehoboam, the son of Solomon, when the ten tribes left the house of David and the tribe of Judah, the term "Israel" was used only when referring to the ten tribes whose capital was Samaria. The term "Judah" meant "the tribes of Judah and Benjamin," which remained loyal to the house of David.

After the destruction of the first temple and the Babylonian captivity, the remnant of the people who were left in Palestine were known as Jews. This is because political Israel had come to an end; and now the people were known by their faith. They were called Jews simply because the center of worship was in Judea. Therefore, the term "Jews" is solely religious. Anyone who embraces the Jewish faith can be called a Jew, but he cannot be called an Israelite or a Hebrew.

GIFTS DECLINED

And he said, What meanest thou by all this drove which I met?
And he said, These are to find grace in the sight of my lord.
And Esau said, I have enough, my brother; keep that thou hast
unto thyself.   Gen. 33:8-9

Customarily, Easterners decline gifts when they are offered, merely for politeness. When a gift is offered, the recipient refuses to accept it, stating he has plenty and thanking the giver; but he knows that the giver will ask him again and again. Thus, the more he declines, the more he will be urged to accept.

Jacob urged his brother Esau to accept his gift not so much because of the Eastern custom but in order to pacify him. Had Esau refused to accept the gift, Jacob would never have been in peace. The refusal to accept a gift means permanent enmity. Esau sooner or later would have sought vengeance from him.

The gift was a token of reconciliation, understanding, and an everlasting peace. The gift healed the wound and repaired the breach which was caused by jealousy.

ESAU WAS INNOCENT

And Jacob said, Nay, I pray thee, if now I have found grace in thy sight, then receive my present at my hand: for therefore I have seen thy face, as though I had seen the face of God, and thou wast pleased with me.   Gen. 33:10

While waiting for an answer from his brother Esau, Jacob was worried and restless. He spent most of the night by the brook *Jabbok* in prayer and supplication. And as he fell asleep he saw himself wrestling with an angel; and the contest continued all night till dawn [Gen. 32:24].

The angel was symbolical of his brother Esau. The Lord had answered Jacob's prayers and revealed the matter to him. Esau had been bitter and hostile toward him, but now he had made his mind up to attempt a reconciliation with his brother and to welcome him. After all, they were twins.

Angel in Aramaic means "God's counsel." Then again, innocent and pious men are often called angels. Esau was innocent like an angel.

Just as the angel blessed Jacob in his vision, so Esau kissed him and embraced him and accepted his gift for reconciliation. "A gift is as a precious stone" [Prov. 17:8].

Jacob acted wisely in presenting himself to Esau as "your servant, Jacob," and in bowing to him seven times.

AN OLD TRICK

And Shechem said unto her father and unto her brethren, Let me find grace in your eyes, and what ye shall say unto me I will give.
                                        Gen. 34:11

The dowry is an ancient Eastern custom as old as the Bible itself. In many parts of the East a dowry is paid in kind to the father of the damsel—a sum of money, or cattle or sheep. Easterners believe the father and mother of the damsel are entitled to a dowry, and that then the husband of the damsel will value her more.

In other words, a dowry is the price of a girl.

Shechem was willing to pay whatever price Jacob and his sons demanded of him. But Jacob's sons lied to the people of Shechem and instead of asking for the dowry, asked them to be circumcised so that they might weaken them and slay them [Exod. 22:16 and 1 Sam. 18:25].

[See also article on "Dowry," Gen. 29:20, 21.]

PRICE OF A BRIDE

Ask me never so much dowry and gift, and I will give according as ye shall say unto me: but give me the damsel to wife. Gen. 34:12

The Aramaic term *mahra* and the Hebrew and Arabic *mahar* mean "the price of the marriage settlement" [Exod. 22:16]. *Mahra* is to be distinguished from the gift of the bridegroom to the bride, or the dowry which was brought by the bride from her wealthy father's house [Josh. 15:18].

Today, according to the Assyrian law, the bridegroom pays the father of the bride. But in Mesopotamia and some other countries, the father of the bride pays the bridegroom. This law seemingly is influenced by the scarcity or abundance of women. Where women are plentiful, the father of the bride pays the bridegroom; and where the marriageable women are scarce, the bridegroom pays the father of the bride. (In the mountainous areas, women are scarce; but in the plains, males are scarce.)

MEETING PLACES

And Hamor and Shechem his son came unto the gate of their city, and communed with the men of their city, saying.   Gen. 34:20

In the East the gates of the walled towns and cities are used for playgrounds, meetings and judgment places. This is because the streets are narrow, and parks and public places are unknown.

[See article "Mature Men," Gen. 23:18.]

FOREIGN GODS

And they gave unto Jacob all the strange gods which were in their hand, and all their earrings which were in their ears; and Jacob hid them under the oak which was by Shechem.   Gen. 35:4

These gods were images which their ancestors had brought from Padan-aram. The people in Mesopotamia worshiped many gods just as Abraham's ancestors did in Ur of Chaldea.

The earrings bore emblems of the pagan deities. These ornaments were a stumbling block to the people, who were surrounded by many pagan and corrupt races.

OAK OF WEEPING

But Deborah Rebekah's nurse died, and she was buried beneath Bethel under an oak: and the name of it was called Allon-bachuth.
Gen. 35:8

Bitimtha dawkhatha means "the oak of weeping." *Bitimtha* sometimes means "terebinth." This name was given as a memorial to Deborah, Rebekah's nurse, who was buried under the oak.

THE SON OF MY RIGHT HAND

And it came to pass, as her soul was in departing, (for she died,) that she called his name Ben-oni: but his father called him Benjamin.
Gen. 35:18

The Eastern text reads: "She called the child's name *Bar-kebai* (the Son of My Sorrow); but his father called him Benyamin (the Son of My Right Hand)." Jacob loved Rachel more than Leah and looked upon her children as his heirs.

"Right hand" in Aramaic is significant of trust, loyalty, and power. [See Mark 16:19: "Sat on the right hand of God."] [See also *Gospel Light*.]

COAT OF LONG SLEEVES

And it came to pass, when Joseph was come unto his brethren, that they stripped Joseph out of his coat, his coat of many colors that was on him.
Gen. 37:23

The Eastern text reads: *cotina di-pidyatha*, "the coat with long sleeves." These coats or *abayas* are generally worn by princes, noblemen, and learned men. The sleeves and front parts of the garments are embroidered with silk of diverse colors. Thus, the color is in the embroidery of the garment and not in the material itself.

The princes and the noblemen never work; therefore, they are attired with a garment with long sleeves. This is a token of honor, dignity, and the position they occupy in society. On the other hand, a poor man neither can afford a coat with long sleeves, nor can he work while wearing it.

Joseph was trained by his father, Jacob, to succeed him as the head of the tribe—in other words, Joseph was elevated to the rank of a crown prince and a scholar. The rightful heir, Reuben, had defiled his father's bed, commiting adultery with one of his concubines. Jacob's other sons were not intelligent enough to be trained for this high office, the office of the chief of the tribe, which was political, religious, and judicial.

It was Jacob who had taught Joseph to interpret dreams and sit in council and manage tribal affairs. Moreover, the chief of a tribe must find grazing places for the flocks and cattle of the tribe. He must provide wells, make treaties with the chiefs of other tribes, and lead his people to war if necessary. He must know something about the law, religion, stars, weather, interpretation of dreams, and many other things which are essential to the welfare of a nomad tribe in lands where the people depend on wells for water, migrate by means of the stars, and communicate one with the other through dreams and visions.

Joseph was the only lad among the sons of Jacob who could occupy such an office, so his brothers were jealous of him. All of them except Benjamin were older than he. The very fact that his father had given him such a cloak of honor proved that he had selected him to train him to take his place.

ISHMAELITES AND MIDIANITES

Then there passed by Midianites merchantmen; and they drew and lifted up Joseph out of the pit, and sold Joseph to the Ishmaelites for twenty pieces of silver: and they brought Joseph into Egypt.
Gen. 37:28

The reference here is to the descendants of Ishmael, the son of Abraham, and an uncle of Jacob. The Ishmaelites and the Midianites were also the descendants of Abraham [Gen. 25:2]. Both races were Hebrew in origin. They traveled together for protection from their enemies, the Amorites, Hittites, and other races who were the primitive inhabitants of Palestine. Both peoples spoke the same language; that is, the language which their father, Abraham, and his tribe had brought from Haran and from Ur of Chaldea.

There were only three generations of the Ishmaelites in the land, but they were a strong people who exerted a tremendous influence over the native peoples. In a short space of time they became princes and rulers over other races whose culture and religions were inferior to those of the Hebrew tribe. The Ishmaelites might have been the leaders of the caravan. Being a warrior people, they were greatly feared by the weak races in Palestine.

CEASED BEARING

*And she yet again conceived, and bare a son; and called his
name Shelah: and he was at Chezib, when she bare him.*   Gen. 38:5

"He was at Chezib," is a mistranslation of the Aramaic word *peskat,*
"she stopped bearing." In Aramaic, when a woman ceases bearing children we say, "She is cut off from bearing," which means she bears no
more.

Shuah bore three sons to Judah, but she stopped bearing children after
the birth of Shelah.

There is no such place in Palestine as Chezib.

A GIANT

*And it came to pass, as he drew back his hand, that, behold, his
brother came out: and she said, How hast thou broken forth? this
breach be upon thee: therefore his name was called Pharez.*

Gen. 38:29

Pharez or *Pheriz,* in colloquial Aramaic, means "a mighty man" or
"a giant." The child was named Pharez simply because he prevailed
against his brother, Zarah. The midwife expected the latter to be born
first, but Pharez prevailed against him and was born first.

Pharez is the ancestor of the kings of Judah.

DREAMS

*And they said unto him, We have dreamed a dream, and there
is no interpreter of it. And Joseph said unto them, Do not interpretations belong to God? tell me them, I pray you.*   Gen. 40:8

In the olden days the chief occupation of the wise and the learned
was to interpret dreams, explain riddles and dark sayings, and to foretell
things to come. This knowledge was handed down from father to son
and from a teacher to his student. Assyrians, Babylonians, and Egyptians
had astrologers, soothsayers, and interpreters of dreams.

Abraham, Isaac, and Jacob communed with God by means of dreams
and visions and revelations, and they understood the meaning of the
symbols which they saw in their dreams. Jacob on his way to Padan-
Aram saw a ladder set on earth and the top of it reached to heaven.

MAGICIANS

And it came to pass in the morning that his spirit was troubled; and he sent and called for all the magicians of Egypt, and all the wise men thereof: and Pharaoh told them his dream; but there was none that could interpret them unto Pharaoh. Gen. 41:8

In biblical days, magicians, like wise men, were employed as counselors to kings and statesmen. Magic was regarded as a high profession, and magicians were highly honored by kings and princes.

The magicians performed magic in kings' palaces to entertain the idle and bored kings and princes.

The Egyptian magicians were noted for their magical performances, for magic was a great art in Egypt. Even the priests were great magicians, and magic played a conspicuous part in their temple rituals.

But the Egyptians were not versed in the interpretation of dreams and visions. This was a totally different field of study, and it was common among the tribal people who dwelt in the deserts, but unknown to highly cultured wise men of Egypt, who relied on human wisdom more than the hidden power of God.

The Israelites could foretell future events and predict years of famine and prosperity, but the art of magic was unknown to them. In other words, they were a simple nomadic people who relied on a higher power. This is why the wisdom of Joseph and Moses was superior to that of the Egyptians.

The Egyptian magicians, like Moses and Aaron, performed many wonders, but the wonders performed by Moses and Aaron were divinely guided and superior [Exod. 8:18,19; 9:11].

A DOUBLE DREAM

And for that the dream was doubled unto Pharaoh twice; it is because the thing is established by God, and God will shortly bring it to pass. Gen. 41:32

The fact that the dream was doubled indicated to Pharaoh that the thing which he had seen was very important and was to come to pass soon. In the East, when a matter is serious, the words are repeated for emphasis. In a dream one might forget certain symbols, but he cannot easily forget all of them. That is to say, if Pharaoh should forget the dream of seven cows, he would remember the dream of the seven ears of wheat, or vice versa.

Even today many Easterners are guided by the dreams and visions they see, and they know the meaning of the symbols.
[See comment on Gen. 28:12.]

RINGS

And Pharaoh took off his ring from his hand, and put it upon Joseph's hand, and arrayed him in vestures of fine linen, and put a gold chain about his neck. Gen. 41:42

The custom of wearing rings and other gold and silver ornaments is as old as the history of man. Kings, princes, governors, and noblemen wore rings as a symbol of authority, wealth, and power. Rings were also indispensable articles in marriage. They were given as a token of the agreement. Moreover, rings, earrings, and bracelets were given to brides as a token of affection and love from their spouses [Gen. 24:30, 53]. Then again, rings were used as signets wherewith imperial edicts, secret documents, and treaties were sealed [Esther 3:12; Dan. 6:17].

The Jews used more rings, earrings, bracelets, and other jewelry than any other race. Such articles were indispensable in Jewish society. They were worn on fingers, ears, and ankles [Isa. 3:18-23].

LIFTING OF HAND

And Pharaoh said unto Joseph, I am Pharaoh, and without thee shall no man lift up his hand or foot in all the land of Egypt.
Gen. 41:44

"Lift up his hand or foot" is an Aramaic idiom which means, "No one shall start to do anything without your approval." Such idioms are derived from the customs and manners of the people. In the East, even today, most of the labor is done with the hands and feet.

Joseph's position was similar to that of a vizier of the Arabian empire. He was second to the emperor and had unlimited powers and authority over the people, so that no one dared to do anything in government without his consent, or to question his wisdom and understanding.

ZAPHNATH-PAANEAH

And Pharaoh called Joseph's name Zaphnath-paaneah; and he gave him to wife Asenath the daughter of Potipherah priest of On. And Joseph went out over all the land of Egypt. Gen. 41:45

Zaphnath-paaneah (Aramaic *panakh*) means "the interpreter of dreams" or "revealer of hidden secrets." It may also mean "the savior of the world." Joseph saved Egypt and many other lands during the severe famine. Joseph was an interpreter of dreams. He was made the chief of astrologers and soothsayers.

GIFTS FOR OFFICIALS

And their father Israel said unto them, If it must be so now, do this; take of the best fruits in the land in your vessels, and carry down the man a present, a little balm, and a little honey, spices and myrrh, nuts and almonds.   Gen. 43:11

When Easterners call on a prince, a high government official, or a holy man, they always present gifts to him, not always as a bribe, but sometimes as a token of honor and respect. This custom is so old and widely practiced that princes, judges, and government officials *expect* some kind of gift from their visitors. To call on them with empty hands is disrespectful, and some of them would be offended. "And the daughter of Tyre shall be there with a gift" [Ps. 45:12].

A gift should not be confused with *shukhda,* "a bribe." The term "bribe" is often translated in the King James as "gift." "For a gift does blind the eyes of the wise, and pervert the words of the righteous" [Deut. 16:19; Exod. 23:8].

Jacob's gift was not a bribe, but a present which was expected by a high government official. When his sons went down to Egypt the first time, Jacob did not expect them to meet high government officials such as Joseph, who was governor general over all the land of Egypt. This is why no gifts were sent by Jacob.

RELIGIOUS DIFFERENCES

And they set on for him by himself, and for them by them-selves, and for the Egyptians, which did eat with him, by them-selves: because the Egyptians might not eat bread with the He-brews; for that is an abomination unto the Egyptians. Gen. 43:32

In many Eastern countries members of one religion refuse to eat bread with the members of another religion. Even today, in some parts of the Near East, Jews, Moslems, and Christians cannot eat together.

Bread is symbolic of friendship; therefore, only those who are on good terms with one another can sit at the same table and break bread together. When two men eat bread and salt together, they consider them-selves friends. But the followers of rival religions cannot be friends; therefore, they cannot eat bread together. If they do, then they are not loyal to their religion. One often hears people saying to one another, "He ate my bread and yet he has done me harm."

The Egyptians, being of different race, culture, and religion could not eat with the Hebrews. Certain animals which the Hebrews ate, such as sheep, were an abomination to the Egyptians, but the Hebrews were a pastoral people [Gen. 46:34].

EASTERN ETIQUETTE

And they sat before him, the firstborn according to his birthright, and the youngest according to his youth: and the men marveled one at another. Gen. 43:33

From time immemorial Easterners have revered and respected gray hairs and seniority. The younger salutes the older and lets him occupy a higher seat at a banquet or a religious feast. At times the younger men stand up while in the presence of their elders.

In the East, chairs and tables are unknown, especially among the nomads. The guests sit upright on the floor, with their legs folded under them, around the cloth which is spread before them. Each person is seated according to his age; the honored guests recline against bedding and cushions.

The sons of Jacob were well brought up and trained by their father. Their fathers and grandfathers had feasted with princes and kings. The tribal people were trained to respect the chiefs of the tribes and the elders, who act as counselors, and to behave in the presence of the rulers. The Egyptians were amazed because they did not expect that these desert men would know anything about good manners.

EXCHANGING SOPS

And he took and sent messes unto them from before him: but Benjamin's mess was five times so much as any of theirs. And they drank, and were merry with him. Gen. 43:34

At a feast or a banquet the best dishes containing delicacies are customarily placed before the host and the honored guests who are seated at the table close to him.

During the meal the host or some of the honored guests take food from the special dishes which are before them and pass them to their friends. The sops of food are wrapped in thin bread and exchanged without hesitation or embarrassment.

At times, a man may taste a sop by eating a portion of it and then passing the rest to one of the guests near him. Easterners are not afraid of germs. In the East, to exchange sops and eat from one another's dish is a great honor and a token of a lasting friendship. When enmity exists between two men, they never exchange sops or eat at the same table.

Judas dipped his hand in Jesus' dish to prove that he was not a traitor. But Jesus knew that he was going to betray him, so he passed a sop to him in order to point him out [Matt. 26:23; John 13:26].

The best and most delicious dishes were placed before Joseph. He was the governor and the host. Before him were special dishes and trays of food which his poor brothers had never seen.

Joseph gave larger portions to his brother Benjamin, simply because he loved him more than his other brothers. Joseph could no longer restrain his affection toward his brother, the son of his own mother.

DIVINING CUP

And put my cup, the silver cup, in the sack's mouth of the youngest, and his corn money. And he did according to the word that Joseph had spoken.

As soon as the morning was light, the men were sent away, they and their asses.

And when they were gone out of the city, and not yet far off, Joseph said unto his steward, Up, follow after the men; and when thou dost overtake them, say unto them, Wherefore have ye rewarded evil for good?

Is not this it in which my lord drinketh, and whereby indeed he divineth? ye have done evil in so doing. Gen. 44:2-5

In the East, kings, princes, and noblemen have individual silver or golden cups for drinking water. Neither the servants nor even other members of the family are allowed to use these cups.

Some of these cups are handed down from one generation to another and, therefore, they are looked upon not only as heirlooms but also as sacred. Some of these cups were previously used by famous kings, high priests, and holy men. This custom of special drinking cups for kings and princes still prevails in the East.

Soothsayers and men and women with familiar spirits used these cups for divination and fortune telling. The cup is filled with water and placed before the fortune teller and the inquirer. The medium then gives an oracle which he claims comes out of the cup. At times, a small voice comes out of the cup revealing hidden things to the inquirer.

The custom of divining by means of the cup is still practiced in the East, and many people believe in it. This is something similar to the use of the crystal ball.

EL, THE GOD

And he said, I am God, the God of thy father: fear not to go down into Egypt; for I will there make of thee a great nation.

Gen. 46:3

The Eastern text reads: "I am *El*, the God of your father"; that is, the God of Isaac.

In patriarchal days, *El* was the name of the God of Israel. In Aramaic, the noun begins with the letter *aleph*, *A*. *A* and *Ae*, another Aramaic letter (in Hebrew pronounced *ein*), are interchangeable in vernacular tongue. *El* might have been derived from *Al*, "upon," which is the root of the adverb *elaiah*, "high." The ancient peoples pictured God as dwelling in high places and riding upon the clouds. [See Exod. 24:16; Lev. 16:2.] "He makes clouds his chariot" [Ps. 104:3].

Such was the concept of the ancients about God and his holy attributes when they named him *El* or *Al*, "the Highest," the One who sees the whole universe beneath him.

When Jacob saw the vision of the ladder and the angels, he called the name of the place *Beth-el*, "the house of God" [Gen. 28:19]. And Jacob's name was changed to Israel, "prince of God" [Gen. 32:28].

The Arabic name for God is *Allah*, the Aramaic *Allah* or *Alaha*, the Assyrian *Elu*. All the gods of the Gentiles were images and idols which were made of silver, gold, stone, and wood. They were all stationary on the ground. *El* was the high and living God whose abode was in heaven, above all creation, and who was not made by the hands of men.

CLOSING OF EYES—DEATH

I will go down with thee into Egypt; and I will also surely bring thee up again: and Joseph shall put his hand upon thine eyes.

Gen. 46:4

"And Joseph shall put his hand upon thine eyes" is an Aramaic idiom which is still in common use, and which means, "He shall close your eyes when you die"; that is, "He shall bury you." When Jacob died, Joseph made the preparations for his burial in the land of Canaan and buried him with his father, Isaac [Gen. 50:1-7].

Even today, one of the highest desires of a father is to have one of his beloved children close his eyes, mourn over him, and bury him. That is why one of Jesus' disciples said to him, "Lord, suffer me first to go and bury my father" [Matt. 8:21, 22]. This man's father was not dead.

What he wanted was to take care of his father, stay home as long as his father lived, and then bury him after his death. [See *Gospel Light* comment on Matt. 8:21, 22.]

SIXTY-SIX SOULS

All the souls that came with Jacob into Egypt, which came out of his loins, besides Jacob's sons' wives, all the souls were three-score and six;

And the sons of Joseph, which were borne him in Egypt, were two souls: all the souls of the house of Jacob, which came into Egypt, were threescore and ten.   Gen. 46:26-27

It is interesting to know that there are sixty-six books in the Bible, equivalent to the number of persons who came out of Jacob's loins and went down with him into Egypt. All persons, including the children of Joseph, were seventy persons.

The number of the elders of Israel was seventy [Exod. 18:25; Num. 11:16]. Jesus also sent forth seventy of his disciples to preach the gospel [Luke 10]. The years of the captivity as foretold by Jeremiah were seventy [Jer. 25:11]. There were seventy shawoay (weeks) in Daniel's prophecy [Dan. 9:24]. The number seventy must have been a lucky number in those days. It is a sacred number.

PASTORAL PEOPLE

That ye shall say, Thy servants' trade hath been about cattle from our youth even until now, both we, and also our fathers: that ye may dwell in the land of Goshen; for every shepherd is an abomination unto the Egyptians.   Gen. 46:34

The Hebrews who went down to dwell in Egypt, like their ancestors, were a pastoral people. They knew no other occupation than raising sheep and cattle.

On the other hand, pastoral life or sheep-raising was an abomination to the Egyptians who lived in the fertile lands and whose occupation was agriculture. This is still true of the mountain and plains people in Palestine and other lands in the Near East. The city people seldom drink sheep milk; they prefer cows' milk.

Joseph knew that the Egyptians were not interested in the lush pasture lands in the land of Goshen, which belonged to the crown. The city people usually are engaged in arts, crafts, farming, and manufacture of household articles which they exchange for butter, wool, cheese, and other products [Gen. 47:3]. They looked down on the nomad people, their occupation, and their way of life.

SLAVERY

Wherefore shall we die before thine eyes, both we and our land? buy us and our land for bread, and we and our land will be servants unto Pharaoh: and give us seed, that we may live, and not die, that the land be not desolate. Gen. 47:19

In biblical days, when families found that all their substance was gone and there was no hope of borrowing money or wheat, they sold themselves and their children, and thus became the slaves of the lenders. Both men and women were traded for money, wheat, and other commodities. Joseph was sold by his brothers for thirty pieces of silver [Gen. 37:28; 45:4].

Slavery prevailed in many Near Eastern, Middle Eastern, and African lands until recent years. Men and women were sold and bought in the markets, and debtors sold themselves to their creditors.

The Mosaic law sanctioned the sale of poverty-stricken Hebrews, but enjoined the purchasers to treat them well [Lev. 25:39-43; Isa. 52:3].

LAYING ON OF HANDS

And Israel stretched out his right hand, and laid it upon Ephraim's head, who was the younger, and his left hand upon Manasseh's head, guiding his hands wittingly; for Manasseh was the firstborn. Gen. 48:14

Laying on of hands in Semitic languages has several meanings:

1. To transmit God's blessings from one person to another. The physical contact helps the person to receive the blessing. The hand symbolizes power and authority.

2. To arrest. "And laid their hands on the apostles, and put them in the common prison" [Acts 5:18]. "When they sought to lay hands on him"—which means "to arrest him" [Matt. 21:46]. In this case, it means they seized them.

3. To appoint or ordain [Acts 13:1-3]. In most cases in the New Testament it is used as a symbol of blessing and healing [Matt. 19:13; Luke 4:40].

4. To signal out a guilty person, hence to accuse.

JACOB REDEEMED

The Angel which redeemed me from all evil, bless the lads;
and let my name be named on them, and the name of my fathers
Abraham and Isaac; and let them grow into a multitude in the
midst of the earth.   Gen. 48:16

The reference here is to the evil which Jacob had done to his brother,
Esau, and to his father, Isaac, when he deceived them about the birthright. [Gen. 27:12-27].

Jacob had also taken justice into his own hands and had acquired
some of Laban's cattle and sheep by some device unknown to Laban
and the people of Haran.

Jacob acknowledged his faults and sins, and sought God's forgiveness.
And God forgave him and blessed him and granted him power to bless
others. The angel of the Lord blessed him and called his name Israel,
"prince of God," and delivered him from all his enemies.

BLESSING WITH RIGHT HAND

And when Joseph saw that his father laid his right hand upon the
head of Ephraim, it displeased him: and he held up his father's
hand, to remove it from Ephraim's head unto Manasseh's head.
                                                   Gen. 48:17

Among Semitic peoples the right hand is symbolical of blessing and
right action; and the left hand is a bad omen. The queen sits on the
right hand of the king, and honored guests on the right hand of the
host. Moreover, the right hand symbolizes power. ". . . with the pleasure
of victory of thy right hand" [Ps. 16:11]. "If I forget you, O Jerusalem,
let my right hand forget me" [Ps. 137:5]. [See Eastern text.]

All blessings are bestowed upon people by placing of the right hand
upon them. Joseph was alarmed when he saw his father had placed his
right hand upon the head of his younger son, so he tried to remove it
and place it on the head of his eldest son, Manasseh; but Jacob knew
what he was doing. Being a seer, he saw that Ephraim would be greater
than Manasseh, Joseph's first-born.

PATRIARCHS—PROPHETS

And Jacob called unto his sons, and said, Gather yourselves to-
gether, that I may tell you that which shall befall you in the last
days.   Gen. 49:1

All the Hebrew patriarchs were prophets. They saw visions, interpreted
dreams, foretold things to come, warned the people of impending dis-

asters, and admonished them to walk in the way of God. All of them were divinely guided, and during the times of famine and disaster were led to safety.

The Lord God had revealed his plans for the salvation of mankind to Abraham, to Isaac, and to Jacob. He had assured them that by their seed (that is, Christ) the nations of the world would be blessed. He also revealed to them what was to take place after them.

Jacob not only could foretell future events, but also knew how to interpret dreams. It was he who taught Joseph how to interpret dreams and reveal hidden things.

The Hebrew patriarchs lived a simple life and they lived close to God, believed in him, and walked in his way. That is why God communed with them and revealed to them things which were hidden from the eyes of other peoples and races who were far stronger and more advanced.

FIRST-BORN

Reuben, thou art my firstborn, my might, and the beginning of my strength, the excellency of dignity, and the excellency of power: Unstable as water, thou shalt not excel; because thou wentest up to thy father's bed; then defiledst thou it: he went up to my couch.
Gen. 49:3-4

The first-born was the heir of his father, his glory and strength. Reuben was Jacob's first-born and the right heir to succeed him, but Reuben had committed adultery with Bilhah, one of his father's concubines. His father Jacob never forgave him for that impious act.

"Unstable as water" is an Aramaic saying which means "undecided" or "undependable." When water is poured on the ground, its course is never straight. Reuben was a weakling. He lacked integrity and moral character.

SCEPTRE

The sceptre shall not depart from Judah, nor a lawgiver from between his feet, until Shiloh come; and unto him shall the gathering of the people be.
Gen. 49:10

The sceptre is the symbol of authority or leadership. Judah was the most brilliant among his eleven brothers. He was a gifted speaker and a statesman. When Joseph wanted to detain Benjamin, Judah stood before Joseph and made an excellent appeal on the behalf of his brother,

Benjamin, which so moved the heart of the governor general that he could no longer restrain his tears [Gen. 44:16-34].

Judah was second only to Joseph in wisdom and understanding. Reuben had committed adultery with one of his father's concubines and, therefore, Jacob had discarded him as an heir. The tribe of Judah was to be the most important of the twelve tribes. Kings and lawgivers were to come forth out of Judah's descendants until the coming of the Messiah. The Aramaic text reads: "Until the coming of the One to whom the sceptre belongs, to whom the Gentiles shall look forward." The word *Shiloh* is not in the Eastern text.

Jacob, as a patriarch and a seer, saw the fulfillment of Israel's mission. His descendants were to rule until the coming of the Great King, the Messiah, who was to establish a universal kingdom and become a light to the Gentiles and to the world in general [See Isa. 9:1, 2].

The term *Shiloh* might be derived from shaal, "to ask." *Sheaila, Shiloh,* "that which the people had prayed for," "a deliverer"; that is, "the Messiah."

Shiloh was a city in Ephraim where the Israelites assembled and erected the tabernacle [Josh. 18:1, 19:51].

In the East when people visit a shrine they present offerings, make wishes, and ask God to grant them the desire of their hearts, as in the case of Hannah described in 1 Sam. 1:10, 11.

See comment on *Shiloh*.

RED WITH WINE AND WHITE WITH MILK

Binding his foal unto the vine, and his ass's colt unto the choice vine; he washed his garments in wine, and his clothes in the blood of grapes:
His eyes shall be red with wine, and his teeth white with milk.
                                                        Gen. 49:11-12

These verses should not be taken literally. The author of Genesis used colloquial expressions. "He washed his garments in wine" and "his eyes shall be red with wine" are figurative speech meaning that he will inhabit a land graced with many vineyards and that he will have plenty of wine to drink.

Easterners often say, "He swims in oil," which means, "He has plenty of butter or olive oil." "He bathes in milk," means, "He has an abundance of milk."

In the East those who have vineyards use considerable wine at the table. In the olden days, wine was used because of the lack of water. Even today, in Italy, France, and Spain, the people use wine on the table instead of water. "Red eyed" in English means "drunkard."

The land of Judah was noted for good vineyards. The Hebron region was the place from which the Hebrew spies brought grapes to Moses and the elders of Israel [Num. 13:23].

"His teeth white with milk" is an Eastern idiom which means, "He shall have an abundance of flocks and plenty of milk."

In biblical days the economy was based on sheep, milk, wool, and other sheep products. Then again, the main diet of the people consisted of milk, buttermilk, cream, cheese, and butter. In many regions where the people live on milk, cheese, and other sheep products, their teeth are white and in good condition.

AN ASS

Issachar is a strong ass couching down between two burdens.
Gen. 49:14

The Eastern text reads: *Gabbara,* "a mighty man." The Aramaic word for "ass" is *khamara.* The letters *kheth* and *gamel* resemble one another when placed before a word. The error was caused by the close similarity of the two Aramaic words. When a manuscript is too old or mutilated, as often they are, letters and words are confused with one another. The scribes and the translators had some difficulty in ascertaining the meaning of some of the words.

The Aramaic reads, "Issachar is a mighty man, couching by the highways." In the East, it would be repulsive to call a person a donkey. On the other hand, no father at his deathbed would call his son a donkey, especially when he blesses him before he dies.

JOSEPH, A CULTURED MAN

Joseph is a fruitful bough, even a fruitful bough by a well; whose branches run over the wall.
Gen. 49:22

The Eastern text reads: "Joseph is a disciplined son" or "a cultured man"; that is, "Joseph has been trained to be the chief of the tribe and a successor to his father, Jacob." This is why Joseph wore a coat of long sleeves embroidered with colors, which made his brothers hate him.

Joseph was trained by his father, Jacob, who had taught him to interpret visions and dreams and to know how to behave in the presence of princes and rulers. As a lad, he had received God's revelations. Joseph was called by God to a great mission to save his people during the famine [Gen. 50:20].

Isaac was trained by Abraham, and Abraham was a learned man and a prophet of God who belonged to a learned Babylonian priestly family.

Joseph's education and his good manners helped him to rise to such a high position in the land of Egypt.

STRETCHED OUT HIS FEET

And when Jacob had made an end of commanding his sons, he gathered up his feet into the bed, and yielded up the ghost, and was gathered unto his people. **Gen. 49:33**

The Eastern text reads: "He stretched his feet on his bed." Jacob was sick in bed when he summoned his sons to his bedside. He had been sick for some time, and when Joseph and his sons came to see him he sat upon the bed [Gen. 48:1, 2].

"He stretched out his feet" is an Eastern idiom which means "he died." In the East when a sick man is near death they stretch out his feet before he is dead.

EGYPTIAN MOURNING

And when the inhabitants of the land, the Canaanites, saw the mourning in the floor of Atad, they said, This is a grievous mourning to the Egyptians: wherefore the name of it was called Abelmizraim, which is beyond Jordan. **Gen. 50:11**

Abel-mizraim means the "mourning" of the Egyptians. *Abilotha* means "mourning," "lamentation," or "to wail for the dead." Easterners mourn for many days and raise their voices in wailing over the dead.

Palestine, at this time, must have been a protectorate under Egypt.

The Hebrews at this time spoke pure Aramaic, which their forefathers had brought from Padan-aram. All of Jacob's children, with the exception of Benjamin, were born in Padan-aram.

See article on "Wailing."

UNDER GOD

And his father refused, and said, I know it, my son, I know it: he also shall become a people, and he also shall be great: but truly his younger brother shall be greater than he, and his seed shall become a multitude of nations. **Gen. 50:19**

The Eastern text more correctly reads: *Tkehet alaha na,* "I am a servant of God" instead of "I am in the place of God." What Joseph meant here is that he also was a human being under the care and guidance of God. His brothers were so frightened that they prostrated themselves before him as they would do when worshiping God.

Joseph saw that his visions of the sheaves and the stars and the moon were fulfilled, but he refused to see his brothers doing obeisance to him, for, after all, he was a human being like each of them.

CHAPTER TWO

EXODUS

INTRODUCTION

THE term "Exodus" is Greek, but is a translation of the Aramaic word *Mapkana,* "the departure," which means "going out without thought of returning."

The Hebrew patriarchs spoke Aramaic. This is clearly seen from their names and the names of localities mentioned during their wanderings in Palestine, Egypt, and Sinai. All the sons of Jacob, with the exception of Benjamin, were born in Padan-aram. They spoke Aramaic.

Exodus is one of the five books of Moses. Undoubtedly Moses wrote the five books which bear his name, but the account of his death was written by Joshua, his scribe and secretary, and naturally Moses could not have written the episode of his journey to Mount Nebo or the account of his own death.

Exodus, like the other books of Moses, is written in minute detail. No later scribe could have produced such a book with numerous ordinances, laws, and statutes. Indeed, the five books of Moses were written as occasions demanded; as they wandered in the desert new problems arose, and hence new laws and ordinances were written and added.

Many Western scholars are led to believe that the five books of Moses were written many years after his death. Some even venture to say that the law of Moses was written during the captivity, that is, a thousand years after Moses' death. This is because the scholars are unaware that writing was prevalent among the Jews during the time of Moses, that Moses had scribes, and that he was called by God to write. In Exodus 17:14 we read: "And the Lord said unto Moses, Write this for a memorial in a book, and rehearse it in the ears of Joshua . . ." God told Moses to write this ordinance so that he might teach it to the people. All of God's commandments and statutes were written after the Lord had commanded Moses to write.

The book of Exodus contains the history of the Israelites and their sojourn in Egypt, God's wonders in Egypt, the crossing of the Red Sea, the erection of the tabernacle, and the establishment of the priesthood and the sacrifices. These are the most important parts of the book, together with the ten commandments and ordinances which the Lord God gave to Moses on Mount Sinai.

MIDWIVES

And the king of Egypt spake to the Hebrew midwives, of which the name of the one was Shiphrah, and the name of the other Puah;

And he said, When ye do the office of a midwife to the Hebrew women, and see them upon the stools, if it be a son, then ye shall kill him; but if it be a daughter, then she shall live. For the midwives feared God, and did not as the king of Egypt commanded them, but saved the men children alive. Exod. 1:15-17

In lands where hospitals and doctors are unknown, midwives help women to deliver their babies. All midwives are women. No male, not even a doctor, is allowed to perform this important task. In some parts of the East, women do not require even the help of a midwife; they deliver their babies unassisted.

Thousands of mothers and their babies perish because of the lack of proper help and the ignorance of untrained midwives. The midwives are untrained and do their work gratis. Every town or little village has one or two women who are known as midwives and who rush to help pregnant women when they are in travail and need assistance.

Pharaoh appointed Hebrew midwives simply because the Hebrew women would have resented Egyptian midwives, who were members of an alien religion. Even today, Moslem midwives attend Moslem women, Christian midwives, Christian women, and Jewish midwives, Jewish women. Eastern governments are magnanimous in their tolerance of minorities and members of different religions. They respect the laws and customs of other races.

Pharaoh knew that the Hebrew midwives would not report the birth of all Hebrew male children, but he respected the Hebrew custom. No doubt the Egyptian midwives would have carried out his imperial orders much more faithfully and drowned all the male children, except for the fact that the Lord caused Pharaoh to be kind and to respect Hebrew customs. Had Pharaoh been as severe an oppressor as Hitler was he would not have appointed Hebrew women, nor would he have respected the Hebrew customs.

MIDWIVES NOT LOYAL TO PHARAOH

Therefore God dealt well with the midwives: and the people multiplied, and waxed very mighty.

And it came to pass, because the midwives feared God, that he made them houses. Exod. 1:20-21

The term "houses" is wrong. The Eastern text reads: "He made them mothers of children," that is, he gave them families. The midwives, being Hebrews, refused to obey Pharaoh's command. They did not report every birth.

It seems that the imperial edict was limited to certain areas. That is to say, Pharaoh's persecution was local. Two midwives [Exod. 1:15] would not have been enough to take care of all the Hebrews in Egypt. On the other hand, the persecution lasted for a short time only. When Moses returned to Egypt he found hundreds of thousands of men, women, and children, which proves that the persecution was not so severe as it might look. God was always with the Israelites.

DAUGHTER OF LEVI

And there went a man of the house of Levi, and took to wife a daughter of Levi. Exod. 2:1

"A daughter of Levi" does not literally mean a daughter of Levi, the son of Jacob, but a girl of the tribe of Levi. We do not know if Levi had a daughter. Easterners always identify a girl by the name of the founder of her tribe or family.

Jesus spoke of a woman whom he healed as a daughter of Abraham. "And ought not this woman, being a daughter of Abraham, whom Satan hath bound, lo, these eighteen years, be loosed from this bond on the Sabbath day?" [Luke 13:16]. This incident happened about two thousand years after Abraham.

Mohammed speaks of the Virgin Mary as the daughter of Aaron, which means she is of the house of Aaron.

MOSES

And the child grew, and she brought him unto Pharaoh's daughter, and he became her son. And she called his name Moses: and she said, Because I drew him out of the water. Exod. 2:10

Mosheh, Moses, is supposed to be a Hebrew name derived from the Hebrew word *moshah*, "to draw out." The Aramaic word "to draw out" is *shalah*. The Hebrew people who went down into Egypt with Jacob were all Aramaic-speaking people. The names of both of Joseph's sons, Manasseh and Ephraim, are of Aramaic origin. So also are the names of all of Jacob's children.

It is unlikely that the Egyptian princess would have given the child she found in the little ark a Hebrew name. The Hebrews were hated, and according to the text, Pharaoh was trying to exterminate them.

The Egyptian princess may have given the child an Egyptian name. Moses might have been a later adoption. The name *Mosheh* might have been given to him when he was in the land of Midian. The Hebrews invariably changed their names when they lived in foreign lands. They do it even today.

Mosheh might originally have meant *Emoh-asheh,* "saved by his mother."

Moses became the savior of his people, and the greatest prophet or leader in the history of the Hebrew people.

MIDIANITES

Now when Pharaoh heard this thing, he sought to slay Moses. But Moses fled from the face of Pharaoh, and dwelt in the land of Midian: and he sat down by a well.   Exod. 2:15

The Midianites were the descendants of Abraham from his wife Kenturah, whom he married after the death of Sarah [Gen. 25:1-2]. Kenturah bore him six children; and all of them became the chiefs of tribes.

The Midianites spoke a Hebrew dialect which was easy for Moses to understand. This is why Jethro, the priest of Midian, rejoiced to see the Israelites delivered from the hand of the Egyptians; and he blessed the Lord who had delivered his people [Exod. 18:9-12].

No doubt the Midianites, like other descendants of Abraham and Lot, in one way or another knew about the Lord God of their ancestors.

On the other hand, Moses had no difficulty in conversing with Jethro and his people. There might have been some slight differences in dialect, such as there are today.

WATERING OF THE SHEEP

Now the priest of Midian had seven daughters: and they came and drew water, and filled the troughs to water their father's flock. And the shepherds came and drove them away: but Moses stood up and helped them, and watered their flock.   Exod. 2:16-17

In the desert where water is scarce and wells deep, watering of the sheep and cattle is a great problem. At times, because of scanty rains, the wells begin to dry up and watering becomes difficult. Every drop of water has to be brought forth out of the deep well and poured out into the trough. During the watering, both sheep and cattle rush to get places around the trough, one pushing another. The flock may not have been watered for several days; and the shepherd too is thirsty.

On the other hand, the well is continuously visited by the herds which come in from the desert, by caravans, and by passing men and women who come to draw water for drinking. At times many herds come at the same time, and when the thirsty animals see the troughs, they stampede; and as some of the beasts are drinking, others are howling and impatient to take their places around the trough.

When one flock is through watering another comes in. In some places, the water is apportioned and watering is orderly. But during the droughts, shepherds fight over the water and at times even slay one another. The powerful and well-armed shepherds are feared by the unarmed and the weak, especially the women shepherds who are at the mercy of the male shepherds, and who wait until other shepherds are through watering.

When these shepherds saw Moses, they knew that he was a nobleman. His apparel and his hands and face showed that he was not an ordinary man.

REUEL

And when they came to Reuel their father, he said, How is it that ye are come so soon to-day?   Exod. 2:18

Reuel was the priest of Midian, and Moses' father-in-law. When Moses fled from Egypt, he went to Midian, where he married Zipporah, one of the seven daughters of Reuel, the high priest of Midian.

In Exodus 3:1 Moses' father-in-law is called Jethro, but in Numbers 10:29 he is called Hobab. The discrepancy between these names has made it hard for Western scholars to know the true name of Moses' father-in-law.

Jethro, Aramaic *yathron* ("they enriched me," or "made me excellent"), is the title of the priest: "Excellency," just as one may call an American priest Venerable or Dean. In the East, when speaking of a priest, sometimes we use the priestly title instead of the name. We would say, "Moses was feeding the flock of the priest, his father-in-law."

Hobab is another father-in-law of Moses. The Hebrews were polygamists. Abraham had many fathers-in-law. Jacob had three and David had more than a dozen. Moses must have married another woman when the Israelites were wandering in the desert. We are told that he married an Ethiopian woman.

JETHRO

Now Moses kept the flock of Jethro his father-in-law, the priest of Midian: and he led the flock to the back side of the desert, and came to the mountain of God, even to Horeb.   Exod. 3:1

Jethro is the title of Reuel, the priest of Midian, Moses' father-in-law.

Jethro is a noun derived from Aramaic *yetar*, "to increase," "to excel," hence "His Excellency" or "the Reverend Reuel."

Easterners often indiscriminately address the priests by their titles or their names. Some biblical authorities believe that there must be some confusion in the names. Reuel is the name, and *yathron*, Jethro, is the priestly title.

THE BURNING BUSH

And the Angel of the Lord appeared unto him in a flame of fire out of the midst of a bush: and he looked, and, behold, the bush burned with fire, and the bush was not consumed.   Exod. 3:2

The burning bush symbolizes trials and difficulties. Both men and animals suffer from thorny bushes and brambles [Gen. 22:13]. In the olden days the wise men and prophets used and understood symbols, metaphors, similes, and figurative speech.

Moses was to suffer many difficulties, but he was to come out victorious. The fact that the bush burned but was not consumed indicated that ultimately Moses would triumph in his great mission [Comment on Judges 9:15].

Moses suffered both in Egypt and in the desert, but he succeeded in leading Israel out of bondage in Egypt. He also gave the world a lasting contribution, the moral law.

Many scholars and archeologists have tried to find an answer to explain this strange phenomenon. Some believe it was a bush with some kind of shiny berries which looked like a blazing fire, or it might have been blossoms of the mistletoe, which grows on acacia bushes. The bush, which is covered with oil glands, bursts into flames. There are no such burning bushes in the area, nor are they ever seen or mentioned by the nomad people or travelers.

Moses, in a vision, saw a bush burning but not consumed; and when he went near it, he heard the divine voice speak to him. Moses was still in the vision. God's revelations and his divine communications are always imparted in visions and dreams.

SHOES REMOVED

And he said, Draw not nigh hither: put off thy shoes from off thy feet; for the place whereon thou standest is holy ground. Exod. 3:5

In the East, owing to much dust, mire, and dirt in the streets, the people take off their shoes when they enter the church or the mosque, or any other holy place where prayers are offered to God. They also remove their shoes when they enter a room or a house which is furnished with rugs. And especially when they are in the presence of a ruler or high religious dignitary.

To remove one's shoes in a house or a holy place is the highest token of respect to the host and to God. Metaphorically, shoes are symbolic of contempt and false belief, and disregard for responsibility [Deut. 25:9; Ruth 4:7].

YAHWEH

And he said, Certainly I will be with thee; and this shall be a token unto thee, that I have sent thee: When thou hast brought forth the people out of Egypt, ye shall serve God upon this mountain.   Exod. 3:12

Yahweh, or as it is pronounced in Aramaic, *yehowah,* means the "ever-living," the "life-giver," the "self-existence," the "eternal," the "creator," or the "one who causes things to be." *Yehowah* is the name of God as it is given in Genesis in the Eastern text.

In Exodus 20:2, it is called *Alahek,* "your God," from the Aramaic word *Alaha* and Hebrew *Elohim* [Exod. 6:3 and Gen. 3:20].

THE LIVING GOD

And God said unto Moses, I Am That I Am: and he said, Thus shalt thou say unto the children of Israel, I Am hath sent me unto you.   Exod. 3:14

The Lord conversed with Moses in the Midianite dialect of the Semitic vernacular speech, which was understood by all the members of the Semitic race in Palestine. The Midianites were the descendants of Abraham [Gen. 25:1-2]. Moses had been in Midian for forty years. No doubt, as a shepherd living in the open country among simple nomads, he had forgotten most of the Egyptian tongue.

The Eastern text reads: *Ahiah Ashar High,* "I am the living God; the God which always has been; the eternal God, the God of Abraham, Isaac, and Jacob."

This term expresses the divine nature and the unity of God, in contrast with the Midianite idols. At the outset, Moses thought he was conversing with a Midianite deity. In those days there were many deities and each country had its own gods or idols. Previously God had revealed himself to the Hebrew patriarchs as *El* and *Elohim;* then as *Yhowh,* from Hebrew *Hayah,* "to be." He was that which always has been, the eternal and the only God. This concept of the unity of God was a contradiction of the Midianite and other pagan deities.

Moses was born and reared in Egypt and now he was in pagan Midian. He wanted to be sure of the deity with whom he was communing.

Moses had heard about the God of his ancestors from his mother and from the Israelites in Egypt. He had been told that the Hebrew God was the living God, the creator of the heaven and the earth.

Ahiah is the name of God as revealed to Moses at Horeb. *Ahiah* means "the living." In western Aramaic, *kh* becomes *h,* thus *khia,* "living," will become *hiah,* Hebrew, *Achai.* Thus, *Ahiah Ashar High* means, "I am the living God," that is, "That which I always have been."

BORROWING CLOTHES

> *But every woman shall borrow of her neighbor, and of her that sojourneth in her house, jewels of silver, and jewels of gold, and raiment: and ye shall put them upon your sons, and upon your daughters; and ye shall spoil the Egyptians.*   Exod. 3:22

In the East during the festivals, weddings, and banquets, people borrow jewelry, clothes, and shoes. Those who do not intend to participate in these occasions lend their apparel and jewelry of silver and gold to those who participate. Some of the holy shrines are two or three days journey, and the worshipers and merrymakers want to be well dressed in the presence of a multitude of strangers and acquaintances.

Borrowing of clothes is so common that the people think nothing of it, and are not surprised to see some of their best garments loaned by the members of their families to their neighbors.

Easterners generally dress in simple garments, but when they attend a banquet or wedding feast, they dress lavishly. Those who have no new garments and jewelry borrow from others. When they are not well dressed, they are not welcome.

Owing to the secrecy of their departure, the Hebrews were unable to take away their own tangible property. They had told Pharaoh that they were going to celebrate a feast to their God and return to Egypt. This is why Pharaoh granted them permission to go. They could take their cattle, gold, and silver, but all their other possessions had to be left behind.

They thought that the only way to reimburse themselves for their heavy losses of land, houses, and other unmovable property would be to take advantage of the custom of borrowing clothing and jewelry from their Egyptian neighbors.

In those days all such acts were done with the knowledge and permission of God, who was the ruler over the people. Anything that the leaders said or did was supposed to be done with the consent of God.

God knew that the Israelites were leaving behind houses, fields, orchards, and vineyards. The Israelites may have arranged to exchange their unmovable property for clothing and jewels as the refugees do today, when they flee.

TAIL

And the Lord said unto Moses, Put forth thine hand, and take it by the tail. And he put forth his hand, and caught it, and it became a rod in his hand. Exod. 4:4

"Tail" is symbolic of weakness and defeat. In Aramaic people often say, "I will hold you with your tail," which means, "I will overcome you."

Then again, when snakes are caught, they are caught by their tails. When a serpent is lifted up by its tail, it is helpless. So when Moses was afraid of the serpent, the Lord told him to hold it by its tail.

The serpent was symbolic of the great Pharaoh, the sea monster, who was feared not only by the Egyptians, but also by other peoples. The serpent was the mortal enemy of the Israelites and other Semitic peoples. Moses was given wisdom and power to handle Pharaoh, and, through God's wonders, bring him to terms. It was a contest between God's power and man's wisdom, and a conflict between a nomad tribe and a great imperial power. But Moses, in his wisdom, was assured of victory.

HAND IN BOSOM

And the Lord said furthermore unto him, Put now thine hand into thy bosom. And he put his hand into his bosom: and when he took it out, behold, his hand was leprous as snow.
And he said, Put thine hand into thy bosom again. And he put his hand into his bosom again; and plucked it out of his bosom, and, behold, it was turned again as his other flesh. Exod. 4:6-7

Generally, magicians put their hand in their bosom when performing their magical tricks. In the East most of them wear three or four shirts, between which they hide the objects.

Since God was directing Moses to perform this wonder, Moses seemingly needed not to put his hand in his pocket and bring it forth again. He could have stretched his hand forth and wrought the wonder of leprosy without putting it back into his bosom. This would have impressed the people more.

On the other hand, we do not know why God should resort to magic and use leprosy as a sign to convince Pharaoh. The healing of a blind man would have been far more impressive, and the Egyptian magicians could not have duplicated the miracle.

Moses was a magician. He had studied the art of magic under the care of skillful Egyptian priests. He knew that Pharaoh, like all Eastern monarchs, would be pleased to see this performance. Probably Moses did not know that the present Egyptian magicians could perform the same acts. He had not been in Egypt for forty years. It is hard to believe that the Living God of Israel would resort to such common means to convince Pharaoh of his great power. After all, Pharaoh was not convinced by these performances which both Moses and his own magicians wrought in his presence.

The whole training of the Egyptian priests was solely based on magic. Objects were changed instantly, fire was brought from the ground, and the doors of the temples were opened and closed in a mysterious way. Some of these works are still performed by the priests who are in charge of the holy sepulchre in Jerusalem. They cause fire to come out from the earth.

The human mind always relies on human agencies, and when these agencies fail, it turns to God. No doubt, God can do anything. There is nothing that he cannot do. All his works are miracles and wonders. God could have taken the Hebrew people and placed them in Palestine without any trouble, but God let things take their own natural course. He sent the Hebrews by way of the desert simply because the shorter route was fortified by strong Egyptian and Philistine garrisons [Exod. 13:17]. One thing we know, God is not the author of leprosy.

MOSES' TONGUE

And Moses said unto the Lord, O my Lord, I am not eloquent, neither heretofore, nor since thou hast spoken unto thy servant; but I am slow of speech, and of a slow tongue.   Exod. 4:10

Some commentators believe that Moses was slow of speech, or shy. Some maintain that he stuttered, and others say that his tongue was defective. Moses did confess that, because of his speech, he was not the man to stand in the presence of Pharaoh.

What was wrong with Moses? We know that Moses was brought up in the palace. He had seen and spoken to princes, generals, and men of nobility; therefore, he could not have been shy, as some people think. What then was wrong with his speech? There are other factors to be examined.

Moses had spent forty years in the land of Midian feeding the sheep of his father-in-law, Jethro. During these years, he had forgotten his Egyptian language and learned the Midianite speech, a dialect of the Semitic languages. Marco Polo, an Italian, forgot his Italian language in twenty years. Some people forget their languages in five or six years. This is why the Lord told him that he would put words in his mouth (inspire him). "And Aaron, your brother, is a good speaker; you must speak to him and tell him what to say, and I will be with his mouth and with your mouth."

Aaron was fluent in his Egyptian language. Moses was instructed by God to speak to him in the Midianite dialect, and Aaron was to interpret it into the Egyptian tongue. Therefore, Moses' difficulty was not the defection in his tongue, but lack of knowledge of the Egyptian tongue. Moses spoke well to Aaron in the presence of the elders. He had no impediment in his speech. God could have healed his tongue or taught him the Egyptian language, but God always works in a natural way. He found an interpreter.

On the other hand, God would not have chosen a stutterer and sent him to speak to Pharaoh. The latter would not have received him in the palace. Moses was not eloquent in Egyptian, but slow of speech. Moses might have had a slight impediment in his speech. Be that as it may, during the forty years in the desert, Moses spoke as a great orator, and no mention of his stuttering is made.

The Aramaic words *leaeg leshana* mean "hesitating in speech," but the same word means "stammer" or "stutterer." *Leaeg mamla* means "dumb," "stutterer," or "stammerer."

KNIVES

Then Zipporah took a sharp stone, and cut off the foreskin of her son, and cast it at his feet, and said, Surely a bloody husband art thou to me.   Exod. 4:25

In the olden days when iron was scarce and steel in its infancy and limited to nations whose learned men had discovered the art of hardening iron, knives and swords were rare. The tribal people still continued to use sharp flint. As late as the beginning of this century, steel knives were rare. When a certain family needed a knife, they went to a shepherd or a wealthy man who happened to have one.

Evidently, steel or iron knives were scarce among the Midianites. This is why Zipporah, the wife of Moses, took a sharp stone to circumcise her son.

Zipporah knew that Moses, her husband, was a fugitive from Egypt. Moses had murdered an Egyptian and fled to Midian. He had told his wife that the Hebrews circumcised their males, but Moses, not thinking of returning to Egypt, had neglected this ancient ordinance. Moses and his wife would not have been welcomed by the Hebrews in Egypt had not Zipporah circumcised their son according to the Hebrew law.

Forty years later, Joshua faced the same situation. He had to circumcise all males who were born in the desert, so he made a sharp knife of flint to circumcise the people who had not been circumcised in the desert. The usage of flint knives might have been an ancient tradition or custom. These knives were called *chereb* in Hebrew, but knives which were used for food were called *makebeth*.

SCRIBES AND WRITING

And Pharaoh commanded the same day the taskmasters of the people, and their officers, saying.   Exod. 5:6

Saprey, in Aramaic, means "scribes" and not "officers." In the East, educated men, those who know how to read and write, generally are placed in charge of workers to distribute the work and receive an account of what has been done during the day. The scribes, in turn, were responsible to officers, or taskmasters, and other higher authorities, who generally could not read and write.

The term "scribes" appears many times in the Old Testament, but it is always wrongly rendered "officers." In the New Testament, however, it is correctly translated.

Even today the nomad tribes employ one or two scribes to write treaties and agreements and to render accounts to the chief of the tribe concerning sheep, butter, wool, and other things that are sold in the markets in the cities.

The Hebrews wrote as early as 1600 B.C.

ELSHADDAI

And I appeared unto Abraham, unto Isaac, and unto Jacob, by the name of God Almighty; but by my name Jehovah was I not known to them.   Exod. 6:3

The Eastern text reads: *El Shaddai,* "the Almighty God." *El* means "God," and *Shaddai* means "strong," or "powerful." The Arabic is *Shaddidan,* "powerful."

In patriarchal days, when religion was in its infancy, gods were known by their character and abilities. There were gods of fertility, gods of rain, gods of insects, and gods of winds and storms. The Hebrew God was *Elshaddai,* "the Almighty God." This is because he was the Creator of all and had power over all things. He was called the "God of gods."

In those early days every tribe relied on its own god for pasture, water, and security. Then again, gods fought for their people and destroyed their enemies.

REDEEM

Wherefore say unto the children of Israel, I am the Lord, and I will bring you out from under the burdens of the Egyptians, and I will rid you out of their bondage, and I will redeem you with a stretched out arm, and with great judgments.   Exod. 6:6

The Aramaic word *parak* means "to save," "to deliver." The Eastern text reads: "I will save you . . ." *Porkana* means "salvation."

The term "redeem" is wrongly used, for God did not have to pay a ransom. Redeem means "to recover by paying a debt," "to ransom by paying a price," "to atone for."

The Aramaic word for redeem is *zban,* "to buy," "to ransom." *Meshikha zabnan min lotta denamosa,* "Christ has redeemed us from the curse of the law." Paul speaks of "the church of Christ, which he purchased (redeemed) with his blood" in Acts 20:28.

The Aramaic text, throughout the Bible, uses two words, save and redeem. Nowhere does it speak of God as paying a price, but instead, as saving by his strong arm and his outstretched hand.

Men redeem one another by paying a price to kings, princes, and governors, but since God is the only power in the universe, there is no one else to pay to [Exod. 15:13].

MARRIED HIS COUSIN

And Amram took him Jochebed his father's sister to wife; and she bare him Aaron and Moses: and the years of the life of Amram were a hundred and thirty and seven years.   Exod. 6:20

Barth dadey means "his uncle's daughter." His father's sister would be his aunt, and the Mosaic law prohibited the marriage of near kin on both sides. In the East a man is permitted to marry his first cousin.

The Eastern text reads: "And Amram took his uncle's daughter, Jokhaber . . ." Jochebed should read *Jokhaber* or *Yokhabor*, which means "the glory is departed from Israel" [1 Sam. 4:21]. *Abar* means "to pass over," "to pass away."

The error was caused by the confusion between the letters *resh* "R," and *daleth* "D." Resh has a dot over it, and daleth a dot under it.

I HAVE MADE THEE A GOD

And the Lord said unto Moses, See, I have made thee a god to
Pharaoh; and Aaron thy brother shall be thy prophet.   Exod. 7:1

The term "god" in this instance means power and authority. Moses was to take the part of God, or be instead of God, in transmitting divine messages to Pharaoh [Exod. 4:16]. Aaron, on the other hand, was to act as a prophet in translating and interpreting Moses' words to Pharaoh and his ministers. Aaron was an eloquent speaker, but Moses spoke Egyptian hesitatingly.

The Aramaic or Hebrew word *nbia* or *nabi* means a "prophet," a "foreteller of events," or a "bearer of news." Moses had almost forgotten the Egyptian language. He had spent forty years in the land of Midian feeding the flocks of his father-in-law, and during this period he spoke the Midianite language, which was close to ancient Hebrew. Thus, the term "god" in this instance should not be confused with a deity or an idol.

Moses, because of the power which God had granted him, had a great influence over Pharaoh and the Egyptians. All the people of the land feared and respected him.

STAFF

For they cast down every man his rod, and they became serpents:
but Aaron's rod swallowed up their rods.   Exod. 7:12

Khotra, "staff," in Aramaic symbolizes power and protection. In the ancient days, when firearms were unknown and steel swords difficult and expensive to acquire, shepherds and travelers carried staffs with them as a means of protection against wild animals and snakes, and for defense against robbers. Jesus admonished his disciples not to carry staffs (staves) with them [Matt. 10:10]. They were to trust in the spirit of the Lord for protection. Rods or wands are generally used by magicians.

The staffs of Moses and Aaron were symbolic of God's power. The Egyptians relied on chariots and swords of steel. God chose weapons which men would reject for defense in the time of danger.

The rods of Moses and Aaron were cut from the trees. They were symbolic of life and power, for they relied on the staff of the Spirit rather than a staff of wood.

Aaron and the Egyptian magicians cast down their staffs in the presence of Pharaoh, and they became serpents. But Aaron's serpent swallowed up the serpents of the Egyptian magicians. Nevertheless, Pharaoh was not convinced, because the Egyptian magicians did the same.

Some authorities say the Egyptian magicians used stiff serpents in performing these acts in the temples. There are certain snakes which become stiff at certain times during the year. We call them *sawya*, "stiff." These are awakened by chanting and piping. Serpents respond to music. Be that as it may, God granted Moses victory over the Egyptian magicians.

RIVER TURNED INTO BLOOD

And Moses and Aaron did so, as the Lord commanded; and he lifted up the rod, and smote the waters that were in the river, in the sight of Pharaoh, and in the sight of his servants; and all the waters that were in the river were turned to blood. Exod. 7:20

Some people in Egypt maintain that erosion from the Ethiopian highlands causes the water of the Nile to become as red as blood. They believe that this change was caused by the red soil. All of Egypt depends on the Nile for its water. Be that as it may, the author of Exodus states that the Egyptian magicians did the same, and therefore, Pharaoh was not impressed by the wonder which Moses and Aaron performed in his presence.

Apparently the Egyptian scientists were familiar with biological warfare. We know that in Arabia, and other adjacent lands, wells and other sources of water are often contaminated and poisoned.

God could do anything, and could also endow his agents with power. But where the Egyptians received their knowledge to perform these wonders is a puzzle to many Bible readers. For to a great extent, they duplicated most of Moses' and Aaron's wonders.

It was the personality of Moses, and the divine power that God had given him, which frightened Pharaoh, his court officials, and his magicians.

FROG PESTS

And the Lord spake unto Moses, Say unto Aaron, Stretch forth thine hand with thy rod over the streams, over the rivers, and over the ponds, and cause frogs to come up upon the land of Egypt.

Exod. 8:5

Egypt is noted for swarms of frogs. The great river Nile is cut into many canals, which irrigate the fertile Egyptian delta. These canals are cut again into smaller ones, and thus, water is distributed among the farmers. The term *mizrin* or *Heb mizrim* means "canals."

When the water is cut off from the smaller canals it becomes stagnant and, because of the heat, frogs swarm and multiply very rapidly. The river is full of them [Verse 11].

Frog pests have been a problem in the land of Egypt. Efforts to destroy them have been made from time to time.

Egypt is flat, and houses built near the banks of the canals are invaded by the frogs. Frogs are found all over, even in bed chambers. This is also true of insects and other things that make life hard for the people. Snakes are found in tents and houses in many lands in the Near East.

Egypt, being a hot land, is an ideal place for the swarms of frogs, flies, and other insects which hatch and grow overnight.

The Egyptian magicians, by some unknown means, also caused the river and the canals to swarm with frogs. But Moses and Aaron had the power to destroy them; something which the Egyptian magicians could not do.

LICE

And they did so; for Aaron stretched out his hand with his rod, and smote the dust of the earth, and it became lice in man, and in beast; all the dust of the land became lice throughout all the land of Egypt.

Exod. 8:17

Lice are common in all primitive lands where soap and water are scarce, poverty prevalent, and bathing rare. At times, clothes have to be put in boiling water in order to destroy the lice. Lice and fleas are also found in bedclothes and on the ground.

There is also another kind of lice, *kalma,* found in wheat storehouses, which destroys the wheat supplies. Still another kind of lice is found on animals. The people in the olden days did not know how to destroy these pests.

MAGICIANS HELPLESS

And the magicians did so with their enchantments to bring forth lice, but they could not: so there were lice upon man, and upon beast.   Exod. 8:18

The Egyptian magicians were able, with their enchantments, to produce lice, but they could not get rid of them as Moses and Aaron were able to do.

The Eastern text reads: "But they could not get rid of it." The translator, for an unknown reason, overlooked the word *lamparakotah*, "get rid of." The early translators might have confused this word with *lmapakotah*, with negative "not to bring it forth."

The Egyptian magicians believed that Moses' act was the finger of God, that is, an act caused by the power of God. Moreover, this wonder proved the superiority of Moses' and Aaron's wonders over the magical acts of the Egyptians.

GOING TO THE RIVER

And the Lord said unto Moses, Rise up early in the morning, and stand before Pharaoh; lo, he cometh forth to the water; and say unto him, Thus saith the Lord, Let my people go, that they may serve me.   Exod. 8:20

"He cometh forth to the water" is an Aramaic idiom which means "he goes to the latrine." This idiom is still used in Aramaic speech, and is often misunderstood by Westerners.

It was easier for Moses and Aaron to meet Pharaoh on his way to his daily duties than to wait months for an appointment and endless oriental court formalities. On such occasions, the king walked alone, and was easily approached by those who wanted to make an appeal to him.

In those days, latrines were unknown. The people relieved themselves by the rivers, in isolated places, and in the ruins of buildings. This ancient custom is still prevalent in some backward lands. A latrine in the Iranian language is called *abidust*, "the place of washing hands."

SWARMS OF FLIES

And the Lord did so; and there came a grievous swarm of flies into the house of Pharaoh, and into his servants' houses, and into all the land of Egypt: the land was corrupted by reason of the swarm of flies.   Exod. 8:24

In the Bible lands flies are more abundant than all other pests. During the summer months streets, houses, and public places are full of them. Flies are responsible for eye diseases. One could see clusters of flies hanging on the ceilings of restaurants, and boys standing over the patrons chasing the flies away from the dishes. Even a few decades ago, Palestinians and Egyptians suffered from flies. Many helpless little children were victims of these flies.

Today, the Egyptian government has taken measures to free the country from these pests. Science and modern sanitary conditions are the answer to these ancient plagues.

The fact that no swarms of flies were in the land of Goshen, where the Israelites were living, was a miracle or a wonder. God protects those who trust in him. Moses had trusted in God.

SACRED ANIMALS

And Moses said, It is not meet so to do; for we shall sacrifice the abomination of the Egyptians to the Lord our God: lo, shall we sacrifice the abomination of the Egyptians before their eyes, and will they not stone us?   Exod. 8:26

The Hebrews were a pastoral people, and they raised large flocks of sheep, of which they sacrificed to God. But sheep were an abomination to the Egyptians. The latter could not even eat with sheep-raising people [Gen. 43:32].

Some of the other animals which the Israelites might sacrifice were sacred to the Egyptians. Swine might have been one of them. For swine are immune to the venom of snakes, since their bodies are protected with fat, and swine will devour snakes.

The Egyptians would have been offended at seeing their sacred animals sacrificed to the God of the Israelites. This would have been an insult to the Egyptian deities. The Hindus protest and fight when they see a Moslem slaughter a cow. Pharaoh had no other choice; he had to permit the Israelites to sacrifice to their God in the desert, far away from the Egyptians.

BLAINS

And the Lord did that thing on the morrow, and all the cattle of
of Egypt died: but of the cattle of the children of Israel died not
one. Exod. 9:6

In verse 10 of this chapter we are told that the blains burst forth upon
men and upon cattle.

It is evident that all the Egyptian cattle did not die. Some of the
cattle, belonging to the Egyptians who feared God, were spared. "He
who feared the word of the Lord among the servants of Pharaoh brought
his servants and his cattle into the house" [Exod. 9:20]. But all the cattle
which were in the open country perished.

MAGICIANS DEFEATED

And the magicians could not stand before Moses because of the
boils; for the boil was upon the magicians, and upon all the Egyp-
tians. Exod. 9:11

The term "magic" means "to magnify"; that is, "to deceive the eye."
The Egyptian magicians performed many wonders in the presence of
Pharaoh, so that the king gave little credence to the wonders which
Moses and Aaron performed. This is why Pharaoh refused to let the
Israelites leave Egypt. The superiority of Moses' wonders over the
wonders of the Eygptians for a while was not sufficient to convince
Pharaoh that God had sent Moses to Egypt to lead his people out.

But Moses and Aaron smote the Egyptians with boils, and even the
magicians, on whom Pharaoh had relied, were stricken, so that they recognized Moses' superiority over them. The magicians were endowed with
deceptive powers.

PHARAOH'S DESTINY

And in very deed for this cause have I raised thee up, for to show
in thee my power; and that my name may be declared throughout
all the earth. Exod. 9:16

"For this cause have I raised you" means "this is your mission." That
is, you were born and made a king for this reason. This does not imply
that God purposely made Pharaoh to be a wicked and stiffnecked king
in order that he might perform wonders and show his power.

Pharaoh, because of his pride and greed, was unwilling to let the Hebrews leave Egypt. There were also political and economic reasons for his stubbornness. The Hebrews were a Semitic people who constantly warred against the Egyptians. Moreover, the Hebrews were digging canals and building cities for Pharaoh.

In Hebrew thinking, every act is governed by God, and since Pharaoh refused to let the people go, it must have been God who hardened his heart. This is because no cause or action can happen without God's knowledge. And since God knew that Pharaoh would not let the people go, then he must have allowed him to act the way he did.

Pharaoh, like other kings, was unwilling to let hundreds of thousands of Israelites, who were working for him, leave Egypt. God's glory and power are manifested through his wonderful creations. It is the human mind which wants to show its glory, honor, and power. Even today, many nations would not permit the exodus of so many people with their sheep, cattle, gold, silver, and other goods. Pharaoh, the king of Egypt, is not the first oppressor, nor the last.

HAIL AND THUNDER STORMS

And Moses stretched forth his rod toward heaven: and the Lord sent thunder and hail, and the fire ran along upon the ground; and the Lord rained hail upon the land of Egypt.   Exod. 9:23

Hail and thunder storms are common in tropical lands, and are accompanied by lightning. They cause severe damage to crops, trees, and cattle. The miracle or wonder is the fact that the land of Goshen was divinely spared the great disaster.

The laws of nature are subject to the laws of God, who guides and controls the whole universe. God spares and preserves those who trust in him, and who work with his laws and not against them.

SWARMS OF LOCUSTS

And Moses stretched forth his rod over the land of Egypt, and the Lord brought an east wind upon the land all that day, and all that night; and when it was morning, the east wind brought the locusts.   Exod. 10:13

Plagues of caterpillars and locusts are very common in Egypt and other Near Eastern lands [Ps. 105:34; Deut. 28:38]. At times, wheat fields, vegetables, grass, and trees are devastated by swarms of locusts, and as a result the people suffer from famine. This was the most severe catastrophe caused by the locusts [Exod. 10:5, 6].

Moses was divinely guided. He knew when the locusts were coming. All his predictions were divinely guided, and took place at the right time. The locusts swarm every seventeen years.

Since the World Wars every effort has been made to bring to an end these devastating plagues. The fight against locusts still goes on in Africa and Asia. Planes, gases, and other modern methods have lessened the disasters caused by the locusts.

BEHIND THE MILL

And all the firstborn in the land of Egypt shall die, from the firstborn of Pharaoh that sitteth upon his throne, even unto the firstborn of the maidservant that is behind the mill; and all the firstborn of beasts. Exod. 11:5

In the olden days wheat was ground with handmills made of granite stones or baked clay. Water-powered mills and windmills were unknown in some lands, especially in low lands where there are no waterfalls, and in Palestine where water is scarce.

The grinding was done by women, just as it is today in many lands in the Near East, and especially among the dwellers of the desert lands.

Most of the grinding work is assigned to blind persons and maidservants. This occupation is considered the lowest occupation. It is almost a disgrace for a man to see his wife seated behind the grinder. Job says if his heart has been deceived by a woman or if he has done any evil to his neighbor, then let my wife grind to another, and let her bake bread in another's oven [Job 31:9,10].

What the author of Exodus means here is that the firstborn of the people, from the highest to the lowest, was smitten. [See also Matt. 24:41; Luke 17:35.]

DIVINELY PROTECTED

But against any of the children of Israel shall not a dog move his tongue, against man or beast: that ye may know how that the Lord doth put a difference between the Egyptians and Israel. Exod. 11:7

"Shall not a dog move his tongue" means that no dog shall bark and no one shall say anything. In the East men often say, "When we entered the town, not even the dogs barked"; that is, the movements of the men were so quiet and stealthy that not even the dogs knew they were in the city.

Dogs are very sensitive to strangers and animals, and are therefore easily awakened. In Eastern thinking the barking of dogs is symbolic of noise, disturbances, and howling.

The smiting of the firstborn of the Egyptians brought forth crying and wailing throughout the land of Egypt, but the land of Goshen was so quiet that not even the dogs barked. The Lord God had spared the first-born of the Israelites from the great slaughter. The blood of the lamb served as a sign to mark the houses of the Israelites from those of the Egyptians. The angel, or the messenger of death, passed by the houses of the Israelites.

THE BLOOD OF THE LAMB

And they shall take of the blood, and strike it on the two side posts and on the upper doorpost of the houses, wherein they shall eat it.   Exod. 12:7

The blood of the lamb was used to distinguish the houses of the Israelites from those of the Egyptians. In the olden days numbers were unknown and houses were identified by marks. When the Hebrew spies promised Rahab to spare her and her relatives, they asked her to place a line made of scarlet thread in the window [Joshua 4:18-21].

When covenants, compacts, and agreements were made, sheep and lambs were slaughtered to seal the treaties, and the people made a feast as a memorial to the covenant. This ancient custom still prevails in biblical lands.

The Lord smote all the firstborn of the Egyptians, even the firstborn of the cattle. The blood on the doorposts was symbolic of life. The Egyptians were plagued, but the Hebrews were to be spared. When the Lord saw the blood on the doorpost, he passed on to the next Egyptian house. Thus, the blood of the lamb became the means of salvation to the Israelites. The flesh of the lamb was eaten during the feast, just as they ate other sacrificial meat. Some people wonder why did God need a red sign in order to distinguish the houses of the Israelites from those of the Egyptians.

God had commanded Moses that the Israelites must observe this ordinance throughout their generations. Later, it became to be known as the Passover, because the Lord had passed over the houses of the Hebrews when he slew the firstborn of the Egyptians.

In the East the feast of the Passover is called the feast of *Pesakh*, that is, the feast of rejoicing. The Hebrews rejoiced when they left Egypt and were free from bondage.

GIRDLES

And thus shall ye eat it; with your loins girded, your shoes on your feet, and your staff in your hand; and ye shall eat it in haste: it is the Lord's passover.   Exod. 12:11

Easterners wear girdles over their garments when they go on a journey. The girdle, or sash, keeps the flowing garment together and thus makes travel easier and faster. The girdle is fastened over the loins, the waist.

The girdle is symbolic of readiness, alertness, and strength. John the Baptist wore a girdle [Matt. 3:4]. Jeremiah was told by God to wear a girdle. ". . . Go and get thee a linen girdle and put it upon thy loins . . ." [Jer. 13:1]. Servants are girded when serving their masters.

The Israelites were to leave in haste. This is why they ate the Passover standing, with their staffs in their hands. They had no time even to bake bread and prepare provisions for the journey. They took their dough before it was leavened, and baked it along their way, just as the tribal people do today [Verse 34].

FEAST OF REJOICING

That ye shall say, It is the sacrifice of the Lord's passover, who passed over the houses of the children of Israel in Egypt, when he smote the Egyptians, and delivered our houses. And the people bowed the head and worshipped.   Exod. 12:27

The Aramaic word *pesakh* means "to rejoice." The stem of the verb is *psakh*. The Hebrews rejoiced when they saw that the firstborn of the Egyptians were dead and their own firstborn spared by the destroyer, who saw the blood on the doorposts and passed by [Verse 13].

Piskhah means "rejoicing." This is because the people ate, drank, and rejoiced. Passover means the destroyer passed over the Hebrew houses when he slew the firstborn of the Egyptians.

SIX HUNDRED THOUSAND

And the children of Israel journeyed from Rameses to Succoth, about six hundred thousand on foot that were men, beside children.
Exod. 12:37

Women and children are not counted in the East [Matt. 14:21; Mark 6:44]. The author of Exodus, according to the Eastern text, states that there were six hundred thousand men who could walk, besides the little ones who had to be carried on the backs of their parents and on animals.

The order for drowning the Hebrew boy babies seemingly was local and of short duration. Had the persecution been widely spread and of long duration, there would have been no Israelites to be oppressed by Pharaoh Rameses, or to be led out of Egypt by Moses. No doubt, some children of the Israelites were cast into the River Nile in a certain city, probably in Memphis, but the decree must have been rescinded.

When Moses fled to Midian the Israelites were oppressed by the Egyptians, that is, they were made to work. Had the decree and persecution lasted for a long time, there would have been no Israelites to be enslaved by the Egyptians.

The Israelites left Egypt a strong people; healthy, prosperous, and armed [Exod. 13:18]. We are told that not one of them was sick or weak. After all, the Egyptians had hearts; they were not as bad as some other races who have oppressed and murdered the Jews.

JUDAISM IS A RELIGION

And when a stranger shall sojourn with thee, and will keep the passover to the Lord, let all his males be circumcised, and then let him come near and keep it; and he shall be as one that is born in the land: for no uncircumcised person shall eat thereof.

One law shall be to him that is homeborn, and unto the stranger that sojourneth among you.　　　　　　　　　Exod. 12:48-49

Judaism is a religion. In biblical days any person who was circumcised could be admitted into the Jewish religion. This is also true of the Moslem religion today. On the other hand, the term Israel, or Hebrew, signifies the race and not religion.

In the East, even today, when a man changes his religion he changes his nationality. When Ruth forsook her people and her god and followed her mother-in-law, Naomi, she forsook her god and embraced the religion of Israel [Ruth 1:16]. Today, when a Christian becomes a Moslem, he immediately renounces his nationality, religion, and customs in order to become a member of the Moslem religion; and after his conversion he is known as a member of the race of the Moslem people among whom he may happen to live.

Many peoples of diverse races, religions, and cultural backgrounds left Egypt with the Israelites, but after they were circumcised, they were admitted into the Hebrew religion. The term Jew was not used at that time, but it came into use after the destruction of the temple, during the second captivity, 586 B.C. As early as the conquest of Palestine by Joshua, many Gentiles, who surrendered peacefully, were spared and later became members of the Hebrew religion [Exod. 12:38].

FIRSTLING OF ASSES KILLED

*And every firstling of an ass thou shalt redeem with a lamb; and
if thou wilt not redeem it, then thou shalt break his neck: and all
the firstborn of man among thy children shalt thou redeem.*

Exod. 13:13

Seemingly, the priests and Levites had no use for donkeys. They
preferred lambs, rams, and he-goats, which they sold or used for food.

In the East donkeys are considered unclean animals, and are only
used as beasts of burden. In some countries, like Midian and parts of
Arabia, donkeys are so plentiful that they could not easily be sold or
exchanged for other animals. That is why their owners are admonished
to break their necks.

REPENT

*And it came to pass, when Pharaoh had let the people go, that
God led them not through the way of the land of the Philistines,
although that was near; for God said, Lest peradventure the people
repent when they see war, and they return to Egypt.*   Exod. 13:17

The Aramaic word for repentance is *tiabotha*, derived from *to-boo*,
"to cease" to do a certain thing, "to return from," "to be sorry," or "to
change one's mind." The Eastern text reads, "Lest the people be afraid."

THE ISRAELITES WERE ARMED

*But God led the people about, through the way of the wilderness
of the Red sea: and the children of Israel went up harnessed out
of the land of Egypt.*   Exod. 13:18

The Aramaic word *mezanin* means "armed." The term "harnessed"
is wrong. The mistranslation is due to the similarity of the word "to
arm" and "to harness."

The Hebrews, or Israelites, left Egypt well-armed with swords, bows,
lances, and spears. They fought against the Amalekites and later the
Levites and slew three thousand rebellious men.

The Israelites could not have left Egypt unarmed. They would have
been devoured by the roaming tribes in the Sinai desert.

The Egyptians, like other Near Eastern governments, allowed their subjects to be armed in order to protect themselves against their natural enemies and to help the nation when it was threatened from the outside.

CLOUD AND FIRE

And the Lord went before them by day in a pillar of a cloud, to lead them the way; and by night in a pillar of fire, to give them light; to go by day and night.   Exod.13:21

Travel in the Arabian desert is beset with many difficulties. At times travelers are lost because of the lack of directions, and they perish of thirst. In the desert, roads are unknown and landmarks and footprints are quickly obliterated by winds. Desert dwellers and expert men who lead the camels travel by the means of stars and the shadows of trees and rocks.

The Lord sent the cloud to show the directions and to protect the people from intense heat. In the East shepherds and the desert experts know the movements of the clouds and their direction, just as they know the movement of the stars. The Lord made stars, clouds, and other signs for the times and seasons and gave man wisdom to understand their movements.

Oil experts in Arabia believe that what the Israelites saw was the glow from the burning oil ignited by heat. In some parts of Arabia where oil is abundant, fires are seen during the night. Be that as it may, the Lord God led the Israelites and aided them by means of miracles and wonders which were natural to him. The cloud protected them from the heat of the sun. The heat in the Sinai desert is scorching, and travel is difficult when clouds are absent. It was the hand of God which wrought these wonders.

THE RED SEA

Speak unto the children of Israel, that they turn and encamp before Pihahiroth, between Migdol and the sea, over against Baalzephon: before it shall ye encamp by the sea.   Exod. 14:2

The reason for the divine command to turn backward, southwest of the Gulf of Suez, was because of the danger of the presence of the Egyptian army which was pursuing them and the Egyptian military outposts at the isthmus. Evidently Pharaoh's army was trying to reach the crossing place before the Israelites in order to block their way, and thus leave them stranded and finally trapped on the western side of the tip of the Gulf of Suez.

Prior to the construction of the Suez Canal, the Bitter Lakes were connected with the Gulf of Suez by high tides. Pharaoh thought that the Hebrews, being a pastoral people and strange in the land, would not understand the tides, and therefore, would try to cross through the isthmus. But Moses, being a shepherd and scientist, knew when the tides were high or low. That is why the Lord directed him southward instead of northward where the crossing was easy.

Moreover, even though the Israelites were armed, they would have been no match for Pharaoh's trained army. On the other hand, women and children would have been frightened to see a battle.

The Bible does not claim that the Hebrews crossed through the Red Sea. According to the biblical text, the Hebrews crossed at a place called Pihahiroth, which in Aramaic is called *Kheritha,* which means a "strait" or "channel" or "shoals." The British admiralty years ago warned British ship captains of the danger of these shoals at high tide. Pihahiroth is on the northern end of the Gulf of Suez, near the Bitter Lakes toward Migdol. This is the place where the journey of the Israelites started.

The Red Sea is more than one hundred miles south of Pihahiroth and Baal-zephon, where the Israelites were told by God to encamp before they crossed the channel. These places are on the northern and further-most tip of the Gulf of Suez. Even the Gulf is about twenty miles wide and very deep. The Red Sea must be several hundred feet deep. On the other hand, the sea is far away from the route to Palestine. Had they crossed the Red Sea, then they would have had to cross the Gulf of Akaba in order to reach the places where they encamped in the Sinai peninsula. Places such as Marah, Elim, Rephidim, and Mount Horeb are not far away from the crossing place, Pihahiroth.

A glance at the biblical map will show that the Israelites neither crossed the Gulf of Suez nor did they go near the Red Sea, but instead they crossed this channel (or shoals) which is plainly mentioned in the fourteenth chapter of the book of Exodus.

It is interesting to know that in Aramaic any body of water, no matter how small, is called a sea. For instance, the river of Egypt, the Nile, is called a sea. The term "sea" means a gathering of waters together, whether it be small or large.

God can do anything, and no one can sincerely doubt his power and wisdom, but why should God direct the Hebrews to cross such a deep sea, at a place far away from their route, when they could cross at the crossing place which is on the route to Sinai and where the channel is narrow and negotiable, especially when the tide is low? Indeed, God would not do something which men would not do, that is direct the people in the wrong way. On the other hand, neither Israelites nor Egyptians would have attempted to cross through the midst of a sea thousands of feet deep and over a hundred miles wide!

In 14:21 we are plainly told how the sea was divided: "and the Lord caused the sea to go back by a strong east wind all that night, and made the sea dry land, and the waters were divided." The waters at the channel were divided when the crossing place, owing to the low tide, became dry land. This was done by the act of God, who caused the wind to throw the water backward until the crossing place appeared. It would not have taken God all night to divide the sea, but it took the wind that length of time.

The miracle in this instance is God's guidance. Moses and the Hebrews trusted in God, whereas the Egyptians trusted in their chariots and horses. They thought they could overtake the Israelites, but before they reached the eastern shore God caused the wind to cease and the tide came back swiftly, covering the Egyptian army.

Centuries ago there were no maps, and Bible students had no knowledge of the crossing place on the Suez channel. This is why millions of people are still taught today that the Hebrews crossed in the midst of the Red Sea. Some people refuse to believe in the whole Bible and to accept this story, not knowing that the Bible never has made such a claim.

As Moses had been a shepherd near this area for forty years, he knew the crossing place, and when he relied on God for guidance, God told him at what time to negotiate the crossing. This is why he instructed the Israelites to rise up early and to bake unleavened bread and eat hastily. Every minute was needed in order to get to the crossing place when the tide was low. God was with Moses in every way.

PHARAOH'S HEART HARDENED

And I will harden Pharaoh's heart, that he shall follow after them; and I will be honored upon Pharaoh, and upon all his host; that the Egyptians may know that I am the Lord. And they did so.
Exod. 14:4

The Lord knew that Pharaoh was so obstinate that he would change his mind again and try to prevent the Israelites from gaining their freedom. It was a great loss to him to see so many thousands of his subject-laborers leave his domain. His innate lust for power and wealth would return once more, but this time for his own destruction.

God's justice and majesty were to triumph over human pride and power. Pharaoh's heart was hardened by his own false pride and greed. Pharaoh simply regretted to see the work on his cities, palaces, and other projects stopped and the Israelites allowed to leave well-armed and with much gold, silver, cattle, and sheep. Pharaoh apparently realized that the Israelites, once on the other side of the Gulf of Suez, would not return to Egypt to lay bricks and do the manual work which was so detestable to the pastoral people.

LOWER TIDE

And Moses stretched out his hand over the sea; and the Lord caused the sea to go back by a strong east wind all that night, and made the sea dry land, and the waters were divided. Exod. 14:21

When Moses stretched out his hands over the sea, imploring God to save the Israelites from the Egyptian army which was in sight of the panic-stricken men and women, the Lord caused the sea to go back by a strong east wind all night, so that the passage was dry. The water now was on both sides of the crossing place, that is the water of the Bitter Lakes and the water at the tip of the Gulf of Suez. When the tide is high, both waters join, and the shoals are submerged.

The miracle in this instance was the wind which the Lord God caused to blow all night at the right time. God could have dried the passage instantly or placed the Israelites on the other side without even walking on the dry land; but instead the Lord guided the people and caused natural forces to be in their favor.

Moses and the Israelites trusted in God, but Pharaoh and his army trusted in the human mind and on the arm of the flesh. This is why the Egyptian army was drowned. While they were in the midst of the passage, the wind changed, the chariot wheels were mired, and the water rushed back upon them.

The Israelites crossed at a place about 185 miles north of the main body of the Red Sea.

WALL OF PROTECTION

And the Children of Israel went into the midst of the sea upon the dry ground: and the waters were a wall unto them on their right hand, and on their left. Exod. 14:22

The Aramaic word *shora*, "wall," is the same word used in speaking of a city wall, a fortification, or a fence.

The reference here is to the two bodies of water north and south, namely, Lake Timsha and the tongue of the Red Sea, which were a strong defense on both sides of the fleeing Israelites.

The Aramaic word for all is *esta. Shora* is used metaphorically to mean protection. We often say, "He has been a wall to me," meaning that he has given me protection. In the East people living in the walled cities are more secure than those who dwell in open towns.

GOD IN THE PILLAR OF FIRE

And it came to pass, that in the morning watch the Lord looked unto the host of the Egyptians through the pillar of fire and of the cloud, and troubled the host of the Egyptians.　　　Exod. 14:24

The Egyptian armies saw the glory of God and his might revealed in the pillar of cloud which led the Israelites by day, and the pillar of fire which gave them light by night [Exod. 13:21].

The Lord's presence was manifested in the camp of Israel, day and night. This phenomenon was a strange sight to the eyes of the Egyptians, so they were alarmed. The Eastern text reads: "The Lord was seen," that is, they saw his glory.

The chariot wheels were mired and could not operate in the muddy passage; the horses became frightened and halted. Thus the Egyptians saw that the Lord God of Israel was a mighty God and began to flee backward. But the waters covered them and they perished. Sisera suffered from the same disaster [Judg. 4:15].

THE WHEELS STOPPED

And took off their chariot wheels, that they drave them heavily: so that the Egyptians said, Let us flee from the face of Israel; for the Lord fighteth for them against the Egyptians.　　　Exod. 14:25

As the captain of the chariots tried to drive the chariots fast in order to cross to the other side while the tide was low, the chariot wheels stuck in the sand or mud in the channel's bed, and the horses were unable to pull them out.

The fear of the Lord God of Israel and the rushing water discomfited the Egyptians. Then Pharaoh's army, his horsemen, and his chariots were caught in the middle of the passage. And when Moses implored the Lord again, the water came back just as the Egyptians were fleeing toward it. Thus the Egyptians were overthrown in the midst of the channel (sea).

SONG OF MOSES

Then sang Moses and the children of Israel this song unto the Lord, and spake, saying, I will sing unto the Lord, for he hath triumphed gloriously: the horse and his rider hath he thrown into the sea.　　　Exod. 15:1

This song was composed on the scene, when the waters of the Red Sea covered the Egyptian army, their chariots and horsemen. In the

East songs of victory and mourning are composed instantly. Poets and professional mourners have no trouble in composing them on the spur of the moment.

On such occasions the poet sings first and the people repeat what he has sung. This song was composed by Moses and was sung by the people as they danced and glorified God. Miriam, the sister of Moses, and the women also started to dance with timbrels in the front of the tents [Exod. 15:20].

The song gives a vivid description of the triumph of the Israelites who trusted in the God of their fathers, and of the sudden defeat of the Egyptian army. This battle decided the fate of the Hebrew people; slavery was left behind and freedom was ahead in the vast desert.

The song of Moses is the first song in the Bible.

GOD'S NOSTRILS

And with the blast of thy nostrils the waters were gathered together, the floods stood upright as a heap, and the depths were congealed in the heart of the sea. Exod. 15:8

The term "blast of thy nostrils" is used figuratively, of course, meaning the blowing of the wind. The reference is to the incident when Moses stretched out his hand over the sea, and the waters were driven back [Exod. 14:21, 22]. The Egyptian defeat was caused by the miraculous east wind.

When people are angry they breathe rapidly. "Keep away from the man whose breath is in his nostrils" means beware of a man who is hasty, he might do anything [Isa. 2:22].

When a ruler is angry it is said, "smoke belched out of his nostrils," or "fire blazed in his face."

This use of the term nostrils suggests God's indignation against Pharaoh and his army which drowned in the Red Sea.

The passage which the Israelites crossed is between the Bitter Lakes and the tip of the Gulf of Suez. These words were written poetically. The waters were not congealed, but gathered in the depths of the sea. The term "congealed" is wrong. The Eastern text reads—"the waves gathered in heaps in the heart of the sea."

The water was driven back with the blast of the east wind which issued before the face of the Lord. "Thou didst blow with thy wind, the sea covered them" [Exod. 15:10]. Both of these verses prove beyond a doubt that the waters were driven back by the force of the east wind. [See also Exod. 14:21.]

BITTER WATER SWEETENED

And when they came to Marah, they could not drink of the waters of Marah, for they were bitter: therefore the name of it was called Marah.

And the people murmured against Moses, saying, What shall we drink?

And he cried unto the Lord; and the Lord showed him a tree, which when he had cast into the waters, the waters were made sweet: there he made for them a statute and an ordinance, and there he proved them.   Exod. 15:23-25

Miracles, such as healing bitter water were still performed in the Near East by some of the holy men who practiced healing and who believed in God's power. Some of these men cast salt in polluted brooks and other water sources when the water was bitter or polluted. Others heal by the means of prayer.

Elisha healed the spring in Jericho by casting salt in it. At times bitterness is caused by pollution. Springs are used for washing as well as for drinking, and even animals are sometimes washed in them [2 Kings 2:19-22]. Prophets and men of God were endowed with power and wisdom to overcome some of the problems which the people could not solve.

Marah is on the route to Mount Sinai. It is called *Ain Nabi*, "the fountain of the prophet." The water is brackish. The fountain is about forty miles from Lake Timshah.

RAINED BREAD

Then said the Lord unto Moses, Behold, I will rain bread from heaven for you; and the people shall go out and gather a certain rate every day, that I may prove them, whether they will walk in my law, or no.   Exod. 16:4

Bread in this instance means "food," that is, the manna which God provided for the needs of the Israelites in the desert [Exod. 16:35].

In Eastern languages the term bread is used collectively, meaning bread, cheese, butter, and other foods.

The people ate so much of the manna that they were satiated. The author of the book of Numbers describes manna as being like coriander seed. It was gathered daily, ground, and made into cakes [Num. 11:7-9].

QUAIL

And it came to pass, that at even the quails came up, and covered the camp: and in the morning the dew lay round about the host.   Exod. 16:13

God can perform any kind of wonder, but the sacred Book explains the miracle in a convincing and miraculous way which anyone can accept and believe. The miracle proves beyond a doubt that when the Israelites complained of the lack of meat the Lord provided them with abundant supplies of quail which flew from the shores of the sea and fell upon the camp.

The Aramaic word *shamaya* and the Hebrew word *shamayim* means "heaven," "sky," or "universe." The flocks of quail came from the sky. Heaven does not contain material things.

The quail mentioned in the Bible came from Europe and other lands to winter in the Arabian desert, just as they come today. Thousands of flocks of quail still winter in the warm Arabian desert. They fly from Europe by hundreds of thousands to the Eastern shores of the Mediterranean Sea. At times they are caught by strong winds and fall exhausted on the ground. They are gathered by natives and stored for food. Today, some of them are canned and shipped to European countries. During the fall months one sees large flocks of quail covering the ground for miles.

The author of the book of Psalms gives us an explicit answer as to how and where the quail came from. He says: "He caused the east wind to blow in the heaven (sky): and by his power he brought in the south wind. He rained flesh also upon them as dust, and feathered fowls like as the sand of the sea: and he let it fall in the midst of their camp, round about their habitations" [Ps. 78:26-29].

According to the book of Numbers, the quail came from the sea, that is from the sea shores. After the flocks had flown over the sea, they had rested on the shores, then they started again for the desert and got caught by a strong wind. "And there went forth a wind from the Lord, and brought quails from the sea, and let them fall by the camp, as it were a day's journey on this side, and as it were a day's journey on the other side, round about the camp, and as it were two cubits high upon the face of the earth" [Num. 11:31].

"About two cubits upon the face of the earth" and "as the sand of the seas" should not be taken literally. In Eastern languages this simply means that the quail fell in abundance. When bread loaves are plentiful on the table, one can hear the people say, "The bread was high to the neck or to the knee." Had the quail fallen two cubits high on the surface of the ground, it would have been difficult, if not impossible, for both cattle and men to move. Of course, the wind might have made deep piles of the quail at certain places. The inspired writers were not concerned about exact figures; these were unimportant, but they were concerned about the spiritual truths.

The miracle of the quail is a divine act of God. It was God who caused the wind to blow, and to bring the quail toward the Hebrew camp. When the people turn to God, he not only meets their needs, but heals their wounds, and leads them to new pastures and new sources of supplies. On the other hand, the miracle is that the hungry people who craved for meat were fed, and not how the quail came.

MANNA

And when the children of Israel saw it, they said one to another, It is manna: for they wist not what it was. And Moses said unto them, This is the bread which the Lord hath given you to eat.

Exod. 16:15

Manna or *mann ho* is an Aramaic saying, meaning "What is it?" The letter *heh,* "H," becomes silent, so the word is pronounced *manno,* "What is it?"

When the Israelites saw manna they did not know what it was, so they exclaimed, *Mann ho?* "What is it?" Even today no one knows what the origin of manna is or where it comes from.

Manna is like coriander seed, white, and the taste of it is like honey in the comb. The Hebrews gathered it from day to day. But on Friday they gathered for the Sabbath day also and it remained fresh. But on the other days of the week when they broke the divine command and gathered more than their daily need and had some left over for the next day, they always found worms in it.

The miracle or wonder is that the Lord God led the Israelites into an area where manna was plentiful. A similar thing, like manna, is found today in Arabia and other regions in the Near East. In northern Mesopotamia it is called *harullah* and is collected and eaten by the people. The author has eaten it many times. It tastes like honey. It falls on certain trees in the early morning and disappears when the sun is hot. [See *Gospel Light,* the article on "Manna."]

MANNA STORED

And they gathered it every morning, every man according to his eating: and when the sun waxed hot, it melted.   Exod. 16:21

The author has eaten manna many times when feeding sheep or traveling in places where manna is found. In some towns northwest of

Mosul manna is still gathered and stored. In this area manna is called *harola*. The Beduoins in the Sinai Peninsula call it *mann es-sama*, "the heavenly manna."

Manna is gathered in the early morning before it is eaten by ants and other insects or dried by the sun's rays.

When manna is not properly sealed in earthen jars it spoils and small black flies appear in it. This is because the manna is contaminated by flies which settle on it and lay their eggs on it. But when it is sealed it can be preserved. Moses told Aaron to fill a pot with it and preserve it so that the generations to come might see it [Exod. 16:33]. Manna can also be preserved in cold places and in fresh-cut grass. The Bedouins collect manna and seal it so that it may be preserved. They mix it with other things and eat it [Comment on verse 23].

REFRIGERATION

And he said unto them, This is that which the Lord hath said, To-morrow is the rest of the holy sabbath unto the Lord: bake that which ye will bake today, and seethe that ye will seethe; and that which remaineth over lay up for you to be kept until the morning.
Exod. 16:23

The Eastern text has an extra word, *karrira*, "cold." It reads: "Keep it cold for yourselves for the morning."

It indicates that the Egyptian and other highly civilized nations knew how to preserve meat and other perishable food stuffs.

Even today, meat, milk, and other perishable food are placed under newly cut grass and are well preserved. Warm water, likewise, when placed in a heap of wheat or freshly cut grass becomes cold like ice water. These ancient methods of preserving food are still practiced among the tribal people. Refrigeration is not a new thing.

On the other hand, ammonia was discovered by the Egyptian priests and used in their temple worship.

SABBATH OBSERVANCE

See, for that the Lord hath given you the sabbath, therefore he giveth you on the sixth day the bread of two days: abide ye every man in his place, let no man go out of his place on the seventh day.
Exod. 16:29

The name Sabbath is derived from a Hebrew word *shabbath*, "to rest" or "to cease from work." The Sabbath was a sign between God and the Children of Israel [Exod. 31:17].

The seventh day was chosen as a day of rest simply because the Lord rested or ceased from his work of creation on the seventh day. "God blessed the seventh day, and sanctified it" [Gen. 2:3]. It is said that the seventh day was sanctified because God had not created anything on that day. The other days were blessed by his work.

The unbroken week continued to be observed from the time of Moses to the present day, always the Sabbath falling on the seventh day. The cycle runs throughout the year independent of the month calendar and the year. The breaking of the Sabbath was punishable by death [Exod. 31:14].

The Sabbath observance always depended on the phases of the moon. It is also said that the Babylonians had a day of rest. Be that as it may, the Sabbath observance was very strict among the Israelites, and later it became the most sacred institution in Jewish religion. Many other important teachings were either neglected or forgotten, but the observance of the seventh day was intensified from one generation to another which, in the course of time, came to be looked upon as a man-made institution.

The Sabbath was a controversial institution during the time of Jesus [Matthew 12:1-9; Luke 13:14]. Jesus said, "the Sabbath was made for man, and not man for the Sabbath" [Mark 2:27]. The Sabbath was observed by Jesus' disciples and his immediate followers prior to the observance of the first day of the week. But as we see from the council of Jerusalem, this Jewish institution was not included in the Christian doctrines and was not enforced on the Gentiles [Acts 15:29].

STRIKE THE ROCK

Behold, I will stand before thee there upon the rock in Horeb; and thou shalt smite the rock, and there shall come water out of it, that the people may drink. And Moses did so in the sight of the elders of Israel.   Exod. 17:6

"Smite the rock" or "strike the rock" has several meanings. First, he bore the rock, and the second, strike the rock on the top of the cover of the hidden wells or sources of water [Num. 21:61].

In Arabia and other arid lands where water is scarce, wells and other sources of water are hidden in order to discourage roaming tribes from encamping, grazing the area, and using the scanty water supplies. Then again, in all parts of the Near East wells are covered to prevent animals and men from falling into them and to keep the drinking water clean. A large stone is put on the top of the well [Gen. 29:2-3].

Large stones are placed upon the mouths of the wells and water sources, and are then covered with earth. Therefore, hidden wells are not easy to locate.

God told Moses where to strike, and when he struck the rock or uncovered the mouth of the well, he found abundant water for the people to drink and for the herds and flocks also.

The author of the book of Numbers gives us a description of the discovery of the water sources. He called the name of the place, *beer*, "well" [Num. 21:16]. The author of the book of Exodus does not go into detail in describing this miracle. God could have brought water out of a rock or a stone.

It was a miracle or a wonder wrought by God to meet the needs of a thirsty people. The Israelites had disputed with Moses and Aaron and were doubtful about the place [Num. 20:10]. Moses was indignant and spoke inadvisedly and smote the rock twice [Num. 20:11; Ps. 106:32, 33]. God's guidance provided the people with food, water, and other necessities of life.

[See article in the *New Testament Commentary*, Lamsa, p. 266.]

ARMED WITH SWORDS

And Joshua discomfited Amalek and his people with the edge of the sword. Exod. 17:13

The children of Israel went forth out of Egypt well armed with all kinds of implements of war. Exodus 13:18 in the King James Version wrongly reads "harnessed." This word means "armed."

Joshua and his army defeated the King of Amalek and his army with the sword. The Israelites also must have had other weapons such as spears, daggers, and bows.

In the East, daggers and swords are worn as decorations. One can see hundreds of peace-loving men walking on the streets or even carrying burdens with their daggers in front of them. Swords are worn on certain special occasions, even during the time of worship.

Then again, when Easterners celebrate a feast they wear their best clothes and jewels, put their daggers in front of them, and gird themselves with their swords and other weapons.

The Israelites may have borrowed some of their weapons from their Egyptian neighbors, but no doubt some of the weapons were their own. They could not have ventured into the desert without arms. Later on, many battles were fought and the Israelites seemed to be well armed.

Swords and other implements of war could not have been forged in the desert. The Hebrews seemingly were not as badly persecuted as it may seem from the reading of the early account of the Exodus. The Egyptians were more tolerant than other races who had persecuted the Israelites. But the persecution in Egypt was the first ever suffered by the Israelites. This is why it was overemphasized.

BOOK

And the Lord said unto Moses, Write this for a memorial in a book, and rehearse it in the ears of Joshua: for I will utterly put out the remembrance of Amalek from under heaven. Exod. 17:14

This is the first reference to writing in the Bible. No doubt, the Hebrews were familiar with the various systems of writing which were invented and used by the Babylonians and the Assyrians. The Semitic culture embraced all kindred people in Palestine, Amalek, Midian, Moab, and Amon.

The Semitic alphabet which Moses used (1600 B.C.) consisted of twenty-two letters. God's revelations could not have been recorded with the cuneiform or pictographs. This is because the Bible contains many abstract words and phrases which cannot be plainly written with a sign system of writing. Moses was a well-trained man and he had spent forty years in the house of the high priest of Midian. Moses used the simplest alphabet so that the holy words of God might be recorded accurately.

The term *sepra* means a "book" or a "scroll."

The ten commandments were written on stone tablets in order to be handed down from one generation to another. The victory over Amalek was written as a memorial to be taught to the people and kept in the book of the tribal chronicles.

Moses no doubt used the Semitic or Babylonian writing, that is, the earliest form of the alphabet. He could not have used either hieroglyphics or pictographs for in so doing he would have violated the second commandment. Then again, the meanings of pictographs and hieroglyphics are not always clear. At times they are conjectural.

The Hebrew tribes always had scribes and learned men. Abraham was a learned man, a member of a cultured Babylonian family.

The alphabet was used by merchants and traders. No doubt Moses used the alphabet to write this memorial. Evidently both cuneiform and the alphabet were used in those days, the former for state documents and the latter for business and religion.

Cuneiform writing might have been a later development from the ancient alphabet just as shorthand is a later development from our present alphabet.

Two thousand years hence the people who study the records of the twentieth century may think that shorthand was first and the alphabet came later.

THE MEANING OF AN ALTAR

And Moses built an altar, and called the name of it Jehovah-nissi.
Exod. 17:15

Madbekha, "altar," is derived from *dabakh,* meaning to offer an animal sacrifice. The Arabic word *madbeakh* means "a place to cook."

Altars were built so that the people might broil meat on them. The animals were slain, skinned, cut into pieces, and placed upon the altars built of stones.

In the wilderness and other isolated places, altars were built of un-polished stones. But in towns and cities the people used griddles. The nomad tribes built stone shrines and altars, which were visited when the tribe returned to the place again.

Some of the ancient localities were looked upon as holy places, be-cause they were founded by the patriarchs and holy men. Such places as Bethel and Shiloh became places for prayer and worship.

The word *nissi* which has been rendered a "sign" or "standard" is *nasi,* "The Lord has tried us" or "tempted us" [Verse 11].

The Hebrews during this period spoke Aramaic, the language which the twelve patriarchs had brought from Haran, Assyria.

Amalek refused to permit the Israelites to pass through his territory, and thus caused the people to wander in the desert for many years. This refusal of passage and the difficulties ahead of the people were a great test, but Moses went through them faithfully.

ELIEZER

And the name of the other was Eliezer; for the God of my father, said he, was mine help, and delivered me from the sword of Pharaoh.
Exod. 18:4

Eliezer is an Aramaic compound noun which means "God has been my help." *Eli* means "God," *ezer,* "help." The root of the verb is *adar* or *edar-daleth.* D is often pronounced as Z.

All Aramaic or Hebrew names have a meaning and refer to a certain incident or occurrence.

GOD OF GODS

Now I know that the Lord is greater than all gods: for in the thing wherein they dealt proudly he was above them. Exod. 18:11

The Midianites were kindred of the Israelites, and they, like the children of Israel, believed in the Lord God. But some of Abraham's descendants took wives of the daughters of Canaan and thus the race was mixed with the native Palestinians [Gen. 36:2].

The Midianites, like other races who were kindred of the Jews, worshiped many gods, but they looked upon the God of their ancestors as a greater God, or the God of gods.

At times, the Israelites likewise believed in pagan deities but looked upon the God of their fathers as the chief God, or the God of gods.

HIGH PLACES

And Moses went up unto God, and the Lord called unto him out of the mountain, saying, Thus shalt thou say to the house of Jacob, and tell the children of Israel; Exod. 19:3

All pagan peoples worshiped on high places. Altars and shrines were always built on top of hills and high mountains. The Lord told Abraham in a vision to take his son Isaac and sacrifice him upon one of the mountains [Gen. 22:2]. Balak, King of Moab, built altars upon a hill [Num. 23:14].

The people in the olden days believed that clouds were the dwelling place of their deity. This is why they sacrificed and prayed on high places. A mountain was closer to the gods than a plain, and the gods could hear them better. Then again, when one is on the top of a mountain he is away from the noise and the turmoil of this world. Indeed, one can concentrate better in a lonely place than in a crowded city. Moreover, the air on the mountain is purer, which helps one to meditate and pray.

Sinai was a holy mountain, and was known as the mountain of God. It is also called Mount *Khoreb*, or *Horeb*, probably meaning "desolate." The mountain is desolate and has some volcanic eruptions. Moses had been on this mountain when he received his call to go to Egypt [Exod. 3:1-12].

Today this mountain is called the mountain of Moses.

EAGLE'S WINGS

Ye have seen what I did unto the Egyptians, and how I bare you on eagle's wings, and brought you unto myself. Exod. 19:4

The Aramaic reads: "And how I bore you as if on eagle's wings." The term "wings" is used metaphorically, meaning "speed." In Eastern language the eagle is symbolic of speed. We often say, "He flew like an eagle."

The Lord God bore Israel in the wilderness as a father would bear his son [Deut. 1:31]. God took care of the Israelites throughout their journeys in the wilderness, providing them with food, water, clothing, and all other necessities of life [Acts 13:18].

SANCTIFICATION

And let the priests also, which come near to the Lord, sanctify themselves, lest the Lord break forth upon them. Exod. 19:22

The priests and the Levites were admonished to wash their clothes, bathe, and sanctify themselves before they appeared before the Lord in the tabernacle of the congregation.

The two sons of Aaron transgressed God's command and were burned in the tabernacle [Lev. 10:1-3].

"Lest the Lord break forth" means "lest he smite you," just as Aaron's sons Nadab and Abihu were smitten.

Drinking of wine and strong drink in the tabernacle of the congregation was also prohibited by a new statute [Lev. 10:9].

MONOTHEISM

Thou shalt not make unto thee any graven image, or any likeness of any thing that is in heaven above, or that is in the earth beneath, or that is in the water under the earth:
Thou shalt not bow down thyself to them, nor serve them: for I the Lord thy God am a jealous God, visiting the iniquity of the fathers upon the children unto the third and fourth generation of them that hate me. Exod. 20:4-5

All pagan peoples worship images and idols of silver, gold, wood, and stone. This is because all the gods of the Gentiles were human deities. They were men who had risen to the rank of deities by the sheer force of power and wealth. Some of them were heroes; others were pious kings, princes, and holy men to whose memories their people built temples, shrines, and statues on the high places.

The identity of some of these pagan gods was completely lost in the past, but their images remained as sacred possessions among the people.

Then again the sun, moon, stars, and planets were also worshiped as gods and their images erected in the places of worship. Indeed, man in his quest to find God worshiped animals, trees, brooks, fish, and other creatures.

The plurality of diverse gods and idols created schism and strife among their worshipers, which at times resulted in bloodshed. Apparently every tribe sought a higher place for the image of its idols and patron gods. Moreover, during the processions and feasts they argued and fought with one another over the question, which god was born first? Even today some Christians fight over the places which their patron saints occupy in their religious processions.

This is why the Lord God told Moses that the Israelites were not to have other gods besides the living God, the Eternal, the Creator of heaven and earth and all that is therein. The pagan images were not gods. They could not walk, they could not even keep flies from their own faces. They were helpless, dumb, blind, and deaf images. The god's of the Gentiles were made by the hands of men, who themselves were created by God.

This prohibition of images and idols and of the worship of many gods has been responsible for the unity and the solidarity of the Jewish people. The Jewish God is a spiritual God. No one can see him and no one can portray him. Therefore, no one can debate what kind of likeness he has. This is why the Jews were free from schism and from theological quarrels and disputes over the person of their God. This concept of a spiritual monotheism also gave them protection from other races. In other words, the God of the Israelites was not a rival of the pagan gods, because no one could see his image and likeness. This gave the Israelites protection when traveling among pagan peoples. Even today Christians in the Near East, as well as Jews and Moslems, adhere to this commandment. They never make pictures or statues of any kind, and use no images or relics in worship. And of course they never worship human gods. The word "jealous" should read "zealous." The similarity of the two Aramaic words was responsible for this error.

SWEARING

Thou shalt not take the name of the Lord thy God in vain: for the Lord will not hold him guiltless that taketh his name in vain.
Exod. 20:7

In the lands where business transactions are done by bargaining, taking of the Lord's name falsely is very common. As the price of an article is unknown, both the seller and the buyer take oaths in the name of the Lord while bargaining. And since neither the prospective buyer nor the merchant trusts the other, bargaining is a necessity.

The merchant starts with a high price, and each time the buyer refuses to purchase the article, he invokes the name of God and reduces the price. The buyer likewise swears by God that the article is too high; and at last he adjures the merchant by holy names, by the head of his son, and by the graves of his fathers to tell the truth about the price.

Moreover, many disputes and litigations are settled by oaths.

Jesus admonished the people not to take the name of God falsely. "But I say to you, swear not at all; neither by heaven; for it is God's throne: . . . Neither shalt thou swear by thy head . . ." [Matt. 5:34-38]. [See also Deut. 5:11.]

HONORING FATHER AND MOTHER

Honor thy father and thy mother: that thy days may be long upon the land which the Lord thy God giveth thee.   Exod. 20:12

Nearly all the Near Eastern people obey this commandment and honor and revere their fathers and mothers. Where houses are large the family ties are preserved for a long time. Children and their children live with their parents under the same roof. Easterners consider it a sacred duty to care for their fathers and mothers and to be guided by them.

Moreover, in some instances, men prefer to leave their wives rather than to part from their parents [Deut. 5:16; Prov. 23:22].

In biblical days those who cursed their fathers or mothers were put to death [Exod. 21:17].

MORAL LAW

Thou shalt not commit adultery.   Exod. 20:14

The Hebrews prior to the Mosaic law upheld the sacredness of marriage and family ties. The seventh commandment must have been imbedded in the early codes such as the code of Hammurabi, king of Babylon, about 2000 B.C., and the Egyptian code of ethics. For instance, when Pharaoh discovered that Sarah was Abraham's wife, he returned her to him and rebuked him for having deceived him [Gen. 12:18, 19]. This is also true of King Abimeleck; he told Abraham why he had brought this sin upon him and his kingdom. He also returned Sarah to Abraham [Gen. 20:9].

We can see that in the olden days the moral law was upheld by most civilized people to insure the solidarity of the family as a social unit. This law embraces all the ordinances relative to sexual morals. Intercourse, both with married and unmarried women, was prohibited. A man not only respected his neighbor's wife, but his daughter and his sister also.

Morality among the tribal people is still very strong, especially the pastoral people who look upon the whole tribe as a family unit.

A SACRED ALTAR

And if thou wilt make me an altar of stone, thou shalt not build it of hewn stone: for if thou lift up thy tool upon it, thou hast polluted it.   Exod. 20:25

Iron is one of the metals which rusts. And it was looked upon as a symbol of pollution. Gold, on the other hand, is the symbol of glory and purity.

The altar was to be built of unhewn whole stones, in Aramaic called *shalmatha*, "whole" or "perfect." *Shalam* means "peace." Iron instruments might cause injuries to the workers and pollute the altar with human blood.

The stones were to be natural, symbolizing the purity, naturalness, and simplicity of the religion of Israel, as compared with man-made pagan religions. The altars of the God of Israel were to be different from lavish pagan altars. That is to say, they were to be simple.

Many of the ancient altars in the countryside were built of unhewn stones [Deut. 27:5].

SLAVERY

If thou buy a Hebrew servant, six years he shall serve: and in the seventh he shall go out free for nothing.   Exod. 21:2

All Israelites were brothers, the free children of Abraham, and therefore they were not supposed to oppress or enslave one another.

The term "buy" in the case of an Israelite was always conditional.

First, the Israelite must offer himself to be sold; second, the buyer was admonished not to treat him like a bondservant or a slave, but as a sojourner, and later the servant could leave with his family [Lev. 25:39-43; Deut. 15:12-18].

When men and women of other races were bought they were made bondservants, and thus they became an inheritance to the children of the buyer.

"But as for your male servants and your female servants whom you may have from among the people that are round about you, of them shall you buy bondmen and bondwomen" [Leviticus 25:44]. This is not all. The Israelites were also admonished to redeem men and women of their race [Lev. 25:47-55].

FEMALE SERVANTS REDEEMED

And if a man sell his daughter to be a maidservant, she shall not go out as the menservants do.

If she please not her master, who hath betrothed her to himself, then shall he let her be redeemed: to sell her unto a strange nation he shall have no power, seeing he hath dealt deceitfully with her.

Exod. 21:7-8

Maidens were also sold to become servants. And at times, their masters took them as wives or concubines. When the master of the female servant was not pleased with her, he was not allowed to sell her. She was permitted to redeem herself.

CURSING OF FATHER AND MOTHER

And he that curseth his father, or his mother, shall surely be put to death.

Exod. 21:17

Cursing of father or mother was punishable by death. The Israelites loved and respected their fathers and their mothers. At times, they forsook their wives but cleaved to their fathers and their mothers. Even today, the paternal ties in a Jewish family are stronger than they are among the Gentiles.

This law was repeated in the books of Leviticus and Deuteronomy [Lev. 20:9; Deut. 27:16].

Jesus said, "For God said, Honor your father and your mother, and whoever curses his father or his mother, let him be put to death" [Matt. 15:4].

COMPENSATION

If he rise again, and walk abroad upon his staff, then shall he that smote him be quit: only he shall pay for the loss of his time, and shall cause him to be thoroughly healed.

Exod. 21:19

The Eastern text reads: "If he rises again and walks in the street with his staff, then the one who struck him shall be acquitted, except that he shall pay for the loss of his time and the physician's fee."

The Aramaic word *asya* means a "healer" or a "physician." *Asa* means "to heal."

Evidently the Hebrews, like other races, had paid physicians and healers who devoted all of their time or a part thereof to cure the people of their illnesses, cleanse them of their leprosy, and set their broken bones.

This type of doctor or healer is still to be found among all the tribal people in biblical lands. They are paid in money, food, or clothing. Some of them receive whatever gifts the sick may offer, and some refuse to accept any gift of money.

The term "physicians" is also used in Genesis 50:2.

SEVERE PUNISHMENT

Eye for eye, tooth for tooth, hand for hand, foot for foot.
                                                           Exod. 21:24

In biblical days all tribal people upheld this law which was the only protection against bandits, thieves, and murderers. In those days force was the only thing the people understood; kindness and nonresistance were mistaken for weakness, just as often they are mistaken even by Christians.

On the other hand, the ancients had fewer laws, fewer ordinances, and no organized police force as we have today. The law meant what it said. The culprit knew that he would be severely punished for his evil acts, so he refrained from doing evil.

These ancient biblical laws are found in the Koran, the holy book of the Moslems. Today in some Moslem lands crime is unknown, and in the others there is little crime. This is because the people respect the law and know that crime does not pay. Even today severe punishment, such as cutting off a foot or an arm, is inflicted on a criminal.

Christians can overcome not only crime but also all the problems of life by following in the footsteps of their Master. The day will come when the word "evil" will not be understood in our vocabulary.
[See Exod. 21:24; Deut. 19:21; Prov. 24:29; Matt. 5:38, 39.]

INNOCENT

If an ox gore a man or a woman, that they die: then the ox shall be surely stoned, and his flesh shall not be eaten; but the owner of the ox shall be quit.   Exod. 21:28

The word "quit" should read "innocent." That is, the owner of the ox shall be declared innocent. The Aramaic word *zaki* means "innocent" or "blameless."

The stoning of the ox was recommended by the Mosaic law so that all the people present might participate in inflicting capital punishment on both men and animals, and that all men present were equally to be responsible for executing the sentence.

THE PRICE OF A MAN

If the ox shall push a manservant or a maidservant; he shall give unto their master thirty shekels of silver, and the ox shall be stoned.
Exod. 21:32

The Aramaic word *nidkor* means to "gore," "pierce through," and to "stab." In this instance the manservant or the maidservant has been killed by the ox.

The price of a man was seemingly set at thirty pieces of silver [Zech. 11:12, 13; Matt. 26:15].

In biblical days thirty pieces of silver was a considerable sum of money.

PITS

And if a man shall open a pit, or if a man shall dig a pit, and not cover it, and an ox or an ass fall therein;
The owner of the pit shall make it good, and give money unto the owner of them; and the dead beast shall be his. Exod. 21:33-34

In the East, until recent days, pits were common in cities and villages, and in some countries they are still in use.

Pits were used to store wheat and other grain supplies. When the grain was used up, the pits were left open to be filled again during the wheat harvest.

These pits were dangerous during the dark hours, and both men and animals sometimes fell into them.

The Hebrew prophets and Jesus used them metaphorically, meaning "traps," that is, evil devices [Prov. 28:10; 22:14]. Jesus said, when the blind leads the blind, both of them fall into the pit [Matt. 15:14]. [See also Isa. 24:18.]

BORROWING AN ANIMAL

And if a man borrow aught of his neighbor, and it be hurt, or die, the owner thereof being not with it, he shall surely make it good.
But if the owner thereof be with it, he shall not make it good: if it be a hired thing, it came for his hire. Exod. 22:14-15

The Eastern text reads: "If a man borrow an animal of his neighbor . . ." The Aramaic word *beaira* means an "animal" or a "beast of burden."

In the East, even today, oxen are borrowed to plow with, and donkeys and mules to carry burdens. If the owner of the animal is not with it and the animal is injured or dies, restitution must be made. This is because the borrower might have been negligent or might have laid a heavy burden on the animal.

But if the owner of the animal is with it, as generally they are, no restitution is made. And if the animal is hired, no restitution is sought. In this case, the owner of the animal is usually with it and if he is not, he has entered into an agreement with the man who had hired his animal. The hire of the animal is sufficient for the restitution thereof.

DOWRY OF VIRGINS

And if a man entice a maid that is not betrothed, and lie with her, he shall surely endow her to be his wife.

If her father utterly refuse to give her unto him, he shall pay money according to the dowry of virgins.   Exod. 22:16-17

The Aramaic term *makhirtha* means "purchased," "acquired for a price," or a "dowry."

Dowries were paid in biblical days and still are paid today according to the beauty and the social standing of the maids. Some of the maids who are daughters of poor men bring a small dowry consisting of a few silver coins, or a few sheep. On the other hand, the daughters of the wealthy and the nobles bring an abundant dowry, according to their beauty and social standing.

The dowry of a virgin girl is always higher than that of one who is not a virgin. In the East the virginity of a girl is important in determining her dowry.

A maid who has lost her virginity by being raped finds it difficult to get married. And when she does marry her father cannot demand a dowry for her. Instead, he would be glad to pay the husband to be, so that the reproach may be taken away from his family. Dowries are determined by expert matchmakers.

USURY

If thou lend money to any of my people that is poor by thee, thou shalt not be to him as a usurer, neither shalt thou lay upon him usury.   Exod. 22:25

The term "my people" means the Israelites, who were known as the people of the Lord. This is because the Lord had set them aside and hallowed them for himself.

The Israelites were admonished not to lend money to one another with interest, but instead to help one another as members of the same race, and the people of the same God.

Even though usury was forbidden among the Israelites, it was permitted when money was lent to foreigners [Lev. 25:35, 36]. The Christians also practiced usury and at times exacted exhorbitant interest. But usury is forbidden among the Moslems.

GARMENTS AS A PLEDGE

If thou at all take thy neighbor's raiment to pledge, thou shalt deliver it unto him by that the sun goeth down:

For that is his covering only, it is his raiment for his skin: wherein shall he sleep? and it shall come to pass, when he crieth unto me, that I will hear; for I am gracious. Exod. 22:26-27

In the East it is not unusual for a man to give one or two of his garments as a pledge to the moneylender as a surety. When poor people lack other valuable articles to give as a pledge, they give their mantles (cloaks). Such pledges are given for a short duration and are redeemed as soon as the debtor is able to pay.

Mantles are worn by day and used as a covering by night. On their journeys people sleep in their mantles. The poor also use their mantles as bedclothes to cover themselves on cold nights.

Pious creditors return such pledged articles even before the debt is paid.

RESPECT TO JUDGES AND RULERS

Thou shalt not revile the gods, nor curse the ruler of thy people.
Exod. 22:28

The Eastern text reads: "Thou shalt not revile the judge, nor curse the ruler of your people."

Paul, during his trial, said to the high priest, "God shall smite thee, thou whited wall!" "Whited wall" means "hypocrite." Those who were there warned him that he had reviled the high priest. Paul immediately apologized, stating that he did not know that he was the high priest [Acts 23:3-5].

The term "gods" is a mistranslation, or possibly a later change from judges to gods. The change might have been made by the priests who went after Baal and other pagan deities. Moses could not have used the term gods, for he knew that the gods of the Gentiles were not gods, but blind and dumb images.

DEAD ANIMALS

And ye shall be holy men unto me: neither shall ye eat any flesh that is torn of beasts in the field; ye shall cast it to the dogs.
                                                                    Exod. 22:31

The Israelites were admonished to abstain from eating the flesh of animals which had died of themselves or been torn by wild beasts, or strangled. This is because the blood of these animals was congealed in them, and the Israelites were commanded not to eat blood. The Hebrews believed that life was in the blood [Gen. 9:4; Lev. 3:17].

Moreover, the Gentiles and savage people ate the meat of dead animals, and some of them drank their blood. At times the veins of the animals were severed and the people drank fresh blood while the animals stood up, bleeding.

The Israelites were sanctified to the Lord and therefore they were to abstain from eating the meat of animals which had died or been torn by wild beasts, and they were not to inflict cruelty on animals as the pagans did. Some savage people still drink blood today.

On the other hand, these laws were sanitary laws. The meat of dead, torn, and strangled animals was often spoiled and, therefore, unfit to be eaten. In Palestine and Arabia, owing to the intense heat, dead bodies decompose rapidly.

These ordinances were also kept by the early Christians and are still observed by Eastern Christians and Moslems [Acts 15:20].

EMPTY-HANDED

Thou shalt keep the feast of unleavened bread: (thou shalt eat unleavened bread seven days, as I commanded thee, in the time appointed of the month Abib; for in it thou camest out from Egypt: and none shall appear before me empty:).   Exod. 23:15

The Aramaic word *srekaaith* means "empty-handed," "in vain," or "without cause." In this instance it means "without gift offerings."

On such feasts as the Passover the people brought food offerings and other gifts which they shared with the poor and the needy.

Even today Easterners never visit a shrine empty-handed. They bring animals, meal-offerings, and other gifts which are shared among the people.

The Passover was a day of rejoicing and thanksgiving, and on this occasion the people were most generous in the sharing of food as a token of their gratitude to God.

Then again, Easterners generally offer their gifts to God before petitioning him for mercy, health, and prosperity.

MEMORIAL OFFERINGS

Three times in the year all thy males shall appear before the Lord God.   Exod. 23:17

The Eastern text reads: *dokhranek*, "your memorial offering," instead of "your males." The Aramaic word for "your males" is *dikhrek*. The two words in Aramaic are almost identical in appearance.

The reference here is to the first fruits of the harvest and the feast of the ingathering [Verse 16]. The first fruits and tithes were offered to the Lord, but they were given to the priests and the Levites. The latter were scattered through all the tribes of Israel.

THE MESSENGER

Behold, I send an Angel before thee, to keep thee in the way, and to bring thee into the place which I have prepared.

Beware of him, and obey his voice, provoke him not; for he will not pardon your transgressions: for my name is in him.
                                                                          Exod. 23:20-21

The reference here is to Joshua who was chosen by God to succeed Moses and to bring the Israelites into Palestine [Josh. 24:8].

The term *malakha* means "angel," "messenger," or "counselor." Joshua was to be more severe than his master, Moses. When *Achar* (Achan) confessed his sins before Joshua and the elders of Israel, Joshua did not forgive him, but he gave orders to stone him together with his family [Josh. 7:19-26]. This act was contrary to the Mosaic Law [Deut. 24:16]. Joshua may have disregarded the Law because of expediency.

The angel of the Lord, that is, the counsel of the Lord, guided the Israelites throughout their journeys.

HORNETS

And I will send hornets before thee, which shall drive out the Hivite, the Canaanite, and the Hittite, from before thee.
                                                                          Exod. 23:28

The Aramaic word *deborey*, "hornets," is used idiomatically, meaning a large and swift army, raiders, or other marauding forces. This is because when hornets attack they fly very fast. In some parts of the Near East flies, mosquitoes, snakes, and other stinging insects and reptiles make life difficult for travelers, armies, and migratory tribes who have little or no protection against them. The Hebrews in the desert were often bitten by snakes.

The reference here is to the Hittites, Canaanites and other inhabitants of Palestine, and not to hornets. No people would leave their land and flee if attacked by a swarm of hornets. When the Hebrews occupied the land, they found all these diverse peoples in Palestine and they had to fight against them [Deut. 7:20].

A PAGAN SPARED

I will not drive them out from before thee in one year; lest the land become desolate, and the beast of the field multiply against thee.   Exod. 23:29

The Israelites were born and reared as nomads in the desert. And, being a pastoral people, they knew little about agriculture and complicated city life. Had they destroyed all the inhabitants of the land, the land would have been left desolate and the wild beasts would have multiplied.

When the ten tribes were carried captive to Assyria, lions and other wild beasts infested several districts in northern Israel [2 Kings 17:25].

The conquest of Palestine was comparatively slow. Many of the inhabitants of Palestine were not conquered until the reign of Solomon. Some remained free even after the reign of Solomon. The Hebrews not only spared some of the inhabitants of the land but also made league with them and, years later, even worshiped their gods.

MOSES WROTE THE COVENANT

And Moses wrote all the words of the Lord, and rose up early in the morning, and builded an altar under the hill, and twelve pillars, according to the twelve tribes of Israel.   Exod. 24:4

The Covenant was dictated by God, but Moses wrote it on tablets or on sheepskin. The art of writing was well developed at this time. Moses had spent forty years in Midian in the house of the high priest of Midian, and the Midianites were a Semitic people. They, like the Moabites, Ammonites, and other Semitic peoples, were influenced by the Aramaic or Syriac culture. At this time Damascus was the cradle of Aramaic (Syriac) culture west of the River Euphrates.

Moreover, Moses had scribes who acted as recorders, judges, and officials over the people. Joshua also was educated by Moses. He wrote upon the stones of the altar which he built on Mount Ebal [Josh. 8:30-32].

As we see from the Bible, all laws, covenants, and ordinances were written on the day in which they were given by God to Moses. Nothing important was handed down from one generation to another orally. The Lord commanded Moses to write so that no portion of the law might be distorted or forgotten [Deut. 6:9; 31:19].

A BOOK

And he took the book of the covenant, and read in the audience of the people: and they said, All that the Lord hath said will we do, and be obedient.   Exod. 24:7

Sepra, "book," in this instance means a "scroll." Books as we have them today were a later invention. *Sepra* also may mean "reading" the material which is written by a *sapra,* "scribe."

The book of the covenant contained statutes and ordinances (which the Israelites had pledged or sworn to obey); a list of ordinances and rules to insure health and cleanliness of body and mind; and moral laws to govern worship, justice, and ethics.

The law, that is the Ten Commandments, was engraved on stone tablets so that they might endure forever.

BLOOD

And Moses took the blood, and sprinkled it on the people, and said, Behold the blood of the covenant, which the Lord hath made with you concerning all these words.   Exod. 24:8

Moses in this instance acted as a priest, in a rite which was only performed by the ordained priests, Aaron and his sons. But since Moses was the founder of the Hebrew system of worship, and later the consecrator of the high priest, he had the authority to serve as a priest. Aaron was not yet consecrated to the office of the high priest.

The blood was symbolic of the confirmation of the covenant. Whenever a covenant or a compact was made between two men or two nations, animals were slain and the people ate the broiled meat and rejoiced [Gen. 31:44-54]. Then again, when a man joined a tribe his blood and the blood of the chief of the tribe or one of its members were mingled. A small cut was made on the arms of the two men.

Blood symbolizes life-giving. The ancients believed that life was in the blood. The pagan drank the blood of the animals, but the Hebrew

sprinkled it on the people as a symbol of atonement. In Mosaic law
blood was forbidden to be used as food [Gen. 9:4; Lev. 7:26]. It was
sprinkled round about the altar [Exod. 29:12]. The blood of the animals
in the Old Testament was symbolic of the blood of Jesus in the new
covenant.

CLARITY—LIGHT

*And they saw the God of Israel: and there was under his feet as
it were a paved work of a sapphire stone, and as it were the body
of heaven in his clearness.*   Exod. 24:10

Clarity and light are symbolic of goodness, purity, holiness, truth, and
understanding; the Hebrew writers associated it with God, who is the
Light of the world. Jesus said, "I am the Light of the world" [John
8:12].

Moses, Aaron, Nadab, and Abihu, and the seventy elders of Israel
saw God seated on a paved work of sapphire stone, clear as heaven in
its clearness. The psalmist spoke of God as the one "who coverest thyself with light as with a garment" [Ps. 104:2].

Just as light is symbolic of holiness and purity, darkness is symbolic
of sin and evil forces [Gen. 1:1].

THEY SAW GOD

*And upon the nobles of the children of Israel he laid not his hand:
also they saw God, and did eat and drink.*   Exod. 24:11

"They saw God" does not mean they saw his figure or that they saw
him as one sees a human being; but they saw his divine presence, his
glory, his majesty, and the beauty of his habitation. Sapphire stones and
the clarity of the space in which they beheld him are symbolic of his
holiness.

God is spirit and he can be seen only with spiritual eyes. No one can
see the face of God and live. God said to Moses, "You cannot see my
face, for no man can see me and live" [Exod. 33:20]. But God showed
Moses his glory. Such spiritual conception of God was beyond the grasp
of mortal men. Hitherto, all they had seen and known were gods with
concrete forms.

The Scriptures also tell us that no one has seen God, but Jesus Christ
[John 1:18].

When men sanctify themselves and are inspired they can see the real presence of God. Ezekiel saw visions of God [Ezek. 1:1]. Other Hebrew prophets beheld his glory and majesty.

SHITTIM

And thou shalt make an altar of shittim wood, five cubits long, and five cubits broad; the altar shall be four-square: and the height thereof shall be three cubits.   Exod. 27:1

The shittim tree is a tree which grows in arid desert regions. Its wood is hard and durable and excellent for chests and such objects as the Ark of the Covenant.

The tree is known as the acacia tree.

AN ORACLE

And thou shalt put in the breastplate of judgment the Urim and the Thummim; and they shall be upon Aaron's heart, when he goeth in before the Lord: and Aaron shall bear the judgment of the children of Israel upon his heart before the Lord continually.
                                                      Exod. 28:30

The reference here is to the sacred oracle by which the Hebrews inquired of God. It was called Urim and Thummim. Urim means "light" and Thummim means "purity and perfection."

The oracle was put in the high priest's breastplate, upon his heart, to guide him in judgment and help him commune with God. (Note: The Hebrew prophets never relied on this material medium; they communed directly with God.)

The Greeks and other pagan people had many oracles in their sacred shrines to which they turned in times of uncertainty and distress; such as the oracle of Dodona in the Epirus, the Shrine of Delphi, and that of Diana of Ephesus.

These shrines were visited not only by the simple and credulous people but also by the wise men, kings, and princes. The shrines received fabulous gifts and thus became very wealthy. All those who inquired of the oracles offered gifts of gold and silver and brought food and wine to the priests.

The oracles were usually ambiguous and therefore subject to diverse interpretations. For example, an oracle which meant victory could also mean defeat. The messages were seldom unequivocal. In a few cases the pagan priests were correct by accident. Moreover, some of them, knowing the situation and having the political power and money, "made accurate predictions."

The Israelites were many times deceived by the pagan oracles. At times, they forsook their God and inquired of the pagan oracles [2 Kings 1:2-4; Isa. 8:19].

ANOINTING

And thou shalt put them upon Aaron thy brother, and his sons with him; and shalt anoint them, and consecrate them, and sanctify them, that they may minister unto me in the priest's office.
                                                              Exod. 28:41

Oil is symbolic of light. In the olden days oil was used to light the lamps in the temples and shrines. Light symbolizes God and law [Exod. 27:20; Lev. 24:2].

Oil comes from the highest realms in the universe, the sun, which was worshiped as the god of nature.

Kings and priests were anointed so that they might able to lead and guide their people in times of need. Their commandments were to be a light to their subjects.

On the other hand, oil is refreshing to the body in lands where water is scarce and bathing is rare or unknown, and it makes one glad [Pss. 23:5; 104:15]. Oil preserves the skin and relieves skin pains. In the East oil and butter are still used as medicines [Luke 10:34].

RANSOM

When thou takest the sum of the children of Israel after their number, then shall they give every man a ransom for his soul unto the Lord, when thou numberest them; that there be no plague among them, when thou numberest them.   Exod. 30:12

The Aramaic reads, *porkan* which means deliverance by payment of money, hence a "ransom." *Porkana* means "salvation." The Hebrew word used here is *kepar*, "ransom." The word ransom is generally used when paying a price to redeem a person. The ransom in this instance was to be given as an offering to God.

Porkan, "deliverance," is used in referring to salvation from sin, from disease, and from an enemy. Ransom was paid for those who had committed murder, and for captives and slaves.

This was some kind of a poll tax which was paid to the sanctuary.

This tax was paid as a means of protection from the enemy. Easterners offer gifts to God so that they may return safely from war or from a journey.

LEGAL TENDER

This they shall give, every one that passeth among them that are numbered, half a shekel after the shekel of the sanctuary: (a shekel is twenty gerahs:) a half shekel shall be the offering of the Lord.
                                                            Exod. 30:13

The shekel of the sanctuary was the only legal tender when tithes were paid to the sanctuary of the Lord. This is because the common shekels wore out through constant exchange and trading.

Also, in the East merchants often file off some of the silver or gold from the coins. This is also true of the weights; there are diverse weights and balances; some large and some small.

This custom prevailed in Eastern countries until recently. The Turkish government discounted ten per cent; that is, a Turkish gold coin worth 100 kroshes, was accepted at the Treasury for 90 kroshes. (Piaster)

The edges were placed on the coins to prevent the merchants from stealing some of the gold.

The shekel was a measure of weight and money [Gen. 23:15; Jer. 32:9]. The temple shekel was sacred; no one dared to tamper with it.

MYRRH

Take thou also unto thee principal spices, of pure myrrh five hundred shekels, and of sweet cinnamon half so much, even two hundred and fifty shekels, and of sweet calamus two hundred and fifty shekels.   Exod. 30:23

Myrrh is an aromatic resin of sweet spices. It was used as an ingredient in the holy anointing oil. It was also used for embalming [Esther 2:12; Ps. 45:8].

FINGER OF GOD

And he gave unto Moses, when he had made an end of communing with him upon mount Sinai, two tables of testimony, tables of stone, written with the finger of God.   Exod. 31:18

"Written with the finger of God" is an Aramaic idiom that means, "They were perfect," or without any defects. We often say, "This article is made by God, human hands cannot make it." What we mean is that the article is perfect. The word finger also means an act.

God is spirit. The ancient writers, often portrayed him as a man with fingers, hands, feet, eyes, and heart, in order to explain his spiritual attributes to men.

God gave Moses strength, wisdom and understanding to engrave the tablets without a flaw. Engraving of so many words on two tablets on a desolate mountain was not an easy job and, it could not have been accomplished without divine help, guidance, and inspiration.

In another passage, the author of Exodus states that the writing was the writing of God, graven upon the tablets [Exod. 32:16].

In Exodus 34:1 we are told that God instructed Moses to hew two tablets, and that he, the Lord, would write upon them. But when the tablets were ready, the Lord commanded Moses what to write. The Lord said to Moses, "Write thou these words . . ." [Exod. 34:27].

The Lord dictated the commandments and ordinances, but Moses inscribed them on the stone tablets. In the East the one who dictates is known as the author of the written material. The Lord God was the author of the commandments and ordinances which Moses wrote on the tablets. Moses simply acted as a scribe. And Moses wrote all the words of the Lord . . . [Exod. 24:4].

GOLDEN CALF

And he received them at their hand, and fashioned it with a graving tool, after he had made it a molten calf: and they said, These be thy gods, O Israel, which brought thee up out of the land of Egypt.   Exod. 32:4

The ox is symbolic of strength and endurance, and was worshiped as a god by the Assyrians. The Assyrian emblem consisted of a man's head, an eagle's wings, and an ox's body and feet, which meant intellect, omnipresence, and strength.

God is symbolic of power, glory, and excellency. Thus, the golden calf was the deity of the material world, and is still the god of those who worship money and material things more than their Creator.

When Aaron made the golden calf, he said, "This is your god, O Israel." That is, gold is the god of this world, and without which no one can be free and happy. Then again material things were their gods in Egypt. All gods of the Gentiles were made of silver and gold, the two most precious metals.

The people who conspired against Moses believed that the future welfare of Israel depended more on gold and silver than on the unseen God, who had conversed with Moses from the midst of a bush.

Throughout centuries gold and silver have meant more to mankind than the Living God and his Truth. The golden calf still stands un-

challenged, and those who aspire to power and false glory still look up
to its shining metal.

ROSE UP TO PLAY

*And they rose up early on the morrow, and offered burnt offer-
ings, and brought peace offerings; and the people.*   Exod. 32:6

Lemishtaayo, "rose up to play" can mean also "quarrel," "fight," or
"sport." In this instance it means that after they ate they started to
quarrel among themselves.

The same saying occurs in 2 Samuel, when the men who were with
Joab and Abner met; Abner said to Joab, "Let the young men now
arise and sport before us." Many of the men were killed including Joab's
brother, Asahel [2 Samuel 2:14-16].

Even today when people are hungry they are quiet, but when they eat
and drink they often start to quarrel or fight.

The quarrel, no doubt, started over the question of whether to return
to Egypt or not. Some of the people were still loyal to Moses, but many
were dissatisfied and rebellious. After they had sacrificed to the calf, they
ate and drank and then they started to quarrel among themselves.

When people are hungry and thirsty they find no time to quarrel, but
when they are prosperous they want to quarrel and fight.

REPENTED

*And the Lord repented of the evil which he thought to do unto
his people.*   Exod. 32:14

The term repented means "returned." That is, returned from his way,
or changed his plans. The term repentance in this instance does not mean
that the Lord repented as though he had done something wrong, or,
that he was intending to do something that he shouldn't do. The change
was wrought by the people's repentance from their evil works. Moses
prayed on behalf of the people and the Lord forgave them.

WRITING

*And the tables were the work of God, and the writing was the
writing of God, graven upon the tables.*   Exod. 32:16

The Hebrews were familiar with the various kinds of writing which
were developed in their ancestral lands, Chaldea and Assyria. Abraham,

Isaac, and Jacob had scribes who wrote deeds, treaties, and agreements and who recorded the history of the tribe. The term scribes is mentioned throughout the Bible, but it has been wrongly translated as "officers."

Apparently, the Jews made more use of the alphabet than other races round about them. They wrote down the commandments and all the ordinances. They were interested in preserving what was valuable, sacred, and enduring, whereas the Assyrians and the Babylonians wrote a great deal on science, astronomy, astrology, and government. Most of the Hebrew writings were sacred, and are now the greatest heritage which the past has bequeathed to us.

The writing was perfect, the work of God [Comment on Exodus 31:18].

FILE

And he took the calf which they had made, and burnt it in the fire, and ground it to powder, and strewed it upon the water, and made the children of Israel drink of it.   Exod. 32:20

The Eastern text reads: "He filed it with a file until he ground it to powder." The file, like many other instruments, was an early invention.

The gold dust then was scattered upon the water; and Moses told the children of Israel to drink of it. The gold no doubt settled to the bottom of the water and might have been preserved.

It would have been difficult, if not impossible, to distribute the gold to men and women who had donated their rings, earrings, and bracelets for the making of the golden calf. On the other hand, men and women who had parted with their gold could no longer think of returning to Egypt. Moreover, the gold was defiled. That is why Moses had to purify it with the fire.

SINNED

And when Moses saw that the people were naked, (for Aaron had made them naked unto their shame among their enemies,).
Exod. 32:25

The Eastern text reads: "And when Moses saw that the people had sinned; (for Aaron had caused them to sin, to have a bad name at the end) . . ." The term naked metaphorically means "ashamed" [Gen. 3:10, 11].

Aaron had caused them to sin in that he had made them worship the golden calf and to sacrifice to it. When Moses saw them, they were ashamed of their evil act.

REBELLION

And he said unto them, Thus saith the Lord God of Israel, Put every man his sword by his side, and go in and out from gate to gate throughout the camp, and slay every man his brother, and every man his companion, and every man his neighbor. Exod. 32:27

For a long time, there had been dissatisfaction with the leadership of Moses and Aaron. The desert hardships, thirst and hunger, caused the people not only to complain but also to revolt against Moses and Aaron, desiring to return to Egypt. "Would to God we had died by the hand of the Lord in Egypt" [Exod. 16:3].

Had Moses not returned from the mountain in time, the leaders of the rebellion would have compelled Aaron to lead them back to Egypt. The calf was made to serve them as a god, to guide them in the place of the God of their fathers.

Moses had to crush this revolt as soon as possible before it got out of his control. The Levites were asked to kill all those who disputed Moses' leadership. The word "brother" here means brothers and other members of their own tribe who were involved in the conspiracy. The Levites knew all the men who were dissatisfied.

In those days every command or ordinance was issued under the name of the Lord. In other words, the Lord was the true ruler of the people, and Moses as a leader carried out God's orders.

SIGN OF MOURNING

And when the people heard these evil tidings, they mourned: and no man did put on him his ornaments.

For the Lord had said unto Moses, Say unto the children of Israel, Ye are a stiffnecked people: I will come up into the midst of thee in a moment, and consume thee: therefore now put off thy ornaments from thee, that I may know what to do unto thee.

Exod. 33:4-5

Ornaments were left off as a sign of mourning and repentance. Easterners, when mourning, leave off their silver or gold daggers, jewels, and costly garments as a token of grief. Likewise, they do not wear ornaments when making supplications before princes and kings, but generally appear in simple garments and with sackcloth.

Moreover, in the olden days, people tore their garments at the hearing of sad news. King David tore his clothes when he heard that Saul and Jonathan were slain [2 Sam. 1:11]. The Israelites, on other occasions, put their ornaments on, especially when they attended feasts and rejoiced before the Lord [Jer. 2:32]. "I decked thee also with ornaments, and I put bracelets upon thy hands, and a chain (necklace) on thy neck" [Ezek. 16:11, 12].

CLOUDY PILLAR

And all the people saw the cloudy pillar stand at the tabernacle door: and all the people rose up and worshipped, every man in his tent door.   Exod. 33:10

The cloudy pillar symbolized the Lord God. "Cloud" in this instance, is a synonym for "mystery." In other words, God appeared in a pillar of cloud because the people could not see his face and live. Moses conversed with God as man to man, but never beheld his face. He saw God's glory as he passed by him [Exod. 33:18-23].

When Moses conversed with God, "the people stood afar off, and Moses drew near to the thick darkness where God was" [Exod. 20:21].

God is spirit and the spirit cannot be seen with the human eyes.

NO ONE HAS SEEN GOD

And he said, Thou canst not see my face: for there shall no man see me, and live.   Exod. 33:20

God is the Eternal Spirit. No one can behold the spirit with physical eyes. The term face is used symbolically, meaning "presence." One can feel the presence of God but cannot see his face, for God has no physical face or form to be seen with human eyes. God said to Moses that his face shall not be seen [Verse 23].

Moses did not ask to see God's face. What he wanted to see was his glory. "Show me thy glory" [Exod. 33:18]. In the book of the Revelation we are told that God's countenance is "like the sun shining in its strength" [Rev. 1:14-17].

John says, "No man hath seen God at any time: the only begotten Son, which is in the bosom of the Father, he has declared him" [John 1:18].

Isaiah, in a vision, "saw the Lord sitting upon a throne, high and lifted up" [Isa. 6:1-5]. But what Isaiah saw was God's glory and his majesty [Ezek. 10:4]. All the prophets and men of God who beheld God's glory and heard his voice can say that they have seen the Lord, but all of their communications with the Lord were in visions and dreams. God is goodness and truth. Jesus said, "He who sees me has seen the Father" [John 14:9].

GOD IS THE AUTHOR OF THE LAW

And the Lord said unto Moses, Hew thee two tables of stone like unto the first: and I will write upon these tables the words that were in the first tables, which thou brakest. Exod. 34:1

"And I will write upon these tables" does not literally mean that God sat down and engraved the tablets with an engraver's tool. God spoke out of heaven and Moses heard his voice and wrote the commandments. In other words, the Lord God was the author of the writing and Moses acted as a scribe. In verse 27 the Lord said to Moses, "Write these words: . . ."

In the East, kings, judges, and governors employ scribes. They dictate to the scribes just as an American businessman dictates a letter to his secretary. Jeremiah's book was written by Baruch [Jer. 36:4]. And the Pauline epistle to the Romans was written by Tertius [Rom. 16:22].

God is the eternal spirit and truth. God could have commanded and the tablets would have been written instantaneously. Indeed it would not have taken God forty days to write ten commandments. But it would take forty days for a good scribe to perform such an important and delicate task. But the Lord guided Moses in performing this task and in producing two perfect tablets containing the Ten Commandments. "And he (Moses) wrote upon the tablets the words of the covenant, the ten commandments" [Exod. 34:27, 28]. It was the work of God: Moses acted as an agent. [See also comment on Exod. 34:28.]

SACRED GROUND

And no man shall come up with thee, neither let any man be seen throughout all the mount; neither let the flocks nor herds feed before that mount. Exod. 34:3

The ground around sacred shrines and sacred groves was generally protected. Grazing was prohibited near the holy places. In the East, even today, the people respect the holy places; even the fruit trees which grow round about a holy place cannot be touched, nor the ground contaminated with filth.

Mount Sinai was a holy mountain not only to the Jews but also to the Midianites. It was called the mountain of God.

PAYING OF DEBTS

Keeping mercy for thousands, forgiving iniquity and transgression and sin, and that will by no means clear the guilty; visiting the iniquity of the fathers upon the children, and upon the children's children, unto the third and to the fourth generation.   Exod. 34:7

In the East children pay debts incurred by their fathers, and at times they are even put to death for the wicked acts of their parents. Debts incurred by the parents may be paid by the third or fourth generation.

The Hebrews, like other Eastern races, believed the children were responsible for the evil acts of their parents. "Thou showest loving kindness to thousands of generations, and recompensest the iniquity of the fathers to the bosom of their children after them" [Jer. 32:18].

But this old concept was to be changed in due time, and the children were no longer to be held responsible for the evil acts of their fathers. "In those days they shall say no more, The fathers have eaten sour grapes, and the children's teeth are set on edge" [Jer. 31:29].

When Jesus was asked about the blind man: "Who did sin, this man or his parents, that he was born blind?" Jesus answered, "Neither hath this man sinned, nor his parents . . ." [John 9:2-3].

The Mosaic law stated: "The fathers shall not be put to death for their children, neither shall the children be put to death for their fathers; but every man shall be put to death for his own sin" [Deut. 24:16]. But Joshua disregarded this ordinance when he ordered the children of Achar (Achan) stoned and burned with fire [Josh. 7:24-25]. This act of Joshua's which was contrary to the Law of Moses might have become a precedent in Israel.

GUILTY CONSCIENCE

And he said, If now I have found grace in thy sight, O Lord, let my Lord, I pray thee, go among us; for it is a stiffnecked people; and pardon our iniquity and our sin, and take us for thine inheritance.   Exod. 34:9

The Aramaic word *teratan*, "conscience," has been confused with *tertan*, "to inherit us." The two words are similar in Aramaic, but are pronounced differently and have different meanings. There are many such words in Semitic languages.

The reference here is to the people's sins, iniquities, and their guilty consciences. Moses was imploring the Lord not to leave the people in the wilderness, but to continue to go with them to the end of their journey [Exod. 3:16-17]. The people had sinned against the Lord and were rebellious toward Moses and Aaron. Many of their leaders wanted to return to Egypt. They had a guilty conscience in the whole matter.

FIRSTLINGS OF ASSES

But the firstling of an ass thou shalt redeem with a lamb: and if thou redeem him not, then shalt thou break his neck. All the first-born of thy sons thou shalt redeem. And none shall appear before me empty. Exod. 34:20

These rigid ordinances were written so that the people might fulfill their obligations to the priests and the Levites, who lived off the temple revenue, such as tithes, vows, and the things which were dedicated to God. This ordinance is also recorded in Exodus 13:13.

The priests and the Levites had little use for donkeys; they were constantly engaged in the service of the temple. Thus, the firstlings of asses were redeemed with lambs, sheep or goats, which the priests used for food.

Undoubtedly, the firstlings of the asses were not slain, but redeemed. The poor owners brought lambs to redeem them. Asses were valuable for the working classes, especially the poor [Num. 18:15]. [See also comment on Exod. 13:13.]

MEMORIAL OFFERINGS

Thrice in the year shall all your men children appear before the Lord God, the God of Israel. Exod. 34:23

It is likely that the Aramaic word *dokhranaik,* "your memorial offerings," has been confused with *dikhraik,* "your males." The letters *yuth* and *nun* are very similar in appearance, especially when they are written in the middle of a word.

The Eastern text reads: "Three times a year shall all your memorial offerings be brought before the Lord, the God of Israel."

The males also went to the place of worship at least once a year. But all the males could not have gone at the same time three times every year. Their enemies would have invaded their border towns. [See Exodus 23:17.]

TENT MAKING

And all the women whose heart stirred them up in wisdom spun goats' hair.   Exod. 35:26

All tents in Palestine, the Arabian desert, and other parts of the Near East are made of goats' hair. Most of the goats are black and their hair is coarse and difficult to be woven.

The hair is first cleaned, then carded. The longer hair is separated to be spun for the tents, and the shorter hair is made into bags which are used as containers for grain, household goods, and for rugs to be used for the floor of the tent.

All of this manual labor is wrought by women who are noted for their skill in carding, spinning by hand, and weaving on wooden looms.

The tent cloth is noted for its durability and it repels water and offers protection from wind, cold, and heat.

WRITING THE COMMANDMENTS

And he was there with the Lord forty days and forty nights; he did neither eat bread, nor drink water. And he wrote upon the tables the words of the covenant, the ten commandments.

Exod. 34:28

In the East, generally the credit for writing goes to the author of the material just as in the case of the Pauline Epistle to the Romans. Paul dictated the epistle but Tertius the scribe wrote it [Romans 16:22].

On the other hand, at times when a written text is copied by a scribe, the credit is given to him, and the book is often identified by his name, even though he is not the author of the material.

According to Exodus 24:12; 31:18; 32:15-16, God wrote the commandments and other laws. Exodus 31:18 declares that they were "written by the finger of God." Likewise in the book of Deuteronomy (5:22) we are told that God wrote the commandments and then delivered them to Moses.

"Written by the finger of God" does not necessarily mean that God has fingers. Finger here is used figuratively. Moreover, the Bible often-times portrays God as a man with fingers, eyes, arms, and feet so that man might understand his attributes. Finger in this case is symbolic of the part which God had in the writing of the commandments and ordinances. In Aramaic we often say, "He has a finger in it," which means he has been interested in it. Then again, "written by the finger of God" means that they were perfect. In the East when articles are perfect we often say, "They are made by the fingers of God because only God can make things perfect."

In Exodus 24:4 we read, "And Moses wrote all the words of the Lord." Moses wrote the law, but God dictated to Moses in a vision. Moses heard God's words, for God spoke to him face to face. Moses fasted forty days and forty nights in order to commune with God.

HIS FACE SHONE

And when Aaron and all the children of Israel saw Moses, behold, the skin of his face shone; and they were afraid to come nigh him. Exod. 34:30

The Aramaic word *azlag* means to "shine," to "radiate." Moses had fasted forty days and forty nights in order to commune with God [Exod. 34:28]. During this period of fasting Moses had overcome all physical weaknesses, so that the spiritual forces in him radiated.

When people fast for a long period, their faces shine and the spiritual forces assert themselves over the forces of the flesh. Their faces become transparent and lighted with spiritual forces.

The Israelites had never seen such a phenomenon before, so they were afraid. Therefore Moses covered his face.

The term *azlag*, "shone," was indicated by horns. Western artists pictured Moses with horns.

THE PLACE OF WOMEN IN WORSHIP

And he made the laver of brass, and the foot of it of brass, of the looking-glasses of the women assembling, which assembled at the door of the tabernacle of the congregation. Exod. 38:8

Beth-makhziah in Aramaic refers to the place where women assembled to pray, that is the place where women appeared before the Lord. *Makhziah* also means a "mirror." The root of the word is *khaza*, "to see." The term mirror is a mistranslation of the word to "appear." This place of worship was set apart for women.

In the East men and women never sit or stand together during the worship. The women pray by themselves in the rear portion of the temple or church. They can see the priests, the singers, and the men praying and worshiping; but they cannot see their faces.

Both the tabernacle and the temple had places of worship for women. Today one sees women praying by themselves in Moslem mosques.

CHAPTER THREE

LEVITICUS

INTRODUCTION

IN the Eastern text, Aramaic, the language of the Hebrew patriarchs, the book of Leviticus is called *Kahney*; that is, "The Priesthood." This is because the priests were in charge of the tabernacle. They offered sacrifices, judged the people, and looked after their health and welfare.

On the other hand, the Levites assisted the priests in their sacrificial, ceremonial, and administrative duties The term "Levites" is derived from Levi, the son of Jacob. Thus, both the priests and the Levites were the descendants of Levi.

The book of Leviticus contains many dietary laws, ordinances, and rituals in the tabernacle which were written by Moses about 1500 B.C., when the Israelites were wandering in the Sinai Penninsula. That Moses is the author of the book, there is not the slightest doubt. The work covers everything in detail. No one could have remembered so many diverse laws, ordinances, statutes, and usages a thousand years after Moses' death.

Then again, these ordinances, statutes, and laws were needed during the time of Moses and, therefore, they had to be written in order to be taught to the people and handed down to the generations to come after them. Tribal people would perish without such laws and ordinances as a guide and lamp to their feet amid their difficulties and trials in vast deserts. Such a book as that of Leviticus was essential in a land where water is scarce and sanitary conditions unknown. Even today, some of these laws and ordinances are still used just as of yore among desert people.

OFFERING OF SACRIFICES TO DEITY

But his inwards and his legs shall he wash in water: and the priest shall burn all on the altar, to be a burnt sacrifice, an offering made by fire, of a sweet savor unto the Lord.   Lev. 1:9

Offering of sacrifices to gods was a universal custom as old as the Bible itself. Cain and Abel offered sacrifices to God [Gen. 4:3-5]. When Noah left the ark he sacrificed to the Lord [Gen. 8:20-21]. Invariably, all pagan peoples, in one form or another, offered sacrifices and gift offerings to their gods.

In the pagan conception of God (polytheism) sacrifices were a necessity. This is because pagan gods were human beings; and they needed food and drink. In those remote days emperors, kings, heroes, and holy men were worshiped as deities.

The Hebrews, like the pagans, offered sacrifices to their God, but their concept of deity was totally different from that of the pagans. The Hebrew God needed appeasement, but was not in need of sacrifices. The Hebrew concept of God was more crystallized. Their God was a spiritual God, the Creator of heaven and earth and all that is therein.

God saw the sacrifices, heard the prayers and supplications of the worshipers, and rewarded the faithful, but the meat and food were eaten by the priests, the Levites, and the people. A small portion of the offering was burned as a token of God's share.

The Hebrews, just like the pagans, thought that God was pleased with the smell of the sweet savor of meat of lambs and rams and oxen. In Hebrew terminology, all these expressions were used metaphorically [Lev. 2:2]. The sacrifices were symbolic, and they reminded the worshipers that they should share with their needy fellow men, and that God had a share in their possessions. After all, the sacrifices were shared with the thousands of worshipers who came from far off places to worship at the holy shrines. All the worshipers had to be fed while they remained in the holy place. This ancient custom still prevails in many lands in the Near East. Sacrifices and gift offerings are shared and given to the poor.

MEMORIAL OFFERING

And the remnant of the meat offering shall be Aaron's and his sons': it is a thing most holy of the offerings of the Lord made by fire.   Lev. 2:3

Dokhraney, "his memorial," means the offering of the person. In 'Aramaic *dokhrana* is another word for *korbana* or *debkha,* an "offering" or a "sacrifice." This is because most of the offerings are offered as a memorial for a certain thing.

The meal offering, therefore, was most holy and was 'eaten only by the priests within the sanctuary. All those who ate thereof were to be clean.

CAKES AND WAFERS

And if thou bring an oblation of a meat offering baked in the oven, it shall be unleavened cakes of fine flour mingled with oil, or unleavened wafers anointed with oil. Lev. 2:4

The Aramaic word *smida* means "the finest wheaten flour," which is used for a meal offering and baked in a *tanora*, "an earthen oven," or in a pan. The oven is about five or six feet deep and about three feet in diameter.

The term "cakes" is a Western word for what today in Aramaic are called *cadeys*, which are made of fine flour.

Cadeys are made in this manner: First, the flour is mixed with warm water or milk, and when it is leavened by placing in it a portion of dough from the previous day, it is left for several hours; then the dough is placed on a wooden board and flattened with a wooden roller. The process of making it is similar to the making of an American pie. A filling, which is made of baked fine flour and butter, is placed between two layers of dough. Then the *cadeys* are placed upright against the sides of the heated oven until they are baked. During the baking process butter or buttermilk is sprinkled on the cakes to make them crusty.

Cakes were placed before the Lord sometimes for a whole night, or a few hours, to be consecrated and were then eaten by priests, Levites, their families, and the singers. Cakes and wafers were usually consumed in the early morning hours before the meat sacrifice was cooked and eaten.

Cadeys or cakes are still made in many biblical lands, and are favored by the people. They are placed before kings, princes, and noblemen. At times they are baked in honor of certain guests.

The Jews baked them unleavened in commemoration of the time when the Israelites left Egypt so hastily that they had no time to wait until their dough was leavened [Exod. 12:34].

PEACE OFFERING

And if his oblation be a sacrifice of peace offering, if he offer it of the herd, whether it be a male or female, he shall offer it without blemish before the Lord. Lev. 3:1

The Aramaic word *shalma*, to "recompense," to "fulfill one's vows," is written exactly like the word *shalama*, "peace." Even though the words are identical, they are pronounced differently.

A recompense offering is a thanks offering to God for his blessings, or for his favors. When Jacob was on his way to Haran, he made a vow in which he vowed to give a tithe to God [Gen. 28:20-22].

Shalama, "peace," also means to surrender; that is, to give up hatred and enmity, and become reconciled. Peace becomes a reality through recompense, which brings harmony between a man and his adversary.

The worshiper was required to make peace with his God and his fellow men. Jesus said, "Leave your offering there upon the altar, and first go and make peace with your brother . . ." [Matt. 5:24, Eastern text]. If one has to make peace with his brother before offering a gift upon the altar, how much more then is it necessary that he should make reconciliation with God.

The recompense or the peace offering is different from the sin offering, thanks offering, and other offerings. Even though all these offerings were made to God for the forgiveness of sins and for God's blessings, each one was offered for a special thing, or for a special favor from God. There were also some differences in the ritual. Each offering had its own ritual.

THE UNCLEAN ANIMALS

Or if a soul touch any unclean thing, whether it be a carcass of an unclean beast, or a carcass of unclean cattle, or the carcass of unclean creeping things, and if it be hidden from him; he also shall be unclean, and guilty.　　　　　　　　　　Lev. 5:2

"Unclean cattle" in this instance means any beast which is not cloven-footed, or an unclean carcass of any animal. Even the carcass of an ox or a sheep would be unclean if it had been strangled or if it died of a natural cause [Lev. 11:24]. Today Jews, Christians, and Moslems comply with this ancient ordinance. They refrain from eating unclean meat.

MEAL OFFERING

If he offer it for a thanksgiving, then he shall offer with the sacrifice of thanksgiving unleavened cakes mingled with oil, and unleavened wafers anointed with oil, and cakes mingled with oil, of fine flour, fried.　　　　　　　　　　Lev. 7:12

Thanks offerings were made up of meal offerings; that is, cereal offerings of unleavened cakes tempered with oil, and wafers tempered with oil. All of these were made of fine flour and pure oil. The meal offering was offered together with the burnt offerings. The priests and their families ate some of these offerings. It was unlawful to leave anything until the next day. What was left over was burned.

SOAP

And the fat of the beast that dieth of itself, and the fat of that which is torn with beasts, may be used in any other use: but ye shall in no wise eat of it.   Lev. 7:24

In the East, even today, the fat of strangled animals and of those which die a natural death is used for soap, and the meat is thrown to the dogs.

The meat of dead animals was unsanitary and people were forbidden to eat it. The intense heat and numerous flies caused the dead bodies to decompose rapidly.

Then again, the Israelites were forbidden to eat the blood of the animals [Gen. 9:4; Exod. 29:12; Lev. 3:17]. The blood of dead animals remains congealed in the corpses. This ordinance also is observed by both Christians and Moslems. The pagans did eat meat containing the blood. That is why the Jews called them "dogs."

The Apostles decreed that the Gentile Christians must abstain from meats offered to idols, and from blood, and from things strangled [Acts 15:29].

CHOICEST MEAT

For the wave breast and the heave shoulder have I taken of the children of Israel from off the sacrifices of their peace offerings, and have given them unto Aaron the priest and unto his sons, by a statute for ever, from among the children of Israel.   Lev. 7:34

In desert lands where water is scanty and grazing poor, the sheep and cattle are generally lean. During the grazing hours, the sheep are constantly in search of grass; and in the evening they return to the fold hungry.

At times one can hardly find a fat sheep in the flock; therefore, fat is rare and expensive. Men and women, when buying meat, beg the butchers to give them a small piece of it.

Fat meat is generally served to prominent men and government officials. This is why when a man gives a banquet, he kills fat sheep or fat oxen [Luke 15:23].

Moses wanted the people to give to the priests and their families not only their choicest sheep and bullocks, but also the fattest sacrificial meat, such as the breast and the fat which is around the kidneys.

Easterners love fat and try hard to obtain it. The other meat is red and lean and is looked upon as of inferior quality [Exod. 29:22-28; Lev. 10:12-15].

SHAVING

And Moses said unto Aaron, and unto Eleazar and unto Ithamar, his sons, Uncover not your heads, neither rend your clothes; lest ye die, and lest wrath come upon all the people: but let your brethren, the whole house of Israel, bewail the burning which the Lord hath kindled. Lev. 10:6

The Aramaic word *peraa*, to "spring up," "bring forth," "requite," or "shave," in this passage means "shave." It should read: "Do not shave your heads." Shaving is an ancient custom. The Hebrews, like other races, had razors [Judg. 13:5].

In the East men and women cut off their hair, tear their clothes, and, at times, even inflict injuries on their bodies while mourning over the dead. But the priests, having been consecrated for the service of the Lord, were not to mourn over the dead, inflict injuries on their bodies, or shave their heads. Hair is symbolic of glory, honor, and beauty.

[See article on mourning.]

STRONG DRINK FORBIDDEN

Do not drink wine nor strong drink, thou, nor thy sons with thee, when ye go into the tabernacle of the congregation, lest ye die: shall be a statute for ever throughout your generations. Lev. 10:9

Wine and strong drink were used in pagan ceremonials. The worshipers ate, drank wine and strong drink, and then danced and committed immoralities. The Hebrews also used wine and strong drink during the feasts [Deut. 14:26].

This new command was given by God after two of the sons of Aaron were burned in the tabernacle. The priests were now to abstain from strong drink when they went into the tabernacle. In the book of Numbers we are told that the Nazarites were to abstain from strong drink [Num. 6:3].

Nevertheless, these ordinances of God were not always kept. The people often forsook God and his laws and went after strange gods. Both Isaiah and Habakkuk condemn drunkenness [Isa. 5:11; Hab. 2:15; Prov. 20:1].

DIETARY LAWS

And the Lord spake unto Moses and to Aaron, saying unto them,
Speak unto the children of Israel, saying, These are the beasts
which ye shall eat among all the beasts that are on the earth.
Whatsoever parteth the hoof, and is cloven-footed, and cheweth
the cud, among the beasts, that shall ye eat. Lev. 11:1-3

The dietary laws were essential in the desert where water is scarce and bathing and sanitary conditions unknown. These laws helped the people to control their appetites and desires, and prevented them from excessive drinking and riotous living.

Moreover, the distinction between the clean and the unclean helped the people to esteem that which was holy, and restrained them from doing evil. In other words, it was a mastery of the soul over the body. If a man cannot control the forces that are within him, how then can he control the forces that are outside of him? The Jews during the Maccabean period chose to die rather than eat prohibited foods.

Food and drink do not defile a man, but in those early days certain meats, such as pork, could not be preserved, nor could it be properly cooked. The Moslem and the ancient Eastern Christians still abstain from eating swine meat and other foods prohibited in the Mosaic law. The abhorrence of swine meat, no doubt, was due to the animal's filthy and indiscriminate mode of living. There must have been a reason at that time to enact these dietary laws. Then again, the swine might have been one of the Egyptians' sacred animals. Swine are immune to snake poison.

[See article on Swine.]

EIGHTH DAY

And in the eighth day the flesh of his foreskin shall be circumcised. Lev. 12:3

When the Lord commanded Abraham to circumcise all the members of his household, Isaac was eight days old and Ishmael thirteen years old [Gen. 17:12].

Therefore, the Jews circumcise their male children when they are eight days old, and the Moslems when they are thirteen years old. This is because Mohammed was a descendant of Ishmael, the son of Abraham.

COVERING OF LIPS

And the leper in whom the plague is, his clothes shall be rent, and his head bare, and he shall put a covering upon his upper lip, and shall cry, Unclean, unclean.　　　　　Lev. 13:45

The Aramaic term "cover his lips" is an Eastern idiom which means, "Keep silent" or "shut your mouth." In order to indicate that they have nothing to say, Easterners cover their lips with their hand.

The lepers were admonished to keep silent, so that they might not engage in conversation with people who might approach them and thus expose them to the dreadful disease.

The lepers warned other people by calling, "Unclean, unclean!" which means, "Keep away from me!"

WOOLEN GARMENT

The garment also that the plague of leprosy is in, whether it be a woolen garment, or a linen garment.　　　　　Lev. 13:47

In the East woolen garments were very common. This is because cotton was rare among sheep-raising people. The people wore woolen garments close to the body. Cotton or linen garments were considered a luxury, and were worn by kings, princes, and the wealthy [Luke 16:19].

The lepers generally rubbed their skin and preferred a rough garment to a soft one. The disease is transferred onto the garment by the means of rubbing and by lice in the garment.

Touching garments of the lepers is feared just as much as touching their skin. People are afraid even to sit upon things that a leper has sat upon. The Hebrew priests, just like the doctors in our own day, were cautious about the spread of this malignant disease and did everything to check it. But the Hebrew prophets healed this dreaded disease by the Word. They were not afraid of it. Jesus touched the lepers when he healed them.

Leprosy is an infection caused by filth and lack of sanitary conditions.

PRIESTS AS DOCTORS

When ye be come into the land of Canaan, which I give to you for a possession, and I put the plague of leprosy in a house of the land of your possession;

And he that owneth the house shall come and tell the priest, say-
ing, It seemeth to me there is as it were a plague in the house:
Then the priest shall command that they empty the house, before
the priest go into it to see the plague, that all that is in the house
be not made unclean: and afterward the priest shall go in to see the
house.   Lev. 14:34-36

Until recent days, in many Near Eastern countries, priests and pious
religious men acted as doctors, lawyers, judges, and counselors in many
important social and political matters. This is because the priests were
the only educated men who could read the books of law and who knew
something about the nature of diseases and their causes and effects.

Leprosy was very common in olden days and still is prevalent in some
backward lands where people are crowded in small houses, and where
sanitary conditions are bad.

Owing to the lack of water and sanitary conditions in biblical lands,
and also the lack of doctors, plagues spread rapidly. But today, because
of American help, this dreadful disease is under control and is gradually
disappearing. Education and hygiene have destroyed all fear of this
malady.

The Hebrew priests had made a thorough study of leprosy and knew
that it was contagious and dangerous. When they examined a leper, they
always isolated the spot to see whether it would spread or not. The
lepers were shut off from the rest of the people until they were pronounced healed. Even infected houses were shut off in order to check
the disease and bring it under control.

VENEREAL DISEASE

Speak unto the children of Israel, and say unto them, When any
man hath a running issue out of his flesh, because of his issue he is
unclean.   Lev. 15:2

These precautions were taken not so much because of the emission
of semen, but because of venereal disease, which was common among the
Baal worshipers. When the Hebrews joined the Baal worship at Baal-
peor, 24,000 men died of this disease. This incident is called the sin of
Balaam, who caused the Israelites to sin and to suffer from venereal
disease [Num. 25:1-9; 1 Cor. 10:8].

Then again, desert people wear few garments, and they sit on bed
coverings. Some parts of their bodies might touch bedclothes that are
infected with venereal disease. The Hebrew priests knew that carelessness
in these matters would cause the disease to spread among the congregation. The people were living in the desert. Water was scarce and
sanitary conditions were hardly known. All of these strict ordinances were
precautions to keep the congregation of God clean and healthy.

HOLY GARMENTS

He shall put on the holy linen coat, and he shall have the linen breeches upon his flesh, and shall be girded with a linen girdle, and with the linen mitre shall he be attired: these are holy garments; therefore shall he wash his flesh in water, and so put them on.

Lev. 16:4

When the high priest ministered in the holy of holies he put on his simple garments made of pure white linen as an example of purity and humility. On other occasions the priests were arrayed in garments made of silk and embroidered with gold thread.

White garments are symbolic of purity. The priests were commanded to bathe and to be pure and pious before they could petition God for forgiveness.

The Hebrew priests in the olden days fasted, abstained from their wives, and humbled themselves before they appeared before God, whose nature is pure and holy.

SCAPEGOAT

And Aaron shall lay both his hands upon the head of the live goat, and confess over him all the iniquities of the children of Israel, and all their transgressions in all their sins, putting them upon the head of the goat, and shall send him away by the hand of a fit man into the wilderness.

Lev. 16:21

This goat is called "scapegoat," one of the two goats which bore the sins or the blame of the people, which were offered on the day of atonement. The priest cast lots upon them, one lot for the Lord and the other lot for Azazael. The one for the Lord was offered for a sin offering [Lev. 16:7-9]. The high priest laid both of his hands upon the head of the other goat, confessed the sins of Israel, and sent it into the wilderness to die of thirst.

The goat died for the sins of the people. In other words, the goat paid for the wrong deeds of the people.

Jesus, in his death for our sins, did away with the animal offering; and, in dying for us, he did away with sin and death [Heb. 7:26-28].

SLAUGHTER OF ANIMALS

What man soever there be of the house of Israel, that killeth an
ox, or lamb, or goat, in the camp, or that killeth it out of the camp,
*   And bringeth it not unto the door of the tabernacle of the con-*
gregation, to offer an offering unto the Lord before the tabernacle
of the Lord; blood shall be imputed unto that man; he hath shed
blood; and that man shall be cut off from among his people.

Lev. 17:3-4

This ordinance was given by God in order to prevent the Israelites
from sacrificing to idols, sacred trees, and other objects in the fields, hills,
and in the countryside, and also for sanitary reasons.

The Baal worship was older than the Hebrew religion, and many of
the Israelites were still idolatrous in their concept of deity. Many of
them believed that there were other gods besides their God, and at
times they forsook their God and his religion and participated in pagan
worship.

On the other hand, tribal people seldom slaughter sheep or cattle for
food, but they often offer thanks offerings at shrines of saints and other
ancient places of worship. Many of these places are far off from towns
and villages. Moses wanted all sacrifices to be slaughtered in front of
the tabernacle so that the people would keep away from the pagan idols
that were found round about them, and also in order to prevent the
worshipers from offering blemished, sick, and strangled animals whose
meat was prohibited by the law from use in sacrifice.

HEBREW MORAL CODE

The nakedness of thy father's wife's daughter, begotten of thy
father, she is thy sister, thou shalt not uncover her nakedness.

Lev. 18:11

In lands where polygamy is practiced, a brother might covet one of
his half sisters; that is, the daughter of one of his father's wives or
concubines.

In the olden days, the Israelites were polygamous. Their kings, princes,
and noblemen married many wives. For instance, King David had many
wives; and Amnon, one of his sons, forced Tamar, his half sister.

FATHER'S SISTER

Thou shalt not uncover the nakedness of thy father's sister: she is thy father's near kinswoman. Lev. 18:12

Marrying of either the father's sister or the mother's sister was forbidden by Mosaic law [Lev. 20:19]. In Exodus 6:20, according to the King James Version, we are told that Amram, the father of Moses and Aaron, married his aunt. But the Eastern text states that he married his cousin. "And Amram took his uncle's daughter Jokhaber . . ." [Exod. 6:20]. Even today, the marrying of an aunt is prohibited by Canon Law.

THE TERM "SEED"

And thou shalt not let any of thy seed pass through the fire to Molech, neither shalt thou profane the name of thy God: I am the Lord. Lev. 18:21

"Seed," in this instance, means "semen." The Eastern text reads: "You shall not let any of your semen be cast into a strange woman to cause her to be pregnant. . . ."

Molech was the Ammonite god, a fire god, also known as Malchom (Aramaic, *malkom*). The Israelites, during the reign of Solomon, worshiped Molech and other pagan gods. Ahaz offered his son by fire [2 Kings 16:3].

God warned the Israelites not to worship him in the manner of the pagan gods. He did not want human sacrifices. He was not even interested in animal sacrifices. He wanted justice and mercy. The pagans did all kinds of abominations in worshiping their gods [Deut. 12:30, 31].

This ordinance is against cohabiting with pagan women. The Israelites were a sanctified people; that is, they were the people of God. But pagans worshiped strange gods and sacrificed their children to them.

RESPECTING FATHER AND MOTHER

Ye shall fear every man his mother, and his father, and keep my sabbaths: I am the Lord your God. Lev. 19:3

The Aramaic word *dekal* means "fear," "reverence," and "respect." *Dekhal min* literally means "to fear them when they discipline and chastise"; that is, "to obey their words." "For the fear of the Lord (Aramaic, "reverence of the Lord") is the beginning of wisdom" [Prov. 9:10].

Jesus admonished his followers to love and honor their fathers and mothers [Matt. 15:4]. Children don't have to be afraid of their fathers and mothers, but they must revere and obey them, for they are God's guardians over them.

When we love and revere God, then we can have a true love toward our parents and our neighbors.

LABORERS UNPAID

Thou shalt not defraud thy neighbor, neither rob him: the wages of him that is hired shall not abide with thee all night until the morning.　　　　　　　　　　　　　　　　　　　　Lev. 19:13

Prior to World War I, savings banks, trust companies, pension funds, and many other institutions which make laborers independent and secure in the Western world were unknown in many parts of the biblical lands. The laborers lived from day to day, and their livelihood depended on the wages they earned each day. When their wages were unpaid, they and their families suffered hunger.

In the East pious men pay those who work for them at the end of each day, so that the laborers may buy food and other necessities for their families. But government officials and wicked and wealthy men often refuse or delay the wages of laborers. Some wealthy and powerful men even conscript men and force them to work without even feeding them. In biblical days there was no law to compel them to pay, nor were there unions to protect the laborer. The corrupt government officials and the wicked rich worked together. The Mosaic law condemned these unjust practices [Deut. 24:15].

Both the prophet Jeremiah and James, the brother of our Lord, condemned the rich who exploited the laborers and withheld wages from the workers [Jer. 22:13; James 5:4].

THE MEANING OF LOVE

Thou shalt not avenge, nor bear any grudge against the children of thy people, but thou shalt love thy neighbor as thyself: I am the Lord.　　　　　　　　　　　　　　　　　　　　Lev. 19:18

Khobba, Aramaic "love," is derived from *khob*, a "debt." In the olden days, ideas or words were represented by ideographs or symbols. At times, the symbols may be identical, but have different meanings, according to the context.

For example, the same word which meant "scholar" or "learned man" also meant "stupid man" or "fool." Centuries later the meanings of some of these words were differentiated by a dot. When the dot is placed *over* a letter the word is read "scholar" or "wise man," but when placed *under* it the word means "stupid" or "fool."

Thus, the meanings of many words were ascertained by the context and the position of the dot. This is true of all ancient languages. For instance, in Chinese, *ai* means "love," but it also means to "covet" or to be "selfish" or "mean."

The Aramaic language uses the term *khobba*, because love is reciprocal; that is, a debt which first we owe to God and then to our fellow men, who are our neighbors. On the other hand, all-embracing love is the inarticulate language of the soul. Love knows no color, recognizes no human barriers, and seeks not its own. This is because love is universal. It is like air, available for all humanity; and like water, for all those who are thirsty.

DIVERSE SEEDS

Ye shall keep my statutes. Thou shalt not let thy cattle gender with a diverse kind: thou shalt not sow thy field with mingled seed: neither shall a garment mingled of linen and woolen come upon thee.   Lev. 19:19

Mingled seeds will not grow well together. Some plants would grow higher than others, and thus prevent the others from growing.

On the other hand, it would be difficult to collect taxes and tithes on mixed produce. In the East taxes on wheat are higher than on barley and other grains. Taxes are levied on fields of wheat and on fields of barley and other inferior grains. Thus, the mixing of seeds would complicate the taxing. A farmer may swear before a tax official that his field is sown with barley simply because a small portion of it is barley and thus he would pay taxes on barley, whereas most of his field is sown with wheat.

This is also true of cattle. Breeding cattle with a diverse kind might produce weak stock. In the East the only unlike animals allowed to be bred together are the ass and the she-horse, which produce the much needed pack animal, the mule. All other cross-breeding is prohibited.

Mixing of linen and wool would create confusion in trading. In some places where linen is scarce, the price of wool is cheap, and in other places where linen is abundant, the price of wool is higher. Thus, the mixing of wool and linen would create many difficulties between the merchants and the consumers. On the other hand, garments made of a mixture of wool and linen do not wear well.

TREES PROTECTED

And when ye shall come into the land, and shall have planted all manner of trees for food, then ye shall count the fruit thereof as uncircumcised: three years shall it be as uncircumcised unto you: it shall not be eaten of. Lev. 19:23

This ordinance was written so that the young trees might be protected and their maturity hastened. The Aramaic reads, ". . . you shall leave them for three years. . . ."

Most of the trees bear fruit in the third year, but their fruit is immature. The first yield of a young tree is generally removed so that the trees may become stronger.

Moses was a scientist. He had acquired considerable scientific knowledge in Egypt. Moreover, the Lord God revealed these ordinances to him, so that he might help the once pastoral people sow and plant in a strange land. It must be remembered that the Israelites who crossed the River Jordan into Palestine knew nothing about agriculture. They had spent forty years in the desert. And the generation which was familiar with orchards, vineyards, and agriculture was dead. The new generation had to be taught.

LONG AND SHORT HAIR

Ye shall not round the corners of your heads, neither shalt thou mar the corners of thy beard. Lev. 19:27

The Eastern text reads: "You shall not let the hair of your heads grow, neither shall you trim the corners of your beard."

Women in biblical lands let their hair grow long. Some of them make their hair look longer by braiding black wool into it. In the East a woman's long hair is symbolic of beauty and dignity, and is admired by men. On the other hand, too long hair for a man is a symbol of disgrace. This is because in the East it is sacrilegious to imitate women's apparel and makeup.

Paul in his epistle to the Corinthians says: "Does not even nature itself teach you that if a man have long hair, it is a disgrace to him? But if a woman have long hair, it is a glory to her; for her hair is given her for a covering" [1 Cor. 11:14, 15].

PAGAN MOURNING

Ye shall not make any cuttings in your flesh for the dead, nor print any marks upon you: I am the Lord.   Lev. 19:28

This was a warning against pagan practices. During festivals and funerals people inflicted injuries to their bodies. In some countries in the Near East, until recent days, the people prayed with knives and swords in their hands, and at times cut themselves, inflicting severe wounds to their bodies as a token of mourning over the death of their saints who were murdered centuries ago.

Even today Eastern women cut off their long hair and punish themselves by smiting their faces and breasts. In the olden days the men tore their garments and shaved their hair as a token of grief over beloved ones who had died [Job 1:20]. Even kings and princes tore their garments when mourning over the death of their friends and relatives [1 Sam. 1:11-12].

This ordinance is also given in the book of Deuteronomy, but it was often violated [Deut. 14:1].

The Israelites were the children of God. They were called and sanctified for a holy mission. They were to beware of pagan customs and practices.

Death has no power over those who are the children of the Living God. "I have said, You are gods; all of you are children of the most High" [Ps. 82:6].

RESPECT FOR ELDERS

Thou shalt rise up before the hoary head, and honor the face of the old man, and fear thy God: I am the Lord.   Lev. 19:32

To rise up before the hoary head, and to honor and respect the elders is inherent among all Asiatic peoples. When a group of elders is seated the young men stand up, and when an elder is speaking the young are silent. In some instances the young never speak unless they are asked to do so.

Then again, in the East the young salute the old and honor them as they would their own father.

"The glory of young men is their strength; and the beauty of old men is their grey hair" [Prov. 20:29, Eastern text].

In the olden days, when schools were unknown, elders served as instructors, judges, and counselors, and they were respected and honored for their wisdom and understanding.

Elders in the East never retire. They are active until they die. Moses was eighty years old when God called him to his great mission, and he died when he was one hundred and twenty years old [Deut. 34:7]. All the children of Israel respected and obeyed their elders. In the Bible the priests or ministers are called elders.

STRANGE WOMEN

Again, thou shalt say to the children of Israel, Whosoever he be of the children of Israel, or of the strangers that sojourn in Israel, that giveth any of his seed unto Molech; he shall surely be put to death: the people of the land shall stone him with stones.

Lev. 20:2

"Molech" is a mistranslation. The Aramaic reads "a strange woman"; that is, a woman of another race or religion.

The Israelites were called by God and set aside as a peculiar people. Therefore, they were not to have intimacy with pagan women and thus mix the holy seed with that of women of pagan religions whose laws and ways of life were contrary to those of the Israelites.

On the other hand, some of the worshipers of Baal were infected with venereal disease. On one occasion when the Israelites joined the Baal ritual and cohabited with the Moabite women, 24,000 Israelites perished with venereal disease [Num. 25:1-9; Deut. 4:3; Josh. 22:17]. [See also "Baal-peor."]

This law is still upheld among some of the people in the Near East. It is against the religious laws to cohabit with a woman who is a member of a rival faith, especially with an unbeliever or atheist [See Lev. 15:2].

SOOTHSAYERS CONDEMNED

A man also or woman that hath a familiar spirit, or that is a wizard, shall surely be put to death: they shall stone them with stones; their blood shall be upon them.　　　Lev. 20:27

Soothsayers, wizards, and men and women who had a familiar spirit were condemned by the Mosaic law and put to death. This is because these people were engaged in black magic and uttering oracles, which caused the people to go astray from the God of Israel. Moreover, the soothsayers terrified the people with their false prophecies and oracles. Therefore, they were considered as a menace to society, especially to an illiterate and credulous people who dwelt in the desert and who were easily victimized. They also pronounced cures and bestowed blessings upon the people for gifts and favors [Num. 22:4-6].

The soothsayers and wizards many times caused Israel to go astray and take up Baal worship [Lev. 19:31; Isa. 8:19].

DESERTED WOMEN

They shall not take a wife that is a whore, or profane; neither shall they take a woman put away from her husband: for he is holy unto his God.   Lev. 21:7

"Put away from her husband" in this instance means "deserted" or "separated" and thus lacking a bill of divorcement. A woman with a bill of divorce is allowed to remarry [Deut. 24:1-2]. The Aramaic word *dashbika*, "deserted," is confused here with divorcement. A divorced daughter of a high priest is permitted to eat holy meat at her father's house. In this case the woman is the innocent party. [See also Num. 30:9.] If the woman was guilty of adultery, then she should be stoned [Deut. 22:20-21].

But when the bill of divorcement has been granted the Aramaic word *neshrey*, "to loose the bond," is used. And the divorced woman is generally called *sheritha*, meaning that her sacred bond is loosened and she is free to marry again.

A high priest is prohibited from marrying a divorced woman who is guilty of fornication [Lev. 21:12-14]. But this law does not seem to apply to a layman.

The words desertion and divorce have caused some difficulty in foreign languages, because the word *shabikta* could be rendered either way. This is because the parties who are divorced no longer live together.

DEAD BODIES UNCLEAN

What man soever of the seed of Aaron is a leper, or hath a running issue; he shall not eat of the holy things, until he be clean. And whoso toucheth any thing that is unclean by the dead, or a man whose seed goeth from him.   Lev. 22:4

Dead bodies were declared unclean for sanitary reasons. In those days the whole family lived under the same roof or in the same tent, and at times even slept in the same bed. The sick person remained with the rest of the family until he died. Rooms were scarce just as they are today in many of these ancient lands.

And as water is scarce in Palestine and the desert, the sick were never bathed and their clothes were seldom washed. Therefore at times the people were so afraid of plagues that they were not allowed to touch the body of a dead person or his garments, or the vessels that he had used during his illness. Moreover, owing to the intense heat, bodies quickly decomposed.

Moses was well versed in hygiene, and he was guided by God. All the laws and ordinances he wrote served as precautions against disease. The scarcity of water and soap made it difficult for people to wash their hands or to bathe.

BRANCHES OF TREES FOR BOOTHS

And ye shall take you on the first day the boughs of goodly trees, branches of palm trees, and the boughs of thick trees, and willows of the brook; and ye shall rejoice before the Lord your God seven days.   Lev. 23:40

The branches of palm trees, the boughs of thick trees, and the willows of the brook were used for the construction of booths. All Israelites were required by law to dwell in booths during the Feast of Tabernacles, which was held on the seventh month and which lasted for seven days.

This feast was celebrated in commemoration of the Exodus when the Israelites left Egypt. For forty years Israel dwelt in booths and tents [Verse 43 and Neh. 8:15]. Even today many nomad people who cannot afford tents live in booths made of tree branches. The willow of the brook is used to bind thick branches together.

The Aramaic word *atrogey* means "citron." This is the only time the word "citron" occurs in the Bible. [See also Neh. 8:15, Eastern text.] Citrons are not mentioned in other Bible versions.

Citrons were known in Palestine. The Chaldeans, Egyptians, and Arameans had communication with Far Eastern countries.

Today Palestine is noted for its prolific and excellent citrus orchards.

BLASPHEMY AGAINST GOD

And he that blasphemeth the name of the Lord, he shall surely be put to death, and all the congregation shall certainly stone him: as well the stranger, as he that is born in the land, when he blasphemeth the name of the Lord, shall be put to death.   Lev. 24:16

Blasphemy against the name of the Lord was punishable by death. Blasphemy consisted of cursing the Lord, belittling him, and making oneself equal with him.

Moses put to death by stoning a man who had blasphemed the God of Israel [Lev. 24:23]. Jesus, when he forgave the sins of a sick man and healed him, was accused of blasphemy. He forgave sins as though he were God [Matt. 9:2-3]. Naboth was accused of having blasphemed against God and against the king, and he was stoned [1 Kings 21:13].

When Jesus said to the high priest, "Hereafter shall ye see the Son of man sitting on the right hand of power, and coming in the clouds of heaven (glory)," the high priest rent his clothes and Jesus was accused of blasphemy, which was punishable by death. "He is guilty of death," said the members of the council [Matt. 26:64-67].

ONE LAW FOR ALL

Ye shall have one manner of law, as well for the stranger, as for one of your own country: for I am the Lord your God. Lev. 24:22

The Eastern text reads: "You shall have one manner of justice; as for a proselyte, so for an Israelite. . . ." The Israelites had one law for both the Israelites and for the proselytes who dwelt among them. This ordinance is still respected in many Moslem lands whose codes of law are based on the Koranic code, which is similar to the biblical code, which was given to Moses by God. They have one law for the Moslem as well as for all those who have embraced Islam. This is because the members of a religion are looked upon as brothers.

To have two kinds of laws or two different yardsticks is not only contrary to the law of God, who is the Father of all races, but would also establish bad precedents for the future. This is because no nation or people can rule forever. History proves that the oppressors have been oppressed by those whom they have oppressed, and the weak races have become strong, and the strong, weak.

The Mosaic law, in this respect, is the fairest code in the world, because it is impartial and offers justice and equality to all the people of all races who turn to God and join the religion of Israel [Deut. 1:16].

The term "strangers" is a mistranslation. It should read "proselytes," that is, the native Palestinians who had embraced the Jewish faith. For example, the Israelites were permitted to practice usury when lending to strangers (non-Jews) but were forbidden to loan with interest to one another [See Exod. 22:25; Lev. 25:35-36].

SOIL CONSERVATION

Six years thou shalt sow thy field, and six years thou shalt prune thy vineyard, and gather in the fruit thereof;
But in the seventh year shall be a sabbath of rest unto the land, a sabbath for the Lord: thou shalt neither sow thy field, nor prune thy vineyard. Lev. 25:3-4

In biblical days fertilization and conservation of the soil were in their infancy. Constant sowing and planting rendered the poor soil useless.

Moreover, Palestinian soil is poor. This is because most of the top soil has been washed away.

A year of rest for the fields gives the soil a chance to regain some of its lost strength. When fields are not sown they are used as pastures for the sheep and cattle. The manure fertilizes the field. This was a sabbath or a rest for both fields and trees.

LAND NEVER SOLD

The land shall not be sold for ever: for the land is mine; for ye are strangers and sojourners with me.　　　　Lev. 25:23

This ancient ordinance is still upheld in many Eastern countries. Land may be leased, but it is never sold. In Iraq, ground for a house is leased for thirty years. This is because the land is looked upon as a family's sacred possession to be handed down from one generation to another. Then again, land is the only tangible property that a family can hold. Money is often confiscated. Sheep and cattle and other possessions are carried away.

On the other hand, arable land being scarce in Palestine, fields are looked upon as precious and secure possessions.

Naboth refused to sell his vineyard to Ahab, the king of Israel. He was willing to die rather than part from the inheritance of his fathers [1 Kings 21:1-3].

BROTHERLY LOVE

And if thy brother be waxen poor, and fallen in decay with thee; then thou shalt relieve him: yea, though he be a stranger, or a sojourner; that he may live with thee.

Take thou no usury of him, or increase: but fear thy God; that thy brother may live with thee.　　　　Lev. 25:35-36

The Eastern text reads: ". . . you shall not look upon him as a stranger or a sojourner. . . ."

The Israelites were admonished to help one another and to loan money to each other without interest [Exod. 22:25].

The Israelites were not allowed to practice usury or loan money at interest to their own people, but they could loan at interest to strangers and foreigners. Today Jews and Christians practice usury, but the Moslems are forbidden to practice it.

The Jews often loan money to one another without interest, but when they loan to a Gentile they charge interest.

[See Deut. 15:7.]

SEVEN A SACRED NUMBER

And if ye will not yet for all this hearken unto me, then I will
punish you seven times more for your sins.   Lev. 26:18

Seven was the figure used by God against those who would slay Cain.
". . . whoever slays Cain, vengeance shall be taken on him sevenfold"
[Gen. 4:15].

Seven is a sacred number: Seven planets, seven candlesticks, seven
wells which Abraham dug in Beer-sheba, seven churches in the New
Testament, and the seven angels.

The seven "planets" known to the ancients were the sun, moon, and
the five true planets, Mercury, Venus, Mars, Jupiter, and Saturn.

The number also was used figuratively, meaning "many times."

The Hebrews were punished many times more than seven times. [See
also Lev. 26:21, 24, 28.]

Jesus admonished his disciples to forgive not only seven times but
seventy times seven [Matt. 18:22].

A LONG DROUGHT

And I will break the pride of your power; and I will make your
heaven as iron, and your earth as brass.   Lev. 26:19

The terms iron and brass are used metaphorically, meaning "hard,"
"parched"; this suggests a severe drought. In the East during a drought
the people say, "The ground is as hard as brass." The "heaven like iron"
means that the air would be dry like iron.

These terms of speech were well understood by the writer as well as
the people to whom he wrote.

When the Israelites forsook the Lord God and went after other gods,
they suffered from long droughts and famines. These droughts at times
lasted for two or three years. During the reign of Ahab, king of Israel,
there was a drought which lasted for three years. But when Elijah prayed
for rain the rain came [1 Kings 18:41-45].

CONFESSION

If they shall confess their iniquity, and the iniquity of their
fathers, with their trespass which they trespassed against me, and
that also they have walked contrary unto me.   Lev. 26:40

Confession is an old institution in religion. People confessed in order
to relieve themselves of the guilt they had committed against God and

against their neighbors. But according to the Mosaic law, confession
and offerings were not enough to absolve a person of his sins. All the
things which he had taken violently or deceitfully were to be restored
before performing the atonement for sin. Good deeds and sincere repentance are better than empty prayers and confessions which do not
help those who have suffered injustices and wrongs. ". . . he shall restore
what he took violently or what he got deceitfully . . ." [Lev. 6:4-5;
Ps. 32:5].

CHAPTER FOUR

NUMBERS

INTRODUCTION

THE author of the book is Moses, who is also the author of the other four books of the Pentateuch which are called by his name.

The book of Numbers deals chiefly with the wanderings of the Israelites in the second year of their journey in the wilderness of Sinai, until they came in view of the Promised Land.

The title of the book is derived from the numbering of the people, *Minyana*, "Numbers." Like the book of Leviticus, Numbers contains many priestly ordinances, laws, and statutes, and history, all of which were written during the years when Israel wandered from one place to another.

The book must have been written in about the 15th century B.C. Numbers, like other books of Moses, deals with the law, justice, and state and religious affairs of the people in the desert.

Moses had scribes who recorded most of the important laws, ordinances, and events which took place under his leadership. He also wrote their goings out [Num. 33:2].

A TRESPASS

Speak unto the children of Israel, When a man or woman shall commit any sin that men commit, to do a trespass against the Lord, and that person be guilty;

Then they shall confess their sin which they have done: and he shall recompense his trespass with the principal thereof, and add unto it the fifth part thereof, and give it unto him against whom he hath trespassed.
                                                          Num. 5:6-7

"Commit a sin," in this instance, means transgression of any of the Ten Commandments or the ordinances. But the reference is to verse 7, which comes under the Eighth Commandment, "You shall not steal."

The goods stolen, and a fifth part added to it as a fine, are returned to the owner or to his heir if the owner is dead.

This ancient biblical ordinance is still upheld among the nomad tribes. Stolen goods are returned and the culprit is punished and fined.

SPIRIT OF JEALOUSY

And the spirit of jealousy come upon him, and he be jealous of his wife, and she be defiled; or if the spirit of jealousy come upon him, and he be jealous of his wife, and she be not defiled.

Num. 5:14

The Aramaic word *rookha,* here translated "spirit," may also mean "wind," "pride," "temper," and "rheumatism." In the East we often say, "The wind has entered into him," which means that he has an urge; or we say, "He has a high spirit," which means that he is conceited, proud.

The reference here is to the man who is moved by suspicion or jealousy because of his wife's unbecoming conduct [Num. 5:30].

The usage of the term "spirit" must be decided by the context. For example, "Blessed are the poor in spirit" [Matt. 5:3] should read, "Blessed are the poor in pride." "A woman was suffering from a spirit of infirmity" [Luke 13:11] should read, "suffering from rheumatism."

THE WATER OF TESTING

And the priest shall take holy water in an earthen vessel; and of the dust that is in the floor of the tabernacle the priest shall take, and put it into the water:

And the priest shall set the woman before the Lord, and uncover the woman's head, and put the offering of memorial in her hands, which is the jealousy offering: and the priest shall have in his hand the bitter water that causeth the curse!

And the priest shall charge her by an oath, and say unto the woman, If no man have lain with thee, and if thou hast not gone aside to uncleanness with another instead of thy husband, be thou free from this bitter water that causeth the curse.   Num. 5:17-19

The water of testing is something like the modern lie detector. Easterners are always afraid of oaths, especially when they are adjured in a church or a holy shrine before the altar. The presence of the priest, the Holy Book, the Bible, and the complex ceremonials frighten the guilty men or women and cause them to confess.

This custom is still in use in ancient churches in the East. Many men and women confess their guilt. Others who do not confess are stricken [Verses 18-22].

THE WRITTEN CURSE

And this water that causeth the curse shall go into thy bowels, to make thy belly to swell, and thy thigh to rot. And the woman shall say, Amen, amen.

And the priest shall write these curses in a book, and he shall blot them out with the bitter water. Num. 5:22-23

The words of the curse are written on paper or on parchment, then washed off with the water of testing or bitter water. It is said that when the person who is on trial drinks the water, he drinks also the words and the curses which are therein.

This practice is still used by men and women who write charms and talismans.

In the olden days the oath was done in the name of the Lord to solve problems that were beyond the understanding of judges and could not be decided in the courts. But today it is practiced for money and other worldly gains.

Innocent men and women are never stricken. They take the water gladly and the truth protects them. But the guilty persons are afraid to drink the water of testing.

THE LAW OF THE NAZARITE

He shall separate himself from wine and strong drink, and shall drink no vinegar of wine, or vinegar of strong drink, neither shall he drink any liquor of grapes, nor eat moist grapes, or dried.

Num. 6:3

This ordinance was given by God to protect the Nazarite from violating his vows. Wine causes men and women to err and to forget their vows. A drunken Nazarite might cut off his hair which serves as a continual reminder of the vow.

Samson lost his strength when he broke the vows. When his hair was gone, his strength was gone, too [Judg. 16:17-19]. The strength was not in the hair, but in the divine promises of which the hair was a sacred token.

REUEL, NOT DEUEL

On the sixth day Eliasaph the son of Deuel, prince of the children of Gad, offered.   Num. 7:42

The Eastern text reads "Reuel." The error is caused by the similarity between the letters *daleth* and *resh;* that is, "d" and "r." *Daleth* has one dot under it, and *resh* one dot over it.

The confusion caused by the location of the dots has been responsible for many errors of this kind.

Reuel is a common name in the Bible. Reuel (Reuben) was the first-born of Jacob. The name of Moses' father-in-law was Reuel.

FIRE OF THE LORD

And when the people complained, it displeased the Lord: and the Lord heard it; and his anger was kindled; and the fire of the Lord burnt among them, and consumed them that were in the uttermost parts of the camp.   Num. 11:1

"Fire" is symbolic of destruction, disaster, and affliction.

In Aramaic it is often said, "May the fire of God kindle in you," which means, "May a disaster or an affliction fall upon you." Then again, when people are afflicted by a disaster, or suffer persecution, or are heavily taxed, it is said, "They are burning," which means, "They are oppressed."

Moreover, lightning is also called "the fire of God," because it comes from the sky (heaven).

When a ruler or government official is angry, it is said, "Fire is kindling in his face," which means, "He is enraged." In the Bible, likewise, God is often portrayed with fire kindling in his face, and fire coming from his nostrils, which means he is angry, or his wrath is kindled.

In those early days all natural calamities were attributed to the action of God. When people suffered from them it was said that God smote them. The fire was brought by the evil deeds which the people had committed against God. In other words, fire came at the right time.

The Hebrews were constantly complaining. They were a difficult people to deal with. This is because they were wandering in a treacherous wilderness full of difficulties, and their hearts were in Egypt, the land of luxuries and plenty. Whenever they turned to God they were guided well and cared for, and everything went smoothly. But when they started complaining and doubting God, they were confronted with unforeseen difficulties.

One has to be guided by a higher power in order to travel safely in a desert land full of dangers. What water there is may be brackish, food is scarce, and the temperature is very high. Such difficulties can be overcome only by God, who directs his people to the right places at the right time, and who warns them of disasters.

An eruption of fire took place at the outer part of the camp, similar to that which destroyed the cities of Sodom and Amorah (Gomorrah). This calamity fell on a section of the camp where the leaders had doubted God, and had challenged Moses as a prophet of God. In the East calamities often strike only certain sections of the land. At times, disease may break out in a part of the city while the rest of the city is safe, as in the case of the disaster which befell Egypt when the firstborn of the Egyptians were destroyed and the Hebrews escaped the disaster.

In biblical days the people relied on God for water, food, health, and guidance in travel. The faithful were guided and warned against wars, disasters, and natural calamities. But the wicked perished. The Bible is full of such examples. Noah was warned about the flood. Lot was told by God to flee from the cities of Sodom and Gomorrah because an eruption was to take place there soon. Joseph was told in a dream to flee to Egypt. Peter and Paul were directed on their journeys in a hostile world. Man can be forewarned of every disaster when he is in tune with God.

THE MIXED PEOPLE

And the mixed multitude that was among them fell a lusting: and the children of Israel also wept again, and said, Who shall give us flesh to eat? Num. 11:4

The reference here is to the mixed people who left Egypt with the children of Israel [Exod. 12:38]. In Aramaic they are called *Khalotta*.

Some of these people were members of Semitic tribes who had migrated to Egypt and who were recruited by Ramses, Pharaoh of Egypt, to work on the cities which he was building. Because of hard labor many of these people had sided with the Israelites. Some of them were born of mixed marriages.

These people were the first to complain. They were not accustomed to the rigors of desert life. They thought that their departure with the Israelites would bring them not only freedom from hard labor but also happiness and prosperity. But, on the contrary, they found life in the desert harder than labor in Egypt.

Both the mixed people and the Israelites were accustomed to eating meat, fruits, and vegetables. The Egyptians are noted for their lavish tables, and the land of the Nile is a land of plenty. As one crop is gathered, another one is ripening, and a new one is planted.

Whereas, in the desert, from April to October or November, the water sources are nearly dried up and grazing is difficult. Vegetables and fruits are unknown except when brought by the sedentary tribes to be exchanged for cheese, wool, butter, and other sheep products. Such business transactions are very rare. The merchants generally become the victims of bandits and government officials.

The generations of the Israelites who were born in Egypt were soft. They had never experienced desert difficulties.

GOD'S PRESENCE

And I will come down and talk with thee there: and I will take of the spirit which is upon thee, and will put it upon them; and they shall bear the burden of the people with thee, that thou bear it not thyself alone. Num. 11:17

"I will come down" does not mean that God was not there. God is Spirit and he is everywhere. In biblical days the people believed that God's abode was in high places and in the clouds. This is why the people built altars on high places.

God did not decrease Moses' spirit when he gave some of it to the elders. When you light a candle from another candle, the light is not decreased, but increased. Moses' spirit was multiplied, simply because his task now was greater than before.

As man's work and his responsibility increases, so does his spirit and understanding increase. Nevertheless, Moses' jurisdiction over the people was decreased. In other words, his duties and functions were less, but the spirit was the same. The term spirit is used simply because all political and religious functions were carried out by the Spirit of God.

This is also true of the laying on of hands. In so doing, the spirit of bishops and patriarchs does not decrease. The Spirit cannot be measured in balances.

QUAIL TWO CUBITS HIGH

And there went forth a wind from the Lord, and brought quails from the sea, and let them fall by the camp, as it were a day's journey on this side, and as it were a day's journey on the other side, round about the camp, and as it were two cubits high upon the face of the earth. Num. 11:31

"Two cubits high" means plentiful. In the East people say, "The bread on the table was several cubits high," which means the bread was abundant. Or, "The food on the table was high to my nose," which means, "I ate plenty." The Aramaic-speaking people never take these sayings literally. They know that the speaker or writer is expressing himself in figurative speech, just as in English one may say, "I met a man who is rolling in money."

If the quail were two feet high, then the whole region, a day's journey around about the camp, would have been covered with quail. In such case it would have been impossible for the flocks and the herds to graze and the people to walk. The flocks and herds generally graze a few miles from the camp.

The flocks of quail came from European countries to winter in the warm Sinai and Arabian deserts, just as they do today. The birds, exhausted by flying over the Mediterranean, fell to the ground. The author of the book of Numbers states that there came a wind from the Lord and brought the quail from the sea.

Many times when the birds are exhausted by flying more than 200 miles nonstop, they fall into the sea or on the beaches as if they are dead. They are picked up by the people and eaten.

The Lord brought the flocks of quail and the wind at the right time when the people were craving meat. God met the need by causing the wind to blow toward the camp.

[See article on quail in Exodus.]

QUAIL GATHERED

And the people stood up all that day, and all that night, and all the next day, and they gathered the quails: he that gathered least gathered ten homers: and they spread them all abroad for themselves round about the camp.   **Num. 11:32**

The Aramaic word *kam* means to "rise up," "stand," "stay," "wait," and to "halt." In this instance it should read "rose up"; that is, they ceased from all other activities and left their tents in order to gather the quail which were lying exhausted upon the ground.

The quail, after they were gathered, were dried and stored.

GRUMBLING

And while the flesh was yet between their teeth, ere it was chewed, the wrath of the Lord was kindled against the people, and the Lord smote the people with a very great plague. Num. 11:33

"While the meat (food) was yet between their teeth" is an Eastern idiom, that means they had plenty of food on hand and lacked nothing.

The Israelites were not accustomed to the desert hardships and food shortages which are common among the nomad people, who are content with scanty supplies of food and water. The Israelites had just come out of Egypt, the land of abundance, where people ate bread, meat, and fruits until they were satisfied, and then stored plenty of supplies for the future. They had quail, manna, milk, cheese, and other sheep products, but their hearts were in Egypt. Food and water were more precious to them than freedom. This is why they were constantly grumbling.

The desert life is different. The people live from day to day, trusting in God, who provides their daily needs. They have no fear of the future. They trust that the same God who met their needs today will take care of them tomorrow.

GRAVES OF LUST

And he called the name of that place Kibroth-hattaavah: because there they buried the people that lusted.   Num. 11:34

The Aramaic reads, *Kabrey di Rigta* (the graves of craving, or lust). It was here that the people tried God when they craved for meat. And while the quail meat was still in their mouths they started to complain. The people were not satisfied with meat. They wanted other luxuries which could not be found in the desert.

Many of the leaders of Israel who questioned God's power and rebelled against Moses died in this place. Therefore, the place was called The Graves of Craving.

VISIONS AND DREAMS

And he said, Hear now my words: If there be a prophet among you, I the Lord will make myself known unto him in a vision, and will speak unto him in a dream.

My servant Moses is not so, who is faithful in all mine house.

With him will I speak mouth to mouth, even apparently, and not in dark speeches; and the similitude of the Lord shall he behold: wherefore then were ye not afraid to speak against my servant Moses?   Num. 12:6-8

All of God's revelations to the Hebrew patriarchs, gentile kings, and to prophets and seers came in visions or dreams during the night: God spoke to Jacob in a dream [Gen. 28:12], to Abimeleck, the king of Philistia [Gen. 20:3], to Laban [Gen. 31:24], to Joseph [Gen. 37:5], to Pharaoh and his servants, and to Solomon and other men.

But to Moses he spoke plainly; that is, in words that could be heard and understood instead of by symbols and dark sayings. This is because Moses had an inner understanding of God and his divine communication.

"Mouth to mouth" means plainly, face to face, without intermediaries [Deut. 34:10].

To Aaron, Miriam, and the prophets he spoke in similitudes, dark sayings, and figures of speech. The prophets and seers knew the meaning of every figure of speech which was imparted in a vision or dream and were able to explain and understand the dark sayings.
[See Job 33:14-16; Daniel, chap. 8.]

SPITTING IN THE FACE

And the Lord said unto Moses, If her father had but spit in her face, should she not be ashamed seven days? let her be shut out from the camp seven days, and after that let her be received in again.   Num. 12:14

Spitting is the most contemptible rebuke in the East, and it is still in common use. Spitting in one another's face precipitates quarrels and disputes among people.

At times, spitting is used as a token of strong rebuke. Fathers and mothers, when rebuking their children for misdemeanors, say to them, "Poo," which means, "I spit on you"; that is, "I condemn your actions." In this case, no saliva is discharged. But in more serious quarrels, the person who spits discharges his saliva on the face of the other person [Deut. 25:9; Job 30:10].

Jesus condemned this contemptuous Eastern habit when he said that no one should say to his brother *Raca,* which, in Aramaic, means "I spit on you" [Matt. 5:22].

When a father spits on his daughter, the daughter remains silent for a long time until she is forgiven. Miriam had spoken against Moses and had criticized him for marrying the Ethiopian woman [Num. 12:1]. Miriam was rebuked by God for her unwarranted action. Moses was the head of the tribe and the prophet. He was looked upon as the father of the Hebrew race. The Lord decreed that Miriam should remain silent at least for seven days. "To be silent" in the Eastern language means "to be ashamed" [Isa. 50:6; Matt. 26:67; Mark 10:34].

BUNCH OF GRAPES

And they came unto the brook of Eshcol, and cut down from thence a branch with one cluster of grapes, and they bare it between two upon a staff; and they brought of the pomegranates, and of the figs.   Num.13:23

The Eastern text reads: *wapsako min taman shaboka, wasgola khad di-anwey,* which means, ". . . and cut down from there a branch with one bunch of grapes. . . ."

The author has visited the place and found many small but prolific vineyards around Hebron, whose grapes are delicious and famous, and the bunches unusually large.

Some biblical authorities believe that there were other clusters of grapes on the branch. Be that as it may, the cluster was no doubt unusually large. They might have brought more grapes on the pole. Apparently, the author of the book of Numbers lays emphasis on the single bunch and uses the singular form, "They carried it."

Even today, in the East, branches of vine are often cut down with grapes on them and carried from place to place. The branch with its fresh leaves helps to preserve the grapes in the hot climate. It is a considerable distance between Hebron and the wilderness of Paran. Moreover, the spies were traveling on foot.

VALLEY OF THE CLUSTER

The place was called the brook Eshcol, because of the cluster of grapes which the children of Israel cut down from thence.

Num. 13:24

The Aramaic reads: *nakhla di segola* (the Valley of the Cluster). The place was called the Valley of the Cluster because from there the spies whom Moses had sent to spy on the land brought a large bunch of grapes to Moses and the children of Israel.

Later, the Hebrews called it *nakhal eshcool*. After the occupation of the land, many names of other ancient localities were changed to new names. *Koriath-arba* was named Hebron.

FEARFUL OF ENEMY

And they brought up an evil report of the land which they had searched unto the children of Israel, saying, The land, through which we have gone to search it, is a land that eateth up the inhabitants thereof; and all the people that we saw in it are men of a great stature.

Num. 13:32

The Hebrews were born and reared in the fertile Egyptian delta where food was abundant and life easy. They were unable to withstand the rigors of desert hardships, thirst, and famines. And having been subjugated by the Egyptians and compelled to work, they knew little or nothing of warfare.

The new generation which was born and reared in the desert was different. They were sturdy and rugged. They knew nothing of the luxurious life which their parents had lived in Egypt. They had never seen watermelons, cucumbers, grapes, garlic, and other foods of which their parents had spoken.

This new generation was more fit to invade and conquer the land of Canaan than the generation which had left Egypt. The inhabitants of Palestine were feared, not so much because they were warriors, but because the Hebrews who came out of Egypt were not skilled in war. And because of fear they exaggerated the strength and the stature of the inhabitants of Palestine.

This is why Moses decided to spend forty years in the desert until the generation which had left Egypt were dead and the new generation ready to take their place. Then again, the generation which came out of Egypt had murmured against God and against Moses, and had broken many of God's ordinances and had gone after other gods.

EASY CONQUEST

Only rebel not ye against the Lord, neither fear ye the people of the land; for they are bread for us: their defense is departed from them, and the Lord is with us: fear them not. Num. 14:9

"They are bread for us" is an Aramaic idiom which means, "We can conquer them very easily." In the East, when a difficult task is described as easy, it is said, "It is like eating bread." This idiom is still used today. This is because eating food and drinking water are two of the simplest and easiest things in a man's life.

The inhabitants of Palestine had weakened themselves by sensual Baal worship and other evil practices. And they were rejected by God because of their evil works. The Israelites were admonished not to be afraid of them, because the natives of the land were so weak that they could be consumed as easily as one consumes a loaf of bread.

When this Aramaic idiom is translated literally it loses its meaning. "For they are bread for us" in English would mean, "They are our very livelihood" or "They will feed us." This is also true of English idioms and mannerisms of speech. When translated literally they lose their true meaning.

ANOTHER SPIRIT

Surely they shall not see the land which I sware unto their fathers, neither shall any of them that provoked me see it:
But my servant Caleb, because he had another spirit with him, and hath followed me fully, him will I bring into the land whereinto he went; and his seed shall possess it. Num. 14:23-24

The Eastern text reads, ". . . because he has my spirit with him. . . ." The Aramaic term *rokha* (spirit) has many meanings. *Rokha* means "spirit," "pride," "temper," "wind," "rheumatism," "inclination," and "behavior." Thus, the term *rokha* must be rendered, not literally, but according to the context. The Semitic language, because of a limited vocabulary, economizes on words. One word may have many meanings. The term *rokha* has been confused many times.

In Aramaic, we often say, "His spirit is soft"; that is, "He is meek or gentle." "He is poor in spirit" means "He is poor in pride, and humble" [Matt. 5:3]. "He has the sickness of the spirit" means "He is afflicted wtih rheumatism." "And, behold, there was a woman which had a spirit of infirmity. . . ." [Luke 13:11].

Caleb, the son of Jophaniah, and Joshua, the son of Nun, behaved properly when Moses sent them to spy out the land of Canaan. They were loyal to Moses and they brought a good report of the land which they had seen. The other ten men, being dissatisfied with the living conditions in the desert and wanting to return to Egypt, were unfaithful to Moses and opposed him.

Of all the men and women who went out of Egypt, only Caleb, the son of Jophaniah, and Joshua, the son of Nun, entered into the Promised Land. They were rewarded for their good behavior, humility, and obedience to Moses, the servant of God. They had inclined their hearts to obey God, but the others were rebellious.

FORTY YEARS

And your children shall wander in the wilderness forty years, and bear your whoredoms, until your carcasses be wasted in the wilderness.

After the number of the days in which ye searched the land, even forty days, each day for a year, shall ye bear your iniquities, even forty years, and ye shall know my breach of promise.

Num. 14:33-34

Forty is one of the sacred and well-known numbers used by the Hebrews. Even today, pastoral people use this number very frequently, and because of the ten fingers, it is easily understood. Some of the simple and illiterate people cannot understand numbers beyond forty.

Forty can be divided into four tens. The number four is symbolic of the four corners of the earth, the four winds, the four seasons, and the four elements. Ten can be divided into fives, and five is symbolic of the five senses and the five books of Moses.

Then again, Moses was forty years old when he fled to Midian. And he spent forty years in Midian and forty years in the wilderness. Both Moses and Elijah fasted forty days. Jesus also fasted forty days.

For each day spent in spying on the land the Israelites wandered in the wilderness a year, because the spies brought a bad report concerning the Promised Land.

WORDING OF MOSAIC LAW

Ye shall have one law for him that sinneth through ignorance, both for him that is born among the children of Israel, and for the stranger that sojourneth among them. Num. 15:29

The term "strangers" should read "proselytes." The Mosaic law is the most just code of law ever penned by man. It is plain and unequivocal. It is one law for the native, for the proselyte, for the poor, and for the rich. It does not show partiality. Justice cannot be bought and sold.

Moreover, Mosaic law is terse. It has no ifs, no buts, and no qualifying clauses which are so common in other laws, which make them difficult and ambiguous. Then again, no other code of law employs as few words and says as much as the Mosaic law. For instance, "Thou shalt not kill." No one can improve on this law; also, "Thou shalt not steal." In Aramaic and Hebrew these laws are stated in two words: *La tiktol, la tignow.* A Western jurist might use several hundred words with many qualifying clauses and ambiguities to write one of these laws.

The superiority of the Mosaic code over other laws is due to God's revelation. The Mosaic code is the inspired Word of God which will continue to be in use to the end of time. Jesus said that not an iota or a dot shall fall from it until it is fulfilled [Matt. 5:18].

Then again, all Mosaic treaties and covenants with other nations were written in the same manner and were honored and respected for many generations [Josh. 9:15-16].

Every nation that is interested in the welfare of its own people first is bound to have laws and treaties that are one-sided. But God's law is a universal law for *all* his children without discrimination. Men discriminate, but God does not respect the persons of people. On the other hand, God's law is true, permanent, and unchangeable. It cannot be revised or amended like human laws.

SEVERITY OF THE LAW

And while the children of Israel were in the wilderness, they found a man that gathered sticks upon the sabbath day.
And they that found him gathering sticks brought him unto Moses and Aaron, and unto all the congregation. Num. 15:32-33

The Mosaic law is one of the severest laws in the world. This is because the law was revealed and written in the wilderness for a nomad people who were illiterate, stubborn, and rebellious.

The desert people could not understand sympathy and forgiveness. They often mistook them for weakness. This is why there is no forgiveness in the Mosaic law and in tribal laws. The culprit has to pay the penalty whether he repents or not.

Jesus would not have put this man to death. He would have forgiven him and told him not to do it again, just as he told the woman who was caught in adultery, "Sin no more." But conditions in the desert were different. Forgiveness, sympathy, and shirking of duty to enforce the law would have led hundreds to transgress the law.

It was not the gathering of the wood, but disrespect of the Sabbath, which made the death penalty mandatory. No doubt the man had been told not to do any kind of work on the Sabbath day, but he disregarded the commandment. His stoning was an example for the others.

Therefore in comparing the Mosaic law with the laws of Jesus Christ we must consider the time and condition. Moses lived 1,600 years before Jesus. He lived at a time when people were illiterate, hostile, and stubborn.

BORDER OF GARMENTS

Speak unto the children of Israel, and bid them that they make them fringes in the borders of their garments, throughout their generations, and that they put upon the fringe of the borders a riband of blue.　　　　　　　　　　　　　　　Num. 15:38

Fringes on the borders of garments were made as a reminder of God's commandments, his ordinances and moral law. Also, fringe made the garment larger and longer, so that it covered the whole body. The desert dwellers, because of intense heat, wear few garments and some of them lack lower garments. Moreover, in biblical lands members of different religions are known by the style and color of their garments.

The Israelites were a peculiar people, called by God to obey his commandments and his statutes. Long garments with fringe served as a reminder that they were God's people, and they were to uphold God's laws and not live like the pagan people who were round about them [Deut. 22:12].

Centuries later the wearing of wide fringes and long garments became a religious custom of the scribes and Pharisees, as a sign of dignity and learning. Jesus condemned them for this because they did it in order to display their piety [Matt. 23:5; Deut. 22:12].

COVENANTS SEALED WITH SALT

All the heave offerings of the holy things, which the children of Israel offer unto the Lord, have I given thee, and thy sons and thy daughters with thee, by a statute for ever: it is a covenant of salt for ever before the Lord unto thee and to thy seed with thee.

Num. 18:19

From time immemorial, salt has been considered a sacred and precious article. When two men ate salt together they never betrayed each other. Easterners often say, "We have eaten bread and salt together," which means, "We have made a covenant with one another." An enemy, or one who has guile in his heart, never breaks bread or eats salt with those against whom he intends to do harm. When they are asked to eat they refuse.

This ancient custom still prevails among the Bedouins in the Arabian desert. When they eat bread and salt with a stranger they protect him and will even die to save him.

Salt was used to seal covenants and agreements. When covenants were made, one or more animals were slaughtered and their meat salted and roasted on fire; then all those who had entered the covenant participated in eating together as a token of everlasting memorial and friendship.

Salt was a precious article in biblical days, and is still precious in some parts of Africa and other lands which are far away from oceans. It was used as a medium of exchange in many lands. Our word "salary" is derived from salt. Romans, as well as other governments, used it as a medium of exchange.

Jesus said, "You are the salt of the earth." Just as salt savors food, so good deeds savor the people around us. But when salt loses its savor it is useless. Jesus' followers were the salt of the earth because they had the Jewish Scriptures, which contain God's truth, the light of the world.

DEAD BODIES

He that toucheth the dead body of any man shall be unclean seven days.

Num. 19:11

Dead bodies were considered unclean by the Israelites. Apparently, this ordinance was written as a precaution against unsanitary conditions which at times prevailed among the tribes, especially in the lands where water is scarce and washing and bathing difficult. Moses was not only a prophet but also a scientist. He was aware of the danger of unsanitary conditions and plagues [Lev. 21:1; Num. 5:1-3]. When Israel joined the Baal worship at Baal-peor, 24,000 men died of the plague [Num. 25:9].

Dead bodies sometimes remained unburied for a day or two, and in hot areas such as Sinai dead bodies start to disintegrate soon.

When Jesus said, "Whoso eateth my flesh, and drinketh my blood, hath eternal life," his disciples misunderstood the metaphor and many of them left him. This was a hard saying to accept [John 6:53-66]. This is because his disciples were loyal to the Mosaic ordinances and they took the words of Jesus literally, just as many Christians take some of the sayings in the Bible literally.

Jesus explained the spiritual meaning of his words. ". . . the words that I speak unto you, they are spirit, and they are life"; that is, Jesus was speaking of his spiritual body and blood, of the hardships he was facing, even the cross. Even today Easterners say, "I have eaten my body and drunk my blood" or "I have eaten my father and mother," which mean, "I have endured many difficulties and trials."

STRUCK THE ROCK

And the Lord spake unto Moses, saying,

Take the rod, and gather thou the assembly together, thou and Aaron thy brother, and speak ye unto the rock before their eyes; and it shall give forth his water, and thou shalt bring forth to them water out of the rock: so thou shalt give the congregation and their beasts drink.

And Moses took the rod from before the Lord, as he commanded him.

And Moses and Aaron gathered the congregation together before the rock, and he said unto them, Hear now, ye rebels; must we fetch you water out of this rock?

And Moses lifted up his hand, and with his rod he smote the rock twice: and the water came out abundantly, and the congregation drank, and their beasts also. Num. 20:7-11

"Struck the rock" in this case means that he struck the rock on the top of the well, or he dug a well in a rocky place. The psalmist says, "He clave the rocks in the wilderness, and gave them drink as out of the great depths" [Ps. 78:15]. "He opened the rock, and the waters gushed out. . . ." [Ps. 105:41].

Moses and Aaron provoked the Lord. When the people disputed with them, Moses said to the people, "Hear now, ye rebels; must we fetch you water out of this rock?" [Num. 20:10].

Moses and Aaron, as well as the princes of Israel, were doubtful. That is why Moses struck twice, instead of once, and the Lord was angry [Exod. 17:5-7; see also the comment on Num. 21:16].

The Lord had showed Moses and Aaron the place where there was abundant water, and had told them what to do. God sees what is hidden from human eyes. God had the power and wisdom to provide water even in an arid land. The Lord could provide water and food in diverse miraculous manners.

The miracle is that the Lord provided water in a desolate place where there was no water. When men turn to God they are led to abundant sources of water and food. When Hagar and her son were dying of thirst, the Lord opened her eyes and showed her the well [Gen. 21:19]. See Commentary on Num. 21:16-19.

WELLS RENTED

Let us pass, I pray thee, through thy country: we will not pass through the fields, or through the vineyards, neither will we drink of the water of the wells: we will go by the king's high way, we will not turn to the right hand nor to the left, until we have passed thy borders. Num. 20:17

In deserts and arid lands wells are the properties of kings, princes, and chiefs of the tribes. Wells are precious, well guarded, and at times hidden in order to conserve the scanty water supply and to prevent marauding tribes from passing through the land.

When a peaceful tribe passes through the territory of another tribe a small tax is levied on it for grazing and for the use of the wells.

The king of Edom was afraid of the Israelites; therefore he refused to grant them permission to pass through his territory. Customarily, tribes share the wells and the grazing lands. But the king of Edom broke the unwritten desert code and refused to let the Israelites go through his territory.

TRIBAL MISTRUST

And the children of Israel said unto him, We will go by the high way: and if I and my cattle drink of thy water, then I will pay for it: I will only, without doing any thing else, go through on my feet. Num. 20:19

Nomad tribes buy their food, clothing, and other necessities of life from sedentary people. Wool, cheese, butter, sheep, and goats are exchanged for grain, clothing, hardware, and household articles.

The king of Edom had heard about the defeat of Pharaoh and his army and was afraid to let the Israelites pass through his territory, fearing that they might occupy his land. In arid lands where water is scarce and grazing poor, the chiefs of the tribes are reluctant to allow strange tribes to pass through their lands, fearing the water would not be sufficient for themselves and for the hosts of strange tribes.

The Israelites were a strong and numerous people. They were feared by all the people who had heard of them [Deut. 2:28].

DEATH OF AARON

Take Aaron and Eleazar his son, and bring them up unto mount Hor:

And strip Aaron of his garments, and put them upon Eleazar his son: and Aaron shall be gathered unto his people, and shall die there.

And Moses did as the Lord commanded: and they went up into mount Hor in the sight of all the congregation.

And Moses stripped Aaron of his garments, and put them upon Eleazar his son; and Aaron died there in the top of the mount: and Moses and Eleazar came down from the mount.   Num. 20:25-28

Both Moses and Aaron died healthy and full of days. Strange as it may seem, Aaron walked to the mountain where he was buried. Apparently, God had revealed to Moses that Aaron was to die on a certain day.

There are some old Eastern traditions that when men reached a certain age they were disposed of. It is said that this custom prevailed among the Assyrians. Aaron was an old man. Moses knew the exact time of his death. So when Moses stripped Aaron of his priestly garments, Aaron saw that the end had come, and he passed away peacefully.

FIERY SERPENTS

And the Lord sent fiery serpents among the people, and they bit the people; and much people of Israel died.   Num. 21:6

The Aramaic word for fiery serpents is *kwawatha kharmaney* (cockatrice). They may have been described as fiery because of their shiny, reddish color. These snakes were so ferocious that even to look at them was so terrifying that some people died of heart attacks.

Even today this species of serpents is still to be found in the Sinai desert and in other regions in the Arabian desert [Deut. 8:15]. The British Army suffered from them in World War I in a region known as *Abu Serhan.* Col. T. E. Lawrence, in his book, *The Seven Pillars of Wisdom,* tells of the British Army's struggle with the snakes.

The Israelites had spoken against God and murmured against Moses and Aaron. Had they remained loyal to God, he would have led them through another region where they would not have confronted the fiery serpents.

BRASS SERPENT

And the Lord said unto Moses, Make thee a fiery serpent, and set it upon a pole: and it shall come to pass, that every one that is bitten, when he looketh upon it, shall live.

And Moses made a serpent of brass, and put it upon a pole; and it came to pass, that if a serpent had bitten any man, when he beheld the serpent of brass, he lived. Num. 21:8-9

This part of the desert, which today is called *Abu Serhan*, is noted for snakes and scorpions.

Moses was told by God to make a serpent of brass and set it upon a pole so that those who had been bitten might look upon it and be healed. The placing of the serpent on the pole was symbolic of the destruction of the deadly serpents. Many of those who were bitten were struck with fear. But when they saw the serpent placed on the pole, they lost their fear and were healed [Deut. 8:15; John 3:14-15]. Years later the brass serpent became an object of worship [2 Kings 18:4].

SPRING OF THE HEBREWS

And they journeyed from Oboth, and pitched at Ijeabarim, in the wilderness which is before Moab, toward the sunrising. Num. 21:11

The Eastern text reads: "And they journeyed from Aboth, and encamped at the *Een di Ebraye* (the spring of the Hebrews) . . ."

The Hebrew tribe during the time of Abraham was known to the people of the land as *Hebraye;* that is, the people who had crossed the River Euphrates. Thus, the spring was called by their name.

In the East springs and wells are called by the names of the men who discover them or by events which take place near them during the grazing season.

BOOK OF WARS

Wherefore it is said in the book of the wars of the Lord, What he did in the Red sea, and in the brooks of Arnon. Num. 21:14

There must have been other sacred writings besides what we have today. Evidently, in the course of time, many books were lost or destroyed. Israel was invaded many times, and the sacred Ark was carried away by the Philistines. Moreover, the temple of Solomon was plundered by Shishak, the king of Egypt [1 Kings 14:25].

Then again, prior to the compilation of the books into our Bible, every scroll contained a separate account of an episode.

The Bible as we know it today was unknown to the Hebrew people. During the time of Joshua writing was in its infancy. Compilations and canonizations of the scrolls were made after the second century B.C.

During wars and persecutions, sacred writings were destroyed or burned by the enemy. It is a miracle that most of the sacred writings were spared and handed down.

BEER—A WELL

And from thence they went to Beer: that is the well whereof the Lord spake unto Moses, Gather the peopel together, and I will give them water.
Then Israel sang this song, Spring up, O well; sing ye unto it:
The princes digged the well, the nobles of the people digged it, by the direction of the lawgiver, with their staves. And from the wilderness they went to Mattanah.   Num. 21:16-18

The Aramaic word for "well" is *beera* (Hebrew *beer*). The reference here is to the rock which Moses struck at Horeb when the people strove with him, asking him to give them water to drink [Exod. 17:5-6; Num. 20:11].

After this miracle Israel fought with Amalek and was almost ready to enter into the Promised Land, but Moses was unable to get permission from the king of Edom to pass through his territory in southern Palestine. Moreover, the spies whom he had sent out brought back a bad report. The Israelites in their journeys had reached the River Arnon, but they had to return to the place where God had said to Moses, "Gather the people together, and I will give them water."

In the book of Numbers Moses explains in detail the episode and the miracle which he performed in the sight of the people. On previous occasions he did not describe the miracle in detail.

In deserts wells are often hidden in order to prevent strange tribes from using them, and their flocks from grazing in the territory. The shepherds and tribal wise men prove the ground in order to find the wells. Then again, at times, they strike in stony places and find water.

During World War I the German and Turkish Armies in Arabia hid the wells or poisoned them. But the British searched for them and found them.

"He brought streams also out of the rock, and caused waters to run down like rivers" [Ps. 78:16].

"Behold, he smote the rock, that the waters gushed out, and the streams overflowed . . ." [Ps. 78:20].

"He opened the rock, and the waters gushed out; they ran in the dry places like a river" [Ps. 105:41].

Moses was led by God to find the precious water which was hidden from the eyes of men.

See the commentary on 1 Corinthians 10:4, *New Testament Commentary*. Also, see article on the "Rock," Numbers 20:7-11.

MEDEBA

We have shot at them; Heshbon is perished even unto Dibon, and we have laid them waste even unto Nophah, which reacheth unto Medeba. Num. 21:30

"Medeba" is a mistransliteration of the Aramaic word *madebra* (wilderness). The name of the city which reached as far as the edge of the desert is *Nekhakh*. In Palestine there are many towns on the edge of deserts, and some in the wilderness itself. They are built near wells or an oasis.

BALAAM

He sent messengers therefore unto Balaam the son of Beor to Pethor, which is by the river of the land of the children of his people, to call him, saying, Behold, there is a people come out from Egypt: behold, they cover the face of the earth, and they abide over against me. Num. 22:5

Balaam was an Aramean-Syrian who had a knowledge of divination and the gift of prophesying. The Arameans were kindred of the Hebrews. Some of them believed in the God of Abraham.

When Laban the Aramean pursued Jacob, the Lord warned him in a dream to deal justly with Jacob [Gen. 31:21-24].

Balaam spoke in his Aramean dialect, and the king of Moab was able to understand him. The Moabites were the descendants of Lot, a nephew of Abraham and a cousin of Laban the Aramean.

When Balaam was determined to deliver the divine oracle, God endowed him with power to speak the truth and to reveal that which is hidden from the eyes of men.

SOOTHSAYERS

*And Balaam rose up in the morning, and saddled his ass, and
went with the princes of Moab.*   Num. 22:21

Balaam was a native of Pethor on the Euphrates, but at this time he
was residing in Syria or the land of Arnon [see verse 36]. The distance
from the Euphrates to the hills behind the Dead Sea would have taken
many days.

In the East, no matter where people live, they are identified by the
land of their nativity. Then again, the soothsayers and the magicians
travel from one place to another, telling fortunes and predicting events
and uttering oracles. They are consulted by kings, princes, and the
wealthy. And some of them are engaged in black magic.

IN A TRANCE

*And God's anger was kindled because he went: and the angel of
the Lord stood in the way for an adversary against him. Now he
was riding upon his ass, and his two servants were with him.*
                                                         Num. 22:22

All the communications between the Lord and the prophets took place
in visions, dreams, or some form of ecstasy. In verse 20 we read, "And
God came unto Balaam at night, and said unto him, If the men come to
call thee, rise up, and go with them; but yet the word which I shall say
unto thee, that shalt thou do." Balaam "saw the vision of the Almighty,
falling into a trance, but having his eyes open" [Num. 24:16].

At the outset Balaam was firm in his convictions and was loyal to God.
But when King Balak increased his reward and sent princes to persuade
him, Balaam was inclined to go. His refusal to go was merely an Eastern
custom. He knew the king would send messengers again and offer more
gifts. Easterners usually refuse when first invited. This is why the king
persevered in asking him to come.

In verse 20 God said to Balaam, "If the men come . . ." God knew
what was in the heart of Balaam. He knew he was eager to go to receive
gifts and honors. In other words, God tried out Balaam. This is why
his anger kindled against him.

"The angel of the Lord" in this case means God's counsel; that is,
God was really opposed to Balaam's mission to curse the Israelites.

A TALKING ASS

And the Lord opened the mouth of the ass, and she said unto Balaam, What have I done unto thee, that thou hast smitten me these three times?   Num. 22:28

Aramaic literature contains many such episodes, such as speaking asses which at times acted as advisers to their masters, and even spoke on their behalf before governors. Balaam was riding on his she-ass, Aramaic *atana*. The Aramaic word for "ass" is *khemara*.

In Aramaic, the term ass means sheer stupidity. We often say, "An ass is wiser than you" or "An ass could have given a better speech than you." Such sayings are general in Eastern speech.

No doubt God can make an animal speak and rebuke its rider. But the incident here might be used parabolically in rebuking Balaam for his stupidity. In other words, the ass knew more than Balaam did. In English we would say, "His conscience bothered him." Balaam was guilty of misconduct in using his prophetic powers for the sake of material rewards and worldly gains. Balaam in his heart wanted to please both God and King Balak.

On the other hand, divine communication generally takes place when the prophet is asleep or in a trance. God came to Balaam at night [Num. 22:20]. And in Num. 24:16 we are told that Balaam saw the vision of the Almighty when he had fallen into a trance. [See article on Visions.]

BAAL WORSHIP

And it came to pass on the morrow, that Balak took Balaam, and brought him up into the high places of Baal, that thence he might see the utmost part of the people.   Num. 22:41

Baal, Aramaic *Baala*, means Lord, husband, or a kind of deity concerned with husbandry or agriculture. In other words, *Baala* was the god of fertility.

Baal or *Baala* was generally worshiped in fertile regions such as Damascus and Lebanon where the soil was rich and water was abundant. There is a great contrast between fertile Lebanon and the poor and dry Judean hills.

Moreover, the worship of Baal was sensual. The people ate, drank, and practiced whoredom in the temples of Baal.

The Israelites, having poor soil and scanty water, often were lured by the sensual Baal worship; time and again they fell victims to it. Baal worship was common in biblical lands. Its altars, temples, and shrines were built on high places, and there people worshiped the god of nature, which they thought had provided them with material things.

SACRIFICES AND DIVINATION

And Balaam said unto Balak, Build me here seven altars, and pre-pare me here seven oxen and seven rams.   Num. 23:1

Sacrifices were used by the Hebrews, as well as by the pagans, for divination. The person who inquired of a deity offered a burnt offering to the god.

The people in those days believed that gods were pleased with the savor of the burnt offerings. The priests and soothsayers lived on what the people offered to their gods.

While the meat was being broiled, the prophet meditated and gave an oracle to the royal inquirer who stood by his offering. Balaam was told by God to speak the truth and to bless Israel, which Balaam did, much to the displeasure of the king of Moab.

ALTARS PREPARED

And God met Balaam: and he said unto him, I have prepared seven altars, and I have offered upon every altar a bullock and a ram.   Num. 23:4

Tayibt (you have prepared) has been confused with *taybit* (I have prepared). The difference between "I have" and "you have" is a single dot over or under the letter "t."

The altars were prepared by Balaam, and God was telling him that he had seen what he had done. God did not prepare the altars, but God heard Balaam and knew what was in his heart. Now God was to tell him what to do.

DUST OF JACOB

Who can count the dust of Jacob, and the number of the fourth part of Israel? Let me die the death of the righteous, and let my last end be like his!   Num. 23:10

Dust in this case means "multitude." In biblical days high figures such as millions and billions were unknown. The people used dust, the sand of the sea, and the stars of heaven when speaking of large numbers [Isa. 40:12].

Balaam was told that Israel was destined to multiply and become a great nation.

GOD IS NOT A MAN

God is not a man, that he should lie; neither the son of man, that he should repent: hath he said, and shall he not do it? or hath he spoken, and shall he not make it good? **Num. 23:19**

The Eastern text reads: "neither the son of man that he should be given counsel . . ."

The Aramaic word *nithmlikh* is derived from *melakh* (to give counsel). What the author of Numbers means here is that God does not need counsel from men.

A MESSIANIC PROPHECY

He shall pour the water out of his buckets, and his seed shall be in many waters, and his king shall be higher than Agag, and his kingdom shall be exalted. **Num. 24:7**

The Eastern text reads: "A man shall rise up from among his sons . . ." The reference here is to the coming of the Messiah whose kingdom is exalted above all kingdoms.

Water is symbolic of light, understanding, and abundance. Just as the people in arid lands are thirsty for water, so are they in need of enlightenment. Rich men who own wells dispense water to the poor and to thirsty travelers. The term "seed" means both offspring and teaching; that is, the seed of Jacob was to spread all over the world, and the Messiah would become the Light of the world.

Agag was a tall king, but the term higher is used metaphorically, meaning "exalted." All these references are relative to the spiritual mission of Israel and not to a political kingdom.

Balaam saw that Israel was called for a great mission, to become a light to the Gentiles. This prophecy was fulfilled in Jesus Christ, who shared the true religion of the Jews with the Gentile world. ". . . there shall come a Star out of Jacob, and a Sceptre shall rise out of Israel . . ." [Num. 24:17].

EXCELLENCY

*God brought him forth out of Egypt; he hath as it were the
strength of a unicorn: he shall eat up the nations his enemies, and
shall break their bones, and pierce them through with his arrows.*
                                                          Num. 24:8

The Aramaic word *bromey* is derived from *rom* (to become high). It
means "high in his excellency." The Aramaic word for a wild bull,
buffalo, and unicorn is *rema*. The first word is written with a preposition
and a genitive; otherwise, the two words are very close to one another
and can easily be confused.

The reference here is to the power and greatness of God, who brought
Israel out of the land of Egypt with a mighty hand. He was to destroy
their enemies, also.

ADVERTISE YOU

*And now, behold, I go unto my people: come therefore, and I
will advertise thee what this people shall do to thy people in the
latter days.*   Num. 24:14

The Aramaic word *melakh* means "to give counsel." The Eastern text
reads: ". . . come, therefore, and I will give you counsel . . ." The
term "advertise thee," as we know it today, is wrong.

In biblical days both pagan and Hebrew kings relied on the counsel
of their prophets, who acted as statesmen in times of war and emergencies.
The king of Moab needed no advertising from Balaam. What he
wanted from him was to curse the children of Israel who were menacing
his border, and to give him counsel how to fight them. Balaam caused
Israel to sin when the people committed whoredom with the daughters of
Moab.

This error also occurs in Ruth 4:4.

STAR OUT OF JACOB

*I shall see him, but not now: I shall behold him, but not nigh:
there shall come a Star out of Jacob, and a Sceptre shall rise out
of Israel, and shall smite the corners of Moab, and destroy all the
children of Sheth.*   Num. 24:17

"A Star" in this case means "hope" and "light." In Aramaic "His star
is out" or "His star is shining" means "His fortune is high" or "His

expectations are bright." On the other hand, "His star is dark" means "His hope is lost."

Easterners travel by stars. They rejoice when they see the star which they follow on their journeys. The stars give light by night as the sun gives light by the day [Jer. 31:35]. In pagan religions stars had something to do with deities. "We have seen his star in the East" [Matt. 2:2].

The term "Sceptre" means "a rule of justice and righteousness" [Gen. 49:10; Ps. 45:6; Heb. 1:8]. All these references are relevant to the messianic hopes of Israel which were to be fulfilled in the future by the Messiah, or *Meshikha*, Christ.

ASSYRIAN POWER

And he looked on the Kenites, and took up his parable, and said,
Strong is thy dwelling place, and thou puttest thy nest in a rock.
Nevertheless the Kenite shall be wasted, until Asshur shall carry
thee away captive.   Num. 24:21-22

The reference here is to the growing power of Assyria, a nation east of the River Euphrates. Assyria hitherto was not even heard of by the common people, but learned men such as Balaam knew of other great races and peoples who inhabited other parts of the world. Moreover, Balaam, being an Aramean, knew about Assyria.

The Kenites were kindred of the Midianites. In Judges we are told that Heber the Kenite, a descendant of Hobab, the father-in-law of Moses, was a member of one of the Midianite tribes [Judg. 4:11]. Migratory tribes often are called by the name of the tribe to which they belong instead of by the name of their race. This is also true of Arab and other tribes in the Near East. Some tribes never use their ethnic name. For example, the Lors and the Bakhtiars are called by the name of the tribe, but their racial name is Irani or Parsi.

Moreover, the Midianites, the Kenites, and the Moabites were not only a kindred people but they also lived close to each other. Balaam could see some of the territory of these people from the top of the mountain.

During the time of the invasion of Palestine by Assyria, many of these races were amalgamated. They were either called Edom or the Arameans of Damascus in Syria. The Assyrian kings conquered all these peoples in the eighth century B.C. Ashur and Eber represented the Semitic power east of the River Euphrates. Eber was the father of the Hebrews [Gen. 10:21; 11:14].

CHINA

And ships shall come from the coast of Chittim, and shall afflict
Asshur, and shall afflict Eber, and he also shall perish for ever.

Num. 24:24

The Aramaic reads *Ketaye. Araa di-ketaye* means the land of "China"
(Gatey), also known as Gog. The people east of Iran (Persia) were
known as Chinese. The Assyrians, Babylonians, Arameans, and Persians
had some contacts with China, the land of many peoples, ". . . the number of whom is as the sand of the sea" [Rev. 20:8]. These are the lands
in the Far East from which spices, ivory, and elephants were brought to
King Solomon. Some authorities think that Chittim is Crete, but the
latter has no ivory, elephants, or spices. China and Mongolia were
known to the Hebrews, Egyptians, and the Arabians. They were called
Gog and Magog [Ezek. 38:2; 39:1, 6; Rev. 20:7-9].

"Chittim" is a plural form of *Ketaye,* Chinese.

The Arameans (Syrians) of *Zur,* Tyre, had markets in all parts of
the known world and they brought spices, frankincense, elephants, and
other things from India and the Far East. On the other hand, these lands
were not too far from Persia and Assyria.

In the twelfth century the armies of Kublai Khan, under the command
of his grandson, Hulago, devastated Persia, Assyria, and most of
Palestine. They were defeated not far from Jerusalem.

China is mentioned in Genesis, Isaiah, Jeremiah and Ezekial.

BAAL-PEOR

And they called the people unto the sacrifices of their gods: and
the people did eat, and bowed down to their gods.
And Israel joined himself unto Baal-peor: and the anger of the
Lord was kindled against Israel.

Num. 25:2-3

Baal-peor, the lord of Peor, was the name of a mountain upon which
the Moabites sacrificed and worshiped their gods. It was on the top of
this mountain that Balaam admonished King Balak to build seven altars
and to sacrifice seven bullocks and seven rams [Num. 23:28-29].

"Joined himself to Baal-peor" means the people of Israel were initiated
at the pagan ceremonies. The Moabites and Midianites through the
counsel of Balaam invited many Israelites to participate in the strange,
alluring, and sensual pagan ritual. The Israelites had just come from
the desert and were ignorant of the dangers of this immoral and licentious

pagan rite. Twenty-four thousand Israelites died with the plague, and the Lord was angry at Israel.

Moses was so enraged that he commanded the judges of Israel to slay every man who had joined Baal-peor [Num. 25:1-5].

PRINCES EXPOSED

And the Lord said unto Moses, Take all the heads of the people, and hang them up before the Lord against the sun, that the fierce anger of the Lord may be turned away from Israel. Num. 25:4

Reshey, in Aramaic, means "chiefs," "leaders," "princes," and "head men." The Eastern text reads: "And the Lord said to Moses, Take all the chiefs of the people and expose them before the Lord . . ." That is to say, "Take all the princes and bring them before the people and expose them publicly before the Lord."

The princes of Israel had been negligent in their duties, and lax in enforcing the law. Consequently, many of the Israelites committed fornications with the Moabite women, and twenty-four thousand people died of disease. Therefore God was angry with the leaders of Israel who themselves had been guilty of this act.

Balaam, after failing to curse Israel, devised a snare in which to entrap thousands of desert Israelites in the mysterious worship which was known as Baal-peor. This was a kind of pagan ritual with immoral practices and pagan rites. The children of Israel committed sins so openly that they even brought Medianite women to their tents openly. The worship of Baal-peor was so common that it was done even in the presence of Moses and the elders. [See verse 6.]

Moses could not have hanged up *all* the people, and the Lord could not have demanded such an act from him, because he would not have wanted to destroy all Israel. But Moses was instructed by God to expose the princes in the daylight; that is, openly, because many of them were involved in the practice of Baal-peor.

The mistranslation was caused by the Aramaic word *reshey* (chiefs, princes) and the word *parsa,* from *paras* (to expose). The translators confused the word "expose" with the word "hang up."

When the shepherds become disloyal and negligent, the sheep go astray. But the shepherds, and not the sheep, are held responsible. God wanted to see the leaders of Israel exposed and punished for the evil of Baal-peor, which caused such widespread death in Israel.

MOUNTAIN OF THE HEBREWS

And the Lord said unto Moses, Get thee up into this mount Abarim, and see the land which I have given unto the children of Israel. Num. 27:12

"Abarim" is a mistransliteration of the Aramaic noun *Ebraye* (the Hebrew). This mountain was called Mount Ebraye simply because the early Hebrews dwelt in that region.

When Abraham and Lot parted from each other and divided the land between them, Lot chose all the lands west of Jordan [Gen. 13:8-12]. At this early time the whole tribe which came from Assyria with Abraham and his nephew Lot were known as *Ebraye*, from the Aramaic word *abar* (to cross over). The Hebrews had crossed the River Euphrates and were known by their kindred on the other side of the river as Hebrews [Num. 33:47].

A SACRED VOW

If a woman also vow a vow unto the Lord, and bind herself by a bond, being in her father's house in her youth;

And her father hear her vow, and her bond wherewith she hath bound her soul, and her father shall hold his peace at her; then all her vows shall stand, and every bond wherewith she hath bound her soul shall stand.

But if her father disallow her in the day that he heareth, not any of her vows, or of her bonds wherewith she hath bound her soul, shall stand; and the Lord shall forgive her, because her father disallowed her. Num. 30:3-5

Even today many Easterners make vows and keep them. A vow is a solemn pledge made before God; therefore, the breaking thereof is a great sin.

The reference here is to a young girl who makes a vow while living with her father and mother. In such a case the father of the girl can cancel the vow.

Even today young women in the East sometimes vow not to marry but to devote all their lives to God's work. But when they become of age and find that they cannot keep the vow, the vow is canceled by their parents and they are permitted to marry. This is because they had vowed when they were too young.

Paul gives permission to the fathers of virgins who had made a vow to let them marry. In 1 Corinthians 7:36 he says:

"If any man thinks that he is shamed by the behavior of his virgin daughter because she has passed the marriage age and he has not given her in marriage and that he should give her, let him do what he will and he does not sin. Let her be married."

[See also Lev. 27:2 Eastern text.]

VOWS OF MARRIED WOMEN

But every vow of a widow, and of her that is divorced, wherewith they have bound their souls, shall stand against her.   Num. 30:9

The Aramaic word *shabikta* is derived from *shebak* (to leave, let go, put away, repudiate, desert; to keep, permit, allow, spare).

The reference here is to a woman who is deserted or put away, but not legally divorced. *Shabikta dwnamosa* is "a legally divorced woman."

Sherita, derived from *shara* (to loosen, untie, revoke) here means "divorced." These terms are so close in their meaning that the divorce question has been difficult for Western people to explain from the Scriptures.

The term *nishrey;* that is, "divorcement by giving divorce papers," is used in Deuteronomy 24:1. *Ketaba shokana* means "a bill of divorce or a bill of release." The Aramaic *dolala* means "legal separation."

In Matthew 5:31 Jesus uses the term *sharey* (divorce, put away forever).

Nishrey also is used in Matthew 19:9. *Nishrey attey* (divorces his wife) is used in Mark 10:11 (Eastern text). Note that the word *nishbok* is not used. When *nishbok* (to leave, desert) is used, it means that the woman had been deserted and then divorced. At times, a woman is deserted or put away, but her husband takes her back again. But once a woman is legally divorced, she cannot be taken back by her former husband.

Luke also uses the term *nishrey* (divorce). "He who divorces his wife and marries another commits adultery; and he who marries the one who is illegally separated commits adultery" [Luke 16:18, Eastern text].

The Catholic and Apostolic Churches of the East, from the earliest times, have permitted divorce on the grounds of adultery and desertion (after 11 years). The innocent party c\u0131n marry again. This is because Easterners understand the difference between a woman who is put out by her husband for no grounds and the one who is legally divorced and given a bill of divorcement.

The vows of widows and of women who were put away were to stand.

This is because these woman were of age; that is, they understood the meaning of the sacred vow.

See the article on "Divorce."

SOUL—SPIRIT

And levy a tribute unto the Lord of the men of war which went out to battle: one soul of five hundred, both of the persons, and of the beeves, and of the asses, and of the sheep.   Num. 31:28

The Aramaic word *naphsha* (Hebrew *nephesh*) in this instance, means "a person." However, *naphsha* also means "breath" and sometimes "soul." The Eastern text reads: "And levy a tribute for the Lord from the men of war who went out to battle; out of all the congregation, one person of every five hundred, both of the persons and of the oxen and of the asses and of the sheep."

Jacob's children and grandchildren who went with him into Egypt are spoken of as souls, but they were living persons and not the souls of dead people. *Naphsha* means "a living person." Even today, we still say, "How many souls are in the family?" meaning persons.

Just as there is a difference between atoms and electrons, there is a difference between the soul and the spirit—one is finer than the other. The core of an atom is the smallest particle thereof.

The soul or life is subject to death, but the spirit is indestructible. Jesus said, "It is the spirit that quickeneth; the flesh profiteth nothing: the words that I speak unto you, they are spirit, and they are life" [John 6:63], which means eternal life.

The soul or life is subject to death and resurrection, but the spirit is the essence of life. The spirit can depart from a person just as it departs from the soul.

Animals have life, and are called *nephshatha* (heads), but they are never identical with men, for men were created in God's image and endowed with his Spirit.

REBEKAH

And they took their journey out of the wilderness of Sin, and encamped in Dophkah.   Num. 33:12

The Aramaic reads *Raphka* (Rebekah). The letters *resh* (r) and *daleth* (d) are identical, with the exception of the dot over or under the letter. When the dot is over the letter it reads "r," and when the dot is under the letter it reads "d."

LOTS

*And ye shall divide the land by lot for an inheritance among
your families; and to the more ye shall give the more inheritance,
and to the fewer ye shall give the less inheritance: every man's
inheritance shall be in the place where his lot falleth; according to
the tribes of your fathers ye shall inherit.*   Num. 33:54

The system of dividing by lots is very old. It must have been used by
other races prior to its adoption by the Israelites.

In many parts of the Near East dividing of the land, dry goods, fish,
and other things by lots is still common. This practice is considered
fair for all the parties concerned.

At the outset the land is measured and marked. Then lots are thrown
on it. Each lot is marked with the name of one of the men who is
concerned in the deal. When the land is divided, everyone is happy,
believing that God caused his lot to fall on his portion.

THORNS IN YOUR SIDES

*But if ye will not drive out the inhabitants of the land from be-
fore you; then it shall come to pass, that those which ye let remain
of them shall be pricks in your eyes, and thorns in your sides, and
shall vex you in the land wherein ye dwell.*   Num. 33:55

The term "thorn" here means grievance, worry, or annoyance. In
the East, even today, we often say, "He has been a thorn in my flesh."
This is because in that part of the world people suffer from thorns and
briers. In the olden days, when surgical instruments were unknown,
thorns remained in the flesh until they decayed. Once the thorn was in,
it was difficult to get it out.

Thorns and thistles are used allegorically, referring to enemies [Ezek.
28:24]. Paul, in his epistle to the Corinthians, speaks of the thorn in
his flesh [2 Cor. 12:7]. Paul had many enemies who tried to discredit
him. Paul had not been with Jesus, and therefore his apostleship was
doubted and even attacked by his enemies. Otherwise, Paul was healthy
and physically strong.

The Israelites were warned against the remnant of the pagan people
in Palestine who were to become a snare to them and a thorn in their
flesh if they should remain in the land. The Israelites were told to destroy
them.

See commentary on Thorn, *New Testament Commentary*, page 314.

SEA OF CHINNERETH

And the coast shall go down from Shepham to Riblah, on the east side of Ain; and the border shall descend, and shall reach unto the side of the sea of Chinnereth eastward.   Num. 34:11

Chinnereth means a "harp," "cithara," or "lyre." This was the old name for the Sea of Galilee, which resembles the shape of a chinnereth, Aramaic *kinareth* (harp, cithara) [Deut. 3:17; Josh. 11:2].

The names of many cities, towns, and other localities were changed by the Israelites after the occupation of Palestine.

TWO WITNESSES

Whoso killeth any person, the murderer shall be put to death by the mouth of witnesses: but one witness shall not testify against any person to cause him to die.   Num. 35:30

The legal concept of having two witnesses stemmed from the ancient tribal custom. When Laban and Jacob made a covenant they made a heap and erected a pillar which was symbolic of two parties entering into an agreement.

"And Laban said to Jacob, Behold this heap, and behold this pillar, which I have set between me and you; this heap is a witness, and this pillar is a witness, that I will not pass over this pillar against you, and that you also shall not pass over this pillar against me or this heap for harm" [Gen. 31:51-52, Eastern text]. The heap and the pillar served as a reminder between Laban and Jacob.

When written agreements and court records were unknown, pillars and heaps of stones, set by the two parties concerned, were the only reminders of a covenant or lasting agreement between the descendants of Jacob and those of Laban.

Heaps of stones and pillars are still found in many places in biblical lands. Evidently, many of them were erected as witnesses to tribal treaties, agreements, and covenants, and in honor of great conquerors. Then again, one witness may lie or be bribed, but it would be more difficult to bribe two men or to persuade them to agree to a conspiracy. One would be suspicious of the other. [See Witnesses, Deut. 17:6.]

CHAPTER FIVE

DEUTERONOMY

INTRODUCTION

THE title of this book is derived from the nature of its contents; that is, the repetition of the law. The Aramaic title of the book is *Tinyan Namosa* (the repetition of the law). This is because Deuteronomy contains many laws and ordinances which are similar to those in other books of Moses, and which were written before it.

The book might have been the one which was found by Hilkiah the scribe during the reign of Josiah [2 Kings 22:8]. Of course, Moses was not the author of chapter 34, in which the episode of his death was inscribed. This chapter was written by Joshua after the death of Moses.

The book of Deuteronomy contains many laws and ordinances, and many occurrences and events which took place when the people had come to the end of their journeys in the plains of Moab.

Many of these laws and ordinances were now needed because new problems had risen and the older ones were left behind. The people were soon to change from a purely pastoral life to a semiagricultural life. Tents were to give way to stone houses, palaces, and temples.

That Moses is the author of the book there is no doubt. No other man could have written it, describing the events in such minute detail. Nor could such laws and ordinances have been handed down orally.

STARS OF HEAVEN

The Lord your God hath multiplied you, and, behold, ye are this day as the stars of heaven for multitude. Deut. 1:10

The Babylonian and Assyrian astronomers knew that the universe was endless and that the number of the stars was infinite. The phrase "as the stars of heaven for multitude" is used figuratively, meaning "many." These statements should not be taken literally, for the stars of the heavens cannot be numbered. Even today, with our mathematical knowledge and calculating machines, we cannot number the stars.

When Moses uttered these words, figures such as million, billion, and trillion were unknown. Therefore, when people spoke of large numbers, they used stars and the sand of the sea to convey their thought.

The Jews are one of the smallest races on the earth. The descendants of Ishmael and Esau have been more numerous than those of Jacob.

See the commentaries on Genesis 15:5 and Deuteronomy 10:22.

ARMY OFFICERS

So I took the chief of your tribes, wise men, and known, and made them heads over you, captains over thousands, and captains over hundreds, and captains over fifties, and captains over tens, and officers among your tribes.   Deut. 1:15

The Aramaic term *reshy-alpey* (the heads of thousands) refers to generals or high-ranking army commanders. Today the term "captain" applies only to an officer who is in charge of 100 soldiers.

The Aramaic term *saprey* means "scribes." In the olden days, when writing was in its infancy and schools unknown, scribes occupied a high position in the tribes as well as in governments; and they were indispensable in tribal and governmental organizations. They had to number the people, keep records, transact business, write letters, and record history.

It is said that the Assyrians were the first to divide their armies into divisions, regiments, and companies. In the course of time the Assyrian system and its military organization was adopted by smaller powers.

TURNING BACKWARD

But as for you, turn you, and take your journey into the wilderness by the way of the Red sea.   Deut. 1:40

The people who had left Egypt had murmured in their tents and spoken unwisely against the Lord. Therefore, they were barred from entering the good land which the Lord had promised them [verse 27]. Now they were commanded to turn backward into the vast wilderness by way of the Red Sea, to wander until the generation which had left Egypt was consumed.

Nevertheless, their children, who had been born in the wilderness and who knew nothing about Egypt and its luxuries, were innocent and fit to enter into the Promised Land [verse 39].

Murmuring against Moses and mistrust of the Lord were responsible for the doom which fell upon the people in the wilderness.

THE EDOMITES RESPECTED

And command thou the people, saying, Ye are to pass through the coast of your brethren the children of Esau, which dwell in Seir; and they shall be afraid of you: take ye good heed unto yourselves therefore:

Meddle not with them; for I will not give you of their land, no, not so much as a footbreadth; because I have given mount Seir unto Esau for a possession. Deut. 2:4-5

The children of Esau, or the Edomites, were the descendants of Isaac and of Abraham, and hence heirs to the promise which God had made with Abraham and Isaac [Gen. 17:21]. Being the descendants of Abraham, they were also granted certain territories in the land which God had promised to Abraham and Isaac and their descendants. On the other hand, even though Esau had sold his birthright, he was the firstborn of Isaac, and his father blessed him, too [Gen. 27:38-39].

In reality, all the descendants of Abraham and Isaac were blessed by God and assured of being great peoples and kingdoms. Moreover, God had blessed both Ishmael and Esau. "And as for Ishmael, I have heard you; behold, I have blessed him, and will multiply him, and will make him exceedingly great; twelve princes shall he beget, and I will make him a great nation" [Gen. 17:20, Eastern text].

The Arabs, descendants of Abraham, believe that they are the children of the promise. Mohammed says that he is the blessing which God bestowed upon Ishmael. Nearly three quarter billion people are blessed by the religion of Islam, which was founded by Mohammed, a descendant of Ishmael, the firstborn of Abraham.

WELLS RENTED

Ye shall buy meat of them for money, that ye may eat; and ye shall also buy water of them for money, that ye may drink.

Deut. 2:6

In the Sinai and Arabian deserts where water is scarce, wells are rented, and water is sold for money or sheep. In these arid regions wells are the property of wealthy landowners or powerful tribes. Then again, in some areas wells are the property of those who dug them.

Strangers and migratory tribes must pay for the use of wells and grazing rights. Some of the tribes refuse to grant grazing permits and the usage of their wells, especially during long droughts, when some of the wells are dry, or when political conditions are uncertain [Gen. 26:15, 25; John 4:6].

MOABITES AND AMMONITES

And the Lord said unto me, Distress not the Moabites, neither contend with them in battle: for I will not give thee of their land for a possession; because I have given Ar unto the children of Lot for a possession. Deut. 2:9

The Moabites and Ammonites were the descendants of Lot, a nephew of Abraham. When the Lord commanded Abraham to leave his country and his kindred, Lot went with him [Gen. 12:4].

When Abraham and Lot parted, Lot chose the land east of the Jordan, and Abraham remained west of the Jordan [Gen. 13:10-12].

Thus, the Moabites, being the descendants of Lot, were protected by the oral or written agreement between Abraham and his nephew Lot. In the olden days agreements and covenants were respected for centuries after they were made [Deut. 2:19, 37].

THIRTY-EIGHT YEARS

And the space in which we came from Kadesh-barnea, until we were come over the brook Zered, was thirty and eight years; until all the generation of the men of war were wasted out from among the host, as the Lord sware unto them. Deut. 2:14

The generation which came out of Egypt was a rebellious one. They had been accustomed to Egyptian luxuries, meats, fruits, and bread.

After their departure from Egypt they confronted many desert difficulties and food and water shortages. They were sorry they had listened to Moses and left Egypt, for they saw no hope beyond the arid desert, and they were not interested in the religion of their forefathers.

Moses knew that these people would be dissatisfied with Palestine, for Palestine, also, is an arid land when compared with the fertile Nile delta. So God advised Moses to wander in the desert until all the men who had left Egypt had died. The new generation which had been born in the desert would be happy to cross over into Palestine.

Palestine is a paradise when compared with the desert. There is some honey, milk, grapes, and a few other fruits and vegetables, but it cannot be compared with Egypt.

Joshua, the son of Nun, and Caleb were the only two men who had left Egypt who were to enter into Palestine. Both of these men were faithful.

GIANTS

That also was accounted a land of giants: giants dwelt therein in old time; and the Ammonites call them Zamzummim;

A people great, and many, and tall, as the Anakims; but the Lord destroyed them before them; and they succeeded them, and dwelt in their stead.   Deut. 2:20-21

The Eastern text reads *ganbarey* (giants). In the East tall men who are physically strong are known as mighty men or giants.

Ganbarey in this instance, is the name of the people who produced giants and valiant men of war like Goliath, Sheshai, Ahiman, and Talmai.

Anakims (giants) were the early inhabitants of Palestine who dwelt in Hebron and other mountain towns in Judah. They were destroyed by Joshua [Josh. 11:21]. Hebron was given to Caleb [Judg. 1:20].

THE AVIMS

And the Avim which dwelt in Hazerim, even unto Azzah, the Caphtorim, which came forth out of Caphtor, destroyed them, and dwelt in their stead.   Deut. 2:23

The Avims (Avites) were the primitive inhabitants of southwest Palestine; they dwelt in Gaza. They were conquered and finally destroyed by the immigrants from Capedoci (*Caphedoki*). In the book of Joshua the Philistines are called Avites [Josh. 13:3].

WOMEN AND LITTLE ONES SLAIN

And we took all his cities at that time, and utterly destroyed the men, and the women, and the little ones, of every city, we left none to remain.   Deut. 2:34

Moses, as a spokesman for God, had admonished the people to destroy all the Amorites west of Jordan. Even the women and the little ones were to be put to the edge of the sword.

One reason for the destruction of the women and the little ones was that the inhabitants of the land had become corrupt in their religion and their way of life, and, as a result, immorality was rampant and disease prevalent among the people. The other reason was the scarcity of land. There was insufficient land for the native inhabitants and for the new-comers, the Israelites.

But the Israelites were united, strong, and determined to possess the land, so they fought valiantly. The Israelites were told not to show mercy on the inhabitants of the land, but to destroy them utterly [Deut. 3:6; 7:2].

These ordinances seem cruel in the eyes of modern readers of the Bible. But it must be remembered that in those early days it was not uncommon for one tribe to exterminate another. Years ago, even Arab tribes in the desert sometimes utterly destroyed each other. Then again, in biblical days everything was done in the name of God, because God was the king or ruler of the tribe. The pagans did the same; and at times the followers of God committed the same crimes against defenseless women and children.

ADDITIONS AND OMISSIONS

Ye shall not add unto the word which I command you, neither shall ye diminish aught from it, that ye may keep the commandments of the Lord your God which I command you.   Deut. 4:2

In the olden days the revealed Word was considered sacred and pure, and therefore no one dared to add to it or to take anything from it. The Scriptures were carefully copied by the Hebrew scribes and were never revised. At times, important marginal notes and captions were unwittingly copied, but no one except the wicked dared to forge the sacred Word.

Even today the Eastern Christians, the Jews, and the Moslems never add or omit a word from their holy books. When a scribe finishes copying a sacred manuscript, other scribes and priests examine it. If a word is added or omitted, the new book cannot be dedicated until the error is corrected. Years ago, even the words and letters were counted [Deut. 12:32].

"Do not add to his words; lest he reprove you, and you be found a liar" [Prov. 30:6].

A great many difficulties in our Western versions of the Bible are due to constant revisions, additions, and omissions from the sacred Word. Indeed, translations are subject to revisions, in order to strengthen the meaning. But additions and omissions are contrary to the Word of God.

AMPLIFICATION

And ye came near and stood under the mountain; and the mountain burned with fire unto the midst of heaven, with darkness, clouds, and thick darkness.   Deut. 4:11

"Unto the midst of heaven" means "high into the sky." In Semitic languages the same word that means heaven also means sky and universe. Easterners, when describing a strange phenomenon, generally amplify it in order to impress the hearer or the reader. In biblical days, all the space above the earth was known as heaven, the dwelling place of God.

We often say, "The smoke went up to heaven." In Deuteronomy 9:1 we read of cities in Palestine which were fenced up to heaven. The walls of these cities could not have been more than twenty or thirty feet high. "Fenced up to heaven" means "very, very high."

HUMAN IMAGES

Take ye therefore good heed unto yourselves; for ye saw no manner of similitude on the day that the Lord spake unto you in Horeb out of the midst of the fire;

Lest ye corrupt yourselves, and make you a graven image, the similitude of any figure, the likeness of male or female.
                                                   Deut. 4:15-16

The warning here is against making an engraved image, or the likeness of the Lord [Exod. 20:4]. Pagan gods were made of gold and silver. Their adherents worshiped them and carried them upon their shoulders. God is the Eternal Spirit. He has no likeness, nor does he dwell in temples made by hands [Acts 17:24-29]. Not even Moses was able to see the face of the Lord, but he saw his presence and glory.

Not only the likeness of God was forbidden to be portrayed, but also the likeness of any beast or any fowl of the air [Exod. 20:3-5]. This is because the pagans lowered themselves and worshiped animals, birds, and images. When Moses was on Mount Sinai the Israelites made a golden calf and started worshiping it as their god [Exod. 32:4; Deut. 9:16].

Moses expressly states that there was no similitude (form), but God's voice was heard. That is to say, the ears of the men who had sanctified themselves and came near the presence of God could hear his words as though they fell from the mouth of a man.

FISH WORSHIPED

The likeness of any thing that creepeth on the ground, the likeness of any fish that is in the waters beneath the earth.

                                                            Deut. 4:18

Man, in his quest to find the true religion, worshiped many kinds of animals, reptiles, and fish.

When religion was in its infancy people believed that every creature was created and governed by a certain god. For example, Baal-zebub was the god of flies; Baal-bak, the god of mosquitoes.

Fish were worshiped by the Assyrians. Ninos, the founder of Nineveh, was the fish god. Nineveh means "a fish." Until recently, some of the Assyrians considered fish so sacred that they never ate it. Then again, in northern Assyria, there were sacred pools where fish were protected and considered sacred.

Moses knew that the pagans worshiped animals, fish, serpents, and heavenly bodies. That is why he warned the Israelites not to worship them. The Egyptians and Assyrians worshiped animals, and the Persians worshiped the sun and stars.

The Israelites oftentimes transgressed God's commandments and went after other gods, worshiped all the host of heaven, and also served Baal [2 Kings 17:16].

SUN AND MOON

And lest thou lift up thine eyes unto heaven, and when thou seest the sun, and the moon, and the stars, even all the host of heaven, shouldest be driven to worship them, and serve them, which the Lord thy God hath divided unto all nations under the whole heaven.

                                                            Deut. 4:19

Ancients recognized the sun as the center of the solar system. The moon and other planets were also associated with its worship.

Indeed, the Babylonian and the Egyptian scientists, who developed the twelve-month calendar based on the sun, must have known that all planets in our universe revolved around it.

The Persians for many centuries worshiped fire simply because fire is symbolic of the sun, which they called the life-giver. Sacred fire was kept constantly burning in the temples and was zealously guarded by the priests. The Incas in Peru likewise worshiped the sun.

The Hebrew prophets and seers knew that the sun, moon, and planets were created by a greater power—God. Therefore, the Israelites were warned by Moses and by later prophets not to worship the sun and the moon and the stars, which in their days were worshiped by the pagans around them, but to keep steadfast in the pure religion of Abraham, and to worship the Living God, the Creator of heaven and earth and all that is therein.

GOD FORSAKES NOT THOSE WHO TRUST IN HIM

(For the Lord thy God is a merciful God;) he will not forsake thee, neither destroy thee, nor forget the covenant of thy fathers, which he sware unto them. Deut. 4:31

God does not forsake those who trust in him, keep his commandments, and do his will. ". . . so I will be with thee: I will not fail thee, nor forsake thee" [Josh. 1:5]. "I . . . will not forsake my people Israel" [1 Kings 6:13]. "When my father and my mother forsake me, then the Lord will take me up" [Ps. 27:10].

It is man who forsakes his Creator. God cannot forsake his children, just as a mother cannot forsake her baby. In every instance, it was Israel who forsook God and broke his commandments. But God searched for his people who had gone astray, like a shepherd who searches for a lost sheep.

"I have been young, and now am old; yet have I not seen the righteous forsaken, nor his seed begging bread" [Ps. 37:25; see also Deut. 31:8].

A REMINDER OF GOD'S WORK

For ask now of the days that are past, which were before thee, since the day that God created man upon the earth, and ask from the one side of heaven unto the other, whether there hath been any such thing as this great thing is, or hath been heard like it?
Deut. 4:32

Moses here reminds the people of the miracles and wonders which God had wrought among them: how he had brought them forth out of Egypt by a mighty hand and by a stretched out arm, how he had fed them with manna, given them water to drink in a dry land, clothed them, and defeated their enemies. There was no previous occurrence similar to this in the history of mankind.

God had been nearer to the Israelites than to any other people. He had led them and favored them, and they had even heard his voice and lived [verse 33].

Therefore the people were admonished not to forget the covenant and the laws that God had given them. And if they did, then they were to be scattered among the nations. Heaven and earth would be witnesses against them if they forsook their God and his way.

GOD SPOKE OUT OF HEAVEN

Out of heaven he made thee to hear his voice, that he might instruct thee: and upon earth he showed thee his great fire; and thou heardest his words out of the midst of the fire. Deut. 4:36

When God gave Moses the Ten Commandments, the ordinances, and the statutes, the people who stood at the foot of Mount Sinai heard God's voice as he conversed with Moses [Exod. 19:18-19].

The Lord spoke out of heaven, but the people heard him from the top of the mountain. Moreover, fire and thunder preceded God's appearance upon Mount Sinai [Deut. 5:24].

God is everywhere. Even though, according to the author of Exodus, God descended upon the mountain, God spoke out of heaven. The author of the book of Exodus, Moses, pictures God as a man descending and ascending so that the people might understand the phenomena. But the book of Deuteronomy gives us a clear concept of a spiritual God who is in heaven. Out of heaven he made the people to hear his voice and to feel his divine presence.

MOSES WAS CLOSE TO GOD

The Lord talked with you face to face in the mount out of the midst of the fire. Deut. 5:4

"Face to face" is an Eastern saying which means "person to person," openly or without intermediaries. God spoke to the people by prophets and seers. But to Moses he spoke as one person would speak to another.

Then again, God spoke to prophets in visions, similitudes, and figurative speech, but to Moses he spoke openly, or mouth to mouth [Num. 12:6-8].

See the commentary on Numbers 12:8.

NEIGHBOR'S WIFE

Neither shalt thou desire thy neighbor's wife, neither shalt thou covet thy neighbor's house, his field, or his manservant, or his maidservant, his ox, or his ass, or any thing that is thy neighbor's.
Deut. 5:21

The Eastern text reads: "You shall not covet your neighbor's wife." The Aramaic word *khabrakh* means also your "friend," "companion," "comrade," and "intimate friend." The Aramaic word for "your neighbor" is *karibakh*. In the East neighbors visit one another and talk to one another's wives, but they seldom can approach a strange woman.

Note that the sister and the daughter of the neighbor are not mentioned.

Adultery is covered in verse 18. The term "adultery" is inclusive and covers any kind of immorality. But verse 21 is specifically aimed against those who covet a neighbor's or friend's wife. In most cases in which a man covets a neighbor's wife he kills her husband, for in the East a man seldom commits adultery with a woman whose husband is alive. But when he covets her, he tries to do away with her husband, as in the case of King David and Uriah [2 Sam. 11:15].

When Abraham went to Egypt during the famine, he told Pharaoh's servants that Sarah was his sister, fearing Pharaoh would put him to death in order to have Sarah for himself [Gen. 12:13]. Isaac for the same reason told Abimeleck that Rebekah was his sister [Gen. 26:7-11].

In the East when a friend covets his friend's wife, his house, or his field, he tries to do away with him just as in the case of Ahab and Naboth [1 Kings 21:9-13].

LOYALTY TO GOD

Ye shall observe to do therefore as the Lord your God hath commanded you: ye shall not turn aside to the right hand or to the left.   Deut. 5:32

"Ye shall not turn aside to the right hand or to the left" is an Aramaic idiom which means "You shall not deviate from the Lord's commandments and his way, but you shall observe every ordinance and walk in the way of the Lord, straightforwardly."

The same idiom was used when the Lord admonished Joshua to be strong and courageous and loyal to the commandment which Moses had given him before his death [Josh. 1:7].

THE CONCEPT OF ONE GOD

Hear, O Israel: The Lord our God is one Lord.   Deut. 6:4

The concept of one God, as revealed to the early Hebrew patriarchs, was almost lost. The Hebrews were the only people who had a clear idea of monotheism. Abraham was a true believer in one God, the universal Father and the Creator of the heavens and the earth.

The Israelites had spent 400 years in Egypt and had seen the Egyptians and other races around them with many gods. In those days people thought that the more gods a nation had, the stronger and more prosperous it was. Each deity presided over a certain thing. There were gods who had control over rain, gods who had authority over flies, and others who had authority over the plagues. The concept of one God was repugnant in the eyes of great nations.

This ancient teaching of one God unified the Hebrew tribes and enabled them to withstand their enemies. When Easterners are divided on the matter of religion they are easily defeated. This is because the Easterners take their religion very seriously, and are willing to die for it. Differences in religious opinions may set a son against his father, a daughter against her mother, and a brother against his brother.

Jesus quoted these words of Moses, saying, "The first of all the commandments is, Hear, O Israel; the Lord our God is one Lord" [Mark 12:29].

WRITING OF LAWS

And thou shalt write them upon the posts of thy house, and on thy gates.   Deut. 6:9

The commandments were written on the stone tablets which were placed in the Ark of the Covenant. But copies were made available for instruction.

Writing was prevalent. Moses had many scribes, and every tribe had its own scribe. The commandments and the ordinances, just like all other portions of the Scriptures, had to be written down in order to be memorized by heart.

Moreover, the Hebrews were told to write these commandments on the doorposts, on the gates, and on their hands [Exod. 13:9, 16].

The Israelites laid strong emphasis on the keeping of the law and the ordinances. Thus, the law became the most important thing in the Jewish religion. The Israelites had been a wandering people in the desert, where few laws were needed, but now they were to enter and possess Palestine. Therefore, these laws and ordinances were a necessity for a newly established state.

A ZEALOUS GOD

(For the Lord thy God is a jealous God among you;) lest the anger of the Lord thy God be kindled against thee, and destroy thee from off the face of the earth.   Deut. 6:15

The Aramaic word *tannana* means "to be zealous and to be provoked to anger." The Lord God of Israel was not jealous of pagan images and idols, which were no gods, but he was zealous to keep his people on the right way and to prevent them from following after false and dangerous deities, whose worship was based on immoral practices and sensualities.

When the Israelites joined the form of Baal worship in Peor, which was known as Baal-peor, 24,000 men died of disease [Num. 25:3-9; Deut. 4:3]. They joined themselves unto Baal-peor and ate the sacrifices of the dead. Thus, they provoked God to anger with their inventions, and the plague broke out upon them [Ps. 106:28-29].

God is zealous to protect, guide, and lead those who trust in him, but there is no one greater than him to be jealous of.

TRIED OUT

Ye shall not tempt the Lord your God, as ye tempted him in Massah.   Deut. 6:16

The Aramaic word *nasa* means to "test," "try out," "tempt." In this instance, it means to test; that is, to try God out, or to test his ability. For instance, in Numbers 11:4 the people questioned God's ability to meet their needs.

The Israelites in the desert wanted to see whether their God could meet their needs or not. Pagan deities were supposd to meet the needs of their worshipers. In the vast and desolate wilderness the people were confronted with many strange problems and difficulties which no one could solve but a mightier power than man. The people were in need of water, food, and other necessities of life.

To tempt a person may mean to try to persuade him to deviate from his course by promising him greater rewards or something that he is otherwise unable to get. For example, Satan tempted Jesus by offering him greater rewards [Matt. 4:7]. But in this case the word means "test." The people put God to the test, or tried him out to see whether he could meet their needs. Nomad tribes rely on God for water, rain, and food.

God tempts no one, nor can he be tempted with evil. "Let no man say when he is tempted, I am tempted of God: for God cannot be tempted with evil, neither tempteth he any man" [James 1:13].

MARRIAGES WITH PAGANS

Neither shalt thou make marriages with them; thy daughter thou shalt not give unto his son, nor his daughter shalt thou take unto thy son.   Deut. 7:3

The prohibition of marriages with the Hittites, Girgashites, Amorites, and the other inhabitants of Palestine was based on religious grounds.

The Hebrews were allowed to marry the Moabites, Ammonites, Arameans (Syrians), and Edomites. These people were not only akin to the Israelites, but also were not as corrupt as the original inhabitants of Palestine. David married the daughter of the king of Gashur, and Solomon married the daughter of the king of Egypt.

Many Israelites were the victims of pagan religions which their alien wives brought with them and taught to their children. The early inhabitants of Palestine were corrupt and degenerate, and marriages with them would have weakened the Israelites.

Israel, during the reign of King Solomon, suffered from intermarriages with pagan people. The alien wives caused him to stray after pagan gods [1 Kings 11:1-8].

A HOLY PEOPLE

For thou art a holy people unto the Lord thy God: the Lord thy God hath chosen thee to be a special people unto himself, above all people that are upon the face of the earth.   Deut. 7:6

Kadisha (Hebrew *kadesh*) means "set aside," "separated," "consecrated." The Israelites were chosen or selected by God for a special mission. In other words, they were called to play the most difficult and dominant part in the divine plan which charted human destiny. Indeed, the Israelites were instruments in God's hand to reveal his love and his purposes to his children.

God was concerned about the other races and peoples just as much as he was concerned about the Israelites. The same God who had blessed Abraham had also blessed Lot and his descendants. The same God who had blessed Isaac had also blessed Ishmael and his children [Gen. 16:10; 17:20].

Many kings and princes, the descendants of Ishmael, have ruled over Arabia and, politically, have played a greater part in human history than the descendants of Isaac did over Palestine. The Arabs, the descendants of Ishmael, were the builders of one of the greatest empires in the world. Mohammed is the founder of a religion which is now established in countries all the way from Africa to India.

But the Israelites' mission was purely spiritual [Rom. 9:6-8]. They were called to bring God's truth and light into a dark world. The call and the blessings were subject to the loyalty and the obedience of the people [Deut. 28].

God does not discriminate between peoples and races, but he chooses certain races for certain purposes because of their qualifications. The Israelites were better qualified in the field of religion than other races. God chooses people for all kinds of purposes and objectives. And when they fail he rejects them and calls others. Those who believe in the faith of Abraham are the heirs to his religion [Gal. 3:29].

ISRAEL PROTECTED BY GOD

And the Lord will take away from thee all sickness, and will put none of the evil diseases of Egypt, which thou knowest, upon thee; but will lay them upon all them that hate thee. Deut. 7:15

Egypt, being a tropical land, had many plagues and diseases which were unknown in Palestine. The Egyptians suffered from swarms of flies and malaria-carrying mosquitoes. Trachoma and other eye diseases were common until recent years. But the plagues of flies and locusts still continue.

The reference here is to the plagues which Moses and Aaron brought upon the Egyptians, especially the boils with blains which broke forth upon men [Exod. 9:10-11].

The Israelites were to be protected from these plagues by means of God's love and understanding. Sanitary conditions, education, and health ordinances which God gave to Moses were to be as a lamp to their feet and a light to their path. "Unless thy law had been my delights, I should then have perished in mine affliction" [Ps. 119:92].

TRIALS

The great temptations which thine eyes saw, and the signs, and the wonders, and the mighty hand, and the stretched out arm, whereby the Lord thy God brought thee out: so shall the Lord thy God do unto all the people of whom thou art afraid. Deut. 7:19

The Aramaic word *nisioney* which is translated "temptations," in this instance, means "trials" and "difficulties." The reference here is to the people's wanderings in the desert and the difficulties they met during their journeys in the vast and desolate wilderness.

RAIDERS

Moreover the Lord thy God will send the hornet among them, until they that are left, and hide themselves from thee, be destroyed.
Deut. 7:20

The term "hornet" is used metaphorically, meaning invaders or swift raiding expeditions. In the East, raiders and oppressors are often called hornets. This is because during the harvest when the nests of hornets are disturbed they drive the reapers away. Then again, the desert raiding parties are as swift as hornets. They strike at their victims and disappear.

The inhabitants of Palestine were to be raided and made tributaries, and thus weakened. When the Israelites invaded the land under Joshua, they found the inhabitants of Palestine weak and divided among themselves.

See the commentary on Exodus 23:28.

GARMENTS LASTED LONG

Thy raiment waxed not old upon thee, neither did thy foot swell, these forty years.   Deut. 8:4

In the East the wearing of old and mended clothes is very common. One can see thousands of men and women in rags. At times there are more patches on a garment than there is original cloth. "Thy raiment waxed not old upon thee" might mean "You never wore old garments."

Rich men and women seldom wear old clothes. They give them to their servants, to beggars, and to the poor. As soon as a garment starts wearing out they give it away and wear a new one.

The Israelites were so abundantly supplied by God that they did not have to wear old garments. Nor did they have to walk barefooted. They had large flocks which supplied them with abundant wool and leather which they made into garments and shoes. In the East when a man has good clothes and a pair of shoes he is considered well-to-do. The Israelites lacked nothing during their wanderings in the desert. God met all of their needs. Such terms of speech are used to show God's care for his people.

IRON AND COPPER

A land wherein thou shalt eat bread without scarceness, thou shalt not lack any thing in it; a land whose stones are iron, and out of whose hills thou mayest dig brass.   Deut. 8:9

Granite, flint, and volcanic stone abound in Palestine. The land is full of hard burned stones, as though a severe volcanic eruption had taken place. Stones are scattered all over the face of the land. "So the Lord . . . made him to suck honey out of the rock, and oil out of the flinty rock" [Deut. 32:12-13].

Many of the metals mentioned in the Bible are found in Palestine. The land has some mineral resources, but not as abundant as other lands. Copper has been found in the Negeb. Brass is a mixture of copper and tin, and may be found in the future.

In biblical days there was little need for metals. A little iron, brass, and copper was sufficient for the needs of the tribal people. Most of their instruments were made of wood.

See the commentary on Deuteronomy 32:13.

A TERRIBLE WILDERNESS

Who led thee through that great and terrible wilderness, wherein were fiery serpents, and scorpions, and drought, where there was no water; who brought thee forth water out of the rock of flint.

Deut. 8:15

The desert in the Sinai Peninsula is noted for its severe droughts, and its scorpions and poisonous snakes. The nomad tribes have to depend on scanty water supplies and brackish wells [Num. 21:5].

Flint rock is difficult to bore and the water is far below. In Aramaic *apek lakh maya* means "who brought you forth water . . ."; that is, he struck water in a dry place, a place that man would not even try to dig. The psalmist declared that God "turned the rock into a standing water, the flint into a fountain of waters" [Ps. 114:8] and "He opened the rock, and the waters gushed out; they ran in the dry places like a river" [Ps. 105:41].

The Lord God led Moses to the places where water was hidden from human eyes and helped him to bore the rock and to bring forth water for the thirsty people. He also revealed to him the location of hidden wells.

What is impossible to man is possible to God. When the Israelites turned to God, all their needs were met. God led them to fertile places where there was grass and sources of water, and when the water was brackish he told Moses how to purify it. But when they forsook God they suffered from thirst and hunger.

See articles on Exodus 17:6; Numbers 21:16; and Psalm 105:41.

HIGH WALLS

Hear, O Israel: Thou art to pass over Jordan this day, to go in to possess nations greater and mightier than thyself, cities great and fenced up to heaven.

Deut. 9:1

"Fenced up to heaven" should not be taken literally. Of course no walls can be erected up to heaven.

"Fenced up to heaven" means "very, very high." The walls might have been twenty or thirty feet high.

Even today the walls of some of the fenced cities in the Near East are no more than twenty to twenty-five feet, and some of them are even less. For instance, the walls of Damascus and Jerusalem are no more than twenty feet high.

In the East such statements are made to convey an idea to the illiterate public, and are well understood.

See the commentary on Deuteronomy 4:11.

WICKED INHABITANTS

Understand therefore, that the Lord thy God giveth thee not this good land to possess it for thy righteousness; for thou art a stiff-necked people.   Deut. 9:6

The land was not given to the Israelites because of their righteousness, but because the original inhabitants of the land had been wicked. No doubt they had been warned but did not repent or turn from their evil ways.

It was because of this wickedness that God had promised their land to the Hebrew patriarchs, who obeyed God's laws and walked in his way. The Hebrews possessed the land, but when they refused to obey their God and walk in his ways, they also lost it. But a small remnant remained, which served God's purposes. In other words, Israel's spiritual mission was fulfilled.

GOD WROTE

And I will write on the tables the words that were in the first tables which thou brakest, and thou shalt put them in the ark.
                                                      Deut. 10:2

"And I will write" means "I will dictate." God spoke out of heaven, but Moses engraved the divine words upon two stone tablets.

In Exodus 34:27-28 we read: "And the Lord said unto Moses, Write thou these words: . . . And he wrote upon the tables (tablets) the words of the covenant, the ten commandments." Moses, through God's guidance, produced two perfect tablets which only God could have produced [Exod. 32:16].

See also the commentaries on Exodus 34:1 and 34:27-28.

CIRCUMCISING OF HEART

Circumcise therefore the foreskin of your heart, and be no more stiffnecked.   Deut. 10:16

Circumcise in this instance is used figuratively. The phrase means "Purify your heart of all evil, rebellion, and stubbornness." The circumcision of the foreskin was not enough. The people had to bring forth good fruits in order to be heirs of God's covenant which was given to Abraham [Gen. 17:10-14].

Judaism was a religion not of rites and ceremonies but of the Spirit. The people were required to change their hearts of flesh into hearts of the Spirit. The term heart means "mind" [See Deut. 30:6].

GOD OF GODS

For the Lord your God is God of gods, and Lord of lords, a great God, a mighty, and a terrible, which regardeth not persons, nor taketh reward. Deut. 10:17

This saying does not mean that there were other gods besides God the creator of heaven and earth. In the olden days the gods of the Gentiles were emperors, kings, and images of wood, silver, and gold. All these gods were created and, therefore, they were not true gods.

To be a god, one has to be able to create, but the Gentile gods not only could not create but themselves were helpless. They were fashioned by man's hands. They could neither walk nor move. "O give thanks unto the God of gods: for his mercy endureth for ever" [Ps. 136:2].

The worship of human gods, images, stars, and other heavenly bodies sprang from human longing to find the Living God, the Creator of the universe. Everything powerful in heaven and on earth was worshiped in one form or another in man's quest for the truth. The images were re-minders of the old deities which had been discarded or forgotten and had become legends.

The Israelites spoke of pagan deities as gods simply because the Gentiles believed in them and called them gods. Then again, the Israelites often forsook their God and went astray after pagan gods and worshiped images and heavenly bodies.

On the other hand, their concept of a spiritual and universal God was not yet fully crystallized. In the early days, Abraham had a true concept of God, the Creator of heaven and earth.

WATERING WITH FOOT

For the land, whither thou goest in to possess it, is not as the land of Egypt, from whence ye came out, where thou sowedst thy seed, and wateredst it with thy foot, as a garden of herbs. Deut. 11:10

In the East, when a field is irrigated, the farmer walks in it barefooted to see that every part is watered. When spades and watering instruments were scarce or unknown, the farmers used their feet to direct the water to dry spots. In some lands this ancient method prevailed until recent days, and in some places it is still in use.

Egypt is irrigated by canals which derive their water from the Nile.

Palestine is irrigated by rain and dew. But during long droughts, when the land is parched, sheep and cattle perish because of the lack of grass and water [1 Kings 18:5].

SACRED TREES

Ye shall utterly destroy all the places, wherein the nations which ye shall possess served their gods, upon the high mountains, and upon the hills, and under every green tree. Deut. 12:2

Some of the pagan altars and shrines were erected under thick green trees, where weary and thirsty travelers rested during the hot hours of the day; and the sick and suffering sought refuge under the cool and refreshing shadows. Some of the sick, because of their faith, were healed; others were helped by the cool breeze.

Tree worship was common in biblical days. People visited some of the trees for healing. They also made offerings to them. And the worshipers cut pieces from their clothes and hung them on the green boughs. Even today, some of the people in Kurdistan and northwestern Iran seek healing from the leaves of these sacred trees. They call them *manasap*. Most of these trees are feared and, therefore, are protected. No one dares to cut off their branches or even touch the fruit thereof. Among these trees are some of the rare mulberry trees with large and thick green leaves. Some of the sacred trees are visited at regular intervals.

Moses admonished the Israelites to destroy everything which the pagans worshiped and which might be a stumbling block in the way of the people [Exod. 34:13]. Gideon cut down the grove that was by the altar of Baal [Judg. 6:28].

COMMON MEAT

Notwithstanding, thou mayest kill and eat flesh in all thy gates, whatsoever thy soul lusteth after, according to the blessing of the Lord thy God which he hath given thee: the unclean and the clean may eat thereof, as of the roebuck, and as of the hart. Deut. 12:15

Animals which were slaughtered in towns were eaten by both the clean and the unclean people. This is because these animals were not taken to the holy place to be killed by the priests and the Levites and offered upon the Lord's altar. In other words, the meat of these animals was common, just like the meat of the roebuck and the hart. (Roebuck and hart were never offered upon the altar of the Lord.)

The unclean men and women were forbidden to eat of any of the sacrifices which were offered to the Lord. They had to cleanse themselves before they could eat of holy offerings. [See laws and ordinances relative to the sacrifices, Leviticus 16:16.]

SIGNS AND WONDERS TO DECEIVE

If there arise among you a prophet, or a dreamer of dreams, and giveth thee a sign or a wonder,

And the sign or the wonder come to pass, whereof he spake unto thee, saying, Let us go after other gods, which thou hast not known, and let us serve them;

Thou shalt not hearken unto the words of that prophet, or that dreamer of dreams: for the Lord your God proveth you, to know whether ye love the Lord your God with all your heart and with all your soul. Deut. 13:1-3

In biblical days a prophet was known by the predictions which he had made and the good works which he had performed, such as healing the sick and giving good counsel to kings and princes. There were too many false prophets who, from time to time, delivered false messages which confused and even frightened the people.

Moses gave this ordinance to guard against these men who acted as statesmen and counselors, for some of them took advantage of the outcome of their prediction, even when their prediction happened by chance or accident. Once the thing which was predicted came to pass, the prophet might advocate changes in government and in religion. And at that time religion and government were one. The false prophet, for his own gains, led the people astray from the way of God to worship false gods. Miracles and signs were the only convincing proofs whereby true prophets and false prophets were distinguished one from another.

Jesus was asked by the priests and Pharisees to show signs so that they might believe that he was the Messiah (Christ). But he refused to do so. Jesus did heal the sick, raise the dead, and open the eyes of the blind, but the Pharisees refused to accept these miracles as acts of God. They attributed them to the power of the devil. What they wanted was signs and wonders.

SEVERE PUNISHMENT

And that prophet, or that dreamer of dreams, shall be put to death; because he hath spoken to turn you away from the Lord your God, which brought you out of the land of Egypt, and re-deemed you out of the house of bondage, to thrust thee out of the way which the Lord thy God commanded thee to walk in. So shalt thou put the evil away from the midst of thee. Deut. 13:5

This severe punishment was prescribed by the law to guard against false prophets, magicians, soothsayers, and alarmists. The faith of some of the simple folk in the East is like that of a child. They take for granted what they hear, especially when it comes from the mouth of a man who wears a cloak of religion, or a prophet.

Some of these false prophets who pretended that the Lord had spoken to them caused the people to go astray after other gods. This statute made the so-called prophets think twice before giving ambiguous oracles and making false predictions.

GOD AS A FATHER

Ye are the children of the Lord your God: ye shall not cut your-selves, nor make any baldness between your eyes for the dead.
Deut. 14:1

The Hebrews looked upon God as the father of their tribe. This is because the people had to look to God for rain, guidance, protection, food, and health, just as children look to their father for food, safety, and protection.

Man was created in the image and likeness of God; therefore man is a child of God and dependent on him, just as a child is dependent on his father and mother.

The Hebrew concept of the fatherhood of God was spiritual. It was different from that of the pagans. The Hebrews believed that God was a spiritual Father. Such terms of speech as "begotten from God" or "Holy Spirit" are alien to the Semitic people. They believe that God, being the Eternal Spirit, never is begotten, nor does he beget. The term "God's children" is common in Eastern languages. God is looked upon as a spiritual Father and protector.

GENTILES NOT UNDER THE LAW

But of all clean fowls ye may eat.
Ye shall not eat of any thing that dieth of itself: thou shalt give
it unto the stranger that is in thy gates, that he may eat it; or thou
mayest sell it unto an alien: for thou art a holy people unto the
Lord thy God. Thou shalt not seethe a kid in his mother's milk.
Deut. 14:20-21

Some of the Mosaic laws and ordinances were relevant only to the Israelites. This was also true of the pagan religion; their ordinances and statutes were pertinent to their own people and had no relation to the adherents of alien religions. As we can see from verse 21, the Israelites were permitted to give the unclean meats to strangers, or to sell it to aliens. This is because the strangers and aliens were not under the law.

Likewise, foreigners were not to be released of debts at the end of every seven years [Deut. 15:1-3].

In the olden days the religious concepts of the people were polytheistic; every tribe or race had its own god, who loved and cared for his own people and hated the other people. At that early time even the Hebrew concept of monotheism was not yet crystallized. *Jahveh* was the God of Israel, and at times he was called the God of gods. That is to say, the Hebrews recognized other gods, but they believed that their God, the Eternal God, was greater than the gods of the Gentiles.

Then again, the Israelites were admonished not to make a covenant with the Gentiles nor with their gods [Exod. 23:32]. Moreover, the Israelites were prohibited from eating blood and the meat of strangled animals. This is because in those early days it was supposed that the life was in the blood [Gen. 9:4; Lev. 3:17]. The apostles, also, at the council of Jerusalem (A.D. 15) decided that the Gentiles must abstain from pollution of idols, from fornication, from things strangled, and from blood [Acts 15:20].

MONEY FOR OFFERINGS

And if the way be too long for thee, so that thou art not able to
carry it; or if the place be too far from thee, which the Lord thy
God shall choose to set his name there, when the Lord thy God
hath blessed thee:
Then shalt thou turn it into money, and bind up the money in
thine hand, and shalt go unto the place which the Lord thy God
shall choose. Deut. 14:24-25

"Bind up the money in thine hand" is an Aramaic idiom which means "Guard it carefully" or "Keep it before your eyes"; that is, "See that it is not used for any other cause."

The tithes were sacred. They consisted of a small portion of the increase, which was devoted to God.

The money was taken to the holy place and used to buy animal offerings and things which the worshiper desired: wine and strong drink, to eat and be merry before the Lord at the holy place, and also for the Levites who ministered to the Lord [Deut. 12:21].

DRINKING

And thou shalt bestow that money for whatsoever thy soul lusteth after, for oxen, or for sheep, or for wine, or for strong drink, or for whatsoever thy soul desireth: and thou shalt eat there before the Lord thy God, and thou shalt rejoice, thou, and thine household.
Deut. 14:26

Both wine and strong drink were permitted by Mosaic law to be drunk by the worshipers at the feasts. But the people drank moderately.

Wine and strong drink were allowed so that the people might rejoice during the day of festivities. This is because in those days feasts and other memorial days were celebrated by dancing, singing, and rejoicing before the Lord.

Drinking was forbidden in the tabernacle of the congregation. Even the priests were not to drink there [Lev. 10:8-9]. But this ordinance was at times transgressed by the priests. They drank heavily outside the holy place [Isa. 28:7-8]. And at the place of worship most of the drinking was done outdoors around the holy place, where the people had encamped [1 Sam. 1:9]. Centuries after, many of the Hebrew prophets condemned the drunkards and the misuse of wine and strong drink.

TRIBAL ETHIC

Of a foreigner thou mayest exact it again: but that which is thine with thy brother thine hand shall release. Deut. 15:3

Tribal laws and moral ethics seldom were applied to the members of strange tribes. This is because tribal people were more or less communal. All the members of the tribe were responsible for one another and for the welfare of the tribe.

During famines and severe droughts the members of the tribe shared with one another [Deut. 15:10-11].

On the other hand, the members of one tribe were not responsible for the welfare of other tribes. The tribal laws, ordinances, ethics, and hospitality were limited to the tribe itself, and denied to other tribes who were their rivals and who fought against them [verse 6].

See also the commentary on Deuteronomy 23:20.

SEASON CALENDAR

Seven weeks shalt thou number unto thee: begin to number the seven weeks from such time as thou beginnest to put the sickle to the corn.
Deut. 16:9

The Aramaic term *shaboaa* means "seven weeks," that is, 49 days. An extra day was added to make it fifty days [Lev. 23:16]. This unit of time was generally used as a division of the ecclesiastical year. This yardstick of time was also used by the pastoral people who depended on the moon and seasons and on the priestly advice in the matters concerning the calendar.

The reference here is to the feast of the harvest and the feast of the ingathering, which fell at the end of the year [Exod. 23:16].

At the feast of the harvest the people brought sheaves of their first-fruits to the priest so that the harvest might be blessed [Lev. 23:10; Deut. 16:10].

During these feasts, the people offered sacrifices to the Lord, ate and drank, and rejoiced before him.

MEMORIAL OFFERINGS

Three times in a year shall all thy males appear before the Lord thy God in the place which he shall choose; in the feast of un-leavened bread, and in the feast of weeks, and in the feast of taber-nacles: and they shall not appear before the Lord empty.
Deut. 16:16

The Eastern text reads *dokhranek* (your memorial offering). And the Aramaic word for "your males" is *dikhrek*. The two words are identical so that at times even a native may confuse one word with another.

Every man was commanded to bring an offering or a gift, according to the blessing which the Lord God had given him. The offerings were brought by the members of the family. Men, women, and children participated in these feasts [Deut. 26:1-2; 1 Sam. 1:4-7].

Memorial offerings and gift offerings generally consisted of sheep, oxen, firstfruits, and grain.

It does not seem possible that all males in Israel could have left their cities and towns and assembled in Jerusalem at the same time. There would not have been room in Jerusalem for the whole male population. Moreover, their deserted towns would have become a prey to their enemies who were round about them.

All males, and most of the women, visited the holy places from time to time. Even today, Eastern Christians and Moslems visit their holy places, some frequently, others once in a lifetime.

SCRIBES NOT OFFICERS

Judges and officers shalt thou make thee in all thy gates, which the Lord thy God giveth thee, throughout thy tribes: and they shall judge the people with just judgment.   Deut. 16:18

The Aramaic word *saprey* (Hebrew *sepher*) means "scribes." Scribes were employed by Moses and Joshua, and by judges and kings. They wrote letters, recorded deeds, and numbered the people [2 Kings 12:10; 2 Chron. 24:11; Isa. 8:1].

Scribes are also mentioned in the New Testament. Here they acted as lawyers, interpreting the law and ordinances of Moses. They were the most learned men in those days [Matt. 2:4; 7:29; Mark 1:22].

STONING

The hands of the witnesses shall be first upon him to put him to death, and afterward the hands of all the people. So thou shalt put the evil away from among you.   Deut. 17:7

"The hands of the witnesses shall be first upon him" means that the witnesses shall start to stone him first. Jesus was probably referring to this law when he said to those who accused a woman of adultery, "He that is without sin among you, let him first cast a stone at her" [John 8:7].

The whole responsibility for stoning rested on the testimony of the witnesses. This is why they had to cast the first stones at the guilty person. After that, all the people were to participate in the stoning, thus putting evil away from among them.

According to the Mosaic law, on the testimony of two or three witnesses a person was declared guilty and then put to death. The witnesses must agree.

During the trial of Jesus, the testimony of false witnesses did not agree and, therefore, the council was unable to convict him [Matt. 26:59-63; Mark 14:55].

KINGS READ THE LAW

And it shall be, when he sitteth upon the throne of his kingdom,
that he shall write him a copy of this law in a book out of that
which is before the priests the Levites. Deut. 17:18

Israel's jurisprudence was based on the law of Moses; that is, the Ten
Commandments, the ordinances, and the statutes. In those early days
copies of the law were rare and scribes few.

Sacred books were found only in the possession of the high priests
and kings, who were the sole authorities in legal matters, and who saw
that the law and ordinances were kept and executed.

When kings were crowned, the high priests read the book of the law
and charged the king with the responsibility of upholding it [2 Kings
11:12; 22:8-13].

Some of the kings were literate; others employed scribes who read to
them.

HUMAN SACRIFICES FORBIDDEN

There shall not be found among you any one that maketh his son
or his daughter to pass through the fire, or that useth divination, or
an observer of times, or an enchanter, or a witch. Deut. 18:10

The sacrificing of sons and daughters to idols was an ancient pagan
rite as old as the Bible. Pagans tried to appease the wrath of their gods
by offering one of their children as a sacrifice to them, or they sometimes
made vows pledging one of their children to the idol.

The offering of children as sacrifices to the gods was a token of loyalty
and devotion to the deity. Moses warned the people against these strange
pagan customs. ". . . for even their sons and their daughters they have
burnt in the fire to their gods" [Deut. 12:31].

Abraham was tempted to make Isaac a burnt offering to God, but the
angel of the Lord warned him not to slay his son but instead to offer a
ram. Abraham had thought that he should express his love and his devotion to God by offering his only son as a burnt offering [Gen. 22:10-13].

The Hebrews offered animal offerings. But once in a while they relapsed
into paganism and sacrificed their children to foreign gods. Jephthah
sacrificed his daughter in order to fulfill his vow [Judg. 11:29-40].

Many children were sacrificed in the Valley of Hinnom where Molech,
the god of the Ammonites, and Chemosh, the god of the Moabites, were
worshiped [1 Kings 11:7-8]. King Ahaz made his son pass through fire
[2 Kings 16:3; Lev. 18:21].

INNOCENT

Thou shalt be perfect with the Lord thy God.　　　Deut. 18:13

The Aramaic word *tamim* means "innocent," "simple," "blameless," "harmless." But in this instance it means innocent or harmless. In Aramaic, generally, the word *gimira* is used for "perfect" [Matt. 5:48].

Moses admonished the people to be innocent and harmless and pure in their minds. No human being can attain complete perfection, but people can learn to be blameless, pious, and innocent before the Lord their God.

Abraham was told by God to be faultless or blameless [Gen. 17:1].

A GREATER PROPHET

The Lord thy God will raise up unto thee a Prophet from the midst of thee, of thy brethren, like unto me; unto him ye shall hearken.　　　Deut. 18:15

Moses predicted the rise of a great Prophet like himself, who would reveal the inner meaning of the law and the prophets, and make the religion of Israel a universal religion. He knew that in the course of time some of his laws and ordinances would be misunderstood, and that God would send another Messenger, even greater than himself, to interpret his books to the world.

Moses also realized that the people would resist any interpretation or teaching which deviated from what he had written. That is why he said, "To him you shall hearken." Messiah's interpretation was to be of divine authority.

The Prophet was to be sent by God in the fullness of time, and he was to rise from among the people.

This prophecy was fulfilled in Jesus Christ, who, as a revealer of God, was the greatest since the days of Moses. He was greater than Moses, in that he spoke with authority. Moses spoke what the Lord commanded him to speak, but Christ in Jesus spoke with divine authority. He never said, "Thus said the Lord," or, "I saw in a vision," or, "An angel of the Lord said to me."

The new Prophet was to proclaim the Lord's highest revelation and to cause the light of God to shine upon other races and peoples.

He was to be Wonderful, Counselor, the Mighty God, the everlasting Father, the Prince of Peace [Isa. 9:6; 11:2].

THE MESSIAH

*I will raise them up a Prophet from among their brethren, like
unto thee, and will put my words in his mouth; and he shall speak
unto them all that I shall command him.*   Deut. 18:18

The reference here is to the coming Messiah, the Saviour of Israel and
of the world. "Their brethren" means men from one of the tribes of
Israel. Some Easterners think that "brethren" means the races which were
kindred of the Israelites. Be that as it may, this prophecy was fulfilled
when Jesus began to preach in Galilee.

Centuries after the death of Moses, Isaiah and other Hebrew prophets
predicted the coming of a Great Deliverer, who was to conquer the world
spiritually and share the Hebrew religion and law with the Gentiles.

Jesus said to the Jews: "Search the scriptures; for in them ye think ye
have eternal life: and they are they which testify of me" [John 5:39].

WARNING AGAINST FALSE PROPHETS

*When a prophet speaketh in the name of the Lord, if the thing
follow not, nor come to pass, that is the thing which the Lord hath
not spoken, but the prophet hath spoken it presumptuously: thou
shalt not be afraid of him.*   Deut. 18:22

This ordinance was written to guard against false prophets who prophesied in the name of the Lord for notoriety.

Many times the Israelites were misled by false prophets who tried to
seek fame and fortune by acting as spokesmen for God and counselors
to kings and princes [1 Kings 22:11-14].

Jonah had prophesied that Nineveh would fall, but when the great
Assyrian capital did not fall, Jonah was angry because he was in danger
of being called a false prophet. But God told Jonah that the people of
Nineveh had repented and that therefore he had spared the city and its
people [Jonah 3:10; 4:9-11].

REMOVING BOUNDARIES AND CURSES

*Thou shalt not remove thy neighbor's landmark, which they of
old time have set in thine inheritance, which thou shalt inherit in the
land that the Lord thy God giveth thee to possess it.*   Deut. 19:14

A landmark is a sharp-pointed stone set between two fields, or a pile
of stones between fields or grazing areas, to determine the boundary be-

tween the lands of different owners. And as land deeds were not clearly defined and recorded, the boundary marks were easily removed. They are removed even today.

When the stones are moved the violator suffers because of the curse that was pronounced when stones were placed between the fields [Deut. 27:17]. Many pious Easterners are afraid even to touch these boundary landmarks, fearing that when they do they will suffer injuries or misfortunes [Job 24:2; Prov. 22:28].

See also the commentary on "Landmarks," Isa. 5:8.

GENERALS

And it shall be, when the officers have made an end of speaking unto the people, that they shall make captains of the armies to lead the people.   Deut. 20:9

Reshai-khelawatha or *rab-khelawatha* means "generals" or other high army commanders; that is, the commanders of divisions and army corps. The captains, just as today, were chiefs of one hundred soldiers, and they were under the authority of the high-ranking officers.

The Hebrew military system was copied from the Midianites and Assyrians [Exod. 18:21]. The Midianites might have borrowed from the Egyptians or the Babylonians.

All of the military ranks and organizations are attributed to the Assyrians, who were versed in military science and whose methods were copied by other nations.

See "Army Commanders."

FRUIT TREES PROTECTED

When thou shalt besiege a city a long time, in making war against it to take it, thou shalt not destroy the trees thereof by forcing an axe against them: for thou mayest eat of them, and thou shalt not cut them down (for the tree of the field is man's life) to employ them in the siege.   Deut. 20:19

The Eastern text of the latter part of this verse reads: ". . . (for the trees of the field are not like men, to flee from before you at the time of the siege)." The reference here is to fruit trees, which are so essential for both the conqueror and the conquered.

In biblical days when food was scarce and transportation difficult the conquering forces lived off the land. Wicked conquerors destroyed all fruit trees and vineyards as a revenge [2 Kings 3:19]. This Mosaic ordinance was violated when Elisha commanded the kings of Israel, Judah and Edom to cut the trees and stop all wells in the cities of Moab.

FIRSTBORN

Then it shall be, when he maketh his sons to inherit that which he hath, that he may not make the son of the beloved firstborn before the son of the hated, which is indeed the firstborn.

But he shall acknowledge the son of the hated for the firstborn, by giving him a double portion of all that he hath: for he is the beginning of his strength; the right of the firstborn is his.

Deut. 21:16-17

The firstborn, being the heir of his father, receives a double portion and the homestead. The other sons were given their portions and sent away. Abraham sent Ishmael away and made Isaac, his secondborn, his heir. Ishmael was the son of Abraham's concubine.

The reference here is to a man with two wives with the same status, but one of them beloved and the other put aside or neglected. If the son of the neglected one is the firstborn, he must remain as the heir and thus receive a double portion.

Jacob bought the birthright from Esau, and thus became the heir of his father [Gen. 25:31-34]. This ancient custom is still upheld in many Near Eastern lands. The firstborn has the preference over the other sons.

See the article on "Birthright," Genesis 25:31.

GLUTTONY AND DRUNKENNESS CONDEMNED

Then shall his father and his mother lay hold on him, and bring him out unto the elders of his city, and unto the gate of his place;

And they shall say unto the elders of his city, This our son is stubborn and rebellious, he will not obey our voice; he is a glutton, and a drunkard.

Deut. 21:19-20

Glutton, in this instance, means extravagant. Easterners resent seeing their children squandering the hard-gathered family substance in riotous eating and drinking. They consider them as lost sheep, because they bring shame upon the family.

Disobedience and disrespect for parents are the real trouble in this case. The Fifth Commandment states, "Honour thy father and thy mother: that thy days may be long upon the land which the Lord thy God giveth thee"

[Exod. 20:12]. It is the breaking of this commandment which makes the above misbehavior a crime punishable by death. The rebellious person was made an example so that other men might live moderately, fear the Lord, and respect their parents.

THE ORIGIN OF THE CROSS

And if a man have committed a sin worthy of death, and he be to be put to death, and thou hang him on a tree:
His body shall not remain all night upon the tree, but thou shalt in any wise bury him that day; (for he that is hanged is accursed of God;) that thy land be not defiled, which the Lord thy God giveth thee for an inheritance.   Deut. 21:22-23

The Eastern text reads *wnezdkep* (and he is crucified). The victims were crucified in order to make them an example to the people. *Kesa* in Aramaic means "wood," and sometimes is used to mean "a forest."

The cross was made of wood found in the desert. The body of the victim was left on the cross until sunset.

Death on the cross was an Eastern custom. Joshua crucified the king of Ai in 1451 B.C. [Josh. 8:29]. The Hebrews may have discarded it and later adopted it from the Egyptians, Babylonians, or Persians. The person who was crucified was called "the accursed of God." Blasphemy against God, murder, and worship of pagan deities were considered crimes worthy of death.

Death was inflicted as a punishment for the shedding of blood [Gen. 9:6; Exod. 21:12]. Most of the guilty persons were put to death by stoning [Lev. 20:2].

Jesus was condemned and crucified for blasphemy. The high priest thought it was blasphemy when Jesus said, "Hereafter shall ye see the Son of man sitting on the right hand of power . . ." [Matt. 26:64].

DISGUISING

The woman shall not wear that which pertaineth unto a man, neither shall a man put on a woman's garment: for all that do so are abomination unto the Lord thy God.   Deut. 22:5

This ordinance apparently was written to guard against immorality and to prevent the people from deceiving one another by disguising themselves in female apparel and vice versa. In the East women are generally neither searched nor molested, but are respected even by bandits.

Wearing of women's raiment by men would encourage spies, thieves, and undesirable people to infiltrate and operate without being detected. Then again, immorality would have increased among the people.

MIXED SEEDS

Thou shalt not sow thy vineyard with divers seeds: lest the fruit of thy seed which thou hast sown, and the fruit of thy vinyeard, be defiled. Deut. 22:9

The Aramaic reads *krabek* (your furrow). The Aramaic word for vineyard is *karma,* and in the possessive case becomes *karmek* (your vineyard). Evidently the scribe (copyist) or the translators confused *krabek* with *karmek.*

The reference here is to the fields and not to the vineyards. In vineyards one finds all kinds of fruit trees.

In the East taxes are levied according to the kind of crops. The levy on winter wheat is higher than on spring wheat, and the taxes on wheat are higher than on rye and barley.

When diverse seeds are sown in the same field, taxes become complicated. A farmer might swear that his field contains barley while it also contains wheat. Then again, in the olden days certain crops and fruits of the vineyards were consecrated to God. When other seeds were sown in the same field or vineyard, the entire crop was consecrated, and hence confiscated. Not long ago, in Turkey, where most of these ancient biblical customs have remained intact, a farmer would plant tobacco in a wheat or barley field and pay taxes on barley. Thus, the government was cheated of higher taxes on tobacco. But when the farmers were caught they were heavily penalized.

In biblical days the land belonged to the Lord. The people had to pay tithes to the priests and the Levites. This law was enacted to guard against defrauding the priests and the Levites and to simplify the gathering of taxes [Lev. 19:19].

PLOWING WITH ASSES

Thou shalt not plow with an ox and an ass together. Deut. 22:10

In some parts of Palestine where poor families cannot afford to have two oxen, an ox and an ass are yoked together when plowing or threshing wheat. And in some lands, men and women pulled the plow.

The Mosaic law prohibited this practice, simply because of cruelty to the ass. The ox is a strong animal of great endurance, but the ass is weak.

GARMENTS OF WOOL AND COTTON

Thou shalt not wear a garment of divers sorts, as of woolen and linen together.   Deut. 22:11

The reason underlying the prohibition of wearing garments of diverse sorts or colors may have been deception and cheating. A garment made of cotton may be sold for a garment of wool. Nomad tribes are ignorant of the value of the dry goods which are woven in cities. In the East, until recently, members of certain races and religions were known by their apparel. This is also true of princes and nobility; they wear garments of diverse colors and materials. Lower classes were prohibited from imitating the princes and nobles, who wore cotton and linen, which were a luxury to the desert people. The latter wore rough wool garments.

Jesus said those who wear cotton garments are found in king's palaces.

The wearing of garments of diverse colors and stuffs would make it hard to distinguish men from women. Where cotton is not grown it is a luxury and is more expensive than wool. Wealthy women generally wear cotton garments of diverse colors [See verse 9].

See the commentary on Leviticus 19:19.

TOKEN OF VIRGINITY

If any man take a wife, and go in unto her, and hate her,
And give occasions of speech against her, and bring up an evil name upon her, and say, I took this woman, and when I came to her, I found her not a maid:
Then shall the father of the damsel, and her mother, take and bring forth the tokens of the damsel's virginity unto the elders of the city in the gate.   Deut. 22:13-15

In the East when a marriage is consummated two or three women, representing the father and the mother of the bride and the father and mother of the bridegroom, witness the token of the virginity (a cloth stained with the blood of the bride).

These tokens are preserved by the parents of the bride so that the husband of their daughter may not reproach her name by stating that she was not a virgin and thus seek to divorce her. When such charges are made, the tokens of virginity are spread before the elders, and the man is punished and fined for having defamed the good name of his wife.

This ancient custom still prevails. Maidens who are not chaste are subject to divorcement.

A VIRGIN

If a damsel that is a virgin be betrothed unto a husband, and a man find her in the city, and lie with her. Deut. 22:23

The Aramaic term *damkhira* means "acquired with a price." *Maher* or Arabic *mahra* means "the settlement price of a woman's dowry"; that is, the money or sheep or cattle given by the bridegroom to the father of the bride. In some lands in the East a bride brings nothing with her to her bridegroom. Even her clothes have to be purchased anew.

Note that in verse 24 the woman is called *atta* (wife). Sometimes a man may marry a young girl, but not consummate the marriage until the maiden has reached a certain age. Even today such marriages are very common in the East.

The Virgin Mary was acquired for a *mahra* to Joseph, but because she was young the marriage had not been consummated. This is why when Joseph found his wife pregnant, by the power of the Holy Spirit, he planned to divorce her or put her away secretly [Matt. 1:19].

Little girls who are married but whose marriages have not been consummated are nevertheless referred to as wives. This is because the state of such marriages is kept a secret.

WHOREMONGER BARRED FROM TEMPLE

He that is wounded in the stones, or hath his privy member cut off, shall not enter into the congregation of the Lord. Deut. 23:1

The Eastern text reads: "No adulterer shall enter into the assembly of the Lord."

Adultery was prohibited by the Mosaic law [Exod. 20:14] and was punishable by death. When Tamar, the daughter-in-law of Judah, was suspected of adultery, Judah commanded that she should be burnt [Gen. 38:24].

According to Deuteronomy, if a man and woman were convicted of adultery both man and woman were stoned [Deut. 22:22-24]. Sodomites were also put to death. Those who broke the moral law were considered apostates, and therefore unworthy to enter into the congregation of the Lord [Lev. 21:9; Deut. 22:21]. This ordinance was applicable to both men and women.

BREAD AND WATER

Because they met you not with bread and with water in the way, when ye came forth out of Egypt; and because they hired against thee Balaam the son of Beor of Pethor of Mesopotamia, to curse thee.
Deut. 23:4

Bread and water, like salt, are tokens of friendliness and loyalty to one another.

When Israel came to the borders of Ammon and Moab, the Moabites and Ammonites violated the accepted etiquette by not greeting Israel with bread and water. Therefore the Ammonites and Moabites were barred from entering into the congregation of the Lord.

The Arab tribes would offer bread and water even to their enemies. The book of Proverbs states: "If thine enemy be hungry, give him bread to eat; and if he be thirsty, give him water to drink" [Prov. 25:21].

TOILET

Thou shalt have a place also without the camp, whither thou shalt go forth abroad.
Deut. 23:12

This passage should read: "You shall have a latrine outside the camp, to which you shall go to relieve yourself."

Latrines or toilets and other sanitary conditions as we have today were unknown in the olden days, and are still unknown in many backward countries. Moses was told to meet Pharaoh as he was going to the water, that is, to the latrine [Exod. 7:15]. In Aramaic we still say "He has gone outside" or "He has gone to water," which means he has gone to the toilet.

This ordinance was given to guard against disease which breaks out in large military camps which are without sanitary facilities. The refuse was covered with earth [verse 13].

One reason for the lack of sanitary conditions was the scarcity of water and the lack of education. In some places sand or stones were used to clean the body [verse 13]. Today these conditions are somewhat remedied.

WHOREDOM CONDEMNED

There shall be no whore of the daughters of Israel, nor a sodomite of the sons of Israel.
Deut. 23:17

Whoredom was prohibited by the Mosaic law, and harlots were put to death. This is also true of sodomites or homosexuals. These destructive evils were prevalent in corrupt Baal worship; therefore, they were not to be found among the Israelites, who were sanctified to the Lord. Whores were those who sold themselves for a hire or fee [verse 18].

In Hosea we read that the Lord told him to take a wife of whoredom, but this is a parable. The term *gomer* from *gemor* (an end) means "the end of Israel."

USURY

Thou shalt not lend upon usury to thy brother; usury of money, usury of victuals, usury of any thing that is lent upon usury:

Unto a stranger thou mayest lend upon usury; but unto thy brother thou shalt not lend upon usury: that the Lord thy God may bless thee in all that thou settest thine hand to in the land whither thou goest to possess it.   Deut. 23:19-20

Even though usury, or any kind of interest on loans, was prohibited by the Mosaic law among the Israelites, the people were permitted to loan money to strangers with interest [Lev. 25:36-37; Ps. 15:5; Isa. 24:2; Deut. 23:19].

The Israelites looked upon each other as brothers, the children of the same father and the members of the same religion; therefore they could not lend money with usury to one another.

In those days laws and ordinances were limited to the people for whom they were revealed and written. The other people of other races did the same; they loaned money to their people without interest, but to the people of an alien race they loaned with interest.

Mohammed prohibited usury. Moslems do not accept usury either from a Moslem or from a non-Moslem.

VOWS MUST BE FULFILLED

When thou shalt vow a vow unto the Lord thy God, thou shalt not slack to pay it: for the Lord thy God will surely require it of thee; and it would be sin in thee.   Deut. 23:21

Vows (Aramaic *nedrey*), were made voluntarily at a time when people sought God's help in matters which they were unable to understand or solve, and in time of distress.

In the East, people who go on a journey, generally make a vow, consisting of an offering or a gift to a shrine, for their safe return and as an expression of gratitude to God. When Jacob fled to Assyria, he vowed a vow [Gen. 28:20-22].

Once a vow is made, it must be faithfully fulfilled as soon as possible. This is because no one is obliged by law to make a vow or to pledge any-thing to God; but when a person willingly makes a vow, there is no reason not to fulfill it. When vows are deferred they are often forgotten.

All vows made in the name of God are binding and must be fulfilled. "When thou vowest a vow unto God . . . pay that which thou hast vowed" [Ecc. 5:4].

PLUCKING WHEAT

When thou comest into the standing corn of thy neighbor, then thou mayest pluck the ears with thine hand; but thou shalt not move a sickle unto thy neighbor's standing corn.　　　Deut. 23:25

Owing to the shortage of bread and other food, Easterners, from time immemorial to the present day, permit travelers, shepherds, and strangers to pluck ears of wheat from their fields. The ears are either eaten raw or roasted over a fire. They also may pick up fruit to eat, but neither wheat nor fruit is supposed to be carried home. That would be stealing and, therefore, against the law. Neither are the strangers permitted to use a sickle to cut the wheat.

Jesus and his disciples, when they were hungry, plucked ears of corn with their hands and ate them [Matt. 12:1].

In Palestine fields are very small and stony, and wheat is scarce and hard to raise. This statute was written to protect small farmers.

BILL OF DIVORCEMENT

When a man hath taken a wife, and married her, and it come to pass that she find no favor in his eyes, because he hath found some uncleanness in her: then let him write her a bill of divorcement, and give it in her hand, and send her out of his house.　　　Deut. 24:1

Prior to the Mosaic law, women had no rights. A man could put away his wife at any time he pleased. In those days women were purchased and sold [Isa. 50:1]. Therefore, they were looked upon as a possession. [Hos. 3:2].

The Mosaic law gave women certain rights unknown to the people of other races; that is, it stated that when a man puts his wife away, he must give her a bill of divorcement.

Prior to the Mosaic law, women were put away or deserted for any cause, such as finding no favor in their husbands' eyes, not bearing male children, or being weak or sick. Note that even in the Mosaic code there is no mention of women leaving or divorcing their husbands. But now, men must have a reason to put them away, and the reason was uncleanness, which means "not virgin." This law is still upheld by Moslems. When a maiden is found not to be a virgin she is put away.

The Mosaic law was the first law we know of that regulated marriage and gave women certain rights unknown hitherto.

This law was not kept during the time of Jesus. This is why Jesus recommended that men should give divorce papers when they put their wives away, and that a divorce must be only on the ground of adultery. Jesus' law was stronger than the Mosaic law [Matt. 5:31-32].

See also the commentary on divorce.

A FORMER HUSBAND

And if the latter husband hate her, and write her a bill of divorcement, and giveth it in her hand, and sendeth her out of his house; or if the latter husband die, which took her to be his wife.

Deut. 24:3

The bill of divorcement was given by the husband so that his unwanted wife might marry another man, and that he might not remarry her. Without the bill, he could take her back. The bill showed why the woman was put away, and it cleared her from any other charge. On the other hand, without the bill, she would have no legal grounds for divorce, and her first husband might claim her again at any time he wished. The bill terminated the marriage contract.

Cases like these are common in the Near East, where women who are put away or deserted and have no legal divorce papers cannot legally marry. And anyone who marries women thus put away without a church divorce commits adultery and is excommunicated.

In the Church of the East men and women who obtain divorce papers and are innocent can marry again and remain in the Church. But when a man wants to marry a woman who has been deserted by her husband, who is separated from him, or who has left him on no legal grounds, they cannot marry.

MILLSTONES

No man shall take the nether or the upper millstone to pledge: for he taketh a man's life to pledge.

Deut. 24:6

In the East it often happens that a mill owner possesses no sheep, cattle, fields, or other property. The care of the mill and grinding of the wheat for the townspeople take all his time.

The mill is valuable property which is handed down in the same family from one generation to another. Both the nether (lower) and upper granite millstones are very costly and often are brought from far off places.

When the stones are taken as a pledge, the mill ceases to operate and the miller's income stops. The townspeople may take their wheat to another mill in the same town or to a nearby town.

ROBE GIVEN AS SECURITY

And if the man be poor, thou shalt not sleep with his pledge.
                                                               Deut. 24:12

Robes and good garments are sometimes sold or given as a pledge for loans. It is not unusual for an Easterner to sell some of his clothes which he wears, or to pledge his robe, or even the rug on which he sleeps, to his creditor.

Some men sleep with their clothes, and cover themselves with their robe or mantle. Especially on a journey, a robe is the only garment to protect a person from the cold. At times one may pledge his coat or any other garment just for a few hours, hoping that he can repay the loan soon. But when he fails to pay, the creditor keeps the pledge. Pious creditors often return the garment to its owner before the sun sets, so that he may use it for his bed. In biblical lands the days are hot but nights are cold.

See the commentary on Exodus 22:26.

LABORERS WERE CHEATED

Thou shalt not oppress a hired servant that is poor and needy, whether he be of thy brethren, or of thy strangers that are in thy land within thy gates.   Deut. 24:14

The Aramaic word *aghra* means (wages) and *agira* (a hired laborer). This should read: "You shall not cheat the wages of a hired laborer who is poor and needy . . ."

In biblical days, just as today, some landowners cheated on the wages of hired men, especially when the hired person was a foreigner. Some employers never paid the men who reaped their fields and dressed their vineyards [Mal. 3:5; James 5:4].

Moreover, some laborers were paid in kind, and their employer might use deceitful weights and balances [Prov. 20:10].

FATHER'S GUILT

The fathers shall not be put to death for the children, neither
shall the children be put to death for the fathers: every man shall
be put to death for his own sin.   Deut. 24:16

The Mosaic code has some similarity to the laws of Hammurabi and
the codes of other nations during the time of the Exodus of the Israelites.
Indeed, there is some similarity between the laws of all nations. This
does not mean that one legal system is a copy of the other. Most of the
similarities are based on human needs; that is, the problems were the
same, just as they are today. On the other hand, the law of cause and
effect operates the same way. True law and justice are like arithmetic—
available to all races and people of the world.

Other nations put children to death for the sins of their fathers. Prior
to the law of Moses the Hebrews might have done the same. After the
death of Moses, Joshua put the children to death for the sin of their
father [Josh. 7:24-26].

Abraham and his tribe, like all the Arabian tribes, had a written or
oral code. The ordinances and statutes were handed down orally, but the
law must have been written. The people were judged according to the
precepts of the Book of the Law. Moses wrote all the laws of the Hebrew
tribes. Hebrew social, political, and ethical life was bound to their religious
belief. Family life was governed by an oral or written code.

Israel, from the time when God called Abraham to the day when Moses
brought down the two tablets from Mount Sinai, was a cultured people,
well trained in ethics. The way of life of the Hebrew tribe was very different from the inhabitants of Palestine. The Hebrews feared God and
therefore had a code of ethics. But when they forsook God, they forgot
the moral law, too. The stoning of the children of Achan (Achar) was
against the Mosaic law.

Apparently, the Assyrian, Babylonian, and Hittite codes had some influence on the Hebrew law and ordinances. This was natural. Abraham
was an Assyrian. And the moral law is a gift of God to all his children.

REDEMPTION

But thou shalt remember that thou wast a bondman in Egypt, and
the Lord thy God redeemed thee thence: therefore I command thee
to do this thing.   Deut. 24:18

The Aramaic word *parkakh* (delivered you) is derived from the Aramaic word *perak* (to save, deliver, break loose, go away).

The Lord God saved Israel from bondage. The term redeem means to pay a ransom. God did not pay a ransom to Pharaoh, the king of Egypt, but he delivered Israel by a strong hand and an outstretched arm. Kings, princes, and rich men redeemed one another by paying a price.

The Aramaic word for redeem is *zeban* (to pay a ransom or a price). There is no power stronger than God to whom God might pay a ransom. God can deliver those who pray to him and trust in him.

THRESHING BY OXEN

Thou shalt not muzzle the ox when he treadeth out the corn.
Deut. 25:4

In lands where modern methods of threshing are unknown and machinery is scarce, threshing is done as of yore. A wooden post is erected in the center of a large circle, to which five or six oxen are tied, side by side.

Wheat or barley sheaves are then placed in the circle, and the oxen are driven over it, until the wheat is treaded out under the feet of the oxen. A boy or a man walks after the oxen for five or six hours. At times, the oxen become so accustomed to this hard task that they walk over the wheat without being driven or guided [Hos. 10:11].

In Palestine wheat and barley fields are small and grain is scarce and precious. Even today some of the farmers muzzle the mouths of the oxen during the threshing hours. Not only in Palestine, but also in other lands where wheat is scarce, this Mosaic ordinance is broken and the mouths of the oxen are muzzled. Nevertheless, when the fields are large and the wheat abundant, the oxen are not muzzled.

Moses wrote this ordinance when Israel was in the desert. He had never been in Palestine. He was born and reared in Egypt, and Egypt is a fertile land with abundant crops. In Egypt no one would think of muzzling his oxen.

In the East it is often said, "A laborer is worthy of his food," just as an ox is worthy of eating wheat while threshing.

God cared for the oxen just as he cares for men. This is because the oxen help man in plowing and threshing, and thus are instrumental in producing food for man.

From this text we learn a great lesson: to be kind to dumb animals and not to subject them to unnecessary suffering. "A righteous man regardeth the life of his beast: but the tender mercies of the wicked are cruel" [Prov. 12:10].

PUNISHMENT FOR INJURIES

When men strive together one with another, and the wife of the one draweth near for to deliver her husband out of the hand of him that smiteth him, and putteth forth her hand, and taketh him by the secrets:
Then thou shalt cut off her hand, thine eye shall not pity her.
Deut. 25:11-12

In the East it is not uncommon to see a wife helping her husband when he strives against his adversary. In such cases the wife of the weak person may try to deliver her husband from his rival by seizing his private parts. In such a case, the person thus attacked by the woman may be severely injured.

DIVERSE WEIGHTS

Thou shalt not have in thy bag divers weights, a great and a small:
Thou shalt not have in thine house divers measures, a great and a small.
But thou shalt have a perfect and just weight, a perfect and just measure shalt thou have: that thy days may be lengthened in the land which the Lord thy God giveth thee.
Deut. 25:13-15

Weights are selected from round, smooth stones which are found in the beds of dried-up rivers or streams. They are stored in a bag to protect them from little children who might play with them when they find them.

Most of the tribal families have their own weights, and some of the families have diverse weights. That is, some are used to buy with and others to sell. Balances also are often dishonest. Some of the merchants, when they cannot cheat the prospective buyer with weights, would try to cheat him with the deceitful balances.

Diverse weights and balances were common in the Near East until recent years, and are still in use in backward countries among the tribal people.

In the olden days governments were not interested in the welfare of their people, and they did not regulate weights and balances; therefore cheating was prevalent, and the buyer was at the mercy of the seller. It often took many hours before the buyer and the seller agreed on the kind of weights and balances to be used in their transaction. And those who sold with small measures, diverse weights, and deceitful balances were sold to with the same measures and balances. "Let me be weighed in an even balance," says Job [Job 31:6]. "A just weight and balance are the Lord's" [Prov. 16:11]. Many of the prophets warned the people against these crooked practices [Amos 8:5].

Dry goods were measured by the arm. Therefore, some shops had two men, one with long arms who bought wholesale, and the other with short arms who sold retail. Jesus said, ". . . and with what measure ye mete, it shall be measured to you again" [Matt. 7:2].

OFFERINGS IN A BASKET

That thou shalt take of the first of all the fruit of the earth, which thou shalt bring of thy land that the Lord thy God giveth thee, and shalt put it in a basket, and shalt go unto the place which the Lord thy God shall choose to place his name there.

And thou shalt go unto the priest that shall be in those days, and say unto him, I profess this day unto the Lord thy God, that I am come unto the country which the Lord sware unto our fathers for to give us.

And the priest shall take the basket out of thine hand, and set it down before the altar of the Lord thy God.   Deut. 26:2-4

Easterners, whenever they visit a holy place or a holy man, take some gifts of their produce, such as food, cheese, fruit, sheep, or any other thing which they can afford to offer. Customarily no one ever appears in a holy place or before a man of God empty-handed. The giver and his wealth are blessed. "Blessed shall be your breadbasket and your dough" [Deut. 28:5, Eastern text].

The gifts are placed in a breadbasket and taken as thanks offerings, which the priests and holy men share with the needy and the strangers. In the East a shrine or a holy place is a sanctuary for the poor, the way-farers, and the strangers. The devout worshipers constantly bring gifts and articles of food, so that the shrine is well supplied and is always able to meet the needs [1 Kings 14:1-4].

When David and his men were hungry they went into the holy place in Shiloh where they were given consecrated bread [1 Sam. 21:4].

". . . and there shall meet thee three men going up to God to Bethel, one carrying three kids, and another carrying three loaves of bread, and another carrying a bottle (skin) of wine" [1 Sam. 10:3].

Even today people bring bread and meal offerings of flour baked in butter to the church, which are given to worshipers after the service is over.

Moses had commanded that the food offerings must be brought in baskets [Exod. 29:3; Judg. 6:19].

When David was made king in Hebron, the people brought abundant bread and other supplies on asses, camels, and mules [1 Chron. 12:40].

In the East there is always a shortage of food, and many people are poor and needy.

JACOB, AN ARAMEAN

And thou shalt speak and say before the Lord thy God, A Syrian ready to perish was my father; and he went down into Egypt, and sojourned there with a few, and became there a nation, great, mighty, and populous.   Deut. 26:5

The term "Syria" is derived from the famous city of *Sur,* a place where dyestuffs were made from shells and plants. For centuries this city was famous for these dyestuffs. The Syrians made material of crimson and scarlet, as well as violet, for kings and royalty. In ancient days the name of the country was called Aramia or Aram.

The reference in this case is to *Aram-nahrin,* Mesopotamia. Jacob went to Haran, a city in Mesopotamia (Assyria), and from thence returned to Palestine; and then, because of severe famine, he went to Egypt [Gen. 31:21; 46:3-8]. "Jacob fled to the land of Aram, and Israel served for a wife, and for a wife he kept sheep" [Hos. 12:12, Eastern text]. All of Jacob's children, with the exception of the youngest one, Benjamin, were born in Haran, Assyria.

Moses here reminds Israel about their racial ancestry in order not to mix with other races in Palestine. Hitherto, the Hebrews under their patriarch had succeeded in preserving their racial purity. Racial purity was essential, because the divine promises of the salvation of mankind were made to Abraham, Isaac, and Jacob. The religion of Israel was to bless the Gentile world in the latter days through the coming of the Messiah, Christ.

WRITING ON STONE

And it shall be, on the day when ye shall pass over Jordan unto the land which the Lord thy God giveth thee, that thou shalt set thee up great stones, and plaster them with plaster.

And thou shalt write upon them all the words of this law, when thou art passed over, that thou mayest go in unto the land which the Lord thy God giveth thee, a land that floweth with milk and honey; as the Lord God of thy fathers hath promised thee.

Deut. 27:2-3

The writing could have been done by engraving on the stones or by writing upon a plastered surface, just as it is done today. The smooth stones were covered with wet plaster and then the writing was inscribed upon the stones with a sharp tool.

The altar was built as a memorial, and the commandments were inscribed upon it to remind the people of God's laws and ordinances that were given to their forefathers.

The altar was erected on the highway which leads to Samaria and the north. No doubt it was a caravan route, just as it is today. It is near the place where the Midianites' caravan passed when Joseph was sold to the Ishmaelites [Gen. 37:28]. The altar was situated in such a prominent place that all passersby could see the sacred writing and some of them could read it to the others. All Hebrew altars and shrines were built in conspicuous and convenient places so that the people might have easy access to them.

The writing was plain so that no one could stumble in reading it. The sentences were short and terse, and there were no qualifying clauses [Hab. 2:2].

WRITING IN A PLAIN STYLE

And thou shalt write upon the stones all the words of this law very plainly.   Deut. 27:8

One of the greatest desires of an Eastern writer is to write plainly, so that what he has written will be understood. Therefore both calligraphy and composition of the material are considered important. This is why the sentences in the Bible are short and direct, especially when it comes to the law, ordinances, and admonitions. There are hardly any qualifying clauses, ifs, or buts.

The Word of God was intended to be clear and terse, so that no one could find excuses to revise it. The Bible is not a book of mystery, like the books of magicians and fortune tellers, which can hardly be understood. Magicians generally charm the people not so much by what the listener understands as by that which he cannot understand. This is because people are more attracted by mysteries than they are by the truth. The truth is too simple and too good to be true.

CURSING FATHER OR MOTHER

Cursed be he that setteth light by his father or his mother: and all the people shall say, Amen.   Deut. 27:16

The Eastern text reads: "Cursed be he who reviles his father or his mother." The Mosaic law states, "Honor thy father and thy mother" [Exod. 20:12; Deut. 5:16].

Then again, the Mosaic code prescribed a death penalty against those who cursed or reviled their father and mother [Exod. 21:17; Lev. 20:9].

Jesus commended this law when he said, "For God said, Honor your father and your mother, and whoever curses his father or his mother, let him be put to death" [Matt. 15:4, Eastern text].

The term "setteth light" does not make sense.

FATHERS' WIVES

Cursed be he that lieth with his father's wife; because he uncovereth his father's skirt: and all the people shall say, Amen.

Deut. 27:20

Polygamy is an ancient custom, as old as the Bible itself. In biblical days men married many wives, and at times some of their grown sons committed adultery with their fathers' concubines.

The reference here is to the men who had sexual intercourse with their fathers' concubines. Reuben, Jacob's son, committed adultery with Bilhah, his father's concubine [Gen. 35:22]. And when Absalom revolted against his father, he committed adultery with all of his father's concubines, who were left behind in Jerusalem [2 Sam. 16:22].

We can see that even before the law was revealed and written, such acts were considered immoral and wicked. The first curse for such an immoral act was pronounced by Jacob upon his son Reuben [Gen. 49:3-4].

BASKET AND DOUGH BLESSED

Blessed shall be thy basket and thy store.   Deut. 28:5

In the East baskets were used as food containers and as tables. "Blessed shall be thy basket" means "Blessed shall be your table." Easterners, after eating, bless the table. And when they eat in their neighbors' houses, they say, "May God bless your table. May your basket always be filled." The Eastern text reads: "Blessed shall be your breadbasket and your dough."

Even today in some parts of the Near East baskets are used for tables and are called *suphra*. These baskets are about three inches deep and five to six feet in diameter, according to the size of the family. Baskets which are used for fruit and for provisions for a journey are made smaller and deeper [Exod. 29:3; Jer. 24:2; Amos 8:1; see also article on "Basket"].

THE LACK OF WINE

Ye have not eaten bread, neither have ye drunk wine or strong drink: that ye might know that I am the Lord your God.

Deut. 29:6

Desert people lack wine, and bread is scarce. The Israelites were in the desert for forty years. Grapes, pears, peaches, and other fruits were rarely seen. These luxuries are rare in the Arabian desert even today. A few raisins and dates were brought by merchants, which they purchased in cities to be exchanged for wool, cheese, and other sheep products.

The Israelites were fed with manna and quail, but they were strong and healthy. They saw that God could provide the comforts of life even in a wasteland. In other words, they had not raised wheat and planted vineyards and worked hard to appreciate what God had done for them.

The people who do not drink wine and strong drink are more peaceful and religiously inclined. This is why the Nazarites were forbidden to drink wine or strong drink or to eat grapes. But the Israelites were rebellious against God and against Moses.

A CORRUPT PERSON

Lest there should be among you man, or woman, or family, or tribe, whose heart turneth away this day from the Lord our God, to go and serve the gods of these nations; lest there should be among you a root that beareth gall and wormwood. Deut. 29:18

The term "root" is used symbolically, meaning "a corrupt person," "an evil man," or one in whose heart paganism is so deeply rooted that he is a menace to the congregation of God.

There were many mixed people who had left Egypt with the Israelites, and many of them still secretly worshiped images and idols. On the other hand, Palestine had many cults. Every race had its own gods and images, which were a snare to the Israelites. The people often fell victim to strange gods, which resulted in plagues, affliction, and bitterness.

ADDING ONE EVIL TO ANOTHER

And it come to pass, when he heareth the words of this curse, that he bless himself in his heart, saying, I shall have peace, though I walk in the imagination of mine heart, to add drunkenness to thirst. Deut. 29:19

The reference here is to the rebellious men and women who, through the imagination of their hearts, became the prey of pagan worship.

Many people in those days were not content with their tribal religion. They tried to find peace and prosperity in other religions. In other words, many of them wanted a religion which came from the imagination and the dictates of their own heart. The tribal people despise regimentation and cults that are forced on them.

"To add drunkenness to thirst" is an Eastern idiom which means "to add one evil to another." In the first place, the person breaks the law; and second, he is entrapped in an evil that is hard to escape.

The people who sought to find peace and prosperity were generally thirsty for the truth. But instead of finding what they wanted, they got drunk with destructive pagan philosophies and sensual worship.

SALTY LAND

And that the whole land thereof is brimstone, and salt, and burning, that it is not sown, nor beareth, nor any grass groweth therein, like the overthrow of Sodom and Gomorrah, Admah and Zeboim, which the Lord overthrew in his anger, and in his wrath.

Deut. 29:23

Many regions in Palestine which contain salt are waste; nothing grows in them. This is especially common around the Dead Sea and the Judean Desert.

Salt is symbolic of desolation and barrenness, and also is used figuratively to represent seasoning and preserving qualities and as a sign of true friendship [Gen. 19:24].

See also the commentary on salt.

PURIFICATION OF HEART

And the Lord thy God will circumcise thine heart, and the heart of thy seed, to love the Lord thy God with all thine heart, and with all thy soul, that thou mayest live.

Deut. 30:6

The term circumcise in this instance means to purify. The Hebrews were called by God for a special mission [Deut. 10:15-16]; that is, they were a peculiar people selected by God in order that he might reveal himself to the human race through them.

Thus, circumcision was a token of separation or sanctification, and was symbolic of the spiritual man. "Circumcise therefore the foreskin of your heart, and be no more stiffnecked" [Deut. 10:16, Eastern text].

Moreover, circumcision was a sign of cleanliness and a reminder of God's covenant with Abraham [Gen. 17:10-14; Lev. 12:3].

Circumcision was supplanted by baptism in water, which symbolizes new birth in Jesus Christ [Acts 15:1-11; Phil. 3:3].

Circumcision of the flesh was not enough. The Israelites had to cleanse their hearts in order to love their God with all their heart and with all their soul, and bring forth the fruits of the Spirit.

MOSES' AGE

And he said unto them, I am a hundred and twenty years old this day; I can no more go out and come in: also the Lord hath said unto me, Thou shalt not go over this Jordan.   Deut. 31:2

Even today, many people in Turkish Kurdistan live to be 115 or 120 years old, and more. The span of life seems to be longer in that part of the world than other lands.

One reason for the long span of life is the pastoral occupation, the out-door life, and simple food. Also, the people in that part of the world have few things to worry about. Banks, insurance companies, doctors, and dentists are unknown, and taxes are low. The people worry for their daily needs only. This was true of the desert Israelites. They were an outdoor people, strong and healthy.

Moses was 80 years of age when God called him and commanded him to go to Egypt to lead the children of Israel out of Egypt. Aaron was 83. Today bishops and ministers retire at 65.

In the East wisdom is determined by age. The people respect the elders simply because they are wise. Wisdom is the outcome of human experience. An elderly person has more experience than a younger one [Deut. 34:7].

MOSES WAS WELL TRAINED

And Moses wrote this law, and delivered it unto the priests the sons of Levi, which bare the ark of the covenant of the Lord, and unto all the elders of Israel.   Deut. 31:9

Moses was well educated in Egypt. He had all the education and wisdom which the Egyptian priests and wise men could offer to a prince. He knew the Egyptian system of writing, as well as the Egyptian code of law.

Apparently, in Midian Moses learned the Semitic alphabet and system of writing. The Hebrews, even though sojourning in Egypt for 400 years, spoke the language of their fathers, which they had brought from Babylon and Assyria. On the other hand, the Midianites were the descendants of Abraham, and, like the Ammonites, Moabites, and Edomites, spoke a Semitic dialect.

Moses learned the Semitic language in the house of his father-in-law, Jethro, the priest of Midian. Moreover, being a prince, he could have studied the Assyrian and Babylonian dialects of Aramaic, which was the language of the Semitic empire, a rival of Egypt.

"HIDE MY FACE"

And I will surely hide my face in that day for all the evils which they shall have wrought, in that they are turned unto other gods.
Deut. 31:18

The Aramaic word *apekh apai* means "I will turn away from them" or "I will not look after them to help them." The term "hide" is a mistranslation. The Aramaic word for hide is *tashi*. God is spirit, and the Spirit is everywhere. There is no place in the whole universe where God is not present, or where God can hide himself.

When people turn away from God they cut off themselves from the Great Power which sustains them and helps them in time of distress.

WRITING COMMON

Now therefore write ye this song for you, and teach it the children of Israel: put it in their mouths, that this song may be a witness for me against the children of Israel.
Deut. 31:19

Many biblical commentators, who maintain that the sacred literature was handed down orally and was not written until many centuries after the death of Moses, have failed to recognize that writing was common in the time of Moses. The Lord commanded Moses to write the song so that he would be able to teach it to the people. Certainly God knew that Moses could read and write. Had Moses failed to record it, he would not have remembered all of it.

Moses wrote the song and taught it to the children of Israel. He had to write it down in order to be able to teach it. Then again, when a song or an ordinance is written, it can be committed to memory. One may have to read it about fifteen times in order to be able to recite it orally. This is why all laws, ordinances, and important revelations were written right after they were revealed.

God commanded Moses to write the commandments and the covenant [Exod. 34:27]. In Exodus 31:18 we read that the commandments were written by the finger of God (which means without fault or flaws). They were written by Moses on the same day in which they were revealed. Other prophets were told to write their visions. Isaiah, Jeremiah, and Habakkuk recorded their visions immediately.

BOOK

And it came to pass, when Moses had made an end to writing the words of this law in a book, until they were finished.   Deut. 31:24

This passage throws light on the authorship of the book of Deuteronomy as well as on the kind of writing.

In the book of Exodus we are told that Moses wrote the law on the tablets. In this passage we are told that he wrote it in a *sepra* (book); that is, a scroll made of skin. Evidently, both sheepskin and tablets were used by the scribes in the olden days. Legal documents and treaties were written on stone tablets so that they could be preserved and handed down from one generation to another. Tablets were generally buried in the ground. But prayers, songs, deeds, and commercial letters were written on sheepskin. Skin was light and easy to carry from one place to another. The scribes used pens [Judg. 5:14]. Isaiah was told to write with a pen on the skin. "Moreover the Lord said unto me, Take thee a great roll, and write in it with a man's pen . . ." [Isa. 8:1].

That Moses is the author of the book is clearly seen from local color, customs, and the way of life in the desert. No one living in Babylon or Palestine could have given us such a vivid description of the events and small incidents which took place in the arid desert. Only an eyewitness could have written the book of Deuteronomy.

Those who challenge Moses' authorship forget that the book of Deuteronomy is a review of the former writing of Moses. This is why he does not describe things at length. As the problems grew more complex, more laws and ordinances were added.

Then again, writing on sheepskin and papyrus was prevalent in Egypt long before the time of Moses.

GENTLE WORDS

My doctrine shall drop as the rain, my speech shall distil as the dew, as the small rain upon the tender herb, and as the showers upon the grass.   Deut. 32:2

The term "dew" is used metaphorically to mean "gentle and clear teaching."

In Palestine and Transjordan, where long droughts are common and water supplies scanty, dew is the only source of life-giving moisture for the vineyards, crops, and herbs, and is symbolic of God's truth and his divine care in the midst of scarcity and want.

God's doctrine is to come not by the means of force or man's knowledge, but as a gift from heaven. The dew falls from heaven gently, without man's efforts. The teaching of God came like the night dew and like the light rain upon the tender grass.

AS THE APPLE OF HIS EYE

He found him in a desert land, and in the waste howling wilderness; he led him about, he instructed him, he kept him as the apple of his eye. Deut. 32:10

Most of Palestine south of Beer-sheba is a barren wilderness. The land is devoid of trees and shrubs, and the people depend on wells for water. During the severe droughts some of the wells dry up. All the south country between Kadesh and Shur is semiwilderness.

Abraham, Isaac, and Jacob grazed their large flocks in this area, simply because they were strangers in the land and would not be permitted to dwell in regions where the water was abundant. At times they had to ask permission from kings and princes to graze and to use the wells.

God took Jacob out of this land where he was struggling for existence and brought him to Egypt, and from thence to Palestine.

"He kept him as the apple of his eye" is an Aramaic idiom which means, "He loved him very much and took care of him." God instructed Israel through his divine revelations, and at last established him in Palestine. "The apple of the eye" is one of the most delicate and important organs of the body. This idiom is still used today in Eastern speech [Ps. 17:8].

GOD CARED FOR ISRAEL

As an eagle stirreth up her nest, fluttereth over her young, spreadeth abroad her wings, taketh them, beareth them on her wings:
So the Lord alone did lead him, and there was no strange god with him. Deut. 32:11-12

The eagle (Aramaic *nishra*) should not be confused with the vulture. In biblical days various species of birds were not identified as they are today. The eagle is described in Micah 1:16 as bald. It might be different from the species mentioned in Matthew 24:28 and Luke 17:37.

The eagle is noted for its keen sight, swiftness, and great power, for an eagle can lift up a lamb or a child; and it can fly higher than other birds. God took care of Israel as an eagle takes care of her young.

The eagle feeds on animal food and it devours both living and dead prey. It was declared unclean [Lev. 11:13].

See also Job 39:27-30; Prov. 30:19; Ezek. 1:10; Rev. 4:7.

ROCKY PLACE

He made him ride on the high places of the earth, that he might eat the increase of the fields; and he made him to suck honey out of the rock, and oil out of the flinty rock;

Butter of kine, and milk of sheep, with fat of lambs, and rams of the breed of Bashan, and goats, with the fat of kidneys of wheat; and thou didst drink the pure blood of the grape. Deut. 32:13-14

The Eastern text reads: "He made him to dwell in a fertile land . . . with fat of fatlings and rams of the breed of rock-goats and goats, with the fat and the best wheat . . ." [Ps. 147:14].

Palestine is a rocky place. The fields are full of stones, and flint is abundant everywhere. Wild bees nest in cracks in trees, in stone heaps, and in the fields. The word "suck" is used figuratively, which means honey was abundant and free for all.

In Palestine olives grow in rocky places and in the flint-covered ground. Easterners use both olive and sheep oil for food. Grazing is poor in Palestine, but olives grow well even in rocky places.

God supplied Israel with abundant food and oil regardless of the poor soil.

THE MIGHTY ONE

Of the Rock that begat thee thou art unmindful, and hast forgotten God that formed thee.

And when the Lord saw it, he abhorred them, because of the provoking of his sons, and of his daughters. Deut. 32:18-19

The Aramaic reads *takipa* (the Mighty One); that is, the Lord God of Israel, who was called the Father of the Hebrew race.

Shekipa, in vernacular Aramaic, means "rock." *Takipa* is quite often rendered "rock," which means "strength or protection" [see "Rock"].

The Eastern text reads: "But you forsook the Mighty One who bore you, and you forgot the God who made you glorious."

The term rock is used figuratively to mean shelter, strength, protection, or salvation. Rock is hard and, therefore, offers a good protection as a shelter from the arrows of the enemy and from the wind, storm, and rain. In Arabia during sand storms travelers and shepherds take refuge under the cover of the rocks in caves. Warriors use them as shelters [Isa. 17:10].

On the other hand, rock, because of its hardness, is symbolic of endurance and truth. In the East it is often said, "His words are like a rock," which means that his words are truthful.

The God of Israel is often called a Rock, which means a Protector. It is he who conceived the divine plan in which the Hebrews played a part. It is he who created them, protected them, and delivered them out of Egyptian bondage. But Israel forgot the God of their forefathers, the Rock of Ages, and went after foreign gods. They had not been mindful of the protecting arm of the God of their salvation.

ZEALOUSNESS

They have moved me to jealousy with that which is not God; they have provoked me to anger with their vanities: and I will move them to jealousy with those which are not a people; I will provoke them to anger with a foolish nation. Deut. 32:21

The Aramaic word *atnon* is derived from *tan* (zeal, zealous desire, emulation, provocation, indignation). But in this instance it should read "zealousness" or "indignation"; that is, "They made me burn with zeal or indignation." "The zeal of thine house hath eaten me up" or "made me indignant" [Ps. 69:9; John 2:17].

God was not jealous of images or false gods, but his anger was provoked because the people wasted their time worshiping objects which were not gods and which could not help them.

SHEOL

For a fire is kindled in mine anger, and shall burn unto the lowest hell, and shall consume the earth with her increase, and set on fire the foundations of the mountains. Deut. 32:22

Hell, in Aramaic and Hebrew, is called *Sheol*, a place under the earth for the departed souls of the dead. *Sheol* means "a place of silence and inactivity," but it is not a place of burning.

The term "hell" is derived from the Greek *Hades*. But Hades has been rendered equivalent to *gehana* (the place of torment).

Sheol is used throughout the Peshitta Bible, the Eastern text of the Bible:

"If I ascend into heaven, thou art there; if I descend into Sheol, behold, thou art there also" [Ps. 139:8].

"Her feet cause men to go down to death; her steps take her to Sheol" [Prov. 5:5].

No Hebrew prophet would speak of God as being in hell, but he can be in *Sheol*, the place of departed souls.

Gehana (hell) is comparatively a new term, used mostly in the New Testament.

VINE OF SODOM

For their vine is of the vine of Sodom, and of the fields of Gomorrah: their grapes are grapes of gall, their clusters are bitter.
Deut. 32:32

"Vine" in this instance is used metaphorically to mean "stock" or "plantation," that is, the race. Israel was called the vine of God which he had planted. "I had planted thee a noble vine" [Jer. 2:21]. Hosea calls Israel an empty vine which had failed to produce fruits [Hos. 10:1].

"The vine of Sodom" and the bitter grapes symbolize teaching that produced corruption and immorality and which caused Sodom's downfall. Sodom was used as an example of God's wrath.

Wicked cities were likened to Sodom and Amorah (Gomorrah), which, because of their evil works, were completely destroyed.

WINE OF DRAGONS

Their wine is the poison of dragons, and the cruel venom of asps.
Deut. 32:33

The reference here is to the pagan teaching and corrupt practices which often caused Israel to go astray after pagan deities. These teachings were as destructive as the venom of dragons. The pagan rituals consisted of eating, drinking, and immoral practices.

Paul speaks of it as "the cup of devils," meaning the teaching of devils [1 Cor. 10:21]. On the other hand, "the cup of the Lord" means the true teaching of God; that is, the cup of salvation. "I will take the cup of salvation, and call upon the name of the Lord" [Ps. 116:13]. Jesus said, "This cup is the New Testament"; that is, the new teaching which was to supplant the old [Luke 22:20; 1 Cor. 11:25].

The cup also was symbolic of the blood of Jesus Christ which was shed on the cross in order to save mankind from false and destructive teachings.

MOSES' DEATH

Get thee up into this mountain Abarim, unto Mount Nebo, which is in the land of Moab, that is over against Jericho; and behold the land of Canaan, which I give unto the children of Israel for a possession:

And die in the mount whither thou goest up, and be gathered unto thy people; as Aaron thy brother died in mount Hor, and was gathered unto his people. Deut. 32:49-50

Even though the Israelites expected Moses to return with Elijah, the book of Deuteronomy explicitly states that Moses died and was buried in a valley in the land of Moab. Tradition states that an angel buried him. Neither his body nor his grave was ever discovered.

In the East when a great man or a holy man dies the people say that God took him. Easterners hate to use the term "death" when referring to a holy man. Then again, when the people curse one another, they say "May God take you away"; that is, "May you die." Such phrases were used in the time of Moses, and at times were misunderstood by simple people. Aaron had died earlier and was buried by Moses and Eleazar in Mount Hor [Num. 20:27-29].

Evidently, Moses was told that his time to die had come, and to be ready to be gathered to his people. Moses must have revealed the matter to Joshua, who later wrote the account of his death.

A FUTURE KING

And he was king in Jeshurun, when the heads of the people and the tribes of Israel were gathered together. Deut. 33:5

The Aramaic word *nehwey* is the future tense of *hewa* (to be). It should read: "And there shall be a king in Israel, when the heads of the people and the tribes of Israel are gathered together."

Moses is speaking of the future, when the tribes of Israel would conquer the land, dwell in it, multiply, and choose a king to reign over them. When the book of Deuteronomy was written, the people were still in the wilderness.

This error is due to the transcription of the book from one alphabet into another, or probably the scribe failed to recognize the tense of the verb *hewa*.

BENJAMIN SECURE

And of Benjamin he said, The beloved of the Lord shall dwell in safety by him; and the Lord shall cover him all the day long, and he shall dwell between his shoulders.   Deut. 33:12

The Eastern text reads: "And of Benjamin he said, The beloved of the Lord shall dwell in safety; and the Lord shall have compassion on him all the day long, and he shall dwell in his bosom." The last phrase is an idiom that means "He shall cuddle him"; that is, embrace him closely in his arms.

When Palestine was divided by Joshua, the lot of Benjamin fell between Judah and Ephraim, the two most powerful tribes of Israel. Nearly all of Benjamin's borders were thus secure from enemies. Benjamin, being the youngest of his brothers, the Lord gave him the most secure portion of the land surrounded by his own people, the Israelites.

STRONG AS AN OX

His glory is like the firstling of his bullock, and his horns are like the horns of unicorns: with them he shall push the people together to the ends of the earth: and they are the ten thousands of Ephraim, and they are the thousands of Manasseh.   Deut. 33:17

"Bullocks and horns" are used figuratively, meaning "strength" and "defense." Bullocks, because of their strength, were worshiped as gods by the Assyrians. Today cows are worshiped in India. In the olden days in biblical lands where elephants were unknown, the ox was looked upon as the strongest of all animals. Today we often say, "He is strong as an ox."

Horns symbolize honor, defense, victory, and ruling power (kingdom) [Dan. 7:7; Hab. 3:4; Luke 1:69]. The unicorn is a wild ox. [See article on "horn."]

THE GADITES AND DANITES BLESSED

And of Gad he said, Blessed be he that enlargeth Gad: he dwelleth as a lion, and teareth the arm with the crown of the head.
And he provided the first part for himself, because there, in a portion of the lawgiver, was he seated; and he came with the heads of the people, he executed the justice of the Lord, and his judgments with Israel.   Deut. 33:20-21

Gad was originally settled west of Judah and Benjamin, on the northern coast of Philistia. But when the Philistines subjugated the Israelites, the

Gadites were driven away from the seacoast. The tribe of Gad had to find another place to dwell, so they sent spies from Zorah, near Ir Shemesh and the valley of Ajalon, to northern Israel [Josh. 19:40] and from there to Laish near the Syrian border [Judg. 18:27-30].

The tribe of Dan was the seventh to receive its lot from the hands of Joshua. But somehow their territory was too little for them. Their lot had fallen close to Ephraim and Judah, the two most powerful tribes, who had taken a generous share of the good land which could be easily fortified against their enemies.

The Gadites had to look for other places. Finally, they found Laish and destroyed its weak inhabitants and settled near the border of Sidon (Zidon) in Syria.

The Gadites were good fighters. Moses likens them to the lions when they devour their prey. Their territory was close to Syria and was hard to defend.

FOOT IN OIL

And of Asher he said, Let Asher be blessed with children; let him be acceptable to his brethren, and let him dip his foot in oil.
Deut. 33:24

"Dip his foot in oil" is an Eastern idiom which means "Let him become very prosperous." In biblical days oil was used as a medium of exchange. And it was still used as such in the Near East until World War II. Oil also may mean butter.

In the East a man with plenty of olive oil or butter is considered wealthy. Easterners, when describing a rich man, say, "He bathes in oil and milk." Olive oil and butter are exchanged for dry goods, wheat, silver, and gold. In the parable of the unjust servant, oil was loaned just as one would loan silver and gold [Luke 16:6].

The land of Asher was fertile and good for grazing. Olives also are plentiful in northern Palestine and Lebanon.

SHOES OF IRON AND BRASS

Thy shoes shall be iron and brass; and as thy days, so shall thy strength be.
Deut. 33:25

"Your shoes shall be iron and brass" is used metaphorically to mean "You will have plenty of good leather to make shoes." In the East the shortage of shoes is one of the greatest problems. Thousands of men, women, and children walk barefooted. Many workers cut grass and work in the fields barefooted. Only the rich and the princes have more than one pair of shoes. Moreover, when the shoes are well made, the merchants say, "They are like iron," which means they are durable.

Then again, in the East, shoes are a sign of prosperity. Those who have shoes are well dressed and fed.

The tribe of Asher was to have oil, food, and leather for shoes. And they were to be healthy and strong all the days of their lives. God's blessings were to provide for all their needs.

GOD RIDES THROUGH HEAVEN

There is none like unto the God of Jeshurun, who rideth upon the heaven in thy help, and in his excellency on the sky.

Deut. 33:26

This should read: ". . . who rides through the heaven to your help . . ."

All pagan gods were helpless and stationary images, which were carried on the backs of donkeys and horses. But the God of Israel had dominion over heaven and earth. Heaven is the place of his abode, and earth is his footstool.

The term ride is used to point out that the God of Israel was a universal God and his presence was felt everywhere.

The Aramaic text reads "Israel" instead of "Jeshurun."

EVERLASTING ARMS

The eternal God is thy refuge, and underneath are the everlasting arms: and he shall thrust out the enemy from before thee; and shall say, Destroy them.

Deut. 33:27

The Eastern text reads: "In the heaven of heavens is the dwelling of our God from everlasting, and below he creates men . . ."

The Aramaic word *zra* (to sow) has been confused with *dra* (arm). These two words have a close similarity. And the Aramaic word *almey* (world) men have confused with *almin* (everlasting).

Moses states that God, who is in heaven and who created the world and men beneath, had promised that he would destroy all the enemies of Israel, and that he would keep that promise. God had power to fulfill his promises.

THE ACCOUNT OF MOSES' DEATH

So Moses the servant of the Lord died there in the land of Moab,
according to the word of the Lord.   Deut. 34:5

No doubt this portion of the book was written by Joshua or one of
his scribes. Moses of course could not have written about his own death.

In the East a book is called by the name of the author of the material.
Moses was the author of the book of Deuteronomy [Deut. 31:24]. Moses
had been told by God that he was not to enter into the Promised Land
[Num. 20:12].

CHAPTER SIX

JOSHUA

INTRODUCTION

THE title of the book in Aramaic is *Eshoo Bar Nun* (Jesus the Son of Nun). Joshua, in Hebrew, means "salvation," or "savior." Joshua saved Israel from the wrath of the kings whose lands they possessed.

Joshua prepared the people to cross Jordan into the Promised Land. He was a pious leader and a great general, who obeyed God's command and was loyal to the prophet Moses.

The book was written about 1450 B.C., after the crossing of the Jordan and the conquest of Palestine. The events are described in such lengthy detail that only an eyewitness could have recorded all these events, battles, and ordinances.

Some biblical authorities place the date of the book in the fifth century. They also doubt that Joshua was the author. This concept is due to the fact that the account of the death of the author, Joshua, like that of Moses, is recorded in his own book.

The material relative to the death and burial of Joshua is the work of a later scribe who added the last episode to the book, as in the case of the book of Deuteronomy, in which the account of the death of Moses was recorded later.

In those early days a book was made of many scrolls, which were written by different scribes. These Eastern practices have been a stumbling block to Western scholars who are unfamiliar with the customs and manners in biblical lands. Joshua was a learned man and a student of the greater teacher, Moses.

PROVISION FOR THE JOURNEY

Then Joshua commanded the officers of the people, saying,
Pass through the host, and command the people, saying, Prepare
you victuals; for within three days ye shall pass over this Jordan,
to go in to possess the land, which the Lord your God giveth you to
possess it.   Josh. 1:10-11

Preparing of provisions for a journey is an ancient Eastern custom as
old as the Bible itself. The women spend a day or two baking bread
and making flour cakes tempered with butter for the journey.

This ancient custom prevailed until recently. Even now, in countries
where Western culture has not yet penetrated, and where public eating
places are rare or unknown, the people prepare provisions for their journeys. The amount of bread and cakes is determined by the days of the
journey and the number of persons.

The Gibeonites deceived Joshua by taking old and dry bread for their
journey, pretending they had come from a far-off country [Josh. 9:5].

Jesus and his disciples took bread and other provisions for their
journeys [John 4:8].

RAHAB

And Joshua the son of Nun sent out of Shittim two men to spy
secretly, saying, Go view the land, even Jericho. And they went,
and came into a harlot's house, named Rahab, and lodged there.
                                                     Josh. 2:1

Rahab (Aramaic *Rakhab*) is probably derived from *rakh* (to be
merciful).

The conquest of Jericho took place about the fifteenth century B.C.
In the Pauline Epistle to the Hebrews Rahab is commended for her
faith [Heb. 11:31].

Rahab, the wife of Salmon, was a different woman. There are only
three generations from Salmon to Jesse, and Jesse was living during the
time of King Saul and David, about 1000 B.C. There must be about
eighty years from Salmon to Jesse. This Rahab is not to be confused with
Rahab the harlot, who entertained the Hebrew spies sent by Joshua from
Shittim.

Rahab (or Rachab) the wife of Salmon, is mentioned in the genealogy
in Matthew 1:5.

In Psalm 87:4 Rahab is the name of a city; also in Psalm 89:10 and in Isaiah 51:9. In the olden days, just as today, cities were called by the names of famous men and women.

In Psalm 87:4 Rahab is likened to Babylon which was destroyed in the sixth century B.C. These names of places should not be confused with the name of Rahab as given in Joshua 2:1.

STALKS OF FLAX

But she had brought them up to the roof of the house, and hid them with the stalks of flax, which she had laid in order upon the roof.   Josh. 2:6

The flax stalks were gathered from the fields and made into a heap on the roof of the house to be used for fuel. Even today, women in the region of Jericho and the desert of Judah gather dry stalks, thorns, and dry grass which the sheep and cattle cannot eat, and store it on the housetops for fuel. At times, these heaps are large enough for two or three men to hide in.

The king's officers believed Rahab's story; after all, she was an inhabitant of Jericho.

CROSSING THE JORDAN

And it shall come to pass, as soon as the soles of the feet of the priests that bear the ark of the Lord, the Lord of all the earth, shall rest in the waters of Jordan, that the waters of Jordan shall be cut off from the waters that come down from above; and they shall stand upon a heap.   Josh. 3:13

Some archaeologists and biblical authorities maintain that the water of the River Jordan was stopped by a landslide caused by an earthquake.

But even an earthquake happening at the time the priests started to cross the river is a divine miracle and not a coincidence. Something miraculous must have happened; otherwise, Joshua would never have recorded the incident. It is true, the Jordan is a small and narrow river. It may look like a creek to Americans and Europeans, but it is a great river to nomadic people who hardly ever see flowing water.

God can do anything. The wonder or the miracle is that the people crossed the swollen river. Joshua trusted in God, and when one trusts in God, miracles and wonders happen.

WALL OF JERICHO

And Joshua adjured them at that time, saying, Cursed be the man
before the Lord, that riseth up and buildeth this city Jericho: he
shall lay the foundation thereof in his firstborn, and in his youngest
son shall he set up the gates of it.   Josh. 6:26

When Easterners curse one another, they usually say "May your firstborn die" or "May God put out your lamp"; that is, "May your heir
die."

The city of Jericho was cursed by Joshua. The army was commanded
to kill all men and women, cattle and sheep, and to burn the city with
fire.

This curse was intended to prevent anyone from building the city
again. It threatened that anyone who started to rebuild its foundation
would be punished by the death of his firstborn son; and if he continued
the work until the gates were hung his youngest son would die.

Jericho is still in ruins. No one has dared to rebuild it. Easterners are
afraid of curses, especially of those which are mentioned in the Holy
Scriptures.

During the reign of Ahab, the king of Israel, Hiel, the Bethelite, defied
the curse and built Jericho. He lost two of his sons [1 Kings 16:33-34].

OLD BREAD

And old shoes and clouted upon their feet, and old garments
upon them; and all the bread of their provision was dry and mouldy.
                                                         Josh. 9:5

Men who go on long journeys take large supplies of bread with them.
Other provisions, such as cheese, perish quickly; therefore they are eaten
on the first stage of the journey. But bread, being dry and thin, is kept
for more than a month. Emigrants from the Near East brought their
bread as far as Ellis Island, New York. Even though the bread becomes
dry and moldy, the hungry travelers eat it.

The inhabitants of Gibeon pretended they had come from a far country so that the Israelites would not know they were their neighbors. Thus,
through deception, they obtained a treaty from Joshua in which they
became allies of the Israelites. And when Joshua discovered that he had
been deceived and that the Gibeonites lived only a short distance from
the land which he had already conquered, he still honored his pledge
not to destroy them. This is because such treaties were made with sacred

oaths. Evidently, Joshua and the elders of Israel had sworn by the name of God.

The Hebrews were noted for keeping their word of honor. When they said something in the name of God, they kept their word.

Many centuries after, the Hebrew kings still honored this treaty between the Gibeonites and the children of Israel. What an example to the governments of our day, who forget their promises and pledges in a short while.

THE SUN STOOD STILL

And it came to pass, as they fled from before Israel, and were in the going down to Beth-horon, that the Lord cast down great stones from heaven upon them unto Azekah, and they died: they were more which died with hailstones than they whom the children of Israel slew with the sword.

Then spake Joshua to the Lord in the day when the Lord delivered up the Amorites before the children of Israel, and he said in the sight of Israel, Sun, stand thou still upon Gibeon; and thou, Moon, in the valley of Ajalon.

And the sun stood still, and the moon stayed, until the people had avenged themselves upon their enemies. Is not this written in the book of Jasher? So the sun stood still in the midst of heaven, and hasted not to go down about a whole day.

And there was no day like that before it or after it, that the Lord hearkened unto the voice of a man: for the Lord fought for Israel.

Joshua 10:11-14

In the olden days, the Hebrews, like many other races, thought that the earth was the center of the universe and that the sun, moon, and other planets revolved around it. This ancient astronomical concept was upheld by the Jews and the Christians until the sixteenth century, and it is still upheld in some primitive lands.

The Chaldeans were the first people to discover that the sun and not the earth is the center of the universe. These people, owing to the heat of the day, depended on the stars and the planets for their travels during the night, and, thus they explored the universe and made a study of the stars and planets by the naked eye. They succeeded in finding that the sun was the center of the universe, and that it took the earth three hundred and sixty days to travel around it. Later, the Egyptians adopted the Babylonian calendar which is based on the solar system.

Hebrews and prophets always attributed the glory and honor to God who led them and fought their battles. When God was on the side of the Israelites even the universe shared in their battles and rejoiced in their victories. In verse 14 the author states, "The Lord hearkened unto the voice of a man: for the Lord fought for Israel." In the book of Judges we are told that "the stars fought from their courses." They fought from heaven against Sisrea by the River Kishon [Judg. 5:20; Ps. 11:13]. This signifies that the stars rejoiced in the victory of God's people and the universe was on their side.

In the East when kings and great men die, the writers in their mourning songs say "the sun was covered with black and the moon refused to give light."

In the Gospels we are told when Jesus was on the cross, the sun became dark as a sign of mourning. Some Bible teachers say this was just an eclipse of the sun and was therefore a coincidence. It was not a coincidence. It was divinely ordained to show that even the universe shared in this great tragedy. Moreover, why should this phenomenon happen at the same hour when Jesus was on the cross?

Today some skeptical people who are doubtful about miracles maintain that the stopping of the sun could not have prolonged the day. This is because the sun does not revolve around the earth, but instead the earth and all planets revolve around the sun. Others say the earth stood still instead of the sun and moon. Be that as it may, a miracle took place during the great battle.

Assuredly God, who is the author of the universe, could have stopped the earth or the sun if He wished to do so, and thus caused a day to be longer by other means, which are beyond human understanding. On the other hand probably Joshua could have seen a second sun setting after leaving the deep valley of Ajalon in pursuit of the Amorites. In mountainous regions the sun sets early in the valley, but later it can still be seen from the top of the mountain.

Joshua had assured the people that the enemy would be conquered before the sun went down.

The miracle in this instance is the great victory which God granted to Joshua. Five kings and their large armies were defeated by Joshua and his army. Indeed, it must have been a long battle which resulted in a glorious victory in which the universe shared. Joshua had assured his army that the enemy would be defeated before the sun went down.

Miracles such as this cannot be explained by human mind. One has to accept them with faith, believing that God's power is unlimited and that God is the author of the universal laws.

ANAK, "GIANTS"

There was none of the Anakim left in the land of the children of Israel: only in Gaza, in Gath, and in Ashdod, there remained.

Josh. 11:22

The Eastern text reads *ganbarey* (giants, mighty men). Prior to the Israelite occupation of the land there might have been more of these mighty men. During the time of Saul and David, Goliath was the great giant of his day. He terrified the armies of Israel, but at last was slain by David [1 Sam. 17:4].

All races had certain powerful men who were known as giants and who defied the armies of their adversaries. Even today in the Near East one can find powerful men who can lift up a heavy burden and place it on the back of a mule. There were two such men in Kudshanis, Kurdistan, in 1941. They were noted for their strength throughout the land. In biblical days, during the wars, victory or defeat was often decided by the triumph or the defeat of these champions.

Before the advent of the gun, giants precipitated the battles. Ancient history is full of such accounts.

HOT SPRINGS

All the inhabitants of the hill country from Lebanon unto Misrephoth-maim, and all the Sidonians, them will I drive out from before the children of Israel: only divide thou it by lot unto the Israelites for an inheritance, as I have commanded thee. Josh. 13:6

The Aramaic reads *maya khamimey* (hot waters) instead of Misrephoth-maim. The hot springs which, during the Roman occupation of Palestine, were used for baths, are in Tiberias. The water is very famous for its healing properties. There are many other hot springs along the edges of the Sea of Galilee.

CALEB'S STRENGTH NEVER FAILED

As yet I am as strong this day as I was in the day that Moses sent me: as my strength was then, even so is my strength now, for war, both to go out, and to come in. Josh. 14:11

"To go out and to come in" is an Aramaic idiom which means to do anything which one is assigned to do—to lead the people out and to bring them back again.

Caleb, even though old, was a strong man. He must have been over seventy-five at this time. But seventy-five years are not too many years for the men of the desert who spend most of their time sleeping in the tents and idling in the camp, and who let the women do the work.

Moreover, Caleb had been loyal both to God and to Moses. In the face of much opposition he gave the people a good report about Palestine.

Therefore the Lord had been with him and had granted him strength and health. Moses was a hundred and twenty years when he died, and yet his eyes were not dim or his strength weakened [Deut. 34:7].

When one works in the interest of God's kingdom he receives strength and health.

SHILOH

And the whole congregation of the children of Israel assembled together at Shiloh, and set up the tabernacle of the congregation there: and the land was subdued before them.   Josh. 18:1

Shiloh was a town situated in the tribe of Ephraim. Here the Israelites gathered together after a large part of Palestine was conquered by Joshua. Here they erected the tabernacle of the Lord and made the city a center of worship [Judg. 18:31].

Shiloh was in the center of the land and easily accessible to all tribes. Therefore it became the mecca of the Israelites, the scene of great feasts and pilgrimages [Judg. 21:19; 1 Sam. 1:3].

The name of the place might be derived from *shaal* (to ask, make a petition, a place of peace).

"I HAVE NOT"

Behold, I have divided unto you by lot these nations that remain, to be an inheritance for your tribes, from Jordan, with all the nations that I have cut off, even unto the great sea westward.
                                                    Josh. 23:4

The Eastern text reads: "Behold, I have not divided to you the land of these nations that remain, in the inheritance of your tribes; but from the Jordan, all the nations that I have destroyed, even to the Great Sea westward, have I divided among you."

This portion of the land which was not conquered was not yet divided. In other words, one cannot divide what he does not possess. Some of the strong Hittite, Jebusite, and Canaanite kingdoms remained unconquered until the reign of David, and were conquered by him for the first time. Until David, the occupation of Palestine by the Israelites was partial and at times the Israelites were completely conquered and subjugated, now by the Syrians, now by the Midianites, and now by the Philistines.

HORNETS-RAIDERS

And I sent the hornet before you, which drave them out from before you, even the two kings of the Amorites; but not with thy sword, nor with thy bow.   Josh. 24:12

Diboriatha (hornet) is used metaphorically to mean raids. This is because desert raiders strike and run like hornets. [See commentary on "Hornet," Exod. 23:28.]

The kingdoms of Sihon and Og, the kings of the Amorites, were conquered by Moses at the battle of Jahaz [Num. 21:21-25]. Og, king of Mathnin (Bashan), was defeated at the battle of Ardai (Edrei) [Num. 21:33-35].

Evidently, these two kings had been weakened by Arab raiders who came from the Arabian desert.

CHAPTER SEVEN

JUDGES

INTRODUCTION

THE name Judges is a literal translation of the Aramaic word *Diany*, or Hebrew *Shapatim*.

The book of Judges is a chronicle of the days when the Israelites were ruled by judges, whom the people had appointed to lead them during the time of their tribulations.

Seemingly, the book is the work of various scribes who acted as recorders under the reign of particular judges. It is interesting to know that the Hebrews, from the time of Moses and Joshua, employed scribes in their tribal organizations as well as in their kingdom.

The book of Judges must have been written between the years 1400 and 1000 B.C. New material which had been handed down orally may have been added to the scrolls which were written by the original scribes.

The book contains some of the most alluring and dramatic episodes of men and women whom God called to lead Israel. The book of Judges gives us an idea of the faith, courage, humility and devotion of these great leaders of Israel who led their people and saved them from their enemies.

The greatest thing in the book of Judges is the democratic government and the democratic institutions of the Hebrew people. The period of Judges may be called the first democratic state that the world ever knew. It preceded all other democracies by many centuries.

Most of these judges were brave and humble, and many of them refused to lead until they were drafted by the people or called by God. During this period most of the issues were decided by the casting of lots. The judges were fair to rich and the poor alike, and they were looked upon not as overlords but as fathers of the tribes.

LACK OF CHARIOTS

And the Lord was with Judah; and he drave out the inhabitants of the mountain; but could not drive out the inhabitants of the valley, because they had chariots of iron.   Judg. 1:19

The Eastern text reads: "And the Lord was with Judah; and they possessed the mountain; but they could not destroy the inhabitants of the valley, because they had chariots of iron."

The error is caused by mistranslation of the Aramaic word *oyiretho* (they possessed) for *oyerith* (he possessed). The letter *wow* (o) is a sign of the third person plural. Without the ending *wow,* it would read "he" third person singular. Errors of this kind are found in other books of the Bible.

It was Judah, and not the Lord, who possessed the mountainous country, but failed to conquer the inhabitants of the valley because they had chariots of iron.

When Judah trusted in God she was able to defeat great armies, even those equipped with chariots of iron. But at times Judah was not with God; therefore she was defeated by her enemies.

The Israelites, being a desert people, were afraid of iron chariots, which they had never seen before. And it was because of this important weapon of war that the Philistines maintained their independence for many centuries, and at times even ruled over Israel.

KORIATH-ARBA

And Judah went against the Canaanites that dwelt in Hebron: now the name of Hebron before was Kirjath-arba: and they slew Sheshai, and Ahiman, and Talmai.

And from thence he went against the inhabitants of Debir: and the name of Debir before was Kirjath-sepher.   Judg. 1:10-11

Prior to the conquest of Palestine by the Hebrews the names of the ancient cities were in Aramaic dialects which were used in Palestine. Many of the inhabitants of Palestine had come there from Mesopotamia and Syria before the advent of the Hebrews. The movement westward had begun after the division of the languages and the dispersion of the people. Apparently the new immigrants were welcomed by the early settlers.

Koriath-arba means "the fourth city" or town; that is, the fourth largest city in that region. During the time of the Jewish kingdom, Hebron was the second city in importance, Jerusalem being first.

Koriath-sephra means "the town of scribes" or "of books." Apparently some of the inhabitants of the town knew how to read and write. The Hebrews called in *Debir-Dabir*. In Aramaic it means a "district governor." This title is still used in Arabic.

The Hebrews changed the names of many towns, cities, and localities, and renamed them after some of their great men, and as memorials of the events which took place there. This practice is prevalent all over the world.

HE BUILT A CITY

And the man went into the land of the Hittites, and built a city, and called the name thereof Luz: which is the name thereof unto this day.   Judg. 1:26

In Palestine and other biblical lands new towns or cities are generally named for the chief of the tribe or one of its founders. In Genesis we are told that when Cain was driven out of the land where he lived he went into the land of Nod and there he built a city which he named after his son [Gen. 4:17].

This native of Luz, later called Beth-el, went to the land of the Hittites, where he dwelt in a tent or a small house. When his descendants increased they built a city and called it Luz after the name of the city from which their father had escaped. They gave the credit for the founding and building of the city to their forefather.

On the other hand, in biblical lands one often comes across small towns or hamlets consisting of one, two, or three houses. There is a town in the region where the author was born called *Yekmala* (one house) because it was inhabited by a single family.

EHUR WAS MAIMED

But when the children of Israel cried unto the Lord, the Lord raised them up a deliverer, Ehud the son of Gera, a Benjamite, a man left-handed: and by him the children of Israel sent a present unto Eglon the king of Moab.   Judg. 3:15

Ehud (Aramaic *Ehur*), the son of Gera, a Benjamite, was not left-handed, but his right hand was maimed. This is why he was selected for the task of assassinating Eglon, the king of Moab.

Ehur was sent with the tribute which the Israelites paid yearly to the king of Moab. Ehur was chosen simply because the king of Moab would not suspect the ruse. Being a man with a maimed hand, the king let him come alone into his presence.

On the other hand, left-handed men were considered good warriors, experts in using sword and sling. Almost everyone could sling stones at a hairsbreadth target and not miss.

KING'S TOILET

When he was gone out, his servants came; and when they saw that, behold, the doors of the parlor were locked, they said, Surely he covereth his feet in his summer chamber.

And they tarried till they were ashamed: and, behold, he opened not the doors of the parlor; therefore they took a key, and opened them: and, behold, their lord was fallen down dead on the earth.

Judg. 3:24-25

The Aramaic reads, ". . . they said, Perhaps he has gone to the toilet in the closet of the upper chamber." So they waited outside, hoping that the king would open the door and come out into the parlor.

Ehur had locked the door, escaped through the porch, and had shut and locked the doors of the parlor.

When the servants waited too long and the king did not yet come out, they were perplexed and alarmed. And when they could wait no longer they unlocked the doors and found their lord slain on the floor.

See verses 20, 21.

SHAMGAR

And after him was Shamgar the son of Anath, which slew of the Philistines six hundred men with an oxgoad: and he also delivered Israel.

Judg. 3:31

The ox goad was used as a weapon. In those days, when steel and iron weapons were rare and difficult to obtain, warriors often used goads, jawbones, and other instruments. At times conquered people were completely disarmed. Even knives and sickles were forbidden.

Samson slew a thousand men with the jawbone of an ass [Judg. 15:15]. Fresh jawbones are heavy. In the East bones of animals which have broken down under heavy burdens are found scattered by the roads.

Shamgar used the ox goad simply because he had no other weapon. Ox goads and sharp objects were placed on the tips of sticks, which were then used as spears.

HOBAB

Now Heber the Kenite, which was of the children of Hobab
the father-in-law of Moses, had severed himself from the Kenites,
and pitched his tent unto the plain of Zaanaim, which is by Kedesh.

Judg. 4:11

Hobab, the father-in-law of Moses, should not be confused with Jethro
or Reuel. Hobab was another father-in-law of Moses. Moses in the
desert took an Ethiopian wife. There were many mixed races which left
Egypt with the children of Israel.

The Israelites, like the Arabs, were polygamists. Even today, some
of the Jews in Israel and Arab countries have two or three wives. Hobab
belonged to one of the Kenite families in Midian. But Heber, a descendant
of Hobab, had withdrawn from the tribe of the Kenites and had pitched
his tents near Rakim (Kadesh).

DEBORAH

And the Lord discomfited Sisera, and all his chariots, and all
his host, with the edge of the sword before Barak; so that Sisera
lighted down off his chariot, and fled away on his feet. Judg. 4:15

Deborah was led by God to choose the rainy season and the Valley of
Kishon for the decisive battle which was to decide the fate of Israel.
Being a prophetess, she knew that chariots with their heavy iron wheels
could not operate on muddy ground in the rainy season. Hebrew prophets
and seers were able to forecast rains and dry seasons.

The Kishon Valley is dry in the summer months and during periods
of long droughts. But during the rainy season the fertile soil turns into
churning mud.

The Hebrew infantry was well trained and light. When they saw that
the chariots were stuck in the mud, they rushed against the enemy from
their hideouts on Mount Tabor, and destroyed both the chariots and
the riders.

This victory was attributed to a woman prophetess, she believed in the
God of Israel, and he guided her to select the right time and the right
place for the battle.

When we think right and commune with God, we are directed and
guided, for the outcome of a battle is in the hands of the Lord.

WHITE ASSES

Speak, ye that ride on white asses, ye that sit in judgment, and walk by the way. Judg. 5:10

White asses are symbolic of purity and dignity. The elders and the men of dignity and humility generally ride on white asses when traveling between the town and the field. The kings of Judah rode on mules when they were anointed and proclaimed kings.

The donkey is symbolic of humility. When Jesus entered Jerusalem he rode on a colt. ". . . behold, thy King cometh unto thee: he is just, and having salvation; lowly, and riding upon an ass, and upon a colt the foal of an ass" [Zech. 9:9; Matt. 21:2-7].

In the olden days, when all honor and glory was given to God as the head of the state, both kings and the elders who were judges and statesmen humbly declined honors. But Gentile kings, princes, and nobles rode on white *horses* amid great pomp and ceremony.

WRITING AN ART

Out of Ephraim was there a root of them against Amalek; after thee, Benjamin, among thy people; out of Machir came down governors, and out of Zebulun they that handle the pen of the writer. Judg. 5:14

In biblical days the art of writing, like the arts of working silver, iron, and brass, was handed down from father to son. Certain families were renowned for having produced many scribes. This ancient custom was prevalent in some parts of the Near East until the dawn of Western civilization and Western missions. Certain towns and families were noted for being scribes, others for being silversmiths, and others for ironwork.

The tribe of Zebulun evidently was noted for producing many scribes which were employed by the government, especially when the people were mustered for war. The term "scribe" in the King James Version has unfortunately been translated as "officers." The Eastern text uses both, "officers and scribes."

Even today scribes are employed in the Near Eastern armies where the majority of people are illiterate. The scribes write letters for the soldiers and read to the soldiers their letters from home, besides working for the government.

GAD, DAN, AND ASHER UPBRAIDED

Gilead abode beyond Jordan: and why did Dan remain in ships?
Asher continued on the seashore, and abode in his breaches.

Judg. 5:17

The Eastern text reads *Gad* instead of *Gilead*. Gad was a tribe, but Gilead is the name of the region beyond the Jordan close to the Syrian border.

Evidently Gad, Dan, and Asher, for some unknown reason, had refused to cooperate with Deborah and Barak. They had been more mindful of their shipping and business than of the war. Deborah, in her song, is seemingly upbraiding them for not having joined the other tribes in freeing Israel from her enemies.

GIDEON

And there came an angel of the Lord, and sat under an oak which was in Ophrah, that pertained unto Joash the Abiezrite: and his son Gideon threshed wheat by the winepress, to hide it from the Midianites.
And the angel of the Lord appeared unto him, and said unto him, The Lord is with thee, thou mighty man of valor.

Judg. 6:11-12

Gideon saw the angel of the Lord in a daytime vision, just as the Lord appeared to Abraham [Gen. 12:7].

Angels, being spirits, appeared only in dreams and visions, and to men who were in ecstasy. The angel of the Lord appeared to Joseph in a dream or a vision [Matt. 1:20-24]. He also appeared and spoke to the Virgin Mary in a vision [Luke 1:26-38].

The Aramaic term *ethgli* (appeared) means that the appearance took place in a vision during the day or night.

The angel of the Lord appeared to Joseph in a dream and warned him to take the child and his mother and flee to Egypt [Matt. 2:13]. At times the term *ethgli* is used without mentioning the dream or vision. This is because *ethgli* is derived from *gla* (to reveal), and a revelation takes place when men are asleep or in ecstasy [Judg. 6:22-23].

Gideon had been praying and wondering why God had forsaken his people and delivered them into the hands of their enemies. At last he found that it was the people who had forsaken the Lord their God and broken his covenant. Gideon was called by God to lead Israel out of chaos.

GIDEON WANTED A SIGN

And he said unto him, If now I have found grace in thy sight,
then show me a sign that thou talkest with me.   Judg. 6:17

In biblical days there were many false gods and false prophets who often misled the people and led them into disaster. Men and women sometimes saw conflicting visions and dreams, making it hard for the people to believe in anyone. All of them claimed that the Lord had spoken to them, but it was obvious that the Lord had *not* spoken to *all* of them.

Gideon, like Moses, asked for a sign so that he could be assured that it was the Lord God of his own people who had communed with him [Exod. 4:1-9]. When the man who had seen a true vision showed a sign or performed a wonder, then the people believed in him [Exod. 4:30-31].

BASKET

And Gideon went in, and made ready a kid, and unleavened
cakes of an ephah of flour: the flesh he put in a basket, and he put
the broth in a pot, and brought it out unto him under the oak, and
presented it.   Judg. 6:19

In the olden days, men and women who visited a man of God for healing or consultation took with them a basket of freshly baked bread, cheese, fruits, and other articles of food as a gift. Even today, in the East, no one would think of visiting a holy man or a bishop or patriarch without offering a gift. Easterners seldom give money to a healer as a gift; they give bread, sheep, cheese, and other articles of food.

The bread and other food is distributed among the poor who gather around the man of God and at times follow him from place to place. This is why Jesus said, "You seek me, not because you saw the miracles, but just because you ate bread and were filled" [John 6:26].

When Saul and his servant found that they had no bread in the bag which they had taken on their journey, they took a coin, a fourth of a shekel, and gave it to Samuel as a gift [1 Sam. 9:7-8].

JEREBAAL

Therefore on that day he called him Jerubbaal, saying, Let Baal
plead against him, because he hath thrown down his altar.
                                                         Judg. 6:32

The Eastern text reads *Nedobaael* (Let Baal judge or plead his own cause against Gideon). Probably the error is caused by the similarity of *nun* (n) and *yoth* (y) or (i) and the similarity of *daleth* (d) and *resh* (r).

Nedon in Aramaic means, "Let him judge." *Nedon-baal* is in construct state form; therefore, *nun* (n) being a weak letter, is dropped.

The Hebrew scribe might have later used *yerebaal* (fighter of Baal) from the Aramaic word *yarob* (to become great). *Yerebael* does not mean to "plead" or to "judge," but, to "become great." It is derived from *rab* (to become great, grow up, increase in power, be exalted). This was the title of the king of Assyria [Hos. 10:6].

And if this was the new name of Gideon, it had been retained as it is in the Peshitta text.

WINE CHEERS GOD AND MAN

And the vine said unto them, Should I leave my wine, which cheereth God and man, and go to be promoted over the trees?
                                                                    Judg. 9:13

The term wine in this instance should not be taken literally. In Aramaic, wine is often used metaphorically, meaning joy, inspiration, teaching, and life-giving. "For this is my blood of the new testament, which is shed for many for the remission of sins" [Matt. 26:28].

The wine of which Jotham spoke in his parable is spiritual wine, the joy and harmony which cheers God and achieves reconciliation between God and man.

God is Spirit, and the Spirit does not drink material wine, nor is there wine or strong drink in the kingdom of God. If there is wine, then there will be marriages, also. Pure wine gladdens men's hearts if used moderately [Ps. 104:15]. Jesus said, ". . . I shall not drink from this fruit of the vine until the day when I drink it anew with you in the kingdom of God" [Matt. 26:29, Eastern text]. The kingdom of God does not contain material things.

By wine, Jesus meant joy. He was to renew the joy which they had at the Passover evening with the new joy which they would receive in the kingdom of God.

BRAMBLE

And the bramble said unto the trees, If in truth ye anoint me king over you, then come and put your trust in my shadow; and if not, let fire come out of the bramble, and devour the cedars of Lebanon.
                                                                    Judg. 9:15

Bramble is symbolic of difficulties, troubles, and annoyances. Shepherds, farmers, and laborers despise thorny bushes and brambles. At times sheep are caught in their thorny branches [Gen. 22:13]. Reapers and workers also suffer from them.

When the Lord appeared to Moses in Midian, he saw a burning bush. The bush symbolized difficulties. It burned, but it was not consumed, which indicated that Moses would suffer but at last would triumph over all his difficulties [Exod. 3:2-4].

The bramble symbolized the wicked people who made Abimeleck king over them. They were to turn against him, and many of them were to be slain. Abimeleck burned the men of Shechem in the tower of Shechem [Judg. 9:49].

Thus, Jotham's prophecy was fulfilled. The men of Shechem chose the bramble (Abimeleck) and Abimeleck destroyed them before he himself was destroyed.

THE BIRTH OF SAMSON

And the angel of the Lord appeared unto the woman, and said unto her, Behold now, thou are barren, and bearest not: but thou shalt conceive, and bear a son.   Judg. 13:3

The angel of the Lord communed with the woman in a vision. The Aramaic word *etikhzi*, like *ethgli* (appeared), means "appeared in a vision."

The angels of the Lord appeared to prophets and men of God in dreams and visions. They appeared in the form of men so that they might commune with them. Angel spirits cannot be seen with human eyes, so they manifest themselves in a human body and converse with men as a man converses with another man.

WINE PROHIBITED

She may not eat of any thing that cometh of the vine, neither let her drink wine or strong drink, nor eat any unclean thing: all that I commanded her let her observe.   Judg. 13:14

Samson's mother was to abstain from wine and strong drink because the Baal worshipers drank wine and strong drinks and then committed fornication in the temple. The Israelites had become victims of Baal worship. Every time they forsook the Lord they went after sensual Baal worship. Baal was the lord of fertility. The land of Baal was irrigated with rivers, streams, and rains. Food and fruits were abundant, and wine plentiful.

The angel instructed Samson's parents that their unborn child was to be a Nazarite, dedicated to the Lord. The angel struck at the root of the evil which had weakened Israel: drunkenness, immorality, and unclean foods, which can weaken any race or people.

INVOKING HOLY NAMES

And Manoah said unto the angel of the Lord, What is thy name, that when thy sayings come to pass we may do thee honor?
Judg. 13:17

The Aramaic word *nekrekh* (to call you, to invoke you) has been confused with *niakrekh* (to honor you). The two words are very similar, and when written by hand can easily be confused one with the other.

Manoah wanted to know the angel's name so that he and his wife might invoke his name during their prayers. In the East, even today, the people, during their prayers, invoke the names of patron saints and angels.

THE TERM "HEIFER"

And the men of the city said unto him on the seventh day before the sun went down, What is sweeter than honey? and what is stronger than a lion? And he said unto them, If ye had not plowed with my heifer, ye had not found out my riddle.
Judg. 14:18

The Eastern text reads: ". . . If you had not enticed my heifer, you would not have interpreted my riddle." Plowed is a mistranslation. Heifer in this instance means "weak-minded." In the East, a weak-minded man is called an ox, and a weak-minded woman a cow or an heifer. This is because oxen and cows must be guided by men; they never learn. When a man loses his mind, it is often said, "He has become an ox." In the book of Daniel we are told that Nebuchadnezzar ate grass like an ox, which means that he lost his mind [Dan. 4:33].

Samson's wife was deceived by the Philistine princes. After all, she was a Philistine and she was interested more in her people than in a leader of the Israelites, who were ruled by her people. She was a weak-minded woman who betrayed her husband because of the fear of her own people.

THREE HUNDRED FOXES

And Samson went and caught three hundred foxes, and took firebrands, and turned tail to tail, and put a firebrand in the midst between two tails.
Judg. 15:4

In this instance, Samson is used collectively. Samson was the ruler over Israel. He had ordered many men to go out and catch foxes for him. Probably he himself never caught any.

In the East all the actions of a tribe are credited and attributed to its chief. For example, Abraham defeated five kings. The army does not get the credit. Even in English, we often say, "Washington defeated the British"; that is, the army under George Washington defeated the British.

Many people doubt the story simply because they cannot realize how one man could catch so many foxes. Samson was merely a symbol for Israel here.

SAMSON'S HAIR

That he told her all his heart, and said unto her, There hath not come a razor upon mine head; for I have been a Nazarite unto God from my mother's womb: if I be shaven, then my strength will go from me, and I shall become weak, and be like any other man.

Judg. 16:17

The Hebrews believed that a man's strength was in his hair. This is because when a man dies, his hair still continues to grow for some time. This is why the Hebrew Nazarites did not shave. The hair was symbolic of divine strength, a sacred token and reminder that the Nazarite was dedicated to the Lord.

As long as Samson's hands felt the hair on his head he felt strong, but when his hair was gone the vow was broken and his strength departed. In other words, the strength was not in the hair, but in the vow and the divine instructions which were given by the angel [Judg. 13:5].

EASTERN HOSPITALITY

And they turned aside thither, to go in and to lodge in Gibeah: and when he went in, he sat him down in a street of the city: for there was no man that took them into his house to lodging.

Judg. 19:15

In lands where hotels, motels, and lodging houses are unknown, travelers lodge with relatives, friends, and acquaintances. Those who have no friends or acquaintances unload their donkeys and sit on the pack in the street until someone invites them to his house [Gen. 19:1-4].

Pious Easterners cannot happily eat, drink, and sleep when they know that strangers are in the street without shelter or food, especially when the latter are members of their own race. Easterners are famed for their hospitality and sharing. Today they are hosts to a stranger or wayfarer; tomorrow they might find themselves in the opposite situation, sitting in the street and waiting to be invited.

Jesus said, "Whatever you wish men to do for you, do likewise also for them; for this is the law and the prophets" [Matt. 7:12]. This is a universal law which cannot be violated: Give and it shall be given to you. When one invites strangers and wayfarers, he is inviting the Lord to his house, and the Lord will open many doors to him and reward him for his act. This belief is strongly upheld by all Easterners, Jews, Christians, and Moslems.

CHAPTER EIGHT

RUTH

INTRODUCTION

THE book of Ruth no doubt grew from oral narratives and folk stories. The fascinating story of a faithful woman, Naomi, and her devout daughter-in-law, Ruth, had impressed itself on the hearts of many faithful men and women in Israel.

At the outset, neither Naomi nor Ruth, her daughter-in-law, were known. They were simple poor folk about whom no one would venture to write. One was an Israelite and the other a Moabite who forsook her people and her gods for the God of Naomi and her people.

Years after, Ruth and Naomi became conspicuous because a descendant of Ruth became the greatest ruler and hero in Israel, King David.

The book of Ruth is a simple folk story written in a simple and innocent style. The episode was so well known that the writer could not omit any part of it.

Both Naomi and Ruth are admired for their faithfulness to the God of Israel in spite of the tragedies that occurred while living in a foreign land. Even during famine and disasters Naomi never forsook the God of her people. Her loyalty to the Hebrew religion and God's commandments was responsible for the conversion of her daughter-in-law, Ruth.

The book, like many other books in the Bible, is the work of a scribe, probably a court scribe.

EASTERN TOLERANCE

Now it came to pass in the days when the judges ruled, that there was a famine in the land. And a certain man of Beth-lehem-judah went to sojourn in the country of Moab, he, and his wife, and his two sons.   Ruth 1:1

During famines and natural catastrophies Easterners forget their political and religious differences and extend their hospitality both to their friends and their enemies. "Who knows?" they say, "Today you need me; tomorrow I may need you."

The Moabites and the Hebrews had been enemies since the days when Joshua conquered Palestine. The Hebrews were the descendants of Abraham, and the Moabites the descendants of Lot, the nephew of Abraham, but border incidents and grazing had kept the old feuds alive.

But now, when the Moabites looked from the other side of the Jordan Valley and saw the land of Israel scorched because of droughts, and heard of the plight and suffering of their kindred tribes, they opened their hearts to the famine-stricken Israelites who crossed the Jordan River to escape the famine that was devastating their land.

There was plenty of food in Moab. The land of Moab depends on heavy dew for irrigation. Thus, the Moabites were willing to extend a helpful hand to a people who were perishing because of a long drought and famine. Christian and Moslem tribes do the same during famines and other disasters. They forget their differences and help one another.

YOUR PARENTS

The Lord grant you that ye may find rest, each of you in the house of her husband. Then she kissed them; and they lifted up their voice, and wept.   Ruth 1:9

It should read "in the house of your parents" instead of "your husbands." The Aramaic word *abahekhon* means "your parents." The Aramaic word for "husbands" is *gabrey;* "your husbands" is *gabrakhon.*

The husbands of Naomi's daughters-in-law were dead. In verse 8 Naomi admonished her daughters-in-law to return to their own land, to the house of their own kinsmen. The term "her mother's house" is a mistranslation.

The two widows had no husbands to return to. In the East when a woman loses her husband she returns to the house of her parents or to her nearest kinsmen.

WHEAT IS GUARDED

And when Boaz had eaten and drunk, and his heart was merry, he went to lie down at the end of the heap of corn: and she came softly, and uncovered his feet, and laid her down.   Ruth 3:7

During the threshing season, the owner of the grain generally eats and sleeps at the threshing floor. Wheat, being dear and scarce, is often stolen by strangers, wayfarers, and at times even by hired workers. Even though the threshing floors are a stone's throw from the town, wheat must be carefully guarded.

Some landlords sleep in the heap; others bury themselves in the straw, leaving their heads out. And as the threshing floors are dark and deserted during the night, it is easy for a woman to sleep near a man without being noticed.

AN ANCIENT ORDINANCE

Tarry this night, and it shall be in the morning, that if he will perform unto thee the part of a kinsman, well; let him do the kinsman's part: but if he will not do the part of a kinsman to thee, then will I do the part of a kinsman to thee, as the Lord liveth: lie down until the morning.   Ruth 3:13

According to the Mosaic law, when a brother died having no child, his wife was not to marry a stranger, but must marry her husband's brother in order that he might raise offspring to his brother [Deut. 25:5].

This law was enacted by Moses in order to keep the land in the family [Ruth 4:1-6]. The maidens of one tribe whose father had no male heir and who had inherited his land were not to marry among other tribes, in order that the land might not change hands from one tribe to another [Num. 27:8-11].

ADVERTISE

And I thought to advertise thee, saying, Buy it before the inhabitants, and before the elders of my people. If thou wilt redeem it, redeem it: but if thou wilt not redeem it, then tell me, that I may know: for there is none to redeem it besides thee; and I am after thee. And he said, I will redeem it.   Ruth 4:4

The Aramaic word *egley* is derived from *gala* (to reveal, inform, make known). "Advertise you" is a mistranslation. It should read "to let you know."

Boaz wanted to inform his kinsmen in the presence of the townspeople relative to the field and Ruth. He wanted to know if his kinsman would be willing to redeem the field and marry Ruth. If not, he himself would redeem the field and marry Ruth [Ruth 4:9-10].

SHOES

Now this was the manner in former time in Israel concerning redeeming and concerning changing, for to confirm all things; a man plucked off his shoe, and gave it to his neighbor: and this was a testimony in Israel.   Ruth 4:7

In the East when the hand of a girl is sought in marriage and the father is willing to give her in marriage, he says, "I will make her a pair of shoes and place her under your feet." For many centuries women were looked down upon and were bought and sold in marketplaces.

Shoes symbolize inferiority: ". . . one whose shoes I am not worthy to remove" [Matt. 3:11, Eastern text].

In the East shoes are considered unclean. When the people enter a mosque or a church they take off their shoes. Then again, the sin of Adam has been blamed on the woman, and women are looked upon as temptations.

The taking off of shoes indicates relinquishing the right to acquire another woman, and to close the matter. The shoes serve as a reminder. Easterners use symbols and examples in order not to forget compacts and agreements. It is equivalent to saying, "I have washed my hands of the case."

CHAPTER NINE

1 and 2 SAMUEL

INTRODUCTION

SAMUEL, or *Shemoel*, means "the name of God." This name was given to him because his mother invoked the name of the God of Israel when she prayed for a child, and God answered her prayer. Thus, *Shemoel* means also "God has heard my prayer."

The two books are called by the name of Samuel simply because the latter was a ruler over Israel and most of these events occurred during his lifetime. Moreover, it was the prophet Samuel who appointed both King Saul and later King David to rule over Israel.

Thus the two books cover most of the occurrences and events during the long ministry of Samuel. The books also relate the stories of the boyhood of Samuel and of David, who became the greatest hero in the history of the Israelites. The two books have a great deal to do with the establishment of the Hebrew monarchy.

Samuel was a great prophet and a true judge over Israel. As a leader he never deviated from the way of God. He upheld the Mosaic law and the ordinances, and led the people during the time of their distress and subjugation under the Philistines.

1 SAMUEL

LORD OF HOSTS

And this man went up out of his city yearly to worship and to sacrifice unto the Lord of hosts in Shiloh. And the two sons of Eli, Hophni and Phinehas, the priests of the Lord, were there.

1 Sam. 1:3

Sabaoth is a title rather than a name. *Sabaoth* (hosts) signified God's authority over the armies—"the Lord God of hosts"; that is, of heavenly bodies, the angelic legions which Isaiah saw ministering to the Lord [Gen. 32:1-2; Isa. 6:1-4].

The term *sabaoth* was used when the Israelites implored God's help against their enemies, when the hand of man had failed. Then again, the Lord God of Israel was the Lord of their armies. The people fought for the cause of God's religion, and in his name.

The term "Lord of hosts" occurs very frequently in the Bible, especially when the prophets spoke of his great power and implored him for help.

MY MOUTH IS ENLARGED

And Hannah prayed, and said, My heart rejoiceth in the Lord, mine horn is exalted in the Lord; my mouth is enlarged over mine enemies; because I rejoice in thy salvation.　　　　1 Sam. 2:1

"My mouth is enlarged" is an Aramaic idiom which means, "Now I can talk back, and say plenty."

Hannah had been barren for many years. Peninnah, the other wife of her husband, had called her "the barren." Other women had gossiped about her and at times reproached her.

Now Hannah could talk back, and could sing and shout with joy. Her horn had been exalted; that is, she had been honored and had become victorious. God had taken away her reproach.

ELI'S SONS MISBEHAVED

Now Eli was very old, and heard all that his sons did unto all Israel; and how they lay with the women that assembled at the door of the tabernacle of the congregation.　　　　1 Sam. 2:22

Eli's sons did not lie with the women that assembled to pray at the door of the tabernacle of the congregation. No matter how wicked they were, they could not have committed such an evil act in the holy place and in the presence of the people who worshiped.

The Aramaic word *mesarin* in this instance means "to treat shamefully," "to dishonor" and "to insult." In other words, Eli's sons accosted some of the women and uttered impious remarks.

Eli's wicked sons accosted women who came to worship and at times reviled them.

STONE OF HELP

And the word of Samuel came to all Israel. Now Israel went out against the Philistines, to battle, and pitched beside Eben-ezer: and the Philistines pitched in Aphek.   1 Sam. 4:1

The Aramaic reads *Kepa di Aodrana* (the Stone of Help, the Rock of Help). The Hebrew equivalent is *Eben-ezer* (the Stone of Help). A large stone is often called a rock. The Aramaic word for rock is *shoaa.*

Eben-ezer is the name of a place where the Israelites defeated the Philistines. Samuel, in commemorating the victory, set a stone between Mizpeh and Shen and called it the "Stone of Help" [1 Sam. 7:12].

HEMORRHOIDS

Wherefore ye shall make images of your emerods, and images of your mice that mar the land; and ye shall give glory unto the God of Israel: peradventure he will lighten his hand from off you, and from off your gods, and from off your land.   1 Sam. 6:5

The Aramaic word *takhorey* means "hemorrhoids" or "piles." They appear in the rectum. But boils may appear on any part of the body.

Takhorey are not to be confused with the boils with which the Egyptians were afflicted [Exod. 9:9]. These, in Aramaic, are called *shokhney* (cancerous boils, blisters), which are quite frequent in lands where unsanitary conditions are prevalent.

ARK OF GOD FEARED

And he smote the men of Beth-shemesh, because they had looked into the ark of the Lord, even he smote of the people fifty thousand and three-score and ten men: and the people lamented, because the Lord had smitten many of the people with a great slaughter.

1 Sam. 6:19

Sacred relics and shrines are highly revered and feared by the people. In the East the Moslems revere and respect Christian holy places, and the Christians likewise respect the Moslem holy places. The Moslems often visit Christian shrines and places of worship, but until recently, the

Christians were prohibited from entering Moslem holy places. Even now, some shrines and places of worship are still restricted to Moslems only.

This custom was true in the olden days, when people believed in many gods and when each nation had its own deities. The pagans feared Hebrew holy places and sacred relics such as the Ark of the Covenant. And the Hebrews not only feared the ancient pagan shrines but also worshiped them again and again.

During the reign of Samuel, the Hebrews now and then worshiped Baal and Ashtaroth. This is why the Hebrews were asked to destroy pagan idols [1 Sam. 7:3-4].

The Philistines had heard of the wonders which the God of Israel had performed by the hand of Moses, and the mystical power of the golden Ark which contained the law and the commandments [verse 6]. Since its capture in the battle, they were afraid of it. And when boil plagues played havoc with them, they attributed them to the Ark, because they had a guilty conscience in fighting against the Israelites and in taking their sacred Ark.

Now the lords of the Philistines had to send it back, but, according to the Eastern custom, they could not send it back empty. They had to send some gifts with it as trespass offerings to the God of Israel, against whom they had transgressed [verse 17].

DREW WATER

And they gathered together to Mizpeh, and drew water, and poured it out before the Lord, and fasted on that day, and said there, we have sinned against the Lord. And Samuel judged the children of Israel in Mizpeh. 1 Sam. 7:6

"Drew water and poured it out before the Lord" should not be confused with the sacred ordinances and ceremonial rites.

In Palestine and the Arabian desert where water is scarce the people draw water from the wells in advance of the gathering. The water is needed for drinking, cooking, washing, and for watering the camels, oxen, and sheep which are brought to be sacrificed.

The Israelites gathered at Mizpeh in large numbers. They came to ask Samuel to seek help from the Lord to be delivered from the Philistines.

Water was provided in advance for the people as well as for the sheep and cattle.

During the summer season the brooks dry up and wells are the only sources of supply. It takes considerable time to draw water into the troughs [Gen. 29:2-10].

FOXES

And he passed through mount Ephraim, and passed through the land of Shalisha, but they found them not: then they passed through the land of Shalim, and there they were not: and he passed through the land of the Benjamites, but they found them not.   1 Sam. 9:4

The Eastern text reads *taley* (foxes). The Hebrew for foxes is *shalim. Shalim* should not be confused with *shalem* or *salem* (Jerusalem). *Taw* at times is pronounced *sh* as in *Athur,* and *Ashur* (Assyria).

GIFTS TO THE MEN OF GOD

Then said Saul to his servant, But, behold, if we go, what shall we bring the man? for the bread is spent in our vessels, and there is not a present to bring to the man of God: what have we?

1 Sam. 9:7

In biblical lands when men and women visit a holy man, a prophet, or a king, they take gifts with them. The size of the gift is determined by the nobility, social standing, and the wealth of the visitor; that is to say, each person gives according to his wealth. Even the poor must take a gift, no matter how small it is.

Nevertheless, in the case of men of God, prophets, seers, and healers, the gifts generally consist of a number of loaves of bread, a little honey, cheese, fish, and other foods; but the bread is more proper than other food staples. In the East bread is regarded as the staff of life. Moreover, bread is considered sacred. "And Jesus said unto them, I am the bread of life: he that cometh to me shall never hunger" [John 6:35].

When Jesse sent David to King Saul, he loaded a donkey with many loaves of bread, a skin full of wine and a kid, and sent them as a gift by the hand of David [1 Sam. 16:20]. Moreover, Gideon bid the angel of the Lord who appeared to him to tarry with him until he could bring a gift; then he brought a basket containing meat and unleavened bread [Judg. 6:18].

When people have no faith in a prophet, or dislike a ruler, they do not offer him gifts. When Saul was anointed king over Israel, some of the people refused to bring gifts. They thought that he was not the right kind of ruler [1 Sam. 10:27]. In the book of Proverbs we read, "A man's gift maketh room for him, and bringeth him before great men" [Prov. 18:16].

When the people from Issachar came to see David they brought loads of loaves of bread on the backs of donkeys, oxen, and in carts.

When Naaman, the captain of the army of the king of Syria, was healed from his leprosy, he brought many costly gifts to Elijah the prophet, but the latter refused them because they were gifts of silver and gold and costly garments [2 Kings 5:15-16].

Gifts are offered as a thanks offering to God for the services rendered by his holy men. The gifts are offered in advance as a token of faith in the men of God, who share them with the poor and the needy.

Saul was embarrassed to appear before Samuel without a few loaves of bread. His servant told him that he had a small silver coin which would be sufficient for a gift.

It is not the amount of the gift that counts, but the spirit and thoughtfulness with which it is given.

PRESENTS TO KINGS

But the children of Belial said, How shall this man save us? And they despised him, and brought him no presents. But he held his peace.   1 Sam. 10:27

Beni khetaha means "wicked" or "sinful men." These men were not convinced that Saul could save them; so they did not bring him any presents.

In the olden days kings received no salary from the state. They were supported by gifts which the people offered to them when they came to see them, and by taxes. Some of the kings had large estates, sheep and cattle, and many menservants and maidservants, who worked for them without wages.

King Saul, instead of taxing the people, confiscating fields and vineyards, and accepting bribes, worked in the field and tended sheep [1 Sam. 11:5].

Then again, when Saul was made king over Israel he was a poor man. Kings spent most of their incomes on guests, banquets, and armed forces.

MUST OBEY THE KING

Now therefore stand and see this great thing, which the Lord will do before your eyes.   1 Sam. 12:16

The Aramaic word *alekon* (against you) has been confused with *ainakhon* (your eyes). *Lamed* (1) and *nun* (n) are very similar.

After the anointing of Saul as king over Israel, Samuel warned the people that they should not provoke God's anger against Israel, but should be loyal to the king. God had heard their supplication for a king, even though their demand for an earthly ruler over them displeased him [verse 15].

THREE THOUSAND, NOT THIRTY THOUSAND

And the Philistines gathered themselves together to fight with Israel, thirty thousand chariots, and six thousand horsemen, and people as the sand which is on the seashore in multitude: and they came up, and pitched in Michmash, eastward from Beth-aven.

1 Sam. 13:5

The Aramaic words *telatha alpin* mean "three thousand." *Telatha* (three) has been confused with *tlathin* (thirty).

The Philistines could not have mustered so many chariots, nor was such a great number of chariots needed to defeat a small and poorly armed force of Israelites under Saul [verse 6].

WILD HONEY

And when the people were come into the wood, behold, the honey dropped; but no man put his hand to his mouth: for the people feared the oath.

1 Sam. 14:26

In many parts of the Near East honey is found in the trunks of old trees, in rocks, and on the ground.

Palestine is a rocky place. In some places rocks and small stones are so abundant that one can scarcely see the soil. Many scientists claim that the soil has been carried away by erosion. Others claim that the abundance of rocks is due to volcanic eruptions.

The climate in Palestine is generally dry and, therefore, very suitable for the swarms of bees, which settle in the rocky places and in small and secure cracks in the rocks. During the summer months one can see honey running on the rocks and in the bark of the trees.

This was more true of the olden days, when Palestine was sparsely settled and forests were abundant. The swarms of bees found new nests in the holes of the trees and in the rocks. ". . . and he made him to suck honey out of the rock, and oil out of the flinty rock" [Deut. 32:13].

Centuries ago, Palestine, even though a poor land, had many flocks and much wild honey. Probably this is why the land was called literally "a land flowing with milk and honey" [Exod. 3:8]. But milk and honey are symbolic of peace, prosperity, and spirituality.

MEAT WITH BLOOD

And the people flew upon the spoil, and took sheep, and oxen, and calves, and slew them on the ground: and the people did eat them with the blood.   1 Sam. 14:32

The Aramaic word *ethlaabo* means "to seize greedily," "to give oneself over to pleasures," or "be gluttonous."

The Israelites were hungry and faint while fighting the Philistines, and when the enemy was defeated, they rushed to slaughter sheep and oxen and to eat the meat with the blood, although it was against the Mosaic law to eat blood.

During the battle there was no one to inspect the meat and to see that all the blood was poured out. The animals were slaughtered and the meat cooked hastily. Kosher meat must not contain any blood.

AN EVIL SPIRIT

But the Spirit of the Lord departed from Saul, and an evil spirit from the Lord troubled him.   1 Sam. 16:14

The term *rokha* (spirit) also means "wind," "pride," and "temper."

The term "spirit" here should not be confused with the Holy Spirit, for the Holy Spirit cannot turn into an evil spirit, nor is there an evil spirit in God that could proceed from him. The term spirit also means "tendency"; that is, a tendency to do evil or an evil inclination.

When the Spirit of the Lord departed from Saul he lost his good graces and began to suspect everyone around him. The change was attributed to God without whose knowledge nothing happens in this universe. The Hebrews, like other races, blamed everything on their God.

King Saul had been disloyal both to Samuel and to God. Wherefore, he lost God's grace and blessing which had been upon him. When these spiritual forces and the blessing he had received during his crowning were gone, the king found himself lacking and lost. Now he was troubled with his own evil thoughts, hatred, and jealousy simply because David, the son of Jesse, was a valiant man and was acclaimed by the people as a great hero. In other words, jealousy and hatred had taken possession of Saul and were driving him crazy.

The Lord knew that Saul was now possessed with an evil spirit which made him jealous of David.

GIFTS TO THE RULERS

And Jesse took an ass laden with bread, and a bottle of wine, and a kid, and sent them by David his son unto Saul.   1 Sam. 16:20

In biblical days, just like today, it was the custom not to send a man to appear before a king empty-handed. Jesse sent bread, a skin of wine, and a kid of goats, not because King Saul was in need, but because he wanted to honor the king not only with words but also with gifts that would prove his loyalty and love for the king.

This ancient custom is still practiced in many Eastern lands. The people never send an ambassador or even a messenger without a gift. [See "Gifts."]

INSANITY

And it came to pass, when the evil spirit from God was upon Saul, that David took a harp, and played with his hand: so Saul was refreshed, and was well, and the evil spirit departed from him.

1 Sam. 16:23

Even today nomadic or backward peoples believe that evil spirits can be driven away by the sound of music or the striking of two pieces of metal one against the other.

Nekhash means an "augurer," a "diviner," or a "worker in brass." From time immemorial it has been known that music charms snakes and domestic animals and frightens evil spirits and wild animals.

Saul, no doubt, had some mental trouble or some form of insanity, which in the olden days men called an evil spirit or force. King Saul was jealous of his kingship and, being a member of the tribe of Benjamin, the least among the tribes of Israel, he was afraid that he might be overthrown by his enemies. The evil spirit took possession of his suspicious mind and at times made him violent [1 Sam. 18:10-11].

When David played the harp, Saul began to think of beautiful musical rhythms and thus recovered from the evil spirit. In other words, he let the evil spirit go.

ARMY PROVISIONS

And carry these ten cheeses unto the captain of their thousand, and look how thy brethren fare, and take their pledge.
Now Saul, and they, and all the men of Israel, were in the valley of Elah, fighting with the Philistines.   1 Sam. 17:18-19

In the olden days armed forces were neither fed nor clothed by the state. Each soldier was supported by his own family, and at times he lived off the land. The soldiers fought to defend their land, and they considered it an honor to die in battle.

Also, the soldiers participated in the spoils, and were permitted to take food and other necessities of life by violence [Num. 31:25-46].

"And the soldiers also asked him saying, What shall we do? And he said to them, Do not molest any man, and do not accuse any man; your own wages should be enough for you" [Luke 3:14, Eastern text]. (Roman soldiers were hired. They received a small salary and also a portion of the booty.)

Prior to World War II, soldiers in some of the Eastern countries were unpaid, but were allowed to plunder citizens and take things by violence. This is why, until recent days, government officials and soldiers were hated and feared. Some governments paid only ten or fifteen cents a month.

Jesse had to supply his sons with provisions. He also sent a few cheeses to the commandant of the army.

FIGURATIVE SPEECH

And the women answered one another as they played, and said, Saul hath slain his thousands, and David his ten thousands.

And Saul was very wroth, and the saying displeased him; and he said, They have ascribed unto David ten thousands, and to me they have ascribed but thousands: and what can he have more but the kingdom?
                                                            1 Sam. 18:7-8

The figures given here should not be taken literally. Thousands and ten thousands, in Eastern languages, mean many. In the olden days, large figures, such as million and billion, were unknown. Not until recent days did the tribal people know or hear of such large figures. Hundred was the highest number which the people used in their daily conversation. Only learned men understood the meaning of thousand and ten thousand.

In biblical days such large figures as thousand and ten thousand were seldom used. Only kings and princes who collected taxes knew the exact meaning of these high numerals. The simple people knew that they were high figures, but they did not know *how* high. Illiterate people who count numbers on their fingers can hardly understand the difference between a thousand and a million.

David could not have killed tens of thousands of Philistines, especially at a time when soldiers fought with swords, spears, knives, or even jawbones of asses, and other crude implements of war.

What the women said was that Saul had slain many Philistines and that David had slain many times more. In those days, battles were decided in a few hours or days. On the other hand, the armies were small and the people could not stay long on the battlefield without water and food.

On such occasions poets magnify their heroes. God was with David. He helped him to defeat the champion of the Philistines who had blasphemed against God, and to rout their armies.

WORRIES

And it came to pass on the morrow, that the evil spirit from God came upon Saul, and he prophesied in the midst of the house: and David played with his hand, as at other times: and there was a javelin in Saul's hand.   1 Sam. 18:10

The evil spirit, in this case, was Saul's worry because David had captured his popularity. It was a depressing spirit which plagued the king. Whenever he heard the echoes of the voices of the women singing and dancing and saying, "Saul has slain his thousands, and David his ten thousands," he was so enraged that at times he became violent and tried to kill David.

But when David played on his harp, Saul forgot his worries over his lost prestige. Now his mind was on the music.

Man cannot think about two things at the same time. The mind is like a baby sitter. It cannot take care of the body and worries at the same time. This is why Jesus said, "Do not worry for your life, what you will eat and what you will drink . . ." [Matt. 6:25]. Eastern text.

BRIDE PURCHASED

And Saul said, Thus shall ye say to David, The king desireth not any dowry, but a hundred foreskins of the Philistines, to be avenged of the king's enemies. But Saul thought to make David fall by the hand of the Philistines.   1 Sam. 18:25

The Aramaic word *mahra* refers to the price paid by the bridegroom to the father of his bride. The bride, in this case, is called *makhirta* (purchased for a price). This custom is still practiced today. Bridegrooms pay a price to their bride's parents in the form of money, cattle, or sheep.

On the other hand, in some countries in the East, such as Egypt and Iran, the father of the bride offers money and rich gifts to the bridegroom. Both systems are still practiced today.

King Saul wanted no money. What he wanted was to do away with his son-in-law-to-be, so he demanded what he thought would be an impossible price for his daughter. But David slew two hundred (one hundred, according to King James Version) Philistines and brought their foreskins to Saul as proof of his victory over the king's enemies.

"Dowry" is another name for the gift which the father of the bride gives to the bridegroom. But in this instance David was to pay a price to Saul for his daughter.

LOYALTY TO THE KING

For he did put his life in his hand, and slew the Philistine, and the Lord wrought a great salvation for all Israel: thou sawest it, and didst rejoice: wherefore then wilt thou sin against innocent blood, to slay David without a cause?   1 Sam. 19:5

The Eastern text reads: "For he put his life at your disposal . . ."; that is, "He risked his life for you when he killed the Philistine giant." The Aramaic word *edaik* (your hand) is confused with *edey* (his hand).

The reference here is to David, who placed himself in King Saul's hands and volunteered to accept the challenge of the Philistine who had defied the armies of Israel. David was but a youth, but he was willing to avenge King Saul and the armies of Israel.

In Aramaic we often say "I have placed myself in your hand," which means "I am at your service." We also say "I have placed my life in my hand," which means "I have exposed myself to danger" [1 Sam. 28:21; Job 13:14].

Jonathan reminded his father, Saul, that David was willing to die for the king.

In Psalm 119:109 (Eastern text), we read: "My soul is continually in thy hands [King James Version reads 'my hand']; I do not forget thy law," which means, "I am willing to lay down my life for the cause of thy law."

THIRD HOUR, NOT THREE DAYS

Then Jonathan said to David, Tomorrow is the new moon: and thou shalt be missed, because thy seat will be empty.

And when thou hast stayed three days, then thou shalt go down quickly, and come to the place where thou didst hide thyself when the business was in hand, and shalt remain by the stone Ezel.
                      1 Sam. 20:18-19

The Eastern text reads: "And when at the third hour you will be wanted very much, then you shall come tomorrow to the place where you hid yourself, and you shall sit down beside the same stone."

This incident took place at the beginning of the month, which was a holiday. The king made a banquet for his warriors and dignitaries. The feast was to take place the next day. The Aramaic word *shaain* means "hours." At the time of the banquet, David's place would be empty, and the king would inquire about him and wonder why he was not at the banquet.

HE BECAME AS A STONE

But it came to pass in the morning, when the wine was gone out of Nabal, and his wife had told him these things, that his heart died within him, and he became as a stone.

And it came to pass about ten days after, that the Lord smote Nabal, that he died.
1 Sam. 25:37-38

"And he became as a stone" is an Aramaic idiom which means that he was stricken, had a heart attack, or became paralyzed. In the olden days our present medical terms were unknown, of course. When a man was stiff and he could not move, it was said, "He has become as a stone." As we see from the text, Nabal died ten days later. Had he actually turned into a stone, he would have died at once. Sayings like these are well understood by all Easterners, who speak in metaphors.

Nabal's anger killed him. Nabal was so bitter against David that the little kindnesses which his wife had done for him caused him to suffer a heart attack.

David was a rebel and was hunted by King Saul. Any kind of hospitality extended to him would be misconstrued by the king, and the act would be considered treason. Thus Nabal, because of fear or rage, had a stroke.

THE MEDIUM OF ENDOR

Then said the woman, Whom shall I bring up unto thee? And he said, Bring me up Samuel.

And when the woman saw Samuel, she cried with a loud voice: and the woman spake to Saul, saying, Why hast thou deceived me? for thou art Saul.
1 Sam. 28:11-12

The term "familiar spirit" refers to knowledge of necromancy, divining, and foretelling. There were many pagans and Israelites who practiced this art, though it was prohibited by the Mosaic law and condemned by the Hebrew prophets. Both Samuel and Saul had sought to destroy all these men and women who were engaged in witchcraft.

The person with the familiar spirit serves as a medium in contacting the dead (or living persons who may be far away) and converses with them. The work sometimes is done by means of contemplation or by a hidden force which is called the familiar spirit; that is, the method acquired through experience. This is because the method is known only to the person who has the gift and the ability of divining.

Even today there are many men and women in the East who act as mediums, predicting events and answering many hidden questions for a price. And they are consulted by governors, noblemen, and the people. These witches do not believe in God.

After the death of Samuel, there was no other prophet in Israel of whom to inquire. The Israelites had gone astray from the religion of their fathers, and many of them were worshiping pagan deities, so that their God was silent. Therefore, Saul had to seek the help of a woman medium who had this familiar knowledge in communing with the dead.

After contemplating, the woman saw the picture of Samuel and then gave the description of him to the king, which made it possible for him to commune with Samuel. Meanwhile, King Saul knew that he had been rejected by God, because he had not obeyed God's voice and carried out his orders. The words that Samuel had uttered in his ears when he was still alive were made audible again to him.

On the other hand, King Saul for some time had seen ahead a dark future, defeat, and death.

REAR GUARD

But David pursued, he and four hundred men: for two hundred abode behind, which were so faint that they could not go over the brook Besor.   1 Sam. 30:10

The Eastern text reads: "And David continued the pursuit with four hundred men; then the two hundred men who were left behind rose up and kept guard, that the raiders might not cross the brook of Besor."

The two hundred men were left as a rear guard to prevent the enemy from crossing the brook of Besor. These men were not so faint that they could not go. They had to protect the rear. This is why David gave them an equal share of the plunder to which they were entitled.

This ancient custom is still upheld among the tribal people. The booty is divided equally among all the raiding force.

NEGEB

We made an invasion upon the south of the Cherethites, and upon the coast which belongeth to Judah, and upon the south of Caleb; and we burned Ziklag with fire.   1 Sam. 30:14

The Eastern text reads: "After we returned from raiding the Negeb of Judah and the Negeb of Caleb and from Ziklag, and we burned the towns with fire."

"Cherethites" should read "Negeb"; that is, the south country. The Cherethites and Pelethites were two army units; namely, the archers and the slingers [1 Kings 1:38, Eastern text].

2 SAMUEL

FAST AS A GAZELLE

The beauty of Israel is slain upon thy high places: how are the mighty fallen!   2 Sam. 1:19

The Aramaic word *tabya* (gazelle) has been confused with the Aramaic word *taba* (good, beautiful). The Hebrew uses the word *saboh* (to be beautiful). The Aramaic word *sabat* means an "ornament" or "adornment."

David, in his famous song, is here likening Saul and Jonathan to gazelles in their swiftness, but they were caught and slain as a fast gazelle is caught and slain by the hunters.

"They were swifter than eagles; they were stronger than lions" [verse 23] are terms of speech still used today in Aramaic and other Semitic languages. We often say, "He is as fast as a gazelle." Eastern poets often liken valiant men to gazelles and eagles.

CHOICEST FIELDS

Ye mountains of Gilboa, let there be no dew, neither let there be rain, upon you, nor fields of offerings: for there the shield of the mighty is vilely cast away, the shield of Saul, as though he had not been anointed with oil.   2 Sam. 1:21

The King James Version's "fields of offerings" should read "choicest fields." The error, in this instance, is caused by confusing the Aramaic words *damparshian* (the choicest) and *porshan* (portion set apart as an offering to God).

Mount Gilboa lies east of the plain of Esdraelon. The mount is about 1,700 feet above sea level and is the highest mountain range between Jazreel and the Jordan Valley.

The fields below the slopes of these rugged hills are very fertile. The plain of Esdraelon was the breadbasket of Israel.

No doubt, the battle between the Israelites and the Philistines took place in the fertile fields below Mount Gilboa. When Israel was defeated, Saul and his sons were overtaken and slain as they fled toward Jordan on their way to Manheim. This is why David likens them to a gazelle.

SWIFTER THAN AN EAGLE

Saul and Jonathan were lovely and pleasant in their lives, and in their death they were not divided: they were swifter than eagles, they were stronger than lions.   2 Sam. 1:23

"Swifter than an eagle" is an Aramaic idiom which means "very fast." These terms of speech are used figuratively and, therefore, should not be taken literally. Not even an Arabian horse can run as fast as an eagle.

In the East, valiant men of war are protrayed as eagles. Saul and Jonathan were mighty men of war. They moved fast on the battlefield. Probably they were faster than other men. In the olden days swiftness in the battlefield was of great importance, especially in mountainous regions. See the commentary on 2 Samuel 1:19.

JOAB'S MOTHER WAS PROMINENT

And they took up Asahel, and buried him in the sepulchre of his father, which was in Bethlehem. And Joab and his men went all night, and they came to Hebron at break of day.   2 Sam. 2:32

The name of the father of Joab, Abishai, and Asahel (Aramaic *Ashael*) is not mentioned in the Bible. The three brothers are always called by the name of their mother Zeruiah (Aramaic *Zoriah*), one of the daughters of Jesse, and a sister of King David.

In the East, when a man dies and his children are young the boys are called by the name of the mother. The name is generally given by the boys' playmates who have not seen, or have forgotten, the father of the orphan boys, but who know the mother. Moreover, in the East, when the mother is more important or prominent than the father, the children are called by her name. Zoriah was the sister of the king; so everyone in Israel knew her.

DOG'S HEAD

Then was Abner very wroth for the words of Ish-bosheth, and said, Am I a dog's head, which against Judah do show kindness this day unto the house of Saul thy father, to his brethren, and to his friends, and have not delivered thee into the hand of David, that thou chargest me to-day with a fault concerning this woman?   2 Sam. 3:8

"Am I a dog's head" is a mistranslation of the Aramaic metaphor *resh kalbey* (the leader or headman of vicious men). In the East, vicious men and gossipers are called *kalbey* (dogs).

The Eastern text reads, "Am I the leader of vicious men in Judah?" Abner implied that he was treated by Ashbashul (Ishboshesh) as though he were a leader of the armed bands of Judah which plagued the Israelites and sought the throne of Israel. Even today, vicious men and gossipers are called *kalbey* (dogs). Paul warned the Philippians to beware of dogs; that is, vicious gossipers [Phil. 3:2].

BILL OF DIVORCE

And he said, Well; I will make a league with thee: but one thing I require of thee, that is, Thou shalt not see my face, except thou first bring Michal Saul's daughter, when thou comest to see my face.

And David sent messengers to Ish-bosheth Saul's son, saying, Deliver me my wife Michal, which I espoused to me for a hundred foreskins of the Philistines.   2 Sam. 3:13-14

Michal (Aramaic *Malchel*) was a legal wife of David. The latter had married her according to the customs, paying a price for her. David had slain two hundred (one hundred, according to King James Version) Philistines for *mahra* (the price of the bride). When David fled, Saul took her and gave her to Phaltiel. The term "espoused" is the wrong word. David had lived with Michal prior to his flight from King Saul, but David had taken her by force and, therefore, her marriage to Phaltiel was illegal. This is because David had not given her a bill of divorce, according to the Mosaic law [Deut. 24:1-4].

On the other hand, Michal was David's first love, but because of his difficulties with his father-in-law, Saul, he had spent little time with her. Now the purpose of the request was more a political move than an expression of love.

Michal had lost her love for David, whom she blamed for the downfall of her father's house and the loss of the kingdom. Then again, David had already married many other wives. The love she had for him when they were young was now dead. Now David was an enemy of the house of her father.

DIED DEFENSELESS

And the king lamented over Abner, and said, Died Abner as a fool dieth?

Thy hands were not bound, nor thy feet put into fetters: as a man falleth before wicked men, so fellest thou. And all the people wept again over him.   2 Sam. 3:33-34

The Eastern text reads, "Abner died like Nabal"; that is, Nabal, the husband of Abigail, who, after the death of her husband, became one of the wives of King David.

Nabal died of rage. When his wife told him that David's men had come to the camp and she had given them provisions, Nabal's wrath was so kindled that he was stricken. Ten days later he died [1 Sam. 25:36-38].

His hands were not tied, nor were his feet chained; that is, Nabal had a chance to defend himself. He died of his rage and not as a captive. This was also true of Abner, the son of Ner. He was slain through a conspiracy. Neither his hands nor his feet were tied. Joab snared him and slew him outside the city. Abner, even though a valiant man, had no chance to defend himself.

SINFUL MEN

And they came thither into the midst of the house, as though they would have fetched wheat; and they smote him under the fifth rib: and Rechab and Baanah his brother escaped.   2 Sam. 4:6

The Eastern text reads "those sons of wickedness" or "those sinful men" instead of "as though they would have fetched wheat." The error is due to the confusion of the Aramaic words *kheta* (sin) and *kheta* (grain of wheat). The words are written alike, but are pronounced differently, making it easy for a foreigner to be confused.

The conspirators did not come to fetch wheat, but to slay the king who was asleep in the house. What would wheat be doing in the king's bedchamber?

A LEAGUE

So all the elders of Israel came to the king to Hebron; and king David made a league with them in Hebron before the Lord: and they anointed David king over Israel.   2 Sam. 5:3

The Hebrew word for "covenant" or "league" is *berith*. The Aramaic word is *kiama;* that is, "a standing agreement between two or more persons." The league or the promise depended on the loyalty of the people to God's way. When Gd was forsaken the agreements and leagues were broken and the promises disregarded.

As long as Israel remained loyal to the way of the God of their fathers, this league was kept; but when King Solomon worshiped foreign gods, and when they revolted against God and made golden calves in Beth-el, the league with the house of David was broken.

The covenant was made while eating together and feasting. The people took oaths and brought witnesses. When there were no other witnesses, God was made the witness [Gen. 21:30; 31:50-52].

BLIND AND LAME PROTECTED

And David said on that day, Whosoever getteth up to the gutter,
and smiteth the Jebusites, and the lame and the blind, that are hated
of David's soul, he shall be chief and captain. Wherefore they said,
The blind and the lame shall not come into the house.   2 Sam. 5:8

The Eastern text reads: "And David said on that day, Whosoever smites a Jebusite and whosoever strikes with a weapon the blind and the lame, he is a hater of David's soul."

When David went to fight against the Jebusites and to capture Jerusalem, the Jebusites reproached David by saying that even the lame and blind would be enough to defeat him, and that he first must destroy them before he could fight against their army. In the East, many times one hears the saying: "A blind or lame man can defeat him." But these words are not taken literally. They are used as a reproach, pointing out the weakness of the person who comes to fight against them.

There were probably four or five lame men in Jerusalem at that time, and naturally they could not defeat David's army, but the Jebusites were so sure of their defenses that they reproached David, saying that the lame and blind could take care of him.

At this time Israel had suffered a severe defeat in fighting against the Philistines. King Saul and his sons were slain at Gilboa. The Philistines were now masters of the land, and the Jebusites also were well fortified. Hitherto, David had been the head of a marauding force leading a small army of discontented men against Saul. But now David had just been made the king over Israel in defiance of the Philistines. Israel was too weak to fight against fortified cities like Jerusalem.

David ordered his generals of the army not to touch the blind and lame because they had nothing to do with what the king of Jerusalem had said, nor were they in a position to fight him. David took the city by a ruse.

Since David was reproached by the blind and the lame, it was decreed on that day that no blind or lame person should enter into the temple of God. David did what a noble man would do—he took the reproach lightly and did not destroy either the blind or the lame.

A PLACE OF WEEPING

And when David inquired of the Lord, he said, Thou shalt not go
up; but fetch a compass behind them, and come upon them over
against the mulberry trees.   2 Sam. 5:23

The term "mulberry trees" is wrong. The Aramaic text reads *bakhim* or *bachim*—derived from *bakha* (to weep)—which means "a place of weeping, mourning, or lamentation."

This name occurs in the book of Psalms, "the valley of weeping." The Aramaic is *aomka dabkhatha* [Ps. 84:6].

VALLEY OF WEEPING

And let it be, when thou hearest the sound of a going in the tops of the mulberry trees, that then thou shalt bestir thyself: for then shall the Lord go out before thee, to smite the host of the Philistines.
2 Sam. 5:24

The Eastern text reads: "And when you hear the sound of marching on the top of the mountain of Bachim, then you shall become strong; for then shall the Lord go out before you to smite the army of the Philistines."

The error in the King James Version is due to the confusion of the Hebrew word *baka*, plural *bakaim*, a species of balsam tree, with *bakha* (to weep). *Emek bakha* means "the valley of weeping" [Ps. 84:6].

This valley of weeping must have been in a place where the Israelites had suffered a defeat or were marched through on their way to captivity. Its present locality is unknown. The term "mulberry trees" is wrong. The Israelite Army could not have marched on top of the mulberry trees. Because of the similarity of the two words, such errors are unavoidable in the Bible. These errors were caused during the transcription from one alphabet into another and during the translation from one language into another.

AN ERROR

And when they came to Nachon's threshingfloor, Uzzah put forth his hand to the ark of God, and took hold of it; for the oxen shook it.
2 Sam. 6:6-7

Uzzah did not sin deliberately. It was through his zeal and ignorance that he touched the Ark of the Lord to support it, fearing it would fall and break. The act was so sudden that Uzzah forgot for a moment that the sacred Ark was untouchable and that even the Levites were forbidden to touch it.

The term "erred" here means "made a mistake." God forgives mistakes when they are committed through ignorance. Seemingly, the fear of having broken the law by touching the sacred relic caused his death.

WHITE BREAD

And he dealt among all the people, even among the whole multitude of Israel, as well to the women as men, to every one a cake of bread, and a good piece of flesh, and a flagon of wine. So all the people departed every one to his house. 2 Sam. 6:19

The Aramaic word *snarka* means "a loaf of fine white bread." Apparently, the translators confused the word with a flagon of wine.

In the East, fine white bread was considered a luxury until recent days. Most of the peasants and the poor ate black bread made from rye and barley.

Princes, governors, and the rich ate white bread made of pure wheat. No king in biblical days could offer a flagon of wine to each person in such a large assembly.

THE HOLY PLACE

Moreover I will appoint a place for my people Israel, and will plant them, that they may dwell in a place of their own, and move no more; neither shall the children of wickedness afflict them any more, as beforetime. 2 Sam. 7:10

The reference here is to Jerusalem which, during the reign of David, was selected as the center of worship. During the reigns of Samuel and Saul the people continued to bring offerings and to worship in Shiloh, Gilgal, and other holy places which had been selected during the period of Joshua and the Judges.

The Lord had promised to choose a city as a habitation for his holy name. David was the man who was to have a permanent grasp on Palestine. Hitherto, the people had been more or less enslaved to the Philistines.

When Jerusalem was declared to be the holy habitation of the Lord, the people ceased to go to Beth-el and Shiloh, and thus these ancient shrines were bereft of their worshipers and deserted. Beth-el was revived by Jeroboam [1 Kings 12:28-29]. Jerusalem was a larger city than Shiloh or Beth-el.

THE KINGDOM

He shall build a house for my name, and I will establish the throne of his kingdom for ever. 2 Sam. 7:13

"Kingdom" in Aramaic means "consulship"; thus, "the kingdom of God" means "the counsel of God." Among the ancient Hebrews a king was merely a counselor who, in time of war, gave advice to his people on important matters pertaining to the affairs of the state. Therefore, the kingdom of God is God's counsel in the realm of the Spirit where harmony, peace, and security reign. On the other hand, the kingdoms of men are founded on the counsel of men, where greed, pride, strife, rivalry, and injustices prevail.

The kingdom of God which was promised to David is a spiritual kingdom ruled by the counsel of God, and not a political kingdom ruled by the counsel and power of worldly men. For political kingdoms are generally acquired by force, bloodshed, bribery, and conspiracy, and God cannot have a part in such kingdoms. But, because man is born with a free will, God, after showing him both evil and good, lets man make his own choice.

The throne of David should not be taken literally. God promised that the house of David should never lack an heir; that is to say, David was to have a successor who would sit on his throne forever. Solomon, in his supplications, reminded God of these promises [1 Kings 8:23-26].

When these passages are taken literally we find that the divine promises relative to the eternal kingdom were not fulfilled. The Jewish kingdom was destroyed in 586 B.C. The last king who sat on the throne of David was Zedekiah. Thus, from the time of the Babylonian captivity to the present day there has been no Jewish king in Jerusalem or anywhere else. But the promises of God to David have not failed, in that the whole world has been blessed by the counsel of God (the kingdom of God) as given to David and Israel. Today almost the whole world is governed by the biblical laws. The moral law, which for centuries was more or less the law of Israel, has become the law of the world.

Therefore the promise is of the Spirit and not of the flesh. Any king, regardless of race and color, who believes in God, carries out God's commands, and acts faithfully is an heir of David; that is, he is an heir to the spiritual kingdom and the divine promises. This is because God's plan is a universal plan. His kingdom is a universal kingdom embracing all races and peoples on this earth. And Israel is simply an agent, like any other agent of God, who is ordained by him to carry out his purposes.

THE MEASURING LINE

And he smote Moab, and measured them with a line, casting them down to the ground; even with two lines measured he to put to death, and with one full line to keep alive. And so the Moabites became David's servants, and brought gifts. 2 Sam. 8:2

The Aramaic word *khawley* means "measuring cords" or "lines." The people were made to lie down side by side. Two measuring lines were marked for the slaughter and a measuring line to be spared.

In those days, the only way to crush the enemy was to reduce the population of the enemy by slaughtering many males and carrying many of the young women away captive. Those who were left were subjected to hard labor and heavy tributes until they revolted [verse 6].

CHERETHITES AND PELETHITES

And Benaiah the son of Jehoiada was over both the Cherethites and the Pelethites; and David's sons were chief rulers. 2 Sam. 8:18

The Eastern text reads: "And Benaiah the son of Jehoiada was over both the nobles and the laborers, and David's sons were the princes."

Bar kherey means "free-born, of noble extraction." In the olden days the people of nobility were not classed among the common people.

Palkhey means "laborers, working classes, the common people," who, during the time of war, served as soldiers. Somehow the translators were unable to recognize these designations of class distinction.

There were no such people or tribes as Cherethites and Pelethites.

KING'S TABLE

And David said unto him, Fear not: for I will surely show thee kindness for Jonathan thy father's sake, and will restore thee all the land of Saul thy father; and thou shalt eat bread at my table continually.   2 Sam. 9:7

In the olden days the houses of kings and princes were open to visitors who came from far-off lands, as well as to their own subjects who came to seek justice or counsel from their rulers. A king was considered the father of the people, and he acted as a counselor in judicial matters, as in the case of King Solomon and Joram, king of Judah.

All those who came to see the king—the noblemen, the prophets, the counselors, and the princes of the realm—ate at his table. Many oxen and sheep were slaughtered every day to feed the people and the foreign visitors. Kings received many lavish gifts from their subjects, but they also entertained very lavishly.

This custom prevailed until World War I. The homes of princes, emirs, and the chiefs of the tribes were always open to the public all day. Hundreds of unexpected guests sat at their tables. Scores of menservants and maidservants were engaged in preparing food. In the East the princes, the rich, and the nobles are proud of their tables, and they love to entertain.

Mephibosheth was a prince. He was a grandson of King Saul. King David kept his promise to Jonathan, the son of Saul, in preserving Mephibosheth and inviting him to sit at his table continually. This was a great honor to Mephibosheth.

FOUR THOUSAND HORSEMEN

And the Syrians fled before Israel; and David slew the men of seven hundred chariots of the Syrians, and forty thousand horsemen, and smote Shobach the captain of their host, who died there.

2 Sam. 10:18

The Aramaic word *arbaa* (four) has been confused with *arbaain* (forty). The Hebrew also reads *arbaaim* (forty).

Forty thousand would be too many cavalrymen to be lost in a battle between two small nations like Israel and Syria (Aram). Four thousand is more accurate. Some of the battles in the olden days lasted only a few days.

In 1 Chronicles 19:18 we read that David slew of the Syrians 7,000 men who fought in chariots, and 40,000 footmen. But, in 2 Samuel 10:18 they are cavalrymen instead of footmen.

WICKED RICH MAN

The rich man had exceeding many flocks and herds:
But the poor man had nothing, save one little ewe lamb, which he had bought and nourished up: and it grew up together with him, and with his children; it did eat of his own meat, and drank of his own cup, and lay in his bosom, and was unto him as a daughter.
And there came a traveler unto the rich man, and he spared to take of his own flock and of his own herd, to dress for the wayfaring man that was come unto him; but took the poor man's lamb, and dressed it for the man that was come to him. 2 Sam. 12:2-4

Such occurrences were very common in biblical lands until recent days, and are still to be seen in some feudal countries.

The rich men not only did not pay taxes and other levies to the government but also they were allowed by kings and princes to collect taxes for themselves from the poor, to confiscate the fields of the widows and the orphans, and to seize their sheep. During the lean years, the poor subjects were required to give one or two of their sheep to the rich man to keep him rich. This custom still prevails in India. Millions of poor Moslems save their money with which they buy costly jewelry and gold to give to their holy men and religious leaders.

It was this type of greedy rich man whom Jesus condemned when he said, "Again I say to you, It is easier for a rope to go through the eye of a needle, than for a rich man to enter into the kingdom of God" [Matt. 19:23-24, Eastern text; see also Job 31:24-25; and the comments in *Gospel Light* on Matt. 19:23-24].

The parable was aimed against King David, of course, who had many wives but who had conspired to have Uriah slain in the battle in order that he (David) might take his only wife. David recognized his folly and repented of his evil. The prophet composed the parable to see how David would react. This is still done by the Eastern diplomats and government officials.

See 2 Sam. 14:17.

YOUR MASTER'S DAUGHTERS

And I gave thee thy master's house, and thy master's wives into thy bosom, and gave thee the house of Israel and of Judah; and if that had been too little, I would moreover have given unto thee such and such things.   2 Sam. 12:8

The Aramaic reads *benat* (the daughters of your master) instead of "your master's house." The letters *yuth* and *nun* are so alike in Aramaic that they are easily confused one with the other. *Yuth* is a little shorter than *nun*. The words *benat* (daughters) and *bet* (house) look alike when written in Aramaic.

RABBATH

And Joab sent messengers to David, and said, I have fought against Rabbah, and have taken the city of waters. 2 Sam. 12:27

Rabbath (Rabbah in King James), the capital of the kingdom of Ammon, can hardly be called "the city of waters." The land of the Ammonites, like Palestine, lacks water. The fields are watered only by the heavy dew which forms at night.

The error here is due to confusion of the Aramaic word *kerita* (town) with the Aramaic word *kevita* (a pond of water).

Rabbath, now called Ammon, was a well-fortified capital city situated on a hill.

CAPTIVES WERE NOT SAWN

And he brought forth the people that were therein, and put them under saws, and under harrows of iron, and under axes of iron, and made them pass through the brickkiln: and thus did he unto all the cities of the children of Ammon.   2 Sam. 12:31

The Eastern text reads: "And he brought forth the people who were in it, and put them in iron bands and in chains, and made them pass through the measuring line . . ."

In those days the people were placed under a measuring line. Then the men under one line were spared and carried captive, and those under the other line were put to death.

The phrases "under saws . . . and under axes" are wrong. No captives were sawn alive or chopped with axes. They were killed with the sword.

Generally, those who were killed were valiant men of war. Those who were spared were the farmers and artisans whose services were needed by the conqueror. Some of these people were left in their native land and subjected to hard work and tributes. Others were carried away as captives.

David did the same thing to the inhabitants of Moab [2 Sam. 8:2].

THE WOMAN OF TEKOAH

Then thine handmaid said, The word of my lord the king shall now be comfortable: for as an angel of God, so is my lord the king to discern good and bad: therefore the Lord thy God will be with thee.   2 Sam. 14:17

The Aramaic word *tishar* means "to be confirmed." The woman of Tekoah had petitioned King David on behalf of her son and had pleaded before him to perform her request [verse 15].

But, in reality, the woman was pleading before the king on behalf of the king's own son, Absalom. She had used the case of her own son as a parable to soften David's heart. Now she wanted the king's command to be confirmed to "deliver her son"; that is, to be confirmed in Absalom.

When King David understood the subtle words of this wise woman, he called Joab and asked him to go to Geshur to bring back his son Absalom.

See 2 Sam. 12:24

FOUR YEARS, NOT FORTY

And it came to pass after forty years, that Absalom said unto the king, I pray thee, let me go and pay my vow, which I have vowed unto the Lord, in Hebron.　　　　2 Sam. 15:7

The Aramaic reads: "And it came to pass after four years . . ." The Aramaic word for "four" is *arbaa,* and the Aramaic word for "forty" is *arbain.* The error is probably caused by the long tail of the letter *ai* or *ayen.*

The entire reign of David in Hebron and Jerusalem was forty years, and Absalom was a young man when he was slain by Joab [2 Sam. 18:5].

Absalom, after slaying his brother, Amnon, fled to Geshur. When he returned from Geshur he was commanded by his father, David, to dwell in his own house. So Absalom dwelt two full years in Jerusalem and saw not the king's face [2 Sam. 14:28]. Had Absalom waited for *forty* years, he would never have seen his father, the king.

ON FOOT

And David went up by the ascent of mount Olivet, and wept as he went up, and had his head covered, and he went barefoot: and all the people that was with him covered every man his head, and they went up, weeping as they went up.　　　　2 Sam. 15:30

Easterners cover their heads when they mourn over the dead or some catastrophe. The covering of the head is an ancient custom and is symbolic of shame, failure, or difficulties ahead. On the other hand, when they dance and rejoice, even women remove their veils.

David was mourning over the sad events which were taking place in his kingdom. His own son had revolted against him and was even seeking his life. In the past he had sinned (in the case of Uriah) and now things seemed to be going against him.

David covered his head and walked on foot (Eastern text) as a token of repentance so that he might receive forgiveness from God. Evidently the king refused to ride on his royal mule. He wanted to humble himself before the Lord and his people. All these evils which had befallen him were the results of some of his blunders in the past.

David was always ready to repent, and the Lord forgave him, just as a father forgives his son.

WILD ANIMALS

For the battle was there scattered over the face of all the country: and the wood devoured more people that day than the sword devoured.   2 Sam. 18:8

Khewat-awa means "wild beasts of the forest," not "the wood." The battle was fought in a junglelike forest full of wild beasts.

Wild beasts were abundant in Palestine and at times they menaced the population [Judg. 14:5-6]. David slew a bear and a lion in Bethlehem [1 Sam. 17:34-36].

Even in the eighth century B.C., the people in Galilee were menaced by wild beasts, especially lions [2 Kings 17:25-26].

GATES AS ROYAL COURTS

Then the king arose, and sat in the gate. And they told unto all the people, saying, Behold, the king doth sit in the gate. And all the people came before the king: for Israel had fled every man to his tent.   2 Sam. 19:8

Small walled cities and towns in biblical lands had neither parks nor other space for public gatherings. City gates and housetops were the only places where people could assemble.

During emergencies, kings, their generals, and dignitaries assembled at the city gate [1 Kings 22:10].

King David was accompanied by his ministers and dignitaries, and surrounded by the people at the gate. [See articles on gates.]

RAFTS

And there went over a ferryboat to carry over the king's household, and to do what he thought good. And Shimei the son of Gera fell down before the king, as he was come over Jordan.   2 Sam. 19:18

The Aramaic word *mabraney* means "rafts." Rafts are made from logs which are cut from trees and at times mounted on inflated goat skins. This kind of raft was used on the Tigris and Euphrates rivers until recent days.

In verse 17 we are told that Ziba, the servant of the house of Saul, his fifteen sons, and his twenty servants made a bridge over Jordan. The Aramaic word *geshar* means, "They made a bridge"; that is, a make-shift one.

The River Jordan is very narrow and at some points a temporary bridge could be constructed in a very short time. But ferryboats could not navigate such a swift and narrow river. When the Bible was translated into English, the translators had never seen the Jordan River. They probably thought it was a navigable river like the Thames.

SATAN

And David said, What have I to do with you, ye sons of Zeruiah, that ye should this day be adversaries unto me? shall there any man be put to death this day in Israel? for do not I know that I am this day king over Israel?   2 Sam. 19:22

The Eastern text reads *Satana* (Satan). *Satana* is derived from the Aramaic word *sata* (to go astray, to mislead). *Satana* is a proper noun, denoting the action of the verb *sata;* that is, the one who causes men to go astray, an adversary, or an accuser [Job 1:6]. He is also called "the devil" and "that old serpent" in Revelation 12:9.

The terms "Satan" or "devil" were not known to the Hebrew patri-archs. Evidently, these terms were used later when the Israelites came in contact with the people who believed in two gods, the god of good and the god of evil. The Babylonians and the Persians accepted the doctrine of dualism, with two powers, good and evil. In the East the kings had ministers who acted as accusers.

There is no mention of Satan or devil in the Bible accounts of God's creations. Everything that God created was good, and God blessed all his creations [Gen. 1:28]. Anything which deviates from the truth and is contrary to good is evil or Satanic.

A PLEA TO JOAB

I am one of them that are peaceable and faithful in Israel: thou seekest to destroy a city and a mother in Israel: why wilt thou swal-low up the inheritance of the Lord?   2 Sam. 20:19

The Aramaic words *parath khebley* mean "one of those who have suffered the pangs of childbirth in Israel." And the Aramaic word *talia* means "a child." Thus, the Eastern text reads: ". . . you seek to de-stroy a child and his mother in Israel . . ."

The woman thought that Joab was ready to destroy all the inhabitants of the city. Many mothers were already bereaved of their sons, who had been slain in the battle fighting on the side of Absalom against King David.

VENGEANCE

And he delivered them into the hands of the Gibeonites, and they hanged them in the hill before the Lord: and they fell all seven together, and were put to death in the days of harvest, in the first days, in the beginning of barley harvest.   2 Sam. 21:9

Seemingly, this was a violation of the Mosaic law which decreed that children must not suffer for the sins of their parents. The Eastern text reads: "And he delivered them to the Gibeonites, and they sacrificed them in the mountain before the Lord; and they fell all seven together, and were slain in the first days of harvest, in the beginning of barley harvest."

In the East, kings generally are afraid of their rivals. At times kings even destroy their own brothers for fear they might try to seize the throne. Abimelech slew seventy of his brothers [Judg. 9:5]. Joram, king of Judah, slew all of his brothers in order to secure the throne for his heirs. This custom prevailed during the reign of the Ottoman sultans. Many of them exterminated all their brothers.

Apparently David was afraid that in the future the sons of King Saul might attempt to seize the throne. These young men had nothing to do with the sins of their father, Saul, nor could they be blamed for the severe drought; it is prevalent in Palestine even today. What the people needed was repentance from their evil deeds.

King Saul had paid for his sins with his own death and the death of his sons in the battle. The Gibeonites, the enemies of King Saul [verse 6], asked for a severe vengeance, which was a violation of the Mosaic code.

GATH, NOT GOB

And it came to pass after this, that there was again a battle with the Philistines at Gob: then Sibbechai the Hushathite slew Saph, which was of the sons of the giant.   2 Sam. 21:18

The Eastern text reads *Gath* instead of Gob. This is a scribal error made during the transcription of the text from ancient Hebrew letters into square characters, or perhaps a scribal error caused by defective script.

GOD OF MY ROCK

The God of my rock; in him will I trust: he is my shield, and the horn of my salvation, my high tower, and my refuge, my saviour; thou savest me from violence.   2 Sam. 22:3

The Aramaic reads *takipa* (strong)—"strong God" instead of "God of my rock." All such phrases are used metaphorically. Rock means strength and surety. Shield is symbolic of divine protection from evil forces [Ps. 3:3]. Horn symbolizes glory and strength, and tower means defense, safety, and alertness against the enemy [Prov. 18:10]. Towers were built sometimes in the city walls and sometimes near the city walls, as the tower of David, which is now in Jerusalem.

David trusted in God and looked upon him as a fortress of refuge, as a warrior's shield, and as a rock during a storm.

FIRE AND SMOKE

There went up a smoke out of his nostrils, and fire out of his mouth devoured: coals were kindled by it.   2 Sam. 22:9

Fire is one of the most powerful and destructive things in the world. It was man's first great discovery in his progress toward civilization.

In this instance fire and smoke are used metaphorically to mean anger and destruction. Just as fire causes smoke and consumes wood, so anger destroys the wicked.

Even today, in the East, when a man is enraged men say "fire kindled in his face" or "fire issued out of his mouth."

All these figures of speech are used to amplify God's wrath towards his enemies and their evil works, and his power to perform wonders [Ps. 18:8].

WINNING PEOPLE

With the pure thou wilt show thyself pure; and with the froward thou wilt show thyself unsavory.   2 Sam. 22:27

Titakam is derived from *aakam* (to be crafty, perverse, crooked). The meaning implied here is to pretend to be like one of them in order to win them to God.

Paul, in his missionary journeys, approached all men on their own level in order to win them to Jesus Christ. In other words, one has to lower himself to the level of the person who is to be converted.

The book of Psalms reads: "With the pure thou shalt be pure; with an upright man thou shalt be upright. With the clean thou shalt be clean; and from the crooked thou shalt turn aside" [Ps. 18:25-26, Eastern text; see also Lev. 26:23-24].

THE LORD IS MY LAMP

For thou art my lamp, O Lord: and the Lord will lighten my darkness.   2 Sam. 22:29

"Lamp" is often used figuratively to mean "light," "enlightenment," "posterity," or "heir." Isaiah spoke of "the salvation thereof as a lamp that burneth" [Isa. 62:1].

In Jerusalem and other ancient walled cities in the Near East one has to have a lamp in his hand when walking in the narrow and crooked streets during the dark hours. "Thy word is a lamp unto my feet, and a light unto my path" [Ps. 119:105].

In Aramaic, we often say, "God has given him a lamp," which means "an heir." "May God lighten your lamp" means "May God preserve your posterity." David thanked God for having given him a lamp, or an heir. ". . . I have ordained a lamp for mine anointed" [Ps. 132:17].

God had been like a lamp to Israel. His laws and ordinances protected the people who walked through the valley of the shadow of death. Then again, God's way was free from obstructions and stumbling blocks. God was the Light and the Salvation of Israel.

See article on "Lamp" [Ps. 119:105].

HIS COUSIN

And after him was Eleazar the son of Dodo the Ahohite, one of the three mighty men with David, when they defied the Philistines that were there gathered together to battle, and the men of Israel were gone away.   2 Sam. 23:9

Bar-dadey means "the son of his uncle." The translators mistook it for a name Dodo.

CHIEF OF THIRTY OFFICERS

And Abishai, the brother of Joab, the son of Zeruiah, was chief among three. And he lifted up his spear against three hundred, and slew them, and had the name among three.

Was he not most honorable of three? therefore he was their captain: howbeit he attained not unto the first three. 2 Sam. 23:18-19

These verses should read: "And Abishai, the brother of Joab, the son of Zoriah, was chief of thirty men. And he lifted up his spear against three hundred and slew them. And he was honored above the thirty men; therefore he became their chief and performed heroic deeds equal to thirty men" (Eastern text).

Abishai, the brother of Joab, was one of the high-ranking generals of David's army. He was a commander over thirty officers because he performed heroic deeds equal to thirty officers. Abishai ranked second only to his brother Joab.

REGIMENTATION RESENTED

And David's heart smote him after that he had numbered the people. And David said unto the Lord, I have sinned greatly in that I have done: and now, I beseech thee, O Lord, take away the iniquity of thy servant; for I have done very foolishly. 2 Sam. 24:10

Easterners resent a census, and they revolt against regimentation and high taxation. A census is viewed with suspicion, and usually is followed with new taxes which result in discontent and revolutions. This is especially true of the tribal people who live in tents and breathe the fresh air of freedom.

The Israelites hitherto had been more or less a tribal people, wandering from place to place without any passports or identification papers. They resented having a census taken.

This is also true of the Bedouin tribes in Arabia. They do not welcome the census or the requirement of passports. They love to wander freely. Both the British and the French governments had difficulty in making these desert people understand modern ways of governing. Being a pastoral people and accustomed to desert life, they also resent making bricks, digging ditches, or even sitting behind a desk in a bank.

The numbering of the people at this time was unwise. The people were still ruled by the princes of their respective tribes and dominated by their tribal traditions and family ties. In other words, they were not ready for regimentation and the costly monarchical system which King David was so eager to establish [verse 1].

CHAPTER TEN

1 and 2 KINGS

INTRODUCTION

THE books of the Kings are records written by the royal scribes who worked at the palace writing important events, and recording deeds, ordinances, and taxes.

The books of the Kings, like the Chronicles, contain important occurrences and episodes, such as wars, famines, revolutions, treaties, changes in the dynasties, and other noteworthy events. They also contain sacred material relative to religion both in Israel and Judah.

The written sources might have been put together during the exile or soon after, when both kingdoms had come to an end and memories of the past had become dear to the hearts of the exiles. Both the kings of Judah and the kings of Israel employed scribes and recorders of deeds, who wrote on sheepskin.

Apparently, the royal scribes omitted some of the events which they considered unimportant and dwelt at length on other matters which they regarded as more important.

The divisions of First and Second Kings and First and Second Chronicles were introduced later. All these books were written on vellum or sheepskin, and they were the property of kings, princes, priests, and the rich, who jealously guarded them.

1 KINGS

DAVID WARMED

Wherefore his servants said unto him, Let there be sought for my lord the king a young virgin: and let her stand before the king, and let her cherish him, and let her lie in thy bosom, that my lord the king may get heat.　　　　　　　　　　　1 Kings 1:2

In biblical lands, steam heating and stoves were unknown. The houses were generally heated with fire which burned in the ovens. Palaces were heated with hearths or by burning coals in a brazier [Jer. 36:22]. Palaces were built with large stones and thick walls, which made it difficult for the servants to warm them.

Jerusalem is cold and damp during the winter months, and the cold is penetrating. Because the land lacks coal and wood, grass is often used to heat the ovens and for baking of bread and cooking [Matt. 6:30; Luke 12:28]. Kings used wood.

David's intentions in this matter were pure. Abishag remained a virgin throughout her life.

A SHILOMMITE OR SHULAMITE

So they sought for a fair damsel throughout all the coasts of Israel, and found Abishag a Shunammite, and brought her to the king.   1 Kings 1:3

The Eastern text reads "a Shilommite"; that is, an inhabitant of Shiloh. No doubt, the error is caused by the confusion between the letters *lamed* (l) and *nun* (n). These two letters are very similar to one another when they fall in the middle of a word. They often confuse foreign translators and at times even the natives.

Shiloh is a town northeast of Jerusalem. In the olden days it was the center of worship; but when the worship was transferred to Jerusalem, Shiloh was deserted and its population diminished.

The women of Shiloh must have been pretty. The name Shilommite (Shulamite) is mentioned in the Song of Solomon 6:13.

SHILOKHA

The king also said unto them, Take with you the servants of your lord, and cause Solomon my son to ride upon mine own mule, and bring him down to Gihon.   1 Kings 1:33

The Eastern text reads *Shilokha*. Gihon might be a later name. The Israelites, like other races, changed the names of some towns and localities [2 Chron. 32:30].

ARCHERS AND SLINGERS

So Zadok the priest, and Nathan the prophet, and Benaiah the son of Jehoiada, and the Cherethites, and the Pelethites, went down, and caused Solomon to ride upon king David's mule, and brought him to Gihon.   1 Kings 1:38

The Aramaic word *kashatey* means "archers," and the Aramaic word *kilaey* means "slingers"; that is, certain units of the archers and the slingers went down with Zadok the priest and Nathan the prophet to anoint Solomon king over Israel.

Evidently the early translators, not having dictionaries, did not know the meaning of these two military terms.

These names have been wrongly connected with the Philistines and the people of Crete. In 1 Samuel 30:14 the reference is to the Negeb.

The Eastern text reads: "So Zadok the priest and Nathan the prophet and Benaiah, the son of Jehoiada and the archers and the slingers went down and caused Solomon to ride upon King David's mule, and took him to Shilokha."

ADONIJAH REJECTED

Then tidings came to Joab: for Joab had turned after Adonijah, though he turned not after Absalom. And Joab fled unto the tabernacle of the Lord, and caught hold on the horns of the altar.

1 Kings 2:28

The Eastern text reads: "Now when the news reached Joab that Adonijah had been slain (for Joab had been leaning toward Adonijah and he was not leaning toward Solomon), Joab fled to the tabernacle of the Lord and took refuge on the horns of the altar."

Joab was with Adonijah when the latter proclaimed himself king over Israel. But Joab was not with Solomon. This is because Adonijah was the crown prince at this time, and thus the rightful heir to the throne [1 Kings 1:5-7; 2:15]. Absalom was dead long before the crowning of Solomon.

Solomon was the son of Bathsheba, David's favorite wife. This is why David granted Bathsheba's request in making her son the king to sit upon his throne.

GOVERNORS

Geber the son of Uri was in the country of Gilead, in the country of Sihon king of the Amorites, and of Og king of Bashan; and he was the only officer which was in the land.   1 Kings 4:19

The Aramaic word *ekhad* (to lay hold, to rule over) has been confused with *khad* (one, the only).

The Eastern text reads: "Geber the son of Uri was in the land of Gilead, the country of Sihon king of the Amorites and of Og king of Bashan; and the governors ruled in the land."

Kayomey means "governors, prefects, superintendents." King Solomon had appointed twelve governors over the land to gather taxes and to supply the king's household and his armies with food and other provisions [verse 7].

AN ARTIST

He was a widow's son of the tribe of Naphtali, and his father was a man of Tyre, a worker in brass: and he was filled with wisdom, and understanding, and cunning to work all works in brass. And he came to king Solomon, and wrought all his work.

1 Kings 7:14

This verse should read, ". . . and his father was an artist . . ." The Aramaic word *zaiar* (an artist, a fashioner, a painter) has been confused with *Zur* (Tyre).

Hiram's father and mother were Israelites of the tribe of Naphtali. His deceased father was an artist in brass. Tyre was noted for its brasswork and for its builders and designers. Even today, Syria and Lebanon are renowned for their brasswork.

THE LORD APPEARED TO SOLOMON

That the Lord appeared to Solomon the second time, as he had appeared unto him at Gibeon.

1 Kings 9:2

The Lord appeared to King Solomon in a vision. All God's appearances to the Hebrew patriarchs, prophets, and holy men were in visions during the night. However, some visions took place in the daytime. "Then he spoke in visions to his righteous one . . ." [Ps. 89:19, Eastern text]. "For God speaks . . . in a dream, in a vision of the night, when deep sleep falls upon men, while slumbering upon the bed; then he opens the ears of men, and humbles them according to their rebelliousness" [Job 33:14-16, Eastern text].

Visions and dreams take place during the silent hours of the night simply because man's mind is then peaceful and at rest.

The Lord does not appear as a man with flesh and blood. He appears in the spiritual image of man.

TADMOR

And Baalath, and Tadmor in the wilderness, in the land.

1 Kings 9:18

The Aramaic reads *Tadmor*, derived from *Tadimor* (to wonder, to surprise); that is, "a place of wonders."

Tadimor is the city of Palmyra. No doubt, Palmyra is a later name derived from palms. In the desert lands even a few palm trees are conspicuous in the eyes of the desert people. Tadmor has many palm trees. This name may have been given after the city was destroyed or deserted.

Tadmor is situated in the desert between Syria and Mesopotamia. King David, after the defeat of Ammon, had extended the frontiers of Israel as far as the River Euphrates. The city of Tadmor was built as a sort of fortification against nomad tribes. Solomon needed a garrison and supplies in the desert in case of war with the kings on the other side of the River Euphrates and the troublesome desert tribes.

Then again, a fortified and well-supplied city was needed on such an important caravan route in Solomon's far-flung domain.

The name of Tadmor, the city of wonders, occurs in both Aramaic and Arabic literature.

ONE SHIP

And king Solomon made a navy of ships in Ezion-geber, which is beside Eloth, on the shore of the Red sea, in the land of Edom.
1 Kings 9:26

The Eastern text reads *sepinta* (a ship). The term "navy" means many ships with their crews, officers, and men. The Israelites, being a pastoral people, knew very little about navigation. One ship was plenty to start with. Even today some Arab states much larger and stronger than the kingdom of Solomon have no navies.

The cargo brought back from Ophir plainly indicates that it was a single ship. One does not need more than one ship to carry four hundred and twenty talents of gold; it could easily be loaded in a small boat.

SOLOMON'S WIVES ENVIED

Happy are thy men, happy are these thy servants, which stand continually before thee, and that hear thy wisdom. 1 Kings 10:8

The Eastern text reads *neshek* (your wives). *Neshek* has been confused with *nashak* (your men).

The queen of Sheba envied the king's wives and his servants, who were in his presence daily.

THE PRICE OF A CHARIOT

*And Solomon had horses brought out of Egypt, and linen yarn:
the king's merchants received the linen yarn at a price.*

*And a chariot came up and went out of Egypt for six hundred
shekels of silver, and a horse for a hundred and fifty: and so for all
the kings of the Hittites, and for the kings of Syria, did they bring
them out by their means.*   1 Kings 10:28-29

Linen is a mistranslation. It should read: ". . . and the king's merchants received a commission on the goods they bought."

The price of a chariot brought out of Egypt was as high as six
hundred shekels of silver, and that of a horse one hundred and fifty
shekels of silver. "Chariot came up" means that the price of chariots
was up.

King Solomon had buyers in Egypt who purchased chariots, horses,
and implements of war for Solomon's army. Israel, at this time, knew
little about the manufacture of iron and steel weapons.

GODDESS ASHTORETH

*For Solomon went after Ashtoreth the goddess of the Zidonians,
and after Milcom the abomination of the Ammonites.* 1 Kings 11:5

Ashtoreth or *Ishtar* was the planet goddess. She was the goddess of
the Zidonians and was also worshiped by the Israelites. During the time
of the prophet Samuel, Israel forsook the Lord God and served Ashtoreth
and Baal [1 Sam. 12:10].

The origin of this goddess was Babylonian. The worship of *Ishtar*
was introduced as a result of the study of stars and other heavenly
bodies. Later, the Persians, the successors of the Babylonians, adopted
this religion.

The name "Esther" is derived from *Ishtar* which means "star." The
Babylonians and Persians worshiped the god of light. In the second
century after Christ the god of light was called *Mazda* (which, in
ancient Persia, means "light"), and the god of darkness, *Akriman*.

A PAGAN GOD

*Then did Solomon build a high place for Chemosh, the abomina-
tion of Moab, in the hill that is before Jerusalem.*   1 Kings 11:7

The Aramaic word *dekheltha* means "a god"; that is, an image of a
pagan god or an object revered by the pagan.

Chemosh was the god of Moab, and Malcom or Molech was the god of Ammon.

The worship of these pagan deities was prohibited by the law of Moses. The Israelites were commanded to destroy them utterly [Num. 33:52].

These pagan gods were an obstacle to the Israelites. Again and again Israel forsook her God and went after pagan gods whose sinful worship was an abomination to those Israelites who remained loyal to the religion of their fathers and the Mosaic law.

A LAMP, AN HEIR

And unto his son will I give one tribe, that David my servant may have a light alway before me in Jerusalem, the city which I have chosen me to put my name there.   1 Kings 11:36

The Eastern text reads *sheraga* (a lamp); that is, an heir. In Aramaic, the term "lamp" is quite often used metaphorically to mean an heir. Easterners in their conversations often say, "May God keep your lamp burning," or, "May the Lord keep your light burning."

The Lord had sworn to David that his descendants would sit on his throne forever. The Lord was to keep his promise through the heirs of David [1 Kings 15:4; Isa. 37:35].

This promise was kept so that the messianic prophecies might be fulfilled. David had been loyal to God and had upheld the true worship.

Today Christ reigns over this spiritual kingdom. David's reign was symbolic of the Messiah's reign—a reign of righteousness. The term "heir" is spiritual. "The lamp," figuratively means the light of the Jewish faith which was to light the Gentile world.

HEAVY TAXES

And the young men that were grown up with him spake unto him, saying, Thus shalt thou speak unto this people that spake unto thee, saying, Thy father made our yoke heavy, but make thou it lighter unto us; thus shalt thou say unto them, My little finger shall be thicker than my father's loins.

And now whereas my father did lade you with a heavy yoke, I will add to your yoke: my father hath chastised you with whips, but I will chastise you with scorpions.   1 Kings 12:10-11

"Loins" is a mistranslation. Fingers could not possibly be thicker than loins. The Eastern text reads: "My little finger is thicker than my father's thumb." This idiom is still used by the Aramaic-speaking people.

The hand is symbolic of action and power. It is often said, "His hand is heavy," which means that he is an oppressor. "His hand is light," means that he is pleasant and his taxes are light.

The Israelites were heavily taxed. King Solomon and his princes and ministers had too many wives, servants, and chariots, which were maintained by taxes and by confiscation of properties by the servants of the king, who preyed upon the helpless citizens.

Rehoboam was inclined to increase taxes and to exert more power over the people than his father Solomon did. He also decided to employ enforced labor in building more magnificent palaces for himself and his wives.

BREAD AS A GIFT

At that time Abijah the son of Jeroboam fell sick.

And Jeroboam said to his wife, Arise, I pray thee, and disguise thyself, that thou be not known to be the wife of Jeroboam; and get thee to Shiloh: behold, there is Ahijah the prophet, which told me that I should be king over this people.

And take with thee ten loaves, and cracknels, and a cruse of honey, and go to him: he shall tell thee what shall become of the child.
                                                    1 Kings 14:1-3

Even today, in many Eastern lands, men and women seek healing from the hands of men of God and inquire of them concerning sick persons and lost articles and animals. When they visit these men, they take a gift with them—a few baskets containing bread, cakes (bread baked with butter and milk), honey, fish, and other articles of food.

Even kings, princes, and wealthy persons adhere to this ancient custom. They send bread to the men of God, just as the poor do. This is because they know that in the presence of God all men are equal.

The king of Israel commanded his wife to go to see the man of God, and to inquire of him concerning the health of their son. And he told her to take bread, honey, and a few other things as a gift. The king could have sent gold and silver, but he knew the prophet of God would refuse it. Such healers would accept bread and other food supplies, however, and would share it with the poor. Jesus commanded his disciples not to carry (Aramaic, accumulate) silver or gold in their purses [Matt. 10:9-11].

Healing cannot be purchased by means of money, but it can be sought by means of faith and belief in the men of God who are endowed with power to heal the sick and to reveal hidden things. [1 Sam. 9:7; 2 Kings 4:42-44].

MATURE MAN

Therefore, behold, I will bring evil upon the house of Jeroboam, and will cut off from Jeroboam him that pisseth against the wall, and him that is shut up and left in Israel, and will take away the remnant of the house of Jeroboam, as a man taketh away dung, till it be all gone. 1 Kings 14:10

The phrase "him that pisseth against the wall" is an Aramaic idiom which is still used today, referring to "mature men." Little boys urinate anywhere, but grown men stand with their faces to the wall and their backs to the people passing by.

In the East, until recent years, public toilets were unknown. The people, in order to relieve themselves, stood or sat near walls, under trees, in fields and ruins, and other places which offered slight seclusion.

Aser osharey, translated in King James as "him that is shut up and left," means "anyone with authority"; that is, all officials in the government who belonged to the royal family of Jeroboam.

The Eastern text reads: "Therefore, behold, I will bring evil upon the house of Jeroboam, and will cut off from Jeroboam every male and him that possesses authority in Israel, and I will glean after the house of Jeroboam as they glean the vines of the vineyard when the gathering of the grapes is over."

The Aramaic word *baar* (glean) has been wrongly translated "dung." The term glean is used here to mean total destruction or annihilation.

ABIJAH

And there was war between Rehoboam and Jeroboam all the days of his life. 1 Kings 15:6

This should read, "And there was war between Abijah the son of Rehoboam and Jeroboam . . ." Rehoboam was dead, and now Abijah was the king over Judah [verses 1, 7, 8].

The Eastern text correctly reads "Abijah the son of Rehoboam."

HADAD AN EDOMITE

Then Asa took all the silver and the gold that were left in the treasures of the house of the Lord, and the treasures of the king's house, and delivered them into the hands of his servants: and king Asa sent them to Ben-hadad, the son of Tabrimon, the son of Hezion, king of Syria, that dwelt at Damascus, saying. 1 Kings 15:18

The Eastern text reads "king of Aram, who dwelt in Damascus." Damascus was the capital of Aram (Syria) but the king was an Edomite.

When King David conquered Edom, and Joab had slain every male in Edom, Hadad, the Edomite of the royal family, fled to Egypt with some of the servants of his father. Hadad, at this time, was only a child [1 Kings 11:15-20].

Later, Hadad married Pharaoh's sister-in-law and found favor in the eyes of the king of Egypt.

When King David and Joab were dead, Pharaoh helped Hadad to return to his land. Hadad, with other men who had fled because of David and who were discontented, gathered in Damascus. Hadad abhorred the reign of Israel over Syria, so he plotted and reigned in Damascus over the Syrians (Arameans) [1 Kings 11:24-25].

Hadad had made a league with Jeroboam, the son of Naboth, a servant of Solomon who had conspired against his Lord and who also had fled to Egypt. Asa, after giving Hadad gold, asked him to break the league which he had made with the king of Israel, which he did, and also helped him against Baasha, the king of Israel [1 Kings 15:18-20].

The Hadad dynasty seems to have reigned in Syria for a long time. Therefore, according to the Eastern text, Syria at times is called Edom; that is, the king was an Edomite. Seemingly, all these nations which had survived David's conquests merged together in order to resist the Israelites. And Hadad, having the support of Pharaoh, the king of Egypt, reigned over them. In the East, kingdoms were often known by the name of the ruling dynasty.

OLD WINE

And his servant Zimri, captain of half his chariots, conspired against him, as he was in Tirzah, drinking himself drunk in the house of Arza steward of his house in Tirzah.   1 Kings 16:9

The Eastern text reads "drinking old wine." In the East, old wine is very scarce, and is generally drunk by kings, princes, and the rich. The poor are content with new wine [Acts 2:13].

Old wine is stored in earthen jars and kept for the winter, spring, and summer months until the new wine is ready. Since wine is scarce and storage difficult, most of the people drink their wines during the winter months, when they are idle, attending wedding feasts and banquets. Nevertheless, kings, princes, and wealthy people have enough wine in storage to last for a few years. Therefore, this wine is called old wine. It is stronger and more delicious than the new.

The king, instead of attending his business, was indulging himself in drinking old wine, until one of his generals slew him in his house built of cedars. *Arza* is an Aramaic or Hebrew word meaning "cedar."

HIS SON DIED

And Ahab made a grove; and Ahab did more to provoke the Lord 'od of Israel to anger than all the kings of Israel that were before 1im.

In h.s days did Hiel the Beth-elite build Jericho: he laid the foundation thereof in Abiram his firstborn, and set up the gates thereof in his youngest son Segub, according to the word of the Lord, which he spake by Joshua the son of Nun. 1 Kings 16:33-34

During the reign of Ahab, Hiel, the Bethelite, rebuilt the accursed city of Jericho. And when he laid its foundation, Abiram his firstborn died; and when he set up its gates, his youngest son Segub died. Joshua had cursed the city and also put a curse on anyone who should rebuild it [Josh. 6:26, and comment on that verse].

When Easterners curse one another, they say, "May your son die," and when they take an oath, they say, "May my firstborn die if I break this agreement."

Jericho was rebuilt, but it was destroyed again. A short distance from the ancient ruins lies the new Jericho, the city where Jesus met Matthew [Matt. 9:9].

RAVENS

And it shall be, that thou shalt drink of the brook; and I have commanded the ravens to feed thee there.

So he went and did according unto the word of the Lord: for he went and dwelt by the brook Cherith, that is before Jordan.

And the ravens brought him bread and flesh in the morning, and bread and flesh in the evening; and he drank of the brook.

1 Kings 17:4-6

The same word which in Aramaic and Hebrew means "a raven" may also mean an "Arab," "dark," "mixture," "swarm," "pledge," "sunset," and "evening." These words are written alike but pronounced differently, and the root of the verb denotes "darkness, gray, and sunset."

For instance, *ereb* (the "b" is aspirated in Aramaic and Hebrew and pronounced as *erev*), means "a raven," and *erab* means "an Arab." The Arabs who live in the desert are slightly darker than the other Arabs and Hebrews.

In biblical days, dots on vowels were not written. The meanings of words such as these were generally determined by the context. Then again, some biblical narratives were handed down orally. Words, even though different in their meaning, sounded alike. Some authorities maintain that an Arab tribe fed Elijah (the tribe of Raven's); others believe that the ravens, the dark birds, fed him. Be that as it may, the miracle is, Elijah was fed and provided with water by God. No one should question God's power and his wisdom.

No reader would expect a raven to be feeding a hungry man. On the other hand, the raven being declared as an unclean bird in Mosaic law, would not be the proper bird to come to the rescue of Elijah [Lev. 11:14; Deut. 14:12-15].

FIRE OF GOD

Then the fire of the Lord fell, and consumed the burnt sacrifice, and the wood, and the stones, and the dust, and licked up the water that was in the trench.   1 Kings 18:38

Lightning is called the fire of God. This is because lightning strikes from above and causes fire and damage on earth. All other fires start from the ground up, but lightning comes down from the sky.

In Aramaic, the same word which means "heavens" also means sky and universe. Oftentimes sheep, cattle, and men are struck and killed by lightning, and in most cases such deaths are attributed to the acts of God, especially when evildoers are struck.

Palestine is noted for droughts. There are times when rain does not fall for two or three years, and the people suffer seriously from the shortage of water; sheep and cattle often die because of the lack of water and grass. When the dry season is over, rain is often accompanied by lightning and severe storms. Learned men and shepherds can generally predict the end of the drought and foretell the start of the rain by examining the skies. The prophets and men of God could predict events and perform miracles and wonders by means of revelations from God who guided them.

In the days of the prophet Elijah there was no rain for three years. Both the king of Israel and the people had left God and had followed Baal and his prophets. During this period Baal worship was firmly established in Israel.

The people had prayed for rain, but in vain. The pagan gods did not hear their prayers. Every brook and fountain had dried up, and most of the cattle and the sheep had perished.

This drought was blamed on Elijah, who had opposed Baal worship and condemned the people for forsaking their own religion. He had also warned them of the impending disasters and the drought, and had not prayed for rain.

When Elijah saw that the drought had had serious effects on the country and that both the people and the cattle were suffering, he was instructed by God to challenge the prophets of Baal, in the presence of the king and the people, to prove that their gods were true gods.

So the prophets of Baal built an altar and laid wood and sacrifice on it. And the priests and the prophets of Baal called to Baal their god to send fire from heaven, but Baal answered not. When they were tired of praying and inflicting injuries on their bodies, Elijah repaired the altar of the God of Israel and placed wood upon it. Then he laid the sacrifice upon the wood and poured water on it. He also made a trench around the altar and filled it with water [verse 32]. Then he called on the God of Israel, and the Lord sent the fire which licked up both the sacrifice and the wood, as well as the water. Lightning preceded the downpour.

The miracle, in this instance, is that God told Elijah what to do and he revealed to him the secrets of the lightning. Note that Elijah chose the highest spot on the mountain and made a trench around the altar and filled it with water, because water is a good conductor of electricity. God and the laws of the universe were on the side of Elijah, because Elijah had trusted in God.

The prophets of Baal failed in their performance because they received no guidance from their false god. Elijah not only succeeded in bringing the lightning from the skies but he also predicted the end of the drought. All this performance was done by means of prayer and trust in God. Elijah was noted for his trust in God. Even when he was alone, he still believed and had confidence in the God of his forefathers.

When one believes and trusts in God and prays with a sincere heart, God will grant his request. Miracles and wonders are acts of God, who is the author of universal laws.

ELIJAH IN DILEMMA

So Ahab went up to eat and to drink. And Elijah went up to the top of Carmel; and he cast himself down upon the earth, and put his face between his knees.   1 Kings 18:42

Easterners, when facing a serious situation or trying to solve a problem, meditate in this manner: They sit on the ground and rest their elbows on their knees and cover their heads with their hands. The head is not literally between the knees, but rather bent over the knees and supported with the elbows. This position symbolizes a dilemma.

Elijah had performed a great miracle before the eyes of the king and the people, but he had also angrily and hastily executed four hundred prophets of Baal. The execution of these palace prophets made him think things over. He knew Jezebel would not be converted or even be impressed by the great wonder and the much needed rain, but that she would seek to avenge the death of the court prophets. Thus, Elijah was contemplating where to flee from the wicked queen, and what to do next.

BINDING AND LOOSING

And the king of Israel answered and said, Tell him, Let not him that girdeth on his harness boast himself as he that putteth it off.
1 Kings 20:11

The Aramaic phrase *asar* means "to bind," "to tie," "to gird." And the Aramaic word *sharey* means "to loosen" or "to untie," "to have authority." The term *asar* also means "an alliance" or "conspiracy."

What the king of Israel meant is this: "He who binds or ties a knot is not as able as he who unties it"; that is to say, "He who destroys is stronger than he who builds."

All the preparations which the king of Syria had made, and all his alliances, were broken. In other words, King Ben-hadad was too presumptuous and too sure of his victory. But, at last, his army was completely destroyed [verses 20-21]. King Ahab trusted in the Lord God of Israel, and the Lord caused the Syrian (Edomite) army to be confused and to flee.

FLOCKS OF KIDS

And the children of Israel were numbered, and were all present, and went against them: and the children of Israel pitched before them like two little flocks of kids; but the Syrians filled the country.
1 Kings 20:27

Flocks of kids are usually much smaller than flocks of lambs. This is because pastoral people raise more sheep for wool and meat, which are the two important products on which the tribal people depend for their livelihood. The meat and hair of goats are not so much in demand. The hair of goats is used only for tents, ropes, and at times for bags. The wealthy classes eat lamb and mutton and drink sheep milk.

The army of Israel was small, like a flock of kids, when compared with the large Syrian army. Israel had suffered several severe defeats during the reign of Omri [verses 13-16, 34].

KING—SOOTHSAYER

Now the men did diligently observe whether any thing would come from him, and did hastily catch it: and they said, Thy brother Ben-hadad. Then he said, Go ye, bring him. Then Ben-hadad came forth to him; and he caused him to come up into the chariot.   1 Kings 20:33

The Eastern text reads: "Now Bar-hadad was a soothsayer, and the men surmised and quickly caught his meaning, and they said, Behold your brother, Bar-hadad."

The Aramaic word *nakhsha* means a "diviner" or "augur." Not knowing the meaning of *nakhsha,* the translators placed some of the words in italics, indicating that those words are not actually in the original text.

Bar-hadad, king of Syria, was a diviner. He knew that the king of Israel was kind and that he would forgive him and let him go.

BELIAL

And set two men, sons of Belial, before him, to bear witness against him, saying, Thou didst blaspheme God and the king. And then carry him out, and stone him, that he may die.

1 Kings 21:10

Belial is a corrupt transliteration of the Aramaic words *benai* (the sons) and *awla* (iniquity); that is to say, wicked or ungodly men.

In the East, false witnesses and evil men are called *benai awla* (the offspring of wickedness) [verse 13].

The letters "l" and "n" are very similar in Aramaic. The Hebrew is *beni-belyael.*

A CANAANITISH WOMAN

And Zedekiah the son of Chenaanah made him horns of iron: and he said, Thus saith the Lord, With these shalt thou push the Syrians, until thou have consumed them.   1 Kings 22:11

The Eastern text reads "the son of a Canaanitish woman." The Mosaic code permitted Israelites to marry foreign women.

DOGS LICKED THE BLOOD

And one washed the chariot in the pool of Samaria; and the dogs licked up his blood; and they washed his armor; according unto the word of the Lord which he spake.   1 Kings 22:38

Ramtha means "hill"; that is, the hill upon which Samaria was built. "Pool" is wrong. To wash a bloody object in a pool would contaminate the water; and that would have made it impossible for the dogs to lick the blood. Moreover, Samaria has no pool of water. The land is semi-arid.

The Eastern text reads: "And they washed the chariot on the hill of Samaria; and they washed his armor; and the dogs licked up his blood, according to the word of the Lord which he spoke."

NO KING IN EDOM

There was then no king in Edom: a deputy was king.

1 Kings 22:47

The Aramaic word *kaem* (to reign) is confused with *kayoma* (governor, prefect). Edom was subjugated by King David and his general, Joab [2 Sam. 8:13-15]. But Edom rebelled during the reign of Joram (or Jehoram), the son of Jehoshaphat [2 Kings 8:20].

The Aramaic reads, "There was then no king who reigned in Edom." Apparently, Edom and *Aram* (Syria) were ruled by Hadad, an Edomite prince who had fled to Egypt, where he married the sister of Tahpenes, wife of Pharaoh [1 Kings 11:14-22]. Many of the kings of Syria were called Ben-hadad or Bar-hadad, "the son of Hadad" [1 Kings 15:18].

2 KINGS

BAAL-ZEBUB

And Ahaziah fell down through a lattice in his upper chamber that was in Samaria, and was sick: and he sent messengers, and said unto them, Go, inquire of Baal-zebub the god of Ekron whether I shall recover of this disease.   2 Kings 1:2

Baal-zebub means "the god of flies." The "d" and "z" are interchangeable in Aramaic speech. Thus, *debub* (flies) becomes *zebub*. In the olden days people believed that insects were controlled by certain pagan deities.

Baal-zebub was the god of Ekron, one of the Philistine gods who was believed to have power over flies. Biblical lands are noted for swarms of flies. The suffering caused by the flies, mosquitoes, and other insects caused the pagans to try to appease the gods who controlled them.

In the New Testament, Baal-zebub is called the prince of devils, who caused the people to suffer. Jesus was accused of working miracles by the power of Baal-zebub [Matt. 12:24; Mark 3:22-26].

Baal-bak probably means "the god of mosquitoes." Lebanon is noted for its mosquitoes.

HAIRY MAN

And they answered him, He was a hairy man, and girt with a girdle of leather about his loins. And he said, It is Elijah the Tishbite.
                                                      2 Kings 1:8

Prophets wore garments made of sheepskins, or coarse material made of wool or the hair of goats. They were men who had given up the world in order to preach justice and righteousness; and many of them spent most of their time in lonely places, in mountains and deserts, and slept in caves.

The garment made from sheepskin had become the official garment of the prophets and symbolized denial of the worldly life. At times even the false prophets, who made an easy living by prophesying, wore rough garments in order to deceive the people [Zech. 13:4].

When the visions of a prophet did not come true, he discarded his hairy, rough garment. Today, we say, "He has lied so much that he has lost his hair."

John the Baptist wore a garment made of camel's hair, and a leather girdle about his loins [Matt. 3:4].

The prophet Elijah spent most of his time hiding from King Ahab and Queen Jezebel and the prophets of Baal.

Garments of this kind were also used by the kings as symbols of authority. Even today, the robes of kings are adorned with ermine.

DOUBLE PORTION

And it came to pass, when they were gone over, that Elijah said unto Elisha, Ask what I shall do for thee, before I be taken away from thee. And Elisha said, I pray thee, let a double portion of thy spirit be upon me.
                                                      2 Kings 2:9

"Double portion," in this instance, means "abundant." Spirit can neither be measured nor weighed in balances.

The Mosaic law states that the firstborn must inherit a double portion of his father's possessions [Deut. 21:17]. Elisha considered himself as the heir of Elijah and, therefore, entitled to a double portion of his master's spirit and power. In other words, he wanted to be recognized as the successor of Elijah.

Elisha was destined to reform Israel, put an end to the house of Omri, and perform many miracles and wonders. Elisha needed a double portion of the power of his master in order to save Israel.

ELISHA HEALED THE SPRING

And the men of the city said unto Elisha, Behold, I pray thee, the situation of this city is pleasant, as my lord seeth: but the water is naught, and the ground barren.

And he said, Bring me a new cruse, and put salt therein. And they brought it to him.

And he went forth unto the spring of the waters, and cast the salt in there, and said, Thus saith the Lord, I have healed these waters; there shall not be from thence any more death or barren land.   2 Kings 2:19-21

In the lands where people wash clothes and bathe in the springs, the water sources become polluted. One can sometimes see worms around the edges of the springs and small streams.

Salt is often used to kill the worms. The prophet used salt as a medium, but God caused the water to be healed from contamination. The prophets and men of God had strong faith in God's power, but at times they used material substances because the people were accustomed to them. Isaiah recommended ripe figs when he healed Hezekiah [2 Kings 20:7; Isa. 38:21]. Jesus used a little clay when he healed the eyes of the blind man.

The Lord showed Moses a tree, and when he cast it into the bitter water, the waters were made sweet [Exod. 15:23-25].

Even today, the spring in Jericho is known by the name of Elisha.

BALD-HEADED

And he went up from thence unto Bethel: and as he was going up by the way, there came forth little children out of the city, and mocked him, and said unto him, Go up, thou bald head; go up, thou bald head.   2 Kings 2:23

Karkha (bald) in this instance could also mean liar, empty skull, or empty head. In vernacular Aramaic we often say, "He has lied so much that he has lost his hair." Easterners never walked bareheaded.

Seemingly, the people of Jericho had doubted Elisha's story that his master had ascended into heaven. They asked him to go with them to search for his master, Elijah; but Elisha refused. Nevertheless, they went ahead and sent fifty men, but they failed to find him [2 Kings 2:16-17].

Evidently the little boys had heard the gossip in the town when some of the men had doubted Elisha's sincerity. But Elisha would never have been offended by being called "bald," nor could the children have known that he was bald-headed. In the East men always cover their heads, even when at home.

The boys certainly would have had to do something more serious than calling him "bald-head" to justify his cursing them. They called him a liar. Elisha had told the truth about Elijah, but the people did not believe him.

MINSTREL

But now bring me a minstrel. And it came to pass, when the minstrel played, that the hand of the Lord came upon him.

2 Kings 3:15

The Aramaic word *nakosha* means a "bell," a "musical instrument," or a "player." Musical instruments were used to quiet the nerves and thus make meditation and communication with the deities easier. On the other hand, the people believed that the sound of music would charm the spirit, and frighten away the evil spirits.

Musical instruments were used by the pagans, also. Even today, snake charmers and diviners resort to this ancient practice.

"After that you shall come to the hill of God where there is a garrison of the Philistines; and it shall come to pass when you arrive there at the city, behold, you will meet a company of prophets coming down from the high place with psalteries and tabrets and tambourines and timbrels before them; and they will be prophesying" [1 Sam. 10:5, Eastern text].

PITS FOR WATER

And he said, Thus saith the Lord, Make this valley full of ditches.

2 Kings 3:16

In arid lands water is often found in pools on the mountain slopes, especially in rocky places, where the water is stored between the rocks. Moreover, Arabs make pools or ditches to collect the rainwater and to hold and conserve the seeping water.

But in this instance there was no rain. Had there been rain on that day, the Moabites would not have been deceived by the color of the water.

The prophet Elisha was guided by God to point out the places to be dug, and the Lord filled the pits with water in a dry land.

The Moabites, not having seen rain falling on that day, thought the water was the blood of their enemies who had fought one another, which often happens in the East.

When men turn to God, they are guided to sources of water, food supplies, and prosperity. Elisha believed in the God of Israel, who in the past had provided water, bread, and meat for his people, Israel.

KINGS APPEASED

Then he took his eldest son that should have reigned in his stead, and offered him for a burnt offering upon the wall. And there was great indignation against Israel: and they departed from him, and returned to their own land.   2 Kings 3:27

Human sacrifice was contrary to the law of Moses. But the pagans continued to burn their children on the altars of their gods as of yore. The Moabites sacrificed to Malcom (Molech).

The king of Moab offered his firstborn, or the crown prince, not on the altar to Malcom, but to the kings who besieged the capital city. He did this as a token of acknowledgment of his guilt in provoking the kings to war against him. His firstborn was the dearest person he had. This is why the king of Israel and his allies departed from him. Nomad people are magnanimous on such occasions. When their enemies sincerely humble themselves and repent, they forgive them and let them go free.

OIL INCREASED

Now there cried a certain woman of the wives of the sons of the prophets unto Elisha, saying, Thy servant my husband is dead; and thou knowest that thy servant did fear the Lord: and the creditor is come to take unto him my two sons to be bondmen.

And Elisha said unto her, What shall I do for thee? tell me, what hast thou in the house? And she said, Thine handmaid hath not any thing in the house, save a pot of oil.

Then he said, Go, borrow thee vessels abroad of all thy neighbors, even empty vessels; borrow not a few.

And when thou art come in, thou shalt shut the door upon thee and upon thy sons, and shalt pour out into all those vessels, and thou shalt set aside that which is full.   2 Kings 4:1-6

This miracle which Elisha performed is similar to that which was wrought by his master, Elijah, when he increased the barrel of flour and the pot of oil [1 Kings 17:16]. In neither case does the author of the book of the Kings explain the miracle. The flour and oil were multiplied. The episode, whether handed down orally or written, was true. Hebrew prophets were credited with great miracles and marvels. They even raised the dead and cleansed the lepers.

The words of a prophet had the power to cause such an increase in the oil and flour. God can do anything. He is the author of all good gifts. He brings the rain, and causes the grain to grow, and provides grass for the sheep, which is turned into milk and butter for food, and wool for raiment.

On the other hand, the men of God in those days exerted a tremendous influence over their people, who trusted them and believed in them. Whatever they asked, or even suggested, the people did.

In the East, people do not try to explain how the oil was increased, but they thank God that the poor woman had enough oil to sell in order to pay the debt of her deceased husband. The prophet, through his faith in God, blessed the oil, and the Lord God multiplied it.

In America, a religious man may bless some of his followers and thus increase the source of their supplies. The increase would come in money, good business, and wisdom to know how to buy and sell. It may result in good investments, but not in oil and flour. Oil and flour were used as mediums of exchange. Thus, the miracle is the increase of the substance and not how the substance was increased. What is impossible to man is possible to God. Faith in God is the only answer to miracles and wonders in the Bible.

SHUNEM

And it fell on a day, that Elisha passed to Shunem, where was a great woman; and she constrained him to eat bread. And so it was, that, as oft as he passed by, he turned in thither to eat bread.

2 Kings 4:8

"Shunem" is wrong. There was no such city in Israel. It should read "Shiloh." The latter is on the way to Samaria and Jezreel. The error was caused by the close similarity between the letters *lamed* (l) and *nun* (n) [1 Kings 1:3; 2 Kings 4:12].

Such errors, caused by the similarity of letters, are prevalent in many parts of the Bible.

Shiloh was the city wherein the tabernacle and the Ark of the Covenant were kept during the time of the Judges. It was the place where the Israelites gathered to make offerings to the Lord their God. The town is about thirty miles northeast of Jerusalem [1 Sam. 1:3].

ADDRESSING THE WOMAN

And he said unto him, Say now unto her, Behold, thou hast been careful for us with all this care; what is to be done for thee? wouldest thou be spoken for to the king, or to the captain of the host? And she answered, I dwell among mine own people.

2 Kings 4:13

Lah (to her) has been confused with *leh* (to him). *Lah* has a dot over the letter *hey* (h), indicating the feminine gender.

The Eastern text reads: "And he said to her, Behold, you have shown us all this respect; what is to be done for you?"

The Shilomite woman was already standing before Elisha [verse 12]. The prophet spoke directly to her, and not to Gehazi, his servant.

THERE WAS NO DECEPTION

Then she said, Did I desire a son of my lord? did I not say, Do not deceive me?   2 Kings 4:28

The Aramaic word *tishal* (to ask) is confused with *teshadal* (comfort, deceive, entice, cajole). Such words with close similarity can easily be confused.

The Shilomite woman (Shilomite is a native of Shiloh) and her husband had taken care of the man of God during his visits to that part of the country, and the man of God had prayed that the woman might have a child.

When the child died, the woman came to the prophet for help, believing he could raise him. And when she spoke to him, she reminded him that she had not asked for the child in the first place. The prophet had not lied to her; he knew that God would give her the child.

PROPHETS RAISED THE DEAD

And when Elisha was come into the house, behold, the child was dead, and laid upon his bed.

He went in therefore, and shut the door upon them twain, and prayed unto the Lord.

And he went up, and lay upon the child, and put his mouth upon his mouth, and his eyes upon his eyes, and his hands upon his hands: and he stretched himself upon the child; and the flesh of the child waxed warm.   2 Kings 4:32-34

Many of the prophets of Israel healed the sick, cleansed the lepers, and raised the dead. They had faith in God, who is the source of life; and they were endowed with wisdom to understand God and to heal.

The prophet Elisha knew the science of restoring life. Like his master, Elijah, he prayed and then stretched himself upon the dead body to warm it [1 Kings 17:20-21]. More than eight hundred years later Jesus Christ healed the sick and raised the dead by his word [Mark 5:41-42].

Natural means apply to the body, and spiritual means to life. The healer has to understand both the soul and the body.

GIFTS OF FOOD INCREASED

And there came a man from Baal-shalisha, and brought the man of God bread of the firstfruits, twenty loaves of barley, and full ears of corn in the husk thereof. And he said, Give unto the people, that they may eat.

And his servant said, What should I set this before an hundred men? He said again, Give the people, that they may last: for thus saith the Lord, They shall eat, and shall leave thereof.

2 Kings 4:42-43

In the East healers and religious men receive gifts of food from men and women who visit them seeking healing and inquiring of God. Everyone who seeks their presence takes with them a small gift of bread, cheese, fish, honey, or other foodstuffs as an offering to God.

The food thus offered is given to the poor, to travelers, and to other visitors.

The men of God, like Jesus, had power to increase the bread and feed the people who had come to see them. How the bread is increased is not explained. One thing we know, the increase comes from God, who is the Creator of all substance, and from people who are willing to share what they have. On the other hand, God can meet all the needs of those who sincerely trust in him.

The people who had come to the prophet were seeking spiritual things. They received material things, too. When we seek the kingdom of God, other things will be added and multiplied for us. No matter from where the supplies come, ultimately they come from God.

Jesus also multiplied the loaves and fish, but the Gospel does not explain how the miracle was performed. Whether the loaves of bread grew larger or whether more people brought baskets unexpectedly, or whether the bread and the fish came from heaven, the need was met by the power of God and the people were fed.

After all, our supplies all come from God. Easterners attribute all the gifts they receive to God. They say, "God has given me sheep, oxen, and grain." They know God can do anything. He can even change the stones into bread if there is a worthy need [2 Kings 4:1-6].

NAAMAN

But Naaman was wroth, and went away, and said, Behold, I thought, He will surely come out to me, and stand, and call on the name of the Lord his God, and strike his hand over the place, and recover the leper.

Are not Abana and Pharpar, rivers of Damascus, better than all the waters of Israel? may I not wash in them, and be clean? So he turned and went away in a rage.   2 Kings 5:11-12

The Jordan is the largest river in Palestine. In the semiarid lands, because of the long droughts and scarcity of water, some of the rivers, springs, and other water sources were looked upon as sacred. The Jordan was the first large body of water that the Hebrews saw when they came from the desert lands into Palestine. The river was sanctified by the wonders of the Lord and the holy Ark of the Covenant, which the priests bore as they crossed it.

Some biblical authorities believe the Jordan's water contains minerals such as phosphorous and potash, and that potash heals leprosy. It is true that the Jordan's waters are rich in minerals, but Elisha was not thinking of the minerals when he admonished Naaman to bathe in the River Jordan seven times. Undoubtedly, Naaman had tried all kinds of medicines but had failed to find a cure.

The prophet, by suggesting something very simple, rebuked the power of the disease. Water is so common that no one would think that it contains any healing power. Easterners generally search for something rare and hard to find. On the other hand, most of the healers suggest medicines that cannot be procured, so the sick and suffering cannot blame them if they are not healed.

The number seven is a sacred number—seven planets, seven days, seven candlesticks.

Naaman, being a pagan, was accustomed to pagan rituals and enchantments. This is why he took Elisha's words derisively. Damascus is graced with rivers and prolific brooks which have transformed the land into a garden. There is no place in Palestine to compare with the beautiful gardens and orchards of Damascus.

The prophets of Israel spoke words that contained the power of healing. Indeed, the same words that can convert a sinner can also heal a sick person and cleanse a leper.

HOLY SOIL

And Naaman said, Shall there not then, I pray thee, be given to thy servant two mules' burden of earth? for thy servant will henceforth offer neither burnt offering nor sacrifice unto other gods, but unto the Lord. 2 Kings 5:17

The earth was to be used in the building of a shrine or a house of prayer, so that Naaman might pray to the God of Israel, who had cleansed him from his leprosy. In the East, when a man is healed by a healer or a preacher of another faith, he forsakes his religion and his place of worship as a token of gratitude to the god who had healed him.

Even today Easterners take soil from sacred shrines and churches which are noted for cures and carry them to their own lands to be placed in their houses. Soil, stones, and water from Palestine and other biblical lands have been carried to Europe, America, and other parts of the world. This is not all. The convert may even exchange his customs and usages for those recommended by the leaders of the new faith which he has adopted.

KING'S AIDE

In this thing the Lord pardon thy servant, that when my master goeth into the house of Rimmon to worship there, and he leaneth on my hand, and I bow myself in the house of Rimmon: when I bow down myself in the house of Rimmon. 2 Kings 5:18

"My lord leans on my hand" is an Eastern idiom which means, "I am his aide," or aide de camp.

Naaman was the highest ranking general in the Syrian army and therefore he was the closest person to the king. He accompanied the king wherever he went. Even when the king went to worship, Naaman went with him as a bodyguard of honor.

In the East kings must constantly be protected from conspirators and rivals. The king of Assyria was assassinated in the temple of his god [2 Kings 19:37]. King Abdullah of Jordan was slain at the entrance of the Mosque of Omar.

The king of Syria relied on Naaman's support and protection, so he made him his aide [2 Kings 7:2, 17].

GEHAZI THE SERVANT

But Gehazi, the servant of Elisha the man of God, said, Behold,
my master hath spared Naaman this Syrian, in not receiving at his
hands that which he brought: but, as the Lord liveth, I will run
after him, and take somewhat of him.   2 Kings 5:20

Easterners customarily decline to accept gifts when offered, but they
know the giver will urge them to accept. After a few customary re-
fusals, the gifts are accepted with gracious words of gratitude.

But, in this particular instance, things were different. Elisha was sincere in his refusal. He could not accept lavish gifts from a pagan general whom he had healed. The prophets generally accepted a basket of
loaves, a little honey, fruit, cheese, or other food supplies, which they
then shared with the poor. On the other hand, they had received the
power of healing freely; and they felt they should use it freely to help
sufferers.

But Gehazi, Elisha's servant, being greedy, went after Naaman, pretending that his master wanted some of the gifts. And the general, not
having begged and implored the prophet to accept his gifts, gladly
parted with whatever Gehazi wanted.

When the prophet saw that his servant had followed after the general
and had lied to him, he cursed him, and he became a leper.

AXE HEAD SWAM

But as one was felling a beam, the axe head fell into the water:
and he cried, and said, Alas, master! for it was borrowed.
And the man of God said, Where fell it? And he showed him
the place. And he cut down a stick, and cast it in thither; and the
iron did swim.   2 Kings 6:5-6

The confusion in this miracle is caused by the mistranslation of two
Aramaic words: *armi* (he pushed it into the water) and *tap* (it stuck
into the axe hole). The Aramaic word for "swim" is *sakha,* but *sakha*
is not in the Eastern text.

The miracle or wonder was performed in this manner: The prophet
was divinely guided to direct the man to recover the axe head. This is
why he asked him to cut off a branch from a tree and push it into the
water of Jordan, where the axe head had fallen. The Lord caused the
tip of the branch to enter the hole of the axe head.

The miracle is that the prophet, through God's guidance, knew where
the axe head had fallen and was thus able to recover it.

No doubt, God could have caused the axe head to swim if he had wanted to do so, but then the prophet would not have told the man to cut a branch from the tree. There was no power in the wood to cause the axe head to swim, but there is power in the Word of God, which is the most powerful thing in the world.

When we turn to God and seek his divine guidance, we are directed and led to do things that seem difficult or impossible. This is because everything is possible to God, and nothing is hidden from his eyes.

SPIRITUAL BLINDNESS

And when they came down to him, Elisha prayed unto the Lord, and said, Smite this people, I pray thee, with blindness. And he smote them with blindness according to the word of Elisha.
2 Kings 6:18

Blindness in this instance means blindness of spiritual vision and not of the eyes. The eyes of these Syrians (Arameans) were open and clear, but their vision was obscured and their minds confused. When people make mistakes or travel on a wrong route, it is said, "They were blind." When Elisha prayed, the Lord blinded their vision so that they were unable to find their way.

In other words, it was not physical blindness, but spiritual blindness that obscured the sight of these Syrians. The physical eye is an instrument through which we see, but vision is centered in the mind. Therefore, when the mind is obscured, the eyes fail to recognize objects.

The Pharisees and scribes were not physically blind, but they were suffering from mental and spiritual blindness. This is why Jesus called them blind guides [Matt. 23:16]. Moreover, Isaiah stated that some of the people in his day had eyes but could not see, and ears but could not hear. They had lost their spiritual vision because they had gone astray after other gods [Ps. 82:5].

KING'S BODYGUARD

Then a lord on whose hand the king leaned answered the man of God, and said, Behold, if the Lord would make windows in heaven, might this thing be? And he said, Behold, thou shalt see it with thine eyes, but shalt not eat thereof.
2 Kings 7:2

"He leans on my hand" is an Aramaic idiom meaning "I am his aide." The "lord" was a bodyguard to the king of Israel.
See comment on 2 Kings 5:18.

FIVE HORSEMEN

And one of his servants answered and said, Let some take, I pray thee, five of the horses that remain, which are left in the city, (behold, they are as all the multitude of Israel that are left in it: behold, I say, they are even as all the multitude of the Israelites that are consumed:) and let us send and see.   2 Kings 7:13

The Aramaic word *rakabey* means "riders" or "horsemen." The five horsemen were to be sent to see if the army of Aram (Syria) had fled.

The Eastern text reads: "And one of his servants answered and said, Let some horsemen take five of the horses that remain; if they are captured, let them be considered a loss like all the army of Israel that has perished; therefore let us send and see."

Most of the horsemen of the king of Israel had been either slain or captured by the forces of Aram.

KING LEANED

And the king appointed the lord on whose hand he leaned to have the charge of the gate: and the people trode upon him in the gate, and he died, as the man of God had said, who spake when the king came down to him.   2 Kings 7:17

"On whose hand he leaned" means "who was his aide."
See comment on 2 Kings 5:18.

FABULOUS GIFTS

And the king said unto Hazael, Take a present in thine hand, and go, meet the man of God, and inquire of the Lord by him, saying, Shall I recover of this disease?   2 Kings 8:8

In biblical days when people went to inquire of a prophet, a seer, or a man of God, or to seek healing from his hand, they always took a present with them. It is against the ancient custom to visit a prophet or a healer empty handed. [See comment on 1 Sam. 9:7 and 1 Kings 14:1-3.]

Easterners have so much faith in a healer or a man of God that they are ready to pay them something in advance. Most gifts of this kind consist of bread, honey, and fruits. Money is seldom given, and at times it is even refused. Elisha refused to accept Naaman's fabulous gifts [2 Kings 5:15-16].

BEN-HADAD SUFFOCATED

And it came to pass on the morrow, that he took a thick cloth, and dipped it in water, and spread it on his face, so that he died: and Hazael reigned in his stead.   2 Kings 8:15

Hazael was so sure that he would become king over Syria that he could not wait until the sick king died. He lied to him by telling him that the prophet of God had told him he would recover.

He placed the thick, wet cloth on the sick and helpless king to suffocate him, and then he could tell the princes and ministers that the king had died a natural death. This was done in order to avoid a revolt.

In olden days, it was believed that when a general disposed of his lord, he automatically became the heir and possessed the divine authority to rule over the people. The heir or the successor was always the slayer.

AHAB'S SISTER

And he walked in the way of the kings of Israel, as did the house of Ahab; for the daughter of Ahab was his wife: and he did evil in the sight of the Lord.   2 Kings 8:18

The Eastern text reads *khatey* (the sister) of Ahab; that is Italiah, daughter of Omri, and sister of Ahab. The Aramaic word for "daughter" is *barta; barteh* (his daughter).

GOD PROMISED TO DAVID

Yet the Lord would not destroy Judah for David his servant's sake, as he promised him to give him always a light, and to his children.   2 Kings 8:19

The Aramaic word *sheragha* (a lamp) is used metaphorically, meaning "an heir." In the East an heir is spoken of as a lamp, or the light of the family. One hears people saying: "May God bless and protect your lamp."

God had promised David to give him an heir to sit upon his throne. From the time the promise was made until 586 B.C., an heir of David ruled over Judah.

A PUBLIC TOILET

And they brake down the image of Baal, and brake down the house of Baal, and made it a draught house unto this day.

2 Kings 10:27

The Aramaic words *beth makhria* (Hebrew *mekhraoth*) mean "a public toilet." In biblical lands, private toilets were unknown until recent days, and even now in some towns they are still unknown. The people go to the fields and ruined places.

The temple of Baal was destroyed and its ruins had become a public toilet. In the olden days, the members of rival religions desecrated the holy places of one another by turning them into public toilets.

The Jewish temple was desecrated by Antiochus Epiphanes and other men who conquered Jerusalem.

See comment on Judges 3:24.

A CHALLENGE

Then Amaziah sent messengers to Jehoash, the son of Jehoahaz son of Jehu, king of Israel, saying, Come, let us look one another in the face.

2 Kings 14:8

"Let us look one another in the face" is an Aramaic idiom which means, "Let us face one another in battle." In other words, this was a challenge to the king of Israel to come out and fight. When Easterners are angry at one another, they say, "I wish I could face him," or, "I wish I could see his face."

In the olden days kings marched at the head of their armies and many of them died in the battle [2 Chron. 25:17].

WITHOUT COUNSELORS

For the Lord saw the affliction of Israel, that it was very bitter: for there was not any shut up, nor any left, nor any helper for Israel.

2 Kings 14:26

The Aramaic words *asar* (bind) and *sharey* (loosen) are often used in referring to "a man in power"; that is, having authority to put people in prison and to set them free. The Eastern text reads: "For the Lord saw the affliction of Israel, that it was very bitter; for there was no one in power, and there was no one to help Israel."

In the East a wise counselor or leader is compared to a man who can bind an intricate knot and loosen it. The phrase *asar-sharey* is often used metaphorically, meaning "able to give counsel, make treaties, interpret law, and overcome difficult problems."

Israel was so crushed by the Arameans (Syrians) that they had lost all of their leaders and counselors.

See comment on 1 Kings 20:11.

AZARIAH

In the twenty and seventh year of Jeroboam king of Israel began Azariah son of Amaziah king of Judah to reign. 2 Kings 15:1

The Eastern text reads "Uzziah the son of Amaziah." Azariah is not mentioned at all. Moreover, there is no king in the genealogy of the kings of Judah called Azariah. Uzziah was the successor to Amaziah. In Matthew 1:8 (Eastern text) he is called Uzziah. Thus, both the Old Testament and the New agree on the spelling of the kings of Judah. Azariah, no doubt, is an error of a scribe or copyist. In Aramaic the names Azariah and Uzziah are very similar. King Uzziah was smitten with leprosy and his son Jotham took over the affairs of the kingdom [verse 5]. After his death, Jotham, his son, reigned in his stead. In verse 32 we read, ". . . began Jotham the son of Uzziah king of Judah to reign . . ." and in verse 34, ". . . he did according to all that his father Uzziah had done."

RICH TAXED

And Menahem exacted the money of Israel, even of all the mighty men of wealth, of each man fifty shekels of silver, to give to the king of Assyria. So the king of Assyria turned back, and stayed not there in the land. 2 Kings 15:20

In the East the rich and those in power never paid taxes. There is nothing more humiliating to a rich or noble man than to have to pay taxes or a tribute. The rich were allowed to collect taxes and employ forced labor.

Taxes are collected from the poor, the widows, and the workers. This is why tax-gatherers were despised and the greedy rich men abhorred by the prophets and barred from entering into the kingdom of God [Matt. 19:24].

This was a very exceptional thing for Menahem, the king of Israel, to do; but he had to break the ancient tradition by taxing even the rich, because the tribute was too much for the poor and the workers of the land to meet.

Today, some reforms have already been carried out in the Near East and the Middle East. In some parts of the East the rich are still tax-free, but in other parts they are slowly learning to support the government by paying taxes.

SYRIAN A WRONG TERM

At that time Rezin king of Syria recovered Elath to Syria, and drave the Jews from Elath: and the Syrians came to Elath, and dwelt there unto this day.   **2 Kings 16:6**

The term "Syrian" is Greek derived from *Sur* (Tyre) the famous Aramean port on the eastern shore of the Mediterranean Sea. The Eastern text of this verse reads "Rezin king of Aram." The capital of the Arameans was the ancient city of Damascus [verse 5].

The term "Syrian" is misleading. This term was unknown prior to the Greek conquest. Moreover, in the New Testament, the term *Aramaye,* meaning Arameans, has been translated "Greeks" in the Western translations of the Bible for an unknown reason, or probably to prove that the Greeks were among the first converts.

LOST TRIBES

In the ninth year of Hoshea the king of Assyria took Samaria, and carried Israel away into Assyria, and placed them in Halah and in Habor by the river of Gozan, and in the cities of the Medes.   **2 Kings 17:6**

The ten tribes of Israel were carried away captive under Sargon and Shalmaneser, kings of Assyria. And they were placed in Halah, in Habor (*Khabor*), and in Gozan.

In the former days some of these lands belonged to the Medes and Parthians. Today most of this region is inhabited by the Kurds, who are the descendants of the Medes and Parthians.

Gozan means "the land of walnuts." The area north of Habor (*Khabor*) is noted for large walnut trees. Gozan, no doubt, is the region north of the River Khabor [1 Chron. 5:26; Isa. 37:12].

Josephus states that the ten tribes were beyond the River Euphrates even in his time. Apparently, the Israelites remained in the fertile regions wherein they were settled, and they became a strong people who played an important part during the reign of the Chaldeans and Persians. They had prospered so much that Haman, the prime minister of Persia, sought to destroy them and confiscate their wealth.

The Jewish community in Babylon not only was the largest but also the wealthiest and most learned. The Jews in Babylon had schools of higher learning. Their savants produced many works. Notable among them is the Babylonian Talmud, which is written in Aramaic.

Prior to World War II, thousands of Jews and members of the ten tribes were still living in the lands where the kings of Assyria had placed them. The writer lived among them. They still spoke Aramaic, which they called *Leshan Galotha*, "the language of the captivity." In 1950, thousands of these people migrated to Israel. Now many of them are in Jerusalem and Galilee. And they still converse in Aramaic.

NEHUSHTAN

He removed the high places, and brake the images, and cut down the groves, and brake in pieces the brazen serpent that Moses had made: for unto those days the children of Israel did burn incense to it: and he called it Nehushtan. 2 Kings 18:4

Nehushtan or *Nikheshtan* is derived from *nakhash* (to divine). *Nehushtan* means "our object of divination"; that is, the brass serpent.

The serpent of brass which Moses had made eight hundred years before had become an object of veneration among the Israelites.

When the Israelites were bitten by snakes in the desert, the victims looked at the serpent of brass which Moses had made and were healed [Num. 21:9].

Images of snakes (as in the case of the black serpent), birds, and fish were prohibited by the Mosaic law. Some of these creatures were worshiped by the pagans. Fish were looked upon as sacred in Assyria. Even today some people never eat them. The name Nineveh means "fish." Snakes, monkeys, and oxen were also worshiped by the pagans as gods.

PALACE FIELD

And the king of Assyria sent Tartan and Rabsaris and Rabshakeh from Lachish to king Hezekiah with a great host against Jerusalem: and they went up and came to Jerusalem. And when they were come up, they came and stood by the conduit of the upper pool, which is in the highway of the fuller's field. 2 Kings 18:17

The Aramaic reads *khakley di kasra* (the palace field). The Aramaic word *kasra* means a "fortress" or "palace," but *kasra* is used when speaking of a royal residence which, in olden days, was fortified. Palaces and the residences of the princes and the rich are adjoined to fields.

The word *kasra* has been confused with *kasor* (fuller) meaning one who scours or fulls cloth. The Hebrew word is *kaser*.

A WEAK ALLY

Now, behold, thou trustest upon the staff of this bruised reed, even upon Egypt, on which if a man lean, it will go into his hand, and pierce it: so is Pharaoh king of Egypt unto all that trust on him. 2 Kings 18:21

"Bruised reed" is an idiom meaning "a weak ally."

The reed mentioned here is the tropical reed, something like bamboo. The stems are used for staffs, canes, and chairs. In the East priests, shepherds, and nobles carry wooden or reed staffs. The elderly priests lean on their staffs when praying.

"And there was given me a reed like unto a rod: and the angel stood, saying, Rise, and measure the temple of God, and the altar, and them that worship therein" [Rev. 11:1].

Egypt was a weak and an untrustworthy ally. Even the Hebrew prophets had warned Judah against such an alliance [Isa. 36:6; Ezek. 29:6-7].

ENTICING IN THE NAME OF GOD

Am I now come up without the Lord against this place to destroy it? The Lord said to me, Go up against this land, and destroy it. 2 Kings 18:25

The Assyrians did not recognize the God of Israel as the God of the world. They had their own gods, and temples larger than the temple of Solomon.

The Assyrian commander knew that the Israelites feared their God, and that when they had gone astray after other gods they were defeated by their enemies. Therefore, the commander of the Assyrian army tried to win the confidence of the people by pretending that his master, the king of Assyria, had an oracle from the God of Israel, and that it was he who had sent him against Judah. There had been some prophecies concerning the rise of the Assyrian power and the invasion of both Israel and Judah [Isa. 7:17]. Israel was already carried away captive to Assyria [verses 10-11].

But Isaiah admonished the people not to be afraid of the words of

Rab-shakeh, which were nothing but blasphemy against the Lord. The Lord had heard the prayer of Hezekiah and had compassion on Judah.

SPEAK IN ARAMAIC

Then said Eliakim the son of Hilkiah, and Shebna, and Joah, unto Rab-shakeh, Speak, I pray thee, to thy servants in the Syrian language; for we understand it: and talk not with us in the Jews' language in the ears of the people that are on the wall.

2 Kings 18:26

The Eastern text reads, "Speak to your servants in the Aramaic; for we understand it."

Aramaic was the lingua franca, and Hebrew the vernacular speech of Judah and Israel. The term "Jews' language" means the Hebrew spoken in Judea. In those days, just as today, every tribe had its own local dialect. Even the dialects of Ephraim and Manasseh differed.

The king, princes, and learned men understood Aramaic, because that speech was the literary tongue of all the cultured people in the Fertile Crescent, Aram, Moab, and adjacent lands. Each tribe or people had its own native dialect, but all of them understood Aramaic, the international speech of that day, and the language of the Hebrew patriarchs. Because the two great Semitic empires of Assyria and Babylon used Aramaic, it was the lingua franca of the day.

On the other hand, the workers, the soldiers, and the common people spoke the Jewish dialect. This is also true of the literary Arabic when compared with the common speech.

WRITTEN ON SKIN

And Hezekiah received the letter of the hand of the messengers, and read it: and Hezekiah went up into the house of the Lord, and spread it before the Lord.

2 Kings 19:14

Letters or epistles were written on sheepskin and not on clay tablets. But treaties, imperial edicts, and other important state documents were usually written on clay tablets, which were then baked and stored away. The Eastern text reads *egratha* (several scrolls).

Writing in Aramaic was prevalent in the eighth century B.C. in Syria, Babylon, and other lands in the Near East and in Assyria. King Hezekiah spread the scrolls before the Lord in the temple.

The letter was written in Aramaic, the literary tongue of that time. Jewish kings, scribes, and learned people understood Aramaic. This written language was to everyday speech as the King James English is to current American speech, or as high German is to low German. Aramaic was the language that Jacob and his sons had brought from Padan-Aram.

FRUITS AS MEDICINE

And Isaiah said, Take a lump of figs. And they took and laid it on the boil, and he recovered.   2 Kings 20:7

In the East, fruits, herbs, and honey are used as medicines. The sweet fruit or honey is placed upon the wound to draw out the poison. It is said that sweets will counteract poisons. This formula is still used by the *hakims* (doctors) in Kurdistan and adjacent lands.

The healing was not accomplished by means of the figs, but rather by the faith which King Hezekiah had in the prophet who spoke and acted in the name of God and showed him a sign.

PEACE, HEZEKIAH'S WISH

Then said Hezekiah unto Isaiah, Good is the word of the Lord which thou hast spoken. And he said, Is it not good, if peace and truth be in my days?   2 Kings 20:19

The Aramaic words *eshtoop den* means "I wish"; that is, "I wish that peace and justice would reign in my days."

"But would that peace and justice shall be in my day!" (Eastern text.)

Hezekiah knew that there was danger ahead. The might of the Assyrian army was felt all over the lands west of the River Euphrates. And now another great military power was rising, the Babylonian Empire.

JUDAH IS DOOMED

And I will stretch over Jerusalem the line of Samaria, and the plummet of the house of Ahab: and I will wipe Jerusalem as a man wipeth a dish, wiping it, and turning it upside down.

2 Kings 21:13

In the lands where food is scarce and the people suffer hunger and thirst, food is not wasted. Every bit of it is eaten, and the dishes are so thoroughly cleaned that they do not need to be washed. On the other hand, owing to the scarcity of water, dishes are wiped with the bread and then turned over so that flies may not alight on them.

In the East three or four persons often ate from the same dish. Knives and forks were unknown. Food was picked up with a piece of bread. The term "wipe," meaning "destruction," is still used, but the Aramaic reads *emkhey* (I will smite). *Emkhey* has been confused with *emshey* (I will wipe). The author of the books of Kings is speaking of the impending disaster which was to befall the kingdom of Judah, just as it already had come upon the kingdom of Israel.

The line of Samaria and the plummet of the house of Arab are used symbolically, meaning, "I will apply the same measures"; that is, the same destruction and captivity.

"I will wipe them" is an Eastern idiom which is commonly used in the vernacular speech, and means, "I will destroy them completely." In those days, doomed cities were measured with the measuring line. Some portions of the city were completely destroyed. Some portions were turned into fields [Isa. 34:11; Lam. 2:8; Amos 7:7-8].

A WICKED KING

And Manasseh slept with his fathers, and was buried in the garden of his own house, in the garden of Uzza: and Amon his son reigned in his stead.   2 Kings 21:18

The Eastern text reads *beganath gaza* (in the garden of the treasury) —where the king's treasures were stored. This garden was close to the royal palace. The error was caused by the confusion of the letters *gamel* and *aey,* or *ain.*

Manasseh, being a wicked king, was not buried in the royal burial ground. King Manasseh had rejected the way of the Lord God of Israel for Baal worship, and had filled Jerusalem with idolatry, whoredom, and bloodshed. Therefore, he was not worthy to be buried with the kings of Judah.

It was during the reigns of Manasseh and his son, Amon, that the temple of the Lord was polluted with immoral pagan practices [Isa. 43:28].

TREASURES IN TEMPLE WALLS

And Hilkiah the high priest said unto Shaphan the scribe, I have found the book of the law in the house of the Lord. And Hilkiah gave the book to Shaphan, and he read it.   2 Kings 22:8

Finding of ancient books, gold, and silver in churches, caves, and fields is very common. In the East, until World War I, sacred books and church treasures were kept in small chambers built into the massive church walls, or buried in caves.

During wars and persecutions, jewels and other costly articles are stored in churches and in caves. These vaults or chambers cannot be easily detected. At times, a whole church building is destroyed by the invaders in order to find the hidden treasures. When priests are killed, or die a sudden death, the location of the treasure is lost.

The Book of the Law had been lying in the strong chamber in the wall for many generations. The book was discovered by workingmen who were repairing the breaches in the temple walls. It might have been hidden during the reign of some of the wicked kings of Judah who introduced Baal worship into the temple, especially during the reign of Queen Athaliah [2 Kings 11:1-3; 2 Chron. 34:15].

STUDYING

So Hilkiah the priest, and Ahikam, and Achbor, and Shaphan, and Asahiah, went unto Huldah the prophetess, the wife of Shallum the son of Tikvah, the son of Harhas, keeper of the wardrobe; (now she dwelt in Jerusalem in the college;) and they communed with her.   2 Kings 22:14

Betinianotha, derived from *tena* (to repeat) means that she was studying the law of Moses or meditating on the Book of the Law. Colleges and similar schools were unknown in those days [2 Chron. 34:22].

In the East one can see learned men repeating the words of the Holy Scriptures, trying to commit them to memory. In biblical days sacred books were rare, and many priests, scribes, and learned men committed them to memory. This ancient custom still prevails in Arabia, Palestine, and other parts of the Near East.

RIBLAH

So they took the king, and brought him up to the king of Babylon to Riblah; and they gave judgment upon him.
                                                   2 Kings 25:6

Riblah, or Riblath, is the ancient name of Antioch. The name of this ancient city was changed by Seleucus Nicator, who called it Antioch as a memorial to his father, Antiochus, in 301 B.C.

Antioch was the capital of the Syrian kingdom which was ruled by a Macedonian general. Owing to its geographical and strategic position, the city was made the seat of the Roman government in the Near East, and subsequently was declared a Roman province.

It was in Antioch that the disciples of Jesus were first called *Mashikhaye* (in the Greek), "Christians."

Antioch was the gateway to the East. During the Roman campaigns against the Parthian and Sassanid Empires (Iran), the Romans mobilized their forces in Antioch. The city is situated in the northeast end of a wide plain. The city has several large natural springs, and the climate is fair.

CHAPTER ELEVEN

1 and 2 CHRONICLES

INTRODUCTION

IN the Peshitta, the title of the books is *Debaryamin* (the acts day by day, the daily words). This title, like the Hebrew, implies that the two books known as Chronicles were written by scribes who kept daily state records and deeds.

Thus, the authorship of the books of Chronicles, like the books of the Kings, can be ascribed to various state scribes and recorders, who were employed by the kings of Judah and Israel.

In many instances the Chronicles are identical with the books of the Kings. The accounts in the books of Chronicles might have been written by the state scribes, and those of the Kings by the palace or royal scribes. This is why some accounts differ slightly from one another.

The scribes recorded every event that they thought important, such as wars, building of cities, famines, disasters, and the reigns of kings.

The books of Chronicles could not have been written by Ezra after the exile, as some biblical authorities maintain. The Hebrews, from the earliest times, employed scribes. Both Moses and Joshua had scribes who recorded all important state deeds, ordinances, tabernacle rituals, and laws.

In Deuteronomy we are told that Moses wrote down all daily occurrences. "And Moses wrote down their goings out and their journeys by the commandment of the Lord; and these are their journeys according to their goings out" [Num. 33:2; see also Exod. 24:4; Deut. 31:9].

1 CHRONICLES

COMMANDER-IN-CHIEF

Of the three, he was more honorable than the two; for he was their captain: howbeit he attained not to the first three.

1 Chron. 11:21

This should read: "He was more honorable than the thirty men, and he became their chief and fought like thirty men."

Abishai, the brother of Joab, was second in the rank only to his brother, Joab. In all expeditions and wars he served as corps commander, and at times as the king's aide [2 Sam. 23:19].

REVOLT AGAINST SAUL

And there fell some of Manasseh to David, when he came with the Philistines against Saul to battle; but they helped them not: for the lords of the Philistines upon advisement sent him away, saying, He will fall to his master Saul to the jeopardy of our heads.

1 Chron. 12:19

The Eastern text reads: "And some of the men of the tribe of Manasseh went over to David when he went to war with the Philistines against Saul to battle; but they would not go with Saul to war to help him, because they hated him, for they had gone and made a secret treaty with the princes of the Philistines, saying, Let us go first and fall on Saul our master."

The Manassites went with David to help him when he went with the army of the Philistines, but they had refused to go with Saul to battle against the Philistines. This is why they were so honored and loved by King David.

KING'S GENEROSITY

And he dealt to every one of Israel, both man and woman, to every one a loaf of bread, and a good piece of flesh, and a flagon of wine.

1 Chron. 16:3

The Aramaic word *snarka* (a fine white loaf) is wrongly translated "a flagon of wine." The translators of the King James Version, not being sure of the word "wine," put it in italics [see also 2 Sam. 6:19].

The bringing of the Ark of the Lord out of the house of Ober-edom was a great event. Hundreds of priests and thousands of Levites were assembled for this occasion. Moreover, the elders and the princes of Israel, with thousands of men, women, and children, had come to Jerusalem to participate in this historic celebration.

King David could hardly have provided all these people with wine. But he provided them with bread, and especially with the kind of white wheat bread which the king and his royal family ate, and which is greatly coveted by the poor.

In the East, until World War I, white bread was hardly known among the common people. It was found only on the tables of princes, foreign missionaries, and the wealthy classes. The poor eat bread made of whole wheat, rye, barley, and millet. Many of the Israelites subsisted on barley bread.

See the commentary on 2 Samuel 6:19.

NOT CUT WITH SAWS

And he brought out the people that were in it, and cut them with saws, and with harrows of iron, and with axes. Even so dealt David with all the cities of the children of Ammon. And David and all the people returned to Jerusalem.   1 Chron. 20:3

The Aramaic word *esar* or *asar* (to bind) is confused with *nesar* (to saw). Undoubtedly, *aleph* (a) the first letter in the Semitic alphabet, has been confused with *nun* (n).

David bound these people and took them captive to Jerusalem.

See the commentary on 2 Samuel 12:31.

DAVID ACTED FOOLISHLY

And God was displeased with this thing; therefore he smote Israel.   1 Chron. 21:7

The Aramaic word *damna,* derived from *mena* (numbered) has been confused with *damkha* (smote). The two words have a close resemblance to one another. The right angle of the letter *kheth* (kh) is similar to the letter *nun* (n).

In verse 1, we are told that Satan provoked David to number Israel [verse 1-3].

Even though God had been with David for the good of Israel and had granted him one victory after another, yet David wanted to rely on the arm of flesh. He wanted to know how many soldiers he could master [verse 5].

King David should have trusted in the Lord. The Lord's battles are not won by means of large armies or by weapons of war, but by God's Spirit, counsel, and by his strong and outstretched arm. See 2 Sam. 24:11.

SIX THOUSAND OVERSEERS

Of which, twenty and four thousand were to set forward the work of the house of the Lord; and six thousand were officers and judges.   1 Chron. 23:4

The Eastern text reads: "Of them David appointed overseers over the work of the house of the Lord, twenty-four men over every thousand workers; and judges and scribes, six men over each hundred workers."

Six thousand are too many to have served as overseers. There were 912. Four thousand porters and four thousand singers could not have been accommodated in the temple, nor was there need for so many porters and singers.

The thousands of porters and singers in verse 5 are not mentioned in the Eastern text. The reference there is to the 912 who are mentioned in verse 4.

THEY SHOULD CARRY

And also unto the Levites: they shall no more carry the taber-nacle, nor any vessels of it for the service thereof.   1 Chron. 23:6

The Eastern text reads: "And he also said to the Levites that they should carry the tabernacle and all the vessels for the service thereof." The Aramaic word *nisheklon* means "shall carry."

The Levites were the only ones entrusted with the care of the taber-nacle of the congregation, and with the carrying of the holy vessels and the instrument of the altar [Num. 4].

According to the Mosaic law, the Levites were to carry all the holy vessels and the tabernacle from the house of David to the place in which the Lord God would choose to dwell (the temple which later was built by King Solomon).

PROPHETS AND SEERS

Now the acts of David the king, first and last, behold, they are written in the book of Samuel the seer, and in the book of Nathan the prophet, and in the book of Gad the seer.   1 Chron. 29:29

Samuel the seer is the same Samuel, the prophet, who lived during the reigns of King Saul and King David.

The term "seer" is an old name given to the prophets. The Aramaic is *khazaya* (seer)—one who can foresee or foretell future events [1 Sam. 9:9].

The reference here is to the books of Samuel, the First and the Second respectively. Nathan also was a prophet living during the reign of David [2 Sam. 7]. Gad was David's seer. When David numbered the people, Gad told David of his folly and the impending disaster. The Lord did not want him to number the people [2 Sam. 24:11].

The books of Nathan the prophet and those of Gad the seer must have been lost during the destruction of Jerusalem in 586 B.C. Many sacred relics and scrolls which were in the Ark of the Covenant and the walls of the temple were lost or burned. Moreover, during the persecution the Israelites suffered considerably. Pagan oppressors destroyed the sacred books first.

Other works of Hebrew prophets, poets, and seers suffered during the persecution, and copies are extinct. In the olden days, copies of the holy books were rare and in the possession of kings, princes, priests, and the wealthy.

GOD WAS WITH DAVID

With all his reign and his might, and the times that went over him, and over Israel, and over all the kingdoms of the countries.
                                                        1 Chron. 29:30

"And the times that went over him" is an Eastern saying which refers to the periods of difficulty, trial, and change through which one passes.

A great many changes took place during the reign of David. Israel was freed from the Philistine oppression, and the latter were completely defeated and almost subjugated. Moreover, Damascus was conquered and the borders of Israel extended to the River Euphrates. Israel was respected by the great powers.

On the other hand, many nations which had fought Israel were gone, and the days of oppression and harassment by their enemies were forgotten. David and his house were strongly established and the kingdom was strengthened.

The Lord had been with David. He had spared his life from Saul, Goliath, and other enemies. David had gone through many difficulties and escaped many hazards, but because of his faith in God, he had come through successfully.

2 CHRONICLES

CLOUD MEANS GLORY

It came even to pass, as the trumpeters and singers were as one, to make one sound to be heard in praising and thanking the Lord; and when they lifted up their voice with the trumpets and cymbals and instruments of music, and praised the Lord, saying, For he is good; for his mercy endureth for ever: that then the house was filled with a cloud, even the house of the Lord.   2 Chron. 5:13

Anana (cloud) is often used symbolically to mean glory, protection, exaltation [Exod. 16:10].

In the olden days, since a cloud was the highest thing above the highest mountains, it was used metaphorically to suggest glory and majesty. ". . . thy faithfulness reacheth unto the clouds" [Ps. 36:5]. Clouds were also supposed to be the habitation of the Lord, or even God's chariots. ". . . who maketh the clouds his chariot" [Ps. 104:3].

Mount Sinai was covered with a thick cloud when Moses was communing with God. The glory of God and his divine presence were manifested in the cloud.

Jesus ascended into heaven in a cloud, and we are told he will come in a cloud [Matt. 24:30; Acts 1:9].

CURVED TRUMPETS

And the priests waited on their offices: the Levites also with instruments of music of the Lord, which David the king had made to praise the Lord, because his mercy endureth for ever, when David praised by their ministry; and the priests sounded trumpets before them, and all Israel stood.   2 Chron. 7:6

The Eastern text reads *karnatha kepepatha* (curved trumpets). This name for these ancient musical instruments occurs frequently in the Peshitta text. It shows that both straight and curved trumpets were used by the priests during the festivals and other solemn days.

The Assyrians, Babylonians, and Egyptians were famous for the invention and manufacture of musical instruments, some of which have been discovered in recent days in Iraq [Dan. 3:5-7].

TWO CALENDARS

And on the three and twentieth day of the seventh month he sent the people away into their tents, glad and merry in heart for the goodness that the Lord had showed unto David, and to Solomon, and to Israel his people.   2 Chron. 7:10

Kisaa, in Aramaic, means "the time of the full moon," which is the fifteenth day of the month. The Eastern text reads: "And on the fifteenth day of the month of Tishrin (October) the king dismissed the people . . ."

The reckoning is based on the calendar which begins in the seventh month—October. The Israelites reckoned their year from October, *Roshah Shanah*.

April was the month in which they went out of Egypt. Thus, *Abib*, "April, the month of blossoms," became the first month of a new era, the era of freedom of rejoicing, the month in which the Israelites celebrated the Passover.

The Church of the East also reckons the year from October. The Israelites had two calendars—one for business and commerce, and the other for their religious observances.

FATHER'S THUMB

And the young men that were brought up with him spake unto him, saying, Thus shalt thou answer the people that spake unto thee, saying, Thy father made our yoke heavy, but make thou it somewhat lighter for us; thus shalt thou say unto them, My little finger shall be thicker than my father's loins.   2 Chron. 10:10

The Aramaic word *crata* means "thumb." This phrase should read: "My little finger is thicker than my father's thumb." The Aramaic word for "loins" is *khassa*. No one would compare a little finger with the loins.

Hands and fingers symbolize power and authority. In Aramaic, it is often said of kings and government officials, "His hand is light," which means he is a good and kind ruler. "His hand is heavy" means he is a harsh and oppressive ruler.

Rehoboam was determined to continue his father's policy in oppressing the people and levying heavy taxes upon them. In other words, he wanted to surpass his father, Solomon, in lavish spending and luxuries which the state was no longer able to bear [1 Kings 12:10].

SON OF A CANAANITISH WOMAN

And Zedekiah the son of Chenaanah had made him horns of iron, and said, Thus saith the Lord, With these thou shalt push Syria until they be consumed.   2 Chron. 18:10

The Eastern text reads *bar Caananeta* (the son of a Canaanitish woman). His father was a Jew, but his mother was a native of Canaan.

In the olden days many Jews married women of other races, some of whom became converts. This error occurs also in 1 Kings 22:11.

See the commentary on 1 Kings 22:11.

AN HEIR

Howbeit the Lord would not destroy the house of David, because of the covenant that he had made with David, and as he promised to give a light to him and to his sons for ever.   2 Chron. 21:7

Shragha (a lamp) is used metaphorically here, meaning "an heir to sit on David's throne."

In the East, an heir is often called the lamp or light of the family.

See the commentary on 1 Kings 11:36.

AN EVIL EYE

For the sons of Athaliah, that wicked woman, had broken up the house of God; and also all the dedicated things of the house of the Lord did they bestow upon Baalim.   2 Chron. 24:7

The Aramaic word *beein* (in her eyes) has been confused with *benin* (her sons). The Eastern text hints that Athaliah taught with a wicked eye; that is, an evil purpose to destroy God's temple and his religion.

Athaliah had no more sons. Her last son was Ahaziah, the youngest son, who was the only son left to Jehoram [2 Chron. 21:17].

All male members of the royal family, the sons of Ahaziah, were destroyed by Athaliah, who proclaimed herself queen and reigned over Judah [2 Chron. 22:10-12].

KING OF JUDAH

For the Lord brought Judah low because of Ahaz king of Israel; for he made Judah naked, and transgressed sore against the Lord.
                2 Chron. 28:19

The Eastern text correctly reads "Ahaz king of Judah." Ahaz was not the king of Israel [verse 27]. Ahaz was the son of Jotham, king of

Judah, who reigned in the seventeenth year of Pekah, the son of Romaliah [2 Kings 16:1].

The Masoretic text, from which Western versions were made, reads "king of Israel." During the time of Jotham and Ahaz in Judah, Menahem, Pekahiah, and Pekah were kings over Israel. No doubt, this is a copyist's error.

WATER SOURCE CONCEALED

He took counsel with his princes and his mighty men to stop the waters of the fountains which were without the city: and they did help him.
So there was gathered much people together, who stopped all the fountains, and the brook that ran through the midst of the land, saying, Why should the kings of Assyria come, and find much water?   2 Chron. 32:3-4

The Aramaic word *kasi* means to "cover, conceal." The Aramaic word for "stop" is *sakar*.

King Hezekiah and his princes hid the scanty water sources in order to discourage the commanders of the Assyrian army from invading Jerusalem and other towns in Judah whose inhabitants depended on small brooks for water.

To hide or to destroy water sources when a land is invaded is an ancient custom. The Turks in World War I hid or polluted the wells in the Arabian desert in order to prevent the advance of the British and Arabian armies. In Palestine, even today, the shortage of water is a great problem [verse 30].

HEZEKIAH'S SICKNESS

But Hezekiah rendered not again according to the benefit done unto him; for his heart was lifted up: therefore there was wrath upon him, and upon Judah and Jerusalem.   2 Chron. 32:25

The Eastern text reads: "And the sickness of Hezekiah was due to the pride of his heart; therefore the wrath of the Lord came upon him and upon Judah and Jerusalem."

The Aramaic word *kerah* means "He fell sick." *Korhana* means "sickness or weakness." The sickness was the result of his false pride. Hezekiah, because of his prominence and wealth, had become proud and selfish, thus bringing God's wrath upon the inhabitants of Judah and Jerusalem.

Sickness is often due to wrong thinking, false pride, and worldly aspiration. When a man's wealth increases, instead of becoming proud, he should give glory to God, who is the Giver of all substance.

CISTERN HID

This same Hezekiah also stopped the upper watercourse of Gihon, and brought it straight down to the west side of the city of David. And Hezekiah prospered in all his works. 2 Chron. 32:30

Temar, in Aramaic, means "buried or hid"; that is, he hid the outlet of the water. The Eastern text reads: "This same Hezekiah also buried the outlet for the waters of the upper spring and brought it straight down to the western cistern of the city of David."

At times, such costly and difficult work was done in order to hide the water from the armies of invaders.

See the commentary on 2 Chronicles 32:3-4.

SACRIFICE TO IDOLS PROHIBITED

Nevertheless the people did sacrifice still in the high places, yet unto the Lord their God only. 2 Chron. 33:17

La (not to do) has been rendered "did." The Eastern text reads: "And not to sacrifice again to strange gods, nor to offer burnt offerings to them, but before the Lord their God only."

King Joash destroyed the shrines on the high places which the kings of Judah and the kings of Israel had built. He also commanded the people not to offer sacrifices and burnt offerings except before the Lord their God.

THE BOOK DISCOVERED

And Hilkiah answered and said to Shaphan the scribe, I have found the book of the law in the house of the Lord. And Hilkiah delivered the book to Shaphan. 2 Chron. 34:15

The Book of the Law; that is, the book of Deuteronomy, was written on parchment. It shows beyond a doubt that "book" means a volume or a number of scrolls which a person can carry in his hand. The Ten Commandments were written on two tablets, so we are told by Moses.

Had the book of Deuteronomy been written on tablets, it would have taken many hundreds of tablets of stone. Undoubtedly, the Hebrews wrote on stone as well as on parchment as early as the fifteenth century B.C. Writing on parchment and papyrus was very common among the Egyptians and other ancient peoples.

The Aramaic term *sepra* (Hebrew *seper*) means "a scroll"; that is, "a book." Books were not bound in those days. Even today, Hebrew sacred writings are found written on separate scrolls [2 Kings 22:8].

EIGHTEEN YEARS OLD

Jehoiachin was eight years old when he began to reign, and he reigned three months and ten days in Jerusalem: and he did that which was evil in the sight of the Lord.   2 Chron. 36:9

The Aramaic word *tmanaesrey* (eighteen) has been confused with *temaniah* (eight).

The Eastern text reads: "Jehoiachin was eighteen years old when he began to reign, and he reigned three months and ten days in Jerusalem . . ." [2 Kings 24:8].

Obviously, a boy of eight years can hardly distinguish between evil and good. But a young man of eighteen can understand to do good or evil. This error was caused by the copyist. In 2 Kings 24:8, the age of Jehoiachin is given correctly as eighteen years old instead of eight.

The Masoretic text also reads "eight years old." The Peshitta is accurate in both instances.

CHAPTER TWELVE

EZRA

INTRODUCTION

THE book of Ezra, like that of Nehemiah and Esther, is a postexilic work. The books of Ezra and Nehemiah contain the narratives of the two most zealous and pious Jews who contributed so much to the second Jewish commonwealth and played a prominent part in the restoration of the remnant and the rebuilding of Jerusalem and the second temple.

The Eastern text, like the Vulgate and the Septuagint, contains Second Ezra, but this book is not read in churches.

All of these postexile books were written in Chaldean or southern Aramaic, which was the literary and imperial language. Ezra, Daniel, and Nehemiah were in government service. The Hebrew language was lost during the 70 years of the exile, and Aramaic, a sister tongue, had become the vernacular of the Jews. Both Ezra and Nehemiah were born during the captivity and educated in Babylon.

All these postexile writings were translated or transcribed into what the people thought to be the original Hebrew. Some of the portions still remain in Aramaic, which was the imperial language in the western provinces of the far-flung Persian Empire. The letters written against the Jews were written and interpreted in Aramaic [Ezra 4:7]. The Persians could not dispense with Aramaic in the provinces west of the River Tigris and Egypt. Aramaic was well established by the Assyrians and the Babylonians, who ruled over the same provinces.

Ezra was a scribe, probably in the service of the government. He was also a teacher of the Mosaic law.

Ezra speaks in the first person [Ezra 7:27-28]. At other places he is placed in the third person.

CYRUS PROCLAMATION

*Now these are the children of the province that went up out of
the captivity, of those which had been carried away, whom Nebuchadnezzar the king of Babylon had carried away unto Babylon,
and came again unto Jerusalem and Judah, every one unto his
city.*   Ezra 2:1

The return of the first Jews from captivity in Babylon under the
leadership of Zerubbabel and Jesuha was in the first year of the reign
of Cyrus, the king of Persia, about 538 B.C. [Ezra 1:1; Neh. 7:6].
Another group came up with Ezra about 458 B.C. The third group
came with Nehemiah in 443 B.C.
All these people who returned comprised the remnant of Israel and
Judah which was destined to return to Jerusalem and Judah. But because of strong opposition from the enemies, the restoration was
gradual [Ezra 4:7].

CONFUSION IN NAMES

*The children of Solomon's servants: the children of Sotai, the
children of Sophereth, the children of Peruda.*   Ezra 2:55

This should read *benai Abar* (the children of Abar) and *benai Shalim*
(the children of Shalim).
The error is caused by the confusion of *abar* (crossing) with *abad*
(a servant). Solomon's servants were registered among their own
families and by their own tribes. All kings of Judah had servants, but
they were registered among their own families and tribes.

TIRSHATHA

*And the Tirshatha said unto them, that they should not eat of
the most holy things, till there stood up a priest with Urim and
with Thummim.*   Ezra 2:63

The Peshitta text reads *reshey di Israel* (the headmen or chieftains
of Israel). The Hebrew word *hatiershatha* which appears in the Masoretic text should read *reshey* (chieftain, prince). Apparently the term
tirshatha is a confusion of *reshey* or *reshaney*. The Hebrew word for
"leader" is *neged,* and the Hebrew word for "chief" is *rosh* (Aramaic
resha).

HINDERERS

And hired counselors against them, to frustrate their purpose,
all the days of Cyrus king of Persia, even until the reign of Darius
king of Persia.   Ezra 4:5

The Aramaic word *meawkaney* (objectors, hinderers) has been confused with the Aramaic word *malkaney* (counselors) who persuaded
the king of Persia to revoke the royal decree and stop the work.

The reference here is to Rehum, Shimshai, and the rest of the native
people west of the River Euphrates. These men were hindering the work
of building the temple [verses 4; 8-16].

LETTERS INTERPRETED

And in the days of Artaxerxes wrote Bishlam, Mithredath,
Tabeel, and the rest of their companions, unto Artaxerxes king of
Persia; and the writing of the letter was written in the Syrian
tongue, and interpreted in the Syrian tongue.   Ezra 4:7

"Syrian" is a misnomer. It should read "Aramaic." This ancient
language was called Syrian because it was the language of *Sur* (Tyre)—
a city on the Mediterranean coast which was visited by Greek sailors
and later conquered by Alexander the Great about 332 B.C.

Aramaic was the language of the Fertile Crescent, and the imperial
language of the two great Semitic empires, Assyria and Babylon. The
Persians could not dispense with Aramaic in their far-flung provinces
west of the River Tigris. Then again, the Jews who had returned from
Babylon and other parts of the Persian Empire spoke and wrote in
Aramaic.

In the Near East it is not unusual to interpret a king's letter or a
government decree. Such letters are generally written by the court
scribes, who use hard words and abstruse terms of speech, unfamiliar
to ordinary readers and illiterate people, and are couched in diplomatic
language which ordinary people cannot understand. This is true of
laws and treaties in our own day. They have to be interpreted in order
to clarify qualifying clauses and ambiguous terms of speech.

The letter was interpreted in order to clarify all the issues which were
involved, so that there should be no more misunderstanding and delay
in the rebuilding of the temple.

A REMNANT

And after all that is come upon us for our evil deeds, and for our great trespass, seeing that thou our God hast punished us less than our iniquities deserve, and hast given us such deliverance as this.

Ezra 9:13

The Eastern text reads: "And after all these things that have come upon us for our evil deeds and for our great sins, seeing that thou our God hast purposed to forgive our sins and to give us a remnant in the world, . . ."

The Aramaic word *sharkana* (a remnant) has been confused with *porkana* (salvation, deliverance). Ezra states that despite all the evil works of the people, the Lord had forgiven them and spared a remnant.

Only a small remnant of the people returned from Babylon. But this remnant served as a nucleus for a new Jewish commonwealth through which God's promises to mankind were fulfilled and God's lamp kept burning.

CHAPTER THIRTEEN

NEHEMIAH

INTRODUCTION

NEHEMIAH was a great Jewish leader with deep religious convictions. His devotion and concern for his race and religion transcended his political and material interest in life.

Nehemiah was living at Shushan Palace (465 B.C.). He had risen to the high position of cupbearer to Artakhshisht, king of Persia, an office which was coveted by princes and nobles of the realm because the cupbearer stood in the presence of the king daily. No one else could enter into his presence without being summoned—not even the queen or his children.

Nehemiah must have been a handsome and educated youth, and a man of integrity and trustworthiness to have been appointed as cupbearer to the great king of Persia because in those days cupbearers often were bribed and kings were murdered by poisoning the wine.

When Nehemiah heard the sad report concerning the state of Jerusalem and the misery of the people who were living in Judah, he was so grieved that he fasted and prayed fervently and made supplications to God confessing the sins of his forefathers who had broken God's covenant and transgressed his commandments. The Lord God answered his prayers and granted him favors in the eyes of the Persian King.

In April of 445 B.C. he obtained permission from Artakhshisht, king of Persia, to go to Jerusalem to rebuild the walls of the city and to supply the timber for the gates and other materials. The king not only granted all his requests but he also granted him power never allowed to any other Jewish leader who had gone to Jerusalem before him. Nehemiah could issue commands to the army and order food supplies from king's treasurers beyond the River Euphrates. Because of his high position he was looked upon as a prince of the realm and all governors and army commanders both revered and feared him.

The first edict to rebuild Jerusalem and the temple was issued by King Cyrus in 538 B.C. and resulted in many Jews returning to Judah with Zerubabel and later with Ezra. But the work of rebuilding the city and the temple was greatly hampered by enemies of the Jews—the Samaritans, and the Gentiles in Galilee. Sanballat, Tubiah, and Geshem the Arabian made every effort to stop the work of rebuilding the walls. These men even conspired to kill Nehemiah, who was also accused of the rebellion against the king of Persia [Ezra 4].

The book of Nehemiah and the book of Ezra are seemingly one book. Some scholars believe that Ezra went to Jerusalem after Nehemiah. I believe that Ezra preceded Nehemiah by a number of years. However, both of them went during the reign of Artakhshisht, king of Persia.

Indeed, Nehemiah was greatly responsible for overcoming the opposition against the Jews and the establishment of the second Jewish commonwealth and rebuilding of Jerusalem which was completed in 445 B.C. Moreover, Nehemiah being well versed in Jewish law and religion helped with the reorganization work and as the governor of the city made new laws and ordinances. Nehemiah was a pious and just man and hospitable toward the poor and oppressed Jew. Some people look on him as a messiah and savior of the Jewish people, but Nehemiah being a humble person refused such honors and preferred to live in a simple way and not as a prince or governor [Neh. 5:14].

NISAN

And it came to pass in the month Nisan, in the twentieth year of Artaxerxes the king, that wine was before him: and I took up the wine, and gave it unto the king. Now I had not been beforetime sad in his presence.　　　　　　　　　　　　　　Neh. 2:1

Nisan is another name for *Abid* (April) the month of the blossoms and greens. This is the name of the first Hebrew month, in which the feast of the Passover was celebrated on the fifteenth day. It was in this month that the Hebrews left Egypt and Pharaoh and his army were drowned in the Red Sea [Exod. 23:15].

Abib, in Aramaic, is called *hababey* (blossoms). The term *nisan* must have been a later adaptation. *Nisan* might mean *bethnesaney* (spring).

A CUPBEARER'S POSITION

Wherefore the king said unto me, Why is thy countenance sad, seeing thou art not sick? this is nothing else but sorrow of heart. Then I was very sore afraid.　　　　　　　　　　　　　　Neh. 2:2

The Persian kings lived in complete isolation. The person of the monarch was so sacred that no one, not even the queen or one of his children, could approach him without being summoned. The Persian court etiquette was rigid in this respect. The rulers, being despots and lavish, had many enemies. No one was trusted, not even the members of the king's household and his ministers [Esther 4:16].

Cupbearers were carefully selected from among the most faithful men. Poisoning in the East was, and still is, common. Our word "assassin" is derived from a Persian word *hashashin,* a kind of poisonous drug. The cupbearer was the most trusted person in the palace and the only one who could freely come before the king's presence. And, being faithful and close to the king, he indulged in conversation and jokes with him.

This is why Nehemiah was so bold as to make such a request from the emperor; and this is why the request was speedily granted. Had the monarch been petitioned by a Jewish delegation, the matter would have been referred to one of the ministers and the appeal delayed or even discarded.

The building of Jerusalem was stopped by Emperor Artaxerxes. The Gentiles in Galilee and Syria had complained to the king, warning him against the rebuilding of such a strategic city as Jerusalem [Ezra 4:5].

The Persian monarch was deeply moved by the sincere appeal which his faithful cupbearer made before him, and the deep concern he had for the city and the graves of his fathers, so evidenced in his sad face. The king promptly granted the request. And Nehemiah wrote another glorious chapter in the history of Israel.

NEHEMIAH PRAYED

Then the king said unto me, For what dost thou make request? So I prayed to the God of heaven.　　　　　　　　　Neh. 2:4

Wsalet means "and you have prayed." The Eastern text reads: "Then the king said to me, For what did you make supplications and pray before the God of heaven?"

The error is caused by the dot over the "t," which would read "you have prayed." The dot *under* the "t" would read "I have prayed."

HUNDRED TOWER

Then Eliashib the high priest rose up with his brethren the priests and they builded the sheep gate; they sanctified it, and set up the doors of it; even unto the tower of Meah they sanctified it, unto the tower of Hananeel.　　　　　　　　　Neh. 3:1

It should read, ". . . as far as the tower of the Hundred; and they sanctified it as far as the tower of Hananael."

Maa, in Aramaic, means "one hundred"; that is, the one hundred tower. Ancient cities had small towers round about the wall.

WEAK WALL

Now Tobiah the Ammonite was by him, and he said, Even that which they build, if a fox go up, he shall even break down their stone wall.   Neh. 4:3

These words were spoken sarcastically, meaning that the wall being so weak, could not serve as a defense. A fox walks very carefully when climbing walls to prey on animals or chickens.

The present wall could hardly be compared with the strong and wide wall of Jerusalem which, in former days, was built by the kings of Judah. The people were very poor, and the work was done hastily.

FORGIVE NOT

And cover not their iniquity, and let not their sin be blotted out from before thee: for they have provoked thee to anger before the builders.   Neh. 4:5

The Aramaic word *tishbook* means "forgive." It should read: "And forgive not their offenses, and let not their sins be blotted out from before thee . . ." "Cover" is incorrect.

Sanballat and Tobiah the Ammonite, had hindered the rebuilding of the temple of God. Nehemiah invokes God not to forgive them or to blot out the offenses and sins which they had committed against him.

KING LOANED MONEY

There were also that said, We have borrowed money for the king's tribute, and that upon our lands and vineyards.   Neh. 5:4

The Aramaic word *Nezap* means "Let us borrow." It should read: "There were those who said, Let us borrow money from the king's tribute, and work our fields and our vineyards, that we may live."

The Aramaic word *Neplokh* means "Let us work our fields and vineyards." The italics in the King James Version show that the translators were not sure of the meaning of the words.

In the East, kings loan money to farmers during famines and disasters. In most cases, the loans are repaid in kind, and the produce, which is sold to the people, is stored in government storehouses. In the olden days Persian kings were magnanimous toward their subjects.

CITRONS OR CITRUS

And that they should publish and proclaim in all their cities, and in Jerusalem, saying, Go forth unto the mount, and fetch olive branches, and pine branches, and myrtle branches, and palm branches, and branches of thick trees, to make booths, as it is written.
Neh. 8:15

The Aramaic word *etrogey* means "citron, orange tree" and "fruit." Oranges were known in biblical days. The term "citrons" occurs twice in the Peshitta. There is no mention of this fruit in other Bibles.

SHOES LASTED LONG

Yea, forty years didst thou sustain them in the wilderness, so that they lacked nothing; their clothes waxed not old, and their feet swelled not.
Neh. 9:21

The Aramaic word *mesaney* means "shoes." The last phrase should read, ". . . and their shoes had no holes in them."

The Aramaic word for "feet" is *rigley*, but this word is not in the Eastern text of this verse.

The Assyrians, until World War I, wore woolen shoes called *rashikey*, which lasted for many years. They are still worn by the tribal people. They are easily mended, and thus will last for years.

The reference here is to God's care, who provides our daily needs, clothes us, and protects us. Those who trust in God lack nothing [Deut. 8:4].

MIXED MARRIAGES

In those days also saw I Jews that had married wives of Ashdod, of Ammon, and of Moab.
And their children spake half in the speech of Ashdod, and could not speak in the Jews' language, but according to the language of each people.
Neh. 13:23-24

During the Babylonian captivity in 596 B.C., some of the Jews of the peasant classes were left in the land to take care of the vineyards and

the trees [2 Kings 25:22]. Many of these Jews married foreign wives.
The temple was destroyed and the national unity broken up. The people
who remained in the land became the prey of the pagan people, and
many of them gave up hope of any restoration.

Children born of these mixed marriages spoke the language of their
mother, which was a dialect of the Hebrew language. The Moabites,
Ammonites, and Edomites were akin to the early Hebrews, and they
spoke different Semitic dialects. Both Nehemiah and Ezra were opposed
to these mixed marriages and the departure from the language of their
forefathers, the ancient Hebrew.

REMEMBER ME, NOT THEM

Remember them, O my God, because they have defiled the
priesthood, and the covenant of the priesthood, and of the Levites.
                                                    Neh. 13:29

The Eastern text reads: "Remember me, O my God, concerning the
rest of the priesthood and concerning the rest of the priests and the
Levites."

The Aramaic word *li* (to me) is the objective case of "I." The
Aramaic word for "them" is *lon.*

Nehemiah prays to God to remember him for the work he had done
in cleansing the priests and the Levites.

Only a remnant of the priests and the Levites had returned from
exile and participated in the rebuilding of the temple.

CHAPTER FOURTEEN

ESTHER

INTRODUCTION

Esther is a Persian name, *Histar*, "the star"; that is, Venus, one of the prominent Babylonian goddesses, whose cult had spread throughout the Near East and Greece. Queen Esther is the principle character in the book which was named for her.

Esther is more admired than all other Jewish heroines. Therefore, there are more scrolls of the book which bears her name than of any other book in the Holy Writ. This is because Queen Esther was willing to die for her people, and because of her devotion to the cause of the Jews she saved them from complete annihilation.

The book of Esther was written about 520 B.C., during the reign of Akhshirash, a Persian king.

The name of God is not mentioned in the book of Esther. And one reason for its omission is the fact that the queen's husband, Akhshirash, was the god of the empire. Had the book been written later than the Persian period, the Jews would have mentioned God's name in it.

Had Esther refused or been afraid to intervene on the behalf of her people, there would have been no Jewish race, no second temple, and no Christianity. The Jews would have perished completely.

But, while Haman was planning to destroy the Jewish people in the vast Persian realm, the Lord God was preparing Mordecai and Esther to act as his agents in saving the remnant, so that his messianic promises might be fulfilled and the world be blessed by the faith of Abraham.

COUCHES

Where were white, green, and blue hangings, fastened with
cords of fine linen and purple to silver rings and pillars of marble:
the beds were of gold and silver, upon a pavement of red, and
blue, and white, and black marble.   Esther 1:6

Arsatha in this instance should read "couches," on which the king, princes, and high state dignitaries reclined. And it should not be confused with the beds on which the people slept at night.

Persia, now known as Iran, has always been famous for its couches, carpets, draperies, and for the arts which made their palaces and divans famous and conspicuous. Moreover, Persian kings entertained lavishly, just as they do today.

In that part of the ancient world the glory and the fame of a king is manifested by his extravagant palaces, vessels of gold and silver, and couches and rugs.

Persia inherited all Assyrian and Babylonian culture. Moreover, Persian kings were interested in beauty and progress.

DRINKING WINE

And the drinking was according to the law; none did compel:
for so the king had appointed to all the officers of his house, that
they should do according to every man's pleasure.   Esther 1:8

In the East during the weddings, banquets, and feasts, drinking of wine is compulsory. Easterners seldom indulge in wine or strong drink, but during wedding feasts and banquets it is compulsory to drink until they are drunk. This is more true of wedding feasts, where the people consider it a great honor to the married party to be drunk at their wedding. On such occasions, generally, all guests are drunk. Even those who refuse to drink are compelled to do so. Pious men are exempted.

The emperor of Persia had to rescind the unwritten law, stating that there must be no compulsion in drinking and that the guest shall drink as he wishes. Only a ruler can do away with an ancient custom which in the Near East is looked upon as a law.

Even though wine and strong drinks are commonly used in weddings and feasts, and are approved by the people, there always have been wise men, prophets, and kings who have realized the danger of indulging in them. Drinking is a bad habit even when wine and strong drinks are used moderately.

The king of Persia was wise in rescinding the law at such an important state banquet. Many conspiracies and revolutions are conceived and carried out when men are drunk with wine. The Bible condemns excessive drinking and drunkenness.

MEHEMNEY, EUNUCHS

> On the seventh day, when the heart of the king was merry with wine, he commanded Mehuman, Biztha, Harbona, Bigtha, and Abagtha, Zethar, and Carcas, the seven chamberlains that served in the presence of Ahasuerus the king.　　　　Esther 1:10

Mehemney (eunuchs) has been left untranslated. The translators thought it was the name of one of the palace attendants.

Eunuchs were employed in kings' harems until the twentieth century. The office of the eunuch still prevails in some of the backward countries.

The Aramaic mehemna means "a trustworthy person." Eunuchs were entrusted with the care of women in the royal palace [Esther 2:8]. Most of the eunuchs were men who had been castrated, though some of them were born eunuchs, that is, without the usual sexual powers and characteristics of males.

EASTERN WOMEN ARE SHY

> But the queen Vashti refused to come at the king's commandment by his chamberlains: therefore was the king very wroth, and his anger burned in him.　　　　Esther 1:12

Until recent days, no stranger could see the face of an Iranian princess or a woman of nobility, not even princes and noble guests. Even the peasant women covered their faces with their black veils and ran away when they saw a stranger.

Covering of the face is an ancient Eastern custom going back to time immemorial. When Rebekah saw her future husband, Isaac, in the field, she covered herself as a token of respect and dignity [Gen. 24:65].

Kings' wives were always veiled; and because of fear they shunned the presence of strangers. Their faces could only be seen by eunuchs, who were appointed by the king to take charge of them.

Queen Vashti was mindful of her dignity as a queen of the world's largest and most powerful empire. She refused to lower herself and to act as an entertainer in the presence of provincial governors, princes, and servants.

Vashti stands as the greatest example of chastity and dignity. For centuries, in the East, women were considered inferior to men. They were presented to honorable guests and princes, and, at times, were asked to act as striptease dancers at banquets. Vashti would not have any of that.

On the other hand, it was divinely planned that Vashti should refuse to obey the imperial command of her husband, who was the human god of the empire, so that Esther might become the queen in her place and thus save her people from the slaughter. Vashti was willing to sacrifice her crown for the sake of womanhood, and Esther was willing to lay down her life, if necessary, for the sake of her people.

WOMEN MUST OBEY

If it please the king, let there go a royal commandment from him, and let it be written among the laws of the Persians and the Medes, that it be not altered, That Vashti come no more before king Ahasuerus; and let the king give her royal estate unto another that is better than she. Esther 1:19

In lands were polygamy is practiced, and other backward lands, men are afraid to give their wives freedom. Women must obey their husbands' every wish, and must never question their wisdom. This is especially true of the wives of princes and noblemen.

The princes were afraid that Vashti's act would become an example to millions of women in the vast empire, who craved freedom and equality, and who were ready to revolt against the tyranny of their husbands, especially those who had large harems [verse 22].

HADASSAH

And he brought up Hadassah, that is, Esther, his uncle's daughter: for she had neither father nor mother, and the maid was fair and beautiful; whom Mordecai, when her father and mother were dead, took for his own daughter. Esther 2:7

Hadassah is an Aramaic name meaning "a bud." The Hebrew word *hadas* means "a myrtle tree." Hadassah was born in captivity and her parents had given her a native name as the Jews do today. Esther is a Persian name which means "star," or Venus, a Babylonian goddess [see Introduction].

Mordecai, being a palace servant, knew most of the king's servants and eunuchs. That is why Esther was left in the custody of the keeper of the women, or the chief eunuch. The Lord gave Esther favor in the eyes of the keeper of women, who helped her to become the queen of Persia and wear the coveted crown [verse 15].

HAMAN

*After these things did king Ahasuerus promote Haman the son
of Hammedatha the Agagite, and advanced him, and set his seat
above all the princes that were with him.*   Esther 3:1

Haman is a Semitic name. *Man* means "what, why." Hebrew might be
the definite article *ha. Hamelek* means "the king." *Manna* means, "What
is it?" I believe Haman was an Edomite.

Some biblical authorities believe that Haman was a Greek and that
therefore he hated the Jews. But this theory cannot be true. During
this period the Greeks were hardly known in the Near East. The
Persian armies had subjugated a part of Greece and crushed all Greek
resistance in other provinces which remained independent.

The Greek conquest of the Near East and the destruction of the
Achaemenian Empire began in 311 B.C., after the battle of Essus.

Haman, the son of Hammedatha, the Agagite, was a descendant of
one of the Semitic races who had been enemies of the Jews. The
enmity between the Jews, Arabians, Syrians, Edomites, and Moabites
was smoldering in the Persian Empire as well as in Palestine [Neh.
6:1-10].

HUMAN DEITIES

*And when Haman saw that Mordecai bowed not, nor did him
reverence, then was Haman full of wrath.*   Esther 3:5

Bowing to anything or anybody besides God, the Creator of the
heavens and the earth, was idolatry in the eyes of the Jews [Exod.
20:3].

Haman was a pagan high official in the realm of King Akhshirash of
Persia (Iran), a mortal man made a deity by the princes of the realm
and the people.

When Jesus was tempted to worship the devil for glory and honor, he
said: ". . . for it is written, Thou shalt worship the Lord thy God, and
him only shalt thou serve" [Matt. 4:10; Deut. 6:13].

Mordecai was requested not only to salute the pagan prime minister of
Iran, Haman, but also to worship him. *Barak osagid* in Aramaic means
"to kneel and worship." This is why Mordecai refused to obey the
command.

Mordecai, being a Jew, a worshiper of the only true God, would
not acquiesce to Haman's request or accept the counsel of his fellow
officials and servants.

Shadrach, Meshach, and Abednego refused to bow and worship the statue of Nebuchadnezzar and his gods [Dan. 3:1-20]. Daniel also refused the command of the king of Iran and was willing to die rather than violate the ordinances of his religion.

Man's difficulties have always sprung from his infidelity and his worship of human deities and false material gods.

We owe our pure concept of a spiritual God to the Jews and, in particular, to men like Mordecai and Daniel.

A DRASTIC ORDINANCE

All the king's servants, and the people of the king's provinces, do know, that whosoever, whether man or woman, shall come unto the king into the inner court, who is not called, there is one law of his to put him to death, except such to whom the king shall hold out the golden sceptre, that he may live: but I have not been called to come in unto the king these thirty days. Esther 4:11

This drastic ordinance was enacted to protect the lives of kings from usurpers and rivals. In olden days, just as today, kings were assassinated by their wives, sons, and other relatives. At times, conspirators connived with one of the king's wives and thus murdered him.

On the other hand, jealousy between wives in large harems would engender hatred against the person of a king who took sides and who favored some and punished others.

Akhshirash had many wives and concubines as well as many servants. Therefore, he was always in danger of being assassinated.

The Lord touched the king's heart so that he held out to Esther the golden sceptre that was in his hand [Esther 5:2].

ESTHER'S DESTINY

For if thou altogether holdest thy peace at this time, then shall there enlargement and deliverance arise to the Jews from another place; but thou and thy father's house shall be destroyed: and who knoweth whether thou art come to the kingdom for such a time as this? Esther 4:14

"For such a time as this" means, "You have come to the kingdom for this cause." Esther was an orphan girl whom the Lord reared and prepared for a great mission. Even though it was unlawful for Queen Esther to appear before the king to petition him on the behalf of her people, nevertheless, she risked her life and appeared before him [Esther 4:10-11].

Just as the wicked Haman was preparing to destroy the Jews, the Lord was preparing Esther to be a deliverer of her people.

No doubt, Jesus must have read these words when he said before Pilate, "And for this cause came I into the world, that I should bear witness unto the truth" [John 18:37].

Moreover, Jesus' cry on the cross was similar to that of Esther. "My God, my God, for this I was spared"; that is to say, "This is my destiny to die for them" [Matt. 27:46, Eastern text].

KING'S SCRIBE

But when Esther came before the king, he commanded by letters that his wicked device, which he devised against the Jews, should return upon his own head, and that he and his sons should be hanged on the gallows.   Esther 9:25

The Eastern text reads: "When Esther came before the king, the scribe would say, Let the wicked plots which were devised against the Jews return upon the head of him who had devised them, and let him and his sons be hanged on the gallows."

The Aramaic word *sapra* (scribe) is omitted in the King James Version but is retained in the Hebrew text. The error is caused by the translator who evidently overlooked the word.

Without the noun scribe, the antecedent is missing. According to the King James Version, the reference is to the king himself; that is, the king, instead of condemning Haman's evil devices and putting his sons to death, condemns his own device and commands his own sons to be put to death.

When Queen Esther appeared before the king, she first saw the scribe, who informed the king of her coming to the king's house. As the queen waited in the scribe's office, the scribe condemned Haman's evil devices as well as those of Haman's sons, who later were hanged by the command of the king.

SEEKING WELFARE

For Mordecai the Jew was next unto king Ahasuerus, and great among the Jews, and accepted of the multitude of his brethren, seeking the wealth of his people, and speaking peace to all his seed.
Esther 10:3

The last portion of the verse should read: ". . . and he sought the good of his people and spoke on behalf of all his race."

The Aramaic word *tabta*, means "good, favor, welfare, interest." It has nothing to do with material wealth or monetary gains. Mordecai was not that type of man. He had been willing to die for his people, if necessary. Moreover, Jewish leaders intercede on behalf of their people without any remuneration.

CHAPTER FIFTEEN

JOB

INTRODUCTION

IT is assumed by some authorities that Job was not a Palestinian Hebrew. Nevertheless, Job was a prophet who believed and communed
with the Living God, the God of Abraham. Job might have been a
Hebrew descendant of Abraham, who lived on the other side of the
River Euphrates.

Job was from the land of Uz in Mesopotamia or southeast Arabia.
Uz was a son of Aram, and the Arameans were a kindred people of
the Hebrews. The Arameans also revered the Lord, the God of Israel,
and for a long time preserved their racial ties with the Hebrews, a branch
of their families which had crossed the River Euphrates with Abraham.
Isaac married Rebekah, a sister of Laban the Aramean. Jacob married his
Uncle Laban's daughters, Leah and Rachel [Gen. 29:15-28].

Job's trials took place in Padan-Aram (Mesopotamia). We are told
that Job's asses, camels, sheep, and cattle were raided by the Sabeans
and Chaldeans [Job 1:15-17]. Had Job been born in Palestine, the
author of the book would have mentioned the name of his father and
his tribe. Uz is mentioned in Jeremiah 25:19-21.

Job, no doubt, was one of the richest patriarchs on the other side
of the River Euphrates; his fame had spread all over the East and his
conduct and faith had been emulated by those who revered God. In
the East wealthy men are known even in foreign lands. Caravans and
wayfarers carry their fame from one place to another. Their possessions
and gold and silver become common topics in towns, cities, and camps.
Job is familiar with mining, astronomy, and other sciences which were
discovered by the Babylonians.

This book is called Job, the book is written about Job and not by
Job himself. Job is placed in the third person: "There was a man in
the land of Uz" [Job 1:1]. However, Job might have dictated the work.

In the East, a book about a ruler is called by the name of the ruler,
and the name of the scribe may never appear in it. Sometimes the
scribe places his name at the end, as a writer or a copyist.

Job must have lived about 800 B.C. He is mentioned in Ezekiel 14:14. Some Bible authorities place the date at 1520 B.C. If this were the case, Moses and Joshua would have written about him. The book, indeed, is inspired and is a dramatic narrative of a pious and wise man whose faith and loyalty to God had never been questioned.

The style of the book of Job has never been duplicated or surpassed. It still stands as the greatest philosophical work. The book is noted for its depth and sublimity. Indeed, the book is written by wisdom that is out of this world; that is, the author was inspired by God to be able to produce such a poetic and philosophical work. The book is the greatest drama ever penned by man, a philosophical and scientific work of a magnitude without equal in thought or in diction. Job knew the earth is round and floating in the air [Job 26:7].

The book of Job answers one of the oldest human riddles: Why does a righteous man suffer? The answer is: There is no such thing as a righteous man. No man born of woman can attain perfection and righteousness. God is the only righteous and perfect one; man is imperfect.

Man is punished by the evil that he does; but he is rewarded for good as well [Blessings and Curses, Deut. 28].

It is very hard to see how a merciful and loving God would take counsel from Satan and grant him power to torture a pious man. But, in a drama, anything can happen, at any time and in any place.

JOB, A PERFECT MAN

There was a man in the land of Uz, whose name was Job; and that man was perfect and upright, and one that feared God, and eschewed evil.   Job 1:1

Sickness was commonly supposed to be a punishment from God for sin. The Jews thought that even natural blindness was the result of sin. But when Jesus healed the blind man he said that neither the man nor his parents had sinned [John 9:3]. Nevertheless, Jesus did imply that some sickness is caused by sin. "Sin no more," he said to the sick man after he had healed him [John 5:14].

In biblical days all kinds of sickness were attributed to evil forces. Such medical terms as insanity were unknown. All lunatics were supposed to be possessed by evil spirits.

Job was punished and afflicted beyond description, but not for his sins. There is not even the slightest suggestion that he was afflicted because of his sins. The author of the book of Job tells us that Job was perfect and upright and one who revered God and eschewed evil.

Therefore, Job could not have been justly punished by a good and just and loving God who rewards pious men with goodness and health, nor could Satan have tempted God.

Whether Job was an actual person, or merely a fictional character in this great drama written by a wise man or a group of wise men, is not important. One thing we know now is that Satan can neither sit in the presence of God nor tempt him with his evil devices. God is purity, goodness, and love, and cannot be tempted with evil.

The most important thing in the book is the fact that there have always been such upright men in the world as Job, who revered God above their possessions, their children, and even their own lives.

The contents of the book show that it was written as a dialogue in the most vivid and dramatic style ever penned by man. Whenever God's sons presented themselves before him, Satan came too. And God conversed with him, but he never said anything to his children.

The book reveals that there is no such thing as a perfect man. Job must have had some kind of sin of which he knew nothing; otherwise, he would not have been plagued with calamities and subjected to such severe tortures. People in the olden days believed that sickness, blindness, and suffering were caused by sin. When Jesus healed a blind man, his disciples wanted to know whether *he* had sinned, or his parents [John 8:2-3].

The book proves that there is no one perfect but God; even Jesus, who *was* perfect, refused to be *called* perfect. The book also proves that those who trust in God cannot be shaken by material losses, calamities, and disease. Job is an example of a pious man who revered God above everything else.

SONS OF GOD

Now there was a day when the sons of God came to present themselves before the Lord, and Satan came also among them.

Job 1:6

"The sons of God" in this instance means "the good men," "believers in God." There were always some men and women who remained loyal to God. They were called the sons of God—spiritual—to distinguish them from the sons of men, or the materialists, or the descendants of Cain [Gen. 6:1-2].

Satan here represents the old adversary, the enemy, who caused man to transgress against his creatures. Satan, the adversary, is included in this episode simply because he is the author of sin and the cause of the fall of man. Satan is envious to see such an upright man as Job trying to do good and refraining from evil.

All of God's conversation in this narrative is with Satan. He seemingly did not even notice and greet his sons, the good men.

In this wonderful drama we see that there were some men who were envious of Job, and who thought that he was a hypocrite, and that he used his religious life and piety to camouflage his improper business activities. Even the so-called friends who came to comfort him came to try to make him confess his evil deeds.

The sons of God were pious men like Job who had been steadfast in the way of God. Probably Job was the most pious among them. This is why Satan, adversary to the truth, singled him out.

SABEANS

And the Sabeans fell upon them, and took them away; yea, they have slain the servants with the edge of the sword; and I only am escaped alone to tell thee.   Job 1:15

Sabeans are a Mesopotamian people, descendants of the ancient Babylonians. Even today, there is a community of them in Iraq. They are also known as the people of St. John the Baptist. They still practice baptism and believe in the teaching of John the Baptist.

The Sabeans are a very peaceful people whose occupation for centuries has been silverwork. They are noted silversmiths, engravers, and craftsmen in the Near East.

In the olden days, the Sabeans, like many other nomad tribes in southwestern Mesopotamia and the Arabian desert, at times raided peaceful agricultural communities. Until the rise of Islam, Arabian tribes raided each other, killing, plundering herds and flocks, and carrying away other booty.

JOB MOURNS

Then Job arose, and rent his mantle, and shaved his head, and fell down upon the ground, and worshipped.   Job 1:20

To rent one's mantle and shave one's head are symbolic acts of mourning over a great calamity. In the East, even today, men tear up their clothes, and women cut off their hair and inflict wounds on their faces as an expression of their deep grief over losing their dear ones, or similar calamities.

When Israel was defeated before the Philistines, the messenger who brought the news of the defeat to Eli had rent his clothes and put earth upon his head [1 Sam. 4:12].

The priests were commanded by Moses not to rend their clothes as a sign of mourning over two of Aaron's sons, who were burned in the tabernacle of the congregation [Lev. 10:6].

A great calamity had befallen Job. His wealth was plundered, his sons and daughters were dead. And by shaving his hair and tearing his clothes he showed his humility and deep grief to the people around him.

JOB'S FRIENDS

Now when Job's three friends heard of all this evil that was come upon him, they came every one from his own place; Eliphaz the Temanite, and Bildad the Shuhite, and Zophar the Naamathite: for they had made an appointment together to come to mourn with him, and to comfort him.   Job 2:11

The three friends of Job were the wisest men in those days and, because of their fame and wisdom, were known in all adjacent lands.

Eliphaz was a native of Teman (south), Negeb, the ancient Edom. The people in this place were renowned for their wisdom and counsel. "There is no more wisdom in Teman; the counsel is perished from the prudent; their wisdom is taken away" [Jer. 49:7, Eastern text].

Bildad the Shuhite and Zophar the Naamathite were members of the Aramean tribes who dwelt in the desert, also known as Naabatites.

The descendants of these tribes were some of the first Arabs in Edom and northwestern Arabia who embraced Christianity. They were converted to Islam in the earliest part of the seventh century.

These wise men tried to induce Job to confess his guilt and seek forgiveness. They believed that Job's punishment was the result of his sins. Job had no guilt to confess; his conscience was clear. As far as he knew, he had done nothing wrong [Job 4:6].

JOB DISFIGURED

And when they lifted up their eyes afar off, and knew him not, they lifted up their voice, and wept; and they rent every one his mantle, and sprinkled dust upon their heads toward heaven.

Job 2:12

"Knew him not" in this instance means "he was so afflicted that they did not recognize him. The three friends could hardly believe that it was Job who sat in ashes, scraping himself with a potsherd.

In the East, when a man is afflicted or reduced to poverty, his friends say, "I saw him, but I did not recognize him." Of course, the three friends who came to see him and comfort him expected to find him deep in grief, but Job's wounds were very great. That is why they lifted up their voices and wept, and they tore their garments.

The tearing of garments is an ancient Eastern custom. During funerals and great tragedies, men tear their garments and women cut off their hair as a token of deep mourning. When Abner was slain by Job, David ordered the army commanders and nobles to tear their clothes and put on sackcloth [2 Sam. 3:31; Lam. 2:10].

SEVEN DAYS OF SILENCE

So they sat down with him upon the ground seven days and seven nights, and none spake a word unto him: for they saw that his grief was very great. Job 2:13

Seven is a sacred number which appears in the Bible quite often: seven wells, seven stars, seven candlesticks, seven virgins, seven churches, and seven angels.

The three friends of Job who had come to comfort him sat in silence for seven days. Easterners, when entering a house of mourning, sit down in silence for a long time. On such occasions no greetings are exchanged. After a long period of quietness, the silence is broken; then one of the men starts to comfort the mourners. At times, the silence is broken by one of the mourners.

The seven days and seven nights of silence prove that these wise comforters were deeply grieved for their friend Job.

CURSING OF THE DAY

After this opened Job his mouth, and cursed his day.
And Job spake, and said,
Let the day perish wherein I was born, and the night in which it was said, There is a man child conceived . . . let it not be joined unto the days of the year, let it not come into the number of the month [verse 6]. Job 3:1-3

According to ancient astrological beliefs, the particular day of one's birth or conception determines one's fate and future.

Astrology, astronomy, and other studies of the heavenly bodies were common among the Assyrians and the Egyptians. They believed time was an important element in man's life, and that it had something to do with his conception, birth, and death. The whole universe, including man, is one organism. These beliefs are still maintained in many parts of the world. But time and space have no place in the realm of the spirit.

Job thought he was conceived on a bad night and born on an unlucky day. That is why he cursed both the day and the night.

Jeremiah also cursed the day in which he was born [Jer. 20:14]. Easterners, when mourning or despondent, often curse the day of their birth and wish they never had been conceived and born. On such dark occasions when life is bitter, death becomes sweeter [verses 4-7].

LEVIATHAN, THE DEVIL

Let them curse it that curse the day who are ready to raise up their mourning.   Job 3:8

The Aramaic word *lewiathan* (leviathan, sea monster, serpent, whale) metaphorically means "the devil." It has been confused with *aoliathan* (lamentation, wailing, mourning for the dead). The two words are similar in Aramaic. The Eastern text reads: "Let them curse it who curse the day, who are ready to stir up Leviathan." (Leviathan, another name for evil forces, is not used in the King James Version.)

Job here is speaking of the awakening of the great monster, the devil, who was responsible for his afflictions.

Undoubtedly, the question of Job's piety and integrity was raised by many of his neighbors and associates. Job was a very wealthy man. The people wondered how he had accumulated so many possessions.

CHILDBIRTH

Why died I not from the womb? why did I not give up the ghost when I came out of the belly?

Why did the knees prevent me? or why the breasts that I should suck?   Job 3:11-12

Prior to World War II, hospitals and maternity wards were unknown in many cities and towns in the Near East, and especially in little villages, sheep camps, and the deserts. Most of the people knew no more about the nature of disease than their ancient ancestors had known.

The old methods of child delivery were still practiced, and they are still common in many isolated and backward countries.

When a pregnant woman is ready to give birth to a child, she is assisted by two midwives, who hold her arms and help her walk around the house or the tent. Some women, however, require no assistance.

In most houses, and especially in tents, privacy is lacking, and there are no beds on which the women may lie. When the child is delivered, the mother has to be careful to prevent the child from falling on the hard ground. Verse 12 should read: "Why was I reared at my mother's knee? Why did I suck the breasts?"

Job wishes his mother's knees had let him drop on the ground so that he might have died.

HIDDEN FUTURE

Why is light given to a man whose way is hid, and whom God hath hedged in?   Job 3:23

"Light" in this instance means "joy, happiness, and delight." Here Job wonders why God gives men wealth and fame and the desire to enjoy life and yet hides his future and hedges him in.

Job's tragedy was very sudden. In the past, God had given him prosperity, children, and fame. But now he found himself hedged in, his wealth gone, and his children slain.

Job wonders why man has no power over his destiny. Why cannot he map his future and see the dangers that are ahead of him? Or, why does man, with all the knowledge with which God has endowed him, lose his direction? Then again, Job wonders why man should suffer and pass away.

Such questions are not new. Throughout the centuries man has been bewildered about certain unhappy events in his life; in particular, sickness, suffering, and death. Today, we know that disease is the result of sin and transgression against God's laws.

FEEBLE KNEES

Behold, thou hast instructed many, and thou hast strengthened the weak hands.

Thy words have upholden him that was falling, and thou hast strengthened the feeble knees.   Job 4:3-4

"Feeble knees" is an Eastern idiom which means literally people with uncertain, weak, shaky, or unsteady feet. In these words Eliphaz was reminding Job that he had strengthened many men who were falling and those who were uncertain of their faith in God and his true way of life.

Many of the men whom Job had helped and strengthened had had experiences like his own. Some of them had suffered severe tragedies; some had been sick; and others had lost their possessions. And now, Job was troubled because of the losses which *he* had suffered and because of *his* disease. Eliphaz seems to be suggesting that one who has been a counselor and instructor to others should practice what he preaches.

FEAR CAUSES SICKNESS

Is not this thy fear, thy confidence, thy hope, and the upright-ness of thy ways?   Job 4:6

The Aramaic word *adlaiah* means "blame, fault, censure"; *adal* means "to find fault." The Eastern text reads: "Behold, your fear is to be blamed, and your trust in the integrity of your way."

Eliphaz states that Job's fears were due to faults or blunders which he had committed. Eliphaz is sure that if Job were not guilty of some sin he would not suffer. ". . . whoever perished, being innocent?" [verse 7].

THE LAW OF COMPENSATION

Remember, I pray thee, who ever perished, being innocent? or where were the righteous cut off?

Even as I have seen, they that plow iniquity, and sow wicked-ness, reap the same.   Job 4:7-8

Eliphaz, like other Easterners, believed in the law of compensation, or cause and effect [Ps. 7:14-17].

Job had been wondering why he was stricken and bereaved of his children. He thought that he had been innocent all of his life, that he had helped the poor and the widows and had wronged no one.

Eliphaz was not quite sure of Job's innocence. He had seen Job's flocks, herds, camels, and other possessions increasing, and now he wondered if Job had acquired all of these earthly goods righteously. Like other rich men, Job's stewards and servants probably had loaned money at interest, had kept the pledges of those who had been unable to pay, and at times may have acted crookedly in order to make more money for their master. In other words, Job might have been a pious man, but what about his servants, shepherds, and cameleers?

Eliphaz believed that no mortal man can be justified before God.

Paul said that you reap what you sow, or you gather what you scatter [Gal. 6:7-8].

FALSEHOOD IS HIDDEN IN MAN

Although affliction cometh not forth of the dust, neither doth trouble spring out of the ground.   Job 5:6

The Aramaic word *shookra* means "falsehood." The Eastern text reads: "For falsehood does not come forth from the dust, nor does iniquity spring out of the ground."

Man's troubles and difficulties come forth from within him; that is, a man charts his own path. There is an Eastern parable: "The worm of a tree is within itself"; that is, man, through good thinking, is rewarded with good things; and, through bad thinking, is punished with bad things.

TROUBLES OF LIFE

Yet man is born unto trouble, as the sparks fly upward. Job 5:7

The Eastern text reads: ". . . as sure as the wild birds fly."

Man is born for trouble, struggle, and hard labor. His span of life is full of sorrows, difficulties, and insecurities which befall him as suddenly as a bird flies.

In the olden days, hard work was looked upon as a curse and the lot of slaves, the poor, and the weak. Most of the men and women of the higher classes shunned work. Even today there are people in the East who would choose to starve rather than do any kind of work.

Here Job is speaking of toil and grinding which one has to go through in order to make a living. Even the rich are not free from trouble and toil [Eccles. 2:22-23], nor is man sure of his future. Truth and righteousness are the only safe guides for directing man's course of life.

NATURE ON MAN'S SIDE

For thou shalt be in league with the stones of the field: and the beasts of the field shall be at peace with thee.   Job 5:23

Such sayings are used metaphorically. "You shall be in league with the stones of the field," means, "Nature will be on your side, and whatever you do will prosper."

In the East, it is often said, "Stones talked to him," or, "Asses gave him admonition."

When a man is at peace with his Creator, the universal forces are on his side, and he can overcome any problem or difficulty.

JOB SEEKS HEALING

Even that it would please God to destroy me; that he would let loose his hand, and cut me off! Job 6:9

The Eastern text reads: "So that God would hearken to cleanse me, and to spread out his hand and make me whole."

Job is pleading with God for help that he might be healed and live. This is consistent with Job's patience and his firm faith in God. ". . . so that I may be restored to my strength without measure; for I have not lied against the words of the Holy One" [Job 6:10, Eastern text].

"Do not withdraw thy help from me; and let not thy dread terrify me" [Job 13:21, Eastern text].

PEACE AND GOOD DEEDS

To him that is afflicted pity should be showed from his friend; but he forsaketh the fear of the Almighty. Job 6:14

The Eastern text reads: "He who withholds peace from his friend, forsakes the worship of the Almighty."

The Aramaic word *dikhlety* means "worship, reverence, fear." In this instance it means "worship." Worship without peace and good deeds is dead, as faith without works is dead. Peace always reigns in the house of the righteous. Peace, like light, must be shared in order to lighten the path of those who seek the way of God.

The Hebrew prophets exhorted the people to extend kindness one to another—to strangers and to widows and orphans.

Jesus said: "For I was hungry, and you gave me food; I was thirsty, and you gave me drink; I was a stranger and you took me in" [Matt. 25:35, Eastern text].

Charity and good works are the manifestations of true religion.

DECEITFULNESS

My brethren have dealt deceitfully as a brook, and as the stream of brooks they pass away. Job 6:15

In Palestine, Arabia, and other arid lands, brooks and streams dry up suddenly. During the severe droughts, springs and streams which once had been prolific suddenly dry up. The shepherds and travelers who visit the springs and streams are greatly disappointed when they find them dry.

The term "deceitful" is used simply because no one can tell when brooks and streams will dry up. This is also true of deceitful and ungodly men—no one knows how long their friendship will last.

Job was disappointed with his friends. He expected comfort, but instead, they heaped scorn upon him. Instead of bringing consolation to his heart, his comforters added mischief to his sorrows [verses 16, 26].

INSINCERE FRIENDS AND COMFORTERS

Which are blackish by reason of the ice, and wherein the snow is hid.

What time they wax warm, they vanish: when it is hot, they are consumed out of their place.

The paths of their way are turned aside; they go to nothing, and perish.   Job 6:16-18

The Eastern text reads: "Those who were afraid of ice, much snow has fallen upon them." This is an Eastern saying which means, "When one was expecting a little trouble, he received much." One can easily walk over the ice, but it is difficult to walk in deep snow.

The reference here is to Job's comforters. He had expected some criticism from them, but they heaped too much upon him.

On the other hand, Job had not sent for his comforters or asked them to do anything for him. When they came, however, he was eager to discuss his misfortune with them. But he found they were like dry brooks which disappoint the thirsty traveler.

SHADOW USED FOR CLOCK

As a servant earnestly desireth the shadow, and as a hireling looketh for the reward of his work.   Job 7:2

In biblical times, when clocks were unknown, the time was determined by the declining shadows of the rocks and trees. The kings and princes used dials like the dial of Ahaz [2 Kings 20:9-11]. The Romans used sand containers to measure time.

The reference is to the servants who work long hours from early dawn to sunset. Being eager to go home, they frequently stop to look at the shadows. "Reward" is wrong. It should read "as a hireling who looks to complete his job."

Clocks and watches were hardly seen until World War I in some of the lands in the Near East and Middle East. The time was determined by the crowing of the rooster and the shadows of the rocks.

In the East, laborers were paid in the evening. But, in some instances, when the employer was a government official or a rich person, the laborer's wages were held for months and even years; and, in most cases, were not paid at all. This custom prevailed until World War I. And it still prevails in backward lands.

"Behold, the wage of the labourers who have reaped your fields, that which you have fraudulently kept back, cries; and the cry of the reapers has already entered into the ears of the Lord of Sabaoth" [James 5:4 (Eastern text); see also Lev. 19:13; Mal. 3:5].

LIFE IS ETERNAL

O remember that my life is wind: mine eye shall no more see good.
                                                              Job 7:7

In Aramaic, the word which means "spirit" also means "wind." This should read: "O remember that the spirit is still alive; even yet my eye shall again see good."

Job believed in immortality of the spirit, life eternal. He knew that the spirit is indestructible.

Rokha (spirit, wind, pride, rheumatism) is often mistranslated. Jesus said, "It is the spirit that gives life; the body is of no account . . . [John 6:63]. "Do not be afraid of those who kill the body . . ." [Matt. 10:28, Eastern text].

Eternal life is compared to the spirit because the spirit is indestructible. But the temporal life is like the wind—it passes away [Ps. 78:39]. James compares life to vapor, which appears for only a little while and then disappears [James 4:14]. Job was speaking of life hereafter.

GOD STOOD BY JOB

So that my soul chooseth strangling, and death rather than my life.
                                                              Job 7:15

The Aramaic word *bakhar* means "to try" or "prove," and metaphorically, "to examine." The Aramaic word for "strangle" is *khenak*. Job here is speaking of his soul which has been purified and drawn out of destruction.

It should read: "Thou hast drawn my life out of destruction, and my bones out of death."

Job's concern is the spiritual man—the spirit—and not the temporal man which passes away like a shadow [Ps. 8:4].

When silver and gold are purified, the impurities perish, but the fine gold and silver come out shining. Job came out happily and victoriously. At last he was vindicated and his temporal losses were restored.

JOB'S PIETY A BURDEN

I have sinned; what shall I do unto thee, O thou preserver of men? why hast thou set me as a mark against thee, so that I am a burden to myself? Job 7:20

The Eastern text reads: "If I have sinned; what have I done to thee, O thou Creator of men? Why hast thou caused me to encounter thee? Thou hast become a burden to me."

The Aramaic word *hwet* (you have become) has been confused with *hwet* (I have become). The difference between these two words is merely in the position of a dot over or under the letter "t."

Job considered himself a pious man who had done nothing wrong to justify his afflictions, and yet, seemingly, God had afflicted him just to test his loyalty. In other words, his righteousness and his loyalty to God had become a heavy burden upon him. He had been subjected to a harsh ordeal to prove his faith in God. Job did not expect to see a good man suffering.

SPIDER'S WEB

Whose hope shall be cut off, and whose trust shall be a spider's web.
He shall lean upon his house, but it shall not stand: he shall hold it fast, but it shall not endure. Job 8:14-15

"Spider's web" is used figuratively, meaning "weakness" or "insecurity." Spiders' webs are so delicate that they are easily destroyed. This figure of speech is still common in Near Eastern languages and literature. It is used by Mohammed in the Koran.

The spider's web not only is weak but also is a trap to insects which take refuge in it. Such are the hopes and evil devices of the wicked. They are destroyed and cut off like a spider's web.

GOD DOES NOT FORSAKE THE RIGHTEOUS

Behold, God will not cast away a perfect man, neither will he help the evildoers.   Job 8:20

God does not cast away or reject the perfect or the upright man who trusts in him. And when he suffers and is persecuted by evildoers, God is with him and helps him overcome his difficulties. God does not forsake the righteous.

The psalmist tells us: "Though he fall, he shall not be utterly cast down: for the Lord upholdeth him with his hand. I have been young, and now am old; yet have I not seen the righteous forsaken, nor his seed begging bread" [Ps. 37:24-25].

"Though he slay me, yet will I trust in him" [Job 13:15]. "Yea, though I walk through the valley of the shadow of death, I will fear no evil: for thou art with me" [Ps. 23:4; see also Ps. 34:8].

When Jesus was on the cross, he said, "My God, my God, for this I was spared!" [Matt. 27:46, Eastern text]. God never forsook him. Even his enemies said he trusted in God and let him deliver him.

SHORT LIFE

Now my days are swifter than a post: they flee away, they see no good.

They are passed away as the swift ships: as the eagle that hasteth to the prey.   Job 9:25-26

The Aramaic word *rakhta* means a "runner" or "courier." "Post," in this instance, means a "messenger" or "postman."

In biblical days letters were conveyed and delivered by fast runners or couriers.

Job is comparing his life to a fast runner who reaches his destination in a short while. His days had passed away as when a swift ship disappears beyond the horizon [Job 10:20].

JOB'S DISCOURSE RESENTED

Should thy lies make men hold their peace? and when thou mockest, shall no man make thee ashamed?   Job 11:3

The Eastern text reads: "Behold, at your words only the dead can hold their peace; for when you speak, there is no one to stop you; and when you mock, there is no one to rebuke you."

Zophar the Naamathite was impatient to sit down and listen to Job's lengthy discourse. Job was a sick man. His comforters had some sympathy and regard for him. When he spoke, no one could stop him and offend him, and when he spoke derisively, no one could rebuke him.

The three men had come to comfort him, but they were unable to tell him that he was wrong in justifying himself and claiming to be righteous [verse 4].

GOD IS UNSEARCHABLE

Canst thou by searching find out God? canst thou find out the Almighty unto perfection?
It is as high as heaven; what canst thou do? deeper than hell; what canst thou know?   Job 11:7-8

The Aramaic word *sopeh* means "the boundaries thereof"; that is, "Can you find the ends or the limits of God?" Since God is the eternal Spirit and the only Creator, he has no beginning or end; and since he is the pervading Spirit, above time and space, there is no place in the universe which is devoid of him.

The Eastern text reads: "Can you understand the deep things of God? Or can you stand at the outer boundary of the Almighty? Do you know the height of the heaven? Or the depth of Sheol? How can you know?"

GOD SEES EVIL THINGS

For he knoweth vain men: he seeth wickedness also; will he not then consider it?   Job 11:11

This should read: "For it is he [God] who knows the beginning of time; and sees wickedness, and considers it."

Zophar states that God is above time and space and that he knows what is to take place, and he also sees wickedness and he considers it.

Some theologians erroneously state that God does not behold evil or sin. The Bible, in many places, states that God saw the evil works of men [Gen. 18:21; Judg. 3:7, 3:12; 2 Kings 3:1-2, 13:2; Isa. 1:16].

God sees and feels anything that is contrary to good. But God does not recognize evil or wickedness as a power apart from himself. Evil or wickedness is contrary to the nature or the essence of God, just as water is contrary to fire and evil to good.

A PURE MAN

For vain man would be wise, though man be born like a wild ass's colt.   Job 11:12

The Eastern text reads: "For a pure man inspires courage, and a mighty man helps others."

A man who is pure in heart sees purity and counsels people for good, but a vain man sees vanity and evil. Thus, the strength of a pure man is like that of a mighty man.

The Aramaic word *ganbara* (a mighty man) is confused with *khamara* (an ass). This error occurs also in Genesis 49:14: "Issachar is a strong ass." It should read: "Issachar is a mighty man."

TOIL IS FORGOTTEN

Because thou shalt forget thy misery, and remember it as waters that pass away.   Job 11:16

The Eastern text reads *tedbedar* (shall scatter or pass away). *Tedbedar* is confused with another verb *titdkhar* (to be remembered). It should read: "Because you shall forget your misery, and you shall be led like running water."

In many Eastern lands, water dries up in the early summer months. Brooks, ponds, and rivers turn into a parched land. The thirsty people forget that once those water sources were prolific. Man's toil is also forgotten and often replaced with joy.

TO SEE CLEARLY

And thine age shall be clearer than the noonday; thou shalt shine forth, thou shalt be as the morning.   Job 11:17

The Aramaic word *khipra* means "pit, ditch, or mine." Job states that when a man makes his heart right and stretches his hands toward God, everything will be in his favor. Evil will flee from him, and he will be led smoothly like running water.

"The pit [or the mine] will be clearer than the noonday, and the thick darkness will be like the morning." Then man sees hope and salvation ahead of him.

Mines, in the olden days, were lighted with butter lamps and candles. At times, however, the miners worked in thick darkness.

When man changes his heart and turns to God, all his difficulties disappear and he is divinely led into straight paths, for God is the light of this world and his Word is a lamp to man's feet.

HUMAN FOLLY

He that is ready to slip with his feet is as a lamp despised in the thought of him that is at ease. Job 12:5

The Eastern text reads: "Who is ready to do away with contempt and iniquity, and to strengthen the slippery feet."

The reference here is to God in verse 4. Job had been a laughingstock to his friends. Even though he was innocent, his friends and acquaintances doubted his sincerity. God was to remove all this contempt and iniquity, and strengthen the slippery feet of his accusers.

No doubt, the meaning of this verse was lost through mistranslation. Job was an Easterner. The book is written in a literary tongue—Aramaic —which was the lingua franca of all the people of the Near East, just as Arabic is today. Such a work as this could not be expressed in a dialect spoken by tribal people.

The Hebrews, as well as the Naamathites and Temanites and other Semitic races in southeast and southwest Arabia, used Aramaic as a literary tongue [2 Kings 18:26].

The term "as a lamp despised" does not make sense. No one hates a lamp, but people often mock and persecute the righteous.

RETRIBUTION

The tabernacles of robbers prosper, and they that provoke God are secure; into whose hand God bringeth abundantly. Job 12:6

The Eastern text reads: "The tabernacle of robbers shall be removed, and the confidence of those who provoke God; for there is no God in their heart."

The error is caused by the resemblance of the Aramaic words *neshanon* (to remove) and *neshamnon* (to be fat, to prosper). The word "abundantly" is emphasized in the original verse, indicating that it is not found in the original text.

Prior to the rise of Islam, many Arab tribes lived by raiding and robbing. They moved their tents from one place to another in order to escape being raided by their victims. Nevertheless, sooner or later justice caught up with them and vengeance was inflicted on them. Their tents were dismantled and taken as booty, and their sheep and cattle plundered. Just as they had plundered others, they were also plundered.

This ancient custom prevailed until World War I, when the British and the Arab governments put an end to it.

Job throughout his discourse has been against the wicked. Job could not have spoken of God as a partner of the wicked.

LIGHT OUT OF THE SHADOW OF DEATH

He discovereth deep things out of darkness, and bringeth out to light the shadow of death. Job 12:22

The Eastern text reads: ". . . and brings the light out of the shadow of death." No shadow can come out of light. The shadow is the absence of light. The prophet Amos says: "They have forsaken him who made Pleiades and Orion, and who turns the shadow of death into the morning" [Amos 5:8, Eastern text].

The reference here is to the times of despair when everything seemingly is hopeless. As long as there is faith there is hope, and God can change any situation. He can bring joy and happiness out of a dark and hopeless situation.

The seed is buried in the dark chambers of the earth, but it sprouts, clothed with majesty and with glory.

FLESH IN MY TEETH

Wherefore do I take my flesh in my teeth, and put my life in mine hand? Job 13:14

"Wherefore do I take my flesh in my teeth, and put my life in mine hand?" is an idiomatic expression which means, "Why am I so afflicted, and why is my life exposed to danger?" [verse 15].

When people are harassed and plundered, they put their finger on their teeth, implying that all they have is what is between their teeth. Job had lost all his possessions and now was suffering from his wounds, which to his friends seemed to be incurable.

Job questions his trials and sufferings. But he knows that whatever he does is under the control of God. So he entrusts everything to God with the assurance that he will be vindicated and declared righteous.

MAN'S LIFE IN GOD'S HAND

Though he slay me, yet will I trust in him: but I will maintain mine own ways before him.   Job 13:15

The last portion of the verse, according to the Eastern text, reads: ". . . because my ways are before him"; that is, "My way of life or my conduct is not hidden from him." Job trusted in God. He knew that his suffering and trials were for good.

At last, Job was vindicated, blessed, and rewarded abundantly for his suffering and losses. Job was tested, but not rejected [Job 8:20]. God does not forsake the righteous, nor those who put their trust in him [Ps. 23:4; 37:24-25].

NEED GOD'S HELP

Withdraw thine hand far from me: and let not thy dread make me afraid.   Job 13:21

This should read: "Do not withdraw thy help from me."

Job implores God to stand by him and help him in his trial and suffering. Without God's help, the dreadful disease would terrify him.

The Aramaic term "hand" in this instance means "help or support." Without God's help Job would have been unable to stand his long suffering and trial.

BORN OF A WOMAN

Man that is born of a woman is of few days, and full of trouble.   Job 14:1

"Born of a woman" is an Eastern idiom which means "weak." Woman is used here as a contrast between those who are born of the Spirit and those who are born of the flesh. People often say, "He is born of a woman," meaning that he is weak and liable to make mistakes.

No doubt, this idiom is based on the fall of man. The book of Genesis states that the woman was tempted first and then ate from the fruit of the forbidden tree and caused Adam to eat, also.

Jesus said, "Among them that are born of women there hath not risen a greater than John the Baptist" [Matt. 11:11].

CLEAN OUT OF THE UNCLEAN

Who can bring a clean thing out of an unclean? not one.

Job 14:4

The Eastern text reads: "Who can bring a clean thing out of an unclean? No one." That is, there is no man who can produce good out of evil, or evil out of good.

Jesus said: "A good tree bringeth not forth corrupt fruit; neither doth a corrupt tree bring forth good fruit" [Luke 6:43].

In the olden days, just as today, some people, to justify their evil acts, claimed that good could come out of evil. But good produces good, and evil produces evil. Every tree is known by its fruits. Moreover, no spring can issue both sweet and bitter water.

MORTAL MAN

But man dieth, and wasteth away: yea, man giveth up the ghost, and where is he?

As the waters fail from the sea, and the flood decayeth and drieth up;

So man lieth down, and riseth not: till the heavens be no more, they shall not awake, nor be raised out of their sleep. Job 14:10-12

The reference here is to mortal man and not to spiritual man, who is immortal and indestructible. Job is speaking of the bodies and not of the souls of men. Job himself believed that in the Spirit we will see God [Job 7:7, Eastern text].

"Till the heavens be no more" means eternity or endless time. The spiritual man is not subject to time and space. He always was and always shall be. Heaven and earth will pass away, but man, being the image of God, is eternal. In chapter 19:26, Job says, "In my flesh shall I see God."

The question of immortality was a live issue then as it is today, but was not well defined during the time of Job. The early Hebrews made little mention of the life hereafter. The life in this world was so hard and harsh that the people thought little or nothing of life hereafter.

ENRAGED

Should a wise man utter vain knowledge, and fill his belly with the east wind?

Job 15:2

"Fill his belly with the east wind" is an Eastern idiom commonly used, which means to utter supposedly great things. When a man is enraged, it is said, "He has wrath or wind in his belly," or "His belly burst with anger." False pride, likewise, is called wind. This is because the sound of the wind is meaningless, and no one knows its destination or its source.

The east wind is noted for being strong [Exod. 14:21].

The Eastern text reads: "Should a spiritually minded man answer with knowledge and then become enraged?"

DECEITFUL RICHES

Because he covereth his face with his fatness, and maketh collops of fat on his flanks.   Job 15:27

The Eastern text reads: "Because he has deceived himself with his wealth, and he places Pleiades above Aldebaran."

The Aramaic word *tarbeh* (his fatness) means "his wealth or riches." The Bible often speaks about the fat of the land.

"He places Pleiades above Aldebaran" means that he falsifies things and does not speak the truth.

Wealth often deceives those who are carried away by it. King Solomon says, ". . . but money brings one low and causes him to go astray in all things" [Eccles. 10:19, Eastern text].

HORN DEFILED

I have sewed sackcloth upon my skin, and defiled my horn in the dust.   Job 16:15

"Defiled my horn in the dust" is an Eastern saying which means, "I have reduced my glory to dust," or, "I have humbled myself." When a man was humbled it was said, "His horn has been broken" [Jer. 48:25].

Horns are symbolic of triumph, excellency, royalty, and strength. Then again, horns are used by animals as weapons. "To exalt one's horn" means to give one strength and victory in battle [1 Sam. 2:1]. It also means to prosper and become great, to become a ruler, and to be exalted.

Job's wealth and glory were gone. His skin was covered with sores. Therefore, his horn (glory) was broken and reduced to dust. "He hath cut off in his fierce anger all the horn of Israel" [Lam. 2:3].

See commentary on Horn.

CANDLE AN HEIR

Yea, the light of the wicked shall be put out, and the spark of his fire shall not shine.
The light shall be dark in his tabernacle, and his candle shall be put out with him. · Job 18:5-6

"Candle" or "lamp" is used metaphorically, meaning "an heir" [1 Kings 15:4]. Darkness is symbolic of mourning. In the East, an heir is known as the light of the family. When he dies, during the mourning days, the people sit in darkness. "Spark of his fire" means "his lifeline." His distant relatives also shall perish.

See the commentary on Lamp, 1 Kings 15:4.

WICKED, NOT BABIES

Yea, young children despised me; I arose, and they spake against me. Job 19:18

The Aramaic word *awaley* (the ungodly, the wicked) has been confused with *aweley* (babies, children, infants). These Aramaic words are written alike, but are pronounced differently.

Job is complaining of wicked men who, when he rose to say something, spoke against him. His counselors also despised him. Job had lost everything he had. His honor and his glory were gone with his wealth. The people no longer respected him.

Babies or children could hardly have spoken against Job, or even known of his suffering or the loss of his wealth.

WRITING ON ROCK AND LEAD

That they were graven with an iron pen and lead in the rock for ever! Job 19:24

At the time of Job, much of the writing was engraved on rocks. Great events and triumphs of emperors were inscribed on stone tablets and on rocks as a memorial forever. Rock symbolizes strength and endurance. Other writing materials, such as sheepskin and papyrus, soon perish. Tablets are broken and parchment deteriorates, but rock lasts for ages.

Today one can see many Assyrian inscriptions on large rocks. Some of them were written in the eighth century B.C. They are still intact. Job wanted his wise words to be engraved with an iron pen on a lead tablet or on a rock to be preserved for posterity. One of the Dead Sea Scrolls is written on copper.

SAVIOUR

For I know that my Redeemer liveth, and that he shall stand at the latter day upon the earth.   Job 19:25

The Aramaic noun *paroka* is derived from *parak* (to save or deliver). *Paroki* means "my Saviour." "Redeemer" is wrongly used, because in redeeming one has to pay a price or a debt.

Paroka (saviour) is one who saves or delivers with his strength without paying a price to anyone. For example, one may jump into a river to save a child from drowning. He would not have to pay a price to anyone. The act of saving is performed because of his love for his fellow men.

Jesus died to save us from evil forces and not to redeem us by paying a debt to the devil. But instead, being powerful, he destroyed the power of the devil and sin. Jesus gave his life voluntarily, like a man who risks his life to save another man from drowning or fire. He said, "I give my life of mine own."

God is our Saviour because he saves us from sin and evil forces when we turn to him [Ps. 19:14]. God, being the Sovereign over the universe, has power to save, but he pays no ransom to anyone.

RESURRECTION

And though after my skin worms destroy this body, yet in my flesh shall see God.   Job 19:26

The concept of a newer and longer life was prevalent in all ancient religions. The Assyrians, the Babylonians, and the Egyptians believed in the immortality of the soul and the life hereafter. They supplied the dead with all the necessities of life, even with seeds and other things.

The Egyptians embalmed their dead many centuries before the birth of Moses. They believed that one day the soul (*ata*) would return to the body.

The concept of immortality evolved among the Jews during the exile in Babylon. Prior to the Babylonian captivity they believed in the immortality of the soul, but during the captivity and thereafter, they began to feel the necessity of another life in a physical body in order to compensate for what they had lost in this life.

"Flesh" (body) here means "a person." Even when the flesh or body is consumed, the Spirit, which is the image of God, shall see God [Job 7:7, Eastern text].

But the resurrection will be a spiritual resurrection; that is to say, we will rise in a spiritual body and in the Spirit and likeness of God [Ps. 17:15]. Isaiah states that the earth shall cast out the dead [Isa. 26:19]. Daniel also speaks of resurrection to the everlasting life and to everlasting condemnation [Dan. 12:2].

Those who have suffered injustices will enjoy life, but the wicked will suffer for what they have done.

Paul says, ". . . and the dead shall be raised incorruptible, and we shall be changed" [1 Cor. 15:52].

THE CHILDREN OF THE WICKED

His children shall seek to please the poor, and his hands shall restore their goods.   Job 20:10

It should read: "His children shall be crushed with poverty, and he shall stretch out his hands toward them." The Aramaic word *tabar* means "to break or crush."

The triumph of the wicked is short, and the joy of hypocrites but for a moment [Job 12:6, Eastern text].

EMBEZZLEMENT

He hath swallowed down riches, and he shall vomit them up again: God shall cast them out of his belly.   Job 20:15

"He hath swallowed down riches, and he shall vomit them up again" is a saying which means that one has acquired riches by embezzlement, extortion, or other corrupt practices, but at last he will pay for it. The Aramaic word for embezzlement is "eat." "You have eaten the houses of widows." The Aramaic reads: "The riches which he had swallowed down . . ."

"God shall cast them out of his belly" means that God will punish him for his unjust acts. We often say, "God will bring his food forth out of his nostrils." Easterners believe in the law of compensation; that is, he who gives alms and does good will be rewarded with good, but he who is unjust and acquires wealth by corrupt means will receive evil as his reward.

POISON OF ASPS AND VIPERS

He shall suck the poison of asps: the viper's tongue shall slay him. **Job 20:16**

"The poison of asps" and "the viper's tongue" are used metaphorically to suggest sickness and death.

Easterners believe that wicked men and, in particular, extortionists and embezzlers of the property of the poor will, in due time, be afflicted with sickness, or will meet a violent death because of their evil deeds [Job 4:7-8].

BROOKS OF HONEY AND BUTTER

He shall not see the rivers, the floods, the brooks of honey and butter. **Job 20:17**

"Brooks of honey and butter" represent prosperity and abundance. When butter and honey are plentiful, we say "they run like a river."

When God's kingdom reigns, everything will be as plentiful as water. Honey and butter will be as abundant as water. The scarcity of food is due to wars, destruction, and greed. Wherever there is harmony and peace, there is prosperity and abundance.

Butter and honey are generally found on the tables of the rich. The poor seldom see butter and honey on their tables.

THE WICKED PERISH

There shall none of his meat be left; therefore shall no man look for his goods. **Job. 20:21**

The Eastern text reads: "There shall none of his posterity be spared; therefore his good will not be remembered."

Zophar the Naamathite argues that the triumph of the wicked is short, and that no matter how much they prosper and how much their excellency mounts up, in the end they shall perish and be forgotten. This is because they had oppressed the poor, committed injustices, and confiscated the property of widows.

The posterity of the pious abides, and the good which they have done on earth never perishes [Job 12:6, Eastern text].

WITH THE MEASURE YOU MEASURE

In the fulness of his sufficiency he shall be in straits: every hand of the wicked shall come upon him.   Job 20:22

The Aramaic words *bekelalta dakil* mean, "With the measure with which he had measured, he shall be recompensed."

In the East, when a man gives short measure, he is in turn given short measure. And when he measures with a long-arm measure or a full-and-shaken wheat measure, he in turn is given generous measure.

Jesus said: "For with the same judgment that you judge, you will be judged, and with the same measure with which you measure, it will be measured to you" [Matt. 7:2; also Mark 4:24 and Luke 6:38, Eastern text].

Zophar is trying to blame Job's troubles on his evil devices. Zophar and his companions firmly believed that Job was being punished for his evil deeds. So they tried to make him confess his guilt. But Job was an upright man.

The Easterners believe in the law of compensation. Both the good and the bad are rewarded accordingly. Sickness and misfortunes are attributed to evil deeds.

DESCENDANTS

How oft is the candle of the wicked put out! and how oft cometh their destruction upon them! God distributeth sorrows in his anger.
                    Job 21:17

"Candle" or "lamp" in Aramaic means "heir or posterity." Thus, "How oft is the candle of the wicked put out," means that the heirs of the wicked often die. In the East people often say: "May the Lord God bless your candle." "May your candle be burning for many generations." "God has given him a lamp."

David's descendants ruled on the throne for nearly four centuries. The prosperous and wicked who persecute the poor and oppress the needy often are left without an heir, and their possessions are inherited by the meek and those they have oppressed.

Jesus Christ said: "Blessed are the meek, for they shall inherit the earth" [Matt. 5:5].

See the commentary on Lamp, 1 Kings 15:4.

CLOTHES AS A PLEDGE

*For thou hast taken a pledge from thy brother for nought, and
stripped the naked of their clothing.*   Job 22:6

In the East, when the poor borrow money, they may have to put up
even their clothes as a pledge. A poor man may give his robe, the one
that he sleeps in at night. The greedy rich who take clothes, robes, and
bedclothes are generally upbraided and even condemned by pious men.
". . . hath not restored the pledge" [Ezek. 18:12].
". . . nor take a widow's raiment to pledge" [Deut. 24:17].
The clothes taken as a pledge from the poor are badly needed both
day and night. "They drive away the ass of the fatherless, they take
the widow's ox for a pledge" [Job 24:3].
Job or his servants had loaned money and taken pledges from the
poor, as all rich people in the East do.

WATER AND BREAD SHARED

*Thou hast not given water to the weary to drink, and thou hast
withholden bread from the hungry.*   Job 22:7

Pious rich men in the East provide water to weary travelers, strangers,
and the poor. At times one can see on a highway a large jar of water
placed in a wall of a memorial monument for thirsty travelers to drink.
Water is still scarce in many parts of the biblical lands, and travelers
and strangers often suffer thirst. This is more true in deserts and among
nomad tribes who depend on wells for water. At times water is found
only in the tents of the rich and the sheiks. And some of them share it
with the thirsty.
Bread also is shared with the hungry and strangers. But some greedy
men withhold both their bread and water from the thirsty and the
hungry.
When bread and water are scarce the people eat and drink secretly
so that they will not have to share it with the needy. "Stolen waters are
sweet, and bread eaten in secret is pleasant" [Prov. 9:17].
On the other hand, pious men offer their bread and water to the
hungry and the thirsty. To give water to the thirsty, and bread to the
needy, is considered one of the most pious acts in biblical lands. This is
because bread and water, so essential to life, are scarce.
Job, in upholding his piety, states, "If I have withheld the poor from
his desire, or have defrauded the widow, or have eaten my bread alone,

and the orphans did not eat of it . . . Because from my youth I was brought up in sorrows, and from my Mother's womb with sighing . . . But they were reared upon my knees and were warmed with the fleece of my sheep . . ." [Job 31:16-20, Eastern text].

ARM

Thou hast sent widows away empty, and the arms of the father-less have been broken.   Job 22:9

"Arms of the fatherless have been broken" is an Aramaic idiom which means they have been "left helpless."

In Aramaic, arms are symbolic of men's strength and power, and when the arms are broken it is symbolic of weakness and hopelessness.

". . . let it (my arm) be broken from the bone" [Job 31:22].

". . . with a stretched out arm . . ." [Jer. 32:21].

". . . by the greatness of thine arm . . ." [Exod. 15:16].

THE HUMBLE

When men are cast down, then thou shalt say, There is lifting up; and he shall save the humble person.   Job 22:29

The Aramaic word *demithmakakh* means "who is humbled." The Eastern text reads: "For it is said, He who humbles himself shall be exalted; and he who is meek shall be saved."

The meek are praised for their humility. The proud shall be humbled, but the meek shall be saved and exalted; and they shall inherit the earth [Matt. 5:5].

To be meek is to be gentle, natural, and tolerant.

THE INNOCENT

He shall deliver the island of the innocent: and it is delivered by the pureness of thine hands.   Job 22:30

The Aramaic word *zakaiah* means "innocent, blameless, guiltless." The Eastern text reads: "The innocent man shall be spared wherever he is, and he shall escape by the purity of his hands."

"Island" is a mistranslation, probably due to a faulty or damaged text.

THE WICKED

Why, seeing times are not hidden from the Almighty, do they that know him not see his days?   Job 24:1

The Aramaic word *awalin* (the ungodly, the wicked) is confused with *zabnin* (times). The Eastern text reads: "Why are the wicked not hidden from the presence of God, and why do those who know him never enjoy their days?"

The ungodly do not hide themselves from the presence of God, because they do not recognize him as their Lord and Creator. They remove landmarks to steal the land from the poor, and violently seize the sheep of the weak, and keep the pledges of the poor and the widows.

What Job means here is, "Why are the wicked allowed to live?" This question was answered by Jesus in his parable of the wheat and the tares. They must stay to the end.

GRAZING RIGHTS

Some remove the landmarks; they violently take away flocks, and feed thereof.   Job 24:2

Removing of landmarks is very common among both the settled tribal people and the nomads. In grazing regions the landmark generally is a heap of stones which can be easily moved a few hundred yards or more to either side of the boundary.

When sheep are found to be grazing without a permit beyond the territory of their owners, they are confiscated. This is because pasture lands and wells are rented or leased for money or sheep.

Some powerful and wicked men, in order to confiscate the sheep of the weak tribes, remove the landmarks and seize the sheep as a fine [Deut. 19:14; Isa. 5:8].

THE OPPRESSORS

They are of those that rebel against the light; they know not the ways thereof, nor abide in the paths thereof.   Job 24:13

The Aramaic word *mediary* (dwelling place, habitation) has been confused here with the Aramaic word *marodey* (rebellious men). The difference between the letters *resh* and *daleth* is a dot placed over or under the letter.

The Eastern text reads: "They were in God's world; but they knew not his ways; nor did they walk in his paths."

These people were in God's world and yet they did not see the ways of God. They took away the bread and the clothes of the poor and forced them to reap their fields and tread their wine presses [verses 9, 10, Eastern text].

MORTAL MAN

How much less man, that is a worm? and the son of man, which is a worm?   Job 25:6

This verse should read: "How much less man, who is dust, and the son of man, who is a worm!"

Rimtha in this instance means "dust." The text uses two words: *rimtha* (dust) and *tolaa* (a worm). *Nasha* (man) and *barnasha* (son of man) are used collectively, meaning "a man, mankind, a human being."

Bildad the Shuhite argues that man cannot be justified with God, seeing that he is born of a woman, who had transgressed against the law. The reference is to Eve.

THE SLAIN MEN

Dead things are formed from under the waters, and the inhabitants thereof.   Job. 26:5

The Eastern text reads: "Behold, the mighty men shall be slain, and they shall lie down quieter than still waters."

"Quieter than water" is an Eastern idiom which means "stillness or silence."

The mighty men, during their lives, had been turbulent and noisy, but in their graves they would sleep quietly.

THE EARTH FLOATING IN THE AIR

He stretcheth out the north over the empty place, and hangeth the earth upon nothing.   Job 26:7

Nearly 2,500 years before Copernicus and Galileo discovered that the sun, and not the earth, is the center of our solar system, Job by the means of divine inspiration declared that God by his omniscient intelligence had hung the earth on nothing.

The Assyrians and Chaldeans, who are noted for their studies of the stars and planets and who were responsible for the development of the calendar, which is based on the solar system, knew that the earth revolved around the sun. The Christians in Mesopotamia in the tenth century were warned not to believe that the sun was the center of the universe. This knowledge reached Europe during the Arab conquest of Spain between the seventh and the thirteenth centuries.

After centuries of study of our vast universe, today man is able to explain some parts of this complex system which for ages was beyond man's grasp.

Today, just as of yore, we know that the revolving and rotating movements of the stars in this complex system are governed by a great power which we call God. The scientists may call it the immutable law created through harmony and a perfect balance between the force of gravity and centrifugal force, or the field created by the motion of the revolving planets.

Only God could have constructed such a complex system governed by an immutable and eternal law. That is why the psalmist cried out: "The heavens declare the glory of God; and the firmament shows his handi-work" [Ps. 19:1, Eastern text].

The Chaldeans, centuries before Galileo, knew that the earth was round and floating like a ball in the air. The Babylonians prior to the departure of Abraham from Ur of Chaldea knew that the earth was a small planet revolving around the sun, and that the sun was the center of our universe.

The Babylonians had developed the 12-month calendar, with 24 hours in a day and the 7-day week. They also knew about the movement of the stars and planets. And their knowledge was fairly good in comparison to our knowledge today, considering their lack of telescopes and other measuring devices which we have at our disposal today.

We have made a little improvement on the calendar, but we are still guided by the findings of the past. The week is still the same, and the number of months and hours has not changed.

Being a pastoral people, the Hebrews' concept of a flat world was tribal. Job was from the land of Uz. Therefore the book is written from the point of view of Chaldean astronomy. Job, no doubt, was a descendant of Abraham, or some kin of the Israelites.

"Hangeth the earth upon nothing" of course implies that it is floating in space, and not stretched out upon the water as the Hebrews thought.

Mar-Isaac, bishop of Baghdad in the eighth century, warned the Christians not to believe the Chaldean doctrine that the earth revolves around the sun.

This ancient astronomical knowledge was passed on by the Babylonians and Assyrians to the Persians, and the latter passed it on to the Greeks during their conquest of Asia Minor and Greece, just as the Arabs were responsible for the transmission of science from the Near East to Spain, and from thence to Europe.

The book of Job is the only book in the Bible which speaks of a round world.

POWERFUL ACTS OF GOD

He divideth the sea with his power, and by his understanding he smiteth through the proud.   Job 26:12

The reference here is to the Red Sea when the Lord caused it to go back by a strong east wind [Exod. 14:21].

When the water over the shoals went back during the night, the sea was divided; that is, as the crossing place became dry land, the waters were suddenly divided into two bodies—the Bitter Lakes and the tip of the Gulf of the Suez. This dry passage was the crossing place of the Israelites.

The Lord God brought the powerful east wind that divided the sea, and he guided the Israelites to cross at the right time.

All races and peoples in Arabia and Chaldea had heard of God's wonders in Egypt, especially those races which were the descendants of Abraham.

A TEMPORARY BOOTH

He buildeth his house as a moth, and as a booth that the keeper maketh.   Job 27:18

The Eastern text reads: "For the wicked had built his house upon a spider's web, and like a booth he had made his shelter."

"Spider's web" is used metaphorically, meaning that the foundation of the house is flimsy. This idiom is still prevalent in Eastern languages. A spider's web is weak and is easily destroyed by the wind and by the larger insects and birds.

The booth mentioned here is the shelter which farmers and vinedressers build in vineyards and in fields where cucumbers and melons are grown. The booth is made of thin branches and covered with grass.

When the cucumbers and grapes have been gathered, the booth is deserted and finally destroyed or burned.

Jonah made such a booth to protect himself from the heat [Jonah 4:5].

A RUINED MINE

The flood breaketh out from the inhabitant; even the waters for-
gotten of the foot: they are dried up, they are gone away from men.

Job 28:4

Mistranslations have obscured the whole meaning of this verse. The
Peshitta, the Eastern text, reads: "They have inherited a ruined mine
from an alien people; they are gone astray from the right path and their
number has diminished from among men."

Job likens the evildoers to miners who had inherited a ruined mine
from an alien people and had gone astray because of the crooked paths.

The former inhabitants of the world had gone astray from God's way
of life. The present inhabitants, metaphorically, had inherited a ruined
mine and the number of good men had diminished. Note, miners are
always exposed to dangers.

A great many people around Job were hypocrites and evildoers
[chaper 27].

MINING DIFFICULTIES

He cutteth out rivers among the rocks; and his eye seeth every
precious thing.
He bindeth the floods from overflowing; and the thing that is hid
bringeth he forth to light.   Job 28:10-11

"Rivers" in this instance means underground rivers or streams which
the miners divert in order to prevent the mines from being flooded.

Mining gold, silver, and precious stones was dangerous in the olden
days just as it is today. But man has been endowed with wisdom and
understanding to divert the course of rivers and streams, not only on
the ground, but also under the ground.

WHERE IS WISDOM FOUND?

By his Spirit he hath garnished the heavens; his hand hath
formed the crooked serpent.   Job 28:13

The Aramaic word *ela* (except) has been confused with the Aramaic
word *la* (no, not, neither). The Eastern text reads: "No man knows the
treasure thereof; neither is it found except in the land of the living."

Job points out that wisdom is beyond human comprehension, and it is found only in the land of the living; that is, in the spiritual realm—where that which we see now as imperfect will be revealed as perfect, and where that which we see in part we will see as a whole.

Wisdom and understanding were revealed to the prophets and men of God through inspiration from the Highest. Wisdom is hidden from human eyes simply because wisdom is perfect and spiritual, and it cannot be easily revealed through impurities.

When we rise in our consciences and penetrate the terrestrial veil, then we can find wisdom and apply it through our understanding.

Only God knows the source of wisdom and only God can make it manifest to men.

WISDOM IS PRICELESS

The topaz of Ethiopia shall not equal it, neither shall it be valued with pure gold.
                                                                Job 28:19

The Eastern text reads: "For the price of wisdom is above everything, and nothing can equal it. The pearls of Ethiopia and the topaz cannot equal it."

Ancient Ethiopia embraced a large portion of southwestern Arabia. This region was famous for its jewels, especially pearls which are common in southern Arabia and along the Persian Gulf. When the queen of Sheba came to see Solomon, she brought him many precious stones, pearls, and other gifts.

The present Ethiopia has no access to the Arabian Sea and the Gulf of Persia, but pearls are imported and exported by pearl merchants.

CANDLE OF GOD

When his candle shined upon my head, and when by his light I walked through darkness.
                                                                Job 29:3

In many Eastern cities where streets are narrow, servants carry lamps or candles in front of their lords or hold them high over their heads so that they may see their way and guide their footsteps safely [Ps. 119:105].

"His candle" here means God's light, his reverence, and his glory. Job was a religious man with strong convictions and faith in God. He was guided and governed by God's law and his ordinances. He was praised by the people and called pious. But now he wondered why this evil had befallen him.

Job, during his suffering and agony, at times complained and lamented his downfall. Now Job was destitute. The candle of God was taken away from him. His glory and his wealth were gone. Now Job was so afflicted that he could not even go to the place of worship.

WEALTHY

When I washed my steps with butter, and the rock poured me out rivers of oil.   Job 29:6

"When I washed my steps with butter" is an Eastern saying which means "when I was very wealthy and had large flocks."

Easterners often say, "He is bathing with butter or milk" which means his sheep produce is abundant. This is similar to the English phrase, "He is rolling in money." In the East, rich men bathe with milk. In the desert lands milk is more abundant than water.

Palestine is a rocky place. The grass is very poor, but God causes the poor land to produce butter and olive oil, since olive trees and goats thrive on rocky places.

Job had lost all of his wealth and popularity, but he never lost his faith in God.

HAND ON MOUTH

The princes refrained talking, and laid their hand on their mouth.
The nobles held their peace, and their tongue cleaved to the roof of their mouth.   Job 29:9-10

In the East, when a king, a prince, or a nobleman speaks, the other men hold their peace and lay their hands on their mouths as a token of respect and admiration for the speaker and for what is said. And when common men speak or answer a question in their presence, they are frightened.

Even the young people pay high respect to elders and nobles. They never utter a word in their presence and, at times, they even hide themselves when they listen to them.

EYES TO THE BLIND

I was eyes to the blind, and feet was I to the lame.   Job 29:15

These phrases are used metaphorically, meaning, "I gave good counsel to those who were spiritually blind, and helped those who were ready to slip to walk straight."

Job was not only a wealthy man who was highly honored, but also he was a pious and wise elder whose counsel was continually sought by many people—especially the weak.

STRAIGHT LIKE A REED

Then I said, I shall die in my nest, and I shall multiply my days as the sand.
                                                            Job 29:18

The Aramaic word for "reed" is *kania,* and the word for "nest" is *kina.* The translators from the Aramaic (or the transcribers) confused *kania* with *kina.* The resemblance between these two words is so close that an occasional error of this kind is inevitable. The letter *youth* (i) or (y) so closely resembles the letter *nun* (n) that at times even a native scribe who is versed in Aramaic might be deceived.

In the East, when a person is straightforward or honest, it is said, "He is like a reed"; that is, he is perfect in his conduct. This is because reeds grow straight. Our word for canon law is derived from the Aramaic word *kania* (reed).

Job had thought that he had been straight and perfect in all his ways, but he found that he was not as pious as he had thought in his heart that he was.

But now Job was going to change his way of life and strive to be perfect like a reed; then he was to multiply descendants and become prosperous and great again.

JOB'S ENEMIES SHAMED

To dwell in the cliffs of the valleys, in caves of the earth, and in the rocks.
                                                            Job 30:6

The Eastern text reads: "Fleeing to dwell in the cliffs of the valleys, in caves of the earth, in crevices."

Job predicts the sudden fall of the wicked men who mocked him and scorned his righteousness. The day would come when, because of fear and shame, they would hide themselves in crags and caves.

Job's fortune was to be restored and all the men who had rejoiced in his calamity would hide themselves because of fear and shame [verse 1].

GIRDED UP

By the great force of my disease is my garment changed: it bindeth me about as the collar of my coat.   Job 30:18

The Aramaic text reads: "I have put on my garment; and girded up myself with my robe."

Job had trusted in God and therefore he was sure of his restoration. The term "disease" is due to mistranslation or defects in the text as is seen from the italics in the King James Version. "Girded up myself with my robe" is an Eastern saying which means "I am ready to start." Job was ready to start to come back. The Lord had revealed to him that his suffering and his trial were not in vain. Job was destined to be greater than in the former days.

SOLITARY LIFE

I am a brother to dragons, and a companion to owls. Job 30:29

The Eastern text reads: "I am become a brother to jackals, and a companion to ostriches."

"A brother to jackals and a companion to ostriches" means "I have become an outcast living in desolate places." Job's fearful disease made many people shun him. Even some of his best friends and acquaintances turned their faces away from him. Job, in order to convey the thought of being deserted by his friends and relatives, describes himself as dwelling in the deserts with jackals and ostriches.

In the East, until recent days, men who were afflicted with an incurable disease were abandoned. Many of them wandered in cemeteries, fields, and forests. This is because hospitals were unknown, and incurable diseases were greatly feared.

JOB HAS LOST HIS FLESH

My skin is black upon me, and my bones are burned with heat.
Job 30:30

The Aramaic word *kepod* means "shrunk"; that is, "My skin has shrunk."

Job here is speaking of his suffering and the loss of his flesh. "My skin shrunk" is an idiom which means, "I have become lean" [verse 31].

Some people maintain that Job's skin turned black as a sign of his guilt. But this is not true. Job was neither perfect nor wicked. But he was a pious and unblemished man. This is why at last he was vindicated.

JOB'S PURITY

I made a covenant with mine eyes; why then should I think upon a maid?
Job 31:1

Rich men in the East were polygamists and, in some lands, still are. They acquired young concubines whenever they wanted them. Some of them took their concubines by force. In some cases men presented their virgin daughters to kings, princes, and rich men.

Job was a pious man. He had lived a pure life. He had never walked in the way of the ungodly or swerved from the way of God. So he had made a vow that he would never try to entice a maid [verses 9-10].

JOB WAS A JUST MAN

Then let me sow, and let another eat; yea, let my offspring be rooted out.
Job 31:8

The Eastern text reads: "But when I sowed, then I ate, and when I planted, then I cultivated and gathered the crops."

In the East it often happens that one man sows and another reaps; one man plants and cultivates and another enjoys the fruit.

In biblical days, when the enemy occupied the land, they gathered the grain and picked up the grapes and the fruits of the trees. Or sometimes wicked men and oppressors confiscated vineyards, orchards, and fields and gathered their produce [Mic. 6:15]. At times, some sow and let others reap. Jesus said, "For in this case the saying is true, One sows and another reaps" [John 4:37, Eastern text].

Job declares that he has not confiscated sown fields by violence, but that he has worked hard for everything he has gained.

Some of these corrupt and unjust practices are still prevalent in many lands which are still ruled by dictators and oppressors. Sown fields and vineyards are still confiscated.

BAKE BREAD FOR ANOTHER MAN

Then let my wife grind unto another, and let others bow down upon her.
Job 31:10

The Aramaic word *appey* (to bake bread) is very similar to *appay* (face). The Eastern text correctly reads: "Then let my wife grind for another, and let her bake bread at another man's place." This literally means, "Let me be so destitute that there will be no wheat or flour in my house."

In the East, the wives of poor men work in the houses of the rich, grinding wheat and baking bread. Wheat is ground at home and the bread is baked daily. This work is done only by women, each one working in her own house preparing food for her own family.

Only poor and destitute men would permit their wives to grind or bake bread for others. They may perform other services for a stranger, but to grind or bake bread would hurt the pride of the husband. This is because when women perform such tasks, they uncover their arms and wear light garments.

DEFRAUDING WIDOWS

If I have withheld the poor from their desire, or have caused the eyes of the widow to fail.
Job 31:16

The phrase "have caused the eyes of the widow to fail" is an Aramaic idiom which means "have defrauded the widow." The Aramaic word *kheshakh* means "darkness." In the East, when a man is defrauded or deceived, we say, "They have darkened his eyes," which means that he has failed to see the value of an article that he has bought or sold.

Until recent years, widows in biblical lands had few legal rights; and in some places they had none. Therefore, they could not transact business or manage property. These tasks are generally performed by men.

Invariably, many widows entrust their money, property, and important business transactions to seemingly pious men, who act on their behalf. Some of these men defraud the widows and orphans. Job insists that he had done none of these evil acts, but that he had fed them and clothed them.

Jesus said, "Woe unto you, scribes and Pharisees, hypocrites! for ye devour widows' houses, and for a pretence make long prayer: therefore ye shall receive the greater damnation" [Matt. 23:14]. "Devoured" in this instance means "embezzled."

Job is upholding his integrity and piety. Job, even though he was rich and looked upon as a prince, regarded and respected the poor and the widows.

JOB'S HOSPITALITY

If his loins have not blessed me, and if he were not warmed with the fleece of my sheep. Job 31:20

The Eastern text reads: "But they were reared upon my knees . . ." The translator evidently misunderstood the words "reared upon my knees."

Job here implies that not only had he fed and clothed the poor and the needy but also that some of them grew up in his house and he had raised them. "Reared on my knees" is an Aramaic idiom which means, "I took care of them from the time of their birth."

In the East it is not unusual to see poor workers and their wives and children living in the house of the rich employer or a landlord. One can see workers' children and the children of their employer playing together.

Job was a wealthy landlord who had hundreds of male and female servants who tended his flocks and herds, some of whom were born and reared in his own house.

SUN WORSHIP

If I beheld the sun when it shined, or the moon walking in brightness. Job 31:26

The sun, because of its warmth and light, was sometimes worshiped as a god. Sun worshipers rose up early in the morning and bowed to the sun as it rose. Even today, the Parsees (Zoroastrian religious sect), or the sun worshipers, do obeisance to the sun as it appears on the horizon. They also worship fire and keep it in their temples. The moon was also worshiped as a deity.

Moses warned the Israelites against doing obeisance to the sun and the moon. He says: "And lest you lift up your eyes to heaven, and when you see the sun and the moon, and the stars and all the host of heaven, should go astray and worship them and serve those things which the Lord your God has provided for all the peoples under heaven" [Deut. 4:19, Eastern text].

Job could not have helped seeing the sun and the moon, but he did not recognize them or worship them as deities [2 Kings 17:16].

GOOD LUCK

And my heart hath been secretly enticed, or my mouth hath kissed my hand.   Job 31:27

"My mouth has kissed my hand" is an Eastern way of speaking of cheating in business.

In the East, when merchants make large, unexpected profits, they kiss the back of their hand as a token of good luck.

Job is trying to prove that he had lived uprightly and that he had done no evil to anyone.

JOB WAS BENEVOLENT

Did I fear a great multitude, or did the contempt of families terrify me, that I kept silence, and went not out of the door?   Job 31:34

The Eastern text reads: "If I have trampled upon the rights of the others (but on the contrary, it is the multitude of families which has ruined me. Nor have I turned away anyone at the door; or engaged in gossip) let the provocations of God lay me low!"

Job had done everything which he thought was righteous in the eyes of God and pious men. He had kept all the ordinances of the law and had done what God had commanded him to do. Now he sums up some of the good deeds which he had done, and also insists that he had not done any evil. He had not engaged in gossip, nor turned the poor from his gate empty-handed. But, on the contrary, he had spent much of his wealth in helping many destitute families.

A WRITTEN SENTENCE

Oh that one would hear me! behold, my desire is, that the Almighty would answer me, and that mine adversary had written a book.   Job 31:35

The last portion of the verse is mistranslated. It should read: ". . . and let him write the sentence in a book."

In verse 34 Job testifies to his benevolence, his integrity, and his righteousness. And now Job is asking God to judge him, and, if he is wrong, to sentence him and write his sentence in a book so that it might be read by the generations to come.

In biblical days, just as today, when men were sentenced, the sentence, as well as the nature of the crime, was written on a scroll. Jesus' crime was that he had made himself a king. "This is Jesus the King of the Jews" [Matt. 27:37].

YOUNG RESPECT THE OLD

Now Elihu had waited till Job had spoken, because they were elder than he.   Job 32:4

According to Eastern etiquette, a younger man must remain silent until all the elders present have spoken.

The elders, generally, are a governing body which directs the affairs of a tribe, town, or city. They sit in council with princes and kings. The older a man is, the more his wisdom and knowledge are respected. This is why the younger men have to keep silent and wait; and in some cases they never have a chance to express their opinions.

When the elders are through speaking and are tired, the younger men may speak and give counsel [verse 16].

IMPATIENT

Behold, my belly is as wine which hath no vent; it is ready to burst like new bottles.

I will speak, that I may be refreshed: I will open my lips and answer.   Job 32:19-20

Elihu could no longer hold his peace. He had waited too long to let the elders share their wisdom with one another. But now he had to speak out and admonish Job. He could no longer restrain himself.

"My belly is as wine which has no vent" is an Eastern idiom which means, "I cannot keep silent any more." Easterners, when they are restrained from speaking or have some secret to impart, say, "My belly is bursting," which means, "I can no longer restrain myself from talking."

New wine stored in goatskins without an opening for fermentation to escape causes the skins to burst. [For information about new wine in old skins, see Matt. 9:17; Mark 2:22; Luke 5:37, Eastern text].

"Bottles" should read "skins." In the East new wine is transported in new goatskins.

GOD SPEAKS ONCE

For God speaketh once, yea twice, yet man perceiveth it not.
In a dream, in a vision of the night, when deep sleep falleth
upon men, in slumberings upon the bed.   Job 33:14-15

The Aramaic reads: "For God speaks once; he does not speak a second time."

The reference here is to visions or revelations; they come once only. Some of the visions are repeated, which signifies that the event will come soon. For example, Pharaoh saw two visions which had similar meanings; that is, the vision of the cows and that of the ears of wheat [Gen. 41:1-7].

God spoke to the Hebrew prophets in visions and dreams. At times one vision explained another.

A large portion of the Scriptures is based on the visions which the men of God saw during the night. The rest are written from experiences and occurrences in the daily life of the people.

The Bible reader must discriminate between a vision and a story based on an actual daily occurrence. Throughout the Bible, God spoke in visions and dreams. He spoke to Abraham, Isaiah, Jeremiah, Noah, and other patriarchs in visions, and, in later days, to Jesus Christ and his apostles.

God speaks to man during the silent hours of the night when man's mind is at rest. This is because during the night the mind does not record events, but instead records spiritual messages. We know that one's sense of time is based on events which take place during the day. Thus, if a man were to sleep one day or a year, he could not tell the difference when awakened. In the realm of the Spirit there is neither time nor space. Things that may happen a hundred years hence may be seen happening now.

The prophets or the men of God rose high in their contemplations in order to be on the spiritual beam and see the things happening below them. They went into deserts and lonely places to contemplate; that is, to detach their minds from earthly things and thus commune with the living God and look into the realm of the Spirit, which is the pattern of the realm of the earth. This is how Daniel foresaw the rise and fall of many empires and kingdoms, from the fifth century B.C. to A.D. 10.

Mary saw a vision; Joseph was warned through visions; Peter and Paul were guided by visions.

Some of the visions are revealed in symbols because symbols can be remembered; for example, the seven cows, the seven ears of wheat [Gen. 41:1-7], the visions which Daniel saw, and the visions of Isaiah and Ezekiel.

God spoke in visions and dreams to his holy prophets. "And the Lord appeared unto Abram, and said . . ." [Gen. 12:7].

Some visions came to men as they fell into a trance, yet their eyes were open [Num. 24:4]. Peter was in a trance when he saw a great sheet let down from heaven by its four corners [Acts 10:11-16; 11:5].

GOD NOT A PARTNER OF EVIL

Therefore hearken unto me, ye men of understanding: far be it from God, that he should do wickedness; and from the Almighty, that he should commit iniquity. Job 34:10

Elihu, like Eliphaz, blames Job for his misfortune and vindicates God. Job has declared himself righteous and seemingly has accused God of having taken his righteousness from him and causing him to suffer. Moreover, Elihu accuses Job of being a companion of the workers of iniquity, of having walked with wicked men, and of having said that it profits man nothing that he should delight himself with God [verse 37].

Elihu, like Eliphaz, believes in the law of compensation; that is to say, every man is rewarded according to his works [verse 11]. He maintains that God does not pervert judgment. Moreover, Elihu believes that Job is receiving only what is due him and that his illness and his trials are the result of some evil deeds that he has done.

GOD SEES ALL AND KNOWS ALL

For his eyes are upon the ways of man, and he seeth all his goings. Job 34:21

Since in the realm of the Spirit there is no darkness, man's ways and deeds cannot be hidden from God, who knows all and sees all. Moreover, God cannot be blamed for man's difficulties and mishaps. They are the result of his own actions and wrong thinking.

When man does good he is bound to be rewarded with good, simply because God is total goodness. But when man does evil, he rewards himself with his evil deeds. God cannot reward anyone with that which he does not possess. For God is not the author of evil.

On the other hand, since God is all in all, he knows all and sees all. Nothing happens without his knowledge. Not even a sparrow or a hair falls without his being aware of it. When evil is done, he knows it and sees it, because anything evil is contrary to his nature [verses 24, 25].

GOD'S EYES ON THE RIGHTEOUS

He withdraweth not his eyes from the righteous: but with kings are they on the throne; yea, he doth establish them for ever, and they are exalted.   Job 36:7

The righteous are constantly before the eyes of God, who sees them and watches over them. God does not forsake the righteous or those who trust in him. The Lord knows the way of the righteous [Ps. 1:6]. The Lord upholds the righteous [Ps. 37:17]. "I have not seen the righteous forsaken" [Ps. 37:25].

Jesus, the only true, righteous, and sinless one in the eyes of God, was not forsaken. He was spared or kept to die on the cross in order to confirm the new gospel which heralded a new way by which to conquer the world—the way of meekness and gentleness, the way of forgiveness, the way which makes men and women free and worthy to be called the children of their Father.

THE RIGHTEOUS ARE DELIVERED

Desire not the night, when people are cut off in their place.
                                                    Job 36:20

The Eastern text reads: "He shall deliver you from those who drive you away in the night, and give peoples for your sake, and the nations for your life."

The reference here is to oppressors who strike during the dark hours of the night and carry away both people and plunder.

The Lord sustains those who trust in him. He delivers them, and he gives wicked people and nations for their sake.

See the commentary on Job 36:7.

GOD'S DWELLING PLACE

Also can any understand the spreadings of the clouds, or the noise of his tabernacle?
Behold, he spreadeth his light upon it, and covereth the bottom of the sea.   Job 36:29-30

In biblical days clouds were considered as the tabernacle or the dwelling place of God. This is because clouds are higher than the highest thing on earth and, in biblical terminology, they are symbolic of glory, honor, and majesty [Ps. 36:5].

The Lord called to Moses out of the cloud which had covered the top of Mount Sinai [Exod. 24:15-18]. "And the Lord descended in the cloud . . ." [Exod. 34:5]. Jesus ascended into heaven in a cloud [Acts 1:9].

The Aramaic reads, ". . . out of the greatness of his tabernacle." "Light," in this instance, means lightnings which lighten even the bottom of the sea.

GOD CARES FOR THE JUST
AND THE UNJUST

The noise thereof showeth concerning it, the cattle also concerning the vapor. Job 36:33

The Eastern text reads: "He shows his possessions [or substance] to his friends, and to the wicked also." The Aramaic word *kinyaney* (his possessions or wealth) also means "cattle." The meaning of this word is determined by the context. The Aramaic word *awaley* has been wrongly rendered "vapor."

What Elihu means here is that God is merciful to all his children— to the good and to the bad. God's blessings are shared with the good and the wicked, just as a human father shares his prosperity with both his obedient and disobedient children. Jesus said: "So that you may become sons of your Father who is in heaven, who causes his sun to shine upon the good and the bad, and who pours down his rain upon the just and the unjust" [Matt. 5:45, Eastern text].

God is patient with the wicked, just as a loving father is patient with his disobedient children. God knows that some of the wicked will see the light and turn from their evil. The thief repented while he was dying on the cross. Paul changed from a persecutor to a man of God, and St. Francis from a sinner to a saint [verse 10].

EQUINOX

How thy garments are warm, when he quieteth the earth by the south wind? Job 37:17

The reference here is to the equinox, when the earth changes its position in its orbit around the sun and the days become longer than the nights.

December is the coldest month in the year in the northern hemisphere, sun is then farthest southward. But after December 22, the rays of the sun begin to grow gradually warmer. Easterners wear woolen robes which are conductive to the heat of the sun's rays. One can feel the warmth of the sun in one's robe.

The Iranians celebrate the day when the light prevails against darkness and heat over cold. March 22 is called *Nowruz* (the new day). The year begins with the returning of the sun to the halfway point in the spring.

The date of Christmas coincides with the ancient Roman holiday celebrating the returning of the sun from its southward trend.

MAN'S KNOWLEDGE LIMITED

Hast thou with him spread out the sky, which is strong, and as a molten looking-glass?   Job 37:18

The last portion of this verse is mistranslated. The Aramaic words *lamsamakho akhda* mean "to support it together." The root of these words is *samak* (to support, lean upon, rely on). The words "looking glass" are not in the Eastern text. It should read: "Were you with him when he spread out the great sky, helping him hold it up?"

Elihu is trying to convince Job that man cannot grasp the wonders of God or make himself equivalent to him in wisdom, power, and majesty. Man is a creature and not a creator, and cannot know the secrets of the complex universe.

GOLD GLEAMS OUT OF THE NORTH

Fair weather cometh out of the north: with God is terrible majesty.   Job 37:22

The Aramaic word *dahba,* pronounced *dahwah,* means "gold." The Eastern text reads: "Golden gleams come out of the north; and light shines from God"; that is, "Out of the northern regions come golden gleams and light of truth and understanding from God."

In biblical days, most of the gold came from Tarshish, Assyria, and other lands north of Palestine [Gen. 2:11]. There is no mention of gold mines in Palestine. Some gold came from Ethiopia.

Gold symbolizes purity, truth, and light. Metaphorically, gold means understanding and enlightenment. This is because through the light of God we are able to see gleams of truth.

EARTH WITH END

Whereupon are the foundations thereof fastened? or who laid the corner stone thereof.   Job 38:6

The Aramaic word *ebreh* means "the ends thereof." The Aramaic word for "foundations thereof" is *shatisaw*. The author here is speaking of the limits of the earth. Job, like all other men, wondered about the earth's outer ends and the vastness of the universe. This question was never answered by the ancient savants. Even today, most of the universe is a mystery to man.

Not until Columbus crossed the Atlantic Ocean did man accept the earth as being round. Our earth was supposed to be flat and endless. In the olden days the Atlantic Ocean was looked upon as the end of the world. But as man's knowledge grew, his concept of the earth and the universe grew also, and it still continues to grow.

Job believed the earth was hanging in the air. "He stretches out the north from the empty place, and hangs the earth upon nothing" [Job 26:7, Eastern text]. But the size and the limits of the globe were a great mystery to Job.

STAR'S SONG

When the morning stars sang together, and all the sons of God shouted for joy?   Job 38:7

"Stars sang" is an Aramaic idiom meaning that the stars radiated abundant light. Moreover, Easterners, when describing harmony and beauty, describe them in poetic and figurative speech.

Stars are likened to human beings, singing and guiding men when traveling in the deserts. Stars are very brilliant in the Arabian desert, and as they appear close to the earth on the horizon, they seem almost to beckon one.

Moreover, it is often said that nature sings, which means nature is harmonious. Then again, the people speak of stars as walking before men, which means men follow the direction of the stars. All the dwellers of the desert travel by the means of the stars [Matt. 2:2].

In the olden days, stars were associated with the birth of kings and great men, and they shared in their victories. This is why the pagans worshiped the stars. "There shall come a Star out of Jacob" [Num. 24:17]. The star, in this instance, means a king; hence, the Messiah— Jesus Christ.

When the sons of God (good men) live in peace and harmony, all nature shares in their joy.

All nature declares the glory of God and sings praises to his name. Nature songs and praises are conveyed in music, beauty, and harmony, and not in words.

WILD GOATS

Their young ones are in good liking, they grow up with corn; they go forth, and return not unto them. Job 39:4

"Corn" is wrong. The wild goats do not feed on corn.

It should read: "They bring up their young ones, until they grow up and are weaned." When the young wild goats are grown up and able to take care of themselves, they are weaned and let go on their own.

BEHEMOTH PROTECTS HELPLESS ANIMALS

Surely the mountains bring him forth food, where all the beasts of the field play. Job 40:20

The Eastern text reads: "He roams about the mountains, and all the wild beasts of the field lie down under his protection."

The reference is to the behemoth (hippopotamus) which, in olden days, was difficult to catch [verses 15-19].

The hippopotamus fights lions, tigers, and large snakes. Wherever the hippopotamus is, the other beasts of the field graze in peace.

NOT AFRAID OF RIVERS

Behold, he drinketh up a river, and hasteth not: he trusteth that he can draw up Jordan into his mouth. Job 40:23

Behemoth is another name for hippopotamus. The Eastern text reads: "Behold, if he plunges into the river, he is not afraid; he is confident, though the Jordan reaches to his mouth."

The hippopotamus is a land and water animal, and it might have flourished in the marshes of the Jordan when the Hebrew patriarchs lived in Palestine. But today, there are none to be found in the Jordan Valley. The writer of the book of Job might have seen the huge animal somewhere else or even heard of it from travelers. The Jordan is the largest river in Palestine, and was well known to the people.

When guns were unknown, a hippopotamus was hard to catch. Spears, arrows, and nets had no effect on him. The animal's skin was too tough for arrows and spears, and its body too large and powerful to be dragged into a net. Therefore, in those early days, a hippopotamus was a great wonder. But today, in the face of modern weapons, he is as helpless as any other animal.

LIMITATION OF HUMAN KNOWLEDGE

Will he make a covenant with thee? wilt thou take him for a servant for ever?   Job 41:4

The Eastern text reads: "Will he make a covenant with you? Or will you count him as a servant for ever?"

The Lord speaks of the strength of the hippopotamus and the impossibility of it being trained by men, like a bird that is trained.

Yet, this large animal is just one of the smallest of God's wonders which man cannot understand or overcome. God revealed to Job how little man knows about the things that are around him, and how many things are beyond his human comprehension.

THE DAY, THE END, THE GLORY

And he called the name of the first, Jemima; and the name of the second, Kezia; and the name of the third, Keren-happuch.
                                                    Job 42:14

Emama (Jemima) means "day, midday, noontide." When his daughter *Emama* (Jemima) was born, Job was living in a new and bright day. The days of his suffering, poverty, and humiliation were past, just as night flees before the dawn.

In the East, most of the names of men and women are significant of events which took place when the person was born. Nearly all biblical names have meanings.

Kesoaa (Kezia) is derived from the Aramaic *kesa* or Hebrew *kaseh,* "the end." The name of this second child signifies the end of Job's trials, tribulations, and misfortunes. Job has come through his trials and sufferings victoriously.

Karna-pokh (Keren-happuch) is a construct state noun meaning, "My glory (horn) has returned to me."

The horn is symbolic of strength and glory. Job's glory and his power were lost during his trials and afflictions, but now his fortunes had returned. Job was once more healthy and wealthy, and had a better understanding of God. The Lord had given him more sons and daughters, and his neighbors had given him gold and silver, and the Lord had increased his substance abundantly.

CHAPTER SIXTEEN

PSALMS

INTRODUCTION

No BOOK in the Old Testament has received such world-wide use as the book of Psalms. Indeed, this sacred portion of the Holy Scriptures has been an integral part of the prayer books of all Christian denominations and is highly revered. For centuries, many men and women have turned to its pages for devotion, inspiration and consolation.

The Psalms, Aramaic *Mazmorey*, derived from *zamar* (to sing praises), Hebrew *mazmar* or *tallim*, came through divine inspiration and, in the course of time, became the inspired songs, praises and fervent prayers of Israel, and later of the Christian religion.

For instance, the Twenty-third Psalm, a Psalm of David, is revered and read by millions of people of many races. This psalm is a praise and prayer wherein God, the Creator of the universe, is portrayed as a loving shepherd, who cares for his flocks day and night, and the people as sheep which need direction, protection and guidance.

Moreover, the book of Psalms, like the books of the Prophets, contains messianic prophecies. The author, King David, foresaw the rejection and the suffering of Christ and His moral victory over death and Sheol.

Apparently, most of the psalms were composed by King David and later written by the court scribes. Some of them were composed during his early youth when he wandered on the hills of Judah and in the desert feeding sheep.

Indeed, David, like many Eastern shepherds, was a poet-musician who spent many of his lonely hours singing, playing music on the harp or lyre, and composing new songs. It was during these lonely hours in the solitude of the hills and valleys that David saw the heavens declare the glory of God and the works of His hand reveal the firmament. Later, he played music before King Saul. The psalms of David were sung and resung, again and again; sometimes by the shepherds, then by the new poets and by the temple singers. Some of the Psalms represent the prayers of Israel for deliverance from her oppressors; others, the joy of triumph over her enemies.

Many of the psalms were composed during the reign of King Hezekiah, some during the exile in Babylon and others at the time of Maccabees, when Israel was harassed by her enemies round about.

The first inspired folk song was the Song of Moses when the Israelites crossed the Red Sea and Pharaoh's army was destroyed. Miriam, his sister, and many women with timbrels danced when this song was sung. We have the Song of Deborah which was composed by Deborah when King Nabin was defeated by Barak. Then we have the inspired Lamentations of Jeremiah, which is a wailing song composed when Jerusalem and the holy temple were destroyed by the Chaldean army.

The book of Psalms is divided into five *seprey* (books), and every book is divided into several *holalies* (praises and hallelujahs). Some of the praises were accompanied with the musical instruments such as psaltry, guitar, and lyre, but most of them were sung without instruments. They were also songs which were used during battle.

COUNSEL OF THE WICKED

Blessed is the man that walketh not in the counsel of the ungodly, nor standeth in the way of sinners, nor sitteth in the seat of the scornful.   Ps. 1:1

The Aramaic word *reyana* means "counsel, decision." This phrase should read: ". . . nor abides by the counsel of sinners." That is, when the sinners plot to do evil, he does not agree with them, nor does he participate in their evil deeds.

One cannot help but find himself in the company of the ungodly, but he should not agree with them when he sees that they are conspiring against their neighbors or plotting to commit crimes against the weak and the poor.

REVOLT OF KINGS

The kings of the earth set themselves, and the rulers take counsel together, against the Lord, and against his Anointed, saying.

Ps. 2:2

The Aramaic word *kam* means "to stand up, rise up, conspire, revolt, halt." In this instance *kam* means "to conspire."

This is a messianic psalm which foretold the rejection and the suffering of Jesus Christ. And it also reminds us about his humanity.

The messianic kingdom with its new laws and its moral principles was opposed by the princes and the kings of this world, because Jesus

Christ tried to cut off their bands and remove their harsh yoke from the people. They revolted because they did not want to come under the bonds of the Spirit and the easy yoke of God [verse 3]. But, at last, Christ's dominion reached to the ends of the earth.

CHRIST FORETOLD

I will declare the decree: the Lord hath said unto me, Thou art my Son; this day have I begotten thee.   Ps. 2:7

The Aramaic reads: "To declare my promise (or covenant). . . ." The reference is to the divine promises which were made by God to Adam and Eve, and to Abraham and David.

"Begotten" should not be taken literally. God neither begets nor is begotten. God is not a man; God is the Eternal Spirit. Begotten here means "made manifest." Messiah Christ existed in the mind of God from the very beginning. John tells us, "The Word [Christ] was in the beginning, and that very Word was with God, and God was that Word" [John 1:1].

Messiah Christ is the eternal promise of God which became manifested in the fullness of time. God, before time, knew man would go astray from the true path of life; therefore, Christ was the preordained promise of God to save mankind. See 1 Peter 1:20.

SPIRITUAL KINGDOM AND SONSHIP

Ask of me, and I shall give thee the heathen for thine inheritance, and the uttermost parts of the earth for thy possession.

Ps. 2:8

The messianic kingdom would have dominion over all the world. But the kingdom is to be a spiritual kingdom that will embrace all nations and peoples of the world.

This universal kingdom was envisioned by the Hebrew prophets, who hailed the Messiah as an Everlasting King. Both the Messiah and his eternal kingdom can only be understood spiritually. Daniel calls it the stone not cut by human hand, which in due time would destroy the realms of the Gentiles and establish the reign of justice and peace.

The word son in Aramaic means "an image or likeness of the father." But it is often used metaphorically, meaning "love." When Easterners love and trust one another, they call each other "my son." This is because a good son occupies the highest place in the heart of his father. God called Solomon "my son." The term son is applied also to members of the same faith.

God is Spirit, and Messiah Christ is his spiritual and eternal son and the heir to the kingdom. God made manifest his love to humanity through Messiah, his son.

KISS THE SON

Kiss the Son, lest he be angry, and ye perish from the way, when his wrath is kindled but a little. Blessed are all they that put their trust in him. Ps. 2:12

"Kiss" in this instance means "to do obeisance." Easterners kiss the hands of noblemen, princes, and holy men, and they bow to them as a token of homage. Then again, during the service, they bow and kiss holy objects as a token of reverence to the holy place where God's name is invoked and prayers offered to him. A kiss is also a sign of approval.

"The Son" here means the Messiah Christ. The people are admonished to acknowledge him, do homage to him, and put their trust in him, so that they may not go astray from his way and bring wrath upon themselves.

COMFORTED ME

Hear me when I call, O God of my righteousness: thou hast enlarged me when I was in distress; have mercy upon me, and hear my prayer. Ps. 4:1

The Eastern text reads: "When I have called thee, thou hast answered me . . . thou hast comforted me when I was in distress . . ."

The Aramaic word *beaolsan* means "distress"; that is, "mental pain" or "pressures of danger." And the Aramaic *arwakht li* means "Thou has comforted me," or relieved me of the anxieties, troubles, and dangers of this life.

The Psalmist proves that God's guidance and help are always ready for those who seek his help with a sincere heart. Then again, the Psalmist had had some experience with God, who had answered his prayers before.

ANGER WITHOUT A CAUSE

Stand in awe, and sin not: commune with your own heart upon your bed, and be still. Selah. Ps. 4:4

Aramaic *regaz* means "be angry." This phrase should read: "Be angry and yet sin not."

Sin in this instance refers to crime. When men are angry at one another, they may strike with a dagger or sword. Anger cannot be easily repressed or controlled, but by meditation and examination of one's own heart, one can agree with his adversary and solve any problem. This is because at times anger is provoked by misunderstanding and may actually have no basis in reason.

Hasty wrath may lead to murder. In other words, anger is the trigger of quarrels and murders. Jesus said, "But I say to you that whoever becomes angry with his brother for no reason is guilty before the court" [Matt. 5:22, Eastern text].

SACRIFICE OF RIGHTEOUSNESS

Offer the sacrifices of righteousness, and put your trust in the Lord.   Ps. 4:5

"The sacrifices of righteousness" in this instance refers to mercy and justice. The Hebrew prophets condemned the animal sacrifices simply because some of the men and women who offered them defrauded the widows, oppressed the poor, and took bribes.

The sacrifices were supposed to absolve the guilty. "The sacrifices of the wicked are an abomination to the Lord; but the prayer of the upright is his delight" [Prov. 15:8, Eastern text].

The psalmist exhorts the people to offer sacrifices of righteousness rather than sacrifice animals. Pagan gods delighted in wickedness, immorality, and human sacrifices. But the God of Israel hates all false worship and the works of iniquity.

Isaiah condemns the multitude of sacrifices: He says, "Of what purpose is the multitude of your sacrifices to me? says the Lord; I am full of the burnt offerings of rams, and the fat of fed beasts; and I do not delight in the blood of bullocks, or of lambs, or of he-goats . . . I do not eat that which is obtained wrongfully, and taken by force" [Isa. 1:11-13, Eastern text; see also Jer. 6:20].

WEEPING BITTERLY

I am weary with my groaning; all the night make I my bed to swim; I water my couch with my tears.   Ps. 6:6

". . . I water my bed and wash my mattress with my tears" is an Aramaic idiom which means, "I was so sorrowful that I wept all night." The Aramaic word *arsi* means "mattress." These sayings are still used today and are never taken literally. We often say, "Rivers of water poured out of my eyes."

This psalm was composed by David when he was in distress because of his sin. He had done away with one of his most faithful soldiers, Uriah [2 Sam. 11:15-17].

King David wept vehemently and repented for his sin, and the Lord forgave him [Ps. 42:3; Isa. 25:8].

GOD IS A RIGHTEOUS JUDGE

God judgeth the righteous, and God is angry with the wicked every day.   Ps. 7:11

The Eastern text reads: "God is a righteous judge; yea he is not angry every day." The translators confused *la* (not) for *leh* (him or his). The Aramaic word for "judge" is *diana,* and the Aramaic word for "judgment" is *dina.* Both words are written alike, but pronounced differently.

The Psalmist here compares God with an earthly judge who at times is very angry. This is more true of the judges in the East in olden days, who were not paid for their services but were allowed to exact all they could get from the men who came before them seeking justice.

The judges' demurrers were always serious. They were angry in order to frighten the disputants and thus exact more money and bribes from them.

"The Lord is merciful and gracious, slow to anger and plenteous in mercy" [Ps. 103:8, Eastern text].

God will judge the wicked, but not the righteous. Only those who have broken the law are tried before an earthly judge. Then again, God being a loving Father, his anger does not abide but a minute. We often portray God as angry, happy, sorry, and jealous simply because men have all these attributes. In other words, God is often pictured as a king, an angry judge, and a warrior. The word wicked is not in the original text; as is indicated in the King James Version by printing it in italics.

SUCKLINGS

Out of the mouth of babes and sucklings hast thou ordained strength because of thine enemies, that thou mightest still the enemy and the avenger.   Ps. 8:2

"Sucklings" is used allegorically to mean "unlearned." In the East, ignorant and illiterate men are often called sucklings or babes. One often hears people say: "You are still a child (or a babe); you have no understanding."

Children and babies are innocent and more ready to accept the truth. Jesus thanked God for the simple men and women who accepted him. "I thank thee, O my Father, Lord of heaven and earth, because thou hast hidden these things from the wise and the men of understanding, and hast revealed them to children" [Matt. 11:25; Luke 10:21].

The truth is often hidden from those who depend alone on human reason, but is revealed to those who, like little children, are willing to learn and are pure in heart.

The Hebrews as a race were humble and trying to seek God's truth and his way. They were a pastoral people whom God called out of other races to praise his name and to proclaim it throughout the world. Not one of Jesus' disciples was a highly educated man. Matthew was the only one who could read and write; the others were unlearned peasants and fishermen who were looked upon by the scribes and Pharisees almost as outcasts.

It was out of the mouths of these men, whose minds were virgin, that the gospel of good news was to be preached and the things which were hidden from the wise and the prudent revealed, so that the learned men could not say they were the founders of the new religion. The glory and honor were given to God.

SON OF MAN

What is man, that thou art mindful of him? and the son of man, that thou visitest him? Ps. 8:4

Aramaic *nasha* (man) is derived from *naphsha* (soul, life, breath). This is because God breathed into Adam's nostrils, and Adam (red soil) became a living soul.

"Son of man" is used frequently in some of the books of the Bible, denoting man's origin—made from the earth, hence weak [Job 25:6]. The term son of man was used to distinguish between mortal man and the immortal spirits and angels, and to point out that man is not God but a weak creature when compared with God.

Ninety times Ezekiel is called "son of man," a human being. Jesus used the term about eighty times. This is because he was human and divine even though in his deity was God. Daniel saw a resemblance "like the Son of man," which means "like a human being" [Dan. 7:13].

GOD FORSAKES NOT THE RIGHTEOUS

And they that know thy name will put their trust in thee: for thou, Lord, hast not forsaken them that seek thee. Ps. 9:10

Easterners never think of God as forsaking them. They forsake God, but they know that he never forsakes them. During times of trouble and trial they always call on God. And when God is slow in answering them they ask death and curse the day in which they were born. "When the poor and needy seek water, and there is none . . . I the God of Israel will not forsake them" [Isa. 41:17, Eastern text].

God never forsakes those who trust in him and defend his cause. See the commentary on "Forsake."

LIFT UP THINE HAND

Arise, O Lord; O God, lift up thine hand: forget not the humble.
Ps. 10:12

"Lift up thine hand" is an Eastern saying which means "fight." When the people speak of a coward, they say, "He cannot lift up his hand."

Easterners, when quarreling, raise their hands as an expression of threatening. We often say, "He has lifted up his hand (or stretched forth his hand) against him" [Luke 22:53].

Paul says that he wishes men would lift up their hands in prayer and not in anger [1 Tim. 2:8].

The psalmist implores God to fight against the wicked, to avenge the poor, and not to forget the humble [verses 13-18].

DOUBLE HEART

They speak vanity every one with his neighbor: with flattering lips and with a double heart do they speak.
Ps. 12:2

"Double heart" is an Aramaic idiom which means hypocritical or insincere; we would say "two-faced."

In the olden days the heart was considered the seat of man's faculties. The term *reyana* (mind) was rarely used in biblical days. At that time life was supposed to be in the blood, and blood passes through the heart.

"But the Lord looketh on the heart" [1 Sam. 16:7]. "A man's heart deviseth his way" [Prov. 16:9].

"Not of double heart" [1 Chron. 12:33] means "sincere, unequivocal, determined."

ANCIENT PUNISHMENT

The Lord shall cut off all flattering lips, and the tongue that speaketh proud things:
Who have said, With our tongue will we prevail; our lips are our own: who is lord over us?
Ps. 12:3-4

"Cut off the lips" is an Eastern saying still in common use. Here the phrase means that God will silence the speech of deceptive men and of those who magnify themselves and utter proud things against God.

In the East, lips, tongues, ears, and noses of culprits and blasphemers were cut off. This form of punishment was prevalent until recent days.

DEVOUR PEOPLE

Have all the workers of iniquity no knowledge? who eat up my people as they eat bread, and call not upon the Lord. Ps. 14:4

Those who "eat up" or "devour my people" are those who oppress and exploit them. In the East, when the people are misgoverned, heavily taxed, and oppressed, it is said, "They have been eaten." When money or other property is embezzled, the people say, "They have eaten the money."

Jesus said, "Woe to you, scribes and Pharisees, hypocrites! for ye devour [*akhliton,* you eat] widows' houses, and for a pretence make long prayer" [Matt. 23:14].

The poor and the needy were oppressed and exploited by those in power who never even remembered the name of God.

CUP OF GOODNESS

The Lord is the portion of mine inheritance and of my cup: thou maintainest my lot.

The lines are fallen unto me in pleasant places; yea, I have a goodly heritage. Ps. 16:5-6

"Cup" is often used metaphorically, signifying trials and uncertainties. In the East, when a man wanted to do away with his enemies or rivals, he invited them to a banquet and poisoned their cup. The fearful and doubtful guests all had to drink from it.

Jesus referred to his arrest at the garden as the "cup." "The cup which my Father hath given me, shall I not drink it?" [John 18:11]. Then again, he said, "Let this cup pass from me: nevertheless not as I will, but as thou wilt" [Matt. 26:39].

The cup which the psalmist speaks of here, however, is the cup of goodness. The Lord's cup is the portion of his goodness and his loving-kindness to those who trust in him and walk in his way. The psalmist is mindful of God's deliverance of Israel from her enemies and the portion of the land which fell to her in good places. Palestine served as a bridge between Egypt and the Fertile Crescent.

HOPE

Therefore my heart is glad, and my glory rejoiceth: my flesh also shall rest in hope. Ps. 16:9

The Aramaic word *sabra* (hope) is derived from *sabar* (to hope, trust, expect) and should not be confused with *sabar* (imagination, illusion, uncertain thought). *Sabra* as used by the psalmist means "expectation of something that will surely come to pass."

The same root *sabar* means "to proclaim good tidings, the gospel." When hope is assured, good tidings are proclaimed or preached. The Aramaic word for gospel is *sebarta* (preaching full of hope).

SHADOW OF THE WINGS

Keep me as the apple of the eye; hide me under the shadow of thy wings. Ps. 17:8

The Hebrew prophets and poets used figurative speech in order to convey the truth to unlearned listeners.

"Wings" in Aramaic are symbolic of protection and speed. During times of danger, cold, and heat, the little birds take refuge under their mother's wings. Her wings offer protection from the early morning cold and the heat of the day. Moreover, when the little ones are menaced by birds of prey they gather under the mother's wings.

The psalmist pictures God as a bird that is constantly mindful of its brood, and ever ready to offer them a shelter when they are in danger.

God has neither feathers nor wings, but his counsel and truth offer an everlasting protection to those who are weary and in danger. In Psalm 91:4 we read: "He shall cover thee with his feathers, and under his wings shalt thou trust: his truth shall be thy shield and buckler."

POSSESSIONS OF THE WICKED

From men which are thy hand, O Lord, from men of the world, which have their portion in this life, and whose belly thou fillest with thy hid treasure: they are full of children, and leave the rest of their substance to their babes. Ps. 17:14

The Eastern text reads: "From the dead that die by thy hand, O Lord; and from the dead of the grave, divide their possessions among the living; fill their belly with thy treasure, so that their children are satisfied and have a portion remaining for their own children."

The psalmist implores God to divide the possessions of the wicked who are slain, among the righteous who are living, so that they may have plenty and leave some of it to their children, that they may, in turn, leave it to their children.

In the olden days, plagues and catastrophes were attributed to the wrath of God.

LIFE HEREAFTER

As for me, I will behold thy face in righteousness: I shall be satisfied, when I awake, with thy likeness. Ps. 17:15

The doctrine of the resurrection was prevalent among the Israelites. The Living God of Israel was the God of the living, and not the God of the dead [Matt. 22:32; Mark 12, 26, 27; Luke 20:37-38]. The Hebrews in their prayers reminded God of his divine promises to their fathers. They also believed that the souls of their fathers were living and that they could intercede on their behalf.

The psalmist believes in a spiritual resurrection; that is, the immortality of the soul. This is because the soul is indestructible. The dead will awake with a spiritual likeness like that of God. We can behold God's majesty only with spiritual eyes and with a spiritual understanding. It is the Spirit which gives life, and the Spirit which seeks God [Job 19:25-27; Dan. 12:2].

ROCK—PROTECTION

The Lord is my rock, and my fortress, and my deliverer; my God, my strength, in whom I will trust; my buckler, and the horn of my salvation, and my high tower. Ps. 18:2

The Aramaic word *takipa* means "the strong one, strength." The reference here is to God, whose strength never fails.

At times "rock" is used figuratively, meaning "strength and protection." In Psalm 31:3, God is called *Beth-gosa* (the house of refuge); it has been rendered "fortress."

In the East, during severe storms and whirlwinds, the shepherds take refuge under rocks [Ps. 18:31; Isa. 17:10].

FLOODS OF TROUBLES

The sorrows of death compassed me, and the floods of ungodly
men made me afraid.   Ps. 18:4

The word translated "floods" in the King James Version signifies difficulties and troubles. Easterners, when speaking of difficult problems and
troubles often depict themselves as surrounded with rushing floods of
water or in the bottom of the sea.

David offers thanks to God who had delivered him from his enemies
and for his goodness to him when he was surrounded with difficulties [Ps.
116:3-4].

THICK DARKNESS

He made darkness his secret place; his pavilion round about
him were dark waters and thick clouds of the skies.   Ps. 18:11

When the Lord descended upon Mount Sinai in fire, the smoke of
the mountain ascended as the smoke of a furnace [Exod. 19:18; Deut.
4:11].

"The darkness" in this instance is symbolic of God's secret place.
No one was to see his face, so that no one could make an image of
the Lord. They saw his glory and heard his voice, but no one beheld
his face [Deut. 4:15-16].

The glory of God was revealed in a cloud upon Mount Sinai. In
Semitic languages "cloud" is symbolic of glory, protection, and omnipresence: "Clouds and darkness are round about him" [Ps. 97:2]. ". . .
who makest the clouds his chariot" [Ps. 104:3]. Jesus is to come in the
clouds of heaven [Matt. 24:30; Mark 13:26].

See the article on "Cloud."

SHUN THE CROOKED

With the pure thou wilt show thyself pure; and with the froward
thou wilt show thyself froward.   Ps. 18:26

The Aramaic word used here is *titpatal* instead of *titaakam* [2 Sam.
22:27].

Patal has many meanings, such as "twist, awry, crooked, forward,
shifty, perverse." But in colloquial speech it means "to shift to one
side, to get out of the way, to turn aside."

This verse should read: "With the clean thou shalt be clean; and from the crooked thou shalt turn aside."

CANDLE GOD'S LIGHT

For thou wilt light my candle: the Lord my God will enlighten my darkness.   Ps. 18:28

"Candle" symbolizes light, truth, and understanding. It is also used metaphorically to mean "an heir." Moreover, light is symbolic of enlightenment, and darkness is symbolic of ignorance.

The true religion of Israel was the light of God which enlightened the dark paths of Israel. As long as this Lamp was burning, the people were happy, prosperous, secure, and full of hope. At times the light of God was temporarily put out by wicked priests, kings, and princes.

This psalm was composed and sung by David as a thanksgiving to God for all his goodness and for the favors he had received during his life. The king implores the Lord to lighten his darkness, remove the dark spots in his life, and grant that his heirs will sit upon the throne of Israel and reign with justice and righteousness.

BRIDEGROOM COMING OUT

Which is as a bridegroom coming out of his chamber, and rejoiceth as a strong man to run a race.   Ps. 19:5

Wedding feasts in the East last from three to seven days, according to the social standing of the bridegroom and the bride [Judg. 14:10].

During the festivities both the bridegroom and the bride remain in the house, surrounded by men and women who dance, eat, drink, and make merry. As the houses are small, some men and women cannot get in, especially the poor, for only those who bring food as gifts can enter and leave freely [Matt. 10:12].

All of those who have been unable to enter into the house wait outside to have a glimpse of the bridegroom when he comes out and walks a distance to refresh himself. In some lands in the East, toilets are still unknown. The bride goes out when it is dark, accompanied by her bridesmaids.

The people rejoice when they see the bridegroom dressed in his wedding garments and ornaments. The bride is covered with a large and long veil [Isa. 61:10].

INSTRUCTION TO YOUNG MEN

The law of the Lord is perfect, converting the soul: the testimony of the Lord is sure, making wise the simple.   Ps. 19:7

The Aramaic word *yalodey* means "children, youths." The term "simple" can be applied also to mean "not intelligent."

In the East, children are taught the law and are required by their teachers to recite it orally. The Law of Moses and the Ten Commandments were one of the first things taught to the Hebrew children. "Hear, O Israel: the Lord our God is one Lord" [Deut. 6:4; Mark 12:29].

The law of the Lord is simple; it is perfect and free from ambiguities and qualifying clauses that would obscure the truth and pervert justice. No other law is truer and plainer than the Law of Moses [verse 9].

REVERENCE OF THE LORD

The fear of the Lord is clean, enduring for ever: the judgments of the Lord are true and righteous altogether.   Ps. 19:9

The word translated "fear" in the King James Version in many instances should read "reverence"; that is, "the reverence of the Lord."

Easterners, when entering into the presence of a king, a prince, or a nobleman, stand in awe as a token of reverence to him because he is the representative of a race or nation. This custom prevails even today. Ministers and high state dignitaries drop to their knees when they pay their respect to the king.

The word "clean" here means "sincere"; that is, without any political or selfish motive. The homage paid to princes and kings is often insincere, motivated by selfish desire for favors and political advantages. But the Ruler of the universe is just, and his decrees are righteous. What he demands from men is purity, a sincere heart, and love and devotion to him and to their neighbors.

DESTINY

My God, my God, why hast thou forsaken me? why art thou so far from helping me, and from the words of my roaring?

Ps. 22:1

The Aramaic word *shabak* means "to keep, leave, forgive, allow, desert." One has to know how the word is used in order to know its true meaning. The Aramaic-speaking people often say: "Leave me bread." "They have killed the men but left the women." "Forgive them." "Allow them to do it." The word is *shabak* in all these instances.

The Aramaic word for "forsake" is *taaa,* which has only one meaning. Another word is *nesha.* Joseph called the name of his firstborn *Manashey* from *nesha* (to forsake, forget) [Gen. 41:51].

Israelites were never forsaken by God, they had forsaken him.

The Hebrew writers used Aramaic and Hebrew indiscriminately. Aramaic was the language of the early Hebrews, the language of the exiles, and the vernacular of the Jews during the time of Jesus and for many centuries after Jesus. It is still used today.

The Hebrew Scriptures used the word *azabatani* which, just like Aramaic, means "to leave"; that is, "to let me leave."

Moreover, Easterners never think of God as deserting them, but are impatient when their prayers are not granted immediately. In time of persecution, oppression, and grief, they ask God to take them away. They wonder why they are allowed to live. At times, they say, "O God, take me away. I am not better than my father." Just as Elijah, Job sought death, but never thought God had forsaken him [Job 3:1-8]. Jeremiah cursed the day wherein he was born [Jer. 20:14-18]. The psalmist is weary of life. Because God has not granted his prayers, he is pursued by his enemies and is discovered.

This verse should read: "My God, my God, why hast thou let me live? and yet thou hast delayed my salvation from me, because of the words of my folly."

TRUSTING IN THE LORD

He trusted on the Lord that he would deliver him: let him deliver him, seeing he delighted in him.   Ps. 22:8

This is a reference to the Messiah, the One ordained by the Lord.

Messiah would trust on the Lord to carry out his difficult mission. He would conquer the world by the Spirit of the Lord, rather than by the arm of man and the weapons of war.

Jesus trusted in the Lord. His faith in God never wavered, not even during his trial or when he was suffering on the cross. Even when he was dying, he said, "Father, into thy hands I commit my spirit" [Luke 23:46]. The priests, Pharisees, Sadducees, and scribes who stood near the cross said, "He trusted in God; let him deliver him now, if he will have him: for he said, I am the Son of God" [Matt. 27:43].

God never forsakes those who trust in him and die for his cause. Jesus on the cross, according to the Aramaic text, cried, "My God, my God, for this I was spared! (or kept)" [Matt. 27:46, Eastern text], which means, "This was my destiny." In other words, Jesus was allowed to suffer as a man, and God did not interfere. Jesus suffered and died as a man, and God was with him, but God did not suffer nor was he buried.

All other versions read: "Why hast thou forsaken me?" This saying is contrary to all Scriptures, for God forsakes no one. He even seeks those who have gone astray; because God is a loving Father, always mindful of his children, and always with those who devote their lives to the spreading of his Word. See 1 Peter 1:19-20.

VICIOUS MEN

For dogs have compassed me: the assembly of the wicked have inclosed me: they pierced my hands and my feet.   Ps. 22:16

The word translated "dogs" in the King James Version is used metaphorically, meaning "vicious men or oppressors." See, for instance, verse 20 (Eastern text): "Deliver my soul from the sword, my only one from the hand of the vicious (dog)."

In the East the shepherd dogs are very vicious. They fight for the sheep against wolves and bears. They devour strangers who dare to approach the flock.

Wicked and vicious men and gossipmongers are often called dogs. Paul in his Epistle to the Philippians exhorts the Christians to beware of dogs; that is, to beware of vicious men, those who assassinate others by means of destructive gossip [Phil. 3:2].

Western commentators who do not understand the metaphor believe the Easterners hate dogs. Dogs are loved by the shepherds and by sheepowners, but in the East, dogs stay with the sheep. They are not kept in houses.

IMMORTALITY

All they that be fat upon earth shall eat and worship: all they that go down to the dust shall bow before him: and none can keep alive his own soul.   Ps. 22:29

The Hebrews, as well as neighboring peoples in Palestine, Assyria, and Egypt, had some glimpse of immortality. The prophets of Israel knew that man's spirit is eternal and indestructible and that there is a resurrection for the good as well as for the bad, so that they might receive their rewards. But the conception of resurrection and life eternal was not crystallized until the time of the captivity. The prophet Daniel was the greatest advocator of the resurrection.

The psalmist believed in immortality. The Eastern text of this verse reads: "All they that are hungry [for truth] upon earth shall eat and worship before the Lord; all they that are buried shall kneel before him; my soul is alive to him." And Job 7:7 in the Eastern text reads: "O remember that the spirit is still alive; even yet my eye shall again see good."

Fat is a mistranslation in the King James Version. The Aramaic word *kapneh* means "the hungry." The Aramaic word for fat is *patmey*. The error might have been due to the confusion of these two words or to defects in the manuscript. No Hebrew psalmist would have used the word fat in this verse. The term fat is often used in referring to wealthy, wicked men who confiscate the property of the poor.

"Hungry" does not always mean hunger for food; it may mean hunger for justice and truth.

The psalmist, according to the King James Version, here denies resurrection.

"Blessed are those who hunger and thirst for justice, for they shall be well satisfied" [Matt. 5:6, Eastern text].

POSTERITY

A seed shall serve him; it shall be accounted to the Lord for a generation.   Ps. 22:30

This is a messianic psalm. Seed here means posterity. The reference here is to the generations to come who would serve Christ and declare his righteousness and his wonders to generations which were yet to be born after them.

TREATMENT OF ENEMIES

Thou preparest a table before me in the presence of mine enemies: thou anointest my head with oil; my cup runneth over.
Ps. 23:5

Easterners are more generous in entertaining their enemies than their friends. They believe friends are always friends, but enemies must be won by means of hospitality, gifts, and favors. "If you meet your enemy's ox or his ass going astray, you shall surely bring it back to him again" [Exod. 23:4, Eastern text].

In the East, tales of hospitality and lavish entertainments are handed down from one generation to another. When an enemy is entertained, piles of bread and dishes of diverse foods are placed before him to convince him that the host loves him and honors him. But if the bread and other foods are not abundant, the guest will rejoice to see that his enemy is so poor that he cannot entertain him lavishly.

Some of the men, when entertaining their enemies, borrow dishes, bread, and other food just to embarrass them and heap coals of fire upon their heads.

"If your enemy be hungry, give him bread to eat; and if he be thirsty, give him water to drink; for when you shall do these things for him, you will heap coals of fire upon his head, and the Lord will reward you" [Prov. 25:21-22, Eastern text].

Good deeds and kindness destroy enmity and bring enduring reconciliation. Acts speak louder and are more powerful than words. Jesus said, "Let your light so shine before men that they may see your good works and glorify your Father in heaven" [Matt. 5:16, Eastern text].

AN ANCIENT BELIEF

For he hath founded it upon the seas, and established it upon the floods.
                                                                              Ps. 24:2

The Hebrews, like other wandering tribal people and small nations, believed that the earth was somehow stretched out upon the waters. In those early days people seldom traveled far away from their own lands, nor did they communicate with the distant nations. In some instances they saw only as far as the horizon and what they saw appeared to be flat and surrounded by the great seas and oceans.

The small races and nations who lived in semidesert lands tending their sheep and cattle had no time to study astronomy neither did they care whether the earth was flat or round. Their main concern was grass and water for their flocks and herds.

The astronomical and geographical research was conducted by the Assyrian, Babylonian, and Egyptian savants, who wanted to solve their agriculture problems. It was they who were responsible for our calendars and the division of time into months, weeks, and hours. It was they who invented alphabets to record time and events. Most of the astronomical and geographical and other scientific knowledge which the tribal people possessed was borrowed from the great nations round about them.

Job states that the earth hangs in the sky [26:7]. The Assyrians and Babylonians who gave us our calendars must have known that the earth was round and that it was not the center of the universe.

But the tribal people were content with what they had. They built no roads and they did not invent anything; they lived a simple life close to nature. That may be one reason the Hebrews were the discoverers of the greatest of all religions, which showered blessings upon humanity.

HILL OF THE LORD

*Who shall ascend into the hill of the Lord? or who shall stand
in his holy place?*   Ps. 24:3

"Hill of the Lord" means Mount Zion. Jerusalem is built upon Mount
Zion, and the temple was built upon Mount Moriah where Abraham
had been commanded in a vision to go and sacrifice his son, Isaac.
[Gen. 22:2]. Judah is a hilly country.

Thousands of men and women, year by year, ascended the "hill of
God" from Jericho, Hebron, Bethlehem, Philistia, and other regions in
the lowlands to worship in the temple of God. All pious men and
women brought their offerings to the temple of God in Jerusalem, which
the Lord God had selected for his dwelling place.

Hills and mountains are symbolic of strength and trust. Trusting in
the living God is as firm as a mountain.

WASH MY HANDS IN INNOCENCE

*I will wash mine hands in innocency: so will I compass thine
altar, O Lord.*   Ps. 26:6

"I will wash mine hands in innocency" means, "I will repent of my
sins." In Aramaic, it is often said, "I have washed my hands of him,"
which means, "I have nothing to do with him," or "I am absolved of
any guilt."

The hand is the agent of the mind, and symbolic of power and action. One has to put away worldly power and repent of evil in order to
come close to the altar of the Lord. Pilate washed his hands of guilt
when he let Jesus be crucified.

AN EVEN PLACE

*My foot standeth in an even place: in the congregations will I
bless the Lord.*   Ps. 26:12

"My foot standeth in an even place" means, "I shall stand firm," or
"I shall not slip or stumble." The foot is used here simply because the
Semitic term for religion is "way." "The way of the Lord" and the term
"walking" are used to mean "good conduct" and "walking in the right
way."

GIFT OFFERING

Give unto the Lord, O ye mighty, give unto the Lord glory and strength.

Give unto the Lord the glory due unto his name; worship the Lord in the beauty of holiness.   Ps. 29:1-2

When the Israelites visited holy places or shrines, they brought with them the choicest of their sheep, rams, and lambs.

Then again, after the victories by which they were delivered from their oppressors they proffered thanks offerings to God and rejoiced over their triumph. They danced, ate, and drank on that day as a token of rejoicing.

Even today, Easterners, when visiting holy shrines or holy men, bring offerings with them—gifts of food, lambs, and sheep. But now they do not drink.

It is said that this psalm was sung after the defeat of the Assyrian army and the deliverance of Jerusalem from the hand of the King of Assyria. The people were exhorted by Hezekiah to come to the house of the Lord and to bring offerings to celebrate the great victory.

OFFSPRING OF RAMS

The Eastern text reads: "Bring unto the Lord the offspring of rams; bring unto the Lord glory and honour. . . . worship the Lord in the court of his holy temple."

This psalm was sung when King Hezekiah was relieved from the seige and oppression of the Assyrian army. The king exhorts the people to bring to the temple of the Lord lambs, sheep, and rams as a thanks offering for their salvation.

The Lord had saved Israel once more [2 Kings 19:35-37; Isa. 37:36-38]. Apparently the song was composed by David, but sung by Hezekiah.

THUNDER

The voice of the Lord maketh the hinds to calve, and discovereth the forests: and in his temple doth every one speak of his glory.
                                                              Ps. 29:9

The Eastern text reads: "The voice of the Lord makes the hinds to tremble [to be disturbed], and uproots the forests."

Thunder was known as the voice of the Lord simply because it is a sound of nature. The Hebrews attributed all natural phenomena to the might of God, who knows all and controls all.

Thunder and lightning are still feared in the East, especially in the flat, desert lands where one cannot find protection. Cedars and other trees are often broken by lightning, and cattle and sheep are killed [verses 5-8].

The voice of the Lord and his rebuke of the Assyrian king broke the army, which resembled a great forest which had besieged Jerusalem, and shook the other forces which were occupying the towns round about it [2 Kings 19:35-37; Isa. 37:36-38].

GOD CONTROLS FLOODS

The Lord sitteth upon the flood; yea, the Lord sitteth King for ever.　　　　　　　　　　　　　　　　　　　　　　　　　　Ps. 29:10

The Aramaic word *aphekh* means "he causes it to go backward, he stops it, he controls it." "Sitteth upon the flood" might have been used metaphorically to mean that he crushes enemy armies.

Floods cause considerable damage in the biblical lands. Sometimes it does not rain for two or three years; and when it does rain, it turns into a deluge, destroying the fields, washing away the soil, and drowning men and animals in the path of violent torrents.

The Lord God turned away the Assyrian invasion which had swept away many kingdoms and people before it. He controlled the power of the Assyrian army and caused it to suffer a severe defeat [2 Kings 19:36].

OUT OF SHEOL

O Lord, thou hast brought up my soul from the grave: thou hast kept me alive, that I should not go down to the pit.　　Ps. 30:3

This psalm is ascribed to Hezekiah, king of Judah, when he was sick. The king was sick to death, and the prophet Isaiah came to see him and told him to set his house in order for he was to die at any time [2 Kings 20:1]. But Hezekiah prayed, and the Lord God healed him [Isa. 38:1-6].

The Eastern text reads: "Thou hast brought up my soul from Sheol; thou hast saved me that I should not join those who go down to the pit [grave]."

The king's recovery was a great miracle, wrought by means of earnest prayer. Sheol was supposed to be a place beyond the jurisdiction of God. It was a terrifying place. The dead were cut off from the living and imprisoned in the depths of the earth. Both Sheol and death were feared in those days. This was because few men were aware of the resurrection. Jesus, through his death on the cross and his resurrection, destroyed the power of Sheol.

DAVID IS TRANQUIL

And hast not shut me up into the hand of the enemy: thou hast set my feet in a large room. Ps. 31:8

"Thou hast set my feet in a large room" means, "Thou hast comforted me and established my feet in tranquility"; that is, "My enemies have not captured me or besieged me."

David, in his early life, was shut up and constantly harassed and pursued by his enemy, Saul. But now the king was free and the ruler over a large kingdom which extended from Palestine to the River Euphrates, and from the border of Egypt to Lebanon.

FORGOTTEN FOREVER

I am forgotten as a dead man out of mind: I am like a broken vessel. Ps. 31:12

The last part of the verse in the Eastern text reads: ". . . I am like something given up for lost." *Mana* in Aramaic means "vessel, dish, thing, something." Copper vessels and dishes are often borrowed and sometimes lost. The nomad people borrow vessels from one another and may forget to return them, or they may lose them during raids in which their camps are plundered.

This psalm is a supplication of the Jews when they were oppressed by their enemies. It could have been sung after the people had returned from Babylon, or during the time of King Hezekiah when Judah and Jerusalem were pressed by the Assyrian army. Judah was seemingly lost and hopeless. She did not know where to turn.

GOD'S PROTECTION

Oh how great is thy goodness, which thou hast laid up for them that fear thee; which thou hast wrought for them that trust in thee before the sons of men! Ps. 31:19

"Before the sons of men" here means "against the opposition of worldly men." Those who revere their God and obey his commandments are often persecuted by those who deny him and do evil in his presence.

But God protects those who worship him and remain loyal to him. He keeps them in his secret place where no one can touch their souls. "Thou shalt hide them in the secret [fortress] of thy presence from the pride of man" [verse 20].

BLOT OUT SINS

Blessed is he whose transgression is forgiven, whose sin is covered.
Blessed is the man unto whom the Lord imputeth not iniquity, and in whose spirit there is no guile.   Ps. 32:1-2

The Aramaic word *kasah* (cover) in this instance means "effaced" or "obliterated," so that God can no longer see them. "Covered" is incorrect. One can cover or hide his sins, but they are still there. Moreover, sins can be covered from men but not from God.

The Hebrew *kippur* (atonement) means to eradicate the sin and blot out iniquity by means of self-denials, prayers, and offerings. *Kipper* means to deny oneself pleasures or to afflict oneself. All this was done to blot out the sins, not to cover them [Prov. 17:9]. In Nehemiah, we read: "And forgive not their offenses, and let not their sins be blotted out from before thee" [Neh. 4:5, Eastern text]. When God covers the sins, then they are blotted out for good [Ps. 85:2].

HARDSHIPS

Many are the afflictions of the righteous: but the Lord delivereth him out of them all.   Ps. 34:19

The Aramaic word *bishathey* (afflictions) also means "hardships" or "evils." This is because Easterners believe a righteous man is subjected to many hardships in this life. This is to say, the wicked make life harder and harsher for the righteous. We often say, "It is hard to be a Christian amidst wicked men."

The righteous has a longer way to go and many difficulties ahead of him, but the Lord delivers him from all of them.

LIONS

Lord, how long wilt thou look on? rescue my soul from their destructions, my darling from the lions.   Ps. 35:17

"Lions" is used here metaphorically to mean oppressors. In the East, dictators and oppressors are often spoken of as lions, leopards, and wild beasts. In the book of Amos they are called "kine" or cows. "Hear this word, ye kine of Bashan . . . which oppress the poor, which crush the needy, which say to their masters, Bring, and let us drink" [Amos 4:1].

The Aramaic word *ykhidoth* means "the only child." The song was composed by David, but, according to the Eastern text, used during the time of the prophet Jeremiah. Be that as it may, Jeremiah was a lone prophet. Jeremiah might have been the only child. His oppressors, the false prophets, are called lions because they wanted to do away with him. The prophet barely escaped death at the hands of many false court prophets and princes who were opposed to his policy. On the other hand, Jeremiah was the only prophet during his time who spoke for God and predicted the fall of Jerusalem. King David was a true and faithful king who put God first.

WINKING WITH THE EYES

Let not them that are mine enemies wrongfully rejoice over me: neither let them wink with the eye that hate me without a cause.
                                                                    Ps. 35:19

The last portion of the verse in the Eastern text reads: ". . . they wink with their eyes but they do not salute," which means that they do not say, "Peace be unto you."

Easterners, when meeting, generally salute one another. The salutation is in spoken words, "Peace be to you." If one of the men happens to be working or carrying a burden, the other says, "My God grant you strength."

Enemies, however, do not salute, but wink with their eyes or nod their head as a gesture of hatred.

This psalm was composed by King David, but according to the Eastern text was sung during the time of Jeremiah when he was accused by false prophets and thrown into prison [verses 11, 26]. Jeremiah was known as a rebel prophet because he did not agree with the false court prophets who had misled Zedekiah, the king of Judah, by their dangerous foreign policy.

THE WICKED FEARS NOT GOD

The transgression of the wicked saith within my heart, that there is no fear of God before his eyes.   Ps. 36:1

The Eastern text reads: "The unjust conceives wickedness within his heart, for there is no fear of God before his eyes." The error in the

King James Version is caused by the confusion in the possessive case or the genetive: *bi* (my heart) and *libeh* (his heart).

The wicked conceives evil in his heart because there is no fear of God before his eyes. He is so wicked that he does not know what righteousness is.

FATNESS AND SPIRITUAL RIVER

They shall be abundantly satisfied with the fatness of thy house; and thou shalt make them drink of the river of thy pleasures.

Ps. 36:8

"The fatness of thy house" and "the river of thy pleasures" are metaphors meaning "truth and spiritual understanding which meet all human desires." "River" also means "rain which causes the earth to produce food" [Ps. 65:9].

Thousands of fat bullocks, he-goats, and lambs were slain in the courtyard of the temple to be offered to God. On such occasions fat meat and wine were abundant, and the people ate and were merry. But after the feast, the people were once more hungry for meat and thirsty for water, which is scarce in the Holy City. "There is a river, the streams whereof shall make glad the city of God, the holy place of the tabernacles of the most High" [Ps. 46:4].

Just as water gives life in a dry place, and the shadow of a tree revives the weary in a dry land, so is the truth and the Spirit of God to those who are hungry and thirsty for justice and spiritual understanding of life. "A pure river of water of life . . ." [Rev. 22:1].

Water is symbolic of light and enlightenment. A river means "truth," the teaching of God which relieves all thirsty souls. God's pleasure is goodness and loving kindness, the observance of his commandments and statutes. "River" also means "abundance" [Isa. 66:12].

God's religion is the River of Life which satisfies all those who are hungry and thirsty for justice and truth. It is like water on parched ground.

See the commentaries on Psalm 46:4 and Isiah 32:1-2.

WICKED RICH

But the wicked shall perish, and the enemies of the Lord shall be as the fat of lambs: they shall consume; into smoke shall they consume away.

Ps. 37:20

The Aramaic reads: ". . . the rich who are enemies of the Lord." The reference here is to the rich oppressors who had defrauded the laborers, oppressed the poor, and taken bribes from the widows. "Behold, the wage of the labourers who have reaped your fields, that which you have fraudulently kept back, cries; and the cry of the reapers has already entered into the ears of the Lord of sabaoth [hosts]" [James 5:4, Eastern text].

The wicked rich also oppressed the widows and the fatherless. Both the wicked and the wealthy oppressors are to be consumed and will vanish like smoke.

In the East the rich were tax exempt and still are in most of the backward countries. They are also allowed to levy taxes on the poor and to confiscate the property of the weak [Prov. 22:7; Matt. 19:23; Mark 10:25; Luke 18:25]. "A little that a righteous man has is better than the great riches of the wicked" [Ps. 37:16, Eastern text].

The pious rich are commended for their good works and blessed by God.

RIGHTEOUS NOT FORSAKEN

Commit thy way unto the Lord; trust also in him; and he shall bring it to pass.   Ps. 37:25

In many portions of the Scriptures we read that God never forsakes the righteous. All the righteous men who cry to the Lord are heard, and the Lord delivers them out of all their troubles [Ps. 34:17]. God never suffers the righteous to be moved [Ps. 55:22].

Moreover, the Lord hears the prayers and the supplications of the righteous who have put their trust in him and taken refuge under his wings. "The Lord is far from the wicked: but he heareth the prayer of the righteous" [Prov. 15:29]. "Blessed is the man that trusteth in him" [Ps. 34:8].

God forsakes no one. He did not forsake Jesus on the cross. When Jesus cried on the cross in Aramaic, he said, "My God, my God, for this I was kept"; that is, "this was my destiny." Jesus had predicted his crucifixion and death, and the prophecies had to be fulfilled. He never questioned God, his Father [Matt. 27:46].

See the commentary on Matthew 27:46 in *Gospel Light.*

DUMBNESS—CONFUSION

I was dumb, I opened not my mouth; because thou didst it.
                                                    Ps. 39:9

"Dumb" in this instance refers to affliction, bewilderment, or confusion. "I was dumb" means "I did not know what to do or say." On such occasions Easterners remain silent.

When David was oppressed by King Saul, he did not complain, hoping the king would change his mind toward him.

In the olden days afflictions and injustices were often blamed on God because he had permitted them to be inflicted by the wicked upon the just.

A PROPHECY CONCERNING MESSIAH

Then said I, Lo, I come: in the volume of the book it is written of me.   Ps. 40:7

Debresh katebey means "in the beginning of the Scriptures"; that is, "the book of Genesis." Messiah Christ was to tread underfoot the head of the serpent, the devil [Gen. 3:15].

A great Deliverer was promised by God to save mankind. Many of the Hebrew prophets envisioned his coming and the establishment of a new and universal kingdom, a reign of righteousness, peace, and justice. This concept runs throughout the Scriptures like a golden thread in a brocade. Messiah was to execute justice not only in Judea but also throughout the world.

"Examine the scriptures; in them you trust that you have eternal life; and even they testify concerning me" [John 5:39, Eastern text; Isa. 4:2; Jer. 23:5; Heb. 10:7].

Messiah, the Anointed One, was the only hope of mankind. Everything else had been tried, but had failed to save mankind and to restore man's lost divinity.

LOOKING AFTER THE POOR

Blessed is he that considereth the poor: the Lord will deliver him in time of trouble.   Ps. 41:1

The Aramaic word *khaar* is derived from *khar* (to look at, behold, regard). But in this case it means "to look after"; that is, "to help them when they are in distress."

In the East, until recent days, the poor were subjected to hard labor, forced to carry burdens, and were heavily taxed; they were discriminated against and their properties often confiscated unjustly. The Mosaic law admonished the people to return the mantle of a poor man, which he had given as a pledge.

"And if the man is poor, you shall not sleep with his mantle. But you shall return to him his mantle again when the sun goes down, that he may sleep in his own mantle, and bless you; and it shall be righteousness to you before the Lord your God" [Deut. 24:12-13, Eastern text].

"But he saves their lives from the sword, and the poor from the hand of the mighty" [Job 5:15, Eastern text].

BREAD OF TEARS

My tears have been my meat day and night, while they con-
tinually say unto me, Where is thy God?   Ps. 42:3

"My tears have been my bread" is an Eastern idiom which means, "I have been sad continually, and tears ran down my cheeks while I was eating." Then again, when people suffer and are afflicted, they say, "I have been eating my bread with the tears of my eyes." None of these expressions are taken literally or are misunderstood. The people know that no one can eat his tears, but they often see men weeping while eating.

Moreover, Easterners often weep while eating and drinking. Their tears mingle with their food and drink. "Thou feedest them with the bread of tears" [Ps. 80:5].

MARKED FOR SLAUGHTER

Thou hast given us like sheep appointed for meat; and hast scat-
tered us among the heathen.   Ps. 44:11

In the East, even today, one can see small flocks of sheep grazing near a city or town. They are generally lambs, rams, goats, and older sheep which will be sold by the owners to sheep merchants to be resold to butchers.

Refrigeration was unknown in Eastern lands, and sheep and goats were killed from day to day.

The butchers count and mark the sheep that are to be slaughtered. At times these sheep are separated from the flock and brought near the city wall to be slaughtered early in the morning.

The psalmist likens the Jews to sheep that are marked to be slaughtered for food. This was one of the darkest periods in the Jewish history. Many Jews were killed by the Gentiles. Others were taken captive.

According to the Eastern text, this psalm was composed and sung during the time of the Maccabees when thousands of Jews were butchered by the Syrians and were compelled by Antiochus to sacrifice to idols. All the Jews who refused to comply with the king's decree were slain.

SECOND PUNISHMENT

Though thou hast sore broken us in the place of dragons, and covered us with the shadow of death. Ps. 44:19

The Eastern text reads: "For thou hast humbled us a second time in the land." The reference here is to the second defeat, this time before the Greeks. First, they were defeated by the Chaldeans and carried away captive to Babylon. And now the Jews were compelled by Antiochus to sacrifice to idols.

The Aramaic word *tinyana* (a second time) has been confused in the King James Version with the Aramaic word *tanina* (a dragon). These two words are written alike but pronounced differently.

This psalm was written after the Jews had returned from Babylon, had built the second temple, and had established the second Jewish commonwealth. After the fall of the Persian empire, the Syrians and other surrounding races started to oppress the Jews. The period under Antiochus was one of the darkest periods in Jewish history. The holy temple was desecrated and Jewish women were violated and put to death.

THERE IS A RIVER

There is a river, the streams whereof shall make glad the city of God, the holy place of the tabernacles of the Most High. Ps. 46:4

The word river in this instance is used metaphorically to mean truth, teaching, or the light of God. The writer of Revelation speaks of "a pure river of water of life" [Rev. 22:1]. Water is symbolic of spiritual enlightenment, and thirst is symbolic of the lack of it. John speaks of "rivers of living water" [John 7:38]. There is no river in Jerusalem. The little brook of Kidron dries up in the early summer, and one can hardly see a trickle of water in the valley.

Israel looked upon God's truth as a place of refuge and strength in the time of trouble. The Jewish state was established on God's promises to Israel and the world, the truth of God which was to leaven the Gentile world—the river of God, the true teaching issued from Jerusalem, the city of peace which God had chosen [Pss. 1:3; 65:9].

Jerusalem, the city of peace, is the center of true worship. The branches of the river ("the streams thereof") are other places which have been enlightened by God's truth from Jerusalem.

The true teaching of God as revealed by the Hebrew prophets was the greatest bulwark round about Jerusalem. Even though the Jewish people suffered hardships and were carried captive, they never lost their faith in the God of Israel. Jerusalem rested on a solid foundation, the Rock of Ages, the truth which issued from Jerusalem and brought light and understanding to the Gentile world.

See the commentary on Ezekiel 47:1-6.

SONG OF RIDDLES

I will incline mine ear to a parable: I will open my dark saying upon the harp.   Ps. 49:4

Eastern poets and musicians play love songs, melodies, and lamentations on harps, violins, and other musical instruments. Moreover, parables, proverbs, and dark sayings are also sung and played on musical instruments.

The dark sayings are songs which contain riddles and are not easily understood by those who lack poetic sense. The singer uses metaphors and similes. He says one thing, but he means another thing. For example, he uses the term "a beautiful garden" when he means "a beautiful woman." When he speaks of a woman's breasts he uses the term "pomegranates."

THE END OF THE WICKED

Nevertheless man being in honor abideth not: he is like the beasts that perish.   Ps. 49:12

The Eastern text reads: "Nevertheless, such a man is not sustained by his honour; his end will be as the beasts, and he will perish."

The psalmist here speaks of a wicked man and not of man in general. In verse 9, the psalmist says, "Do good for ever and you shall live for ever, and not see corruption." But both the wise and the fools will die and perish and their graves shall be their only habitation.

THE DEMENTED

This their way is their folly: yet their posterity approve their sayings. Selah.   Ps. 49:13

The latter part of this verse should read: ". . . in the end, demented, they will graze like cattle."

The Aramaic words *bepomhon neraon* mean "they will graze like cattle." This saying is still in use in Aramaic. We often say, "they eat grass," meaning that they are devoid of knowledge, like cattle.

We are told that Nebuchadnezzar ate grass like an ox, which means that he lost his mind [Dan. 4:32-33].

See also the commentary on Daniel 4:32.

GOD OF GODS

The mighty God, even the Lord, hath spoken, and called the earth from the rising of the sun unto the going down thereof.
                                                                    Ps. 50:1

The Eastern text reads: "The God of gods, the Lord . . ."

The Hebrews, like other races in Palestine and Syria, believed in many gods. At times they looked upon the God of Israel as the greatest among all gods, since the gods of Gentiles were made of wood, silver, and gold. In other words, they believed in pagan deities, but they took for granted the superiority of their own God. Nevertheless, during some periods they forsook their God and went astray after pagan gods and images which had become a snare to them [verse 22].

But the idea of the one and only God, the Living God of Israel, always persisted and was constantly preached by the prophets. These words in the psalm were aimed at those who believed in pagan gods.

FIRE

Our God shall come, and shall not keep silence: a fire shall devour before him, and it shall be very tempestuous round about him.   Ps. 50:3

In the olden days, fire was considered the most powerful thing in the world. This is because fire was the first discovery which man had made in his progress; fire consumed forests, burned dwellings, and melted iron and brass.

God often appeared in fire, symbolizing light, power, and purity. All metals are purified by fire. God appeared to Moses in the burning bush [Exod. 3:2]. Moreover, the Lord led the Israelites by a pillar of fire [Exod. 13:21]. God spoke to Moses and the elders of Israel on Mount Sinai out of the midst of fire, and the people heard his voice, but they did not see him [Deut. 4:12]. God's words were as strong as fire and his messengers were as a flaming fire.

Fire was worshiped and is still worshiped by the Parsees in India, who are a remnant of the ancient Iranian religion, the Zoroastrians or fire worshipers. Fire is often used to symbolize God's vengeance, for instance, when the wicked cities were destroyed [Gen. 19:24; Deut. 32:22].

In Aramaic, fire is symbolic of anger. We often say, "Fire issued from his face," which means, "His anger blazed like fire."

GOD NEEDS NO ANIMAL SACRIFICES

These things hast thou done, and I kept silence; thou thoughtest that I was altogether such a one as thyself: but I will reprove thee, and set them in order before thine eyes. Ps. 50:21

The Eastern text reads: ". . . you thought that I was wicked like you; but I will reprove you, and correct these sins before your eyes."

The Jews are reproved for trusting in ceremonies and animal sacrifices instead of remembering to obey God's commandments and to do mercy and execute justice to the poor and the needy.

God wanted the sacrifices of thanksgiving for the blessings that he had given them, and for the good they had done in his name. He was not in need of meat offerings. All animals and birds belong to him. What God wants is justice and peace.

FORMED IN INIQUITY

Behold, I was shapen in iniquity; and in sin did my mother conceive me. Ps. 51:5

According to the Hebrew terminology, everything was sinful when compared with God, the Holy One of Israel. Perfection and goodness were to be attained only by the observance of God's law and his ordinances. "Who can bring a clean thing out of an unclean? not one" [Job 14:4]. All men born of women were considered sinners [Luke 7:28].

Man, through his sin and disobedience, had fallen from the grace of God. He is to cleanse himself of his sins by means of baptism in order to become a new creation [verse 7].

Women who gave birth to children were pronounced unclean for forty days, after which they were sanctified. The firstborn males also were redeemed and sanctified.

The psalmist here speaks collectively. The reference here is to all Israel. The people who were captive in Babylon confessed their sins and asked mercy and forgiveness.

The people were in captivity because of the sins of their fathers. The idea of being shaped or formed in sin refers to the fact that the people had been rebellious and unwilling to repent and return to God.

HUMBLED

Make me to hear joy and gladness; that the bones which thou hast broken may rejoice. Ps. 51:8

The Eastern text reads: "Satisfy me with thy joy and gladness, that my broken spirit may rejoice."

The term "broken spirit" is used figuratively, meaning humbleness or humility. In the East, when men or women are sad or worried, it is said their spirit is broken, which means their pride has been hurt. The Aramaic word *rokha* (spirit) also means "pride, wind, rheumatism." But in this instance it means "pride."

This psalm was sung by the people who were in Babylon. They confess their sins and iniquities and ask forgiveness. They have been humbled in the land of their captivity, and now they ask God to grant them joy and gladness and to create a new heart in them.

GOD DESIRES MEEKNESS

The sacrifices of God are a broken spirit: a broken and a contrite heart, O God, thou wilt not despise. Ps. 51:17

"Broken spirit" means humbleness, humility. And "broken heart" here refers to the people's grief over the loss of spiritual values. When a man's pride is lost, he becomes humble and gentle. Jesus said, "Blessed are the humble, for theirs is the kingdom of heaven" [Matt. 5:3, Eastern text].

God is not pleased with animal sacrifices. What God required of the Israelites was to be humble, to execute justice, and do mercy. "I will take no bullock out of thy house, nor he goats of thy fold. For every beast of the forest is mine, and the cattle upon a thousand hills." [Ps. 50:9-10; see also Micah 6:6-8].

SCATTERED BONES

There were they in great fear, where no fear was: for God hath scattered the bones of him that encampeth against thee: thou hast put them to shame, because God hath despised them. Ps. 53:5

"Scattered the bones" is an Eastern idiom that means "he has destroyed them or broken their power." Easterners often say, "I will break up your bones," or, "I will crush your bones."

The reference here is to the enemies of the Jews who sought to destroy them. In biblical days the carcasses of the slain were left in the field. The flesh was eaten by wild animals and birds of prey, and the bones were scattered in the fields [Ezek. 37:1-2].

TEARS IN THE BOTTLE

Thou tellest my wanderings: put thou my tears into thy bottle:
are they not in thy book?   Ps. 56:8

The Eastern text reads: "O God, I have declared my faith unto thee; record thou my tears before thee in thy book."

Easterners, more than other people, mourn over their dead. They weep bitterly and at times even cut themselves and beat their faces and chests. The Aramaic reads: "Record [or place] my tears before thee in thy book."

Clothes and other articles worn by the deceased are often kept as a memorial. In the olden days, tears poured out over dear ones were put into small alabaster bottles as a reminder of mourning and grief. The Israelites wanted their tears to be recorded in God's book as a memorial of their suffering and repentance.

". . . and the Lord God will wipe away tears from off all faces" [Isa. 25:8; see also Rev. 7:17].

The psalmist here reminds God of the hardships which the Israelites had suffered from the nations which were round about them. The people beseech God for rest and peace [Mal. 3:16].

SCURRILOUS GOSSIP

Their poison is like the poison of a serpent: they are like the
deaf adder that stoppeth her ear.   Ps. 58:4

"Poison of asps" is an Eastern idiom frequently used in both vernacular and literary Aramaic speech.

Lies, accusations, and defamation of character are often called poison because of their evil effects. These wicked gossipers never stop to reason but, like serpents, they strike unawares.

The Jews, during the time of the Maccabees, suffered many persecutions from the hands of the surrounding pagan nations, who lied and connived against them, and sought their destruction.

MELT LIKE WAX

As a snail which melteth, let every one of them pass away: like
the untimely birth of a woman, that they may not see the sun.
        Ps. 58:8

The Aramaic word for "wax" is *shoaa,* and the word for "snail" is *sheda,* which also means "a demon." Snails, clams, and oysters are called *shedy*, and are considered as unclean. Neither Christians, Jews nor Moslems eat them.

The Eastern text reads: *shoaa* (wax). "Like the wax that melts, and drips before the fire, let them be destroyed." That is, "Let the wicked melt and pass away like the wax on the candle which burns and drips before the fire." Then it continues: "Fire has fallen from heaven and they did not see; the light of truth [sun] has been given and they did not understand."

The word "woman" in the King James Version is due to the confusion between the Hebrew word *aish* (fire) and *esha* (a woman).

Wax is often used in the Bible as a means of illustration. "As smoke is driven away, so let them vanish; as wax melts before the fire, so let the wicked perish at the presence of God" [Ps. 68:2]. Micah uses the same analogy—"like wax before the fire" [Micah 1:4]. But "snail" has never been used as such an analogy; no one would say, "The wicked will pass away like a snail."

DIFFICULTIES INCREASED

Before your pots can feel the thorns, he shall take them away as with a whirlwind, both living, and in his wrath.   Ps. 58:9

The Eastern text reads: "Let their thorns be increased, and fear of wrath shake them violently." A thorn or brier is used metaphorically to mean snares, difficulties, grievance, sorrows or afflictions.

"He has been a thorn in my flesh" means, "He has caused me to suffer" [2 Cor. 12:7; Prov. 26:9]. "And there shall be no more a pricking brier unto the house of Israel, nor any grieving thorn of all that are round about them" [Ezek. 28:24].

Moreover, when Easterners curse a place they say, "Let thorns grow in you." "Thorns shall come up in her palaces" [Isa. 34:13].

The psalm, according to the Eastern text, was composed concerning the snares which the Gentiles had laid in the way of the Maccabees, but, like other psalms, could be applied to any other similar situation.

A GREAT TRAGEDY

O God, thou hast cast us off, thou hast scattered us, thou hast been displeased; O turn thyself to us again.

Thou has made the earth to tremble; thou hast broken it: heal the breaches thereof; for it shaketh.   Ps. 60:1-2

This psalm was composed during the period of the Maccabees, when the Jews were harassed and persecuted by the Syrian kingdom. The people felt that they were forsaken and cast off by their God.

The second verse is composed poetically. The great catastrophes which had befallen their people had made them tremble. This is because this period was a period of tense persecution and upheaval in the history of Israel. The Jews were forced to eat swine meat, to work on the Sabbath day, and the temple was polluted by the soldiers. Many other abominations were committed against the people by the Gentile armies.

In the East, when a great tragedy takes place we say, "the earth shook" because of the impact of evil [verse 3].

WASHPOT—SERVITUDE

Moab is my washpot; over Edom will I cast out my shoe: Philistia, triumph thou because of me.   Ps. 60:8

"Moab is my washpot" is an Aramaic idiom which means "my lowest servant or slave." In the East, washpots are not very clean and are used for washing feet, clothes, and at times as toilet utensils. The psalmist here looks upon Moab as the dirt under his feet.

"Over Edom will I cast out my shoe" is another Eastern idiom, meaning "Edom will pay tribute to me or serve me." In the East shoes are considered unclean. When men enter a house they take off their shoes. Servants remove the shoes of rich men and high government officials. Edom was to be reduced to servitude.

This psalm contains hope for restoration and freedom from their oppressors. The Jews sincerely repented and then sought mercy from their God. At last, the Jews, during their dark hour, turned to God for help. Only God could defeat their strong enemies round about them.

ROCK OF COMFORT

From the end of the earth will I cry unto thee, when my heart is overwhelmed: lead me to the rock that is higher than I.
For thou hast been a shelter for me, and a strong tower from the enemy.   Ps. 61:2-3

The Eastern text reads: ". . . for thou hast led me upon a rock and hast comforted me." Verse 3 agrees with verse 2. The Lord has answered the prayer of the people. This psalm might have been sung at the time when the Persian kings had granted the exiles permission to rebuild the temple.

"Rock" is used metaphorically, meaning "assurance, strength, protection." "God is my rock" in Aramaic means, "God is my protection," or the truth on which my faith rests. During storms and hurricanes people take refuge in caves and under rocks. "I will put you in a cave of the rock" [Exod. 33:22]. "He is the Rock [or strength]" [Deut. 32:4; see also Matt. 7:24].

GIFTS TO TEMPLE

I will go into thy house with burnt offerings: I will pay thee my vows.   Ps. 66:13

Whenever the Israelites went to the temple they took gifts with them as thanks offerings to the Lord. They never went empty-handed. Even when they visited prophets and men of God they took gifts consisting of bread, honey, parched wheat, fruits, and other things.

The gift offerings and animal sacrifices were eaten by the priests, the Levites, and the worshipers. In those days there were no restaurants or hotels. The people brought animal and cereal offerings to the holy places, and the offerings were cooked and eaten by the priests and the worshipers [1 Sam. 1:4; 2:13-17].

When men and women vowed a vow to the Lord, when the days of the vow were fulfilled, they brought a free-will offering to God [Deut. 23:21-24].

GOD'S WAY

That thy way may be known upon earth, thy saving health among all nations.   Ps. 67:2

The Aramaic word *aorkhakh* (thy way) also means "thy religion." Even today, in Aramaic we say, "What is your way?" meaning "What is your religion?" The other name for "religion" is *dina* (right judgment, justice). This is why the term religion does not appear in the Bible; the term way has been used all through the Sacred Book.

God's way is truth, justice, peace, and understanding. It leads men into the paths of righteousness, and finally into the kingdom of God.

When God's way, or his religion, is known to all nations, the reign of God will be hastened. God's religion is not yet known to all nations of the earth. There are too many ways of man-made religions in this world which are far better known and wider spread than God's way, but they lead the people to destruction and misery.

DIVIDE THE SPOIL

Kings of armies did flee apace: and she that tarried at home divided the spoil.   Ps. 68:12

In the East when an army is defeated the soldiers of the victorious army and the citizens plunder the camp of the enemy and divide the spoil. This ancient biblical custom prevailed until recent years, and is still practiced among the nomad tribes and backward peoples.

The Aramaic reads: ". . . and the household of God shall divide the spoil."

According to the Eastern text, this psalm was sung by David when he was bringing up the Ark of God from the house of the Gittite and while he was dancing. David had defeated the Philistines and broken their oppressive yoke from the necks of his people. But the words of this psalm were also used by Moses and Joshua when they related the wonders of God in their days. This psalm is a war song. It was recited before the army charged against the enemy [verse 1].

SLEEP AMONG THE THORNS

Though ye have lain among the pots, yet shall ye be as the wings of a dove covered with silver, and her feathers with yellow gold.   Ps. 68:13

The word "thorns" in this instance is used metaphorically, meaning "grievances" and "tribulations." In the East when the people are oppressed and heavily taxed, they say, "We live in thorns," or, "He has been a thorn to me."

Some of the birds' nests are made of thorns and grass, but are inlaid with soft and warm feathers. The psalmist portrays the Israelites as living in thorns, and God's mercy and protection as the feathers of doves, which protect the young in the nest.

Israel was harassed from all sides. The Philistines, the Moabites, the Ammonites, and the Arameans (Syrians) were all like thorns. And at times the Israelites were subjugated by their enemies, and yet they were protected by their God, who gave them grace in the eyes of the foreign rulers. This is because during these periods the people repented and turned to God and forsook their evil ways. In God there is no want, no need, no fear. When God is with a people or a nation, who can be against it?

HILLS LEAP

Why leap ye, ye high hills? this is the hill which God desireth to dwell in; yea, the Lord will dwell in it for ever.   Ps. 68:16

The Eastern text reads: "What do you want, O you mountains of Bashan? This is the ridge which God desires to dwell in . . ."

The term "mountain" is used figuratively, meaning "the people who dwell in the mountain."

The reference here is to the proud mountains of Bashan, which were ruled by the vicious dictators who oppressed the people.

DIVISION OF SPOILS

Thou hast ascended on high, thou hast led captivity captive: thou hast received gifts for men; yea, for the rebellious also, that the Lord God might dwell among them.   Ps. 68:18

The Eastern text reads: ". . . thou hast carried away captives; thou hast blessed men with gifts; but rebellious men shall not dwell before the presence of God."

In the East, during raids rebellious men who had disagreed with the council receive no portion of the spoil. The Israelites, also, after their victories, divided the plunder among the warriors.

We know that God would not bestow gifts on the men who had rebelled against him and transgressed his commandments and his divine plan. The error in the King James Version, no doubt, is due to mistranslation.

Israel had many enemies and David's reign was fraught with many dangers and rebellions [verse 21].

DEPTHS OF THE SEA

The Lord said, I will bring again from Bashan, I will bring my people again from the depths of the sea.   Ps. 68:22

"Depths of the sea" is an Aramaic saying which means "far-off lands." In the olden days the people thought the sea could not be measured and that its depth was endless. It also means "out of difficult situations." The Eastern text reads "cliffs" instead of "Bashan."

Bashan was on the frontier of Syria and, therefore, the first land to be occupied by the invading armies which came from Mesopotamia and Persia. During these invasions, many people took refuge in cliffs and caves [Isa. 2:21; Jer. 49:16].

The Lord God of Israel had assured his people of his strong hand. He could protect them and gather them, no matter where they had been carried away or where they had been hiding.

A GREAT SLAUGHTER

That thy foot may be dipped in the blood of thine enemies, and the tongue of thy dogs in the same. Ps. 68:23

When Easterners describe a great slaughter they say, "The blood was high to the knee." In the olden days wars were fought with swords and spears at close range in the streets, in fortresses, and in the battle-fields. Blood sometimes flowed like streams of water.

In the East most of the dogs are not fed and have no owners. They roam around and eat anything they can get. They lick blood and eat dead bodies in the field. When the chariot in which Ahab was slain was washed, the dogs licked up the blood [1 Kings 22:38].

FOUNTAIN OF ISRAEL

Bless ye God in the congregations, even the Lord, from the fountain of Israel. Ps. 68:26

"Fountain" here refers to "the truth, teaching and the life-giving religion" of Israel. Water is symbolic of light and truth, and a fountain thus means "an everlasting truth."

The fountain or truth of God issued from the hills of Judea, which irrigated the whole Gentile world [Ezek. 47:1-3].

"ZEAL HAS EATEN ME UP"

For the zeal of thine house hath eaten me up; and the reproaches of them that reproached thee are fallen upon me. Ps. 69:9

"Eaten me up" is an Eastern idiom which means "has made me coura-geous, has moved or provoked me, or has forced me to act." Jesus quoted this psalm when he said, "The zeal of thine house hath eaten me up!" [John 2:17]. In Psalm 119:139 we read: "My zeal hath consumed me."

Zeal for good works, justice, righteousness, and freedom make men and women so courageous that at times they are even willing to die for God's way of life.

Paul, prior to his conversion, was so zealous for the Jewish religion and law that he was determined to suppress Christianity [Ps. 119:139; Acts 22:3; Phil. 3:6].

TABLE AS A SNARE

Let their table become a snare before them: and that which should have been for their welfare, let it become a trap. Ps. 69:22

In the East when a man plans some kind of conspiracy he prepares a lavish table with abundant varieties of food and drink and invites the prospective conspirators into his house.

In the olden days, tables generally were made of skins and cloth and were spread on the floor before the guests. This custom remained until World War I. Even now in some Eastern lands wooden tables are hardly known.

After eating and drinking, the host opens the subject, reveals his devices, and seeks agreement from the guests at his table. The well-fed and drunken guests generally agree to almost everything that the host proposes.

At times these plots and conspiracies are soon discovered and the culprits severely punished. In such cases the table is called a snare, because the shrewd host had enticed the guests by the means of food and wine.

The reference here is to the table of the enemies of the Jews, who were constantly conniving against them.

ORAL PRAISES

My mouth shall show forth thy righteousness and thy salvation all the day; for I know not the numbers thereof. Ps. 71:15

The Aramaic word *saprotha* may mean "the office of a learned scribe, the learning of grammar, or a scribe learned in law." The Eastern text reads: ". . . for I cannot read." In the East, priests, deacons, and singers generally sing from the book. The unlearned offer oral praises and thanksgiving which are different from those composed by the poets and song composers.

The psalmist here states that he praises the Lord orally because he is uninstructed or unlearned and thus unable to praise God by reading in the temple.

Even today, many illiterate Easterners pray and praise God orally. They know the prayers by heart.

THE ISLANDS

They that dwell in the wilderness shall bow before him; and his enemies shall lick the dust.   Ps. 72:9

The Eastern text reads: "They that dwell on the islands shall bow before him . . ." The reference here is to the large islands beyond the Mediterranean—Britain and Ireland. These islands were known to both the Israelites and the Arameans. The latter, being a great naval power, had colonies and mines in these islands [Isa. 23:1-3].

The inhabitants of these islands resisted invasion and many of them remained independent for many centuries.

The reference here is to the Messiah, Christ the King of kings. All kings of the earth were to bow before him. Today all the kings and lords of the islands humble themselves before the King of kings and offer prayer to him [verses 10-15].

MESSIANIC KINGDOM

There shall be a handful of corn in the earth upon the top of the mountains; the fruit thereof shall shake like Lebanon: and they of the city shall flourish like grass of the earth.   Ps. 72:16

The Aramaic reads: "He shall multiply like wheat upon the earth; his seed [offspring] shall spring up on the mountain tops, as on Lebanon . . ."

The reference here is to the remnant of Israel and the establishment of the messianic reign throughout the world [verses 7-11].

According to the Eastern text, this prophecy is about King Solomon and the blessings which the Lord had bestowed upon Israel. The peaceful reign of Solomon, which was granted by God, symbolizes the messianic kingdom. Solomon's kingdom extended from the great sea to the River Euphrates only, but today the messianic kingdom embraces the whole world.

A MARGINAL NOTE

The prayers of David the son of Jesse are ended.   Ps. 72:20

Verse 20 in the King James Version is a marginal note inserted into the text by the scribe. Similar insertions are to be found at the beginning and the end of other portions of the Scriptures.

These insertions, or marginal notes, were made to facilitate the reading of the lesson. For example: "Thus far is the judgment of Moab" at the end of chapter 48 of Jeremiah. "The prophecy concerning the fall of Babylon, which Isaiah the son of Amoz saw" [Isa. 13:1]. "The prophecy concerning the fall of Moab" [Isa. 15:1]. "The prophecy concerning the fall of Damascus" [Isa. 17:1]. Isaiah did not write these phrases.

This verse proves beyond a doubt that the Peshitta has nothing to do with the Masoretic text from which other translations were made, nor with the Greek text, but that it is a copy of the original Hebrew, as many leading scholars in the East have stated.

If the Peshitta had been transcribed from the Masoretic text or translated from the Septuagint, verse 20 would have been included. The copyist would not have omitted it, but this verse is not included in the original Peshitta, and verse 19 ends with "Amen and amen," which means that it is the end of the psalm.

BLEMISH

Their eyes stand out with fatness: they have more than heart could wish.   Ps. 73:7

The Aramaic word *tarba* means "fat or grease." The Eastern text reads: "Their iniquity comes through like grease; they do according to the evil dictates of the heart."

The evil works of the wicked come through like grease on a garment. Fat is also symbolic of wealth. In biblical days the wealthy classes oppressed the poor, robbed widows, and misused the power which they had gained by the means of wicked riches. Their wickedness could not be hidden from the eyes of the people. It remained on them as a spot on a garment. This is also true of good works; they shine like costly stones.

THE PROUD UNGODLY

They set their mouth against the heavens, and their tongue walketh through the earth.   Ps. 73:9

"They set their mouth against the heavens" means they boast and blaspheme against God. Riches acquired unjustly cover their eyes, and human pride compasses them.

"Their tongue walketh through the earth" means that they gossip and brag about their wealth and power. These are the ungodly who for a time prosper and are powerful, but sooner or later are uprooted and their place is remembered no more. These are the ungodly who prosper by the means of violence and who believe that there is no eternal judgment, nor are they aware of the presence of God in human affairs.

ABUNDANCE AFTER CAPTIVITY

Therefore his people return hither: and waters of a full cup are wrung out to them. Ps. 73:10

The Eastern text reads: "Therefore will my people return hither, and they shall have everything in abundance."

The reference here is to the people who had returned from captivity. Now they are praising God, who had been gracious to them while they were still in captivity, and had given them favor in the eyes of pagan kings and princes who had helped them on their way. Some of the people had doubted the prophecies concerning the restoration and thought that God was not aware of what was taking place. But now the people were to have abundance of prosperity and their enemies were to be confounded and ashamed.

RICHES ACQUIRED UNJUSTLY

Surely thou didst set them in slippery places: thou castedst them down into destruction. Ps. 73:18

The Eastern text reads: "Thou didst appoint their portion according to their deceitfulness; thou didst cast them down when they exalted themselves."

In Hebrew thinking, nothing could be done or could take place without God's knowledge and permission. Hence, since the ungodly prospered and became powerful, God must have allowed them to have riches and power so that they might later slip and destroy themselves. Though riches are a great temptation to those who acquire them unjustly and use them wrongly, they can be a blessing to the pious.

God never causes anyone to go astray or to slip. Man's downfall can be blamed only upon himself. God had endowed man with a free will, and given him the power to choose good or evil.

DESTRUCTION OF THE SECOND TEMPLE

A man was famous according as he had lifted up axes upon the thick trees. Ps. 74:5

The Eastern text here is totally different from other versions. It reads: "Thou knowest this as the exalted one who sits on high; they have hewn down the doors with axes as they would cut the trees of the forest."

The complaint here is against the severe treatment of the Jews and the destruction of the second temple by Antiochus Epiphanes during the Maccabean period. The temple doors were cut down with axes and hammers, just as one would cut down a tree in the forest. They also defiled the holy sanctuary. The pagans had no regard for the house of God and his holy habitation, which they profaned [verse 6].

The Jews were also oppressed and many of them were carried away captive. Others were forced to eat swine meat.

The psalm is a prayer for relief, and an appeal to God, reminding him of his covenant and his mercies in the past.

CARVED WORK

But now they break down the carved work thereof at once with axes and hammers.   Ps. 74:6

When the holy sanctuary was entered by the pagan armies the doors were broken with axes and hammers, and all the work of the craftsmen was destroyed. The pagans cut it down as though they were cutting down the trees of the forest. [verse 5]. The whole sanctuary was ransacked and burned with fire.

There were many wreaths of chain work on the capitals of the temple pillars. All the woodwork of brass, silver, and gold was destroyed [Exod. 26:1; 1 Kings 7:17-21].

Temples, with their fabulous gold and silver treasures, were a great temptation to pagan rulers. When Herod's Temple (the third temple) was destroyed by Titus in A.D. 69, millions of dollars in gold coins, gold bars, and much silver and other costly articles were taken away and carried to Rome.

THE HEADS OF THE DRAGONS

Thou didst divide the sea by thy strength: thou brakest the heads of the dragons in the waters.
Thou brakest the heads of leviathan in pieces, and gavest him to be meat to the people inhabiting the wilderness.   Ps. 74:13-14

The Hebrew prophets and poets often used figurative speech and metaphors when describing dictators and oppressors. The reference here is to Pharaoh and his army. Dragons and sea monsters are symbolic of great dictators and oppressors [Rev. 12:3]. When the Israelites crossed to the other side of the Gulf of Suez, the Egyptian army was drowned in the channel (the crossing place).

The Israelites and the Bedouins in the desert plundered what was left of the Egyptian camp, and took the garments and weapons of Pharaoh's warriors which were strewn along the seaside.

WINE AND DREGS

For in the hand of the Lord there is a cup, and the wine is red; it is full of mixture; and he poureth out of the same: but the dregs thereof, all the wicked of the earth shall wring them out, and drink them.

Ps. 75:8

The Eastern text reads: "For in the hand of the Lord there is a cup, full of a mixture of the dregs of wine . . ."

In the East, red wine is generally preferred over white. When princes, governors, and noblemen are entertained, the host serves red wine. Red wine can easily be mixed with poison or *hashhash* (a kind of dope) without being detected by the guests.

Mixing of poison with wine is very common in many lands, and it has been in practice since biblical days. Delilah, no doubt, tempered the wine with *hashhash* and gave it to Samson before he fell asleep upon her knees [Judg. 16:19].

Wine and dregs are used metaphorically. The wine and the cup are symbolic of God's wrath and his fury and his vengeance, which were to be poured out against the wicked [Job 21:20]. "For thus says the Lord of hosts, the God of Israel, to me: Take the wine cup of this fury from my hand, and make all the nations to whom I send you drink it." The nations who had been drunk with power were to face destruction. They were to drink from the cup which now was in the hand of the Lord [Jer. 51:7].

See also the commentary on "The Cup."

THE SECOND AFFLICTION

All the horns of the wicked also will I cut off; but the horns of the righteous shall be exalted.

Ps. 77:10

The Aramaic word *tinyana* means "a second time"; that is, a second visitation, or a second punishment. The reference here is to the second captivity or the second visitation.

The Babylonian captivity was the second affliction of Israel. The ten tribes had been carried captive to Assyria in 722 B.C. Now Judah was captive in Babylon. And because of oppression the people became reconciled to their God and, therefore, they were mindful of his wonders in the olden days.

WATERS WERE AFRAID

*The waters saw thee, O God, the waters saw thee; they were
afraid: the depths also were troubled.* **Ps. 77:16**

The reference here is to the crossing of the Red Sea [Exod. 14:21-22].
The Lord caused the sea to go back all night by a strong east wind. The
statement that the waters "were afraid" is used poetically. The wind
also brought a heavy rain, accompanied by thunder and lightning, which
lightened the earth.

The depths of the sea were also disturbed by the strong wind and
the torrents of rain. Nature itself shared in the great victory over the
Egyptian army.

The psalmist is describing God's mighty power not only over the
Egyptian army but also over the forces of nature. In other words, he
made nature to be on the side of the Israelites and against the Egyptians.
We may state it in this manner: Moses was so divinely guided that
nature was on his side. He and his people arrived at the crossing place
at the right time, when the forces of nature were favorable to them.
The Egyptians, not being divinely guided, came at the wrong time, when
the forces of nature were against them.

Jesus rebuked the strong wind and stilled the storm. Nature is on the
side of those who are with God.

"THY WAY IN THE SEA"

*Thy way is in the sea, and thy path in the great waters, and thy
footsteps are not known.* **Ps. 77:19**

In the desert lands, tribal movements and armed forces are traced
by the imprints of their horses and camels. But God's ways and his
footsteps are hidden from the eyes of the flesh and can only be discerned spiritually.

"Thy way is in the sea" is an Eastern idiom which means "No one
knows your way or can see the imprints of your footsteps." That is to
say, "Your ways are unpredictable." Ships leave no imprints on the
surface of the sea, and birds leave no tracks in the air, nor can their
paths be seen. Such are the hidden ways of God and his footsteps through
time [Hab. 3:15]. But one can hear his small voice in the sea, on the
land, and in the air.

Job says, "Touching the Almighty, we cannot find him out." God's
ways are hidden from the eyes of men; they are not like men's ways.
At times we fail to understand God's plans and purposes simply because
we judge them by our human standards.

Just as God cannot be seen with the eyes of the flesh, his ways can only be understood and discerned spiritually. ". . . for there shall no man see me, and live" [Exod. 33:20].

Nothing happens in the whole universe without God's knowledge.

WATER STANDING AS A HEAP

He divided the sea, and caused them to pass through; and he made the waters to stand as a heap. Ps. 78:13

The Eastern text here reads: ". . . he made the waters to stand as in skins." In desert lands, during wars, water is carried in skins on the backs of donkeys, mules, and camels and piled up at the camp.

The strong east wind caused the water of the Gulf of Suez to go back [Exod. 14:21]. The waters piled up in a heap because of the force of the east wind. But when the wind ceased the water returned to its place.

Strong winds often drive water backward and cause it to pile up; during severe storms the wind often dries up small bodies of water.

When the Israelites crossed the tip of the Gulf of Suez, the Lord caused the water to stand up in a heap as though it were in sheepskins. And when the Egyptians tried to pursue them, the wind ceased and the waters rushed back, drowning all the Egyptians.

God has power over all forces of nature which he has ordained. When one is in harmony with God, all the forces of nature are on his side. Moses and his people were guided to cross at the right time, when the forces of nature were on their side.

WATER MIRACULOUSLY PROVIDED

He clave the rocks in the wilderness, and gave them drink as out of the great depths.
He brought streams also out of the rock, and caused waters to run down like rivers. Ps. 78:15-16

The Aramaic word *tera* means "to cleave, make a breach, pierce, cut, split."

The reference is to the wandering of the Israelites in the wilderness where water is scarce and hard to find. Moses was guided by God to find hidden wells [Num. 21:16]. He also was divinely led to dig wells in rocky places, and at times to bore the flint rocks in search for water.

Moses trusted in God and therefore overcame all the desert difficulties. What was hidden from the eyes of the people was divinely revealed to him. When the psalmist says that God "caused waters to run down like rivers" he means that the water came out abundantly. When rocky places are bored, the water sometimes gushes out because of geological formations.

The miracle is that Moses, through God's help, was able to supply his thirsty people with water in a dry land. When man is divinely guided, what is impossible becomes possible.

QUAIL

He caused an east wind to blow in the heaven: and by his power he brought in the south wind.
He rained flesh also upon them as dust, and feathered fowls like as the sand of the sea.
And he let it fall in the midst of their camp, round about their habitations.   Ps. 78:26-28

Large flocks of quail which migrate from Europe to the Arabian desert were caught between two strong winds and fell to the ground exhausted. When the quail cross the Mediterranean Sea they are sometimes exhausted and fall helpless on the beaches and nearby land. Thousands of them may drown in the sea.

The fact that the Lord caused the winds and brought the quail at a time when the Israelites were craving meat was a miracle. All acts of God are miracles and wonders in the eyes of men.

See the commentary on "Quail," Exodus 16:13.

GOD WAS NOT JEALOUS

For they provoked him to anger with their high places, and moved him to jealousy with their graven images.   Ps. 78:58

The Aramaic reads: "For they provoked him to anger by sacrificing on high places, and made him indignant with their graven images." The Aramaic words for "jealousy" and "indignant" are identical.

God could not have been jealous of images made of wood, stone, silver, and gold. There was nothing in these false gods made by men to make anyone jealous. God was indignant because the people had broken his commandments and were worshiping false deities which he had warned their fathers not to worship. The people also offered their children as burnt offerings to these pagan idols, so God was angry with them.

The worship of images was forbidden, because images were made by men and sold for a profit, but men were created by God in his own image and likeness.

BREAD OF TEARS

Thou feedest them with the bread of tears; and givest them tears to drink in great measure. Ps. 80:5

"Bread of tears" in this instance means oppression, high taxation, and persecution. In the East when people are harassed, highly taxed, and misruled, they weep and groan under their heavy burdens. They sow, but the others reap; they plant, but others eat the fruit of their trees.

One can hear people say, "This is the bread of tears." This is because they weep when they see their children hungry and crying for bread. When the fathers and mothers eat and are aware of the lack of bread, tears run over their cheeks and mingle with the bread.

VINE OUT OF EGYPT

Thou hast brought a vine out of Egypt: thou hast cast out the heathen, and planted it.

Thou preparedst room before it, and didst cause it to take deep root, and it filled the land.

The hills were covered with the shadow of it, and the boughs thereof were like the goodly cedars.

She sent out her boughs unto the sea, and her branches unto the river. Ps. 80:8-11

"Vine" in this instance is symbolic of Israel. Hebrew prophets and poets used poetic terms of speech, parables, metaphors, and allegories when describing important events. "My well-beloved hath a vineyard in a very fruitful hill" [Isa. 5:1].

At the outset, God took Abraham from Ur of Chaldea and brought him to Palestine. When he was uprooted from thence, he was planted in Egypt. After four centuries God took the Israelites out of Egypt and planted them in Palestine. Most of the other races in Palestine were cast out in order to make room for Israel because she was the vine of God.

"Vine" is here also symbolic of teaching. Teaching spreads like the branches of a vine. And just as the vine branches must abide with the vine, so the disciples and followers of a teacher of religion must abide in him in order to receive guidance and understanding.

Jesus said, "I am the vine, ye are the branches" [John 15:5].

When the hedges were broken down, the wild beasts trampled on God's vine (Israel) and broke its branches; that is, when God's commandments were transgressed and his way forgotten, pagan doctrines and practices destroyed the fences around the vineyard of God. The true religion was the only defense which Israel had against the strong nations round about her.

THE BOAR

The boar out of the wood doth waste it, and the wild beast of the field doth devour it.   Ps. 80:13

In the East nearly all vineyards are fenced or hedged to protect the vines from sheep, goats, and wild animals. In some of the vineyards men keep constant watch, especially during the night. Bears, boars, and other wild animals might sneak in and destroy the plants.

The boar and wild beasts here are used symbolically, meaning false prophets who had introduced pagan teachings into the Jewish religion, and pagan enemies who sought the destruction of Israel.

SONS OF GOD

I have said, Ye are gods; and all of you are children of the Most High.   Ps. 82:6

Prior to the flood, the descendants of Seth were good, and they were known as the sons of God; that is, the good men. The sons of Seth, the good men, were tempted by the beautiful daughters of men; that is, the descendants of Cain [Gen. 6:2].

Man was created in the image and likeness of God; therefore, the true man is a child of God. (The term "God" is derived from the German word "good.") In the East, even today, good men are addressed as the sons of God, and bad men are called the sons of the devil, or Satan. Jesus admonished his disciples to pray to God and to address him as their Father, who is in heaven.

GOD'S WAYS

Blessed is the man whose strength is in thee; in whose heart are the ways of them.   Ps. 84:5

"The ways of them" is a mistranslation. It should read, "in whose heart are thy ways"; that is, "God's way" and not the way of men.

The way of God is the true religion, which is based on justice and truth. When men walk in the way of God they are blessed, protected, and caused to prosper in all that they undertake. On the other hand, man's way of life leads to greed, hatred, war, and destruction.

THE VALLEY OF WEEPING

Who passing through the valley of Baca make it a well; the rain also filleth the pools. Ps. 84:6

Aumka debkhatha means "the valley of weeping." The Eastern text reads: "They have passed through the valley of weeping, and have made it a dwelling place; the Lawgiver shall cover it with blessings."

The valley of weeping must have been a place through which the captives were carried away into exile, or a valley in which some massacre had taken place in the olden days. Then again, when children were taken from their parents to be sold as slaves, both the parents and their children wept vehemently.

"SELAH"

O Lord God of hosts, hear my prayer: give ear, O God of Jacob. Selah. Ps. 84:8

The term "selah" has been a riddle to students of the Bible. No doubt, the meaning of this word was understood in biblical days, when both Aramaic and Hebrew languages were spoken by the Jews. (Selah does not occur in the Eastern text.)

The term "selah" occurs in the book of Psalms, other portions of the Bible, and in Jewish liturgical books. Various explanations have been given as to its meaning. Some authorities believe the term "selah" was used as an indication to lift the voice in a doxology. In the olden days, psalms were sung with musical accompaniments.

"Selah" might have been written with the letter *sadeh* instead of *semkat*. The psalms were composed orally and then written, and the two letters would be pronounced alike. "Selah" with *sadeh*, in this instance, would mean "to incline the ear, give heed, pray."

I am inclined to think that it means "heed, give attention, or be ready."

Some of the psalms were sung during battles. "Selah" might have meant, "Be ready to charge" or "Give ear to the command." In Turkish military drills the term "selah" was used, meaning "Be ready." When this word was uttered the soldiers placed their guns in position as though they were ready to charge. (In the Turkish language, the term "selah" was used for weapon or gun.)

That "selah" was used as a rubric, there is no doubt. Many times rubrics and titles were incorporated into the verses by the scribes, translators, and copyists. It may have been used as a marginal note later.

THE LORD IS A SUN

For the Lord God is a sun and shield: the Lord will give grace and glory: no good thing will he withhold from them that walk uprightly. Ps. 84:11

The Eastern text reads: "For the Lord God is our supply and our helper . . ." The sun supplies all human needs. In the East, God is often likened to the sun. This is because the sun is the source of life-giving energy, heat, and light, and is thus symbolic of God. In other words, these attributes of the sun are similar to the attributes of God: life, truth, and love. Just as the whole universe depends on God for its existence, so man and the universe depend on God for their harmony and well-being.

When God's truth is manifested, darkness and falsehood flee.

Jesus said, "I am the light of the world; he who follows me shall not walk in darkness, but he shall find for himself the light of life" [John 8:12, Eastern text].

THERE IS NONE LIKE GOD

Among the gods there is none like unto thee, O Lord; neither are there any works like unto thy works. Ps. 86:8

The Israelites feared other gods, but they believed that *Jahveh*, their God, was the greater god. The God of Israel was called the God of gods.

It took the Hebrew prophets centuries of teaching and warning to destroy polytheism in the minds of the people. Despite God's admonitions and revelations, the belief in pagan gods and idolatry persisted until after the second captivity. The weird pagan rituals and immoral Baal worship was a great temptation and a stumbling block to the children of Israel. The Eastern text reads: "There is none like thee, O Lord my God . . ."

RESURRECTION

Wilt thou show wonders to the dead? shall the dead arise and praise thee? Selah.
Shall thy loving-kindness be declared in the grave? or thy faithfulness in destruction? Ps. 88:10-11

The question of resurrection and life hereafter was not yet crystallized when the early (pre-exile) psalms were written. This question came to be the subject of debate during the exile and the postexile. The belief in resurrection was taught by some of the early prophets and by Job.

"Thy dead men shall live, their dead bodies shall arise. Those who dwell in the dust shall awake and sing, for thy dew is a dew of light, and the land of the giants thou shalt overthrow" [Isa. 26:19, Eastern text].

"Although devouring worms have covered my skin and my flesh, yet, if my eyes shall see God, then my heart also will see the light; but now my body is consumed" [Job 19:26-27; see also Job 7:7, Eastern text].

During the time of the Hebrew patriarchs there was little faith in the life hereafter. The people seemingly were content with one life. The early Hebrews considered death an end, believing that when a man died he was cut off from the Living God. People continued to live only through their posterity or the nation.

Resurrection was proclaimed more openly by Daniel during the exile. The people who had suffered injustices were to rise up and enjoy a new life, and the wicked were to rise up to be condemned for their evil deeds.

This doctrine was upheld by the Pharisees, but disputed by the Sadducees. Jesus, like Daniel, Isaiah, and Job, proclaimed the resurrection of the dead and eternal rewards.

"THE PROUD" NOT "RAHAB"

> Thou hast broken Rahab in pieces, as one that is slain; thou hast scattered thine enemies with thy strong arm.   Ps. 89:10

"Rahab" in the King James Version should not be confused with Rahab the harlot in Joshua 2:1.

The Eastern text of this verse reads: "Thou hast humbled the proud as those that are slain . . ."

There was a city called Rahab, but like many other cities, it was destroyed and never rebuilt [Ps. 87:4]. In Isaiah 51:9, Rahab is confused with *rabba* (great).

See the commentary on Isaiah 51:9.

UNDERSTANDING OF GOD

> Blessed is the people that know the joyful sound: they shall walk, O Lord, in the light of thy countenance.   Ps. 89:15

The Eastern text reads: "Blessed is the people that understand thy glory . . ."; that is, the people who praise the Lord instead of praising idols which were made of silver and gold.

The people who understand God's glory understand his laws and ordinances, and walk in his way. The blessings come from loyalty to the true God, the Creator of the heavens and earth, who knows the thoughts of men and rewards them according to their deeds.

SPEAKING IN VISIONS

Then thou spakest in vision to thy holy one, and saidst, I have laid help upon one that is mighty; I have exalted one chosen out of the people. Ps. 89:19

All God's communications and revelations with his holy prophets and seers were in visions.

The reference here is to the Messiah, who was predicted by the prophets and holy men as the Saviour of Israel and of the world. The Messiah was exalted above all the kings and princes of the world, and he was endowed with power and wisdom. Messiah, Christ, is the heir of the Davidic kingdom, the spiritual realm of God [Jer. 33:17].

DOMINION—POWER

I will set his hand also in the sea, and his right hand in the rivers. Ps. 89:25

The hand, in Semitic languages, is symbolic of power and dominion. It is also used as a token of blessing [Ezra 7:9; Neh. 2:18] and for chastisement [Deut. 2:15; Job 2:10].

"I will set his hand also in the sea, and his right hand in the rivers" means that he shall have dominion over the islands in the sea and the lands of the rivers, namely Egypt and Assyria. This suggests that the kingdom will be a great land and sea power.

This is a messianic psalm. The reference here is to the dominion which the Messiah will have over the world and his everlasting throne [verses 28, 29]. In biblical days, neither Israel nor Judah was a great naval power. Today the messianic kingdom embraces all lands, islands and great rivers.

Messiah, Christ, is the everlasting King and the High Priest [Jer. 33:17-18].

MAN NOT CREATED IN VAIN

Remember how short my time is: wherefore hast thou made all men in vain? Ps. 89:47

The Aramaic reads: ". . . for thou hast not created all men in vain." The error was caused by the mistranslation of negative *la* (not). The first part of the verse reads: "Remember me from the time I was created"; that is, "God is mindful of man from the time he forms him." He is also mindful of man's destiny, for God created him for a purpose, to play a part in this life.

Man has a spiritual mission on this earth. He was not created in vain or by chance. Therefore, God is constantly mindful of man, whom he created in his own image and likeness.

According to the Eastern text, this is one of the psalms of David, which was sung by the people who were in Babylon, asking God for comfort and blessings, and reminding him of their mission in life.

TEMPORAL LIFE

Thou carriest them away as with a flood; they are as a sleep: in the morning they are like grass which groweth up. Ps. 90:5

The Eastern text reads: "The span of their life will be as a sleep; in the morning they are like grass which changes." The reference here is to generations which come and pass away as a sleep.

Man in his growth changes like grass, which today is green and tomorrow is yellow and dry.

In the East grass sometimes grows on the walls of the houses, on housetops, and other places in the towns. This grass grows quickly, but when the sun is hot, it withers [Jas. 1:10-11]. Such is the temporal life; it withers like the grass on the housetops, which today is and tomorrow is gone.

SINS BEFORE GOD

Thou hast set our iniquities before thee, our secret sins in the light of thy countenance. Ps. 90:8

"Thou hast set our iniquities before thee" means, "Thou art constantly mindful of our evil deeds." This is because nothing that man does is hidden from God. The Eastern text reads: ". . . the sins of our youth" instead of "our secret sins."

God does not put evil things in his presence, but he sees and feels every human action that is contrary to the good. Whenever the children of Israel went backsliding, God saw that his laws and ordinances were violated. On the other hand, when men and women did good in his presence, he likewise was cognizant of it. Evil and wickedness prevail when goodness is lacking.

Human sins and iniquities remain in the presence of God until man repents and seeks forgiveness. Then they are no longer in the presence of God. But God sees and remembers even the sins of our youth.

SHADOW—DIVINE PROTECTION

He that dwelleth in the secret place of the Most High shall abide under the shadow of the Almighty. Ps. 91:1

In Semitic languages, "shadow" is often used figuratively, meaning "protection." The term "shadow" originally was derived from the shadow of the trees under which weary travelers and the sick sought refuge and relief during the hot hours of the day. In the olden days, just as today in some Eastern countries, trees are venerated and visited as sacred shrines by the sick and the suffering. In biblical days trees and groves were worshiped. The tree, through the inner forces therein, produces a cool shadow which helps the weary travelers and the sick.

In the East, when a king is good to his people they say, "We are under a good shadow," meaning "protection." On the other hand, dark shadows are symbolic of fear and uncertainty. "The valley of the shadow of death," for instance, means "instant death." In Psalm 23, God's shadow is his divine guidance and protection. "A secret place" in Aramaic means "fortress," the place where the warriors defend the town; that is, the strongest and most secure place in a town or a city. "Fortress," in this instance, means "protection." Kings and princes have secret places to hide themselves from their enemies, but God has no secret place, nor does he need protection.

GOD'S FEATHERS ARE HIS MERCY

He shall cover thee with his feathers, and under his wings shalt thou trust: his truth shall be thy shield and buckler. Ps. 91:4

The psalmist here portrays God as a loving mother bird which tenderly shelters its brood under its soft feathers, and covers them with her wings. The psalmist, being a shepherd and living in the outdoors, had carried newly born sheep under his thick woolen mantle and had seen, during times of danger, little birds taking refuge under their mother's wings.

Wings are symbolic of mercy, grace, protection, and trust. God has no wings, but he protects his children with his goodness and loving kindness, which are symbolic of everlasting wings constantly spread over all his creation, and especially over those who take refuge under them, for God is our refuge and our everlasting fortress.

CONSPIRACY

Nor for the pestilence that walketh in darkness; nor for the destruction that wasteth at noonday.   Ps. 91:6

The Aramaic word *miltha* in this instance means "conspiracy." "Pestilence that walketh in darkness" is a mistranslation of the Aramaic idiom, *miltha damhalkha bekheshokha* (the conspiracy that spreads in darkness).

Conspiracies are generally devised in secret and spread during the dark hours of the night when most of the people are asleep. In the East most conspiracies and revolutions start at night when the victims are sleeping peacefully in their homes.

VIPER AND ADDER

Thou shalt tread upon the lion and adder: the young lion and the dragon shalt thou trample under feet.   Ps. 91:13

"Viper and adder" are used symbolically, meaning "deadly enemies" or "evil forces." The lion and the dragon, metaphorically, are the wicked men and the oppressors who rebel against God and oppress his people.

Serpents and other deadly reptiles are symbolic of Satan, evil forces, and of men who are the enemies of God and his truth. Jesus told his disciples that they could handle serpents and drink any deadly poison, which means that they could handle the enemies of the Gospel and overcome all kinds of attacks and defamation of their names [Mark 16:18]. In Genesis, the devil is called "the serpent" [Gen. 3:1].

The reference here is to Messiah, who had the power to bruise the head of Satan and overcome all obstacles in his way, and to prove that, in the end, the truth triumphs over evil forces.

THE RIVERS ARE FULL

The floods have lifted up, O Lord, the floods have lifted up their voice; the floods lift up their waves.   Ps. 93:3

The Eastern text reads: "The rivers are full flowing, O Lord; the rivers have lifted up their voice; the rivers are flowing with purity." Floods, generally, are symbolic of calamities.

"The rivers" are symbolic of great powers and abundance. They could mean Assyria or Beth-Nahrin, the land between the two rivers, the Tigris and Euphrates.

Assyria had invaded all the lands west of the River Euphrates. Nearly all kingdoms, both large and small, were conquered or made tributaries. Thousands of men and women were carried away captive. The Assyrian power, like a flooded river, was sweeping everything ahead of it. Jeremiah, in his visions, saw the rise of Babylon like a swollen river sweeping everything ahead of it.

"The rivers have lifted up their voice" means that the Assyrians have lifted up their voices and defied the other nations and their gods [2 Kings 19:10-13].

But in the later years, when both Assyria and Babylon were gone, the rivers were flowing with purity. Persian kings were magnanimous in their decrees granting the restoration of the Jews. This psalm is a prophecy concerning God's abundant help to restore the exiles to their homeland.

MATERIAL THOUGHTS

The Lord knoweth the thoughts of man, that they are vanity.
Ps. 94:11

The Eastern text reads: ". . . they are like a breath." The Aramaic word *laha* means "breath" or "vapor." This metaphor is used to indicate that man's thoughts and aspirations are of short duration. This is because man's life is so short when compared with spiritual values which endure forever.

Man's material and temporal thoughts vanish like breath and like vapor, but his spiritual ideas and aspirations endure forever and are handed down from one generation to another.

GOD OF GODS

For the Lord is a great God, and a great King above all gods.
Ps. 95:3

The early Hebrews believed in the existence of other gods—the gods of the Gentiles—but they maintained that the God of Israel was the God of gods, a greater God. The Hebrew religion was different from that of the Gentiles in that they believed in one God, and because he was a mighty God they felt they had no need for other gods. But after defeats they often turned to pagan deities for help.

On one occasion when they lost the battle against the Moabites, they blamed it on their God, believing that he was a God of the mountains and therefore could not direct a battle in the plains.

The Israelites again and again went after the pagan deities and forsook the God of their fathers, the Living God. It took many centuries of defeats, two captivities, and much suffering before their pure concept of God was crystallized.

In other words, the Hebrews were monotheistic in their concept of God. The God of Israel was the Creator of the heavens and the earth and all that is therein.

GIFT OFFERINGS

Give unto the Lord the glory due unto his name: bring an offering, and come into his courts.   Ps. 96:8

The Israelites never visited their holy places with empty hands. They also took an offering of the flocks or herds, or a basket of bread or fruits.

Even today, the Easterners, when they visit holy places or men of God who act as healers, take offerings or gifts with them.

The offerings were used to take care of the priests, the Levites, and to feed the needy ones who came from long distances to worship [Mal. 3:10]. This ancient custom still prevails in the church of the East.

Some of the offerings were known as thanksgiving offerings, peace offerings, and sin offerings, while others were in payment for vows [Lev. 1:9]. See "Thanks Offerings."

GOD IS THE AUTHOR OF LAWS

His lightnings enlightened the world: the earth saw, and trembled. The hills melted like wax at the presence of the Lord, at the presence of the Lord of the whole earth.   Ps. 97:4-5

The reference here is to the appearance of God's glory upon Mount Sinai. Mount Sinai was in smoke because the Lord God descended upon it in fire. The whole mountain quaked. There were also thunder and lightning and a thick cloud [Exod. 19:16-18].

"Earth" in this instance refers to the ground or the earth in the vicinity of Mount Sinai. Such terms of speech as "the earth melted" are used metaphorically in describing the presence of the Lord and the glory of his majesty as compared with the mountains, hills, and even the earth itself. The whole earth could have shaken.

In biblical days thunder, rain, winds, and quakes were looked upon as the acts of God. This is because the people believed, and many still believe, that they were acts of God. God is the author of all universal laws.

HEAVENLY HARMONY

The heavens declare his righteousness, and all the people see his glory.   Ps. 97:6

The reference here is to universal harmony. All planets and other heavenly bodies travel harmoniously in their own orbits. No planet gets out of its orbit without causing disturbances in the universe. Sun, moon, and stars are so firmly established that we can hardly notice a change in their long courses.

Our concept of peace, justice, righteousness, and harmony is derived from the heavenly order. Jesus said, "Thy will be done in earth, as it is in heaven" [Matt. 6:10]. If every man would mind his own business and travel on his own path, many of the difficulties and evils of this world would be eliminated.

THE LIGHT OF GOD

Light is sown for the righteous, and gladness for the upright in heart.   Ps. 97:11

The Aramaic word *denakh* means "has shone"; that is, "light has shone on the righteous." The righteous are always associated with the light, which is symbolic of truth, understanding, and good works; and the wicked are associated with darkness, which is symbolic of ignorance and evil forces.

Evidently the error in the King James Version must have been caused by a defective manuscript, which had suffered from constant use and humidity, or it might be a printer's error. "Shone" and "sown" might be easily confused.

The righteous are always blessed by God. Their offspring prosper and they are spared during times of calamity. The light of God causes the darkness to flee.

EATEN ASHES LIKE BREAD

For I have eaten ashes like bread, and mingled my drink with weeping.   Ps. 102:9

In many parts of biblical lands, Arabia and other regions, where the tribal peoples migrate from one place to another, ovens are unknown and bread is baked on coals of fire. The baking is done so hastily that at times the dough is mixed with ashes. When the nomad peoples are hungry they eat the ashes which are on the bread. "For I have eaten ashes like bread" means, "I was poor and hungry." The poor and hungry do not stop to examine the food they eat. At times, they weep when they eat and drink, and their tears mingle with the water and bread. "My tears have been my bread . . ." [Ps. 42:3; see also Psalm 80:5].

THE LORD CLOTHED THE EARTH

Thou coveredst it with the deep as with a garment: the waters stood above the mountains.
At thy rebuke they fled; at the voice of thy thunder they hasted away.
They go up by the mountains; they go down by the valleys unto the place which thou hast founded for them.
Thou hast set a bound that they may.   Ps. 104:6-9

About two-thirds of the surface of the earth is water. The water covers high mountains in the ocean, some of which are higher than some of the mountains on the land. The reference here is to the seas and lakes which were formed on the tops of the mountains. In verse 9 the psalmist praises God's wisdom for setting bounds that the water may not cover the earth. One will never be able to explain the wonders of God, his wisdom and his creative power. Valleys, plateaus, plains, and hills were all formed by God.

According to the book of Genesis, the lands which now lie under the oceans and seas once were dry and, therefore, could be seen. But the Lord commanded that all the waters should gather together in different places [Gen. 1:9-10].

The Lord clothed the earth with glory and majesty. The great oceans and seas around us are full of beauty and life. Water is one of the four precious elements which makes life possible and the earth beautiful.

SPIRITUAL JOY

And wine that maketh glad the heart of man, and oil to make his face to shine, and bread which strengtheneth man's heart.
                                          Ps. 104:15

"Wine" is another word for "joy." The moderate use of wine was permitted during the feasts. Wine was, and still is, moderately used with food, especially in places where water was scarce or polluted. But wine and strong drink were forbidden by Mohammed. Only a few Moslems drink wine.

When Abraham returned from defeating the five kings, Melchizedek, king of Salem, brought forth bread and wine to greet Abraham and to rejoice with him in his triumph over the five kings. Wine was drunk as a symbol of joy [Gen. 14:17-18; 1 Sam. 1:24; Eccles. 10:19; Eastern text].

In the book of Judges we are told that wine cheers God and man, which means that it rejoices God and man when it is consecrated and drunk as a symbol of communion with God. We all know that God is the Eternal Spirit, and Spirit does not use wine in order to rejoice. Jesus said, "But I say unto you, I will not drink henceforth of this fruit of the vine, until that day when I drink it new with you in my Father's kingdom" [Matt. 26:29]. This means, "I shall not have this joy until I meet you in heaven." The term "wine" in the book of Judges is used to signify eternal joy. This is because bread and wine were offered by Easterners to their guests as a token of hearty welcome and rejoicing. This is why wine was used in offerings, symbolizing the joy of being in the presence of God [Exod. 29:40; Lev. 23:13].

Jesus also sanctioned the use of wine by drinking it and giving it to his disciples at the Lord's Supper [Matt. 26:29]. But in the East, wine was made from grape juices. No alcohol was mixed with it. Even before World War I, the alcoholic content was very small.

The Scriptures condemn the excessive use of wine. It was prohibited to the Nazarites [Num. 6:3]. Many of the prophets, Jesus and his apostles condemned drunkenness [Isa. 5:11; Eph. 5:18; 1 Tim. 3:3; Titus 1:7; 1 Pet. 4:3]. Drinking today is a cause of great evil.

Easterners consume considerable butter and olive oil. Some men drink them like water. They believe that oil makes men's faces shine. Bread is known as the staff of life. In the East no table is complete without high stacks of bread upon it. No matter how much other food is upon the table, the lack of bread would cause the host considerable embarrassment.

A SMALL TRIBE

When they were but a few men in number; yea, very few, and strangers in it.
When they went from one nation to another, from one kingdom to another people.   Ps. 105:12-13

When the Hebrews crossed the River Euphrates they were a small tribe. For many years they continued to wander from one place to another, seeking grass and water for their large flocks and herds.

In biblical days there were many small kingdoms in Palestine. Even small sedentary tribes were known as kingdoms. Joshua in a short space of time conquered thirty-one kingdoms, but the whole area of these kingdoms would not be more than three or four thousand square miles. At times even a city with a few villages around it was called a kingdom. For example, the kingdom of Jericho and *Ai*. They consisted of a few hundred acres of grazing land.

Everywhere the Hebrews went, God was with them and the kings of these small kingdoms. Gentiles welcomed them, traded with them, and did them no harm.

No doubt the grace of God went in advance of the Hebrew patriarchs who were called by him to play the greatest and the most important part in human history.

TO DISCIPLINE

To bind his princes at his pleasure; and teach his senators wisdom. Ps. 105:22

The Aramaic word *nerdey* means "to instruct, chastise, or discipline." "Bind" is a wrong translation.

The Eastern text reads: "To discipline [instruct] the governors at his pleasure and to teach the elders wisdom."

In the olden days kings, princes, governors, and elders acted as judges in settling disputes among the people. They were guided by the law of God and the Holy Scriptures. Every prince and elder was trained in the laws and ordinances.

The prophet Samuel and other Hebrew judges acted as judges, teachers, and arbitrators. All the kings of Israel and Judah were judges and were accessible to their subjects. Even poor men and women appeared before them for judgment.

This psalm is an admonition to the people and a reminder of the glorious past when God's favor was with Israel.

PROSPEROUS AND HEALTHY

He brought them forth also with silver and gold: and there was not one feeble person among their tribes. Ps. 105:37

This passage appears somewhat contrary to what we read in the first chapter of the book of Exodus, where the Israelites were poverty-stricken, oppressed, and living in misery. In Exodus 13:18 we are told that Israel went up armed out of the land of Egypt. The suffering and oppression might have been exaggerated. The Aramaic word *dakhrih* is derived from *karah* (to be ill or weak, to suffer pain). It sems that the people were well-to-do, healthy, and happy. Then again, we must not forget that God was on their side. Their faith in him protected them from disease.

The Hebrews, like other nomad people in the Near East, looked with disdain on labor. Pastoral people consider any kind of labor and regimentation as oppression. This is because nomad tribes live in tents and have no knowledge of laying bricks, making roads, or digging canals. They also abhor houses and palaces.

After all, the Egyptian oppressors seemingly were not as bad as the oppressors of our day. In this century, under Christian governments, the Jews in Europe were murdered and starved to death. But the Egyptians, in biblical days, even loaned the Israelites their jewelry of gold and silver, costly garments, and other articles. The Israelites left Egypt as strong, prosperous, and healthy people. Indeed, the Egyptians were not as bad as they are pictured in the early portion of the book of Exodus.

ROCK BORED

He opened the rock, and the waters gushed out; they ran in the dry places like a river.   Ps. 105:41

The reference here is to Exodus 17:6 and Numbers 21:16. The Aramaic text reads: *tarana* (flint). The word "open" means "He uncovered" or "bored through" the hard rock.

Many of the water sources were hidden under rocks to conserve the water. Then again, water was often struck in dry, flinty places where the people did not expect to find any water. Even during World War I wells were hidden, poisoned, and filled to prevent the enemy from advancing. Wise Arab shepherds know where the water is. Prophets and men of God are divinely guided to find it.

Everything is possible to God, who is the Creator of the universe and all that is therein. What is hidden from the eyes of mortal man is known to God.

See the commentary on Numbers 21:16.

REVOLT AGAINST MOSES

The earth opened and swallowed up Dathan, and covered the company of Abiram.   Ps. 106:17

The reference here is to the revolt in the wilderness under the leadership of Dathan and Abiram [Num. 16:31-32; Deut. 11:6]. These men challenged Moses and Aaron and questioned their leadership. Many leaders and laymen who were unable to face the desert hardships and were discontent tried to persuade the people to return to Egypt. They blamed their plight on Moses and Aaron.

Moses placed the matter in God's hands and asked his enemies to come forth before the Lord with their censers in their hands to see which groups the Lord would choose. And as they started to offer incense, an earthquake took place, and the ground opened under the revolters so that they were swallowed, both they and their families. This incident proved that Moses and Aaron were innocent and that God was with them [Num. 16:1-35].

Moses was divinely guided about the earthquake just as Lot was guided in his days when Sodom and Gomorrah (Amorah) were destroyed by the earthquake and fire [Gen. 19:24-25]. All these regions in Arabia contained oil and pitch, and eruptions like this are not uncommon. But when people are guided by God, they are warned to escape disaster. The people who were swallowed by the earth did not believe in God and had revolted against his commandment. That is why they perished. It was a great wonder and a triumph for Moses and Aaron, because it happened when the rebels came to offer incense before the Lord. The rebel leaders were Reubenites. They were not permitted to offer incense. When men and women break God's laws and rebel against him, strange things happen whereby they are punished.

EGYPT

Wondrous works in the land of Ham, and terrible things by the Red sea. Ps. 106:22

"In the land of Ham" means Egypt. The Egyptians were the descendants of Ham from his son Mizraim. Ham himself never dwelt in Egypt, but his descendants migrated southward. The descendants of Japheth went northward, and the descendants of Shem, the firstborn, remained in their ancestral land.

The term *ham* in Aramaic means "heat." When we say "Hamites," we mean "the people of the hot regions."

SACRIFICE FOR THE DEAD

They joined themselves also unto Baal-peor, and ate the sacrifices of the dead. Ps. 106:28

The reference here is to Baal-peor, or the Baal of Peor, when some of the Israelites took part in this pagan immoral ritual at Shittim. Twenty-four thousand died with disease. The Israelites participated in the sacrifices which the Moabites were offering to their pagan gods and the sacrifices for the dead. The Lord's anger was kindled against Israel.

The sacrifices were an ancient institution. The pagans sacrificed animals in memory of the departed ones. They also offered their children as burnt offerings to their idols. Many of these ancient customs were borrowed and practiced by the Israelites when they forsook their God and went astray after pagan deities.

See the commentary on "Baal-peor" [Num. 25:1-3].

AGRICULTURE

They did not destroy the nations, concerning whom the Lord commanded them.   Ps. 106:34

The Hebrews, prior to the occupation of Palestine by Joshua, were commanded by Moses to destroy all the inhabitants of Palestine who worshiped images and sacrificed to idols. But when the Hebrews conquered a land, they knew nothing about agriculture or the city life. The generation which had left Egypt was dead, and the new generation which was born and reared in the wilderness was ignorant of sowing, planting, and raising crops. They knew nothing about agriculture and the seasons of planting.

For a long time, then, the Hebrews depended on the natives of the land for plowing, sowing, and pruning the vineyards. This is why they did not destroy the worshipers of Baal, the god of agriculture. These inhabitants of the land, despite their pagan practices, were highly experienced in raising crops, building, and other arts unknown to the nomads. They were indispensable to the Hebrew conquerors. This is also true of the Turks when they conquered lands in the Near East. Being a nomad people, they spared the inhabitants of the land, treated them well, and entrusted them with high government tasks, such as trading, raising food, manufacturing and banking. The desert Arabs even today know nothing about raising crops. Some of them have never seen a wheat or barley field.

Had the Hebrews destroyed the inhabitants of the land, they would have confronted many difficulties in building cities, planting trees, and vineyards, pruning, grafting, and many other things of which the desert people are ignorant. In those days textbooks were unknown and knowledge was handed down from one person to another.

HUMAN SACRIFICES

Yea, they sacrificed their sons and their daughters unto devils.
Ps. 106:37

The Canaanites, like other pagans, sacrificed some of their children whom they had vowed to demons. The children were slain and burned on the altars. This ancient custom of sacrificing to demons (*shedy*) was prevalent in Palestine. Four centuries earlier, Abraham had been admonished to offer a ram instead of his son Isaac. The Hebrews never sacrificed their children to idols when they were in Egypt. Seemingly, human sacrifices started after the conquest of Palestine. The Israelites went astray after the gods of the Gentiles.

Pagan worship, pagan practices, and sacrifices, introduced by some of the kings of Israel and Judah, persisted until the second captivity, 586 B.C.

The Mosaic code states that every Israelite shall redeem all the first-born males. This law was revealed and written so that the Israelites might not sacrifice their children to idols. Then again, the Ten Commandments prohibited the worship of other gods and images [Exod. 20:1-6]. Nevertheless, the Israelites left their pure worship for pagan practices.

DRY RIVERS

He turneth rivers into a wilderness, and the watersprings into dry ground.   Ps. 107:33

In Palestine, Jordan, and other lands adjacent to the Arabian desert most of the rivers, brooks, and other sources of water dry up in the early summer months. During the long droughts water becomes so scarce that cattle and sheep perish from the lack of water.

In the East long droughts are attributed to the sins of the people. During the reign of King Ahab there was a drought which lasted for three years. Many flocks of sheep and herds of cattle perished [1 Kings 18:5]. This is also true of the long droughts of today, when wells dry up the sheep and cattle die. The dry rivers are called "wadies."

SATAN ON RIGHT HAND

Set thou a wicked man over him: and let Satan stand at his right hand.   Ps. 109:6

Easterners believe that every person has a guardian angel on the right hand and Satan on the left. The angel guides men in the way of God, but Satan causes them to go astray.

"Let Satan stand at his right hand" means, "Let them receive wrong counsel," or "Let Satan become his counselor."

MESSIAH, KING AND PRIEST

The Lord said unto my Lord, Sit thou at my right hand, until I make thine enemies thy footstool.   Ps. 110:1

The reference here is to Messiah, a greater King than David. The psalmist saw that a spiritual ruler was to replace the political kingdom of David, and he was to conquer and rule all the enemies of the Jews, not with force but with the arm of God, with truth and understanding. And God was to make the Messiah both Lord and Christ [Acts 2:34-36].

The Jewish leaders rejected Jesus of Nazareth on the ground that he was not from the house of David [John 7:40-42]. But Jesus challenged their literal interpretation of this psalm, proving that these words were spoken about himself, the Messiah, and not about David [Matt. 22:41-46; Luke 20:41-43; Mark 12:35-37].

"Right hand" is an Aramaic idiom meaning "power" or "trust," that is, all things in heaven and on earth were to be entrusted to Christ. The enemies are those who had departed from God's way of life and his truth. In due time, error was to be defeated and the truth was to triumph once and for all time.

Christ was to rule over the new theocracy. He was destined to be a King and Priest forever in the order of Melchizedek, the king of Shalem (Salem). No one knows who ordained this Melchizedek; nevertheless, he was a priest and king when Abraham defeated the five kings. "And Melchizedek king of Salem brought forth bread and wine: and he was the priest of the most high God" [Gen. 14:18; Heb. 7:1-2].

JORDAN DRIVEN BACK

The sea saw it, and fled: Jordan was driven back.
The mountains skipped like rams, and the little hills like lambs.
What ailed thee, O thou sea, that thou fleddest? thou Jordan,
that thou wast driven back?   Ps. 114:3-5

These words are expressed poetically and therefore should not be taken literally. "The sea saw it, and fled" means that the sea was turned back by means of a strong wind [Exod. 14:21].

Some authorities attribute this event to the holding back of the Jordan by landslides damming the narrow river. The Jordan is a small river, but the first body of water which the Israelites saw when they came from the Sinai Desert. Water is very scarce in the desert, and some of the natives do not know what a river is. Only two men of those who had left Egypt entered into the Promised Land.

The Lord God cleared every obstacle before them. God caused the waters to go backward;. the river Jordan was dried up so that they might cross. The Hebrews were born in the desert and had never seen rivers.

"The mountains skipped liked rams, and the little hills like lambs" means that the earth rejoiced at the presence of the Lord [verse 7]. All nature shared in the great joy, simply because the Israelites had left Egypt trusting in God. God was able to overcome all the difficulties in their way.

ROCKY PLACE

Which turned the rock into a standing water, the flint into a fountain of waters. Ps. 114:8

The reference here is to Exodus 17:6, when Moses struck the rock; that is, found the water system which had been hidden by the roaming tribes, or struck a new well in a rocky place.

The Lord God told Moses where to prove the ground, and when Moses struck the rock on the top of the well, the princes and the nobles of the people who were with him uncovered the well with their staves [Num. 21:16-18].

Flint is abundant in Palestine and in the Sinai Desert, where water is scarce and droughts common. ". . . who brought thee forth water out of the rock of flint" [Deut. 8:15].

God was able to discover what was hidden from the eyes of men. When Moses turned to God and prayed, God directed him to the places where there was water, grass, and food. God, as a loving Father, is always ready to lead and to answer the prayers of those who seek his divine aid.

See the commentary on Numbers 21:16.

BUILDERS AND STONES

The stone which the builders refused is become the head stone of the corner. Ps. 118:22

Builders in the East refuse to use large, heavy, unhewn stones in walls. This is because they are heavy to lift and it takes a long time to hew them. After a conference with the owner of the house they may agree to use them for foundation stones.

In the East stones and all other materials for building are provided by the owner of the house. The builders are hired to set the stones together;

therefore the builders and the owner of the project must agree on the type of stones to be used in the walls. Generally the owner of the building wishes to see large stones hewn and placed in the walls where they will be seen. The builders argue that the large stones should be placed on the corner. The builders know better than the owner of the house.

The large and unhewn foundation stones are more important than the smooth stones that rest upon them. They bear the weight of the whole building.

Truth is the foundation of a religion, because everything rests upon it. But there are certain important truths that cannot be understood, and therefore they are rejected.

Jesus Christ was the Stone which the builders had rejected but he became the Cornerstone of a new church [Matt. 21:42; Isa. 28:16]. Jesus' teaching was alien to the ears of the Jewish priests and scribes. It was hard for them to love their enemies and to pray for those who hated them.

PROCESSIONS

God is the Lord, which had showed us light: bind the sacrifice with cords, even unto the horns of the altar. Ps. 118:27

The Eastern text reads: "O Lord, our God, enlighten us; bind our festival processions as an unbroken chain, even to the horns of the altar."

"Bind our festival processions" means to make them orderly and permanent; that is, "Keep our ritual in perfect order throughout all generations."

The Israelites, during their festivals and thanksgiving for victory, marched in an orderly manner to the altar where the thanks sacrifice was offered.

The people implore the Almighty to give them light and understanding so that they may continue to worship him, pray before him, and make offerings to him continually, orderly, and faithfully without fear [Isa. 33:20].

THE FAITHFUL

My soul breaketh for the longing that it hath unto thy judgments at all times. Ps. 119:20

The Eastern text reads: "My soul is pleased and desires thy judgments at all times." The Aramaic word *saba* means "to be pleased, to be desirous, or to long for something."

The psalmist here implies that his soul longed to keep God's judgments at all times.

Many Hebrews in exile were forced to break the ordinances of their God and to bow to images. But most of them remained loyal, and some of them, like Daniel, were willing to die for the way of their God rather than break his commandments.

A SOLEMN OATH

My hands also will I lift up unto thy commandments, which I have loved; and I will meditate in thy statutes.   Ps. 119:48

"My hands also will I lift up unto thy commandments" means, "I will implore thy commandments," or "I will take an oath with thy commandments." Easterners when praying lift up their hands above their heads. Lifting up of the hand may be a gesture or threat of striking or punishing. But in this case the term "hand" is used figuratively. When people make a solemn oath, pledge, or vow, they lift up one or both hands. The lifting of the hand signifies that what is to be uttered is the truth.

"And Abram said to the king of Sodom, I have lift up mine hand unto the Lord, the most high God" [Gen. 14:22], which means "I have sworn by God." "My mouth hath kissed my hand" [Job 31:27]. When people exonerate themselves of guilt, they wash their hands.

BOTTLE IN THE SMOKE

For I am become like a bottle in the smoke; yet do I not forget thy statutes.   Ps. 119:83

The Eastern text reads: "I have become like a frozen sheepskin," which means, "I have suffered all disgrace" or "I was harassed."

In the East sheepskins are used as containers for water, milk, and wine. During cold seasons, in the early morning when the temperature is low, empty sheepskins may become frozen. The skin becomes wrinkled and hard like a stone. Bottles made of glass were unknown in biblical days. Even today, sheepskins are still used as containers among the nomads and the migratory tribes in Kurdistan, Iran, and the Arabian desert.

Easterners, when describing the difficulties, humiliations, and persecutions they have gone through, or awful tales they have heard, say, "My skin wrinkled on my bones." This idiom is still in use today in vernacular speech. The psalmist is asking God for his speedy judgment on those who persecute him. In other words, Israel is praying for vengeance against her enemies.

WISE ELDERS

I understand more than the ancients, because I keep thy precepts.
Ps. 119:100

Easterners look up to the elders for wisdom, counsel, and guidance. In some parts of the East, where primitive customs and manners still prevail, the words of an elder are respected and obeyed as the words of a book of law. In these ancient parts of the world, age and gray hair speak with authority, and the counsel of the young man is scorned.

Job says, "With the ancient [elders] is wisdom; and in length of days understanding" [Job 12:12]. "Days should speak, and multitude of years should teach wisdom" [Job 32:7].

The psalmist understood more than the elders, because he was guided by God's commandments. In truth there is no age, but age is important because young men lack experience and are unfamiliar with God's laws and ordinances.

"A LAMP UNTO MY FEET"

Thy word is a lamp unto my feet, and a light unto my path.
Ps. 119:105

Light is symbolic of enlightenment and education, and darkness is symbolic of ignorance and lawlessness.

The streets in the ancient cities of biblical lands are narrow and crooked, and the pavement rough. Even in the daytime one has to watch his steps while walking. Moreover, there are holes and rubbish in the streets which often cause people to fall and injure themselves.

In the ancient days, just as today in some parts of the East, city ordinances were unknown and the streets were neither swept nor repaired—except when a ruler, a prince, or a member of the royal family planned to visit the city. Then the streets were cleaned and repaired in honor of the royal visitor.

In the evening and during the dark hours of the night, when men are walking in the city they generally carry a lamp with them. Noblemen are led by a servant who carries a lamp in his hand. The bearer of the lamp bends one arm down so that the light of the lamp may fall at the feet of his master, and as he walks ahead, he bends down once in a while, turning the light of the lamp to the path ahead of him to see if there are any holes or rubbish in the road.

The ancient lamp is a small, earthen vessel in the shape of a small saucer. The wick is on one end and the oil or butter on the other. They are generally made in an oval shape.

God's laws and his words lighten our path and keep our feet from falling into temptations. Life is full of difficulties and is dark and crooked, like a dark and crooked path. God's laws and his ordinances direct our steps to the straight path of life and protect us and lead us into safety, for only through his light do we see the light.

TRUSTING IN GOD

My soul is continually in my hand: yet do I not forget thy law.
Ps. 119:109

The Eastern text reads: "My soul is continually in thy hands. . . ." The Aramaic word *naphash* (soul) also means "life." And, at times, it used to mean "the spirit." The reference here is to life. The psalmist has entrusted his life into the hand of God, and therefore he is able to keep his commandments.

A man's life without God's helping is not secure, nor can one walk in the way of God without entrusting his life into God's hands. This is because life is full of difficulties, and God's truth has many enemies and much opposition. Many of those who have tried to walk in God's way have been persecuted and put to death.

The Aramaic word *edek* (thy hands) has been confused with *edi* (my hand).

Jesus quoted this phrase when he said, "Father, into thy hands I commend my spirit" [Luke 23:46]. When we entrust our spirit into the hands of God we are sure of ultimate victory over opposition and the forces of evil.

"MY EYES LOOKED FOR SALVATION"

Mine eyes fail for thy salvation, and for the word of thy righteousness.
Ps. 119:123

The Aramaic word *saki*, means "hoped, longed, looked forward, expected." "Fail" is a mistranslation. This verse should read: "My eyes look forward [or hope] for thy salvation."

In the East, when people are in danger, they look around them to see if any help is coming. And when no help comes, then they look up to heaven and implore God to save them.

"Eyes" in this instance are used figuratively, meaning "mind." The eyes are the agents of the mind. What the psalmist means here is that Israel had been looking forward for God's salvation and deliverance from the hands of the oppressors.

In times of oppression and distress the people lifted up their eyes and looked to Zion for salvation and for the reign of God.

TIME TO REPENT

It is time for thee, Lord, to work: for they have made void thy law.   Ps. 119:126

This verse should read: "It is time to serve the Lord; for they [the wicked] have nullified thy law" (Eastern text).

When wickedness was prevalent the prophets and the pious called on the people to turn to God and to keep his laws.

The Lord, like a loving Father, was always ready to receive those who repented and turned to him. The psalmist calls not on God to work, but on the people to repent and serve the Lord. It is never too late to repent. God was always ready to receive the penitent. On the other hand, the suffering and hardships were caused by the people who had forsaken God's law and had gone after pagan gods.

UNDERSTANDING FROM GOD

The entrance of thy words giveth light; it giveth understanding unto the simple.   Ps. 119:130

The Aramaic reads: "Make plain thy word and enlighten and give understanding to the simple."

The terms "children" or "babies" are used in referring to the unlearned, the simple people. Jesus said the truth was hidden from the learned, but revealed to the simple, the little children.

Without understanding from God and the power of the Holy Spirit, we cannot unlock the Scriptures and grasp their inner meaning.

WEPT BITTERLY OR VEHEMENTLY

Rivers of waters run down mine eyes, because they keep not thy law.   Ps. 119:136

"Rivers of waters ran down my eyes" is an idiom which means "I wept vehemently," or, "I washed my bed with my tears." Such sayings are common in Eastern languages and are well understood by the people even today. The people know that no one can wash a bed with tears, literally.

The psalmist was sorry and wept when he saw that the people were not heeding God's admonitions and keeping his commandments. He mourned over the lack of religion and the failure to keep the law of God. This is because religion and God's law were the dearest things in the hearts of the faithful Jews. They meant more than their children, their wives, and their earthly possessions.

PREVENTED THE DAWNING

I prevented the dawning of the morning, and cried: I hoped in thy word.   Ps.119:147

"I prevented" here means "I went before" or "rose up before dawn." This word was well understood a century ago, but now it has become obsolete and hard to understand. It means "preceded," "went before," or "in advance." In a number of other passages it is translated "I rose up early and sent prophets." It should read, "I sent prophets in advance."

Easterners pray at dawn, and some pray at midnight when "the heavens declare the glory of God" [verse 148; also Ps. 119:1].

PRAYER SEVEN TIMES

Seven times a day do I praise thee, because of thy righteous judgments.   Ps. 119:164

Seven is a sacred number among the Hebrews and is often used symbolically. God ended his work on the sixth day, and rested on the seventh day [Gen. 2:2]; Pharaoh in his dream saw seven cows and seven ears of corn [Gen. 41:2-7]; seven priests with seven trumpets marched seven days around Jericho [Josh. 6:4].

The number seven was a well-known number and was used frequently in the Bible.

In the East people pray many times a day. Some of the pious men and women pray at midnight, in the morning, at noon, and in the evening. The Moslems pray five times a day. But in praying it is not the hour or the number of times that counts, but sincerity and pious devotion. Great is the power of the prayer of the righteous.

LONG SOJOURN

*Woe is me, that I sojourn in Mesech, that I dwell in the tents
of Kedar!* Ps. 120:5

"Mesech" is a mistranslation. This verse should read: "Woe to me,
that my sojourn is prolonged." The Jews were carried captive to Assyria
and Babylon. Many of them longed for the return to Zion.

LOOKING UP TO ZION

*I will lift up mine eyes unto the hills, from whence cometh my
help.* Ps. 121:1

The reference here is to Jerusalem and Mount Zion, the city which
God had chosen for his holy habitation. Jerusalem is built on Mount
Zion, the highest mountain, which is situated on the southwesternmost
part of the city, the hill of the Jabosites.

The holy temple was built on Mount Moriah. The terms "hills" and
"mountains" are often used indiscriminately in the Bible. "Why leap
ye, ye high hills?" [Ps. 68:16].

"Yet have I set my king upon my holy hill of Zion" [Ps. 2:6]. From
Zion was to come salvation for the oppressed people of Israel. Thus,
the people look to the high hills for the salvation of Israel.

High hills are symbolic of God's glory, power, and majesty, which
are higher than all the realms of men. In the olden days the people
worshiped in high places in order to be closer to God.

ISRAEL ESTABLISHED

*He will not suffer thy foot to be moved: he that keepeth thee will
not slumber.* Ps. 121:3

The Aramaic word *zaweta* (moved) also means "tremble." "His foot
moves" is an Eastern idiom which means, "He is not firm." In other
words, he is trembling because of fear and uncertainty. But "his foot
is firm" means that he is well established and confident.

Israel was to be re-established in Palestine. The captives were to
return once more, and now they were to be re-established permanently,

so that nothing could ever disturb them or cause them to move from one place to another.

This prophecy was fulfilled during the reign of the Persian kings when the second Jewish commonwealth was established in the fourth century B.C.

WAITING FOR GOD'S HELP

Behold, as the eyes of servants look unto the hand of their masters, and as the eyes of a maiden unto the hand of her mistress; so our eyes wait upon the Lord our God, until that he have mercy upon us.   Ps. 123:2

To "look to the hand" of masters and mistresses is an Aramaic idiom which means to "depend upon" them—to wait for their masters or mistresses to give them their hire and food, and to extend favors to them. Moreover, in Aramaic, the term *eida* (hand) also means "help" or "aid."

In the East servants wait patiently for the master or mistress to give them orders, food, clothing, and their wages. Servants respect and revere their masters and mistresses.

The psalmist here portrays Israel as depending upon the hand of God for direction, guidance, mercy, and blessing.

SOW IN TEARS

They that sow in tears shall reap in joy.   Ps. 126:5

In many lands in the Near East where grain is scarce, farmers hide some of the grain for seed. Seed stores and salesmen are unknown. Every farmer takes care of his own seed.

Generally, wheat supplies are exhausted during the long winter months. The spring months are the hardest months of the year for the family to get through. Nearly all the scanty provisions which the family has stored are gone, and bread and other food supplies become very scarce. Bread is carefully rationed, so much for each person. As the scanty supply of wheat is exhausted, the children cry for bread, but there is little or no bread to give them.

In the spring when the farmer sows the wheat, he weeps, for though his children are crying for bread he must use what grain is left for seed and not for bread. So as he scatters the precious seed in the ground, tears run down his cheeks.

On the other hand, during the months of harvest, the sowers and reapers and their families are happy. The bread supplies are once more replenished and everybody rejoices. ". . . they joy before thee as those who rejoice in the harvest . . ." [Isa. 9:3, Eastern text].

In America a farmer may worry during harvest, not knowing where to store his new and abundant supplies of wheat, or what to do with the grain that is left from the year before.

In the East the farmers usually receive only a small portion of the crops. Most of the produce is taken by the owner of the land. Moreover, high taxes and tithes reduce the farmer's portion. In some cases their wheat supplies are plundered.

The Jews were subjected to many hardships and privations by their ruthless foreign oppressors. But they always looked to the bright day, the day of God's deliverance and the day of abundance.

GOD'S PROMISE TO DAVID

The Lord hath sworn in truth unto David; he will not turn from it; Of the fruit of thy body will I set upon thy throne. Ps. 132:11

The Lord had promised David, saying, "There shall not fail thee a man [an heir] in my sight to sit on the throne of Israel."

This promise is conditional. The descendants of David who were to sit upon his throne were admonished to take heed to their ways, so that they might not depart from the way of the Lord. They were told to walk before him faithfully as David had walked [1 Kings 8:25].

The "seed of David" also means the teaching of David; that is, the things for which David stood. Despite his many weaknesses, King David's faith in God never wavered, nor did he serve other gods. David was the symbol of true loyalty to God.

Zedekiah was the last descendant of David who sat upon his throne. From the year of 586 B.C., when Judah was conquered by the Chaldean army, to the present day, no descendant of David has ever reigned in Jerusalem. This is because David's descendants forsook their God and went after pagan gods. They also made alliances with pagan kings, so they disqualified themselves as the true heirs of David.

Spiritually, these promises were fulfilled through Jesus Christ, the King of kings. The Davidic kingdom is symbolic of a universal state and of the kingdom of God and his reign of justice.

COLLAR OF HIS ROBE

It is like the precious ointment upon the head, that ran down upon the beard, even Aaron's beard: that went down to the skirts of his garments.   Ps. 133:2

The Aramaic word *bar sora* means "the collar." The Eastern text reads: ". . . the beard . . . that went down to the collar of his robe."

In biblical lands, the collar of some of the robes comes down to the man's breast.

The Aramaic word for "skirt" is *shipola*. No man could grow a beard to reach to the skirt of his garment. Most beards are trimmed short. But the priests grow long beards which come down to the collar of their robe as a token of dignity. Even today, the beards of the elderly priests reach to the collar of their robes.

JACOB CHOSEN

For the Lord hath chosen Jacob unto himself, and Israel for his peculiar treasure.   Ps. 135:4

God chose Jacob, not because he hated Esau, but because the latter was not interested in the promises which God had made to his grandfather Abraham. Esau was more interested in hunting than in religious devotion and sacred family traditions.

On the other hand, Jacob, from the outset, was interested in the spiritual religion, laws, and ethics of his forefather, Abraham, which he wanted to hand down from generation to generation, so that the messianic promises might be fulfilled and his religion become a light to the Gentile world.

God did not reject Esau. Esau disqualified himself. This is why his birthright was given to Jacob. Being the firstborn, he had the chance to carry on the spiritual mission of his people, but he rejected it, simply because the material world meant more to him.

Jacob was loved more by his mother, and Esau more by his father. God does not respect the faces of persons. He chose the one who was qualified for his purposes. Nevertheless, Esau was also blessed. Twelve kings and princes came out of his loins. God declared his Word to Jacob, his statutes and his judgments to Israel [Ps. 147:19].

KINGS

I will praise thee with my whole heart: before the gods will I sing praise unto thee.   Ps. 138:1

The Eastern text reads: ". . . before the kings will I sing praise to thee." The term "gods" was generally used when speaking of the idols which were worshiped in God's place, or human deities [Deut. 32:16]. Moreover, the men who represented God were sometimes called gods [Exod. 4:16; 7:1]. The term "god" was also used for good people, the children of God. "I have said, You are gods; all of you are children of the most High" [Ps. 82:6, Eastern text].

The prophets and poets of Israel, when praising their God, spoke of him as God of gods, King of kings, and Lord of lords. At times, the Israelites were misled by false prophets and priests who, for the sake of worldly gain and sensualities, had embraced pagan religion and had worshiped pagan gods. The pagans had many gods.

Most of the kings and emperors were worshiped as gods. The true concept of a spiritual and universal God was crystallized.

HUMAN CONDUCT

Thou knowest my downsitting and mine uprising; thou understandest my thought afar off. Ps. 139:2

"My downsitting and mine uprising" means "my conduct of life" or "my behavior." In the East when a noble or wise man is praised men say, "He knows how to sit down and how to rise up"; that is, he is cultured and knows etiquette. Noblemen, pious men, and the cultured never sit in the chief places. They sit in the low places or stand until they are seated by the host.

Easterners are known and esteemed for their correct behavior. "But I know thy abode, and thy going out, and thy coming in . . ." [2 Kings 19:27].

The psalmist here implies that the Lord knows the conduct of men and the thoughts of their hearts [verses 7-10].

DESCENDING INTO HELL

If I ascend up into heaven, thou art there: if I make my bed in hell, behold, thou art there. Ps. 139:8

"Hell" is wrong. The Aramaic and Hebrew word is *Sheol* (the resting place for departed souls). The word for hell is *gehenna,* derived from the valley of Hinnom. *Gehenna* was a place outside the walls of Jerusalem where rubbish was burned, a place where the pagans had sacrificed their children to idols. Therefore, hell is a fearful place prepared for the wicked, and not a place for God to visit.

The Eastern text reads: ". . . if I descend into Sheol, behold, thou art there also."

The Hebrews thought that Sheol was the place of the dead, an isolated place beyond the jurisdiction of the living God. "In Sheol who shall give thee thanks?" [Ps. 6:5]. Today we know that there is no place in the universe that is not under the jurisdiction of God, no place that is hidden from his presence.

GOD IS EVERYWHERE

If I take the wings of the morning, and dwell in the uttermost parts of the sea;
Even there shall thy hand lead me, and thy right hand shall hold me.

Ps. 139:9-10

Prior to the eighth century B.C., some of the Hebrew prophets, such as Amos, Hosea, and Isaiah, proclaimed the universality and omnipresence of God. The eternal and living God was no longer a local deity like pagan gods, but the God of all nations and people, the Lord of the mighty empires and the small kingdoms. On the other hand, in the past, Abraham, Isaac, and Jacob knew that their God was the only Creator of the heavens and the earth and all that is therein.

Years later this pure concept of the universality of God was lost. The Hebrews had spent 400 years in Egypt, and the Egyptians were idolators. They had many gods with diverse duties and jurisdictions. The Egyptians were opposed to the idea of a single deity.

The Hebrew prophets knew that no man could escape or hide himself from the presence of God. Nearly all great Hebrew prophets believed in the universality of their God. But prior to the eighth century B.C., the Hebrews believed that their God was the Creator of the heavens and of the earth, but they also thought of the pagan deities as lesser gods. In other words, Jehovah was the God of gods.

With this clear Hebrew concept of the universality of God so plainly expressed in the above verses, we can see that no Hebrew prophet could have hidden himself or fled from God. And when they did, they did it in a vision or in a dream like those of Ezekiel and Daniel. All communication between God and the prophets took place in visions and dreams.

Jonah stated that the Hebrew God, Jehovah, "made the sea and the dry land" [Jonah 1:9].

LIGHT OF GOD

If I say, Surely the darkness shall cover me; even the night shall be light about me.
Yea, the darkness hideth not from thee; but the night shineth as the day: the darkness and the light are both alike to thee.

Ps. 139:11-12

This passage should read: "If I say, Surely the darkness shall be as light upon me; even the night shall be light before my face."

Darkness and light are relative terms. Darkness is caused by the turning of the earth. Darkness is symbolic of ignorance, evil, and paganism, and light symbolizes God's truth and his way of life. When one knows the truth, even the night shall be light before his face. Just as light dispels darkness, so truth dispels error. And just as the darkness is the absence of light, evil is the absence of truth.

PRAYER AS INCENSE

Lord, I cry unto thee: make haste unto me; give ear unto my voice, when I cry unto thee.

Let my prayer be set forth before thee as incense; and the lifting up of my hands as the evening sacrifice.   Ps. 141:1-2

This psalm was sung by the exiles who were in Babylon. They implored God to stand by them and to strengthen them, that they might not incline to evil things in a strange land.

The Aramaic word for incense is *bisma*, and the Aramaic word for health and satisfaction is *basam*. When incense is cast on the fire, the smoke with its aroma rises up to heaven. Their prayer and supplication was to rise up above all the materialism, confusion, and paganism in Babylon.

The evening sacrifice referred to here was a meat offering that consisted of lambs which were offered daily, in the evening and in the morning [Exod. 29:38-41; Num. 28:4].

RIGHTEOUS TEACHERS

Let the righteous smite me; it shall be a kindness: and let him reprove me; it shall be an excellent oil, which shall not break my head: for yet my prayer also shall be in their calamities. Ps. 141:5

The Eastern text reads: "Let the righteous teach me and reprove me; let the oil of the wicked not anoint my head since my prayer has been against their evils."

Easterners never refuse chastisement and reproof from the mouths of pious men; they look upon it as dew on dry land. But they refuse admonition and discipline from the wicked. In the East the righteous elderly men and teachers of religion discipline men and women who have gone astray, and they correct and punish the youth. The parents are pleased and grateful when their children are chastised and punished by the elders.

Oil is used for healing. In the East, where Western medicine is unknown, oil is poured on wounds. The heads of guests are anointed with oil to refresh them. Because water is scarce, bathing in some of the arid lands is unknown. People anoint their heads and parts of their bodies with butter or olive oil to prevent the skin from cracking [Luke 7:46].

Pious men would refuse the admonition and the hospitality of the wicked, because they condemn the evil deeds of such men.

A STRONG HAND

When their judges are overthrown in stony places, they shall hear my words; for they are sweet.   Ps. 141:6

This should read: "When their judges are stopped [or hindered] by a strong hand . . ." the reference here is to the wicked judges and oppressors who perverted justice and thus defrauded the poor. Only a strong hand, the hand of God, could restrain these wicked judges from oppressing the people. God was the only hope of the pious men who longed for justice and righteousness. Nothing else could stop the oppression, extortion, and prevailing evil. Under such circumstances the words of the law of God were sweet.

The oppressors perverted justice and used violent means to exploit the people and to defraud the weak and the needy.

VENGEANCE UPON THE DEAD

Our bones are scattered at the grave's mouth, as when one cutteth and cleaveth wood upon the earth.   Ps. 141:7

The Eastern text reads: "Like the ploughshare that scatters the earth, let their bones be scattered at the mouth of the grave."

When cities were occupied by the enemy forces, dead bodies were often dug out of their graves and burned or otherwise desecrated. Moreover, the graves of kings and princes were sometimes dug up by treasure seekers, and they would leave the bones of the dead scattered around the graves. The sepulchers of the princes and kings usually contained costly objects of gold, silver, and precious stones. For centuries, therefore, sepulchers and graves of the kings have been violated by treasure hunters.

Josiah took the bones of the pagan priests out of their sepulchers and burned them [2 Kings 23:16-18].

The Jews who were oppressed were cursing their enemies and seeking God's vengeance upon them, and even upon their dead bodies.

DWELLING IN DARKNESS

*For the enemy hath persecuted my soul; he hath smitten my
life down to the ground; he hath made me to dwell in darkness,
as those that have been long dead.* Ps. 143:3

This is not the song of a poet as it may seem, but a song of the
people who were in Babylon, beseeching God's mercy and protection in
the land of their enemies. All references are to the state; that is, to
Israel. The term "servant" means the exiles (Israelites) who were captive in Babylon. The psalm might have been composed by King David
and sung by the exiles.

Political Israel was crushed and the people were in despair in a
pagan land. The enemy had destroyed both the state and the temple
and done away with the law, which was the light and the very life of the
Jewish people. Now the Israelites were living in darkness, in lands where
paganism was the official religion. The hopes of restoration were dim,
and the people felt that there was nothing worthwhile to live for.

Now the exiles were remembering the glorious past, the days of old
when they were living in their own land and worshiping in God's temple.

STRANGE CHILDREN

*Send thine hand from above; rid me, and deliver me out of
great waters, from the hand of strange children.* Ps. 144:7

The Aramaic word *awaley* (wicked or ungodly men) has been confused with *aweley* (little children or babies). The Aramaic word for
wickedness is *awla;* the Hebrew is *awel.* These words in Semitic languages
are written alike but pronounced differently. The word for child or baby
has two dots under it, and the word for wicked or ungodly men has
one dot under it.

When the Old Testament was translated into Greek about 300 B.C.,
vowels and dots were unknown. They were introduced in the fifth century after Christ by the learned men in the church of the East (wrongly
called Nestorian) and later were adopted by the Jews. Note that the
Aramaic and the Hebrew alphabets are the same. Thus the words were
confusing and difficult for the translators, especially to foreigners.
At times, flies placed more dots on a manuscript than had been placed
there by the scribe! Western versions were based on Hebrew or masoretic
texts of the ninth century, and these texts contained dots or vowel signs.
The oldest Aramaic texts of the Peshitta, written in Estrangelo characters,
have no vowels.

No one would even think to pray for deliverance from the hands of children. The people ask God for complete delivery from their enemies [verse 11].

SON OF MAN

Put not your trust in princes, nor in the son of man, in whom there is no help.   Ps. 146:3

"Son of man" in this instance means an ordinary human being; that is, a man should put his trust in God instead of trusting in a human being.

The Aramaic words *bar-hasha* (son of man) and *barnasha* (a human being, or humanity in general) are similar. *Barnasha* is often used collectively, meaning "mankind."

The title *breh-dnasha* (the Son of man) was frequently used by Jesus when he referred to himself [Mark 2:10; 14:62]. Jesus used this term more often than the title "Son of God." He did this as a token of his humility and as proof that he was both a perfect man and a God. *Breh-dnasha* (the Son of man) was used by Jesus about forty times, The term was used by the prophet Ezekiel [Ezekiel 2:1].

Earthly man was made from dust, and into dust he returns. But spiritual man is the image and likeness of the living God. Physical man, being weak and subject to temptations, cannot be relied upon for help. Therefore, God is man's only hope, his trust and his salvation [Pss. 131:3; 146:5]. Then again, man's help is temporal, but God's help endures from one generation to another.

SPIRITUAL BLINDNESS

The Lord openeth the eyes of the blind: the Lord raiseth them that are bowed down: the Lord loveth the righteous.   Ps. 146:8

Hebrew prophets healed the sick, cleansed the lepers, raised the dead, and performed other wonders, but there is no mention in the Bible that they ever opened the eyes of the blind.

When Jesus opened the eyes of a man who was born blind, the Jews rejected the miracle and tried hard to prove that the blind man had not been born blind and therefore was not healed by Jesus. This is because they had never heard that anyone could open the eyes of a blind person. It was hard for them to believe that a prophet from Galilee could perform greater miracles than those wrought by their great prophets,

Elijah and Elisha. But the man *was* born blind and he *was* healed by Jesus.

The blind man argued to prove that Jesus must be a man of God to have opened his eyes: "From ages it has never been heard that a man opened the eyes of one who was born blind. If this man were not from God, he could not have done this" [John 9:32-33].

"Blind" is often used to mean dull-minded. This expression was used by both Isaiah and Jesus. "Eyes they have, but they cannot see." "Their eyes have become blind and their hearts darkened, so that they cannot see with their eyes and understand with their hearts; let them return and I will heal them" [John 12:40, Eastern text].

"I was eyes to the blind," declared Job, by which he meant that he was a guide to men who were carried away with the material world [Job 29:15]. Spiritual blindness is worse than physical blindness. A physically blind man may have keen spiritual sight and be pleasing in God's sight, but a spiritually blind man cannot even know God. He is blind to truth and justice, and his evil influence may lead others astray.

CHAPTER SEVENTEEN

PROVERBS

INTRODUCTION

THE Aramaic *mathley* means "parables or proverbs." *Mathley* is something devised by the mind—a mental picture. Parables, axioms, and riddles are devised by the learned and the wise. Easterners, during their discourses, debates and preaching, use parables and proverbs in order to convey their meaning and to impress that meaning vividly on the minds of their hearers. Some of the great teachers and preachers never speak or preach without first telling a parable or composing a proverb. This is because pictures were prohibited by the Mosaic law.

The book of the Proverbs, no doubt, was composed largely by King Solomon, the wisest king in Israel. This is why the book bears his name. They are called the Proverbs of Solomon, the son of David, the king of Israel. There was only one king in Israel by the name of Solomon.

Solomon prayed for wisdom and understanding instead of praying for wealth and power, and the Lord granted him his prayer and gave him both wisdom and riches. Nevertheless, some of these sayings might be the works of other wise men which Solomon had collected.

Most of the sayings in the book of Proverbs are expressed in axioms in order to leave a lasting impression on the mind of the reader. The parables and proverbs served to guide the young and the old in their ways of life and to warn them against evils.

Jesus illustrated most of his teachings by parables, metaphors, and figures of speech; in fact, he hardly ever spoke without parables. This is why the Four Gospels are more widely read and understood than all other portions of the Bible put together.

THE LAW OF COMPENSATION

*Therefore shall they eat of the fruit of their own way, and be
filled with their own devices.*   Prov. 1:31

"Therefore shall they eat of the fruit of their own way" is an idiom
in Semitic languages which means that they shall be punished by the
results of their own evil devices. This is because good men receive good
rewards and bad men receive evil rewards. It is the law of compensation.
One reaps what he has scattered. That is, if one sows wheat, he reaps
wheat; and if he sows tares, he reaps tares; for nothing can change the
essence of a seed or the essence of an act.

In the East it is often said, "I will make him eat a beating," which
means, "I will punish him." The term "eat" is also used for embezzlement.

"Woe to you, scribes and Pharisees, hypocrites! for you embezzle the
property of widows, with the pretense that you make long prayers; because of this you shall receive a greater judgment" [Matt. 23:13, Eastern
text].

The Hebrew prophets and poets were familiar with the law of compensation, for they had seen it work in their own tribal life.

REVERENCE TO GOD

*Then shalt thou understand the fear of the Lord, and find the
knowledge of God.*   Prov. 2:5

The Aramaic word *dikhelta* (reverence, fear, worship) in most cases
should read "reverence"; that is, "the reverence of the Lord God."
Dikhelta also means worship, and worship is reverence to God. *Dighlatha
di ammey* refers to the worship or the images of the Gentiles.

In the East kings and princes demand great reverence from their subjects and officials. The people bow to the ground and then stand up in
awe in their presence. This is because pagan kings were worshiped as
gods and therefore were greatly feared.

God is a loving Father, who loves and cares for his children. The
Scripture admonishes us to revere him, to put him in the first place in our
hearts, and to walk in his ways. When we reverence a person, we also
love him. But when we fear a man we hate him in our heart. Reverence
produces love, but fear creates hatred. To be afraid of God would do no
one any good.

Today millions of people are afraid of dictators, and the more they
are afraid of them, the more they hate them.

We must revere God because he is our Father and our Creator. We revere our human parents, but we are not afraid of them. The reverence of God is the foundation of all wisdom.

WISDOM

Happy is the man that findeth wisdom, and the man that getteth understanding.   Prov. 3:13

Wisdom and understanding are two separate things. Wisdom is the source of knowledge, and understanding is knowing how to use wisdom. Therefore, wisdom without understanding is dangerous.

For instance, atomic energy is a blessing to mankind, but without understanding, man may use it for his own destruction. This is also true of money and power. One has to gain knowledge and understanding in order to use them properly and constructively. For example, when religion is understood, it is a great blessing to humanity; but when it is not understood it is a curse. Peace, harmony, and brotherly love are fruits of the understanding of religion and worship. On the other hand, strife and religious wars are the fruits of misunderstanding. Wisdom must be tempered with the love of God which passes all human understanding.

THE WICKED BLESS THEMSELVES

The curse of the Lord is in the house of the wicked: but he blesseth the habitation of the just.   Prov. 3:33

The wicked prosper, but not by the blessing of the Lord. They bless themselves and flourish for a time, but sooner or later they are cut off. The Lord, being longsuffering, grants them time to repent, and when they refuse to mend their evil ways, they destroy themselves.

Job says: "The tabernacle of robbers shall be removed, and the confidence of those who provoke God; for there is no God in their heart" [Job 12:6, Eastern text]. Justice sooner or later catches up with the wicked.

"I will bring it forth, saith the Lord of hosts, and it shall enter into the house of the thief, and into the house of him that sweareth falsely by my name, and it shall remain in the midst of his house, and shall consume it with the timber thereof and the stones thereof" [Zech. 5:4].

"The ungodly are not so: but are like the chaff which the wind driveth away" [Ps. 1:4].

WINE

For they eat the bread of wickedness, and drink the wine of violence. Prov. 4:17

"Wine" is here used metaphorically, meaning "extortion," "rage," and other evil things which dominate the lives of the wicked and cause them to oppress the poor and the needy.

Wine was used for drink offerings and for human rejoicing. Wine causes men's hearts to rejoice, but it also destroys them when they drink to excess. "Wine is a mocker, strong drink is raging: and whosoever is deceived thereby is not wise" [Prov. 20:1].

People can be drunk with wine, with inspiration, with hatred, pride, anger, and with other evil things.

See the article on "Drunkenness."

LOOK STRAIGHT

Let thine eyes look right on, and let thine eyelids look straight before thee. Prov. 4:25

"Let thine eyes look right on" is an Eastern saying which means "Be honest and sincere, and look people straight in their eyes." Eyes are the windows of the soul. Pious and sincere persons are not ashamed to look straight into the faces of other people.

On the other hand, liars and crooked persons cannot look straight even into the faces of their friends. They look down because they are hypocrites and are ashamed of their evil acts.

EVIL PATHS

Ponder the path of thy feet, and let all thy ways be established. Prov. 4:26

The Eastern text reads: "Keep your feet away from evil paths; then all your ways shall be firm." Evil paths is another name for broad and dangerous ways which are full of temptation, the ways which lead one to destruction. Jesus said, "Enter ye in at the strait gate: for wide is the gate, and broad is the way, that leadeth to destruction, and many there be which go in thereat: because strait is the gate, and narrow is the way, which leadeth unto life, and few there be that find it" [Matt. 7:13-14].

One who keeps away from evil paths will avoid all the stumbling blocks in his way.

The word "way" is an Eastern term which means "religion," the way of life and human conduct.

IMMORALITY DISCOURAGED

Drink waters out of thine own cistern, and running waters out of thine own well.

Let thy fountains be dispersed abroad, and rivers of waters in the streets.   Prov. 5:15-16

This is an Eastern saying that is used commonly in vernacular speech and means "Love your own wife and keep away from other women." Water, in this instance, is symbolic of love between a husband and his wife and the children that are born to them [verses 17, 18]. "Drink waters out of thine own cistern, and running waters out of thine own well" means "Keep faithful to your own wife and have no relations with strange women."

"Rivers of waters in the streets" means many children playing in the streets. Love, like precious water, must be zealously guarded. The author of the Proverbs here warns the Israelites not to waste their semen with strange women because the children they beget would not be their own. Adultery was strongly condemned by the Mosaic law, and the Israelites were warned against cohabiting with strange women. They were the holy offspring of Israel, called and sanctified for a holy mission. They were not to mix with other races. Because of their calling they were to keep their posterity pure and holy.

In Palestine and the Arabian desert, water is so scanty and precious that some men are reluctant to let strangers and, at times, even their neighbors, draw water from their wells.

BECOMING SURETY

Thou art snared with the words of thy mouth, thou art taken with the words of thy mouth.

Do this now, my son, and deliver thyself, when thou art come into the hand of thy friend; go, humble thyself, and make sure thy friend.   Prov. 6:2-3

The Eastern text reads: "Then you are snared with the words of your mouth, you are caught with the words of your lips. Do this now, my

son, and deliver yourself because, for the sake of your friend, you have
fallen into the hands of your enemies; go, therefore, and stir up your
friend for whom you have become surety to meet his obligation."

King Solomon is admonishing his son in case he has become a surety
to his friend and thus has fallen into the hands of his enemies. The
son is told to stir up his friend to pay the debt for which he had become
a surety.

In the East, a good man's word is accepted as surety. And at times a
man may become surety for his friend who, being poor, is unable to
give a pledge.

The good man may incur the enmity of the lender because of the
failure of his friend to pay his debt. Most lenders would hold the pledge
at a high rate of interest until the debt was paid, either by the borrower
or by the one who has been a surety for him. On the other hand, some
borrowers take advantage of the good men who become surety for
them, and they refuse to pay the debt.

SLUGGARDNESS

*So shall thy poverty come as one that traveleth, and thy want as
an armed man.*   Prov. 6:11

The Eastern text reads: "And then poverty shall come upon you, and
distress shall overtake you; become a successful man."

The reference here is to a sluggard who spends most of his days in
idleness, playing, and sleeping. These men sooner or later are overtaken
by poverty and want. Neither a traveler nor an armed man have anything to do with poverty. The translators were unable to translate certain Semitic words and terms of speech in this verse. The Aramaic word
tadrekhakh (shall come upon you, shall catch up with you) has been
confused with "the traveling man" or "an armed man." Fortunately,
in the East, traveling men and soldiers are better off than other people.

In the Near East some people are poverty-stricken simply because
they are heavily taxed and exploited. But a great many are poor because
they are unwilling to work. Some, who consider themselves noble, would
choose death rather than work in the field or in the street.

LAW IS A LIGHT

*For the commandment is a lamp; and the law is light; and re-
proofs of instruction are the way of life.*   Prov. 6:23

In the East lamps and candles were used not only to lighten the dark
houses but also to lighten the paths in the crooked, narrow streets during

the night. Even today, men and women carry lamps or candles while walking in the night.

God's commandments are likened to a lamp, because life is full of difficulties and stumbling blocks. One has to have the light of God in order to be sure of his steps.

See the commentary on Psalm 119:105.

A REMINDER

Bind them upon thy fingers, write them upon the table of thine heart.   Prov. 7:3

"Bind them upon thy fingers" is an Eastern idiom which means, "Do not forget them." In the East people bind a string on the finger as a reminder of an admonition or of something to be done.

The Israelites, like other Near Eastern people, carried amulets containing passages from the Scriptures to protect them from evil spirits, and as signs to remind them of promises and vows. The amulets are still used in Palestine and other parts of the East [Deut. 6:8].

The reminder is placed in a small silver amulet and fastened to a chain or silken cord and worn around the neck or placed in a necklace and worn by women.

HARLOT'S ENTICING

For at the window of my house I looked through my casement.
And behold, there met him a woman with the attire of an harlot,
and subtil of heart.   Prov. 7:6, 10

The Eastern text reads: *adikath* (she looked out) and *adiketh* (I looked out). The difference between these two words is a single dot over or under the letter "t."

The reference here is to a bad woman who sits at the window, trying to entice young men. In the East, as women cannot converse with men, harlots beckon with their eyes and nod their heads to men who pass by their houses. They seldom walk in the streets, nor do they dare to talk to men.

In some places the harlots sit at the door of their houses. They are also found in camps and small villages; some of them sit on the highways far off from the villages [Gen. 38:14].

PRUDENCE THE PRODUCT OF WISDOM

*For wisdom is better than rubies; and all the things that may be
desired are not to be compared to it.*
*I wisdom dwell with prudence, and find out knowledge of witty
inventions.*   Prov. 8:11-12

It should read: "I, Wisdom, have created prudence . . ." The
Aramaic word *bereth* (I have created) has been confused with *beth*
(house, dwelling place). Prudence and knowledge are the products of
wisdom.

Wisdom is the source of power, honor, glory, and riches. Then again,
justice and righteousness are determined by wisdom and understanding.
Wisdom is more precious than rubies and other costly stones. Only with
wisdom can we distinguish between evil and good, false and real. King
Solomon, in his prayer, asked for wisdom because wisdom is more
precious than gold and silver. When one possesses wisdom, he possesses power, glory, riches, and understanding.

WISDOM, THE SOURCE OF GOOD

*My fruit is better than gold, yea, than fine gold; and my
revenue than choice silver.*   Prov. 8:19

From time immemorial the world's economic systems, wealth, and
commerce have been based on wisdom and understanding. Wisdom has
made silver and gold the mediums of exchange. Moreover, all our inventions are fruits of wisdom.

Our banks, our institutions, and our industries are all managed by
men of understanding.

STOLEN WATER AND SECRET BREAD

Stolen waters are sweet, and bread eaten in secret is pleasant.
                                                  Prov. 9:17

Where water is brackish and wells and brooks dry up during the
early summer, water is precious and at times is stolen. The people who
dwell in arid lands may suffer thirst, and the sheep and cattle may
perish because of the lack of water. In many cities in the Near East
water is sold in the market places.

In Europe and America, where the people are blessed with abundant water, no one would think or even dream of stealing water. But in Bible lands and Arabia, during droughts when wells and springs dry up and water is hard to obtain, thirsty people often steal water. The water is usually stored in a skin that is hung on a pole in the tent. At times it is hidden under bedclothing, for it is so scarce that it is given only to little children. The adults may go to sleep thirsty.

The stolen water is sweet simply because the person who steals it is suffering from thirst and it is obtained without paying anything for it.

The reference here is to stolen love—those who neglect their wives and satisfy their desires by secretly loving the wives of others. Anything which is stolen or deceitfully obtained tastes sweet, but sooner or later it turns bitter.

In the East when men are on a journey they try to conserve their provisions. According to the Eastern custom, whenever a man sits down to eat he must invite all those who happen to be near him. Therefore, some men, in order to avoid inviting other men to share their scanty supply of bread, eat secretly. That is, they do not sit down; they eat while they are walking. The loaves of bread are kept under their garments. Other food supplies are kept in their large sashes. The person who eats secretly enjoys the bread because he knows some of the men who are with him are hungry.

Bread, being scarce on a journey, tastes good, but when bread is abundant, it is no longer a delicacy.

RICHES

The blessing of the Lord, it maketh rich, and he addeth no sorrow with it.   Prov. 10:22

Riches are the result of spiritual understanding of life and the keeping of God's commandments. In other words, God blesses those who walk in his ways and do his will. He entrusts wisdom to one and riches to another to be distributed to his children. Thus, riches are gifts of God, that man may rejoice in his labor, have his portion in this life, and offer thanks to his Creator. "The Lord gave, and the Lord hath taken away," says Job [Job 1:21]. God sets one up high and puts down another.

The Hebrew patriarchs who walked in God's way were blessed with wealth. Their sheep and cattle multiplied exceedingly, and they were led by God to green pastures and prolific wells.

Extreme wealth is just as dangerous as extreme poverty. When riches multiply, some people forget God. They may attribute their wealth to their own power and wisdom, and thus are destroyed by them [Deut. 8:13-14; Matt. 13:22; Mark 10:22].

The secret of wealth is not the quantity thereof, but the joy, the blessing, and the contentment which it brings to those who possess it.

GOLD CANNOT REDEEM

Riches profit not in the day of wrath: but righteousness deliver-eth from death.   Prov. 11:4

"The day of wrath" is "the Day of the Lord"; that is, the day of reckoning when every man will be rewarded according to his deeds. On that day, silver and gold will not count, nor will it ransom those who possess it. "They shall cast their silver into the streets, and their gold shall be despised; their silver and their gold shall not be able to deliver them in the day of the wrath of the Lord . . ." [Ezek. 7:19]. On that day, works and righteousness shall count for the deliverance of the soul.

Noah was spared because of his righteousness when the rest of the people perished in the flood [Gen. 7:1].

GOOD COUNSEL

Where no counsel is, the people fall: but in the multitude of counselors there is safety.   Prov. 11:14

The Eastern text reads: "A people who have no leader shall fall; but in the multitude of counsels there is deliverance."

The Aramaic word *medabrana* means "a leader, ruler, high priest." The Aramaic word for counsel is *molkana,* derived from *melakh* (to give counsel).

Israel was often portrayed as a flock without a shepherd [1 Kings 22:17]. Whenever the people lacked a good ruler and faithful counselors, they suffered defeats, exile, poverty.

Indeed, the rise and fall of a kingdom or a people is in the hands of those to whom the people have entrusted themselves, their welfare, and their future.

THE PIOUS MAN

The merciful man doeth good to his own soul: but he that is cruel troubleth his own flesh.   Prov. 11:17

The Eastern text reads, "The pious man does good to his soul." The Aramaic word *khasia* means "unblemished, pious, one whose sins are forgiven." The Aramaic word for "merciful" is *merakhmana.*

The pious man does good to his own soul by his good behavior, charity, and character. But the evil man destroys his own body by his evil conduct.

A pious man whose sins are forgiven is greater than a merciful man. Even the wicked have mercy toward one another. But the pious is unblemished in all his way.

MERCIFUL GRAIN DEALERS

He that withholdeth corn, the people shall curse him: but blessing shall be upon the head of him that selleth it.   Prov. 11:26

Etta means "deceit or villainy." The Eastern text reads: "He who holds back grain in the day of distress shall fall into the hands of his enemies; but a blessing shall be upon the head of him who sells it." During famines and droughts, many wicked rich men refuse to sell their grain. They store it and keep it to sell at a high price. They know that when the people are hungry they will pay any price for food. In the East most of the grain and other food supplies are in the hands of the wealthy and greedy land owners. They refuse to sell until the people are at the point of starvation [Gen. 41:56].

The Egyptians lost their houses, their cattle, and their fields during the famine, but the lives of the people were spared [Neh. 5:1-5].

Easterners believe that what is gathered deceitfully and unjustly will be scattered away by God's justice like dry stubble before the wind.

A GOOD TREE

The fruit of the righteous is a tree of life; and he that winneth souls is wise.   Prov. 11:30

"Tree" is used here figuratively, meaning "family"; that is, "the tree of life" or one's posterity.

Vine is symbolic of a race, and cedar of a ruler. Good men who trust in God and obey his commandments are likened to the trees planted by the waters, which spread out their roots by the stream and give good fruit in their seasons [Ps. 1:3; Jer. 17:8]. "The trees of the Lord are full of sap; the cedars of Lebanon, which he hath planted" [Ps. 104:16].

A good tree brings forth good fruits, and a bad tree bad fruits. Jesus sometimes spoke of men figuratively as trees [Matt. 7:17]. The importance of a tree is the fruit thereof, and not the tree itself. When a tree fails to bring forth good fruit, it is cut down [Matt. 7:19]. This is also true of men and women. They are judged by their works. And the wicked are cut off from the face of the earth [Prov. 12:7; Job 12:6, Eastern text].

WICKED ARE OVERTHROWN

The wicked are overthrown, and are not: but the house of the righteous shall stand.   Prov. 12:7

The wicked may prosper for a while, but sooner or later they are destroyed and are no more.

This passage confirms what Job wrote. "The tabernacle of robbers shall be removed, and the confidence of those who provoke God; for there is no God in their heart" [Job 12:6, Eastern text]. But the rendering of that verse in the King James Version is a contradiction of Proverbs 12:7.

POSTERITY

The light of the righteous rejoiceth: but the lamp of the wicked shall be put out.   Prov. 13:9

"Light" in this instance means "posterity," and the lamp is symbolic of the heir; that is to say, the posterity of the righteous shall rejoice, but the posterity of the wicked shall be extinct.

"Lamp" is used quite often to mean an heir. In the East we often say "God has given him a lamp," and, "May God preserve your lamp." In 1 Kings 15:4, we read: "Nevertheless for David's sake did the Lord his God give him a lamp in Jerusalem, to set up his son after him, and to establish Jerusalem."

When families mourn over the death of their heir or a beloved person, their tents are dark. They sit in darkness as a token of mourning.

WORSHIP OF RICHES

Much food is in the tillage of the poor: but there is that is destroyed for want of judgment.   Prov. 13:23

In the King James Version the Aramaic word *aomrah* (life span, manner of life) has been confused with *eborah* (wheat, food). The Eastern text reads: "Those who do not understand the manner of life are destroyed by riches; yea, many men are destroyed completely."

The wise king speaks of men whose worship of wealth has deprived them from enjoying their lives. And many men lose their lives in pursuit of riches and material things. Life is more important than all things around it. The spiritual and eternal life should not be jeopardized for the sake of material things that are temporal. [See Eccles. 10:19, Eastern text].

HOUSEHOLD OF THE WICKED

The house of the wicked shall be overthrown: but the tabernacle of the upright shall flourish.   Prov. 14:11

"House" in this instance means "household." In the East overlords and oppressors have large households and many servants. Moreover, some of them have their own private tax collectors and armies. These wicked men had enriched themselves at the expense of the poor. They believed they would continue to exert power forever.

The houses and the tabernacle of the wicked are overthrown at the end, but the upright shall flourish [Job 8:15].

"The tabernacle of robbers shall be removed, and the confidence of those who provoke God; for there is no God in their heart" [Job 12:6, Eastern text].

Note that verse 11 is longer in the Eastern text. "A heart which has understanding knows its own bitterness; and a stranger does not share in its joy." (This portion is missing in the King James Version.)

RICH IN WISDOM

The crown of the wise is their riches: but the foolishness of fools is folly.   Prov. 14:24

Aothra (riches) is often used figuratively, meaning "rich in wisdom, intelligence, and understanding." *Miathra* means "excellent." In the East, learned men are addressed as *Miathra,* "Excellency," which denotes their vast scope of knowledge.

On the other hand, not all wise men are blessed with material things. In the East men who are in search of knowledge and understanding generally neglect their business affairs and overlook the material world. Some of these wise religious men are so engrossed in their studies that they are poverty-stricken. But nevertheless, they are highly respected for their wisdom. Thousands of men and women are blessed by their wisdom and understanding.

PEOPLE ARE IMPORTANT

*In the multitude of people is the king's honor: but in the want
of people is the destruction of the prince.*　　Prov. 14:28

The Aramaic reads: "In the abundance of population is the king's
honor; but in the destruction of the people is the ruin of the king."

The reference here is to the increase of population, and the welfare
and prosperity of the people. During famines and plagues many people
perish and, consequently, the king becomes impoverished and weak.
Isaiah says: "Thou hast multiplied the people, and thou hast increased
its joy" [Isaiah 9:3, Eastern text].

ANGER KILLS

*A sound heart is the life of the flesh: but envy the rottenness
of the bones.*　　Prov. 14:30

The Aramaic *de mepaig* is the active participle of *paag, piga* (to cool,
abate, mitigate). The Eastern text reads: "He who cools down his anger
is a healer of his own heart; but wrath is the rottenness of the bones."

The reference here is to the man who controls his anger and thus
heals his heart. For anger and resentment are two destructive forces
which result in pain and suffering. Job says: "For anger kills the foolish
man, and enmity slays the silly one" [Job 5:2, Eastern text].

THE WICKED ARE OVERTHROWN

*The wicked is driven away in his wickedness: but the righteous
hath hope in his death.*　　Prov. 14:32

The Aramaic reads: ". . . he who is confident that he is without sin
is a righteous man." The word "death" is not found in the Eastern text.

The reference here is to men who have done good deeds throughout
their lives and are confident in their hearts that at the end they will be
rewarded for their good works and thus declared pious. But the wicked
are overthrown in their wickedness. They remember the evil that they
have done, and expect nothing but ultimate judgment, condemnation,
and destruction.

SPIRITUAL TRUTHS

A wholesome tongue is a tree of life: but perverseness therein is a breach in the spirit.   Prov. 15:4

The latter part of the verse is mistranslated in the King James Version. The Eastern text reads: ". . . and he who eats of its fruit shall be filled with it."

The Aramaic word *akhel* means "eat." *Akhel* has several other meanings, such as "devour, decay, embezzle."

The fruits of a wholesome tongue are spiritual truths and a wise counsel, which lead men to the way of God. The souls of those who heed the admonitions of wise and pious men are satisfied with spiritual food.

LOYALTY TO FRIENDS

Every one that is proud in heart is an abomination to the Lord: though hand join in hand, he shall not be unpunished. Prov. 16:5

The Aramaic word *moshit* is derived from *yeshat* (to stretch out). The Eastern text reads: "Every one who is proud in his heart is an abomination to the Lord; and he who stretches out his hand against his neighbor shall not be pardoned because of this evil."

"Stretch out his hand against his neighbor" in this instance means to do evil or harm to his neighbor. One can be on guard against his enemies, but few men suspect that their friends or neighbors would harm them. An enemy can be forgiven, but a friend cannot be forgiven or declared innocent when he does evil to his friend.

EARLY RAIN

In the light of the king's countenance is life; and his favor is as a cloud of the latter rain.   Prov. 16:15

The latter part of the verse should read: "And his favor is like a cloud of the early rain." The Aramaic word *bakherata* means "the first." The early rain is most welcome in the Eastern countries, and is received with joy by both farmers and the pastoral people. This rain is held by a thick cloud and lasts for many days. It softens the parched ground for the sower and causes grass to grow. On the other hand, the later (latter) rains often destroy the ripening crops.

Easterners watch for the rain patiently, especially when the land has suffered a long drought [1 Kings 18:14-45]. Droughts are very common in Palestine. Sometimes they last two or three years.

The unexpected favor of a king is like the appearance of a cloud heralding the downpour upon the parched ground. People rejoice to receive favors and commendations from their rulers. They also rejoice when they see the cloud which heralds the early rain.

WISDOM IS PRECIOUS

How much better is it to get wisdom than gold! and to get understanding rather to be chosen than silver! Prov. 16:16

Wisdom is more precious than costly jewels. Without wisdom and understanding, man would not be able to discern the value of things. He would not know the difference between pearls and glass beads. He invents new things to meet his growing needs.

All values of material articles are determined by wisdom and understanding. It is wisdom which declares gold more valuable than silver and brass. Wisdom is the essence of prosperity and happiness.

Jesus said, "And yet wisdom is justified by its works" [Matt. 11:19, Eastern text].

The works of the wise are manifested and praised, and the works of fools detested and scorned.

DISGRACE COMES FIRST

Pride goeth before destruction, and a haughty spirit before a fall. Prov. 16:18

The Aramaic reads: "Disgrace goes before destruction, and pride before misfortune." That is to say, a wicked man is disgraced before his fall, and his pride is gone before his misfortune.

In the olden days, when justice caught up with wicked people they were humiliated in the presence of the people before they were reduced to poverty and put to death [Esther 6:10-13].

POOR IN PRIDE

Better it is to be of an humble spirit with the lowly, than to divide the spoil with the proud. Prov. 16:19

"An humble spirit" in this instance means a meek or humble person. In the East men who are unassuming and unconscious of their noble racial ancestry are known as *rokha makikhta* (humble men).

Jesus said, "Blessed are the humble"; that is, "the humble, those who have no racial pride" [Matt. 5:3, Eastern text].

The Aramaic word *rokhah* (pride) means also "spirit, temper, wind, and rheumatism." At times, *rokha* is also used meaning "a person." "It is better to be humble and lowly in pride than he who divides spoil with the mighty."

SELF-CONTROL

He that is slow to anger is better than the mighty; and he that ruleth his spirit than he that taketh a city.   Prov. 16:32

The Aramaic reads: ". . . he who conquers himself than he who takes a city." The Aramaic word *naphsha* (soul) also means "self"; *naphshey* (himself).

In the East men who control their anger and restrain themselves from doing evil hastily are considered wise. Many good men are noted for their patience and self-control.

"Be not hastily angry" [Eccles. 7:9]. Anger is condemned by Jesus Christ. ". . . whosoever is angry with his brother without a cause shall be in danger of the judgment" [Matt. 5:22]. Isaiah says, "Shun the man who is hasty for of what account is he?"   [Isa. 2:22, Eastern text].

FEASTING

Better is a dry morsel, and quietness therewith, than a house full of sacrifices with strife.   Prov. 17:1

The Aramaic term "sacrifices" in this case means "feasting." In the East when men are blessed and their substance multiplied, they offer sacrifices to display their wealth.

Sheep and oxen are slaughtered and the meat is distributed among the people, who feast and make merry. And the house of the rich man is full with guests. The women are busy cooking and baking bread, and servants serving food. Wealthy Easterners are lavish in their banquets. On the other hand, the poor seldom offer sacrifices and other offerings, nor do they entertain.

In the East generally there is more quarreling and strife in the houses of the rich, where money is abundant and food plentiful, than in the houses of the poor. This is because many of the rich men in the East marry more than one wife, but most of the poor must settle for one. Therefore, in the houses of the rich one is not surprised to see strife and rivalry between women and children who are jealous of one another. Many women whose husbands have more than one wife prefer to live in poverty and to work hard rather than to live in a household where there is constant quarreling and strife.

Peace of mind is more important than riches. For without peace one finds no contentment, and without peace of mind life becomes meaningless. Then again, peace and harmony can create wealth, but riches cannot buy peace.

MEDITATION

Let a bear robbed of her whelps meet a man, rather than a fool in his folly.   Prov. 17:12

The Eastern text reads: "Meditation and reverence are suitable for a wise man; but a fool meditates in his folly." There is nothing in the Eastern text about a bear. The translators may not have been able to understand the Semitic words *napel renya odekheltha legabra*.

In the East a bear whose whelps (cubs) are captured or killed by hunters is considered to be very dangerous. The bereaved mother bear will attack any person she sees, thinking that he has robbed her of her cubs. Thus, both bereaved and wounded bears are greatly feared by hunters and travelers.

A fool cannot meditate or give counsel. There is nothing in his secret treasure to bring forth but folly [Prov. 18:2]. His friendship and counsel may cause a great deal of damage or even endanger the lives of those with whom he associates, for a fool will give advice in his folly. But the mind of the wise pours out wisdom and good counsel.

WORDS ARE AS DEEP WATER

The words of a man's mouth are as deep waters, and the wellspring of wisdom as a flowing brook.
It is not good to accept the person of the wicked, to overthrow the righteous in judgment.   Prov. 18:4-5

Just as deep waters cause men to drown, so the deceitful words of a man may cause men difficulties and sorrows. The reference here is to damaging words and false testimony in courts. Pious men do not respect the person of the wicked, nor pervert justice for the sake of a bribe or because of fear. They are like deep and turbulent water round about a person who cannot swim. The word is probably the most powerful thing in the world. It goes on and on, and can be used for good and for evil.

But words of wisdom and truth are like the gentle water of a spring which refreshes thirsty and weary travelers and laborers.

THE POWER OF A BRIBE

A man's gift maketh room for him, and bringeth him before great men.
                                                          Prov. 18:16

In biblical lands, the term "gift" is another name for "bribe." Many recipients of bribes prefer to call them gifts. The word gift occurs many times in the Bible and it should be distinguished from the true meaning of a gift or present which is offered voluntarily without thought of any gain or advantage.

In the olden days, judges, governors, and other government officials were seldom paid for their services; they depended on gifts or bribes for their livelihood.

When people wanted to visit a certain high judge or official, they sent a gift in advance of their arrival; some men took the gifts with them, but those who went empty-handed were not received. This is why the wicked judge refused to see the widow until she wore him out by calling on him again and again [Luke 18:1-5].

Ezekiel upbraids Jerusalem for corruption, bloodshed, and bribes. "In thee have they taken gifts to shed blood" [Ezek. 22:12]. ". . . and their right hand is full of bribes" [Ps. 26:10]. A very few people refused to accept bribes [Isa. 33:15].

The bribes blinded the eyes of the judges and government officials, and perverted justice. True presents are always presented with the right hand as a token of loyalty and sincerity.

A BROTHER IS PROTECTION

A brother offended is harder to be won than a strong city: and their contentions are like the bars of a castle.   Prov. 18:19

The Eastern text reads: "A brother helped by a brother is like a city helped by its fortifications; and his helpers are like the bars of a castle." The King James translators used italics simply because they were not sure of the meaning of the words in Latin or Greek versions.

A brother who is dependent for help from his brother is like a city which is dependent on its fortifications. Easterners often say, "My brother has been a fence to me," which means that he is a defense and protection.

In the East a brother renders help to his brother. They lend money to one another and fight for each other. This is a sacred obligation that no brother can easily shirk. Brotherly love and kindness are highly recommended by the Scriptures [Heb. 13:1; 2 Pet. 1:7].

HASTY FEET

Also, that the soul be without knowledge, it is not good; and he that hasteth with his feet sinneth. Prov. 19:2

The Eastern text reads: "He who has no knowledge of his own soul, it is not good for him; and he who is hasty with his feet sins."

A person must first examine himself before he passes judgment on others. At times some men overestimate themselves and think they are better and more righteous than they are. When a person does not know himself, how can he understand the people around him?

A man with "hasty feet" is ready to commit crimes or do other evil things. This idiom is still used in the East. Many people regret what they have done hastily. It is always wise to examine the matter before taking any action.

"Be not rash with thy mouth, and let not thine heart be hasty to utter any thing before God" [Eccles. 5:2].

A RICH LIAR

The desire of a man is his kindness: and a poor man is better than a liar. Prov. 19:22

The latter portion of the verse, according to the Eastern text, reads: ". . . and a poor man is better than a rich man who lies." That is to say, a poor man who makes his living honestly is better than a rich man who acquires his riches by cheating and lying and other deceitful means.

In the East every businessman is suspected of lying and cheating. Measuring short and having diverse weights and balances is a great problem. This is because the merchants and prospective buyers bargain and take oaths. And many of them lie about prices in order to make large profits. The poor buyer is always at the mercy of the rich seller. Then again, the rich are always suspected of being crooked.

WINE A MOCKER

Wine is a mocker, strong drink is raging: and whosoever is deceived thereby is not wise.   Prov. 20:1

Most of the Easterners, especially pastoral and nomad peoples, seldom drink wine or strong drink. And those who do drink, drink comparatively less than Western people. But when the Easterners drink at banquets and feasts, they drink until they are dead drunk. And when they are drunk, they stagger through the streets cursing and uttering shameful remarks. Then they are mocked by the people, who gather around them to amuse themselves.

When a man is drunk he does not know what he is doing. Some men while drunk even expose their bodies and do other evil things. When Noah was drunk, he slept in his tent uncovered. And his sons, Shem and Japheth, covered him [Gen. 9:21]. Lot, when he was drunken, slept with his daughters, not knowing what he was doing, and both of his daughters conceived and bore sons by him.

Isaiah condemns drunkenness. He says, "Woe unto them that are mighty to drink wine, and men of strength to mingle [mix] strong drink" [Isa. 5:22]. "But these also have erred with wine, and with strong drink are gone astray; the priests and the prophets have erred with strong drink, they are overcome with wine, they stagger with strong drink, they err in judgment with drunkenness, they eat immoderately" [Isa. 28:7, Eastern text; see also Gen. 19:32-35; Prov. 23:20-22].

SURETY FOR DECEITFUL GAIN

Bread of deceit is sweet to a man; but afterward his mouth shall be filled with gravel.   Prov. 20:17

The Eastern text reads: "He who becomes surety for a man by means of deceitful gain will afterwards have his mouth filled with gravel."

At times greedy men became surety for bandits, murderers, and men of bad reputation and credit. Even though they knew that the person for whom they had become a surety was a risk, they did it because of the large sum of money they received and for political reasons. And when the crooked men failed to carry out their promises and pledges, the man who had become surety for them had to make good the losses. This is true even today. At times, even honest and pious men are victimized.

"Gravel" is an Eastern idiom which means that the person cannot give an answer or exonerate himself for his evil deed. In the East small stones and gravel are often found in bread and food, and, at times, they cause people to choke. This is because wheat which comes from the threshing floor contains gravel, soil, and other impurities.

CURSING FATHER OR MOTHER

Whoso curseth his father or his mother, his lamp shall be put out in obscure darkness. Prov. 20:20

Cursing father and mother was a capital crime and punishable by death. "He who curses his father or his mother shall surely be put to death" [Exod. 21:17; Lev. 20:9, Eastern text].

The Aramaic word *sheraga* (lamp) is used metaphorically, meaning "posterity or heir." In Aramaic a son or an heir is often called "the lamp." "Nevertheless for David's sake did the Lord his God give him a lamp in Jerusalem, to set up his son after him" [1 Kings 15:4].

The Lord is displeased with haughty eyes, a proud heart, and the posterity of wicked men. When the Lord rejected wicked kings, their posterity was cut off. Those who cursed their father or their mother were counted among the wicked. Their posterity was to be cut off.

VOWS FULFILLED

It is a snare to the man who devoureth that which is holy, and after vows to make inquiry. Prov. 20:25

The Aramaic word *nader* means "to vow or make a vow." The Eastern text reads: "It is a snare for a man who vows to give something to a holy place, and regrets after he has vowed."

The Scriptures admonished the Israelites to fulfill their vows as soon as possible. Even today, Easterners are afraid to delay or cancel their vows. Generally, vows are made by people who are sick or in difficulties, or traveling, or praying for the birth of a male child. The animals or money vowed are given to the priests or distributed among the poor. The vow is a reminder of God's favor and his blessings in the time of need. God does not need the things that are vowed, but the poor people who know about the vows look forward for the meat of the animals and bread.

"When you vow a vow to God, do not delay in fulfilling it; for he has no pleasure in fools; but as for you, pay that which you have vowed. It is much better that you should not vow than that you should vow and not fulfill it" [Eccles. 5:4-5, Eastern text].

"And you shall make your prayer to him, and he shall hear you, and you shall fulfill your vows" [Job 22:27, Eastern text].

SICKNESS RESULT OF EVIL

The blueness of a wound cleanseth away evil: so do stripes the inward parts of the belly.   Prov. 20:30

The Eastern text reads: "Misery and torment befall the evil men; and wounds smite the inner parts of their bodies."

It is commonly believed that evil sooner or later manifests itself on the body of evildoers, and misery and torment take possession of it. In other words, wicked men receive their evil rewards just as good men receive their good rewards in this world.

Evil obscures the mind, which is the lamp of the body. When the mind is clear, the whole body is lighted and well. But when the mind is obscured by evil thoughts and acts, the body is in darkness and is helpless to heal itself. Jesus said, ". . . when thine eye is single, thy whole body also is full of light" [Luke 11:34]. "Single" means clear. When one's mind is clear, his body is strong and well.

A QUARRELSOME WOMAN

It is better to dwell in a corner of the housetop, than with a brawling woman in a wide house.   Prov. 21:9

Easterners, when lacking a place in the house, live anywhere they can find a place to put their heads. Indeed, it is not unusual to see men and women eating in the streets, or holding councils and sleeping on the housetops [Matt. 10:27]. Dwelling places have always been scarce in biblical lands. One can see small houses crowded with three or four families. The family traditions are so sacred that as long as the father and mother are living, both their married and unmarried sons live with them.

"It is better to dwell in a corner of the housetop, than with a brawling woman in a wide [spacious] house" means that it is better to remain single and to sleep anywhere than to be married to a quarrelsome woman and live in a spacious house with luxuries.

LACK OF GIFT STIRS WRATH

A gift in secret pacifieth anger: and a reward in the bosom, strong wrath.   Prov. 21:14

The last portion of the verse is mistranslated in the King James Version. It should read: ". . . but he who is sparing with his gifts stirs wrath."

"Gift" in many cases means "bribe." In the East prior to World War I bribery was prevalent. Many litigations and disputes were settled in advance by means of bribes.

When people transgressed the law and incurred the anger of the officials, they often pacified the officials' anger by means of lavish gifts. Small gifts, or bribes, were rejected and those who offered them were rebuked and punished.

In biblical days, "tribute" was often called "a gift." Kings in Palestine presented gifts to the kings of Assyria, Babylon, and Egypt in order to win their favor and to get protection against their enemies. But when they failed to present gifts, they were invaded and more heavily taxed.

Bribery is condemned by the Mosaic law and the prophets. Bribes obscure the eyes of judges and other government officials, and pervert justice.

See the article on "Bribes."

WEALTH

There is treasure to be desired and oil in the dwelling of the wise; but a foolish man spendeth it up. Prov. 21:20

The Eastern text reads: "A coveted treasure and ointment are in a dwelling place; but the wisdom and understanding of men shall dispense it." That is to say, they will spend it wisely. The reference here is to the houses of pious men who revere the Lord and who are blessed with abundance [Ps. 112:3; Prov. 15:6].

"Treasure" in this instance means a good accumulation of silver, gold, and precious stones. In the East, until recent days, men stored gold and silver in the houses or buried in fields or caves. Banks were unknown; therefore, a house or a field was the safest place to store money.

From time immemorial, oil and butter have been an important part of the economy in biblical lands; especially in the olden days when money was scarce and buried in the ground or lying idle in the treasures of the rich. Olive oil and butter were used, and still are used in some areas, as a medium of exchange [Mic. 6:7].

Jesus spoke of the unjust steward who reduced the debts of his Lord, which he had loaned to the people in oil [Luke 16:5-8].

The men who have a treasure of silver, gold, and oil are wise and rich. They spend it with wisdom and understanding. The unwise spend their money and oil in riotous living and suddenly become poor [Prov. 21:17-18].

KNIFE ON YOUR THROAT

And put a knife to thy throat, if thou be a man given to appetite.

Prov. 23:2

"Knife" in this instance is used allegorically to mean "poison." When people eat something bad or poisonous, they say, "It cuts me like a knife." The poison injures the throat of the victims who eat it in food or drink it in wine.

In many Eastern lands, when a person wishes to do away with his enemies, he gives a lavish banquet in their honor and poisons their food or drink. The poison is secretly placed in the plate or the cup of the particular victim whom the host wants to do away with.

Kings, princes, and rich men generally employ food-tasters, who try the food first. Some men examine the food secretly before they put it into their mouth. Years ago this practice was so general that many men who were invited to such banquets were afraid and reluctant to accept.

Doing away with one's enemies by means of poison is an old oriental custom. Alexander the Great was poisoned at a banquet in Babylon. Mohammed was poisoned by a woman whose relatives were slain in the battle against him. Hundreds of prominent men and government officials have met with such a horrible death.

Jesus in his prayer asked God to let the cup pass away from him [Matt. 26:39]. Because of poisoning men at banquets, the term "cup" has become symbolical of treachery, and guests at banquets are often fearful and hesitate to drink.

BEWARE OF HYPOCRITES

Eat thou not the bread of him that hath an evil eye, neither desire thou his dainty meats.

Prov. 23:6

The Aramaic word *khawara* means "hypocrite," and this verse should read: "Do not eat with a hypocrite, neither desire his food." This is because hypocrites are dangerous to associate with [verses 7, 8].

In the East some wicked men use their tables to snare the innocent. They entertain lavishly for ulterior purposes. Some of them do away with their enemies and rivals by poisoning their food. "Let their table become a snare before them," says the psalmist [Ps. 69:22]. This is because many plots and conspiracies are planned at the table, and at times the conspirator himself is caught and punished [Ps. 141:4].

SWALLOW PITCH

*For as he thinketh in his heart, so is he: Eat and drink, saith he
to thee; but his heart is not with thee.*   Prov. 23:7

The Eastern text reads: "For he is like him that swallows pitch; in
like manner you will eat and drink with him, but his heart is not with
you."

"Swallows pitch" is an idiom which means that he is a superb liar;
he can make you believe that he is your sincere friend, whereas he is
your enemy. Pitch is hard to swallow, but a liar can convince the
people that he can do it. In the East, magicians claim that they can
do what the people cannot do. A liar is the same, and his big lies
seemingly are convincing.

HYPOCRITES REJECT TRUTH

*The morsel which thou hast eaten shalt thou vomit up, and
lose thy sweet words.*
*Speak not in the ears of a fool: for he will despise the wisdom
of thy words.*   Prov. 23:8-9

"Vomit up" is an Eastern idiom which means, "You shall pay for it,"
or, "It shall be exacted from you by force or deceitful means." That is,
when one eats the bread of an hypocrite and associates with him, he
puts himself in danger. Sooner or later he will pay for it double.

The good counsel which the guest has given will also be lost. This
is because fools and hypocrites despise the truth and words of wisdom.
Jesus said, "Do not give holy things to the dogs; and do not throw your
pearls [words of wisdom] before swine [fools], for they might tread
them with their feet, and then turn and rend you" [Matt. 7:6, Eastern
text].

A HARLOT IS A TRAP

*For a whore is a deep ditch; and a strange woman is a narrow
pit.*   Prov. 23:27

The Aramaic word *gomasa* means "a deep pit used as a trap." The
whore traps men by her smooth words and cunning, until they are caught
in her net.

The "strange woman" here means any woman not his own wife. The strange woman is likened to a narrow and dry well with mud in its bottom. In the olden days, dry wells were used to imprison men. Once a man is in it, it is hard to pull him out. Jeremiah spent many days in a muddy well. It took many strong men to pull him out.

"These are wells without water . . ." [2 Pet. 2:17, Jer. 38:6-10].

RED EYES

Who hath woe? who hath sorrow? who hath contentions? who hath bubbling? who hath wounds without cause? who hath redness of eyes?
Prov. 23:29

Redness of eyes is symbolic of drunkenness and also of material prosperity. When Jacob blessed his son, Judah, he said, "He washed his garments in wine, and his clothes in the blood [juices] of grapes: His eyes shall be red with wine, and his teeth white with milk" [Gen. 49:11-12]. This saying is still in use in vernacular speech—"His eyes are red; he is drunken."

The woe here is against those who drink wine to excess, and who mix wine with strong drink. These men have woes and sorrows which wine and strong drink have brought upon them. "For at the last it bites like a serpent and stings like an adder [verse 32, Eastern text; see also Prov. 20:1].

RED WINE

Look not thou upon the wine when it is red, when it giveth his color in the cup, when it moveth itself aright.
Prov. 23:31

The Eastern text reads: ". . . but meditate on righteousness."

In the East red grapes are scarce, and therefore red wine is more coveted and enticing than the white wine which is abundant. During banquets and wedding feasts, red wine sells at a premium. Then again, red color is popular in biblical lands. Most of the women are arrayed in red garments with stripes. And during feasts, banquets, and weddings, most women wear red. "O daughters of Israel, weep over Saul, who clothed you in scarlet and dyed garments" [2 Sam. 1:24, Eastern text].

The author of the Proverbs admonishes us not to be covetous after the color of red wine, but to think of righteous things and good works which are edifying.

A DRUNKARD IS LOST

Yea, thou shalt be as he that lieth down in the midst of the sea, or as he that lieth upon the top of a mast. Prov. 23:34

The last portion of the verse, according to the Aramaic, reads: "or as a sailor in a tempest."

"Lieth down in the midst of the sea" is an Eastern idiom which means that he is lost, or does not know what he is doing. The reference here is to drunkenness. Drunkards lose their senses [verses 29-32]. In a raging storm, sailors lose direction and do not know what to do [verse 35]. In the olden days ships were small and the sea hazards many. Compasses were unknown. The sailors relied on the sun and stars for finding their way.

Wine bites like a serpent and leaves its mark on the victim.

See the commentary on "Drunkenness."

WISDOM CRUSHES THE FOOL

Wisdom is too high for a fool: he openeth not his mouth in the gate. Prov. 24:7

The Aramaic word *ramiah* (to crush) is confused in the King James Version with the Aramaic adverb *ramah* (high). This verse should read: "Wisdom crushes a fool." Wisdom cannot grace the mind of a fool, because he does not value it.

"He openeth not his mouth in the gate" means that he never gave counsel when he sat with the elders at the gate. In the East, important meetings and councils are held at the gate of the city where the people gather to discuss the affairs of the town, settle disputes, and receive the judgments of the rulers [Ruth 4:1-4; 1 Kings 22:10]. Squares and parks are unknown, and the streets are too narrow for gatherings. The gate is the only adequate place for meetings of this nature.

The wise and prudent men try to show their knowledge at the gate. This is because the words spoken at the gate are published in the town and countryside and are quoted by the wise men. On such occasions fools are rebuked when they start to speak or give counsel.

See the commentary on "The Gate."

ADMONITION TO KINGS

My son, fear thou the Lord and the king: and meddle not with them that are given to change.   Prov. 24:21

The Eastern text reads: "My son, fear [revere] the Lord and give good counsel; and meddle not with the fools." The Aramaic word *amlikh* is a verb meaning "to give counsel, to reign." King Solomon is here advising his son to reverence the Lord when he reigns over the people. The term "king" in Aramaic means "a counselor." At the outset, kings were chiefs of the tribes. They gave counsel and led the tribal people during their wanderings.

Without wisdom and reverence for the Lord, no ruler would execute justice. When kings and princes revere God they are afraid to do evil and to oppress the poor.

Moreover, Solomon admonishes his son not to meddle with fools. Nevertheless, his son, Rehoboam, who reigned in his place, rejected the good counsel of the elders who had acted as counselors to his father, and he accepted the counsel of young men who had grown up with him [1 Kings 12:13-14].

GOLDEN RULE

Say not, I will do so to him as he hath done to me: I will render to the man according to his work.   Prov. 24:29

This verse is the foundation of the Golden Rule. Jesus said: "But I say to you that you should not resist evil; but whoever strikes you on your right cheek, turn to him the other also" [Matt. 5:39, Eastern text].

King Solomon, in his long reign as a king and judge over Israel, found out that to render evil for evil did more harm than good. His statement here was a departure from the Mosaic law. ". . . but life shall be for life, eye for eye, tooth for tooth, hand for hand, foot for foot" [Deut. 19:21; see also Exod. 21:24].

The author of the Proverbs admonishes the people to leave vengeance to God, who is the only true Judge. Many of the Hebrew prophets found out that evil for evil was the cause of Israel's long struggle with the Gentile world. They also disagreed with Mosaic ordinances and man-made laws.

Jesus went further in reversing the Mosaic ordinances in that he admonished his followers not to resist evil, but to turn their other cheek to those who smote them. ". . . Love your enemies, bless anyone who curses you, do good to anyone who hates you . . ." [Matt. 5:44, Eastern text]. "Do not say, I will recompense evil; but wait for the Lord that he may save you" [Prov. 20:22, Eastern text]. A good man does not wish to do to others that which he does not wish to be done to him.

SLUGGARD

So shall thy poverty come as one that traveleth; and thy want as an armed man. Prov. 24:34

The Eastern text reads: "So shall poverty come upon you, and want shall overtake you suddenly like a runner."

The sluggard at last becomes the victim of poverty and want which, in due time, catch up with him. In biblical days, letters and other royal messages were dispatched by fast runners.

ETIQUETTE

Put not forth thyself in the presence of the king, and stand not in the place of great men:
For better it is that it be said unto thee, Come up hither; than that thou shouldest be put lower in the presence of the prince whom thine eyes have seen. Prov. 25:6-7

In the East uncultured men sometimes try to stand in high places when in the presence of kings and princes. These places belong to the wealthy and to noblemen. Indeed, in the East it makes a great deal of difference where a guest stands or sits. Customarily the ministers of state, princes, and noblemen do not sit down in the presence of a king unless they are asked to do so.

This is also true of assemblies, wedding feasts, and banquets. Some men come very early and occupy the high places where food is more abundant. The host is generally busy welcoming the guests, chatting with them, and seeing that the food is abundant. But when all the guests are seated and some of the prominent guests have arrived, he may ask those who have occupied the prominent seats to get up and move to lower places. This is an embarrassing moment for those who must rise in the presence of seated guests and walk to a lower seat.

The wise noblemen sit low so that they may be asked to rise up and sit higher. This is considered a great honor. The guest is accompanied by the host, and all other guests watch.

Jesus knew Eastern etiquette. He admonished his disciples not to occupy higher seats in the synagogues and at wedding feasts, but to sit in low seats so that the host might ask them to rise up and go to sit in higher places [Luke 14:8-10].

THE UNRULY PERSON

As he that taketh away a garment in cold weather, and as vinegar upon nitre, so is he that singeth songs to a heavy heart. Prov. 25:20

The Eastern text reads: "As he who takes away a garment from his neighbor in cold weather, as one who drops sand on the string of a musical instrument, as he who afflicts a broken heart, as a moth on a garment, and as a boring-worm on a tree: such is the effect of sorrow on a man's heart."

In the East, good mantles or robes are given by the poor as pledges of surety when borrowing money from a stranger. And some of the wicked moneylenders would take the robe of the borrower as a pledge even on a cold day. Thus the lender has no mercy upon the poor borrower, for the latter needs his garment more on a cold day, just as much as he needs the money he borrows. The poor and the strangers sleep with their garments. They lie on the floor and cover themselves with their robes or mantles.

The Mosaic law forbids keeping of a neighbor's mantle or raiment during the night. ". . . you must give them back to him by sunset" [Exod. 22:26-27, Eastern text].

"Dropping of sand on the string of a musical instrument" is an Aramaic idiom which means "wasting time." This is because sand cannot stand on the string of a musical instrument. It is just like saying, "placing an orange on a telephone wire."

The broken heart needs no affliction. Sorrow is likened to a moth on a garment and a boring-worm on a tree. They cause suffering within the person. In the East we say, "They eat the inside."

DOING GOOD TO YOUR ENEMY

If thine enemy be hungry, give him bread to eat; and if he be thirsty, give him water to drink:
For thou shalt heap coals of fire upon his head, and the Lord shall reward thee. Prov. 25:21-22

"Heap coals of fire upon his head" is an Eastern idiom which means to embarrass him or cause him to suffer. In the East nothing would embarrass an enemy more than having to accept the bread and water from one whom he has hated or wronged. The enemy guest burns inside; that is, he regrets the wrongs he has done to the host. And on such occasions the guest may confess his evil deeds, forget the enmity, and become a sincere friend of the host [Ps. 23:5; Rom. 12:20].

Moreover, in the East during droughts and famines and natural calamities, enmities are forgotten and food and water are shared. This is especially true of tribal people who are constantly dependent on one another.

Jesus even went further in admonishing his disciples and followers to love their enemies, and do good to those who hate them [Matt. 5:44].

THORNS IN HAND OF A DRUNKARD

As a thorn goeth up into the hand of a drunkard, so is a parable in the mouth of fools.   Prov. 26:9

The Eastern text reads: "Thorns spring up in the hand of a drunkard . . ."

Biblical lands are noted for thorns and briers. Barren fields and grazing lands are full of thorns. Shepherds, reapers, and men and women who walk barefooted suffer from them.

Then again, during the wintertime all those who handle dry grass suffer from thorns. Leather gloves were unknown in that part of the world. Indeed, thorns are a problem summer and winter.

The author of Proverbs uses this analogy simply because a drunkard's difficulties multiply day by day. His substance is wasted in drinking, and sooner or later he finds himself facing money problems; but at first he does not feel the pinch of poverty, just as he does not feel the thorn when it goes into his hand if he is drunk.

This is also true of the fool; he does not know how to relate a parable so that those who listen to him may understand its meaning.

THE FOOL REPEATS HIS FOLLY

As a dog returneth to his vomit, so a fool returneth to his folly.
Prov. 26:11

In the East, dogs are seldom fed, especially in lands where dogs are considered as unclean. Except in the case of shepherds who live outdoors, dogs are not wanted. The dogs roam around the city hungry, howling and searching for food in vain.

At times, dogs find dead animals which are thrown away, and they eat until they are satiated. Some of them vomit the food and later when they are hungry, eat it again.

The fool, likewise, repeats his mistakes and folly. He refuses to learn a lesson from them, and he abhors discipline and correction.

A SLOTHFUL

The slothful hideth his hand in his bosom; it grieveth him to bring it again to his mouth. Prov. 26:15

"Hides his hand in his bosom" is an Eastern idiom which means, "He is lazy." In the East idle men generally keep their hands in their bosoms or pockets. One often hears people saying, "His hands are in his pocket," which means that he is unwilling to work.

"It grieves him to bring it again to his mouth" means, "He is so lazy that he would rather stay hungry than lift his hand to his mouth." This portion of the verse is used sarcastically in denouncing the slothful.

OIL AND OINTMENT

Ointment and perfume rejoice the heart: so doth the sweetness of a man's friend by hearty counsel. Prov. 27:9

The Eastern text reads: "As oil and perfume rejoice the heart, so does the sweetness of a man's friend by hearty counsel."

In the East ointment is made of oil, perfume, wax, and balm, and is placed on sores to keep the skin soft and to heal it.

Because of the scarcity of water to drink, bathing is very rare and in some places unknown. Sores on hands and feet and other parts of the body are very common, and they often become infected and are wide open. A little oil or ointment softens the dirt and removes it from the skin.

This is also true of the good counsel given by a faithful friend. It relieves the person of his worries and troubles. The good counsel sinks into the mind and heals it, just like oil sinks into dry skin and cures the wound.

FLATTERY

He that blesseth his friend with a loud voice, rising early in the morning, it shall be counted a curse to him. Prov. 27:14

The Aramaic word *beshopra-notha* is derived from *shapar* (flattery). It is confused in the King James Version with *shapraiotha*, derived from *shapar* (early dawn). Flattery is condemned in the Near East, and looked upon as a brand of hypocrisy.

The flatterers usually speak loudly when showering praises upon their unworthy friends. Flattery is deceitful and harmful both to the flatterer and to him who is flattered.

A QUARRELSOME WOMAN

A continual dropping in a very rainy day and a contentious woman are alike.   Prov. 27:15

In many parts of the biblical lands, houses are covered with timber and branches of trees, and the branches are covered with straw and earth. During the rainy season, water may drip from the ceiling into the house. Vessels are placed on the floor to catch the water. Beds are also moved from one place in the house to another to escape the dripping. The roof is so weak that no one knows where the next drops will fall.

Moreover, during the rainy season families may suffer considerably from the drippings; clothes and valuable articles are spoiled and bedclothing soaked in water. There is an Eastern parable which is very common: "He fled from the rain and sat under the dropping," which means, "He fled from a minor annoyance to suffer from a greater one."

In the East quarrelsome women are feared like a dripping ceiling. They are an annoyance to their husbands as well as to their neighbors. They always find fault and are dissatisfied with life.

NO TWO HEARTS ARE ALIKE

As in water face answereth to face, so the heart of man to man.
                                              Prov. 27:19

The Aramaic word *damin* means "to be alike or resemble." The last part of the word resembles the Aramaic word for water. Note that in the King James Version the word "answereth" is placed in italics simply because the translators were not sure of the meaning of the verse.

The Eastern text reads: "As faces do not resembles faces, so hearts do not resemble hearts."

It is said that no two persons look alike. The author of the Proverbs states that no two hearts are alike. Probably no two people think alike. God has created everything in its own pattern. No two things look exactly alike.

GOOD SHEPHERD

Be thou diligent to know the state of thy flocks, and look well to thy herds.   Prov. 27:23

The Eastern text reads: "When you are feeding the sheep, know their faces and set your mind on the flock."

This is true of all good and experienced shepherds in the East. They know both the names and the faces of their own sheep, and of most of the flock which is entrusted to them. The women who milk the sheep know their own sheep by their faces and call them by their names. When a sheep is lost, they search the whole flock for it, and when they fail to find it, they rush to the shepherd.

The sheep, likewise, know the shepherd and their owners; and they follow them; but they refuse to follow a stranger.

Jesus must have read this passage in the original Old Testament written in ancient Aramaic. He says: "And when he has brought out his sheep, he goes before them; and his own sheep follow him, because they know his voice. The sheep do not follow a stranger, but they run away from him, because they do not know the voice of a stranger" [John 10:4-5, Eastern text].

"I am the good shepherd, and I know my own, and my own know me" [John 10:14, Eastern text].

CONFESSING OF SINS

He that covereth his sins shall not prosper: but whoso confesseth and forsaketh them shall have mercy.   Prov. 28:13

The term "confessing" means "to acknowledge." That is, to reveal what he has done and, if possible, make restitution. Confessions were made in court, in public, before God, and in the house or in a place of worship. "I have acknowledged my sin unto thee, and mine iniquity have I not hid from thee . . ." [Ps. 32:5, Eastern text]. True confession must be followed by sincere repentance.

When a person confessed his sins, he pledged that he would not commit them again. Habitual sinners can hardly obtain mercy. The Mosaic law demanded confession before one could receive mercy from God. "If they shall confess their iniquity and the iniquity of their fathers, with their wickedness with which they transgressed against me, and also that they have walked contrary to me" [Lev. 26:40, Eastern text].

James says, "Confess your faults one to another" [James 5:16, Eastern text].

When a person confesses his sins he is relieved of the burden of bearing them every day. Confession must come from a sincere heart, and forgiveness of sins cannot be purchased with money. One has to repent from his heart in order to receive forgiveness and mercy from God.

WICKED AS A MAJORITY

Where there is no vision, the people perish: but he that keepeth the law, happy is he. Prov. 29:18

The Eastern text reads: "When the wicked men multiply, the people are ruined; but he who keeps the law, blessed is he."

The error in the King James Version is probably due to copyists who confused the Hebrew word *khazan* (vision) with *khayaz* (to cut asunder). The Aramaic word is *me-terra* (to break in pieces, to cause to ruin).

Corrupt politics, immorality, drunkenness, and evil deeds have been the cause of the fall of many great empires and kingdoms. When the wicked multiply and become a majority, they take over and then start to destroy what the good men have built.

TAMPERING WITH THE SCRIPTURES

Add thou not unto his words, lest he reprove thee, and thou be found a liar. Prov. 30:6

This ordinance was given so that the people might revere the inspired Word and refrain from adding to it or changing it. The Ten Commandments were to be handed down from one generation to another, intact, without revisions, additions or changes. The words which the Lord uttered on Mount Sinai were perfect and eternal.

On the other hand, if one person or a church is permitted to change the Word of God, then everyone else would have the right to change it to suit his own purpose.

The ordinances and statutes were also to be safeguarded against forgeries, additions, omissions, and unnecessary revisions so that the truth which the law contains might be preserved intact.

The Moslems, Jews, and Eastern Christians (wrongly called Nestorians) never dare to change a letter in their Scriptures, nor have they ever revised any portion thereof; nor do they ever add or omit a word. This is because revisions and deliberate forgeries have been the causes for many disputes, false theological doctrines, and divisions among the Western Christians.

In the Near East when a sacred book or a Bible is copied, every word of the copy is compared with the text from which it is copied. Even the letters are counted, so that no error might creep into the Scriptures.

"You shall not add to the commandment which I command you, neither shall you take from it, but you must keep the commandments of the Lord your God which I command you" [Deut. 4:2, Eastern text].

"Everything that I command you, that you must be careful to do; you shall not add nor take from it" [Deut. 12:32, Eastern text].

"I testify to every man who hears the words of the prophecy of this book, If any man shall add to these things, God shall add to him the plagues that are written in this book; and if any man shall take away from the words of the book of this prophecy, God shall take away his portion from the tree of life and from the holy city and from the things which are written in this book" [Rev. 22:18-19, Eastern text].

KNIVES

There is a generation, whose teeth are as swords, and their jaw teeth as knives, to devour the poor from off the earth, and the needy from among men.

Prov. 30:14

In the East table knives and forks were unknown until recent years. The people used their front teeth as knives to cut off pieces of meat.

The reference here is to the oppressors who devour the poor and the needy. These men are known as having sharp teeth like swords. In American slang they are called "sharks."

When the Israelites forsook the way of the Lord and transgressed his commandments, their rulers and judges became wicked. They devoured the poor and corrupted justice. These wicked men had no knowledge of God, neither did they fear the Most High [Ps. 10:4].

In the East when princes or government officials defraud or exploit their people it is said, "They have devoured [eaten] the poor and the weak."

Job says, "And I broke the jaws of the wicked, and snatched the prey out of his teeth" [Job 29:17, Eastern text].

Jesus used the same Aramaic metaphor: "Woe to you, scribes and Pharisees, hypocrites! for you embezzle [Aramaic 'eat'] the property of widows . . ." [Matt. 23:13, Eastern text].

YOUNG MEN

The way of an eagle in the air; the way of a serpent upon a rock; the way of a ship in the midst of the sea, and the way of a man with a maid.

Prov. 30:19

The Eastern text reads: ". . . and the way of a man in his youth." *Balemothey* (in his youth) is confused with *alemtha* (a maiden). In the East, until recent days, unmarried men never kept company with women, and in some parts of the East this ancient custom still prevails. Marriages are arranged by the parents of the bridegroom and those of the bride.

Young men find it difficult to make decisions or to know what to do or what not to do. It takes a long time before a young man comes to himself. In the East, when people speak of young men, they say, "They are in the air"; that is, they do not know what they are doing, or they do not know the head from the tail. This is why in the East, until young men reach the age of thirty, they cannot speak in the council. Jesus was thirty years old when he began to preach and teach. This is why we know so little of his early life.

WRATH PRODUCES STRIFE

Surely the churning of milk bringeth forth butter, and the wringing of the nose bringeth forth blood: so the forcing of wrath bringeth forth strife.   Prov. 30:33

The second clause is a mistranslation. The Aramaic word *khetta* means "a grain of wheat," and it should read: ". . . and if you press your hand on a raw grain of wheat, it will bring forth juices; thus out of the strife goes forth judgment."

Butter is made up by churning. The buttermilk is placed in a goat's skin which is hung on a tripod. Two women stand, one on each side of the tripod, and shake the skin until the butter is separated from the buttermilk. This process takes about an hour.

The author of the book of Proverbs likens the storing of wrath to the churning of buttermilk. Wrath and anger generate power, which, in due time, bring forth strife.

One should not allow room in his heart for wrath, for wrath is like a double-edged sword; it cuts both ways.

WINE TO MOURNERS

Give strong drink unto him that is ready to perish, and wine unto those that be of heavy hearts.   Prov. 31:6

The Aramaic word *abiley* means "mourners"; that is, those whose hearts are heavy and sorrowful. The root of the verb is *abal* (to mourn). The Eastern text reads: "Let strong drink be given to those who mourn, and wine to those who are of heavy heart."

Easterners mourn over their dead for a long period [Gen. 50:3; Num.

20:29; 2 Sam. 3:31]. Some of the mourners, because of their grief, inflict injuries upon their bodies. They also wear old garments and are silent and sad.

In some places the mourners are comforted after the burial; they are given food and drink.

Wine is given to the mourners so that they may forget their grief [Ps. 104:15; Eccles. 10:19]. Easterners, except at weddings and feasts, drink very little wine. Pastoral and nomad peoples drink milk and buttermilk. In some areas, wine is never drunk, and strong drink is unknown. Milk and buttermilk are their only drink.

A VIRTUOUS WOMAN

She perceiveth that her merchandise is good: her candle goeth not out by night.   Prov. 31:18

People in biblical lands a few decades ago went to bed at sunset and rose up at dawn. And the people worked from dawn to sunset. Some of the people went to bed at seven or eight in the evening. Therefore, lamps were lighted for only a short duration. Only the extravagantly rich may keep their lamps burning all night.

"Her lamp does not go out all night" is an Eastern saying which means that she works during the night to the early morning hours. Industrious women worked at night, spinning, weaving cloth and rugs, sewing, and doing other housework.

When the virtuous woman found that her merchandise was good and in plenty of demand, she worked during the night to supply the need. The woman was pious, wise, and industrious; she had prospered and was emulated.

KNOWN IN THE GATE

Her husband is known in the gates, when he sitteth among the elders of the land.   Prov. 31:23

In olden days trials were held at the town gate, where most of the elders and nobles were gathered. The houses were too small and the streets too narrow for such assemblies. Then again, because the woman baked bread and cooked food, the house was often filled with smoke.

In the East city gates are used for gatherings of the elders and noblemen and for other meetings. When the king of Israel and the king of Judah wanted to discuss war against Syria, they met at the gate [1 Kings 22:10].

Until recently, many trials were held in the gate or other open places where noblemen were able to assemble. The judges were appointed from among the noble elders who sat at the gate. When Boaz wanted to settle the question of Naomi's field he went and sat at the gate. "And he took ten men of the elders of the city, and said, Sit ye down here. And they sat down" [Ruth 4:2].

When Hamor and Shechem, his son, wanted to discuss with the people of their city the question of circumcision, they went to the gate [Gen. 34:20].

Noblemen and prosperous men are usually found idle at the gate. The husband of the virtuous woman was well dressed and well fed. He wore new garments and new girdles which his wife had made for him. Consequently he was well known and admired in the town.

A SKILLFUL WOMAN

She maketh fine linen, and selleth it; and delivereth girdles unto the merchant.   Prov. 31:24

In the Near East, until recent days, girdles, gloves, and stockings were made by women during their spare time and sold to merchants. Most of the other clothing articles were woven on looms by men weavers.

Women retained the price of the articles they made as their own possession. In the East the family purse is kept by men. Some women gave the money thus gained to their husbands, or spent it on their children, or made it into necklaces, earrings, and bracelets for their daughters.

Wise, pious, and skillful women of this type are admired and emulated in biblical lands.

CHAPTER EIGHTEEN

ECCLESIASTES

INTRODUCTION

THE Aramaic term for the Ecclesiastes is *Kohlat* (the voice, the words); that is, "the preaching." It is the words of the Preacher, the son of David, king in Jerusalem. The first verse confirms the authorship of the book, King Solomon, son of David, the author of the Proverbs and of the Song of Solomon, and the wise king of Israel.

The author, King Solomon, through his long experience as a ruler, and hard study, and being a wealthy ruler, had tasted all phases of life. And at last, he found that life is vanity, that all things under the sun are temporary and that man comes into this world naked and goes out naked. The book of Ecclesiastes, like the book of Proverbs, contains wise sayings, axioms, admonitions, and instructions.

THE PREACHER

The words of the Preacher, the son of David, king in Jerusalem.
Eccles. 1:1

The book of Ecclesiastes in Aramaic is called *Kohlat;* that is, "the voice or the preaching." This is because the theme of the book is like a sermon, containing advice and admonitions, and transmitting the experiences of one generation to another.

The author of the book is King Solomon, the son of David, who reigned in his stead in Jerusalem. King Solomon was noted for his wisdom and understanding [Eccles. 2:9]. When God appeared to him in Gibeon in a dream by night, he said to him, "Ask what I shall give thee?" Solomon asked for wisdom and understanding [1 Kings 3:4-14]. Moreover, when the queen of Sheba heard of the fame of Solomon and his wisdom, she came to see him and to prove his wisdom with her dark sayings, axioms, and riddles [1 Kings 10:1].

Solomon had a full share of this life. He knew much and saw plenty. He had abundant riches and a thousand wives. He had all that his heart desired, but at last when his material desires were gone, he found himself empty, despondent, and dissatisfied [verse 8].

HUMAN TOIL

What profit hath a man of all his labor which he taketh under the sun?   Eccles. 1:3

The Aramaic word *amel* means "he toils." This verse should read: ". . . at which he toils under the sun." "Taketh" is a mistranslation.

"Sun" means "light." In the East when electricity was unknown all work was done during the day. The dark hours of the night were used for rest. Only a few women worked during the dark hours.

All man's gains are left where they are wrought. One generation goes and another comes, but all man's labor and gains are left upon the earth.

MAN CANNOT CHANGE NATURE

That which is crooked cannot be made straight: and that which is wanting cannot be numbered.   Eccles. 1:15

The Eastern text reads: "The chaotic [or crooked] cannot be made orderly; and he who is lacking knowledge cannot be supplied with it."

The Aramaic word *mithmlaio* (to be supplied) has been confused in the King James Version with *mithmnaio* (to be numbered). The only difference between the two words is the former has the letter "l" where the latter has "n." These two letters are often confused. The "n" is slightly shorter than "l." The error must have occurred during the transcription, when the alphabet was changed, or it is a copyist's error.

What the author of Ecclesiastes says is this: What is lacking, that is, what we do not have now, cannot be supplied. Man can create from the things which God has already created. But man cannot create the substance for new things, nor can he change the essence of the things which God has created [Eccles. 7:13].

ETERNAL VALUES

I said in mine heart, Go to now, I will prove thee with mirth; therefore enjoy pleasure: and, behold, this also is vanity. Eccles. 2:1

During the time of Solomon men had very little conception of life hereafter. Those who died were either cut off from life and the living God, or they lived on in their posterity.

Solomon, during his peaceful and prosperous reign, gave himself to luxuries and indulged in everything that his heart desired. Pleasures, wine, and joys of this earthly life were the only realities to him [Eccles. 2:10]. Nevertheless, with all the wealth he had, fame, wives, wine, and luxuries, he found his life empty and boring [verses 3-12].

Everything that King Solomon had is gone and forgotten, even the magnificent temple that he built. The only thing he left behind his riotous life is his profound writings. The only permanent thing that man can bequeath to posterity is the good he leaves behind him. And, in that good he lives forever; for good, like God, is eternal and indestructible.

UNDERSTANDING

I sought in mine heart to give myself unto wine, yet acquainting mine heart with wisdom; and to lay hold on folly, till I might see what was that good for the sons of men, which they should do under the heaven all the days of their life.   Eccles. 2:3

The Aramaic word *sacolthanotha* means "understanding" and it also means "folly or stupidity." With a dot *over* the third letter the word is pronounced *sacolthanotha* (understanding), and with a dot *under* the same letter, the word is aspirated and thus is pronounced *sakholthantha* (folly, stupidity).

Solomon is speaking of wisdom and understanding, for wisdom without understanding is dangerous. One can be wise, but he has to know how to use his wisdom; that is, understanding guides man and warns him when he produces something remarkable and powerful but dangerous. Wisdom can create an atomic bomb, but understanding will declare it a dangerous device.

Solomon could not have sought wisdom and yet held onto folly. Through understanding, Solomon found that all human wisdom was folly, and that there was nothing material under the sun to strive for or in which to find lasting happiness [verse 17].

MANY SERVANTS

I made me great works; I builded me houses; I planted me vineyards.   Eccles. 2:4

The Aramaic word *abdey* (servants) is confused in the King James with *abadey* (works). Both words are written alike, but pronounced differently. Solomon had many servants, eunuchs, court attendants, butlers, and herdsmen.

King Solomon built his magnificent royal palace and the costly and beautiful temple in Jerusalem.

In the East all rich men, princes, and kings are noted for the number of their servants and the ministers, singers, and musicians, and the palaces they maintain.

BUTLERS AND WAITRESSES

I gathered me also silver and gold, and the peculiar treasure of kings and of the provinces: I gat me men singers and women singers, and the delights of the sons of men, as musical instruments, and that of all sorts. Eccles. 2:8

The Aramaic word *shakyatha* means "waitresses" or "female butlers." The Eastern text reads: ". . . and I appointed for myself butlers and waitresses."

The Bible mentions butlers, but this is the first mention of waitresses. Nehemiah was a butler who waited on Artakhshisht, king of Persia [Neh. 2:1].

Waitresses were employed by King Solomon to wait on the queens and princesses in his palace. The king had everything in the world that money could buy, and that power could acquire. But at the end of his life he found that everything was vanity and very fleeting [verse 2].

TIME

To every thing there is a season, and a time to every purpose under the heaven. Eccles. 3:1

The Aramaic word for "time" is *zabna,* but is pronounced *zawna,* and the Aramaic word "to buy" is *zaban,* pronounced *zawan.*

In the realm of the Spirit, there is no time and space. Time is relative to the movements of the earth, moon, stars, and other planets. The author of Genesis tells us that all of these heavenly bodies were created to lighten the world, and for marking the days, months, and years.

Man buys time by working and creating events. Time is more precious than gold. All things are reckoned by time. Time can make an article precious, and time can also depreciate the value thereof. Time graces the heads of kings with crowns; and time sends them away, disgraced and empty-handed.

Man must not waste his time in foolishness, for time is precious, and is like a one-way street. It comes only once and never returns.

GOD'S WORKS UNCHANGEABLE

I know that, whatsoever God doeth, it shall be for ever: nothing can be put to it, nor any thing taken from it: and God doeth it, that men should fear before him. Eccles. 3:14

God's laws and works are from everlasting to everlasting, and are unchangeable. No one can alter one of God's laws, or change the essence of the things that he has created; nor can anyone add to or take from what he has created.

God has done this so that men may revere him and glorify his holy name. The term "fear" should be "revere." God is revealed through his marvelous works. Heaven and earth declare his glory, and men wonder about the work of his hands.

THE PERSECUTED

That which hath been is now; and that which is to be hath already been; and God requireth that which is past. Eccles. 3:15

The Aramaic word *redipa*, derived from *radap* (to persecute, pursue, urge on) in this instance means "the persecuted"; that is, "God will seek him who is persecuted and the outcast." The persecuted are driven away by their enemies, but the Lord always succors and gathers those who are persecuted and driven away unjustly. God always avenges those who trust in him.

IMMORTALITY

For that which befalleth the sons of men befalleth beasts; even one thing befalleth them: as the one dieth, so dieth the other; yea, they have all one breath; so that a man hath no preeminence above a beast: for all is vanity. Eccles. 3:19

During the time of King Solomon the Hebrew concept of immortality was not yet crystallized. In the olden days the Hebrews, like the pagans, thought that death was the end. There was a slight glimpse of life hereafter, but it had not yet become a doctrine.

The only preeminence which man has over the animals is his free will. Moreover, man has the Spirit of God in him, and therefore he is God's own child. Man's spirit is eternal and indestructible, because the spiritual man was created in the image and likeness of God, and he was perfect and immortal. Death came through transgression of the law and sin.

A MISERABLE KING

For out of prison he cometh to reign; whereas also he that is born in his kingdom becometh poor. Eccles. 4:14

The Eastern text reads: "Out of prison he has come to reign, because also in his own kingdom he had been born miserable."

The reference here is to the foolish king who has not been brought up well.

In the East at times foolish kings are imprisoned and branded insane by their own rival brothers. Generally, when a king died his several sons fought over the throne and the strongest one among them slew or imprisoned the others. Many of the imprisoned princes became insane. Then when the dynasty lacked an heir one of these stupid or insane men would be brought out and set on the throne. The king has been born and reared in a palace with hundreds of rival women and unfriendly half-brothers.

FULFILLING OF VOWS

Better is it that thou shouldest not vow, than that thou shouldest vow and not pay.
Suffer not thy mouth to cause thy flesh to sin; neither say thou before the angel, that it was an error: wherefore should God be angry at thy voice, and destroy the work of thine hands?
Eccles. 5:5-6

The Eastern text reads "before God" instead of "before the angel." In the East it is considered a sin to vow a vow and not fulfill it. This is because a vow is a solemn promise made under the name of God, pledging and consecrating something to him. It is a sacred oath which cannot be violated, a promise to God which has to be met. God does not require that anyone make vows in the first place. It is much better not to vow than to vow and then delay to fulfill it, or to say, "I did not mean it," or, "It was an error."

When people are at peace and secure, some of them forget, defer, or even conceal, their vows. They may say their vow was vowed erroneously. Sometimes the vows are beyond the ability of the person who had vowed them and, therefore, they are not performed. Such violations are considered as an offense before God. This is because in the East, people meet their obligations and pay their taxes and debts.

Today, just as of yore, Easterners make vows and then offer gifts of meat, bread, money, and other things to fulfill those vows.

See the article on "Vows."

PATIENCE AND TIME

Better is the end of a thing than the beginning thereof: and the patient in spirit is better than the proud in spirit.   Eccles. 7:8

Time is the only thing which can determine the course of events. Some events are preordained; others are due to cause and effect.

Many things which men call tragedies have a meaning in life, and in the end one may find that they turned out to one's advantage. For example, the selling of Joseph to the Arabians, who in turn sold him in Egypt, at the outset seemed a tragedy for himself and his father, Jacob. But later it proved to be a blessing and salvation to Jacob, his sons, and their families. It seems that the tragedy was a part of the divine plan. For, had Joseph not been sold, the Hebrew tribe would have perished of famine, like other tribes which perished during the severe drought. Joseph himself acknowledged it as a part of the divine plan: "Now do not be grieved, nor displeased with yourselves, that you sold me here: for it was to provide for you that God sent me before you" [Gen. 45:5, Eastern text].

James says: "Blessed is the man that endureth temptation: for when he is tried, he shall receive the crown of life . . ." [James 1:12].

Therefore, patience and time are the key to many things which happen in life. Patience can solve many problems in life, avert wars and tragedies, and lead man into the true path of life. But to be patient, one has to be humble and wait for the fulfillment of things, and not be disturbed by their beginning [Isa. 30:15].

WISDOM BETTER THAN WEAPONS

Wisdom is good with an inheritance: and by it there is profit to them that see the sun.   Eccles. 7:11

The Eastern text reads: "Wisdom is better than weapons; yea, it is better for those who see the light of the truth."

This parable is still in use in some parts of the Near East. One hears: "Wisdom is better than a gun." This is because wisdom offers protection to those who possess it, just as a weapon offers protection to the one who carries it with him.

Wisdom is invaluable to those who know the truth and rely on God for protection, health, and prosperity.

In Aramaic "sun" metaphorically means "the truth," "the true light of God." The sun is seen by all God's creatures. Even the wicked see the sun, but the truth is hidden from them.

THE WISE MEN

Who is as the wise man? and who knoweth the interpretation of a thing? a man's wisdom maketh his face to shine, and the boldness of his face shall be changed.   Eccles. 8:1

The Eastern text reads: "Who is like the wise man? And who knows the interpretation of a thing? A man's wisdom makes his face to shine, but he who is impudent shall be hated."

A wise man is like a deep sea that cannot be measured with a line. The thoughts and imagination of his mind are like remote mountains that can be seen only from a distance.

True wise men are humble and lovable. Wisdom makes their faces to shine, that is, to radiate; in the East the people rejoice to hear a wise man speak, and they respect his counsel. But impudent and foolish men are hated when they speak or give counsel, and they cannot look straight into the face of the people.

IMMORTALITY IS ESSENTIAL

Then I commended mirth, because a man hath no better thing under the sun, than to eat, and to drink, and to be merry: for that shall abide with him of his labor the days of his life, which God giveth him under the sun.   Eccles. 8:15

When this book was written ideas of immortality were in their infancy and very few people thought seriously of another life. In those early days life was uncertain and beset with so many difficulties and sorrows that people were reluctant even to consider the possibility of another life—on earth, or anywhere else.

Therefore, the kings, princes, and the rich tried to make the best of everything. Their slogan was: "Today we eat, drink, and be merry, and tomorrow we shall die." Nevertheless, they failed to find satisfaction even in riotous living. Thus, the philosophers and wise men concluded that eating, drinking, and the joys of this life were the only portions which man has on earth. But even that was vanity, because sooner or later man loses all his desire for the material things. And just as he came naked into this world, so naked he goes out of it. Thus, all joys of life are temporal, and life is meaningless without the hope of resurrection and life hereafter.

WONDROUS WORKS OF GOD

Then I beheld all the work of God, that a man cannot find out the work that is done under the sun: because though a man labor to seek it out, yet he shall not find it; yea further; though a wise man think to know it, yet shall he not be able to find it. Eccles. 8:17

God's works are so great, marvelous, and unsearchable that man shall never be able fully to understand their nature and objectives. This is because man himself is one of God's many wonders. Indeed, God's wisdom is so great and his works so wondrous that there is no way to search out his wisdom and to expound his understanding. The psalmist says: "When I thought to know this, it was too painful for me" [Ps. 73:16].

There are too many things which are wrought under the light of the sun which man cannot discover or understand. Every day reveals new wonders of God. Nevertheless, man, during his short stay in this world, has found, understood, and made use of some of them. Hundreds of things which were a mystery in the days of Solomon are now well understood, and many others are partially known. Every day reveals new things and every night brings forth new knowledge. Man lives in a progressive revelation. As one curtain is lowered, another curtain goes up [Job 5:9; Ps. 73:16; Isa. 40:28].

FLIES AND OINTMENT

Dead flies cause the ointment of the apothecary to send forth a stinking savor: so doth a little folly him that is in reputation for wisdom and honor. Eccles. 10:1

In biblical lands, jars containing oil, honey, and ointments are often left uncovered, or the cover is not securely placed. Owing to the unsanitary conditions and lack of water, flies are so abundant that they get into such things.

When ointment, honey, and butter are contaminated with flies, they are rejected by prospective buyers. This is also true of a man who has wisdom and is honorable. One mistake or folly will be easily noticed by his followers and admirers. Wisdom and knowledge are like precious ointment; they must be kept secure and pure so that they may be imparted to generations to come.

HEART—MIND

A wise man's heart is at his right hand; but a fool's heart is at his left. Eccles. 10:2

"Heart" in this instance means "mind." That is to say, "A wise man thinks wisely." To say that a man "walks on the right hand" means that he goes straight. Right hand is symbolic of faithfulness, straightforwardness, and power. Left hand is symbolic of error, wrong thinking, and mistrust.

Jesus said, ". . . and he shall separate them one from another, as a shepherd divideth his sheep from the goats; and he shall set the sheep on his right hand, but the goats on the left" [Matt. 25:32-33].

The hearts of all men and women are of course in the same place, whether they are wise or foolish. Right hand and left hand are used symbolically, meaning, the right way and the wrong way; that is, the right thinking and the wrong thinking; the good and the bad; the ones who are chosen and the ones who are rejected. But it is the mind that is responsible for good and for evil. The mind is the master and the guardian of the body.

BLIND AND PIT

He that diggeth a pit shall fall into it; and whoso breaketh a hedge, a serpent shall bite him. Eccles. 10:8

"Pit" is often used figuratively for "evil or mischief." What this verse says is that whoever tries to do evil to his neighbor will himself become the victim of evil.

Pits were common in biblical days, and are still to be seen in many isolated places where Western civilization has not yet penetrated. The pits are dug to be used as storage for wheat, turnips, and cheese. Some of the pits are about twelve feet deep and ten feet in diameter. Pits are often left empty and open. Pits were dug sometimes in secret places by hunters in order to trap wild game. They were also dug by conspirators who wanted to do away with their enemies. These types of pits are generally covered and concealed so that even the man who dug them may fall into them [Ezek. 19:8].

A grain pit may be dug in a village only a few feet from the house of its owner. During the winter and in the spring months when the pit is empty, both men and animals might fall into it, especially during the dark hours of the night [Exod. 21:33-34]. Jesus called the Pharisees, "blind guides" [Matt. 23:16-17]. When a blind man tries to lead another blind person, both of them may fall into a pit [Matt. 15:14; Luke 6:39].

"Hedge" in this instance means boundaries or landmarks. In some lands hedge is the only landmark between two fields. Easterners are afraid to trespass the boundaries between houses and remove the landmarks between the fields. Snakes generally are found in hedges and in heaps of stones which are used as landmarks.

BUYING AND SELLING

The labor of the foolish wearieth every one of them, because he knoweth not how to go to the city.   Eccles. 10:15

The Eastern text reads: "The labor of fools wears them out because they do not know how to buy and sell in the city."

"Knoweth not how to go to the city" is an Eastern idiom that is still used today. It does not mean that the foolish cannot walk to the city, but that they are not wise enough to buy or sell in the city.

In the East, until recent days, there were no commission houses or middlemen. Farmers, artisans, and pastoral people brought their produce to the city where they sold it or exchanged it themselves.

Bartering and bargaining are extremely difficult, especially for farmers and men and women who come to the cities from far off villages and country places. These simple peasants are often cheated. Even today, many Easterners, when buying or selling, seek the services of shrewd and experienced businessmen. The articles to be sold or exchanged have certain values, and the price is determined through bargaining. The foolish and the simple are easily fooled by shrewd and wise merchants.

There is a somewhat similar American idiom—"He has gone to town"—which would be hard for the Easterner to understand.

EATING IN THE MORNING

Woe to thee, O land, when thy king is a child, and thy princes eat in the morning!
Blessed art thou, O land, when thy king is the son of nobles, and thy princes eat in due season, for strength, and not for drunkenness!   Eccles. 10:16-17

Easterners seldom eat much breakfast. They arise early to go to work. They are satisfied with just enough to break their fast. "Breakfast" in colloquial Aramaic is called *taamta* (to taste). A morsel or a mouthful of bread and a little cheese or buttermilk is sufficient for a breakfast. Meat, cereals, and eggs are seldom eaten. The heavy meal is eaten at noon.

Today many men in the East break their fast with a cup of Turkish coffee, a piece of bread, and a little cheese. But those who drink alcoholic liquors start the day with a heavy meal. This is because when Easterners drink, they also eat; and the more they eat, the more they drink. Breakfast is eaten not so much because they need the food but because of the wine or strong drink.

When the Apostles were charged with being drunk [Acts 2:13-15], Peter said, "For these are not drunken, as ye suppose, seeing it is but the third hour of the day [9 A.M.]."

BREAD CAST UPON THE WATER

Cast thy bread upon the waters: for thou shalt find it after many days. Eccles. 11:1

"Cast your bread upon the waters; for you shall find it after many days," means, "Do good to others and some day when you are in need they will come back to help you."

It often happens that when a person is returning from a journey, in the last stage of his journey, while he is eating beside a winding stream or a river, he throws a few dry loaves of bread upon the water, thinking he will not need them. Hours later, as he continues on his journey toward his home town, he may become hungry and may find floating on the water the same loaves he had thrown away. Of course he picks them up and eats them.

At times the road is beset with difficulties and travelers are delayed. There are many winding streams in some lands. The Jordan is a winding river.

But the thought here is that good comes back again to the person who does good. It may not come the same day, but it will come some day when the person is in need. David recompensed Biham, the son of Barzilai, for what his father had done for David [2 Sam. 19:31-40].

The law of compensation is an immutable law. It is just as sure as the shining of the sun. Good always produces good, and evil produces evil. Man reaps what he sows. Jesus said, "Give, and it shall be given unto you. . ." [Luke 6:38].

THE WAY OF THE WIND

As thou knowest not what is the way of the spirit, nor how the bones do grow in the womb of her that is with child: even so thou knowest not the works of God who maketh all. Eccles. 11:5

The same Aramaic word that means "spirit" also means "wind, pride, rheumatism" [Luke 13:11, Eastern text].

Rokha in this instance means "wind." This is because no one knows its way; that is to say, no one knows where it originates or where it goes.

Modern scientific instruments, such as radar, have revealed some of the hidden secrets of the wind. The translators of the King James Version no doubt misunderstood the meaning of the term *rokha*.

Jesus quoted this passage when he said: "The wind blows where it pleases, and you hear its sound; but you do not know whence it comes and whither it goes; such is every man who is born of the Spirit" [John 3:8, Eastern text]. This proves that Jesus, his apostles, and their contemporaries were using the Peshitta, or the original Hebrew Bible. The term *rokha* has been mistranslated many times.

The works of God are more mysterious than those of the wind. Things do not happen because of chance. There is a hidden reason in everything that happens.

OLD AGE

While the sun, or the light, or the moon, or the stars, be not darkened, nor the clouds return after the rain.   Eccles. 12:2

In this instance "sun" symbolizes beauty, glory, and majesty. Stars and moon denote fortune and success. In the East when a man's beauty fades and his glory passes away, it is said, "His sun has set and his stars have disappeared behind the horizon," which means, "He has lost his good looks, power, and fortune." Clouds symbolize sorrows; they stop the light of the sun.

The author of the book of Ecclesiastes is writing about men who have advanced in years and are fast declining in strength, fame, beauty, and wealth.

In the olden days, just like today, it was commonly believed that the stars had something to do with a man's rise and decline, and with his birth, strength, and fortune [Matt. 2:2]. Astrology is one of the oldest sciences, and is just as ancient as the Bible. The people in the olden days traveled by the stars and, at times, were warned and guided by them.

PARTS OF THE BODY

In the day when the keepers of the house shall tremble, and the strong men shall bow themselves, and the grinders cease because they are few, and those that look out of the windows be darkened.
Eccles. 12:3

This is one of the most poetic passages in all the writings of King Solomon. The members of the human body are described subtly in allegories.

"The keepers of the house" are the legs, "the strong men" are the arms, "the grinders" are the teeth, and "those that look out of the windows" are the eyes. Many of King Solomon's sayings are written in figurative language and were well understood by the readers [verse 12].

In olden days, all wise men were able to understand proverbs, riddles, and dark sayings and the interpretations thereof.

The author of Ecclesiastes is speaking of old age, when man's legs and arms become feeble and his eyes become dim [verse 1]. The reader is admonished to remember his Creator when he is young, strong, and sound in health, and not to wait until after he is so old and burdened with his physical body that he cannot pray and is too weary and poor to offer sacrifices.

DEAFNESS

And the doors shall be shut in the streets, when the sound of the grinding is low, and he shall rise up at the voice of the bird, and all the daughters of music shall be brought low.　　Eccles. 12:4

"The doors" in this case mean "old age," when the old man cannot go out and his hearing becomes so dull that the sound of the grinding of the handmill is low, and the noise of singing, dancing, and rejoicing of young women is hardly audible. That is, the old man is no longer able to recognize musical tones and melodies [2 Sam. 19:35].

In the East many families live together. Dancing, grinding, and cooking are done under the same roof. The old men live together with the young and at times become nervous and greatly disturbed. During the night even the sound of the chirping of a bird may awaken them.

THE ALMOND TREE

Also when they shall be afraid of that which is high, and fears shall be in the way, and the almond tree shall flourish, and the grasshopper shall be a burden, and desire shall fail: because man goeth to his long home, and the mourners go about the streets.
Eccles. 12:5

The almond tree is symbolic of man's maturity and fruitfulness. The almond tree produces abundant blossoms. The Aramaic reads: ". . . the almond tree shall blossom, and the locust shall be multiplied, and fragrance shall scatter, and trouble shall cease . . ."

"The almond tree shall blossom" means that man shall begin to beget many children. "The locust" and "fragrance" are symbolic of children, grandchildren, and great-grandchildren, which some of the old men see before they pass away. The daughters marry and spread the fame of the old man abroad. In the East some men marry at the age of nine or ten and live to be 120 or 130. By the time they are old, the house is filled with children, grandchildren, and great-grandchildren.

King Ahab and Gideon had 70 male children each. Even after World War I there were some Near Eastern kings and princes with 500 to 600 children.

Man is in trouble and struggles from the day of his birth to the day of his death. And when he goes to his everlasting house, all troubles and worries are left behind him.

PITCHER BROKEN

Or ever the silver cord be loosed, or the golden bowl be broken, or the pitcher be broken at the fountain, or the wheel broken at the cistern.
Eccles. 12:6

"The pitcher" here symbolizes the earthly life, the body in which the soul dwells. Man is often likened to a vessel. This is because vessels are made of clay, and man's body was created from the red earth. In the East water is brought from wells, cisterns, and brooks upon the heads or the shoulders of women. It often happens that as a maiden places the vessel on her shoulder or on her head, it falls and breaks near the well. The maiden then returns home sad and empty-handed. In that part of the world such a vessel is important. Some women even cry over a good vessel. But once it is broken at the well, the fragments are left there.

Silver cord or thread is used for the weaving of costly brocades. It runs through the cloth from one end to the other. When it is cut off, the weaver stops weaving. The golden bowl is a family heirloom. Allegorically, the thread and the bowl mean life. This is because life is more precious than all man's possessions on earth.

CHAPTER NINETEEN

SONG OF SOLOMON

INTRODUCTION

THE title of the book is clearly stated in the first verse, which was added to the book by the copyist or the compiler. For many centuries these songs have been known as the *Song of Solomon, the King of Israel.*

King Solomon was a wise man, a poet and philosopher, who knew every part of his land and every phase of life. He was a lover of nature and a born poet. The author of the book is familiar with the beauty of the land in northern Israel and Lebanon. That is why he mentions Tirza, Carmel, and Lebanon. Lebanon is one of the most beautiful lands in the world. The country is graced with fertile valleys, lush fields, trees, vines, and cedars. Streams and brooks are also abundant. The region of Tirza and Galilee is also beautiful and prolific when compared with the stony land of Judah.

The book is rich in poetic philosophy in which deep and sincere love is generously and vividly expressed.

The early church authorities believed that Solomon's songs were composed about the Christ and his bride, the church. Be that as it may, the Song of Songs deserves its caption. Its style and beauty have never been surpassed. Indeed, only a wise and experienced king like Solomon, who had made a deep study of nature, the world, and man, could have written such a song as this, with its profound and lasting spiritual meaning.

SUNBURN

Look not upon me, because I am black, because the sun hath looked upon me: my mother's children were angry with me; they made me the keeper of the vineyards; but mine own vineyard have I not kept. Song of Sol. 1:6

The sun is very hot in Palestine and Arabia during the summer months. In that part of the world the days are warm and the nights cold. Consequently, the vineyard keepers and the men and women who live an outdoor life with their flocks are sunburned.

During the summer season, when grapes are ripening, the whole family leaves the town home and moves into small cottages or booths that are constructed in the vineyard. They do this to escape the heat and to protect the vineyard from thieves and travelers who might steal the grapes.

"Vineyard" is also used allegorically, meaning "my beloved." Israel was called God's vineyard. "Now I will sing to my well-beloved a song of my beloved concerning his vineyard. My well-beloved had a vineyard on the corner of a fertile land" [Isa. 5:1, Eastern text].

The vineyard and the garden, metaphorically, also mean "a beloved one" or "wife."

THE WATCHMEN

The watchmen that go about the city found me: to whom I said, Saw ye him whom my soul loveth?   Song of Sol. 3:3

In the East the streets of the walled cities were patrolled by the night guards, who walked in the dark and crooked streets beating a drum as a warning that the people could not walk in the streets during the night hours.

Only city officials, noblemen, and those who in advance had obtained the name of the night could walk freely. Every night was given a name, and those who failed to know the name of the night were detained by the night watchmen. This custom prevailed until after World War I.

PALACE IN LEBANON

King Solomon made himself a chariot of the wood of Lebanon. He made the pillars thereof of silver, the bottom thereof of gold, the covering of it of purple, the midst thereof being paved with love, for the daughters of Jerusalem.   Song of Sol. 3:9-10

The Aramaic word *magdla* means "a palace or tower"; but the King James Version mistakenly reads "chariot." The Eastern text reads: "King Solomon made himself a palace of wood of Lebanon."

"He built also the house of the forest of Lebanon; its length was a hundred cubits and its breadth fifty cubits and its height thirty cubits, upon four rows of cedar pillars, with cedar beams upon the pillars" [1 Kings 7:2, Eastern text].

The reference here is to the house which Solomon built of wood (cedar) of Lebanon. Solomon ruled over all the lands from the Great Sea (Mediterranean) to the River Euphrates.

ENCOURAGED BY HIS BELOVED

Thou hast ravished my heart, my sister, my spouse; thou hast ravished my heart with one of thine eyes, with one chain of thy neck. Song of Sol. 4:9

The Aramaic text reads *labewteni* (you have encouraged me). The same word means also "comforted or consoled."

In the East maidens are very shy. They seldom see or talk to their fiances. But the more retiring they are, the more they are sought by their lovers. But when a girl is in love she may secretly encourage her lover to see her. On such an occasion the girl may make signs with her eyes.

"HONEY" USED FIGURATIVELY

Thy lips, O my spouse, drop as the honeycomb: honey and milk are under thy tongue; and the smell of thy garments is like the smell of Lebanon. Song of Sol. 4:11

"Honey" in this instance is a metaphor meaning "sweet speech." Honey drops gently from the honeycomb, and as it drops, those who see it are eager to eat it.

In the East we often say, "His words are like honey; his speech is sweet." Milk, because of its whiteness and purity, in Eastern languages is symbolic of wisdom, innocence, and sincerity. Milk is a natural food prepared by God for babies and little children who cannot yet eat other food. Words spoken with sincerity are like pure milk and are sweet like pure honey which drips from a honeycomb.

Isaiah says, "Butter and honey shall he eat" [Isa. 7:15]. "My son, eat thou honey, because it is good; and the honeycomb, which is sweet to thy taste" [Prov. 24:13]. The words of wisdom are sweet to the ear of the wise, just as honey is sweet to the palate.

GARDEN A WIFE

A garden enclosed is my sister, my bride; yea, a garden guarded, a fountain sealed.   Song of Sol. 4:12

The Aramaic term "garden" is used figuratively, meaning "a wife." In the East a wife is often called a garden and the husband, "keeper of the garden." Even today, the term garden, meaning a wife or a beloved one, is still used by Eastern poets and song composers. "I am come into my garden . . ." means "I am with my beloved." Song of Sol. 5:1.

HEART FAINTING

My beloved put in his hand by the hole of the door, and my bowels were moved for him.   Song of Sol. 5:4

In the Near East both doors and keys are made of wood. There is a hole about a foot long and six inches wide between the doorpost and the door. The wooden lock is constructed in this hole in the side of the door. One has to put his hand into the hole in order to reach the lock. As the wooden key is large and the hole in the lock long, the opening causes noise. Bandits and robbers use keys made of stiff hair when they steal, so that those who are in the house might not be awakened.

In this case, the girl waits on her bed, expecting her beloved to place the key into the lock.

"My bowels were moved for him," means, "My heart was moved for him when I heard the noise of the key."

VISITING AT NIGHT

I sleep, but my heart waketh: it is the voice of my beloved that knocketh, saying, Open to me, my sister, my love, my dove, my undefiled: for my head is filled with dew, and my locks with the drops of the night.   Song of Sol. 5:2

In the East no one can visit his sweetheart in the daytime. Easterners gossip if they see a man talking to a virgin, and such gossip is destructive to the reputation of the maiden and her parents.

Nevertheless, some lovers dare to visit their beloved ones during the dark hours of night, when the streets are empty and everyone is asleep.

The dew here is symbolic of late hours when the dew falls on the ground. The two lovers meet in a secret place near the door, in the silence of the night, when the dew is falling on the ground.

NIGHT WATCHMEN

The watchmen that went about the city found me, they smote me, they wounded me; the keepers of the walls took away my veil from me.
I charge you, O daughters of Jerusalem, if ye find my beloved, that ye tell him, that I am sick of love.   Song of Sol. 5:7-8

All walled cities in the Near East have night watchmen who guard the shops and market places until dawn. Two or three of them go together about the city, beating on a small drum in a peculiar sound which announces their presence.

When the watchmen meet strangers in the street they arrest them. Even the inhabitants of the city who happen to be late are liable to arrest and a beating if they fail to know the number or the sign of the night.

All those who think that they might be late home at night ask for the sign of the night so that they might not be arrested. Then again, some of the guards are stationed on the wall near the city gates, and the doors of the gate are closed and locked.

At times spies and dangerous men try to enter the city disguised in women's attire. When the night guards suspect them, they remove their veils. Today, in most cities, the night watchmen have been replaced by policemen.

The maid was so much in love with her beloved that she sought him regardless of the dangers and difficulties during the night hours when even men dared not walk abroad and confront the night watchmen.

BEAUTIFUL AND DESIRABLE

Thou art beautiful, O my love, as Tirzah, comely as Jerusalem, terrible as an army with banners.   Song of Sol. 6:4

The Eastern text reads: "You are beautiful and desirable, O my beloved, comely as Jerusalem, and esteemed [or revered] as one chosen among beauties."

The term "Tirzah" in the King James Version is a mistranslation of the Aramaic word *sebyana* (delight). Tirzah was the name of the youngest daughter of Zelophehad [Num. 26:33]. The first capitol of the northern kingdom was named Tirzah, and Jeroboam, the founder of the kingdom, dwelt there. King Jeroboam may have beautified the city, but this would have been after the death of King Solomon. In the East fair women are often likened to beautiful cities.

BLACK HAIR

Turn away thine eyes from me, for they have overcome me: thy hair is as a flock of goats that appear from Gilead. Song of Sol. 6:5

Women with black hair are greatly admired in biblical lands and other parts of the Near East. Blond hair is so rare that men or women who do have blond hair are looked upon as strangers.

The few blond and blue-eyed men and women who are found today in Palestine and Arabia are the descendants of Roman soldiers and the Crusaders.

Goats in biblical lands are very black. A flock of goats look beautiful when led by the shepherd to and from the mountain. The black color stands out conspicuously against light brown earth and faded grass. In the same way a fair maiden with long black hair stands out among women.

PUBLIC CHARIOT

Or ever I was aware, my soul made me like the chariots of Amminadib.   Song of Sol. 6:12

The Aramaic reads *bemarkabtha di amma* (the public chariot). The Eastern text reads: "And being unfamiliar with the place, I sat in the public chariot which was ready." Evidently, chariots and wagons were used for transportation during the glorious reign of King Solomon.

The Assyrians and Babylonians used wagons for transport of military supplies, and chariots for war. The Egyptians were noted for the manufacture of beautiful gilded chariots. Joseph sent Egyptian wagons to bring his father, Jacob, and his brothers and their families from the land of Canaan to Egypt about 2000 B.C. [Gen. 45:19]. About 1000 B.C., during the reign of King Solomon, the Hebrews used both chariots and wagons.

The term *amminadib* is a mistransliteration of *di amma* (of the people); that is, "a public chariot."

DAMASCUS

Thy navel is like a round goblet, which wanteth not liquor: thy belly is like a heap of wheat set about with lilies.
Thy two breasts are like two young roes that are twins.
Thy neck is as a tower of ivory; thine eyes like the fishpools in Heshbon, by the gate of Bath-rabbim: thy nose is as the tower of Lebanon which looketh toward Damascus.   Song of Sol. 7:2-4

The Aramaic *bartha* (pronounced bath), meaning "daughter," is often used for "a city." For example: *Bath Babel* means "the daughter of Babylon" [Jer. 50:42; 51:33], "the daughter of Zion" [Ps. 9:14], and "Harken, O my daugther" [Ps. 45:10].
Barth sagiaey (the daughter of many) means "the city with many inhabitants." During the time of King Solomon, Damascus was a great metropolis and the oldest city in the world. The city is like an emerald encased in a yellow gold setting. The city is like a paradise in the heart of the arid desert. The other Aramaic word for "many" is *rabey*. In Semitic languages parts of the body are often portrayed metaphorically.

KISSING

O that thou wert as my brother, that sucked the breasts of my mother! when I should find thee without, I would kiss thee; yea, I should not be despised.   Song of Sol. 8:1

In biblical lands girls cannot commune with or court their lovers, nor can they kiss them prior to their marriage. The only male a girl can openly converse with is a close relative; and the only one she can kiss is her brother or possibly a close cousin.
When girls meet their brothers returning from a journey they kiss them, but they are not allowed to speak or to keep company with their lovers or strangers. All arrangements for a marriage are made by the parents [Song of Sol. 4:9; 5:2].

UNDER THE APPLE TREE

Who is this that cometh up from the wilderness, leaning upon her beloved? I raised thee up under the apple tree: there thy mother brought thee forth; there she brought thee forth that bare thee.
        Song of Sol. 8:5

"Under the apple tree" means under the protection of the shadow of an apple tree. In the East during hot summer months, babies and small children are put under fig or apple trees to protect them from the sun. The shadow of an apple tree is considered cool and refreshing. The sick and the weary also seek the protection of the shadow of the trees, especially that of the apple tree. For many centuries trees were worshiped. Jesus said to Nathaniel, "When thou wast under the fig tree, I saw thee" [John 1:48].

The apple is symbolic of love, beauty, and tender care [Deut. 32:10]. "Keep me as the apple of the eye; hide me under the shadow of thy wings" [Ps. 17:8]. Beloved ones are spoken of as the apple of the eye. "Let not the apple of thine eye cease from shedding tears" [Lam. 2:18, Eastern text]. In the East during marriage feasts the bridegroom throws an apple at the bride. This is because an apple is more coveted than any other fruit.

UNMATURED GIRLS

We have a little sister, and she hath no breasts: what shall we do for our sister in the day when she shall be spoken for?
Song of Sol. 8:8

"She hath no breasts" means of course that she has not matured. In the East mature women are known by the size of their breasts. "In the day when she shall be spoken for" means when she is sought in marriage, or betrothed. It should read: ". . . in the day when they shall seek her hand."

In the East girls who are ready to be married cannot be seen either by their prospective bridegrooms or by the matchmakers. Those who arrange a marriage for a son have to take a chance. It is like buying an article without seeing it. Then again, women can be rejected or divorced on account of certain deficiencies in their bodies. Easterners like fat women with large breasts [verse 10].

The sister in this case is refused on the grounds of her lack of breasts. They will take care of her and wait until she has matured.

LARGE BREASTS

I am a wall, and my breasts like towers: then was I in his eyes as one that found favor.
Song of Sol. 8:10

In the East the larger the women are, the more they are preferred. Not many years ago, women used to wear many garments just in order to look big and fat. On the wedding day the bride is attired with many garments and covered with a heavy veil.

Moreover, women with large breasts are considered beauties and are preferred by kings, princes, and the wealthy classes. This is also true in many European countries and in some parts of South America.

VINEYARDS LEASED

Solomon had a vineyard at Baal-hamon; he let out the vineyard unto keepers; every one for the fruit thereof was to bring a thousand pieces of silver.   Song of Sol. 8:11

The Eastern text reads: ". . . and its fruits were abundant." *Baal-hamon* is a translation of the Aramaic word *ebey* (its produce). Baal was the god of fertility and farming, but the reference here is to the abundant fruits.

Solomon's vineyard was very fertile. The Aramaic reads: ". . . he let out the vineyard to keepers; a man offered for its fruits a thousand pieces of silver."

In the East vineyards, orchards, and large gardens belong to wealthy landowners and princes. When the fruit is ripe many vineyards, orchards, and produce fields are leased to contractors who in turn hire workers to watch over them, gather the fruit thereof, and sell it in the market for a profit. The rich seldom bother with the fruit. They prefer to lease their vineyards and orchards to professional contractors, who take care of them or lease them to others for a profit.

In Aramaic the vineyard is symbolic of one's beloved, and the song is a vivid poetic description of the relationships of lovers. Easterners, in such cases, use poetic and figurative speech which is easily understood by the unlearned public.

Many Christians consider this poetry a figurative expression of the relation between Christ and his church. Jesus loved his church so much that he died for it. The Song of Solomon thus has a profound spiritual meaning for those who read it spiritually.

CHAPTER TWENTY

ISAIAH

INTRODUCTION

ISAIAH, Aramaic *Eshaya,* stands out as the greatest prophet and states-man in the history of Israel and Judah. This prophet came from a different background. He was respected by kings and princes. He was well educated and versed in foreign policy and the internal affairs of his own people.

Isaiah lived during the reigns of four kings of Judah; namely, Uzziah, Jotham, Ahaz, and Hezekiah. He was put to death during the reign of Manasseh when Judah, like Israel, had forsaken the way of God and had gone astray after pagan gods, and when God's sanctuary was polluted with pagan sacrifices and immoral worship. Isaiah, like Jesus, was rejected and put to death. It is said he was sawed in two between two wooden planks.

The prophet saw the rise and the decline of the small kingdoms west of the River Euphrates, and the struggles between Judah and the con-federate states, Israel and Aram (Syria). And he lived until he saw the rise and expansion of the imperial power of Assyria.

Many social, religious, and political changes took place during the lifetime of Isaiah. This is why the material in his book and its message is so varied. This explains also why, in the course of time, the prophet grew more spiritual; he saw that Judah could no longer defend herself against the mighty empires which were rising on the Eastern horizon—Assyria and Babylon, and other neighboring states.

Isaiah changed his prophecy of a conquering political Messiah, as envisioned by some of the Jewish prophets and statesmen, to that of a suffering servant. He saw that other races and people who now were in power were also ruled by the God of Israel, and that the same God had given them power to punish the wicked nations [Isa. 10:5]. He saw that Assyria was the rod of God's anger and a staff in his hand to punish the wicked nations, including Israel and Judah. Isaiah saw that the light of Israel must shine on the Gentile nations and that the Jewish religion must become universal in order to save Israel and Judah [Isa. 9:1-5].

Isaiah is the author of all the books that bear his name. He wrote the scrolls of his book at different periods of his ministry. But as he grew he changed his message and gradually saw a universal state ruled by the God of Israel. He also saw that God's light must shine upon the pagan people. In other words, Isaiah had a new concept of religion— a universal concept—and a new view of the Messiah. The triumph of the messianic kingdom was to be achieved by means of meekness, love, and the arm of God, instead of by hatred and the sword.

The Messiah whom Isaiah saw was to be rejected and killed, simply because the priests would oppose such a radical concept. Sharing the Jewish faith with the Gentile world would be resented both by the people and their religious leaders. And yet, this new policy was the only hope for the salvation of the Jewish state and of all mankind, and for the establishment of a universal state to replace the kingdoms of this world.

Isaiah lived about the eighth century B.C. He was in Jerusalem when the Emperor Sennacherib invaded Judah and when the Assyrian army was smitten.

Bible students must remember that scribes added new material, what in the East we call marginal notes, to the book of Isaiah. For instance: "The burden of Babylon which Isaiah the son of Amoz did see" [Isa. 13:1]. These and many similar phrases were not written by Isaiah. They were originally marginal notes which later were incorporated into the book. These notes were made to facilitate the reading of the book by the priests and scribes. This custom still prevails in the East.

Some Bible authorities wonder how Isaiah could have named King Cyrus by name, when Cyrus actually was not born until two centuries after Isaiah died. The name Cyrus might originally have been inserted as a marginal note and later incorporated into the text. But of course the prophet could have known the name of the king through a revelation. After all, Isaiah was a prophet who acted as a spokesman for God. No doubt, the prophet foresaw the downfall of Assyria and Babylon and the rise of the Persian empire, just as Daniel foresaw the rise and fall of great imperial powers which ruled centuries after his death. There is only one book of Isaiah, and not three. Jesus read from the book of Isaiah and said that the prophet's prophecy has been fulfilled.

Isaiah, like Hosea and Jeremiah, used metaphors, parables, and allegories. His wife, the prophetess, and his son, Maher-shalal-hash-baz, are used in a parabolic sense, describing the speedy conquest of Syria and Israel by the king of Assyria. In the Aramaic Eastern text the name of the child is *Mesarhib-shabey-otakib-bas*, which means "to hasten the captivity, and to record the spoil" [Isa. 8:1].

The book of Isaiah is the most important book in the Old Testament because it gives a new perspective and clear concept of the Messiah, his rejection, his suffering, and his triumph. Its message is of a universal appeal. According to Isaiah, Messiah will be a light to the Gentiles and to the people who dwell in darkness. "The people who dwelt in darkness will see a great light." This light was the teaching of the Mosaic moral law and of the Hebrew prophets which was to be preached by Jesus in Galilee and shared with the Gentile world.

The book of the prophet Isaiah is inspiring and consoling. Jesus quoted from it many times. It was from the book of Isaiah that he read when he proclaimed himself the Messiah [Luke 4:17-20, Isaiah 61:1-4].

COTTAGE

And the daughter of Zion is left as a cottage in a vineyard, as a lodge in a garden of cucumbers, as a besieged city. Isa. 1:8

Koprana (cottage, booth, lodge) is a small shelter made of branches of trees. Four posts are sunk into the ground, and then the walls are made of small branches, and the roof is covered with the grass and leaves.

Generally, the cottage is placed in the center of the vineyard, so that the watchman can see the whole vineyard and thus guard it from thieves and travelers who might break in and steal the grapes.

This "booth" is also a shelter to protect the workers from the heat of the sun during the day, and is used for a sleeping place during the night.

In some places in Palestine one sees booths built of stones which are gathered from the fields and then covered with the branches of trees. Palestine is a dry land. There is hardly any rain during the summer months. The booths offer a comfortable place for the workers to rest in the vineyard.

When the grapes have been gathered, the booth, once a place of feasting and dancing, is deserted and left forlorn. When one looks at it he feels sad to see it left alone and empty. Sometimes such booths are burned by shepherds, travelers, and bandits [Job 27:18].

Hedges are built around the vineyards and gardens to prevent men from stealing the cucumbers and grapes. Some of the hedges are made of dry briers, others of small stones.

The daughter of Zion, Israel, was to be deserted just as a cottage is deserted in the autumn. The hedges were to be burned. Hedges here means the fences which were to be breached by the enemy [Lam. 2:6].

FALSE DEVOTION

Bring no more vain oblations; incense is an abomination unto me; the new moons and sabbaths, the calling of assemblies, I cannot away with; it is iniquity, even the solemn meeting. Isa. 1:13

To sacrifice to deities and to offer gifts to kings and holy men was an ancient and universal custom. Pagans appeased their angry and hungry gods by means of incense and sacrifices. They also brought gifts to kings and offered incense and sacrifices to human deities.

Sacrifices, gifts, offerings, and incense were used as reminders that the people should offer thanks to the Lord, praise his name for his goodness and loving-kindness, and share with the poor and the needy of the land. But later they became the center of worship, even replacing the love of God, justice, and mercy. As a result of this change, injustices, hatred, and evil prevailed, and the true meaning of the sacrifices was completely lost. At times, the animals offered to God had been stolen or violently taken from the weak and the poor to be devoured by the priests, elders, and princes. The Eastern text of the latter part of this verse reads: "I do not eat that which is obtained wrongfully, and taken by force."

God was not pleased with such a false devotion which was carried to extremes of pomp and ceremony at the expense of the poor. What God wanted was justice and mercy, rather than the meat offerings, wine offerings, and the incense which the priests themselves enjoyed. Many of the prophets of Israel opposed the use of sacrifices and rituals simply because the true meaning thereof was completely lost and the institution had become corrupt and useless.

JUSTICE

Learn to do well; seek judgment, relieve the oppressed, judge the fatherless, plead for the widow. Isa. 1:17

This verse should read: "Learn to do good; seek justice, do good to the oppressed, plead for the fatherless, plead for the widows."

In the East the fatherless and the widows are often oppressed and their property confiscated. They have no one to plead their cause, nor do they have money with which to bribe the judges and officials to obtain justice. On the other hand, unpaid judges, tax gatherers, and officials are always in need of money, and so they refuse to take the cases of orphans and widows and secure justice for them [verses 22-23].

The parable of the widow, which was told by Jesus, proves that the widows and orphans were oppressed and neglected in those days [Matt. 23:13; Mark 12:40]. Widows and orphans are under God's protection. When injustices are done to them, God is angry at the judges and rulers [Deut. 10:17-18; Jer. 49:11].

The prophets of all great religions have warned their followers against injustices to the weak, the orphans, and the widows, who look to God to plead their cause and to avenge the wrongs which are committed against them.

DROSS IN SILVER

Thy silver is become dross, thy wine mixed with water. Isa. 1:22

When justice and righteousness are forgotten, and corruption prevails, businessmen cheat one another. The silver merchant mixes dross with his silver, and the wine merchant mixes water with his wine. Moreover, they use diverse weights and balances in order to defraud one another.

The prophet here is referring to the corrupt conditions which prevailed in Jerusalem.

Silver and dross are used allegorically, meaning good and evil. There was the holy temple, there were the sacrifices, and there was the supposedly holy priesthood. But there was also corruption in government, bribes, and oppression.

The city was once a faithful city, but now its princes and judges had become as thieves, and sought bribes and refused to plead the cause of those who could not afford to offer bribes.

BRIBE

Thy princes are rebellious, and companions of thieves: every one loveth gifts, and followeth after rewards: they judge not the fatherless, neither doth the cause of the widow come unto them.

Isa. 1:23

"Gift" in this case means "bribe." In the East, as well as in many other parts of the world, bribery is common. Officials of the government, judges, princes, and governors expect bribes from those who seek their help to plead their cause.

Years ago, bribes were sent in advance in order to pervert judgment and to seek favors. Nevertheless, some honorable rulers and pious judges refused to accept bribes. Samuel, while addressing the people, said, "Of whose hand have I received any bribe?" [1 Sam. 12:3]. "Their right hand is full of bribes" [Ps. 26:10].

RESTORATION

*And I will restore thy judges as at the first, and thy counselors
as at the beginning: afterward thou shalt be called, The city of
righteousness, the faithful city.*   Isa. 1:26

The reference here is to the Hebrew judges in the olden days, when
justice and righteousness reigned, when the people were pious and bribes
were unknown. During that time the judges were selected from among
the pious men in the land, and the counselors were prophets and men
of God who admonished the people to keep God's commandments and
ordinances, and to beware of pagan teachings and practices. Now the
city was full of corruption, extortion, and murders [verse 21].

The prophet laments the situation. He compares the people in his
days with the people in olden days, especially during the reign of the
Judges when the law was well kept and the people adhered to the way
of God.

WITCHCRAFT

*For they shall be ashamed of the oaks which ye have desired,
and ye shall be confounded for the gardens that ye have chosen.*
                              Isa. 1:29

The Aramaic word *petakhrey* means "idols." "Oaks" is a mistranslation. The Aramaic word *ginyatha* (witchcraft) has been confused with
the Aramaic word *genyatha* (gardens). Both words are written alike but
pronounced differently.

Oak trees were worshiped in biblical days. The thick foliage of an oak
was a great relief to the weary and the sick who sought refuge under
their boughs during the hot hours of the day. Other beautiful and green
trees were also worshiped, but not so much as those which grow in
barren lands and are few.

In the hot-weather lands where trees are scarce, any green thing is
appealing to the eye of the weary and thirsty traveler and to the sick.
In some arid areas one can see trees decorated with pieces of cloth torn
from the robes of men and women who have sat under their refreshing
shadows. The people offered a little gift—a piece of their garments—
which they tied on the branches. Most of these trees are called sacred
and are therefore protected. No one dares to break a limb or even
damage a leaf. Moreover, sick people visit them from time to time. In
biblical days the Hebrews, as well as other races, worshiped green trees
and groves.

But the reference here is to the prevailing witchcraft which was practiced by false prophets and soothsayers.

MOUNTAIN

And it shall come to pass in the last days, that the mountain of the Lord's house shall be established in the top of the mountains, and shall be exalted above the hills; and all nations shall flow unto it.

And many people shall go and say, Come ye, and let us go up to the mountain of the Lord, to the house of the God of Jacob; and he will teach us of his ways, and we will walk in his paths: for out of Zion shall go forth the law, and the word of the Lord from Jerusalem.   Isa. 2:2-3

"Mountain" in this instance means Israel and the truth for which it stood. The prophecy is concerning the remnant of Israel which was to be spared and reestablished once more upon Mount Zion, the place which the Lord God had chosen as an habitation for his holy name.

During the time of the prophet Isaiah, Israel was harassed by the great nations round about her. Both Judah and Israel had become tributary to the mighty kings of Assyria. In due time both kingdoms, Israel and Judah, were to be destroyed and the people carried away captive. The people had forsaken their God, had made alliances with pagan nations, and had trusted in foreign kings and worshiped their pagan gods.

Nevertheless, the time was to come when a spiritual Israel would rise out of the ruins of political Israel, which would exalt Jerusalem above all other cities of the world and the true religion of Israel above all pagan religions. For the law and a new Word of God were to be proclaimed from Jerusalem. At last truth was to destroy error [Dan. 2:38; Mic. 4:1; Zech. 14:8-9].

MESSIANIC FULFILLMENT

And he shall judge among the nations, and shall rebuke many people: and they shall beat their swords into plowshares, and their spears into pruning hooks: nation shall not lift up sword against nation, neither shall they learn war any more.   Isa. 2:4

The reference here is to the messianic fulfillment. The moral law and the ordinances which God had given to Moses on Mount Sinai were to be shared with the Gentile world, and the light of God was to shine in the dark lands where people groped in ignorance, in order that they might know the way of God, be judged at the last day.

The great Gentile nations were to learn justice and mercy and to beat their swords into plowshares and their spears into pruning hooks.

The truth of God and the increase of knowledge and brotherhood would do away with greed, worldly ambitions, fear of poverty, and war. Then no nation would lift up the sword against another nation, nor learn the art of war any more. Meekness, kindness, and gentleness would take the place of the greed, hatred, and the implements of war.

CHILDREN OF STRANGERS

Therefore thou hast forsaken thy people the house of Jacob, because they be replenished from the east, and are soothsayers like the Philistines, and they please themselves in the children of strangers. Isa. 2:6

The phrase "because they be replenished from the east . . ." should read: "because they are self-satisfied as in the olden days, and they practice augury like the Philistines, and they have reared many alien children." The alien children were taken captive during the wars and some of them were brought up as members of the family. It was against the law to mix thus with pagan people. The Israelites tried to keep their race holy and pure, but, at times, owing to marriages with alien women and the adoption of children, this was impossible.

The Aramaic word *kadim* means "as before, as of old, as of yore." The Aramaic word *kadim* has been confused with the Hebrew *kedam* (east). The Israelites, whenever they were hungry and in distress, turned to God, but when they were filled they forsook him and broke his commandments.

The rearing of strange children was discouraged by the Mosaic law. During the wars they were permitted to spare some of the virgin females, but they were told to destroy all the males.

"Now therefore kill every male among the little ones, and kill every woman that hath known man by lying with him. But all the women children, that have not known a man by lying with him, keep alive for yourselves" [Num. 31:17-18].

The Israelites were to remain a pure race. Marriages with women of other races were discouraged. They were prohibited from giving their daughters to the uncircumcised [Gen. 34:14]. Even after the captivity they were not permitted to marry Gentile women [Ezra 9:1-2].

DWELLING IN ROCKS

Enter into the rock, and hide thee in the dust, for fear of the Lord, and for the glory of his majesty. Isa. 2:10

"Enter into the rocks, and hide in the dust" is an Eastern saying which means, "Flee for your life, be ashamed and confounded."

Palestine has many caves which are used as hiding places in time of war. In some regions where houses are scarce and difficult to find, many families live in caves. Then again, shepherds and travelers often abide in caves.

The Lord God of Israel was going to judge the nations and rebuke the people. Jerusalem would be exalted in that day, and the glory of the Lord would be manifested. The wicked would be judged, the proud humbled, and the idols destroyed. It is a day of reckoning wherein many wicked men would hide themselves from the impending disaster.

CEDARS OF LEBANON

And upon all the cedars of Lebanon, that are high and lifted up, and upon all the oaks of Bashan,
And upon all the high mountains, and upon all the hills that are lifted up.　　　　　　　　　　　　　　　　　Isa. 2:13-14

"Cedars" in this instance is used metaphorically to mean "great men." And "the oaks of Bashan" symbolize strong men. "High mountains" are symbolic of proud kings, princes, and rulers who had boasted of their power.

Many of the Hebrew prophets spoke and wrote in parables and used hyperbole, similes, and metaphors in order to convey their ideas to the simple folk. On the other hand, this was the only kind of language by which they could express such high and spiritual ideas, ideas that would be difficult to convey in an abstract way. Even today Eastern people use the same similes and hyperboles found in the Bible. A proud man is called a mountain and a strong man is likened to a tall cedar or a hard oak.

TEMPER

Cease ye from man, whose breath is in his nostrils: for wherein is he to be accounted of?　　　　　　　　　　　　　　　Isa. 2:22

"His breath in his nostrils" is an Aramaic idiom which means that he is impatient, hasty, or impulsive; this refers to a person who does not think things over, but acts without thinking. This idiom is still used among Aramaic-speaking people.

When a man is hasty or impatient he talks with his breath in his nostrils. Easterners consider impatient men dangerous. Leaders and judges who are impulsive are greatly feared and are considered impractical.

Easterners generally think things over before they act, especially the wise men. They let a matter cool off for a while before they make a decision.

CHILDREN

And I will give children to be their princes, and babes shall rule over them.   Isa. 3:4

"Children" here is a wrong translation. The Aramaic reads: "And I will appoint young men to be their princes, and mockers shall rule over them."

Young men are feared as rulers because they easily fall victims of wicked counselors and ruthless government officials. Athaliah was the only woman who ruled over Judah, and she was so wicked that she introduced Baal worship and even slew her own grandchildren [2 Kings 11:1-3].

"Woe to you, O land, when your king is a child, and your princes eat in the morning!" [Eccles. 10:16, Eastern text].

LEADER AND HEALER

When a man shall take hold of his brother of the house of his father, saying, Thou hast clothing, be thou our ruler, and let this ruin be under thy hand:

In that day shall he swear, saying, I will not be a healer; for in my house is neither bread nor clothing: make me not a ruler of the people.   Isa. 3:6-7

In the East leaders, mayors, governors, and even kings are chosen from among the rich. This is because the houses of the rulers and princes are open to the public, even to strangers and travelers. Therefore, one has to have abundant bread and other material things in order to accept such a high position. When people lack money, food, and clothing, they decline these honors.

Strangers and travelers, when traveling, stop in the houses of mayors and other high officials. Moreover, during the meal hours, hungry town people may come uninvited into the houses of the leaders. At times, men who accept these high offices become impoverished, especially the pious men who refuse to accept bribes or to exact heavy taxes from their subjects.

The prophet paints a dark picture. The conditions in Israel were to be so bad that men would even decline high honors because they would be unable to set food before those who called on them, or to entertain foreign officials and dignitaries.

"Healer" is used in the King James Version to mean leader or counselor; that is, one who leads the people in the right path and solves their problems. When wrong things are corrected, men say they are healed. Healers and leaders, when they are good, are a great comfort to their people in times of distress.

CHILDREN WILL RULE OVER THEM

As for my people, children are their oppressors, and women rule over them. O my people, they which lead thee cause thee to err, and destroy the way of thy paths. Isa. 3:12

The Aramaic word for "baby" and "child" is written exactly like the word for "wicked, ungodly, oppressors, iniquity." But when the word is used to mean a baby or child, the scribe places two dots under it. When he intends to use the word for oppressor, wicked, or ungodly, he places one dot under it.

The word is *awla*. The meaning of this word is determined by the position of the dots. Sometimes flies lay specks on a manuscript, which look like dots placed there by the scribe, and consequently those words which have double meanings are confused. Foreigners who are unfamiliar with these dots are often bewildered when they translate from the ancient Semitic languages into modern languages. Such errors have been the cause of murders and divisions. The Aramaic text reads: "The princes shall pluck my people out . . ." (that is, the ungodly oppressors).

No prophet would have used children as an analogy of oppression. Jesus said, "Allow the little children to come to me, and do not stop them; for the kingdom of heaven is for such as these" [Matt. 19:14, Eastern text].

MODESTY

Moreover the Lord saith, Because the daughters of Zion are haughty, and walk with stretched forth necks and wanton eyes, walking and mincing as they go, and making a tinkling with their feet. Isa. 3:16

In the East women wear many bracelets on their arms, anklets on their ankles, and ornaments on their brows. Some anklets have bells on them [Ezek. 16:10-14].

These ornaments were worn by women so that they might be seen by the people. They also made noise when women walked, and thus aroused curiosity and attention. Pious women were to be simple, modest, and chaste, says the prophet, so that they might become an example to the pagan women.

Paul admonished Christian women to be simple in their attire and to refrain from wearing too many bracelets and trinkets and other jewels [1 Tim. 2:9-10].

HOPE FOR THE REMNANT

In that day shall the branch of the Lord be beautiful and glorious, and the fruit of the earth shall be excellent and comely for them that are escaped of Israel.

And it shall come to pass, that he that is left in Zion, and he that remaineth in Jerusalem, shall be called holy, even every one that is written among the living in Jerusalem. Isa. 4:2-3

The Aramaic word *dinkhey* is derived from *denakh* (to shine forth). The Eastern text reads: "In that day shall the glory and honor of the Lord shine forth, and the fruit of the earth shall be excellent and comely for the remnant of Israel."

During the time of the invasion of the land by the Assyrian kings, Israel was oppressed and burdened with tributes and taxes. The Lord had humbled Zion to the ground. The wound was so great that even the women had to put away their beautiful garments, bracelets, and other ornaments and wear sackcloth. The hearts of the people were gloomy. But even in the midst of the gloom and despair the prophets saw a ray of light and hope.

Isaiah is speaking here of the remnant of Israel which would be spared. The Lord would shine forth upon them and would shelter them as of yore.

The glory of God would shine forth in Jerusalem again when the city was purged of its evil. The remnant of Israel in Jerusalem would be called holy, and Israel would be established again.

The remnant is what counts. The Lord God always leaves a small remnant so that his true religion may be reestablished again and his lamp kept burning.

GOD'S PROTECTION

And there shall be a tabernacle for a shadow in the daytime from the heat, and for a place of refuge, and for a covert from storm and from rain. Isa. 4:6

Palestine is hot during the summer months. The temperature rises high during the day and drops low during the night. During the middle of the day the people take refuge in houses, tents, booths, and other shelters that have been built to protect them from the heat. The shepherds sit under the shadow of trees, bushes, and rocks.

When the Israelites were in the desert of Sinai, the Lord went before them by day in a pillar of cloud to lead the way, and by night in a pillar of fire to give them light [Exod. 13:21].

"The tabernacle" is here used metaphorically, meaning "protection." The Lord will serve as a shelter to protect Israel not only from the heat but also from their oppressors.

VINEYARD OF GOD

> *Now will I sing to my well-beloved a song of my beloved touching his vineyard. My well-beloved hath a vineyard in a very fruitful hill:*
>
> *And he fenced it, and gathered out the stones thereof, and planted it with the choicest vine, and built a tower in the midst of it, and also made a winepress therein: and he looked that it should bring forth grapes, and it brought forth wild grapes.* Isa. 5:1-2

Isaiah, like other Hebrew prophets, spoke and wrote in parables and in figures of speech. This was the only way he could convey his message to the simple and illiterate people who could not grasp abstract terms of speech, and who were misled by their wicked kings, princes, and false court prophets.

"The vineyard" means Israel. The "well-beloved" is the Lord God, who had a vineyard in a very fruitful hill. "The hill" is Mount Zion. The Lord fenced the vineyard (Israel) and gathered the stones that were in it. Judea is full of stones. One has to gather the stones and make them into heaps or fences before he can plant the vines.

"The stones" are symbolic of pagan doctrines, and "the fence" symbolizes God's protection from evil forces. "The tower" is symbolic of watchmen, who were the prophets and men of God who looked after Israel and protected it from wild beasts, the false prophets. But even though the vineyard, Judah, was well taken care of, it did not produce good grapes, but instead, it produced wild grapes.

Jesus quoted this parable which was used by Isaiah about the eighth century B.C. [Matt. 21:33; Isa. 1:8].

REMAINING LANDMARKS

> *Woe unto them that join house to house, that lay field to field, till there be no place, that they may be placed alone in the midst of the earth!* Isa. 5:8

The Aramaic text reads: "Woe to those who trespass the boundaries between houses, who remove the landmarks between the fields . . ."

The Aramaic word *makrewin* means "to bring near"; that is, "to change the position" of a boundary or a landmark in order to steal the land of the neighbors [Micah 2:1-3].

To remove a landmark was against the Mosaic law. "You shall not remove your neighbor's landmark, which they of old time have set in your inheritance . . ." [Deut. 19:14]. "Do not remove the old landmark; nor enter into the field of the fatherless" [Prov. 23:10; see also Prov. 22:28, Eastern text].

Some people removed the boundaries and the landmarks in order to seize the land from the poor and the weak. ". . . they violently take away a flock" [Job 24:2, Eastern text].

In the East landmarks are still removed, especially when the owner of a field is absent. As surveying is unknown, landmarks and boundaries are not recorded in books. Therefore stealing of land is common, and quarrels over landmarks are frequent.

Moses placed a curse upon anyone who removed a landmark. "Cursed be he who removes his neighbor's landmark. And all the people shall say, Amen" [Deut. 27:17, Eastern text].

STRONG DRINK

Woe unto them that rise up early in the morning, that they may follow strong drink; that continue until night, till wine inflame them!   Isa. 5:11

Easterners seldom drink wine or strong drink, but during feasts and weddings they may drink very heavily. The people start the day with music, drinking, and eating. On such occasions the guests rise up early and drink excessively until they are drunk [Eccles. 10:16-17; Prov. 23:29-30; Isa. 28:7-10].

RIGHTFUL OWNERS

Then shall the lambs feed after their manner, and the waste places of the fat ones shall strangers eat.   Isa. 5:17

The Aramaic word *amorey* means "dwellers, inhabitants, sojourners." In this instance it should read "the inhabitants"; that is, the remnant of the Jews who were to return from captivity. The fields and the grazing lands were to be the property of their original owners.

"Strangers" is a wrong translation. After the restoration, righteousness would reign in the land and the Jews would be the rightful owners of the lands and the fields they had lost during captivity. Now their sheep and lambs were to graze freely as of old.

MIXING DRINKS

Woe unto them that are mighty to drink wine, and men of strength to mingle strong drink:
Which justify the wicked for reward, and take away the righteousness of the righteous from him!   Isa. 5:22-23

Mixing of drinks is just as old as the Bible itself. The people in the olden days mixed light wines with strong drinks in order to get drunk quickly. Drunkenness was prevalent in the olden days just as it is today. Noah was the first man to make wine and get drunk [Gen. 9:21].

When the people were at ease and prosperous they ate and drank. The government officials who were idle, living on extortion, bribes, and on the poor, spent most of their time eating and drinking. They mixed strong drinks with wine just as people do today. Even the priests and the prophets had become the victims of strong drink, so that they could not administer justice and interpret the law and visions. ". . . the priests and the prophets have erred with strong drink, they are overcome with wine, they stagger with strong drink, they err in judgment with drunkenness, they eat immoderately" [Isa. 28:7, Eastern text].

SPEEDY CONQUEST

None shall be weary nor stumble among them; none shall slumber nor sleep; neither shall the girdle of their loins be loosed, nor the latchet of their shoes be broken.   Isa. 5:27

The prophet is here portraying the speed of the Assyrian army, which was to invade the land. The troops would march without stopping to sleep and rest. "Neither shall the girdle of their loins be loosed" means that they will never halt in their march.

Easterners loosen their girdles when they sleep or stop for rest. The breaking of the latchet of the shoes causes delay. But the Assyrian army was to have neither hindrances nor delays on their march against Israel, Judah, and the other nations west of the River Euphrates.

This prophecy was fulfilled when Sennacherib, King of Assyria, came up against Israel and Judah. The Assyrian march *was* speedy. All small and great nations west of the Euphrates were invaded. Some were subjugated, others reduced to tributaries [Isa. 36:1-22; 2 Kings 18:13-19].

KING UZZIAH

In the year that king Uzziah died I saw also the Lord sitting
upon a throne, high and lifted up, and his train filled the temple.

Isa. 6:1

"I saw also the Lord" means that the Lord appeared to the prophet
in a vision. "High and lifted up" is symbolic of his glory and majesty.
"Throne" is symbolic of power and judgment [1 Kings 22:19]. God's
appearances always took place in a vision [Ezek. 10:1-2]. No one ever
has seen God, with the exception of Jesus Christ.

In 2 Kings 15:6-7 Uzziah is called by mistake Azariah. There is no
such king in the genealogy of the kings of Judah. The Eastern text is
consistent in both books. The king's name is Uzziah.

UNCLEAN LIPS

Then said I, Woe is me! for I am undone; because I am a man
of unclean lips, and I dwell in the midst of a people of unclean
lips: for mine eyes have seen the King, the Lord of hosts.
Then one of the seraphim flew to me, having a live coal in his
hand, which he had taken with the tongs from off the altar . . .

Isa. 6:5-6

Tamma sipwatha (unclean lips) is an Eastern term meaning "sinful."
This is because words of blasphemy, curses, and lies are uttered by the
lips. On the other hand, such phrases are commonly used as a token of
humility, and, therefore, should not be taken literally. Easterners never
say they are holy or good, but they always say that they are miserable
sinners and unworthy servants.

The prophet, while standing in the divine presence and the majesty
of God in his vision, felt his human weaknesses and smallness. "A live
coal" is symbolic of purification, for in the East all metals are purified
by fire.

STUBBORN

And he said, Go, and tell this people, Hear ye indeed, but under-
stand not; and see ye indeed, but perceive not.
Make the heart of this people fat, and make their ears heavy, and
shut their eyes; lest they see with their eyes, and hear with their
ears, and understand with their heart, and convert, and be healed.

Isa. 6:9-10

The Eastern text of verse 10 reads: "For the heart of this people is
darkened and their ears are heavy and their eyes closed, so that they

may not see with their eyes and hear with their ears and understand with their heart and be converted and be forgiven." This verse in Aramaic is reflexive or passive; that is, their eyes, ears, and hearts have been closed by love of the material world.

God is telling the prophet that the heart of the people is darkened or hardened, and their ears have become dull. They can hear, but they cannot understand; they can see, but they cannot perceive [John 12:42, Eastern text]. God did not close their eyes nor stop their ears. They had brought this upon themselves through their disobedience and transgression against God's law and his ways of life. God is always ready to receive those who are ready to repent sincerely and return to him.

THE IMPENDING DISASTER

But yet in it shall be a tenth, and it shall return, and shall be eaten: as a teil tree, and as an oak, whose substance is in them, when they cast their leaves: so the holy seed shall be the substance thereof.   Isa. 6:13

The Eastern text reads: "And they that remain in it shall be a tenth, and again they shall be burned and shall be made like the terebinth or like an oak which is fallen from its stump. The holy seed is the source thereof."

The prophet predicts the destruction that would befall the land during the Assyrian invasion and the first captivity. One tenth of the people would be spared, but even these would be consumed by fire. Both Israel and Judah would fall like an oak which is fallen from its stump. But a shoot in the stump would be spared.

When the ten tribes were carried away captive to Assyria in 722 B.C., only Judah and a small portion of Benjamin were left. And even these were carried away captive by Nebuchadnezzar, the king of Babylon, in 586 B.C. The prophet saw the fall of both Israel and Judah. But he also was sure of a small remnant remaining, for Israel was the holy seed.

PALACE'S FIELD

Then said the Lord unto Isaiah, Go forth now to meet Ahaz, thou, and Shear-jashub thy son, at the end of the conduit of the upper pool, in the highway of the fuller's field.   Isa. 7:3

The latter part of this verse in the Eastern text reads: ". . . which is in the highway of the palace's field." The Aramaic word *kasra* means "palace, citadel, fortress."

In the East palaces are surrounded by large grounds planted with flowers and trees.

Evidently the King James translators failed to know the meaning of the word *kasra*, Arabic *el-kaser* (the palace). Some of them thought it was the name of dyestuff.

King Ahaz was walking near the palace grounds, and the prophet was commanded and directed by God to go and meet King Ahaz.

TROUBLEMAKERS

And say unto him, Take heed, and be quiet; fear not, neither be faint-hearted for the two tails of these smoking firebrands, for the fierce anger of Rezin with Syria, and of the son of Remaliah.

Isa. 7:4

"Smoking firebrands" is an Eastern idiom that means troublemakers. The ends of the firebrands are charred in fire. A firebrand is used to move the wood around in the oven or hearth. A troublemaker is called a firebrand because he stirs up troubles between the people.

Israel and Syria had made an alliance to fight Judah and to oppress and lay tributes on the weak nations around about them.

Isaiah was to tell the king not to fear the kings of Israel and Syria, because they were nothing but weak, half-burned firebrands.

VIRGIN

Therefore the Lord himself shall give you a sign; Behold, a virgin shall conceive, and bear a son, and shall call his name Immanuel.

Isa. 7:14

The term "virgin" in Aramaic means "purity and chastity." An unmarried girl is addressed as *petolta* (virgin). A young, unmarried maid may be called *alemta* (virgin), in Hebrew *alma*. But the term *petolta* is given to a girl who has taken a vow not to marry or have relations with a man.

The term "virgin" may not be important in the West, but in the East it is very important, because when a man marries, his parents pay a dowry to the father of the damsel. The dowry is stipulated according to the social standing and nobility of the virgin. In some cases beauty also enters in, but the virginity of a girl is the most important part of the contract in a marriage.

The dowry of a virgin is twice that of a widow. On the other hand, unmarried girls, whether they be young or old, if they are not virgins, no one would take them in marriage. They are looked upon as unclean. And if they should be given in marriage, they are given without a dowry. Thus, in the East it is important for a bride to be a virgin from the standpoint of the marriage and the name of her family. This is because when a girl loses her virginity her father cannot give her in marriage, and at times such girls are killed [Deut. 22:23-25]. In the Bible days they were stoned because they had brought shame upon the family of their fathers.

Therefore, in the East maidens must keep their purity and must be betrothed in faithfulness; that is, they must be chaste and pure when given in marriage.

It is important for a man to keep his virgin daughter pure and chaste in order that he may give her in marriage. No father wants his daughter to remain in his house unmarried except when she has taken a vow. Philip the evangelist had four virgin daughters [Acts 21:9; see also 1 Cor. 7:36-38].

Moreover, in the East kings, princes, and high priests marry virgin girls only, and the virginity of the girls has to be ascertained. In the book of Leviticus we are told that the Jewish high priest can marry only virgin women [Lev. 21:13; Esther 2:3-4].

It often happens that young girls are given in marriage to older men because of inheritance laws. In such cases the marriage may not be consumated. When it is consumated the token of virginity is displayed before witnesses to prove that the girl is a virgin. In some places the token is hung on the front of the tent. "If any man take a wife, and go in unto her, and then hate her . . . and say, I took this woman, and when I lay with her, I found her not a virgin; then shall the father of the damsel, and her mother, take and bring forth the tokens of the damsel's virginity to the elders of the city at the gate" [Deut. 22:13-15]. Many of these women remain virgins for a long time even though they are married. The prophet Joel calls such husbands "the husbands of her youth" [Joel 1:8].

The virgin mentioned in Isaiah 7:14 is a pure damsel who had never known a man. She is a young and pure girl; that is, a virgin girl. On the other hand, a girl can be young and yet not a virgin, and any young woman can give birth to a child, but such a birth would not be looked upon as a sign or wonder. But the birth of which Isaiah speaks is a special birth, a miraculous birth, in that God intervenes in it. A virgin would conceive and give birth to Messiah. This is why the prophet Isaiah calls it a sign.

One must know the political and social conditions in Israel and Judah. During the time of Isaiah, Israel was defiled. The temple of God was polluted and the women were raped by foreign soldiers. Corruption, immoral Baal worship, and drunkenness prevailed. And the moral conditions in Israel were very low.

But the prophet is hopeful of a brighter future [Isa. 9:6]. He predicts a period of restoration, peace, and prosperity, when Israel would be redeemed and cleansed of her sins. And at that time a virgin will give birth to a great Deliverer, the Messiah in whom God will reveal his power and his purposes. This great Leader must be born of a pure and spiritual mother. The spiritual ruler would be conceived by the power of the Holy Spirit.

Emmanuel is an Aramaic name which means "God is with us." *Emman-ho* (with us) and *El* (God). God was to spare Judah from the hand of the king of Assyria [Isa. 9:6; Matt. 1:23; Luke 1:35].

HONEY AND BUTTER

Butter and honey shall he eat, that he may know to refuse the evil, and choose the good. Isa. 7:15

"Honey and butter" are symbolic of harmony, meekness, peace, and prosperity. The butter mentioned here is made from sheep and goat's milk. In the East cow's milk is seldom used for drinking or for butter. Only the poor and the strangers depend on it for milk and butter and other milk products. The rich and those who are well-to-do drink sheep and goat's milk, and use butter made from the sheep milk.

Sheep are the most gentle of all animals, and they are weak. They never resist their enemies, nor do they protest when they are led to the slaughter. Isaiah likened Messiah to a sheep—"He was led as a lamb to the slaughter" [Isa. 53:7].

The bee, which produces honey, is an insect that minds its own business. He gathers nectar from flowers, which are the most beautiful things in God's creation. Colors are symbolic of peace, harmony, wisdom, and prosperity. In them the beauty of nature and God's handiwork are generously manifested. King Solomon says, "My son, eat thou honey, because it is good; and the honeycomb, which is sweet to thy taste" [Prov. 24:13; Song of Sol. 5:1].

Then again, neither the sheep nor the bees steal or interfere with other animals or insects. Thus, butter and honey symbolize a period of peace and prosperity. This is because wherever there is milk and honey there is peace, and milk, butter, and honey are abundant; everyone is happy. On the other hand, during wars and revolutions, sheep are slaughtered by the government, and the invading armies drown the bees, eat the honey, and burn the hives.

The reign of Messiah was to inaugurate the period of peace, prosperity, and happiness. Under his rule the people were to become harmless. Instruments of war were to be broken and forged into farm implements.

Easterners believe that when they drink milk, eat butter and honey and other sheep products, and abstain from meat and strong drinks, they become pure and wise and less subject to physical passions. This is why Jesus, the Hebrew prophets, Paul, and other men of God fasted when they tried to commune with God. On the other hand, many pastoral people in the East seldom eat meat. They hate to see their sheep or lambs slaughtered, for they love them. They prefer to eat butter and honey [Isa. 7:22].

All sheep-raising people are noted for their hospitality and sincerity, and their fear of God. They are closer to nature and to God than the rich who live by commerce or agriculture in the cities and towns.

Most of the prophets and men of God were called from among the people who were engaged in raising sheep, keeping bees, and doing other outdoor work. Messiah was another great leader to come from among simple and pastoral people. He was to eat milk and honey, that he might know to refuse evil and choose the good. Palestine was known as the land of milk and honey.

FLIES AND BEES

And it shall come to pass in that day, that the Lord shall hiss for the fly that is in the uttermost part of the rivers of Egypt, and for the bee that is in the land of Assyria.

And they shall come, and shall rest all of them in the desolate valleys, and in the holes of the rocks, and upon all thorns, and upon all bushes.   Isa. 7:18-19

"Flies" and "bees" in this instance are used allegorically, meaning "large armies." The reference is to the Egyptian and Assyrian armies which were to invade Palestine just as swarms of locusts and flies sometimes invade the land and devour the grass and crops. Invading armies and raiders are also sometimes depicted as hornets [Deut. 7:20; Josh. 24:12].

In the East, when describing a great army, we often say they are "like ants," or "like flies," or "like the sand of the sea." These invading armies were so large that some of the soldiers would dwell in caves. All the nations and peoples in Palestine were to be humiliated.

This invasion took place in 722 B.C., when Assyria invaded all the lands west of the River Euphrates, and another occurred in the sixth century B.C., when the Chaldeans and the Egyptians fought for political ascendancy in Palestine and Syria.

MAHER-SHALAL-HASH-BAZ

Moreover the Lord said unto me, Take thee a great roll, and
write in it with a man's pen concerning Maher-shalal-hash-baz.
                                                            Isa. 8:1

The Eastern text reads: ". . . To hasten the captivity, and to record
the spoil." "Take a large scroll and write on it plainly" is symbolic of
the importance of the message. "With a man's pen" is an Eastern idiom
which means with large letters. At times, the term "man" signifies
strength. There were no women scribes in those days.

The writing was to be plain and large, so that it could be easily read
and understood. King's decrees and edicts were written plainly and with
large letters so that they might be easily read and understood. This was
an important announcement and a great event. This is why the prophet
speaks in parables.

The reference here is to the first captivity which took place during
the reign of Tiglath-Pileser, king of Assyria, when Israel was carried
away captive. The prophet was so sure of the impending disaster that
he prophetically saw the Assyrian army despoiling the cities, and their
scribes recording the booty to be divided among the soldiers.

The prophet had his vision recorded and witnessed by Uriah, the
priest, and Zechariah, the son of Berechiah [Isa. 8:2]. The prophecy
was recorded before the Assyrian invasion took place. Otherwise no
one would believe that the prophet had seen the impending disaster.
Moses warned against prophecies which are proclaimed when the events
have already taken place.

The name Maher-shalal-hash-baz is the transliteration of the Aramaic
words *Mesarhib-shabey-otakib-bas,* which means "to hasten to take captives; speed to take away the spoil." This was the name which the
prophet gave to his son which the prophetess had born to him in his
dramatic parable relative to the Assyrian invasion [Isa. 8:3].

ISAIAH'S MARRIAGE

And I went unto the prophetess; and she conceived, and bare a
son. Then said the Lord to me, Call his name Maher-shalal-hash-
baz.   Isa. 8:3

Hebrew prophets used parables, metaphors, and similes in order to
make their messages plain to simple people who could neither read nor
write, and who could not understand abstruse terms of speech.

"I went in to the prophetess; and she conceived" is a parable describing the reality of a prophecy relative to a sudden invasion. (The prophet had relations with the prophetess in a vision.) The Lord spoke to Isaiah in a vision, and visions are often revealed in a symbolic language. The name of the conqueror is called "To hasten the captivity, and to record the spoil." Both Damascus and Samaria were to be conquered and plundered by the king of Assyria.

The prophet predicted the sudden invasion and the destruction of both kingdoms, the kingdom of Israel and the kingdom of Syria.

The prophet Hosea used a similar parable [Hos. 1:1-5].

THE MIGHTY CONQUEST

Now therefore, behold, the Lord bringeth up upon them the waters of the river, strong and many, even the king of Assyria, and all his glory: and he shall come up over all his channels, and go over all his banks.

Isa. 8:7

"The waters of the river" in this instance are used figuratively, meaning "a mighty and sweeping invasion" which was to come like a torrential rain, leaving destruction in its path.

The Assyrians were known as the people of the rivers—*Beth-nahrin* (the house of the rivers); that is, the land between the Euphrates and Tigris rivers.

The Assyrian army was to cross the Euphrates and all its channels, and encamp on the banks of its tributaries. The tributaries also mean the other tributary races who would join the mighty army of the king of Assyria. This invasion took place about 722 B.C. The Assyrian armies swept over all Palestine and Syria and at last occupied Egypt, plundering and carrying away captives.

PAGAN ALLIANCES

Associate yourselves, O ye people, and ye shall be broken in pieces; and give ear, all ye of far countries: gird yourselves, and ye shall be broken in pieces; gird yourselves, and ye shall be broken in pieces.

Isa. 8:9

The Aramaic word *zoo* means "tremble, quake, be afraid." The Eastern text reads: "Tremble, O you people, and you shall be broken in pieces."

The prophet warns the people not to trust in foreign alliances or to lean on the arm of flesh. Counsels, prophecies, and alliances were in vain. The impending calamity was on its way. Nothing but sincere repentance could change its course. Judah had made alliances with Egypt, trusting in horses and chariots, which the Assyrian general sarcastically called "the staff of this bruised reed, . . . Egypt" [2 Kings 18:21].

The houses of Israel, Judah, Ephraim, and Syria were to suffer. The kingdoms, instead of trusting in the Lord, had gone whoring after pagan gods and were too stubborn to repent and turn back to the God of Israel [verses 13, 19].

MEN WITH FAMILIAR SPIRITS

And when they shall say unto you, Seek unto them that have familiar spirits, and unto wizards that peep and that mutter: should not a people seek unto their God? for the living to the dead?

Isa. 8:19

The prophet here warns against those who inquire of soothsayers and the wizards who shriek and mutter when they deliver an oracle.

The Eastern text reads: ". . . these men are not God's people, who inquire of the dead concerning the living."

The prophet warns the people against soothsayers, magicians, and men and women who had familiar spirits and who advised the people to depart from their God and join pagan cults which practiced immorality and magic.

Magicians, soothsayers, and those with familiar spirits were condemned to death by the Mosaic law [Lev. 19:31; 20:27]. King Saul and Samuel tried to destroy them completely [1 Sam. 28:9].

Pagan wizards, false prophets, and magicians were a stumbling block in the way of Israel and Judah.

REJOICE, O LAND OF GALILEE

Nevertheless the dimness shall not be such as was in her vexation, when at the first he lightly afflicted the land of Zebulun, and the land of Naphtali, and afterward did more grievously afflict her by the way of the sea, beyond Jordan, in Galilee of the nations.

Isa. 9:1

The Aramaic word *sarhebat* is derived from *rehab* (to hasten, speed, accelerate, quicken); that is, "rejoice."

In vernacular speech, *rehab* means "to be surprised" or "to become exhilarated with a sudden joy."

The land of Zebulun, the land of Naphtali, and Galilee of the Gentiles were surprised with the sudden joy. The people who dwelt in darkness had seen a great light; that is, the light of God, the truth. The Messiah (Christ) Jesus was to be reared in Galilee, and his gospel of truth was first to be preached on the shores of the Lake of Galilee.

These lands were conquered by Tiglath-Pileser, the king of Assyria, in 733 B.C. "The way by the sea, the country beyond the river Jordan" means the road to Syria and the great city of Damascus.

The prophet prophesied that these lands and their Gentile inhabitants would be the first who would see the great light. Jesus preached both in Galilee and Syria.

These Gentiles were brought by the Assyrian kings and settled in northern Galilee [2 Kings 17:24]. They worshiped the Lord God of Israel, but they also venerated their own pagan gods [2 Kings 17:29-34].

When Ezra was building the second temple the descendants of these people offered to help the Jews, but Ezra and the Jewish fathers refused to accept their help because of their mixed race [Ezra 4:1-4]. Jesus also was rejected on the grounds that he was from Galilee. "Search and see that no prophet will rise up from Galilee" [John 7:52, Eastern text].

JOY IS INCREASED

Thou hast multiplied the nation, and not increased the joy: they joy before thee according to the joy in harvest, and as men rejoice when they divide the spoil.   Isa. 9:3

The Eastern text reads: ". . . and thou hast increased its joy." The last part of the verse confirms the first part: "They joy before thee as those who rejoice in the harvest, and as men rejoice when they divide the spoil."

In biblical lands where droughts, famine, and food shortages are common, the people rejoice in the harvest. Their wheat supplies are usually exhausted before the harvest, and they are hungry. Even today Easterners rejoice and celebrate during the harvest season. The harvest was a time of joy to the Israelites. They celebrated and made a feast, offering the firstfruits of their produce to the Lord [Exod. 22:29; Lev. 2:12; Num. 18:12-13].

On the other hand, in the early spring many families are short of food and they are hungry. The sower weeps when he scatters the precious seed on the ground. "He who goes forth and weeps, bearing precious seed, shall doubtless come again with rejoicing, bringing his sheaves with him" [Ps. 126:6, Eastern text].

ASSYRIAN EXPANSION

For thou hast broken the yoke of his burden, and the staff of his shoulder, the rod of his oppressor, as in the day of Midian.

Isa. 9:4

The reference here is to Assyria. The Assyrian kings were on the march. Both Damascus and Samaria were to be captured and plundered by the Assyrian Army [Isa. 8:4-9]. Even the land of Judea was to be invaded and caused to suffer.

But at the end, the yoke and the staff of Assyria were to be broken, just as the yoke of the Midianites was broken in the olden days [Judg. 7:24-25].

Assyria was looked upon as God's agent to execute judgment and to punish the wicked nations, but when this assignment had been fulfilled, Assyrian rule was to come to an end [Isa. 10:5-7].

THE PRINCE OF PEACE

For unto us a child is born, unto us a son is given: and the government shall be upon his shoulder: and his name shall be called Wonderful, Counselor, The mighty God, The everlasting Father, The Prince of Peace.

Isa. 9:6

Isaiah here predicts the coming of the Messiah, the Saviour of Israel and of the world. The Lord had already broken the yoke of the oppressor of Israel, the king of Assyria. Both Israel and Judah were oppressed, and Israel was carried away captive to Assyria, and Judah had become a tributary. But Judah survived the great calamity.

The remnant of Israel was to be spared. God was interested in this remnant which kept his torch burning [Isa. 10:22].

The term "son" in Semitic languages is often used metaphorically to mean joy, love, victory, or a change from bad to good. The birth of a male child is looked upon as a good omen.

Messiah Christ was to become the Light of the world. The Gentile nations who dwelt in darkness would see the Light (truth). He was to be the Wonderful Counselor, the Mighty God, the Prince of Peace. The term "king" in Semitic languages means "a counselor." Only a mighty counselor could establish a universal and enduring kingdom to embrace all races and people. He would give the world the true wisdom, a true and just government, the lasting peace which the world cannot give, and, at last, a universal kingdom. In his days not only Israel and Judah would be saved, but also the Gentiles [Jer. 23:6]. Daniel calls him the "Ancient of days"; that is, the One expected since the olden days [Dan. 7:13].

"For unto you is born this day in the city of David a Saviour" [Luke 2:11]. Jesus said, "All power is given unto me in heaven and in earth" [Matt. 28:18].

UNRIGHTEOUS DECREES

Woe unto them that decree unrighteous decrees, and that write grievousness which they have prescribed;
To turn aside the needy from judgment, and to take away the right from the poor of my people, that widows may be their prey, and that they may rob the fatherless!   Isa. 10:1-2

"Unrighteous decrees" means arbitrary decrees; that is, unjust laws and statutes which were enacted to defraud the weak, the orphans, and widows.

At times the Mosaic laws and ordinances were interpreted in such a manner as to suit the princes and those who were in power. In biblical days, just as today, laws and ordinances were subject to various interpretations and conclusions. But in biblical times reading and writing were limited to scribes, priests, and a few learned men. The unlearned could not challenge the unrighteous decrees.

ASSYRIA GOD'S AGENT

O Assyrian, the rod of mine anger, and the staff in their hand is mine indignation.
I will send him against a hypocritical nation, and against the people of my wrath will I give him a charge, to take the spoil, and to take the prey, and to tread them down like the mire of the streets.   Isa. 10:5-6

According to the prophet Isaiah, Assyria was God's agent, given power to execute judgment upon the wicked nations.

Prior to the eighth century B.C., God had very little to do with pagan nations like Assyria. But when Israel and Judah came in contact with such a great empire, were unable to fight against it, and were forced to pay tribute to pagan rulers, the Hebrew prophets realized that Assyria must have received her commission and power from their God, who was the only God who ruled over the world. Therefore they concluded that Assyria must be his agent in order to execute judgment because Israel and Judah had departed from his way [verses 10-11].

THE SMALL REMNANT

And shall consume the glory of his forest, and of his fruitful field, both soul and body: and they shall be as when a standard-bearer fainteth.
And the rest of the trees of his forest shall be few, that a child may write them.   Isa. 10:18-19

"Forest" in this instance is a metaphor meaning "people." Strong nations are often likened to a forest. "Trees" are symbolic of men and women.

"As when a standardbearer fainteth" is a mistranslation. This should read: "And they shall be as if they never had been." "The rest of the trees" means "the rest of the people." They would be so few that a child could number them. In many Eastern lands trees in the orchards are numbered and recorded to facilitate the leasing of an orchard to the husbandman.

During a census all the names of males of a certain age are written by the government scribes. After the fall of Jerusalem and the captivity of Judea very few peasants were left in the land to dress the vineyards and to cultivate the land [Isa. 10:34].

A MIGHTY CONQUEROR

And it shall come to pass in that day, that his burden shall be taken away from off thy shoulder, and his yoke from off thy neck, and the yoke shall be destroyed because of the anointing.
                                                         Isa. 10:27

The Eastern text reads *moshkha*, which, metaphorically, means "bull"; that is, "a strong king, or a mighty conqueror."

Moshkha has been confused with the Aramaic word *mishkha* (oil). The two words are very close to each other.

The prophet here predicts the rise of a mighty ruler who will break up the yoke of the oppressor, just as a bull breaks a yoke when it is harnessed to it.

The reference here is to the Anointed One; that is, the Christ who would overthrow the rule of the oppressor, conquer the world, establish a universal kingdom, and usher in the reign of peace and justice [verse 33].

ANSWER ME O ANATHOTH

Lift up thy voice, O daughter of Gallim: cause it to be heard unto Laish, O poor Anathoth.   Isa. 10:30

Anai (answer me) has been confused in the King James Version with *ana* (the poor, the one who is afflicted, a hermit). It should read, ". . . give ear, O Laish; answer me, O Anathoth."

The Lord will have compassion on the remnant of Israel. The oppressor was soon to be overthrown.

A SHOOT—AN HEIR

And there shall come forth a rod out of the stem of Jesse, and a Branch shall grow out of his roots:

And the Spirit of the Lord shall rest upon him, the spirit of wisdom and understanding, the spirit of counsel and might, the spirit of knowledge and of the fear of the Lord.   Isa. 11:1-2

"Rod" or "shoot" in this instance means "an heir"; that is, a spiritual heir to rule over the true and messianic kingdom, the religion of Israel. David is often referred to as symbolizing power, strength of character, and true obedience to God. For it was David who united Israel and extended her territory to the great River Euphrates. King David was obedient to God. He blundered many times, but he always repented.

The reference here is to the coming of the Messiah and the establishment of God's reign of justice and his universal kingdom. Messiah was to become the spiritual heir of the kingdom, and not a political ruler as the Jews expected. The seed of David also means the teaching or the faith of David.

This prophecy was fulfilled through Jesus Christ. For wisdom, justice, and righteousness were fully expressed through his teaching. The true religion of the prophets was quickly revived. The whole chapter speaks of a new world, a new order which, in due time, will be ushered into the world by the Messiah.

ROD OF HIS MOUTH

But with righteousness shall he judge the poor, and reprove with equity for the meek of the earth: and he shall smite the earth with the rod of his mouth, and with the breath of his lips shall he slay the wicked.   Isa. 11:4

"The rod of his mouth" is a Semitic idiom which means "with his words." The rod is generally used to lead the sheep and the lambs, and is therefore symbolic of discipline and correction. It is often said, "His words are as sharp as a sword."

The Messiah was to smite the earth with his words; that is, he would condemn all evil practices, injustices, greed, and oppression. "The breath of his lips" is symbolic of a wind which, at times, kills people in their sleep. (There *is* a kind of poisonous wind which often kills people.)

The whole verse reveals that the Messiah would condemn the world for its evil acts, and that he will destroy the evil by means of his meekness and his teaching, and not by force.

GIRDLE OF HIS LOINS

And righteousness shall be the girdle of his loins, and faithfulness the girdle of his reins.   Isa. 11:5

"Girdle" symbolizes strength, readiness, and alertness. During times of fear men wear their girdles day and night.

Girdles are worn to hold the looser garments together. Then again, men with girdles walk faster and are ready to defend themselves when in danger. Servants put their girdles on when waiting on their masters.

Girdles are made of woven materials in diverse colors. Some are made of leather. A container inside the girdle is used as a purse for money and other valuable articles.

The prophets used girdles of leather [2 Kings 1:8; Matt. 3:4].

Then again, girdles are worn by travelers so that they might be able to carry bread and other provisions between their garments. Swords and daggers are also fastened between the girdle and the upper garment [2 Sam. 20:8].

The reference here is to the Messiah, who was to be girdled not with leather and linen girdles but with righteousness and faithfulness. His strength was to be spiritual strength. His armor was to be meekness and the spirit of the Lord, and the spirit of wisdom and understanding.

WOLF AND LEOPARD

The wolf also shall dwell with the lamb, and the leopard shall lie down with the kid; and the calf and the young lion and the fatling together; and a little child shall lead them.   Isa. 11:6

"The wolf and the leopard" are symbolic of wicked oppressors. "The lamb and the kid" symbolize the pious and innocent people. "The calf and the young lion and the fatling" are symbolic of a reign of righteousness and equality under which oppression and injustices would cease, and justice and harmony would reign; that is, the Assyrians and the Egyptians, who are portrayed as wild animals, would be tamed and would live with the Israelites and other weak nations without harming them.

Eastern writers and preachers always use symbols and figures of speech in order to convey what they want to say. These things were to take place during the messianic era, when the kingdoms of the earth would be transformed into the kingdom of God. This change was not to be sudden, but rather a slow process of transformation. The kingdom of God cannot come by observation, but it is like a seed. It grows slowly, but steadily.

The term "child" in this instance is used metaphorically, meaning "a simple counselor" or "unlearned adviser." In Aramaic and other Near Eastern languages, it is often said, "It is so easy that a little child can do it," or, "He is like a child," which means that he is weak.

"The wolf, the leopard, and the young lion" are great powers such as Assyria, Egypt, Elam, and Ethiopia. "The lamb, the kid, and the calf" are small powers, such as Judah, Israel, and Edom which were often devoured by the great powers.

Messiah would establish the reign of justice, peace, and brotherly love, which ultimately would end the reign of tyranny and injustices, and hasten the kingdom of God. The world then would have no use for human wisdom and wise counselors who see only one side of the truth, and the diplomats who usually have two yardsticks of justice. An unlearned man, simple and honest like a child, will give counsel both to the great and the small nations. Every nation will be satisfied with what it has. Then wars will cease and the reign of God will begin [verses 7, 11].

THE END OF OPPRESSION

And the cow and the bear shall feed; their young ones shall lie down together: and the lion shall eat straw like the ox. Isa. 11:7

"The lion shall eat straw like the ox" is an idiom which means that the powerful nations who invaded and devoured small nations would be satisfied with what they have. The lion symbolizes a great power. Many great nations have used it as their emblem and as a symbol of strength.

The ox, on the other hand, is a weaker animal when compared with the lion. It does not prey on other animals, and is satisfied with grass.

The lion will always eat meat, for it has no teeth to chew the grass. But the lion here is a devouring nation which lives on spoil taken from small nations. The devouring nations will be satisfied with that which the Lord has provided for them.

The time will come when the great nations will use their strength and knowledge for the good of all mankind. Then prosperity will be so abundant that there will no longer be any need for plundering the weak and defenseless nations [verse 6].

ASP AND COCKATRICE

And the sucking child shall play on the hole of the asp, and the weaned child shall put his hand on the cockatrice' den.   Isa. 11:8

These sayings should not be taken literally. They are used allegorically. "Asp" and "cockatrice" in this instance are symbolic of deadly enemies. In the new era these men would become so meek and harmless that even simple men could mix with them and deal with them. The terms "suckling child" and "weaned child" mean innocent men and women, suggesting that they can handle the wise and wicked men who hitherto had been like asps and cockatrices.

In the East, especially among the tribal people who live in tents, little children often handle snakes and are not bitten. The snake knows that little babies are innocent and therefore does not harm them. In many Eastern languages the term "snake" is used in speaking of an enemy.

Jesus told his disciples that they could handle serpents and drink poison but would not be harmed, which means that they would overcome their enemies and withstand false charges without being destroyed. These sayings often are taken literally by American and European Christians, and at times innocent and credulous men and women are bitten by poisonous snakes.

In the fullness of time the earth will be filled with understanding and knowledge of God, and evil will be destroyed forever.

ROOT OF JESSE

And in that day there shall be a root of Jesse, which shall stand for an ensign of the people; to it shall the Gentiles seek: and his rest shall be glorious.   Isa. 11:10

"A root" in this instance means a branch growing from the stem of the Jewish religion which would be as an ensign of the people, and the Gentiles would rally to it.

This prophecy was fulfilled in Jesus Christ, who restored the true religion of Israel, and to whom the Gentiles came for knowledge of God and salvation. The term "root of Jesse" is of the Spirit and not of the flesh, for even David called the Messiah, "My Lord." "The Lord said to my Lord, Sit at my right hand, until I put your enemies under your feet"

[Matt. 22:44; Mark 12:36; Luke 20:42-43, Eastern text; see also John 7:40].

Jesus began his ministry in Galilee, the land of the Gentiles [Isa. 9:1-2].

THE POWERFUL REMNANT

But they shall fly upon the shoulders of the Philistines toward the west; they shall spoil them of the east together: they shall lay their hand upon Edom and Moab; and the children of Ammon shall obey them.　　　　　　　　　　　　　　　　　　　　　　　　　*Isa. 11:14*

This should read: "But they shall fly upon the shoulder of the Philistines on the sea . . . "; that is, the remnant of Israel and Judah which was to be restored would dominate the Philistian coast and use Philistian labor for rowing their ships.

In the olden days ships were rowed by the arms of sailors, especially the galleys. Slaves and subjugated peoples were often assigned to this hard task.

The Philistines, as well as the Edomites, Moabites, and Ammonites, were to be subjugated by the remnant of the Israelites, who would enslave them and lay heavy tributes upon them.

A HIGHWAY FOR REMNANT

And there shall be a highway for the remnant of his people, which shall be left, from Assyria; like as it was to Israel in the day that he came up out of the land of Egypt.　　　　　　　　　　　　　　　*Isa. 11:16*

"An highway" in this instance refers to an understanding between the government and the remnant of the Jews who were in Babylon—liberation of the people from bondage. The highway is also symbolic of freedom and escape. Then again, during the periods of peace, there was considerable traffic between Assyria and Egypt.

The remnant which was in Babylon would be granted permission by the Persian kings to return to their own land. And the highway would be open to them and guarded by the imperial forces. Persia would aid them and lead them just as God had guided them and aided their forefathers when they left Egypt. God would grant them favor in the eyes of the Persian kings.

This prophecy was fulfilled during the reign of Cyrus, who issued an edict giving the Jews permission to return to their own land. About the year 445 B.C. Nehemiah started to build the wall of Jerusalem. Some of the captives had returned previously, but the work of restoration was hampered for some time by the Gentiles.

God did for the remnant which was in Assyria just as he had done for the Hebrews who were in Egypt centuries before [Exod. 14:29]. All the future hopes for a universal kingdom lay in the remnant.

WATER OF SALVATION

Therefore with joy shall ye draw water out of the wells of salvation.
Isa. 12:3

The term "water" is used metaphorically, meaning "truth and spiritual understanding." The Jews were thirsty, not for material water but for living water; that is, the truth which sets men free from error and directs them to the true paths of life and eternal salvation. Truth is pure as running water. God's teaching and his true worship were likened to a fountain of living waters. And pagan teaching was portrayed as dry wells, broken cisterns that can hold no water [Jer. 2:13].

Jesus said, ". . . If any man is thirsty, let him come to me and drink" [John 7:37]. He also said to the Samaritan woman that, had she asked of him, he would have given her living water; that is, the truth. But the woman misunderstood him [John 4:10-11; Ezek. 47:1-8].

THE FALL OF BABYLON

The burden of Babylon, which Isaiah the son of Amoz did see.
Isa. 13:1

The Aramaic word for "burden" is *mobla* (something carried on the backs). *Mashkla* means the "fall" or "capture"; that is, "the prophecy of an oracle concerning the fall of Babylon." In the East we still say, "The city is *shekelta*"; this means that the city has fallen or has been conquered. *Shakal* also means "to lift up." The Hebrew word is *messa* (a heavy weight).

These words were originally written by a later scribe as a caption to facilitate the reading of the scroll. The term "burden" does not clearly convey the meaning. The prophet foresaw the fall of Babylon long before the city actually fell to the Persian Army in 538 B.C.

These captions were originally written in the margin, but later were copied into the text. In the olden days, when paper was unknown and parchment scarce, notes were written on the margins of the scrolls. This ancient custom still prevails in the Near East.

Isaiah foresaw the rise and fall of Babylon and Assyria. During his lifetime Assyria had already shown a great many signs of weakness. There were dynastic difficulties and revolts in the far-flung empire. On the other hand, Babylon was extending its influence beyond the River Euphrates and making contacts with Syria, Judah, and other small kingdoms west of the great river.

Isaiah saw the fall of Babylon, just as he had foreseen the fall of Assyria. The prophet, like Daniel, had a long-range vision and a deep understanding of the rise and fall of great imperial powers.

The prophecy is written by Isaiah himself, or dictated to a professional scribe. There are not two or three Isaiahs, as some Bible authorities claim. There is only one Isaiah, who lived during the reigns of Uzziah, Jotham, Ahaz, and Hezekiah, kings of Judah. Isaiah grew from a nationalistic political statesman into a spiritual prophet. He clearly saw the coming of the Messiah and the establishment of a universal kingdom which would embrace the whole of mankind. But before this kingdom was to start, several Gentile imperial powers were to rise and fall. Babylon was one of the greatest empires in the olden days.

THE FALL OF KING OF BABYLON

How art thou fallen from heaven, O Lucifer, son of the morning! how art thou cut down to the ground, which didst weaken the nations!
Isa. 14:12

The Aramaic word *ailel* (to howl, cry out) has been confused with the Hebrew word *helel* (brightness). The term "Lucifer" means morning star, but it does not appear in the Eastern text.

The Eastern text reads *ailel* (howl, mourn). The reference here is to the king of Babylon whose impending fall is foretold by the prophet. The king of Babylon, like the kings of Assyria and Egypt whose doom was predicted by the prophets, is told to howl and mourn over his fall.

The king of Babylon had lifted himself to heaven but would come down into Sheol. This passage has nothing to do with the falling of an angel, a star, or Lucifer. It refers to the fall of Babylon and its tyrant ruler who had lifted up himself and compelled the nations to worship him as a god. The whole chapter is about the fall of the king of Babylon [verse 4].

All the kings who had oppressed the Israelites unjustly were overthrown.

THE BRANCH—THE HEIR

But thou art cast out of thy grave like an abominable branch, and as the raiment of those that are slain, thrust through with a sword, that go down to the stones of the pit; as a carcass trodden under feet.
Isa. 14:19

The Aramaic word *norba* (shoot) in this instance is used metaphorically, meaning "an heir." In Aramaic an heir is often called "shoot."

This is because an heir is like a tender shoot which grows out of the root of a dying tree.

Eastern poets and composers of lamentation, in their mourning songs, call the heir the beautiful shoot or branch.

The "abominable branch" is a weak or bad shoot which grows at the root of the tree. This shoot is cut off and the root of the tree dug out and sold for fuel. The owner of the tree sees that the shoot is weak and not worthy of the ground which it occupies.

Nebuchadnezzar was the scion of the Babylonian empire, but it had become like a rotten tree which is ready to be cut down, with shoots so weak that they live for only a short time. The great king of Babylon saw a vision concerning his downfall. In his night vision he saw a high and strong tree cut down [Dan. 4:10-15].

BABYLON SHORN OF POWER

Prepare slaughter for his children for the iniquity of their fathers; that they do not rise, nor possess the land, nor fill the face of the world with cities. Isa. 14:21

The Aramaic word *kraba* (war) has been confused with the Aramaic word *korya* (cities). The Eastern text reads: ". . . nor fill the face of the world with war."

Babylon is denounced because of war, slaughter, and suffering which she had brought upon the earth through her military campaigns. Babylon had destroyed many cities like Jerusalem.

COCKATRICE

Rejoice not thou, whole Palestina, because the rod of him that smote thee is broken: for out of the serpent's root shall come forth a cockatrice, and his fruit shall be a fiery flying serpent. Isa. 14:29

"The serpent's root" means the Assyrian empire. Assyria was to be destroyed, but out of Assyria were to come other oppressor nations, namely, Babylon and Egypt, which were to cause still more destruction and plunder in Palestine, Syria, Edom, and other adjacent lands [Isa. 27:1; Ezek. 29:2-5].

Babylon is called a "flying serpent," that is, speedy in punishing the nations. In the East when a man walks fast it is said "he flies"—"He flew like lightning," or, "He flew like a bird." Nebuchadnezzar was to be swift in punishing the nations. And Egypt was to challenge the might of the king of Babylon. And consequently Palestine was to become a battleground between Nebuchadnezzar and Pharaoh, the king of Egypt.

Thus, the prophet warns the inhabitants of Palestine not to rejoice over the fall of Assyria because other oppressors were on the scene.

SMOKE—ANGER

Howl, O gate; cry, O city; thou, whole Palestina, art dissolved: for there shall come from the north a smoke, and none shall be alone in his appointed times   Isa. 14:31

"Smoke" in this instance is symbolic of anger, burning, disaster, and destruction. Just as smoke spreads and darkens the air, so the land was to be covered by the invading armies from the north. The anger of the Assyrian kings was to kindle in all the cities [Rev. 9:2].

"The smoke" is Assyria. The Assyrian armies were to invade the whole of Palestine. The land would be dimmed and the joy gone. The Assyrian invasion began in the year that King Ahaz died. Ahaz had made an alliance with the king of Assyria [2 Kings 16:7-9]. But after the death of Ahaz, seemingly, the alliance was broken and Judah was invaded.

WEEPING BITTERLY

Therefore I will bewail with the weeping of Jazer the vine of Sibmah: I will water thee with my tears, O Heshbon, and Elealeh: for the shouting for thy summer fruits and for thy harvest is fallen.
                                                    Isa. 16:9

"I will water thee with my tears, O Heshbon, and Elealeh" means, "I will weep bitterly for you." Easterners when speaking of vehement weeping say, "Rivers of waters flowed from my eyes," or, "I watered my bed with my tears," or, "I washed my bed with my tears" [Ps. 6:6].

BELLY—BOWELS

Wherefore my bowels shall sound like a harp for Moab, and mine inward parts for Kir-haresh.   Isa. 16:11

Karse (my belly) in this case means "my heart." "Inward parts," or "kidneys" mean tender mercies. Easterners often say, "My heart burned for them; my kidneys kindled with fire." All these sayings are used allegorically, signifying sorrows and bitter weeping. The kingdom of Moab was to be invaded by the king of Babylon and punished for its sins.

DAMASCUS, AN ANCIENT CITY

The burden of Damascus. Behold, Damascus is taken away from being a city, and it shall be a ruinous heap.   Isa. 17:1

Darmsook (Damascus) is known as the oldest inhabited city in the world. Damascus was an old city when Abraham passed through it on his way to Palestine. The city might be one of the earliest of all human settlements.

Damascus was conquered by King David [2 Sam. 8:5-6]. Later the Assyrian kings took it and carried its inhabitants captive [2 Kings 16:9]. But the ancient city was not destroyed. Damascus escaped many disasters and flourished both under the reign of the Israelite kings as well as under the Assyrian kings. The city might have been damaged to some extent, but apparently remained intact. Evidently the city was indispensable to the conquerors. For Damascus is a heaven in the heart of a desert land. Its abundant waters, its fruits and lush fields were needed by all those who conquered it.

Jeremiah also predicted the destruction of Damascus. "Damascus is weakened, and she turns to flee; trembling has seized her; anguish and pangs have taken her like a woman in travail. How is the glorious city ruined, the city of joy!" [Jer. 49:24-25, Eastern text].

Other prophetic denunciations of this ancient city which oppressed Israel are to be found in Amos 1:3, 5 and in Zechariah 9:1.

The city might have been razed and rebuilt, but Damascus has always been a city of culture and beauty in the Arabian desert.

See the commentary on Jeremiah 49:25.

A SMALL REMNANT

Yet gleaning grapes shall be left in it, as the shaking of an olive tree, two or three berries in the top of the uppermost bough, four or five in the outmost fruitful branches thereof, saith the Lord God of Israel.   Isa. 17:6

"Gleaning" is used metaphorically and means the "remnant." Olives in Palestine are smaller than those in Greece, Italy, and Spain, and when they are gathered a great many of them are left on the branches.

The prophet reminds the people of future events when Israel and Judah will be carried away captive and a small remnant will be left. The prophet likens the remnant to ears of wheat that are overlooked by the reapers, and to the olives that remain after the tree is shaken. Some of the berries are left on the top of the outermost branches.

This impending disaster was due to fall upon the people because they had forsaken their God and gone astray after other gods and trusted in foreign alliances.

CLEAR DAY

For so the Lord said unto me, I will take my rest, and I will consider in my dwelling place like a clear heat upon herbs, and like a cloud of dew in the heat of harvest.　　　　Isa. 18:4

The Aramaic word *nahra* means "river." The Aramaic word *yoma* (day) has been confused with *khoma* (heat)—"the midday heat upon the river."

The harvest season is a hot season with intense heat, and many reapers seek shelter under trees, in caves, and in the shade of sheaves. At times the heat is broken by the shadow of a cloud.

THE MEDES

And the Egyptians will I give over into the hand of a cruel lord; and a fierce king shall rule over them, saith the Lord, the Lord of hosts.　　　　Isa. 19:4

This should read: "And I will deliver the Egyptians into the hands of the cruel Medes; and a fierce king shall rule over them, says the Lord of hosts."

The Aramaic word *Madaya* (a Mede) is very close to the Aramaic word *maraye* (lords). The only difference is a dot over or under the letter *daloth* or *resh*.

Egypt was conquered by Cambyses, the king of Persia.

NILE DRIED UP BY ENEMY

And the waters shall fail from the sea, and the river shall be wasted and dried up.　　　　Isa. 19:5

Whenever a conqueror threatened to conquer and destroy Egypt, he tried to change the course of the River Nile, for Egypt without the Nile would be desolate. Egypt is rich because the Nile not only irrigates millions of acres of good earth, but also because it continues to enrich the land with the rich soil which it brings from the south.

Egypt was to be invaded and the Nile's course reversed by the Assyrian or Babylonian armies. This threat was feared when Italy conquered Ethiopia in 1936.

When the river's course was changed, cotton, flax, and papyrus dried up and the fish died. Egypt was conquered by both the Assyrian and the Chaldean kings.

DRUNKENNESS

And they shall be broken in the purposes thereof, all that make sluices and ponds for fish.   Isa. 19.10

The Aramaic word *shakhra* (strong drink) has been mistaken with the Hebrew word *seker* (dams, sluices) in the King James Version.

The Hebrew text reads *sheker* (to make drunk, to intoxicate). The Masoretic text reads *sheker* (strong drink). The error is due to the mistranslation of the Hebrew word *sheker* (strong drink) [Lev. 10:9; 1 Sam. 1:15].

The Hebrew word *seker* (dams, sluices) is spelled with the letter *semkath*, but *sheker* is spelled with the letters *sheen* or *seen*.

Isaiah here condemns drinking. He accuses the priests and the prophets of drunkenness.

"But these also have erred with wine, and with strong drink are gone astray; the priests and the prophets have erred with strong drink, they are overcome with wine, they stagger with strong drink, they err in judgment with drunkenness, they eat immoderately. For all tables are full of vomit and filthiness, so that there is no place clean" [Isa. 28:7-8, Eastern text].

Drunkenness, to a large degree, has been responsible for the fall of many great nations. The drunkard kings and leaders, being overcome with wine and strong drink, failed to do justice; therefore, they were rejected by God. Both Israel and Judah were in such a state. They were carried away with wine, strong drink, and immoral pagan practices, and their time to be destroyed had come.

HEAD AND TAIL

Neither shall there be any work for Egypt, which the head or tail, branch or rush, may do.   Isa. 19:15

The Aramaic word *nebed* (will do) is the imperfect of *ebad* (to do) and is confused in the King James Version with *ebad* (a work). The Eastern text reads: "Neither shall there be any leader for the Egyptians who can make head or tail of it, or tail or head."

The prophet hints that the time would come when there would be no man of understanding who would be capable of helping Egypt or to solve her problem. The Aramaic idiom *resha odonba* (head and tail) means "the most important and the least important things." This saying is still used where Aramaic is spoken.

THE LANGUAGE OF CANAAN

In that day shall five cities in the land of Egypt speak the language of Canaan, and swear to the Lord of hosts; one shall be called, The city of destruction.   Isa. 19:18

Canaanite languages were spoken in the eastern borders of Egypt. The Egyptians always welcomed migratory tribes who, because of famine, came and settled in eastern Egypt. They were used as a buffer against invading armies from the East.

Egypt was the breadbasket for the famine-stricken Canaanites and Semitic tribes, who from time to time sought refuge in the land of the Pharaohs, especially during long periods of drought in Palestine and Arabia, when food became scarce and famine was severe. Abraham, Isaac, and Jacob went to Egypt because of famine.

These migrating Semitic tribes kept their own languages, religions, and cultures, and because of their religions and peculiar customs they had no intercourse with the Egyptians and other African people. On the other hand, the Egyptians never forced their religion and language on the minorities who took refuge in their land. This is because the Egyptian religion was a secret religion. The less the people knew about it, especially the wise foreigners, the better it was for the priest.

The Hebrews spent nearly four hundred years in Egypt, but when they left they still spoke the language of their forefathers; that is, Aramaic, the language which Jacob and his children spoke when they migrated to Egypt. This is clearly seen from the names of localities in the desert and the terms of speech used by the Hebrews during their wanderings in the desert. Moreover, Joseph gave his two sons Aramaic names, *Manasseh* and *Ephraim*. The first means "to forget," and the second "to increase." These words are still used in Aramaic today. Joseph was born in Mesopotamia. His mother was an Assyrian and his father, Jacob, had spent twenty-one years in Assyria.

The language of Canaan was a mixed dialect made up of Phoenician and the northern and eastern dialects of Aramaic, such as Assyrian, Babylonian, the desert dialects, and Syrian. The Canaanites were the early settlers of Palestine. They were the early emigrants from the Euphrates Valley, who crossed the River Euphrates seeking grass for their large flocks. The Canaanites were the descendants of Canaan, the second son of Noah [Gen. 9:18].

The Hebrew dialect of Aramaic contributed much to the language of the Canaanites. The early Hebrews who came from Haran spoke the northern dialect of Aramaic, the Assyrian Aramaic. The Aramean or Syrian dialect also exerted tremendous influence on the languages of the smaller races. Damascus was the center of culture and learning. Then again, the Israelites conquered the land and subjugated its people.

Isaiah was living in a period when Assyrian power was spreading northward, eastward and southward. Many kingdoms in Palestine and Syria were already paying heavy tributes to Assyria. Egypt was to be defeated and conquered by the Semitic-speaking nations, and the speech of Canaan (Western Aramaic) was to become the language of five cities in Egypt. Moreover, the "language of Canaan" in this verse refers to the language of the Hebrews who were dwelling at this time in Canaan. Be that as it may, all the languages in Palestine were closely related. The people of one race could converse with those of another without any difficulty.

Israel and Judah were to enter into an alliance with Egypt to fight against Assyria, but Egypt was to be defeated and its people oppressed. Many of the inhabitants of Palestine were to flee to Egypt. Jeremiah went with a remnant which left for Egypt. And the prophet warned them, stating that the king of Babylon would conquer Egypt, also [2 Kings 25:26; Jer. 42:15-18]. Both the Assyrians and Babylonians ruled over Egypt at different times [Isa. 19:23, Eastern text].

AN ALTAR IN EGYPT

In that day shall there be an altar to the Lord in the midst of the land of Egypt, and a pillar at the border thereof to the Lord.

And it shall be for a sign and for a witness unto the Lord of hosts in the land of Egypt: for they shall cry unto the Lord because of the oppressors, and he shall send them a saviour, and a great one, and he shall deliver them. Isa. 19:19-20

The Aramaic word for "altar" is *madbkha*, derived from the Aramaic word *dabakh*, which means "to offer a sacrifice." *Madbkha* is the place where the sacrifice is cooked or broiled.

"Altar" is symbolic of worship and devotion, and a pillar stands as a witness. In the East pillars are erected as memorials to treaties and agreements between two parties or nations [Gen. 31:51-52]. The pillar, in this case, was set as a reminder of the contract between Jacob and Laban. In those early days there were no books or libraries wherein deeds and treaties could be kept; in fact, written treaties were unknown. Most agreements were oral and were witnessed by several witnesses. A heap of stones or a pillar was erected as a memorial to the treaty. As long as the heap of stones stood intact and the pillar was there, the treaty was in force.

The "pillar" in this verse refers to a treaty or agreement between Egypt and Israel. The "altar to the Lord" signifies that the true religion of Israel would be practiced in Egypt. This was to come later when both the Israelites and the Egyptians would have a better understanding of God. Both peoples were crushed by the Assyrians and Babylonians.

Today there are many Jewish synagogues and hundreds of Christian altars in the land of Egypt. Then again, the Moslem religion, which is the state religion in Egypt, is very close to the Hebrew religion during the time of Isaiah. It is interesting to know that today there are no more altars of the ancient religion of Egypt in the land of Egypt. The God of Israel has become the God of the Egyptians and the God of the Assyrians.

UNDERSTANDING BETWEEN NATIONS

In that day shall there be a highway out of Egypt to Assyria, and the Assyrian shall come into Egypt, and the Egyptian into Assyria, and the Egyptians shall serve with the Assyrians. Isa. 19:23

Aurkha (highway) means "religion," hence, justice and understanding. "A highway between Assyria and Egypt" is symbolic of good will, good relations. The desert between Assyria and Egypt is a natural highway, but the prophet is speaking of a spiritual highway, the true religion. This prophecy concerns the fall of Egypt [verses 1-5]. The Egyptians were to be restored and their wounds healed by the Lord God of Israel.

In the East when people are not on good terms they do not visit one another, but when good will and friendliness reign between them they visit and trade with one another. The Eastern text reads: ". . . and the Egyptians shall serve the Assyrians."

The Assyrians and the Egyptians had been rivals for centuries. They had been fighting over Palestine and other lands on the borders of the two great empires. But the time was to come when the Assyrians and the Egyptians would forget their enmity and work together and trade with one another. The whole world was gradually to be blessed by God through moral law and the promises which he had made to Israel. Thus, Israel was God's agent in a world-wide plan of salvation. The prophet Isaiah here sees very clearly good relations between various races and Israel's mission.

Israel has been a blessing to both the Assyrians and the Egyptians. Both races have accepted the God of Israel, his religion and his laws. The Bible has been the light to the Gentile world [verse 24].

READY FOR WAR

Prepare the table, watch in the watchtower, eat, drink: arise, ye princes, and anoint the shield.   Isa. 21:5

In the East raids are preceded by conferences and lavish banquets. The war lords and their chieftains sit in council to map strategy while the soldiers eat and drink.

"Anoint" means to "ordain" or "select"; that is, to choose the shields. Then again, some of the shields of gold and brass were burnished with oil.

The description of the feasting is typical of an Eastern army on the day before the march, excited and confident of victory.

THE LORD IS THE WATCHMAN

And he cried, A lion: My lord, I stand continually upon the watchtower in the daytime, and I am set in my ward whole nights:
Isa. 21:8

The Eastern text reads: "Then the watchman cried into my ears, saying, I the Lord stand continually in the daytime, and I stand upon my watchtower every night."

The Aramaic word *edna* (ear) has been confused in the King James Version with *aria* (lion). The letters "r" and "d" are differentiated by a single dot over or under the letter, and the letters *yuth* and *noon* are very similar. *Yuth* is slightly shorter.

According to the Eastern text, the Lord God was continually watching, day and night. It was the Lord who was revealing the forthcoming events to the prophet.

The term "watchman" is used simply because in the East all walled cities have watchmen who stand upon the towers [2 Sam. 18:25; 2 Kings 9:17; Isa. 21:5].

THE SIEGE OF BABYLON

O my threshing, and the corn of my floor: that which I have heard of the Lord of hosts, the God of Israel, have I declared unto you.   Isa. 21:10

The Aramaic word *blai*, derived from *bla*, is a negative particle used with *min* (without, for lack of). This verse should read: "There is no one to reap and no one to thresh . . ."

Babylon was sorely besieged by the Persian armies. The people were unable to harvest their fields and gather their fruits. The threshing floors were outside of the city wall, and because of the siege no one was able to leave the city to harvest the fields and thresh the wheat. Babylon, like Samaria and Jerusalem, fell because of the famine. The gods of Babylon were defeated; they were unable to relieve their adherents of famine and suffering.

Then again, Babylon was trampled upon by the foreign soldiers and threshed like a threshing floor [Jer. 51:33].

VALLEY OF VISION

The burden of the valley of vision. What aileth thee now, that thou art wholly gone up to the housetops? Isa. 22:1

The prophecy concerns the Valley of *Khizion* (vision).

The reference here is to one of the beautiful and fertile valleys in Judea [verse 4]. The prophet mourns because of the impending calamity which was to befall the daughter of his people (Jerusalem) [verse 10].

The army of Elam was to march from Babylon to Egypt, conquering all the nations in its path, small and great. And Judah was not to be spared.

The first kings of Persia were magnanimous toward their subjects, especially toward the Jews. But the later kings started to persecute the Jews and conquer their land. The change in the policy was due to the dynastic changes.

WATER SITUATION

And ye have numbered the houses of Jerusalem, and the houses have ye broken down to fortify the wall.
Ye made also a ditch between the two walls for the water of the old pool: but ye have not looked unto the maker thereof, neither had respect unto him that fashioned it long ago. Isa. 22:10-11

The Aramaic word *meleton,* derived from *mela* (to fill) is confused with the Aramaic word *meneton,* derived from *mena* (to number). Because of the similarity of "l" and "n," the two words are almost identical and at times hard to distinguish. The Eastern text reads: "And you have supplied the houses of Jerusalem with water . . ."

Until recent years Jerusalem depended on rainwater, which was stored under the houses. Other sources of water were scanty, and they dried up during severe droughts.

During wars, houses were sometimes filled with water. The city was besieged by enemy forces so that no one could go out or come in.

The inhabitants of Jerusalem, instead of relying on the Lord their God, trusted in material things and in man-made defenses and fortifications. In the olden days they trusted in God, and he delivered them from their enemies. But now they were trusting in their own strength and in foreign alliances.

KEYS OF HEAVEN

And the key of the house of David will I lay upon his shoulder; so he shall open, and none shall shut; and he shall shut, and none shall open. Isa. 22:22

"Key" means authority, true knowledge, and trustworthiness. In Aramaic we often say, "He has the key to the situation," which means he has found a solution to a certain problem. "Key" is also used as a symbol of authority and power. "He has the key," means he can declare certain things to be lawful and others unlawful; that is, to bind or to loose, or to prohibit or to permit, or to forgive.

On the other hand, in the East when a person is well trusted, he is given the key to the house.

The prophet saw that a great change was to take place, which would cause the people to return to the true religion of Israel. King David was guided by God and, therefore, had wisdom and understanding to lead the people in the right way.

The Messiah, who was the true heir to the kingdom of David, was to be endowed with knowledge and given authority to teach the way of God. Jewish traditions and man-made doctrines were to be supplanted with the true teaching which was to embrace the whole world.

Jesus also gave his disciples authority to bind and to loose. "I will give you the keys of the kingdom of heaven; and whatever you bind on earth shall be bound in heaven, and whatever you loose on earth shall be loosed in heaven" [Matt. 16:19, Eastern text].

FALL OF TYRE AND ZIDON

Behold the land of the Chaldeans; this people was not, till the Assyrian founded it for them that dwell in the wilderness: they set up the towers thereof, they raised up the palaces thereof; and he brought it to ruin. Isa. 23:13

The Eastern text reads: "Behold the land of the Chaldeans; this is the people, and not the Assyrians, who destroyed it; they appointed spies who spied on her palaces, and they brought it to ruin."

The prophet is prophesying against *Zur* (Tyre) and Zidon [verses 1-4]. He states that these two cities were destroyed by the Chaldeans and not by the Assyrians. This is because the Assyrian kings in the eighth century B.C. had invaded Syria, Palestine, and Egypt, but they had not taken the well-fortified city of *Zur* (Tyre).

The Babylonian power and its influence over the nations west of the River Euphrates was growing very fast during the time of the prophet Isaiah. It was during the time of Isaiah that Merodach-baladan, the son of Baladan, king of Babylon, sent letters and gifts to King Hezekiah [Isa. 39:1].

In the seventh century B.C., Babylon revolted against Assyria and ruled in its stead. The Assyrians and Chaldeans were closely related, were natives of the same land, and spoke the same language—Aramaic— also called Chaldean and Assyrian. The first Babylonian kingdom was older than that of Assyria.

DEDICATED THINGS

And her merchandise and her hire shall be holiness to the Lord: it shall not be treasured nor laid up; for her merchandise shall be for them that dwell before the Lord, to eat sufficiently, and for durable clothing. Isa. 23:18

In biblical days, when accursed cities were overthrown and their inhabitants put to the sword, gold, silver, tin, and costly garments were dedicated as an offering to the Lord. No one, not even generals of the army, were allowed to take anything of the booty. This is because it belonged to the Lord for the use of his holy temple and for the maintenance of priests and the Levites, who served therein. These men did not go to war.

When Jericho fell before the armies of Joshua, all gold, silver, and precious objects, as well as clothing, were dedicated to the Lord. Achor (Achan) sinned by stealing some of the devoted things. He was put to death, together with all his family [Josh. 7:20-26].

TYRE'S FLEET GONE
AND VINES DESTROYED

The new wine mourneth, the vine languisheth, all the merry-hearted do sigh. Isa. 24:7

The Eastern text reads, "The grain mourns . . ." Tyre imported considerable wheat from other countries. When King Solomon began to build the temple, Hiram, the king of Tyre, gave him cedar trees in exchange for wheat. Solomon sent twenty thousand measures of wheat and twenty thousand measures of pure oil year by year [1 Kings 5:11].

Tyre was a great merchant city, but its people did not have sufficient food supplies. Now the fleet was gone, and grain lay stored in warehouses to be shipped, but there were neither ships nor sailors [Isa. 23:2-5].

In the East during wars and revolutions nature shares in man's calamities and suffering. Fruit trees and vines are cut down by the invading armies for fuel. It is said that when Mongolian emperors invaded Mesopotamia all the date palms were cut down and all the vineyards destroyed. The invading armies depend on trees and vines for fuel and kindling. Sometimes the trees are cut down by the enemy in order to make it hard for the people to rebuild the towns.

Wine is symbolic of joy and gladness. And because wine makes men's hearts merry [Ps. 104:15], all the vines were cut off. Now the joy of the land was gone, and everything looked dark and gloomy. Tyre, the beauty of the Zidonians, was made a heap [Isa. 23:1-6; 25:2]. The young wandered in the streets with sad faces. The mirth was gone and the sound of music was silent. The people were not so much mourning for wine as for the vineyards and the land which was devastated by the enemy's armies.

A MYSTERY

From the uttermost part of the earth have we heard songs, even glory to the righteous. But I said, My leanness, my leanness, woe unto me! the treacherous dealers have dealt treachery. Isa. 24:16

The Eastern text reads: ". . . the glory [might] of the righteous, saying, It is a mystery to me, it is a mystery to me, woe to me, the wicked have dealt treacherously, . . ."

The Aramaic word *raz* means "mystery, a secret"; that is, something that one cannot understand. The prophet is complaining of the wicked; that is, the treacherous leaders and princes who were oppressing the righteous. The glory of the righteous was crying for justice, but they could not understand why their cries were not heard, and why the evildoers were in power. The nation had gone astray after pagan gods so that now they had wicked leaders. The whole earth languished.

PITS ARE DANGEROUS

And it shall come to pass, that he who fleeth from the noise of the fear shall fall into the pit; and he that cometh up out of the midst of the pit shall be taken in the snare: for the windows from on high are open, and the foundations of the earth do shake. Isa. 24:18

Until recent days pits were very common in biblical lands. Grain supplies were stored in pits a few yards away from the houses. During the winter, when all the grain had been used for bread, the pits were left open to be used again the next fall.

Falling into the empty pits was common. During the evening and night hours it often happened that both men and animals fell into these empty pits. Jesus said that when a blind man leads another blind man, both will fall into the pit [Matt. 15:14]. "O blind guides" [Matt. 23:16, 24]. Then again, Jesus spoke of animals falling into a pit [Luke 14:5].

Moses warned against open pits: "And if a man shall open a pit [that is, empty it of wheat], or if a man shall dig a pit, and not cover it, and an ox or an ass fall therein; the owner of the pit shall make it good . . ." [Exod. 21:33-34].

Pits are symbolic of man's own evil acts. A man may dig a pit to trap another and himself fall into it [Prov. 28:10]. Then again, the evil acts of some men and women are like empty and uncovered pits, which are dangerous during the dark hours and the time of calamities, when men cannot clearly see the obstacles ahead of them, and during heavy storms and earthquakes. "The mouth of a strange woman is a deep pit; he with whom the Lord is angry shall fall into it" [Prov. 22:14, Eastern text].

THE ALIENS BLOTTED OUT

Thou shalt bring down the noise of strangers, as the heat in a dry place; even the heat with the shadow of a cloud: the branch of the terrible ones shall be brought low.   Isa. 25:5

The Eastern text reads: "Thou shalt blot out the pride of aliens as the shadow at noonday, and as the heat is blotted out by the shade of a cloud; thus the branch [the heir] of the mighty ones shall be humbled."

The Aramaic word *nokhraye* in this instance means "alien people" who had oppressed Israel and Judah. The change will be sudden, just as the shadow is blotted out at noonday and as heat is blotted out by the shadow of a cloud.

"Branch" as a metaphor means an heir. ". . . the branch of my planting . . ." [Isa. 60:21]. "And there shall come forth a shoot out of the stem of Jesse, and a branch shall grow out of his roots" [Isa. 11:1, Eastern text].

OTHER LORDS

O Lord our God, other lords besides thee have had dominion over us; but by thee only will we make mention of thy name.
They are dead, they shall not live; they are deceased, they shall not rise: therefore hast thou visited and destroyed them, and made all their memory to perish.   Isa. 26:13-14

"Other lords," in this instance, means other kings and princes. The Jewish state had paid tribute both to Egypt and Assyria, but some of the people had remained loyal to their own God, the living God of Israel.

Many of these Gentile human deities were worshiped as true gods and were called lords. But the Jews always refused to bow down to human gods and to man-made images. They saw that these human gods could not create, nor raise the dead, nor heal the sick, and that, sooner or later, they were challenged, overthrown, and succeeded by other mortal men who also posed as gods.

The remnant of the Jews was always loyal to the God of their forefathers, the Creator of the heavens and of the earth, the everlasting and eternal God.

BEING WITH CHILD

We have been with child, we have been in pain, we have as it were brought forth wind; we have not wrought any deliverance in the earth; neither have the inhabitants of the world fallen.

Isa. 26:18

"We have been with child" means, "We have hoped for good." "We have been in pain like those who brought forth wind" means, "Our hopes were in vain," or miscarried.

Israel and Judah had expected great things to be wrought through them, but thus far nothing had happened. Not only had they failed to conquer the Gentile nations, but now they were even oppressed by them, because both Israel and Judah had been unfaithful and stiff-necked. Instead of trusting in their God, they trusted in pagan kings and pagan gods, and made alliances with pagan nations. They did not adhere to the old and true pattern, to walk in the way of their God and keep his commandments and his statutes.

RESURRECTION OF THE DEAD

Thy dead men shall live, together with my dead body shall they arise. Awake and sing, ye that dwell in dust: for thy dew is as the dew of herbs, and the earth shall cast out the dead.   Isa. 26:19

Even as far back as the eighth century B.C., the Hebrews had some idea of the immortality of the soul. The Hebrew prophets believed that the soul was indestructible, and that since man was God's image and his likeness, he also was indestructible.

The Eastern text reads: ". . . for thy dew is a dew of light, and the land of the giants thou shalt overthrow." Sheol was supposed to be unconquerable and beyond God's jurisdiction. But even Sheol was to be conquered by the Messiah. The earth can retain only dust, but it must cast out the soul which cannot be held in material form.

The true resurrection was preached by Jesus Christ who defied death and Sheol [John 11:23-25]. This doctrine was also preached by the Apostles [Acts 17:18; 1 Cor. 15].

CROOKED SERPENT

In that day the Lord with his sore and great and strong sword shall punish leviathan the piercing serpent, even leviathan that crooked serpent; and he shall slay the dragon that is in the sea.
                                                            Isa. 27:1

"Leviathan, that crooked serpent" means an oppressor. Pharaoh, the king of Egypt, is likened to a great dragon (sea monster) who controlled the River Nile [Ezek. 29:3-4]. *Niniveh* also means "a fish"; that is, a large fish; hence, leviathan.

The prophet predicts the day of the restoration when Israel will be planted again in Palestine and the people protected from their enemies. The great powers which had destroyed Israel would be punished and finally destroyed [Isa. 14:25].

VINEYARD OF RED WINE

In that day sing ye unto her, A vineyard of red wine.   Isa. 27:2

The reference here is to Israel. Israel is often called a vineyard, the vine which God brought out of Egypt and planted in Palestine [Ps. 80:8]. In the Eastern languages men and women are often portrayed as vineyards and gardens. "Now will I sing to my well-beloved a song of my beloved touching his vineyard" [Isa. 5:1]. The Aramaic pronoun is masculine, *leh* (to him); that is, to Israel. *Lah* could mean a woman.

Red wine is scarce and is considered the best wine, and it is symbolic of blood and life. Israel was to be restored again and protected as the husbandman protects a good vineyard.

BRIERS AND THE THORNS

Fury is not in me: who would set the briers and thorns against me in battle? I would go through them, I would burn them together.
                                                            Isa. 27:4

The Eastern text reads: "You have no hedge; who then did set in you the briers and the thorns? I will blow at the vineyard from near and will burn it together." The Aramaic word *shora* means "hedge, fence, wall."

Weeds and briers are symbolic of pagan teachings and image worship. The fences of the vineyard (Judaism) were broken down and pagan teachings and alien customs and practices were introduced into the once pure Jewish worship.

The Lord would blow at the vineyard, Israel, and burn it, together with the weeds and thorns which had grown in it.

When weeds, briers, and thorns cover a vineyard, its owner burns it and plants new vines or some other crop.

ISRAEL GATHERED

And it shall come to pass in that day, that the great trumpet shall be blown, and they shall come which were ready to perish in the land of Assyria, and the outcasts in the land of Egypt, and shall worship the Lord in the holy mount at Jerusalem.   Isa. 27:13

The Aramaic reads: ". . . those who were lost in the land of Egypt and those who were scattered in the land of Assyria . . ." The reference here is to the Israelites who were carried away captive by the Assyrian kings in 721 B.C., and scattered in Assyria, Mesopotamia, Media, and other lands east of the River Euphrates [2 Kings 17:18-24]. When Jerusalem was destroyed by the Chaldean army, the Jews fled with Jeremiah to Egypt in the year 586 B.C. [2 Kings 25:25-27].

Isaiah foresaw the restoration of the remnant of the house of Israel and of the house of Judah. Messiah was to gather the scattered people from the house of Israel. Jesus called them "the lost sheep of the house of Israel" [Matt. 10:5-6].

DRUNKARD EPHRAIM

Woe to the crown of pride, to the drunkards of Ephraim, whose glorious beauty is a fading flower, which are on the head of the fat valleys of them that are overcome with wine!   Isa. 28:1

"Drunkard" in this instance is used metaphorically, referring to one who is carried away with his own sense of power, pride, and glory. The Israelites had become drunk with power and false religious zeal, the Baal worship. In the East when people are carried away with their false pride and power we say, "they are drunken." The Aramaic *gedala mesara* means "shameful diadem of the strength of his glory."

Ephraim was situated in one of the most fertile portions of Palestine. The land was graced with wheat fields and vineyards. Wine was abundant. Then again, the people boasted of their power and glory. They were the descendants of Ephraim, the second son of Joseph, whom Jacob had blessed, predicting that he would become a great people [Gen. 48:5-22].

Moreover, the name of Israel, the prince of God, was bestowed upon Ephraim and his descendants. Therefore, Ephraim was the crown of the pride of Israel, but had defiled himself by worshiping pagan gods. Now he was wearing upon his head a shameful diadem. Ephraim had been unfaithful. He made alliances with pagan nations, and had utterly forsaken the Lord God of Israel and his everlasting covenant.

DRUNKENNESS CONDEMNED

But they also have erred through wine, and through strong drink are out of the way; the priest and the prophet have erred through strong drink, they are swallowed up of wine, they are out of the way through strong drink; they err in vision, they stumble in judgment.
                                                              Isa. 28:7

The princes, judges, and false prophets started the day early by eating and drinking. And when they sat in councils the prophets were so drunk that they could not see or interpret visions. The priests were out of their way, because of excessive drinking, behaving shamefully [1 Sam. 2:22-23]. The drunken judges also erred in judgment. They perverted justice.

Excessive eating and drinking were responsible for the downfall of Israel, and have caused many other nations to stumble and fall. At times even the priests overdrank.

After two of the sons of Aaron were burned while ministering in the tabernacle, Moses prohibited the use of wine and strong drink in the tabernacle [Lev. 10:9].

Wine in the olden days was fermented, just as it is today. In the East wine is made of grapes. No alcohol is mixed with it. Grape juice was unknown in those days, and was unknown until recent times.

There is no doubt that the wine which the Hebrews drank was intoxicating. The priests and the prophets were often drunk, and the tables were filled with vomit and filthiness as is sometimes the case during wedding feasts and banquets [verses 8-10].

"Wine is a mocker, strong drink is raging: and whosoever is deceived thereby is not wise," says the author of Proverbs [Prov. 20:1].

VOMIT

For precept must be upon precept, precept upon precept; line upon line, line upon line; here a little, and there a little. Isa. 28:10

The Eastern text reads: "For filth is upon filth, filth upon filth; vomit upon vomit, vomit upon vomit; a little here, a little there."

Banquets were held in large houses. Washrooms and toilets were unknown, and in some parts of the East are still unknown. The drunkards vomit in the house, some of them even upon the tables. In the East on such occasions the people eat too much and drink until they are drunk, for the food and wine are abundant.

Then again, not having toilets, filth is seen in front of the houses, scattered all over town, here a little and there a little. This condition is still common in places which are still backward. Nevertheless, today the Moslems do not drink wine nor strong drink. But non-Moslems still drink intoxicating wine and spirits.

THE CORNERSTONE

Therefore thus saith the Lord God, Behold, I lay in Zion for a foundation a stone, a tried stone, a precious corner stone, a sure foundation: he that believeth shall not make haste.   Isa. 28:16

The cornerstone is the foundation stone, a large, unhewn stone.

The Eastern text reads: ". . . he who believes shall not be afraid."

The psalmist called it the stone which the builders refused, because large stones were too heavy to be lifted up and were therefore used for the foundations or as cornerstones [Ps. 118:22].

Jesus also referred to the stone which the builders rejected, how it became the cornerstone [Matt. 21:42].

Messiah was the cornerstone which the priests and Pharisees would reject, but God would make him the cornerstone of his church. Truth was the cornerstone of the Jewish faith. When a building is destroyed the cornerstone may still remain, as it is too heavy to be removed. Truth cannot be destroyed. Christian truth is based on the true hopes of Judaism; that is, the messianic kingdom and the reign of justice.

See "Cornerstone" in *Gospel Light*, Matthew 21:42.

THE CLOTH IS SHORT

For the bed is shorter than that a man can stretch himself on it: and the covering narrower than that he can wrap himself in it.
    Isa. 28:20

The Eastern text reads: "For the cloth is too short, and the warp grows weak and is insufficient for a garment."

The Aramaic word *mishtitha* (a weaver's shuttle, warp, or web), in this instance "warp," has been confused in the King James Version with *shewitha* (bed, mattress).

These words are used in a poetic sense. The time for the vengeance of the Lord was near, and the days of oppression and injustice were over, like a web when it is cut off from the loom. The prophet reminds the people of a new foundation, a precious cornerstone. The time remaining before his coming was short, just like a weaver's web, when it nears the end. The Gentile nations were to be punished, and judgment and justice were to overflow like water.

THRESHING INSTRUMENT

Bread corn is bruised; because he will not ever be threshing it, nor break it with the wheel of his cart, nor bruise it with his horsemen.
                                                                    Isa. 28:28

The Aramaic word *gargara* means "threshing instrument," not "cart." This instrument is one of the oldest of man's inventions and has survived to the present day without any change or improvement.

A *gargara* is constructed like a sledge. It has two axles covered with short and sharp iron teeth, which roll over the wheat. A man or boy sits on top of the sledge to direct the oxen, which pull the threshing instrument around the circular threshing floor.

The Eastern text reads: "Grain is threshed for our sakes because man would not otherwise be threshing it, nor break it with many wheels of his threshing instruments, nor crush it under the feet of his oxen."

ARIEL

Woe to Ariel, to Ariel, the city where David dwelt! add ye year to year; let them kill sacrifices.
                                                                    Isa. 29:1

Ariel is a construct state noun meaning "the land of God"—*Ar* (land) and *El* (God). The city is Jerusalem which was besieged and destroyed by the Chaldean army [Ezek. 4:1-2].

Isaiah saw this vision about the year 712 B.C. At this time the Assyrians were on the march southward, northward, and westward. Sargon was murdered and Sennacherib, his son, first marched against Babylon, then against Egypt, and then against Judah and many other small kingdoms that had made alliances with Egypt. Judah's alliance was condemned by the prophets, who had a clear insight of the situation and the weakness of Egypt.

The Assyrian armies marched through Syria, Palestine, and other lands on their way to attack the army of Pharaoh. Many cities and towns in Israel and Judah (Ariel, the land of God) were destroyed. Jerusalem was destroyed later by the Babylonian king, the successor of the Assyrians.

ZION

And the multitude of all the nations that fight against Ariel, even
all that fight against her and her munition, and that distress her,
shall be as a dream of a night vision.   Isa. 29.7

The Eastern text reads "Zion" instead of "Ariel." The reference here is to Mount Zion, Jerusalem [verse 8].

Ariel is a later name which means "the land of God"—*ar* (land) and *El* (God). "Ariel" was used in a poetic sense. Jerusalem and Mount Zion are known as the land of God. This is because the temple, or the house of God, was built in Zion.

See the commentary on Isaiah 29:1.

HUNGER AND THIRST

It shall even be as when a hungry man dreameth, and, behold,
he eateth; but he awaketh, and his soul is empty: or as when a
thirsty man dreameth, and, behold, he drinketh; but he awaketh,
and, behold, he is faint, and his soul hath appetite: so shall the
multitude of all the nations be, that fight against mount Zion.
Stay yourselves, and wonder; cry ye out, and cry: they are
drunken, but not with wine; they stagger, but not with strong drink.
                                                    Isa. 29:8-9

In lands where poverty is dominant and water scarce, many people sleep either hungry or thirsty. In some areas water is scarcer than food.

In the East it is not unusual to dream of eating food or drinking water. One can subdue his hunger, but thirst is more difficult to overcome. When one has eaten a good meal but slept thirsty, he will see continuous visions and dream dreams of drinking water all night. Such dreams of eating and drinking cause much suffering to hungry and thirsty persons.

The prophet likens the Gentile plots against Jerusalem to the dream or vision of a hungry or thirsty person who longs to eat or drink but cannot find either food or water. And when he awakens he is still hungry or thirsty. The Gentile kings were drunken with power.

People can be drunken with power, with greed, with false aspirations. In the East when people are carried away by the material world, money, or pride, it is often said, "They are drunk, but not with wine, nor with strong drink."

Strong drink is extracted from raisins, and is more than 100 proof. It makes those who drink it stagger.

SPIRIT AND SLEEP

For the Lord hath poured out upon you the spirit of deep sleep, and hath closed your eyes: the prophets and your rulers, the seers hath he covered.   Isa. 29:10

"The spirit of deep sleep" means dullness of mind. The prophets, the seers, and the rulers of the people no longer could see true visions. Their eyes were closed by false teaching, corruption, and materialism. They had eyes, but they could not see. They prophesied, but they erred. They saw visions, but were unable to understand them.

"Spirit" here means the power which drives people this way or that way. We often say, "He is moved by a good spirit," or by an evil spirit, or by the wind. Anything erroneous is attributed to an evil spirit or some power. The term *rokha* (spirit) also means wind, pride, and rheumatism.

The people had lost their spiritual sight. They were unable to understand the books of the law and the prophets. Their eyes were closed to spiritual things.

SPIRITUAL TRUTHS

And the vision of all is become unto you as the words of a book that is sealed, which men deliver to one that is learned, saying, Read this, I pray thee: and he saith, I cannot; for it is sealed.   Isa. 29:11

"Sealed" in this instance does not mean closed and sealed with a wax seal, as was the custom when an important letter or an official document was dispatched.

"Sealed" here means that it was written in a language that could not be understood by ordinary readers, or even by learned men. Such a book or letter is generally composed in a code. The writer and those who know the code can read it, but strangers cannot. Such writings are still in existence in Aramaic. One of them is the Book of *Makamet*, which was composed by Mar Abdishoo, metropolitan of Zoba and Armenia. Only those who know the secret and the style of writing can read it.

When the book was delivered to the learned man and he was asked to read it, the book was opened, but the scribe could not understand its meaning. "I am not learned," does not mean, "I cannot read," but, "I cannot explain the contents." Take, for example, the name of Nero Caesar in Revelation 13:18. It is written in code form—666. The number is the name of Nero Caesar in Aramaic. See the comment on Revelation 13:18, *New Testament Commentary*.

The people had lost their vision, their ability to understand spiritual truths. Jesus likewise found that the Pharisees and the learned men in his days did not understand the Word of God. They could read it, but they could not interpret it. Spiritual truths were like sealed letters to them.

DOCTRINE OF MEN

Wherefore the Lord said, Forasmuch as this people draw near me with their mouth, and with their lips do honor me, but have removed their heart far from me, and their fear toward me is taught by the precept of men. Isa. 29:13

During the time of Isaiah the kings of both Israel and Judah had made alliances with pagan kings, and they trusted in the arm of man. Consequently, pagan doctrines and pagan practices were introduced into the true religion of Israel. Traditions, ordinances, and the teachings of the elders had supplanted the Word of God. The people revered God with their lips only, but in their hearts they trusted in pagan kings and in the pagan idols that they had built on the high places. God was near their mouth, but far away from their heart [Jer. 12:2].

The people had become a hypocritical people. They said one thing and did another. All their acts were contrary to the teaching of God [Ezek. 33:31].

Jesus quoted these passages when he condemned the scribes and Pharisees. "Woe to you, scribes and Pharisees, hypocrites! for you embezzle the property of widows, with the pretence that you make long prayers; because of this you shall receive a greater judgment. Woe to you, scribes and Pharisees, hypocrites! for you have shut off the kingdom of heaven against men; for you do not enter into it yourselves, and do not permit those who would to enter. Woe to you, scribes and Pharisees, hypocrites! for you traverse sea and land to make one proselyte; and when he becomes one, you make him the son of hell twice more than yourselves" [Matt. 23:13-15, Eastern text].

PERVERSE COUNSELORS

Woe unto them that seek deep to hide their counsel from the lord, and their works are in the dark, and they say, Who seeth us? and who knoweth us? Isa. 29:15

The Aramaic word *mithakmin* (to act perversely) has been confused with *mithamkin* (to dig deep) in the King James Version. The difference between the two words is the position of a single letter. But the two words are derived from two different roots. The Eastern text reads: "Woe to them who act perversely to hide their counsel from the Lord; . . ."

The prophet here denounces those who had turned aside and become perverse, and who dealt crookedly and tried to hide their evil devices from the Lord. Their evil works were committed in darkness, because they thought the Lord could not see them nor know what they were doing.

THE POTTER

Surely your turning of things upside down shall be esteemed as the potter's clay: for shall the work say of him that made it, He made me not? or shall the thing framed say of him that framed it, He had no understanding?
Isa. 29:16

The Eastern text reads: "Surely you are esteemed as the potter's clay; . . ." *Mithhapkhin* means "turning upside down" or "topsy-turvy."

The prophet admonishes the people that man is like clay in the hands of a potter, who shapes it any way he pleases; and that the work cannot question the wisdom of its maker. So man cannot question his Maker's wisdom and purposes.

Many changes were taking place during the time of the prophet Isaiah. Some great nations were falling and others were in the making to take their place. Assyria was to be replaced by another imperial power— Babylon—and far beyond, Persia was rising. Small nations were being crushed by the great empires. On the other hand, both Israel and Judah were to be destroyed and then rebuilt through the remnant. The nations were like clay in the hands of God. The prophet saw that all these changes were for the ultimate good. And at the end, God's own kingdom was to embrace all lands.

INSINCERE OFFERINGS

Woe to the rebellious children, saith the Lord, that take counsel, but not of me; and that cover with a covering, but not of my Spirit, that they may add sin to sin.
Isa. 30:1

The Eastern text reads: "Woe to the rebellious children, says the Lord, who take counsel, but not of me; and who offer wine offerings, but not of my spirit, that they may add sin to sin"; that is, they worship pagan gods and offer offerings to the idols.

After the destruction of Jerusalem, the Jews, despite the counsel of Jeremiah, fled to Egypt and there they denounced Jeremiah, departed from God's way, and worshiped the queen of heaven [Jer. 44:15-19; 43:1-4].

Moreover, during the lifetime of the prophet, Judah sent presents or offerings to pagan kings, seeking their help. And the sacrifices which they offered to God were not from their hearts. It was the ancient customs and traditions that made them offer these offerings.

SHADOW OF PHARAOH

That walk to go down into Egypt, and have not asked at my mouth; to strengthen themselves in the strength of Pharaoh, and to trust in the shadow of Egypt!
Therefore shall the strength of Pharaoh be your shame, and the trust in the shadow of Egypt your confusion.   Isa. 30:2-3

"Shadow" means protection. In lands where the climate is hot, people take refuge under the shadow of rocks and trees. One often hears people say, "We live under the comforting shadow of our ruler."

Judah had made an alliance with Egypt against Assyria. Egypt itself was weak, and was not to be trusted. The prophet, being a great statesman, was against the alliance with Egypt, because Egypt was weak and therefore, could not offer protection to the people who had made league with her against the king of Assyria. Egypt was like a bruised reed. "Now, behold, you have trusted upon the staff of the broken reed, even on Egypt, on which if a man leans, it will go into his hand and pierce it; so is Pharaoh king of Egypt to all who trust in him" [2 Kings 18:21, Eastern text].

Even as far back as the time of Isaiah, many Jews were leaving for Egypt, fearing the Assyrian invasion. The Assyrian power was continuing to spread all over the lands west of the River Euphrates. The news of the fall of other nations had frightened many Jews and made them seek refuge in Egypt.

To take refuge in Egypt was contrary to God's command [Deut. 17:16]. The Israelites were no more to return to Egypt to dwell. But both Israel and Judah trusted more in Egypt than in the Lord their God.

On the other hand, the king of Assyria had a mission to fulfill. (He was the rod of God.) "O Assyrian, the rod of mine anger, and the staff in their hand is mine indignation" [Isa. 10:5].

EDUCATION OF THE PROPHETS

Now go, write it before them in a table, and note it in a book, that it may be for the time to come for ever and ever.   Isa. 30:8

Isaiah, like some of the other Hebrew prophets, was well educated and could read and write. Writing was common among the higher classes and priests. Moses and Joshua wrote, and the people were exhorted to write the words of the law on the doorposts, walls, and other places, so that they might commit it to memory [Exod. 34:27-28]. Moses wrote this law. We read about writing in Deuteronomy 17:18; 31:9; and 31:19-23.

When Habakkuk saw his vision, God told him to write it [Hab. 2:2].

Nevertheless, some of the prophets were illiterate. They prophesied, but their visions were written by scribes. For instance, the book of Jeremiah was written by Baruch, a professional scribe. Even today, many learned priests and bishops in the Near East cannot write. They dictate to scribes.

The prophet was admonished to write his prophecy concerning Judah's alliance with Egypt and her trust in Pharaoh on tablets, so that it could be read, and in the Book of the Covenant for a testimony in the future. The prophet was so sure and firm in his policy that he was not afraid to record it in a book.

WEAK STATESMEN

And though the Lord give you the bread of adversity, and the water of affliction, yet shall not thy teachers be removed into a corner any more, but thine eyes shall see thy teachers.   Isa. 30:20

The Aramaic word *matianekhon* means "those who have caused you to go astray," "those who have deceived you." The root of the word is *taa* (to deceive, mislead, cause to err). The Aramaic word for teacher is *malpana*. And the Eastern text Peshitta reads: ". . . yet he will not gather any more those who have caused you to err, and your eyes shall see the misfortune of those who have caused you to err."

The reference here is to the princes, false prophets, and leaders of the people who had been responsible for the alliance with Egypt and the calamity which had fallen upon the people. All these wicked leaders were doomed to remain and die in exile [verses 1-4].

The remnant was to be restored and Jerusalem rebuilt and inhabited [verse 19]. But the rebellious leaders and prophets were to perish [verses 1-3].

LIGHT OF THE SUN

Moreover the light of the moon shall be as the light of the sun, and the light of the sun shall be sevenfold, as the light of seven days, in the day that the Lord bindeth up the breach of his people, and healeth the stroke of their wound.   Isa. 30:26

"Sun" is symbolic of deity, and it was worshiped by many nations in the East. Even today there is a sect in India, called fire worshipers, who still worship the sun because they believe all life comes from and depends upon the sun, and that the sun is the center of the universe.

"The light of the moon shall be as the light of the sun" symbolizes the eradication of evil and ignorance. The moon depends for its light upon the sun which, in turn, reflects it upon the earth. The time would come when the light of the moon would be as bright as the sun, which means that people will no longer stumble in darkness; night and day will be alike because of the light of God.

Seven is a sacred number; recall the seven planets (sun, moon, and the five nearest planets), the seven days of the week, the seven wells of Abraham, and the seven candlesticks.

The Lord would once more heal the wounds of Israel and restore them from their captivity. All this points to the messianic fulfillment when justice and peace will reign and all nations of the earth will see the light of God, which will be sevenfold greater than the light of the sun.

ROCKY HABITATION

And he shall pass over to his stronghold for fear, and his princes shall be afraid of the ensign, saith the Lord, whose fire is in Zion, and his furnace in Jerusalem.   Isa. 31:9

The reference here is to the king of Assyria who, after the fall of Nineveh, would flee to his rugged mountains (Kurdistan).

Nahum says: "Your friends slumber, O king of Assyria; your allies have deserted; your people are scattered on the mountains, and they have none to gather them" [Nahum 3:18, Eastern text; Isa. 31:8].

A small remnant of the Assyrian people have remained in northern Iraq until the present day. The Assyrians have preserved their ancient customs and Aramaic language until the present day.

TEMPEST

And a man shall be as a hiding place from the wind, and a covert from the tempest; as rivers of water in a dry place, as the shadow of a great rock in a weary land.   Isa. 32:2

Storms, whirlwinds, and tempests are very violent in the deserts. This is because the desert is waste and treeless, and the wind develops great momentum. There is nothing in its way to hamper its fury. Many of the desert storms are violent and destructive. Isaiah describes the fury of the Lord as a destroying storm [Isa. 28:2; Ezek. 13:11].

During storms and tempests the people take refuge under rocks, in caves, and in any other places that offer protection. And in summer months, when the heat is intense, desert travelers and the weary and sick also take refuge under the shade of the rocks. This is why the Lord is often portrayed as a rock and a place of refuge [Isa. 4:6; 25:4].

ANOTHER GOLDEN RULE

Woe to thee that spoilest, and thou wast not spoiled; and dealest treacherously, and they dealt not treacherously with thee! when thou shalt cease to spoil, thou shalt be spoiled; and when thou shalt make an end to deal treacherously, they shall deal treacherously with thee.

Isa. 33:1

"Cease" is a wrong translation. The Eastern text reads: ". . . when you seek to plunder, they will plunder you; and when you seek to deal treacherously, they shall deal treacherously with you."

The Hebrew prophets fought for justice and righteousness, and warned against plundering, dealing treacherously, extortion, short measures, and deceitful balances.

This verse is another Golden Rule. It also confirms the law of compensation: When a man sows evil, he reaps evil; and when he sows good, he reaps good. Those who take the sword perish by the sword, and those who plunder are plundered.

GOD IS LIGHT

But there the glorious Lord will be unto us a place of broad rivers and streams; wherein shall go no galley with oars, neither shall gallant ship pass thereby.

Isa. 33:21

The Eastern text reads: "For there the name of the Lord is glorious to us; he will be for us a place of light, an enlightenment, and an open space made by the hand; wherein the authority of a prince shall not reign, neither shall the mighty one be able to invade it."

The Aramaic word *nahira* (a light) has been confused in the King James Version with *nahra* (a river). And *nahirotha* (enlightenment) has been mistaken for *nahrawatha* (rivers, streams).

God is often spoken of as the Light of the world [Exod. 10:23]. ". . . Lord, lift thou up the light of thy countenance upon us" [Ps. 4:6], which means the spiritual enlightenment through which we see the image of the spiritual man. Jesus spoke of himself as the Light of the World [John 8:12; Luke 2:32].

When we walk in the light we never stumble. "Bible" means the law, the light. Throughout its pages one finds guideposts that lead men to God.

ISRAEL RESTORED

Thy tacklings are loosed; they could not well strengthen their mast; they could not spread the sail: then is the prey of a great spoil divided; the lame take the prey.
And the inhabitant shall not say, I am sick: the people that dwell therein shall be forgiven their iniquity.   Isa. 33:23-24

The prophet uses a ship with its "tacklings" (riggings, mast, and sail) in portraying the great fortunes which awaited the remnant. The ship is so heavily laden with spoil that the tacklings are loosed, because they could not well strengthen their mast. The ship might be a fishing boat. The plunder is so great that the ship is almost unable to bear it [John 21:6].

When spoil is taken in abundance, even the lame gets his share. In the East plunder is divided among the raiders; but when there is too much, some of it is given to the lame and to the blind who cannot participate in the raids.

In that day Israel will call upon the name of the Lord and declare his wonders among the Gentiles. The Lord will again make Jerusalem his holy habitation. In that day the Lord's anger will be turned away from Jerusalem, and Israel will be forgiven and comforted [Isa. 12:1-6].

THE SWORD OF THE LORD

For my sword shall be bathed in heaven: behold, it shall come down upon Idumea, and upon the people of my curse, to judgment.
The sword of the Lord is filled with blood, it is made fat with fatness, and with the blood of lambs and goats, with the fat of the kidneys of rams: for the Lord hath a sacrifice in Bozrah, and a great slaughter in the land of Idumea.   Isa. 34:5-6

The Bible often speaks of the sword of the Lord. The Lord has no sword. "Sword" in this instance is used to indicate God's power. In the olden days a sword was the most feared implement of war, and when a town was occupied by the enemy, its inhabitants were put to the edge of the sword. "The sword of the Lord" is the punishment which the people bring upon themselves [Deut. 32:41; Judg. 7:18].

"My sword shall be bathed in heaven" means, "My sword shall be sharpened and burnished in heaven." The Aramaic reads, *titerwey* (will get drunk), which means "well-sharpened." "Sword" is symbolic of destruction and slaughter. When the people prepare for war they clean their swords, oil them, sharpen them, and burnish them. Moreover, during wars and conquests, the victorious armies slaughter thousands of sheep, fatlings, and lambs for food. The slaughter is done by the sword. The meat and the fat are cut with the edge of the sword and cooked for the armed forces.

The prophet here portrays a complete destruction of the enemies of Judah—the people, the herds, and the flocks.

EDOM BURNED

And the streams thereof shall be turned into pitch, and the dust thereof into brimstone, and the land thereof shall become burning pitch.
                                                              Isa. 34:9

All the regions south of the Dead Sea contain pitch and brimstone. Moreover, wherever there is pitch there is some oil. In some parts of the Near East oil is so close to the ground that it is collected and used for fuel. Pitch, likewise, drips from rocks during the hot summer months.

The fire is caused by the earthquakes and by careless persons, especially shepherds, who make a fire wherever they go. And at times a fire may be caused by heat, combustion, or sudden eruption, like the eruption which took place in Sodom and Amorah (Gomorrah) during the time of Abraham [Gen. 19:24-25].

Edom was doomed because she had done unjustly and had sided with the oppressors of Israel. And yet, Edom (that is, Esau) was the brother of Jacob.

TRIUMPH OF GOD'S TRUTH

And the parched ground shall become a pool, and the thirsty land springs of water: in the habitation of dragons, where each lay, shall be grass with reeds and rushes.
                                                              Isa. 35:7

"Parched ground" means paganism which in due time would see the light of the God of Israel. Paganism was to go, and the true religion of Israel was to become the religion of the world. The Hebrew prophets always used metaphors in order to convey their message to the illiterate and simple people who did not understand abstract terms of speech.

The world around Palestine was like parched and desolate ground. God's truth was to irrigate the world and cause abundant fruits to be brought forth. The Word of God, like a seed, would fall into good ground, which in due time would yield a hundredfold.

Desolate places in the deserts are to be graced with knowledge which will spring up like a fountain. And those who have been thirsty for justice will drink thereof. Knowledge and the reverence for God shall spring up abundantly, like reeds and rushes by the rivers.

TRUE UNDERSTANDING

And a highway shall be there, and a way, and it shall be called The way of holiness; the unclean shall not pass over it; but it shall be for those: the wayfaring men, though fools, shall not err therein.

Isa. 35:8

"Highway" is used figuratively, meaning "understanding" or "the way"; that is, a true and holy religion wherein there will be no crookedness, deception, or injustice, and from which the wicked will be excluded.

Moreover, the light of God will lighten the dark and crooked paths so that no man will stumble and no thieves can hide by the way. Knowledge and wisdom will increase, and human needs will be met, so that there will be lasting peace between the nations, and no need for war [Isa. 11:1-10].

STAFF OF BROKEN REED

Lo, thou trustest in the staff of this broken reed, on Egypt; whereon if a man lean, it will go into his hand, and pierce it: so is Pharaoh king of Egypt to all that trust in him.   Isa. 36:6

"Staff of this broken reed" is an idiom which means weakness and unreliability. When a man leans against a staff of reed, it breaks and may even pierce the hand of the person who leans upon it.

The reference here is to Egypt. Judah had made an alliance with Egypt against the king of Assyria.* The prophet likens Egypt to a staff of broken reed because Egypt was weak.

The general of the Assyrian army upbraided King Hezekiah for trusting in Egypt. He called Egypt a bruised reed. "Now, behold, thou trustest upon the staff of this bruised reed, even upon Egypt, on which if a man lean, it will go into his hand, and pierce it: . . ." [2 Kings 18:21].

Ezekiel speaks of a staff of reed as a symbol of weakness. "And all the inhabitants of Egypt shall know that I am the Lord, because they have been a staff of reed to the house of Israel" [Ezek. 29:6; Matt. 12:20].

* And later Judah made a treaty against Babylon.

Israel, instead of trusting in God, had put her trust in Pharaoh, the king of Egypt, and the weak Egyptian army, which was defeated before the army of Assyria and later by Nebuchadnezzar, the king of Babylon, at Charchemish by the River Euphrates.

ARAMAIC LANGUAGE

Then said Eliakim and Shebna and Joah unto Rabshakeh, Speak, I pray thee, unto thy servants in the Syrian language; for we understand it: and speak not to us in the Jews' language, in the ears of the people that are on the wall.   Isa. 36:11

The Eastern text states that the general of the Assyrian army was asked to speak Aramaic, which was the common language of the Near East at that time. This was the language of Aram-nahrin and also of Padan-Aram which, in the course of time, became the official tongue of the Assyrian, Babylonian, and Persian empires. And it was also spoken by the Hebrews.

Syriac is derived from *Zur,* and is the dialect of Aramaic spoken in Syria, which in biblical days was called Aram, with Damascus as its capital. Syriac is the Greek term for Aramaic; that is, the language of the people of *Zur,* Tyre. Syriac is a misnomer. [See *Pen-Smith Aramaic Dictionary.*]

All the learned Hebrew princes, statesmen, and prophets understood Aramaic, which was the language of their forefathers [Gen. 15:7; Deut. 26:5].

Today most learned Americans understand Elizabethan English, but the common people do not. The fact that Rabshakeh, the commander of the Assyrian army, spoke the language of the Hebrews proves that the two languages at that time were closely related, just as American English is closely related to the English spoken in England, the mother country.

Rabshakeh spoke in the vernacular speech, or the common tongue, simply because he wanted the armed forces and the workers to understand him. Today, all cultured Arabs read and write in the literary Arabic, but the peasants speak their own dialects of Arabic [2 Kings 18:26].

SUN WENT BACK

Behold, I will bring again the shadow of the degrees, which is gone down in the sun dial of Ahaz, ten degrees backward. So the sun returned ten degrees, by which degrees it was gone down.

Isa. 38:8

In biblical days the Hebrews and other pastoral peoples believed that the sun traveled around the earth, and the earth was stationary and the center of the universe. This concept was held until the Western astronomers with their telescopes discovered that it is the earth that revolves around the sun, and that the sun is the center of the solar system.

But the Chaldean and Egyptian astonomers knew that the earth was only one of the small planets, and that the sun was the center of our planetary system. This is why they were able to develop a calendar of 364 days. They were well versed in all the movements of the earth, moon, and stars.

In the time of King Hezekiah only the prophets and learned men knew about the equinox and the movements of the stars and planets. On December 21, shadows decline and on June 21, they lengthen.

It is true, God could have stopped the sun, but the sun's motion has nothing to do with the shortness or the length of our days. Then we may infer that he stopped the rotation of the earth.

Hezekiah was tempting God. In some mysterious way, the prophet divinely caused the shadow to go backward. God is the author of universal laws and had power over them. It might have been June 22. This is the time when figs ripen. At any rate, the miracle is that Hezekiah's life was lengthened and he was healed [2 Kings 20:8-11].

HEZEKIAH'S SCROLL

The writing of Hezekiah king of Judah, when he had been sick, and was recovered of his sickness.　　　　　　　　　　　　Isa. 38:9

This verse is the title of the scroll which contained the account of Hezekiah's illness. In olden days the title of the material was written at the beginning of the scroll or on the margin, and often was read and translated as a portion of the Scripture itself. This custom still prevails in biblical lands. Occasionally scribes are warned not to copy the marginal matter.

King Hezekiah is the author of the material, but evidently the writing itself is the work of a court scribe. The term *katabeh* means "his scroll" or "his writing." But kings always employed court scribes.

A WEAVER'S WEB

Mine age is departed, and is removed from me as a shepherd's tent: I have cut off like a weaver my life: he will cut me off with pining sickness: from day even to night wilt thou make an end of me.　　　　　　　　　　　　Isa. 38:12

Sira or *siras* in Aramaic means "the thread of a loom," Greek *seira*. This is the warp which is tied up above the loom. *Nola* in Aramaic means "a weaver's beam," or the web that is nearly ready to be cut off, or finished. In the East looms are constructed in the houses where the people live. As the weaver works, the people in the house watch the web every day and look forward to the day when the finished product will be cut off and taken from the loom.

King Hezekiah here speaks of the web of life—the span of life when it comes to an end, and the temporal life, which is like a shepherd's tent. Today it is struck, and a few days or weeks later it is dismantled and removed.

This passage was composed by Hezekiah, king of Judah, when he was sick [verses 9-11]. "He will cut me off with pining sickness," is not in the Eastern text. It should read: ". . . my life has shrunk like a shoelace and as a weaver's web which is nearly ready to be cut off; from morning even to night thou hast delivered me to my fate."

HEZEKIAH IN DOUBT

Like a crane or a swallow, so did I chatter: I did mourn as a dove: mine eyes fail with looking upward: O Lord, I am oppressed; undertake for me.   Isa. 38:14

The Eastern text reads: "What shall I say? He has both spoken to me, and himself has done it, and has caused my sleep to flee because of the bitterness of my soul." The translators, in the King James Version, had confronted some difficulties in rendering the verse.

King Hezekiah was not only suffering from physical sickness, but also was pressed by the Assyrian armies, which had destroyed many nations in the path of their march into Egypt and had made tributaries of the others. The uncertainty of the political situation made his soul bitter. He did not know whether he should turn to Assyria, or keep his alliance with Egypt. Hezekiah had sought the Lord's help and his deliverance from his oppressors. At last he was healed, his days lengthened, and he was delivered from the Assyrian army.

VALLEYS EXALTED

Every valley shall be exalted, and every mountain and hill shall be made low: and the crooked shall be made straight, and the rough places plain.   Isa. 40:4

All these sayings are used metaphorically. Valleys and low places are symbolic of meek and weak peoples who were crushed under the feet of the proud and strong nations. Mountains and hills are the haughty and arrogant nations and peoples who were to be humbled. The crooked and rough places symbolize injustices, high taxation, and other evils which brought misery upon the people. They were to be made straight.

All great nations who had oppressed Israel were to be humbled. A new order was to supplant the old, an order of righteousness and justice. At last Jerusalem's iniquities are pardoned and a new era is ahead of the people. The kingdom of God is near, says the prophet.

MAN LIKE GRASS

The voice said, Cry. And he said, What shall I cry? All flesh is grass, and all the goodliness thereof is as the flower of the field:
The grass withereth, the flower fadeth; because the spirit of the Lord bloweth upon it: surely the people is grass.
The grass withereth, the flower fadeth: but the word of our God shall stand for ever. Isa. 40:6-8

"Grass" in this instance means the temporal life. ". . . they are like grass which groweth up. In the morning it flourisheth, and groweth up; in the evening it is cut down, and withereth" [Ps. 90:5-6]. Then again, grass is tender and beautiful and is clothed with beauty and majesty, but it fades away and is cut down [Matt. 6:30].

Grass is used here symbolically because it fades quickly and is cut down and later some of it is used for fuel.

Man's days are like the grass [Ps. 37:2; 1 Pet. 1:24].

Man is tender and beautiful like the flower of the field, but his days upon the earth are numbered. He grows like the flower and then fades away and is cut down. His temporal life comes to an end. Then again, man comes and goes, but the Word of God endures forever [verse 8].

THE GREAT SHEPHERD

He shall feed his flock like a shepherd: he shall gather the lambs with his arm, and carry them in his bosom, and shall gently lead those that are with young. Isa. 40:11

The shepherd gathers the newly born lambs and holds them in his arms. The little lambs do not respond to the voice of the shepherd; they have to be gathered and brought to the fold.

Moreover, the sheep that are with their young cannot walk fast. It takes several weeks before the lamb's legs are strong enough to keep up with the flock; therefore, the shepherd is gentle and patient with the sheep who, because of their young lambs, walk slowly. Moreover, the sheep that suckle their lambs are fed in the evening.

The sheep and lambs are symbolic of God's people, and the shepherd is God himself, who has compassion on the weak, who searches for those who are lost, and who feeds the hungry with spiritual food.

EVERLASTING

Hast thou not known? hast thou not heard, that the everlasting God, the Lord, the Creator of the ends of the earth, fainteth not, neither is weary? there is no searching of his understanding.

Isa. 40:28

The Hebrew God was a spiritual and everlasting God, but the gods of the Gentiles were temporal and mortal human deities, who grew old and died. They were images of wood, silver, and gold which were broken or discarded and eventually replaced by new ones.

The God of Israel is a permanent God, from eternity to eternity. All other gods pass away, but he endures forever. Moreover, the God of Israel is the substance or the essence of life, and hence the Creator of the heaven and of the earth and all that is therein. The prophet here compares the God of Israel with the helpless and hopeless pagan deities [verse 19].

Then again, the prophet reminds the people of the character of the God of Israel, his promises which endured forever, and his everlasting covenant which was good throughout all generations.

In the religion of Israel time was irrelevant. God was above time and space; and, being eternal and the life-giver, he was the Sovereign and the Lord of all. This is because the Hebrew God was a spiritual and eternal God. In the realm of the Spirit it is the destiny of a nation that counts. Israel worked and waited for the fulfillment of the promise, the messianic kingdom.

ISRAEL'S ENEMIES DEFEATED

Behold, I will make thee a new sharp threshing instrument having teeth: thou shalt thresh the mountains, and beat them small, and shalt make the hills as chaff.

Isa. 41:15

In the olden days threshing was done with oxen or by sledges spiked with sharp iron spikes. The threshing instrument was one of the first machines invented by man. It was an improvement on the older method, which was done by trampling or treading the wheat under oxen's feet.

The sledge is made of wood with two wooden axles beneath it. The axles are covered from one end to the other with sharp iron spikes about three inches wide and eight inches long. As the sledge is driven by oxen, the axles turn over the sheaves of wheat.

These threshing instruments are still in use in some parts of the Near East. They were very common before World War I.

The enemies of Israel were to be threshed like wheat; that is, crushed and punished severely, and scattered as chaff is scattered before the wind. "Arise and thresh, O daughter of Zion: for I will make thine horn iron . . ." [Mic. 4:13].

WATER SHORTAGE

When the poor and needy seek water, and there is none, and their tongue faileth for thirst, I the Lord will hear them, I the God of Israel will not forsake them.   Isa. 41:17

For centuries water has been one of the most difficult problems in Palestine and other Bible lands west of the River Euphrates. Water is very precious. At times there are long periods of drought in which cattle and sheep die and men suffer thirst just as in the days of Elijah and Ahab.

During such periods the poor suffer most. The wells are usually the property of rich individuals, and water is sold. Prior to World War II one could see water sold on the streets. Then again, when a tribe passes through the territory of another tribe, they must buy water for the sheep, cattle, and men.

The poor have nothing with which to buy water. Many of them suffer thirst and may even have to steal water from their neighbors. King Solomon says that stolen water is sweet [Prov. 9:17; Isa. 44:3].

The poor and the needy pray for rain, and God answers their prayers and meets their daily needs.

AN ABOMINABLE CHOICE

Behold, ye are of nothing, and your work of nought: an abomination is he that chooseth you.   Isa. 41:42

Gebithkhon (choosing you) has been confused here with *gabovekhan* (he that chose you). The Eastern text reads: "Behold, you are nothing, and your works are corrupt; choosing you is an abomination."

The prophet here condemns the choosing or the selection of the people, because they had been abominable. The chosen is God, who selected a good vine, but it became a bad vine. The Hebrew patriarchs whom God chose were good, but their descendants revolted against him, broke his commandments, and departed from his way.

MY SERVANT

Behold my servant, whom I uphold; mine elect, in whom my soul delighteth; I have put my Spirit upon him: he shall bring forth judgment to the Gentiles.   Isa. 42:1

Messiah here is called the servant of God; that is, the one who does God's work and publishes his Word. The Aramaic word for "servant" is *awda,* and the word for "work" is *awada.* Both words are derived from the root *abad,* in which the "b" is aspirated and hence becomes "w."

"Servant" here should not be confused with "slave." Moses was called the servant of God. This is because a servant is obedient to his master and carries out his orders.

Jesus spoke of God as his God and his Lord. He also said, "Why callest thou me good? there is none good but one, that is, God" [Mark 10:18; Luke 18:19]. Then again, Jesus was obedient to God even to his death on the cross. The Messiah was to reveal the love of God and the reign of justice, not by his power, but through his humility and suffering. In the East faithful servants would die for their masters. Messiah was to surrender his will to the will of God. He was to lower himself and take the form of a servant in order that he might become an example to us.

Isaiah uses Eastern expressions which the people understood. Eastern ambassadors and high government officials are known as the servants of the king. Jesus of Nazareth was a spokesman for God.

HE SHALL NOT CRY

He shall not cry, nor lift up, nor cause his voice to be heard in the street.

A bruised reed shall he not break, and the smoking flax shall he not quench: he shall bring forth judgment unto truth.

He shall not fail nor be discouraged, till he have set judgment in the earth: and the isles shall wait for his law.   Isa. 42:2-4

This is a messianic passage. "He shall not cry, nor make a sound," means that he will not campaign, nor cry or blow a trumpet to mobilize an army and start a revolt. In biblical days, uprisings and revolts were generally heralded by the sound of trumpets and the crying of the messengers, who went from town to town heralding the news and trying to enlist the people. When Ehud slew Eglon, the king of Moab, he blew the trumpet in the mountain of Ephraim, announcing the revolt against the Moabites [Josh. 6:4-5; Judg. 3:27-28].

Messiah was to inaugurate a new way, the way of God. He was to change the world, not by means of arms, but by the Word of God—by becoming a light to the Gentiles, who were groping in darkness.

Isaiah knew that Messiah would be so meek and gentle that the people would shun him as a leader and saviour. He was to be so weak in the eyes of the people that he would not extinguish a flickering lamp nor break even a bruised reed.

But even though Messiah was so meek and weak in the eyes of the Jewish leaders, he could not be discouraged in putting his plan forward. Nothing, not even death, could deter him from his path.

The Jews, like other races, were looking for strong leaders to deliver them from their enemies. In those days, just like today, force was considered the only way to meet force. To conquer the world by means of meekness was unknown and seemed strange to the leaders. The prophets were the only ones who foresaw the new way of meekness and gentleness which would slowly but ultimately lead the world to a just and everlasting peace.

Messiah was God's small but powerful voice. He would triumph where others had failed.

WILDERNESS REJOICING

Let the wilderness and the cities thereof lift up their voice, the villages that Kedar doth inhabit: let the inhabitants of the rock sing, let them shout from the top of the mountains.   Isa. 42:11

Many parts of the wilderness are inhabited by nomad tribes. Petra in the land of Edom was a city whose houses were hewn in the rocks. Moreover, many Israelites lived in the wilderness for forty years. Even today in some parts of the wilderness one can see thousands of sheep, goats, and camels, and hundreds of black tents made of the hair of goats. And still, many nomad peoples dwell in caves as of yore.

The reference here is to the desert dwellers and the people who dwell in caves and the villages of Kedar. Joy would come to them through the reign of Messiah, the Prince of Peace, who would prevail against the enemies of God and bring forth judgment to the Gentiles [verse 1].

Today many parts of Judea, Edom, and Arabia, which a few decades ago were wastelands, now are meadows. Wisdom and understanding have turned many dry lands into standing pools of water. Today because of abundant water the Jews and the Arabs are singing and shouting with joy [Isa. 43:19; 44:3].

A MIGHTY WARRIOR

The Lord shall go forth as a mighty man, he shall stir up jealousy like a man of war: he shall cry, yea, roar; he shall prevail against his enemies.   ˙ Isa. 42:13

In the olden days the mighty men of war went forth out of the ranks of their armies to challenge the army of the enemy. At times a single combat decided the battle, as in the case of David and Goliath [1 Sam. 17:3-4].

The Eastern text reads: ". . . he shall stir up zealousness like a man of war . . ." When a mighty man went forth to challenge the enemy, he cursed their king and their god, thus stirring up zealousness among the armed forces.

Israel rejoiced in the strength of her God, who went forth ahead of the armies of Israel, challenging the pagan deities. The term "mighty" is used to indicate God's triumph over his enemies. "The Lord is a mighty warrior: the Lord is his name" [Exod. 15:3, Eastern text].

THE LORD'S PATIENCE

I have long time holden my peace; I have been still, and refrained myself: now will I cry like a travailing woman; I will destroy and devour at once.
I will make waste mountains and hills, and dry up all their herbs; and I will make the rivers islands, and I will dry up the pools.
                                                   Isa. 42:14-15

The Aramaic word *ethwar* (to confound) has˙ been confused with *ethbar* (to destroy, break up). The Eastern text reads: "I have for a long time held my peace; I have kept silent, I have been patient like a woman in travail; I have remained speechless and completely confounded."

The Lord had been patient and silent, but now he will come forth like a mighty warrior ready to destroy his enemies.

Mountains and hills are symbolic of mighty kings and emperors. When the rivers dry during the droughts, islands are formed in the midst of them. A great change was to take place. The blind men, who knew only one path, now would be led by a new way which they had never known.

GLORIFY IN SHIPS

Thus saith the Lord, your Redeemer, the Holy One of Israel;
For your sake I have sent to Babylon, and have brought down all
their nobles, and the Chaldeans, whose cry is in the ships. Isa. 43:14

The Aramaic word *meshtabkhin* means "glorify themselves in ships";
that is, Babylon was proud of its navy and merchant marine, which navigated all the known seas. And her merchants filled the markets with all
kinds of merchandise. Jeremiah says, "O thou that dwellest upon many
waters, abundant in treasures . . ." [Jer. 51:13]. The Chaldeans took
pride in their ships and commerce.

All the markets of Babylon were to be laid waste because of the lack
of ships' trade, and the prosperous merchants were to mourn its fall.

Persia, the successor of Babylon, also became a great naval power,
threatening Asia Minor, Greece, and the Aegean Islands.

RIVERS IN THE DESERT

Behold, I will do a new thing; now it shall spring forth; shall
ye not know it? I will even make a way in the wilderness, and
rivers in the desert.
The beast of the field shall honor me, the dragons and the owls:
because I give waters in the wilderness, and rivers in the desert, to
give drink to my people, my chosen.   Isa. 43:19-20

No place in the world is water desired and valued more than in the
desert lands, where people often go to sleep thirsty, and sheep and cattle
perish because of the lack of water. In these lands water is bought and
sold, and is precious in the eyes of the people.

The highest aspiration of the inhabitants of the deserts is to find
prolific wells and other sources of living or running water for their flocks.
The people dream of rivers, brooks, and wells with abundant water [Isa.
42:11].

The prophet compares the world of his days to the deserts where the
people are in constant fear of droughts. The rivers are symbolic of true
religion, enlightenment, and abundance, which in due time will usher in
the reign of knowledge, peace, harmony, and prosperity. When permanent
peace is established and greed and war eradicated, the deserts can be
turned into blooming gardens [Ps. 46:4; 36:8; Isa. 32:12].

CHOSEN PEOPLE

This people have I formed for myself; they shall show forth my praise. Isa. 43:21

The Aramaic word *gabeth* (I have chosen) has been confused with *gableth* (I have formed). The Eastern text reads: "This people whom I have chosen for myself, they shall drink."

The Israelites were called or chosen by God for a great mission. God's divine promises to mankind were to be fulfilled through them [Rom. 1:6; 8:28]. The whole world was to be blessed by the teaching that God had revealed to the Hebrew patriarchs, which years later was proclaimed by the Hebrew prophets and shared with the Gentile world by Jesus Christ and his disciples.

God's choice in this instance does not mean that God shows partiality to the Israelites. Israel was chosen or called to play an important part in God's divine plan of salvation. Israel was a prominent actor in a world-wide drama. And Israel, despite persecution and suffering, has played her part well.

SWEET CANE

Thou hast bought me no sweet cane with money, neither hast thou filled me with the fat of thy sacrifices: but thou hast made me to serve with thy sins, thou hast wearied me with thine iniquities. Isa. 43:24

Sweet cane was used in the manufacture of frankincense, in the sacred oil that was used for the anointing of the priests, and in the sweet incense, beaten small, which the high priest burned upon the altar [Exod. 30:7-9; Lev. 16:12].

THE PRINCES HAD POLLUTED

Therefore I have profaned the princes of the sanctuary, and have given Jacob to the curse, and Israel to reproaches. Isa. 43:28

The Aramaic word *towisho* is third person plural, "They have polluted or profaned." *Towshet* means, "I have polluted." The Eastern text reads: "Your princes have profaned the sanctuary . . ." The letter *waw* at the end of the word is the sign of plural, "they."

Since God is goodness and purity, he could not have polluted the princes of his sanctuary. The reference here is to Baal worship which was introduced into the holy temple by some of the wicked priests and kings of Judah, especially by Kings Manasseh and Amon. The priests committed fornication in the holy place. This immoral worship was a part of the pagan ritual.

When Josiah cleansed the temple he destroyed the immoral worship and had the images burned and the priests and Sodomites slain [2 Kings 23:4-7].

DULL IMAGINATION

He feedeth on ashes: a deceived heart hath turned him aside, that he cannot deliver his soul, nor say, Is there not a lie in my right hand? Isa. 44:20

Raaey kitma is an Aramaic idiom which means "dull imagination" or "people who have no understanding." *Kitma* (ashes) is used in the King James Version simply because there is nothing in it to feed on. All organic and inorganic matter is burned.

SIGNS OF DIVINERS

That frustrateth the tokens of the liars, and maketh diviners mad; that turneth wise men backward, and maketh knowledge foolish. Isa. 44:25

It should read: "Who makes void the signs of the diviners and despises their divinations . . ." The Lord God of Israel is the author of all creation. Nothing can happen in the universe without his knowledge.

The God of Israel had the power to make void the divinations and signs of wise men, and to contradict and despise their human wisdom and understanding [verse 24].

Signs were wrought by means of magical performances. The magicians and the diviners showed false signs to convince the people of their great powers. God's truth exposed them and proved that they were liars and their wisdom was foolish.

This is why Jesus refused to show signs like the diviners of his day. But he wrought true miracles and wonders which were the acts of God for the good of men.

CYRUS THE PERSIAN

That saith of Cyrus, He is my shepherd, and shall perform all my pleasure: even saying to Jerusalem, Thou shalt be built; and to the temple, Thy foundation shall be laid. Isa. 44:28

King Cyrus was the first Persian king who conquered Babylon and overthrew the Chaldean empire. He is known as the founder of the Persian empire.

According to Daniel, when Bel-shazzar, the last Chaldean king, was slain, Darius the Mede reigned in his place [Dan. 6:5-31]. Daniel places Darius first. So this Daniel prospered in the reign of Darius, and in the reign of Cyrus the Persian [Dan. 6:28]. It was during the reign of Cyrus that the true Persian dynasty was established. The Medes were the inhabitants of Media and the Persians of Paras.

The two great prophets of Israel, Isaiah and Jeremiah, had predicted the fall of the Chaldean empire and the rise of the Persians [2 Chron. 36: 22-23]. Jeremiah had also predicted the return of the remnant from Babylon after seventy years [Jer. 29:10]. This prophecy was fulfilled in the first year of the reign of Cyrus, king of Persia. ". . . the Lord stirred up the spirit of Cyrus king of Persia, that he made a proclamation throughout all his kingdom and put it also in writing, saying, Thus says Cyrus king of Persia: All the kingdoms of the earth has the Lord God of heaven given me; and he has charged me to build him a house in Jerusalem, which is in Judah" [2 Chr. 36:22-23, Eastern text].

Some commentators doubt that Isaiah wrote this portion of his prophecy. They claim that this material was written by a later man. God could have revealed the name of Cyrus to Isaiah just as he revealed many deep secrets to Daniel, or, when the prophecy was fulfilled, Cyrus' name might have been recorded on the margin of the scroll, and later incorporated into the prophecy. This practice is still common in the Near East. Isaiah is the author of the whole book. Like Daniel, he could foresee the rise and fall of great empires which came after him.

CYRUS CALLED GOD'S ANOINTED

Thus saith the Lord to his anointed, to Cyrus, whose right hand I have holden, to subdue nations before him; and I will loose the loins of kings, to open before him the two-leaved gates; and the gates shall not be shut. Isa. 45:1

Cyrus is here called *messiah* (the anointed one). Most of the kings of Judah were anointed with oil. The anointment symbolized ordination and divine appointment and command to rule over the people of God. The anointed king was invested with power from above to execute justice and to do mercy. Oil is symbolic of the light of God.

"Anointed," in this instance, means "ordained or appointed." Some of the pagan nations also practiced anointing with oil. Elijah anointed Hazael king over Syria [1 Kings 19:15].

We have no evidence that the Assyrian, Babylonian, and Persian kings were anointed with oil. Cyrus was appointed and given power by God to save the remnant of Judah, rebuild the temple, and establish the second Jewish commonwealth, which was to prepare the way for the coming of the Great One, the Messiah.

CREATE HARDSHIPS

I form the light, and create darkness: I make peace, and create evil: I the Lord do all these things.   Isa. 45:7

The Aramaic word *bishta* (evil) in this instance means "difficulties, hardships, misfortunes." In Aramaic anything that is imperfect or unpleasant is called *bisha* (evil); that is, "not good." The trees which bear fruits that do not taste good, or are not pleasant to the eye, are called evil trees. Jesus said, "Either produce like a good tree good fruits, or produce like a bad tree with bad fruits; for a tree is known by its fruits."

In Hebrew terminology, everything is under the control of God and hence, nothing can happen without his knowledge and permission. No, not even a hair falls from a man's head without God's knowledge. Hence, since God controls and knows everything, nothing can happen without his knowledge and consent. And since he permits things to happen; therefore, he is the author thereof. But God cannot be the author of evil. He is the author of darkness simply because he formed the earth and caused it to revolve on its axis. Then again, darkness is the absence of light created by the motion of the earth.

Everything which God created was good, and still is good. God created no evil. Evil is man's own creation. Hardships, difficulties, and depressions cannot be blamed on God. They are the result of the law of cause and effect. Man reaps what he has sown and gathers that which he has scattered. On the other hand, man has the power to create his own world. He can make his life healthy, holy and easy, or he can violate the law of cause and effect and bring sickness, evil, and difficulty. Moreover, since God is a good God and, his essence is light, life, and truth, he would not create evil. There is no darkness in light and no error in truth.

Jeremiah speaks of good figs and of bad or evil figs [Jer. 24:1-5].

Both Israel and Judah had faced many hardships which were brought upon the people by bad kings, false prophets, and by the breaking of God's commandments.

MEN OF STATURE

Thus saith the Lord, The labor of Egypt, and merchandise of Ethiopia and of the Sabeans, men of stature, shall come over unto thee, and they shall be thine: they shall come after thee; in chains they shall come over, and they shall fall down unto thee, they shall make supplication unto thee, saying, Surely God is in thee; and there is none else, there is no God.   Isa. 45:14

The reference is to the merchants of Ethiopia and of Sheba, a province of ancient Ethiopia. Sheba is in southern Arabia. The region was famous for its spices, gold, pearls, and precious stones. The queen of Sheba once came to Jerusalem to see Solomon [1 Kings 10:1-10; Ps. 72:10; Isa. 60:6; Jer. 6:20; Matt. 12:42].

The Ethiopians and men of Sheba are of high stature.

Sabeans are a different people. They are the remnants of the Chaldean tribes in Mesopotamia and in the Arabian desert. Prior to the introduction of Christianity and Islam, all these tribes, including the Arab tribes, were pagans. Some of them tenaciously held to old Babylonian cults.

Today, the Sabeans are known as the people of St. John the Baptist. There are more than ten thousand of them in Iraq. They were converted from paganism by the disciples of John the Baptist.

The Sabeans are men of stature and strength, and have beautiful eyes and well-expressed personalities. They live a secluded and peaceful life. Most of them are engravers and silversmiths.

A SHELTER

Verily thou are a God that hidest thyself, O God of Israel, the Saviour. Isa. 45:15

The Aramaic word *setar* means "a covert, shelter, or hiding place." The Eastern text reads: "Truly thou art a shelter, O God, the God of Israel, and his Saviour."

The term *setar* is here used in the sense of protection. In the East when people fought one another they sought a shelter to protect themselves from the arrows of the enemy.

God never hides himself from his children. But in time of trouble, man takes refuge under the protection of his Creator.

"Keep me as the apple of the eye, hide me under the shadow of thy wings" [Ps. 17:8].

"I will abide in thy tabernacle for ever: I will trust in the covert of thy wings. Selah" [Ps. 61:4].

CALLING A BIRD

Calling a ravenous bird from the east, the man that executeth my counsel from a far country: yea, I have spoken it, I will also bring it to pass; I have purposed it, I will also do it. Isa. 46:11

The Aramaic term *tera* (bird) is used metaphorically, meaning "a mighty king, a ruler, as swift as a bird." In Aramaic, we often say, "He is as fast as a bird."

The reference here is to Cyrus, the king of Persia, who was to overthrow the Babylonian Empire and free the Jews. Cyrus' conquest was to be speedy.

Isaiah was living at the time when the kings of Assyria were threatening Judah and all the lands west of the River Euphrates. Another realm was to rise and pass away—the realm of Babylon, or the image of gold. And the realm of Persia, or the image of silver, was to rise up and execute vengeance against Babylon. Persia is east of Babylon.

THEY HAVE POLLUTED

I was wroth with my people, I have polluted mine inheritance, and given them into thine hand: thou didst show them no mercy; upon the ancient hast thou very heavily laid thy yoke.   Isa. 47:6

The Aramaic word *tawisho* is a reflexive verb which means, "They have polluted"; *tawsheth* means "I have polluted." It should read: "They have polluted my inheritance . . ." The princes and the unfaithful priests had polluted the land by erecting shrines for pagan gods and introducing abominable customs and practices of pagan nations whom God had overthrown before the children of Israel.

God is Spirit and purity. There is nothing in him to pollute the people. The error in the King James Version was caused by the mistranslation of the Aramaic word *tawisho* (They have polluted).

See the commentary on Isaiah 43:28.

CALLED FROM THE WOMB

Listen, O isles, unto me; and hearken, ye people, from far; The Lord hath called me from the womb; from the bowels of my mother hath he made mention of my name.   Isa. 49:1

"Called me from the womb" means "has ordained me before my birth." The Aramaic text reads: ". . . from the womb, and from the body of my mother . . ." The Aramaic word *karsa* literally means "belly" or "stomach." The reference is to the body.

In the East children are often dedicated to God before they are even conceived. Women vow to give one of their offsprings to the Lord, as in the case of Hannah [1 Sam. 1:11]. Women who make a vow refrain from eating certain foods and from drinking wine and strong drink.

Isaiah was called by God to a great mission before his birth. His mother, like Hannah, might have dedicated him for the service of the Lord to bring Israel again to God [verse 5].

Jeremiah, likewise, was called before his birth to be a warner to Judah and a prophet to the Gentiles [Jer. 1:5; Isa. 49:5].

NOT LABORED IN VAIN

Then I said, I have labored in vain, I have spent my strength for nought, and in vain: yet surely my judgment is with the Lord, and my work with my God.   Isa. 49:4

The Eastern text reads: "I have not said to the descendants of Jacob that I have labored in vain, nor that I have spent my strength for nought. Surely my judgment is before the Lord, and my work before my God."

Isaiah states that his preaching and his admonitions to his people are not in vain. The prophet hints that through his prophetic teaching, hard work, and persecution, he had succeeded in bringing back a remnant of the people to God.

In verse 5, according to the Eastern text, he assures both Judah and Israel of restoration and reconciliation with God. The reference here is to the remnant of both Judah and Israel, which was to return from captivity, and the coming of the Messiah, who was to be the light to the Gentile world [verses 6-7].

ISRAEL GATHERED TOGETHER

And now, saith the Lord that formed me from the womb to be his servant, to bring Jacob again to him, Though Israel be not gathered, yet shall I be glorious in the eyes of the Lord, and my God shall be my strength.   Isa. 49:5

Ekanish means "I will gather." This verse should read: ". . . and gather Israel together . . ." Jacob is the name and Israel is the title, which includes all the tribes of Israel.

Messiah was to gather the scattered people from the house of Israel [verse 6]. Jesus admonished his disciples to go first to the lost sheep from the house of Israel; that is, the ten tribes who were carried away captive by the Assyrian kings in 722 B.C. [Matt. 10:5-6].

A UNIVERSAL KINGDOM

And he said, It is a light thing that thou shouldest be my servant to raise up the tribes of Jacob, and to restore the preserved of Israel: I will also give thee for a light to the Gentiles, that thou mayest be my salvation unto the end of the earth.   Isa. 49:6

From the outset, the messianic kingdom is coupled with a universal religion. In other words, Messiah must save the whole world in order to save the Israelites. Jewish leaders and some of the prophets and seers were interested in the salvation of Israel only. They had no concern about the Gentile nation who persecuted them and, at times, carried them away as captives.

Isaiah saw that all Jewish troubles were due to the ignorance of the Gentile world, and the only solution to the old problem was to give the Gentiles the law, justice, and truth that God had revealed to Moses and the prophets of Israel.

Messiah's mission was universal. He was to become a light to the Gentile world. He would share the Jewish religion and Jewish ethics with them, and thus open their eyes to justice and God's truth.

Thus, the salvation of the Jews was relevant to the salvation of the Gentiles. In other words, the Jews could not live by themselves in the midst of many pagan nations, who had no knowledge of God and who had not seen the light of truth.

True Christianity, based on the teaching of Jesus and that of his disciples, is a fulfillment of messianic prophecies which would usher in a new reign, the reign of God.

". . . I have put my spirit upon him; he shall bring forth justice to the Gentiles" [Isa. 42:1, Eastern text].

SUFFERING MESSIAH

Thus saith the Lord, the Redeemer of Israel, and his Holy One, to him whom man despiseth, to him whom the nation abhorreth, to a servant of rulers, Kings shall see and arise, princes also shall worship, because of the Lord that is faithful, and the Holy One of Israel, and he shall choose thee.   Isa. 49:7

This is a messianic prophecy concerning the rejection, suffering, and humiliation of Messiah, Christ. Messiah was to be rejected, mocked, and despised by the people, priests, and the rulers of this world. But in due time the descendants of the same people and their rulers would pay homage to him, and princes also would worship him, because the Lord had chosen him to be the Saviour. And Messiah would pour out his blood on the cross for the sake of a sinful humanity.

Jesus *was* rejected and mocked. The soldiers ironically placed a reed in his hand symbolizing the sceptre; and they put a crown of thorns on his head and bowed their knees before him, saying, "Hail, King of the Jews!" [Matt. 27:29].

The governor and the soldiers who mocked him, placed the crown of thorns upon his head, and crucified him did not know that a few centuries later the crown of Jesus Christ would be worn by the Roman emperors. But the prophet Isaiah saw that the suffering Messiah would ultimately triumph over the evil forces and the princes and lords of this world.

CHINA

Behold, these shall come from far: and, lo, these from the north and from the west; and these from the land of Sinim. Isa. 49:12

Sinim is another name for Cathay (China). The Aramaic is *Sanim*. In the later Aramaic literature, China is called *Sin* or *Seen*. The letter *zadeh* (strong s) and *semketh* (s) are used interchangeably. *Sinim* might be the Hebrew plural for *Seen*, China. The term Cathay (China) occurs in the book of Numbers 24:24 and Jeremiah 2:10.

Today the Aramaic-speaking peoples call the Japanese and Chinese *Gatayey* from *Gog-Gatay,* and *Chinayey* from *Sinayey.*

Cathay, Gog and Magog, China and Mongolia, are mentioned in several books in the Bible [Gen. 10:4; Ezek. 38:2; Rev. 20:8].

GOD DOES NOT FORGET

Can a woman forget her sucking child, that she should not have compassion on the son of her womb? yea, they may forget, yet will I not forget thee. Isa. 49:15

In the East, until recent days, milk bottles and baby foods were unknown. The mothers nursed their babies until they were able to eat common food. Like all mothers, they are constantly mindful of the nursing and the welfare of their little ones.

Easterners believe that a mother instinctively knows the hour of nursing her child, and that no mother can forget to nurse her child.

This analogy is used by the prophet in assuring the people of God's faithfulness and love toward them. A mother, through negligence or sleep, may forget her suckling child, but God would not forget Zion. God's love toward those who believe in him and keep his commandments is more abundant than that of a mother toward her suckling child. God does not forsake those who trust in him. He is also constantly mindful of those who have gone astray [verse 16].

INSCRIBED ON THE HAND

Behold, I have graven thee upon the palms of my hands; thy walls are continually before me. Isa. 49:16

"I have graven thee upon the palms of my hands" is used figuratively, meaning, "I remember you continually." The reference is to Zion, the mountain which the Lord God had chosen for his everlasting habitation. The Aramaic reads "inscribed."

Tattooing was very common among ancient people. Signs and talismans were tattooed on the palms of the hand, the arms, and the brows. Moreover, tokens were tied on the fingers and forehead as reminders.

God never forgot Jerusalem, the city of his holy sanctuary. Even a mother may forget her child, but God was constantly mindful of his promises to the Hebrew patriarchs, to the prophets and to the world. Justice and peace were to spring forth out of Jerusalem, and salvation was to come from Zion. Jesus said to the woman in Samaria, ". . . for salvation is of the Jews" [John 4:22].

EAT THEIR OWN FLESH

And I will feed them that oppress thee with their own flesh; and they shall be drunken with their own blood, as with sweet wine: and all flesh shall know that I the Lord am thy Saviour and thy Redeemer, the Mighty One of Jacob. Isa. 49:26

"I will feed them that oppress thee with their own flesh; and they shall be drunken with their own blood" is an idiom commonly used in Aramaic speech to mean "I will cause them to endure hardships and to suffer because of their evils." Many of the Gentile nations had oppressed Israel and Judah, and they were to be recompensed for their evils.

During siege and famine many men and women ate their children. "And thou shalt eat the fruit of thine own body, the flesh of thy sons and of thy daughters . . ." [Deut. 28:53-57; Jer. 19:9].

During a severe famine when Samaria was besieged by the Syrian army, two women conspired to eat their own little sons. The son of one of them was eaten, and when the other refused to slay her son for food, the former complained to the king of Israel. And when the king heard the case, he rent his clothes [2 Kings 6:28-30]. It was against the Mosaic law even to touch a dead body. And the Israelites were forbidden from eating the blood of animals. Savages and pagans ate blood.

Easterners in their conversation often say, "I have eaten my flesh and drunk my blood to build this house," which means, "I have suffered many difficulties to build the house."

See the commentary on Jeremiah 19:9; see also *Gospel Light*, page 342.

ISRAEL NOT REJECTED

Thus saith the Lord, Where is the bill of your mother's divorce-
ment, whom I have put away? or which of my creditors is it to
whom I have sold you? Behold, for your iniquities have ye sold
yourselves, and for your transgressions is your mother put away.

Isa. 50:1

The reference here is to Deuteronomy 24:1. The Mosaic law states
that when a man puts his wife away, he must give her a written bill of
divorcement [Deut. 24:1; Matt. 5:31].

God is often portrayed as the husband, and Israel as a wife. Israel,
because of her transgression and iniquities, sold herself to strangers; that
is, to pagan gods. God had not given her a bill of divorcement; that is,
he had not put her away.

The prophet uses figurative speech to point out the unfaithfulness of
Israel to God. Yet God has not rejected Israel; he still loves the people
whom he had chosen. And regardless of Israel's sins, he has not forsaken
the people, nor sold them to other gods. Whenever the people repented
and returned to him, he was ready to receive them. This was the only way
to make the people understand [Hos. 2:1-6].

THE NEW TEACHING

The Lord God hath given me the tongue of the learned, that I
should know how to speak a word in season to him that is weary:
he wakeneth morning by morning, he wakeneth mine ear to hear as
the learned.

Isa. 50:4

The Eastern text reads: ". . . he wakens me in the morning; in the
morning he causes my ears to hear the teaching."

Easterners believe that in the silent morning hours one can be closer
to God than at any other time. This is why pious men rise up early in
the morning to pray and to meditate. "He wakeneth mine ears" means,
"He gives me spiritual understanding to hear his inner voice." Man has
eyes, but often he cannot see the truth; he has ears, but he cannot hear
the inner voice of God. Only in silence and meditation can one hear the
silent and inarticulate voice of God.

The prophet was given the tongue of the learned. His eyes and his ears
were opened so that he might deliver his ominous message to his people.
In the outset, the prophet, like other court prophets, believed in a political
Messiah and a political kingdom. The Messiah was to be a great conqueror. But now the prophet sees a totally different picture. He sees a

meek, spiritual Messiah, who would be despised, rejected, and put to death. But the prophet did not rebel. He remained faithful to what God had revealed to him. Isaiah was put to death during the reign of Manasseh, the king of Judah.

DISCIPLINE

I gave my back to the smiters, and my cheeks to them that plucked off the hair: I hid not my face from shame and spitting.
                                                                    Isa. 50:6

The reference here is to the prophet's early discipline and training. In the East a good child or student accepts punishment and discipline gladly. At times teachers may strike a student on his cheek or pluck out his hair. Some students are even injured and may lie in bed for weeks. Also, when a student is rebellious, the teacher not only strikes him but even spits in his face.

The prophet has accepted all the humiliation which a good student goes through in order to have the tongue of the learned and the understanding of the wise. To inaugurate the new messianic concept, the "servant suffering."

Messiah Christ was also to be smitten on his cheek, humiliated, and his enemies were to spit in his face because of his teaching [Matt. 26:67].

KINDLING WOOD

Behold, all ye that kindle a fire, that compass yourselves about with sparks: walk in the light of your fire, and in the sparks that ye have kindled. This shall ye have of mine hand; ye shall lie down in sorrow.
                                                                    Isa. 50:11

The Eastern text reads: "Behold, all of you are like kindling wood and the sparks of the kindling"; that is, the people, because of their evil doings, were good for nothing but to be used as kindling to start the fire which was to consume the land.

The prophet uses kindling wood, flames, and sparks allegorically, meaning the people were worthless, and responsible for the impending disaster. In the East even today we say "They are the kindling wood to light the fire," which means, "They have started the fight."

The people were to suffer because of the disaster which they themselves were bringing upon the nation. Judah and all Palestine were to be invaded by the Assyrian and Chaldean armies. Judah was the kindling. The great conflict between Assyria and Egypt was over Judah. The people would suffer because of the fire which they had started.

HEBREW RACE

Hearken to me, ye that follow after righteousness, ye that seek the Lord: look unto the rock whence ye are hewn, and to the hole of the pit whence ye are digged.   Isa. 51:1

The Aramaic word *tora* (mountain) has been confused in the King James Version with *tarana* (flint, hard stone, rock).

The Eastern text reads: ". . . look to the mountain from which you were hewn . . ."

The reference is to Abraham, the founder of the Hebrew race. The Lord had called Abraham, blessed him, and multiplied his seed. The Jews were descendants of Abraham and heirs to the divine promises.

The prophet admonishes the people to look back into the glorious past and remember Abraham, the servant of God, who was the founder of their race and religion.

A BRIGHT FUTURE

For the Lord shall comfort Zion: he will comfort all her waste places; and he will make her wilderness like Eden, and her desert like the garden of the Lord; joy and gladness shall be found therein, thanksgiving, and the voice of melody.   Isa. 51:3

The Aramaic word *baney* (to build) has been confused with *nebaya* derived from *baya* (to comfort, to console). The two words resemble one another closely. The letters "n" and "y" when in the middle of the word are very similar.

The prophet assures the people that Jerusalem, which later was to be destroyed by the Chaldean army, would be rebuilt and the waste places would be like Eden, the garden of the Lord.

The Garden of Eden is in the basin of the River Tigris. The region is graced with all kinds of trees and vegetables which grow naturally. Eden also means delight, happiness, and abundance.

Messiah was to usher in a new era of happiness, peace, and prosperity.

A SEVERE DECREE

Awake, awake, put on strength, O arm of the Lord; awake, as in the ancient days, in the generations of old. Art thou not it that hath cut Rahab, and wounded the dragon?   Isa. 51:9

Pesak piska means a "decree," or the passing of a sentence. The Eastern text reads: "Awake, awake, put on strength, O arm of the Lord; awake as in the ancient days, as in the generations of old. Surely it was thou that didst decree a severe sentence that didst slay the dragon."

Rabba means "great"; that is, "God decreed a great sentence." The reference is to Egypt, the great sea monster which dwelt in the Nile.

Rabba (great) and *Rahab* have been confused in the King James Version. The two words closely resemble one another. At times defections in the manuscripts make it difficult to distinguish words which resemble one another.

The Lord God had decreed a severe decree against the great powers, the oppressors who had harassed his people and laid his land waste. They were to drink from the same cup of trembling which they had given to the small nations [verse 22].

A WILTED BEET

Thy sons have fainted, they lie at the head of all the streets, as a wild bull in a net: they are full of the fury of the Lord, the rebuke of thy God. Isa. 51:20

The Aramaic word *silka* means "beets." The Eastern text reads: ". . . they are faded like a wilted beet . . ." The beet plants grow erect, and when well waterèd are lush and green. The phrase is used metaphorically in dscribing the conditions in Judah, the sorrows of the people, and the dark future ahead of them.

Judah was so afflicted that she looked like a wilted beet plant, symbolizing desolation, destruction, and famine, which were found everywhere [Lam. 2:11-12]. This idiom is still used by Aramaic-speaking people.

The Lord's rebuke had humbled the once proud kingdom. Jerusalem had drunk from the cup of fury, but now the Lord had taken the cup of trembling out of her hand and it would be given to those who had oppressed her [verse 22].

DRUNK, BUT NOT WITH WINE

Therefore hear now this, thou afflicted, and drunken, but not with wine. Isa. 51:21

"Wine" is often used figuratively in the Scriptures. The same word that means wine also means joy, inspiration, teaching: the wine of joy, the wine of sorrows and affliction, the cupful of dregs, the cup of trembling [Isa. 51:22].

In the East we often say, "He is drunk with power." "I will give you the cup of poison." When things are done in extreme it is said they are drunk, which means they are mad. "Babylon has been a golden cup in the Lord's hand that made all the earth drunken of her wine; all the nations have drunk, and therefore the nations stagger with drunkenness" [Jer. 51:7, Eastern text]. Babylon was drunk with the power and wealth she had gotten by plundering.

CUP OF TREMBLING

Thus saith thy Lord the Lord, and thy God that pleadeth the cause of his people, Behold, I have taken out of thine hand the cup of trembling, even the dregs of the cup of my fury; thou shalt no more drink it again.
Isa. 51:22

"Cup" is symbolic of treachery. "Cup of trembling" is the poison cup from which those who were doomed were forced to drink. The doomed convict took the cup in his trembling hands and drank the poison in the presence of the prison officials. This was one form of capital punishment. Socrates, the great Greek philosopher, died in this manner. He was given a cup of hemlock.

In the East when one wants to do away with his enemies he gives a banquet in honor of the man of whom he wants to dispose. Then the host instructs one of his faithful servants to poison the cup.

The guest of honor, not knowing what the intentions are, trembles when the cup is offered to him. He either has to drink it, flee, or murder the host.

Many men were disposed of in this manner. In Iran and many other Eastern countries, this custom still prevails. The Iranians used hashish. That is where we get out our English word "assassin." Princes and kings have cup or food testers, but ordinary men must either drink or flee.

Jesus knew about this ancient custom when he said, "O my Father, if it be possible, let this cup pass from me" [Matt. 26:39-42].

Israel was made to drink many bitter cups. She was lured into crooked alliances which caused her miseries. Now the Lord was to give the cup to her enemies. Their turn for punishment was soon to come.

SHAKE THE DUST

Shake thyself from the dust; arise, and sit down, O Jerusalem: loose thyself from the bands of thy neck, O captive daughter of Zion.
Isa. 52:2

"Dust" is symbolic of inactivity, mourning, and bondage. In the East when people mourn they throw dust over their heads and garments [Lam. 2:10].

On the other hand, the clothes of prisoners are usually dirty and dusty, because they sleep on the ground with their clothes on.

"Shake thyself from the dust" means, "Free yourself and start to act."

The remnant of the Jews was to be restored and Jerusalem rebuilt. The nation was to regain her freedom and rededicate herself to God. The idol worship and pagan rituals were to be discarded and the true religion of God restored.

Then again, dust is symbolic of evil and falsehood. Jerusalem was to purge herself of her evil ways.

FEET BLESSED

How beautiful upon the mountains are the feet of him that bringeth good tidings, that publisheth peace; that bringeth good tidings of good, that publisheth salvation; that saith unto Zion, Thy God reigneth!
Isa. 52:7

"Feet" here is symbolic of good omen, blessing, and good news. In the East when a traveler or messenger arrives in a town or a sheep camp the people greeting him say, "May your feet be blessed," which means, "You may have good news," or, "You have come in peace." One often hears people say, "His feet are bad," which means he is the bearer of bad news, or he brings bad luck.

The messengers and bearers of news are noted for running, and the people are eager to hear the news [2 Sam. 18:19-21, 27].

A PEACEFUL DEPARTURE

Depart ye, depart ye, go ye out from thence, touch no unclean thing; go ye out of the midst of her; be ye clean, that bear the vessels of the Lord.

For ye shall not go out with haste, nor go by flight: for the Lord will go before you; and the God of Israel will be your rereward.
Isa. 52:11-12

The prophet reminds the people of the hasty flight of their forefathers from Egypt. The Israelites rose up early; they did not wait even for their dough to leaven [Exod. 12:34].

The Israelites fled at night when they left Egypt with Moses, but now they were to depart from Babylon in peace, protected by the king's army.

The return of the remnant from Babylon would be different from the exodus. The exiles would be accompanied by the imperial forces. They would be supplied with provisions for their long journey. They would return to Jerusalem with gold, silver, and the temple vessels.

The day would come when war would be abolished and every nation would live in peace and security in its own land. This era of peace and tranquility was predicted by the other Hebrew prophets. And it will ultimately come when the teaching of the Hebrew prophets and of Jesus Christ will be understood, practiced, and made universal. This era, also, is called the Kingdom of God.

PURIFICATION

So shall he sprinkle many nations; the kings shall shut their mouths at him: for that which had not been told them shall they see; and that which they had not heard shall they consider.

Isa. 52:15

The Aramaic word *medakey*, means "he shall cleanse"; that is, he shall cleanse or purify the people of their sins.

"Shut their mouths" means keep silence, be speechless and astonished because of God's power and wisdom, and the new things which the people would see and hear [Ezek. 36:25].

Messiah was to purify many nations with his baptism of water and of the Holy Spirit. The people would become a new creation, a new Adam saved by the death of Jesus Christ.

SIMPLE AS A CHILD

For he shall grow up before him as a tender plant, and as a root out of a dry ground: he hath no form nor comeliness; and when we shall see him, there is no beauty that we should desire him.

Isa. 53:2

The Aramaic reads *yaloda* (an infant, babe, suckling). This term is used by the prophet in describing the Messiah, who was to be simple, innocent, and pure, like a child.

The Messiah was to lack all the human qualities that make a man look like a worldly leader. Therefore he would be despised, rejected, and denied by those who were looking for a strong political leader to restore the kingdom of David. These people even seven centuries later would be looking for a militant leader who would overthrow the Gentile kingdoms. And all this change was to come suddenly.

Isaiah saw that the world could be conquered only through meekness, gentleness, and loving-kindness. But he also saw that it would take a long time before the people would understand the change from a strong political Messiah to a meek and spiritual Messiah. The new concept of the servant and suffering found a definite expression among the Hebrew prophets. Jesus was rejected on the ground that he possessed no militant qualities. The leaders of the Jewish religion despised him and abhorred his doctrine of meekness and the turning of the other cheek. The priests and the princes had also rejected their holy prophets.

SMITTEN OF GOD

Surely he hath borne our griefs, and carried our sorrows: yet we did esteem him stricken, smitten of God, and afflicted.   Isa. 53:4

"Smitten of God" is an Eastern idiom that is still in constant use in the vernacular speech. The term "smitten of God" denotes the most severe punishment, a punishment that men cannot inflict on one another. In Aramaic, people who are afflicted, oppressed, and heavily taxed are called stricken or smitten of God. Moreover, this idiom at times is used when speaking of meek men. We often say, "Do not hurt him; he is smitten of God."

Because God permitted Jesus to suffer humiliation and death on the cross, the prophet calls him "smitten of God, and afflicted." Jesus had to die so that God's love toward his children might be revealed. "For God so loved the world, that he gave his only begotten Son, that whosoever believeth in him should not perish, but have everlasting life" [John 3:16].

Jesus suffered for our sins and our iniquities. His suffering on the cross has destroyed the power of evil forces and sin. And through his stripes we are healed [verses 5, 6, 10].

AS A SHEEP BEFORE THE SHEARERS

He was oppressed, and he was afflicted, yet he opened not his mouth: he is brought as a lamb to the slaughter, and as a sheep before her shearers is dumb, so he openeth not his mouth.

Isa. 53:7

Sheep are dumb before the shearer, just as a man is quiet and happy in a barber's chair. The sheep are not only relieved of the heavy fleece which they carry on their backs during the hot summer months but also of sheep lice (a red bug which breeds in the wool and thrives on the blood of the helpless sheep).

Sheep, more than any other animal, are helpless against lice which torment them day and night. When they are shorn of their heavy wool, they are relieved of bugs and dirt which accumulate in the fleece. They lie before the shearer motionless and enjoy the gentle touch of the shears on their bodies.

Messiah is likened to a sheep or a ewe before the shearer, simply because he went to the cross without any protest. He did not even open his mouth. He was willing to die so that men might live and find the true way to everlasting salvation.

"Lamb" is symbolic of purity and innocence. This is because the lamb is the weakest and gentlest of all the offspring of animals. The newly born lambs are taken in the arms of men and women, and are loved by the shepherds.

The lamb was the most favored animal recommended in Mosaic ordinances for sacrifice [Exod. 29:38-41]. Jesus was often called the Lamb of God: "Behold the Lamb of God" [John 1:29]; as "a lamb without blemish" [1 Pet. 1:19]; and "the Lamb slain from the foundation of the world" [Rev. 13:8].

Lambs are too young to know anything about slaughter. They follow the butchers just as they follow the shepherds who love them. Jesus went to the cross without protest. Like a lamb to the slaughter, he accompanied the soldiers who were to crucify him.

Isaiah knew that any departure from the old messianic concept would mean rejection, humiliation, condemnation, and the cross. He also knew that Messiah would accept the challenge and defy the old traditions and doctrines, and willingly go to the cross in order to fulfill the prophecies and to accomplish his divine mission. Messiah would save the world through the Spirit of God, suffering, and the cross, and not by the means of weapons and force.

Jesus, through his death on the cross, destroyed the power of death and sin, and rose in glory and majesty.

TRIALS IN LIFE

He was taken from prison and from judgment: and who shall declare his generation? for he was cut off out of the land of the living: for the transgression of my people was he stricken. Isa. 53:8

The Aramaic word *dara* (with the genitive *dareh*) means "generation, trials, struggles." In this instance it means his trials or his warfare against the evil forces and his enemies. In Aramaic, when we say trial or warfare, we double the letter *resh* (r). Thus, *dareh* (his generation) becomes *darreh* (his warfare, his trials). The two words are written alike. The doubling is done in pronounciation.

The prophet in this chapter tries to depict Christ's suffering, his humiliation and affliction. Messiah would be put to death and, therefore, according to the Jewish theology of the time, he would be cut off from the land of the living. He would die for the transgressions of the people who had forsaken the way of God. And his struggles and trials are so many that no one can describe them or relate them.

The reference here is to the trial, affliction, and suffering of Jesus Christ, which Isaiah foresaw. The prophet knew that Messiah would be rejected by the priests [verses 3-5].

MESSIAH HUMBLED

Yet it pleased the Lord to bruise him; he hath put him to grief: when thou shalt make his soul an offering for sin, he shall see his seed, he shall prolong his days, and the pleasure of the Lord shall prosper in his hand. Isa. 53:10

The Aramaic word *danmakkhey* is derived from *mak* (to humble, humiliate, become meek). "Bruise him" is a wrong rendering. The Aramaic word *saba* means "to prefer, seek, consent, wish."

God, because of his love for us, consented to allow Christ to be humiliated and crucified for our sins. God, from the very beginning, knew that Messiah Christ would be rejected, humbled, and crucified by sinful men. Jesus, in his parable of the vineyard and the wicked husbandmen, placed the guilt for his rejection and his humiliation on the unfaithful husbandmen, who had rebelled against the owner of the vineyard, God [Mark 12:1-8; Luke 20:9-15].

Thus, the rejection and humiliation of Jesus Christ was blindly caused by the high priests and some of the Pharisees and scribes. A righteous man was to die the death of a sinner in order that sin might be destroyed. God had sent prophets in advance to bring the people to the true way of life, but they were also rejected, humbled, and slain. At last, God sent Messiah, his Son, with assurance that his death and suffering might cause the hearts of men to change and be brought back into his fold.

A BRIGHT FUTURE

Sing, O barren, thou that didst not bear; break forth into singing, and cry aloud, thou that didst not travail with child: for more are the children of the desolate than the children of the married wife, saith the Lord. Isa. 54:1

"Desolate," in this instance, refers to a woman who had not been beloved by her husband. And the term *beailta* means a woman who has been favored by her husband.

In the East men who marry more than one wife usually prefer one over all the others; that is, one of them becomes the favored and, therefore, is loved more, and the others are neglected or loved less.

Jacob married Leah and Rachel, and he loved Rachel more than Leah.

But when the Lord saw that Leah was not favored, he opened her womb, but Rachel was barren. Thus Leah, who was less loved, had more children than the one who was favored [Gen. 29:31-32].

Judah and Jerusalem were to be made desolate and their inhabitants carried away captive, but they were to be inhabited again. The Lord would remember them, favor them, and multiply them again.

During the time of the prophet Isaiah, the future of Israel was so dark that her survival was doubtful. But the prophet saw a bright future.

ISRAEL NOT FORGOTTEN

For the Lord hath called thee as a woman forsaken and grieved in spirit, and a wife of youth, when thou wast refused, saith thy God.

Isa. 54:6

The Aramaic *shabikta* means "deserted or left." In the East women are often deserted or left by their husbands for no reason. Then again, in the lands where polygamy is practiced, many men neglect some of their wives and favor the others. Jacob favored Rachel and neglected Leah [Gen. 30:15]. The women try to outdo one another in order to win favor in the eyes of their husbands [Gen. 30:20].

God had, for a time, left Israel, just as a husband leaves or deserts his wife. But he was to claim Israel again with love and loving-kindness as of yore. Israel had been unfaithful to her God; that is, they had broken his covenant and forsaken his way. But because of the remnant and God's promises to Abraham, the race was to be spared, restored, and multiplied again.

In reality, God was always seeking Israel. "Can a woman forget her sucking child . . . ? Yea, they may forget, yet will I not forget thee" [Isa. 49:15].

A NEW PROMISE

For this is as the waters of Noah unto me: for as I have sworn that the waters of Noah should no more go over the earth; so have I sworn that I would not be wroth with thee, nor rebuke thee.

Isa. 54:9

Yomatha (days) has been confused in the King James Version with *yammatha* (seas, waters).

The prophet reminds the people of God's covenant with Noah after the destructive flood [Gen. 9:11]. The verse should read: "This is like the days of Noah to me; for as I have sworn that the waters of Noah should no more go over the earth . . ."

God had sworn that he would not be angry with Israel, nor rebuke the people. The nation was so crushed and afflicted that the remnant had learned a good lesson from the past.

GOD'S PROMISES ARE SURE

For the mountains shall depart, and the hills be removed; but my kindness shall not depart from thee, neither shall the covenant of my peace be removed, saith the Lord that hath mercy on thee.

Isa. 54:10

The Aramaic word *nethmakkhon* means "brought low, humbled." This verse should read: "For the mountains shall be brought low and the hills bent downward. . ." This is an Eastern saying denoting the permanency of a promise or an oath, for people know that no one can cause a mountain or a hill to flatten out or bend down.

Jesus said, "For truly I say to you, Until heaven and earth pass away, not even a yoth or a dash shall pass away from the law until all of it is fulfilled" [Matt. 5:18, Eastern text].

Isaiah thus assures the people of God's love toward them and the permanency of his everlasting covenant. The Lord had forsaken them for a while, but now he reassures them of his loving kindness toward them [verses 6-7; also Ps. 89:33-35]. But in reality they had broken his covenant and forsaken him.

BROUGHT BACK BY GOD

Behold, they shall surely gather together, but not by me: whosoever shall gather together against thee shall fall for thy sake.

Isa. 54:15

Mithpnin min edai means "brought back by my hand." This refers to the people whom the Lord had caused to return to Jerusalem. They were to become a house of refuge for those who had remained in Judah.

This verse should read: "All those who are brought back by my hand shall enter into you; and they shall be as a place of refuge to your inhabitants."

The Lord was determined to restore and rehabilitate the remnant. He had control over everything. Nothing could alter his plans or stand against him.

GOD'S ABUNDANCE

Ho, every one that thirsteth, come ye to the waters, and he that hath no money; come ye, buy, and eat; yea, come, buy wine and milk without money and without price. Isa. 55:1

The prophet strongly assures his hearers of the restoration of the remnant of Israel to the land of their fathers. They would replenish the land once more and prosper. The Lord God would take Israel back to himself as a man who takes back a wife whom he has deserted. Israel no more would be forsaken by her God [Isa. 54:4-9].

Moreover, the remnant would be blessed with prosperity which would reign in the land in such abundance that the inhabitants would be unable to store the surplus food.

"Yea, come, buy wine and milk without money and without price" is symbolic of extreme prosperity. In the East when food is plentiful, it is sold very cheap or even given away, especially perishable food. The term "waters" symbolizes the Truth, the right religion: "Therefore with joy shall ye draw water out of the wells of salvation" [Isa. 12:3].

Just as water is refreshing to the thirsty, so the truth revives the weary souls of those who have gone astray from the living God, seeking comfort and material security from false gods. Jesus said, "If any man thirst, let him come unto me, and drink" and ". . . out of his belly shall flow rivers of living water" [John 7:37, 38; see also Jer. 2:13].

FAITHFUL EUNUCHS

Neither let the son of the stranger, that hath joined himself to the Lord, speak, saying, The Lord hath utterly separated me from his people: neither let the eunuch say, Behold, I am a dry tree.
For thus saith the Lord unto the eunuchs that keep my sabbaths, and choose the things that please me, and take hold of my covenant. Isa. 56:3-4

Eunuchs were men who worked in the harems of kings, princes, and wealthy men. Most of these men were made eunuchs against their will. Some were prisoners of war whom the conquerors had brought from foreign lands. Some were born eunuchs, and others made themselves eunuchs in order to enter into the kingdom of heaven.

During the time of Isaiah eunuchs were looked upon as pious men and were well respected by the people as well as by the rulers. The eunuchs were very religious. They observed the Mosaic law and ordinances very strictly. The Aramaic term for eunuch is *mehemna* (faithful). This is because eunuchs were faithful to their masters, who entrusted their wives and children, their secrets, and their important household affairs to them. Some of them held high offices in government [Acts 8:27]. It is said that Paul was a eunuch. Jesus spoke of different classes of eunuchs [Matt. 19:12].

Jeremiah was rescued from the dungeon by Ebed-meleck, the Ethiopian, a faithful eunuch who was employed in Zedekiah's palace [Jer. 38:7-13].

BLIND LEADERS

His watchmen are blind: they are all ignorant, they are all dumb dogs, they cannot bark; sleeping, lying down, loving to slumber.

Isa. 56:10

"Watchmen" in this instance means religious and political leaders, governors and rulers, who were entrusted with the welfare of the people.

These false prophets, princes, and leaders were blind and ignorant and dumb, like dogs who cannot bark and who lie down in the camp; that is, the leaders were indifferent. They did not care what happened to the people [Phil. 3:2].

Good leaders, like good shepherds, take good care of their people and watch over them like good dogs who protect the sheep and bark at strangers and beasts of prey who come near the fold.

Jesus called these leaders "blind leaders of the blind." He said, "And if the blind lead the blind, both shall fall into the ditch" [Matt. 15:14].

A FORGIVING GOD

For I will not contend for ever, neither will I be always wroth: for the spirit should fail before me, and the souls which I have made.

Isa. 57:16

The Eastern text reads: ". . . for the spirit proceeds from before me, and the breath, I have made it."

God's anger does not abide forever, for he is the author of the spirit and the breath of man. "God is a righteous judge; yea, he is not angry every day." Princes and judges were always angry with the people who displeased them or broke their words. But God is a loving and forgiving Father. He cannot hold the offenses of his children forever. Israel was to be healed and restored to her former glory. There was no other lord or god who was compassionate like the God of Israel [Mic. 7:18]. The reference here is to the true man, the spiritual man, who was created in the image and the likeness of God.

Israel had forsaken the way of God. The priests, false prophets, leaders, and judges were calling evil good, and good evil. Drunkenness and injustices prevailed in the land, which made God angry against his people [Isa. 5:20-25].

PEACE, PEACE

I create the fruit of the lips; Peace, peace to him that is far off, and to him that is near, saith the Lord; and I will heal him.

Isa. 57:19

"Peace" is a key word that is constantly used in daily conversation and which introduces two strangers to one another. Whenever two Easterners meet, they greet one another by saying, "Peace be unto you." And the greeting is returned by the same words, "To you be peace." When the magic words of peace are offered and received, the strangers become close neighbors, or even brothers. This greeting of peace establishes confidence and good relations between the two strangers.

The term *shallam* (peace) means, "I surrender to you." When two strangers surrender to one another, they surrender to God.

God had been wroth with Israel, but he was to return to them again and heal them and revive the heart of the contrite ones so that they could make peace with their God. Political and stubborn Israel was crushed. The spiritual Israel, or the remnant, was to be blessed so that they might bless the world.

A SINCERE FASTING

Behold, ye fast for strife and debate, and to smite with the fist of wickedness: ye shall not fast as ye do this day, to make your voice to be heard on high.

Isa. 58:4

There is considerable debate over the feasts and fasts. Written calendars were rare and in some towns unknown. Time was measured by means of shadows, sundials, and cocks. The elders and priests argued about the exact time of the observance and the way the fast should be observed. Especially on cloudy days, when the sun could not be seen, it was difficult to agree on the time.

Paul warned the Colossians relative to the observances [Col. 2:16-19]. Even today, during fasts and feasts, there is considerable vain talk concerning certain men and women who fast from everything. They are praised for their strict observance, while others are condemned for being lax on such occasions.

Jesus warned his disciples to abstain from such manner of fasting. He admonished them to fast secretly and not to appear sad so that men might know they were fasting, nor to blow a trumpet to let the whole town know that they were fasting. This is what the hypocrites did when they fasted.

Fasting is good when one fasts sincerely in order to weaken the physical forces within him so that he may strengthen his soul.

Fasting was introduced to help the poor and the needy, and to let those who had plenty understand the meaning of hunger and want.

KINDNESS TO PRISONERS

Then shalt thou call, and the Lord shall answer; thou shalt cry, and he shall say, Here I am. If thou take away from the midst of thee the yoke, the putting forth of the finger, and speaking vanity.
Isa. 58:9

In the Eastern text the latter part of this verse reads: "If you remove deceit from your midst and release the prisoners and cease speaking falsehood."

The Aramaic phrase *oteshrey lakhbishey* means "and release the prisoners," the defeated and conquered soldiers. In the East prisoners were kept in dungeons and bound in chains. Bread and water were given by measure. Indeed, death is better than life in a prison.

LORD'S HANDS ARE NOT SHORT

Behold, the Lord's hand is not shortened, that it cannot save; neither his ear heavy, that it cannot hear.   Isa. 59:1

In Semitic languages the Lord God is often pictured like a man with hands, feet, eyes, ears, and fingers. This is done in order to explain the attributes of God in a symbolic way. Easterners understand symbolic expressions much more than words. Then again, a symbol impresses itself on the mind, but words are easily forgotten. In other words, a spiritual idea is portrayed in physical or human terms.

"The Lord's hands are not shortened," is an Aramaic expression which means, "He is not helpless." One often hears people say, "This year my hands have been short," which means, "I have been in want." On the other hand, when a man is prosperous and generous, it is said, "His hands are stretched out," which means he distributes his wealth generously. In the East, when people pray to God, asking his blessings, they say, "Stretch out thy hand, O Lord God."

The Hebrews had gone after other gods, expecting better material re-wards. At times they saw their neighboring Gentiles, who worshiped pagan gods, more blessed with material things than themselves; therefore, they forsook their God and worshiped pagan idols. They forgot the Lord God of Israel who had fed their forefathers in the desert and supplied them with water in the dry places. Isaiah is upbraiding the people for having been unfaithful to the God of their forefathers and for seeking material prosperity from pagan gods.

CORRUPT RULERS

They hatch cockatrice' eggs, and weave the spider's web: he that eateth of their eggs dieth, and that which is crushed breaketh out into a viper.   Isa. 59:5

The prophet condemns corrupt officials, princes, and evildoers. They are likened to cockatrices and spiders. This is because their malicious works are like the poison of adders, and their evil devices with which they entrap the innocent are likened to the spider's webs.

The works of iniquity are dangerous both to those against whom they are devised and to those who devise them. The evildoers fail at the end and are caught in their own corrupt works.

THE TRUTH WAS HIDDEN

Yea, truth faileth; and he that departeth from evil maketh himself a prey: and the Lord saw it, and it displeased him that there was no judgment.   Isa. 59:15

The Eastern text reads: "Yea, truth is hid, and understanding has de-parted from our mind . . ."

The truth never fails, but at times it is hidden from the eyes of the wicked, or is covered so that the people may not know the difference.

The people during the time of Isaiah were in difficulties simply because the truth was hidden or buried in the cold sacrificial ashes. The princes and their false prophets had placed their trust in foreign alliances, and the priests had gone after Baal worship.

Had Israel known the truth, the truth would have made her free from her oppressors.

GOD'S HELP

And he saw that there was no man, and wondered that there was
no intercessor: therefore his arm brought salvation unto him; and
his righteousness, it sustained him.					Isa. 59:16

The Aramaic reads: ". . . and wondered that there was no one to
help . . ." The Aramaic word *adar* means "to give help, to succor" [Isa.
63:5].

"Arm" means strength and trust; that is, trust in God.

When Israel saw that she had no helper, she turned to God—her
strength in time of need and the everlasting arm of protection. ". . . his
right hand, and his holy arm, hath gotten him the victory" [Ps. 98:1].

DARKNESS—DISASTER

For, behold, the darkness shall cover the earth, and gross darkness
the people: but the Lord shall arise upon thee, and his glory shall be
seen upon thee.					Isa. 60:2

"Darkness" is symbolic of disaster, sorrow, and despair. When Eastern
poets eulogize dead kings and princes, they say, "The sun refused to give
its light" or "The sun became dark, and the moon failed to give its light."

Then again, darkness is used figuratively, meaning punishment and
hardship [Matt. 22:13; 2 Pet. 2:4].

Darkness also means ignorance and superstition. The ignorant and
ungodly grope in darkness like the blind [Deut. 28:29; Prov. 4:19].

The pagans were to suffer a calamity, but Israel would walk in God's
light. The glory of God would shine upon the people again. Difficulties,
sorrows, and suffering would be replaced with happiness, and poverty
with prosperity [verses 16-22].

LARGE ARMIES

So shall they fear the name of the Lord from the west, and his
glory from the rising of the sun. When the enemy shall come in like
a flood, the Spirit of the Lord shall lift up a standard against him.
					Isa. 59:19

This should read: "So shall they revere the name of the Lord from the
west, . . ."

"Floods" sometimes are used symbolically, meaning large armies which boasted of their power and numerical superiority. They marched upon the weak nations like a flood, destroying everything in their paths. Eastern prophets and poets pictured these invading armies as the surging waters of floods, sweeping everything before them.

In Psalm 93:3 we read: "The floods have lifted up their voice; the floods lift up their waves." The suffering caused by the invading armies of the oppressors would cause the people to turn to God for help and to revere his name as the King of kings. The messianic kingdom would embrace the people of the East as well as those of the West.

MILK—WEALTH

Thou shalt also suck the milk of the Gentiles, and shalt suck the breast of kings: and thou shalt know that I the Lord am thy Saviour and thy Redeemer, the Mighty One of Jacob.   Isa. 60:16

"Milk" is symbolic of wealth and God's blessings. Among the pastoral people a man's wealth is measured by the number of his sheep and goats, and by the large caldrons in which milk is boiled. The Hebrews and the nations that were around about them were all pastoral people whose medium of exchange was butter, cheese, sheep, and goats. The prophets spoke and wrote in the terms of speech which were common expressions and well understood by the simple folk. Today we speak of gold, silver, stocks, oil fields, and coal mines.

"The milk of the Gentiles" means the wealth of the Gentiles. The Jews who were carried away captive were to find favor in the eyes of the Gentile kings and princes. The Gentiles were to give precious gifts of silver and gold to the exiles who were to return to Palestine. All those who had suffered for their faith, but had remained loyal to their God, were to be reimbursed for their losses. They would return to Palestine with a new understanding of God. Milk is the purest and most natural food, and symbolic of God's truth.

In Eastern languages, when people offer lavish gifts and generous assistance to others, or are robbed of their goods, it is said, "They have been milked."

PERPETUAL SUN

Thy sun shall no more go down; neither shall thy moon withdraw itself: for the Lord shall be thine everlasting light, and the days of thy mourning shall be ended.   Isa. 60:20

In Aramaic symbolism the sun is symbolic of God. In the liturgical books of the Church of the East we read: "The Eternal Sun [meaning

God], let us give thanks and worship him, who is surrounded by the three *kenoney* (attributes)."

"Sun" is also used figuratively, meaning light of God, truth, and justice. When there is light there is understanding, justice, and happiness. "And it shall come to pass in that day, says the Lord, that I will cause the sun to go down at noon, and I will darken the earth in the daylight" [Amos 8:9, Eastern text]. Darkness symbolizes evil forces, ignorance, and injustices.

In the future the remnant of Israel was to be under the light of God. Violence, persecutions, and injustices were to come to an end, and justice and truth were to reign forever. These prophecies were to be fulfilled after the coming of the Messiah [Mal 4:2; Rev. 21:23].

CAPTIVES RELEASED

The Spirit of the Lord God is upon me; because the Lord hath anointed me to preach good tidings unto the meek; he hath sent me to bind up the broken-hearted, to proclaim liberty to the captives, and the opening of the prison to them that are bound.

Isa. 61:1

"Captive" refers to the men who were enslaved to the stereotyped doctrines and dogmas of Judaism, which had replaced the Word of God and the true meaning of the Scriptures with man-made theological concepts.

The messianic teachings of the Word of God, the new interpretation and the fulfillment of the law and prophecies, were to set the people free from bondage, fear, and condemnation, and to release those who were bound in chains of ignorance and superstition.

The prophet proclaims the liberty of the soul and mind, and not a political liberty. For the Messiah did not free the Jews from the political and oppressive power of the Gentiles.

Jesus read this passage at the synagogue in Nazareth [Luke 4:16-22]. Then he said to them: "Today this Scripture has been fulfilled in your ears [hearing]." The Eastern text adds the word "forgiveness," and it reads, ". . . to strengthen with forgiveness those who are bruised"; that is, liberty was to come through true repentance. The people must seek forgiveness for the evils which they had committed and which had led them into bondage.

The day of vengeance would take place after the gospel has been preached and false theological concepts eradicated. The evil works in the world would be condemned and exposed with the light of the gospel of Jesus Christ. When truth comes, falsehood disappears. Evil destroys itself.

THE ACCEPTABLE YEAR

*To proclaim the acceptable year of the Lord, and the day of
vengeance of our God; to comfort all that mourn.*   Isa. 61:2

"The acceptable year of the Lord" means the year which the Lord had
chosen for the day of vengeance and reckoning; and the day wherein to
comfort those who had suffered injustices and had mourned because of
the heavy burdens they had been bearing under the reign of the wicked
kings, princes, and priests. The mourners were to be comforted in that
day [Isa. 61:3; Matt. 5:4].

During the time of Moses and the Judges, the acceptable year was
known as the Year of the Jubilee, or the Year of Atonement and Redemption. It was the fiftieth year, when both the land and the people
rested. Slaves were freed and properties returned to their owners [Lev.
25:9-13].

The Year of the Jubilee was symbolic of the acceptable year of the
Lord wherein not only slaves were to be freed and fields returned to their
owners, but also all humanity was to be redeemed to God's plan of
salvation, which was to be wrought by the Messiah, Jesus Christ. It was
to be a new year and a new day not only for the Jews but also for the
Gentiles.

When Jesus read this portion of the Scriptures, he said, "The Spirit of
the Lord is upon me; because of this he has anointed me to preach good
tidings to the poor; and he has sent me to heal the brokenhearted, and
to proclaim release to the captives and sight to the blind; to strengthen
with forgiveness those who are bruised and to preach the acceptable
year of the Lord" [Luke 4:18-19, Eastern text].

Malachi foresaw also this day. He saw the destruction of the wicked
and the new and glorious day for the righteous [Mal. 4:1-3].

RAMS OF RIGHTEOUSNESS

*To appoint unto them that mourn in Zion, to give unto them
beauty for ashes, the oil of joy for mourning, the garment of praise
for the spirit of heaviness; that they might be called Trees of
righteousness, The planting of the Lord, that he might be glorified.*
                                                        Isa. 61:3

This verse should read: ". . . beauty instead of ashes, perfume instead
of mourning, a cloak of beauty instead of the spirit of heaviness; they

shall be called men of righteousness . . ." The term *dikhrey* means "male rams." Unblemished lambs, rams, and bullocks were offered as burnt offerings to cleanse the people of their sins.

Innocent and pious men are often called the lambs of God or the sacrifices offered to God. This is because the lambs, rams, and other animals that were offered were unblemished. Israel, after obtaining forgiveness, was to wear garments of glory and anoint herself with perfume, and rejoice in the presence of God, her Saviour.

GARMENTS OF SALVATION

I will greatly rejoice in the Lord, my soul shall be joyful in my God; for he hath clothed me with the garments of salvation, he hath covered me with the robe of righteousness, as a bridegroom decketh himself with ornaments, and as a bride adorneth herself with her jewels.   Isa. 61:10

"Garments of salvation" means good deeds; that is, the good works which will bring salvation. "Garment" here signifies beauty, joy, and good works. In olden days when people sinned they wore sackcloth and garments of repentance. There were also the garments of vengeance for those who had transgressed God's laws [Isa. 59:17].

In the other world the righteous will be clothed with their good works, white and unblemished clothes; and the wicked will be clothed with black garments of shame. Adam and Eve covered themselves and wore garments because they had transgressed the law. They found themselves naked and, therefore, were ashamed [Gen. 3:9-21].

LIGHT OF GOD

For Zion's sake will I not hold my peace, and for Jerusalem's sake I will not rest, until the righteousness thereof go forth as brightness, and the salvation thereof as a lamp that burneth.   Isa. 62:1

"Lamp that burneth" in this instance means an everlasting salvation. The lamps in the temple of God burned day and night, symbolizing God's presence in his holy place. When the temple was destroyed the lamp was put out.

"Lamp" is used figuratively for the light of God, justice, righteousness, and truth. Where there is light people never stumble, and there is peace and understanding. Jesus said, "I am the light of the world [John 9:5]. See the commentary on "Lamp," Psalm 119:105.

JUDAH HAD GONE ASTRAY

Thou shalt no more be termed Forsaken; neither shall thy land any more be termed Desolate: but thou shalt be called Hephzibah, and thy land Beulah: for the Lord delighteth in thee, and thy land shall be married. Isa. 62:4

Shabekta is a woman who has been forsaken or deserted by her husband, but not divorced. The Aramaic word for "divorced" is *sharitha;* that is, "one whose marriage bond is loosened."

The reference here is to the land of Judah, which, during the second capitvity in 586 B.C., was forsaken and had become desolate.

Judah was to be restored and Jerusalem rebuilt. The truth of God was to shine forth once more as a burning lamp.

The land was no more to be called desolate but God's delight, for the Lord was to be delighted in it. Moreover, the land was to be cultivated by husbandmen once more.

The Lord had not forsaken Judah; it was Judah who had forsaken him. God was to visit his people again and redeem their land.

RIDING ON AN ASS

Behold, the Lord hath proclaimed unto the end of the world, Say ye to the daughter of Zion, Behold, thy salvation cometh; behold, his reward is with him, and his work before him. Isa. 62:11

The Eastern text reads *Parokekh* (your Saviour). *Parokekh* has been confused with *porkanekh* (your salvation).

The reference here is to the Messiah, the Mighty Counselor and the Prince of Peace, who would gather the scattered people from the house of Israel [Isa. 11:11-16; 40:9-11].

Jesus quoted Zechariah when he said, "Tell the daughter of Zion, Behold your King is coming to you, meek, and riding upon an ass, upon a colt, the foal of an ass" [Matt. 21:5, Eastern text; also Zech. 9:9].

The ass is the most stupid and despised animal in the East. Jesus rode upon an ass as a token of his meekness and humility. In the East kings ride upon white horses.

See the commentary in *Gospel Light,* Matthew 21:5.

RED APPAREL

Who is this that cometh from Edom, with dyed garments from Bozrah? this that is glorious in his apparel, traveling in the greatness of his strength? I that speak in righteousness, mighty to save.
Wherefore art thou red in thine apparel, and thy garments like him that treadeth in the winevat? Isa. 63:1-2

In the East kings, princes, and the wealthy wear colorful garments with stripes. Kings generally are dressed with purple—a color between crimson and violet. Bozrah was noted for its crimson and other colorful apparel.

"Red" is symbolic of murder and bloodshed [Rev. 6:4]. In the East grapes are trodden under the feet of men. The grapes are placed in a large wooden container or wine press, then the treader removes his shoes and stockings and treads over them until all the juice is squeezed out of them.

As the treader moves in the large wine press, the red juices splash on his garments, so that all of his apparel is red. Easterners cannot take off their apparel and expose their bodies while treading grapes or doing other kinds of manual work.

Then again, one often hears people saying, "His hands or his clothes are red," which means he has shed blood.

The Lord is likened to a treader of grapes. He was to tread and trample the oppressors and the wicked in his fury. Their blood, like the juices of grapes which splash on the garments of the treader of the wine press, will splash upon his apparel [verse 6; also Lam. 1:15].

DRUNK WITH MY FURY

And I will tread down the people in mine anger, and make them drunk in my fury, and I will bring down their strength to the earth.
Isa. 63:6

"Made them drunk in my fury" means they are confused. Wine and strong drink create confusion and cause men to err. The people often say, "They are drunk with power," which means carried away with power.

The nations who helped the oppressors to destroy Judah were themselves to be destroyed and trampled under the feet of invading armies.

GOD DOES NOT AFFLICT

In all their affliction he was afflicted, and the Angel of his presence saved them: in his love and in his pity he redeemed them; and he bare them, and carried them all the days of old. Isa. 63:9

The Aramaic word *la* means "did not." The Eastern text reads: "In all their troubles he did not afflict them." That is to say, in all Israel's troubles, trials, and difficulties in the wilderness and in Palestine God did chastise them, but did not afflict them severely. Instead he sent his angel to comfort and save them.

The afflictions, trials, and difficulties were brought upon the people by their backsliding and disobedience to God's laws and ordinances.

At times God took action himself, and on some occasions he sent his angel [Exod. 23:20; 32:34]. God looked upon Israel as a man looks upon his family. In other words, God was the Father of the Hebrew tribes. Therefore he is portrayed as a loving Father, guiding them, caring for them, and disciplining them.

THE DAYS OF OLD

Then he remembered the days of old, Moses, and his people, saying, Where is he that brought them up out of the sea with the shepherd of his flock? where is he that put his Holy Spirit within him? Isa. 63:11

The Eastern text reads: "Then he remembered the days of old, of Moses his servant. Just as when he brought up out of the sea the shepherd of his flock, and as he put his holy Spirit within Moses."

The prophet here reminds the people how Israel had been unfaithful and backsliding, from the days of Moses when they murmured against the shepherd of the flock (Moses) and against the Lord; and how the Lord remembered the days of old and his servant, Moses, who was faithful to him during all his life, and how God forgave the people for his sake.

The reference to bringing them up out of the sea of course means the Lord helped them to cross the canal near the Bitter Lakes, when the Egyptian army pursued them. The Lord caused the sea to go back by a strong east wind all that night, and the tip of the Gulf of Suez was made dry. The Hebrews crossed, but when the Egyptian army tried to cross, the wind ceased and the waters rushed back, and the whole Egyptian army was drowned [Exod. 14:21-28].

The Lord saved Israel in a miraculous way by the hand of Moses, the shepherd, that is, the leader of Israel [Exod. 14:30].

See the commentary on Exodus 14:21.

LOOK DOWN FROM HEAVEN

Look down from heaven, and behold from the habitation of thy holiness and of thy glory: where is thy zeal and thy strength, the sounding of thy bowels and of thy mercies toward me? are they restrained?   Isa. 63:15

The ancients believed that the heaven was higher than the earth; therefore, they maintained that God's habitation is in heaven from whence he watches men.

In Aramaic and Hebrew the same word that means "heaven" also means "sky" and "the universe." God is everywhere. The term heaven means peace and harmony. In Aramaic, we often say, "This is heaven," which means, "We are living in peace and tranquillity."

This deistic concept of God was changed. The Lord God of Israel was everywhere. He was both in heaven and on the earth. There is no place where he is not, nowhere that a person can hide from his presence.

According to the teaching of Jesus Christ, God is everywhere. He is manifest in the whole universe. He can be worshiped not only in Samaria and Jerusalem, but also in any other place [John 4:21-25].

"The sounding of thy bowels" in the King James Version should read "thy tender mercies."

GOD AS A FATHER

But now, O Lord, thou art our Father; we are the clay, and thou our potter; and we all are the work of thy hand.   Isa. 64:8

Israel looked upon God as the Father of the Hebrew tribes. This is because God led and guided Abraham, Isaac, and Jacob as a father would lead and guide his children. He also protected them and met their needs as a loving father. Israel is called by God, his son, even his firstborn; that is, the first to whom God's truth was fully revealed [Exod. 4:22].

This was a spiritual rebirth, a new revelation to a world living in sin and darkness, and worshiping false deities. The sonship of Israel was attained by the grace of God, who had called them and revealed to them his truth.

But the true sonship was to be sealed through a new revelation and an everlasting covenant, which later was to be written by Jesus Christ.

Thus, the true sonship was to be attained through a new rebirth and complete victory over the evil forces [Gal. 4:2-8]. Today we are made the children of God by adoption through Jesus Christ, who is the firstborn [Eph. 1:5].

Man is like the clay in the hand of a potter. He cannot say, "Form me into this vessel or that vessel." God knows the heart of every man, and he selects them accordingly.

CAVES AND TOMBS

A people that provoketh me to anger continually to my face; that sacrificeth in gardens, and burneth incense upon altars of brick;
Which remain among the graves, and lodge in the monuments; which eat swine's flesh, and broth of abominable things is in their vessels.
                                                                                        Isa. 65:3-4

The Aramaic word *mearey* means "caves." Monuments have no place in which to lodge. This passage should read: ". . . who sit in tombs and lodge in caves."

In many parts of Palestine people still sit in tombs and dwell in caves. In some places one can see the outer portion of the cave covered with curtains made of the hair of goats. Some caves are large enough to accommodate a good-sized family.

Moreover, in the East people spend some time in the cemeteries holding meetings or loitering. And in some places cemeteries serve as public parks.

In Egypt during certain times of the year the living sleep and eat in tombs as a token of reunion with the dead. These places are known as "the cities of the dead." Some of the tombs in Cairo are large enough for several families.

The reference here is to the Israelites, who had forsaken their God and joined pagan cults, who ate swine meat, sacrificed in gardens, and slept in caves and tombs [Isa. 1:29].

GRAPES A BLESSING

Thus saith the Lord, As the new wine is found in the cluster, and one saith, Destroy it not; for a blessing is in it: so will I do for my servants' sake, that I may not destroy them all. Isa. 65:8

The Aramaic word *totita* means "a small portion of the cluster." There is no English equivalent to *totita*.

Totita is a very small cluster of mature but small grapes. The amount of grapes in the cluster is so small that often the husbandmen destroy them or leave them for the gleaners, hungry travelers, and the poor.

The prophet uses *totita* on the vine as an allegory, meaning "the remnant." Just as there is a blessing in the little cluster, the small cluster contains a small amount of new wine. And wine is symbolic of teaching, joy, and inspiration. So there was a blessing in the remnant of Israel. The true teaching and the messianic promises were preserved in the small cluster.

"Wine" in this instance means "grape juice." In the East grapes are eaten with bread as a meal. Some are made into raisins and stored for the winter. Only a small portion of the produce of the vineyard is made into wine.

Political Israel was destroyed, but the leaven, or the wine of God, was to be preserved until the law and the prophets were fulfilled.

The small remnant of Israel was to be a blessing to mankind. They were to carry on the torch and thus keep the light of God burning until the coming of the Messiah.

A NEW EARTH

For, behold, I create new heavens and a new earth: and the former shall not be remembered, nor come into mind. Isa. 65:17

"New heavens and a new earth" means a world full of justice and righteousness, a new order wherein the kingdom of God and Christ will have dominion over the kingdoms of this earth. In the East when peace and righteousness reign, and injustices are done away with, the people say, "This is the reign of God, the new earth."

The prophet in his vision sees a new Jerusalem established on justice, a city of rejoicing wherein the people will no longer remember the wars, the captivities, the trials, and the suffering which they had gone through in the past.

The new order, or a new concept of religion, was to be ushered in by the reign of the Messiah, the Prince of Peace. The old wine was to be forgotten. The truth was to replace sacrifices, ritualism, and all man-made doctrines and dogmas. The old religious order was to give way to the new. In the new order there would be no separation from God [Rev. 21:1]. The messianic kingdom would prepare the way for an everlasting kingdom, which will eradicate evil forces and herald the reign of God [2 Pet. 3:13].

Only God can create a new earth and a new order. Man has failed and will always fail until he turns to his Creator, who has power and dominion over all things.

A LONG SPAN OF LIFE

There shall be no more thence an infant of days, nor an old man that hath not filled his days: for the child shall die a hundred years old; but the sinner being a hundred years old shall be accursed.

                                                                Isa. 65:20

Child mortality is very high in the Near East, especially in lands where there is a scarcity of water and where sanitary conditions are poor. Six or seven children out of ten die in their infancy. In some areas only those who are strong survive; the others die before they reach the age of ten. Until World War II the population of the tribal people and the backward races remained static. Only the strong survived; the weak were eliminated.

The "old man" in this instance means a mature person, one who is thirty years and up. Hard work, poverty, and malaria and other climatic diseases cause the death of many mature men. Seventy years and up is considered an old age, when men and women are willing to leave this life.

In the new order a child will live until he is a hundred years old, and an old man will die full of days and years. The messianic teaching would improve the living conditions. Disease would be conquered and evil gradually eradicated. But the sinners, even though they may live to be a hundred years old, would be accursed; that is, they will suffer for the evil they have done. But the good will pass into life eternal without sickness and suffering.

The new heavens and the new earth will usher in an order of justice, freedom, peace, understanding, and prosperity. This is the fulfillment or the messianic kingdom.

WOLF AND LAMB

The wolf and the lamb shall feed together, and the lion shall eat straw like the bullock: and dust shall be the serpent's meat. They shall not hurt nor destroy in all my holy mountain, saith the Lord.

                                                                Isa. 65:25

"Wolf and lamb" are used allegorically, meaning an oppressor and a weak nation. The weak nations were devoured by the great and cruel nations, as wolves and lions devour helpless lambs.

"The lion" is symbolic of strength and viciousness. It is the most feared of the animal kingdom, and the lamb is the meekest. Lambs never resist their enemies.

"The lamb" here is Israel and "the wolf and lion" are the great powers which devoured her.

"The lion shall eat straw like the ox" means the great powers shall be humbled and satisfied with that which they have. In the messianic kingdom, the strong and the weak will live together in peace. The wise and the powerful no longer will plunder the weak.

THE HUMBLE

For all those things hath mine hand made, and all those things have been, saith the Lord: but to this man will I look, even to him that is poor and of a contrite spirit, and trembleth at my word.

Isa. 66:2

"Poor" in this instance means humble, poor in pride, meek and gentle —those whose minds are devoid of racial superiority and are willing to go the extra mile.

God was to reject the pride of the mighty men because they had failed in establishing justice and order. Humbleness, meekness, and gentleness were the new weapons whereby the world was to be transformed into the kingdom of God. The psalmist says that the Lord is near to them that are brokenhearted, and he saves those who are humble in spirit. (See the commentary on Matthew 5:3.)

Messiah was to introduce, for the first time, the weapons of the Spirit; that is, the Word of God, which would create a new heart and write a new covenant, not on stone tablets but upon human hearts. Such a change was to take place in the process of time and was to grow like a mustard seed.

SACRIFICES CONDEMNED

He that killeth an ox is as if he slew a man; he that sacrificeth a lamb, as if he cut off a dog's neck; he that offereth an oblation, as if he offered swine's blood; he that burneth incense, as if he blessed an idol. Yea, they have chosen their own ways, and their soul delighteth in their abominations.

Isa. 66:3

Hebrew prophets ate meat and participated in feasts and festivals where animals were sacrificed and eaten. Moreover, every Israelite had to eat the Passover meat [Num. 9:11-12].

Jesus and his disciples also observed the Passover and ate thereof on the Passover day [Matt. 26:19; Mark 14:12; Luke 22:7-8].

Nevertheless, some of the Hebrew prophets might have abstained from eating meat, just as the Nazarites abstained from drinking wine, as in the case of Samson [Judg. 13:14] and Jonadab, the son of Rechab [Jer. 35:5-6]. Moreover, ascetic life was an ancient custom. Many people, for one reason or another, abstained from eating meat or drinking wine and strong drink. Eating meat and drinking wine and strong drink was a part of pagan rituals, which existed centuries before Moses.

The prophet was so bitter in his attacks against the sacrificial system which had become so corrupt, that he denounced all sacrifices. This is because the sacrifices during the time of Isaiah had become an abomination to the Lord. The meat of lambs, rams, and bullocks was just like the meat of swine in his presence. The sacrifices were offered to God but were eaten by the priests and the people whose hearts were far away from God and his way. Moreover, at this time most of the people had gone astray after Baal. The meat they offered was as offensive to God as the meat of swine and dogs. What God wanted was justice and a sincere heart. God was not pleased with the smell of the broiled meat.

PROSPERITY

That ye may suck, and be satisfied with the breasts of her con-
solations; that ye may milk out, and be delighted with the abund-
ance of her glory.   Isa. 66:11

"Ye may suck" in this instance means, "You shall become rich and well nourished." Jerusalem is portrayed as a mother who gives suck to her child.

After the restoration of the remnant Jerusalem is to become a peaceful and prosperous city. The Gentiles will offer help to the Jewish exiles, and glory and wealth will pour out like a river.

CHAPTER TWENTY-ONE

JEREMIAH

INTRODUCTION

JEREMIAH, the son of Hilkiah, was another Hebrew prophet well versed in foreign policy during his day. Jeremiah was of the priests who dwelt in Anathoth, a town near Jerusalem. His father, Hilkiah, was a priest.

Jeremiah lived about 620 B.C., at a time when the whole Palestine area and surrounding countries were threatened by another imperial power—Babylon—a nation whose rise the Hebrew prophets had dreaded. Even though Jeremiah was called by God to admonish the people, the princes, the kings, and the statesmen, he was not a palace prophet. Neither did the princes and the leaders of the nation recognize him as a spokesman for God, and they did not heed his appeal to cancel the crooked alliances with Egypt and other pagan nations.

Jeremiah was too young and inexperienced to be taken seriously and to be acceptable as a court statesman and prophet. The palace was crowded with false prophets, ungodly leaders, and statesmen who had no faith in God. These men had recommended alliances with Egypt and other pagan nations. It was they who made the alliances and broke them. The prophets of God were seldom consulted. The nation was contaminated with the Baal worship; the holy temple was polluted with the pagan practices, and thus the Word of God was precious.

Jeremiah saw a great storm coming from the north. Babylonian armies were to march through Syria and Israel and to come southward against Jerusalem. But the more the impending invasion was delayed, the more Jeremiah became a laughingstock of the princes and the people. Everybody mocked him and derided him [Jer. 21:7]. The king and the princes relied on Egypt, and Assyria was still to be feared. Assyria, even though weakened by her Eastern enemies, was still in power until the fall of Nineveh in 612 B.C.

When Babylon began to fill the vacuum created by the fall of Assyria, she imposed her ascendency over all small kingdoms beyond the River

Euphrates. After all, Babylon was the heir of Assyria. Nevertheless, Jeremiah never doubted his mission, never changed his prophecy, and never denied what he had said. But he stood firm. He knew that Nineveh would fall and that the Chaldean armies were preparing to march or were on their way. He knew the Chaldeans would not permit Egypt to occupy the lands that were beyond the River Euphrates, especially Palestine and Syria.

Indeed, Jeremiah was an educated young priest, but, like most of the educated Eastern priests and learned men, he could not write well. He dictated his book to Baruch, a professional scribe and one of his faithful followers. Jeremiah, despite the Jewish alliance with Egypt, was so sure of the fall of Jerusalem that he let his book be read by the princes and by Jehoiachim, king of Judah, but the latter burned the scroll. The prophet then asked Baruch to write another scroll.

Jeremiah, like Isaiah, wrote several oracles against foreign nations who had aided Babylon in her conquest of Judah and the destruction of Jerusalem. He also prophesied against Babylon, Egypt, and other lands.

Jeremiah was in a dungeon for a long time, but when the city fell he was in prison in a courtyard. The prophet was accused as a Babylonian spy or sympathizer. He was released by the Chaldean army. For a while he stayed at Mizpah until he went with some of the rebellious people to Egypt. It is said that he was stoned in Egypt.

I AM A CHILD

Then said I, Ah, Lord God! behold, I cannot speak: for I am a child.
Jer. 1:6

"I am a child," is an Eastern idiom meaning, "I am too young" or "too inexperienced." Customarily, Easterners decline when appointed to go on a mission. They say, "I am a child; I am a sinner; I have no bread and clothing; or I am an unworthy man" [Isa. 6:5].

In the East *young* men seldom sit in council or admonish the people. They learn until they are of age. Not until a man is thirty can he sit in the council or give advice in political and religious matters. Easterners respect age and prefer the elders who are experienced men in such important matters. This is why we know nothing about Jesus from the time when he was brought into the temple at the age of twelve until he was thirty. During all of that time Jesus was working, studying, and listening, as all young men in the East do. Even though God speaks to young men, the elders doubt them and, at times, scorn them.

Jeremiah was twenty-four years old when God spoke to him. He had a clear vision of the downfall of Judah and the destruction of Jerusalem, but he knew that the religious leaders and false prophets who acted as statesmen would scorn him, call him a false prophet, and jeer at his prediction. In other words, Jeremiah was too young to be taken seriously.

Jeremiah, like Samuel, was ordained from the womb to prophesy against the great empires. God's Word was precious and the impending disaster was drawing near. On the other hand, all the palace prophets had gone astray after pagan worship.

ROD OF AN ALMOND

Moreover the word of the Lord came unto me, saying, Jeremiah, what seest thou? And I said, I see a rod of an almond tree.

Then said the Lord unto me, Thou hast well seen: for I will hasten my word to perform it.　Jer. 1:11-12

The prophet speaks in allegories. The rod is symbolic of punishment, discipline, and chastisement.

The almond tree signifies the speedy and harsh punishment that was to be inflicted upon Judah. Almond trees blossom before other trees, and they are heralds of spring. In Palestine they blossom in January, and the blossoms appear before the leaves. Then again, almond branches are used for rods.

Jeremiah was ridiculed as a prophet simply because Assyria was weakening and Babylon was not strong enough to challenge Egypt, the nation upon which Judah had put its trust.

But the prophet was sure of the speedy march of the Babylonian army, just as he was sure of the blossoming of an almond tree in the springtime.

SEETHING POT

And the word of the Lord came unto me the second time, saying, What seest thou? And I said, I see a seething pot; and the face thereof is toward the north.

Then the Lord said unto me, Out of the north an evil shall break forth upon all the inhabitants of the land.　Jer. 1:13-14

"Seething" is used symbolically to represent a great power ready to march. In Aramaic, when a person is powerful and prosperous, we say, "He is seething"; that is, He has too much power and wealth. Babylon now was ready, and its spirit of conquest was boiling like a caldron full of milk.

The prophet sees Babylon as a seething caldron ready to pour out its armies and its wrath upon Judah and Jerusalem. Just as Assyria had done to Israel, so Babylon was to do to Judah. Jerusalem was to be destroyed and the people carried away captive to Babylon. Now Assyria was gone and Babylon was mobilizing all her allies in the north who had helped her to crush Assyria.

SHADOW OF DEATH

Neither said they, Where is the Lord that brought us up out of the land of Egypt, that led us through the wilderness, through a land of deserts and of pits, through a land of drought, and of the shadow of death, through a land that no man passed through, and where no man dwelt?

Jer. 2:6

"Shadow of death" is an Eastern idiom meaning danger, anxiety, or sudden death. In the East when people travel in deep valleys that are infested with bandits they say, "They travel in the valley of the shadow of death." Often the bandits lurk in their ways. This is also true of the deserts and wastelands where water is scarce, and at times both the people and their herds perish from thirst.

The lives of the Hebrews who left Egypt were in constant danger, because of the lack of food and water and because of snakes, diseases, and other desert difficulties. They wandered for forty years, not knowing where to go until the mighty hand of God led them to the Promised Land [Ps. 23:4].

During the time of the prophet the people, like their forefathers, had forsaken the God of their forefathers and forgotten his wondrous works in the land of Egypt and the desert. Now they had put their trust in Egypt and in pagan idols. The prophet is upbraiding them for their unfaithfulness to their God. They were doing what their fathers had done before them.

PASTORS—LEADERS

The priests said not, Where is the Lord? and they that handle the law knew me not: the pastors also transgressed against me, and the prophets prophesied by Baal, and walked after things that do not profit.

Jer. 2:8

"Pastors" is another name for the shepherds, rulers, and leaders of the people. God also is called the Shepherd. "The Lord is my shepherd; I shall not want" [Ps. 23:1]. "Give ear, O Shepherd of Israel" [Ps. 80:1]. Jesus was known as the Good Shepherd because he laid down his life for his flock. The term *raawatha* (shepherds, rulers, leaders) is still in use among the Aramaic-speaking people.

The reference here is to the kings of Israel and their princes and counselors who had forsaken the Lord God of Israel and had caused their people to go astray like sheep without a shepherd. The prophet condemns the rulers, the priests, and the false prophets for teaching the people to worship gods which were *not* gods and for introducing the abominable Baal worship in the temple of God.

DISLOYALTY

Hath a nation changed their gods, which are yet no gods? but my people have changed their glory for that which doth not profit.
Jer. 2:11

The Gentiles who worshiped idols and images had been loyal to their false gods. They had not changed them for the gods of other nations.

The prophet upbraids the Israelites because they had changed their glory, the Living God of Israel, for pagan idols and high places which did not profit them. They had forsaken the fountain of the living waters and had gone after dry wells and broken cisterns [verse 13].

THE LIVING WATER

For my people have committed two evils; they have forsaken me the fountain of living waters, and hewed them out cisterns, broken cisterns, that can hold no water.
Jer. 2:13

"Living water" here means God, the Lifegiving Truth, the Fountain of life, the Well of salvation [Isa. 12:3]. "For with thee is the fountain of life: in thy light shall we see light [Ps. 36:9].

Both Israel and Judah had forsaken the Lord God, the fountain of the living water, and had searched for and found false religions which were like broken cisterns and dry wells, having nothing to offer to the weary and thirsty travelers.

In the East during wars and revolutions cisterns are broken and wells destroyed or poisoned [Eccles. 12:6].

Wells were scarce in Palestine and were owned by the tribes. Some wells in towns were held in common, others were the property of the wealthy landowners.

The prophets and the apostles were like wells of living water; that is, the true religion. And the dry wells were like a false religion which has nothing to offer to its adherents.

SHRINES ON HIGH PLACES

For of old time I have broken thy yoke, and burst thy bands; and thou saidst, I will not transgress; when upon every high hill and under every green tree thou wanderest, playing the harlot.

Jer. 2:20

Pagan idols were generally placed on high places so that the people might see them, make offerings to them, and pray before them. Moreover, shrines and the houses of idols were also erected upon high places and used for the immoral practices of Baal worship.

The Israelites again and again adopted Baal worship with its immoral practices, and forsook the true religion of their fathers. Even children were sacrificed to these abominable pagan gods. Baal worship with its immoral practices was the cause of the downfall of both Israel and Judah.

PERVERSE WAYS

How canst thou say, I am not polluted, I have not gone after Baalim? See thy way in the valley, know what thou hast done: thou art a swift dromedary traversing her ways.

Jer. 2:23

The last portion of the verse should read: ". . . you have lifted up your voice, O you perverse in her ways." The term "her ways" means "your corrupt practices" and refers to the worship of idols and to the child sacrifices offered in the Valley of Hinnom. Jerusalem had polluted herself by the worship of other gods besides the Lord.

Israel had tried all other gods. They had run after false prophets and false religions, forgetting the true God of their fathers. But now they were lifting up their voices, calling on the God of their fathers to save them from the impending disaster to come. But the city and its inhabitants had polluted themselves with the pagan practices, and their cries were in vain.

WILD ASS

A wild ass used to the wilderness, that snuffeth up the wind at her pleasure; in her occasion who can turn her away? all they that seek her will not weary themselves; in her month they shall find her.

Jer. 2:24

The prophet likens Judah to a wild ass which runs in the wilderness at its pleasure. These asses run in the direction of the wind and are fast. No one can catch them to turn them back.

Judah had gone after Baal worship and thus had polluted herself with the abominable pagan practices. Many prophets and men of God had tried to turn her back to her God, but they had not been able to catch up with her. The wind (the influence) of paganism had driven her away into the wilderness and led her into destruction. The wild asses can be traced only by their footprints. Judah was found only through her pagan practices, houses of idols, and altars on the high places [verse 23].

NO DISCIPLINE

In vain have I smitten your children; they received no correction: your own sword hath devoured your prophets, like a destroying lion.
Jer. 2:30

In the East children are beaten and at times severely punished as a means of discipline. "He who spares his rod hates his son; but he who loves his son disciplines him diligently" [Prov. 13:24]. "Chasten your son while there is hope, and let not your soul share his dishonor" [Prov. 19:18].

The Lord had chastised Israel, but in vain. Even the prophets whom he had sent to guide them were slain with the sword. Nearly all great Hebrew prophets who admonished the people to remain loyal to the way of their God were persecuted or even slain by the orders of the kings and priests who had gone astray from the way of God. And now discipline was in vain. Judah was to meet a fate like Israel's, and Jerusalem was doomed.

A FORGIVING GOD

They say, If a man put away his wife, and she go from him, and become another man's, shall he return unto her again? Shall not that land be greatly polluted? but thou hast played the harlot with many lovers; yet return again to me, saith the Lord. Jer. 3:1

In the olden days when a woman was divorced it was unlawful for her husband to take her back again. This law was enacted by Moses in order to warn the people against divorcing their wives hastily for minor offenses, jealousy, and anger [Deut. 24:1-4].

Prior to the Mosaic law, women's status was inferior to that of men. Women were purchased for a price, and their husbands put them away at any time they pleased. The price of a virgin was twice the price of a widow. Some men did not even trouble themselves to obtain written divorces, and some of them married women who had been deserted but not divorced.

Jesus also admonished his followers against easy and unjust desertions and divorces [Matt. 5:31-32].

The prophet portrays Judah as the unfaithful wife of God, who had deserted him and played the harlot with pagan gods. Instead of trusting in God, Judah had made alliances now with Assyria, now with Egypt, and now with other pagan nations, thus relying on the arm of man. Notwithstanding that, both Assyria and Egypt had coveted the gold of Judah, and the precious vessels which were in the temple were a menace to her.

These treacherous alliances weakened the faith of the people in the God of Israel and encouraged them to worship pagan idols. Thus, the land was defiled by human sacrifices and other corrupt pagan practices [Jer. 3:8].

SHAMELESS LIKE A WHORE

Therefore the showers have been withholden, and there hath been no latter rain; and thou hadst a whore's forehead, thou refusedst to be ashamed.

Jer. 3:3

"Whore's forehead" is an Eastern idiom common in many languages; it refers to a woman who is shameless. In the East harlots are considered women with no integrity or self-respect, because they approach men and try to entice them. They also sit along the highways [Gen. 38:14]. The harlots walk with their foreheads up, but good women are shy, and they look down when they see men [verse 2].

The harlot in this instance is Judah, who had deserted the Lord God of Israel and made alliances with foreign kings. The Hebrew prophets always used allegories in order to convey their messages or oracles to the simple people. Judah had been bold in making dangerous alliances with pagan powers.

PLAYED THE HARLOT

The Lord said also unto me in the days of Josiah the king, Hast thou seen that which backsliding Israel hath done? she is gone up upon every high mountain and under every green tree, and there hath played the harlot.

And I said after she had done all these things, Turn thou unto me. But she returned not. And her treacherous sister Judah saw it.

And I saw, when for all the causes whereby backsliding Israel committed adultery, I had put her away, and given her a bill of divorce; yet her treacherous sister Judah feared not, but went and played the harlot also.

Jer. 3:6-8

"Played the harlot" means "worshiped strange gods." Most of the pagan shrines were built on hilltops, mountains, and other high places.

Moreover, some of the altars were erected under sacred green trees [Jer. 2:20].

Both Israel and Judah, metaphorically, are the wives of God, but they had been unfaithful to him, and had played the harlot with pagan gods. And after Israel refused to repent and return, God put her away and gave her a bill of divorce, hoping that her sister, Judah, might learn a lesson from Israel.

Thus, Judah's condemnation was greater. Divorce was allowed in the Mosaic law. Jesus made adultery and incompetency the only causes for divorce [Deut. 24:1-4; Matt. 5:31-32; 19:9-12; Mark 10:11-12].

A WOMAN'S LOVER

Surely as a wife treacherously departeth from her husband, so have ye dealt treacherously with me, O house of Israel, saith the Lord.

A voice was heard upon the high places, weeping and supplications of the children of Israel: For they have perverted their way and they have forgotten the Lord their God.   Jer. 3:20-21

The Aramaic word *khabrah* (her lover) has been confused in the King James Version with the Aramaic word *gabrah* (her husband). The two words are very similar, especially when the letter *kheth* is at the beginning of a word.

The prophet here is referring to a woman who lies to her husband about her lover. Israel had lied to God. Israel had pretended that the alliances with pagan nations were a necessity to strengthen the state, and that the worship of Baal would bring prosperity to the nation. The kings and the false prophets had been unfaithful to God and had lied against him.

I HAVE DECEIVED

Then said I, Ah, Lord God! surely thou hast greatly deceived this people and Jerusalem, saying, Ye shall have peace; whereas the sword reacheth unto the soul.   Jer. 4:10

The Eastern text reads: ". . . I have greatly deceived this people and Jerusalem." The Aramaic word *ataeth* with a dot under the "t" means, "I have deceived," but with a dot over the "t" would read, "Thou hast deceived." Thus, the pronoun of many verbs is determined by the position of the dot.

The translators into Western languages were misled by the dot for one reason or another. Probably the manuscript was defective, as many of them are. On the other hand, centuries ago dots were not used as frequently as they are used today; the scribe simply took it for granted that the reader would understand the pronoun. He assumed that no one would think that God would deceive the people and Jerusalem.

Jeremiah for some time had been preaching peace, but now to his great surprise he found that there was no peace and that war was at hand.

Jeremiah, like many other prophets, was not aware of the impending danger of war between Egypt and Babylon. But when the danger was near, the Lord spoke to him and told him to warn the nation and the king that the war was imminent.

Jeremiah never could have stated that the Lord had deceived the people and Jerusalem. Jeremiah was a faithful prophet of God and, in delivering this message to the nation and the king, he acted as a spokesman for God. On the other hand, no true prophet of God would ever think that God would deceive the people, and he would never doubt the faithfulness of God. But the prophet was humble enough to confess his fault for having said there would be no war. Many of the world's statesmen thought there would be no Second World War. They doubted that Germany would dare to start another war. But when Germany did declare war against Poland, the wise men of Europe had to confess their mistakes.

THE EARTH WITHOUT FORM

I beheld the earth, and, lo, it was without form, and void; and the heavens, and they had no light.

I beheld the mountains, and, lo, they trembled, and all the hills moved lightly.

I beheld, and, lo, there was no man, and all the birds of the heavens were fled.

I beheld, and, lo, the fruitful place was a wilderness, and all the cities thereof were broken down at the presence of the Lord, and by his fierce anger.   Jer. 4:23-26

The prophet here depicts a dark picture of the impending disasters which were to befall the nations. Easterners believe that the universe shares in man's victories, as well as in his defeats and tragedies.

In the olden days, when everything went well and the Israelites triumphed over their enemies, men would say the earth rejoiced, the mountains danced, and the hills skipped like the lambs. In the book of Judges we are told how the universe assisted the Israelites in the battle against the Canaanites. "The stars fought from their courses; they fought from heaven against Sisera by the river Kishon" [Judg. 5:20, Eastern text]. The sun was stayed by Joshua [Josh. 10:12]. And it was brought backward as a sign for King Hezekiah [2 Kings 20:11].

But during times of disaster men would say the sun turns black and the stars and moon refuse to give their light. It is said that the sun was darkened at the death of Alexander the Great and at the crucifixion of Jesus.

The reference here is to all the lands west of the River Euphrates, including Judah and its capitol city, Jerusalem. The lands were to be overrun by the Chaldean Army. The historic city and the temple were to be destroyed. The whole universe would mourn the fall of the holy city and the temple [verse 28].

HARLOTS' HOUSES

How shall I pardon thee for this? thy children have forsaken me, and sworn by them that are no gods: when I had fed them to the full, they then committed adultery, and assembled themselves by troops in the harlots' houses.   Jer. 5:7

The Aramaic word *ethkatasho* (they fought) has been confused with *ethkanosho* (they assembled themselves) in the King James Version. It should read: ". . . and they fought one another in the harlots' houses."

The prophet here condemns the leaders of the people for their disloyalty to the God of their fathers and for the injustices which they had committed [verse 1]. The princes and the prophets had gone astray. Some of them fought in harlots' houses over the wine and harlots. In the East, drinking places and harlots' houses are dangerous meeting places.

During the reigns of wicked kings in Judah immorality was prevalent. The priests and the prophets not only were lax in enforcing the Mosaic law but they themselves had joined pagan esoteric rites and were frequent visitors in brothels or harlots' houses.

WHIRLWIND

And the prophets shall become wind, and the word is not in them: thus shall it be done unto them.   Jer. 5:13

The Aramaic word *alaala* (whirlwind) means "confused, empty, or meaningless." This is because the whirlwind makes noise and creates disturbances.

The prophets of Israel were to prophesy and see visions, but their words were to have no meaning. They were to create confusion among the bewildered people. The Lord would take wisdom and understanding away from them and they would err in their prophesies, for most of the prophets during this period were prophesying falsehoods in order to please the princes and the king. Jeremiah was warning the nations to beware of the false prophets and seers whose prophecies were to bring calamities upon the nation.

A CAGE

As a cage is full of birds, so are their houses full of deceit: therefore they are become great, and waxen rich.   Jer. 5:27

In the East, where shotguns were unknown, birds and other game were snared or trapped by a wooden trap [Isa. 42:22]. The birds then are placed alive in cages and taken to the market place to be sold.

Snares, traps, and pits are used symbolically, meaning crookedness and injustice. The fatherless, the meek, and the widows were trapped like innocent birds, and their properties confiscated. Deceitful ordinances were enacted and false witnesses hired to oppress the poor, the weak, and the fatherless, and compel them to give up their properties, as in the case of Naboth [1 Kings 21:1-13; Jer. 5:28].

FALSE PROPHESIES

The prophets prophesy falsely, and the priests bear rule by their means; and my people love to have it so: and what will ye do in the end thereof?   Jer. 5:31

"The priests bear rule by their means" signifies the priests upheld or supported the false visions which the false prophets saw. In other words, the priests and the prophets had conspired against the people. The prophets prophesied soothing prophecies of peace and prosperity and caused the people to go astray after pagan gods, and the rebellious priests defrauded them. Since the days of the prophet Isaiah, the kings of Judah and their princes, prophets, and priests had put their trust in pagan kings and had turned to pagan gods for help. As a result, the Jewish ethic was weakened by wine, strong drink, and immoral practices.

Isaiah said that both the priests and the prophets had erred through wine and strong drink so that they stumbled in judgment [Isa. 28:7].

DAUGHTER OF ZION

I have likened the daughter of Zion to a comely and delicate woman.   Jer. 6:2

"Daughter of Zion" means "Jerusalem, the beautiful city of God." Jerusalem is built on Mount Zion. Cities are often called daughters or virgins.

Jerusalem was admired for her beauty as a beautiful and comely virgin is admired in the East. But Jerusalem was to be invaded and destroyed by foreign armies which were to come from the north and encamp round about her.

This prophecy was fulfilled when Nebuchadnezzar, the king of Babylon, came with his great army against Jerusalem. The beautiful city was turned into ruins and the holy temple was destroyed [2 Kings 25:1-9].

ARMY COMMANDERS

The shepherds with their flocks shall come unto her; they shall pitch their tents against her round about; they shall feed every one in his place. **Jer. 6:3**

"Shepherds" in this instance is used allegorically, meaning kings, princes, and generals. "Flocks" means armies.

The reference to shepherds and flocks is used here in order that the people may grasp the imminent danger. They knew that when cities were destroyed the shepherds made sheepfolds of the ruins for their flocks. Then again, the armies, like shepherds and their camps, dwelt in tents round about the besieged cities. Jerusalem was to be besieged, captured, and destroyed by the Chaldean army [2 Kings 25:1; Jer. 6:4].

WATCHMEN

Also I set watchmen over you, saying, Hearken to the sound of the trumpet. But they said, We will not hearken. **Jer. 6:17**

"Watchmen" often symbolizes "prophets." "Son of man, I have made you a watchman to the house of Israel . . ." [Ezek. 3:17, Eastern text]. "Your watchman shall lift up their voices . . . for they shall see eye to eye, when the Lord shall bring again Zion" [Isa. 52:8, Eastern text].

Moreover, rulers and prophets are also looked upon as watchmen. This is because they watch and care for their people just as shepherds watch and care for their flocks [Jer. 6:3].

God always sent prophets in advance to warn the people of the impending disasters which their own evil works were bringing upon them. But they refused to repent and turn away from their evil ways.

FALSIFICATION

How do ye say, We are wise, and the law of the Lord is with us?
Lo, certainly in vain made he it; the pen of the scribes is in vain.

Jer. 8:8

The latter half of this verse in the Eastern text reads: "Lo, surely the lying pen of the scribes has made it for falsehood."

The reference here is to the falsifications which were wrought by the pen of disloyal scribes and false prophets who tried to interpret the word of the law to suit their own prophecies and foreign policies. The change of a dot or a letter could alter the meaning of the whole sentence.

The unfaithful scribes at times forged words and wrote false comments on the law. Jesus questioned some of the portions of the law, especially the unjust divorce. "He said to them, Moses, considering the hardness of your hearts, gave you permission to divorce your wives; but from the beginning it was not so" [Matt. 19:8, Eastern text].

I AM BLACK

For the hurt of the daughter of my people am I hurt; I am black;
astonishment hath taken hold on me. Jer. 8:21

The Aramaic word *ethkamreth*, derived from *kemar* (sorrowful, gloomy, dark) is here used metaphorically, meaning sorrowful, sad, or mourning. Black is symbolic of mourning. Also, when a person is embarrassed or dismayed it is said his face has turned black. In English we say his face has turned red. "All faces shall be dismayed and confounded" [Joel 2:6, Eastern text].

The reference here is to the conquest of Judah and the destruction of Jerusalem, which was the symbol of the national glory [Jer. 9:1].

PURIFY THEM

Therefore thus saith the Lord of hosts, Behold, I will melt them,
and try them; for how shall I do for the daughter of my people?

Jer. 9:7

The Aramaic word *sarap* means "to assay, examine, test" and thus "to refine." Isaiah says: "And I will turn my hand against you, and purge away your rebellious men, and remove all your iniquities" [Isa. 1:25, Eastern text].

The daughter of Zion had been deceitful in her dealings with her God. She had become like silver that is covered with dross. Therefore, Judah and Jerusalem were to be purged of their sins. The city and towns were to be made desolate and without inhabitants. The houses of idols and the altars on the high places were to be destroyed. The nation was to be invaded, uprooted, and carried away captive to Babylon.

Some of the wicked men who had transgressed the law of God were to perish by the sword, some by famine, and others were to be carried away captive to Babylon. The land was to be bereaved of its inhabitants. The Lord was to avenge himself of them [verse 9]. But after the purge the remnant was to return again to the land of Israel.

WORMWOOD

Therefore thus saith the Lord of hosts, the God of Israel; Behold, I will feed them, even this people, with wormwood, and give them water of gall to drink. Jer. 9:15

During famine and siege the hungry people eat grass and bitter plants, and drink stagnant water. During severe droughts or disasters caused by locusts even the bark of trees is eaten.

Wormwood is noted for its bitterness. It tastes like hemlock. Wormwood is often used metaphorically to mean affliction, mourning, and sorrow. In the olden days, wormwood was mixed with wine and, like hemlock, was given to condemned men.

When Easterners suffer a calamity or mourn over the dead they say, "I have drunk *merary* (bitterness)" [Deut. 29:18]. In the book of Lamentations Jeremiah says: "He has filled me with bitterness, he has made me drunken with wormwood" [Lam. 3:15, Eastern text].

Judah was to drink of the bitter cup which Babylon held in her hand, the cup which made the nations drunk with bitterness and sorrow. Judah, like Israel, was to be conquered and destroyed and the people carried captive to Babylon [verses 16, 17].

GODS OF THE GENTILES

For the customs of the people are vain: for one cutteth a tree out of the forest, the work of the hands of the workman, with the axe. Jer. 10:3

The Aramaic word *dighlatha* is "an object of worship," generally used for a false god, an idol. The root is *dekhal* (to revere, fear, worship).

Dikhlatha were images of false gods which the Gentiles made from wood and covered with silver and gold. Then they bowed down to them and worshiped them as gods.

"For the gods of the Gentiles are nothing; they are cut from a tree in the forest, the work of the hands of a carpenter, things made with a plane. They are decked with silver and with gold; men fasten them with hammers and nails, so that they may not fall apart" [Jer. 10:3-4, Eastern text].

These false gods which were made by human hands could not be compared with the Lord God of Israel, the Creator of heaven and earth.

GODS

Thus shall ye say unto them, The gods that have not made the heavens and the earth, even they shall perish from the earth, and from under these heavens. Jer. 10:11

Dighlatha (gods) also means images or idols, and other pagan objects of worship.

The pagans worshiped men and man-made gods, which were no gods and could not create anything. Moreover, all pagan deities were helpless. They had to be borne upon the shoulders of men and fastened tightly in the temples so that the people could not steal them.

All these pagan deities were to be destroyed, says Jeremiah. All the pagan altars and shrines in Judea were burned or destroyed by the Chaldean army [verses 3, 4].

TABERNACLE SPOILED

Woe is me for my hurt! my wound is grievous: but I said, Truly this is a grief, and I must bear it.

My tabernacle is spoiled, and all my cords are broken: my children are gone forth of me, and they are not: there is none to stretch forth my tent any more, and to set up my curtains. Jer. 10:19-20

The prophet here is speaking collectively. The tabernacle is symbolic of the kingdom of Judah, which is soon to be overthrown by the Babylon army, and the people carried away captive. This is a grievous wound which cannot be healed.

The tabernacle is dismantled; that is, the reign of the Kingdom of David is over. The cords are broken; that is, all the sacred bands which united the Jews are temporarily broken, and the people are taken captive.

Then again, the tabernacle is symbolic of the earthly habitation. When a family, a tribe, or a kingdom rises to power it is said, "The tabernacle

has been raised," and when they are destroyed, it is said, "The tabernacle
has been dismantled."

Now there was no one to pitch the heavy tent and to set up the curtains. The king, the princes, the nobles, and the artisans were all to be
carried to Babylon. The prophets and the priests were to die in the
captivity. Judah and Jerusalem were to be bereaved [verse 22].

A REPORT

Behold, the noise of the bruit is come, and a great commotion
out of the north country, to make the cities of Judah desolate,
and a den of dragons. Jer. 10:22

The Eastern text reads: "Behold, the noise of the report is come . . ."
The reference is to the news, the rumor, which was to come from the
north. For some time there was fear of an invasion from the north country. Some people believe that this invasion was to come from the countries north of Assyria, probably the Cythians, who had helped the king
of Babylon to overthrow Assyria. But Jeremiah meant the Chaldean
army. All these invasions came from the north through Syria and
Lebanon. The Chaldean armies marched northward through Assyria and
crossed the Euphrates north of Syria. Because of the scarcity of water
and desolate terrain, the army could not have taken the short southern
route.

The news of the invasion had already reached Palestine, but it took
a long time before the king of Babylon was ready to march. In those days
it took years to prepare for a great invasion. There were many military
problems to be worked out before the army could march, such as
arrangements for transport, food, water, and military organization. Sometimes it took several years to prepare. The delay of this invasion made
the princes and the king of Judah discount Jeremiah's prophecy.

THE WAYS OF THE LORD

O Lord, I know that the way of man is not in himself: it is not in
man that walketh to direct his steps. Jer. 10:23

The Eastern text reads: "I know that the ways of the Lord are not
like the ways of men; he does not walk as a man directing his steps."

The prophet warns of the impending catastrophe which was to come
from the north, a disaster that would lay Judah waste. Many of the
prophets, princes, and statesmen who were closer to the palace had

scorned this prophecy. They could not see how God could permit such a great disaster to fall upon his people, and how he could break his divine promises.

The prophet warns that the Lord's ways of doing things are not like those of men; that is, the Lord sees things differently and not as a man who seeks counsel from the wise men and is interested in his personal advantage. In other words, the Lord does not operate as men do. Therefore, one has to understand his way and his long suffering.

DEVOURED JACOB

Pour out thy fury upon the heathen that know thee not, and upon the families that call not on thy name: for they have eaten up Jacob, and devoured him, and consumed him, and have made his habitation desolate.   Jer. 10:25

"Eaten up Jacob" is an Eastern idiom which means they have "oppressed" or "devoured" him. In the East when high tributes and taxes are taken from the people by the rulers it is said, "They have eaten them." And when money is misappropriated or embezzled it is said, "They have eaten the money." Jesus condemned the Pharisees for embezzling the property of the widows. [Matt. 23:13.]

The Gentile nations had oppressed both Israel and Judah. They had imposed high taxes and tributes on the people, and now they were conquering the land and destroying all that was dear to Jacob.

MESSENGERS IN ADVANCE

For I earnestly protested unto your fathers in the day that I brought them up out of the land of Egypt, even unto this day, rising early and protesting, saying, Obey my voice.   Jer. 11:7

The Aramaic words *kadmeth o-shadreth* are mistranslated "rising early" in the King James Version. The Eastern text reads: ". . . I sent messengers in advance, warning them, saying, Obey my voice." God neither slumbers nor sleeps, and one could therefore not speak of him as "rising early" in the morning.

God always warns people in visions and in dreams of impending disasters which are to befall them.

All of the Hebrew prophets were God's messengers sent to admonish the people to turn away from their evil ways. Some heeded his messengers, and other did not [Jer. 25:3-4].

IMMORAL WORSHIP

What hath my beloved to do in mine house, seeing she hath wrought lewdness with many, and the holy flesh is passed from thee? when thou doest evil, then thou rejoicest. Jer. 11:15

It was during the time of the prophet Jeremiah that the holy temple was polluted by wicked princes and kings of Judah, who made alliances with pagan nations and introduced the immoral Baal worship into the holy temple in Jerusalem. Both harlots and sodomites committed immoral acts in their pagan ritual in the temple [Isa. 43:28; Ezek. 16:25]. This happened especially during the reigns of Amon and Manasseh. Josiah cleansed the temple and burned the sodomites and harlots.

Because of these evil practices the sacrificial meat on which the priests depended for their livelihood was soon to be taken away. This prophecy signifies the destruction of the temple and the end of the sacrifices which took place during the lifetime of Jeremiah, when the temple was destroyed by the Chaldean army while the prophet was in prison in Jerusalem.

WINESKINS

Therefore thou shalt speak unto them this word; Thus saith the Lord God of Israel, Every bottle shall be filled with wine: and they shall say unto thee, Do we not certainly know that every bottle shall be filled with wine? Jer. 13:12

The Aramaic word *grab* means "wineskin." In the Near East, until recent days, glass bottles and tin containers were unknown. Wine, milk, and oil were transported in goatskins. "Neither do they pour new wine into worn-out skins so as to rend the skins and spill the wine, . . ." [Matt. 9:17, Eastern text].

"Every wineskin shall be filled with wine" is an Eastern idiom which means that in every battle the people would be drunk with hatred, which leads to excessive slaughter.

"Wine" in this case is symbolic of drunkenness and confusion. When people are drunk they do not know what they are doing. Both terms, "wine" and "drunkenness" [verse 13], are used metaphorically, meaning "hatred and confusion." The priests, the prophets, and the kings of

Judah would be drunk, like men who drink wine and strong drink before they are put to death. Judah was to drink from the bitter cup, as Israel did, and then go into captivity.

DRUNKENNESS

Then shalt thou say unto them, Thus saith the Lord, Behold, I will fill all the inhabitants of this land, even the kings that sit upon David's throne, and the priests, and the prophets, and all the inhabitants of Jerusalem, with drunkenness. Jer. 13:13

"Drunkenness" here means a state of lethargy or insensibility. When men are drunken with wine or strong drink they are in a state of stupor.

The kings, princes, priests, prophets, and all the inhabitants of the land were to lose their sensibility and wander as a drunken man. They were already drunk with power, false worship, and worldly aspirations. "They are drunk, but not with wine," says Isaiah. They were drunk with pagan teaching and immoral Baal practices.

Judah, like Israel, had refused divine guidance in her foreign policy and had gone after foreign gods and made foreign alliances. Both the people and the kings had lost their vision and were groping in darkness.

NAKEDNESS

Therefore will I discover thy skirts upon thy face, that thy shame may appear. Jer. 13:26

This should read: "Therefore I also will cause your skirts to be uncovered and lifted over your face . . ." "I will cause your skirts to be uncovered" is an Eastern saying which means, "I will humble you by causing you to be defeated by your enemies." These terms of speech are common in daily conversation, especially when people are quarreling or fighting.

In the East, until World War I, most of the women covered their faces, as well as all other parts of their bodies. To uncover a woman's legs or arms was an offense. Women were disgraced when their legs were seen. This custom still prevails in many Moselm lands.

Judah and Jerusalem were to be humiliated as a woman who is violated by an enemy, exposed to shame, and humbled in the eyes of her neighbors. Judah was to be defeated and destroyed by the same people in whom she had put her trust, the Chaldeans, her lovers (her allies) [Jer. 13:22; Hos. 2:10].

DEARTH OF WATER

Judah mourneth, and the gates thereof languish; they are black unto the ground; and the cry of Jerusalem is gone up. Jer. 14:2

Palestine is noted for the shortage of water. There are times when no rain falls for two or three years, and both men and beasts suffer because of the lack of water, grass, and food. Abraham went to Egypt because of a famine, which was caused by the lack of rain [Gen. 12:10]. Isaac, likewise, went to Philistia because there was a famine in Palestine [Gen. 26:1].

The Eastern text of this verse reads: ". . . they are fallen on the ground, . . ." This phrase should not be taken literally. "Fallen on the ground" means that the people are mourning because there are few men and women going forth and coming in. In the East we often say, "May your house burn" or be in ruins, or, "May your door fall."

The gates of Jerusalem were empty. The people were too hungry and thirsty to leave their houses and walk to the gates. When Jerusalem was besieged by the Chaldean army, both bread and water were rationed. The people, because of their unfaithfulness to their God and his law, had brought these calamities upon themselves. Drought and famine were blamed on the sins and the wickedness of the people [1 Kings 17:1-16].

JUDAH WAS DOOMED

Then said the Lord unto me, Though Moses and Samuel stood before me, yet my mind could not be toward this people: cast them out of my sight, and let them go forth. Jer. 15:1

"Stood before me" in this case means "interceded for the people before me." In the East ministers of state, princes, and noblemen never sit down in the presence of kings unless they are asked to do so. They stand on their feet when they make a petition or appeal to the ruler on behalf of the people.

Judah was led astray by false prophets who predicted a brighter future and assured the people that they should never see the sword. The rebellious people had built altars on high places and sacrificed their children to the idols. Therefore, if even such prophets as Moses and Samuel, two of the greatest Hebrew prophets, stood before the Lord and implored him and appealed to him, he would not spare the people unless they returned from their evil ways.

NOT TO BE SPARED

*Thou hast forsaken me, saith the Lord, thou art gone backward:
therefore will I stretch out my hand against thee, and destroy thee;
I am weary with repenting.*   Jer. 15:6

Eshbok, derived from *shabak* (to keep, spare, allow, leave) in this
instance means "to spare."

"I am weary with repenting" is a mistranslation. Instead this phrase
should read: ". . . and I shall not spare you again."

Israel and Judah were to be scattered throughout the lands [Jer. 15:7;
16:13].

A DIFFICULT MISSION

*Woe is me, my mother, that thou hast borne me a man of strife
and a man of contention to the whole earth! I have neither lent on
usury, nor men have lent to me on usury; yet every one of them
doth curse me.*   Jer. 15:10

The Eastern text reads: "Woe is me, my mother, that you have borne
me a judge, a rebuker to the whole earth. I am neither a debtor, nor a
creditor; yet all of them curse me."

The Aramaic word *dayan* (a judge) has been confused with *dina*
(judgment); hence the mistaken idea of strife between two parties.

The prophet is complaining here that he was born to become a judge
and a rebuker of princes and prophets who had been the cause of the
downfall of Judah, those who were urging the king to rely on pagan
alliances. The prophet's burden was so heavy and his task so difficult
that he says, "Woe is me." He wonders why God had placed such a heavy
burden upon him. All the princes and the court prophets had put their
trust in Egypt.

In the East moneylenders often charge exorbitant interest; therefore
they are hated and are often cursed. The men who fail to pay their debts
are likewise despised and cursed by the moneylenders.

Jeremiah was hated and cursed simply because he was against his
government's foreign policy. He had warned Judah against making alliances with pagan nations and putting her trust in Egypt.

A HARSH RULER

Shall iron break the northern iron and the steel?   Jer. 15:12

The Eastern text reads: "For he is hard as iron and as brass."

The reference here is to the enemy from the north; that is, the Chaldean army which was to march from the north through Syria.

The Aramaic word *dakshey* means "rough, severe, harsh, violent." The king of Babylon was hard and harsh in his dealings with the conquered people, especially those who had revolted against him and made alliances with his adversary, Pharaoh, the king of Egypt [verse 11].

A MIRAGE

Why is my pain perpetual, and my wound incurable, which refuseth to be healed? wilt thou be altogether unto me as a liar, and as waters that fail?   Jer. 15:18

The Aramaic words *maya kadabey* mean "a mirage." Mirages in the Arabian desert are very common. One sees large bodies of water and waves, and for a short space of time may believe that he is approaching a great lake. But the closer he comes to it, the farther away the mirage goes.

Jeremiah had prophesied against Judah, warning the king and the princes, and admonishing them to trust in the Lord God and keep away from pagan nations whose help they sought. But because of his unpleasant message and foreign policy he was rebuked and persecuted.

It took some time before the king of Babylon started to invade all the lands west of the River Euphrates and to crush both Judah and Egypt. Just as a weary traveler who is anxious to come to a body of water, the prophet was anxious to see his prophecy fulfilled and the wicked kings and princes of Judah punished. This is because the more the impending calamity was delayed, the more the prophet was hated and persecuted.

The prophet never wavered. He never doubted God. He was sure of the impending disaster, just as he was sure of the dawning of the day. The prophet could have never thought of God as a liar.

PEN OF IRON

The sin of Judah is written with a pen of iron, and with the point of a diamond: it is graven upon the table of their heart, and upon the horns of your altars.   Jer. 17:1

"Pen of iron" and the "point of diamond" are allegorical, meaning that the people's sins are deep-rooted. In the olden days pens of iron and points of diamond were used for engraving upon stone, rock, metal tablets, seals, ornaments, and other objects of art. Job says, "Oh that my words were now written! . . . That they were engraved with an iron pen on lead or in the rock for ever!" [Job 19:23-24, Eastern text].

Judah had committed too many sins and provoked the Lord in making alliances and relying on pagan rulers, instead of trusting in the Lord God of Israel, who had delivered them from their enemies and caused them to inherit the land. These foreign alliances always had strings on them. They were instrumental in introducing pagan worship and pagan practices. The weak nations became the prey of the strong powers who, under the pretense of false alliances and protectorates, sooner or later subjugated the people and enslaved them to their imperialistic rule. God was opposed to Judah's alliances with pagan nations and to her reliance on foreign help to save his people and their land from the aggressors. Trusting in the arm of man was tantamount to a denial of the God of Israel [Jer. 17:5; Isa. 30:1].

HUMAN ARM

Thus saith the Lord; Cursed be the man that trusteth in man, and maketh flesh his arm, and whose heart departeth from the Lord.   Jer. 17:5

Trusting in human power and man's wisdom was contrary to the law of God. Whenever Israel trusted in foreign alliances she was defeated and humiliated. Human strength and human wisdom are foolishness in the eyes of God.

When Moses struck the rock twice, trusting in his human wisdom and ignoring the divine command to strike once and thus sanctify the Lord in the presence of the princes and the people, God was displeased with him [Num. 20:11-12].

Jesus taught his disciples and followers to pray to God and to trust him, just as a son trusts his father. Treaties and promises are often canceled or forgotten. The human arm fails, but God's arm and his promises never fail those who trust in him. God does not forsake the righteous nor those who put their trust in him. "Woe to the rebellious children, says the Lord, who take counsel, but not of me . . ." [Isa. 30:1, Eastern text].

TRUSTING IN GOD

For he shall be as a tree planted by the waters, and that spreadeth out her roots by the river, and shall not see when heat cometh, but her leaf shall be green; and shall not be careful in the year of drought, neither shall cease from yielding fruit.   Jer. 17:8

The Aramaic reads: ". . . and it shall not be afraid when heat comes . . . and shall not be afraid in the year of drought . . ." In biblical lands trees, like cattle and sheep, suffer during the droughts. But the trees which are planted near the banks of the streams survive the droughts and continue to bear fruit. Water is often found deep in the beds of dry rivers and wadies.

When men and women trust in the Lord they are protected in the time of adversity and are not afraid when calamities befall their land. The Lord guides them and protects them and meets their needs and grants them favor in the eyes of their oppressors. God's help and strength is never hidden from the eyes of those who trust in him and obey his laws. God is the River of Life. His mercies and his loving-kindnesses are never withheld from those who look to him in the time of distress.

But those who trust in the arm of man are like plants and trees in parched places in the wilderness. They suffer during calamities and are not guided to the right way.

WRITTEN IN THE EARTH

O Lord, the hope of Israel, all that forsake thee shall be ashamed, and they that depart from me shall be written in the earth, because they have forsaken the Lord, the fountain of living waters.

Jer. 17:13

The Eastern text reads: ". . . those who revolt against thee shall have their names written in the dust. . . ." "Written in the dust" means obliterated, forgotten, or brought to naught. Marks and imprints in the earth are quickly lost, but writing on tablets of stone, iron, and brass endure for many generations. In biblical days all important imperial decrees, state documents, and memorials were engraved on hard stones and rocks. On the other hand, commercial documents and deeds were inscribed upon baked clay tablets.

The prophet reminds the people that to trust in man is like writing on the sands or in the earth, which is easily obliterated or lost. But those who trust in God abide forever. History proves that all treaties and alliances are sooner or later broken and forgotten, but the nations who have put their trust in God have remained longer than those who have trusted in the arm of man [verse 1]. Judah, like Israel, had put her trust in pagan alliances and pagan kings. They had forgotten the strong arm of the God of their fathers. They were soon to cease to be a nation. Their political policies were to be obliterated as camel footprints are obliterated in shifting sands by the winds. Jerusalem was to become desolate.

EATING OF CHILDREN

And I will cause them to eat the flesh of their sons and the flesh of their daughters, and they shall eat every one the flesh of his friend in the siege and straitness, wherewith their enemies, and they that seek their lives, shall straiten them. Jer. 19:9

During the long siege of the cities some of the men and women ate their own children. The famine was so severe and of such long duration that the famine-ravaged inhabitants found nothing in the city to eat. After they had eaten everything they had and even the bark of the trees, they ate their children. During these sieges even an ass's head was sold for eighty pieces of silver [2 Kings 6:25].

Moses, centuries before, had warned against these calamities and exhorted the people to remain loyal to the religion of their fathers and to obey God's laws: "And if ye will not for all this hearken unto me, but walk contrary unto me . . . ye shall eat the flesh of your sons, and the flesh of your daughters shall ye eat" [Lev. 26:27, 29; Deut. 28:53-57].

During the reign of King Jehoram, the son of Ahab, the people conspired to eat their children. A woman boiled her child and shared it with another woman, hoping to eat the other woman's child the next day. But when the woman refused to boil her child and share it with her, she appealed to the king [2 Kings 6:28-29].

The Israelites suffered many severe famines because of the long sieges simply because they had departed from the way of their God, and had made alliances with pagan kings and worshiped pagan gods.

PASHUR CONDEMNED

And it came to pass on the morrow, that Pashur brought forth Jeremiah out of the stocks. Then said Jeremiah unto him, The Lord hath not called thy name Pashur, but Magor-missabib.
Jer. 20:3

The Eastern text reads: ". . . The Lord has not called your name Pashur, but [*totaba*] a stranger and a beggar"; *totaba* means "one living in a foreign land in poverty."

Pashur, the son of Amariah the priest, was taken captive by the Chaldean army and he died in Babylon. Pashur had smitten Jeremiah and put him in prison.

Pashur was governor of the house of the Lord and was angry at Jeremiah because he had prophesied that Jerusalem would fall into the hands of the Chaldeans. Seemingly, Pashur, like the princes and court prophets, had been pro-Egypt. Jeremiah urged the princes and the king to make peace with Nebuchadnezzar and not to rely on the Egyptian army [Jer. 27:6-13].

A REFUGEE

For thus saith the Lord, Behold, I will make thee a terror to thyself, and to all thy friends: and they shall fall by the sword of their enemies, and thine eyes shall behold it: and I will give all Judah into the hand of the king of Babylon, and he shall carry them captive into Babylon, and shall slay them with the sword. Jer. 20:4

The Aramaic word *totaba* means "a stranger, sojourner"; that is, a refugee. "Terror" is wrong.

Pashur and all his friends were carried away captive to Babylon by the Chaldean army. They died in poverty in Babylon [verse 3].

COMFORTED

O Lord, thou hast deceived me, and I was deceived: thou art stronger than I, and hast prevailed: I am in derision daily, every one mocketh me.   Jer. 20:7

The Aramaic word *shadal* means "to cajole, persuade, comfort, entice, win." When a child cries his mother tries to cajole him; that is, to comfort him. This word is used idiomatically. The Aramaic text reads: "O Lord, thou hast comforted me, and I am comforted."

This comfort came to the prophet from the Lord, because Jeremiah was persuaded that what the Lord had spoken through him against Jerusalem and Judah would really take place. The prophet knew that the words of the Lord never fail.

In the face of severe opposition from the court prophets and princes and priests, Jeremiah had predicted the fall of Jerusalem and the defeat of the Egyptian army. The other prophets and the princes had advised the king to make an alliance with Egypt and to defy Babylon. This policy Jeremiah opposed very strongly. Therefore he was ridiculed and mocked daily [verse 10]. But the Lord had revealed to him all that was to take place in Judah. The fact that he was sure that the words of the Lord would come to pass was a comfort to him in time of persecution.

Jeremiah could never have felt that he had been deceived by the Lord or enticed to advocate a dangerous policy which would result in disaster. No prophet has ever expressed doubt of the words of the Lord or spoken of him as a deceiver. In verse 11 the prophet states, "But the Lord is with me as a mighty terrible one: therefore my persecutors shall stumble, and they shall not prevail: they shall be greatly ashamed . . ."

At times some of the prophets were deceived by false messages, and the Lord permitted them to be deceived. But the Lord never deceived anyone who spoke in his name [1 Kings 22:23]. All those who have spoken God's truth have been hated and persecuted, but they all won at last.

LABORERS EXPLOITED

Woe unto him that buildeth his house by unrighteousness, and his chambers by wrong; that useth his neighbor's service without wages, and giveth him not for his work. Jer. 22:13

In the olden days there was no law to protect the workers and to compel the wealthy employers and landlords to pay them. Some employers held the wages for years, while others refused to pay at all, or even to feed the laborers. These injustices to the poor laborers prevailed until recent years.

Both prophets and apostles condemned the greedy rich for the bad treatment of those who labored for them [James 5:4]. Moses made it a mandatory law, but the greedy rich still refused to pay. ". . . the wages of him who is hired shall not remain with you all night until the morning" [Lev. 19:13; Deut. 24:15, Eastern text].

In the East the laborers have no other income. They live from day to day. And when they are idle they and their families suffer from hunger.

See the commentary on Leviticus 19:13.

A REBELLIOUS KING

Shalt thou reign, because thou closest thyself in cedar? did not thy father eat and drink, and do judgment and justice, and then it was well with him? Jer. 22:15

The reference here is to Shallum, the son of Josiah, king of Judah, who reigned instead of his father. Shallum was the fourth son of Josiah.

Josiah did good in the eyes of the Lord. He repaired the temple and destroyed the high places, slew the priests of Baal, and rededicated the temple of God [2 Kings 23:4-9]. But Shallum did evil in the sight of the Lord. He trusted in his foreign alliances and money; and he was living comfortably in the magnificent palace which his fathers had built. Shallum was rebellious, like some of his predecessors.

The prophet reminds Shallum how the Lord God had been with his father Josiah, how he had made him prosperous and given him fields and vineyards because he had executed justice and upheld the true religion.

CARRIED BY THE WIND

The wind shall eat up all thy pastors, and thy lovers shall go into captivity: surely then shalt thou be ashamed and confounded for all thy wickedness. **Jer. 22:22**

This should read: "All of your shepherds shall be smitten by the east wind . . ." The term shepherds here refers to the kings and princes who were to be carried captive to Babylon.

In the East when things are destroyed we say, "They were scattered or carried away by the wind." The east wind is violent and often destructive [Exod. 14:21].

The reference here is to the second captivity. The king, princes, and leaders of Judah were to be carried away captive to Babylon.

In Aramaic, rulers, princes, and bishops are often called shepherds.

THE END OF DYNASTY

Thus saith the Lord, Write ye this man childless, a man that shall not prosper in his days: for no man of his seed shall prosper, sitting upon the throne of David, and ruling any more in Judah. **Jer. 22:30**

This prophecy concerns the royal house, the house of David. The descendants of David, the kings of Judah, had nullified the covenant which the Lord God had made with David concerning his descendants who were to sit on the throne of Israel. The kings of Judah had departed from God's way and followed after pagan gods and pagan customs which were contrary to the law of Moses.

Because of the rebellious kings, the powerful and rich dynasty which was founded by David had to come to an end. The prophet saw that after the fall of Jerusalem there would be no more kings to sit upon the throne of David.

Ezekiel, a contemporary of Jeremiah, had prophesied to the same effect: "Clap your hands because this calamity is justified; if the royal family is rejected, it shall be no more, says the Lord God" [Ezek 21:13, Eastern text].

The destruction of Jerusalem and the captivity of Judah were justified. The kings of Judah had turned deaf ears to God's prophets and had slain some of them and persecuted others. They had also polluted both the temple and the land with their pagan worship and immoral practices [Isa. 43:28].

DISLOYAL SHEPHERDS

Woe be unto the pastors that destroy and scatter the sheep of my pasture! saith the Lord.   Jer. 23:1

"The pastors" here refers to the kings, princes, and leaders, and "the sheep" are the people. In the East the people, like sheep, must be led, cared for, and protected from wicked leaders, corrupt judges, oppression, and other things which make life harsh and miserable.

The Hebrew kings and leaders had neglected the people and let them become the prey of their enemies. Moreover, corruption, bloodshed, and injustices were prevalent in the holy city, as well as in the provinces. Consequently, the harassed people were scattered in foreign lands, seeking relief and places of refuge.

The Lord was to seek vengeance upon the kings and princes, and appoint new leaders for the remnant of people, leaders who would gather them, care for them, and feed them in righteousness, and make them to lie down in peace and tranquillity [Ezek. 34:1-5].

See the commentary on Ezekiel 34:1.

OUR RIGHTEOUSNESS

Behold, the days come, saith the Lord, that I will raise unto David a righteous Branch, and a King shall reign and prosper, and shall execute judgment and justice in the earth.   Jer. 23:5

Wickedness and injustice prevailed in Israel during the time of the prophet Jeremiah. The kings of Judah had rebelled against the true religion of their fathers. The princes, the priests, and the court prophets had gone astray from the way of the Lord. Baal worship had taken strong roots in the land. The poor were oppressed and the widows robbed of their possessions. Thus, the political future of Judah was dark and hopeless. Messiah, a Righteous King, who would restore justice and truth, was the only hope of the remnant.

The reference here is to Messiah Christ. Jeremiah, like Isaiah, predicted the coming of a new day when pagan practices would be put to an

end, the true religion of Israel restored, and righteousness established
once more.

PROPHETS AND PRIESTS PAGANIZED

*For both prophet and priest are profane; yea, in my house have
I found their wickedness, saith the Lord.*   Jer. 23:11

The Aramaic word *ethkhanapo* means, "they have become pagans."
It has been confused with *ethtanapo,* which means "polluted" or "profaned."

During the time of the prophet Isaiah the temple was polluted with
the immoral Baal worship and human sacrifices which were offered to
pagan gods. King Manasseh, the son of Hezekiah, built again the
high places and restored pagan worship, and fulfilled Jerusalem with
innocent blood [2 Kings 21:1-9]. Moreover, both the priests and the
false prophets had sanctioned pagan worship in order to please the
wicked and rebellious kings of Judah who had forsaken the worship of
the Lord for Baal worship. They became prophets and priests of the
pagan shrines.

Isaiah says that the princes had polluted his sanctuary [Isa. 43:28,
Eastern text; see also Ezek. 8:9-16; Zeph. 3:4].

THE BURDEN OF THE LORD

*And when this people, or the prophet, or a priest, shall ask thee,
saying, What is the burden of the Lord? thou shalt then say unto
them, What burden? I will even forsake you, saith the Lord.*

*And as for the prophet, and the priest, and the people, that shall
say, The burden of the Lord, I will even punish that man and his
house.*   Jer. 23:33-34

"The burden of the Lord" in this instance means "the message from
the Lord concerning the people." The term burden is often used in referring to the punishment decreed by the Lord, such as the burden of
Babylon, the burden of Tyre, the burden of Edom.

There were many false prophets who had prophesied security, prosperity, peace, and easy times. Jeremiah had predicted the invasion of
Judah by the Chaldean army and the destruction of Jerusalem. This was
"the burden of the Lord," but the people, the priests, the false prophets,
and the princes doubted Jeremiah's knowledge and integrity, and they
mocked him and persecuted him [Jer. 20:7]. Now the prophet is admonished by the Lord not to say anything except that the Lord would

punish all those who spoke of the burden of the Lord and perverted his words. All the court prophets and statesmen who had misled the kings of Judah were either slain or carried captive to Babylon.

The princes, the prophets, the priests, and the people had been so unfaithful that the Lord had rejected them. There was no use delivering messages to such a stiffnecked people except to remind them of the impending calamity which was to befall them. In such situations silence is golden.

BASKETS OF FIGS

The Lord showed me, and, behold, two baskets of figs were set before the temple of the Lord, after that Nebuchadrezzar king of Babylon had carried away captive Jeconiah the son of Jehoiakim king of Judah, and the princes of Judah, with the carpenters and smiths, from Jerusalem, and had brought them to Babylon.

Jer. 24:1

The fruiting of the fig tree is different from that of other trees. They put forth their leaves and fruit at the same time. Both the leaves and the little figs develop together.

Before the fruit is ripened and ready to be taken to market, some of the immature figs drop off. This is because the tree cannot nourish all of them. These figs do not taste good and are known as bad figs. They are gathered from the ground by the poor and taken home in baskets. Then again, when the good figs are gathered and placed in baskets, some of the small and green figs are left to be gathered later.

Kopey (baskets) were made of tender willow branches, palm leaves, and other materials. These baskets, even today, are used as containers for fruit, bread, cheese, and other provisions [John 6:13]. Baskets were also used for presenting offerings of firstfruits and bread at the temple or shrines [Exod. 29:3].

Moreover, baskets were used as containers for family food. Then again, bread and other food are set in a basket and placed before the people [Deut. 28:5]. Large baskets were used, and are still used, to carry grapes to the market place and manure into the fields. Paul was lowered from the wall of Damascus in one of these baskets which are used for carrying manure [Acts 9:25].

The baskets of figs here are symbolic of the Jews, some of whom already had been carried away into captivity in Babylon, while the others were waiting to be carried captive to Babylon. Baskets of ripe summer fruit are the sign of the end. Summer fruits are the sign that summer is over and the hard winter is ahead. The end of Judah had come like the end of summer fruits. Jerusalem and Judah were to be bereaved of their people. Hebrew prophets always used such metaphors so that the people might understand their messages, and, if possible, repent and turn from their evil ways.

EVIL FIGS

Then said the Lord unto me, What seest thou, Jeremiah? And I said, Figs; the good figs, very good; and the evil, very evil, that cannot be eaten, they are so evil.   Jer. 24:3

The same Aramaic word that means "evil" also means "bad" or "spoiled." In Aramaic we often say "a good tree" or "a bad tree." For example, walnuts which have a hard shell are called "evil walnuts," and the walnuts with a soft shell are called "good nuts." Jesus said, "by their fruit you will know them" [Matt. 7:17-20].

Good figs were symbolic of the people who were carried away captive to Babylon when Jehoiakim, the king of Judah, was carried captive. These were the good people whom the Lord had spared as a remnant. On the other hand, the bad or rotten figs were the Jews who were still in Jerusalem with Zedekiah, the king of Judah. They were so bad that they were to be destroyed, and, like spoiled figs, they were to be cast away to be trampled upon. The forthcoming disaster was to be greater than the first. Thousands of people were to be slain [verses 8, 9]. These parables brought the word of the Lord close to the hearts of the people.

WARNING IN ADVANCE

From the thirteenth year of Josiah the son of Amon king of Judah, even unto this day, that is the three and twentieth year, the word of the Lord hath come unto me, and I have spoken unto you, rising early and speaking; but ye have not hearkened.

And the Lord hath sent unto you all his servants the prophets, rising early and sending them; but ye have not hearkened, nor inclined your ear to hear.   Jer. 25:3-4

"Rising early and speaking" and "rising early and sending" are mistranslations of the Aramaic words *kadmeth o-shadreth* (I sent messengers to warn you in advance). See also Jeremiah 11:7.

God neither sleeps nor slumbers. He is always awake and alert, watching all his creations. On the other hand, God always warned Israel and Judah by sending prophets to them in advance, warning them of impending disasters so that they would have no excuse.

Some of the prophets and messengers of God were well received and their admonitions heeded; but some were rejected, and others slain.

NEBUCHADREZZAR

Behold, I will send and take all the families of the north, saith the Lord, and Nebuchadrezzar the king of Babylon, my servant, and will bring them against this land, and against the inhabitants thereof, and against all these nations round about, and will utterly destroy them, and make them an astonishment, and a hissing, and perpetual desolations.   Jer. 25:9

"Nebuchadrezzar" is an error. It should read "Nebuchadnezzar." The latter was a son of Nabopalassar, founder of the Babylonian empire, who revolted against Assyria and made Babylon his capital.

King Nebuchadnezzar is noted for his campaigns against Syria, Israel, Judah, and other nations west of the River Euphrates. He also made Babylon with its hanging gardens one of the wonders of the world, and built magnificent temples and palaces throughout the realm.

This king was also noted for defeating the Egyptian army under the Pharaoh Necho at Carchemish in 605 B.C. He conquered Palestine in 596 B.C. and carried King Jehoiachim captive. In 586 Nebuchadnezzar destroyed Jerusalem, burned the temple, and carried away more captives.

Jeremiah recognized Nebuchadnezzar as the agent of the Lord, ready to punish Judah for its many backslidings, the introduction of Baal worship, and the evil doings of some of the kings of Judah who sat on the throne of David. Hitherto, the kings and princes had doubted Jeremiah's prophecy in regard to the rise of Babylon as a world power. But now Babylon had replaced Assyria and was on the march toward Jerusalem and Judah. Even Egypt, in which Judah had put her trust, was to be conquered by the Chaldean army and made a tributary.

DURATION OF EXILE

And this whole land shall be a desolation, and an astonishment; and these nations shall serve the king of Babylon seventy years.
And it shall come to pass, when seventy years are accomplished, that I will punish the king of Babylon, and that nation, saith the Lord, for their iniquity, and the land of the Chaldeans, and will make it perpetual desolations.   Jer. 25:11-12

The number seventy is a sacred number, and is often used figuratively. Lamech was to be punished seventy and sevenfold [Gen. 4:24]. Cainan lived seventy years [Gen. 5:12]. All the persons . . . who came into Egypt were seventy [Gen. 46:27]. Moses chose seventy elders [Num. 11:16]. "Tyre shall be forgotten for seventy years" [Isa. 23:15]. Jesus sent out seventy disciples [Luke 10:1]. Jesus also states that one should forgive his brother (neighbor) not only seven times, but seventy times seven [Matt. 18:22].

According to Ezra 1:1, Cyrus began to reign when seventy years were fulfilled.

According to history, the fall of Jerusalem was in 586 B.C. Nebuchadnezzar died in 561 B.C. Nabonidus died in 539 B.C., and Xerxes in 464 B.C.

PARTHIANS

And all the kings of the north, far and near, one with another, and all the kingdoms of the world, which are upon the face of the earth: and the king of Sheshach shall drink after them. Jer. 25:26

The Aramaic reads *Areshkaia* from *Arshak*, the name of the founder of the Parthian Empire. It should read: "the king of the Parthians." Sheshach is a mistranslation of *Areshkaia*. There was an Egyptian king named Shishak who ransacked the temple about 950 B.C. [1 Kings 14:25].

The Parthians were to rule after the Babylonians, and then they were to be succeeded by the Persians, or the Achaemenian Empire [Jer. 51:41]. The Parthians inhabited a region southeast of the Caspian Sea. They were a warlike race. They fought against the Romans for more than two centuries. The Parthians were a people racially akin to the Persians and the Medes.

THE CUP OF POISON

Therefore thou shalt say unto them, Thus saith the Lord of hosts, the God of Israel; Drink ye, and be drunken, and spew, and fall, and rise no more, because of the sword which I will send among you.
And it shall be, if they refuse to take the cup at thine hand to drink, then shalt thou say unto them, Thus saith the Lord of hosts; Ye shall certainly drink. Jer. 25:27-28

"The cup" is symbolic of punishment, which was to befall the nations. All the nations which had acted wickedly and had oppressed and exploited the weak nations were to drink from the same cup, the cup of poison.

In the olden days men who were convicted of crimes or treason against the state were given a cup full of hemlock. The victims had to take it from the hand of the prison warden and drink it. Socrates took the cup, drank the poison, and died.

Then again, in the East, when a governor or a ruler wishes to do away with his adversary, he poisons the cup and gives it to him to drink. Of course no one can refuse to accept the cup from the hand of a ruler or his cupbearer. The prophet here declares that all the kings of the earth will drink from the cup of vengeance.

Jesus prayed that the cup might pass away from him. "O my Father, if this cup cannot pass, and if I must drink it, let it be according to thy will" [Matt. 26:42, Eastern text].

See the article on "Cup" in *Gospel Light,* Matthew 26:42.

THY LOVERS

All thy lovers have forgotten thee; they seek thee not; for I have wounded thee with the wound of an enemy, with the chastisement of a cruel one, for the multitude of thine iniquity; because thy sins were increased.
                                                                        Jer. 30:14

The term "lovers" in this instance means the allies of Judah—Egypt and Assyria [Ezek. 16:26-29].

Despite the warnings of God's prophets against foreign alliances, the kings of Judah, their princes, and their false prophets who acted as their advisers, made alliances with pagan nations, refusing to trust in the God of their fathers and to heed the admonitions of his holy prophets who sought their good.

Now it was too late to remedy the situation. The wound was too grievous and there was none to plead the cause of the people. Now Judah was deserted by her allies and those in whom she had trusted.

THE BEDOUINS

Thus saith the Lord, The people which were left of the sword found grace in the wilderness; even Israel, when I went to cause him to rest.
                                                                        Jer. 31:2

Beshebya (in exile or captivity) has been confused with *shilya* (rest, tranquillity, stillness, quietness).

The Eastern text reads: ". . . The people who escaped from the sword found compassion in the wilderness when Israel went into exile."

The prophet here is referring to the captivity in which Jehoiachim and his princes and mighty men of war were carried away captive, together with some of the people. The second captivity of Judah took place during the reign of Zedekiah, the last king of Judah, 586 B.C.

Some of the people who escaped the sword fled into the Arabian desert and took refuge among the Bedouin tribes. The latter, even though usually hostile, are hospitable toward those who seek refuge in their camps. All Arabs are noted for their kindness toward strangers and refugees who seek their protection. The Lord God gave the exiles favor in the eyes of these desert people.

A BULLOCK

I have surely heard Ephraim bemoaning himself thus; Thou hast chastised me, and I was chastised, as a bullock unaccustomed to the yoke: turn thou me, and I shall be turned; for thou art the Lord my God. Jer. 31:18

Bullocks are hard to break in and put yokes upon. They violently refuse to come under the yoke, so they have to be beaten and forcibly subdued.

Ephraim is likened to a bullock who had been crushed because he had refused to accept God's way, his covenant, and his commandments.

Ephraim was the beloved heir of Joseph and the strongest tribe in Israel. God loved Ephraim and therefore chastised him in order to bring him to the right way. Ephraim, like a strong bullock which is not accustomed to the yoke, refused discipline and had to be punished severely.

Ephraim had groaned under foreign yoke and tributes, and the Lord heard his groaning. Ephraim wanted to repent and turn to God, but it was too late. But Judah had plenty of time to repent and turn from her evil ways. Judah had seen what had happened to Israel. The prophet warns them that they shall soon face a similar fate.

LOYALTY TO GOD

How long wilt thou go about, O thou backsliding daughter? for the Lord hath created a new thing in the earth, A woman shall compass a man. Jer. 31:22

Nikbta means "a woman or female," and the Eastern text reads: "A woman shall love her husband."

The reference here is to the faithfulness of a woman to her husband.

In the new order, there would be no whoring and no polygamy. A man will be satisfied with one woman, and a woman with one man.

Metaphorically, Israel is often likened to a woman who had been unfaithful to her husband and had played the harlot with other men. In the new order Israel shall love her God and be loyal to him, just as a faithful wife is loyal to her husband.

The prophet assures the people of the restoration of Israel. The remnant is to be spared and brought back again to Israel. And the Lord is to bless the habitation of righteousness and the holy mountain, for out of Zion was to come forth salvation.

PALESTINE REPOPULATED

Behold, the days come, saith the Lord, that I will sow the house of Israel and the house of Judah with the seed of man, and with the seed of beast.   Jer. 31:27

"I will sow" means that God will populate the house of Israel and the house of Judah with the offspring of man and the offspring of beast.

After the first and second captivities the population of both Israel and Judah was depleted. Most of the people were carried away captive to Assyria and Babylon. Others had taken refuge in neighboring lands. Moreover, sheep and cattle were slaughtered and eaten by the invading armies, and some of the sheep and cattle carried away as prey. The land was bereaved and left desolate of its people and its herds of cattle and flocks of sheep.

But in the new day, the Lord was to replenish them again and care for the remnant of Israel and Judah [verse 22].

A NEW COVENANT

Behold, the days come, saith the Lord, that I will make a new covenant with the house of Israel, and with the house of Judah.
Jer. 31:31

The reference here is to the second covenant, the Gospel of Jesus Christ, which was to supplant the Mosaic rituals and ordinances which had failed to teach the nation reverence for God, justice, and righteousness. The new covenant was to be written, not upon stone tablets but upon human hearts [verse 33].

The old covenant which God made with the Hebrews in Sinai was limited to the Israelites. But the new covenant was to be universal, and would embrace the people of every race and color. The knowledge of God was to spread all over the world. And both the Jews and the Gentiles were to become the heirs of the new covenant. The Hebrew Scriptures and religion were to be shared with the Gentile world. Jeremiah, like Isaiah, saw the need for the conversion of the Gentile races who dwelt in darkness. They must see the light of God in order to have compassion on the Jews and other minorities. God was to write a new agreement and devise a new plan for the salvation of man.

WRITTEN ON HEARTS

But this shall be the covenant that I will make with the house of Israel; After those days, saith the Lord, I will put my law in their inward parts, and write it in their hearts; and will be their God, and they shall be my people.
Jer. 31:33

"Heart" is used metaphorically, meaning "mind." The Hebrews thought that the heart was the seat of the mental faculties.

The prophet reminds the people of breakable stone tablets on which the Mosaic law and ordinances were written, and which were hardly seen by the people, but were jealously and securely kept in the holy and untouchable Ark of the Covenant. Even though these laws were carefully guarded, they were often broken by the people.

The new covenant will be written on human hearts so that it may be handed down from one generation to another. The words of the new covenant were to transform human hearts and minds, and create new men.

This covenant was fulfilled when Jesus delivered his historic sermon on the Mount near Tiberias. And it was sealed with his blood on the cross.

JUDAH'S RESTORATION ASSURED

And I bought the field of Hanameel my uncle's son, that was in Anathoth, and weighed him the money, even seventeen shekels of silver.
Jer. 32:9

Jeremiah was so sure of the restoration of the remnant that he did not hesitate to buy the field of his uncle. The prophet was the closest relative of his uncle Nahmael and, therefore, had the first right of redeeming the field.

Evidently the property had been sold and now it was time to be redeemed, according to Mosaic law [Lev. 25:48-52; Ruth 4:4-6].

When Jeremiah purchased the field, Anathoth was occupied by the Chaldean army. The prophet, by this act and through a divine vision, assured the people of Judah's restoration [Zech. 8:11-15].

Hebrew prophets not only reassured the people by words, but also by evident acts. Jeremiah was looked upon as an agent of the Chaldean army, trying to weaken the hands of the people who were resisting Nebuchadnezzar, the king of Babylon. This is why the prophet was imprisoned and humiliated by his enemies, the court prophets, who were in power.

WRITING IN JARS

Thus saith the Lord of hosts, the God of Israel; Take these evidences, this evidence of the purchase, both which is sealed, and this evidence which is open; and put them in an earthen vessel, that they may continue many days.   Jer. 32:14

The Aramaic word *ashtarey*, derived from *shatar*, means "a deed," or handwritten business document such as a bill of sale [verses 9-16].

Buying and selling of land was an ancient practice. The first deal recorded in the Bible is that between Abraham and Ephron [Gen. 22:15-20]. The purchase was secured in the presence of witnesses and the elders at the gate.

When writing became common, deeds were written on clay tablets, stones, and parchment. Then the deeds, sacred scrolls, and other valuable documents were placed in jars and buried in the ground, or placed in caves.

The Dead Sea scrolls were preserved in jars. (The author was offered several of these empty jars for $25 in 1953.)

Jeremiah bought the field and kept the deed to demonstrate his confidence that the remnant would return again to Judea.

ONE HEART

And I will give them one heart, and one way, that they may fear me for ever, for the good of them, and of their children after them.   Jer. 32:39

"One heart" means "one mind" or one way of thinking, reasoning, and revering God. The Hebrews had too many prophets and seers, as well

as too many ideas of religion. The people were divided because of true
and false divination and diverse ways of worship. The prophet was
opposed to the heavy burdens which the priests and Levites had laid
upon the people. It was because of taxation and temple revenues that
King Jeroboam built new shrines in Bethel and Dan. And this act caused
a great division between Israel and Judah.

In due time the veil of mystery was to be removed and the truth of
God brought forth, shining like the sun. The new Israel would be united
and of one mind.

A COVENANT WITH DAVID

*Then may also my covenant be broken with David my servant,
that he should not have a son to reign upon his throne; and with
the Levites the priests, my ministers.*

*As the host of heaven cannot be numbered, neither the sand of
the sea measured; so will I multiply the seed of David my servant,
and the Levites that minister unto me.*   Jer. 33:21-22

"Covenant" in this case refers to the regularity of the sun and the
moon, the everlasting signs of God which were created "to divide the
day from the night . . . and for seasons, and for days, and years" [Gen.
1:14].

A covenant is a witness, an agreement or sign between the two parties
concerned. Moreover, it is a reminder of the promises, oaths, and agreements entered into. On such occasions Easterners raise up heaps of
stones as a witness, just as in the case of Laban and Jacob [Gen.
31:44-49].

In the olden days God had promised to Abraham, Isaac, and Jacob
that he would give them the land of Canaan. And later he made a
promise to King David that there should never depart an heir from
his throne.

The promise to Abraham was that by his seed (teaching), all the nations of the earth would be blessed. Abraham was called by God "Father
of many nations" [Gen. 15:4-5]. This covenant was not only for the
descendants of Abraham but also for the descendants of Ishmael and
Esau. For Ishmael and Esau were also blessed, and the whole world.
For all the nations of the earth were to be blessed by this divine plan
and promise.

According to Jeremiah, even the Levites were included in this covenant.
They are to minister before the Lord forever.

The wording of this covenant, both in Jeremiah and First Samuel,
shows that this covenant was unconditional. Nevertheless, in 1 Kings
2:4, the covenant is conditional in that the descendants of David are
required to walk before the Lord in truth.

God kept his word, but the descendants of David refused to walk in the way of the Lord, and many of them worshiped pagan gods. This is why for the past twenty-five centuries there has been no heir of David on his throne, nor a Levite to minister in the temple.

Today God's signs, the sun and the moon, are still here, witnessing to God's faithfulness, but the house of David came to and end in 586 B.C. Thus, this covenant is of the Spirit and not of the flesh. The seed, in this case, means the faith, the religion of Abraham and David. But the promise, or covenant, was fulfilled in Jesus Christ, who is the heir of the truth which God revealed to Abraham and his descendants, so that they might be revealed to the world. The promise is of the Spirit and not of the letter. Today Christ is reigning as the Prince of Peace, seated on the throne of David, which is symbolical of justice and loyalty to God.

BURIAL

But thou shalt die in peace: and with the burnings of thy fathers, the former kings which were before thee, so shall they burn odors for thee; and they will lament thee, saying, Ah lord! for I have pronounced the word, saith the Lord.   Jer. 34:5

The Aramaic word *arkedo* (to mourn) has been confused with *awkedo* (to burn). The two Aramaic words in the manuscript closely resemble one another.

King Zedekiah was not to die by the sword, but he was to die in peace, and the people were to mourn over him just as they had mourned over his fathers, the former kings of Judah. King Zedekiah, for a while, turned to God. He freed the slaves and executed justice, but afterward both the king and his princes changed their minds and enslaved the men and women they had freed.

But King Zedekiah, because of his unfaithfulness to God, did not die in peace, nor was he mourned by the people in Jerusalem. When Jerusalem was taken by the Chaldean army, Zedekiah was captured. His eyes were put out, and he was bound in chains and carried captive to Babylon. The king died in the prison in Babylon [Jer. 52:8-11]. Had the king remained loyal to the covenant which he had made with God, he would have died in peace in Jerusalem.

Some of the kings who had done evil were not given a proper burial or buried in the kings' burial ground. At times kings who had conspired and were captured were hanged or crucified and left unburied. The bodies of King Saul and his sons were mutilated and left unburied [1 Sam. 31:9-10].

THE RECHABITES

And I set before the sons of the house of the Rechabites pots full of wine, and cups; and I said unto them, Drink ye wine.

But they said, We will drink no wine: for Jonadab the son of Rechab our father commanded us, saying, Ye shall drink no wine, neither ye, nor your sons for ever. Jer. 35:5-6

There were many movements in Palestine and Arabia that discouraged the drinking of wine, planting of vineyards, and building of houses. These were the peaceful desert dwellers, who hated city life and who looked to God for salvation. The desert dwellers seldom drink wine or strong drink. They drink milk and buttermilk, and they love to dwell in open tents where they can see the beautiful blue Arabian sky and the brilliant stars.

As vines cannot grow in the desert, these people hardly know anything about wine or strong drink, and some of them never have seen it.

The Rechabites were a strict desert-dwelling family who roamed around with their sheep and cattle. Jonadab, the son of Rechab, had commanded his sons not to drink wine, or build houses, or sow seeds, but to dwell in tents [verses 7-8].

Jonadab wanted his descendants to keep away from the corrupt city life where crime and pagan worship prevailed. He wanted his descendants to remain in the desert so that they might preserve the true religion of their fathers.

The Rechabites had kept the ordinance of Jonadab, so they refused to drink wine when Jeremiah offered it to them. The prophet had heard about the Rechabites and he knew they would not break the covenant which Jonadab their father had made. But the people of Jerusalem had broken God's covenant and his ordinances.

DURING THE FAST

Therefore go thou, and read in the roll, which thou hast written from my mouth, the words of the Lord in the ears of the people in the Lord's house upon the fasting day: and also thou shalt read them in the ears of all Judah that come out of their cities. Jer. 36:6

During the feasts and fasts Easterners are usually idle. This is because the people fast from morning to evening. They abstain from both food and water, so of course some of them look weak and sad. Jesus said,

"When you fast, do not look sad like the hypocrites; for they disfigure their faces, so that it may appear to men that they are fasting . . ." [Matt. 6:16, Eastern text].

On such occasions the people are either engaged in prayer or are passing the time on the housetops, in the market places, and around the holy places, discussing the Scriptures and political questions, and debating other matters. The fasting day is ended with prayers in the holy places. Then again, at such times many people come from towns, small villages, and far-off country places to pray and worship. This is why the prophet was told to read the scroll on a fasting day. The Lord wanted his message to be heard by as many people as possible.

Even today the Moslems regularly fast, abstaining from all food and water.

DUNGEON

When Jeremiah was entered into the dungeon, and into the cabins, and Jeremiah had remained there many days.   Jer. 37:16

The Aramaic word *goba* means "a well, cistern, pit." Wells and cisterns are found in many courtyards of ancient walled cities. In some places the people depended entirely on wells, and in others, wells were used during the sieges. Even today the old city of Jerusalem still depends on wells and rain for water.

Jeremiah was lowered into the well. To put a prisoner into a well was one of the worst punishments to inflict on him. The princes did this, thinking that the prisoner would recant and support their war policy [Jer. 38:6]. Then again, wells or dark underground cells are secure places to confine dangerous prisoners, especially those who have followers.

Some of these wells are entirely dried up during the summer months, others are full of mire. Then again, because of the lack of fortified prisons, some of the old wells and cisterns are used for dungeons.

PRISONERS

Then took they Jeremiah, and cast him into the dungeon of Malchiah the son of Hammelech, that was in the court of the prison: and they let down Jeremiah with cords. And in the dungeon there was no water, but mire: so Jeremiah sunk in the mire.

Jer. 38:6

Hamelek in Hebrew means "the king." The Aramaic reads *Bar-malka* (the son of the king).

In the East, owing to the lack of prisons, until recent days prisoners were held in kings' and princes' palaces, and in the courtyards of judges and other government officials. Jails were few, as most culprits were executed when they were caught. In the East crime is not tolerated. The criminals are either severely punished or immediately executed.

In Jerusalem only princes and high army commanders had large enough palaces to accommodate prisoners. Jeremiah had not committed any crime. He had simply disagreed with the court prophets, princes, and counselors, but his disagreement with foreign policy did not warrant his execution. The Mosaic law demanded evidence and two witnesses in order to convict a man and put him to death. But the prophet was looked upon as a friend of the king of Babylon and therefore he was greatly feared.

KING'S HOUSEHOLD

Even men, and women, and children, and the king's daughters, and every person that Nebuzar-adan the captain of the guard had left with Gedaliah the son of Ahikam the Son of Shaphan, and Jeremiah the prophet, and Baruch the son of Neriah.   Jer. 43:6

Beth (household) has been confused with *benath* (daughters). The error is caused by the close similarity of the two words. The letters *nun* (n) and *yoth* (y) are identical when they fall in the middle of a verb.

Because of this error, many Bible students are led to believe that one of the daughters of King Zedekiah was taken to Egypt by Jeremiah and that from thence she was taken to England. Women, especially princesses, generally are taken captive by conquering armies. Indeed, no royal princess would have escaped the eyes of the officers of the king of Babylon.

The king's household consisted of male and female servants, concubines, and cooks. All the king's sons were put to death [Jer. 39:6-7; 2 Kings 25:7].

A SHEPHERD'S CLOAK

And I will kindle a fire in the houses of the gods of Egypt; and he shall burn them, and carry them away captives: and he shall array himself with the land of Egypt, as a shepherd putteth on his garment; and he shall go forth from thence in peace. Jer. 43:12

The prophet warns that the remnant of the Jews which was spared by the Chaldean army should not go to Egypt. Nebuchadnezzar, the king of Babylon, was soon to start another campaign against the already weakened Egyptian army. He had already overthrown the Egyptian dominion over Palestine and Syria, and was making preparations to occupy Egypt itself. The king of Babylon had occupied all the countries "from the river of Egypt to the river Euphrates" [2 Kings 24:7]. Later the army of Pharaoh Necho (Pharaoh the lame) was defeated in Carchemish, where Pharaoh was slain by the Chaldean army [Jer. 46:2].

The prophet here hints at the easy conquest of Egypt by the Chaldean army. The Eastern text reads: ". . . and he shall conquer the land of Egypt as easily as a shepherd puts on his woolen cloak . . ."

The shepherd's cloak is made of lamb's wool about one-half inch thick. It serves as his bed during the night, and during the day it is used to protect him from wind, rain, and sandstorms. The coat is so thick and stiff that the shepherd can put it on in an instant.

The prophet was sure that Egypt would fall like all other lands. The Egyptians had suffered many defeats when fighting against Assyria. See verses 8-11.

PEOPLE ARE DIVINELY WARNED

Howbeit I sent unto you all my servants the prophets, rising early and sending them, saying, Oh, do not this abominable thing that I hate.   Jer. 44:4

The Aramaic words *kadmet oshadret* mean "I sent in advance"; that is to say, God warned the people about their evil doings by the prophets whom he sent in advance. A similar word originally meant "prevented," but this word has become obsolete. "Prevent" now means "hinder" instead of "go before."

No nation or people were ever overthrown without being warned by God in advance, so that they might repent and return to him. But when they refused to turn from their evil ways, they were rejected, defeated, and destroyed by their own evil works [2 Chron. 36:15].

See also the commentary on Jeremiah 25:3.

YOU HAVE BUILT

Thus shalt thou say unto him, The Lord saith thus; Behold, that which I have built will I break down, and that which I have planted I will pluck up, even this whole land.   Jer. 45:4

Dabnet (which you have built) has been confused with *dabnet* (which I have built).

The same error occurs in the word "plant." It should read, "and that which you have planted."

The first and second personal pronouns are distinguished only by a single dot over or under the letter *tau* (t). In the case of the first person, the dot is placed under the letter, and in the case of the second person, the dot is placed over the letter. This error occurs in many places and therefore gives the wrong meaning [Jer. 4:10].

THE FALL OF PHARAOH

As I live, saith the King, whose name is The Lord of hosts, Surely as Tabor is among the mountains, and as Carmel by the sea, so shall he come.　　　　　　　　　　　　　　　　　Jer. 46:18

The Aramaic word *tabara* (breaking up, landslide) has been confused in the King James Version with Mount Tabor. The reference here is to the fall of Pharaoh, the king of Egypt, whose fall is likened to a mountain slide, especially to slides on the side of Mt. Carmel which drop sharply into the sea.

Pharaoh was to suffer a great defeat in the battle against Nebuchadnezzar, the king of Babylon. Pharaoh Necho actually was defeated and slain by Nebuchadnezzar, king of Babylon, at Carchemish by the River Euphrates. Judah had foolishly put her trust in Egypt.

FLOOD

Thus saith the Lord; Behold, waters rise up out of the north, and shall be an overflowing flood, and shall overflow the land, and all that is therein; the city, and them that dwell therein: then the men shall cry, and all the inhabitants of the land shall howl.　　Jer. 47:2

The Aramaic word *alemey* means "young men, young soldiers."

Turbulent water or flood symbolizes an invasion and a swift conquest of the land. Just as a flood damages towns and fields and causes loss of life to both men and animals, so an invading army destroys and burns property, slaughters animals for food, cuts the trees for fuel, and plunders the land through which it passes.

Jeremiah predicted that an invasion of the land would come from the north. The Babylonian army actually did take the Euphrates route northward and then marched down through Syria and Lebanon [verse 3]. Such a large army could not have relied on the wells in the desert for water.

A SCRIBAL NOTE

Yet will I bring again the captivity of Moab in the latter days, saith the Lord. Thus far is the judgment of Moab. Jer. 48:47

"Thus far is the judgment of Moab." This is a scribal note which has been inserted into the text by a reader or scribe.

Ancient biblical texts were not divided into chapters, paragraphs, and verses. Scribes and priests sometimes made notes while preparing the portion of the Scripture to be read on certain occasions. This practice is still in use in the Near East. Manuscripts contain many notes made by the priests and learned men in order to facilitate the reading.

Not having paper, the learned men made notes on the margin, which later were copied into the new texts. In Psalm 72:20, "The prayers of David the son of Jesse are ended," is a marginal note; it is not a part of the text.

THE FALL OF AMMON

Concerning the Ammonites, thus saith the Lord; Hath Israel no sons? hath he no heir? why then doth their king inherit Gad, and his people dwell in his cities? Jer. 49:1

Milcom (Aramaic *Malcolm*), the god of the Ammonites, is confused in the King James Version with *malkehon* (their king).

The prophecy in this instance is against the Ammonites who had conspired with the enemies of Judah and now had become heirs to some of the towns and cities of Judah.

Milcom is the name of the Ammonite deity, which time and again had become a stumbling block to the Israelites. The prophet foresees the fall of Ammon, just as he had seen the fall of Judah and the destruction of Jerusalem.

DAMASCUS WAS DOOMED

How is the city of praise not left, the city of my joy! Jer. 49:25

Damascus is famous for its beauty, its gardens, orchards, and fertile fields. The city is like an emerald in a golden setting, for Damascus is a large and beautiful garden or paradise in the arid Arabian desert.

But Damascus still remains as the oldest inhabited city in the world.

The city was denounced by Hebrew prophets, but somehow it escaped destruction and it has remained to the present day. Nineveh, Babylon, Rabath, Ammon, and Hishbun are in ruins, but Damascus is still the capital of Aram (Syria).

See the commentary on Isaiah 17:1.

LOST SHEEP

My people hath been lost sheep: their shepherds have caused them to go astray, they have turned them away on the mountains: they have gone from mountain to hill, they have forgotten their resting place. Jer. 50:6

When the shepherds are unfaithful and negligent, the sheep scatter on the hills and mountains and are lost. Hired shepherds sometimes leave the sheep alone on the hills while they rest, eat, and drink in camp.

Sheep must be led from the camp to the mountains and hills, and back to the camp. Sheep are the most senseless of animals. They must be guided. When the shepherd is absent, they scatter and are easily lost. They cannot find their way to the camp.

Judah is likened to the sheep, and her kings, princes, and false court prophets are symbolic of unfaithful and hired shepherds. Owing to misgovernment and injustices, many Jews had already scattered into foreign lands and were like the lost sheep with little hope of restoration. Men, like sheep, need good leaders, prophets, and men of God to guide them and protect them in their ways.

Jesus spoke of the ten tribes which were taken captive to Assyria as lost sheep from the house of Israel. "But above all, go to the sheep which are lost from the house of Israel" [Matt. 10:6, Eastern text].

HE-GOATS BEFORE FLOCKS

Remove out of the midst of Babylon, and go forth out of the land of the Chaldeans, and be as the he goats before the flocks. Jer. 50:8

Goats always go ahead of the flock. They are faster than sheep and are always hungry and eager to start grazing. Moreover, goats always explore new places in search of grass, and they often stray from the ranks. The sheep, on the other hand, follow one another, straying neither to the right nor to the left. Many flocks are led by a large he-goat.

The reference here is to the Jews who were in Babylon. These Jews were carried captive with Jehoiakim, king of Judah, before the fall of

Jerusalem in 586 B.C. The prophet is admonishing them to leave Babylon as soon as possible to escape the impending disaster which was to befall the beautiful and prosperous metropolis. Many of the Jews had prospered in Babylon and, like sheep, were satisfied with their lot. The Babylonians, like the Persians, were magnanimous toward the captives whom they had brought from other lands. They were left free to worship their own gods, to trade, plant vineyards, build houses, and participate in government and business. Many of these Jews scoffed at Jeremiah's message and chose to remain in Babylon. These were also some of the Jews of the first captivity, who were carried captive to Assyria and Chaldea by the Assyrian kings in 722 B.C.

GIVEN HAND

Shout against her round about: she hath given her hand: her foundations are fallen, her walls are thrown down: for it is the vengeance of the Lord: take vengeance upon her; as she hath done, do unto her.   Jer. 50:15

"She hath given her hand" is an ancient Eastern idiom that is still used. It means, "She has surrendered unconditionally"; that is, "she has ceased to offer resistance." This idiom is also used in another way with a different meaning. When a girl consents to marry, it is said, "She has given her hand"; that is, "she has surrendered to the will of her parents."

In Aramaic the term "hand" symbolizes power, friendship, and agreement. But when people give their hand, they accept unconditional terms imposed on them.

Babylon was doomed as a great city. Her fall was pronounced by the prophet in a dramatic way. This prophecy was fulfilled when Babylon fell before the armies of Persia about 538 B.C. [Isa. 46:1].

THE REBELLIOUS CITY

Go up against the land of Merathaim, even against it, and against the inhabitants of Pekod: waste and utterly destroy after them, saith the Lord, and do according to all that I have commanded thee.
                                                    Jer. 50:21

The Aramaic word *memarmeranitha*, derived from *marr*, means "provocative, rebellious, bitter." In the King James Version it was assumed to be the name of a city.

The reference actually is to Babylon, the rebellious and oppressive city that had plundered many nations, captured their silver and gold, and made herself the queen of the nations.

BECOME AS WOMEN

A sword is upon their horses, and upon their chariots, and upon all the mingled people that are in the midst of her; and they shall become as women: a sword is upon her treasures; and they shall be robbed.   Jer. 50:37

The term "women" in this instance signifies physical weakness and nonresistance. This is because women are physically weaker than men, and they seldom fight to defend themselves. "They shall become as women" means, "They will be cowards."

In the East when a man refuses to fight the people say, "He is a woman." The valiant men of Babylon who had conquered many lands were to become cowards in the time of the decisive battle for the beautiful and famous imperial city. The glorious city which had conquered many nations and enslaved their people was to surrender to tribal armies [Jer. 51:31-33].

GOLDEN CUP

Babylon hath been a golden cup in the Lord's hand, that made all the earth drunken: the nations have drunken of her wine; therefore the nations are mad.   Jer. 51:7

Gold is symbolic of glory and majesty. In the story of Daniel [2:32] the image's head was of fine gold. Kings and princes use golden cups when entertaining. Wine is often poured into a large golden cup and passed around.

Gold is used as a symbol of enticement. People are often lured by means of this shiny metal which symbolizes power and glory.

Wine here means the teachings of the Chaldeans, that is, the doctrine of might. The nations who drank from this wine had become drunken with power and greed. Their eyes were closed to God's truth. The kings and princes who sat at Nebuchadnezzar's court had become mad with the new wine. The prophet portrays Babylon as God's agent to punish Judah, who had departed from him, and the other nations who had oppressed the weak nations and plundered their lands. The cup is symbolical of conspiracy and treachery. In the East cups are sometimes poisoned and then given to any guests who happen to be the enemies of the host.

All the nations who had drunk from the cup which Babylon held in her hand were destined to be destroyed, and then Babylon itself was to fall.

DESTROYING MOUNTAIN

Behold, I am against thee, O destroying mountain, saith the Lord, which destroyest all the earth: and I will stretch out mine hand upon thee, and roll thee down from the rocks, and will make thee a burnt mountain. Jer. 51:25

Mountains are symbolic of great kings, dictators, and oppressors, who are hard to be defeated or removed. In Aramaic, despotic rulers are called mountains because it is almost impossible to alter their decrees.

The reference here is to Nebuchadnezzar, the king of Babylon, who was looked upon as a mountain by the small powers in Palestine, Syria, and Elam, the nations which he crushed on his way to Egypt.

The great mountain, the imperial Babylon, was to be removed by the Most High God, the Creator of heaven and earth [Jer. 51:29-30; Zech. 4:7]. What was impossible for men was possible to God.

ARMENIA

Set ye up a standard in the land, blow the trumpet among the nations, prepare the nations against her, call together against her the kingdoms of Ararat, Minni, and Ashchenaz; appoint a captain against her; cause the horses to come up as the rough caterpillars. Jer. 51:27

Jeremiah, in his prophecy relative to the fall of Babylon and the end of the Chaldean realm, predicted that an invasion was to come from the north, that is, from Armenia and Georgia and the combination of the northern races which today are called Russians. Note that less than two centuries earlier all these northern races had been under the dominion of the great Assyrian empire. Babylon was the successor of the imperial Nineveh; but Babylon had not succeeded in crushing the small kingdoms in the north.

At this time these northern races were stronger than the scattered Persian tribes. And the Medes and Parthians were with them.

Armen in Aramaic means "Armenia." The translators into other languages, not knowing the meaning of the word, called it "Minni."

THE FALL OF BABYLON

*And the passages are stopped, and the reeds they have burned
with fire, and the men of war are affrighted.*   Jer. 51:32

The Aramaic word *agmey* means "pools, standing water"—hence, a
bastion made of moats. The Eastern text reads: "And that the crossings
are seized and the bastions are burned with fire and all the men of war
are in confusion."

Wood and timber were used in construction of fortifications. These
materials were burned when the city defenses were destroyed.

A BODY OF WATER

*Therefore thus saith the Lord; Behold, I will plead thy cause,
and take vengeance for thee; and I will dry up her sea, and make
her springs dry.*   Jer. 51:36

The Eastern text reads: "I will dry up the sea of Babylon. . . ."
Babylon was situated on many waters at the junction of the Tigris and
Euphrates rivers. The city was the center of commerce for many nations.

Babylon had moats and warehouses where the merchandise was un-
loaded. But Babylon is not by the sea. "Sea" in this instance, means simply
river or waters. In Aramaic, any large body of water can be called a
sea. At times, even ponds are called *yamta* (lake) or *yama* (sea).

CUP OF VENOM

*In their heat I will make their feasts, and I will make them
drunken, that they may rejoice, and sleep a perpetual sleep, and
not wake, saith the Lord.*   Jer. 51:39

The Eastern text reads: "With venom I will prepare their drinks . . ."
The Aramaic word *khimta* (venom, wrath) resembles *khima* (heat). The
two words were confused by the translators of the King James Version.

The term "venom" is used to indicate the severe vengeance of the
Lord upon the king and the princes of Babylon, the vengeance of
Jerusalem. They were to drink from the cup of gold from which they
had forced other nations to drink and get drunk [Jer. 51:7].

When Babylon fell before the Persian army, King Belshazzar and his princes, generals, and governors were feasting in the palace. The king had ordered the sacred vessel (which his father Nebuchadnezzar had brought from Jerusalem) to be used for wine [Dan. 5:23].

In that very night the city was captured and Darius, the Mede, took the kingdom [Dan. 5:30-31]. Belshazzar and his princes and his nobles were slain while they were drunk at the feast. They slept a perpetual sleep, never to be awakened with music again.

THE ROYAL CITY

How is Sheshach taken! and how is the praise of the whole earth surprised! how is Babylon become an astonishment among the nations!   Jer. 51:41

The Eastern text reads *areshkheta* (royal city, chief city). The name of the city is derived from the name of *Arshak,* the founder of the Parthian empire which succeeded the Chaldean or the Babylonian empire. This name must have been used after the fall of Babylon. Later scribes may have substituted the Parthian name for Babel, Babylon. This name could not have been used by Jeremiah [Jer. 25:26]. Sometimes when important cities were conquered their names were changed. For example, Koriath-arba was renamed Hebron [Josh. 14:15].

Sheshak is a corrupt spelling of the Aramaic word *Areshketa* (royal).

THE SEA

The sea is come up upon Babylon: she is covered with the multitude of the waves thereof.

Her cities are a desolation, a dry land, and a wilderness, a land wherein no man dwelleth, neither doth any son of man pass thereby.   Jer. 51:42-43

"The sea" in this instance is used metaphorically, meaning the surrounding nations which have conquered Babylon. In Aramaic, when a man or a nation is hopeless, we say, "They are in the midst of the sea, tossed by the waves."

Babylon was compassed by her enemies round about, like a ship that is tossed in a violent storm. The once beautiful city, and the glory of the Chaldeans, was reduced into a wilderness, a land without an inhabitant.

It is said that the Persian conquerors damned the river, and then let it flow over the city. Be that as it may, Babylon, because of corruption and oppression, was easily overthrown by small kingdoms.

BEL OR BAAL

And I will punish Bel in Babylon, and I will bring forth out of his mouth that which he hath swallowed up: and the nations shall not flow together any more unto him; yea, the wall of Babylon shall fall.   Jer. 51:44

Bel was one of the many Babylonian gods. Many of the treasures of gold and silver which the Babylonian kings had plundered from the conquered nations were put in the temple of Bel. Jeremiah predicts that all these treasures will be taken out of the temple of Bel.

Bel is another name for Baal, the agricultural god of Lebanon and Syria. Baal was worshiped with sensualities, tortures, and human sacrifices. In Syria, Lebanon, Palestine, and other adjacent lands, most of the temples, altars, and shrines of Baal (Bel) were built upon high places and beside highways. All the Syrian and Palestinian deities were originally imported from Babylon.

The idols at times were carried on the shoulders of men, or on the backs of animals. "Bel has fallen down, Nebo is overthrown; their idols were loaded as burdens upon beasts, yea, upon weary beasts and cattle" [Isa. 46:1, Eastern text].

CHAPTER TWENTY-TWO

THE LAMENTATIONS
OF JEREMIAH

INTRODUCTION

THE style of writing differs from the book that bears the name of the author. This is because the book of Jeremiah was actually written by Baruch, a professional scribe. But the book of Lamentations, seemingly, is the work of the prophet himself. No doubt, Jeremiah was a learned man, but he was not a professional scribe like Baruch. In the East learned men seldom write. They employ scribes whose business is writing from dictation and copying. For example, Paul's letter to the Romans was written by Tertius [Rom. 16:22].

Jeremiah was an eyewitness to the seige and destruction of Jerusalem and the temple. The prophet laments the awful destruction of the once beautiful and prosperous city. The prophet wrote in a simple manner for the simple folk, who weep when the professional minstrels sing at funerals. The Lamentations, or eulogies, are written in a distinct style. Each song begins with an Aramaic or Hebrew letter of the alphabet.

The tone of all the songs is wailing. The beautiful city, the holy temple, and the walls had been destroyed, and a great calamity had befallen the people. The priests, princes, and nobles were reduced to beggars, and the remnant of the people were left like sheep without a shepherd. It was for these simple people whom the king of Babylon had left in the land that the book of Lamentations was written, as it is portrayed in the song. After the singing of each lament the reader stops and the people cry. Such songs of wailing as the book of Lamentations of Jeremiah were composed extemporaneously by the professional singers during a tragedy.

WOMEN RAVISHED

The ways of Zion do mourn, because none come to the solemn feasts: all her gates are desolate: her priests sigh, her virgins are afflicted, and she is in bitterness.   **Lam. 1:4**

The Aramaic word *memakkhan* (to humble, afflict) in this case means "humiliated or ravished."

In the East, during wars, women are raped by the foreign soldiers as an expression of vengeance against their vanquished enemies.

The virgins of Jerusalem and Judah had become the victims of the Chaldean army and their ruthless mercenaries, the Moabites, the Ammonites, the Edomites, and other nations which had joined the Chaldean army.

IMPIOUS ALLIES

I called for my lovers, but they deceived me: my priests and mine elders gave up the ghost in the city, while they sought their meat to relieve their souls.   **Lam. 1:19**

"Lovers" in this instance means "allies"; that is, the nation on whom Judah had put her trust, namely Egypt [Ezek. 16:26].

Both Israel and Judah had refused to trust in the Lord God of their fathers, who had brought them out of the land of Egypt. Despite God's warning they had gone and made alliances with pagan nations who later turned on them and destroyed them. Moreover, they had exchanged the glory of God for that of silver and golden idols, and his way for the corrupt pagan way [Ezek. 8:9-10; 16:26]. The Lord their God had let them suffer with their own evil devices. His prophets had warned them against pagan alliances, but they had refused to heed their warning.

"The presence of the Lord has divided them; he will no more regard them; they did not respect the persons of priests, they did not have compassion on the elders" [Lam. 4:17, Eastern text].

SWALLOWED

The Lord hath swallowed up all the habitations of Jacob, and hath not pitied: he hath thrown down in his wrath the strongholds of the daughter of Judah; he hath brought them down to the ground: he hath polluted the kingdom and the princes thereof.

He hath cut off in his fierce anger all the horn of Israel: he hath drawn back his right hand from before the enemy, and he burned against Jacob like a flaming fire, which devoureth round about.

Lam. 2:2-3

Blaa (swallowed) is used metaphorically, meaning "devoured or completely destroyed." The Lord had permitted Nebuchadnezzar, king of Babylon, to destroy Jerusalem, burn the temple, lay waste the towns, and carry away the people as captives to Babylon.

Both Judah and Israel were laid low, and the glory of Jacob had departed. Jerusalem, the glorious city which God had selected as a place for his holy temple, was in ruins, the sanctuary of the Lord was polluted by the Gentile armies, and the holy vessels were taken to Babylon.

JUDAH'S GLORY GONE

Mine eyes do fail with tears, my bowels are troubled, my liver is poured upon the earth, for the destruction of the daughter of my people; because the children and the sucklings swoon in the streets of the city.

Lam. 2:11

The Aramaic word *ekara* (honor, glory) idiomatically means "pride." In the East we often say, "My honor is poured out on the ground."

The Hebrew word for honor or glory is *keber* from *kabar* (to become great, thick and weighty). The Hebrew word for "liver" is *kabad* (Aramaic *kabda*). The only difference between these two words is the position of the dot over or under the last letter. Because of the similarity of the words, such errors are unavoidable.

The prophet in his lamentation is speaking about the honor or the pride of the state which was trampled upon by the foreign armies. The beautiful temple was destroyed, the historic city was in ruins, and the women had been raped. The pride of Judah was low to the ground.

WEEPING VEHEMENTLY

Their heart cried unto the Lord, O wall of the daughter of Zion, let tears run down like a river day and night: give thyself no rest; let not the apple of thine eye cease.

Lam. 2:18

The prophet is admonishing the people to weep and mourn over the destruction of the daughter of Zion, Jerusalem.

"Let tears run down like a river" is another Eastern idiom which means, "Weep bitterly or vehemently" [Jer. 14:17].

"The apple of my eye" is an Aramaic idiom which means "my dearest one." Easterners often call their dear ones "my eyes," or "the light of my eyes." The eye is the most precious organ of the body. A blind man would give everything he has to have the sight of his eyes restored [Deut. 32:10; Zech. 2:8]. Light is the most precious thing in the world. God is often called the Light of the World. Now, darkness covered Jerusalem and Judah. The light of God was temporarily put out. The golden candlestick, which burned continually, was taken to Babylon. The ark was destroyed, and what was dearest and most sacred to the prophet was gone.

See the commentary on Deuteronomy 32:10.

JUDAH HARASSED

He hath inclosed my ways with hewn stone; he hath made my paths crooked.   Lam. 3:9

The Aramaic word *kobey* (thorns, briers) has been confused in the King James Version with *kepey* (stones).

Kobey, (thorns), pronounced *kowey*, is used here symbolically, referring to sorrows and difficulties. Jerusalem was destroyed, the temple was burned, and the people were taken captive to Babylon. The remnant was left as sheep without a shepherd. Besides the Chaldean army, other nations plundered the land and trampled upon the small remnant.

In the East thorns and briers are used to fence vineyards and gardens. Thorns and briers are also used metaphorically, meaning grievances, hardships, and enemies.

A WOLF

He was unto me as a bear lying in wait, and as a lion in secret places.   Lam. 3:10

The Aramaic words *deba* (wolf) and *diba* (bear) are identical in Aramaic, except that *deba* has an *aleph* (a) and *diba* is rarely written with an *aleph*.

Wolves are subtle. They lie in wait, but bears seldom attack if they are not provoked.

According to the prophet Jeremiah, the Lord has brought this great calamity upon the people and upon Jerusalem as a punishment for their backsliding and evil works [verses 9-17].

But the great disaster was brought by the kings, princes, priests, and impious prophets who had left the God of their fathers and had forsaken his ways. The prophet himself had warned them and implored them to return to God and to his ways. But they had turned a deaf ear to all the messengers of God.

MOUTH IN THE DUST

He sitteth alone and keepeth silence, because he hath borne it upon him.
He putteth his mouth in the dust; if so be there may be hope.
Lam. 3:28-29

"He puts his mouth in the dust" is an Aramaic idiom which means, "He does not boast or speak of great things."

Jerusalem was destroyed and the pride of the nation was humbled. Now the people were to sit down, weep, and keep silent, and meditate upon the glorious past. The sins of the fathers were visited on their children. The people were suffering because their priests and leaders had caused them to go astray after pagan gods and had departed from the way of the God of Israel.

TURN THE OTHER CHEEK

He giveth his cheek to him that smiteth him: he is filled full with reproach.
Lam. 3:30

"He giveth his cheek to him that smiteth" means, "He turns the other cheek." When weak or subjugated people strike back they are usually wounded or slain. Conversely, to turn the cheek means to accept a lesser evil. There are times when silence is golden, and turning of the cheek gives a new lease on life. Jesus apparently was referring to these words when he said, ". . . but whosoever shall smite thee on thy right cheek, turn to him the other also" [Matt. 5:39].

In the East when people are defeated they are reproached and struck on their cheeks. The victim does not dare to strike back, but instead he leaves everything to God.

WEEPING

Mine eye runneth down with rivers of water for the destruction of the daughter of my people.
Lam. 3:48

"Mine eye runneth down with rivers of water" is an Eastern idiom which means, "I weep bitterly." In the East we often say, "Rivers of water run down from my eyes," and, "I washed my mattress with my tears." "I am weary with my groaning; and every night I water my bed and wash my mattress with my tears" [Ps. 6:6, Eastern text].

Such sayings are never taken literally and are well understood both by the learned and the unlearned people [Lam. 2:18].

WEEPING VEHEMENTLY

Mine eye affecteth mine heart, because of all the daughters of my city.
Lam. 3:51

"My eyes run down like streams of water" is an Eastern idiom which means, "I weep vehemently." The people sometimes say, "I washed my clothes in my tears." David says, "Every night I . . . wash my mattress with my tears" [Ps. 6:6, Eastern text]. "I will water thee with my tears" [Isa. 16:9]. "Oh that my head were waters, and mine eyes a fountain of tears, that I might weep day and night for the slain of the daughter of my people!" [Jer. 9:1].

Mary Magdalene washed Jesus' feet with her tears. She wept bitterly and her tears fell on Jesus' feet [Luke 7:38].

These sayings should not be taken literally. In the East they are easily understood [Ps. 119:136].

DROWNED

Waters flowed over mine head; then I said, I am cut off.
Lam. 3:54

"Waters flowed over mine head" means, "I was surrounded with all kinds of difficulties." In the East when a man is in trouble, he says, "I am sunk in the water" or "sunk in mire," which means buried in troubles. These sayings are still used in Aramaic speech as of yore. ". . . and the floods compassed me about: all thy billows and thy waves passed over me" [Jonah 2:3].

Israel was in troubled waters. Jerusalem was in heaps, the holy temple burned, and the king, his princes, and the noblemen slain. The wound was very severe. This was the greatest catastrophe in the history of Judah.

THEIR CONDUCT

Behold their sitting down, and their rising up; I am their music.
Lam. 3:63

The Eastern text reads: "Behold their conduct and their behavior I do understand, because of their devices." "Their sitting down and their rising up" is an Eastern idiom referring to their conduct, etiquette, and manners. In the East people's behavior and good or bad conduct are known by the way they sit down with other people at councils and feasts, and by their rising up. Jesus admonished his disciples not to sit in high places without having been asked by the host.

The reference here is to the Jewish leaders and princes who, even after the fall of Jerusalem, were unwilling to change their ways and listen to him. Their conduct was still bad, for they showed no signs of repentance.

"I am their music" is another Eastern idiom which means, "They gossip about me." Jeremiah had been against Judah's foreign policy. He had told the king and the princes not to rely on Egypt, but to surrender to the king of Babylon. Some of the leaders had blamed him for the defeat, thinking that he had weakened the morale of the armed forces.

SCARCITY OF WATER

The tongue of the sucking child cleaveth to the roof of his mouth for thirst: the young children ask bread, and no man breaketh it unto them.   Lam. 4:4

Water is very scarce in Palestine, and especially in Judea where, during the droughts, wells, brooks, and other water sources dry up.

Jerusalem depends on rain for its water. During the rainy season water is stored under houses and other places to be used during the summer and autumn months. And when the drought lasts two or three years both men and cattle suffer from thirst.

Moreover, during wars when cities are besieged, wells and water sources outside the city are destroyed to prevent the enemy from using them. The people depend entirely on the stored water and wells for drinking.

During the siege of Jerusalem both food and water were so scarce that many people, especially the little ones, perished from thirst and hunger. But on such occasions thirst is worse than hunger.

WATER PURCHASED

We have drunken our water for money; our wood is sold unto us. Lam. 5:4

In villages and other country places water is never bought or sold. Drinking water is fetched from streams, wells, and brooks; and wood for fuel is gathered from the fields. Nevertheless, in desert places where water is scarce, tribes pay a small rent for the use of wells, especially when cattle and sheep are watered. Prior to World War I in many cities in the Near East water was sold in the streets.

On the other hand, in large towns where the wells are far off and the streams that run through the cities are polluted, both drinking water and fuel are bought for money. Wood for fuel is brought from long distances on the backs of camels, donkeys, mules, and men and women, and is sold in the market places.

The Jews were besieged by their enemies. And because of the destruction caused by the invading armies, everything in the cities and towns was scarce and had to be purchased.

The Jews who had fled to foreign lands and those who were taken captive had to buy all the necessities of life. They had lost their towns, lands, orchards, and wells. Apparently, some of them had been able to hide their money and valuables.

GIVEN HAND

We have given the hand to the Egyptians, and to the Assyrians, to be satisfied with bread.   Lam. 5:6

"We have given the hand" is an Aramaic idiom which means, "We have surrendered to our enemies."

Judah had surrendered her sovereignty to the Assyrians and the Egyptians for the food and help they expected to receive.

See the commentary on Jeremiah 50:15.

ARE NOT

Our fathers have sinned, and are not; and we have borne their iniquities.   Lam. 5:7

"Are not" is an Aramaic way of saying dead; that is, "our fathers are no more on this earth."

The people now were suffering because of the sins of their fathers [Jer. 16:11-12]. "The fathers have eaten sour grapes, and the children's teeth are set on edge" [Ezek. 18:2].

The inhabitants of Judah wondered why they should pay for the sins which were committed by their fathers. They forgot that what one generation sows, the next generation reaps, and that there is a law of cause and effect, the law of compensation.

Had their fathers remained loyal to God's law and his commandments, Judah would have been spared and Jerusalem would not have been destroyed.

HARDSHIPS

Our skin was black like an oven, because of the terrible famine.
Lam. 5:10

Black is an unlucky color—it symbolizes death, mourning, suffering, distress, and difficulties. In Aramaic, people who suffer from famine or persecution say, "Our days are black." Black also signifies disgrace and humiliation. "Our skin is black" means, "We are humbled" or "harassed."

After the destruction of Jerusalem the Jews suffered many difficulties. There was a severe famine in which the rich, the noble, and the humble people all suffered. Many people discarded shame and went begging. Others obtained their bread at the peril of their lives [verse 9].

VIRGINS RAVISHED

They ravished the women in Zion, and the maids in the cities of Judah.
Lam. 5:11

The reference here is to the Babylonian army which had defeated Judah, destroyed Jerusalem, and ravished both the women and virgins in the cities as well as in country places.

During wars the women became the victims of the invading armies. As soon as a town was taken some of its women were violated and others carried away captive and sold in market places.

CHAPTER TWENTY-THREE

EZEKIEL

INTRODUCTION

EZEKIEL (Aramaic *Khazkiel*) means, "God has armed me" or "clothed me with armor." The prophet was armed with the truth and strengthened by God so that he might be able to carry his heavy burden during such a turbulent period. He was sent to deliver a weighty message to a people who had turned deaf ears to God's prophets and had become like scorpions and snakes.

Ezekiel was one of the captives who were carried to Babylon with Jehoiakim, the king of Judah, in 597 B.C. The prophet lived among other Jewish captives on the banks of the River Chebar.

The prophet Ezekiel was a priest, the son of Buzi, a Jerusalemite. He started to prophesy during the first captivity of Judah, but he was born a priest-prophet. His main prophecies were before and after the destruction of Jerusalem by Nebuchadnezzar, the king of Babylon.

Ezekiel, like his contemporary Jeremiah, was so sure of his prophecies concerning the fall of Jerusalem and the destruction of the temple that he enacted an allegory in a dramatic manner. He portrayed the city on a tile and laid seige against it [Ezek. 4:1-2]. His vision of a creature with four faces and four wings over the chariot was symbolic of the omnipresence of God's Spirit. The prophet was asked to eat a scroll, which meant he was given wisdom to prophesy. Moreover, the prophet was brought in a vision to Jerusalem to measure the temple of God which was to be rebuilt again. He was so sure of the restoration of the remnant that he gave the people a sketch of the temple and a plan for rebuilding Jerusalem.

Ezekiel, like Jeremiah and Isaiah, prophesied against many pagan nations who had oppressed Israel and had helped the Chaldean army to capture and destroy Jerusalem. The prophet, like Jeremiah, disapproved of Judah's foreign policy and her reliance on pagan nations for her salvation [Ezek. 16:26-30].

The prophet's vision of the dry bones which rose up again assured

793

him of the survival of a remnant and the second Jewish commonwealth and the rebuilding of Jerusalem and the temple. In due time the God of Israel was to triumph over the Gentile world, and the enemies of the Jews were to be defeated. The temple had been destroyed, but the truth for which the temple was built was indestructible. The truth was to issue like water out of the foundation of the temple, and this truth was to heal the nations [Ezek. 47:1-10].

Even though the prophet was sincere and terse in his allegories relative to the rebuilding of Jerusalem and the temple, the people refused to accept his words. Because there were so many false court prophets, people had lost their faith even in the men of God. It is said that Ezekiel was slain by people to whom he had been sent to prophesy.

RIVER KEBAR

Now it came to pass in the thirtieth year, in the fourth month, in the fifth day of the month, as I was among the captives by the river of Chebar, that the heavens were opened, and I saw visions of God.
                                                                    Ezek. 1:1

Chebar (Aramaic *Kebar*) means "abound, great." The reference here is to the River Euphrates which is often called "The Great River." The Mediterranean Sea is known as "The Great Sea."

Some commentators believe that Chebar was a canal in Babylon. The River Euphrates is more likely. Captives and refugees are generally settled in country places far from the cities. The princes and the nobles were brought into the cities to be watched.

THE STRANGE EMBLEM

As for the likeness of their faces, they four had the face of a man, and the face of a lion, on the right side: and they four had the face of an ox on the left side; they four also had the face of an eagle.
                                                                    Ezek. 1:10

The eagle is known as the king of the bird kingdom, and it symbolizes speed and omnipresence. This is because eagles fly faster and soar higher than other birds.

This emblem was used by the Assyrians and probably other races, just as the emblem of an eagle today is used by many nations.

The face of a man means intellect. This is because man is the most intellectual of all God's creations. He can plan his future, create new things, and overcome his difficulties.

A lion symbolizes dominion. The lion is known as the king of the animals, and has dominion over the animal kingdom. A lion can devour other beasts. Therefore, a lion is symbolic of mighty and imperial power. The portrait of a lion appears on the emblems of many nations.

The ox, because of its endurance, was considered the strongest animal and therefore was worshiped as a god by the Assyrians. Some of the Assyrian tribes never ate ox meat until World War I. Note that every face of the image represented a new concept of an imperial power with an aspiration to become a world power.

The divine message was revealed to Ezekiel through this symbol. For all divine messages were imparted in a vision or a dream during the night. The Lord was to speak to Ezekiel and reveal to him things to come. The strange image signifies the omnipresence of God and the speed and the power with which he sends his messages.

SON OF MAN

And he said unto me, Son of man, stand upon thy feet, and I will speak unto thee. Ezek. 2:1

Bar-nasha (son of man) is an Aramaic term of speech meaning a human being, a son of man or an ordinary man. This term is used as a token of humility and as a reminder that men are human beings liable to mistakes and weaknesses. One often hears people saying, *Bar-nasha eleh,* which means, "It might happen." This is because man's knowledge is limited. He does not know what the future has for him.

On the other hand, princes and noblemen are generally addressed, according to their titles, as "my lord"; but simple and humble men are addressed as *bar-nasha,* which means an ordinary man.

Many times Jesus called himself Son of man. He used this term more frequently than the term Son of God. This is because he wanted the people to know that he was human and divine, and that the people should not expect to see him change the world in an hour. He even refused to be called good, and yet he was good.

In the olden days good men were called the sons of God, and the other men the sons of men [Gen. 6:2-4].

The prophet used this term as a token of humility, acknowledging that he was not an angel but a human being who was called to a great and difficult mission and to bear a heavy burden in delivering God's message to his people.

WRITTEN WITHIN AND WITHOUT

But thou, son of man, hear what I say unto thee; Be not thou rebellious like that rebellious house: open thy mouth, and eat that I give thee.

And when I looked, behold, a hand was sent unto me; and, lo, a roll of a book was therein;

And he spread it before me; and it was written within and without: and there was written therein lamentations, and mourning, and woe. Ezek. 2:8-10

The Aramaic *ethpashtath* means "stretched out." "Sent" in the King James Version is a mistranslation. Hand is symbolic of power; and the scroll written from within and without signifies the past and the present. The prophet was given power to see and to explain the past, thus showing how Israel had erred, and to prophesy future events.

The scroll in the stretched-out hand contained the mysteries that the prophet was to reveal to his people. The writing on the scroll consisted of lamentations and mourning, signifying the fall of both Jerusalem and Judah. The writing within the scroll pointed out the present sins of the people, and that on the back pointed out the blunders of their fathers that caused them to suffer.

EAT THE ROLL

Moreover he said unto me, Son of man, eat that thou findest; eat this roll, and go speak unto the house of Israel.

So I opened my mouth, and he caused me to eat that roll.

And he said unto me, Son of man, cause thy belly to eat, and fill thy bowels with this roll that I give thee. Then did I eat it; and it was in my mouth as honey for sweetness. Ezek. 3:1-3

"Eat the scroll" in Semitic languages means, "Study it, analyze it, and make it a part of you." It is often said, "I have eaten my lesson or drunk it like water," which means, "I have learned it by heart."

In the East sweetness in a vision or a dream is often interpreted as a symbol of bitterness and sorrows. The scroll contained a message full of denunciation, condemnation of the sins of Israel, and mourning over the city. It was not an easy thing for the prophet to deliver such a weighty message to a people who were in exile and who had repudiated all the men of God who had admonished them to repent and turn from their evil doings.

But the prophet was told to study the prophecy and to make it a part of his life. The words in the scroll were bitter and harsh, but someone had to deliver them to the rebellious and obstinate people who had refused all of God's admonitions and rejected his prophets.

DIVINELY INSPIRED

Then the spirit took me up, and I heard behind me a voice of a great rushing, saying, Blessed be the glory of the Lord from his place.

I heard also the noise of the wings of the living creatures that touched one another, and the noise of the wheels over against them, and a noise of a great rushing.

So the spirit lifted me up, and took me away, and I went in bitterness, in the heat of my spirit; but the hand of the Lord was strong upon me.   Ezek. 3:12-14

"The spirit took me," means, "I was carried away in a vision." The prophet was taken by the Spirit to see the people in the captivity at Tel-abib, by the river of Chebar [Ezek. 3:15]. Later the prophet is lifted by the Spirit and brought to the east gate of the Lord's house [Ezek. 11:1].

On all these occasions the prophet was in a vision and divinely inspired to prophesy the fall of Jerusalem, the destruction of the holy temple, and the restoration of the remnant. In other words, the prophet was in the realm of the Spirit, looking on everything from above. In the Spirit there is neither space nor time. The Spirit of the Lord revealed everything to him, even the restoration of the remnant of Israel which was to take place years later [Ezek. 11:17-18].

HAND UPON HIM

And the hand of the Lord was there upon me; and he said unto me, Arise, go forth into the plain, and I will there talk with thee.
                                                Ezek. 3:22

Laying hands on a person is an Aramaic idiom which has several meanings. In every case, the meaning is determined by the context, the verses immediately preceding or following.

". . . and when they had prayed, they laid their hands on them"; that is, they gave them power or authority [Acts 6:6]. God told Moses to lay his hands upon Joshua, the son of Nun [Num. 27:18]. Then again, in the East, people lay their hands on the animals which they have devoted to God. Moreover, when a girl becomes engaged, it is said they have laid hands upon her. This means she is designated to be given in marriage. On the other hand, when a person is arrested or it is found that he has committed a crime, it is said, "They have laid hands upon him." "And they laid hands on them, and put them in hold [detained them] unto the next day . . ." [Acts 4:3; Ezek. 3:25].

But in this instance laying on of hands means the granting of power and authority so that the prophet might embark on his mission. The Lord was also to show him how to deliver his message and how to approach the rebellious people, and to tell him that they would bind him with chains.

THE SPIRIT ENTERED INTO ME

Then the spirit entered into me, and set me upon my feet, and spake with me, and said unto me, Go, shut thyself within thine house.

But thou, O son of man, behold, they shall put bands upon thee, and shall bind thee with them, and thou shalt not go out among them.
                                                            Ezek. 3:24-25

"The spirit entered into me" means that the prophet was in a vision. Another way of saying the same thing would be "the Spirit of the Lord was upon me," that is, "I prophesied." All the occurrences in these verses took place in a vision while the prophet was in a deep sleep or in a trance. God often speaks to men in a dream or in a vision during the night [Job 33:15].

The prophet was carried away by the Spirit to see the city and to measure the temple. "In the visions of God brought he me into the land of Israel, and set me upon a very high mountain . . ." [Ezek. 40:2]. In a vision, things occur fast. One can build the Empire State Building in a minute, or see the whole world, for the Spirit knows neither space nor distance.

The Eastern text reads: ". . . they shall put chains upon you, and shall bind you with them . . ."

A DRAWING ON TILE

Thou also, son of man, take thee a tile, and lay it before thee, and portray upon it the city, even Jerusalem:

And lay siege against it, and build a fort against it, and cast a mount against it; set the camp also against it, and set battering rams against it round about.
                                                            Ezek. 4:1-2

This is the first reference in the Bible to a design or an architectural drawing of a city. The Assyrians used tile or brick for writing, and for maps and drawings of cities and palaces. Temple drawings might have been sketched on the tile by King Hiram and King Solomon.

Even today, in remote regions where paper is scarce, the people use soil or sand when making maps, drawing plans, dividing property, or directing the shepherds to new grazing areas.

Hebrew prophets either explained things by means of words or acted them out. The prophet was so sure of the fall of Jerusalem that he was not afraid to portray the historic and holy city besieged by the Chaldean army. The Lord had revealed to him the impending disaster which was to fall upon the historic city. The prophet was told to draw this plan in order to convince the people who were in exile who still had confidence in Egypt and did not believe that Jerusalem would fall.

DISLOYALTY TO GOD

Therefore thus saith the Lord God; Because ye multiplied more than the nations that are round about you, and have not walked in my statutes, neither have kept my judgments, neither have done according to the judgments of the nations that are round about you.
Ezek. 5:7

The Aramaic word *ethkhashwton* is derived from *khashab* (to think, count, number, reckon). "Multiplied" is a mistranslation. In this instance the word means "to regard" or "to be considerate." The reference is to the pagan statutes and ordinances of which the Jews were mindful. They had been warned by Moses, by Joshua, and by the prophets against following pagan statutes and laws which were contrary to the statutes and ordinances which Moses had given them.

The people had forgotten the statutes and ordinances of the Lord God and were worshiping pagan gods. They were more considerate of pagan ordinances than of the pure worship of the God of their fathers.

In other words, the prophet complains because the people were obeying pagan ordinances instead of the laws of their God.

BUYER AND SELLER

The time is come, the day draweth near: let not the buyer rejoice, nor the seller mourn: for wrath is upon all the multitude thereof.

For the seller shall not return to that which is sold, although they were yet alive: for the vision is touching the whole multitude thereof, which shall not return; neither shall any strengthen himself in the iniquity of his life.
Ezek. 7:12-13

In the East a buyer rejoices when he is able to buy the merchandise that he desires. In biblical lands, buying and selling and other business transactions are rare as compared with the Western countries. Credit is unknown. All business transactions are in cash or barter. Then again, the buyer may wait a long time in order to acquire that which he desires; and when he does acquire it he rejoices over the deal.

On the other hand, most of those who sell wheat, cattle, sheep, and fields are forced to sell, and therefore they are sad and mourn when they sell and part with the things they love. They sell to pay taxes and to meet other urgent needs. At times the seller is forced to sell for whatever he can get for his goods, land, or animals.

When fields were sold they were returned to the seller in the year of Jubilee. The prophet predicts a day of vengeance and a dark and hopeless future wherein both the buyer and the seller would perish.

AS APPEARANCE OF GOD

Then I beheld, and lo a likeness as the appearance of fire: from the appearance of his loins even downward, fire; and from his loins even upward, as the appearance of brightness, as the color of amber.
Ezek. 8:2

The Eastern text reads: ". . . and from his loins and upward, brightness, as the appearance of God"; that is, a glorious appearance which cannot be described for its beauty—something which human imagination cannot comprehend or grasp.

VISION OF GOD

And he put forth the form of a hand, and took me by a lock of mine head; and the spirit lifted me up between the earth and the heaven, and brought me in the visions of God to Jerusalem, to the door of the inner gate that looketh toward the north; where was the seat of the image of jealousy, which provoketh to jealousy.
Ezek. 8:3

The prophet's soul was lifted up between earth and heaven and carried away to Jerusalem in a divine vision. And in the vision the prophet saw himself walking on the streets of Jerusalem and viewing the holy city from different directions. Then he saw the abominations which were committed in it. And he also was shown the image of lust which provoked lust; that is, a pagan statue of a nude woman, and other images that the unfaithful kings of Judah had placed in the house of the Lord. The prophet was brought to Jerusalem by the Spirit to see the temple and the immoral pagan worship.

In most cases God appeared to his holy prophets in visions and dreams when the prophets were at rest and in the stillness of the night [Job 33:15].

See also the articles on "Visions."

TEMPLE POLLUTED

He said furthermore unto me, Son of man, seest thou what they do? even the great abominations that the house of Israel committeth here, that I should go far off from my sanctuary? but turn thee yet again, and thou shalt see greater abominations.　　　Ezek. 8:6

This vision was seen while Ezekiel was in captivity [verses 2-3]. In his vision he saw the sad condition which prevailed in the holy temple at Jerusalem. The prophet in his vision made a detailed survey of the conditions in Judah, especially the pagan worship, which had caused Judah and Jerusalem to lie low.

The temple, long before the first captivity of Judah, was profaned by the immoral pagan worship and idolatry which were set up in the sanctuary, even in the holy place [Isa. 43:28, Eastern text].

These visions were seen by the prophet from a far-off land. Ezekiel places the blame and responsibility for the captivity upon the people of Judah, who had continued their backsliding and who had introduced the immoral pagan worship into the temple of God. The prophet, in order to dramatize the apostasy and the evils of his people, depicts everything in detail as though he were actually in Jerusalem [Ezek. 8:9-10; 10:1-22].

These visions were a warning to the people who were in Babylon of the calamities which were to befall the people who were still in Judah and Jerusalem and who relied on the temple and God's past agreements with their fathers, which they had already broken.

GIRDLES OF SAPPHIRE

And, behold, six men came from the way of the higher gate, which lieth toward the north, and every man a slaughter weapon in his hand; and one man among them was clothed with linen, with a writer's inkhorn by his side: and they went in, and stood beside the brazen altar.　　　Ezek. 9:2

The Eastern text reads: ". . . and his loins were girded with girdles of sapphire . . ."

These beautiful and costly girdles of sapphire blue were worn by kings and princes of the realm. Some of these jeweled belts are still used today. They signify authority.

The man with the sapphire girdle was an angel or prince of God who was commissioned to cleanse the temple of the Lord and to execute judgment.

The priests and the elders of Israel had polluted the temple of God by introducing in it pagan rituals and sensual Baal-worship practices [Isa. 43:28]. Only those who were marked were to be spared [verse 4].

The vision reveals that Judah, like Israel, was rejected and the glory of God had departed from the temple which soon was to be destroyed by the Chaldean army [verses 6-7].

The remnant; that is, those who had remained loyal to God, who were tormented and who sighed on account of the abominations, were to be marked and thus spared. In the East sheep and lambs are marked either for the slaughter or to be spared. The remnant was marked to be spared and to return to Jerusalem and rebuild the temple [verse 3].

PROPHECY

And the Spirit of the Lord fell upon me, and said unto me, Speak; Thus saith the Lord; Thus have ye said, O house of Israel: for I know the things that come into your mind, every one of them.
Ezek. 11:5

"The Spirit of the Lord fell upon me," means, "I was in a vision." At times it is said, "And the Spirit entered into me" [Ezek. 2:2; 3:24]. On some such occasions it is said, "I was in the Spirit."

True prophecy comes through the Spirit; that is, the Spirit of God. God is the eternal Spirit, and his words can be understood only in a spiritual manner, in a vision. One has to rise high into the realm of the Spirit in order to be able to commune with God and to hear the small inner voice.

See the article on "Visions."

STONY HEART

And I will give them one heart, and I will put a new spirit within you; and I will take the stony heart out of their flesh, and will give them a heart of flesh.
Ezek. 11:19

"Stony heart" is an Aramaic idiom meaning stubborn, obstinate or stiffnecked. When a man is stubborn it is said that "he has a heart of stone" or that "his heart is hard as flint."

Then again, when men are stricken or paralyzed it is said, "He has become like a stone," which means he is paralyzed [1 Sam. 25:37-38].

Both Israel and Judah were stubborn and difficult to deal with. After having seen so many miracles and wonders which God performed before their eyes, they still left him and went after strange gods. And their departures from the true religion of their forefathers caused them to be taken into captivity.

On the other hand, the people were always difficult in their dealings with the prophets and men of God. They refused to heed their admonitions and turn from their evil ways. And at times they even murdered the messengers of God who were sent to warn them and lead them into the way of God.

FALSE PRIDE

Son of man, prophesy against the prophets of Israel that prophesy, and say thou unto them that prophesy out of their own hearts, Hear ye the word of the Lord;

Thus saith the Lord God; Woe unto the foolish prophets, that follow their own spirit, and have seen nothing!   Ezek. 13:2-3

The Aramaic word *rookha* (spirit) also means pride, rheumatism, and wind. But, in this instance, it means "pride." "Blessed are the humble [poor in pride]" [Matt. 5:3, Eastern text].

These false prophets spoke in the name of the Lord in order to make the people believe in their divinations. They were proud of the counsel they had given to princes and kings. But the Lord had revealed nothing to these false prophets, nor did they see visions. They prophesied the things that pleased the king, the princes, and the people. They preached peace, prosperity, and security even when war was imminent and the people were in danger. They did this because of their false pride. In most instances, during critical times, the kings and the princes took the advice of the false prophets and rejected God's counsel which was given by the true prophets.

UNTEMPERED MORTAR

Thus will I accomplish my wrath upon the wall, and upon them that have daubed it with untempered mortar, and will say unto you, The wall is no more, neither they that daubed it. Ezek. 13:15

Jerusalem was noted as a walled city. The historic and holy city had several walls and other fortifications which were strengthened from time to time.

Untempered mortar is mortar that has not been given the proper consistency and hardness. For example, tempered steel is given the desired hardness. Thus, the untempered mortar is symbolic of the weakness of the city, its defenses, and its untrustworthy alliances. The daubers of the wall were the false prophets, who preached peace and security and caused the people to rely on foreign alliances, and the princes who trusted in fortifications.

All these false assurances were likened by God to a weak wall daubed with untempered mortar [Ezek. 13:10; Jer. 29:9].

VICIOUS BEASTS

If I cause noisome beasts to pass through the land, and they spoil it, so that it be desolate, that no man may pass through because of the beasts.
                                                                                        Ezek. 14:15

The Aramaic reads "vicious beasts"; that is, beasts of prey. When a city is made desolate it becomes the dwelling place of wild beasts and unclean birds and reptiles [Jer. 51:37-38].

When cities and towns lie in ruins and without inhabitants, wild beasts increase so that even travelers cannot pass through them. Moreover, the vicious beasts attack the sheep camps and devour any children, sheep, and cattle that happen to be in their way [Lev. 26:22].

When the cities of the northern kingdom were destroyed and the Israelites carried captive to Assyria and the people of other races were brought from the other side of the River Euphrates and settled in their place, they found that the land was already filled with lions and other wild beasts so that they could not live safely in it [2 Kings 17:25-26].

VINES FOR FUEL

Son of man, What is the vine tree more than any tree, or than a branch which is among the trees of the forest?
Shall wood be taken thereof to do any work? or will men take a pin of it to hang any vessel thereon?   Ezek. 15:2-3

In the East when vineyards are pruned the cut branches of the vines are gathered and stored for fuel. In Palestine there is a shortage of fuel. Women collect vine branches, thorns, briers, and dry stubble for baking, cooking, and heating. Since nothing can be made from the wood of the vine, it is used for kindling and for fuel.

Vine is symbolic of Israel, "For the vineyard of the Lord of hosts is the house of Israel . . ." [Isa. 5:7]. "Yet I had planted thee a noble vine . . ." [Jer. 2:21; Matt. 20:1; Mark 12:1]. Israel and Judah were destroyed just as fire destroys dry vine twigs. Even though they were planted as a vine by God, husbanded and watered, they had brought forth wild grapes. They had failed to keep God's commandments and live up to the promises they had made. They had become so corrupt that they were good for nothing. Therefore, the vine (Israel) was to be used for fuel; that is, destroyed by the king of Babylon [Isa. 9:19].

LARGE FLESH

Thou hast also committed fornication with the Egyptians thy neighbors, great of flesh; and hast increased thy whoredoms, to provoke me to anger.   Ezek. 16:26

Judah is often portrayed as the unfaithful wife of God who had left him and gone after pagan gods and made alliances with pagan nations [Ezek. 8:10; 16:30-32]. "Great flesh" is an idiom meaning "men of large sex organs." This saying is still used in several Near Eastern languages. When a woman leaves her husband and goes after a stranger, it is said, "She has gone after him because his sex member is larger."

The prophet is accusing Judah of her unfaithfulness to God whom she had deserted and gone whoring after idols and had made alliances with Egypt and Assyria. Thus, the term "large flesh" is used metaphorically, meaning more advantages. The prophets used all kinds of allegories and similitudes in order to impress the people.

See the commentary on Ezekiel 23:20.

JUDAH AS A HARLOT

They give gifts to all whores: but thou givest thy gifts to all thy lovers, and hirest them, that they may come unto thee on every side for thy whoredom.

And the contrary is in thee from other women in thy whoredoms, whereas none followeth thee to commit whoredoms: and in that thou givest a reward and no reward is given unto thee therefore thou art contrary.   Ezek. 16:33-34

A degenerate person is likened to a harlot who has lost her beauty and charm and runs after her lovers and pays them to commit fornication with her. This is because in Bible lands the lovers pay the harlot and they try hard to find her. But when a harlot has become well known for her evil acts, even those who have committed adultery with her hide away from her; and those who in the past have paid her now demand a payment from her in order to consent to be with her.

The harlot is Judah, and the lovers are the foreign nations, Egypt and

Assyria, upon whom she has relied for peace and security. Judah, like Israel, had left God and gone after foreign gods just as a woman leaves her husband and goes after strange lovers. She had offered little children on the altars of Baal and filled Jerusalem with pagan abominations.

But now Judah was so weak that no respectable power would make an alliance with her. She had to pay for her security, but the nation in which she had put her trust was also a weak power which had suffered several defeats.

JERUSALEM A HARLOT

Wherefore, O harlot, hear the word of the Lord:
Thus saith the Lord God; Because thy filthiness was poured out, and thy nakedness discovered through thy whoredoms with thy lovers, and with all the idols of thy abominations, and by the blood of thy children, which thou didst give unto them. Ezek. 16:35-36

Jerusalem, like Babylon, is called the harlot; that is, the unfaithful city in which treachery and deceit were wrought and much innocent blood shed. Moreover, the backsliding people worshiped pagan idols and sacrificed their children to them.

"Lovers" means allies; that is, the kings with whom Judah had made alliances. These very nations had sought the destruction of Jerusalem. God had constantly warned both Israel and Judah not to trust in foreign aid and the arm of flesh. Both the kings of Israel and the kings of Judah had refused to hearken to God's counsel which was given by the holy prophets. They followed after the devices of their own hearts and the teaching of false prophets who again and again had caused them to go astray from the way of God. Now Baal worship was common, and images and idols were seen in the temple and on all high places. "Nakedness" means humiliation. Jerusalem was to be captured and burned by the Chaldeans, and Judah was to be humbled.

PARABLE OF THE EAGLE

And the word of the Lord came unto me, saying,
Son of man, put forth a riddle, and speak a parable unto the house of Israel;
And say, Thus saith the Lord God; A great eagle with great wings, long-winged, full of feathers, which had divers colors, came unto Lebanon, and took the highest branch of the cedar.

Ezek. 17:1-3

The eagle mentioned here is Nebuchadnezzar, the king of Babylon. An eagle is symbolic of a great imperial power, and its wings symbolize omnipresence. Diverse colors are diverse peoples and nations within the realm of Babylon.

In 721 B.C., Shalmaneser, the king of Assyria, came against Lebanon, Syria, and Samaria. The Lebanese, Syrians, and Israelites were carried as captives to the rich lands of Mesopotamia and Iran. Babylon succeeded the realm of Assyria. The latter was gone and now Babylon was seeking to subjugate all the lands that formerly had paid tribute to Assyria and had made alliances with Egypt [2 Kings 24:12-17].

The "seed of the land" is some of the population thereof. "Great waters" are the rivers Euphrates and Tigris. The Jews were carried away captive, and grew up and prospered, but remained a subjugated people. The "top of his young twigs" which were cropped represent Jehoiakim, the king of Judah, who was removed by Nebuchadnezzar, king of Babylon, and replaced by Zedekiah [2 Kings 24:15-17].

The second eagle, in verse 7, is Egypt, in whom Judah trusted. "This vine did bend her roots toward him" means that the Israelites looked to Egypt for deliverance from Babylon.

Those changes would not bring peace and prosperity to Judah, for in the end Jerusalem would fall and the vine would dry up.

FOWL OF EVERY WING

> Thus saith the Lord God; I will also take of the highest branch of the high cedar, and will set it; I will crop off from the top of his young twigs a tender one, and will plant it upon a high mountain and eminent:
> In the mountain of the height of Israel will I plant it: and it shall bring forth boughs, and bear fruit, and be a goodly cedar: and under it shall dwell all fowl of every wing; in the shadow of the branches thereof shall they dwell.   Ezek. 17:22-23

The reference here is to the messianic fulfillment and the true religion of Israel which, in due time, was to become a universal religion. The branch of the high cedar is the religion of Israel, which was the highest concept of God. The seed, true religion, was preserved in the remnant, which at this time was germinating in Babylon. A tender branch of it was to be planted on the highest mountain of Israel. A great many Jews were to return to dwell in Israel.

This tree, religion, was to bear goodly fruits, and under it were to dwell all fowl of every wing, which means people of every race and color. In due time all these races were to embrace the true religion proclaimed by the Hebrew prophets and fulfilled by the Messiah.

This prophecy was fulfilled through Jesus Christ. Today people of many races and colors have surrendered to him and have taken refuge

in the religion of Israel which represented the spiritual and eternal life.
See the parable of the seed, Matthew 13.

SOUL THAT DIES

*Behold, all souls are mine; as the soul of the father, so also the
soul of the son is mine: the soul that sinneth, it shall die. Ezek. 18:4*

"The soul that sinneth, it shall die" means the soul that departs from
God's way shall die. The term *naphsha* (soul) in Semitic languages
means also "person, spirit, life." God is like a vine and men the branches
thereof. And the branches must abide in the vine or die.

When a person or a soul is not conscious of the living God, that
person or soul is dead. We cannot think of resurrection and eternity
without belief in an eternal and living God. The idols were temporal
images made by men. Their worshipers had no concept of immortality
and hence no high ideals of morality and sanctity which give hope for
life hereafter. Immorality in the Baal worship was the result of man's
concept of temporal life. The priests of Baal believed only in one life.
They ate, drank, and committed immoral acts because that was the only
joy they could derive out of this temporal life. To these worshipers of
Baal, death was the end, and all man's rewards were in this life.

The prophet sees hope of salvation for those who would continue in
God's way, refrain from the worship of idols, give bread to the hungry,
and live a pious life. The people would be judged according to their
works.

GOOD WORKS

*And hath not oppressed any, but hath restored to the debtor his
pledge, hath spoiled none by violence, hath given his bread to the
hungry, and hath covered the naked with a garment.   Ezek. 18:7*

All Hebrew prophets emphasized good works as the highest evidence
of piety and spiritual religion. The priests, on the other hand, demanded
observance of the law, rituals, sacrifices, and the keeping of the ecclesiastical ordinances. They were not concerned with charity, mercy, and kindness.

Jesus referred to these words when he said, "For I was hungry, and
you gave me food; I was thirsty, and you gave me drink; I was a stranger
and you took me in . . ." [Matt. 25:35-46, Eastern text].

True religion is expressed not in observance of customs and traditions, but in spiritual works. Only those who believe in God and eternal life sincerely believe in charity.

HIGH MOUNTAINS

That hath not eaten upon the mountains, neither hath lifted up his eyes to the idols of the house of Israel, hath not defiled his neighbor's wife.   Ezek. 18:15

"Eaten upon the mountains" refers to participation in pagan rituals and sacrifices, which were customarily conducted in shrines on hilltops and mountains. Some of the ruins of pagan altars and shrines remain to the present day on the tops of high hills and mountains. In the olden days the people thought they could be nearer to God on the top of the mountains. Some of them believed that his dwelling was actually on the tops of the high mountains.

The temples and shrines of Baal were usually built on high places, and the worshipers participated in sensual rituals. Baal worship had been a stumbling block to the Israelites, but some of them always remained loyal to their God and his ordinances.

See the commentary on Numbers 25:2.

LIONESS

And say, What is thy mother? A lioness: she lay down among lions, she nourished her whelps among young lions.   Ezek. 19:2

The lioness in this instance means Judah, who had made alliances with surrounding kings. The term "lion" usually means a king.

Judea raised two kings, Jehoahaz and Eliakim, the sons of Josiah. Jehoahaz was dethroned and put in bonds by Pharaoh Necho, the king of Egypt, and Eliakim, his brother, was made king in his stead and his name was changed to Jehoiakim. After his death, Jehoiachim, his son, reigned in his place. But Nebuchadnezzar, king of Babylon, took him captive to Babylon and made his uncle, Mattaniah, king over Judah, changing his name to Zedekiah. Thus, Judah became a protectorate of Babylon [2 Kings 23:31-37; 24:17].

This was the most critical period in the history of Judah. For a long time the people were harassed, first by Assyria, then by Babylon, and then by Egypt. The kings, princes, and court prophets were so confused that they did not know where to turn for help. They had also forsaken their God and his prophets and had gone after pagan gods, hoping thus to reconcile the pagan kings.

LIFT UP MY HAND

And say unto them, Thus saith the Lord God; In the day when I chose Israel, and lifted up mine hand unto the seed of the house of Jacob, and made myself known unto them in the land of Egypt, when I lifted up mine hand unto them, saying, I am the Lord your God.   Ezek. 20:5

"Lifted up my hand to them" is an Aramaic idiom which means, "I swore to them." In the East when a person takes an oath or makes an agreement he lifts up his right hand. At times, when taking an oath by the altar or on the Bible, people raise their hands toward the holy object. When swearing by God they lift up their right hand toward heaven. Then again, when Easterners make supplications to God they lift up their hands toward heaven. In this instance God is portrayed as a monarch taking an oath. God's promises to the Hebrew patriarchs were made in divine visions; that is, they saw God as they would see an earthly ruler.

The reference here is to promises which God had made to Abraham and other Hebrew patriarchs [Gen. 17:7; Exod. 6:7-8].

GOD'S LAWS ARE GOOD

Wherefore I gave them also statutes that were not good, and judgments whereby they should not live.   Ezek. 20:25

"I gave them" in this instance means, "I allowed them to do what they wanted"; that is, "I was through with them." The reference is to the rebellious people in the desert who transgressed God's laws and ordinances, and chose to walk after pagan gods and their statutes. "So they walked according to the desires of their own hearts and according to their own counsels" [Ps. 81:12, Eastern text].

God does not give men statutes or laws that are not good, but when men rebel against him and act contrary, he permits them to follow after the evil devices of their own heart. This is because God has endowed man with freedom and the right to choose good or evil. God had warned Israel, but Israel had refused to heed his admonitions and to keep God's laws and ordinances. The evil which befell them was the result of their own stubbornness, backsliding, and breaking of the covenant which they had made with God.

REMNANT PURGED

*As I live, saith the Lord God, surely with a mighty hand, and
with a stretched out arm, and with fury poured out, will I rule
over you:*

*And I will bring you out from the people, and will gather you
out of the countries wherein ye are scattered, with a mighty hand,
and with a stretched out arm, and with fury poured out.*

*And I will bring you into the wilderness of the people, and there
will I plead with you face to face.*   Ezek. 20:33-35

This prophecy concerns the remnant of Israel which was scattered
among the Gentiles. They were to be gathered from among the nations
and brought into their own land and there ruled with a mighty hand
and with an outstretched arm ready to punish them with fury.

The people were once more to be taken into the wilderness to be disciplined and purged of their evil works. "For he shall return to refine
and purify the people like silver; and he shall cleanse the sons of Levi
and purge them like gold and silver . . ." [Mal. 3:3-4, Eastern text].

"Wilderness" is used metaphorically, meaning "starting all over." It
took the Israelites who entered into the Promised Land forty years of
training, discipline, and cleansing in an arid land before they were able
to cross the River Jordan into the Promised Land.

The remnant which was to be gathered from among the nations was
to go through the same processes as their fathers had, centuries before.
They were to repent of their evil ways and shake off the dust of materialism and paganism which they had acquired in foreign lands.

Now Israel was in the second stage of her journey. Now they will be
prepared to enter into a new covenant, written on their hearts, and into
the true land of promise where they will become God's people, and
God will be their God.

GREEN TREE AND DRY TREE

*And say to the forest of the south, Hear the word of the Lord;
Thus saith the Lord God; Behold, I will kindle a fire in thee,
and it shall devour every green tree in thee, and every dry tree:
the flaming flame shall not be quenched, and all faces from the
south to the north shall be burned therein.*   Ezek. 20:47

"Tree" is often used to mean "men." In biblical language man is
often likened to a tree, and humanity to a forest. "Green tree" in this

instance is symbolic of innocent persons, and dry trees represent the wicked. Jesus spoke of good trees and bad trees, meaning good men and bad men [Matt. 7:17].

The fire, that is, the impending punishment, was to be so severe that it would destroy everything. Both the good and the bad would suffer. Often the righteous suffer because of the sins of the wicked.

Jesus said, "If they do these things in a green tree, what shall be done in the dry?" [Luke 23:31] which means, "If they can bring so much suffering upon an innocent person, how much more upon a wicked person!" Jesus was good and innocent, and yet he suffered the death of a sinner [verse 48].

SET THY FACE

Son of man, set thy face toward Jerusalem, and drop thy word
toward the holy places, and prophesy against the land of Israel.
Ezek. 21:2

"Set thy face" means "Be ready and point out the place." "Drop thy word" means to pour out condemnations. The prophet was thus admonished to make Jerusalem and the temple the targets of his attacks. Jerusalem was to be delivered into the hand of the Chaldean army, and the temple was to be destroyed [verse 12].

The city and the temple were the most sacred institutions in Israel. But the kings and princes of Judah had been corrupt and rebellious, and the priests had gone astray from the true religion of their fathers and had taken up pagan worship. The kings had trusted in pagan kings and pagan alliances so that even the sacred temple and the holy city were not to be spared.

THE END OF THE ROYAL FAMILY

Because it is a trial, and what if the sword contemn even the
rod? it shall be no more, saith the Lord God.   Ezek. 21:13

Evidently the translators of the King James Version mistook the Aramaic word *sharbta* (family) for *shabta* (rod). The reference here is to the royal family which, because of many evils which were committed by the kings of Judah, was to be rejected and never be established again.

From the time of Manasseh and Amon to Zedekiah, the last king of Judah, the people had worshiped Baal and had introduced immoral pagan worship into the Holy of Holies [Ezek. 20:29, Eastern text].

Judah, like Israel, was thus rejected by God. The people were carried away captive to Babylon, and the long-established royal house of David came to an end. The royal family was rejected during the days of the prophet Ezekiel, and since then there never has been a king from the house of David. The kings of Judah, the descendants of David, had broken the covenant which God had made with David, by which God had promised that one of his heirs would always sit upon his throne. But the covenant was conditional. The descendants of David were required to walk in the way of the Lord and to keep God's commandments. Jerusalem was spared many times for David's sake [2 Kings 20:5-6; Isa. 37:33-35]. But now the kings of Judah had gone too far in their evil ways.

LIVER

For the king of Babylon stood at the parting of the way, at the head of the two ways, to use divination: he made his arrows bright, he consulted with images, he looked in the liver.   Ezek. 21:21

The Eastern text reads: ". . . he shoots an arrow, he inquires of his idol, he sees his triumph." The Aramaic reads *khaza beshokhey* (He saw his glory, victory).

The Hebrew word for "glory" is *kabada* and the word for "liver" is *kabad*. The Aramaic word for "liver" is *kabda*. The biblical Hebrew, with the exception of certain words and idioms, was very close to the Aramaic, the language which the Hebrew patriarchs spoke.

Kabda (liver) might easily be confused with the Hebrew word *kabada* (glory). In other words, Nebuchadnezzar, the king of Babylon, saw that he would win the battle. He shot an arrow, then he followed the right counsel or the left counsel, according to the direction of the arrow at the parting of the road. The Aramaic indicates that he saw that he would triumph in the battle.

Had the Aramaic translator translated the Hebrew word *kabad* (liver), the Aramaic would read *kabda;* but the Aramaic text reads *shokha* (glory, triumph). Had the original word been liver, then the author would have told what happened after the divination. Neither the Hebrew nor the King James versions conveys the meaning or points out the outcome of the divination, whereas the Aramaic text does reveal the result of the divination.

Some authorities maintain that this passage refers to the practice of certain diviners of foretelling events by examining the liver of an animal.

Prior to such divination an animal was killed as an offering to a god or idol in order to receive a good omen. The Hebrews also offered such offerings when they went to their holy places or inquired of God [1 Sam. 13:9; 1 Kings 14:1-3].

CURSING FATHER OR MOTHER

In thee have they set light by father and mother: in the midst of thee have they dealt by oppression with the stranger: in thee have they vexed the fatherless and the widow. Ezek. 22:7

The Eastern text reads: "In you have they cursed father and mother . . ."

The fifth commandment reads: "Honor your father and your mother, that your days may be long upon the land which the Lord your God gives you" [Exod. 20:12, Eastern text]. "Cursed be he who reviles his father or his mother . . ." [Deut. 27:16, Eastern text].

During the time of the prophet Ezekiel the commandments of the Lord were broken and his ordinances transgressed. Many of the people were worshiping pagan gods and therefore did not respect their parents.

Jesus condemned the violation of the law. He said, "Why do you also disregard the commandment of God on account of your tradition; for God said, Honor your father and your mother, and whoever curses his father or his mother, let him be put to death" [Matt. 15:3-4, Eastern text].

EAT UPON THE MOUNTAINS

In thee are men that carry tales to shed blood: and in thee they eat upon the mountains: in the midst of thee they commit lewdness. Ezek. 22:9

"They eat upon the mountains" refers to worship and sacrifice on the high places. Most of the pagan altars and idols were built on high places, hills, and on the tops of mountains. The worshipers offered sacrifices, ate broiled meat with bread, drank wine and strong drink, and danced and committed all kinds of lewd and immoral acts.

The reference here is to Jerusalem which had forsaken the Lord God and had engaged in pagan religious practices upon the hills and on the high places in Judea.

See the article on "High Places" [Deut. 12:2-3, 1 Kings 14:22-24].

FATHER'S NAKEDNESS

In thee have they discovered their fathers' nakedness: in thee have they humbled her that was set apart for pollution. Ezek. 22:10

This verse should read: "In you have they uncovered the nakedness of their father's concubines," which means that the men of Jerusalem have committed adultery with their fathers' wives or concubines.

The Israelites, like other Semitic races, practiced polygamy. Many wealthy men and princes had several wives. Even today the Jews in the Near East marry more than one wife.

At times one of the elder sons might commit adultery with one of hi father's wives. Reuben, the son of Jacob, committed adultery with Bilhah, his father's concubine [Gen. 35:22; 49:4, Lev. 18:8; 20:11].

HALF SISTER

And one hath committed abomination with his neighbor's wife;
and another hath lewdly defiled his daughter-in-law; and another
in thee hath humbled his sister, his father's daughter. Ezek. 22:11

"His father's daughter" in this instance means his half-sister, the daughter of one of his father's wives or concubines.

In the olden days, when men married many wives, family ties were weak. A man's wives frequently quarreled among themselves and, consequently, their children often hated each other. Moreover, in those days pagan men married their own sisters and other close relatives, which was forbidden in the law of Moses. For example, the Pharaohs married their own sisters.

Amnon, the son of David, defiled his half sister, Tamar [2 Sam. 13:10-14]. Absalom, another son of David, defiled his father's concubine [2 Sam. 16:21-22].

Such evil deeds were contrary to the law of God and were punishable by death [Lev. 20:10-14]. These abominable practices which prevailed in Jerusalem and Judah were introduced by the wicked kings of Judah, by false prophets, and by the priests of Baal.

"STRIKE MY HANDS"

Behold, therefore I have smitten mine hand at thy dishonest gain
which thou hast made, and at thy blood which hath been in the
midst of thee.   Ezek. 22:13

The Eastern text reads: "Behold, therefore I will strike my hands together with anger because of the iniquity which you have done and because of the blood which has been shed in the midst of you." "Strike my hands together" is an Aramaic idiom, an expression of surprise or shock. Easterners, when they are shocked or surprised, strike one hand on the other and shake their heads as a sign of disapproval and disgust at what has been done.

WEAK ALLIANCES

And her prophets have daubed them with untempered mortar,
seeing vanity, and divining lies unto them, saying, Thus saith the
Lord God, when the Lord hath not spoken.   Ezek. 22:28

"Untempered mortar" symbolizes weakness and instability. Houses
daubed with untempered mortar cannot stand heavy rain, nor is the
plaster thereof secure.

Israel is likened to a house plastered with untempered mortar, weak
and unstable in her foreign policy. The false prophets had daubed their
defenses with untempered mortar; that is, they had seduced the people
with lies and assured them of peace and security when there was
neither peace nor security in sight. They spoke in the name of the
Lord when the Lord had not spoken to them. But the people had forsaken God's strong assurances and accepted the deceptive and weak
assurances of pagan rulers. They sought the false prosperity which the
priests of Baal had promised them [Ezek. 13:10].

See the commentary on Ezekiel 13:15.

AHLAH AND AHLIBAH

The word of the Lord came again unto me, saying,
Son of man, there were two women, the daughters of one mother:
And they committed whoredoms in Egypt; they committed
whoredoms in their youth: there were their breasts pressed, and
there they bruised the teats of their virginity.   Ezek. 23:1-3

The two women are symbolic of the northern kingdom, Israel, and
the southern kingdom, Judah. Both Israel and Judah had violated God's
covenant and had made alliances with Assyria, Egypt, and Babylon.
Instead of trusting in the God of their fathers, they trusted in foreign
nations and in the assurances of the prophets of Baal, Malcom, and
other pagan gods.

Hebrew prophets often used parables and metaphors when dealing
with serious political and religious problems in order to convey their
ideas to people [Hos. 1:3-7]. The Aramaic reads: ". . . there were
their breasts fondled, there was their virginity broken." That is to say,
Ahlah (Samaria) and Ahlibah (Jerusalem) had been disloyal to God
from their youth. Israel had gone astray after pagan gods when the
people were in Egypt, and now they had gone astray after the gods of
Babylon and Syria.

The nations in whom Israel and Judah had trusted violated them, just as a man violates a woman. That is, instead of helping them during the time of their distress, they exploited them and took advantage of their weakness. Judah imitated Israel in provoking the Lord; therefore, she was facing the same fate.

Compare Jeremiah 3:6-8 and Ezekiel 16:46.

SAMARIA AND JERUSALEM

And Aholah played the harlot when she was mine; and she doted on her lovers, on the Assyrians her neighbors,
Which were clothed with blue, captains and rulers, all of them desirable young men, horsemen riding upon horses. Ezek. 23:5-6

Ahlah and Ahlibah are used figuratively, meaning Samaria; that is, Israel and Jerusalem, or Judah [verses 1-4].

Both Israel and Judah are likened to two unfaithful married women who had broken the law and played the harlot. Both nations had forsaken the Lord God of their fathers and had made alliances first with Assyria, then with Egypt, and then with Babylon, to their ultimate disadvantage and destruction. They had acted treacherously against God, like a woman who acts treacherously against her husband.

Ahlah (Israel) paid tribute and made a treaty with Pul, the king of Assyria [2 Kings 15:19]. And Ahaz, the king of Judah, made an alliance with Tiglath-pileser, king of Assyria, to help him against Syria [2 Kings 16:7-9]. Thus, both Judah and Israel paid the kings with whom they made alliances. This is why they are likened to harlots who paid their lovers [Jer. 3:1; Ezek. 16:33-36; 44-46].

FOREIGN ALLIANCES CONDEMNED

Neither left she her whoredoms brought from Egypt: for in her youth they lay with her, and they bruised the breasts of her virginity, and poured their whoredom upon her.
Wherefore I have delivered her into the hand of her lovers, into the hand of the Assyrians, upon whom she doted. Ezek. 23:8-9

The term "whoredoms" should not be taken literally. The term is used metaphorically, meaning evil, unfaithfulness, and worship of foreign gods [verse 3].

What the prophet means here is that the Israelites were corrupted from their youth, from the time when they were in Egypt. The Israelites had

been a pure tribal people living a nomad life in tents. But while sojourning in Egypt they acquired many corrupt habits of the city people
and became the victims of pagan teachings.

The reference here is to the alliances that Israel and Judah had made
with foreign nations; namely, Assyria, Babylon, and Egypt. The wicked
allies are compared to lovers, and Israel and Judah to a woman who
commits whoredom; but instead of being paid, she pays her lovers.

"Discovered her nakedness" is another Aramaic idiom which refers to
the fact that she (Israel) was humiliated by her allies, as is usually the
case when small nations trust in a great power.

Ezekiel uses the same allegory as Hosea, but with a different picture
[Hos. 1:1-10].

ASSYRIAN ARMY

Then I saw that she was defiled, that they took both one way.
Ezek. 23:13

The Eastern text reads: "Then I saw that the ways of both of them
were defiled." The reference is to Ahlah and Ahlibah; that is, Samaria
(Israel) and Jerusalem (Judah) [verses 1-5].

"Way" in Semitic languages means religion, which is the way of life.
Both the kings of Israel and Judah had left their own religion, gone
after foreign gods, adopted alien worship, and thus corrupted themselves [verse 7]. Moreover, instead of trusting in the Lord their God,
they had put their trust in the strength of the Assyrian army—the
gorgeously blue-clothed soldiers, handsome young men riding on horses.

PICTURES OF THE CHALDEANS

And that she increased her whoredoms: for when she saw men
portrayed upon the wall, the images of the Chaldeans portrayed
with vermilion,
Girded with girdles upon their loins, exceeding in dyed attire
upon their heads, all of them princes to look to, after the manner
of the Babylonians of Chaldea, the land of their nativity.
Ezek. 23:14-15

The Aramaic word *samaney* means "medicines"; that is, colors obtained from herbs and other dyestuffs. Vermilion is a red pigment obtained from cinnabar, the red sulphide of mercury.

The Chaldeans were noted for engraving and painting. They portrayed pictures of their gods, kings, and handsome and valiant soldiers dressed in colorful apparel upon the walls of their palaces. Apparently, some of these pictures were made on tablets, cloth, and other material, and were sent to foreign lands as propaganda, or were bought by merchants [verse 16]. Some of the descendants of the Chaldeans, now known as Sabeans, are noted for their skill as engravers and workers in silver and gold. There are about ten thousand of them in Iraq.

Both Israel and Judah are likened to unfaithful women who had left their husbands and committed adultery with strangers. This language was the only one by which the prophet could help the people understand the folly of their kings, princes, and false prophets [Ezek. 5:11].

GREAT OF FLESH

For she doted upon their paramours, whose flesh is as the flesh of asses, and whose issue is like the issue of horses.   Ezek. 23:20

The Eastern text reads: ". . . whose male organs are like those of asses, and whose privates are like those of horses." Such expressions are common in Eastern speech, and such remarks are often made about unfaithful women who leave their husbands and go after their lovers.

See the commentary on Ezekiel 16:26.

THE CUP OF PUNISHMENT

Thus saith the Lord God; Thou shalt drink thy sister's cup deep and large: thou shalt be laughed to scorn and had in derision; it containeth much.
Thou shalt be filled with drunkenness and sorrow, with the cup of astonishment and desolation, with the cup of thy sister Samaria.
Ezek. 23:32-33

"Cup" here means punishment, vengeance, and defeat; that is, the cup of trembling. In the olden days, criminals were made to drink a cup full of hemlock poison. Isaiah calls it the cup of fury of the Lord [Isa. 51:17]. "Take the wine cup of this fury at my hand, and cause all the nations, to whom I send thee, to drink it" [Jer. 25:15].

Jesus said, ". . . let this cup pass from me: nevertheless not as I will, but as thou wilt" [Matt. 26:39].

See the commentary on "Cup" [Matt. 26:39, *Gospel Light*].

A LESSON TO OTHERS

Thus will I cause lewdness to cease out of the land, that all women may be taught not to do after your lewdness.

And they shall recompense your lewdness upon you, and ye shall bear the sins of your idols: and ye shall know that I am the Lord God. Ezek. 23:48-49

"Women" in this instance is used figuratively, meaning other capital cities, or nations. Just as Ahlah (Samaria) and Ahlibah (Jerusalem) are punished for their lewdness, so the nations which played harlot with them and deceived them are also to be punished for their evil part in the destruction of Israel and Judah [Ezek. 16:41].

All the capitals of the nations were to drink from the cup of the Lord's fury and pass away [Jer. 25:15-16].

NO MOURNING

Son of man, behold, I take away from thee the desire of thine eyes with a stroke: yet neither shalt thou mourn nor weep, neither shall thy tears run down. Ezek. 24:16

The Aramaic word *righta* (desire) is here used figuratively to mean a beloved wife. "The desire of thine eyes" means your physical desire. Easterners often call their wives "light of my eyes" or "desire of my heart."

The prophet was told not to mourn over his beloved wife, neither to eat the bread which the mourners brought to him, but to act as though nothing had happened [verse 17].

Then the prophet was to tell the people that, just as he had been bereaved of his beloved one, so also would they be bereaved of the desire of their eyes. Both Jerusalem and the temple would be destroyed and their sons and their daughters would fall by the sword. The catastrophe would be so great and sudden that the people would not mourn their dead, just as the prophet had not mourned over his wife. On such occasions the dead are left unburied and the people who are left are seized with such astonishment that they do not know what they are doing. Death and life become meaningless. Ezekiel was to be a sign to the people.

COVERING OF LIPS

Forbear to cry, make no mourning for the dead, bind the tire of thine head upon thee, and put on thy shoes upon thy feet, and cover not thy lips, and eat not the bread of men.   Ezek. 24:17

In the East when people mourn over the dead they cover their lips with one of their hands and keep silent as a sign of mourning. The mourners sit down silent for hours [Job 2:13]. "Tire" is an obsolete English word which, years ago, meant "dress." The Eastern text reads: ". . . put on your robe and put shoes on your feet . . ." The close relatives of the dead person may even remove their shoes and walk barefooted. Women may cut off their hair, and some of the people tear their clothes and put ashes upon their heads. And on such occasions they eat only simple food, abstaining from wine, meat, and many other things as a token of grief.

Now, the impending disaster was to be so great that both the young and the old would be put to the sword and the people would have no time to mourn over the thousands of dead, because their grief would be so great. Jerusalem also would be destroyed, and the holy temple, the glory of Judah, profaned by the Gentiles [verses 21-22].

The removing of shoes is not a sign of mourning, but is a sign of reverence. Easterners, when they enter a house or a holy place, remove their shoes as a token of respect and cleanliness.

In the East funeral houses are unknown. Mournings are conducted in the houses of the dead persons. All the mourners must remove their shoes before entering the house or the room where the dead body lies. This is because a part of the burial service and the reading of the Scriptures take place in the house.

The prophet was told that the impending disaster was to be so sudden and so great that the people, because of grief, would not mourn over their dead. This is because there were to be too many dead bodies. On such occasions, ritual and customs are done away with and many people are buried in one grave. Others are left unburied, with no one to mourn and lament over them. This prophecy was fulfilled when Jerusalem was captured by the Chaldean army, the temple destroyed, and the remnant of the people carried captive to Babylon.

Ezekiel's wife was to serve as an example to the Jews who thought they were secure in Judah, and a reminder of what was to happen to thousands of people in Jerusalem and other cities in Judah.

CRETE

Therefore thus saith the Lord God; Behold, I will stretch out mine hand upon the Philistines, and I will cut off the Cherethim, and destroy the remnant of the seacoast.   Ezek. 25:16

The Eastern text reads: ". . . I will destroy Crete" (*Kretey*). Crete is one of the largest islands in the eastern Mediterranean Sea or the Grecian Archipelago. Crete and Cyprus were important islands in the economy of Palestine.

In the olden days Crete was famous for its temple of Minas and for its Minoan culture. Jews from Crete were present on the Day of Pentecost [Acts 2:11]. Titus was made bishop of Crete [Titus 1:5-13].

PRINCES OF THE SEA

Then all the princes of the sea shall come down from their thrones, and lay away their robes, and put off their broidered garments: they shall clothe themselves with trembling; they shall sit upon the ground, and shall tremble at every moment, and be astonished at thee.   Ezek. 26:16

"Princes of the sea" is another name for the kings of the islands. Tyre was famous for her foreign markets and her merchant fleet which navigated all known seas and took her merchandise to Ireland, Britain, and other far-off lands, and brought back tin, gold, silver, and other metals [Ezek. 27:25-36].

All these islands depended on Tyre for cloth, hardware, and other manufactured goods. In the olden days Tyre was the mistress of the seas and the mart of commerce. Her rich merchants were princes and honorable men of the world. The city was famous for its fabulous treasures of gold and silver and its palaces of ivory. Tyre was the queen of the seas, situated on a small island near the seacoast [Isa. 23:8].

ARVAD

The inhabitants of Zidon and Arvad were thy mariners: thy wise men, O Tyrus, that were in thee, were thy pilots. Ezek. 27:8

In biblical days Arvad was one of the important cities of the kingdom of Zur (Tyre or Phoenicia). The last two names were given by the Greeks. Zur is the name used by the Hebrew prophets. The city, being close to the sea, was famed for its sailors and navigators.

The city was very old in its origin and is mentioned in the book of Genesis as the city of the Arvadites [Gen. 10:18]. They were the descendants of Ham [1 Chron. 1:8-17].

Arvad was next to Tyre in importance, fortifications, and men of war [verse 11].

TARSHISH

Tarshish was thy merchant by reason of the multitude of all kind of riches; with silver, iron, tin, and lead, they traded in thy fairs.
                                                          Ezek. 27:12

Tarshish might have been the name of far-off islands and the coasts thereof; namely, Ireland and Britain. Great Britain is famous for its iron. Undoubtedly, these islands were known to the people of Tyre who had navigated all the known seas and established markets for their wares and brought back raw materials for her industrious inhabitants. These islands were known as the far-off islands at the end of the known world [Isa. 66:19].

The Arameans (Syrians), also known as Carthaginians, had built cities in these islands and other far-off places from which they brought spices, ivory, silver, gold, tin, iron, and lead.

The term *Eire* (Ireland) in Aramaic, the language of Tyre, means "air." Britain is a Hebrew name which means "the second covenant." "The kings of Tarshish and of the isles shall bring presents" [Ps. 72:10].

Tar in Aramaic means "a door" and *sheghish* means "violent, troubled, boisterous, perturbed." Ireland is noted for its rough seacoasts. Thus, Tarshish means "the door to the turbulent sea."

Isaiah predicted that the ships of Tarshish would bring back the Jews to Palestine with their gold and silver [Isa. 60:9]. After World War II thousands of Jews were brought to Palestine by British ships.

The ships of Tarshish were the ships which brought raw materials or ores from Tarshish. They must have been large ships to stand the weight of the ores [Ps. 48:7; Isa. 2:16]. Isaiah predicted that some of the remnant of the Israelites would go to Tarshish [Isa. 66:19].

Tarshish is also the name of a semiprecious stone, the chrysolite.

JAVAN, THE GREEKS

Javan, Tubal, and Meshech, they were thy merchants: they traded the persons of men and vessels of brass in thy market.
                                                          Ezek. 27:13

Javan (Aramaic *Yavan*) means Ionians, or Greeks. Javan was one of the sons of Japheth [Gen. 10:2]. "And the sons of Javan [were] Elishah, and Tarshish, Kittim (Cathay, China), and Dodanim" [Gen. 10:4]. The Aramaic word for Greeks is *Yonaye*.

Isaiah prophesied that some of the remnant of Israel would go to Tarshish, Pul, and Lud, ". . . to Tubal, and Javan, to the isles afar off, that have not heard my fame, neither have seen my glory; and they shall declare my glory among the Gentiles" [Isa. 66:19]. All these nations traded with Tyre. I believe Tarshish is Spain, Britain, and Ireland. They were far-off islands at the end of the known world.

Tarshish might be derived from the Aramaic *Tarsheghis: tar* (door) and *sheghis* (turbulent, agitated). This is because the sea beyond Spain and Portugal is turbulent, and Gibraltar is the door to the sea.

TYRE LIKE EDEN

Thou hast been in Eden the garden of God; every precious stone was thy covering, the sardius, topaz, and the diamond, the beryl, the onyx, and the jasper, the sapphire, the emerald, and the carbuncle, and gold: the workmanship of thy tabrets and of thy pipes was prepared in thee in the day that thou wast created.

Ezek. 28:13

"Eden" in Aramaic means time and delight; that is, temporary delight. The term "Eden" is used metaphorically, meaning "a delightful place." Zur (Tyre) was noted for its wealth, luxuries, and beauty. Tyre was a small Babylon situated on the eastern shore of the Mediterranean Sea. It was the world's greatest commercial city [Ezek. 26:16].

Tyre was doomed, like Sodom and Gomorrah (*Amorah*). The king of Tyre was to be humbled like Nebuchadnezzar, king of Babylon, and the kings of other Gentile nations which had destroyed Israel, plundered their cities, and burned the temple, and carried their people captive [Isa. 14:12-15]. The king of Zur (Tyre), like Nebuchadnezzar, because of his wealth and power, lifted up his heart and made himself a god. He was to fall to the ground, and the fate of his beautiful city was to be worse than that of Samaria and other cities which were overthrown by the Assyrian kings. These powerful Gentile kings were the personification of evil forces that had destroyed many nations and, at last, were to be destroyed by stronger nations.

Tyre was destroyed by the army of Nebuchadnezzar, king of Babylon [verse 18]. But the city must have been rebuilt. It was destroyed again by Alexander the Great about 311 B.C.

GRIEVING THORN

And there shall be no more a pricking brier unto the house of Israel, nor any grieving thorn of all that are round about them, that despised them; and they shall know that I am the Lord God.
Ezek. 28:24

"Grieving thorn and pricking brier" are used allegorically, meaning annoyances, enemies, and troubles. The reference here is to Israel's enemies. "But if you will not destroy the inhabitants of the land from before you, then it shall come to pass, that those who are left of them shall be splinters in your eyes, and spears in your sides . . ." [Num. 33:55].

The Israelites were warned against the original inhabitants of Palestine, who were to become like thorns and briers to the people [Josh. 23:13]. Paul speaks of the thorn in his flesh, by which he means an annoyance, grievance, or sorrow. This ancient idiom is still used in Near Eastern languages. We still say, "He has been a thorn in my flesh."

All the Gentile nations who had helped the king of Babylon against Judah were to be destroyed. Just as they had treated Judah, so they would be treated.

OPENING OF THE MOUTH

In that day will I cause the horn of the house of Israel to bud forth, and I will give thee the opening of the mouth in the midst of them; and they shall know that I am the Lord.   Ezek. 29:21

"The opening of the mouth" in this instance means boldness and daring and implies "talking back." Hitherto, Israel had been the victim of great powers like Assyria, Egypt, and Babylon. She had accepted everything that was unjustly imposed on her without opening her mouth and protesting. When a person is humble and meek, it is said, "He did not open his mouth." Then again, mourners cover their mouths with their hands as a token of silence and grief. Israel had been silent like the mourners. She did not open her mouth in the time of her oppression.

But the day was coming when both Egypt and Babylon would drink from the bitter cup and pass away. And a new day was to dawn, the day when the Lord would restore the fortune of Israel and raise the horn of salvation. Then Israel would become bold in her dealing with her enemies. Jesus, in his humility and affliction, was likened to a sheep before the shearers. He did not open his mouth.

CLOUDY DAY

For the day is near, even the day of the Lord is near, a cloudy day; it shall be the time of the heathen.   Ezek. 30:3

"Cloudy day" here is used metaphorically, meaning a bad day or a rainy day. Cloud also suggests glory and protection from the heat. The exact meaning of the metaphor is generally determined by the context. The cloud in the wilderness was for protection from the heat, but here it is symbolic of disaster, an ominous day [Ezek. 34:12].

Then again, clouds indicate the end of the dry season and the long droughts [1 Kings 18:44-45]. On such occasions desert dwellers and shepherds take refuge in caves and under the edges of large rocks.

THE WILDERNESS OF SEEN

And I will pour my fury upon Sin, the strength of Egypt; and I will cut off the multitude of No.   Ezek. 30:15

The Eastern text reads: "And I will pour out my fury upon Seen," the wilderness between Elim and Sinai. Here the people, because of the lack of food, murmured against Moses and Aaron in the wilderness, and the Lord sent them manna [Exod. 16:1].

The land of Seen is a portion of Egypt that lies northeast of Sinai. The arid wilderness served as a defense against the Assyrian and Babylonian armies. "No" was a city or province in Egypt.

DARKNESS AND CLOUD

At Tehaphnehes also the day shall be darkened, when I shall break there the yokes of Egypt: and the pump of her strength shall cease in her: as for her, a cloud shall cover her, and her daughters shall go into captivity.   Ezek. 30:18

The darkness and cloud in this instance mean disaster, sorrow, and distress. Easterners when describing a calamity say, "The day is dark; a cloud covered the sky." Just as the light is symbolic of joy, knowledge, and tranquillity, so darkness, in the Semitic languages, means disaster [Ezek. 32:7].

Egypt was soon to face one of the greatest disasters in her history. The Egyptian delta was to be conquered by the armies of the king of Babylon. The Egyptian armies on whom Judah had relied for help were to be defeated and carried captive to Babylon, together with young men and maidens, and their land devastated [verses 25-26].

LEBANESE

Behold, the Assyrian was a cedar in Lebanon with fair branches, and with a shadowing shroud, and of a high stature; and his top was among the thick boughs.   Ezek. 31-3

"Cedar" is an idiom which means "the choicest people, handsome and tall." Even today, when describing a handsome person, we say, "He is like a tree." The Assyrians and Chaldeans were noted for their fine figures and their beauty. The Mesopotamians are tall and handsome as compared with the inhabitants of Palestine and Syria [Ezek. 23:5-6].

The Assyrians, during their campaigns in Syria, Palestine, and Egypt, occupied Mount Lebanon. In biblical days the mountain served as a fortress for the invading armies. Moreover, Lebanon is beautiful, fertile, and has abundant water, fruit trees, orchards, and tall cedars.

The present inhabitants of Lebanon closely resemble the Assyrians. They are sturdy, tall, and agile. They spoke Aramaic until the sixteenth century. Even today Aramaic, the Assyrian language, is still spoken in some Lebanese and Syrian villages. Moreover, Aramaic is the ecclesiastic language of the Maronite Roman Catholic Church.

BODIES TURN INTO DUST

And I will lay thy flesh upon the mountains, and fill the valleys with thy height.   Ezek. 32:5

The Aramaic word *rimthakh* (your dust) has been confused with *ramtakh* (your height, your hill). In Aramaic the two words are identical, but they are pronounced differently.

The prophecy is concerning the destruction of Pharaoh's army in which Judah had trusted for deliverance despite the warnings of the prophet of God. Pharaoh's army was defeated at Mahbug (Carchemish) by the Euphrates. The bodies of the Egyptian soldiers were strewn on the ground. "Fill your valleys with your dust" means, "I will inflict a heavy slaughter upon your army."

CONQUEST OF EGYPT

Then will I make their waters deep, and cause their rivers to run like oil, saith the Lord God.　　　　　　　　Ezek. 32:14

The term *mishkha* (oil) is used here to indicate the smoothness of the rivers. This is because oil runs very smoothly when poured out on the ground. Swollen rivers are hard to cross and very destructive, and they flow for only a short while.

Still waters are symbolic of peace. Egypt would surrender to the army of Nebuchadnezzar peacefully.

Egypt was an eternal enemy of Israel. Now Egypt was to be overthrown by the mighty Chaldean army. Even nature would share in its destruction. The Nile would be easily crossed by the Chaldean army. The Egyptians would hardly offer resistance. The remnant of Israel henceforth would find rest and peace.

SCATTERED SHEEP

As a shepherd seeketh out his flock in the day that he is among his sheep that are scattered; so will I seek out my sheep, and will deliver them out of all places where they have been scattered in the cloudy and dark day.　　　　　　　　Ezek. 34:12

During the grazing season when the flocks are small they are mixed together. The shepherds rotate in shepherding. This is more true of the flocks of lambs and ewes. They are generally mixed until the fall.

When the grazing is over the shepherds separate their flocks [Matt. 25:32]. The sheep know their shepherd's voice, and when he calls them they follow him. When sheep are lost or gone astray, the chief shepherd searches for them until he finds them and brings them back to the fold [Ps. 119:176].

Sheep here means Israel and Judah. The Lord will seek and gather the remnant from among the other nations. The shepherds of Israel, the kings and princes, had dealt wickedly with the people. They had let them scatter. They had neglected the weak and devoured the strong. They had acted like unfaithful shepherds [verse 2].

The Lord himself would shepherd Israel and lead them to good pastures and to the mountains of Israel [verses 13-15].

"The Lord is my shepherd" [Ps. 23:1]. Jesus said, "I am the good shepherd: the good shepherd giveth his life for the sheep" [John 10:11].

JUSTICE TO ALL

I will seek that which was lost, and bring again that which was driven away, and will bind up that which was broken, and will strengthen that which was sick: but I will destroy the fat and the strong; I will feed them with judgment.   Ezek. 34:16

The Eastern text reads: ". . . I will protect the fat and the strong . . ." The unfaithful shepherds often killed the fat sheep for meat, and neglected the others.

Even today bad shepherds often kill the fat sheep and report them to their owners as lost. They also sell the good sheep and report them as stolen.

Now the Lord was to feed his people and seek those who were taken captive to Assyria, Babylon, and other far-off lands. He would also relieve them of their suffering, heal their wounds, and protect the rich from being exploited by the wicked princes and kings. Moreover, the Lord would look after all of them with justice.

EWES AND RAMS

And as for you, O my flock, thus saith the Lord God; Behold, I judge between cattle and cattle, between the rams and the he goats.   Ezek. 34:17

"Cattle" is used symbolically, meaning oppressors. In the Bible oppressors are often called oxen or cows [Amos 4:1]. The Aramaic reads: ". . . I will judge between ewe and ewe, and between ram and ram."

In the East shepherds discriminate between cattle and cattle and between the sheep and goats. The good cattle are grazed on good pastures where they graze and lie down, but bad cattle are put in places where grazing is poor.

Moreover, milking-sheep are fed after grazing on the hills and fields. They are given dry grass before they enter the fold. But goats are not fed.

Jesus, like Ezekiel, was familiar with sheep and the manner in which the shepherds fed them and separated them. ". . . and he shall separate them one from another, as a shepherd divideth his sheep from the goats" [Matt. 25:32]. Even though Jesus was born and reared in a carpenter's house, he spent his early years as a shepherd. This is why he knew so much about the sheep, the soil, the birds, and the flowers.

The time was to come when the good shepherds of Israel, the leaders, would separate the good from the bad just as shepherds separate the sheep from the goats. The Lord himself would be the chief shepherd who would direct the other shepherds and lead the sheep to good pastures and places wherein they would be secure [Ezek. 34:12]. Justice and righteousness would be restored.

WEAK SHEEP

Therefore thus saith the Lord God unto them; Behold, I, even I, will judge between the fat cattle and between the lean cattle.
Because ye have thrust with side and with shoulder, and pushed all the diseased with your horns, till ye have scattered them abroad.
                                                              Ezek. 34:20-21

The Eastern text reads "ewes" instead of cattle. ". . . Behold, I myself will judge between the fat ewe and the lean ewe."

The prophet here uses Eastern symbolism. Sheep are often used figuratively, meaning people.

The fat ewes are the princes and the wicked government officials who oppressed the poor and exploited the widows and the fatherless. The strong sheep thrust with their sides and shoulders, and push the weak with their horns until they drive them away. "Disease" is a mistranslation; it should read "weak."

The Lord is to judge between the princes and the strong men, and the helpless poor and widows who were oppressed, heavily taxed, and exploited. The Lord God was to set over them a righteous prince who would govern with justice and equality—a ruler like his servant David.

ONE SHEPHERD

And I will set up one shepherd over them, and he shall feed them, even my servant David; he shall feed them, and he shall be their shepherd.   Ezek. 34:23

The reference here is to the restoration of the remnant of Israel which was to be gathered from among the Gentile nations. The remnant would return to Israel after the seventy years of captivity in Babylon and other Gentile lands. Nevertheless, this remnant, after a brief period of freedom, peace, and security, was to be subjugated again by the Gentile powers and scattered and driven away by the Romans.

This prophecy was to be fulfilled with the coming of the Messiah, who was to lead Israel into the way of righteousness. The Lord was now to set up one shepherd over the people of Israel, who would feed them with truth and righteousness. And Israel was no more to be divided.

In the messianic kingdom there will be one king and one kingdom, the kingdom of heaven.

The other shepherds, the political leaders, had been disloyal. They had sold out some of the sheep, eaten the fat ones, and neglected the rest of the flock and let it scatter.

Jesus said, "I am the good shepherd." He was ready to lay down his life for the sake of the sheep (people) [John 10:11].

A NEW STOCK

And I will raise up for them a plant of renown, and they shall be no more consumed with hunger in the land, neither bear the shame of the heathen any more.   Ezek. 34:29

The Eastern text reads: "And I will raise up for them a plantation of peace." "Plantation" in this instance is used figuratively, meaning a new generation, or a new stock. Israel is often likened to a vine, an olive tree or cedar, and to tender plants [Ps. 128:3; Isa. 53:2].

The new generation, that is, the remnant, would turn to the Lord, and the Lord would look kindly upon them and care for them as his people. Consequently, peace and prosperity would reign in the land. The Lord would forgive his people and he himself would become their Shepherd and their God. Famine and oppression would cease, and the nations would see the light of God and would seek him and pray to him [Zech. 8:20-27].

BLOODSHED

Son of man, when the house of Israel dwelt in their own land, they defiled it by their own way and by their doings: their way was before me as the uncleanness of a removed woman.

Wherefore I poured my fury upon them for the blood that they had shed upon the land, and for their idols wherewith they had polluted it.   Ezek. 36:17-18

"Their own way" means their own religion or worship. The term "way" in Semitic languages means religion, or the way of worship. Many of the Israelites who worshiped Baal sacrificed some of their children to idols. Others shed innocent blood.

"The uncleanness of a removed woman" means the menstrual blood, which was considered unclean in the Mosaic law [Lev. 15:19]. The Eastern text reads: ". . . their way was before me like the uncleanness of a menstruous woman."

DRY BONES

The hand of the Lord was upon me, and carried me out in the
Spirit of the Lord, and set me down in the midst of the valley which
was full of bones,
And caused me to pass by them round about: and, behold, there
were very many in the open valley; and, lo, they were very dry.
Ezek. 37:1-2

The prophet was lifted up and carried in the Spirit of the Lord to
see the harassed and starved captives and the predicament in which
they were living. "The hand of the Lord was upon me" means "I saw a
vision" or "I prophesied."

"Dry bones" in Semitic languages are symbolic of misery and starvation. Even today, when one refers to refugees and famine-stricken people
who are suffering and hopeless, it is said, "They are dry bones," which
means they are famine-stricken and ready to die, or they are already
dead.

"Dry bones" is used because when the bodies of men are found dead
from starvation or murdered by bandits, the bones are dry. "My bones are
burned as an hearth" [Ps. 102:3].

The bones which the prophet saw in his vision represent the children
of Israel who were carried captive by the Assyrian kings in 721 B.C.
And other captives who were carried away with Ezekiel during the
captivity of Jehoiakim, king of Judah, prior to the fall of Jerusalem.
These captives of Judah were settled in Mesopotamia in areas that were
hot and unsuitable for habitation. The people were crushed under the
foreign yoke and thus had become so hopeless that they had no thought
of restoration. They were like dry bones scattered in a desert land.

The prophet was taken in the Spirit and shown the pitiful condition
of his people and the hopeless situation in which they were living. After
the prophet saw the dry bones God revealed to him that those dry bones,
the children of Israel, would live again and return to their land. Many
of the captives had been given the hope of restoration.

See the commentary on Ezekiel 37:3-4.

DRY BONES RAISED

And he said unto me, Son of man, can these bones live? And I
answered, O Lord God, thou knowest.
Again he said unto me, Prophesy upon these bones, and say unto
them, O ye dry bones, hear the word of the Lord.   Ezek. 37:3-4

When the prophet saw the people in this valley suffering, hungry and
thirsty and dying, he wondered if there was any more hope for their

return to Israel. Then the Lord showed him in a vision that the slain and dead people were to live again. He saw sinews, flesh, and skin coming upon the bones, and finally breath came into them and they lived.

This vision was symbolic of the children of Israel who had been carried away captive to Babylon. They were to be granted a new life, strengthened, and restored to their homeland again. If the Lord God could raise dry and dead bones, how easy it would be to strengthen, heal, forgive, and restore his people, Israel.

BONES RAISED TO LIFE

Therefore prophesy and say unto them, Thus saith the Lord God; Behold, O my people, I will open your graves, and cause you to come up out of your graves, and bring you into the land of Israel.
Ezek. 37:12

"Cause you to come up out of your graves" means "I will get you out of your horrible condition." In Aramaic "grave" is symbolic of misery and suffering. It is often said, "He is on the brim of the grave," which means that he is in a difficult situation. "He is dead" means he has lost out and become hopeless.

Some of the lands where the Israelites were settled were infested with snakes, scorpions, and mosquitoes. Even today they are known as malarial regions. Prior to World War II a whole tribe perished because of the unsanitary conditions and the attacks of malaria.

Such sayings should not be taken literally. The children of Israel were humbled and were on the point of starvation, living in a strange land among hostile people. Owing to the difficult situation, their leaders had lost hope of restoration. The refugees were like dry bones, seemingly without any life in them. But in the eyes of God there was life, hope, and restoration waiting for Israel. God could get them out of this hopeless situation and lead them back again into their own land [Ezek. 36:24-25].

What is impossible to man is possible to God. If God could raise the dead from the grave, he could surely strengthen the weakened and starved Israelites who had become like dry bones. The prophet Ezekiel portrays the remnant in an allegorical manner to show that God can restore his people.

Israel was to come out of the pit or grave into which her leaders had brought her, because God's promises to Abraham and David were to be fulfilled.

This divine plan of the restoration of Israel was revealed to the prophet in a vision during the night. He saw the bones in the valley in a vision, and he saw the flesh and sinews coming on them in a vision, and this vision was fulfilled. Israel was resurrected from death when the remnant of Israel returned from captivity during the Persian reign.

THE LAND OF GOD AND MAGOG

And the word of the Lord came unto me, saying,
Son of man, set thy face against Gog, the land of Magog, the
chief prince of Meshech and Tubal, and prophesy against him.

Ezek. 38:1-2

Gog and Magog are the Aramaic names for China and Mongolia. The prince of Magog was the chief prince of Meshech (Moscow). And Tubal (Tobolsk) is a city in Siberia.

Most of the Russians are of Mongolian origin. In Biblical days the Mongols, Moscovites, and the people of Tubal were nomads who preyed on agricultural communities and, at times, fought against the civilized nations.

These powerful tribes were known to Babylonians, Persians, and the remnant of Israel who were scattered east of Persia. Moreover, the Syrians and the Babylonians traded with these nations in the Far East.

These nations from the Far East invaded Persia and Palestine in the twelfth century, but at last were defeated near Jerusalem. They may again, under the leadership of China or Russia, try to conquer the world as they did during the reign of Kublai Khan and his grandson, Hulago Khan, and other Mongol overlords. The battle between the Asiatic powers and the European powers may be called the Battle of Armageddon and the advent of the kingdom of God [Rev. 16:12].

These nations are the descendants of Japheth, the third son of Noah [Gen. 10:2], and are a warlike people like their brethren, the early Teutonic tribes.

WITHOUT WALLS AND GATES

And thou shalt say, I will go up to the land of unwalled villages;
I will go to them that are at rest, that dwell safely, all of them
dwelling without walls, and having neither bars nor gates.

Ezek. 38:11

In Palestine, Arabia, and Syria many tribal people (Bedouins) live in tents. In some places tents are pitched so close to one another that the camps resemble towns without walls, gates, or bars. In some of these places locks and keys are unknown. The people live peacefully in open country without walls and defenses. Stealing is forbidden and the culprit who does so is punished severely and made an example by cutting off one of his hands.

The reference here is to Magog (Mongolia) and Gog (China) who were to invade Palestine, Arabia, Syria, Mesopotamia, and many other defenseless lands to plunder and to carry away captives. This prophecy was fulfilled in the thirteenth century. These nations will triumph, but finally will be defeated and conquered by God's truth [Ezek. 39:2-6].

GOG AND MAGOG DEFEATED

And I will turn thee back, and leave but the sixth part of thee, and will cause thee to come up from the north parts, and will bring thee upon the mountains of Israel. Ezek. 39:2

"Sixth" is a mistranslation of the Aramaic word *shepolai* (outskirts, outermost parts). The error is caused by the confusion of the word *shepolai*, with the Aramaic word *sheta* (six). Such errors are unavoidable when translating from an ancient language and a defective manuscript.

The kings of Gog and Magog were to be gathered together and brought to Palestine to be defeated [verse 1].

All these invasions came from the north. The Bulgarians, Hungarians, the Seljuk Turks, and the Ottoman Turks came from the north. All these invaders were of Mongol and Tartar origin. All these nations suffered severe defeats. The Seljuk Turks and the Ottoman Turks conquered the Near East and the biblical lands but were themselves defeated in the end.

JAPAN

And I will send a fire on Magog, and among them that dwell carelessly in the isles: and they shall know that I am the Lord. Ezek. 39:6

The Eastern text reads, ". . . the people who dwell peacefully in the islands . . ."

The reference here is to the Japanese people. The Japanese, prior to their contact with the Western powers, were a peaceful people living securely in their islands. They had been living in isolation for many centuries. They had nothing to do with other races and kingdoms.

Gog is the Aramaic word for China (*Gatey*) and Magog for Mongolia. The Japanese were known as the isolated people whose ports were closed to the world. They were opened by Commodore Perry.

In biblical days Syrian ships navigated the Indian Ocean and reached the far-off islands in both the Atlantic and the Pacific.

Chinese or Mongolian armies invaded the land of Israel in the thirteenth century [Ezek. 38:18; 39:1].

VULTURES AND WILD BEASTS

And, thou son of man, thus saith the Lord God; Speak unto every feathered fowl, and to every beast of the field, Assemble yourselves, and come; gather yourselves on every side to my sacrifice that I do sacrifice for you, even a great sacrifice upon the mountains of Israel, that ye may eat flesh, and drink blood.
Ezek. 39:17

The picture depicted by the prophet symbolizes a great slaughter which was to take place. In the olden days when one warrior threatened another he said, "I will give your flesh to the fowls of the air, and to the beasts of the field" [1 Sam. 17:44]. This is because in those days dead bodies were left in the battlefield unburied and were eaten by the vultures and wild beasts [Isa. 18:6; Rev. 19:17].

The reference is to the large armies of Gog (China) [verse 2]. This army was to invade Palestine but was to be defeated. A large Mongolian army was destroyed in Palestine in the thirteenth century.

Israel was to triumph over her enemies and glorify God for the victory [verse 13]. The bodies of the enemy were to be given to vultures and wild beasts.

HIDING OF FACE

And the heathen shall know that the house of Israel went into captivity for their iniquity: because they trespassed against me, therefore hid I my face from them, and gave them into the hand of their enemies; so fell they all by the sword.
Ezek. 39:23

"Hiding of face" is a Semitic idiom which means refusal to see the petitioner or the rejection of an appeal. In the East when a judge or a government official is unwilling to hear a certain complaint he refuses to see the persons who come to see him. He does not allow them to come before his presence

The Jews had trespassed against their God and had broken his covenant and transgressed his commandments. When they prayed to God he hid his face from them; that is, he refused to hear them. He knew that their repentance was insincere. Therefore they were left without guidance and finally defeated by their enemies.

HIGH IN CONSCIOUSNESS

In the visions of God brought he me into the land of Israel, and set me upon a very high mountain, by which was as the frame of a city on the south.   Ezek. 40:2

"In the visions of God" means in true prophecies or true revelations. Ezekiel was carried away captive prior to the fall of Jerusalem. He was among the captives by the River Chebar when he saw his visions. The prophet was brought in the Spirit and set upon a very high mountain north of the city. Mount Olivet is the highest mountain in the holy city. The city itself was built on Mount Zion.

"A very high mountain" is used allegorically. There are no really high mountains in Judea. The highest might be about 5,000 or 6,000 feet high. The term mountain in this instance is used metaphorically, meaning high in consciousness, so that he might see the whole site of the city, just as one might see it from a plane. Most of Jerusalem can be seen from Mount Olivet. The prophet knew Mount Olivet, but in his divine vision he was raised in his consciousness higher than a mountain, so that he might see the entire city, the disaster which had fallen upon it, the immoral condition, the wickedness which was committed therein, and the future restoration of the remnant.

Jesus, too, was set upon a very high mountain and shown all the kingdoms of the earth [Matt. 4:8-9]. The Mount of Temptation can hardly be called a high mountain. It is like a hill when compared with Mount Lebanon or Mount Ararat. The evangelist here speaks of a mental mountain, that is, human aspirations where one can see and covet the material world and all that goes with it.

Ezekiel rose up in his consciousness to see the calamity which had befallen the city and to prophesy concerning the remnant.

HIGH PRIEST

It is for the prince; the prince, he shall sit in it to eat bread before the Lord; he shall enter by the way of the porch of that gate, and shall go out by the way of the same.   Ezek. 44:3

The Aramaic word *medabrana* (ruler, judge, prefect, chief priest) in this instance should read "the high priest," who was the only one permitted by the ordinance to offer offerings and to eat in the holy place. See the commentary on Ezekiel 45:16-17.

CIRCUMCISE YOUR HEART

In that ye have brought into my sanctuary strangers, uncircumcised in heart, and uncircumcised in flesh, to be in my sanctuary, to pollute it, even my house, when ye offer my bread, the fat and the blood, and they have broken my covenant because of all your abominations.   Ezek. 44:7

"Circumcise your heart" is an idiom which means, "Cleanse your heart of evil and turn to God." Circumcision was given before the law of Moses. It was a tribal ritual or a racial mark. Those who were circumcised belonged to God. Circumcision was symbolic of cleanliness because the Hebrews were told to abstain from idol worship, immorality, and other pagan practices.

When their ways were evil, they were called uncircumcised of heart [Lev. 26:41]. "Behold, their ear is uncircumcised" [Jer. 6:10]. Heart in Semitic languages means mind. Circumcision of heart means change of heart. Then again, circumcision was an outward sign, a reminder of the inner change. When men walked not in the ways of God, circumcision was of no effect.

This is also true of baptism, which is an outward sign of an inner cleansing of the heart, that is, being born again into a new life.

SHEKEL

And the shekel shall be twenty gerahs: twenty shekels, five and twenty shekels, fifteen shekels, shall be your maneh.   Ezek. 45:12

The reference here is to the standards of weights. "Shekel" means weight. In Bible times silver was weighed in the balance or scale. Minted coins were unknown. The fifteen shekels or weights were equivalent to the mina. A mina was equal to 50 shekels. The shekel of the sanctuary was the standard, or the royal shekel. No damaged shekels were acceptable as offerings. Shekel was a Babylonian weight. A talent was 3,000 shekels.

See the article on "Weights" [Ex. 30:13, Lev. 27:25].

HIGH PRIEST

All the people of the land shall give this oblation for the prince in Israel.

And it shall be the prince's part to give burnt offerings, and meat offerings, and drink offerings, in the feasts, and in the new moons, and in the sabbaths, in all solemnities of the house of Israel: he shall prepare the sin offering, and the meat offering, and the burnt offering, and the peace offerings, to make reconciliation for the house of Israel. Ezek. 45:16-17

The Aramaic word *medabrana* means "ruler, high priest, governor." But the prophet here speaks of the high priest who was the spiritual ruler over the temple services, priests, Levites, and the temple. In other places he is called *rab-kahney* (the chief priest).

The Mosaic law prohibited the offering of the sacrifices by laymen. The sons of Aaron and their descendants were the only ones who were entrusted with this sacred ritual. This was especially true of the sin offering, which was offered by the high priest only once a year [Lev. 16:34].

Uzziah, a king of Judah, was stricken because he burned incense in violation of the law [2 Chron. 26:16-21]. The law stated ". . . that no stranger, which is not of the seed of Aaron, come near to offer incense before the Lord" [Num. 16:40; 18:7].

On the other hand, there were no more princes and kings after the fall of Jerusalem in 586 B.C. After the building of the second temple by Zerubbabel the office of the high priest gained more prominence, especially during the period of the Maccabees when the high priests became actual rulers over the people both in political and religious matters.

The prophet speaks of the new temple which was to be built and the high priests who were to rule over the people and offer sin offerings and other burnt offerings. During the Roman period the high priests had the title of *ethnarch*, the head of a race.

All the references here are to the high priest. The term "prince" is wrong. Kings and princes were forbidden from offering sacrifices [2 Chron. 26:16-21].

See the commentary on Ezekiel 45:16-17.

TRUTH SURVIVES

*Afterward he brought me again unto the door of the house; and,
behold, waters issued out from under the threshold of the house
eastward: for the forefront of the house stood toward the east, and
the waters came down from under, from the right side of the house,
at the south side of the altar.*   Ezek. 47:1

Water is symbolic of truth, light, and understanding. The Hebrew
temple had been destroyed, but the foundation was still there. And the
foundation of a religion is not its temples and rituals, its altars and
shrines, but the truth which it represents. The temple was demolished by
the Chaldean army, and the lamp of God was temporarily put out.

But the prophet, in his vision, saw that a fountain of water gushed
out on the east side of the temple, which gradually became a river of
healing water, with trees on both sides of it. The prophet saw that the
truth was there, and that it would soon heal Israel of all her wounds
which were caused by pagan worship. Truth is indestructible. New truths
were to be revealed to the Hebrews in exile. The truth, the leaven of
Judaism, was to issue like a river that would irrigate the whole Gentile
world. The psalmist says, "There is a river [truth], the streams whereof
shall make glad the city of God, the holy place of the tabernacles of the
most High" [Ps. 46:4].

Moreover, the water is the living water, the truth which Zechariah
saw flowing into the sea (humanity) continually [Zech. 14:8; John
4:10; 6:35]. The beginning was to be in Jerusalem [Luke 24:47]. Religion was to have a new meaning in the life of Israel. Something greater
than the temple was hidden in the rocky foundations, that is, the messianic promises. The captivity would purify the people and bring them
back to the simple teaching of the prophets.

Babylon was to become the center of Jewish learning, and the synagogues were to spread the truth of God and thus remove the false teachings and traditions that had caused the downfall of Israel.

On the other hand, from henceforth Israel's mission was to be spiritual,
and her religion was to become a universal religion.

This truth was hidden from the eyes of the priests and the elders
who had confused God's truth with the temple rituals, ordinances, and
sacrifices, which were temporal and, therefore, destructible.

The right side of the house means right religion; that is, the truth for
which the temple stood. The water issued eastward, symbolizing that
the true teaching was to be established first in the East and then heralded
to the West. The Jews were to be taken to Babylon, which was southeast of Jerusalem.

A new form of Judaism was to rise in Babylon, which would be like
water in a thirsty and desolate land. Just as the water which issued from

the threshold of the temple caused the trees to grow in the barren lands and healed the water of the sea, so the new Jewish teaching was to heal and irrigate the Gentile world.

The prophet, in his vision, saw that a new spiritual and powerful religion would spring forth from the foundation of the temple. Christianity issued from the ruins of the Jewish temple in Jerusalem and spread first into the east and then into the whole world. All of Jesus' disciples went eastward preaching among the Jews of the exile [Matt. 10:56].

TRUE JUDAISM

Then said he unto me, These waters issue out toward the east country, and go down into the desert, and go into the sea: which being brought forth into the sea, the waters shall be healed.

Ezek. 47:8

Water symbolizes the truth which was imbedded in the Jewish religion. This truth was to heal all pagan religions and become universal. The temple rituals and the sacrificial and ceremonial religion was gone forever. Now the truth which was the foundation of the Jewish faith was to shine forth.

The true religion was to rise up in the East. The prophet Malachi says, "For from the rising of the sun even to its going down, my name is great among the Gentiles . . ." [Mal. 1:11, Eastern text]. The majority of the Jews were in Babylon and Assyria. New interpretations of the prophets of Israel were to be published with a better and truer understanding, and new spiritual aspirations were to rise up among the Jews in Babylon to destroy the pagan teaching that their fathers had adopted in Palestine. Captivity was to purge Israel and cleanse her of her sins.

"The waters shall be healed" means that the teaching that had been corrupted with pagan practices shall be purified and made into a universal religion. Judaism, in due time, would be refined as a man refines silver and gold [Mal. 3:1-4].

True Judaism is the foundation upon which both Christianity and Islam are built.

CONVERSION OF PAGAN WORLD

And it shall come to pass, that every thing that liveth, which moveth, whithersoever the rivers shall come, shall live: and there shall be a very great multitude of fish, because these waters shall come thither: for they shall be healed; and every thing shall live whither the river cometh.

Ezek. 47:9

Irrigation of the desert signifies the spread of the true teaching of God. Desert and barrenness symbolize paganism and ignorance. Judaism, during the time of the prophet Ezekiel, was contaminated with Baal worship and other forms of idolatry.

The water (truth) which issued from the threshold of the temple would heal Judaism, that is, would purify it. All races and people in the path of the river would live a new life. Fish are symbolic of people. Jesus said to Peter, "I will make you fishers of men" [Matt. 4:19].

Judaism was to send out new messengers of the gospel into the world to preach the true gospel, the gospel of salvation. But some of the areas were to resist the gospel and continue to live in paganism [verse 11].

See also the commentary on Ezekiel 47:1.

SALTY SPRINGS

> But the miry places thereof and the marshes thereof shall not be healed; they shall be given to salt. Ezek. 47:11

The Eastern text reads: "But the water in its springs and mouths shall not be fresh, but it shall become salt." These springs are close to the mouth of the River Jordan which empties into the Dead Sea. These springs, or miry places and marshes, are symbolic of lands which would refuse to be healed, that is, to be purified and converted to the true religion which would spring up from the threshold of the temple—the teaching of the Messiah, which in due time was to be heralded to the world.

Many Jews, Edomites, Ammonites, Moabites, and other people who were in the path of this healing water were converted by the apostles and by their Jewish disciples. But some of them resisted the fresh and healing water (teaching) and were unwilling to be purified. These would remain in the salty marshes, lifeless. Nothing grows in salt.

TREES OF RIGHTEOUSNESS

> And by the river upon the bank thereof, on this side and on that side, shall grow all trees for meat, whose leaf shall not fade, neither shall the fruit thereof be consumed: it shall bring forth new fruit according to his months, because their waters they issued out of the sanctuary: and the fruit thereof shall be. Ezek. 47:12

The term "trees" is used here allegorically, meaning men or the planting of the Lord. Men are often likened to trees [Ps. 1:3; Jer. 17:8]. The river which issued forth out of the sanctuary is the life-giving truth which was to purify and sanctify the remnant of Israel who were the leaven of Judaism.

The fruit symbolizes good works and righteous deeds. The righteous were to eat of the tree of life which is in the midst of the paradise of God [Rev. 2:7]. And its leaves were to be used for medicine.

In the East even today the leaves of certain trees are used for medicine and for curing leather. When the Israelites were unable to drink the bitter water at a place called Marah (bitter), the Lord showed Moses a tree. And when Moses cast some of its branches into the water the water was made sweet (healed) [Exod. 15:25]. God's truth was to dispel darkness, and his words of life were to heal the wounds of all the nations [Isa. 61:3; Rev. 22:2].

CHAPTER TWENTY-FOUR

DANIEL

INTRODUCTION

THE book of Daniel is the most important book of the exilic period. The author of the book is learned, wise, and pious. It is the work of a handsome and wise man who had dedicated his entire life to the cause of his people, a devout man who never swerved from the way of God and his commandments, neither to the right nor to the left.

The prophet Daniel took up where his contemporary Ezekiel had left off. And his prophecies are of a far-reaching range. Being a prophet-statesman, Daniel saw the rise and the fall of great empires, some of which were slowly appearing on the horizon while others were in the making.

The Jewish rabbinical school seemingly refused to classify the book of Daniel in importance among the books of the *Nebiyim* (The Prophets) like Isaiah and Jeremiah. However, they did place it among the major prophets, following the book of Ezekiel. The book of Daniel is seldom read in churches. Some of the rabbis ranked Daniel among the *Ketabin* (The Books or "The Writings"). Be that as it may, Jesus called him a prophet and quoted from his book [Matt. 24:15]. Ezekiel pays tribute to Daniel's wisdom [Ezek. 28:3]. And Josephus calls him one of the greatest Jewish prophets. Daniel indeed was beloved by his people and greatly honored by the kings whom he served so faithfully.

As we can see from his own book, Daniel was one of the victims of the first captivity. It is known as the first captivity of Judah, when Nebuchadnezzar, king of Babylon, took Jerusalem in the third year of the reign of Jehoiakim, king of Judah, and carried the king and many princes and noblemen captive to Babylon. In 597 Daniel was one of the young men of the royal seed. And he was one of the handsome, well-favored, and wise men who were chosen to be educated in science and the learning of the Chaldeans so that they might stand before King Nebuchadnezzar [Dan. 1:3-6].

The Assyrians and Babylonians were the inventors of several writing systems—the sign language, the cuneiform, and the present alphabet. Daniel and his companions studied these ancient and complicated instruments of writing. As far as the language was concerned, they could speak it, just like the Arabs in Palestine can converse in Iraqian, Arabic, and vice versa.

Daniel was a Nazarite, or he became a Nazarite during the captivity. He refused to eat meat and other delicacies which were prepared for him and his student companions in the king's kitchen. He preferred to eat vegetables and assured the chief of eunuchs that he would look better and be stronger and healthier.

Daniel lived a long life and stood before the world's greatest potentates of his days: Nebuchadnezzar, king of Babylon; Belshazzar his son; Darius the Mede; and Cyrus, king of the Medes and Persians. He served as governor, chief of the wise men (counselor), and as a high-ranking minister.

All the above kings showered great honors upon him and gave him lavish gifts because of his great wisdom and spiritual understanding.

The prophet was a well-educated man and, like Joseph, gifted in the interpretation of dreams and visions. The Lord his God had revealed to him some of the most difficult and hidden secrets, which made him famous and feared in the eyes of the pagan wise men and seers.

Daniel's messianic prophecies are clear and therefore easy to understand. His vision of a messianic and universal kingdom is so evidently expressed [Dan. 7:27], and the vision of the stone cut out without hands which smote the image upon its feet and broke them to pieces [Dan. 2:34].

The major part of the book of Daniel is historical and the rest is prophetical. The prophetic portion was revealed in a symbolic language and figuratively. This is why the book is difficult to understand, especially to the Western readers who are unfamiliar with the symbols and figures of speech characteristic of the Semitic languages.

Daniel wrote in the Chaldean or southern Aramaic language, which in his time was the imperial tongue of the vast Chaldean empire and which remained the same during the Persian Period, 561-538 B.C. Daniel was trained in Chaldean languages, and he wrote for the Jews who were in Babylon. All these Jews spoke and wrote in Aramaic. During the captivity Chaldean Aramaic had supplanted their Hebrew dialect, a sister tongue. Both the Babylonian and the Palestinian Talmuds were written in Aramaic. The Jews had a large and prosperous colony in Babylon, and the greatest rabbinical school was there about 560 B.C.

After the return of the first exiles under the leadership of Zerubbabel to Jerusalem and Judah and the rebuilding of the temple in 538-516 B.C., the Hebrew leaders started to revive the Hebrew dialect. Thus, the books of the prophets which had been written in Babylon were transcribed into the Hebrew dialect. Some portions were left in their original setting. All the Hebrews in the captivity had become a Chaldean or Aramaic-speaking people. Daniel, Nehemiah, and Esther did not know any Hebrew. Ezra, being a priest and scribe, could read both Hebrew and Aramaic.

LEARNING

Children in whom was no blemish, but well-favored, and skilful in all wisdom, and cunning in knowledge, and understanding science, and such as had ability in them to stand in the king's palace, and whom they might teach the learning and the tongue of the Chaldeans. Dan. 1:4

The Chaldeans were noted for their studies of science, literature, philosophy, medicine, astronomy, and astrology. The Babylonian Empire, which was revealed to Daniel as the golden image, had excelled all the kingdoms of the earth in wealth, culture, and learning. The Babylonians and Assyrians were the originators of our calendar, the alphabet, chariots, and many other things which gave rise to the present sciences and Western culture. The alphabet was the very core of human progress and the key to new knowledge.

Daniel and his young fellow Israelites were to be taught the Chaldean or southern dialect, which was the imperial language of the vast realm of Babylon and the language of the former empire, the empire of Assyria. These young students, after their training, were to be appointed overseers over taxes, tributes, and official business. Some of them were to become governors over cities inhabited by the Israelites; others were to stand before the king as secretaries and scribes. Eastern potentates always preferred native officials, interpreters, and governors. Moreover, some of the young men were made eunuchs and kept in the palace in charge of the king's household. Others were made cupbearers and servants.

VEGETABLE FOOD

Prove thy servants, I beseech thee, ten days; and let them give us pulse to eat, and water to drink. Dan. 1:12

The Aramaic word *zaraoney* means "vegetables or grown seeds." In the East vegetables and fruits are dried during the summer and stored for the winter. The Nazarites and the men and women who abstain from meat, milk, and butter eat fresh and dried vegetables and fruits.

No doubt Daniel was a Nazarite of deep religious devotion. He chose to eat vegetables and drink water rather than to eat meat and other delicacies and to drink wine from the king's table.

Daniel knew that vegetable food was better than meat and the palace delicacies, and that it would help to arouse the spiritual forces which were dormant in him. The remnant of the Jews in Babylon needed a spiritual leader to guide them and lead them during the darkest period in the history of Israel.

On the other hand, plants and trees are wiser than men and animals who devour them. Plants can convert sun, carbon dioxide, and water into energy. After all, food is manufactured by plants and trees, which know the inner secrets of nature. Wine and meat, on the other hand, arouse the physical forces in man and, at times, cause him to go astray. Then again, the vegetable and plant kingdom is closer to nature and, hence, to God than the animal kingdom.

Jesus likened the kingdom of God to a mustard seed instead of to a lion or an elephant, because the mustard seed is endowed with more wisdom and power than the animals which depend on it for food.

Daniel, because of his faith in God, ate a simple diet and was ten times wiser than the other wise men who ate meat and drank wine from the king's table. Trusting in God is the key to his rich treasure of wisdom and understanding.

CHANGES IN TIME

And he changeth the times and the seasons: he removeth kings, and setteth up kings: he giveth wisdom unto the wise, and knowledge to them that know understanding. Dan. 2:21

"Changes the times" is an Eastern saying which refers to good times and bad times, prosperous years and lean years. The people often speak of good times and hard times. That is to say, when the people are good there is a period of peace and prosperity, and when they are bad the times change from good to bad.

The change is caused by human action in accordance with the law of cause and effect. The Easterners, however, attribute all the changes to God, not that he is the author of evil times, but because God controls all things and yet permits the change. There is no time in the realm of the Spirit. Time is relative. Man has the power to use time for creating good things and building houses, or for doing evil and destroying. Time is an element at man's disposal. He can use it as he pleases. King Solomon says, "To everything there is a season, and a time for every purpose under the sun: A time to be born and a time to die; a time to plant and a time to pluck up that which is planted; a time to kill and a time to heal; a time to tear down and a time to build up . . ." [Eccles. 3:1-8, Eastern text].

Time comes and goes, but men continue upon the face of the earth. God changes the rulers of this world. He promotes one and humbles another. He raises one and puts down another [Ps. 75:7].

STONE NOT CUT BY HAND

Thou sawest till that a stone was cut out without hands, which smote the image upon his feet that were of iron and clay, and brake them to pieces.   Dan. 2:34

Stone is symbolic of truth. "Cut out without hands" here refers to the true religion, not devised by the mind of men, but revealed by God. Stones were hewn and polished by hand and used for the temples; thus, the temples were man-made places of worship. Moreover, in the East, stones are used as weapons against wild beasts as well as against men. David killed Goliath with a smooth stone picked from the dry bed of a stream [1 Sam. 17:40].

A new religion was to spring up from the ruins of the Hebrew temple, and a new law was to be written on the hearts of men instead of on breakable stone tablets. It was to be a perfect religion revealed not by men but by God. The reference is to the teaching of Messiah which was to overthrow both paganism and imperial Rome and make the religion of the prophets of Israel the religion of the world. Christianity, the messianic teaching, was to destroy paganism both in the East and the West. All nations of the world were to be healed by the truths that were to issue out of the foundation of the Jewish religion and its temple [Ezek. 47:1]. Jesus' teaching was free from man-made dogmas and doctrines. It was clear, powerful, and perfect.

The diverse image represented the pagan realms of Babylon, Persia, Greece, and Rome. The feet of iron and clay were symbolic of the Roman Empire, the last great pagan empire to be broken by Christianity or by the teaching of Jesus Christ, which was not devised by the wisdom of men but by the power of God. Truth cannot be created by human minds; it must come from God.

The stone became a great mountain; that is, a great spiritual kingdom which at its inception was foreseen by the Hebrew prophets [Isa. 2:2-3; Mic. 4:1; Zech. 14:8-9].

THE DIVERSE IMAGE

Then was the iron, the clay, the brass, the silver, and the gold, broken to pieces together, and became like the chaff of the summer threshingfloors; and the wind carried them away, that no place was found for them: and the stone that smote the image became a great mountain, and filled the whole earth.   Dan. 2:35

The weird image which Nebuchadnezzar, the king of Babylon, had seen in his vision was symbolic of the four great imperial powers—Babylon, Persia, Greece, and the Roman Empire.

Babylon, the image of gold, was noted for its arts, sciences, gaieties, and hanging gardens. Gold symbolizes glory and majesty. Babylon, until the seventeenth century, was never surpassed for its beauty, culture, and imperial power.

The Persian reign is symbolized by the image of silver, which is a precious metal but inferior to gold. The Persian reign was strong and glorious but not like that of Babylon. The Chaldeans were great savants, inventors, scientists, and builders.

The kingdom of brass is Greece, which was strong like brass. But brass, even though durable, cannot be used to hammer other metals.

The fourth kingdom, iron, is the Roman Empire. Iron was the strongest metal until steel was discovered. All other metals could be hammered by iron. But the iron seen in the vision was not pure. It contained some clay, which is symbolic of weakness.

The Roman Empire was strong in its military organization and laws, but it was weak morally. Its main objective was solely to conquer and plunder and rule over weaker nations. The fabulous spoils created rivalries between the numerous contenders to the much-coveted imperial throne. The empire was neither monarchy nor republic and, therefore, it was weak and easy to be broken by the stone cut without human hands, Christian truth.

PROMINENT MEN WORSHIPED

Then the king Nebuchadnezzar fell upon his face, and worshipped Daniel, and commanded that they should offer an oblation and sweet odors unto him.   Dan. 2:46

In the East kings, princes, noblemen, wise men, and holy men are greeted with animal sacrifices and incense. When they enter a town, the people kill oxen and sheep in their honor, offer presents, and do obeisance.

When Paul and Barnabas healed a lame man in Lystra, the people of the town brought oxen and garlands to the gates to offer sacrifices to them. Barnabas and Paul tore their garments and said, "We are men like you" [Acts 14:13-16].

These gifts or sacrifices are offered as a token of gratitude and in recognition of their extraordinary powers and favors.

The Near Eastern kings are very liberal in bestowing honors upon faithful officials, especially upon the learned men and wise statesmen.

SEVEN SEASONS

Let his heart be changed from man's, and let a beast's heart be given unto him; and let seven times pass over him.   Dan. 4:16

The Aramaic word *edan* (time, season) in this case it means "season"; that is, a unit of time, three months, or seven seasons.

Even before the development of the present calendar, which is based on the movements of the solar system, the moon and the change of seasons were used to determine time.

The calendar of 365 days was in use in Babylon during the time of Daniel, but the old yardstick for measuring time was still used, especially by wise men, pastoral people, and nomad tribes. The priests also used seasons of seven weeks; that is, forty-nine days. And another day was added to make them 50 days. And the forty-nine years were reckoned from one jubilee to another. Seven seasons could be reckoned as seven seasons of the year. A season is about three months or ninety days, or a quarter of the year, which was 360 days.

See the commentary on Daniel 7:25.

ATE GRASS

And they shall drive thee from men, and thy dwelling shall be with the beasts of the field: they shall make thee to eat grass as oxen, and seven times shall pass over thee, until thou know that the Most High ruleth in the kingdom of men, and giveth it to whomsoever he will.   Dan. 4:32

"To eat grass as oxen" is an Eastern idiom which means to lose one's senses or to become demented. The ox is considered one of the most stupid animals in the animal kingdom. It takes a long time to train an ox. Even today the Aramaic-speaking people say, "Leave him alone; he is an ox," which means he is crazy. Some people wrongly believe that King Nebuchadnezzar actually turned into an ox in order to eat grass.

Nebuchadnezzar had proclaimed himself as the god of the world. Kings, princes, and the nobles of the great Babylonian realm had worshiped his golden statue. God had granted him favors, power, and glory, and made him like a tall cedar tree in the midst of the forest. But Nebuchadnezzar, like other dictators, never gave thanks to God [Dan. 5:20]. Therefore the tree was to be cut down. First, the great king of kings was to lose his senses and become like an ox in order to teach him that there is a God in heaven. In other words, the king of Babylon was the victim of too much power, gold, and glory.

Nebuchadnezzar lost his mind and ate grass like an ox, and lived outdoors like a beast; and his body was wet with the dew of heaven [Dan. 5:21]. But when seven seasons were fulfilled, Nebuchadnezzar acknowledged the Most High God. Then his understanding returned to him and he was restored to his throne.

WRITING ON THE WALL

In the same hour came forth fingers of a man's hand, and wrote over against the candlestick upon the plaster of the wall of the king's palace: and the king saw the part of the hand that wrote.

Dan. 5:5

Most of the state feasts and banquets take place in the evening when the people are free from their daily work.

As the banquet was going on and the people were eating and drinking at the royal palace in honor of Belshazzar, the king of Babylon, the fingers of a man's hand appeared and wrote opposite the candlestick upon the plaster of the palace wall.

Both the hand and the writing were projected on the plastered wall by means of a mysterious shadow. God thus divinely revealed the downfall of the Babylonian Empire. This was the first moving picture in the history of mankind. How it was done no one can explain, but the writing was seen over against the candlestick. God can do anything.

King Belshazzar had defiled the sacred vessels of the God of heaven. The writing on the wall meant the sudden destruction of the Babylonian Empire, the image of gold [Daniel 5:25].

THE MEANING OF THE WRITING

And this is the writing that was written, Mene, Mene, Tekel, Upharsin.

Dan. 5:25

The Aramaic reads: *Menen* (or *Menin*), *menen, takel, parsen: Menen* (God has numbered the days of your kingdom), *Takel* (It is weighed in the balances and is found wanting), *Parsen* (Your kingdom is destroyed and given to the Medes and Persians).

The above is an interpretation and not a direct translation of the few words which appeared on the plastered wall of the palace.

Parsen is derived from *paras* (to spread out, scatter). The term Persians means "the scattered people." This is because Persia was made up of many powerful nomad tribes.

The writing on the wall revealed that the end of the glorious Babylonian kingdom had come and that another nation was called by God to rule over the vast realm.

DANIEL'S RANK

Then commanded Belshazzar, and they clothed Daniel with scarlet, and put a chain of gold about his neck, and made a proclamation concerning him, that he should be the third ruler in the kingdom.   Dan. 5:29

Daniel was given the rank of third ruler or viceroy in the kingdom. This was a high place, second only to that of the queen. At the royal banquets the queen always sat on the right hand of the king; and next to her sat the highest official, the prime minister or a prince of the realm.

Some authorities believe that Belshazzar at that time was only a prince and therefore he was second in rank. Daniel tells us that Belshazzar was the king. Daniel would not have called him a king had he been only a prince [Dan. 5:1].

Biblical evidence is far superior to doubtful archeological findings. Dumb and deaf tablets cannot surpass the inspired and living evidence in the Bible.

AN EXCELLENT SPIRIT

Then this Daniel was preferred above the presidents and princes, because an excellent spirit was in him; and the king thought to set him over the whole realm.   Dan. 6:3

"An excellent spirit" in this instance refers to good demeanor, good behavior, or straightforwardness.

Daniel revered the Lord and kept his commandments and his ordinances. He was a pious and strict Jew who did good and refrained from evil. He fasted and prayed for the restoration of his people. Being deeply religious and loyal to the faith of his forefathers, he was endowed with wisdom and understanding. So he behaved well in the court of the king of Babylon and was highly respected by the palace officials.

Daniel was trained in the law of Moses and reared with Jewish moral ethics. He could discriminate between right and wrong. Other counselors and officials had no knowledge of Hebrew moral law, nor did they revere the God of heaven; therefore they were partial in their decisions. They sought honors and wealth, and accepted bribes.

WINDS AND BEASTS

Daniel spake and said, I saw in my vision by night, and, behold, the four winds of the heaven strove upon the great sea.

And four great beasts came up from the sea, diverse one from another. Dan. 7:2-3

The number four means completeness. The four corners of the earth mean the four creative elements: fire, soil, water, and air. The wind is symbolic of movements and changes which were to take place to bring forth four great powers. The four beasts symbolize the four absolute monarchies or dictatorships. One beast was, and the other three were yet to come.

The first beast is the Chaldean empire, the image of gold. The lion means strength and dominion. Eagle wings symbolize the omnipresence or the wide spread of the kingdom of Babylon. The realm was soon to be shorn of its glory and power, and its rulers, who were worshiped as deities, reduced to mortal men.

THE SECOND BEAST

And behold another beast, a second, like to a bear, and it raised up itself on one side, and it had three ribs in the mouth of it between the teeth of it: and they said thus unto it, Arise, devour much flesh. Dan. 7:5

The second beast, the bear, is symbolic of the Persian empire, the image of silver. The bear is a weaker animal when compared with the lion or the leopard. The Persian empire was vast, but not as glorious and powerful as the others. Most of the Persian kings were magnanimous and tolerant toward their subjects. They granted them religious freedom and equality, and the people were neither heavily taxed nor crushed.

The bear kills only one sheep at a time, whereas other wild beasts devour many, not because they are hungry, but just because of their desire to exercise their power.

The Persian kings were more or less satisfied with what they had. They were less war-minded than the Assyrian and Babylonian kings.

THE THIRD BEAST

After this I beheld, and lo another, like a leopard, which had upon the back of it four wings of a fowl; the beast had also four heads; and dominion was given to it. Dan. 7:6

The leopard is symbolic of the Grecian empire which began with the reign of Alexander the Great. The leopard is sturdy and rugged, and second only to the lion in strength.

The four wings of the fowl symbolize vast dominion over the earth. The number four means omnipresence, world-wide conquest. This kingdom was to be more powerful and widespread than the other two, but it was to be of short duration.

The four heads are the four kings which rose after the death of Alexander. The vast realm was divided among his generals into four kingdoms—Seleucia, Syria, Egypt, and Greece.

THE FOURTH BEAST

After this I saw in the night visions, and behold a fourth beast, dreadful and terrible, and strong exceedingly; and it had great iron teeth: it devoured and brake in pieces, and stamped the residue with the feet of it: and it was diverse from all the beasts that were before it; and it had ten horns. Dan. 7:7

The fourth beast is the Roman Empire, the fourth great realm to rule over the world. The Romans conquered and subdued the people completely, and made them tributaries. The Chaldeans and the Persians were magnanimous toward their conquered subjects. Many men of the conquered nations held high offices in the imperial government and were highly honored by the kings of Babylon and Persia, as in the case of Daniel, Nehemiah, Ezra, Mordecai, and other Israelites appointed to high office.

The Romans, on the other hand, were different from the other kingdoms. They plundered, devoured, and destroyed. The beast was diverse and exceedingly dreadful. The Romans crushed every semblance of national resistance and ruled over the conquered races with an iron hand.

Iron is symbolic of strength because all other metals are hammered with iron. The ten horns are symbolic of ten kings who were to rise after the fall of imperial Rome. Daniel, in his long-range vision, saw the rise and fall of great empires, and the rise of new dynasties which actually came into power centuries after his death.

THE ANCIENT OF DAYS

I beheld till the thrones were cast down, and the Ancient of days did sit, whose garment was white as snow, and the hair of his head like the pure wool: his throne was like the fiery flame, and his wheels as burning fire.   Dan. 7:9

The Ancient of days is the Messiah, Jesus Christ, whose kingdom is to be an everlasting kingdom and a world-wide dominion which will replace the world powers, the beasts. He is called the Ancient of days because all past generations had prayed, waited, and expected the coming of the reign of justice. Then again, God's promises to Eve, to Abraham, and David were made centuries before Daniel.

Messiah is God's promise to Adam and Eve; he bruised the head of Satan [Gen. 3:15]. He is also the mystical promise which God made to the Hebrew patriarchs and to David. The seed of Abraham, that is, the truth for which Abraham stood and taught, was to become a world-wide religion.

The white garments symbolize truth. Pure wool is symbolic of purity in religion. The fiery flame and the flaming wheels mean speed. The new teaching would spread not by human means but by the forces of the Spirit [verse 14].

BOOKS OPEN

A fiery stream issued and came forth from before him: thousand thousands ministered unto him, and ten thousand times ten thousand stood before him: the judgment was set, and the books were opened.   Dan. 7:10

The stream of fire is symbolic of the new teaching which would purify the nations and remove the dross. Millions of people were to gather round him, and the wicked were to be judged in his presence.

"The books" here mean the law of God which was given to Moses. In the olden days when people were tried the judge opened the book, in which all punishments were prescribed. This custom still prevails in the Near East in lands where judges and lawyers are unknown. A scribe opens the Holy Bible or the Koran, the sacred book of the Moslems, and reads the statute relative to the offense.

MESSIAH ENDOWED WITH POWER

I saw in the night visions, and, behold, one like the Son of man came with the clouds of heaven, and came to the Ancient of days, and they brought him near before him.

And there was given him dominion, and glory, and a kingdom, that all people, nations, and languages, should serve him: his dominion is an everlasting dominion, which shall not pass away, and his kingdom that which shall not be destroyed.   Dan. 7:13-14

In biblical days no one had ascended above the clouds. Not even birds could fly that high. Clouds, in Aramaic, are symbolic of glory and triumph. Coming "upon the clouds of heaven" suggests "in a glorious manner." "Riding on the clouds" symbolizes the overcoming of every difficult problem, and the triumph over all evil forces.

Even today we often say, "He is riding on the clouds." The term "heaven," in Semitic languages, also means "sky." In the Gospels we are told that Jesus will come again riding on the clouds [Matt. 24:30].

God can do anything. Christ can come in any way he wishes. But the most important thing is that he *will* come, and not *how* he will come.

The Ancient of days is the Messiah, Christ, who was given power, dominion, and glory. The man who came is an angel whom Daniel saw in a human form. The angel was the messenger of God who came and stood before the Messiah, announcing his glorious reign.

DANIEL TROUBLED

I Daniel was grieved in my spirit in the midst of my body, and the visions of my head troubled me.   Dan. 7:15

The Eastern text reads *mashkbai* (my bed, bedroom). *Mishka* in Aramaic means "skin." Evidently the translators of the King James Version confused the two words. That is why they translated *mashkbai* as "in the midst of my body."

Daniel was troubled by the vision which he saw in his sleep upon his bed. Apparently he could not discern the meaning of the vision immediately.

RAM AND HE-GOAT

Then I lifted up mine eyes, and saw, and, behold, there stood before the river a ram which had two horns: and the two horns were high; but one was higher than the other, and the higher came up last.

I saw the ram pushing westward, and northward, and southward; so that no beasts might stand before him, neither was there any that could deliver out of his hand; but he did according to his will, and became great.   Dan. 8:3-4

The ram is symbolic of the Persian Empire. After the fall of the Babylonian Empire the Persian kings extended the borders of the new realm beyond those which were established by the Chaldean kings. The Persian kings conquered many lands in the north, south, and east. They tried to excel the glory of the Babylonian Empire and to put down all revolts against the empire (the image of gold).

The ram is a beautiful and powerful animal, but is too fat and therefore slow in motion. Persians, like many other Eastern races, are noted for slowness and indecision. The Persians as a whole are a peace-loving people. Like a ram, they would not attack if left alone.

A he-goat, on the other hand, is rugged and sturdy. The he-goat was the Grecian Empire. Greece is a mountainous land good for goats. The Greeks were an aggressive people interested in plundering and destroying. The king of the Greeks was to defeat the king of Persia and for a brief period rule all the known civilized world from Macedonia to the Indus River.

ALEXANDER THE GREAT

And as I was considering, behold, a he goat came from the west on the face of the whole earth, and touched not the ground: and the goat had a notable horn between his eyes.   Dan. 8:5

The he-goat is Alexander the Great. A goat is symbolic of swiftness and ruggedness. Greece is a mountainous and rugged country.

Alexander the Great was known as a king with a golden horn. A horn symbolizes imperial power, and gold denotes glory and excellency.

Alexander, the Macedonian king, is the he-goat; Darius, the king of Persia and Media, is the ram with two horns. A ram is fat and slow in motion but the he-goat is rugged and swift. The Macedonian army was small, poor, and badly fed as compared with the vast and well-fed

Persian army, but it was faster and stronger than the slow Persian army. After the defeat of the Persian army at the Battles of Issus and Arbela, the Macedonian expeditionary force never gave the Persian army a chance to regroup and reorganize until the whole Persian Empire was conquered by the small but rugged and mobile Macedonian cavalry.

A LITTLE HORN

And out of one of them came forth a little horn, which waxed exceeding great toward the south, and toward the east, and toward the pleasant land.   Dan. 8:9

After the death of Alexander the Great in 323 B.C. the Grecian Empire was divided among his four generals. The little horn is the Egyptian portion of the empire which fell to Ptolemy. The notable horn was Alexander the Great [verse 5].

This kingdom, through marriages and alliances, gained control over Palestine, "The Pleasant Land." The Jews again lost their hard-won freedom. The daily sacrifice was done away with, and the temple and sanctuary were destroyed.

GABRIEL

And I heard a man's voice between the banks of Ulai, which called, and said, Gabriel, make this man to understand the vision.   Dan. 8:16

Gabri-el (Gabriel) is an Aramaic name meaning a man of God; *gabra* (man) and *El* (God). The Hebrew equivalent would be *Adam-Alohim.*

Daniel was carried away captive when he was a youth. He was educated in the royal palace in Babylon, and he spoke Aramaic, the imperial language of the Assyrian and Babylonian Empires. Daniel wrote in Aramaic, but years afterward a portion of his book was transcribed into the Hebrew dialect which was revived by Ezra after the captivity.

Gabriel appeared to Daniel in the form of a man, to give him wisdom so that he might be able to interpret the dream which he had seen [Dan. 9:21-22].

Angels are God's counsels given to men. They are also known as God's messengers. Angels are spirits depicted with wings and human bodies, so that men can understand their missions. The angel spoke in Aramaic, the language of the prophet.

See the commentary on "Angels."

SUDDEN ATTACK

And through his policy also he shall cause craft to prosper in his hand; and he shall magnify himself in his heart, and by peace shall destroy many: he shall also stand up against the Prince of princes; but he shall be broken without hand. Dan. 8:25

The Aramaic word *shilya* is derived from the root *shlai* (stillness, quiet, suddenly, unexpectedly, at once). But in this instance it means "suddenly, unexpectedly." The Aramaic reads: ". . . and suddenly he shall destroy many. . . ."

No king can destroy other nations or kingdoms by means of peace and tranquillity. This king was to strike instantly against his enemies. In other words, he was going to do what Hitler did when he attacked Poland, Czechoslovakia, and Russia.

A SECRET VISION

And the vision of the evening and the morning which was told is true: wherefore shut thou up the vision; for it shall be for many days. Dan. 8:26

The vision was like a sealed book. It was to be opened and to be fulfilled in the future. The prophet was warned not to disclose its meaning, because the time for the restoration of the remnant had not yet come [Dan. 10:14]. The remnant was to be restored, but many political changes were to take place before the restoration would become a fact. Thus the vision was sealed for the time being.

Jeremiah had prophesied that the whole land of Judah would be a desolation and that the people would remain in Babylon for seventy years [Jer. 25:11-12].

Jerusalem was rebuilt during the reign of the Persian kings, but the temple was polluted during the Grecian reign, and the people were subjected to many hardships and finally were enslaved by the Romans in 67 B.C. In A.D. 70 Titus destroyed the temple and sealed the fate of the Jews.

SEVENTY UNITS OF TIME

Seventy weeks are determined upon thy people and upon thy holy city, to finish the transgression, and to make an end of sins, and to make reconciliation for iniquity, and to bring in everlasting righteousness, and to seal up the vision and prophecy, and to anoint the Most Holy. Dan. 9:24

The Eastern text reads: "Seventy times seven weeks are determined upon your people and upon your holy city, to finish the transgressions and to make an end of sins and for the forgiveness of the iniquity and to bring in everlasting righteousness and to fulfill the vision of the prophets and to give the most holy to Messiah."

The Aramaic *shaboa* is a division of the ecclesiastical year; that is, seven weeks, or 49 days. According to the Eastern text, the fulfillment was to take place after seventy *shaboey,* or seventy times seven weeks.

Read also verses 25 and 26. According to verse 25, 490 weeks were to elapse before these things were to take place. The term "seventy times seven" was prevalent in Hebrew or Aramaic speech [Gen. 4:24; Matt. 18:22]. Daniel in his long and mysterious vision saw the fall of the Persian empire and the rise of the Grecian empire, and the rivalry between the king of the North (Syria), king of the South (Egypt) [Dan. 11:2-45]. The Jews were to suffer agony and the temple was to be polluted [Dan. 11:31-34].

The Jews were in Babylon about seventy years. The second temple was built seventy years after the second captivity [Jer. 25:12].

"After seventy years are completed at Babylon I will deliver you and perform my good word toward you in bringing you back to this country" [Jer. 29:10, Eastern text; see also 2 Chron. 36:21].

A SUDDEN REVOLT

> *And in his estate shall stand up a vile person, to whom they shall not give the honor of the kingdom: but he shall come in peaceably, and obtain the kingdom by flatteries.* Dan. 11:21

The Eastern text reads: "And in his place shall rise up a vile person, to whom they shall not bestow the royal honor; but he shall come suddenly and seize the kingdom by fraud."

The Aramaic word *beshiliah* means "'suddenly, quietly, unexpectedly." See the commentary on Daniel 8:25.

WRITTEN IN THE BOOK

> *And at that time shall Michael stand up, the great prince which standeth for the children of thy people: and there shall be a time of trouble, such as never was since there was a nation even to that same time: and at that time thy people shall be delivered, every one that shall be found written in the book.* Dan. 12:1

In the olden days, the same as today, there were scrolls in which men's deeds were recorded. The good expected a reward, and the wicked punishment. "Let them . . . not be written with the righteous" [Ps. 69:28, Eastern text].

Kings also kept the books of records of the chronicles, which from time to time were read before the monarchs [Esther 6:1-3].

In this instance the term "book" is used symbolically. God knows all human deeds, good and bad. He does not have to keep books. The sins of the people are written on themselves; they bear black marks which can be easily recognized. The good are to be rewarded and the wicked punished.

EVERLASTING REWARDS

And many of them that sleep in the dust of the earth shall awake, some to everlasting life, and some to shame and everlasting contempt.
                                                        Dan. 12:2

The prophet Daniel was one of the exiles who were brought from Judah by Nebuchadnezzar, king of Babylon. Daniel had seen much suffering and many injustices inflicted upon his people. The oppressors thought there is no other life beyond this life, and therefore that there is no eternal judgment and punishment.

Daniel saw that there must be an eternal judgment with a final condemnation of the unjust and the oppressors, and eternal rewards for the oppressed.

Those who had suffered persecution and injustices were to rise up to be compensated for their earthly losses. Life is immortal both to the wicked and to the righteous. The righteous will rise up to receive rewards, and the wicked will rise to be judged and sent to eternal condemnation [Isa. 26:19].

A SEALED BOOK

But thou, O Daniel, shut up the words, and seal the book, even to the time of the end: many shall run to and fro, and knowledge shall be increased.
                                                        Dan. 12:4

The contents of the vision were sealed simply because the events had not yet taken place and, therefore, would not be understood by the reader.

Many changes were to take place, and new nations were to come into power before these things were to be fulfilled at the time of the end; that is, at the end of days. The book was to be opened by the Lamb, Jesus Christ [Rev. 6:3-12].

The vision deals with the resurrection both of the wicked and of the righteous, and with rewards and punishment [Dan. 12:2; Matt. 25:46].

CHAPTER TWENTY-FIVE

HOSEA

INTRODUCTION

HOSEA, the son of Beeri, prophesied in the northern kingdom during the reign of Jeroboam II, 782-743 B.C., at a time when Israel was prosperous and powerful. The reign of Uzziah began in 756 B.C. and that of Hezekiah in 720 B.C. The prophet must have lived for a long time. It is said that he prophesied more than eighty years. He must have begun his prophecies before Isaiah, who also prophesied from the reign of Uzziah to that of Hezekiah. Hosea spent most of his time in Israel.

The prophet saw the impending danger from the foreign alliances which both the kings of Israel and the kings of Judah had made with pagan nations. Indeed, Hosea was a great student of the foreign policy of his day. He was strongly opposed to dangerous alliances with pagan states [Hos. 12]. Moreover, the prophet foresaw the fall of the northern kingdom.

The unfaithfulness of Israel and Judah to their God is depicted in a pictorial manner so that even the unlearned man in the street would understand the predicament the two states were in. In his allegory, Hosea is told by God to take a wife of whoredoms and children of whoredoms, symbolizing Israel and Judah, who had departed from the Lord and made alliances with foreign nations. Just as Gomer and her daughters have become unfaithful, so Israel and Judah have become unfaithful to God and engaged in whoredom with foreign kings.

In the allegory or parable Hosea is placed in the third person by the scribe. This is because the book is written by a scribe to whom the prophet had dictated his message. The name of the first child born to Hosea is called Jezreel, the city where Jehu, the king of Israel, destroyed the house of Ahab. The name of the second child is *La-ethrakhmath* (not beloved), "for I will no more have mercy upon the house of Israel." The name of the third, a son, is called *La-ammi* (not my people), "for you are not my people and I will not be your God."

The children of Gomer are asked to plead with the unfaithful wife to repent from her whoredom. The term "Gomer," Aramaic *Gamar* (to finish, to come to an end) means the end of Israel and Judah had come. Idolatry and whoredom with foreign nations were the cause of their downfall.

The second parable is that of the adulterous woman. The prophet is told again to take another woman who was an adulteress. He bought her for fifteen pieces of silver and an homer and a half of barley. Israel was to be without a king for many days [chapters 3-5].

Whoredom was prohibited by the Mosaic law. Harlots were stoned. Hosea, being a prophet of God, could not have bought a harlot and taken her as his wife. But he could do it in a parable, and the people took it as a parable.

Hosea, like Jeremiah, Ezekiel, and other Hebrew prophets, used allegories and parables in order to convince the Israelites of the situation which they had brought upon themselves through their unfaithfulness to their God.

Through these metaphors and allegories Hosea was able to show that both Israel and Judah had departed from God and the true religion of Israel and were doomed to be destroyed by the same nations upon whom they trusted for deliverance and security.

Hosea, like other prophets, condemns the priests, the kings, and the prophets, and blames them for the downfall of Israel and Judah. He calls on the people to return to the Lord, and he sees hope for the restoration of the remnant.

WIFE OF WHOREDOMS

The beginning of the word of the Lord by Hosea. And the Lord said to Hosea, Go, take unto thee a wife of whoredoms and children of whoredoms: for the land hath committed great whoredom, departing from the Lord.   Hos. 1:2

"Wife of whoredoms and children of whoredoms" are used figuratively, meaning Israel's unfaithfulness to God. This is because Israel had gone astray after other gods and had begotten children who worshiped idols.

The conversation between God and Hosea took place in a vision. Gomer (Aramaic *Gamar*), daughter of Diblaim, was a notorious harlot which, in this instance, is used symbolically, meaning Israel. It was during the time of the prophet Hosea that the mighty Assyrian Empire was pushing westward. Both Israel and Judah were forced to make alliances, first with Assyria, then with Egypt, and then with Syria and Babylon. As a result of these pagan alliances, pagan gods and pagan worship were introduced both in Israel and Judah.

Hebrew prophets, in order to illustrate their point, used all kinds of allegories and symbolisms. Israel is likened to Gomer because she (Israel) had whored with strange gods. Hosea begot two children; that is, two messages from God concerning Israel and Judah, *La-ethrakhmath* and *La-ammi*. *La-ethrakhmath* means "not beloved" and *La-ammi* "not my people." Jezreel is mentioned here because it was in this city that Jehu destroyed the house of Omri. And what had happened to the house of Omri was to happen to the house of Jehu.

These passages should not be taken literally.

THE END

So he went and took Gomer the daughter of Diblaim; which conceived, and bare him a son.   Hos. 1:3

Gomer (Aramaic *Gamar*) means "the end." The prophet portrays God as a faithful husband and Israel as an unfaithful wife who had played harlot.

The end of the bloody house of Jehu had come. He was to pay for the blood which he had shed in Jezreel when he destroyed the house of Ahab and spared none of his descendants and relatives. The house of Jehu, like the house of Ahab, had forsaken the way of the Lord, and now was to meet the fate of the other dynasties which preceded it. Now the Lord no longer had mercy on the house of Israel. Both the kings and the people had revolted against him and turned to strange gods. Therefore Israel was to be utterly destroyed.

This type of symbolism is found in Isaiah, Ezekiel, and other books by the prophets, who tried to illustrate their stern warning messages in living parables and examples.

JEZREEL

And the Lord said unto him, Call his name Jezreel; for yet a little while, and I will avenge the blood of Jezreel upon the house of Jehu, and will cause to cease the kingdom of the house of Israel.
                                                           Hos. 1:4

Jezreel is the name of a city in the region of the plains of Esdraelon not far from Samaria. It was in this city that Naboth, the Jezreelite, was put to death by Ahab, the king of Israel [1 Kings 21:1-14]. And Jehu, general of the armies of Israel, slew Joram, the king of Israel, near the field of Naboth and cast his body into the field. And he also slew Ahaziah, king of Judah, who fled and died in Megiddo [2 Kings 9:24].

Later, Jehu slew all the sons of Ahab in Samaria and Jezreel. He also destroyed both the wicked and the innocent, the young and the old, all the relatives of Ahab.

During the time of the prophet Hosea, the house of Jehu had also gone astray from the Lord, just as other houses of the kings of Israel had done. The house of Jehu was soon to come to an end, and a weakened Israel was to be conquered by the Assyrians and the people carried away captive.

FENCES OF BRIERS

Therefore, behold, I will hedge up thy ways with thorns, and make a wall, that she shall not find her paths.   Hos. 2:6

In the East many vineyards and gardens are fenced with briers, thorns, and brambles. Wire fencing was unknown in those days and still was not known until recent years. Fences of dry briers and thorns prevented both men and animals from entering the vineyards and gardens.

Some vineyards are fenced with mud walls, and thorns are so placed upon the walls that no one can enter them. Moreover, the paths are protected with piles of dry thorns.

Thorns, here, are used metaphorically, suggesting the difficulties and trials which both Israel and Judah were to go through. And these hardships were brought upon themselves through their own evil acts and backslidings.

FALSE ALLIES

And now will I discover her lewdness in the sight of her lovers, and none shall deliver her out of mine hand.   Hos. 2:10

"Lovers" is used figuratively to mean allies. Both Israel and Judah had made alliances with Assyria and Egypt. And later Judah turned to the Chaldeans for her security. Judah had doted upon them as a woman is doted upon by her lovers [Ezek. 23:13-19].

The prophet condemns these cheap alliances which were purchased with money, temple treasures, and temple revenues, and which were disastrous to both Israel and Judah. The people should have put their trust in their God who had saved them in the past and would have saved them without chariots, swords, and bows [Hos. 1:7].

See also the commentary on Ezekiel 16:33-36.

JEWELS

And I will visit upon her the days of Baalim, wherein she burned incense to them, and she decked herself with her earrings and her jewels, and she went after her lovers, and forgat me, saith the Lord.

Hos. 2:13

In the East when people visit holy shrines and participate in feasts they deck themselves with jewels and wear costly garments. On such occasions men and women are permitted to mingle, dance, and eat together.

The term "lovers" here means the pagan nations and Baal worship which caused the people to go astray from their religion and forget the way of their God.

When the Israelites left Egypt they borrowed jewels of silver, jewels of gold, and clothes from their Egyptian neighbors. They told the Egyptians that they were going to hold a feast to their Lord [Exod. 3:22; 12:35-36].

See also the commentary on Exodus 3:22.

HARDSHIPS

And I will give her her vineyards from thence, and the valley of Achor for a door of hope: and she shall sing there, as in the days of her youth, and as in the day when she came up out of the land of Egypt.

Hos. 2:15

The Eastern text reads: ". . . that it may open her understanding; and she shall be humbled there . . ."

The Aramaic word *socalah* (understanding) has been confused here with *sorah* (hope).

Judah is likened to a woman who had deserted her husband and committed adultery with strangers [verse 13].

The desert is symbolic of hardships, and the valley of Achor (Aramaic *Achar*) in this instance is symbolic of punishment and vengeance. Achar, the son of Zerah, was stoned to death for stealing some of the goods which were dedicated to the Lord [Josh. 7:25-26].

Jerusalem and Judah would have to suffer a similar fate before they would leave their evil ways and turn to the Lord their God. They had stolen temple vessels and God's tithes and given them to Baal. The severe punishment would reveal to them their evil ways and give them understanding to turn to God.

MY MAN

And it shall be at that day, saith the Lord, that thou shalt call me Ishi; and shalt call me no more Baali.   Hos. 2:16

Ishi is the Hebrew term for a man or a husband. Some women in the East when addressing their husbands call them "my man." Others call them "my lord." *Baali* means "my lord." *Baala* (Baal) was the god of agriculture. In other words, he was the landlord. The lands in Syria and Lebanon where Baal was worshiped were fertile and the water abundant. This is why the Israelites again and again forsook their God and worshiped Baal.

Israel was to call God "my man"; that is, "my protector." The name of Baal was to be forgotten. The time was coming when God would look on the Israelites as his own children and they would look to him as their Father.

CLOUDS AND RAIN

And it shall come to pass in that day, I will hear, saith the Lord, I will hear the heavens, and they shall hear the earth;
And the earth shall hear the corn, and the wine, and the oil; and they shall hear Jezreel.   Hos. 2:21-22

The reference here is to the rain. The Aramaic reads: ". . . I will answer the heavens, and they shall answer the earth," which means, "I will provide the clouds with moisture." "And they shall answer the earth" means that the clouds will pour out rain upon the parched ground, so that the grain and vine may flourish and the people may be supplied with food.

The Aramaic word *shamaya* (heavens) also means sky and universe. But in this instance the reference is to the clear Palestinian sky and to the long droughts which often cause famine and suffering. Such calamities were blamed on the sins of the people.

In biblical lands during the droughts clouds and rain are looked upon as God's blessings poured down upon the earth for the benefit of men. They are heralded with a great joy, dancing, and feasting.

THE REMNANT MULTIPLIED

And I will sow her unto me in the earth; and I will have mercy upon her that had not obtained mercy; and I will say to them which were not my people, Thou art my people; and they shall say, Thou art my God.   Hos. 2:23

"And I will sow her unto me" is an Eastern saying which means, I will plant her and thus cause her to multiply like the seed of wheat.

Sow also means "to create." Men are often spoken of as seed and God as a sower. In Deuteronomy 33:27 the Eastern text reads: "In the heaven of heavens is the dwelling of our God from everlasting, and below he creates men. . . ." The Aramaic word *zraa* (to sow, plant) has been confused with *draa* (arm) in the King James Version of this verse, which reads: "underneath are the everlasting arms."

The reference is to the remnant of Israel. The people who had been rejected and called "not God's people" were to be called "God's people" again.

Sow also means "to scatter." In Aramaic it is often said, "I will sow them like seed." This is because the precious seed which is carefully kept in bags is scattered upon the ground. Israel was scattered, but the remnant was to be gathered again and multiplied and established in Palestine [Zech. 10:9; 13:9].

HOSEA'S MARRIAGE

Then said the Lord unto me, Go yet, love a woman beloved of her friend, yet an adulteress, according to the love of the Lord toward the children of Israel, who looked to other gods, and love flagons of wine.   Hos. 3:1

The Aramaic word *rakhma* (fond, desire, delight) is written similar to the Aramaic word *rakhma* (friend). Both words are derived from *rekham* (mercy, compassion, affection). This should read, "Go again, love a woman who is fond of doing evil things and an adulteress."

Nevertheless, such sayings in the Bible are not to be taken literally. The woman who is fond of doing evil things and an adulteress is used as a parable portraying Israel's relation to God.

Israel is portrayed as a woman who forsakes her husband or her chastity and goes after strangers. Hosea did not actually marry an adulteress, as it may seem from his book. Adultery was forbidden in the Mosaic law, and violators were punishable by stoning [Deut. 22:22-24]. Then again, the seventh commandment reads: "Thou shalt not commit adultery" [Exod. 20:14].

All Hebrew prophets used parables and metaphors in order to convey their deep and serious messages to their people. Israel is often likened to a harlot, a vineyard, and a tree. Jesus also used parables and metaphors [Matt. 13].

Had Hosea actually married a harlot, both he and the harlot would have been stoned. Even before the Mosaic law was given, the Hebrews upheld the moral law [Gen. 38:24].

ARGUING WITH PRIESTS

Yet let no man strive, nor reprove another: for thy people are as they that strive with the priest. Hos. 4:4

In biblical days priests acted as judges, doctors, and arbitrators. Since the Hebrew religion was a theocracy, the priestly office was both civil and religious. The priests judged the people, convicted the guilty, and imposed fines on those who had violated the law and the ordinances and those who brought blemished animals to be offered to the Lord. The priests were guided by the Mosaic law, ordinances, and the precedents that had been set by Moses, Joshua, and the judges.

The guilty persons often resented the sentence and argued with the priests over religious matters, such as blemished and unblemished animals, measures, weights, balances, the quality of flour for meal offerings, and many other things. Persons guilty of disobedience to the priests were put to death [Deut. 17:12].

EATEN SIN

They eat up the sin of my people, and they set their heart on their iniquity. Hos. 4:8

"They eat up the sin of my people" is an Aramaic idiom which means, "They have devoured or oppressed my people." In the East when the people see a person oppressed or wronged they say, *khetey ela* (It is his sin); that is, "He is treated wrongfully; and the evildoer will be punished for the sin which he has committed." This saying is very common among the Aramaic-speaking people. But when translated literally it loses its meaning.

Hosea here condemns the wicked leaders of his people who preyed on the poor and the fatherless and shed the blood of the innocent [Amos 4:1].

WHOREDOM AND WINE

Whoredom and wine and new wine take away the heart.
My people ask counsel at their stocks, and their staff declareth unto them: for the spirit of whoredoms hath caused them to err, and they have gone a whoring from under their God. Hos. 4:11-12

This reference is to Baal worship, which consisted of sensualities and the drinking of wine. "The spirit of whoredom," in this instance, means "inclination"; that is, going whoring after corrupt and dangerous Baal practices.

Baal-peor, or the sensual ritual of Baal, had in the past lured many people to join the pagan worship. See the commentary on Numbers 25:2-4.

In the East men generally carry a staff in their hand. The staff is used for protection from wild animals and snakes. During the night the staff is used to feel the road and point out directions. Moreover, staffs were used for divinations. Moses and Aaron and the Egyptian magicians used staffs when they wrought miracles before Pharaoh [Exod. 7:10-12]. In the olden days the people venerated sacred staffs and wands. They also worshiped images made of wood and stone [Jer. 2:27].

When the Hebrews forsook their God and departed from their religion they, like pagans, practiced witchcraft, worshiped images, and venerated staffs and wands of holy men. Gehazi was told by the prophet Elisha to lay his staff upon the face of a dead child [2 Kings 4:29-31]. The staff with which Moses smote the sea was kept in the Ark of the Covenant.

ASHAMED OF BAAL WORSHIP

The wind hath bound her up in her wings, and they shall be ashamed because of their sacrifices.   Hos. 4:19

The Eastern text reads, "Let the wind rend asunder their robes; let them be ashamed of their altars."

Wind in this instance means a strong whirlwind or the destructive east wind. However, in Aramaic, the term wind is often used metaphorically, meaning fortunes. We often say, "The wind is on his side" or "The wind is against him."

The alliances which Judah and Israel had made with pagan nations, like violent east winds, were to rend their robes and uncover their nakedness.

The time was coming when fortune would turn against them and they would be ashamed of the trust they had put in foreign kings and pagan idols.

ALIEN CHILDREN

They have dealt treacherously against the Lord; for they have begotten strange children: now shall a month devour them with their portions.   Hos. 5:7

The reference here is to the strange or alien children which the Israelites had begotten of pagan women and brought up. Evidently some of the Israelites had transgressed the law of Moses in marrying foreign women and rearing alien children. The children of such marriages were not reared according to the Mosaic law and ordinances. Foreign women exerted a tremendous influence upon their Jewish husbands, as in the case of King Solomon and his foreign wives. Many men who married pagan wives became the victims of Baal worship and pagan practices.

These unfaithful men, even though they should take their flocks for burnt offerings and go to seek the Lord their God, would not find him [verse 6].

SACRED LANDMARK

The princes of Judah were like them that remove the bound: therefore I will pour out my wrath upon them like water. Hos. 5:10

Even today, removal of landmarks between fields is considered one of the most sinful acts in the Near East. The ancient landmarks and boundaries are highly respected. The people are afraid to remove a landmark, fearing the curse which was invoked by those who had partitioned the land. Nevertheless, there are certain men who, despite the sacred ban and the curse, remove the landmarks and boundaries and steal the land.

The landmark is a smooth stone placed between two adjoining properties. At times a stone or landmark may be accidentally removed from its place by a plow.

All those who violate this law are called wicked. The Mosaic law reads: "Cursed be he who removes his neighbor's landmark. And all the people shall say, Amen" [Deut. 27:17, Eastern text; see also Deut. 19:14].

See the commentary on Isaiah 5:8.

THE KING OF KINGS

When Ephraim saw his sickness, and Judah saw his wound, then went Ephraim to the Assyrian, and sent to king Jareb: yet could he not heal you, nor cure you of your wound.   Hos. 5:13

The Eastern text reads *malka deyareh* (the great king); that is, the king of Assyria. In the olden days this title was given to emperors who ruled over many lands. Later, another title came into use, *melekh malkey* (the king of kings) or emperor. [Hos. 10:6].

Ephraim, meaning Israel, had made an alliance with Assyria. The great king of Assyria found conspiracy in Hosea, king of Israel, and therefore went to war against him [2 Kings 17:4].

NO TRUE PROPHETS

Therefore have I hewed them by the prophets; I have slain them by the words of my mouth: and thy judgments are as the light that goeth forth.   Hos. 6:5

The Aramaic word *pesak* (to cut, hew, make an end, decree) in this instance means "to make an end"; that is, "cut them off from the land."

There were times in Israel when the Word of the Lord was precious because there were no true prophets or seers. This is because the prophets of God were either slain or driven away. And many of these so-called prophets had prophesied lies and had led the people astray from the way of God.

During times of calamity the people were so confused that they were unable to discern between the true prophets and false prophets.

The Lord God had cut off the false prophets from the land. He had nullified their wisdom. Many of them whose prophecies had failed were slain by the angry people.

AS AN OVEN HEATED

They are all adulterers, as an oven heated by the baker, who ceaseth from raising after he hath kneaded the dough, until it be leavened.   Hos. 7:4

Oven is used metaphorically here, meaning strong passion. The passion of the rulers to do evil is compared to a heated oven. They are also likened to a baker who, when he had kneaded the dough, waits until it is leavened. The Eastern text reads: ". . . the baker who kneads the dough ceases from going to the city, and waits until it is leavened." That is, the baker did not go to the market place, fearing the oven would cool off.

In Aramaic the people with passion to commit adultery, murder, and other evils are called "hot" [verse 7]. It is often said, "They are as hot as ovens."

QUARREL OVER WHEAT

And they have not cried unto me with their heart, when they howled upon their beds: they assemble themselves for corn and wine, and they rebel against me.   Hos. 7:14

The Eastern text reads: "And they have not cried unto me with their heart, but they howled upon their beds; they quarrel over wheat and wine, and they have rebelled against me."

Mithkathshin (to fight) has been confused in the King James Version with *mithkanshin* (to assemble).

The people defrauded one another while buying and selling, and fought over grain and wine. The priests and the Levites were very particular in selecting tithes of wheat, wine, and animals. They wanted the choicest of the produce of wheat and wine and the unblemished lambs, rams, and bullocks. Likewise, landlords, creditors, and government officials quarreled over their portions and gifts. At times the wheat was seized at the threshing floor and the farmer was left empty-handed.

Even though the people had the law and the prophets, and good discipline, they had perverted themselves with their own evil devices. Therefore they were rejected [Hos. 9:1-3].

MISSING THE MARK

They return, but not to the Most High: they are like a deceitful bow: their princes shall fall by the sword for the rage of their tongue: this shall be their derision in the land of Egypt. Hos. 7:16

The Aramaic word *al* (for) has been confused in the King James Version with *Elaiah* (the Most High); that is, "God."

The Eastern text reads: "They have perverted themselves for nothing; they have become like a deceitful bow; their princes shall fall by the sword because of the boldness of their tongue; such shall be their entanglement in the land of Egypt."

The people had gone after Baal and corrupted themselves with pagan gods and immoral customs for nothing. Their alliances with pagan kings were not only unprofitable but also dangerous. In other words, their alliances were to become pits and traps into which they would fall. Their seers and counselors were like a deceitful bow; they missed the mark, they blundered in their foreign policy.

ISRAEL TO BE RELIEVED
OF ITS BURDEN

Yea, though they have hired among the nations, now will I gather them, and they shall sorrow a little for the burden of the king of princes. Hos. 8:10

The Eastern text reads: "Though they shall be delivered up to the Gentiles, I will gather them, and they shall rest a while from the burden of the kings and the princes."

Ephraim (Israel) had forsaken the law of his God when he made alliances with the Assyrian kings. And now some of the people were burdened with heavy taxation and tributes which the Gentiles had laid upon them.

The prophet sees an end of the exile and predicts the restoration of the remnant of the people.

GIFTS FROM THRESHING FLOORS

Rejoice not, O Israel, for joy, as other people: for thou hast gone a whoring from thy God, thou hast loved a reward upon every cornfloor.   Hos. 9:1

When wheat and barley are threshed, gifts of the new wheat and barley are offered to the priests, judges, and princes. The old wheat is exhausted and even the rich people and the princes wait impatiently for the new crop.

At times these gifts are demanded from the poor farmers in advance. Some wicked government officials confiscated the wheat of the poor and the meek at the threshing floor, fearing that the priests, the landlords, and the creditors would seize it first. The priests, too, demanded many offerings and thus made it hard on the people of the land [verses 13-14].

BRIBES OF GRAIN

The floor and the winepress shall not feed them, and the new wine shall fail in her.   Hos. 9:2

When wheat is threshed, princes, corrupt officials, and creditors come to the threshing floor to receive bribes and gifts and to be paid for their loans. And the poor and helpless farmers give away a portion of their wheat to princes and officials in order to save the rest from being confiscated by the money and seed lenders.

Then again, bribes of wheat, oil, and wine are paid to tax collectors and government officials in order to keep the taxes low and to receive favors. Until a few decades ago, in some Near Eastern countries, tax collectors received no salaries for collecting taxes, but they were allowed to accept bribes and to collect more than that which was levied by the central government. Taxes were paid in kind.

The prophet is condemning these malpractices which robbed the poor people of the fruits of their labor.

EAT UNCLEAN THINGS

They shall not dwell in the Lord's land; but Ephraim shall return to Egypt, and they shall eat unclean things in Assyria. Hos. 9:3

The reference here is to swine meat, blood, meat of dead animals, and other things which were forbidden to the Israelites by the Mosaic law [Lev. 11]. The captives, because of dire need, were to be forced to eat whatsoever they could find in the land of their captivity.

Assyrians, Syrians, and other races ate swine meat and certain other meats, fish, and foods which were an abomination to the Jews. Both Israel and Judah were to pay for their disloyalty to God and the true religion of their fathers. They were to live in foreign lands amidst adversities, want, and uncleanness.

BREAD OF MOURNERS

They shall not offer wine offerings to the Lord, neither shall they be pleasing unto him: their sacrifices shall be unto them as the bread of mourners; all that eat thereof shall be polluted: for their bread for their soul shall not come into the house of the Lord.
Hos. 9:4

In the East when a person dies his relatives kill a sheep or an ox and bake bread to feed the mourners who gather in the house of the deceased. On such occasions all the people of the town share in the grief. At times the mourning lasted for many days. When Aaron died the people mourned for him for thirty days [Num. 20:29].

Food on such occasions is not considered clean. This is because if a person touched the dead he became unclean. Moreover, bedclothes and vessels used for the funeral became unclean. These were placed in hot water and sanctified by the priest.

This ancient custom still prevails. The mourners are fed in the house of the departed one. They eat silently with tears in their eyes. The whole atmosphere is very sad. And while the people are eating one of the professional women mourners raises her voice with a sad lamentation, and the people start weeping again, especially the close relatives of the dead person.

The exiles were to live in strange lands and were to eat their bread with tears in their eyes. They would mourn over the glorious past and weep over the lands and other precious and sacred possessions which they had left behind.

THORNS IN TABERNACLES

For, lo, they are gone because of destruction: Egypt shall gather them up, Memphis shall bury them: the pleasant places for their silver, nettles shall possess them: thorns shall be in their tabernacles.

Hos. 9:6

In biblical lands when camps are removed thorns and weeds start to grow in what once had been a pleasant home. Many of the tribesmen return to encamp where they had been before. But when they fail to come back, the ground, upon which once stood proud tents filled with men, women, and children, looks sad, barren, and destitute.

Most of the refugees who went into Egypt dwelt in tents outside of towns. Even today in Palestine, Jordan, Syria, and other Eastern lands, one sees hundreds of tents of Arab refugees, Bedouins, and strangers encamping outside the cities. In these lands there always has been a shortage of housing.

Many Israelites who fled to Egypt died there, and their precious possessions of gold and silver were left to the Egyptians.

BAAL-PEOR

I found Israel like grapes in the wilderness; I saw your fathers as the first ripe in the fig tree at her first time: but they went to Baal-peor, and separated themselves unto that shame; and their abominations were according as they loved.

Hos. 9:10

"Like grapes in the wilderness" means rugged, pure, and rare. Grapes are seldom found in the wilderness, but when they are found they are good, and delicious. It happens that grapes or their seeds left by travelers grow into small vines and bear fruit. Wild figs grow in many waste lands. The term "wilderness" at times means uninhabited land.

The Lord found Israel in a desert land and in the waste wilderness, and he led them and kept them pure as the apple of the eye [Deut. 32:10]. But Israel corrupted herself with Baal worship.

Baal-peor, was a religious ritual of sensual nature connected with the Baal worship. Baal was the god of agriculture and the producer of abundant crops. The cult offered its worshipers all kinds of sensualities in order to attract them to Baal worship.

During the time of the Exodus, the Baal-peor ritual led many Hebrews astray from the worship of their God. There were 24,000 men who died from disease [Numbers 25:9]. When Balaam had failed to curse the

Hebrews, he enticed the people to participate in the obscene rites [Num. 25:2-3; Deut. 4:3; Ps. 106:28].

See the commentary on Baal-peor, Numbers 25:2-3.

A GREAT KING

It shall be also carried unto Assyria for a present to king Jareb: Ephraim shall receive shame, and Israel shall be ashamed of his own counsel.   Hos. 10:6

Yareb is derived from *rab* (to become great, grow in power, increase, be exalted, rise to high honor). *Rabba* means "great."

This was one of the titles of the king of Assyria—*Malka rabba* (the great king) [2 Kings 18:19; Hos. 5:13].

See the commentary on Hosea 5:13.

DIVISION OF PLUNDER

Therefore shall a tumult arise among thy people, and all thy fortresses shall be spoiled, as Shalman spoiled Beth-arbel in the day of battle: the mother was dashed in pieces upon her children.   Hos. 10:14

The Aramaic phrase *bizta dashlama* means "the plunder of peace." In biblical days when peace was concluded the spoils were divided. The word *bizta* (spoil) has been transliterated in the King James Version. And the Aramaic word *Beth-el*, a town northeast of Jerusalem, has been confused with *Beth-arbel*. There is no such town in Palestine. Arbel is in Assyria, east of the city of Nineveh.

Beth-el was a central and holy place where people met to inquire of God and where spoils were divided. Easterners usually fight over the division of the plunder [1 Sam. 30:22]. When the spoil is divided in a holy place, the warriors behave properly. Moreover, a portion of the plunder is given to the priests or dedicated to God [Num. 31:37-41].

CORDS OF MEN

I drew them with cords of a man, with bands of love: and I was to them as they that take off the yoke on their jaws, and I laid meat unto them.   Hos. 11:4

The Eastern text reads: "I drew them with cords of a man, with the bands of love; and I was to them as one who takes off the yoke from their neck, and I bent over them and fed them."

The prophet Hosea reminds the people of the time when they were living in bondage under the Egyptian yoke. God drew them with the cords of a man; that is, it took strong cords to pull them out of the land of Egypt. "Cords of a man" means large and strong cords which mature Eastern men use to carry burdens. The boys and girls use little cords.

The Lord took off the Egyptian yoke from the necks of the Israelites and, as a Father, cared for them and fed them in the desert for forty years.

Israel no longer was to return into the land of Egypt, but because of their transgressions against the way of God, they were to be carried away captive to Assyria.

CRAZY

Ephraim feedeth on wind, and followeth after the east wind: he daily increaseth lies and desolation; and they do make a covenant with the Assyrians, and oil is carried into Egypt. Hos. 12:1

"He feeds on wind" is an idiom which means, "He is crazy," or "He has gone astray." East wind is used figuratively, meaning Assyria. Ephraim has rejected the counsel of the prophets of Israel and has made two secret alliances, one with Assyria and the other with Egypt [2 Kings 17:4; Isa. 36:7].

The prophet condemns Israel's foreign policy, for they bought alliances with gold, silver, and oil. The people trusted more in Assyria and Egypt than in the Lord God of Israel. But neither Assyria nor Egypt would save them [Hos. 14:3].

THE SCALES OF DECEIT

He is a merchant, the balances of deceit are in his hand: he loveth to oppress.   Hos. 12:7

In many parts of the East balances are scarce and generally are found only in the houses of the rich and well-to-do merchants who belong to the upper class. At times, when the poor people want to buy or sell, they come to the merchant's house to have the articles weighed. The merchant acts as a wholesale dealer. He buys from the producers and sells to the consumers. Thus, both the seller and the buyer are at his mercy. The balances are often tampered with, according to the transactions, and the persons from whom he buys and those to whom he sells.

Such corrupt practices were general and, to some extent, are still general in many parts of the world. This corrupt practice was abhorred by the Hebrew prophets. "How can they justify themselves with the wicked scales and with the bag of deceitful weights?" [Mic. 6:11, Eastern text].

See also the commentary on Amos 8:5.

GOD FED THEM

I did know thee in the wilderness, in the land of great drought.
Hos. 13:5

The Eastern text reads: "It was I who fed you in the wilderness, in a desolate land which is uninhabited."

The Aramaic word *reaetakh*, derived from *reaa* (to feed, to tend sheep) means, "I have fed you," and is used metaphorically, meaning to rule or to govern.

The error is caused by the confusion of the position of the dot. The letters *resh* (r) and *daleth* (d) are distinguished from one another only by the position of the dot. The translators of the King James Version mistook *raa* (to feed) for *daa* (to know).

God fed or shepherded the Israelites in the wilderness, a land devoid of water and beset with many difficulties.

REPENTANCE

Take with you words, and turn to the Lord: say unto him, Take away all iniquity, and receive us graciously: so will we render the calves of our lips.
Hos. 14:2

The Aramaic reads: "Pledge loyalty, and turn to the Lord your God; and pray to him, that he may forgive your iniquity and receive blessings; then he will recompense you for the prayer of your lips." The Aramaic word *perey* means "fruits"; that is, the fruits of prayer and repentance.

The people are exhorted not to put their trust in Egypt or Assyria but to return to the Lord their God and to petition him with pledges of repentance and ask him to take away all their iniquity so that they may receive forgiveness as the fruit of their earnest prayers and supplications. "Let the priests, the ministers of the Lord, weep between the porch and the altar, and let them say, Spare thy people . . ." [Joel 2:17].

CHAPTER TWENTY-SIX

JOEL

INTRODUCTION

THE prophet Joel prophesied about 800 B.C., a few decades before Amos. We are uncertain about the exact time when the prophet began to prophesy. Indeed, the prophet must have lived during the period when the imperial power of Assyria was felt in all lands west of the River Euphrates. Then again, the day of gloom and judgment came during the Assyrian conquest under the great King Sennacherib, who invaded Judah and captured all fortified cities. During this invasion the land of Judah was laid waste, the trees were cut, the produce of the land was destroyed, and both the land and the cattle languished [Joel 1:5-12].

The prophet portrays a dark picture of the impending disaster which was to come upon the land. This is why he calls husbandmen, vinedressers, and priests to lament and gird themselves in sackcloth, to repent and turn to the Lord.

Joel, like other prophets, sees the restoration of the remnant, and the eventual punishment of the Gentile nations who had helped the Assyrians in destroying Judah and selling the children to Greeks and Sabeans [Joel 3:6-8]. The day of vengeance was at hand, when the enemies of Judah would be recompensed for their evil works. Just as they had sold the children of Judah to foreigners, their children would also be sold in the same markets.

The prophet admonishes the people to beat their plowshares into swords, and their pruninghooks into spears and be strong in the day of battle against their oppressors [Joel 3:10].

After the restoration and the sanctification of the people, Baal worship would come to an end and its false prophets be cut off from the land. Then the Lord would pour out his Spirit upon the people and cause them to see true visions and dreams. The true prophets of God would multiply in the land, the people would be led to the way of God, and prosperity would reign again.

BLACK FACES

Before their face the people shall be much pained: all faces shall gather blackness.   Joel 2:6

"Their faces shall gather blackness" is an Aramaic idiom expressing dismay, confusion, and shame. When a man commits an evil act it is said, "His face is black"; and when he does a good deed it is said, "His face is white." Chaste men and women are called white-faced, while liars are spoken of as men with black faces.

The prophet foresees the conquest of Judah and the fall of the historic and holy city, Jerusalem. He is announcing the day of thick darkness, the day of mourning. The faces of false prophets, rebellious priests, and the princes who had trusted in pagan kings and pagan idols would turn red on that day because they would be caught in their own evil devices. They would be dismayed and confounded because of their evil counsels [Joel 2:1-3].

ABUNDANCE

And the floors shall be full of wheat, and the vats shall overflow with wine and oil.   Joel 2:24

The Aramaic reads: "the wine presses shall overflow." A wine press is a large earthen or wooden vessel in which the grapes are squeezed. When grapes are abundant the wine presses overflow with juices. But in lean years and during droughts the wine presses are dry.

The prophet Joel, like Isaiah, Jeremiah, and other prophets, sees a brighter future for the remnant which would be gathered. The Lord will give rain in its due season. Bread and grapes will be abundant as in former days when Israel was loyal to her God and walked in his way [verses 26-28].

BOYS AND GIRLS SOLD

And they have cast lots for my people; and have given a boy for a harlot, and sold a girl for wine, that they might drink. Joel 3:3

The Eastern text reads: ". . . have given boys for the price of harlots . . ." When Judah was conquered and Jerusalem destroyed, many of the Jews who were carried away captive were sold as slaves. When plunder and captives were divided, the victorious armies cast lots on both the people and the sheep and cattle.

The harlots seldom had their own children. Boys were given as a price to harlots by the men who committed adultery with them. Evidently the boys had fallen in the lot of the wicked. The girls, likewise, were sold to merchants for wine. In those days money was scarce. Food, articles, sheep, wool, clothes, and slaves were bartered and exchanged [2 Kings 5:2].

SHEBA OR SEBA

And I will sell your sons and your daughters into the hand of the children of Judah, and they shall sell them to the Sabeans, to a people far off: for the Lord hath spoken it.   Joel 3:8

The Aramaic word *sheba* is the name of a kingdom in Arabia; namely, the kingdom of Sheba. In Hebrew it is called *Seba*. The name is derived from Sheba, the eldest son of Cush, son of Ham [Gen. 10:7; 1 Chron. 1:9]. When Aramaic uses *sh,* Hebrew and Arabic use *s.* This linguistic difference existed in Israel also. The people of the tribe of Ephraim could not pronounce *sh,* but other tribes did [Judg. 12:5-6].

The Gentile nations who had oppressed Judah were to be measured with the same measure and made to drink from the same cup. Just as they had sold the children of Judah to the Greek merchants, so their children were to be sold to the Sabeans (or Shabeans).

WEAPONS OF WAR

Beat your plowshares into swords, and your pruning hooks into spears: let the weak say, I am strong.   Joel 3:10

The picture of deliverance given by the prophet Joel is contrary to that portrayed by the prophet Isaiah. According to the prophet Joel, Messiah would be a political leader, a mighty man of war like David, who would arm the nation to such extent that even plowshares would be beaten into swords, and pruninghooks into spears.

On the other hand Isaiah says Messiah will not only restore Israel but also inaugurate the reign of justice and everlasting peace. According to Isaiah, war would end forever and the people would beat their swords into plowshares and their spears into pruninghooks [Isa. 2:4].

We can see that the prophetic words uttered by Joel are exactly opposite to those spoken by Isaiah. This is because Joel is depicting a political kingdom of Israel in the pattern of the powerful kingdom of David and limited to the people of Israel. Whereas, Isaiah, through his vision and inner understanding, sees a spiritual and universal kingdom not only for the Jews but also for the Gentiles. In this kingdom meekness and loving-kindness were to supplant the weapons of war.

The prophecy of Isaiah was fulfilled in Jesus Christ who, through his meekness and his death on the cross, inaugurated the reign of justice, peace, and prosperity, and laid down the foundation of a lasting and universal kingdom which is to embrace all nations upon the earth.

SPIRITUAL PROSPERITY

And it shall come to pass in that day, that the mountains shall drop down new wine, and the hills shall flow with milk, and all the rivers of Judah shall flow with waters, and a fountain shall come forth of the house of the Lord. Joel 3:18

The whole picture here is metaphorical and, hence, spiritual. Wine is symbolic of God's teaching, and milk symbolizes prosperity and peace. Wherever there is an abundance of wine and milk there is peace and prosperity. During wars and revolutions sheep are slaughtered for food, and vines are cut and burned for fuel.

New wine is the new teaching which will embrace the whole world. It is the teaching of the Messiah—a new message of peace and understanding which will take the place of war, famine, and suffering when the people turn to God. Water is symbolic of enlightenment, and the fountain the source of the new teaching which shall flow out of the New Jerusalem and the spiritual Israel. Even the desert people and the barbarians will see the new light [Ezek. 47:1].

See also the commentary on Ezekiel 47:1.

CLEANSING

For I will cleanse their blood that I have not cleansed: for the Lord dwelleth in Zion. Joel 3:21

The Aramaic word *taba* (or *tawa* with the letter *tau*) means "to avenge." And the Aramaic word *ekhasey* from *khasi* (to make atonement, pardon, purge, absolve) in this instance means "to absolve." "Cleanse" is wrongly used in the King James Version.

The Eastern text reads: "For I will avenge their blood, and I will not absolve the offenders; and the Lord will dwell in Zion."

The Egyptians and the Edomites who had oppressed Judah were to be destroyed. The Lord was to seek vengeance against them [Nah. 1:2].

This prophecy was fulfilled when Nebuchadnezzar, king of Babylon, conquered Egypt and all the other small kingdoms in the path of his march in 586 B.C.

CHAPTER TWENTY-SEVEN

AMOS

INTRODUCTION

Amos' prophetic ministry began about 783 B.C., during the reign of Uzziah, king of Judah, and Jeroboam II, king of Israel. Amos prophesied a few years before Isaiah and was a contemporary of Hosea. The prophet was not the father of Isaiah as some authorities claim. The name of Amos in Aramaic and Hebrew is different from that of Amos, the father of Isaiah. Amos is spelled with *ai* and *semketh,* and the name of the father of Isaiah is spelled with *aleph* and *zaddi.*

Amos was a Jewish herdsman from the town of Tekoa a short distance from Jerusalem. He was also a gatherer of wild figs. As we can see from his book, the prophet was a simple man and had no education, nor did he make a claim to the mantle of a prophet. "Then Amos answered and said to Amaziah, I am not a prophet, neither a prophet's son; but I was a shepherd and a gatherer of wild figs; and the Lord took me as I followed the flock, and the Lord said to me, Go, prophesy against my people Israel" [Amos 7:14-15, Eastern text].

Amos daringly prophesied against Israel, and even went to Bethel, the seat of religion in Israel. The prophet was warned by Amaziah, the priest of the shrine of Bethel, to leave Israel and go to his own land, Judah, and prophesy there.

The prophet first predicts God's vengeance upon the nations who had oppressed Israel. Syria, Edom, Philistia, Moab, Ammon, and Tyre were to drink from the cup of the fury of God. What they had done to Israel would be done to them. Then Amos prophesied against Israel because the people had gone astray after Baal worship and trusted in pagan kings [Amos 2:68]. During the reigns of both Uzziah and Jeroboam, Israel and Judah were more or less secure and prosperous, but the Baal worship had taken deep roots in Israel, and the impending disaster against the wicked nations was on its way [Amos 3:1-7]. And Israel was to share the punishment, for the princes and kings had oppressed the poor and crushed the needy, and had refused to do justice [Amos 4:1-4].

Amos, like other prophets, sees a brighter future for the remnant. The Lord would raise again the tabernacle of David. The spiritual Israel would triumph. A universal kingdom ruled by Messiah Christ would embrace all the peoples of the earth. Israel would be restored and the messianic prophecies would be fulfilled.

OLD WINE

And they lay themselves down upon clothes laid to pledge by every altar, and they drink the wine of the condemned in the house of their god.   Amos 2:8

The Eastern text reads: "And they laid themselves down in filthy clothes on the sides of every altar, and they drank old wine in the houses of their gods." "Laid to pledge" is a mistranslation in the King James Version. The rich moneylenders who take robes and other clothing as a pledge never *use* the pledged articles unless the owner of the pledge fails to pay his debt.

The worshipers of Baal and other pagan gods drank old wine, which is considered better than new wine. After they became drunk and vomited, they slept in their filthy garments in the houses of the gods, or the houses of prostitution where the Baal worshipers met, ate, and drank, and committed adultery.

When the Israelites conquered Palestine they destroyed the Amorites and other races who worshiped idols and indulged in the sensual pagan rites. And now, after years of discipline and sanctification, Israel itself was corrupted by the pagan idols and worship which their forefathers had destroyed.

ISRAEL'S MISSION

You only have I known of all the families of the earth: therefore I will punish you for all your iniquities.   Amos 3:2

God in diverse manners had revealed himself to all his creations, but he was more fully known to the Hebrew race, which he had called for a spiritual mission to be a blessing to the rest of his children. Therefore Israel was more responsible to God than other races, and her punishment was to be more severe than that of the races to whom he was still unknown.

God judges people according to their knowledge and understanding. He holds responsible those to whom he has revealed himself. And Israel had disobeyed him and gone astray from his way. Israel had been faithless and stiffnecked in all her dealings with God. Nevertheless, regardless of Israel's unfaithfulness to God, Israel was always able to keep the fire of God burning.

There was always a remnant which remained loyal to God. This remnant was the children of the promise and, hence, the true children of Abraham; for all those who left Egypt were the children of Abraham, and Israelites, but only two of them entered into the Promised Land. The rest, because of their disobedience, died in the arid desert. God through his mercy spared a remnant so that his promises to the Hebrew patriarchs who had been faithful to him might be fulfilled, so that in the fullness of time the Gentile world also might be blessed and a universal kingdom established.

EVIL MEANS HARDSHIPS

Shall a trumpet be blown in the city, and the people not be afraid? shall there be evil in a city, and the Lord hath not done it?
                                                    Amos 3:6

Bishta (evil) in this instance means hardship or disaster. The Hebrews attributed both good and evil, both peace and war, to God. Since God knows all and controls everything, nothing happens without his knowledge. And since he allowed it to happen, they thought he was the author of it. But God is not the author of evil, disease, famine, and other calamities. They are all the result of man's disobedience to God's laws and his way.

Wars, depressions, and disasters are the result of human actions. In other words, man brings disaster upon himself. This is because man is free to do good, and he is also free to do evil. God warns men of every impending disaster by sending his holy men, but he does not force his way upon people. In other words, man has power to build and power to destroy.

See the commentary on Isaiah 45:7.

VICIOUS OPPRESSORS

Hear this word, ye kine of Bashan, that are in the mountain of Samaria, which oppress the poor, which crush the needy, which say to their masters, Bring, and let us drink.   Amos 4:1

"Kine," meaning "cows," is used metaphorically to mean oppressors. In Semitic languages, oppressors and dictators are likened to animals and vicious beasts. This is because animals have no knowledge of good and evil, and the strong animals prey on weaker ones. This is also true of oppressors, persecutors, and dictators. They oppress the weak and the needy. The cows of Bashan were noted for their fatness and strength.

The author of the Psalms also used animals figuratively to mean oppressors: "Many bulls have compassed me: strong bulls of Bashan have beset me round" [Ps. 22:12].

The authors of the Bible use vicious animals, such as lions, leopards, and wolves, symbolically in order to make their point clear. Lions, leopards, and bears are used in Ezekiel and Daniel to represent kings and emperors. Dogs are symbolic of gossip and vicious men. Paul, in his epistle to the Philippians, told the people to beware of dogs, which means to beware of gossipers and vicious men who were attacking the Christian doctrine.

Amos is addressing his words to the wicked princes and leaders of Israel who dwelt in the mountain of Samaria. It was the wicked princes and landowners who were oppressing the people and crushing the needy, so that they might have more money to lavish upon themselves. Cows neither oppress the people nor drink wine. The prophet condemned these oppressors. In due time they were to be captured, carried captive, and tamed by stronger men than they.

ARMENIA

And ye shall go out at the breaches, every cow at that which is before her; and ye shall cast them into the palace, saith the Lord.

Amos 4:3

The Aramaic word *atta* means "woman." The Eastern text reads: "And every woman shall run to the breach which is before her; and they shall be cast away to the mountain of Armenia, says the Lord."

The prophet depicts a gloomy picture for the wicked men of Bashan who oppressed the poor. They were to be carried away captive to the land of Armenia, which at this time was under the hand of Assyria.

This prophecy was fulfilled when the king of Assyria carried away captive the ten tribes of Israel to Assyria, Babylon, Persia, and Armenia in 722 B.C. [2 Kings 18:9-12]. Many of the descendants of these tribes remained in Assyria, Iran, and Armenia until World War I. And some of them are still there. They still speak Aramaic, which is called *Lishan-galotha* (the language of the captivity).

BLUNTNESS

And I also have given you cleanness of teeth in all your cities, and want of bread in all your places: yet have ye not returned unto me, saith the Lord.

Amos 4:6

The Aramaic word *kahiotha* (being set on edge, bluntness) is used metaphorically here to mean shortage of food. In the East when bread and other foods are scarce people eat unripe fruits which set their teeth on edge, as they say.

The Israelites had been unfaithful to God's covenant; therefore they had brought many misfortunes upon themselves. There had been a long drought in the land and a shortage of food and a scarcity of water [verse 7].

JUSTICE PERVERTED

Ye who turn judgment to wormwood, and leave off righteousness in the earth.   Amos 5:7

The wormwood plant is noted for its bitterness and therefore it is used here metaphorically, meaning bitterness or grievances.

Justice was perverted in Israel, and the cause of the widow and the fatherless neglected. The innocent men and women who expected to rejoice because justice was on their side often left the court with bitterness in their hearts. The judges were so corrupt that they forsook the cause of the righteous and accepted bribes from the wicked [verse 15]. The prophet condemns these corrupt practices and warns Israel of the impending disaster which was to befall even Gilgal and Bethel, the holy places of Israel.

The Mosaic law is the most just and clear code ever given to mankind. But, like other codes, it was corrupted by impious judges, false prophets, and greedy priests who sold justice and truth for bribes [verse 10].

GOD'S POWER OVER THE UNIVERSE

Seek him that maketh the seven stars and Orion, and turneth the shadow of death into the morning, and maketh the day dark with night: that calleth for the waters of the sea, and poureth them out upon the face of the earth: The Lord is his name.   Amos 5:8

The prophet admonishes the people to turn away from false gods and image worship and to seek the Lord God of Israel, the Creator of the Pleiades and Orion (two great constellations of stars) and the earth, the God who has power over the universe.

"The shadow of death" is used symbolically to mean an impending disaster. In the East when people are threatened or are in danger they say, "We are living under the shadow of death," by which they mean that they may die at any time. The God of Israel was the only God who could change an impending disaster into morning; that is, into joy. Pagan gods were helpless images of wood, stone, silver, and gold.

The prophet reminds the people of the rain which God caused to be poured out upon the parched ground to bring relief from droughts.

THE POOR HATED

They hate him that rebuketh in the gate, and they abhor him that speaketh uprightly.   Amos 5:10

The Eastern text reads: "They hate the poor at the gates . . ." The Aramaic word for "the poor" is *miskena;* the word for "rebuker" is *maksana.*

The reference here is to the poor who sought justice at the gate. The ungodly men and corrupt judges hated to see them come before their presence because they had no bribe in their hands to offer them [verse 12]. They also despised the upright who spoke the truth and pleaded the cause of the poor and the widow, as in the case of the widow and the wicked judge [Luke 18:2-5].

In olden days parks and assembly places were scarce or unknown. Controversies and legal suits were settled at the city gates where the people gathered together [Ruth 4:1; 2 Sam. 15:2].

See the commentary on Ruth 4:1.

WHEAT CONFISCATED

Forasmuch therefore as your treading is upon the poor, and ye take from him burdens of wheat: ye have built houses of hewn stone, but ye shall not dwell in them; ye have planted pleasant vineyards, but ye shall not drink wine of them.   Amos 5:11

"Burdens of wheat" means sacks of wheat. The wheat is threshed in the fields and brought home in sacks on the backs of men, donkeys, and mules.

The sacks are often confiscated by strong men and corrupt government officials. Then again, wheat is transported from one country to another by means of caravans. The caravans often are held up and robbed of both animals and wheat. This practice was very common in biblical lands until World War I.

The wicked princes and oppressors were to be punished for the injustices they had committed against the poor and the needy. They would not dwell in their palaces of hewn stones, nor drink wine of the vineyards they had planted with forced labor.

PLACES OF JUDGMENT

Hate the evil, and love the good, and establish judgment in the gate: it may be that the Lord God of hosts will be gracious unto the remnant of Joseph.   Amos 5:15

City gates are often used for gatherings and judgment places. This is because the gates are always crowded with people. During the morning hours people gather at the gates and laborers wait to be hired. In other words, the gates serve as places of public assembly where business is transacted and lawsuits are settled.

"Then shall the father of the damsel, and her mother, take and bring forth the tokens of the damsel's virginity unto the elders of the city in the gate" [Deut. 22:15].

In the olden days kings also sat in council at the gate, surrounded by the counselors, prophets, princes, and the elders [1 Kings 22:10].

PROFESSIONAL MOURNERS

Therefore the Lord, the God of hosts, the Lord, saith thus; Wailing shall be in all streets; and they shall say in all the highways, Alas! alas! and they shall call the husbandman to mourning, and such as are skilful of lamentation to wailing.   Amos 5:16

Professional mourners are still common in many Eastern lands. The Jews hire mourners and singers during funerals, and people of other races do likewise.

The professional mourners are famous for their skill in composing lamentations. They are born poets who compose wailing songs extemporaneously. They are hired to help the people weep over the dead.

Amos, like Joel and other prophets, sees the impending disaster which is to befall the people who are at ease, eating and drinking.

FOR THIS CAUSE

Woe unto you that desire the day of the Lord! to what end is it for you? the day of the Lord is darkness, and not light. Amos 5:18

The Aramaic *lemana* means "for this cause" or "for what end." This word was used by Jesus when he cried on the cross, *"Eli, Eli, lemana shabakthani!"* ("My God, my God, for this I was spared.") [Matt. 27:46, Eastern text].

The dark day of the Lord was reserved for a purpose, the utter destruction of the wicked. In other words, the evils of the people were to bring upon them a day of darkness, gloom, and destruction.

SNAKES IN HOUSES

As if a man did flee from a lion, and a bear met him; or went into the house, and leaned his hand on the wall, and a serpent bit him.

Amos 5:19

In many Eastern countries it is not an unusual occurrence to find snakes in the walls of houses. Some towns are so infested with snakes that one can see them on the ceilings and walls, on the floors, and at times even in the beds.

This is why Jesus said, "For who is among you, a father, if his son should ask him bread, what! would he hand him a stone? and if he should ask him a fish, what! would he hand him a snake instead of a fish?" [Luke 11:11, Eastern text]. In Europe and America it would be difficult for a father to find a snake to give to his son even if he wanted to.

Houses in the East are old and contain many holes. The walls are not tight. Snakes, birds, and lizards nest in the walls. Many of the snakes are poisonous.

STAR GODS

But ye have borne the tabernacle of your Moloch and Chiun your images, the star of your god, which ye made to yourselves.

Amos 5:26

Malcom was an Ammonite fire god. People burned their firstborn child as an offering to this false deity. The Israelites were forbidden to worship these false gods and to offer their children to them, but they disobeyed God's commandments and went after them to their own destruction. They also worshiped the stars and other heavenly bodies and swore by them. Ashtaroth was a star goddess, often worshiped by the Israelites [Judg. 2:13; 1 Kings 11:5]. They also worshiped other stars and planets, and the sun and the moon.

Even King Solomon with all his wisdom and God's blessings worshiped these strange foreign deities which were introduced by his pagan wives, especially Malcom, the god of the Amonites [1 Kings 11:5]. The people sacrificed their children to gods in order to appease their wrath. At times they also tried to appease the anger of kings by sacrificing their firstborn to them [2 Kings 3:27].

BOWLS

That drink wine in bowls, and anoint themselves with the chief
ointments: but they are not grieved for the affliction of Joseph.

Amos 6:6

"That drink wine in bowls" is an Eastern idiomatic expression which means, "They are addicts to wine." The addicts drink from large bowls which ordinarily are used for food. Even today bowls are used for drinking wine during banquets and marriage feasts. The earthen or wooden bowls are passed around from one guest to another.

These words were spoken against the men who were at ease in Zion and who indulged in eating, drinking, and anointing their heads with oil, not knowing that the hour of reckoning was at hand, nor grieving over the fall of Joseph, that is, Ephraim. ("Ephraim" in this instance means "Israel.") Ephraim was the second son of Joseph, and Israel was often called Ephraim.

Israel, or the northern kingdom, fell first before the power of the Assyrian army.

A PLAGUE

And a man's uncle shall take him up, and he that burneth him,
to bring out the bones out of the house, and shall say unto him that
is by the sides of the house, Is there yet any with thee? and he shall
say, No. Then shall he say, Hold thy tongue: for we may not make
mention of the name of the Lord.

Amos 6:10

The Aramaic word *karib* (near to him) has been confused in the King James Version with the Aramaic word *makrib* (to offer a burnt offering). The verbs are identical, but are pronounced differently. The Eastern text reads: "And a man's uncle or one who is near to him shall carry the dead body out of the house; and he shall say to him who is in the house, Is there any one else in the house with you? And he shall say, There is no one, because they have perished; for they did not mention the name of the Lord."

The Aramaic word *sap,* derived from *sop* (to perish, come to an end, be consumed) has been confused with *spa, sipta* (lip brim) and has been rendered, "Hold thy tongue."

Jerusalem was doomed and the inhabitants were to perish [verses 8-9]. The people had forsaken the Lord and had worshiped images and idols. They died because they had not called upon the name of the God of their fathers, but instead they invoked the names of pagan idols who were unable to deliver them in the time of their tribulations.

CITY, NOT HORNS

Ye which rejoice in a thing of nought, which say, Have we not taken to us horns by our own strength?   Amos 6:13

The Aramaic word *keritha* means "town." And the Aramaic word for "horns" is *karnatha*. The letters *yoth* (y) and *nun* (n) are very similar and are often confused by careless copyists and translators who are not proficient in Semitic languages. Then again, when manuscrips are damaged by humidity, these small letters are hard to distinguish one from another, especially when they fall in the middle of a word. "Horns" should read "towns" or "cities." This error occurs also in Habakkuk 3:4.

The reference here is to the capture of a town or city. Some warriors claim the honor for themselves instead of giving it to God.

See the commentary on Habakkuk 3:4.

PLAGUE OF LOCUSTS

Thus hath the Lord God showed unto me; and, behold, he formed grasshoppers in the beginning of the shooting up of the latter growth; and, lo, it was the latter growth after the king's mowings.   Amos 7:1

This should read: ". . . behold, a plague [or a swarm] of locusts coming up in the beginning of springing up of the latter growth . . ."

The locust is symbolic of famine and destruction. The vision reveals that the punishment of Israel was at hand. All the pagan shrines, idols, and altars were to be overthrown, and the house of Jeroboam was to be punished for having caused Israel to sin.

The land was to be left desolate like a field that is mowed.

THE END OF ISRAEL

Thus hath the Lord God showed unto me: and behold a basket of summer fruit.   Amos 8:1

The Hebrew prophets, like Jesus, spoke in parables and used similies in order to impart spiritual ideas and interpret visions and difficult sayings. They explained what they wanted to say by something that was familiar to everybody.

"A basket of summer fruit" in this instance symbolizes the end. When the end of summer is nearing, the husbandmen gather their fruits, place them in large baskets woven of branches of willow trees, load them on the backs of donkeys, and bring them to the market places to be sold for money or exchanged for goods. When one sees donkeys loaded with baskets of summer fruits he knows that the summer is over and that the vineyards and orchards are deserted.

Israel is oftentimes likened to a vineyard or an orchard and God to a husbandman [Isa. 5:1; Matt. 20:1; 21:33; Mark 12:1].

The end of Israel was at hand. The victorious Assyrian armies were on the march to execute judgment and to carry Israel away as captives. The sins of the people had hastened their doom. Israel was ripe to be gathered. Many people would be slain and others would be led into captivity.

CROOKED BUSINESS

That we may buy the poor for silver, and the needy for a pair of shoes; yea, and sell the refuse of the wheat?   Amos 8:6

The Aramaic word *nezabin* (to sell) is confused with the Aramaic word *nizbin* (to buy). The two words are identical, and when the vowel system was unknown it would have been very difficult to know whether the prophet meant buy or sell. The Eastern text reads "sell": "That we may sell to the poor for silver, and pay the needy with the refuse of the wheat, and sell the refuse which is left on the floor of the storehouses."

The prophet is speaking of the oppressors who devoured the poor and the needy. These men sold short with deceitful measures and balances [verse 5]. They sold wheat to the poor for silver, and paid the needy laborers with the refuse of the wheat which was left on the floor of the storehouses. The crooked merchants were not interested in buying the poor, they only wanted to cheat them by giving them short measure and selling bad wheat. This practice is still prevalent in many lands.

The Israelites were permitted to buy poor men and women of their own race; however, they were not to be treated as bondservants or slaves, but as hired servants. On the other hand, the Israelites were to offer themselves to be sold to their own people [Lev. 25:39-43; Deut. 15:12-13].

Wicked merchants and landlords cheated the poor and the needy who were at their mercy.

DIG INTO HELL

Though they dig into hell, thence shall mine hand take them; though they climb up to heaven, thence will I bring them down.
Amos 9:2

The Eastern text reads: "Though they go down into Sheol, thence shall my hand bring them up . . ."

The Aramaic word for "hell" is *gehana*. Sheol is a place of rest for departed souls. Sheol is supposed to be a deep place in the earth where the souls of the departed ones are waiting for the resurrection.

Then again, Sheol is considered a place for the wicked [Pss. 9:17; 16:10]. Sheol should not be confused with "hell" [Matt. 5:22; Luke 12:5].

Moreover, Sheol was supposed to be a place beyond the jurisdiction of God. Amos, however, admonishes the people that they cannot escape from God, and that wheresoever they go, God is there. "If I ascend into heaven, thou art there; if I descend into Sheol, behold, thou art there also [Ps. 139:8, Eastern text; see also Jonah 2:2].

During the time of the prophet Amos, the God of Israel was no longer a tribal God, but the God of the whole universe, who had jurisdiction over all nations and peoples, no matter how near or how far off they were. It was during this period that the Hebrew prophets saw more clearly that their God was a universal God and that even such a great power as that of Assyria was also under his jurisdiction. The God of Israel was to punish the Gentile kings just as he was to punish Israel and Judah.

UNIVERSALITY OF GOD

And though they hide themselves in the top of Carmel, I will search and take them out thence; and though they be hid from my sight in the bottom of the sea, thence will I command the serpent, and he shall bite them.
Amos 9:3

In the eighth and seventh centuries B.C. the Hebrew prophets began to see that the God of Israel was the God of the world. During the patriarchal days the Hebrew belief in the universality of God was clearer than in the time of the judges and the kings, when the Israelites went astray after pagan gods. At times they thought that the God of Israel was just one of the many gods with limited powers. At other times they thought he was greater than other gods. Amos proclaimed the universality of God just as Abraham had about fourteen centuries before. Amos helped the latter prophets in their vision of a universal kingdom ruled by Messiah Christ.

The jurisdiction and the power of the pagan gods was limited to the area in which they were worshiped.

But in the eighth century B.C. the Hebrew idea of the universality of God became crystallized. Now the prophets saw that the God of Israel was the only God, the only ruler over the nations, and that it was he who had given power to the kings of Assyria to conquer other nations [Isa. 10:5], that no one could hide himself from his presence, no, not even in heaven or in Sheol or in the bottom of the deep sea. They saw that even the sea and all that is in it are under his dominion [verse 2].

Jonah also knew that the God of Israel was the only God, and the only Creator, who had made the sea and the dry land, and that no one can escape from his presence [Jonah 1:9].

CHAPTER TWENTY-EIGHT

OBADIAH

INTRODUCTION

THE name Obadiah means "the servant of God." The book of Obadiah was written in the sixth century B.C., about the time of the fall of Jerusalem in the year of 586 B.C.

The prophet predicts God's vengeance against Edom because of the cruelty to the Jews during the siege of Jerusalem by the Chaldean armies. The Edomites were the descendants of Esau, the brother of Jacob. But the Edomites were far more cruel to the Jews than the other Gentile peoples. He also condemns Judah's alliances with pagan nations who had deceived and betrayed the Jews in the time of their distress [verse 7].

The prophet also proclaims the day of the Lord upon all the heathen nations who had helped the Chaldeans to destroy the Jewish state and to oppress and plunder the people. Their evil acts were to be returned upon them; that is, as they had done to the Jews, so it was to be done to them.

Obadiah, like other Hebrew prophets, gives hope to the Jewish remnant. The prophet states that the exiles of Jerusalem who are in Spain shall possess the cities of the south. At the end, Judah will be restored, Zion will triumph, and the kingdom will be the Lord's.

PUNISHMENT OF EDOM

For as ye have drunk upon my holy mountain, so shall all the heathen drink continually; yea, they shall drink, and they shall swallow down, and they shall be as though they had not been.

Obad. 1:16

"Drunk upon my holy mountain" means "You have rejoiced over the downfall of Israel." In the East when one sees his enemies utterly destroyed, he celebrates by eating and drinking.

Now the day of the Lord was at hand. The pagans (the Chaldean army) were to feast in the land of Edom. They shall drink until they shall be confounded. Edom shall be subdued and plundered and humbled. Just as they feasted and rejoiced when the Israelites were harassed, so they would be in distress. The same calamity which had befallen Judah would befall them. "They shall be as though they had not been" means "They will drink so much of the fury of God that they will not know what they are doing."

Edom was to be punished for joining the armies of the oppressors of Israel, casting lots upon Jerusalem, and plundering the people. What Edom had done to Israel would be done to her.

ESPANIA

And the captivity of this host of the children of Israel shall possess that of the Canaanites even unto Zarephath; and the captivity of Jerusalem, which is in Sepharad, shall possess the cities of the south.

Obad. 1:20

The Eastern text reads: ". . . and the exiles of Jerusalem who are in (*Espania*) Spain shall possess the cities of the south (Negeb)."

Spain, the ancient Iberia, is not far from Palestine by the sea. The rise of the Assyrian power in the eighth century B.C. made many Israelites flee to other lands around the Mediterranean Sea. And after the fall of Samaria in 722 B.C., many Israelites fled to far-off lands which were beyond the reach of the Assyrian kings. *Sepharad* is another name for Spain.

The Israelites, like the Sidonians, no doubt, had markets in Spain, especially the tribes of Dan and Asher, who were engaged in ships [Judg. 5:17]. Then again, Solomon's ships traded with Tarshish; and, no doubt, Tarshish is a region in southwestern Spain [Gen. 10:4; 1 Kings 10:22; Ezek. 38:13; 1 Chron. 1:7]. Tarshish is mentioned in the Bible many times. It was a land with which the Hebrews were familiar.

Tar might be an abbreviated form of the Aramaic word *taraa* (a door). *Shish* might be derived from *shegash* (rough, disturb, to rage—as the sea). The letter *gamel* is often dropped, and, hence, *shagish* becomes *shish* (raging or turbulent). Thus Tarshish is the door to the raging or the turbulent ocean. Spain was the door to this mysterious great sea.

The Spaniards were the descendants of Javan, the grandson of Japheth [Gen. 10:4].

THE REMNANT

And saviours shall come up on mount Zion to judge the mount of Esau; and the kingdom shall be the Lord's. Obad. 1:21

The Aramaic reads *perikey* (saved). The reference here is to the messianic kingdom which was to overthrow the Gentile rule and establish the kingdom of God. Obadiah, like many other Hebrew prophets, believed that only a great Saviour could remedy the situation. This Saviour, Messiah, was to be sent by God to establish a new kingdom founded on justice and righteousness. All other efforts and alliances had failed. The heathens were to be rebuked and subdued. Esau is symbolic of the pagan world and the injustices which were to be done away with. The prophet is bitter against the Edomites, the children of Esau, who had plundered his people and sold Jewish captives to foreign merchants.

The Jewish remnant regained their freedom and established a second Jewish commonwealth and remain to the present day as a people. But the Edomites lost both their independence and their race.

This prophecy was fulfilled through Jesus Christ, who rebuked the world for its evil and injustices and laid the foundation of God's kingdom on earth. He told his disciples and followers to seek first the kingdom of God and his righteous reign.

CHAPTER TWENTY-NINE

JONAH

INTRODUCTION

JONAH lived during the reign of Amaziah, king of Judah, about the eighth century B.C. [2 Kings 14:25].

Seemingly Jonah, like many of the other Jewish prophets who preceded him, was a nationalistic prophet. He had no use for the pagan nations, nor did he know at the outset that the God of Israel had any compassion upon the Gentiles. Jonah thought the God of Israel was the God of the Hebrew race alone and was interested only in his own people.

But during Jonah's time the power and influence of the Assyrian kings were spreading in all other lands west of the River Euphrates. The Jews, even though fighting for a righteous cause, were unable to escape from the power of the Assyrian Empire and to free themselves from the heavy burdens which the Assyrian kings had laid upon them. During this period the Jews began to realize that their God was also the God of the Gentiles and that it was he who had given power to Assyria to punish other nations because of their evil-doings.

The book of Jonah, like those of other Hebrew prophets, is inspired and is based on the visions and revelations which Jonah saw. In the East a vision or divine revelation is far superior to a story. The people believe in visions and dreams, but they refuse the warnings which are given by men who have not seen a vision. Even though Jesus was the Son of God, the priests and Pharisees refused to listen to him. This is because Jesus never said he had seen a vision, but he spoke directly from God. Jonah was asked by God in a vision to go to Nineveh, the wicked city, to preach to its people so that they might repent and be spared. Meanwhile, Jonah had predicted the fall of Nineveh and the destruction of the Assyrian Empire and, therefore, he was unwilling to go. He wanted to see his prophecy fulfilled and Nineveh destroyed rather than to see the wicked city forgiven. So Jonah fled to Tarshish (Spain).

Some Eastern writers believe that Jonah fled in a vision. Some maintain that Jonah actually went to Nineveh. Some writers say the large fish was preceded by a procession of other fishes, sea monsters, and musicians.

Jonah, being a prophet of God, would have known that the God of Israel was everywhere. At least, the Hebrew prophets knew that their God was the Creator of the heaven and the earth, and that no man could escape from his presence or hide from him.

Whether the book of Jonah is based on a revelation that he saw or is prose work based on an actual experience, would make no difference. The book, being the work of a holy prophet, is inspired in either case. But even such an experience with God would have had to come through divine revelation. "God appeared," in Aramaic, means that the prophet saw a vision or communed with God. God is the Spirit, and he can only be seen or felt in a spiritual way or in a vision. In visions and dreams God instructed prophets and admonished priests, kings, and princes.

No one, not even a skeptic, would doubt the power of God. God could have kept Jonah in a fish not only for three days but even for three centuries. The book states that God created a large fish—large enough to take care of Jonah. After all, God is the Creator of all fishes and creatures both on the land and in the sea.

That the story of the book of Jonah is based on a vision is seen in Jonah 4:10 when God said to Jonah, "Thou hast had pity on the gourd, for the which thou hast not laboured, neither madest it grow; which came up in a night, and perished in a night." A gourd plant cannot grow in a day and give shade. It takes about ninety days to develop into a large plant with full grown leaves. But in a vision it can grow and wither in one night. Of course God could have caused the plant to grow and wither instantly. God can do anything when there is a need. The important thing in this book is that Jonah obeyed the command of God, and carried his instructions and preached to the wicked city the words of life and salvation.

The main purpose of the book of Jonah is to reveal to the people in his day the fact that the God of Israel is the universal God, the God of the whole world, and that the Assyrians are his people, also. But the most important point in the book is that the God of Israel is a forgiving God, who has mercy even upon the wicked inhabitants of Nineveh, and that he forgave them simply because they repented from their evil ways.

The story of Jonah probably is the first story in the whole Bible wherein a wicked nation has been forgiven. The law of Moses was very severe. Sinners and transgressors were seldom forgiven; they were stoned. It is through the book of the prophet Jonah that we learn of God's love and forgiveness, even to a pagan people. The God of Israel is the God of the universe and the Creator of all races and People. The miracle in the story is the repentance of the people of Nineveh who heeded the warning of the prophet of God and turned away from their evil way.

Jesus quoted from the book of Jonah just as he quoted from other prophets whose books are based on the visions they saw. A large portion of the Sacred Word is based on visions, dreams, and revelations which came directly from God. It was in a vision that God told Hosea to marry an evil woman and an adulteress. The woman was symbolic of an evil nation, Israel. Then again, the lowering of Jonah into the sea was symbolic of the rejection and death and burial of Jesus Christ. His being three days and three nights in the belly of the large fish is symbolic of Jesus' burial for three days and three nights in the grave. His coming out of the fish symbolizes Jesus' resurrection. And Jesus' disciples christianized the pagan Assyrians, while Jesus was preaching in Galilee.

NINEVEH

Now the word of the Lord came unto Jonah the son of Amittai, saying,
Arise, go to Nineveh, that great city, and cry against it; for their wickedness is come up before me.   Jonah 1:1-2

It was at this time that the universality of God was revealed to the Hebrews. Before, whenever they defeated their enemies, they attributed their victories to God, and their defeats to God or to their own evil works. But now they were crushed by a mighty empire. They knew that Assyria could not be defeated by their small, untrained, and ill-equipped tribal armies. God only could defeat such imperial powers as Assyria and Egypt.

The prophets began to see that it was their God who had given power to these pagan kings who oppressed them. And they saw that the pagans also were children of God.

Nineveh means "a fish." A fish was one of the gods of Assyria. Some of the Assyrian tribes never ate fish and in some parts of the country sacred fish in ponds were revered and feared by the people.

In the olden days Nineveh was a great city, probably the largest city in the ancient world. And, being large, strong, and prosperous, Nineveh was a wicked city [Nah. 2:8]. Metaphorically, a fish or a whale means trouble, difficulty and dilemma. Even today when a man is host in a city it is said "He has been swallowed by the city." When a man is in a dilemma, we say "He is at sea," or "in the sea."

JONAH'S REFUSAL

But Jonah rose up to flee unto Tarshish from the presence of the Lord, and went down to Joppa; and he found a ship going to Tarshish: so he paid the fare thereof, and went down into it, to go with them unto Tarshish from the presence of the Lord.
                                                    Jonah 1:3

Jonah, being a prophet, knew that the God of Israel was the God of the universe. He was everywhere. But in a vision one is apt to do anything. Jonah knew that the God of Israel was the Creator of the heaven, the earth, and the seas. When he was asked about his country and race, he said, "I am a Hebrew; and I worship the Lord the God of heaven, who has made the sea and the dry land" [Jonah 1:9, Eastern text]. The prophet must have known that even Tarshish was under the jurisdiction of the Hebrew God.

This concept of fleeing from the presence of God was maintained in the early days, when the true concept of the universality of God was lost and when the God of Israel was looked upon as a local God. Nevertheless, great Hebrew prophets and seers knew that their God was the only Creator of heaven and the earth. Be that as it may, Jonah was reluctant to go to Nineveh. He would rather go to Spain to a strange people than to the wicked city, the capital of Assyria.

JONAH'S VOW

But I will sacrifice unto thee with the voice of thanksgiving; I will pay that that I have vowed. Salvation is of the Lord.

Jonah 2:9

The Aramaic word *porana* (vengeance, punishment, recompense, a payment of a debt) in this instance should be read as "pay." (See the Eastern text.) The difference is caused by the close similarity of the two words *porana* (payment) and *porkana* (salvation).

Jonah, here, is speaking of the vow which he had vowed and which he was going to fulfill. The Israelites never canceled or delayed their vows. Jonah, in the belly of the great fish, remembered the prayer of King Solomon wherein he implored God to hearken to the prayer and supplication of all of those who prayed toward the temple which he had built for his glorious name [1 Kings 8:29].

Jonah's prayer was answered, and the Lord commanded the fish to vomit him up on the dry land. Jonah now realized that he must obey God and listen to the counsel of the Most High. He also knew that the God of Israel was a merciful God ready to forgive those who truly repented and returned to him. The people of Ninevah repented from their evil ways and turned to God the Creator of heaven and earth.

THREE DAY'S JOURNEY

And Jonah began to enter into the city a day's journey, and he cried, and said, Yet forty days, and Nineveh shall be overthrown.

Jonah 3:4

The ancient Hebrew tongue must have been close to the Aramaic spoken in Assyria, so that the people of Nineveh could understand the preaching of Jonah. The differences in these languages are like the differences between American English, British English, and Canadian English. Otherwise God would not have asked Jonah to go to a people of a strange speech. Jonah, being a prophet, could speak the Assyrian Aramaic or the lingua franca. Some of the Hebrew prophets were learned men who acted as statesmen and counselors to princes and kings who had dealings with foreign nations.

Abraham, Isaac, and Jacob and all his children spoke Aramaic. Jacob's children were born in Padan-aram, Mesopotamia. Thus, Jonah was not going to a totally strange race, but to a people of the great Semitic race and culture.

GOURD

So Jonah went out of the city, and sat on the east side of the city, and there made him a booth, and sat under it in the shadow, till he might see what would become of the city. Jonah 4:5

In the East strangers, wayfarers, and poor travelers, when they are unable to find lodging in the city or the village, often take refuge under the shadow of trees and vineyard fences covered with leaves of plants— especially during the hot hours of the day when the sun's rays are almost vertical and very penetrating. And when trees are not found the people take refuge in abandoned booths or whatever other shelters they can find.

Gourds and squashes are very abundant in Assyria. They cover fences and hedges around the vineyards which, during hot hours of the day, are generally visited by strangers and wayfarers.

Jonah was a stranger in the large imperial city, and, being a Jew, at the outset was not welcomed by the people of Nineveh. Therefore, like other strangers, he found shelter outside the city. And the Lord caused a gourd to grow and cover the roof of the booth so that the prophet might be protected from the hot rays of the sun. And through the parable of the gourd the Lord God revealed to Jonah that he had compassion on Nineveh and its people and that he was sorry for them. Then the prophet saw clearly that God had pity upon the people of Nineveh, just as he was concerned and grieved over the withered gourd. Then Jonah knew why Nineveh was not destroyed and his prophecy had not come true. And now he could answer those who might accuse him of being a false prophet.

A FORGIVING GOD

Then said the Lord, Thou hast had pity on the gourd, for the which thou hast not laboured, neither madest it grow; which came up in a night, and perished in a night.   Jonah 4:10

In verse 6 we are told that "the Lord God commanded a tender shoot of gourd to spring up, and it sprang up and came over Jonah, and became a shade over his head." Jonah at this time was staying on the east side of the city of Nineveh, and he had no shelter to protect him from the intense Mesopotamian heat. Nineveh is a hot city during the summer months. The temperature rises so high that people take refuge in houses and under green trees and other shelters until the heat is spent and the air cools off.

Note that the gourd sprang up and grew in one day, and withered the next day. The Lord said to Jonah, "You have had pity on the gourd for the which you did not labor nor did you make it to grow; which sprung up in a night and withered in a night" [Eastern text].

The parable of the gourd reveals the love and tender kindness of the Lord to his children who repent and return to him. The city of Nineveh was doomed to fall, but its people and ruler repented and therefore were forgiven. Jonah had wanted to see the wicked city (which soon was to oppress and overthrow his people) destroyed rather than forgiven. Otherwise his prophecy would not come true, and he would be classified as a false prophet. Moses warned the Hebrews against false prophets. He says, "When a prophet speaks in the name of the Lord, and the thing does not come to pass, nor follow; that is the thing which the Lord has not spoken, but the prophet has spoken it presumptuously; you shall not be afraid of him" [Deut. 18:22, Eastern text].

Jonah's prophecy concerning the fall of Nineveh had embarrassed him. He had to know why God had revealed to him that Nineveh would fall within forty days and then changed his mind. So the prophet was displeased [Jonah 4:1]. In other words, Jonah was more concerned about his prediction and his reputation than about saving a pagan city and its inhabitants.

LEFT HAND AND RIGHT HAND

And should not I spare Nineveh, that great city, wherein are more than sixscore thousand persons that cannot discern between their right hand and their left hand; and also much cattle?   Jonah 4:11

The phrase "cannot discern between their right hand and their left hand" is an Eastern idiom which means "too young to discern between good and evil." The term denotes the things on the left hand (evil) and the things on the right hand (good). Another common phrase is "head or tail."

Nineveh was a capital city which had a large population. Many of its people were wicked. They had fought and conquered and plundered other peoples. Nevertheless, there were also in the city little children and innocent men and women who had done no evil, and some of whom were too young to discern between good and bad.

Two centuries later the kings of Nineveh defied the God of Israel and invaded first Israel and then Judah . . . and hearken not unto Hezekiah when he persuadeth you, saying, The Lord will deliver us [2 Kings 18:32-35].

CHAPTER THIRTY

MICAH

INTRODUCTION

THE book of Micah is one of the twelve books that are called Minor Prophets. Micah prophesied in the days of Jotham, Ahaz, and Hezekiah, kings of Judah.

Micah lived in the eighth century B.C. and was a contemporary of Isaiah. The book was written prior to the fall of Samaria in 721 B.C. Like Amos and many other Hebrew prophets, Micah was a peasant who had seen too many evils, oppressions, and injustices. He denounced sacrifices, self-righteousness, and the false confidence of the people, and admonished them to do justice, mercy, and kindness, the very things which the Lord requires of his followers.

The prophet warns Judah that she may face the fate of Israel. The prophet lived at a time when Assyrian power was expanding and nation after nation was becoming the prey of the Assyrian army. Jerusalem, because of its transgressions, would fall like Samaria. At the end of his book the prophet sees a brighter future because of God's mercies and the promises he had made to the patriarchs. All the enemies of Israel and Judah will be defeated and confounded. They will lick dust like serpents and will be afraid of the Lord God of Israel. The remnant of Judah will be spared so that the messianic prophecies might be fulfilled.

Moreover, Micah, like Isaiah, sees the ultimate triumph of God's truth and justice and the abolishment of war.

MELT LIKE WAX

And the mountains shall be molten under him, and the valleys shall be cleft, as wax before the fire, and as the waters that are poured down a steep place.

For the transgression of Jacob is all this, and for the sins of the house of Israel. What is the transgression of Jacob? it is not Samaria? and what are the high places of Judah? are they not Jerusalem?

Therefore I will make Samaria as a heap of the field, and as plantings of a vineyard: and I will pour down the stones thereof into the valley, and I will discover the foundations thereof.

Mic. 1:4-6

Wax is symbolic of weakness and because of its softness has been used figuratively, just as flint, iron, and brass are used metaphorically to mean hardness and stubbornness. Wax also is symbolic of meekness.

The wax mentioned here is candle wax. Candles made of wax were used and are still used in many parts of the East. As the wick burns, the flames cause the wax to melt and drip.

The prophet predicts the terrible judgment which would come first upon Israel and Judah and then upon all other wicked nations. All high places and altars of idols shall be trodden down and trampled upon. Great nations who are strong and secure like high mountains shall be humbled. They will melt like wax and flow like waters that run down a steep place. Samaria will be made as a plowed field and as a place for the planting of vineyards.

Today Samaria is no longer a city. The once beautiful and prosperous capital city now is graced with olive orchards, vineyards, and fields.

See Psalm 58:8, "Wax, Not Snail"; also see Psalm 22:14; 97:5.

A REBELLIOUS CITY

For the inhabitant of Maroth waited carefully for good: but evil came down from the Lord unto the gate of Jerusalem.   Mic. 1:12

Mirdath has been confused in the King James Version with *marrah,* or *mirtha* (bitter).

There is no such town in the Bible as Maroth. It should read *mirdath* (rebellious), that is, "a rebellious inhabitant."

The reference is to the rebellious city of Jerusalem which had rebelled against the Lord God of Israel, broken his commandments, forsaken his way, and followed after pagan gods. Both Samaria and Jerusalem had been unfaithful to God. Both capitals were notorious for corruption, injustices, and wickedness. The inhabitants of these cities were prosperous government officials, judges, and wealthy merchants who oppressed the poor and the orphans [Mic. 3:2-3]. They were to be punished for their crimes and other evil deeds.

JERUSALEM WILL MOURN

Make thee bald, and poll thee for thy delicate children; enlarge
thy baldness as the eagle; for they are gone into captivity from thee.
Mic. 1:16

Eastern women, when they mourn over their dear ones, cut off their
hair and inflict injuries on their bodies. In the East long hair is symbolic of beauty, and short hair symbolizes mourning and humiliation.
Then again, the hair of unfaithful women is cut off as a punishment. And
men are punished by shaving their beards [2 Sam. 10:4].

Jerusalem was to mourn over her kings, princes, and nobles who were
to be carried away captive. The day was coming when her beautiful
temple and palaces would be reduced to ruins.

The reference here is to Jerusalem. Its inhabitants were to be carried
away captive to Assyria [2 Kings 17:6]. The historic city was to be bereaved of its inhabitants as a woman who has been bereaved of her
children.

PROPERTIES CONFISCATED

Woe to them that devise iniquity, and work evil upon their beds!
when the morning is light, they practise it, because it is in the power
of their hand.

And they covet fields, and take them by violence; and houses, and
take them away: so they oppress a man and his house, even a man
and his heritage.
Mic. 2:1-2

Prior to World War I, fields, houses, vineyards and other properties in
the East were often confiscated by kings, princes, and government officials. In the olden days the people, especially the poor, were enslaved to
the rulers and often exploited by the princes and the rich.

The plan of confiscation of the properties is generally conceived during the still hours of the night, when the wicked oppressors eat and drink,
and then executed in the daylight. False charges are brought against the
owners of the fields, houses, and vineyards. And false witnesses are hired
to testify against them—as in the case of Ahab, king of Israel, and Naboth
the Jezreelite who was put to death and whose vineyard was confiscated.
The king had to hire false witnesses against Naboth [1 Kings 21:1-3].

The case is usually tried by the friends of the rulers or the conspirators.
And during such trials the weak and the poor have no chance. They can-

not stand in judgment against their oppressors. Thus, their fields and houses are confiscated unjustly. This is why in the East rulers, princes, taxgatherers, and rich oppressors were feared and hated by the people.

CARRIED BY FALSEHOOD

If a man walking in the spirit and falsehood do lie, saying, I will prophesy unto thee of wine and of strong drink; he shall even be the prophet of this people. Mic. 2:11

"Walking in the spirit" means "carried by the spirit or the wind." No one can walk in the spirit. In Aramaic the word for spirit also means wind, pride, and rheumatism. We often say, "He has been moved or carried away by the wind" (*rokha*). Just as the men of God were moved by the Spirit, so the false prophets were moved by the wind of falsehood. In other words, pride, lies, and falsehood are the fruits of an evil spirit.

The reference here is to the false prophets who predicted periods of prosperity, peace, and luxuries when there was no prosperity, and when war was at hand. It is easy to predict peace and prosperity, but hard to warn the people against impending calamities. This is why true prophets were slain, but false prophets were often employed as royal counselors.

EAT THE FLESH

Who also eat the flesh of my people, and flay their skin from off them; and they break their bones, and chop them in pieces, as for the pot, and as flesh within the caldron. Mic. 3:3

"Eat the flesh of my people, and flay their skin from off them" is an Eastern idiom which means "to devour the property of the people." When a man is forced to work hard or is oppressed, he often says, "They have eaten my flesh," by which he means, "They have subjected me to hardships." In Aramaic one can often hear people saying, "I have eaten my body and drunk my blood," which means, "I have been subjected to hard work." At times the people say, "I have eaten my father and mother." "They have eaten us," means, "They have taxed us heavily and confiscated our fields and houses" [Mic. 2:1-2]. "Chop their bones to pieces" means they were crushed, not physically but mentally. All such statements are idiomatic, and Easterners have no trouble in understanding them.

In biblical days, when fortified cities were besieged for long periods, some of the people ate their children [Deut. 28:52-54; 2 Kings 6:25-31].

GREEDY LEADERS

The heads thereof judge for reward, and the priests thereof teach for hire, and the prophets thereof divine for money: yet will they lean upon the Lord, and say, Is not the Lord among us? none evil can come upon us.   Mic. 3:11

In the olden days, chiefs of the tribes, judges, and priests received no wages for their labor. Like Moses, they worked in the interest of the people. This ancient custom still prevails among the tribal people. The chiefs of the tribes, judges, and religious men receive no fixed salaries for their services, but they accept presents and tithes.

The prophet accuses the leaders of his people, the judges and the priests, of corrupt practices and disloyalty to their God and the people. They worked for hire, received bribes, and corrupted justice; and yet, they told the people that the Lord was among them.

When priests and prophets work for hire and respect the faces of the persons who appear before them, God departs from among them. God has no part in evil, nor is he with the men who are disloyal to his teaching.

Jerusalem was doomed because of the corruption, bloodshed, briberies and other evil works of its princes, judges, prophets, and priests [verse 12].

MOUNTAIN OF THE LORD

But in the last days it shall come to pass, that the mountain of the house of the Lord shall be established in the top of the mountains, and it shall be exalted above the hills; and people shall flow unto it.   Mic. 4:1

"Mountain" in this instance is symbolic of a nation or kingdom. The reference here is to Israel and Judah and the truth represented by them. On the other hand, Judah and Jerusalem were known as Mount Zion.

The prophet foresees the salvation of the remnant of his people and the rebuilding of Jerusalem, which later would become the beacon light of the world and the center of worship.

The fortunes of Jerusalem are to rise again, but this time the mountain of the Lord will be higher than all mountains; that is, the spiritual realm of God is to be exalted by all the nations of the world. The messianic kingdom, the stone not cut by human hand, will ultimately demolish pagan images and restore God's reign of peace and harmony [Isa. 2:2-3; Dan. 3:34-35].

SWORDS DESTROYED

And he shall judge among many people, and rebuke strong nations afar off; and they shall beat their swords into plowshares, and their spears into pruning hooks: nation shall not lift up a sword against nation, neither shall they learn war any more. Mic. 4:3

The reference here is to the coming of the Messiah, the great Deliverer of Israel. All human efforts had failed to assure Israel's sovereignty. Israel and Judah now were confronted by great powers such as Assyria and Egypt. Hitherto, Israel had confronted only small nations, and if they were unable to defeat them they could at least live with them in peaceful coexistence. But now, large foreign armed forces and new implements of war were unknown to the Hebrews. All foreign alliances had failed to strengthen them against Assyria.

Now the nation was looking forward to the fulfillment of the messianic promises which were made to Eve, Abraham, and David.

When the Messiah, the great Saviour, was to come, all the Gentile nations were to be defeated and the fugitives of Israel gathered from many far-off lands and brought to Jerusalem. This prophecy, like others in Isaiah and other books of the Bible, point to the coming of Jesus Christ and the establishment of a universal kingdom based on justice, freedom, and righteousness. In such a spiritual order the people will have no use for swords, spears, and other implements of war. God's Spirit and his mighty arm will be their weapons [Isa. 2:4].

TRIUMPH OF REMNANT

Now gather thyself in troops, O daughter of troops: he hath laid siege against us: they shall smite the judge of Israel with a rod upon the cheek. Mic. 5:1

The Eastern text reads: "Now you shall go forth in a raid, O daughter of mighty raiders, for they have risen against us and have smitten the shepherd of Israel [ruler] with a rod upon his cheek."

The reference here is to Jerusalem which was afflicted by the Assyrian army during the reigns of Ahaz and Hezekiah, kings of Judah [Jer. 26:18; Mic. 1:1]. "Smitten" means "humbled and harassed." The kings of Israel and Judah prior to the captivity had become vassals, now to the kings of Assyria, now to the kings of Syria, and now to the kings of Egypt. Both states had weakened and fallen into disgrace.

Both Judah and Israel had become tributaries to the kings of Assyria. But at the end, Judah was to triumph once more and the people were to raid those who had plundered them and humbled their kings. A new ruler was to rise, one greater than David and Solomon, and his dominion would reach the far-off ends of the world. The Jewish priests, scribes, and Pharisees believed the great Saviour would be born in the little town of Bethlehem, the city of David [Matt. 2:6; John 7:42].

DEW—TEACHING

And the remnant of Jacob shall be in the midst of many people as a dew from the Lord, as the showers upon the grass, that tarrieth not for man, nor waiteth for the sons of men.   Mic. 5:7

"Dew" in this instance means "teaching." The remnant of Jacob was to be scattered among the Gentiles, and thus become like dew to the herbs. The Gentile world was thirsty for a true religion, just as tender herbs are thirsty for dew and rain.

During the long droughts, vineyards, plants, and grass are watered by the heavy night dew which falls on the parched ground. Just as the parched land in Palestine is thirsty for dew and water, so the Gentile world was thirsty for the teaching of the Hebrew prophets that was to be proclaimed by the remnant of Judah, which was scattered among them [Deut. 32:2].

Captivity served as a meeting ground between the Israelites and the Gentile world. The Jews in exile were thus able to share their spiritual culture, law, and religion with the Gentile world. On the other hand, the Jews borrowed many good things from the Gentiles, such as finance, architecture, science, and commerce. Prior to the captivity, the Jews were a pastoral people.

We can see that in all the lands where the Israelites were scattered, God's hand was with them. Many of them were promoted to high offices in the government. Some became the most prosperous businessmen. Everywhere they went they prospered and were like a lion among the beasts of the forest [verse 8].

SHITTIM AND GILGAL

O my people, remember now what Balak king of Moab consulted, and what Balaam the son of Beor answered him from Shittim unto Gilgal; that ye may know the righteousness of the Lord.   Mic. 6:5

Shittim was the last encampment place in the wilderness. It was at Shittim that the people sinned in the pagan worship of Baal-peor and 24,000 of them died with disease.

Balak, king of Moab, while consulting Balaam, offered burnt offerings to the Lord, but the Lord never heard his prayer or granted his petitions [Num. 22:5; 25:1].

It was at Gilgal that all the males were circumcised. Gilgal means a circle. It was here that the Lord removed the reproach of the Egyptians. "This day have I rolled away the reproach of Egypt from off you. Wherefore the name of the place is called Gilgal unto this day" [Josh. 5:9].

TRUE OFFERINGS

Will the Lord be pleased with thousands of rams, or with ten thousands of rivers of oil? shall I give my firstborn for my transgression, the fruit of my body for the sin of my soul? Mic. 6:7

Most of the Hebrew prophets were opposed to the sacrifices and temple rituals which had obscured the truth and caused the people to forget the law, justice, and mercy. The priests and Levites had gone to extremes in their sacrificial demands. "Of what purpose is the multitude of your sacrifices to me? says the Lord. . . . I do not delight in the blood of bullocks, or of lambs, or of he-goats" [Isa. 1:11]. "I will take no bullocks out of your house nor he-goats out of your folds" [Ps. 50:9, Eastern text].

"Ten thousands of rivers of oil" means "abundant oil." When oil is plentiful, we say, "We have rivers of oil." Oil was offered to God to be mixed with the meal offerings. Oil also means butter. Both olive oil and butter are used for baking in the East. And in the olden days they were used as the medium of exchange.

At times the Israelites, like the pagans, sacrificed their children to idols and made them pass through fire [2 Kings 16:2-4]. The Mosaic law prohibited human sacrifices [Lev. 18:21].

What God wants is not sacrifices and worship alone, but justice and mercy, which are the fruits of the true religion. God abhorred human sacrifices, and the fat of oxen and rams which were offered by men who had forsaken his true religion. The meat of the animal sacrifices was eaten by the priests and the Levites, who assisted the priests in making the offering, and the rest was eaten by the people. God is not in need of sacrifices. What God wants is justice and mercy. This is because God as a loving Father wants to see all his people well and happy [verse 8].

TRIBE

The Lord's voice crieth unto the city, and the man of wisdom shall see thy name: hear ye the rod, and who hath appointed it.
Mic. 6:9

The Aramaic word *sharbtha* has many meanings, such as "tribe, family, generation, race, and nation." In the King James Version this word has been confused with *shabta,* meaning "rod, staff." In this instance it should be read "tribe," meaning "the tribe of Judah and Israel." Micah was prophesying against Judah and Israel, the tribe or family called by God to be the instrument through which he would enlighten the world.

The prophet reminds the people of the iniquities which were committed in the land. He condemns their wicked scales and short weights, and their lies, which were soon to bring a calamity upon them.

BAGS OF DECEITFUL WEIGHTS

Shall I count them pure with the wicked balances, and with the bag of deceitful weights?   Mic. 6:11

In small towns, villages, and sheep camps, weights are stored in bags made of wool. The bag serves as a container to keep the weights together and to protect them from the little children who might break them when they play with them.

The bag usually contains many diverse weights, some heavy and some light [verse 10]. They are usually kept in a dark corner of the house or the tent. The owner of the weights uses light ones when he sells and heavy ones when he buys. The customers do not know that the merchant has more than one weight, since the others are concealed in the bag, so they trust his word.

Jesus, likewise, was aware of the short measures and deceitful scales. He said, ". . . with what measure you measure it will be measured to you again and will increase, especially to them who hear" [Mark 4:24, Eastern text].

Both Israel and Judah were paying dearly for their corrupt practices, injustices to the poor, and their crooked measures, weights, and balances.

See the commentaries on Hosea 12:7 and Amos 8:5.

ISRAEL WEAKENED

Woe is me! for I am as when they have gathered the summer fruits, as the grape gleanings of the vintage: there is no cluster to eat: my soul desired the first ripe fruit.   Mic. 7:1

After the grapes are picked and the vines gleaned by the poor, the vineyard looks destitute. The booth is taken down and the coveted place which once was guarded zealously by the watchman is forsaken, and the song of the husbandmen and the wine pressers and all the mirth is gone.

The vineyard is symbolic of Israel. The once prosperous and powerful nation now was been reduced to servitude and burdened with heavy tributes. The husbandmen, or the leaders of Israel who had been disloyal, had gone astray from their God. Corruption and injustice in government had weakened the very structure of the government.

Israel and Judah now resembled a vineyard whose hedges were broken and its grapes gleaned. The strong defenses were reduced, and the gold and silver were sent as presents and tributes to foreign nations. The prophet laments the pitiful condition in which he found his people [verse 4].

MOTH-EATEN

The best of them is as a brier: the most upright is sharper than a thorn hedge: the day of thy watchmen and thy visitation cometh; now shall be their perplexity. Mic. 7:4

The Eastern text reads: "They have rejected the best part of them, and have become like rags which are eaten by the moth . . ."

The prophet upbraids the leaders and the people for having forsaken their calling and their spiritual religion, which were the best they had, and for having gone after pagan idols and corrupt pagan practices. The once holy people had become evildoers. The prince, the judge, and the prophet accepted bribes and perverted justice for the sake of material things.

After this punishment and captivity, their salvation would come. But now they were mourning because their days were counted, and they were soon to be carried away captive.

CHAPTER THIRTY-ONE

NAHUM

INTRODUCTION

Nahum, or *Nakhum*, is derived from the Aramaic word *Nakham* (to revive, to resurrect).

Nahum was an Elkoshite. Even today, there is a town in Mesopotamia, Iraq, which is called Alkosh and is inhabited by Assyrian Christians. For many years Alkosh had been the center of learning in that part of the ancient world.

We do not know whether Nahum was an inhabitant of Alkosh, or a native Palestinian. He might have been one of the exiles of 721 B.C., or one of the descendants of the exiles who were settled in the region of Alkosh. The Eastern Christians for centuries have believed that Nahum was a native of Alkosh. Be that as it may, Nahum prophesied before the fall of Nineveh. The prophet is so familiar with the minute details and the life in the great capital city that he writes as one who had lived close to it and seen its wickedness [Nah. 2:1-4].

The date of the book is about 700 B.C., during the reigns of Hezekiah and Manasseh, kings of Judah during the period in which the king of Assyria carried away captive the ten tribes of Israel. The prophet no doubt saw that Assyria was beset with revolutions and discontentment. He also was close enough to see the rise of the Persians and the Medes.

We must not forget that the book of Nahum, like many other books in the Bible, is based on a vision which the prophet saw. It is called "The Book of the Vision of Nahum the Elkoshite." Nahum saw the fall of Nineveh. And, being familiar with the city and the riotous life of its inhabitants, he gives us a graphic picture of its fall. "The noise of the whip and the noise of rattling of the wheels and of the snorting of horses and of bounding chariots!" [Nah. 3:2].

The whole prophecy of Nahum is against the wicked city of Nineveh. Seemingly, the Lord was through punishing Israel and Judah, and now he was ready to visit Assyria, Syria, and Edom.

Nineveh fell in 612 B.C. and the prophet foresaw its fall just as Jeremiah foresaw the fall of Jerusalem, Babylon, and other cities.

A ZEALOUS GOD

The burden of Nineveh. The book of the vision of Nahum the Elkoshite.

God is jealous, and the Lord revengeth; the Lord revengeth, and is furious; the Lord will take vengeance on his adversaries, and he reserveth wrath for his enemies.   Nah. 1:2

This should read: "God is zealous." The Aramaic word *tanana* means "zealous." The root of the word is *tan* (to be zealous or to burn with zeal, emulation, and indignation). *Tanana* means "to envy, be jealous." These words are so similar in appearance that the only way to ascertain their true meaning is by pronunciation and by context. There are similar words in English whose meanings can be determined only by context, for example: fresh, light, read, close, led, sow, saw.

There is nothing in the world greater than God. God is zealous, always trying to bring men to his true way, always caring for and guiding his children. Jesus said, "The zeal for thy house has given me courage" [John 2:17; see also Exod. 20:5; Deut. 4:24].

RUBBISH

For while they be folden together as thorns, and while they are drunken as drunkards, they shall be devoured as stubble fully dry.
                                    Nah. 1:10

The Eastern text reads: "Because from the lowest among them up to their rulers they are rebellious, they stagger in their drunkenness; they have eaten and are filled with dry rubbish."

The reference here is to the kings, princes, and nobles of Assyria who had been rebellious and become drunk with power and wealth, as well as with wine and strong drink. The Assyrians had conquered many nations and brought their gold and silver to Nineveh. Sennacherib and his general defied the God of Hazekiah and lowered him to the level of pagan gods which they had destroyed. They also warned the people not to put their trust in their God [2 Kings 18:34-35]. The kings of Assyria were to pay for their blasphemous utterances against the God of Israel, who had given them power to punish his people [Isa. 10:5].

The Aramaic word *khabta* (stubble, brushwood, husks) in this instance means "dry stubble." There are certain plants in Assyria which are eaten during the spring when they are tender. During famines and shortages of food people eat dry plants and other herbs.

The prodigal son ate husks when he was hungry and destitute [Luke 15:11-24]. During prosperous years these dry plants or husks are fed to animals.

The term *khabta* (dry rubbish) is used metaphorically, meaning false glory or useless teaching. The Assyrians laid emphasis on their military power, training, and new weapons of war.

JUDAH WILL DWELL IN PEACE

Behold upon the mountains the feet of him that bringeth good tidings, that publisheth peace! O Judah, keep thy solemn feasts, perform thy vows: for the wicked shall no more pass through thee; he is utterly cut off.   Nah. 1:15

The Aramaic word *nebad* (to do) has been confused with *nebar* (to transgress, pass over, cross).

The Eastern text reads: "Behold, upon the mountains, the feet of him that brings good tidings, that publishes peace! O Judah, keep your solemn feasts and perform your vows; the wicked shall no longer transgress against you, for he is utterly destroyed."

The letters *resh* (r) and *daleth* (d) are distinguished by a single dot over or under the letter. The wicked could pass through Palestine, but they could do no more evil in it as in the past.

The nation between two great rivers was soon to be conquered. Its strength had been spent in bloody wars and expansion. "Thus says the Lord: Against the watersheds of many waters, they have run down and vanished . . ." [Nah. 1:12, Eastern text]. The Lord had broken the heavy yoke of the oppressor from off the neck of Israel.

ASSYRIAN ARMY

He shall recount his worthies: they shall stumble in their walk; they shall make haste to the wall thereof, and the defense shall be prepared.   Nah. 2:5

The Eastern text reads: "The soldiers are obedient to their officers; they stumble as they march; they make haste to the wall, and the battlements are prepared."

The Assyrian army was noted for its training and discipline. The soldiers and their officers were valiant and obedient.

The Assyrians originated the system of military organization based on corps, divisions, and regiments. They had generals of ten thousand, colonels, captains, and lieutenants. Their system was copied by other nations. Assyrian power was feared by all nations west of the River Euphrates. The rise of Assyrian power is mentioned by Balaam in the book of Numbers in the fifteenth century B.C. [Num. 24:22].

The prophet, as a native of Alkosh, northwest of Nineveh, is so familiar with the Assyrian army and the doomed city that he is writing as though he were watching the battle.

THE FALL OF NINEVEH

The gates of the rivers shall be opened, and the palace shall be dissolved.   Nah. 2:6

Nineveh was built on the eastern bank of the River Tigris opposite the new city of Mosul.

Nineveh was noted for having abundant water [Nah. 2:8]. The city is not far from the sources of the River Tigris. The city was founded by Nimrod [Gen. 10:11].

It seems likely that the irrigation dams north of the city were broken by the Scythian and Chaldean armies, and that most of the defenders were drowned. The same strategem was used by the Persian army when they took Babylon in 538 B.C.

Nineveh fell in 612 B.C.

THE QUEEN OF ASSYRIA

And Huzzab shall be led away captive, she shall be brought up, and her maids shall lead her as with the voice of doves, taboring upon their breasts.   Nah. 2:7

The reference here is to the queen of Assyria who, accompanied by her maids and horsemen, fled northward into the inaccessible mountains of Kurdistan.

The legends of this flight continue to the present day. It is said that many of the Assyrian princes and noblemen fled into northern Assyria. They had summer houses, palaces, and fortifications in the northern region, which extended as far as Van and Urmiah. Then again, a great many Assyrian herdsmen and some of the tribes of Israel inhabited the northern region [Amos 4:3, Eastern text; see also Nah. 3:18]. Their descendants lived in Kurdistan until World War I, when they fled into Iraq.

THEBES

Art thou better than populous No, that was situate among the rivers, that had the waters round about it, whose rampart was the sea, and her wall was from the sea?   Nah. 3:8

The Eastern text reads: "Are you better than Jawan of Ammon, which is situated by the rivers, that had waters round about her, whose rampart was the sea, and water her wall?"

This refers to Thebes, the ancient capital of Egypt and the center of the ancient religion of the god Ammon. The city had fabulous treasures, which were offered by the people to the god Ammon. Thebes was plundered by the Assyrian king Ashurbanipal about 666 B.C.

Thebes was situated by the waters. The reference to Thebes' defenses is to the cities in the lower delta. Thebes, being the capital and a wealthy city, stood as the symbol of the whole Egyptian Empire. The names of the capitals of kingdoms are often used in speaking of the whole land. We often say "Washington" when we speak of the United States of America.

COWARDS

Behold, thy people in the midst of thee are women: the gates of thy land shall be set wide open unto thine enemies: the fire shall devour thy bars.   Nah. 3:13

"Your people in the midst of you are women" is an Eastern idiom which means, "Your people are cowards." Even today we often say, "He is a woman; he is afraid to fight back."

The hitherto valiant Assyrian army was to lose its courage and flee like women.

CHAPTER THIRTY-TWO

HABAKKUK

INTRODUCTION

THIS book, like many other books in the Bible, is based on a vision which the prophet saw. The Aramaic text reads *khizwa* (a vision). The prophet was asked to write the vision so that he might proclaim it to the people [Hab. 2:2]. St. John was also asked to write the vision which he saw concerning the new Jerusalem [Rev. 21:5]. Then again, the vision was for the years to come.

Habakkuk, like Micah, condemns injustices, violence, and ungodliness. During his time the law of God was discarded and wickedness prevailed in the land. Many people worshiped Baal and offered human sacrifices to idols. Moreover, morality was at a low ebb. Habakkuk, like Jeremiah, predicted the rise of Babylon as a great imperial power.

The book must have been written before the invasion of Palestine by the army of Nebuchadnezzar about 640 B.C., during the reign of Josiah. The prophet is a contemporary of Jeremiah and Ezekiel. And he gives us a vivid picture of the Chaldean army and its swift cavalry. Injustices, wickendness, and drunkenness must have been prevalent during this period.

Chapter 3 is a long prayer, a reminder of a glorious past. The prophet derives comfort from the fact that the Lord is the strength of Israel.

LUCK

Then shall his mind change, and he shall pass over, and offend, imputing this his power unto his god.   Hab. 1:11

The Aramaic word *rokha* (spirit, pride, rheumatism, wind) in this instance means "wind", that is, luck, victory or fortunes. In the East we often say, "Their wind now is blowing, but someday it will change its course and blow against them." Then again, when threshing floors are

923

winnowed, the workers wait until the wind is favorable. This is also true of sailing ships.

The reference here is to the victorious Chaldean army which was to subdue one nation after another. But when they had fulfilled their mission in punishing other nations, the wind (their luck) would change its course and they would lift up themselves against the Most High God and be punished and overthrown.

GOD IS AWARE OF EVIL

Thou art of purer eyes than to behold evil, and canst not look on iniquity: wherefore lookest thou upon them that deal treacherously, and holdest thy tongue when the wicked devoureth the man that is more righteous than he?   Hab. 1:13

The Aramaic word *awaley* (the wicked men, the ungodly) is confused in the King James Version with the Aramaic word *awla* (iniquity). Both words are written alike but pronounced differently. *Awaley* has two dots over the word, but *awla* has no dot. The same word also means a baby or child, but in the case of "child," two dots are placed under it.

God sees evil, but does not recognize it. Habakkuk here means that God does not tolerate evil, nor does he want to see the faces of wicked men. In other words, God knows what is going on in his world, but he despises evil and refuses to look at the faces of wicked men or allow them to come into his presence. This is because evil separates us from God. It stands as a barrier between man and his Creator. Because God is eternal good and purity, his nature is contrary to that of evil.

In Judges we read: "And the children of Israel did evil in the sight of the Lord" [Judg. 3:7, 12]. Jehoram wrought evil in the sight of the Lord [2 Kings 3:1-2]. "Put away the evil of your doings from before my eyes" [Isa. 1:16].

Habakkuk knew that God is always aware of man's evil doings. Therefore this verse must not be construed to mean that God does not, or cannot, see evil.

PLAIN WRITING

And the Lord answered me, and said, Write the vision, and make it plain upon tables, that he may run that readeth it.   Hab. 2:2

In Aramaic when a letter or document is written very clearly, we say, "I can read it like water" which means it is plain, and there is nothing in it to cause me to stumble. Moreover, when describing a brilliant student, we often say, "He can read the book like water." This is because water runs smoothly and evenly. And when a writing is clear and plain, one reads it without stopping.

Habakkuk, like Moses, John, and other prophets, is instructed by God to write his vision and to make it so plain that anyone who reads it can understand it clearly. "That he may run that readeth it" means that he who reads it may not halt or stumble, and that he may understand it without any interpretations.

God's Word was delivered to the prophets in a clear and terse manner so that the people might not find excuses and say, "I was unable to understand it." Indeed, what today seems difficult and obscure in the Bible once was plain and well understood. The prophets and men of God wrote in the vernacular of the people. They used simple words in order to convey the inner message of the Word of God. They were more interested in the truth than in the style of writing. This is why their works are more widely read than the works of other religious writers and philosophers.

See the article on "Visions."

BLOODY CITIES

For the stone shall cry out of the wall, and the beam out of the timber shall answer it.

Woe to him that buildeth a town with blood, and establisheth a city by iniquity!

Hab. 2:11-12

"The stone shall cry out from the wall, and the nail in the wood shall answer it," is an Aramaic idiom which means that even material things would condemn the injustices and oppression.

"Blood" here means oppression, confiscation of the property of the poor, and the slave labor which was so common in biblical lands.

Prior to World War I many rulers and princes in the East conscripted labor and built towns and palaces. Cities built in this manner were called blood cities, and wealth acquired unjustly was called blood money. Then again, the laborers were not paid, and some of them died because of the hard labor and lack of food [James 5:1-6].

DRUNKARDS

Woe unto him that giveth his neighbor drink, that puttest thy bottle to him, and makest him drunken also, that thou mayest look on their nakedness!

Thou art filled with shame for glory: drink thou also, and let thy foreskin be uncovered: the cup of the Lord's right hand shall be turned unto thee, and shameful spewing shall be on thy glory.

Hab. 2:15-16

Easterners seldom drink. Those who do indulge in wine or strong drink generally drink while they are eating, and they drink moderately. Wine is used at the table, but strong drinks are seldom used except at weddings and banquets, when men are compelled to drink until they are drunk.

At times strong drinks are given to weak-minded men until they are drunk so that other people may be amused by them. This is because in the East drunkenness is so rare that when a man is drunk he arouses considerable curiosity. No one would miss the occasion of watching him misbehaving and hearing him curse. This is especially true at weddings and banquets, where the people look for entertainment.

The author of the book of Proverbs states: "Wine is grievous, drunkenness is shameful; and whosoever drinks excessively is not wise" [Prov. 20:1, Eastern text].

When Noah was drunk, his son Ham saw his nakedness [Gen. 9:12-23]. Moreover, Lot was drunk when he slept with his two daughters [Gen. 19:30-36].

On the other hand, wine and strong drink were the cause of the downfall and corruption of many of the leaders, prophets, priests, and wise men in Israel. Isaiah condemns drunkenness, and the priests, prophets, and wise men who erred in the interpretations of their visions because of their drunkenness. There was vomit and filth everywhere [Isa. 28:7-8].

Drunkenness was censured by all the prophets. Moses made it a crime punishable by death [Deut. 21:20-21]. Habakkuk warns against giving wine or strong drink to a drunken man [Hab. 2:15]. This is because drunkards uncovered their nakedness.

The Eastern text reads: ". . . drink yourself also and stagger . . ." The reference here is to the cup of the Lord, the cup of vengeance and punishment, which is often used figuratively, meaning the cup of the Lord's fury, or the cup of consolation [Jer. 16:7]. But in this instance it is the cup of fury and bitterness [Isa. 51:17; Jer. 51:6-7; Matt. 26:39].

See also the commentary on "Cup."

FALSE WORSHIP

Woe unto him that saith to the wood, Awake; to the dumb stone, Arise, it shall teach! Behold, it is laid over with gold and silver, and there is no breath at all in the midst of it.

Hab. 2:19

The prophet warns the people against the pagan images and idols which were made of wood and stone and overlaid with silver and gold. They were the work of man's hands, deaf and dumb. "They worship the work of their own hands, that which their own fingers have made" [Isa. 2:8].

Idolatry was forbidden [Exod. 20:3-4; Deut. 4:16-19]. But when the people forsook the Lord their God, they worshiped images of wood, stone, gold, and silver. Moreover, they implored the images to bless them and their crops and sheep. Baal was a god of fertility. Gold and silver were symbolic of prosperity. "What profit is a graven image that its maker has fashioned? The molten image is a false doctrine . . ." [Hab. 2:18, Eastern text].

SILENCE

But the Lord is in his holy temple: let all the earth keep silence
before him.   Hab. 2:20

The prophet here infers that other gods were not gods, and that the only true God is the God of Israel who dwells in his holy temple in Jerusalem. Why then should the people make noise in prayers, chants, and supplications to deaf and dumb images? [verses 18-19].

Man has to commune with God in silence. God is constantly speaking, and his voice is heard throughout the universe. Only in silence can one understand the inarticulate tongue of the Spirit. Jesus taught that when you pray you should enter into your closet, shut the door, and pray in secret [Matt. 6:6]. One has to meditate and shut the door of his mind to false images and alien and destructive thoughts in order to hear the small voice of God.

JERUSALEM, GOD'S CITY

And his brightness was as the light; he had horns coming out of
his hand: and there was the hiding of his power.   Hab. 3:4

The Aramaic word *keritha* (town, city) has been confused in the King James Version with *karnatha* (horns). The two words are so nearly identical that even an Aramaic scholar might confuse one word with the other. The only difference between the two words is the letters *yuth* and *nun*, which are very close. *Yuth* is slightly shorter than *nun*. Errors like this were made during the changes of the alphabet and when texts were copied.

The Eastern text reads: "And his brightness was as the light; in the city which his hands had established shall he store his power."

The reference here is to Jerusalem, the city which God's hands had established. Peace and salvation are to come from Jerusalem, that is, from the capital of the land which has given the world prophets and men of God.

CURTAINS OF MIDIAN

I saw the tents of Cushan in affliction: and the curtains of the land of Midian did tremble.   Hab. 3:7

The Midianites were semi-nomadic people. They were noted for their large tents and camps. Though a pastoral people, they migrated from one place to another, carrying their curtains and other belongings with them on the backs of donkeys and camels.

The Midianites were invaded and completely defeated by the Israelites under the command of Moses and Joshua [Num. 31:7-12]. Cushan refers to the Ethiopians who inhabited the eastern shores of the Red Sea. During the times of the judges the Midianites again oppressed the Israelites, and were defeated by Gideon [Judg. 6:2-7]. But the nomad people always regained their strength; that is, the enemy defeated and destroyed the sedentary population, but could not catch up with the roaming tribes. When the battle was over, some of the nomad tribes returned and dwelt in towns.

Habakkuk is reminding the people of God's glorious victories in the past when he led Israel out of the land of Egypt and defeated all their enemies round about them.

OPPRESSORS

Was the Lord displeased against the rivers? was thine anger against the rivers? was thy wrath against the sea, that thou didst ride upon thine horses and they chariots of salvation?   Hab. 3:8

"Rivers" in this instance means "powerful nations" like Egypt and Assyria. Egypt was known as the land of the Nile, and Assyria was called the land of many waters [Nah. 2:6-8]. And the Philistines inhabited the coastal cities. And the realm of the Chaldeans was between the two great rivers, Tigris and Euphrates. Some of these nations trembled before the armies of Israel when Moses led the people out of Egypt.

Now Israel was harassed by the surrounding Gentile nations, and confusion, oppression, and violence prevailed in the land [Hab. 1:2-3].

The armies of the great nations were likened to swollen rivers, rivers which sweep everything before them; but the Lord defeated great and small nations before the armies of Israel. The present oppressors were to be defeated, too, and punished for their evil deeds.

WONDROUS WORKS

The mountains saw thee, and they trembled: the overflowing of the water passed by: the deep uttered his voice, and lifted up his hands on high.   Hab. 3:10

The prophet reminds the people of God's victory over the pagan nations when he brought forth Israel out of Egypt, and when the Lord caused the sea to go back by a strong east wind [Exod. 14:21-29]. "The deep uttered his voice, and lifted up his hands on high," means that the sea raged and the water was piled up by the force of the wind which the Lord God caused to blow.

The people, during the time of Habakkuk, had forgotten God's works and his glorious miracles and wonders which he wrought in Egypt and in the land of Canaan when Moses and Joshua defeated the Amorites. They had gone after pagan gods and trusted in pagan nations for their deliverance.

UNIVERSE SHARED

The sun and moon stood still in their habitation: at the light of thine arrows they went, and at the shining of thy glittering spear.
Hab. 3:11

In biblical days the people believed that the earth was the center of the universe and that the sun and moon were created to give light upon it. This ancient concept was upheld by learned Hebrews, Greeks, and other people, and it was also upheld by the Christian theologians until modern science proved that the sun, and not the earth, is the center of our solar system. But the Assyrians and the Chaldeans, who originated the present calendar of 365 days, knew that the sun was the center. At this early time the Hebrews were a pastoral people, and the Greeks and other Gentiles were known as barbarians. Mesopotamia was the cradle of civilization.

Habakkuk, like other Hebrew prophets, uses metaphors and poetic terms of speech in describing God's great power and the Israelites' triumphs over their enemies. The sun, moon, stars, lightning, and all the forces of nature shared and rejoiced in the victory of the people of God. ". . . the stars in their courses fought against Sisera" [Judg. 5:20]. The light of the stars may have helped the Israelites, but the stars took no actual part in the battle. Such terms of speech are very common in the Eastern languages.

See the commentary on Joshua 10:12-14.

GOD WALKING THROUGH THE SEA

Thou didst walk through the sea with thine horses, through the heap of great waters.   Hab. 3:15

The reference here is to Exodus 13:21: "And the Lord went before them by day in a pillar of a cloud, to lead them on the way; and by night in a pillar of fire, to give them light; so that they might travel by day and by night" (Eastern text).

The Lord's presence and glory were revealed in a cloud which led the people on their way into the trackless desert. The Spirit of the Lord walked through the sea to protect and comfort the Israelites when they were pursued by the Egyptian army. The term "horses" is used metaphorically, ascribing glory and majesty to God. Moreover, horses symbolize strength and speed. Prior to the introduction of railroads and cars, the horse's endurance and speed was never challenged. In the East kings never walk on foot. They either ride on horses or in chariots. (Note the reference to "chariots of fire" in 2 Kings 2:11 and 6:17.) God's presence and his footsteps are everywhere—in the sea, on the land, and in the air.

CHAPTER THIRTY-THREE

ZEPHANIAH

INTRODUCTION

Z EPHANIAH probably was the son of Helakiah, or Hillciah, the high priest during the reign of Josiah, king of Judah about 641 B.C. The Eastern text traces him to Helakiah and not to Hizkiah. The fact that the prophet's ancestry is traced thus far proves that he was a descendant of a well-known family [2 Kings 22:4].

Zephaniah prophesied during the reign of Josiah, after the reformation and the cleansing of the temple in 621 B.C., but before the fall of Nineveh in 612 B.C.

The book deals with God's vengeance and the great day of the Lord when God's wrath would be poured out upon the nations of the earth and upon Judah and Jerusalem. Judah had gone back to idolatry during the reigns of Manasseh and Amon, his son, kings of Judah. This was one of the worst periods in the history of Judah. Jerusalem was filled with the blood of innocent people, and oppression prevailed. Even the holy temple was polluted with immoral Baal worship and pagan images. All the prophets of this period condemned the kings, princes, priests, and false prophets for their unfaithfulness to the God of Israel and for their corrupt practices and injustices.

Both the leaders and the people had provoked God's indignation against the land. Zephaniah predicts the destruction of Judah and Jerusalem by the Chaldean army. This destruction was widespread and from the Almighty, and such a calamity looked like the end of the world. This is because the end of the Jewish state, Jerusalem, and the temple was at hand. The most precious thing in the world would be trampled under the feet of the pagan armies.

The prophet also predicts the fall of Nineveh, the capital of Assyria, and those of other nations which previously were condemned by Isaiah and other prophets. Jerusalem is likened to Nineveh, the saved city of Jonah. Nineveh repented and was spared, but Jerusalem refused to draw near her God and to heed the words of his messengers [Zeph. 3:1-2].

931

Jesus also upbraided the historic city for not receiving God's messenger who sought its welfare, and for slaying the prophets of God [Matt. 23:37].

Zephaniah exhorts the people to repent, and he gives assurance to the remnant.

BAAL WORSHIP DOOMED

I will also stretch out mine hand upon Judah, and upon all the inhabitants of Jerusalem; and I will cut off the remnant of Baal from this place, and the name of the Chemarims with the priests.
                                                        Zeph. 1:4

The Aramaic word *al* in this instance means "against" instead of "upon." To stretch out his hand upon the land would mean that God intended to protect and to bless Judah.

During the reigns of Manasseh and Amon, kings of Judah, the people had forsaken the Lord God of Israel and were worshiping pagan deities and pagan images. Moreover, the immoral Baal worship was introduced into the temple of God. Even the Holy of Holies was polluted. When Josiah cleansed the temple he did away with most of the pagan worship. He also removed the immoral practices and slew the priests of Baal [2 Kings 23:4-25].

Even the remnant of Baal worship was to go, together with its priests and prophets, and Jerusalem was to be rehabilitated again and the enemies of Israel punished.

The Aramaic word *komrey* (high priests) has been transliterated "Chemarims" in the King James Version. The Hebrew priests were called *kahney*.

DISTINCT APPAREL

And it shall come to pass in the day of the Lord's sacrifice, that I will punish the princes, and the king's children, and all such as are clothed with strange apparel.
                                                        Zeph. 1:8

In the Near East members of every race and religion have their own distinct apparel. Until recent days it was unlawful for the members of one race to wear the clothes of another race. The styles and colors of the clothing, hats, and turbans were so different that one could easily distinguish the members of one race from those of another. Moreover, at times it was considered sacrilegious to wear the apparel of an alien race or of the members of a rival religion.

Kings, princes, and their children were imitating pagan nations. They had departed from the simple way of their forefathers and were wearing foreign garments and living in luxury.

UNRIGHTEOUS WEALTH

In the same day also will I punish all those that leap on the threshold, which fill their masters' houses with violence and deceit.
                                                      Zeph. 1:9

The Eastern text reads: "In that day I will punish all those who do violence and those who plunder, who fill their storerooms with things acquired by means of extortion and deceit."

The Aramaic word *madanehon* (their storerooms) is confused in the King James Version with the Aramaic word *marehon* (their masters). The only difference between these two words is the dot which is placed over or under the letters *daleth* (d) and *resh* (r). With the dot above it would be "r," and with the dot beneath, it would read "d."

The prophet condemns the men who acquired wealth by means of violence and deceit, who seized the property of the widows and the fatherless.

NO BRIBE CAN CHANGE GOD

Neither their silver nor their gold shall be able to deliver them in the day of the Lord's wrath; but the whole land shall be devoured by the fire of his jealousy: for he shall make even a speedy riddance of all them that dwell in the land.   Zeph. 1:18

In biblical days many men trusted in their silver and gold for deliverance in time of tribulation. Kings and princes paid heavy ransoms to gain their freedom when they were captured by their enemies. But man cannot bribe his Creator or pay him a ransom for his life.

"He will not regard any ransom; nor will he listen, though you increase the bribe" [Prov. 6:35, Eastern text]. "None of them can by any means redeem his brother, nor give to God a ransom for him" [Ps. 49:7].

When God's vengeance is to come, men and women will cast their silver and gold in the street. Riches shall not be able to deliver anyone in the day of judgment [Ezek. 7:19]. The Koran states: "All the gold and silver in the world cannot save a sinner from eternal punishment." One has to repent and seek forgiveness and make reconciliation with God while he is alive. God cannot be appeased with lavish gifts and money. The law was revealed to guide man during his life, and the prophets were sent by God to admonish and discipline men and women so that they might have no excuse in the Judgment Day.

Jesus settled this question with the parable of Lazarus and the rich man [Luke 16:20-26].

THE SEACOAST PUNISHED

Woe unto the inhabitants of the seacoast, the nation of the Chere-thites! the word of the Lord is against you; O Canaan, the land of the Philistines, I will even destroy thee, that there shall be no in-habitant.   Zeph. 2:5

Both Philistines and Canaanites inhabited the eastern coast of the Mediterranean Sea. Cherethites are the inhabitants of the island of Crete, the seat of the Minoan culture.

All the lands on the seacoast which had escaped other invasions were to be conquered, plundered, and destroyed by the Chaldean armies. Later the coast was to be used for pastures by the inhabitants of Judah.

Many of the peoples in Palestine who helped the army of the oppressor destroy Israel were to be destroyed and made to drink from the same bitter cup from which Babylon had made Judah and other nations drink.

COUNSELORS

Therefore, as I live, saith the Lord of hosts, the God of Israel, Surely Moab shall be as Sodom, and the children of Ammon as Gomorrah, even the breeding of nettles, and saltpits, and a per-petual desolation: the residue of my people shall spoil them, and the remnant of my people shall possess them.   Zeph. 2:9

The Aramaic word *malokhhen* (their counselors) has been confused in the King James Version with *milkhen* (their salt).

The reference here is to the wise counselors who were to be deprived of their wisdom. Neither Moab nor Ammon would have suffered from the lack of salt. Both countries are close to the Dead Sea, which is one of the three seas in the world which are noted for their salt.

But nations suffer when they lack prophets and wise counselors. Both Moab and Edom, because of wrong counselors, had forgotten their racial ties to Israel. They had oppressed the children of Israel and Judah in the day of their defeat and tribulation. They had destroyed the temple and cast lots for plunder and slaves.

WANTON PRIESTS AND PROPHETS

Her prophets are light and treacherous persons: her priests have
polluted the sanctuary, they have done violence to the law.
Zeph. 3:4

The Aramaic reads: "Her prophets are wanton (*pakhzin*) and treacherous persons." The prophet Zephaniah, like Jeremiah and Ezekiel, condemns the false prophets who had misled the people and polluted the
holy temple with pagan worship. "For both prophets and the priests
have become pagans; yea, even in my house have I found their wickedness, says the Lord" [Jer. 23:11].

The priests also had become disloyal and had falsified the law and its
ordinances for the sake of bribes and material gains. They were so carried away and blinded with the pagan practices that they could not tell
the difference between the holy things and the polluted, and between the
clean and the unclean [Isa. 43:28; Ezek. 22:26].

JEWS IN ETHIOPIA

From beyond the rivers of Ethiopia my suppliants, even the
daughter of my dispersed, shall bring mine offering.   Zeph. 3:10

Zephaniah was living during the reigns of Manasseh and his son Amon,
kings of Judah. Amon had forsaken the Lord God of his fathers and introduced all forms of pagan worship in Jerusalem, polluted the temple,
and filled Jerusalem with innocent blood.

Zephaniah prophesied that the land would be destroyed and the people
dispersed [Zeph. 1:2-7]. When Jerusalem fell before the Chaldean army
a great many of the Jews fled to Egypt and Ethiopia. Many of these
refugees went by sea. Some of the descendants of these Jews were to
come to worship in Jerusalem [Isa. 45:14; Mal. 1:11; Acts 8:27].

Even today there is a strong Jewish colony in Ethiopia. The king of
Ethiopia claims to be a descendant of the house of David and the tribe
of Judah.

CHAPTER THIRTY-FOUR

HAGGAI

INTRODUCTION

HAGGAI is one of the postexilic prophets. He was born in Babylon during the reign of the Persian kings. He began to prophesy in 520 B.C., the second year of Darius, king of the Medes and Persians.

Some of the Jews had already returned to Judah during the reign of Cyrus (*Kurush*), 536 B.C. Cyrus had issued a decree giving the Jews permission to return to their own land and to rebuild the temple of the God of Israel. Nevertheless, the work was delayed because of the opposition of the Samaritans and other races which were in Galilee [Ezra 4:7-8].

Both Haggai and Zechariah strengthened the hands of the people and exhorted them to proceed with the work, assuring them of divine help and stating that the new temple would in due time surpass the old one in beauty and grandeur. The rich and magnanimous kings of Persia were generous in their gifts of gold, silver, timber, and other materials. Moreover, the Jews had prospered in Babylon.

BAG WITH HOLES

Ye have sown much, and bring in little; ye eat, but ye have not enough; ye drink, but ye are not filled with drink; ye clothe you, but there is none warm; and he that earneth wages, earneth wages to put it into a bag with holes.　　　　　　　　　　Hag. 1:6

To put money into "a bag with holes" is an Eastern saying which means to squander money or spend it right away. In English we would say he has "a hole in his pocket." That is to say, "the money comes and goes fast."

In the East money is kept in purses made of cloth, and the purse is fastened to the girdle. At times the cloth wears out and the heavy silver

936

and copper coins drop out. Then again, in the East when a man is extravagant people say, "He has a purse without a bottom."

The exiles who had returned were lacking God's blessings. They sowed much, but they brought little home. The more they worked, the more they lacked supplies. This is because they were not mindful of God, and had neglected the work of rebuilding his temple. Nor had they kept God's commandments and his ordinances, which Moses, his servant, had commanded them to keep.

DROUGHTS BLAMED ON WICKED PEOPLE

Therefore the heaven over you is stayed from dew, and the earth is stayed from her fruit.   Hag. 1:10

In the olden days famine, plagues, and droughts were blamed on wicked people. When the king, the priests, and the people were loyal to their religion, executed justice, and pleaded the cause of the poor and the orphans, everything was well with them. The rains came in due season and the land yielded abundantly. But when they departed from the way of God, forsook him, and did evil, nature was against them, so they suffered from long droughts, famine, and other calamities.

There was a long drought and famine in Israel in the day of King Ahab and Elijah, and not until Elijah prayed to God, and the people repented, did the rain fall upon the parched ground [1 Kings 17:1; 18:1].

When man revolts against God and his laws he also revolts against the laws of nature. This is because all life is governed by God.

UNRIPE GRAPES

And I called for a drought upon the land, and upon the mountains, and upon the corn, and upon the new wine, and upon the oil, and upon that which the ground bringeth forth, and upon men, and upon cattle, and upon all the labor of the hands.   Hag. 1:11

"The new wine" in this instance means "the growing, unripe grapes which often are destroyed by severe hailstorms, droughts, and invading armies." Wine which is stored in sheepskins and jars is generally secure.

Easterners seldom keep old wine more than a few years. Generally, the old wine is exhausted before the grapes for the new wine are picked. This is more true of the poor people and laborers who live from day to day. At times, new wine is used even before it is fermented.

The prophet warns the people and pleads with them to be loyal to God's law. Failure to heed his counsel would bring disaster upon vineyards, olive orchards, wheat, cattle, sheep, and men. This is because in biblical lands the people look to God for rain, for dew, and for the protection of crops from locusts and other pests.

SACRIFICIAL MEAT TAKEN HOME

If one bear holy flesh in the skirt of his garment, and with his skirt do touch bread, or pottage, or wine, or oil, or any meat, shall it be holy? And the priests answered and said, No.   Hag. 2:12

During the feasts, when sheep and oxen are killed at the shrines, sacrificial meat, bread, and meal offerings are carried home for the members of the family who have not been able to visit the shrine and to participate in the feast. This is also true of the harvest banquets and wedding feasts where food is abundant.

The boiled meat is wrapped in thin loaves of bread and placed between men's garments, or in the skirts of their robes.

It was against the Mosaic law to let the consecrated offerings touch the human body or any unclean things. This is because some of the men or women who carried consecrated offerings home might be unclean or might have touched unclean things.

The people were unclean because of their evil deeds and unfaithfulness to the ordinances and the religion of their fathers.

CHAPTER THIRTY-FIVE

ZECHARIAH

INTRODUCTION

ZECHARIAH means, "The Lord has remembered me." The prophet was living at a time when the Jews thought that because of their sins they had been rejected and forsaken by the Lord, the God of their fathers. The prophet Zechariah was one of the exiles from Judah. Apparently he returned from Babylon with Zerubbabel during the reign of Cyrus, king of Persia, in 537 B.C.

Zechariah was a contemporary of Haggai. He began where Haggai left off. Both these prophets prophesied at a time when the exiles were in danger of being destroyed by their enemies round about them. The work of restoration and rehabilitation of the Jewish people was retarded by the neighboring adversaries of Judah. The Jews were weak and barely armed and at times were discouraged.

The prophet fired their hearts with faith and zeal by telling them that the Lord was to fight their battles and save them, not with weapons of war but by his Spirit. The prophet's vision strengthened the hands of the people.

Zechariah, like other prophets, foresaw the day when Judah was to be purged of her sins, her idols broken, and the false prophets removed from the land. Moreover, the neighboring Gentile nations were to be punished for the hardships they had inflicted on the Jews.

RED HORSE

I saw by night, and behold a man riding upon a red horse, and he stood among the myrtle trees that were in the bottom; and behind him were there red horses, speckled, and white.　　　Zech.1:8

The red horse is symbolic of war and slaughter [Zech. 6:1-9; Rev. 6:4]. Speckled and white horses signify an intermittent period of anxiety and uncertainty. In other words, restoration would not be an end of Jewish problems and difficulties. The people were to face new difficulties and trials. New problems were to be confronted by the second commonwealth.

The prophet here depicts a time in which the Gentile nations are punished for the evils they had committed against Judah. The Lord was to pour out his indignation upon the Gentiles who had helped the Chaldean army to destroy Jerusalem [Zech. 6:8]. The remnant of the Jews was to be restored to their land and the temple rebuilt [Zech. 6:10-15].

ZION REBUILT

Cry yet, saying, Thus saith the Lord of hosts; My cities through prosperity shall yet be spread abroad; and the Lord shall yet comfort Zion, and shall yet choose Jerusalem.   Zech. 1:17

Nebney (shall build) is derived from *bena* (to build) and has been confused in the King James Version with *nebaya* from *baya* (to console, comfort). The two words are so similar in the Aramaic script that at times even a native might slip.

Zechariah prophesied during the time of the Babylonian captivity. Jerusalem was now in ruins, but it was to be rebuilt 84 years later, during the time of Nehemiah. This mistranslation occurs also in Isaiah 51:3.

HORNS

Then lifted I up mine eyes, and saw, and behold four horns.
And I said unto the angel that talked with me, What be these?
And he answered me, These are the horns which have scattered Judah, Israel, and Jerusalem.   Zech. 1:18-19

Horns are symbolic of strength and glory. The term horn is frequently used in the Bible, denoting strength and honor. Animals use their horns as weapons, and men exalt themselves because of their strength [Deut. 33:17]. "Horn" is also used to suggest rejoicing, prosperity, and triumph. Horns were used by the armed forces and priests as bugles.

"To lift one's horn" means "to be triumphant." In Luke 1:68-69 we read that "the Lord . . . hath raised up an horn of salvation for us . . ." But one has to be careful how this metaphor is interpreted.

In the book of Daniel horns represent kings [Dan. 7:8]. "I will make the horn of David to bud" means that God will give him an heir to sit on his throne [Ps. 132:17].

The horns which Zechariah saw were the Gentile powers who had conquered Israel and Judah and scattered the people. They were to be cast out. The Gentile powers were to be broken, and the nations who had destroyed Israel and Judah were to be humbled and overthrown.

CATTLE IN THE CITY

And said unto him, Run, speak to this young man, saying, Jerusalem shall be inhabited as towns without walls for the multitude of men and cattle therein.   Zech. 2:4

Even today in many backward countries sheep and cattle are kept in walled cities as well as in open cities and towns. Buffalo, oxen, and donkeys live under the same roof with their owners. This is because herds are the only precious possession of these primitive people. However, in some cases buffalo and oxen are kept in the house to help keep it warm, as well as to protect the animals from thieves and robbers.

The Hebrews were a pastoral people whose possessions were flocks and herds, and they remained such until the time of the second captivity.

The prophet was shown in a vision that Jerusalem was to be rebuilt again. God was to spare and rehabilitate the remnant. The new city was to be so large that many people would prefer to live outside the walls because of the abundance of sheep and cattle.

After World War I a new city was built round about the ancient Jerusalem, outside the walls.

A NEW DAY

Hear now, O Joshua the high priest, thou, and thy fellows that sit before thee: for they are men wondered at: for, behold, I will bring forth my servant the Branch.   Zech. 3:8

"Branch" in the King James Version is a mistranslation. It should read "the rising of the sun." The Aramaic reads *dinkha* [Zech. 6:12].

"The rising of the sun" is used symbolically, meaning the change of conditions from bad to good. In the East we often say, "The sun will shine again." The sun is symbolic of joy, prosperity, and the dawning of a new day.

Zechariah sees a hopeful future, a new day, a day of peace and tranquillity, when the remnant of Israel would return to Palestine and everyone would live in peace under his vine and under his fig tree.

The period of peace and prosperity was to be introduced by Messiah, the Prince of Peace. The restoration and rebuilding of Jerusalem were preparations for the messianic reign and the kingdom of God. A new day was ahead, the day when all prophecies would be fulfilled.

TWO OLIVE TREES

And two olive trees by it, one upon the right side of the bowl, and the other upon the left side thereof. Zech. 4:3

Seven golden candlesticks are symbolic of the light of God, that is, the restoration of the pure religion of Israel and the rebuilding of the temple.

The number seven represents the seven major heavenly bodies then known. The candlestick in the temple of Solomon had seven branches, each branch standing for one of these heavenly bodies. Gold is symbolic of purity.

Trees in the Bible are used figuratively to mean men. Olive trees, because of their precious medicinal oil, are considered sacred trees, and oil is the symbol of truth, light, and healing.

The two olive trees are the two new Jewish leaders, Zerubbabel and Joshua, the priests, the two spiritual and truthful leaders. These men were ordained by God for a great mission to rehabilitate the remanant and to rebuild the temple so that the true religion might be restored and the messianic promises, which were the ultimate hopes of Israel, fulfilled.

A DIFFICULT TASK

Who art thou, O great mountain? before Zerubbabel thou shalt become a plain: and he shall bring forth the headstone thereof with shoutings, crying, Grace, grace unto it. Zech. 4:7

The term "mountain" in Semitic language may mean "an unsurmountable problem." In the East when a thing seems hard or impossible we say, "It is a mountain."

Zerubbabel had a great and difficult task ahead of him. He was ordained by God to rehabilitate the people and to rebuild the temple of Solomon. This was not an easy task for a people who had been hated and defeated, and whose hopes for the future were seemingly frustrated.

But God was able to do what was difficult for men to do; and he was to do it, not by means of power, but by his Spirit.

Jesus said that if you have faith like a mustard seed, you can remove a mountain; that is, you can overcome any problem [Matt. 17:20].

FLYING SCROLL

Then I turned, and lifted up mine eyes, and looked, and behold a flying roll. Zech. 5:1

"Flying scroll" is symbolic of a hasty edict. In the East royal decrees and edicts were written on a scroll made of the skin of sheep, and sent by runners or riders on swift horses [Esther 8:10].

Curses, lamentations, and excommunications, likewise, are written on scrolls and are read to the men against whom they are sent [Ezek. 2:9].

CHARMS AND CURSES

And he said unto me, What seest thou? And I answered, I see a flying roll; the length thereof is twenty cubits, and the breadth thereof ten cubits.

Then said he unto me, This is the curse that goeth forth over the face of the whole earth: for every one that stealeth shall be cut off as on this side according to it; and every one that sweareth shall be cut off as on that side according to it. Zech. 5:2-3

In the East curses, charms, and talismans are still written on small and large scrolls, some of which men and women carry in their garments. Others they keep in the house for the protection of the family from evil eyes, envy, and the curses of their enemies.

The scrolls contain both prayers and curses—prayers to bless the owner of the scroll, and curses to curse the enemy. The scrolls of curses are usually buried near the house of the persons against whom the curses are directed. The name of the accursed and those of his ancestors are written therein.

The large scroll which the prophet Zechariah saw contained curses for those who were doing evil, the thief, and those who were taking the name of the Lord falsely. The Gentiles were to be measured with the same measure they had measured to the Jews. The sins of the whole world were placed in an ephah. All wicked nations were to be punished as Babylon was punished. Babylon was to stand as an example of God's fury against the wicked nations. Judah and Jerusalem were to be purged of evil [verse 4].

THE FOUR CHARIOTS

And I turned, and lifted up mine eyes, and looked, and, behold,
there came four chariots out from between two mountains; and the
mountains were mountains of brass.
In the first chariot were red horses; and in the second chariot
black horses;
And in the third chariot white horses; and in the fourth chariot
grizzled and bay horses.   Zech. 6:1-3

The number four symbolizes completeness: the four corners of the
earth and the four winds, for instance.

The mountains of brass indicate that the chariots were headed for the
north country, Greece. Brass is symbolic of the mountainous Grecian
Empire. The four chariots are symbolic of four kingdoms after the death
of Alexander the Great—Seleucia, Syria, Egypt, and Greece.

The red horses are symbolic of war and bloodshed. Black means death
and mourning. Black is a colorless color; hence, lifeless. Therefore it has
been commonly used for mourning.

The white horses are symbolic of victory. Victorious kings, when
entering a city, ride on white horses. A grizzled, gray, or pale horse means
famine.

The vision is similar to the vision of the four horses which John saw
[Rev. 6:2-8].

The fury of the Lord was to be poured out upon the nations. And after
these things had taken place the remnant of the Jewish race was to return
to their land and the temples were to be rebuilt.

The temple was rebuilt during the reign of the Persian kings. Then
the Greeks invaded and defeated Persia. The Jews were harassed again
and their holy temple defiled by Antiochus Epiphanes, king of Syria. 175-
163.

During the conflicts and changes in dynasties many people were killed
and many died from famine.

ZEALOUS FOR THE REMNANT

Again the word of the Lord of hosts came to me, saying,
Thus saith the Lord of hosts; I was jealous for Zion with great
jealousy, and I was jealous for her with great fury.   Zech. 8:1-2

The Eastern text reads "zealous" instead of "jealous." The Lord was
zealous for Zion. He had not forgotten his inheritance and his divine
promises to the Hebrew patriarchs and to David. Political changes and

the rise of new dynasties may deter, but they cannot change God's plan of salvation and the establishment of a universal kingdom, the kingdom of heaven.

Many of these changes were taking place so that the remnant of Israel might be purified and restored to its own land.

The Lord had overthrown the oppressive rule of Babylon. The Jews had found favor in the eyes of the Persian kings who reigned over the great realm of Babylon. In other words, while these changes were taking place, God was not idle. He was zealously working in the interest of the small remnant [Zech. 1:14].

TAKE HOLD OF THE SKIRT OF HIM

Thus saith the Lord of hosts; In those days it shall come to pass, that ten men shall take hold out of all languages of the nations, even shall take hold of the skirt of him that is a Jew, saying, We will go with you: for we have heard that God is with you.
Zech. 8:23

To "take hold of the skirt" is an expression of entreaty or begging. Easterners, when begging one for mercy and favors, take hold of the skirt of the other person's robe.

When a sick woman, because of the crowd, was unable to speak to Jesus, she touched his garments, begging him to heal her. Jesus recognized her plea, and he healed her [Mark 5:30].

Zechariah, like Isaiah and other Hebrew prophets, saw the glorious days of the restoration of the remnant, and the importance of a spiritual Israel and a new religion free from man-made temples and doctrines. Many nations were to visit Jerusalem, the city of peace, seeking the true religion which was envisioned by the prophets and fulfilled by the Messiah, Christ.

Today thousands of men and women of all races, creeds, and colors visit Jerusalem, the city of peace, seeking peace and consolation.

NOTHING IS HIDDEN FROM GOD

The burden of the word of the Lord in the land of Hadrach, and Damascus shall be the rest thereof: when the eyes of man, as of all the tribes of Israel, shall be toward the Lord.   Zech. 9:1

The Eastern text reads: "The word of the Lord against the land of Hadrach and against Damascus, which shall be a gift to him; for to the Lord are revealed the ways of men and of all the tribes of Israel."

The error is caused by confusion between *gelen,* derived from *gela* (to reveal) and *ainey* (*eyes*). The letters *gamel* (g) and *ai* (*ain*) and *nun* and *yoth* are very similar to one another.

The prophet states that the Lord knows the hearts of all men and that nothing is hidden from him. The whole chapter is about the destruction of the oppressive nations who had acted wickedly against Judah in the time of her tribulations.

STRANGERS

And a bastard shall dwell in Ashdod, and I will cut off the pride of the Philistines.   Zech. 9:6

The Aramaic word *nakhraye* means "strangers, aliens," and not bastards. Philistia was to be conquered by a strange people.

The whole land of Philistia was completely conquered by the Romans in 67 B.C. The Philistine stock was assimilated. Some of the fortified cities in Philistia held or gained their freedom during the reign of the Hebrew kings and other invaders. The Romans coveted all the maritime provinces.

Palestine became a melting pot during seven centuries of Roman occupation. The land in Philistia was productive and the coastal cities were ideal for the Roman legions and for the shipping of salt, grains, and other merchandise.

AN ASS

Rejoice greatly, O daughter of Zion; shout, O daughter of Jerusalem: behold, thy King cometh unto thee: he is just, and having salvation; lowly, and riding upon an ass, and upon a colt the foal of an ass.

And I will cut off the chariot from Ephraim, and the horse from Jerusalem, and the battle bow shall be cut off: and he shall speak peace unto the heathen: and his dominion shall be from sea even to sea, and from the river even to the ends of the earth. Zech. 9:9-10

The ass is the humblest and the most despised animal in the Near East. This is because an ass lacks beauty and is a stupid animal. In the East a person who lacks grace, good manners, and understanding is called an ass.

Kings, princes, and noblemen ride on horses and mules. Elderly men and some dignitaries prefer large white donkeys.

The reference here is to Messiah, Christ, who was to be clothed with righteousness and humility in order to reach all colors and all classes of people. The chariot and the horse on which earthly rulers relied for salvation and glory were to be rejected. The true salvation was to come from God. The Messiah was to establish a universal kingdom founded on justice and meekness. His dominion was to cover the whole world. And heathen peoples were to be invited to join his dominion. Messiah was to be a new type of king—a spiritual and meek ruler reigning over the great universal realm, the kingdom of God.

ISRAEL SCATTERED

And I will sow them among the people: and they shall remember me in far countries; and they shall live with their children, and turn again. Zech. 10:9

"I will sow them" in this instance means, "I will scatter them among the nations." In Aramaic we still say, "He has sowed them," which means, "He has scattered them." "I will take them to a place of which they know nothing."

The Israelites were to be scattered among the Gentiles as precious seed is scattered upon the ground. They were to live in strange lands wherein customs, manners, and languages were different. But in due time their descendants were to be gathered and brought back to Palestine. The reference here is to the people who were to be carried away captive to foreign lands, and to their descendants who were to be forgiven and restored to their land. Israel was to leaven the whole Gentile world. The teaching of the Hebrew prophets has been a great blessing to the whole world [Hos. 2:23].

SEA WITH AFFLICTION

And he shall pass through the sea with affliction, and shall smite the waves in the sea, and all the deep of the river shall dry up: and the pride of Assyria shall be brought down, and the sceptre of Egypt shall depart away. Zech. 10:11

"The sea" is often used metaphorically, meaning "many troubles and difficulties." In the East when the people are facing insurmountable problems they say, "We are in the sea," or "in deep water."

Assyria is surrounded by the two great rivers, the Euphrates and the Tigris. The city of Nineveh is built on the banks of the Tigris. Egypt is situated on the south shore of the great Mediterranean Sea with the Nile as its lifeline. Both these lands relied heavily upon the waters of the rivers and the commerce they made possible.

During wars dams were often destroyed, and at times the courses of rivers were changed. All Assyrian and Egyptian wealth came from the rich soil brought down by the rivers [Isa. 19:4-10; Jer. 51:36; Ezek. 30:12].

LITTLE FLOCK

Thus saith the Lord my God; Feed the flock of the slaughter.
Zech. 11:4

The Aramaic word *katinta* (lean) has been confused in the King James Version with the Aramaic word *katilta* (slaughter). The letters *nun* and *lamed* are very similar and can easily be confused.

The Eastern text reads: "Feed the lean flock." The reference here is to the small and weak remnant which had returned from capitvity. The Lord God was watching over them. Jesus called his followers a little flock. He said, "Do not be afraid, O little flock; for your Father is pleased to give you the kingdom" [Luke 12:32, Eastern text].

STAFF AND CORD

And I will feed the flock of slaughter, even you, O poor of the flock. And I took unto me two staves; the one I called Beauty, and the other I called Bands; and I fed the flock. Zech. 11:7

The Eastern text reads: "So I fed the lean flock, for there were many sheep; and I took two staffs; the one I called Pleasant and the other I called Cord, and I fed the flock."

The prophet took two staffs, and one he called Pleasant, which is symbolic of tranquillity and peace. When the sheep behave the shepherds seldom use their staffs. The other staff was called Cord, which suggests the rod which the shepherd of lambs used. Every shepherd carries a staff and a rod. The lambs are too small to be beaten with the staff. "Thy rod and thy staff they comfort me" [Ps. 23:4].

The staff and the rod were used more for protection than to beat the sheep and the lambs with them. The shepherd generally uses his staff to kill snakes and to protect the sheep from wild animals, and at times to punish the goats.

The rod is generally used to train the newly born lambs and to direct them in the right paths. When Jesus drove the merchants from the temple he used a cord made of grass [John 2:15].

The Jews were to be led gently, protected from their neighboring enemies, but at times chastised. The prophets were their spiritual leaders, who guided them in times of tribulation.

See also the commentary in *Gospel Light,* John 2:15.

THIRTY PIECES OF SILVER

And I said unto them, If ye think good, give me my price; and if not, forbear. So they weighed for my price thirty pieces of silver.

And the Lord said unto me, Cast it unto the potter: a goodly price that I was prized at of them. And I took the thirty pieces of of silver, and cast them to the potter in the house of the Lord.

Zech. 11:12-13

The Aramaic word *aghri* means "my wages, fee, hire." The price of a person was determined by the Mosaic law, which states, "If the ox gores a manservant or a maidservant, the owner shall give to their master thirty shekels of silver and the ox shall be stoned" [Exod. 21:32, Eastern text].

The Eastern text of this verse reads: "And the Lord said to me, Cast it into the treasury . . ." *Beth gaza* means "the treasure house"; that is, "the treasury in the Lord's house."

Jesus was sold by Judas for thirty pieces of silver [Matt. 26:15].

Joseph was sold for twenty pieces of silver [Gen. 37:28].

BANDS BROKEN

Then I cut asunder mine other staff, even Bands, that I might break the brotherhood between Judah and Israel.   Zech. 11:14

The reference here is to the cord, staff, or rod which is often used as a measuring line [Rev. 11:1].

The breaking of the cord or rod symbolizes the breaking of the bands between the house of Israel and the house of Judah. This is because Israel was not to be restored any more, but Judah was to constitute the core of the remnant which the Lord had spared. And from henceforth all Israelites were to be called Jews.

Hebrew prophets always illustrated their points by means of parables and metaphors. For example, when a prophet wanted to declare that the reign of a harsh king had come to an end, he made a yoke and broke it in the presence of the people. Easterners are much more readily convinced when they see words portrayed in action. Parables make a deep impression on them and help them to remember something for many years to come. On the contrary, abstract words are easily forgotten.

BAD SHEPHERDS, GOOD SHEPHERDS

For, lo, I will raise up a shepherd in the land, which shall not visit those that be cut off, neither shall seek the young one, nor heal that that is broken, nor feed that that standeth still: but he shall eat the flesh of the fat, and tear their claws in pieces.

Zech. 11:16

In biblical lands a good shepherd always seeks the sheep that are gone astray, lost, or stolen. He heals those which are injured; and he even lays down his life for the sake of his flock. But the hired shepherds flee for their lives and leave their sheep to be devoured by beasts of prey or stolen by thieves.

The Lord was to raise up a shepherd (ruler) in the land who would neglect the sheep, who would not search for the lost, nor heal the wounds of those who were injured, nor lead the sheep to pasture [Ezek. 34:12].

The shepherd in this instance means a ruler. In the East kings, princes, bishops, and leaders are called shepherds. This is because they lead their people and care for them just as the shepherd leads his flock, cares for it, and protects it from thieves and beasts of prey. This is more true of the tribal people. The chief of the tribe leads his people just as a shepherd leads his flock.

The people in the future would be so bad that their leaders would also be bad. This is because their leaders were to be selected from among themselves. Wicked people never select honest and good leaders who will do away with evils, high taxation, and injustices. They select wicked leaders like themselves. In other words, God never appoints wicked men to lead his people, but he allows the people to choose their own leaders. When the people are good, their rulers are good, also. ". . . O my people, your leaders have caused you to err, and disturbed the way of your paths" [Isa. 3:12, Eastern text].

FOOLISH SHEPHERD

Woe to the idol shepherd that leaveth the flock! the sword shall be upon his arm, and upon his right eye: his arm shall be clean dried up, and his right eye shall be utterly darkened.   Zech. 11:17

The Aramaic word *bora* means "simple, foolish, unlearned, rude." In this instance it should be read "foolish." The foolish shepherd is the one who goes after pleasure and neglects his flock. "The shepherd" here means the ruler or prince.

"The sword shall be upon his arm" means that his strength will be wasted by his enemies until he is devastated. His power and influence will cease, and his trust in his allies will be hopeless. He will be so utterly destroyed that he will not see any hope of salvation.

CUP OF TREMBLING

Behold, I will make Jerusalem a cup of trembling unto all the people round about, when they shall be in the siege both against Judah and against Jerusalem. Zech. 12:2

"Cup of trembling" means a cup of wine mixed with poison. In the East many princes, governors, and prominent men are poisoned during banquets and dinners. Some of those who are suspicious of the poisoning tremble when the cup is handed to them.

The days were to come when Jerusalem would be a cup of trembling to the nations who would come to fight against it and besiege it. They would tremble because the capital city and Judah would be defended by God himself [verses 3-6].

A STRONG JERUSALEM

And in that day will I make Jerusalem a burdensome stone for all people: all that burden themselves with it shall be cut in pieces, though all the people of the earth be gathered together against it. Zech. 12:3

The Eastern text reads: "And it shall come to pass in that day, I will make Jerusalem a stone for all the people to trample on; all who trample on it shall be cut in pieces, though all the people of the earth be gathered together against it."

A stone or a rock in Semitic languages is symbolic of strength and power.

Jerusalem would be so fortified that it could defy all those who sought to conquer it. The nations would try to trample on it as in the past, but they would be cut in pieces. On that day the Lord would be with Judah and he would help Jerusalem to defeat her enemies [verses 4-6].

AS GOD

In that day shall the Lord defend the inhabitants of Jerusalem; and he that is feeble among them at that day shall be as David; and the house of David shall be as God, as the angel of the Lord before them. Zech. 12:8

"And the house of David shall be as God" means "they shall have dominion." In the book of Exodus we read: ". . . and thou shalt be to him instead of God" [Exod. 4:16]. Moses was to direct and guide Aaron.

The spiritual house of David was to have power to defeat the enemies of Israel, just as God had defeated them in the olden days [Zech. 14:3]. Both Judah and Jerusalem were to be restored by the strong hand of God. And Judah and Jerusalem were to be feared by the Gentiles who had oppressed them.

After the exile there were no more kings from the house of David. The last king Zedekiah, was put to death by Nebuchadnezzar, king of Babylon, in 586 B.C. The house of David means the messianic promises. In other words, the new Jerusalem was to be ruled and defended by the Messiah, the heir to the messianic promises.

MOURNING

In that day shall there be a great mourning in Jerusalem as the mourning of Hadadriman in the valley of Megiddon.
And the land shall mourn every family apart; . . . Zech. 12:11-12

In the East men and women do not mourn together. The women sit apart. This is because during the mourning the women uncover their breasts and beat upon them. Some of the women cut off their hair, and others inflict wounds on their bodies. The men, likewise, sit apart, mourn and sing mourning songs and lamentations. Some of them tear their garments. Some put ashes on their heads as a symbol of grief.

Judah and Jerusalem were to mourn over the glorious past when Jerusalem was feared and respected by great powers. Now the city was in ruins and the population was like a small and weak flock in the midst of wolves. But greater hardships and tribulations were yet ahead of the people.

FOUNTAIN—TRUTH

In that day there shall be a fountain opened to the house of David and to the inhabitants of Jerusalem for sin and for uncleanness.
Zech. 13:1

A fountain is symbolic of purity and truth. This is because water flows pure and clear from its source, and fountain water is free from contamination. Then again, water means light and understanding. Muddy waters are symbolic of confusion and difficulties.

Clear water from a fountain symbolized the cleansing of Israel from idol worship. The people were to be cleansed from their sins and abominable pagan practices. Both the greatest and the least of the people were to be washed with pure water right from the source [Isa. 1:16-17].

Cleansing by water is symbolic of the inner cleansing. John the Baptist cleansed the people by water in order to symbolize the removal of their sins.

ROUGH GARMENTS

And it shall come to pass in that day, that the prophets shall be ashamed every one of his vision, when he hath prophesied; neither shall they wear a rough garment to deceive. Zech. 13:4

In biblical days many of the prophets wore garments made of camel's hair as an insignia of their office. Some covered their bodies with lambskins, and others wore rough garments, because most of them traveled from one place to another, sleeping in caves, under trees, and in open country. Some of them lived in deserts and rugged mountains, spending much time in meditation.

Elijah and Elisha wore heavy mantles and rough garments. John the Baptist wore raiment of camel's hair and a leather girdle about his loins [Matt. 3:4].

Rough garments and lambskins offer warmth and comfort in the desert lands where the temperature drops to sixty during the night, and they protect the body from thorns, bramble bushes, and briers. These rough garments in the course of time came to be symbolic of the denial of worldly comforts of life. The prophets wanted to live close to nature in order to be able to commune with God.

False prophets also wore rough garments to resemble the true prophets, so that they might deceive the people with their false oracles and visions. The people were warned against them. Jesus warned his disciples and followers against these men: "Be careful of false prophets who come to you in lamb's clothing, but within they are ravening wolves" [Matt. 7:15, Eastern text].

All these false prophets who had prophesied easy times, peace, and prosperity were to be exposed.

MADE ZEALOUS

But he shall say, I am no prophet, I am a husbandman; for man taught me to keep cattle from my youth. Zech. 13:5

The Aramaic word *atnani* is derived from *tan* (to be moved, to burn with zeal and indignation). In this instance it means "He made me zealous." In other words, the false prophet, when caught prophesying falsely, has an alibi.

Seemingly, the Aramaic word *atnani* has been confused in the King James Version with *aknanni,* from *kana* (to own cattle).

LEADERS PUNISHED

Awake, O sword, against my shepherd, and against the man that is my fellow, saith the Lord of hosts: smite the shepherd, and the sheep shall be scattered: and I will turn mine hand upon the little ones.
                                                                 Zech. 13:7

Allaney is derived from *al* (above, upon); hence, "the dignitaries, or great ones," not "little ones," as in the King James Version. In ecclesiastical terms, it means patriarchs, prelates, pontiffs, and other high temporal and ecclesiastic authorities.

The prophet is predicting the punishment of false prophets, great men, and political and religious leaders, and the destruction of pagan temples and idols.

The Lord was to purge the remnant of all of its evils and purify it as gold and silver are purified [verse 9].

THE DAY OF RECKONING

Behold, the day of the Lord cometh, and thy spoil shall be divided in the midst of thee.   Zech. 14:1

"The day of the Lord" in this instance means the Judgment Day or "the day of reckoning." Jerusalem was to be delivered into the hands of the Gentiles, houses were to be plundered and demolished, and women ravished.

The prophet foresaw the fall of Jerusalem and the dispersion of the people. He also foresaw the period of rehabilitation and peace, when the Lord will be King over all the earth.

The political kingdoms are to pass away before the new world order will be established. The old Jerusalem as well as the Gentile kingdoms are to give way to the new Jerusalem and a new order [verse 9].

Every time a disaster falls upon the people, that is a day of judgment or of reckoning and punishment. Jerusalem had rejected the prophets and the men of God who had sought its peace and warned her against her evil doings. The day of the Lord's judgment was at hand. The old Jerusalem, which was filled with the blood of the innocent, would give way to the new Jerusalem, the city of peace and righteousness.

Jerusalem was destroyed by Titus in A.D. 69. Both the city and the temple were plundered, and women were ravished by the soldiers. Jesus also foretold the doom of the historic city and its beautiful temple, and the dispersion of the people [Matt. 24:2; Mark 13:14-20].

PLACE OF DISASTER

And ye shall flee to the valley of the mountains; for the valley of the mountains shall reach unto Azal: yea, ye shall flee, like as ye fled from before the earthquake in the days of Uzziah king of Judah: and the Lord my God shall come, and all the saints with thee.   Zech. 14:5

The Eastern text reads: "And you shall flee to the valley of the mountains; for the valley of the mountains shall reach the place of disaster, and you shall flee as you fled from the earthquake in the days of Uzziah king of Judah; and the Lord my God shall come in, and all his saints with him."

The error in the King James Version ("all the saints with thee") is caused by the confusion in Aramaic pronominal suffixes. *Amey* means "with him" and *amakh* means "with you." When *heh* (h) and *kap* (k) are not clear the translator is at a loss. Moreover, the word *aolsana* (disaster, distress, calamity) has been confused with *azal* (to go) [Mark 13:14-20].

The saints will enter into heaven with the Lord; that is, he will separate them from the wicked and lead them into heaven.

CONTINUOUS LIGHT

And it shall come to pass in that day, that the light shall not be clear, nor dark:
But it shall be one day which shall be known to the Lord, not day, nor night: but it shall come to pass, that at evening time it shall be light.   Zech. 14:6-7

This passage should read: "And it shall come to pass in that day there shall be no light, but cold and ice." Cold and ice are symbolic of hardships and persecutions, and darkness means ignorance. The lamp of God which burned continually in Jerusalem would be put out by the oppressors. But the dark and cold day would be followed by a day in which the light of God would shine continually [Rev. 21:23].

That day will be a long day, and it will be known as the day of the Lord. There will be continuous light both day and night. This is because the Lord will be judging the world, and the Lord knows neither day nor night, but only light, which is symbolic of truth. All human acts will be brought to light and all secrets revealed [verse 9].

THE LIVING WATER

And it shall be in that day, that living waters shall go out from Jerusalem; half of them toward the former sea, and half of them toward the hinder sea: in summer and in winter shall it be.

Zech. 14:8

"The living water" is used metaphorically here, meaning "the true teaching," a universal religion which was to issue out of Jerusalem. Water also means light and understanding, which are the products of a true and universal religion [Ezek. 47:1; John 4:14].

The Lord God would be king over all the earth, and the remnant of the Gentiles who had fought against Jerusalem would worship him and go up to Jerusalem from year to year to keep the feast of the tabernacle.

The vision is similar to the one which Ezekiel saw: ". . . and, behold, water issued out from under the threshold of the house eastward . . ." [Ezek. 47:1]. Both of these great prophets saw the advent of a true and universal religion from Jerusalem, which was to embrace the whole world, and the reign of God as the King over all nations [verse 16].

GIFTS FOR THE TEMPLE

In that day shall there be upon the bells of the horses. Holiness unto the Lord; and the pots in the Lord's house shall be like the bowls before the altar.

Zech. 14:20

The Eastern text reads "bridle of the horse." In the East some bridles contain bells, talismans, and other decorative objects.

In biblical lands one often sees gorgeously decorated and embroidered saddles with bells sewn to the fringe of the trappings. Moreover, some of the bells are fastened to the harness beside the horse's neck. Some of these bells are talismans, others are for noise in order that other horsemen may follow in the same path during the night hours, and others are merely for decorations. Some bells are embellished with decorative script containing holy verses from the Bible or the Koran.

The pots in the Lord's house were made of pure brass, but those which were used for the service of the altar were of pure gold.

The prophet sees a bright future wherein the people will be prosperous as in the olden days when the treasures of the ancient city were coveted by the kings and the princes of the world.

Vessels of gold and silver and bells of gold were to be consecrated to the Lord by the visitors who would come to worship. Easterners often leave jewelry, silk cloth, and objects of gold in the holy places which they visit. They are placed on the wall of the temple, some of which are dedicated offerings.

Jerusalem was the holy city of God. Both the city and the temple were to be rebuilt, and holy offerings were to flow to Jerusalem [Isa. 23:18].

CHAPTER THIRTY-SIX

MALACHI

INTRODUCTION

MALACHI (Aramaic *Malakhi*) means "my angel, my messenger," or "my counselor." Malachi was living during the Persian period. He prophesied at the time of the second Jewish commonwealth, when the temple had been built again and the Jews were returning to their motherland.

Malachi encouraged the people and strengthened their hands at a time when they were harassed by their enemies and facing an uncertain future. Then again, many Jews had married foreign wives and were unfaithful to their religion. The prophet condemns the priests for offering blind animals and other blemished sacrifices and polluted offerings to the Lord [Mal. 1:6-9]. He predicted the coming of God's messenger to prepare the way [Mal. 3:1]. The messenger was John the Baptist [Matt. 11:7-10].

The prophet also helped the work of Ezra and Nehemiah 443-432 B.C.

A RAM

But cursed be the deceiver, which hath in his flock a male, and voweth, and sacrificeth unto the Lord a corrupt thing: for I am a great King, saith the Lord of hosts, and my name is dreadful among the heathen. Mal. 1:14

The Aramaic word dikhra means "a male or a ram." Its meaning is determined by the context.

In this case the prophet is referring to a ram and not to a male. At times people vowed to offer some of their choicest animals to the Lord, but when the time came to fulfill their vows, they brought blemished rams or ewes. The Levitical law demanded that the animals thus offered must be unblemished. Either a ram or a ewe was acceptable.

REBUKE YOUR SEED

Behold, I will corrupt your seed, and spread dung upon your faces, even the dung of your solemn feasts; and one shall take you away with it.
                                                        Mal. 2:3

The reference here is to the seed of wheat and barley which at times is destroyed by droughts or eaten by locusts. The Aramaic reads: "Behold, I will rebuke the seed of the ground . . ."

"Spread dung upon your faces" is an Eastern saying which means, "I will cause you to be ashamed because of the failure of the harvest."

The people will be so poverty-stricken that they will be ashamed even at the feast because of the lack of sacrifices and food.

PUNISHMENT

The Lord will cut off the man that doeth this, the master and the scholar, out of the tabernacles of Jacob, and him that offereth an offering unto the Lord of hosts.
                                                        Mal. 2:12

Labrey olebar brey means "his son and his son's son." The King James phrase "master and scholar" is wrong. The Eastern text reads: "The Lord will destroy the man who does this, and also his son and his son's son out of the tabernacle of Jacob . . ."

The Lord would destroy the men and even their grandsons if they should serve strange gods.

COVERING ALTAR WITH TEARS

And this have ye done again, covering the altar of the Lord with tears, with weeping, and with crying out, insomuch that he regardeth not the offering any more, or receiveth it with good will at your hand.
                                                        Mal. 2:13

"Covering the altar of the Lord with tears" means "weeping bitterly." Easterners weep when they repent and pray for forgiveness. One often sees men and women praying at an altar with tears running down their cheeks.

In biblical days when people came to pray and seek forgiveness they brought gifts with them, which they placed on the altar. They prayed and often wept as they offered their gifts to God.

Hannah wept when she prayed in the house of the Lord in Shiloh [1 Sam. 1:10].

Some people wept because they knew that they had not wholeheartedly repented from their sins and that therefore their offerings would not be acceptable to the Lord. Sincere repentance was better than false tears.

GOD'S MESSENGER

Behold, I will send my messenger, and he shall prepare the way before me: and the Lord, whom ye seek, shall suddenly come to his temple, even the messenger of the covenant, whom ye delight in: behold, he shall come, saith the Lord of hosts.　**Mal. 3:1**

All holy prophets and seers were messengers of God who were sent to guide the people and teach them his way. But God's messengers were rejected and slain. And at last God's promises of his blessings to mankind were to be fulfilled through the long-expected Messiah, who would prepare the way of the Lord and bring reconciliation between God and man.

Jesus, in his parable of the vineyard and the wicked laborers, revealed God's divine plan of salvation and his love for his children [Matt. 20:1]. The messengers, that is, the prophets whom he sent, were slain, but at last he sent his own Son, hoping that they would be ashamed in his presence and repent; but instead they slew him also.

Messiah, through his suffering and death, was to reveal God's love to his children and prepare the way for God's reign of justice, peace, and harmony [Isa. 53:1-12].

THE COMING OF THE MESSIAH

And he shall sit as a refiner and purifier of silver: and he shall purify the sons of Levi, and purge them as gold and silver, that they may offer unto the Lord an offering in righteousness.　**Mal. 3:3**

The Aramaic word *nehpokh* means, "He shall return." The Eastern text reads: "For he shall return to refine and purify the people like silver . . ." In the days of old, silver and gold were refined by fire. All the dross and impurities were burned. Today it is done with acid.

The reference here is to the coming of the Messiah [verse 1]. The Messiah was to purge the nation of its sins, and the priests and the Levites of their transgressions against the law. They were to be purified so that they might serve the Lord as in olden days, when the tribe of Levi had dedicated itself to God and when the Jewish religion was pure and spiritual. The Aaronic priesthood and its temple was to give way for Christ's priesthood and a new temple not built by the hands of men.

GOD IS UNCHANGEABLE

For I am the Lord, I change not; therefore ye sons of Jacob are not consumed.
Mal. 3:6

The Eastern text reads: "For I am the Lord, I change not; but you sons of Jacob have not departed from your iniquities."

The Aramaic word *abarton,* derived from *abar* (to cross, to pass) here means "to depart." "You have not departed from your wickedness."

The Lord, being good, is unchangeable, but man is changeable. He can change from bad to good and from good to evil. But Israel, despite God's warnings, oppression, and captivity, had been unwilling to change and to turn to the Lord.

A FAITHFUL SON

And they shall be mine, saith the Lord of hosts, in that day when I make up my jewels; and I will spare them, as a man spareth his own son that serveth him.
Mal. 3:17

The Eastern text reads: ". . . on that day when I will assemble the people; and I will have pity on them as a man pities his own son who serves him."

The reference is to the remnant of Israel who had remained loyal to God's covenant and had served him faithfully. This remnant was to be restored and pitied just as a father pities his own son who serves him wholeheartedly. God's divine promises were to be fulfilled through this remnant which was to return to Jerusalem. The people were to face greater tribulations and hardships than those they had suffered in Babylon. But the remnant was to be spared.

STUBBLE AND OVEN

For, behold, the day cometh, that shall burn as an oven; and all the proud, yea, and all that do wickedly, shall be stubble: and the day that cometh shall burn them up, saith the Lord of hosts, that it shall leave them neither root nor branch.
Mal. 4:1

In Palestine and the Arabian desert, where wood is scarce and coal unknown, ovens are heated with dry thorns and stubble. Dry grass, thorns, and stubble are gathered from the fields and stored in houses for fuel. One sees women collecting the stubble and thorns and bringing them in on their backs.

When the earthen oven is heated, bread is placed on the sides thereof to be baked. Food is cooked on the top of the oven and later placed in the oven to be kept warm.

The wicked are likened to the stubble which is consumed daily in the oven. Jesus also spoke of the grass of the field which today is and tomorrow falls into the fireplace (oven) [Matt. 6:30; Luke 12:28].

HEALING IN THE WINGS

But unto you that fear my name shall the Sun of righteousness arise with healing in his wings; and ye shall go forth, and grow up as calves of the stall.　　　　　　　　　　　　　Mal. 4:2

"Sun of righteousness" here means "the reign of justice." Wings symbolize protection. The wings of the sun are the warm rays and cooling shadows which strengthen and revive the sick and the weary. The sun was known as the life-giving body. This is why the sun was worshiped by many pagan nations. And without heat and light nothing can grow.

During the hot and cold hours of the day, little birds seek protection under the wings of their mothers.

Israel was to be free from all her enemies round about her. The Lord was to be their sun and protection. Justice and righteousness were to reign in the land.

REINCARNATION

Behold, I will send you Elijah the prophet before the coming of the great and dreadful day of the Lord.　　　　　　　Mal. 4:5

The Jews expected Elijah to come before the day of the Lord. The great prophet was to prepare the way for the coming of the Messiah. Moses had told the Israelites that a great prophet would come, and he had admonished the people to listen to him [Deut. 18:18].

"Elijah the prophet" here means "the spirit of Elijah", that is, a new prophet like Elijah, with strength and courage to reform the people and cause them to turn to the God of Israel. Elijah had been dead a long time, but his spirit was still alive. The spirit never dies, and the cause for which men of God give their lives is never forgotten.

The unlearned men and women expected Elijah to return in the flesh. Even during the time of Jesus, Elijah was expected to return in person at any time. Some of the people said that John was one of the prophets, and some took him for Elijah, and others for Christ [John 1:21].

Jesus said that Elijah already had come and that John was Elijah, whom the people were expecting to return in advance of Messiah [Matt. 11:13-15].

According to the teaching of the Hebrew prophets, the reincarnation is of the spirit and not of the flesh, for the spirit is eternal and immortal, but the body turns into dust. Jesus said, "It is the spirit that gives life; the body is of no account" [John 6:63, Eastern text].

Later on during his discourses, Jesus threw more light on this subject when he said, "There be some standing here, which shall not taste of death, till they see the kingdom of God" [Luke 9:27]. The spirit of his disciples who stood near him when he said these words is still living and more active than it was during the time of Jesus. Elijah's spirit dwelt in the prophets who carried on Elijah's mission. John the Baptist was Elijah. He came ahead of Jesus to prepare the way and to call the people to repentance.

INDEX

Aaron, 206
Abijah, 351
Abimeleck, 57-59
Abominable choice, 683-684
Abraham, 39-40, 42-43, 47, 58, 62-63, 64
Abram, 47 *see also* Abraham
Abundance, 504, 881
Acceptable year, 718
Adam, 8
Adders, 518
Adding evils, 270-271
Additions and omissions, 228
Adonijah, 345
Adultery, 141, 232-233, 257, 269
Advertise, 214, 308
Afflictions, 722
Agriculture, 527
Ahlah, 816-817
Ahlibah, 816-817
Alexander the Great, 857-858
Aliens, 660, 870-871
Alliances, 634-635, 785, 816, 817-818, 865-866
Almond trees, 601-602, 731
Alphabet, 136
Altars, 137, 142, 212, 653-654, 958-959
Ammonites, 226, 776
Amora (Gomorrah), 36-37, 41-42
Amos, 885-897
Amplification, 229
Anak, 289-290
Anathoth, 640
Ancient of days, 855
Angels, 51, 53-54, 79, 81, 149
Anger, 464-465, 561, 620-621, 648
Animals, 29, 33, 116, 145-146, 148, 169, 176, 337, 492 *see also* Beasts of prey
Anointing, 154
Another spirit, 199-200
Appeasement, 79
Apple of his eye, 275
Apple tree, under the, 609-610

Aramaic language, 377, 678, 905-907
Arameans, 267
Ararat, Mount, 31-32
Archers, 344-345
"Are not," 791
Ariel, 666-667
Ark of God, 312-313, 329
Armament, 882-883
Armenia, 780, 888
Arm, human, 438, 752
Armies, 715-716, 818
Army officers, 224, 741
Army provisions, 318-319
Artists, 346
Arvad, 822-823
As God, 951-952
Asher, 299
Ashtoreth, 348
Asps, 435, 643
Ass of Balaam, 211
Asses, 97, 123, 163, 211, 255, 298, 720, 734-735, 946-947
Assyria, 215, 637, 638-639, 818, 920-921
Astronomy, 3, 5-6, 28-29, 33, 440-442, 456-457, 478, 678-679, 929
Attack, sudden, 859
Aunts, marrying of, 177
Avims, 227
Axe head swam, 368-369
Azariah, 373

Baal, 211-212, 783, 870, 932
Baal-peor, 216-217, 876-877
Baal-Zebub, 358-359
Babylon, 645-646, 647, 655-656, 781
Bag with holes, 936-937
Bags of deceitful weights, 916
Bake bread for another, 449
Balaam, 209, 211
Bald-headed, 360-361
Bands broken, 949
Bargaining, 65
Baskets, 269, 300, 760-761, 894-895
Bastards, 946

963

Bearing, cessation of, 85
Beasts of prey, 804, 836, 853-855
Beautiful and desirable, 607-608
Beauty of women, 41, 73-74, 607-608
Became as a stone, 322
Become as women, 779
Becoming surety, 552-553
Bedouins, 764-765
Beer (well), 208-209
Beer-sheba, 61-62
Bees, 632
Beets, 701
Behemoth, 459-460
Behind the mill, 119
Being with child, 661
Bel, 783 see also Baal
Belial, 357
Belly, 648
Beloved, encouraged by, 605
Benjamin, 280
Betrothal customs, 67 see also Marriage
Bills of divorcement, 260-261, 326 see also Divorce
Binding and loosing, 356
Birds, 692-693
Birthrights, 69
Bitter water, 130
Black, 742
Black faces, 881
Black hair, 608
Black sheep, 75-76
Blains, 117
Blasphemy, 184-185
Blast of thy nostrils, 129
Blemish, 503
Blessings, 49, 94, 269, 280-281, 550, 703
Blindness, 328, 597-598, 711
Blood, 33-34, 151-152, 317, 358, 831
Blood of the lamb, 120
Bloody cities, 925
Bluntness, 888-889
Boars, 511
Bodies into dust, 827
Bodies of water, 781
Body, parts of the, 600-601
Bones, 493, 832-834
Books, 136, 151, 207-208, 274, 391, 392, 855-856, 860-861 see also Writing
Booths, 184-442
Born of woman, 429
Borrowing, of animals, 145,
Borrowing, of clothes, 106-107
Bottle in the smoke, 532-533
Boundaries, 251-252
Bowels, 648

Bowls, 893
Brambles, 301-302
Branches, 646-647, 941-942
Brass serpent, 207
Bread, 43, 130, 258, 287-288, 330, 350, 383-384, 437-438, 488, 510, 599, 875
Breasts, 610-611
Bribes, 566, 616, 874, 933-934
Bridegroom, 473
Brides, 68, 82, 320-321 see also Marriage; Wives
Briers, 662-663, 865
Brooks of honey and butter, 435
Brotherly love, 186
Brothers, 566-567
Brought back, 709
Builders and stones, 530-531
Bullocks, 765
Burdens, 60-61
Burial, 770
Burning bush, 104
Butlers, 591
Butter, 631-632
Buying and selling 598, 799-800

Cages, 73
Cain, 23, 24-27
Cakes and wafers, 168
Caleb, 290-291
Calendars, 3, 6, 28-29, 33, 247, 929
Calling a bird, 692-693
Canaan, language of, 652, 653
Canaanitish women, 357, 389
Candles, 432, 444-445, 473
Cannibalism, 697, 754, 911
Captives, 335, 717
Carved work, 505
Cattle, in cities, 941
Caves, 724
Cedars of Lebanon, 620
Chaldeans, 818-819
Challenges to battle, 372
Chariot wheels, 128
Chariots, 294, 348, 608
Charms, 943
Cheating, 895
Cherethites, 332
Chief of thirty officers, 342
Child, simple as, 704-705
Childbirth, 416-417
Children, 545-546, 610, 619, 621-622, 754, 870-871, 881-882
China, 216, 696
Choicest fields, 324
Chosen people, 688
Christ, 463-464 see also Messiah
Chronicles, 382-392

Circumcision, of foreskin, 48-49, 172
"Circumcision," of heart, 240-241, 271-272, 838
Cisterns, 391
Cities, 295, 894, 925, 941
Citrons, 184, 401
Clarity, 152
Clean out of unclean, 430
Cleansing, 883-884
Clear day, 650
Climate, 77
Closing of eyes, 91-92
Cloth too short, 665-666
Clothes, 70-71, 83-84, 106-107, 147, 173, 175, 202, 238, 256, 262, 436, 539-540, 719, 721, 773-774, 932-933
Clouds, 124, 387, 826, 867
Cloudy pillar, 160
Coat of long sleeves, 83-84
Cockatrices, 643, 647-648
Cold and heat, 77
Collar of his robe, 539-540
Comfort, 755-756
Comforted me, 464
Commander-in-chief, 383
Commandments, 164-165
Common meat, 242-243
Compensation, 143-144, 418, 549
Conduct, 789-790
Confessions, 187-188
Confiscation, 910-911
Confusion, 486-487
Conquerors, 639
Conquests, 199, 626, 634
Conscience, 162-163
Consciousness, 837
Conspiracy, 518
Continuous light, 955
Copper, 238-239
Cord, 948-949
Cords of men, 877-878
Cornerstones, 655
Corruption, 270, 714, 878-879
Cottage, 614
Couches, 404
Counselors, 372-373, 669-670, 934
Cousins, 111-112, 341
Covenants, 150-151, 203, 766-767, 769-770
Covering of lips, 821
Cowards, 922
Craftsmen, 346, 505
Cream, 52
Creation, 2
Crete, 822
Crooked serpent, 662
Crookedness, 472-473, 895

Cross, 254
Cupbearers, position of, 398-399
Cups, 90, 469, 702, 763-764, 779-780, 781-782, 819, 951
Cursing and curses, 143, 191, 251-252, 268-269, 943
Curtains of Midian, 928
Curved trumpets, 387
Cyrus, 394, 689-690

Damascus, 609, 649, 776-777
Dan, 299
Daniel, 844-861
Danites, 280-281
Darkness, 4, 545, 715, 826-827
Daughters, of Lot, 57
Daughters of your master, 334
David, 343-344, 384-385, 386, 482, 539, 769-770
Day, 460
Days of old, 722-723
Dead, 183-184, 203-204, 364-365, 526-527, 544, 661-662
Deafness, 601
Death, 27, 91-92, 732
Deborah, 297
Debts, 162
Deceit, 59, 363, 420-421, 737-738, 878-879, 916
Deceitful bow, 873
Decrees, 638, 700-701
Dedan, 69
Dedicated things, 658
Demented, 490-491
Departure, 703-704
Descendants, 436
Deserted women, 183
Deserts, rivers in, 687
Destiny, 474-475
Destroying mountain, 780
Deuel, 192
Devotion, 615
Devour people, 469
Devoured Jacob, 746
Dew, 914
Died defenseless, 326-327
Dietary laws, 172
Difficult tasks, 942-943
Difficulties increased, 495
Dig into hell, 895-896
Disaster, 628, 715, 955
Discipline, 524, 699, 735
Disgrace, 563
Disguising, 254-255
Disloyalty, 733
Distinct apparel, 932-933
Diverse seeds, 179-180
Diverse weights, 265-266

Divinations, 212
Divine inspiration, 797
Divine protection, 119-120, 517
Divine warnings, 774
Diviners, 689
Divining cups, 90
Divorce, 183, 219-220, 260-261, 326, 735
Doctors, priests as, 173-174
Doctrine of men, 669
Dog's head, 325-326
Dogs licked the blood, 358
Dominion, 515
Double heart, 468
Double portion, 359-360
Dowries, 74, 76, 81, 82, 146
Dragons, 7, 505-506
Draught house, 372 see also Sanitation
Dreams, 71-72, 85, 86-87, 196-197
Dregs, 506
Drew water, 313
Drinking, 246 see also Wine
Dross in silver, 616
Droughts, 187, 937
Drowning, 789
Drunkenness, 253-254, 575, 579, 651, 663-664, 701-702, 721, 748, 919, 925-926 see also Wine
Dry rivers, 528
Dull imagination, 689
Dumbness, 486-487
Dungeon, 772
Dust, 22, 702-703
Dust of Jacob, 212-213
Dwelling in darkness, 545
Dwelling in rocks, 619-620
Dynasty, end of, 757-758

Eagles, 138-139, 325, 806-807
Earth, 440-442, 458, 478, 522, 738-739
East, term, 38-39
Eat the flesh, 911
Eat the scroll, 796-797
Eaten ashes like bread, 521-522
Eaten sin, 869
Eaten upon the mountains, 809, 814
Eating grass, 850-851
Eating in the morning, 598-599
Eating own flesh, 697
Eber, 37
Eden, garden of, 13
Edom, 358, 676, 898-899
Edomites, 225
Eglon, 295-296
Egypt, 98, 526, 653-654, 828
Ehur, 295-296
Eighteen years old, 392
Eighth day, 172

El, 91
Elders, 181-182, 533
Eli, 311
Eliezer, 137
Elijah, 355-356
Elisha, 360
Elshaddai, 47, 110-111
Embezzlement, 434
Emblem, 794-795
Empty-handed, term, 148-149
End, 460
End (Gomer), 864
Enemy, 198-199, 477-478, 578-579
Enragement, 430-431
Enticing in name of God, 376-377
Ephraim, 663-664
Equinox, 456-457
Erech, 36
Error, of Uzzah, 329
Esau, 70-71, 81
Espania, 899
Espousal consent, 67-68 see also Marriage
Essence, formless, 2-3
Esther, 403-409
Eternal values, 589-590
Eternity, 2
Ethiopia, Jews in, 935
Etiquette, 89, 577
Eunuchs, 405, 710-711
Even place, 479
Everlasting, 282, 682, 861
Evil, 4, 17, 22-23, 270-271, 425, 551-552, 570, 887, 924
Evil eye, 389
Evil spirits, 317
Ewes and rams, 829-830
Excellency, 214
Excellent spirit, 852
Exile, duration of, 762-763
Exogamy, 56-57, 235-236, 401-402, 870-871
Eyes to the blind, 445-446
Ezekiel, 793-843
Ezra, 393-396

Faithful son, 960
Faithfulness, 531-532
False devotion, 615
False pride, 803
False worship, 926-927
Falsehood, 419, 911
Falsification, 742
Familiar spirits, 635
Fast as gazelle, 324
Fasting, 712-713, 771-772
Fathers and mothers see Parents

Fatness and spiritual river, 485
Fear, 418
Feast of rejoicing (Passover), 121
Feast of Tabernacles, 184
Feasting, 564-565
Feeds on wind, 878
Feet, 98, 241-242, 281, 567, 703
Female servants, redemption of, 143
Feminine gender, 364
Fences of briers, 865
Fiery serpents, 206-207
Figs, baskets of, 760-761
Figs, evil, 760-761
Figurative speech, 64, 319-320
Files, 158
Finger of God, 155-156, 164-165
Fire, 192-193, 340, 354-355, 491-492
Firmament, 4
Firstborn, 95, 253
Fish, worship of, 230
Five horsemen, 370
Flattery, 580-581
Flesh in my teeth, 428
Flies, 116, 632
Flies and ointment, 596
Flocks of kids, 356
Floods, 30-31, 481, 775
Floods of troubles, 472
Flying scroll, 943
Food, gifts of, 365
Fools, 575, 579
Foot, watering with, 241-242
Foot in oil, 281
For this cause, 891-892
Foreign gods, 82 see also Pagan gods
Forgotten forever, 482
Formed in iniquity, 492
Former husbands, 261
Forty years, 200
Fortune, 923-924
Fountain of Israel, 500
Fountains, 952-953
Four beasts, 853-855
Four chariots, 944
Four thousand horsemen, 333
Four winds, 853-855
Four years, 336
Fourth beast, 854-855
Fourth generation, 45
Fowl of every wing, 807-808
Foxes, 303-304, 314
Friends, loyalty to, 562
Frogs, 114
Fruit trees, 252-253
Fruits as medicine, 378
Fuel, vines for, 804-805
Future, 700, 707-708
Future king, 279

Gabriel, 858
Gad, 299
Gadites, 280-281
Galeed, 78
Galilee, 635-636
Garden of Eden, 13
Garments, 147, 202, 238, 256, 719 see also Clothes
Gates, as royal courts, 337
Gath, 339
Gazelle, 324
Gehazi, 368
Generals, 252
Genitals, 805, 819
Gentiles, 35-36, 244, 743-744 see also Pagan gods
Gentle words, 274-275
Giants, 85, 227, 289-290
Gideon, 299-300
Gifts, 80, 88, 314-315, 318, 350, 365, 480, 497, 520, 570-571, 874, 956
Gihon 15
Gilgal, 914-915
Girded up, 447
Girdles, 121, 641, 801-802
Given hand, 778, 791
Glorify in ships, 687
Glory, 460
Gluttony, 253-254
God (See also Lord)
    abundance, 710
    agents, 638-639
    appearance, 800
    ascent, 50
    as author of laws, 161, 520-521
    awareness of evil, 924
    bribes, 933-934
    disloyalty to, 799
    dwelling place, 455-456
    enticing in name of, 376-377
    eyes on righteous, 455
    as father, 244, 723-724
    feathers, 517
    forgiveness, 711-712, 735-736, 906
    hand, man's life in, 429
    help from, 429, 715
    highest, 44
    immutability, 960
    invisibility of, 160-161
    laws, 810
    light of, 521, 542-543, 674-675, 719-720
    loyalty to, 765-766
    mercy, 517
    messengers, 959
    mindfullness, 696
    names of, see Names of God
    none like, 513

God (*cont.*)
    nostrils of, 129
    not jealous, 509
    as not a man, 213
    not partner of evil, 454
    omnipresence, 542
    omniscience, 454, 945-946
    powerful acts, 442
    presence, 194
    promises, 708-709
    protection of, 482-483, 623-624
    reverence to, 549-550
    rides through heaven, 282
    righteousness, 466, 467-468
    sins before, 516-517
    smitten of, 705
    speaks once, 453-454
    spoke out of heaven, 232
    trusting in, 534, 752-753
    truth, 676-677
    understanding, 514-515, 535
    universality, 896-897, 889-890
    as unsearchable, 425
    vineyard, 624
    vision of, 800-801
    waiting for His help, 538
    walking through sea, 930
    as warrior, 686
    ways of, 497, 511-512
    wondrous works, 596
    works unchangeable, 592
    wrote, 240
    zealousness, 234-235, 919
God of gods, 137-138, 241, 491, 519-520
God of my rock, 340
God of the World, 61-62
Gods *see* Pagan gods
Gog, 834, 835
Gold, 457, 557
Golden calf, 156-157
Golden cup, 779-780
Golden rules, 576-577, 674
Gomorrah, 36-37, 41-42
Good, 17, 22-23, 420, 451, 555, 557, 582, 808-809 *see also* Evil
Gossip, 494
Gourd, 905, 906
Governors, 345-346
Grain, 558, 874
Grapes, 197-198, 724-725, 937-938
Grass, 681, 850-851
Graves of lust, 196
Grazing rights, 439
Great king, 877
Great of flesh, 805, 819
Greeks, 823-824
Green tree and dry tree, 811-812

Grieving thorn, 825
Grumbling, 195-196
Guests, divine, 51, 53
Guilt, 162-163, 263

Habakkuk, 923-930
Hadad, 351-352
Hadassah, 406
Hagar, 59-60
Haggai, 936-938
Hair, 180, 608
Hairy man, 359
Half-sisters, 815
Ham, 29-30
Haman, 407
Hands, 87, 93, 94, 107-108, 445, 528, 544, 696-697, 713-714, 778, 791, 796, 797-798, 810, 815, 906-907
Hardships, 483, 691, 792, 866, 887
Harlots, 554, 573-574, 736-737, 739, 805-806
Hasty feet, 567
He shall not cry, 684-685
Head and tail, 651-652
Healers, 621-622
Healing in wings, 961
Health, 524-525
Heap of stones, 77-78
Heart, 240-241, 271-272, 581, 597, 606, 767, 802-803, 838
Heaven, keys of, 657
Heaven, looking down from, 723
Heavenly harmony, 521
Hebrews, 700 *see also* Israel; Jews; Judah; Remnant
He-goats, 777-778, 857
Heifer, term, 303
Heirs, 349, 389, 432, 640, 646-647
Hell, 541, 895-896 *see also* Sheol
Hemorrhoids, 312
Hezekiah, 378, 390-391, 679, 680
Hiddekel, 16
Hide my face, 273
High places, 138, 734, 809, 837 *see also* Mountains
High priests, 837-838, 839
High walls, 239-240
Hill of the Lord, 479
Hills leap, 499
Hinderers, 395
His son died, 353
Hobab, 297
Holy garments, 175
Holy names, 303 *see also* Names of God
Holy people, 236-237
Holy places, 330

Holy soil, 367
Honey, 316, 605, 631-632
Hope, 470
Hornets. 149-150, 237-238, 292
Horns, 431, 894, 940-941
Hosea, 862-879
Hospitality, 52, 54, 304-305, 450
Hot springs, 290
Household of the wicked, 560
Households of kings, 773
Houses of harlots, 739
Human bodies, 203-204
Human conduct, 541
Human deities, 407-408
Human folly, 427
Human images, 229
Human knowledge, limitation of, 460
Human sacrifices, 62-64, 249, 527-528
    see also Offerings; Sacrifices
Human toil, 589
Humbleness, 438, 493, 563-564, 727
Hundred tower, 399-400
Hunger and thirst, 667-668
Husbands, 261
Hypocrites, 572, 573

I am a child, 730-731
I am black, 742
I have deceived, 737-738
I have not, 291
Idols, sacrifices to, 391 see also Pagan
    gods
Images, 7-8, 229, 848-849
Immoral worship, 747
Immorality, 552
Immortality, 476-477, 592-593, 595-
    596, 861
Impatience, 452
Incense, prayer as, 543
Incest, 57
Inheritance polluted, 693
Injuries, punishment for, 265
Innocence, 144-145, 250, 438
Insanity, 318, 878
Inscribed on hand, 696-697
Insincere friends, 421
Intermarriage see Exogamy
Iron, 238-239
Isaiah, 612-728
Ishmael, 46, 59-60
Ishmaelites, 84
Islands, 502
Israel, 79-80, 123-124, 237, 275-276,
    500, 537-538, 663, 675, 682-683,
    694, 698, 708, 873-874, 886-887,
    894-895, 916-917, 947 see also
    Remnant

Jacob, 71, 74-75, 94, 212-213, 214-
    215, 267, 540, 746
Jars, writing in, 768
Japan, 835-836
Javan, 823-824
Jealousy, 190
Jeremiah, 729-783, 784-792
Jericho, wall of, 287
Jerusalem, 806, 817, 910, 927-928, 951
Jethro, 104
Jewels, 866
Jews, in Ethiopia, 935
Jezreel, 864-865
Joab, 325, 338-339
Job, 410-460
Joel, 880-883
Jonah, 901-907
Jordan, 286, 529-530
Joseph, 97
Joshua, 284-292
Joy increased, 636
Judah, 378-379, 389-390, 720, 749,
    767, 768, 786, 787, 805-806, 920
Judaism, 122, 841
Judges, 147-148
Judgment, places of, 891
Just and unjust, 456
Justice, 615-616, 829, 889

Kardu, Mountains of, 31-32
Kebar, 794
Keys of heaven, 657
Kindling wood, 699
Kingdom, 330-331
King of Judah, 389-390
King of kings, 871
Kings, 249, 296, 314, 315-316, 318,
    321, 332-333, 357, 362, 367, 369,
    379, 383-384, 400-401, 462-463,
    540-541, 576, 593, 646, 756-757,
    773, 877
Kinsmen, 308
Kiss the son, 464
Kissing, 609
Knife on your throat, 572
Knives, 63-64, 109-110, 572, 584
Knowledge, limitations of, 457
Knowledge, tree of, 14
Known in the gate, 586-587
Koriath-Arba, 294-295

Laban, 74-75
Labored in vain, 694
Laborers, 178, 262, 756 see also Serv-
    ants; Slavery
Lambs, 726-727
Lame and blind, 328
Lamps, 341, 349, 533-534

Land, selling of, 186
Landmarks, 624-625, 871
Languages, division of, 37-38
Large flesh, 805, 819
Latrines *see* Sanitation
Laws, 185, 191, 234, 553-554
Lead, writing on, 432-433
Leaders, 621-622, 711, 732-733, 912, 954 *see also* Kings; Rulers
Leagues, 327
Learning, 846
Leasing, of vineyards, 611
Lebanon, 604-605, 620, 827
Left and right hand, 906-907
Legal tender, 155
Leopards, 641-642
Leprosy, 173-174
Lesson to others, 820
Letters interpreted, 395
Levi, daughter of, 101
Leviathan, 416
Levites, term, 166
Lewdness, 820
Liars, 567
Lice, 114-115
Life, tree of, 13-14
Life eternal, 422
Life hereafter, 471
Life span, 726
Lift up my hand, 810
Lift up thine hand, 468
Light, 3, 152, 428, 542-543, 672-673, 955
Lioness, 809
Lions, 483-484
Lips, 173, 627, 821
Little flock, 948
Little horn, 858
Liver, 813
Living God, 105-106
Living water, 733, 956
Loans, from kings, 400-401
Locusts, 118-119, 894
Look straight, 551
Looking behind, 55-56
Lord (*See also* God)
 burden of, 759-760
 hands, 714-714
 of hosts, 310-311
 mountain of, 912
 patience, 686
 reverence of, 474
 as sun, 513
 sword of, 675-676
 term, 11
 trusting in, 475-476
 as watchman, 655
 ways of, 745-746

Lost sheep, 777
Lost tribes, 374-375
Lot, 56
Lots, 221
Love, 178-179, 186
Lovers, 737, 764
Loyalty, 233, 321, 562
Luck, 923-924
Lust, graves of, 196
Luz, 295

Magicians, 86, 115, 117
Magog, 834, 835
Maher-shalal-hash-baz, 633
Malachi, 957-962
Male sex organs, 805, 819
Mamre (Moreh), 40
Mankind, 12, 28-29, 515-516, 681
Manna, 130, 132-133
Manners, 89, 577
Marginal notes, 502-503
Marriage, 18, 41, 56-57, 67-68, 74, 76, 81, 82, 111-112, 141, 177, 219-220, 235-236, 256, 257, 260-261, 269, 308, 309, 320-321, 326, 401-402, 632-633, 868
Master's daughters, 334
Material thoughts, 519
Mature men, 65, 351
Meal offering, 169-170
Measuring lines, 331-332
Meat, 170-171, 242-243, 317, 938
Medeba, 209
Medes, 650
Meditation, 565
Meekness, 493
Meeting places, 82
Mehemney, 405
Melt like wax, 494-495, 908-909
Memorial offerings, 149, 163, 167-168, 247-248
Men of stature, 691-692
Mene, Mene, Tekel, Upharsin, 851-852
Meshech, 34-35
Messengers, 149, 746-747, 959
Messiah, 213, 251, 487, 529, 618-619, 637-638, 684, 695, 707, 855, 856, 900, 913, 959-960
Messianic kingdom, 502
Micah, 908-917
Midianites, 84, 102, 928
Midwives, 100, 101
Mighty One, 276-277
Milk, 96-97, 716
Millstones, 261-262
Mind, 597
Mines, 443

Minstrels, 361
Mirages, 751
Mission, 750
Mist, 12
Mixed marriages *see* Exogamy
Mixed people, 193-194
Mixed seeds, 255
Mixing drinks, 626
Moabites, 226
Modesty, 622-623
Money, 245-246
Moneylending, 146-147, 259
Monotheism, 39, 44, 76-77, 139-140, 233-234, 491, 896-897
Moon, 230-231
Moral codes, 57, 59, 141, 176
Mortal man, 430, 440
Mortar, 803-804
Mosaic law, 201-202
Moses, 101-102, 108-109, 128-129, 150-151, 232, 272-273, 279, 283, 525-526
Moth-eaten, 917
Mothers and fathers *see* Parents
Mountains, 218, 618, 809, 837, 891, 912, 942
Mourning, 98, 159-160, 181, 585-586, 820, 875, 952
Mouths, 311, 640-641, 788, 825-826
Music, 26-27
My eyes looked for salvation, 534-535
My man, 867
My mouth is enlarged, 311
Myrrh, 155
Mystery, 659

Naaman, 366
Nahum, 918-922
Nakedness, 19, 20, 748, 814-815
Names, confusion in 394
Names of God, 11, 12, 47, 91, 105-106, 241, 276-277, 491, 519-520, -867
Nations, understanding between, 654
Nature, 419-420, 589
Nazarite, law of, 191
Nebuchadnezzar, 762
Negeb, 323-324
Nehemiah, 396, 397-402
Nehushtan, 375
Neighbor's wife, 232-233
New covenant, 766-767
New day, 941-942
New earth, 725
New stock, 831
New teaching, 698-699
Night, visiting at, 606-607
Night watchmen, 607

Nile, 650-651
Nineveh, 903, 921
Nisan, 398
Nostrils, of God, 129
Not to be spared, 750
Numbers, 189-222
Numerals, large, 45

Oak of weeping, 83
Oaths, 44, 66, 532
Obadiah, 898-900
Obedience, 315-316, 406
Offerings, 24, 62-64, 149, 163, 167-170, 245-246, 247-248, 249, 266-267, 480, 492, 520, 670-671, 915
see also Sacrifices
Officials, 88
Oil increased, 362-363
Oil and ointment, 580
Old bread, 287-288
Old people, 452, 600
Old wine, 352, 886 *see also* Wine
Olive oil, 281
Olive trees, 942
Olives, 32
On foot, 337
One God, concept of, 233-234 *see also* Monotheism
One heart, 768-769
One shepherd, 830-831
Opening of the mouth, 825-826
Oppression, 439-440, 642-643, 887-888, 928
Oracles, 153-154
Oral praises, 501-502
Ordinances, 308, 408
Other lords, 660-661
Ovens, 872, 960-961
Oxen, threshing by, 264

Pagan gods, 76-77, 137-138, 139-140, 167, 211-212, 278, 348-349, 450, 734, 735, 736-737, 743-744, 809, 870, 873, 892, 932
Pagans, 150, 181, 235-236, 634-635, 841-842
Palace fields, 375-376, 628-629
Palestine, 766
Parable of eagles, 806-807
Parents, 141, 143, 177-178, 263, 268-269, 307, 325, 388, 569, 814-815
Parthians, 761
Pashur, 754-755
Passover, 121, 148-149
Pastoral people, 92-93
Pastors, 732-733
Patience, 594
Patriarchs, 94-95

Peace, 168-169, 378, 420, 712
Pelethites, 332
Pen of iron, 751-752
People, importance of, 561
Perpetual sun, 716-717
Persecuted, 592
Persians, 689-690
Perverse ways, 734
Pharaoh, 117-118, 126, 671, 775
Pillar of fire, 128
Pillar of salt, 56
Pillars of stone, 72
Pious men, 557-558
Pison, 15
Pitch, 42, 573
Pitcher broken, 602
Pits, 145, 361-362, 597-598, 659-660
Place of disaster, 955
Place of weeping, 328-329
Plagues, 893, 894
Plain writing, 924-925
Plantation, 831
Plants, 5, 9
Played the harlot, 736-737
Pleaded with her, 75
Plowing, with asses, 255
Plucking wheat, 260
Plunder, 877
Poison, cup of, 763-764
Poison of asps, 435
Polygamy, 269
Poor, 333-334, 487-488, 890
Poor in pride, 563-564
Possessions of the wicked, 470-471
Posterity, 477, 559
Potters, clay, 670
Power, 515
Praises, 501-502
Prayer as incense, 543
Prayer seven times, 536
Preacher, 588-589
Pregnancy, 53
Presence, of God, 194
Presents to kings, 314, 315, 318
Pretty eyes, 73-74
Prevented the dawning, 536
Price of man, 145
Pride, 503-504, 514, 803
Priests, 173-174, 759, 837-838, 839, 869, 935
Prince of Peace, 637-638 see also Messiah
Princes exposed, 217
Princes of the sea, 822
Prisoners, 713, 772-773
Processions, 531
Prominent men, 849
Promises, 708-709

Prophesies, 213, 740, 802
Prophets, 94-95, 250, 251, 364-365, 385-386, 671-672, 759, 872, 935
Prosperity, 524-525, 728
Protection, 471
Proverbs, 548-587
Provisions, 285, 318-319
Prudence, 555
Public chariots, 608
Punishment, 144, 244, 265, 468-469, 489, 819, 898-899, 954, 958
Pure man, 426
Purification, 271-272, 704, 742-743

Quail, 131-132, 194-195, 509
Queen of Assyria, 921

Rabbath, 334
Races, 29-30
Rafts, 337-338
Rahab, 514
Rahab, the harlot, 285-286
Raiders, 237-238, 292 see also Hornets
Rain, 562-563, 867
Rams, 480, 718-719, 829-830, 857, 957
Ransom, 154
Rape, 785, 792
Ravens, 353-354
Rear guard, 323
Rebekah, 220
Rebellion, 159, 778-779, 909
Rebuke your seeds, 958
Rechabites, 771
Reckoning, day of, 954
Red apparel, 721
Red eyes, 574
Red horse, 939-940
Red Sea, 124-126
Red wine see Wine
Red with wine, 96-97
Redeem, term, 111
Redemption, 263-264
Refrigeration, 135
Refugees, 755
Regimentation, 342
Reincarnation, 961-962
Religious differences, 88-89
Remember me, 402
Reminders, 231-232, 554
Remnant (of Israel), 396, 623, 639, 644-645, 649-650, 811, 867-868, 900, 913-914, 944-945, 948, 960 see also Israel
Repentence, 123, 157, 535, 879
Report, 745
Restoration, 617
Resurrection, 433-434, 513-514, 661-662

Retribution, 427-428
Revolt against Saul, 383
Reuel, 103, 192
Reverence, to God, 549-550
Revolt, 525-526, 860
Rib, term, 17-18
Riblah, 380
Riches, 333-334, 373-374, 431, 485-486, 504, 556-557, 559-560, 567, 933
Righteousness, 424, 455, 465, 486, 543-544, 758-759, 842-843
Right hand, Satan on, 528
Rings, 87
Rivers, 113, 115, 489-490, 518-519, 528, 687
Robes, 262
Rocks, 432-433, 471, 496-497, 525, 619-620
Rocky places, 276, 530, 673
Rods, 640-641, 731, 948-949
Rose to play, 157
Rough garments, 953
Royal city, 782
Royal courts, gates as, 337
Royal family, end of, 812-813
Rubbish, 919-920
Rulers, 318, 714, 750-751 see also Kings
Ruth, 306-309

Sabbath, 10-11, 133-134
Sabeans, 413
Sacred animals, 116
Sacred ground, 161
Sacred trees, 242
Sacrifices, 167-170, 212, 249, 391, 465, 492, 526-527, 727-728 see also Offerings
Sacrificial meat, 938
Salt, 203
Salty land, 271
Salty springs, 842
Salvation, water of, 645
Samaria, 817
Samson, 302, 304
Samuel, 310-342
Sanctification, 139
Sanctuary polluted, 688-689
Sanitation, 48-49, 115, 258, 296, 351, 372
Sarah, 49-50, 57-58
Satan, 19-21, 70, 338, 528
Saul, 383
Saviour, 433
Saws, 335, 384
Scapegoats, 175
Scattered bones, 493

Scattered sheep, 828
Sceptres, 95-96
Scribes, 110, 248, 409, 776 see also Writing
Scriptures, tampering with, 583-584
Scrolls, 943 see also Writing
Sealed, 668-669
Sealed book, 861
Sea of Chinnereth, 222
Sea monsters, 7
Seas, 499-500, 781, 782, 822, 947-948
Seasons, 5-6, 32-33, 247, 850 see also Calendars
Second affliction, 506
Second beast, 853
Second temple, 504-505
Secret bread, 555-556
Secret visions, 859
Seeds, 5, 9, 48, 177, 179-180, 255, 958
Seeing clearly, 426-427
Seen, 826
Seers, 385-386
Seething pot, 731-732
Selah, 512
Self-control, 564
Serpents, 19-21, 206-207
Servants, 142, 143, 145, 262, 590-591, 684 see also Slavery
Servitude, 496
Set thy face, 812
Seth, descendants of, 27
Seven, as sacred number, 187
Seven days of silence, 415
Seven seasons, 850
Seventh day, 10-11
Seventy units of time, 859-860
Sex organs, male, 805, 819
Shadow, 517
Shadow of wings, 470
Shadows, used for clock, 421-422
Shake the dust, 702-703
Shame, 20
Shamelessness, 736
Shamgar, 296
Shaving, 171
She had done, 68
Sheba, 69
Sheba (Seba), 882
Sheep, 102-103, 705-706, 828, 830
Shekels, 838
Shelter, 692
Sheol, 277-278, 481-482 see also Hell
Shepherds, 681-682, 758, 773-774, 830-831, 950-951
Shiloh, 291
Shilokha, 344
Shilommite, 344
Shining face, of Moses, 165

Ships, 347, 687
Shittim, place, 914
Shittim, wood, 153
Shoes, 105, 281-282, 309, 401
Shoots, 640
Short life, 424
Shrines, 734
Shulamite, 344
Shun the crooked, 472-473
Shunem, 363
Shyness, 405-406
Sickness, 418, 570
Signs and wonders, 243
Silence, 927
Silver, 616, 949
Simple as child, 704-705
Sin, 158-159, 327, 483, 516-517, 582-583, 869
Six hundred thousand, 121-122
Six thousand overseers, 385
Sixth day, 10
Sixty-six souls, 92
Skillful women, 587
Skirts, taking hold of, 945
Sky see Astronomy
Slain men, 440
Slaughter, 227-228, 500
Slavery, 93, 142, 881-882 see also Servants
Slingers, 344-345
Slothfulness, 580
Sluggardness, 553, 577
Small tribes, 523-524
Smoke, 648
Snakes, 892
Soap, 170
Sodom, 41-42, 53-54, 278
Soil conservation, 185-186
Sojourn, 537
Solitary life, 447
Solomon, 346, 347, 603-611
Son of Canaanitish woman, 389
Son of man, 467, 546, 795
Son of my right hand, 83
Song of Moses, 128-129
Song of riddles, 490
Song of Solomon, 603-611
Sons of God, 412-413, 511
Sonship, 463-464
Soothsayers, 182-183, 210, 357
Sops, exchange of, 89-90
Sorrows, 21-22
Soul, 220, 808
Sow in tears, 538-539
Span of life, 424, 726
Speech, 16
Spider's web, 423
Spirit, 220, 798

Spirit of sleep, 668
Spiritual blindness, 369, 546
Spiritual joy, 522-523
Spiritual kingdom, 463-464
Spiritual prosperity, 883
Spiritual truths, 562, 668-669
Spitting, 197
Spoil, division of, 498, 499
Spring of the Hebrews, 207
Staffs, 112-113, 677-678, 948-949
Stalks of flax, 286
Stars, 214-215, 223-224, 458-459, 892
Statesmen, 672
Sticky, 435
Stolen water, 555-556
Stones, 267-268, 312, 322, 530-531, 848
Stoning, 248
Stony heart, 802-803
Storms, 118
Straight like reed, 446
Strangers, 182, 545-546, 619, 946
Strife, 585
Strike my hands, 815
Strike the rock, 134-135, 204-205
Strong as ox, 280
Strong drink, 171, 246, 625 see also Wine
Strong hand, 544
Stubble, 960-961
Stubborness, 627-628
Studying, 380
Sucklings, 466-467
Sudden attack, 859
Sudden revolt, 860
Sun, 230-231, 288-289, 450, 672-673, 678-679, 716-717, 961
Sunburn, 603-604
Surety, 552-553, 568-569
Swallow pitch, 573
Swallowed, 785-786
Swearing, 140-141
Sweet cane, 688
Swifter than eagle, 325
Swords, 135, 913
Syrian, term, 374

Tabernacles, 744-745, 876
Table, as snare, 501
Tadmor, 346-347
Tail, term, 107
Tarshish, 35, 823
Taxes, 349-350, 373-374
Teaching, 48, 543-544, 698-699, 914
Tears see Weeping
Tears in the bottle, 494
Teeth on edge, 888-889
Tekoah, woman of, 335

Temper, 620-621
Tempests, 673-674
Temple walls, 379-380
Temples, 497, 801, 956
Temporal life, 516
Tent making, 164
Testing God, 235
Thebes, 922
They saw God, 152-153
They should carry, 385
Thick darkness, 472
Third beast, 854
Third hour, 321-322
Thirty-eight years, 226-227
Thirty pieces of silver, 949
Thorns, 221, 498, 579, 662-663, 825, 876
Three day's journey, 904-905
Three hundred foxes, 303-304
Three thousand, 316
Threshing, 264, 666, 874
Thumb, of father, 388
Thunder, 480-481
Thy way in the sea, 507-508
Tides, 126, 127
Tile, drawing on, 798-799
Time, 5-6, 591, 594, 847, 859-860
Tirshatha, 394
Toil forgotten, 426
Toilets see Sanitation
Tolerance, 306-307
Tombs, 724
Tragedy, 495-496
Trances, 210
Tree of knowledge, 14
Tree of life, 13-14
Trees, 5, 9, 180, 242, 252-253, 558-559, 601-602, 609-610, 620, 731, 811-812, 842-843, 942
Trespasses, 189-190
Trials, 237, 706-707
Tribal ethics, 246-247
Tribal mistrust, 205-206
Tribe, 915-916
Troublemakers, 629
Trust, in God, 231
Truths, 562, 676-677, 714, 840-841, 952-953
Turning backward, 224-225
Turning other cheek, 788
Two calendars, 388 see also Calendars
Tyre, 657-659, 824

Unclean animals, 169
Unclean food, 875
Unclean lips, 627
Under God, 98
Understanding, 590, 677

Ungodly, proud, 503-504
Universal kingdom, 694-695
Universe, 929
Unrighteous wealth, 933
Unripe grapes, 937-938
Unruly persons, 578
Untempered mortar, 803-804
Unwalled villages, 834-835
"Us," term, 39
Usury, 146-147, 259
Uzza, 329
Uzziah, 627

Valley of the cluster, 198
Valley of vision, 656
Valley of weeping, 329, 512
Valleys exalted, 680-681
Vegetables, 846-847
Vegetation, 5, 9
Venereal disease, 174, 182
Vengeance, 34, 339, 544
Venom, cup of, 781-782
Vicious men, 476
Villages, unwalled, 834-835
Vines, 278, 510-511, 804-805
Vineyards, 611, 624
Vipers, 435, 518
Virgins, 146, 256, 257, 629-631, 792
Virtuous women, 586
Visions, 196-197, 515, 859
Visiting, at night, 606-607
Vomit, 664-665
Vows, 218-220, 259-260, 569, 593-594, 904
Vultures, 836

Wages, 73
Waitresses, 591
Walls, 127, 239-240, 287, 400, 834-835
War, 655
Warnings, 761-762, 774
Wash hands in innocence, 479
Washpot, 496
Watchmen, 604, 607, 655, 741
Water, 72-73, 130, 190-191, 241-242, 390, 437-438, 507, 508-509, 645, 656, 657, 683, 749, 790-791
Weak allies, 376
Weak sheep, 830
Weak wall, 400
Wealth, 445, 571, 716 see also Riches
Weapons, 135, 594-595, 882-883
Weavers, 679-680
Webs, of weavers, 679-680
Weeping, 328-329, 465-466, 512, 535-536, 648, 786-787, 788-789, 958-959

Weights, 265-266
Welfare, 409
Wells, 46, 61, 66-67, 70, 205, 208-209, 225-226, 733, 790
Wheat, 260, 307-308, 872-873, 890
Whirlwind, 739-740
White asses, 298
White bread, 330
White with milk, 96-97
Whoredom, 257, 258-259, 736, 863-864, 869-870
Wicked, 240, 333-334, 432, 434, 435, 439, 462, 470-471, 484-486, 490, 550, 559, 560, 561, 583, 937
Widows, 449-450
Wife, as garden, 606
Wife of whoredoms, 863-864
Wild animals, 337, 459, 734-735, 836
    see also Beasts of prey
Wild honey, 316
Wilderness, 239, 685-686, 826
Wilted beet, 701
Wind, 599-600, 757, 853-855
Wine, 43, 57, 96-97, 171, 246, 270, 278, 301, 302, 303, 352, 383-384, 404-405, 506, 551, 568, 574-575, 585-586, 625, 626, 651, 658-659, 662, 701-702, 747-748, 869-870, 881, 886, 893, 926, 937-938
Wine of dragons, 278
Wineskins, 747-748
Wings, healing in, 961
Winking, 484
Winning people, 340-341
Wiping out, 378-379
Wisdom, 443-444, 550, 555, 560, 563, 575, 594-595
Witch of Endor, 322-323
Witchcraft, 617-618
With the measure you measure, 436

Witnesses, 222
Wives, 18, 55, 232-233, 269, 347, 606
Wolves, 641-642, 726-727, 787-788
Woman of Tekoah, 335
Womb, called from, 693
Women, 41, 76, 165, 180, 182, 183, 219-220, 227-228, 357, 405-406, 570, 581, 586, 587, 607-608, 735, 737, 779, 785, 792, 820
Wondrous works, 929
Woolen garments, 173
Words as deep water, 565-566
Work, as curse, 21-22
Wormwood, 743
Worries, 320
Worship, 165, 926-927
Wrath, 585
Wrestling with angel, 79
Writing, 110, 136, 150-151, 157-158, 191, 234, 267-268, 273, 298, 377-378, 432-433, 633, 753, 767, 768, 796, 798-799, 851-852, 860-861, 924-925, 943

Yahweh, 105
Yerebaal, 300-301
You have built, 774-775
Young men, 474, 584-585
Youth, respect for elders, 452

Zaphmath-paaneah, 87-88
Zeal has eaten me up, 500-501
Zealous God, 234-235, 919
Zealousness, 277, 953
Zechariah, 939-956
Zephaniah, 931-935
Zeruiah, 325
Zidon, 657-658
Zion, 537, 667, 740-741, 940